Monty Python's Flying Circus

Monty Python's Flying Circus

An Utterly Complete, Thoroughly Unillustrated, Absolutely Unauthorized Guide to Possibly All the References

From Arthur "Two Sheds" Jackson to Zambesi

Volume 1
Episodes 1–26

Darl Larsen

TAYLOR TRADE PUBLISHING
Lanham • New York • Boulder • Toronto • Plymouth, UK

Published by Taylor Trade Publishing
An imprint of The Rowman & Littlefield Publishing Group, Inc.
4501 Forbes Boulevard, Suite 200, Lanham, Maryland 20706
www.rowman.com

10 Thornbury Road, Plymouth PL6 7PP, United Kingdom

Distributed by National Book Network

First Taylor Trade Edition 2013

British Library Cataloguing in Publication Information Available

Library of Congress Cataloging-in-Publication Data

Larsen, Darl, 1963–
Monty Python's flying circus : an utterly complete, thoroughly unillustrated, absolutely unauthorized guide to possibly all the references from Arthur "Two Sheds" Jackson to Zambesi / Darl Larsen. — First Taylor trade edition.
volumes cm
Includes bibliographical references and index.
ISBN 978-1-58979-712-3 (pbk. : alk. paper)
1. Monty Python's flying circus (Television program)—Dictionaries. I. Title.
PN1992.77.M583L37 2013
791.45'72—dc23

2012050135

™ The paper used in this publication meets the minimum requirements of American National Standard for Information Sciences—Permanence of Paper for Printed Library Materials, ANSI/NISO Z39.48-1992.

Printed in the United States of America

For Nycole, Keir, Emrys, Brynmor,
Eamonn, Dathyl, Ransom, and Culainn,

and

WPW

Contents

Acknowledgments

Dr. William P. Williams, University of Akron, continues to be a tireless supporter since our days together at Northern Illinois University, and I thank him again and again for his assistance and friendship.

Thanks are also extended to these Brigham Young University entities: the Center for the Study of Western Europe, the Kennedy Center for International Studies, the College of Fine Arts and Communications, and the Theatre & Media Arts Department—providing generous research and travel grants, research sabbaticals and assistants, and wholehearted support for the completion of this project. The wonderful Harold B. Lee Library offered access to databases; their Interlibrary Loan department found every book or recording I requested, no matter how obscure; and this library thankfully maintains a collection that made research for this edition achievable.

The good folks at the BBC's Written Archives Collection in Caversham Park were both gracious and helpful, allowing unfettered access to production files for the *Flying Circus* episodes for the original edition of this work, upon which this edition builds. My own research assistants included Emma Hoskisson, Jason Hagey, Chelsea Gibbs, and Brett Stifflemire; this edition simply could not have been accomplished without their hard work.

Fellow BYU professor Daryl Lee contributed translations to unpack the Pythons' Jabberwock French. I'd also like to thank my colleagues here in the BYU Theatre & Media Arts department who acted as supporters from the first edition to this project, including Amy Jensen, Tom Lefler, Rodger Sorensen, Kelly Loosli, Sharon Swenson, Dean Duncan, Tom and Courtney Russell, Jeff Parkin, Eric Samuelsen, Brad Barber, and Megan Sanborn Jones. Thanks also to Mark Ellsworth, as well as Tomasz Dobrogoszcz, Miguel Angel Gonzalez Campos, Kevin Kern, and all the faculty and student participants at the 2010 Monty Python Conference at the University of Łódź, Poland; their combined support pushed this book to completion. And a special thanks to Randy Malamud, whose collegiality and friendship I treasure.

Also, warm thanks to my parents Norbert and Patricia Larsen, and editors Stephen Ryan at Scarecrow Press and Rick Rinehart at Taylor Trade.

And lastly, a thanks to my family including my wife, Nycole, and our wonderful children—Keir (and Misti), Emrys, Brynmor, Eamonn, Dathyl, Ransom, and Culainn. They gave me all the time and support I needed, and I'm grateful.

Introduction or "Notes on a Dead Parrot"

The above was a subtitle for a lecture I was asked to give ostensibly to try and explain my area of scholarship to a roomful of English majors and professors. The title more completely read "Notes on a Dead Parrot: Monty Python and/as Scholarship." (The lecture went pretty well—I showed clips.) It seems incongruous from the start—Monty Python and scholarship. Also, the "and/as" isn't an academic handstand but an acknowledgment of the necessary but slippery relationship between the terms. Monty Python isn't Shakespeare or Milton, it's not occasional poetry or courtly revels, and it isn't your standard, sober subject matter for academic study. After all, the Pythons imprecate and deflate all manner of stuffed-shirt-types in their work, from Cambridge dons to monarchs and popes to bowlered representatives of "The City." In one of their feature films they even kill a "Very Famous Historian" as he attempts to apply historical, narrative order to the medieval farrago of uppity peasants and foul-tempered rabbits.

But in the process of determining a thesis subject with the eminent Dr. William Proctor Williams at Northern Illinois University, we were led to another acknowledgment—that the Pythons owe an atavistic debt to the "University Wits" and to Shakespeare of the English Renaissance stage. This led to a successful dissertation in 2000 and then a book, *Monty Python, Shakespeare and English Renaissance Drama* (2003). The challenges encountered when I studied the sixteenth- through eighteenth-century English works of the stage and page (Spenser, Skelton, Dekker, Dryden, et al.) prompted another book project, this one a unique annotation. *Monty Python's Flying Circus: An Utterly Complete, Thoroughly Unillustrated, Absolutely Unauthorized Guide to Possibly All the References from Arthur "Two Sheds" Jackson to Zambesi* (2008) was meant to first dissect the layers and clusters of references and meanings, and then lay bare the interconnectedness between the Pythons' comedy and the world of history, culture, and literature. That hardcover edition serves as the foundation and jumping-off point for this new work.

And so this project continues to be of two minds, at least. One goal was to perform a simple identification of names, faces, places, musical cues, uncredited actors, slang terms, colloquial expressions, etc., with the hope being that the interested reader and viewer could better appreciate the fractured, polyglot, multilevel nature of the Pythonesque world. More significantly, though, are the deeper dives into that created world, where mini-essays provide explications that surface glossings can't fathom. It was this second thread that wove itself throughout not only the late 1960s and 1970s London, but back through the tapestry of English history and mythology, into Number 10 Downing Street and Westminster and Her Majesty's courts system, into the living rooms and ducks-on-the-wall kitchens of Hull and Bristol, across the green belts of Bucks and Berks and the beaches of Oban and Paignton, and onto the brightly lit stages of recent British television history.

It then becomes possible to go deep *and* far, making connections between the world of the 1960s and classical or existentialist philosophy, for example, and consistently identifying allusions, intertextualities, references, classical and modern parodies and imitations, etc. In this way I will satisfy the demands of myriad reader/viewers, demonstrating the cultural significance of these constructions that become Monty Python's social history.

And now the nuts and bolts. This new project is divided into two volumes—episodes 1–26 and 27–45, respectively, meaning Seasons 1 and 2, then Seasons 3 and 4. The glossings for the episodes in both volumes are provided alphabetically in an encyclopedic format. A reader or viewer interested in finding a particular reference (e.g., "Crunchy Frog" or "Scott of the Sahara") can access the index, of course, but can also turn directly to the particular episode and look up the term, spoken phrase, or name in its alphabetic order. Each episode is also headed with a thumbnail list of every significant scene, animation, and link (transition), all in the order they appear in that particular episode. A quick scan of the thumbnail listing at the beginning of Episode 15 will confirm that both "The Spanish Inquisition" and "The Semaphore Version of *Wuthering Heights*" are indeed part of that second season episode. This will help the viewer as well as the reader, of course. A reader wondering where the "Icelandic Honey Week" sketch is found in Episode 45 can quickly see that it's sandwiched between "The Most Awful Family in Britain" and the opening titles. If you know the sketch but not its episode, the same sketch title (or animation or link) can also be looked up directly in the new "Sketch, Animation, and Link Listing." This list identifies in alphabetical order every different or new section, large and small, in the broadcast episodes, down to the knight-and-chicken links and animated tidbits. The multiple appendices for this edition are made to be as focused and helpful as possible, and include complete listings, by episode, of all stock film and music sources included in the archived records. The index is meant to be as comprehensive as possible. *All* the names, places, dates, and references cited by the Pythons, visible in the images or mentioned in the printed script are indexed. Also, the inferences and references produced by textual analyses are indexed and cross-referenced to other Python work, and to history, literature, and culture. It's a giant, marvelous index. Entries are also cross-referenced to other episodes wherever necessary. Quotations from characters are cited using quotation marks, while stage directions, scene descriptions, and many titles are indicated by the use of italics.

Factual, production information culled from the BBC's Written Archives Collection is cited by folder number (e.g., T12/1,084). Neither the printed *Flying Circus* scripts nor the taped episodes comprise a *locus classicus* for our purposes—both are referenced as needed. Finally, the abbreviation "PSC" (Printed Script Commentary) at the beginning of an annotation means the word or phrase being referenced comes directly from the printed script itself and would not be available to the viewer, just the reader. These strange, "in-house joke" phenomena will be discussed in several annotations.

This new edition has an awful lot of "new" about it. From the day I submitted the first edition in late 2007, I've thought about all the things I should have included, of course, and this new edition couldn't come fast enough. The identification and analysis of the many animated sequences was a major goal for this new work. The printed versions of the *Flying Circus* scripts generally avoid describing the animated sequences at all—the cartoons tend to be fluid, full of unattributed and undocumented material, and are a stream-of-consciousness labyrinth. Animator Terry Gilliam borrowed characters and backgrounds from newspapers, magazines, period catalogs, and advertisements as well as art, architecture, and history books; he used Edwardian-era photos and postcards; he shot or borrowed London-area photographs, which he then colored and manipulated to create worlds that did not exist. Dozens of these images and references have been identified and discussed in this edition, and many aren't as random as they may first appear. There are also many new cross-references from the *Flying Circus* episodes to other works the Pythons completed during this period—including a special May Day celebration mini-episode produced for European television, two *Fliegender Zirkus* German-language episodes made for Bavarian television, and *Monty Python's Big Red Book*, all produced in 1971. There are also dozens of new or edited entries made possible thanks to ongoing, evolving research. For example, more specific connections are made between a rambling, recognizably canted speech in a courtroom setting in Episode 3 and T.S. Eliot's *The Waste Land*. There are also many more references to contemporary persons, activities, and the zeitgeist of the period from contemporary newspaper pages (the Pythons' response to Enoch Powell's racially charged speech in 1968 mirrored op-ed page anger during the same period); more moments of art imitating life, including parliamentary discussion of slippery door-to-door salesmen and their code of conduct (Ep. 5); many more identifications of film shooting (and photo) locations—alien blancmanges change men into Scotsmen at 19 Southmere Terrace, Bradford (Ep. 7), funeral workers struggle up Harrogate Street, also in Bradford (Ep. 11), Erik Njorl rides through downtown Twickenham (Ep. 27), the Tudor Job Agency can be found at 280 Uxbridge Road (Ep. 36), the lovable losers in *Up Your Pavement* amble up Cowick Street in Exeter (Ep. 42); and more identifications of not only Gilliam's artwork materials (including each Civil War figure and photo employed), but identification of, often, a copy of the actual source titles Gilliam borrowed from his local library for photocopy purposes. Lastly, glaring mistakes have been corrected where necessary, including Bradford Stadium being called Brentford Stadium, *sorry*, and the correct spelling of "Leibniz," among others.

All this in mind, this edition is a far more complete, correct, and readable experience. It's hoped that this venture into an admittedly popular-culture-meets-academia world will be appreciated for what it is—a close, rigorous but still friendly reading of a cultural phenomenon. Shakespeare was the talented, ambitious "upstart Crow" in 1592, and Hitchcock was for many years simply a competent director of pulpy genre films—both have transcended those early straits to become the respected, acculturating institutions they are today. Whither Monty Python? The *OED* accepted "Pythonesque" into its 1989 edition, after all. There were dozens of funny and influential shows on British television, but *Flying Circus* managed to live well beyond not only its natural lifespan and other shows' popularity—but its "Englishness" has ingrained itself into our cultural lexicon along the way. The following pages explore *Monty Python's Flying Circus*'s longevity, complexity, and reflexivity, and promise an illuminating read.

SEASON ONE

Episode 1: "Whither Canada?"

"It's" Man ocean intro; *Animation: Titles* (calm Cleese v/o); "Good Evening" and sit on a pig; Crossed-Out Pig; "It's Wolfgang Amadeus Mozart" ("famous deaths" of Genghis Khan; scoreboard with Eddie Waring; "request death"; death of Admiral Nelson); Evening Class: Italian Lesson; *Animation: Escaping Pig and Whizzo Butter*; Whizzo Butter and a dead crab on-the-street interview; *"It's the Arts"*: The Films of Sir Edward Ross; Shoot the Pig Link; Pigs 3 Nelson 1; Arthur "Two Sheds" Jackson interview; Tough Interviewers link; Bicycling Picasso map link; Picasso Cycling Race (modern artists at the Tolworth Roundabout); Pig head link from the *"It's the Arts"* studio; *Animation: "Sit up!" photos*; Dead Pig link; **The Funniest Joke in the World** (Ernest Scribbler; Britain's great pre-war joke; German V-Joke); Referee whistle into "It's" Man closing credits

• A •

"A272 . . . Hindhead" — ("Picasso/Cycling Race") The A272 is far south of Hindhead, which *is* on the A3—the A3 continues on north and east into London.

"AA" — ("Picasso/Cycling Race") British Automobile Association, established in London in 1905. The organization doesn't regularly follow celebrity bicycle races, and will be mentioned prominently again in Ep. 44, when Mrs. S.C.U.M. (Jones) is wondering where to pay her AA bill after the impending nuclear holocaust.

"angel-drawers" — (*"It's the Arts"*) A variation of other terms like "angel face," and may also be an ironic term, since Ross doesn't appear terribly angelic or cherubic (see *OED*). This sketch is also an early indication of the "thesaurus sketch" structure as often created by the Cleese and Chapman writing team—in this instance multiple terms of endearment. The homoerotic subtext is apparent, though this subtext will be undercut by the interviewer's loss of interest as the interview concludes, then re-engaged in the exchange between interviewers off-camera.

In *At Last the 1948 Show* (1967), Cleese and Chapman had contributed a similarly homosocial linking element set in a courtroom, where the barrister (Cleese) asks: "Where were you on the evening of the 14th of July?" Chapman responds defensively, "Why?" Cleese then answers, petulant and pouty, "Well, I waited up all night for you and you never came home!"

Python's penchant for undercutting almost any proposition forwarded by the text/performance will become a hallmark of the show's structure.

animation — (PSC; link out of *"It's the Arts"*) Prior to this Gilliam animation mentioned in the printed script, a five-section collage of artists and artwork appears, with the screen divided into fourths and a circular frame in the middle. In each of these spaces is projected a motion picture image. The upper left image appears to be a filmed image of Henry Moore at work (1898–1986), an English sculptor of the human form, including *Reclining Figure* (1939) (Wilkinson, *ODNB*). The bottom right image is a painter using a wide trowel or spatula, and could be Franz Kline (1910–1962), an American abstract expressionist. The lower left image could be violinist Yehudi Menuhin (1916–1999), who will be mentioned again in Ep. 31, as a judge in the "Summarize Proust" competition. The central image is a symphony orchestra, and could be the Royal Philharmonic Orchestra in the Royal Albert Hall. This collage is probably meant to serve as the closing "shot" for the *It's the Arts* program begun much earlier. The Gilliam animation interrupts before any credits can roll.

The music used underneath this arts image is from "Saturday Sports" by Wilfred Burns, played by the National Light Orchestra. "Saturday Sports" was the well-known theme of the BBC television show *Sportsview* (1954–1968), which featured Brian Johnston, the wildly popular cricket commentator mentioned later in Eps. 21 and 45. Music used in the ensuing animation (accompanying Gilliam's animated photos) includes "All the Fun of the Fairground" played on the 89-key "marenghi" fair organ (WAC T12/1,082). The titles/credits for *Sportsview* were structured much like the paneled titles used in *It's the Arts*.

All of the music and film stock cues used in the show are listed, by episode, in the appendices: appendix A lists stock film clips and still images and appendix B lists recorded and live music cues.

"Ardennes" — ("The Funniest Joke in the World") Why the six-month delay, if the joke was ready by January? The Battle of the Ardennes was fought between 16 December 1944 and 16 January 1945. In July 1944, the Battle of the Bulge (becoming the more popular name for the period) was under way, the last German ground offensive on the Western Front, and American and British forces were enjoying some success before a slowdown in autumn 1944. In Python's world, then, the Killer Joke turned the tide of war on the Western Front, effectively ending the Nazi threat in Europe.

"Awful" — (PSC; "The Funniest Joke in the World") This type of joke—a set-up followed by rim-shot payoff—is the very kind of comedy that the Pythons had said they were reacting against as they fashioned *Flying Circus*. Whenever a character in *FC* makes or attempts to make such a joke, he/she is stopped mid-payoff (often fatally), or punished after the fact. In Ep. 18, when the Gents are trying to escape being "caught on film," one urges the others to "Run this way!" One (Idle) answers: "If I could run that way —." He is cut off by the raised fingers of the others, meaning that kind of joke won't be tolerated, and he stops, understanding completely.

In this the Pythons are also moving away from one of their hero groups, the Goons, who were not above delivering, without apology, these kinds of puns and "boom-boom" jokes in the mélange of their physical and cerebral comedy. Example: A character (played by Harry Secombe) is hiding inside the piano in the sketch "Napoleon's Piano." He is discovered, and another character (played by Peter Sellers) asks him what he's doing in the piano. "I'm hidin'," the man answers. "No, you're not," the questioner retorts. "Haydn's been dead for years." The audience responds well to this set-up–payoff joke structure, and the show moves briskly forward.

• B •

"Battersea" — ("Picasso/Cycling Race") South side of the Thames in Wandsworth borough. The nearest major circular (roundabout) seems to be somewhat west and south of Battersea at the confluence of the A27 and the A3205 in Wandsworth Town.

The mammoth, iconic, four-stacked Battersea Power Station is clearly visible over the housetops in Ep. 12, during the "Upperclass Twit" sketch.

Raymond Baxter type — (PSC; "Picasso/Cycling Race") Baxter (b. 1922) introduced the *University Challenge* program on BBC in 1963, and was a presenter on *Tomorrow's World*, a BBC science and technology program, from 1965–1977. His "type" wears a winter coat, hat, horn-rimmed glasses, and small mustache. He cuts a similar figure to the "Eddie Waring" caricature depicted earlier.

beach — ("It's Man" introduction) The beach where the "It's Man" comes ashore is located at Poole Harbour, Dorset, about ninety miles southeast of London. Palin takes viewers back to this setting some twenty years later in the *Pythonland* special show made for the BBC in 1989.

The Pythons and BBC scheduled multiple location shots for this type of excursion, shooting as many exterior locations for future episodes (links and entire sketches/films) as possible. In this same sand dune area, for instance, several exteriors for "The Funniest Joke in the World" and the "Genghis Khan" scenes were shot.

"Berkshire" — ("The Funniest Joke in the World") Home to Windsor Castle, Eton College, and some of England's most prestigious families, Berkshire is an area bounded by Hampshire, Wiltshire, Oxfordshire, Buckinghamshire, and Surrey in the south-central part of England. The Pythons probably chose Berkshire as the Joke's burial place due to nearby Salisbury Plain's military installations and training grounds.

This shot was not recorded in the Berkshire countryside, but in the meadows outside of Saxmundham, Suffolk, on 22 August 1969 (WAC T12/1,083).

"biblical laments" — ("The Funniest Joke in the World") Laments are conventional, ritualized forms of mourning, and here referring to the *Book of Lamentations* in the Old Testament, which details the Chaldean destruction of Jerusalem.

The Chaldeans will be significant again, mentioned in Ep. 43, "Police Helmets."

bizarre things happen — (PSC; "Opening Titles") Gilliam's modus operandi for constructing his title and interstitial animations included both "found" images and created images and sequences. The found images included cutouts from art books, magazines, advertisements, newspapers, and even comic books, as well as postcards and unidentified family photos. More Gilliam-penned backgrounds and purpose-drawn characters also appeared as the series progressed. In this opening sequence (which was changed after season one ended, then again after season two, etc.), the identifiable "found" images in these first season title animations include the following, in essentially the order each appears:

1. The husband bouncing his wife is a retouched, manipulated version of *Govaert van Surpele and His Wife* (1636–1638), by Jacob Jordaens (1593–1678), a celebrated Flemish baroque artist. Gilliam has reversed the sitting position of the wife from the original.
2. The three lovelies emerging from the man's head are likely from Gilliam's collection of "naughty" postcards. Some of these postcards and photos can be seen in *Ronnie Barker's Book of Bathing Beauties* (London: Hodder & Stoughton, 1974).
3. A retouched (wheeled) version of the painting *Cardinal de Richelieu* (c. 1640) by Philippe de Champaigne (1602–1674). This work is also part of the National Gallery collection.
4. A background (behind the Cardinal), perspectival drawing of an abbey nave by Jan Vredeman de Vries (1527–c. 1604), labeled as Plate 47 in de Vries' collection *Perspective*, originally published in 1604 and 1605. The Dover edition had been published in 1968 (and which Gilliam may have owned), the year before *Flying Circus* was first written and produced.
5. A cutout of what looks to be a Liverpool-Manchester train and passenger car from the 1830s. The nude draped across the passenger car could be from any of the men's magazines (*Mayfair, Spontan, Tip Top*) seen later in Eps. 9 and 36.
6. A single, tinted frame from the 1896 Thomas Edison film *The Kiss*, starring May Irwin and John Rice.
7. A model (cutout) from a Madame Dowding corset advertisement found in 19th-century magazines and newspapers. (This model pulls one of her straps, inflating her corset like a Mae West life jacket, and pops her head off.)
8. The corset model's head disrupts the five floating cherubs, which are borrowed from the Nicolas Poussin (1594–1665) painting *Adoration of the Shepherds* (c. 1633).
9. The reclining nude (with the headband) is also likely from the Barker collection of naughty Edwardian photos, while the buildings behind and around her are from another J.V. de Vries's perspective drawing, specifically Plate 42. The far background buildings and a midground bridge have been removed, as have all the streets between the buildings. Gilliam will use de Vries's work again in Ep. 17 (in the "How to Give Up Being a Mason" animation) and in *Holy Grail*, during the "Bloody Weather" animation. The reclining nude is used again by Gilliam on page 18 of *Monty Python's Big Red Book* (Methuen, 1971).

The final images in this opening title sequence are the foot crushing the *Monty Python's Flying Circus* title, and the image of God "shushing" from above. The foot is from the Bronzino painting *An Allegory with Venus and Cupid* (c. 1540–1550), and the God figure is lifted from *The Immaculate Conception* by Carlo Gravelli (1492). Gilliam borrowed Cupid's right foot for the title sequence. Both the Bronzino and Gravelli have been displayed in the National Gallery in London for many years.

The "bizarre things happen" script comment means that the Pythons doing most of the writing (Chapman, Cleese, Idle, Jones, and Palin) would have been given only the scarcest of outlines for the proposed Gilliam animation sequence, and many times all they knew was that Gilliam was working on something thematically connected to the episode.

"black oval shapes" — (PSC; "Picasso / Cycling Race") This description could be referring to abstract Kandinsky paintings like *Black Spot I* (1912), *Ravine Improvisation* (1914), or *Cossacks* (1910–1911). *Cossacks* has been in the Tate's collection since 1938. Kandinsky gave himself over to abstract painting with the formation of the Munich group Der Blaue Reiter / The Blue Rider (1911–1914).

"blimey" — (PSC; "Famous Deaths") A common corruption of "blame me" or "blind me," and probably earlier from "God blame me" and / or "God blind me." Also, certainly incongruous and anachronistic that Mozart would utter such a word, since it is very much a British slang and wasn't coined (according to the *OED*) until the 1890s.

blow-up behind — (PSC; "Arthur 'Two-Sheds' Jackson") During this transition into the "Two-Sheds" Jackson interview on the typical two-chair set, a portion of the "Allegro Vivace" section of Beethoven's Symphony No. 4 plays beneath.

BP screen — (PSC; linking element) *B*ack *P*rojection screen. A projector throws a filmed image from behind onto a see-through screen, thus "back projection" or "back projected." This technology has become outdated with the advent of TV chroma-key technology, etc.

"Brancusi" — ("Picasso/Cycling Race") Constantin Brancusi (1876–1957) was actually a sculptor, which really would have been a feat during a bicycle race. He was an abstractionist, and in the *FC* text he is cleverly described as "making a break on the outside." His *Bird in Space*, for example, wasn't even recognized as a work of art when it came to the United States for the first time in 1927, and was taxed (at a 40 percent rate) as a piece of industrial metal (*Time*, 7 Mar. 1927). The Tate Gallery first collected a Brancusi sculpture in 1959.

"Braque" — ("Picasso/Cycling Race") Georges Braque (1882–1963) was a colleague and competitor to Picasso, and practiced a more lyrical Cubism. He featured the bird motif in a number of his later works, including *Falconeers*, *Frontispiece* (1952), and especially *Untitled (3 birds)* (1955), *Untitled (flock birds)* (1955), and *Untitled (black bird)* (1955). Braque also produced the painting *Bicycle* (1952), depicting a bicycle in a forested area, with flowers and an open field in the background. This last painting may even have had some influence on the juxtaposition of bicycling and painting in the Python creation process for this episode. The Tate collected Braque works as early as 1926, and acquired at least two in the 1960s.

"Buffet, Bernard" — ("Picasso/Cycling Race") Painter and printmaker Buffet (1928–1999) was influenced by the existentialist movement; his work was also Passion-oriented, and influenced by the hardships of the post-WWII era. In 1970 the Pope asked for and received—from the artist—a collection of Buffet works depicting the life of Christ. Buffet may be the most marginally known of all these artists, at least in the UK, which may just mean that he was a personal favorite of one of the Pythons.

The Tate Gallery collected Buffet's *Portrait of the Artist* (1954) in 1955, and then it would be thirty years before a second Buffet work would join the Tate's significant collection of Modern Art.

". . . but which the Germans could" — ("The Funniest Joke in the World") This scenario is reminiscent of wartime endeavors on both sides of the battle, including radar, the Manhattan Project for atomic weaponry, the German atomic research programs (heavy water [D_2O] research, etc.), as well as rocket and jet air warfare technology, etc.

• C •

caption — (PSC; "Famous Deaths") These captions are superimposed on the screen. Python's use of historical figures and settings will become essential to the structure and humor of *FC*. In this case, the incongruity of an eighteenth-century composer hosting a television show provides the jumping-off point for the sketch's humor. In most cases, there is no attempt to explain or account for the presence of long-dead figures, or characters separated by geography, time, or culture, as they interact or just appear in modern settings. This also becomes a Python trope, and reflects the significant influence that seminal Modernist works like Eliot's *The Waste Land*—where class and accent, the past and present, and even cultures and languages interact in a sort of ever-present, decaying London—exhibited in the works of Monty Python. Eliot's play *Murder in the Cathedral* (1935) will be referenced in Ep. 28.

Under this particular caption can be heard music from one of Mozart's quartets, "Pression No. 3," probably referring to Quartet No. 3 (WAC T12/1,082, 5 Oct. 1969).

"Carr, Vicki" — (closing credits) An American-born singer, Carr had performed in 1967 at a Royal Command Performance for Queen Elizabeth.

"Chagall" — ("Picasso/Cycling Race") Russian-born Marc Chagall (1887–1985) combined influences of Expressionism, Cubism, the bright colors of Fauvism, etc., and his early experiences of simple folk life and persecution as a Jew.

The Tate Gallery acquired at least seven Chagall paintings between 1942 and 1953, all of which are still part of the museum's impressive collection of Modern Art.

"Chichester" — ("Picasso/Cycling Race") Town on the A27 in West Sussex county, eighteen miles east of Portsmouth, and north of Chichester Harbour. In Ep. 10, Ron Obvious (Jones) will attempt to eat the Chichester Cathedral. The Chichester Festival is mentioned in Ep. 25, when a Shakespearean actor overplaying the Richard III role is admitted into hospital, to be operated on "just in time."

clearly labelled — (PSC; "The Funniest Joke in the World") This sign-carrying acts as both a means of instant identification and a source for incongruous humor. The silliness of the self-conscious signs may also help shake the stigma that depictions of the Nazis might still have engendered on British television and for British viewers, especially in comedic settings.

In the earliest days of cinematic animation, artists like Winsor McCay, William Nolan, and Raoul Barré regularly employed long-standing comic strip conventions, including labels and thought/dialogue balloons, etc. While at Warner Bros. in the 1930s Tex Avery used some of these same conventions, especially the sign-holding character ("Corny gag, isn't it?"). In this Gestapo scene the signs appear much like those used in the 1952 Bugs Bunny/Marvin Martian cartoon *Hasty Hare* (dir. Chuck Jones). After being captured by the Martians, Bugs is trussed up and labeled "One Overconfident Earth Creature." Later Bugs escapes and ties up Marvin and his dog, K-9, their labels reading "Two Disgruntled Martians."

"Cleveland, Carol" — (closing credits) Unofficial cast member Cleveland (b. 1942) appears here in the credits for Ep. 1, but not in the actual episode. She appears first in Ep. 2, which actually was recorded first but aired second. The credit sequence may have been created for the initial episode, then appended to this episode as it moved into the premier spot.

Cleveland had also posed with the Pythons for several of their publicity photos during the writing and recording of the initial episodes. This inclusion was clearly the BBC's attempt to broaden the show's demographic potentialities, and to be in line with the mixed cast structures of recent successful comedy shows such as *Do Not Adjust Your Set* (1967–1969), *At Last the 1948 Show* (1967), and the American hits *Your Show of Shows* (1950–1954) and *Laugh-In* (1968). The television work of Sid Caesar (b. 1922) and Imogene Coca (1908–2001) came to British audiences' attention for the first time in July 1958, when *Sid Caesar Invites You* appeared on the BBC. (The *Times*, by the way, gave the show a "right padding.")

"comfort" — (PSC; "Arthur 'Two-Sheds' Jackson") Homosocial or homosexual? The significant number of allusions to male homosexuality in *FC* become all the more intriguing as the homosexuality of Graham Chapman is considered. Chapman himself plays some of the most "flaming" and outré characters and, conversely, shoots and kills the admittedly gay Algy (Palin) in Ep. 33, the "Biggles Dictates a Letter Sketch."

The significance of the Stonewall riots in June 1969 in Greenwich Village, New York, have to be considered when discussing the presence of obvious or even flamboyant gay characters in popular culture, and for our purposes, on public television. When New York police raided the known gay bar, the Stonewall Inn, beating cross-dressed and effeminate patrons and sparking a series of street riots, the once-hidden world of sexually active gay men (and, to a lesser degree, lesbians and the transgendered) was splashed across newspapers and evening news reports (see D'Emilio; Duberman). Just two months later the Pythons would record their first episodes, and the following month (October 1969) those episodes begin to air. Essentially, the very public and disturbing police and mob actions gave indirect license to the Pythons (and other creative entities, of course) to cross what may have been formerly an unfordable Rubicon—the redemptive depiction and gentle comedic ribbing of gay characters.

Finally, the "Queer TV Database" lists gay characters appearing or who have appeared on British television, and the absences are quite telling. There are none listed for the 1950s, just seven for the 1960s (none of which seemed to be flaunting their sexuality), then twenty-seven in the decade of the 1970s. (The seven in the 1960s include roommates Bert and Ernie of *Sesame Street* fame, so the delimiting factors for inclusion in the database might be questionable.)

commentator — (PSC; "The Funniest Joke in the World") This man (Jones) is dressed in typical period attire for a newscaster—suit, tie, horn-rimmed glasses—so we are still in the present, assumedly. The timeline will quickly dissolve, however, and we will be back in the WWII era for the balance of the sketch.

"commissioned painting" — ("Picasso/Cycling Race") Probably the most famous of Picasso's commissioned works was the mural requested by the Spanish Republican government in 1937—a work which ultimately became *Guernica*—for the Spanish Pavilion of the Paris Exposition. Picasso also painted the commissioned work *Stage Curtain for the Ballet "Parade"* (1917), and even the dove symbol commissioned by the Communist Party for the World Peace Congress in 1949.

Additionally, BBC Radio and TV had been commissioning musical pieces, radio serials, and television shows since their beginnings, though admittedly few modern art paintings.

(cyclists pass in front of him) — (PSC; "Picasso/Cycling Race") This frantic race set-up—cyclists whizzing past to the announcer's play-by-play—was earlier employed by the Goons in "The Great Bank Robbery" (15 Nov. 1956):

> Announcer (Sellers): Well, hello folks. Here we are at Cobb's Corner, a bare half mile from the finishing post of the Tour de Britain five-day bass drum race. And here, here comes Stirling Moss beating a 1926 all wood British racing drum, followed closely by Sheila van Damm beating her highly tuned father, and . . . What's this now? Yes! Yes! My goodness me, they're really coming along here! It's a wonderful day! You can see them all beating their drums as they come . . .! Yes, that was the Italian ace—Giuseppe Fred Sapone, thundering into the straits of the sticks of a very fast sports drum. So over now to the finishing line!

Both Stirling Moss (b. 1929) and Sheila van Damm (1922–1987) were racing drivers, and van Damm was also well known to both the Goons and the Pythons as the owner, with her father, Vivian van Damm (1895–1960), of the Windmill Theatre, where several of the Goons received their show business baptisms, and where comedians, musicians, and nude tableaux vivants and acts graced the stage.

• D •

"d'Arc, Jean" — ("Famous Deaths") Joan of Arc (1412–1431), also called Saint Joan, answered a divine call and led the French army to victory at Orléans during the Hundred Years' War. She was captured by the English (with the help of French collaborators), and was burned at the stake. Transcripts of the trial are extant (and fascinating), and were the basis of Carl Dreyer's celebrated 1932 film on Joan. She was canonized in 1920.

"Day, Robin" — (*"It's the Arts"* and "Arthur 'Two-Sheds' Jackson") Later in this same episode, when another Interviewer (Idle) is having trouble with an interviewee (Arthur "Two-Sheds" Jackson, played by Jones), the interviewers will gang up and throw Jackson from the studio set. This overtly aggressive and physical characterization is almost certainly based on the reputation earned by well-known Independent Television News (ITN) and BBC interviewer Robin Day (1923–2000), who created for himself an intense, pointed interview style, especially with previously almost untouchable government figures—including heads of state, members of Parliament, and even PM Macmillan in February 1959—asking direct questions and accepting only similarly direct and ingenuous answers. Day is credited with inventing the modern television interview. (For more on Day see his entry in the *ODNB*.) He stood for Parliament for the Liberal Party from Hereford in 1959, and lost. (The Liberal Party will be the focus of Ep. 45.)

See the fine columns/obituaries written about Day and published in *The Guardian* (8 Aug. 2000). In the setting of the sketch, the interviewers become almost Western heroes cleaning up Dodge or Tombstone.

"Dead March" — (PSC; "The Funniest Joke in the World") Actually called "Funeral March," this version of the Beethoven work was arranged by Mayhew Lake (WAC T12/1,082).

"De Kooning" — ("Picasso/Cycling Race") Willem De Kooning (1904–1997), a Dutch painter, was also a member of the New York School (see Pollock note below) and an "action" painter, alternating between "abstract and figural painting" (Tansey, 860).

By 1969 the Tate Gallery could claim three De Kooning works as part of its collection, two of which were donated in 1969 by the painter himself, through the American Federation of Arts. The paintings which the Pythons could have viewed during this period in the Tate were completed in 1966–1967, some of the latest work cited in this sketch.

"Delaunay" — ("Picasso/Cycling Race") Robert Delaunay, born in France (1885–1941), is credited with introducing vibrant colors into Cubism, leading to Orphism. Like Kandinsky, Delaunay was also a member of the Blue Rider movement.

The Tate had purchased two Delaunay works prior to the writing of this episode, one in 1958 (*Study for "The City,"* 1909–1910), and the other in 1967 (*Windows Open Simultaneously*, 1912).

"Derby-Doncaster rally" — ("Picasso/Cycling Race") Derby and Doncaster are about fifty miles apart, and the presumed route might be north on the A38 to the A61 to the A630, and into Doncaster. No such race appears to have existed.

"Der ver . . ." — ("The Funniest Joke in the World") A swipe at Germany's wartime propaganda beamed into Great Britain over the radio waves, where in this case the English syntax seems to have confused the Nazi translators:

> Radio Voice: There were two peanuts walking down the street, and one was a salted . . . peanut.

The confused looks on the faces of the Ma and Pa Britain listeners (Chapman and Idle) tell the whole story, and may have been the actual response of many Brits and especially Londoners who heard the Third Reich's attempts at persuasion by broadcast propaganda.

Words in the joke like "ver" ("were"), "valking" ("walking"), "peanuts" ("peanuts"), "von" ("one"), and "vas" ("was") are not, of course, actual German words, but Python's jabberwocky German.

There were significant attempts at such broadcast propaganda by the Third Reich during the war, including UK citizen William Joyce, known as "Lord Haw-Haw," who made light of the German threat to Great Britain in the late 1930s, and was listened to (and enjoyed) by millions in the UK. He was also an active, vocal member of the British Union of Fascists before the war, and would become a naturalized German during the war. Joyce would be hanged for treason after the war. According to a surviving BBC internal memo dated 16 November 1939, the BBC's counteraction to these popular and subtly effective propaganda broadcasts was to create its own homespun version of the war effort, and broadcast at the same times as the enemy. (See the "BBC at War" sections of bbc.co.uk.)

Deutschland Über Alles — (PSC; "The Funniest Joke in the World") "German, Germany Above (Over) All." German national anthem (1922–present), with music by Haydn, and text by von Fallersleben. This version is drawn from the album *Hitler's Inferno: In Words and Music 1932–1945—Marching Songs of Nazi Germany* (WAC T12/1,082).

"Dibley Road" — ("The Funniest Joke in the World") No such road exists. The setting, however, seems to be the same one used in the "Dull Life of a City Stockbroker" sketch in Ep. 6, as well. Production notes for the episode indicate that this is 48 Ullswater Road, Barnes (WAC T12/1,083).

According to Palin, this name ("Dibley") comes from the "Gwen Dibley's Flying Circus" title that Palin had brought to the table as one possible name for the show (Morgan 1999, 26).

"Different Gestapo Officer" — (PSC; "The Funniest Joke in the World") The transparent use of signs, names, and labels to make one thing or person into another is a Python staple, and was probably a holdover from the vaudeville and music hall stages, and even Warner Bros. cartoons. Cf. the "Dead Parrot" sketch in Ep. 8, "The Chemist Sketch" in Ep. 17, and the "Conquistador Coffee Campaign" sketch in Ep. 24 for similar sign usage.

"Dobson's" — (linking element into "The Funniest Joke in the World") A name possibly borrowed from the Beerbohm 1911 novel, *Zuleika Dobson*. See entry for "know what I like" in Ep. 4 for more on this intriguing possible connection.

This entire sketch is something of a rare linking element to the eventual WWII-era setting of the latter part of the "The Funniest Joke in the World" sketch, foreshadowing the military applications of the lethal joke. It is rare because very few of the *FC* linking elements are anything more than a single person or image, completely decontextualized and distinct from the narrative action at hand. This one is much more of a smoothing device to propel us into the WWII setting of the following and abnormally lengthy sketch. The famous picture of Churchill flashing the "V for victory" hand sign adorns the wall behind, and the link between his ample face and the pigs on the map can't be missed. (Remember, Churchill would fall out of the public's favor very quickly after the war ended, being seen as an innovative wartime leader but a peacetime throwback to the Victorian era. Labour and Clement Attlee picked up 239 seats in the sweeping 1945 General Election, as well as almost 50 percent of the popular vote, and the Conservatives were out of power until 1951.)

Curiously, there is also a small "action figure" standing next to the map table, one clearly requested in the design requirements for the episode. The figure is a striped-shirt robber type, with mask and a gun, and made of balsa wood. It's well out of place, visually and thematically, and not referenced in the short scene at all (WAC T12/1,082). Cleese will dress just this way, however, in the "Bank Robber (Lingerie Shop)" sketch in Ep. 10. The model will finally appear in Ep. 13, in the "*Probe-Around* on Crime" sketch.

"Dufy, Raoul" — ("Picasso/Cycling Race") Dufy (1877–1953) created bright, colorful paintings (Fauvist and Impressionist influences), many of scenes of pleasure. See Tansey.

By late 1969 the Tate Gallery held two Dufy watercolors, *Olive Trees by the Golfe Juan* (c. 1927) and *Deauville, Drying the Sails* (1933).

• E •

"Eddie" — (PSC; "Famous Deaths") The written script earlier identifies this character as an "Eddie Waring figure," though he is clearly supposed to be Eddie himself by the time Mozart (Cleese) thanks him. He is an "announcer type" or "presenter" characteristic of British TV then and now, thus a key figure in *FC's* television parody format. See the note for Waring below.

"Edward the Seventh, King" — ("Famous Deaths") Edward VII (1841–1910) was Queen Victoria's eldest son, and is the only participant on the list to have died a somewhat natural death, which probably accounts for his low score (see "back marker" below). After his father Albert's death in 1861, Edward took on larger responsibilities as his mother grieved in seclusion, though political control was kept from him until he ascended the throne in 1901. His son, George V, succeeded him in 1910. See the *ODNB*.

Edward is slighted as the "back marker": "One who starts from scratch or has the least favorable handicap in a game, match or race" (*OED*). "Bertie's" death was much less dramatic, memorable, and/or tragic than any of the others, his life was characterized by his own epicurean profligacies, being blamed by his mother for his father's early demise, and he finally had the wretched bad luck of following his mother, the iconic and beloved Victoria, onto the throne.

It's likely no coincidence that as recently as late March 1969 the *Times* was reporting on a monograph celebrating the advent of the new Kinemacolor film process in Britain, and that one of the more spectacular color films from 1909 was the funeral of Edward VII (24 Mar. 1969: 15).

Episode 1 — This episode was actually recorded second, on 9 July 1969, then broadcast first on 5 October 1969. (The subtitle "Whither Canada?" is also the lone reference to Canada in the episode.) The stated budget for this episode was £4,000, then £3,800 for each subsequent show, according to Michael Mills of Light Entertainment. He would end the 31 July 1969 budget memo, written to John Howard Davies and Ian MacNaughton: "You have heard the word of the Lord . . . please heed it." (By way of comparison, the fourth and final season episodes had bloated to more than £100,000 per episode) (WAC T12/1,083).

Also, this episode was taped at the BBC Television Centre on Stage 6, with very few extras or walk-ons. The show was often bumped around from soundstage to soundstage as other more known or respected shows needed the space. On several occasions the show actually had to leave TV Centre and tape, for example, at Golders Green Hippodrome or Ealing Television-Film Studios. There are mentions of these somewhat capricious shuttlings in the day-to-day memos and notes found in the BBC's Written Archive Collection.

Lastly, this episode was sub-subtitled at the end of the typed graphics credits page, "A new comedy series for the Switched On." This subtitle did not appear in the finished episode (WAC T12/1,082).

"Ernst, Max" — (Picasso/Cycling Race") Ernst (1891–1976) was originally a Dadaist, then moved to Surrealism and the freedom of "chance associations" in his work (Tansey, 830).

There were four Ernst works available for viewing in the Tate Gallery in 1969.

"evergreen bucket kickers" — ("Famous Deaths") An indication that Lord Nelson continues to be a fascinating (and much-trumpeted) English historical figure, looming large in the elementary and secondary school history classrooms, undoubtedly. The phrase means simply a "favorite" or "popular" ("evergreen") public figure death, in this case one that has burrowed its way into English culture.

Nelson's name would have been in the news fairly recently, and spectacularly, when the Nelson Pillar in Dublin (erected in 1808) was blown up by Irish Republican forces in 1966, and had to be demolished completely. There are extant a number of political cartoons addressing the subject, including one from Keith Waite (*Sun*, 9 Mar. 1966), wherein Lord Nelson unexpectedly alights from his lofty column to read, concernedly, the Dublin newspaper headlines.

"Ewhurst" — ("Picasso/Cycling Race") City in Surrey County on the B2127, and where Picasso is seemingly way off course when he crashes. His attempted shortcut "through Dorking via Gomslake and Peashall" is either cheating or simply impossible, since the towns in question are actually "Gomshall" and "Peaslake," with Dorking farther along the A25.

• F •

"fairy" — ("Arthur 'Two-Sheds' Jackson") Slang for a male homosexual. The term isn't used nearly as often in *FC* as some other homosexual put-downs, like "poof" and its derivatives. The term wouldn't be as significant except that the interviewers are about to share—off-camera but within earshot—a very homosocial/homosexual moment. In the context of this scene, then, a "fairy" is a man who allows himself to be given the bum's rush (pun slightly intended) by more "butch" gay men. The term will be used again, and prominently, in Ep. 33 when Captain Biggles (Chapman) asks Ginger (Gilliam) if he's gay, and in Ep. 13, where policemen become fairies with magic wands.

film of Hitler rally — (PSC; "The Funniest Joke in the World") This series of Hitler images is taken from a Pathé newsreel, Ref. No. 139, while the crowd scenes are lifted from "WWII Nuremberg Rally" footage from Associated British Pathé (BBC WAC T12/1,082).

This speech sequence is originally from *Triumph of the Will* (1935), and was delivered to the Reich Labor Service on the second day of the 1934 Nazi Party Congress gathering at Nuremberg. The shots aren't sequential, since the Pythons needed an edited version that sounded and looked like a set-up and pay-off structure for a music hall joke. Hitler's first line is approximately two-thirds of a complete sentence: "And in particular no one will live in Germany. . . ." The young man's enthusiastic response: "We are the Reich's young men," is followed by the punch line, which is actually fairly boring, and just a portion of this stirring sentence: "The whole nation will be educated by you."

"Fontwell" — ("Picasso/Cycling Race") On the A27 in West Sussex, five miles west of Arundel. The A29 doesn't run to or from Chichester, however, being a north-south route between Bognor Regis and Fontwell. Picasso would then have to stay on the A29 northward to Billingshurst, where the A29 meets the A272, a major east-west road.

• G •

"gate in the country overlooking a field" — ("Flying Sheep") This scene—gentlefolk leaning against a white fence in an idyllic northern setting, admiring the fields of green—is a tableau drawn almost directly from the more pastoral moments of novelist Thomas Hardy and perhaps especially D.H. Lawrence. Both authors will be specifically revisited in later episodes

(Eps. 17 and 2, respectively), and their *ethoi* referenced throughout *FC*.

In Lawrence's *Sons and Lovers* (1913), mother Gertrude and beloved son Paul strike a similar pose as they watch cricketers, and as Gertrude falls in love with her youngest son.

"Geneva Convention" — ("The Funniest Joke in the World") International agreements were made beginning about 1864 in Geneva, Switzerland, regarding conduct of combatants during times of war. Other kinds of Geneva Convention agreements include acceptable treatment of prisoners of war, civilians, and non-combatants, etc.

"Gerard's Cross" — (PSC; "Italian Lesson") Actually misspelled, it is correctly "Gerrards Cross," and is found in the county of Buckinghamshire, four miles northwest of Uxbridge, west of Greater London. This mention of a Greater London suburb elicits a laugh from the cobbled-together studio audience (who don't laugh much at all during this initial episode), perhaps just because the name is familiar. During this period, Gerrards Cross would have been located somewhat awkwardly, viz., its status as a recently incorporated town (1859), and its emerging attractiveness for London belt commuters.

"Gericault" — ("Picasso/Cycling Race") Theodore Gericault (1791–1824) is seemingly well out of place in this bicycling group of modern artists, as he preceded most of the other artists mentioned by several generations. He was influenced by Michelangelo and Rubens and worked in the Romantic movement. Perhaps Gericault's (and Romanticism's in general) fascination with the physiognomy of death and the insane allows his inclusion by the Pythons. (See Tansey 733–37.) Gericault is the only artist in this race to not have a significant, continuing presence in London museums or galleries during the Pythons' lifetimes. A 1965 *Times* article mentions this paucity in London galleries, the critic writing excitedly about the arrival of the "Géricault to Courbet" exhibition (at the Roland, Browse and Delbanco), where "no fewer than three works by Géricault" can be seen (8 June 1965: 13).

Gilliam's wonderfully visual mind — (PSC; "Whizzo Butter" link) Terry Gilliam's animated sequences appear throughout the *FC* series, and continue on into the feature films. At the time of the script rehearsals, Gilliam would have been off alone working on animated links, without consulting other cast members. He would have had a copy of the script, but none of the other Pythons knew, prior to taping, just what the links might look like or contain, thematically. This is why these scripts can only mention Gilliam and his work, and almost never describe it (though the collected scripts' editor, Roger Wilmut, could well have inserted descriptions, but chose not to). See Morgan's *Monty Python Speaks!* or Gilliam's *Gilliam on Gilliam* for more on Gilliam's animation process.

"gramophone records" — ("The Funniest Joke in the World") Both the gramophone (a vintage record player) and records are now considered at least classics, and antiquated. At the time, available technology for sound projection would have been limited to phonograph-type players and reel-to-reel tape players. By Ep. 26, a reel-to-reel player is used for similar sound projection.

This same kind of antiquated player will be mounted on a bicycle and used to broadcast Nazi propaganda and music in the "Minehead By-Election" sketch. See Ep. 12.

"Grazie . . . gentilezza" — ("Italian Lesson") Approximate translations for these sometimes mangled Italian phrases are as follows (only the translated lines are included):

Giuseppe: Il cucchiaio ("The spoon")
Teacher: Molto bene, Giuseppe ("Very well, Giuseppe")
Giuseppe: Grazie signor . . . grazie di tutta la sua gentilezza ("Thank you, Sir . . . thank you for your kindness")
All: Sono Inglese di Gerrard's Cross ("I am an Englishman from Gerrard's Cross")
Teacher: Sono Italiano di Napoli ("I am an Italian from Naples")
Mariolini: Ah, capisco, mille grazie signor ("Ah, I understand, many [thousand] thanks, sir")
Francesco: Per favore, Signor! ("Please, Sir!")
Francesco: Non conosgreve parliamente, signor devo me parlo sono Italiano di Napoli quando il habitare de Milano ("I don't understand this language, Sir. Why do I have to say I am an Italian from Naples when I live in Milan?")
Francesco: Milano è tanto meglio di Napoli. Milano è la citta la più bella di tutti . . . nel mondo ("Milan is much better than Naples. Milan is the most beautiful city in the world.")

As it turns out, the Pythons did fairly well with their probably limited Italian language skills, with only the "Non conosgreve" section exhibiting some "improper Italian," according to Maria Krull, Northern Illinois University, who provided these translations.

***"Guernica* . . . Vallauris"** — ("Picasso/Cycling Race") These are titles of Picasso works as rattled off by the cyclist Reg Moss (Chapman). *Guernica* is titled after the Spanish city bombed in 1937 by German planes as training for the nascent Nazi Blitzkrieg. *Guernica* is actually a mural painting, because of its size (approx.

11′6″ × 25′8″). *Les demoiselles d'Avignon* (actual title) is from 1907 and measures 8′ × 7′8″. At Vallauris, France, the National Picasso Museum contains the celebrated 1952 works *War* and *Peace*.

Secondly, how and why a sprint cyclist would have such intimate knowledge of the history of modern painting can only be answered by referring to Python's penchant for allowing characters (like the Pepperpots, for instance) access to knowledge well beyond their presented position or social station. Coal miners in Ep. 15 will understand classical architecture and European martial/treaty history, for instance; Pepperpots will argue about the true meanings of "freedom" in Sartre's existential masterworks in Ep. 27; and perhaps most famously, Middle Ages peasants will be given intricate knowledge of anarchosyndicalist political structures in the feature film *Monty Python and the Holy Grail* (1975).

"Guilford" — ("Famous Deaths") A town in Surrey, England, at a ford across the River Wey. Guilford is about 28 miles from London, so at least 228 miles from Hull, which means the Pythons probably just pulled names out of a hat when writing this section. With Palin hailing from the north, and several of the others raised in the Midlands, it's easy to see how certain place names might have been chosen based on childhood neighborhoods and regions.

Guilford will be mentioned again during the Picasso sketch ("the Guilford Bypass") as it actually sits astride the A3. No worthwhile bypass seems to have existed in this area, however, since the A3 dissects Guilford, and all other roads are much smaller.

"Guiseppe" — ("Italian Lesson") It's already clear that almost everyone in the classroom is Italian, and only the teacher seems to have missed this point. The irony of teaching introductory, conversational Italian to native Italians is the obvious joke, and it's compounded by Python's characteristic "comic misunderstanding" trope, thanks to the teacher's failure to recognize his students' nationalities. This comic misunderstanding occurs when peasants refuse to recognize kings, in the Python world, or when Thomas Dekker's lower-class characters consort with upper-class characters on the same social level, and without self-consciousness, in *The Shoemaker's Holiday* (1599). The tradition is also carried on in myriad eighteenth-century plays (e.g., Sheridan's *The Rivals*) and novels (Fielding's *Tom Jones*). See Larsen's *MPSERD*.

• H •

Ham House — (PSC; "The Funniest Joke in the World") The home of the Duke and Duchess of Lauderdale in the late seventeenth century, located in Ham, on Ham Street, Richmond, Greater London. It's not absolutely certain from the shot itself whether they actually used the location, since it is a rather tight close-up, though Ham House figures prominently in Ep. 2, so the re-use of the location would be likely. (See notes for "Osborne" in Ep. 2.) BBC production notes confirm that Ham House was, indeed, secured as the setting for several scenes (WAC T12/1,083).

"Harriers" — ("Picasso/Cycling Race") Interesting allusion, since the Manchester Harriers are and were a track-and-field club, not a cycling concern. (A harrier is a dog or a cross-country runner.) This YMCA club has been in existence since 1882.

"HEAVEN!" — ("Whizzo Butter" animation) The final word displayed in Gilliam's Whizzo Butter ad, the music behind this hard-sell moment is a sped-up version of the "Hallelujah Chorus" taken from "Handel's *Messiah* Highlights No. 44" (WAC T12/1,082).

"hedgehog" — (*"It's the Arts"*) An important member of the Python bestiary, by Ep. 14 an enormous hedgehog named Spiny Norman is stalking the notorious criminal Dinsdale Piranha.

The fact that Robin Day has a hedgehog isn't so surprising when looking forward to Praline's (Cleese) encounter with a Post Office Worker (Palin) in Ep. 23. There, it's revealed that Praline himself has a pet halibut, and that prominent public figures such as Sir Gerald Nabarro, Dawn Palethorpe, Alan Bullock, Marcel Proust, and Kemal Ataturk also claim special and oddly named pets. See notes to Ep. 23 for entries on each of these people.

"hospital" — ("The Funniest Joke in the World") This is also shot while on the dunes at Bournemouth, using the same tent seen in the "Genghis Khan" scene. "Mouse Problem" Vox Pops will also be shot on these dunes for Ep. 2. This kind of doubling, especially on locations where film shooting is scheduled, reduced production costs (or kept costs near what the BBC would allow), and will be seen throughout the run of the show. Note, for example, the various shots throughout the first, second, and third season that feature the rugged highlands of Scotland near Glencoe (including, for instance, the "Lemon curry?" inserts in Ep. 33).

"Hull" — ("Famous Deaths") Hull is 200 miles north of London, on the North Sea.

• I •

Indian-style background music — (PSC; "Famous Deaths") According to the music copyright requests for this episode, this piece is called "Tratalala Rhythm" (WAC T12/1,083).

"international cycling fame" — ("Picasso/Cycling Race") At the end of the Picasso sketch, Picasso has fallen and failed to successfully combine his art and cycling. The incongruous elements of this scene create humor, of course, but there's more here. The Python choice of modern painting (and art) and abstractionism overall is significant. The goals of the various movements in modern art (and the Modernist movement in general) tended to be (a) the examination and even shattering of the boundaries of figurative representation, and (b) to push outward the limits of what had been accepted as appropriate media and subject matter in the arts. This is true of painting as well as literature, film, music, and all the plastic arts. Python played with the plasticity of their medium—they understood well the manipulative elements—making demands of both the medium and the audience as they took their Modernist-*cum*-Postmodernist television presentation and re-presentation to new limits. What was said of Brancusi in his use of whatever sculpting material he selected could be said of Monty Python: they "extracted from the material . . . its maximum effect" (Tansey, 840).

interrogating him — (PSC; "The Funniest Joke in the World") This scene is perhaps inspired by similar scenes in films like Rossellini's *Rome: Open City*, or even popular BBC shows like *Spycatcher* (1959–1961), where Nazis were ferreted out by the intrepid Lt.-Col. Pinto. (The hero's name—Pinto—may also have inspired the Pythons as they named their own inspectors: Thompson's Gazelle, Fox, Baboon, Tiger, etc. See entries in Eps. 25 and 29 for more.)

"It's . . ." — (opening credits) Just after this utterance a bell sounds (probably a glockenspiel) and the show's theme music begins, the "Liberty Bell March" by John Philip Sousa, an American composer of martial music. The music was chosen, according to Palin and Gilliam, as these two sat and listened to many title song possibilities, with Gilliam saying that the initial bell sound was the clincher for him (see Johnson's *The First 20 Years of Monty Python*, 21–22).

"It's" man . . . back to the sea — (closing credits) This is one of the few episodes with such an identifiable beginning and ending, a neat book-ending, perhaps attributable to the show's position (first episode) in the series. Palin retreats here back into Poole Harbour, Dorset.

It's the Arts — ("*It's the Arts*") Would become a generic arts program title in a number of *FC* episodes, including Ep. 1 (*It's Wolfgang Amadeus Mozart*), Ep. 6, and Ep. 10, *It's a Tree* sketch. The titular use of "It's" is borrowed by Python from many British television shows, including *It's a Knockout* (BBC1, 1966).

• K •

"Kandinsky" — ("Picasso/Cycling Race") Russian-born Wassily Kandinsky (1866–1944) was one of the first pure abstractionists in modern painting. See the "black oval shapes" entry above for more on Kandinsky and his presence in London galleries.

The laundry list of twentieth-century artists competing in this race is significant, as these artists would have been shaking up the world of art, design, advertising, architecture, and even morality and culture as the Pythons were growing up and shaping their own sensibilities. Interesting also that Pythons would characterize the world of modern art as a heated contest, reflecting the competitive environment created and nurtured by the mass culture art world of the period. In fact, once the *l'art pour l'art* ("art for art's sake") period arrived in the postwar era, and especially into the 1960s, competition for gallery space and, therefore, commercial and public exposure, intensified significantly. See Hughes's *The Shock of the New* for a discussion of this phenomenon.

Also, here is a fine example of significant knowledge given to seemingly insignificant characters, like a Pepperpot (Palin), who in this case is able to identify modern painters by sight, and will later correct commentator Trench (Cleese) as to the proper nationality of German expatriate Kurt Schwitters. (Cf. Shakespeare's use of Dogberry and his associates in *Much Ado*, as well as Python's use of the Pepperpots to discuss philosophy, politics, art, and literature throughout *FC*.)

"Khan, Genghis" — ("Famous Deaths") Mongol conqueror (c. 1162–c. 1227) who is credited with the consolidation of nomadic tribes into a unified Mongolia. His empire eventually extended to the Adriatic Sea.

The larger-than-life Khan—along with Lord Nelson, Mozart, Attila, Stanley Baldwin, Churchill, Ramsay MacDonald, and others—is just the type of historical figure the Pythons will consistently re-contextualize into contemporary settings, or surprise with modernity in their own time. This results in a constant "context smashing" (a Roberto Unger term) where the understood settings, preconceptions, structures, and even verisimilitudes are broken apart by the purposeful decontextualizing of, for example, historical figures (Unger, 63). In such a postmodern world—where fragmentation is the only constant—the Pythons can posit and undercut, posit and undercut, rendering narrative instability the "stable" norm. This cult of context smashing becomes the new context, of course, and the new norm must then be overthrown as well. The pressure for more and newer contexts to continually smash will contribute to the Pythons' eventual demise—the same fate, ironically, of most Modernist movements as their reactions to traditional art forms and subject matters were co-opted by mass culture (often in the form of commercial art).

This tent scene was shot on the location trip to the southern coastal town of Bournemouth in July 1969 (WAC T12/1,083).

"Kingston" — ("Picasso/Cycling Race") Officially Kingston upon Thames, the city is several miles north of Tolworth, and west of Wimbledon Common. Explorer Brian Norris (Palin) will "discover" the Kingston Bypass as he searches for the most likely Surbiton to Hounslow migration trail (see Ep. 28).

"Kiss me, Hardy!" — ("Famous Deaths") These famous last words were originally reported by Robert Southey in his *Life of Nelson* (1813). Thomas Hardy was Nelson's flag captain, and reportedly kissed Nelson on the forehead as the admiral lay dying. (Note the leap from a modern building [see "top window" note below]). Nelson also suffered a violent death, meaning he would rank high on the scoring board. See the note for Nelson below.

"Klee, Paul" — ("Picasso/Cycling Race") Swiss-born Klee (1879–1940) employed "forced associations and distortions" as he commented on the modern world and human foibles, and may have questioned the efficacy of a technology-driven society (Tansey, 832–33). Along with Kokoschka and Schwitters, Klee and the Swiss-Germans are at the back marker of the race.

The Tate Gallery had collected five Klee paintings by 1969, most purchased in 1946 as a part of a broad expansion into the neglected area of European Modernism by the Gallery. The Contemporary Art Society (founded in 1910) arranged for the purchase of many of these Modernist works, including race participants Dufy, Klee, Picasso, and Toulouse-Lautrec.

"Kokoschka, Oskar" — ("Picasso/Cycling Race") Austrian artist Kokoschka (1886–1980) was an Expressionist whose works drew on high Romanticism (the late eighteenth and early nineteenth century) (Tansey, 812). In the episode's cycling race Kokoschka is dropping off the pace, as is Klee, perhaps as the move toward abstraction in art (and away from the traditions of Romanticism) becomes more and more pronounced.

Kokoschka could boast two works owned by the Tate Gallery by 1969.

• L •

Lederhosen Teutonic figure — (PSC; "Italian Lesson") Here Chapman is wearing the traditional lederhosen costume of European Alpine regions, complete with cocked feather hat. This costume will reappear on both Palin and Idle as they play vigorous Bavarian waiters in "The Restaurant Sketch" for the second *Fliegender Zirkus* (Bavarian TV) episode. The German/Teuton is certainly an Other, and characterized by stereotypical dress, as are the Italians in the room. (In Ep. 29, the Welsh women's national costume will be used for the men singing the "Money" song, accompanied by a Welsh harpist.) This type of visual shorthand for character typing is common throughout *FC*, and is carried over from live stage (music hall and burlesque), radio, and television traditions.

The costume people working for the show at the BBC were given the following instructions for this character: "Leiderhousen [*sic*]. The full apple strudle [*sic*] bit" (WAC T12/1,082).

"Léger, Ferdinand" — ("Picasso/Cycling Race") French artist Léger (1881–1955) developed "machine art," influenced by the original Cubists, which illustrated a fascination with the beauty of machinery, and would have reflected the interests of the Futurists of this period as well. (Futurist prophet F.T. Marinetti will be discussed in the notes to Ep. 14, for his early version of a "Silly Walk.") Léger's 1919 painting *The City* was on the "monumental scale" (7′7″ × 9′9½″) cautioned against by Reg Moss (Chapman) early in the sketch.

The Pythons could have traveled to Edinburgh or Manchester to see Léger works during this period, but there were also four Léger works available for viewing at the Tate Gallery, all donated in 1949–1950. Léger had also painted *The Four Cyclists* in 1943–1948, *Big Julie* (1945), *Leisures on Red Background* (1949), and *The Acrobats* (1952)—*all* prominently featuring bicycles and riders.

"Lincoln, A." — ("Famous Deaths") American Abraham Lincoln (1809–1865) was the sixteenth president of the United States, and was shot and killed at Ford's Theatre by John Wilkes Booth, an actor and ardent supporter of slavery. Eddie (Idle) characterizes Lincoln as "little," though he was actually abnormally tall for his era. Lincoln would sign his correspondence, normally, as "A. Lincoln," the same way the Pythons list him on the scoreboard.

• M •

Man — (PSC; opening titles) In this first episode, the introductory character played by Michael Palin is not called the "It's Man," merely "Man." In Ep. 2 he becomes the "It's Man" in the script, and remains so throughout his appearances in *Flying Circus*. This opening—featuring the "It's Man" in myriad situations and settings—became Python's signature introduction, and was also used through *most* of the *FC* episodes. Interestingly, by the middle of the second season (Ep. 19 and beyond), the intro either moves further into the episode, even near the end at times, or is eliminated entirely. As the troupe became more comfortable in its writing ability and with the medium itself, manipulation and undercutting became more prevalent, especially in regard to the accepted television formats of the time.

The "It's Man" doesn't appear in Eps. 19, 21, 26, or 34, nor does he appear in the abbreviated fourth season at all (Eps. 40–45). In Ep. 43, the "Hamlet" episode, Palin will appear in an "It's Man"–type link—where he emerges from an explosion, blackened, but not ragged and tatty, with his own hair, and says "And then"—as if he's a more dignified or Shakespearean transitional element than the "It's Man." Frankly, the "And then" man's appearance makes no sense at all in the context of the show, because the transition is to black, the end of the show.

"Marat" — ("Famous Deaths") Jean-Paul Marat (1743–1793) was a French politician, physician, and journalist, and was the leader of the Montagnard faction during the French Revolution. While resting in a medicinal bath (13 July 1793) he was stabbed to death by Charlotte Corday, a Girondin (royalist) conservative from Normandy (*EBO*).

The well-known death portrait (found in the Musées Royaux des Beaux-Arts, Brussels) painted by Jacques-Louis David is featured in Ep. 25, where characters in famous paintings call a strike and leave the paintings for picket lines. In life Marat also denounced Jacques Necker, who is prominently mentioned in Ep. 40, "The Golden Age of Ballooning."

"Miro" — ("Picasso/Cycling Race") Joan Miro (1893–1983) was an "organic" Surrealist, and eventually became more interested in subject matter, as did many Surrealists (Tansey, 830).

In 1969, the Tate held only one Miro painting, *Women and Bird in the Moonlight* (1949), which had been purchased in 1951.

"Mondrian, Piet" — ("Picasso/Cycling Race") Painter Piet Mondrian (1872–1944) led the Dutch abstract "De Stijl" ("The Style") art movement, and his influence was felt and mimicked broadly in art, architecture, and graphic design. He is a "Neo-Plasticist" because he believed "that plastic art affirms that equilibrium can only be established through the balance of unequal but equivalent oppositions" (*Gardner's*, 824). His work moved away from representation and into abstraction.

Two Mondrian paintings, including the well-known *Composition with Yellow, Blue and Red* (1937–1942), were part of the Tate's collection in 1969.

"Monty Python's Flying Circus" — (opening titles) In these first episodes, John Cleese speaks this line in a very straightforward, sober tone of voice. The delivery of the title (vocally) will change by Ep. 8, though will continue to be voiced by Cleese until the end of the second season, when Palin takes over from Ep. 27 on. (The tag line is not spoken in Eps. 19 or 26.) See notes to titles in Ep. 2. Using Cleese for this announcing task was likely a move promoted by the BBC itself, since he was easily the most recognizable of the new group. (Cleese had already been well received on *That Was the Week That Was* [1962–1963] and *The Frost Report* [1966–1967].) For the popular BBC-4 radio program *I'm Sorry I'll Read That Again* (1964–1973), it had been Cleese announcing the title whenever he appeared in the episode.

The song underneath is a version of John Philip Sousa's "Liberty Bell" theme, as recorded by the Band of Grenadier Guard (WAC T12/1,082, 5 Oct. 1969). This would become the show's (and Pythons') signature song, as well as the traditional version used throughout the series. The end theme will only change in Ep. 45 fittingly, when "Liberty Bell" is played haltingly on a guitar.

Moss, Reg — (PSC; "Picasso/Cycling Race") These scenes were shot on and around the Walton-on-Thames roundabout and shopping precinct in Walton, Surrey (WAC T12/1,083).

Mozart — ("*It's Wolfgang Amadeus Mozart*" and "Famous Deaths") Wolfgang Amadeus Mozart (1756–1791), the well-known Austrian composer. Colin Mozart (Palin), the son of Wolfgang, will appear in Ep. 21 as a ratcatcher.

In 1970, Peter Cook and Dudley Moore—who had, as part of the groundbreaking 1961–1964 satirical stage show *Beyond the Fringe* greatly influenced the Pythons—would create a recurring "Ludwig" (as in Beethoven) musical sketch for their *Not Only . . . But Also* comedy show.

• N •

"National Film Theatre" — ("*It's the Arts*") Mentioned as the venue for Sir David Ross's film retrospective, the NFT is located on London's South Bank, and hosts internationally acclaimed film festivals, including the London Film Festival.

"Nelson, Admiral" — ("Famous Deaths") Viscount Horatio Nelson (1758–1805) won the Battle of Trafalgar, making Britain safe from foreign invasion for perhaps the first time in her history. He lost his life to a sniper's bullet in the battle, allegedly uttering the famous "Kiss me, Hardy" as he died.

The cast of the original *Beyond the Fringe* (1960) satirical show (university wits Alan Bennett, Peter Cook, Jonathan Miller, and Dudley Moore) had included a lengthy sketch on Nelson and specifically the awkwardness of his purported last words (to wit: Hardy has to leave his command position, make his way to the wounded Nelson under fire, kiss him, etc.). Most of the Pythons had seen the show (which premiered in 1960 in Edinburgh, then moved to the Fortune Theatre in London in 1961), and have admitted to being quite influenced by it.

A very short allusion to this obviously seminal and contested historical moment can also be found in the *Do Not Adjust Your Set* episodes, co-written by Idle, Jones, and Palin (and Denise Coffey and David Jason), from 1967. The children's show was produced by Humphrey Barclay for Associated Rediffusion TV, then Thames TV.

"Nicholson, Ben" — ("Picasso/Cycling Race") The only Englishman facing Picasso in this race, Nicholson (1894–1982) is characterized as an austere geometric abstractionist, influenced by studying with Mondrian (see note on Mondrian above), and teaming with sculptor Barbara Hepworth. For more on Nicholson, see Sophie Bowness's article on the artist in the *ODNB*.

Not surprisingly, the Tate holds more works by British native Nicholson than any of the other (foreign) race participants. Approximately two dozen drawings, paintings, and collages, many presented by the artist himself, were part of the Tate collection by late 1969.

Ben Nicholson and his work had been the subject of an arts magazine television program in June 1969, and a Nicholson retrospective was featured in the Tate in June–July 1969.

• O •

"Oh ja . . . Ach!" — ("Italian Lesson") German to English translations for this scene: "Excuse me, sir. What is the word for stomachache?" and "Oh, yes. Thank you very much. Ah, the German classroom. I see!"

In medical terms, "mittelschmerz" is generally an abdominal pain in women associated with ovulation.

There is also a character named Mrs. Mittelschmerz in "Stake Your Claim," who claims to be able to "burrow through an elephant." This sketch can be heard on the Monty Python album *Another Monty Python Record* (side 2), and seen (and heard in German) on the first *Fliegender Zirkus* episode.

"organ and tympani" — ("Arthur 'Two-Sheds' Jackson") Interesting combination of instruments, especially since the composition is being called a "symphony" (meaning at least wind, string, and percussion, and in some numbers), which at least hints at a full orchestral arrangement. No mention of what kind of organ; tympani are tunable kettledrums.

• P •

patriotic music . . . crescendo — (PSC; "The Funniest Joke in the World") According to surviving BBC payroll paperwork, bit-part players Cy Town and Lesley Weekes also appeared in this longer-than-usual sketch, filming their portions on 18 August 1969. Town would go on to appear on *Doctor Who* many times, often in costume as a monster, while Weekes had appeared on *Z Cars* earlier in 1969 (WAC T12/1,083).

See IMDb.com for more on these and other actors appearing in bit parts. Most of the extras and walk-ons who appeared in *Flying Circus* have not yet been credited (beyond the WAC records)—these appearances will be highlighted throughout these annotations.

"Peenemünde" — ("The Funniest Joke in the World") This is the infamous Nazi "V" rocket base in northeast Germany, where German scientists (including many who would later work in the American space program, such as Werner Von Braun) had been building and testing V-1, V-2, and even V-10 rockets—initially for attacks on England, but to eventually combat the Russians and Americans. The V rocket program became a significant target for the Allies late in the war, since the Germans were well ahead of the rest of the world in rocket and atomic technology, and the war could have ended very differently had Peenemünde not been bombed so effectively by the Allies from 1943. Soviet troops overran the base in 1945, and took many scientists into the fledgling Russian space program.

Pepperpots — (PSC; linking element into "Whizzo Butter") A name probably based on the character Mrs. Pepperpot, created by Norwegian children's author Alf Prøysen. Mrs. Pepperpot never knew when she was going to shrink down to Pepperpot size and shape, a roundish pepper container. As rendered by the Pythons, these characters wear frumpy print dresses, wigs, carry purses, and speak in falsetto tones.

Additionally, playwright Terence Rattigan (1911–1977) wrote this character description in the preface to the second volume of his *Collected Plays* (1953):

> [T]here follows a simple truth, and for the purpose of its illustration let us invent a character, a nice, respectable, middle-class, middle-aged, maiden lady, with time on her hands and the money to help her pass it. She enjoys pictures, books, music, and the theatre and though to none of these arts (or rather, for consistency's sake, to none of these three arts and the one craft) does she bring much knowledge or discernment, at least, as she is apt to tell her cronies, she "does know what she likes." Let us call her Aunt Edna . . . Aunt Edna is a universal. (xi–xiii)

Rattigan will be mentioned (and played by Cleese) in Ep. 30, where he is killed with a spear gun by HRH the Dummy Princess Margaret.

Lastly, there is another image of the pepperpot that may have informed, at least unconsciously, the totality of the Python housewife character who became known as a "Pepperpot." Lady Violet Bonham-Carter (1887–1969), daughter of Liberal Prime Minister H. H. Asquith (fl. 1908–1916), lists the fascinating contradictions of the Edwardian age, and includes the feminine but politically committed "suffragettes, hurling bricks at 10 Downing Street, attacking ministers, armed with dog whips, hatchets, and *pepperpots*" (audio transcription, *Eyewitness 1910–1919*, "Death of Edward VII and Political Battles of 1910"). In this instance, then, the traditional housewife as found in both the Edwardian era and the Pythons' world is capable of the odd "slit up a treat" when crossed.

"Picasso" — ("Picasso/Cycling Race") Pablo Picasso (1881–1973) was a noted Spanish painter, sculptor, printmaker, etc., and considered by many to be the most significant figure in Modern Art, and Modernism in general. Python's description of Picasso and his influence on the world of art mentioned later in the episode is spot on, with the exception, perhaps, of his bike-and-painting expertise.

This cross-referencing of Picasso and cycling could certainly be an oblique reference to Picasso's celebrated bicycle-seat-and-handle-bars sculpture, *Head of a Bull*, from 1943.

There were approximately a dozen Picasso works available for viewing in the Tate collection by 1969, most bequeathed in 1933. Also, between April and June 1969 there were a number of articles in London papers discussing the record prices modern artwork was commanding, with names like Nicholson and Kokoschka being tossed about, and auctions set aboard the QE2, etc.

pig — (PSC; link into "*It's Wolfgang Amadeus Mozart*") Pigs become a recurring motif in this episode, and the references even cross over to Ep. 2 (or *from* Ep. 2, since these first two episodes were flip-flopped before broadcast). The pig appearances will include animation, props, audio (squeals), and a caption later in the episode.

"Pigs 3, Nelson 1" — (PSC; link into "Arthur 'Two-Sheds' Jackson") Not only prolonging the pig theme, but also the sport and scoring motif evident from the "Famous Deaths" sketch at the beginning of the episode. See Ep. 2 for the wrestling match to determine the existence of God.

"pig's head" — (PSC; "Picasso/Cycling Race") This is an actual pig's head, as asked for by designer Roger Limington (WAC T12/1,082).

pillbox — (PSC; "The Funniest Joke in the World") A concrete bunker created as a defensive and/or observation position, often with gun slits. These can still be seen throughout the coastal regions of Britain, Wales, Scotland, etc.

"Pollock, Jackson" — ("Picasso/Cycling Race") American artist Pollock (1912–1956) was a member of the "New York School" of the late 1940s and 1950s, and much of his work falls into the "action painting" category; he often poured or dripped on a canvas on his studio floor.

In the Tate collection there were two Pollock works by 1969, both of the "poured" variety.

"pre-war joke" — ("The Funniest Joke in the World") Perhaps one of Python's most scathing political moments, this allusion peels back the scab on a still-painful pre-WWII wound. Then-Prime Minister Neville Chamberlain (1869–1940) had secured promises (the Munich Agreement) from "Herr Hitler" that German advances to that point (including the threats toward Czechoslovakia) would not continue, nor would Germany threaten the sovereignty of the rest of Europe and the world—a policy of appeasement. By 1 September 1939, of course, the "peace in our time" policy was in tatters, as Nazi tanks rolled through Poland. Chamberlain never politically escaped that onerous accomplishment, and the image (newsreel footage of worthless paper in hand) has become iconic. Not a wartime PM, he was replaced by the unpopular Churchill when the elder statesman lost Conservative support in 1940. Chamberlain died a short time later.

It's likely that Chamberlain and perhaps the entire "Funniest Joke" idea appears here thanks to two major and related events of 1968–1969. First, in late 1968 and early 1969 the government records pertaining to Chamberlain's three meetings with Hitler and the PM's briefings to the Cabinet were unsealed, thirty years after the momentous events of 1938, including the regrettable "peace in our time" pronouncement. Major

British papers reported on the secret documents' revelations, depicting the too-trusting Chamberlain ever at a loss with the scheming, fatally underestimated Hitler. Secondly, significant coverage of the former Prime Minister's centenary year followed later in 1969. All the major British newspapers also carried stories on Chamberlain's legacy, many appearing in March 1969, just as the Pythons were writing the first season.

The satirical cast of *Beyond the Fringe* (Bennett, Cook, Miller, and Moore) had also skewered Chamberlain in their stage show first performed in 1961 in Edinburgh, then later in London and New York. (Listen to "The Aftermyth of War" sketch on *The Complete* Beyond the Fringe CD [EMI, 1996].)

This Chamberlain newsreel image came from VisNews (Ref. No. 1450), according to the archival sources request/copyright forms (WAC T12/1,082). The BBC seemed to have been quite careful in checking for and paying for (when necessary) copyrighted material, including photos, film clips, music clips, and sounds of all kinds. The major exception to this would be animator Gilliam's contributions, which are not accounted for in the WAC records, though there are several complaints about those animated sequences in the records. See the Python files in the BBC's Written Archives Collection, Caversham Park.

There had also been an earlier attack along these same lines, when in a 1942 speech Michael Foot (1913–2010), editor of *The Evening Standard*) compared the oppressive, first-strike actions of Churchill's wartime government against the freedom of the newspaper industry to Hitler's actions during the "appeasement" days. In 1940, Foot had co-published *Guilty Men*, a direct attack on Chamberlain and appeasement.

• Q •

"Q Division" — ("The Funniest Joke in the World") A division of Scotland Yard. Jack Slipper (1924–2005)—who became "Slipper of the Yard" after apprehending (then losing) the Great Train Robbers in 1963—was a member of Q Division. The Pythons' oft-heard "So-and-So of the Yard" declamations have been borrowed from at least two sources: Slipper, of course, who took many opportunities to appear in front of news cameras, becoming something of a media celebrity in the 1960s and 1970s, but also the earlier Det. Insp. Robert Fabian of *Fabian of Scotland Yard* (1954) fame. Fabian (d. 1978) sported the trench coat, hat, and pipe ensemble, and usually appeared at the end of each fictionalized episode.

"Quando Caliente del Sol" — ("Italian Lesson") The popular song "When the Sun Is Hot . . ." is performed here by guitarist Miguel-Lopez Cortero, who was paid £10/50 for his services (WAC T12/1,082).

• R •

"Richard the Third" — ("Famous Deaths") Richard (1452–1485) was the famed Plantagenet king later vilified by Tudor apologists, whose inflated villainy also made great dramatic fodder for Shakespeare. Richard died at Bosworth Field (22 August 1485), the ultimate War of the Roses. This battle and Richard's death allowed for the establishment of the Tudor dynasty under Henry VII. See Ross's *Wars of the Roses*.

"Ross" — (*"It's the Arts"*) The Sir Edward Ross character could be based on any number of distinguished and knighted British film directors, including Richard Attenborough (*Oh! What a Lovely War*), Alfred Hitchcock (*The Birds*), David Lean (*Doctor Zhivago*), even Michael Powell (*Peeping Tom*), etc. Attenborough will be sent-up (as "Dickie Attenborough") in Ep. 39, "The British Showbiz Awards" sketch.

Also, this "interviewer and guest" format (three camera set-up) is utilized and satirized throughout *FC*, and has been a staple on British television since its inception.

"Royal Festival Hall" — (*"It's the Arts"*) Situated on the banks of the Thames alongside the Hayward Gallery and opened in 1951, the one-hundredth anniversary of the Great Exhibition. The RFH has primarily been used for music, dance, and lecture series, as opposed to film retrospectives.

• S •

"Salisbury Plain" — ("The Funniest Joke in the World") An open chalk plateau in Wiltshire and Berkshire, the Plain is home to significant prehistoric monuments, including Stonehenge. This area has been used for military exercises for many years as well, which is why the Pythons would have interred the deadly joke here.

"Schwitters, Kurt" — ("Picasso/Cycling Race") Schwitters (1887–1948) was a German collage artist (the Pepperpot is quite correct) and a Dadaist. Schwitters put his "Merz Pictures" together from garbage piles, bits of masonry and stone, found items, etc. Schwitters, then, might not actually belong in the race (which might be why he's in last place), since he was not a painter, but a committed collagist.

There was only one Schwitters work, *Opened by Customs* (1937–1938), purchased by the Tate during this period. And even though Schwitters was a German, as pointed out by a helpful Pepperpot (Palin), a retrospective of his work was mounted in London ten years after his death, at Lord's Gallery, 26 Wellington Road, St. John's Wood. Schwitters lived in England after 1940, having escaped Nazi forces through Norway.

scoreboard — (PSC; "Famous Deaths") The scoreboard created for this sketch does, indeed, look like the original scoreboard on the Eddie Waring–hosted *It's a Knockout* show. (*It's a Knockout* is featured on the 10 and 17 May 1969 *Radio Times* covers.) See the entry for "Eddie Waring" for more.

The *Sunday Times* published a scoreboard not unlike this in March 1969, revealing the popularity (as determined by readers) of the royal family. The complete scoreboard looked like this, as reprinted in *Private Eye*:

> The results were scored as follows: a great deal, plus 1; quite a lot, plus 1/2; not very much, minus 1/2; not at all, minus 1; don't know, zero. This is how it turns out:

Score	
The Queen	63
Prince Philip	55
The Queen Mother	48
Lord Mountbatten	41
Prince Charles	39
Princess Alexandra	36
Princess Anne	26
Princess Margaret	2
Duke of Kent	26 (Ingrams, 227)

"Scotland Yard" — ("The Funniest Joke in the World") Headquarters of the Metropolitan Police, originally at Whitehall, and founded by Sir Robert Peel in 1829. The building (completed in 1967) is found at Broadway and Victoria Street in Westminster.

"Scribbler" — (PSC; "The Funniest Joke in the World") "Ernest Scribbler," or, literally, one who is serious about his writings. This is an allusion to the Scriblerus Club, the ur–Monty Python learned literary troupe including Alexander Pope, Jonathan Swift, John Gay, Thomas Parnell, and John Arbuthnot. The five contributed to the *Memoirs of Martinus Scriblerus*, which was begun in 1713 and eventually published in 1741, and which ridiculed erudition and scholarly jargon. Pope occasionally used Martinus Scriblerus as a pseudonym, as did George Crabbe. (See Drabble's *Oxford Companion to English Literature*.)

"slit your face" — ("Whizzo Butter" advert) Another possibility of violence from a seemingly harmless source, this phrase is adapted elsewhere in *FC* as the slangy "slit (you) up a treat" (cf. "Operating Theatre" and Ep. 14's "The Piranha Brothers"). In Ep. 8, seemingly innocent grandmothers will rampage through London in "Hell's Grannies," and there is also a certain killer rabbit in *Holy Grail*, to name just two other such innocuous threats.

sound effect — (PSC; "The Funniest Joke in the World") With the Gestapo man (Chapman) providing his own sound effects, the result is like bringing the ever-present sound effects technicians out of the offstage areas, or in the case of television, off-camera, and into full view. It also underscores the artificiality of the violent acts as presented in all movies and television—the soundtrack and visual elements are always separate and distinct, and must be artificially generated, then carefully synchronized for the illusion of reality to be achieved.

The Pythons, remember, were raised listening to the radio, including the sound effects–laden *The Goon Show*, as well as working and writing for the university revues at Cambridge and Oxford (as well as performing audio-only routines, including Cleese's work on *I'm Sorry I'll Read That Again*, and each of the Pythons' LP record albums). The Goons made a regular point of identifying for the listening (and studio) audience the machinery behind the magic—whenever an LP-based sound effect was used, or when characters pretended to leave a room by walking away slightly from the microphone, etc. The radio dramas of the 1930s and 1940s on the BBC also employed a rich panoply of sound effects, and audience expectations of a certain level of verisimilitude could be fulfilled. By the same token, when the expectations of verisimilitude are fully in place for any art form, defying those same conventions becomes possible and—in silly comedy like the Goons delivered—even expected.

This becomes the Pythons' sort of raison d'être, creating, for example, as believable a medieval world as they can for the film *Monty Python and the Holy Grail*, then consistently undercutting that reality with anachronisms and general silliness.

"squawk" — (PSC; "Famous Deaths") Genghis Khan (1162–1227) dies here, almost the way the "Dead Parrot" sketch (Ep. 8) explains the demise of the bird in question, including the preference of the Norwegian Blue for "kipping on its back," and its supine condition being blamed on a "long squawk." Also, Cleese dies in the exact same manner later in this episode (lunging backwards into sudden death) as a Nazi hearing for the first time the "Funniest Joke in the World." In reality, Khan actually died rather peacefully, at the old age of 65.

All that is missing from these deaths is the iconic flower clutched at the chest, and these would have been more like the deaths of animated characters. Screwy Squirrel dies just this way, for example, in Tex Avery's MGM cartoons. Cleese as a Nazi also very clearly calls out Woody Woodpecker's signature cry (voiced originally by Gracie Lantz, wife of Woody creator Walter Lantz) as he dies.

The Goon Show pioneered this cartoony-ness, an animated awareness that Peter Sellers characterized years later as being key in developing the show and writing the episodes with Harry Secombe, Michael Bentine, and Spike Milligan—writers and performers also emerging from collective service in WWII—setting the show apart from anything that had come before. Sellers remembers:

> We wanted to express ourselves in a sort of surrealistic form. We thought in cartoons, we thought in blackouts, we thought in sketches. We thought of mad characters. We thought of—take a situation and instead of letting it end normally, let it end the other way—twisted around. (Audio transcription, "The Last Goon Show")

Bentine had remembered he and Sellers visiting "Cameo" theaters just after they'd met. The Cameo News Theatre on Charing Cross Road showed news and cartoons, and had opened in 1936 with a set of Disney titles. This cartoony approach to structure and subject was adopted and adapted to include the visual elements the television medium would allow—the self-conscious signs (both held by characters and generated electronically), knowing glances, fourth-wall-shattering asides, pratfalls, the character squash and stretch, even, which had previously only been allowed in the cartoon world—as the Pythons created *Flying Circus*.

As early as 1959 American theatrical and television cartoons were airing on British TV screens, including *Huckleberry Hound* (July 1959, Granada TV), and *The Bugs Bunny Show* (ABC Midland and Northern TV), *The Flintstones* (Southern TV and South Wales and West of England TV), and *The Bullwinkle Show* (Granada), all appearing in 1961–1962. Early American theatrical cartoons, including Betty Boop titles from the Fleischer Bros., had been gracing British cinema screens since 1935.

"stock film" — (PSC; "The Funniest Joke in the World") Stock film is generally film shot for one purpose, then used for another purpose, or used generically (for news footage, documentaries, commercials, even underfunded feature films). The BBC archives millions of feet of film (and now video) footage (and still photographs) from government information films, how-to films, documentary films, captured wartime footage, BBC TV and Radio performances, news footage, etc.

The Pythons plundered these archives whenever, for example, an establishing shot might be needed, such as the title shot for the "Spanish Inquisition" sketch (Ep. 15) showing the surface works of a chimney-sprouting textile mill, presumably in Yorkshire; a photo of the plans for the Crystal Palace (Ep. 29); and the ubiquitous "Women's Institute" film clip, which appears in many episodes. (See the note for the Women's Institute in Ep. 2.)

All the stock films cues cited either in the printed scripts or in the WAC records are listed—by episode—in appendix A: Stock Film Clips and Still Images.

"Strewth!" — ("Famous Deaths") Historically, a necessary contraction of "God's truth," the type of oath that from at least Elizabethan times would not have been permissible on the English theatrical stage. In a more contemporary instance, a character in the 1969 film *Battle for Britain* (dir. Guy Hamilton; released just weeks before the first *FC* season went on the air) utters the invective as he plunges his Spitfire into combat. See also similar invectives like "zounds" ("by God's wounds") and "s'blood" ("God's blood"). This term is used almost exclusively in *FC* by Chapman, and will be heard in Ep. 2 as the cycling Arthur Figgis (Chapman) realizes Arthur Frampton (Jones) actually has three buttocks.

Generally, BBC jitters over viewers' sensibilities led to synonyms or more metaphorical language rather than straight-out cursing or oaths ("coitus" and "intercourse the penguin" as invectives in Ep. 27; a raspberry instead of "sod" in Ep. 17). Television morality watchdog groups were also quite active during this period, including Mary Whitehouse (see entries in Eps. 8 and 32 notes), meaning there was always the niggling possibility of civil or even criminal action against blasphemers, contributors to public delinquency, etc. See Hewison's *Monty Python: The Case Against* for more on the Pythons' legal and censorial struggles.

Lastly, one of *The Goon Show* characters—William the Gardener—shouts "Strewth!" when he is startled awake in "The Pevensey Bay Disaster" (3 Apr. 1956).

"St Stephen" — ("Famous Deaths") Called the first Christian martyr, Stephen was charged with blasphemy by the Sanhedrin and stoned to death for his faith c. AD 36. The end of Stephen's ministry, life, and his concurrent vision are found in Acts 6–7.

"studio ain't" — ("Arthur 'Two-Sheds' Jackson") Play on the oft-heard "This town ain't big enough for the two of us" from both Hollywood Western lore (apocryphal or otherwise) and especially cartoons spoofing those Westerns. (Bugs Bunny utters the phrase in *Bugs Bunny Rides Again* (1948), then rapidly builds a metropolis around the western town to provide more room for both of them.) The iconic cowboy figure appears occasionally in *FC*, including Cleese's all-in-black mustachioed cowboy "Southerner" who dispenses homilies to buck up Arthur Pewtey (Palin) in Ep. 2, the "Marriage Guidance Counsellor" sketch, as well as the "Cheese Westerns" sketch in Ep. 33, and in both of the *FZ* episodes.

• T •

"taken the A272" — ("Picasso/Cycling Race") The humorous incongruity here, then, isn't just the fact that an internationally known artist is trying to paint a major work while riding a bicycle, but that a celebrity like Picasso (still alive in 1969) would use a road like the A272, and that he has to negotiate local traffic congestion. A similar bit of Python incongruity appears in the 1983 feature film *ML*, when an alleged "mosquito" bite on a British soldier—officer class—is recognized, even the raging Zulu Wars just outside the tent come to a complete halt.

"tea boy" — ("*It's the Arts*") A "gofer" at the lowest level, this certainly refers to the guild-like tradition of working up through the film studio ranks in the early days of British (and even Hollywood) studio cinema, but could also reference more directly the following: Alfred Hitchcock, who began his film career as a title designer for silent films; David Lean, who started as a clapper boy and wardrobe assistant; and Michael Powell, who worked myriad odd jobs as a studio gofer before directing. See the note for "Ross" for additional comments.

"thirteen years" — (PSC; "The Funniest Joke in the World") This is from the *printed* script's description of what Ernest Scribbler's mother "understands" as she reads the deadly joke note: ". . . *thinking it is a suicide note—for he has not been doing well for the last thirteen years.*" It is intriguing to read just how much non-visual, even non-essential information is included in these scripts meant for performance. Many of these ancillary elements can be characterized as editorializations, or asides for the discriminating reader only (the other Pythons?). These moments are a fascinating conceit on the writers' part, since the tidbits (1) do not end up on screen, and (2) would be completely lost without actually reading the performance texts. They often read as almost inside jokes available to and decipherable by other Pythons.

This is even more curious as we take into consideration the fact that Python was writing for itself, as Shakespeare did for the King's Men, and not for anyone else (technical BBC folk aside), as opposed, say, to Ben Jonson, who wrote knowing that his work would be published and actually read. Some of these moments—asides—would seem to be "givens" in this case—*understood*—but they're included anyway.

"this week's request death" — ("Famous Deaths") As early as 1967 there were radio shows on BBC Radio 1 playing listener requests. In the earlier *The Goon Show*, Neddie announces a series of requests from listeners who have allegedly written to the show:

> Neddie (Secombe): Now, first of all, for Mrs. Heironymous Clun of 4, The Villas, Cleethorpes Sinks, here is the very record she hasn't asked for. The Rites of Spring, by Ripsi-Korsettsoff played by the Gulf Stream Tearoom Quartet from the oblique position. . . . And now, Private Wretch of the 4th Mudguards has asked for a record of his sergeant falling down a manhole. And here it is, accompanied (without orchestra), by Geraldo. . . . Now on the serious side, Elsie Sprugg and Gladys Legg of Rowton House Champagne Bar have asked for a record of Sir Gwilym Cludge conducting the Four in Jeopardy with knee-bracket accompaniment and silent dogs with the Massed Bands of the Hybrid Spahi's Banjo Society and the 4th Coolies Harmonica Chorus recorded in the natural surroundings of the living room of Jim Davidson's Saxophone Parlour and Part-Time Egg Hatchery with a solo by Rawicz and Landauer. Well, Elsie and Gladys, we haven't got it. But! Here is a record of Fred Clute and his Nubian Monsters playing cribbage! . . . Finally, Miss Frewina Kellogg would like to hear Sabrina sing. (transcribed excerpts from "The Great Tuscan Salami Scandal," 21 Feb. 1956)

Other actual request shows from the period included *Memories for You* (BBC Home Service and Light Programme, Victor Sylvester's Ballroom Orchestra), *Housewives' Choice* (BBC Light Programme, 1946–1967), *Two-Way Family Favourites* and *Children's Favourites* (both mentioned as quite influential by many of Britain's postwar rock stars, including David Bowie and Eric Clapton), as well as *At Your Request* (Sandy MacPherson at the organ).

tinkling — (PSC; "*It's Wolfgang Amadeus Mozart*") The music being played is Mozart's "L'Oiseau-lyre: Gigue in G," according to the music requests for this week's show (WAC T12/1,082).

"Tolworth roundabout" — ("Picasso/Cycling Race") There is a significant roundabout in Tolworth where the A3 and the A3210 meet, though according to archival sources, this scene was shot in Walton-on-Thames, Surrey, on 17 July 1969 (WAC T12/1,083). The WAC records weren't specific (as often happened, they likely found the location after arriving on scene), but the location is Marshall's roundabout on Walton

Bridge Road, Shepperton, not far from downtown Walton-on-Thames.

"top window" — (PSC; "Famous Deaths") This dummy is thrown from an upper floor of one of the Wellington Close towers in Walton-on-Thames. In Ep. 16, Carol Cleveland will perform a striptease as part of the "And now" Man section of the titles in this same building. Neither of these location uses are accounted for in the WAC records. These blocks are just a few hundred yards from the business center of Walton, where the troupe shot exteriors for many first season episodes.

"Toulouse-Lautrec" — ("Picasso/Cycling Race") Toulouse-Lautrec (1864–1901) was a painter and poster maker, haunting and capturing the nightlife of Paris. He also was quite short of stature, which is why he is depicted riding a tricycle, and not a bicycle like everyone else. He is included by the Pythons, most likely, simply because of his size, and is effectively used in place of a verbal punchline. Toulouse-Lautrec will be revisited via a still photo—where he is wearing a "slenderizing garment" while painting—in Ep. 28, "Trim-Jeans Theatre."

This same gag—including Toulouse and the bicycle bell—is heard earlier in the *Goon Show* episode "The £50 Cure" (23 Feb. 1959). The writers/producers of *The Yellow Submarine* include a very brief cameo of a Toulouse-Lautrec character, glimpsed as John, George, Ringo, and Fred search for Paul.

In 1969 the Tate could claim two Toulouse-Lautrec works, one donated in 1940, the other in 1961.

"train-spotting" — ("Arthur 'Two-Sheds' Jackson") The practice of watching for trains and recording their numbers is still a popular hobby in the UK. Referenced again in Ep. 7, the "You're No Fun Anymore" sketch.

"Two-Sheds" — ("Arthur 'Two-Sheds' Jackson") This is a clear incongruity, where classical arts figures are given handles and nicknames as if they were sports figures or organized crime members. Also, the epithet has a certain "Two Gun" ring to it, as if from a Zane Grey novel, Hollywood Western, or crime drama.

Naming and the power of names/words do become very influential in the Python oeuvre. Here Jackson (Jones) won't be able to escape the implications of his nickname—it will define him and eventually cause a terminal disruption in the interview. Similarly, in Ep. 19 the character Raymond Luxury Yacht (Chapman) announces that though his name is spelled one way it should actually be pronounced "Throatwobbler Mangrove"; in Ep. 22 the new member (Jones) of the faculty at an Australian University isn't named Bruce, so his name is changed to Bruce to be in line with all the other faculty members. Also, see the power of words/ names like "mattress" in Ep. 8, and "witch," "Ni," and especially "it" in the feature film *Holy Grail*.

For a discussion of Shakespeare's version of this same phenomenon, see Larsen's *MPSERD*, and specifically Richard III's abilities as a maker/director. For example, at the height of his powers, if Richard *says* someone is a traitor, that person *becomes* a traitor, and can be dealt with accordingly. A married woman can become an available woman; a cousin can become a foe; rightful heirs can become seditious, etc. Richard is perhaps the ultimate "maker" in English literary history.

• U •

"Unknown Joke" — ("The Funniest Joke in the World") "Unknown soldier" tombs are in many countries; in England the tomb is located in Westminster Abbey.

The subjects treated in this initial episode—Britain's "darkest days" of WWII, television mores and formats, unattractive and even threatening middle-class women, homosexuality, a collage of modern art and sport, and Nazi aggression—anticipate Python's interest in pushing the bounds of subject matter and decency on television, as well as the value of vulgarity and shock in entertainment. These subjects and characters will reappear throughout the series, as well.

• V •

"Vicky" — ("Picasso/Cycling Race") Not normally a man's name, but there was a well-known cartoonist active just prior to this period, pen-named "Vicky." His real name was Victor Weisz (1913–1966), and he was a significantly left-of-center artist who had committed suicide in 1966. Vicky drew for several papers, including the *Daily Mail*, the *Evening Standard*, and the *New Statesman*. His leftist stance and sometimes acid-tipped pen probably endeared him to the young Pythons. There are two portraits of Weisz in the National Gallery collections. Weisz's collection of approximately 4,000 comic strips can be viewed at the British Cartoon Archive.

The Goons would occasionally employ this kind of effeminizing naming, as well. In "The Last Tram (From Clapham)" (23 Nov. 1954) a chauffeur (played by the bandleader Ellington) appears, and Neddie calls him "Gladys," eliciting a hearty laugh from the audience. He answers to "Gladys" for the balance of the show.

viking . . . knight—(PSC; "Picasso/Cycling Race") This Viking, played by various members of the cast, appears throughout the *FC* series as a completely non sequitur linking element. Some of the links shot during this first season (and filmed in Scotland) will appear much later in the third season, as well. The knight also acted as a linking element and/or—using a rubber chicken as a mace—as the punishment for a delivered punchline, not unlike the archetypal vaudeville stage "hook" that appeared when a failed act was to be terminated (or the oversized hammer that will appear in *FC* later). The knight's "slapstick prop" appearances gradually wane as the Pythons mature in their utilization of links and transitions.

Terry Gilliam often plays the knight, and was paid a bit extra for the "walk-on" appearance, according to BBC records.

"V-Joke" — ("The Funniest Joke in the World") A play on the German "V"-rocket program. See "Peenemünde" note above. It is quite fitting that later in the episode the German V-Joke falls flat (misses its target, simply bemusing British homefront radio listeners), since not only did many of the V-rockets miss significant targets, but during the war years German scientists—pursuing the same atomic weaponry ends as the Allies—relied in error on the capabilities of heavy water and carbon, rather than uranium, causing disastrous delays in German atomic research.

"Vott" — (PSC; "The Funniest Joke in the World") An example of the written form of the kind of fractured English Python demands of many of its Others, in this case foreigners, Germans (and evil Nazis, to boot). The troupe members adopt rather caricatured Germanic accents, which affects nearly all their dialogue and even its delivery, though this pervasiveness is only hinted at in the printed form of the scripts. (The Nazis and their Germanic accents are much more hyperbolized here than, say, the earlier Mozart dialogue.)

In this verbal shorthand, the Pythons are much like their Goon ancestors. The Goons did not have the visual element to rely on, however, so dressing a character like a City Gent or a Rustic would make little difference to a radio audience. They would employ often outrageously over-the-top accents to instantly identify nationalities and various Brits, including (East) Indians (Babu Banerjee), French (Moriarty), Germans (Naughty Prisoner), and every accent from English aristocrats to Yorkshire laborers to "Cockney idiots."

This is also not unlike Shakespeare and his approach to Katherine's foreigner status, as well as her maid, in *Henry V*. Shakespeare illustrates Katherine's "foreigner-ness" by skewing her English, reducing her lines, often, to nearly baby-talk. She asks: "Is it possible dat I sould love de ennemie of / France?" (5.2.169–70). After Henry gives her his much longer response, she counters with "I cannot tell wat is dat" (5.2.177). Her last words in butchered English (she does have one more speech in French) come soon after: "Den it sall also content me" (5.2.250). Her woman Alice is painted with the same brush, and though Alice is able to translate Henry's English into French, her accented English is nearly indecipherable; "*Oui*, dat de tongeus of de mans is be full of deceits: dat is de Princess" (5.2.119–20). (For more on this phenomenon, see *MPSERD* 67.)

The primacy of the English language is trumpeted here, as is English-ness. Marston performs the same lingual gymnastics in regard to a foreigner in *The Dutch Courtesan*, wherein Francischina can be heard to utter: "O mine aderliver love, vat sall me do to re- / quit dis your mush affection?" (1.2.87–88). Francischina's accent also seems to come and go as the play moves on, much like Python's characters can massacre some words and leave others alone. Cf. Python's take on the Japanese accent in Ep. 29, "Erizabeth L," or a Caribbean accent later in the same episode, both mangled by Jones.

• W •

Waring, Eddie — (PSC; "Famous Deaths") Game show co-host (with David Vine) on the BBC in the 1966–1987 show called *It's a Knockout* (another "*It's*"-titled show, see notes to Ep. 10). This was the Brit version of the pan-European show *Jeux sans Frontières* (*Games without Borders*). The cast members of *I'm Sorry I'll Read That Again* (*ISIRTA*)—where Cleese wrote and performed—had been lampooning Waring for several years, including the episodes "Telephone" and "Taming of the Shrew." See notes for Eddie Waring in Ep. 2.

wartime planning room — (PSC; link into "The Funniest Joke in the World") This would have been a very familiar setting for especially UK viewers, as many WWII films featured these planning room scenes. The most recent would have been the myriad scenes featured in the big budget, Hollywood-funded (by United Artists and Harry Saltzman, who will be parodied in Ep. 6) blockbuster *Battle of Britain*. Instead of pigs being pushed around, of course, the primarily female operatives would manipulate models of planes to indicate Luftwaffe movement and RAF response.

"wartime radio" — (PSC; "The Funniest Joke in the World") Television broadcasts were halted abruptly by the BBC on 1 September 1939 (reportedly during a Mickey Mouse cartoon), and wouldn't return until June 1946, so radio became the critical source of information for the homefront audience during WWII. Broadcast propaganda was extremely significant during the war, naturally, and emanated from almost all of the major countries involved. Specifically, Germany broadcast English-language propaganda (negative battlefield reports, fascist doctrine and programming, etc.) from the earliest days of the war, and even back into Hitler's early days as National Socialist dignitary (see the earlier entry for "Der ver" for more on these broadcasts). The BBC also broadcast foreign-language programs into occupied countries throughout the war, and the evening news reports and addresses from Churchill became staples of the wartime listener's diet, especially during the Battle of Britain. (There is a poignant, haunting moment in the initial scenes of Rossellini's *Rome, Open City*, where, as Nazi troops bang on a door downstairs, an illegal and secreted radio can be heard droning out the familiar "This is London calling" broadcast.) This image of earnest citizens crouched around a radio would have been well known to the Pythons, all born between 1939 and 1943, most (excepting Gilliam, of course) having at least some memory of the war years in Britain.

"watching generals" — (PSC; "The Funniest Joke in the World") Many of these military scenes were shot 17–18 July 1969 at Pirbright Army Camp, Brookwood, Woking, Surrey (WAC T12/1,084, 19 Oct. 1969).

"Wenn . . . gersput!" — ("The Funniest Joke in the World") Idle would later call the joke "written-down gibberish," as it was intended only for easy memorialization, not translation or meaning (Johnson, *20 Years*, 51).

"Whizzo Butter" — ("Whizzo Butter" advert) Parodying television commercials will become a staple in Python's *FC* episodes. This particular instance is obviously modeled after the "Can you tell Stork from butter?" margarine advertising campaign in the UK circa 1956. Leslie Crowther was often the interviewer looking for comments from the man on the street, with "7 out of 10" generally choosing Stork over butter. (Crowther will be referenced again in Ep. 42, when his *The Black and White Minstrel Show* is featured.) A July 1968 *Times* article discussed the effectiveness of this Stork interview campaign, offering salient points not lost on the Pythons:

> One of the most intriguing campaigns, however, has been Stork margarine, relying on the consistent use of virtually the same platform—Can you tell Stork from butter? During the decade 1957–1967 Stork's share of an almost static market has risen from about 34 per cent to about 45 per cent, and to as much as 80 per cent in the medium grade section of the market. The effectiveness of tasting tests and their impact on sales indicated that the campaign's intrinsic interest and novelty, element of challenge, always new participants and the neo-theatrical situation worked, given slightly new variations of the theme to sustain viewer interest an identification. (Wilfred Altman, 2 July 1968)

The Whizzo name and advert patter would have been quite familiar, then, to not only the Pythons, but a potential *Flying Circus* viewing audience. Acton, Ealing, and Walton-on-Thames were often used for location shooting, especially early in the series, as all three were in close proximity to BBC TV Centre and Ealing TFS.

Later, in Ep. 6, the Whizzo Chocolate Company will be memorably featured for offering such tidbits as "Crunchy Frog" and "Anthrax Ripple."

The Whizzo Butter interview scene was shot in the London suburb of Walton-on-Thames, specifically at the then fairly new Town Centre of Walton-on-Thames, which had opened in 1965. (The Milkman Vox Pop seen later in Ep. 3 was also shot at Town Centre.) Though demolished or built over by 2007, this shopping destination had been opened to great fanfare by Bond girl Honor Blackman and beaming local officials in 1965, just four years before this episode was shot. The official opening and dedication were captured by a film crew, and the surviving archival film is called *Walton on Thames Development 1965*, from British Pathe. There is a short memo in the WAC files asking for permission to shoot this scene outside the FJ Wallis store in Acton, but the location of the finished shot was obviously changed at some point to Town Centre.

"Wisborough Green" — ("Picasso/Cycling Race") Wisborough Green is on the A272 between the A283 to the west and the A29 to the east. This mish-mash of directions isn't surprising, or even original to the Pythons. For example, look at Shakespeare's directions, as provided in *Richard III*, for another route:

> From Northampton to London: "Last night, I [hear], they lay at Stony-Stratford / And at Northampton they do rest to-night. / Tomorrow, or next day, they will be here" (2.4.1–3).

Following these directions it certainly would not be tomorrow or the next day; one would find the Irish Sea quicker than the city of London. Phyllis Rackin offers that Shakespeare's dubious geography was certainly "careless," but "only because he had better things to do with his settings than plot their locations on a map . . ." (*MPSERD*, 80) (All Shakespeare citations, unless otherwise indicated, are culled from G. Blakemore Evans's *The Riverside Shakespeare* [1974], and as nearly as possible employ the typesetting and spellings employed therein.)

The Pythons, too, had more on their collective minds as they wrote this sketch than geographical correctness, with the humor revolving around the specter of Picasso biking and painting through English suburbia. Throughout *FC*, there are instances of nearly accurate historical/academic citations and namings, such as *Horace* Walpole being given credit for *Rogue Herries* (Ep. 33) and the precise page (468) of Trevelyan's discussion of the Treaty of Utrecht in Ep. 26, among many others. (It was *Hugh* Walpole who wrote *Rogue Herries* [1930], and Trevelyan discusses the Treaty of Utrecht on page *486* in his 1952 edition. See notes for Eps. 26 and 33 for more.) It's clear that the Pythons more often than not relied on fairly accurate memorialized versions of history and people as they wrote.

One glaring exception will be seen in Ep. 37, where the Pythons quite obviously quote from a significant passage from G.M. Trevelyan (also the 1952 edition) and his discussion of Frederick William and the Seven Years' War.

"with him" — ("Picasso/Cycling Race") In the Picasso painting/cycling sketch, it is only at this moment that this event or publicity stunt becomes an actual race. Prior to this, Picasso was seemingly alone, performing a Guinness-type bike stunt. Now the narrative has transmogrified the stunt into a full-out race, and Picasso becomes just another participant.

This stream-of-consciousness structure is borrowed from Modernist writers well known to the Pythons, including Gertrude Stein, James Joyce, and Virginia Woolf. The sheer number of Modernist painters, sculptors, essayists, novelists, philosophers, and thinkers as well as Modernist public figures and the Modernist ethos in general informs everything the Pythons do in *FC* as they move away from and react to traditional broadcast TV material, formats, and subject matter. The shuffling between Modernism and Postmodernism in the Python oeuvre will be noted throughout.

"writes" — (The Funniest Joke in the World") The music beneath this intro is "Baywood Villa" (WAC T12/1,082).

Episode 2: "Sex & Violence"

"It's" Man dunes intro; *Animation: Titles* (calm Cleese v/o); Part 2: Sheep—Rustic, City Gent and Flying Sheep (Harold the clever sheep); Commercial possibilities of avine aviation; French lecture on sheep-aircraft; Pepperpots and French people; *Animation: "I think therefore I am"*; "And now for something completely different" link; A man with three buttocks; "And now for something completely different" link; A man with three buttocks (continental version); "And now for something completely the same" link; Women's Institute footage—A man with two noses—WI footage; Butlin's redcoat intro; Arthur Ewing and his Musical Mice; Marriage Guidance Counsellor (Deirdre and Arthur Pewtey); Knight-and-rubber-chicken link and "So much for pathos!"; *"The Wacky Queen"* film; Working-class playwright; "And now for something completely different" link; "A Scotsman on a horse" and WI link; A man with two noses reprised; *Animation: Harold the flying sheep link*; The Wrestling Epilogue: "A Question of Belief"; *Animation: Carnivorous pram and Rodin's "The Kiss"*; "The World around Us": *The Mouse Problem* (the Amazing Kargol and Janet; Mouse Problem Vox Pops); "It's" Man closing credits

• A •

"accounts" — ("Marriage Guidance Counsellor") This last phrase seems to be leading to the possibility of a shared sexual experience on a twice-monthly basis for the Pewteys, but quickly caroms off into the keeping of financial accounts. Ep. 15 will look at the possibility of putting a tax on "thingy," meaning sexual activity, and the conclusion is that chartered accountancy could certainly become more interesting at that point. The Pewteys' sex life may vaguely be the point of discussion throughout Arthur Pewtey's long-winded explanation. There is almost a "nudge" moment from Mr. Pewtey, as if he's using a euphemism for his sexual prowess ("after-dinner speaker"), though it again becomes clear rather quickly that he's speaking more gibberish than anything else.

"Aldridge, Arthur" — ("The Mouse Problem") "The late" Arthur Aldridge (by name only) appears in Ep. 3 as a dead witness in a coffin. Cleese and Chapman earlier used this same name in writing a character for *At Last the 1948 Show*.

"all run down" — ("The Mouse Problem") Certainly some orgiastic implications here, especially in English Renaissance terms. Eric Partridge in *Shakespeare's Bawdy* glosses "climb," citing Marston and Chapman again: "To climb a woman's legs (as though they were the limbs of a tree) and then to 'enjoy' her" (*EH* 2.2.366). This "climb" is in this sketch performed all together, as in the mass orgies described by witnesses to the Profumo affair, and the "all run down" suggests a mass climax, as well.

The sordid events of the much later (and completely serious) film *Eyes Wide Shut* (1999; co-written and directed by Stanley Kubrick) bears striking resemblance to this sketch, and the film itself may have been based at least obliquely on the events surrounding the Profumo scandal. Kubrick was, interestingly, making his own dark, turgid comedy (*Dr. Strangelove*) in England at the time this scandal broke, and was fresh off of another sexually charged film, *Lolita* (1962).

"'ampstead" — ("Working-Class Playwright") May be a reference to King's College, Hampstead, London. King's College is a city school, therefore more erudite and refined than Barnsley College, located in Barnsley, South Yorkshire. Barnsley was a major mining town in the nineteenth century. King's College is also affiliated with the National Theatre, specifically, and not the Royal Court Theatre. Barnsley, being a provincial college, would have been the preferred setting, ironically, for another "Angry Young Man" novelist, Kingsley Amis, author of *Lucky Jim* (1954) and *That Uncertain Feeling* (1955). See Drabble's *Oxford Companion to English Literature*. The Romantic poets set up camp in Hampstead in the nineteenth century, too, creating a more artistic sensibility for the region.

Lastly, the 1969 film *Kes*, directed by Ken Loach and set in the harsh, unforgiving Barnsley area, may have unusually forced this Yorkshire region into the public view during this period.

"And now for something completely different" — ("A Man with Three Buttocks") Cleese and Chapman would actually bring this phrase with them from *At Last the 1948 Show*, where it was voiced by Aimee MacDonald, the linking girl and presenter for the show (listen to *At Last the 1948 Show* Album). This particular utterance (by Eric Idle as the Announcer) is one of the rare times that a troupe member other than Cleese speaks these words as either a linking or introductory element. The line doesn't become a catchphrase for the troupe until the second season (appearing in only two episodes of the first season, Eps. 2 and 9 [where Palin actually says it once, and Cleese, twice]), and is then uttered exclusively by Cleese in Eps. 14–17, 19–20, and 22–26. Idle says it again in Ep. 21, then it changes to just "And now," spoken by Cleese, in Eps. 27, 31, and 39. In many episodes, then, it doesn't appear at all, in any form.

animation — (PSC; link into "The Mouse Problem") This sequence features an animated talking head of Sir Gerald Nabarro, the mustachioed Conservative and frequent target of the Pythons, *Private Eye*, et al. This is his first appearance in the series. See the note for "Sir Gerald" in Ep. 11 for more on the flamboyant politician.

Animation: Harold the flying sheep link — (PSC) In this short linking animation, Harold is shot down by an antique cannon over a southeast view of London. St. Paul's can be seen in the center of the city.

Arkwright — (PSC; "Marriage Guidance Counsellor") In the costuming production notes for the show, Palin's Arthur Pewtey character is to be dressed in a "Herbert Arkwright" suit. The name "Arkwright" has appeared prominently earlier in the *ISIRTA* "Incompetence: The Story of the Arkwright Family" sketch, a sketch that has some connection to the "Trouble at mill" section of the "Spanish Inquisition" sketch in Ep. 15. In *ISIRTA*'s version, Mr. Arkwright is the owner of the Fozz Wackett textile mill, and speaks with a noticeable, clipped Yorkshire accent. See notes to Ep. 15 for more.

"Arternoon" — (PSC; "Flying Sheep") Colloquial (and a printed approximation of an accent) version of "afternoon." The suggestion is that there is a coarse Northern accent being used, which is the case, but the accent can be heard on much more than just the odd word. Note the occasional textual mentions, like "Arternoon," "Ar," "'tis," and "Eh."

"Arthur" — (PSC; "Musical Mice") It should be apparent by now that the first name "Arthur" has some significance to Python, as they've named so many characters in just the first two episodes with that very name. "Arthur" will continue to be a favorite throughout *FC* and even into the feature films, such as *Holy Grail*. It could be that Alun Owen's influential screenplay for *Hard Day's Night* (1964; directed by Richard Lester)—wherein George tells a reporter that his hair is called "Arthur"—served as one inspiration.

Specifically an "Arthur" character appears in Eps. 1, 2 (seven different characters), 3, 4 (the episode subtitle and a character), 5, 6, 9 (six different characters), 10, 14, 19 (five different mentions), 20 and 21 (two characters each), 22, 24 (two characters), 27 (three mentions), 31 (three mentions), 35 (two characters), 36 (four characters), 39, and 41.

"attracted to mice" — ("The Mouse Problem") This looks very much like a nod to the then-current Dr. Thomas Harris book *I'm OK You're OK*, released in 1969. These mice-men, in Harris's co-opted "Transactional Analysis" scenario, would be the "not-OK" types who resort to secretive, ritualistic behaviors, including withdrawal and games to avoid the pains of intimacy with "OK" types. Mr. Jackson's comment that he felt more at ease with other mice seems to put us firmly in this new and dynamic world of interpersonal relationships. Interestingly, Harris quotes Kierkegaard and Sartre in his work, both of whom the Pythons also reference (and put great stock in, clearly). Harris's work was based on Eric Berne's earlier book (*Games People Play*, 1963), which may also have influenced this sketch (in its original iteration prior to *FC*).

• B •

"beating about the bush" — ("Marriage Guidance Counsellor") These clichés anticipate the ones Mr. Pewtey will receive shortly from the American Southerner. The sexual connotation of the word "bush" (slang for female pubic hair) is important, especially if

Pewtey's problem is his inability to sexually satisfy his young, nubile wife. The phrase itself refers to the act of one hunter scaring fowl out of brush or bracken, while another hunter waits with a snare or weapon to finish the job. The literary meaning of the term—to "expend labour of which the fruit is not gained by oneself" (*OED*)—applies aptly to Pewtey as he provides the prey, his wife, unwittingly, to the on-the-hunt marriage counselor.

"Belloc, Hillaire" — ("The Mouse Problem") Belloc's first name was actually spelled "Hilaire." Born in France, Belloc (1870–1953) was a naturalized Englishman, and even stood for Parliament for the Liberal Party in 1906. A noted Edwardian poet and historian, Belloc was an ardent Catholic apologist and attacked high finance (even to the point, some said, of bigotry and anti-Semitism). See "Defender of the Faith" from *The New York Press* by William Bryk, 16 March 2000, and Belloc's entry (penned by Bergonzi) in the *ODNB*.

Why Belloc is included with Caesar and Napoleon as a closet mouse isn't clear, though it should be noted that all three qualify as "others" based on their non-Englishness, which may be all that's necessary. Belloc's clearly being used as a punchline of sorts—but there's no smoking gun as to why. It could be that any Frenchman who is of the papist faith and writes children's rhymes must be a closet sexual deviant, a "disgusting little pervert," the brush Python employs often in *FC* to paint "othered" authority figures. (The mention of Belloc's name also produces a significant laugh from the studio audience, even though he's been dead sixteen years by this time.)

Additionally, Belloc was much in the news in 1968 and 1969; his early "pietous" work called *The Old Road*—identifying stops along the supposed British pilgrim's path—fell prey to more modern (and much more skeptical) scholarship (C. Martin, *Times*, 6 Sept. 1969), some well-publicized auctions of complete sets of his works, and even many employments of his name for crossword puzzle purposes.

"The Bells of St. Mary's" — ("Musical Mice") A popular film and song title, the 1945 film starred Bing Crosby and Ingrid Bergman. Crosby sang the title song as well. The film was directed by Leo McCarey.

"blast" — (link into "The Wrestling Epilogue") This somewhat tame imprecation is taken textually as an order, as off-screen we hear "Sir!" (Jones). The cannon fires in response, yet another example of the significance of language and the word, of the power of words in the Python world. It's also a great example of the fluid nature of Python's narrative structure, where bits of earlier material (here, flying sheep) can resurface, and even, in the case of the "Icelandic Saga" sketch in Ep. 27, can intrude, Viking-like, on another narrative.

"blue cheese films" — ("The Mouse Problem") Blue (or bleu) cheese is whitish cheese with veins of blue mold. "Blue" films are off-color, vulgar, or obscene (or pornographic) films. The color blue is also often associated in England with the Conservative Party (see *OED* and the "blue corner" note below), which adds a level of meaning to this already multivalent sketch.

"blue corner . . . red corner" — (PSC; "The Wrestling Epilogue") The corners in the wrestling ring are identified by the color of spit buckets in each. It should be no surprise that the red corner is located at the announcer's left, based on the political spectrum, and that it is the academic who occupies that leftist/socialist position. The monsignor—as a representative of the church—would be characteristically more conservative, thus on the right, politically.

There are also many instances of political pundits fretting over Labour "going red," or forsaking Socialism for Communism, especially prevalent in the UK in the post-Bolshevik Revolution years. And as the Tories tended to be the landed gentry and moneyed merchant class, their "blue"-bloodedness was also a consistent appellation, especially in the post-Victorian era.

"books about belief" — ("The Wrestling Epilogue") In the 1960s a number of religious books were penned by establishment figures such as Rudolf Bultmann, Paul Tillich, Dietrich Bonhoeffer, and perhaps especially Bishop John Robinson's *Honest to God* (1963).

Robinson (1919–1983) was the Bishop of Woolwich in South London. These books popularized "radical theologian discussion" in the UK, and Robinson was an important secular theologian (William P. Williams, communication to the author). Robinson, a "demythologizer," called for new assertions of faith that would transcend and replace old beliefs that had few adherents in modern England—he saw the need for a new "image of God" more real "to people of a secular scientific world" (James, *ODNB*). The firestorm that followed pitted luminaries such as the Archbishop of Canterbury against Robinson in what may have seemed to be epic wrestling matches for the soul of Man.

"Brian" — ("French Lecture on Sheep-Aircraft") Brian is another name that appears repeatedly in the Python oeuvre. A Brian-named character appears in Eps. 2, 4, 9, 11, 13–14 (three characters), 19 (four characters), 20–23, 29, 36–37, 40–41, 43, and 45.

There are many possibilities for the high status this name seems to occupy in Python, including *FC* staff member Brian Jones, and various BBC television commentators sharing the name. The titular character in the feature film *Life of Brian* (1979) is also a Brian (played by Chapman). The most likely, however, refers to Captain Brian Trubshaw, British test pilot and first pilot of the Concorde SST, whom the Queen referred to openly as "my Brian." Cf. the entry for "Trubshawe" below.

"Brie . . . Gouda" — ("The Mouse Problem") Brie and Camembert are both soft cow's milk cheeses from northern France; Cheddar is a hard English cheese; and Gouda is a cheese from The Netherlands generally made in wheels. Cf. "Cheese Shop" sketch from Ep. 33, which features Mr. Mousebender (Cleese) trying to buy cheese from proprietor Wensleydale (Palin), who actually has no cheese to sell.

"Brighton" — ("Marriage Guidance Counsellor") Resort town on the southern coast of England, less than an hour from London. Popularized in the 1750 book by Richard Russell, Brighton became an important resort destination after its publication.

Brighton became even more popular during the privations of the postwar years, as strict limits were imposed on how much British currency could be taken from the country. Many middle-class travelers found that their bank holiday and even summer excursions had to become in-country visits, so the lake country, holiday camps (e.g., Butlin's), and southern seaside destinations like Paignton, Bournemouth, and Torbay boomed in popularity (see the entry for "holiday money" below, as well as Morgan's *Britain since 1945*).

"botty" — ("A Man with Three Buttocks") Another slang for "bottom." Not the first satirists to fixate on the human buttocks, see the rather protracted tale told by the Old Woman in *Candide*, chapters 9, 10, and 12, who lost one buttock (a "rumpsteak") to her captors, and bore "half a backside" ever after.

"bum" — ("A Man with Three Buttocks") This is one of the naughty words which in Ep. 17 the BBC Man (Palin) announces will not be allowed to be mentioned on the show again.

• C •

caption — (PSC; "The Wrestling Epilogue") Title cards like these were requested from the graphics department at TV Centre on a weekly, as-needed basis, and at least initially described as being like cards "the BBC usual [*sic*] do," meaning these cards were a normal part of BBC production, broadcast, and viewing during this period, and part of the humor would be that the silly titles appeared official (WAC T12/1,083).

cards — (PSC; "Marriage Guidance Counsellor") Perhaps (1) a comment on the cost of these generated titles, which in Ep. 6 are jokingly calculated from the beginning of the show; and (2) another way to remind the audience that a link is under way, that a show is being produced and watched. The artifice of the text is not only forwarded, but it seems that the audience is actually being dared to lose interest, to be distracted by the constant reminders of the show's constructedness. Animator Tex Avery pioneered this sign-holding forwardness in his Warner Bros. and later MGM cartoons, borrowing the convention from *fin-de-siècle* comics and political cartoons.

carnivorous pram — (PSC; animated link into "The Mouse Problem") The baby carriage or pram (from "perambulator") eats old ladies who look in to coo at the baby. This motif—a lethal threat from a seemingly harmless entity—has been seen before and will be recurring, found in Ep. 20, where killer sheep are on the loose; Ep. 7, where a blanc mange eats humans; and most memorably in *HG*, as the white rabbit guarding the cave of Caerbannog kills several knights.

"Charlie Gardener" — ("The Wacky Queen") "Charlie" is a slang name that in Britain was reportedly assigned to all night watchmen during the reign of Charles I, and was also used pejoratively to refer to any bumbling, inept person (*OED*). The Goons use it frequently, especially the scheming Hercules Grytpype-Thynne (Sellers) and Moriarty (Milligan), as they identify their next target for ill-gotten gain. This is not necessarily a term that would be found in a Hollywood film or even a wartime newsreel or human interest short.

"chartered accountant" — (PSC; "The Mouse Problem") In Ep. 10 chartered accountants are described as "appallingly dull fellow[s], unimaginative, timid, lacking in initiative, spineless, easily dominated, no sense of humour, tedious company and irrepressibly drab and awful." For dullness, in the Python oeuvre, no profession exceeds chartered accountancy. This is why in the featurette *The Crimson Permanent Assurance* (1983), chartered accountants can incongruously become pirates, pillaging financial concerns worldwide, and why in Ep. 15 a proposed tax on sexual relations could certainly "make chartered accountancy more interesting."

"Chateau La Tour" — ("Working-Class Playwright") The working-class father's substance abuse of choice happens to be a highly respected (and quite expensive) fine red wine, not tobacco, opium or hashish, or whiskey, as might be typical.

"choice" — ("The Mouse Problem") The Vicar (Cleese) is implicated here as advocating and perhaps even participating in aberrant behavior—akin to the Bishop (Jones) leering at the hint of physicality in Ep. 7, the vicar (Idle) rifling the donations box in Ep. 6, the vicar with his nude lady in Ep. 17 (also Idle), the sherry-swilling vicar (Palin, Ep. 36)—and especially as he gestures like a mouse after he finishes speaking.

city gent — (PSC; "Flying Sheep") A bowler hat and dark conservative suit (with vest), an umbrella, and a purposeful look and walk comprise the uniform of the "City Gent" in the Python oeuvre. (The costumers called for "bowler hat and brolly.") This is significant in that by the late 1960s this "uniform" had been out of style for some years, and would have been much more common in the postwar years. The Pythons, then, were relying on a type that might have been out of sight, but certainly not out of mind, and would certainly have been the "look" of the conservative city businessman as the Pythons grew up. "City" refers to the City of London, that one-square-mile area where so much of the financial business of the UK is transacted, and City Gent types are thick.

This visual dichotomy in the sketch—between city and country folk—sets up a motif that Python will revisit over and over again, offering a visual, shorthand way for character (or caricature) depiction, and which also serves the narrative demand for brevity. This typological approach allows Python to present characters without resorting to the usually necessary (and often lengthy) character development, in favor of a pseudo-physiognomic assessment, followed by either narrative support for that assessment (with all the attendant cultural biases, expectations, etc.) or a narrative undercutting. In this case, the Rustic (Chapman) seems to have both more and more significant knowledge than the City Gent (Jones). The Python world allows for this typing, as later seen in Ep. 28, when all it takes to qualify as a woman or child in the "women and children first" abandonment of a sinking ship is for a grown man to dress like a woman or child (or "Flemish Merchant" or "Red Indian" or "Space Man").

This typology is not unlike the descriptive names Ben Jonson gave to some of his characters, including Drugger, Dapper, Dol Common, Mosca, Volpone, Zeal-of-the-Land-Busy, and Sir Politic Would-Be. Even the Elizabethan dramatists' penchant for making all bastards evil, simply because they are bastards (like *Much Ado*'s Don John), or all foreigners untrustworthy because they are foreigners (Aaron the Moor in *Titus Andronicus*) is a precursor of this typological dramatic practice.

Peter Ackroyd notes in *London: The Biography*, that London has always intermixed pantomime and life, which explains "why London has always been considered to be the home of stock theatrical characters—the 'shabby genteel,' the 'city slicker,' the 'wide boy.'" He continues: "In print-shop windows of the mid-eighteenth century there were caricatures of London 'types'" (142). The Pythons would have found their stock characters not in print shop windows, but in pantomimes, on the radio, in film and TV, and in the pages of *Private Eye*, where Bond author Ian Fleming (called "Phlegm") is characterized as a "bored city gent" who's turned to fantasy writing (Ingrams, 56).

Cleveland, Carol — (PSC; "Marriage Guidance Counsellor") This is the first appearance (by a character, not just a passerby) of a female in *FC*. Cleveland is included because she is a beautiful, buxom (real) woman, not a Pepperpot, and she is the object of lustful affection, not scorn or ridicule. This does set the trend for the balance of the series, because—with rare exceptions—the female characters in *FC* are not allowed to rise above the level of either dimwitted mark or bathing beauty, or dimwitted bathing beauty (as in the "Science Fiction" sketch, Ep. 7). Cleveland here is also nearly mute, excepting her ability to titter. She is certainly objectified here, and her second appearance—in Ep. 2, "The Mouse Problem"—will be equally objectified (and equally silent). Prior to joining the cast of *MPFC*, Cleveland had appeared in an equally objectified guest role in a 1966 *Avengers* episode ("A Touch of Brimstone"). Co-starring in that episode was Peter Wyngarde (b. 1933), who will be mentioned by Mrs. Trepidatious (Chapman) in Ep. 37, "What the stars foretell . . ."

It really won't be until Ep. 5 that Cleveland is allowed to be involved in the narrative in a contributive way—in other words, almost like one of the boys:

> Woman (Cleveland): I think it's silly to ask a lizard what it thinks, anyway.
> Chairman: (*off*) Why?
> Woman: I mean they should have asked Margaret Drabble.

See notes to Ep. 5, the "A Duck, a Cat and a Lizard (Discussion)" sketch.

"clever sheep" — ("Flying Sheep") An oxymoron, and indicative of much of Python's incongruous humor. It will often be the seemingly least clever types (Pepperpots, plumbers, peasants) who display the most profound intelligence and canniness in the Python world.

"commercial possibilities" — ("Flying Sheep") He may be a Rustic, but he is also a wily businessman, able to appreciate nuances missed by the City Gent. This will become the case for many lower-class types depicted by the Pythons, including the peasant Dennis (Palin) in *HG*, and many Pepperpots in *FC*. It is the Pepperpot in Ep. 1, after all, who is able to identify that collagist Kurt Schwitters is not English, but German.

Compère — (PSC; "Musical Mice") This unctuous character appears (played by either Palin or Idle) many times in *FC*, and is essentially a greasy emcee at an equally grungy nightclub. Dressed in garish red, he is meant to resemble entertainment hosts—known as "Redcoats"—at Butlin's Holiday Camps (founded 1936–1966), where affordable family vacations and entertainment could be had. These would have been the kinds of destinations that British families were able to afford in the lean postwar years. Also, the kitschy and bizarre "documentaries" *London in the Raw* (1965) and *Primitive London* (1967) feature dank, sweaty clubs like this one, featuring equally greasy compère types.

For the second season the Pythons shot some footage at the Butlin's Holiday Camp in Bognor. See the notes for "Lake Pahoe" in Ep. 32.

"conjuror" — ("The Mouse Problem") A magician, a user of sleight-of-hand tricks or prestidigitation.

"continental version" — ("A Man with Three Buttocks") Referring to the practice of recording multiple versions of a particular radio/television show, episode, etc., one for British audiences, and one for a French or German audience, for example. (The continental versions were often more racy than would have been allowed on "Auntie Beeb," too.) Also, the BBC had for years provided broadcast material in scores of languages for the far-flung corners of the Empire. The Pythons would later themselves be asked to record two episodes of *FC* for German television, the first, at least, in German and subtitled in English. The new *Fliegender Zirkus* episodes featured a combination of new and already-broadcast sketches.

Credits — (end credits) A typed caption/title card was part of the end credits prior to filming/taping, but was not included in the episode. The note reads: "The second exploration into short, sharp, modern humour" (WAC T12/1,083). The Pythons, producer John Howard Davies, or director MacNaughton may have decided that post-commentary would be missed by most viewers, or they simply ran out of time and sacrificed the card. It also might be that, given JHD's rather droll assessment of the previous week's show (he called it "rubbish"), the producers felt the shows couldn't possibly live up to the boastful tagline (WAC T12/1,082).

• D •

deep Southern American voice — (PSC; "Marriage Guidance Counsellor") This look (black hat, mustache, black cowboy gear) as well as the affected drawl is very much a result of the significant presence on British TV of such American Western staples as *The Lone Ranger* (BBC, 1957), *Gunsmoke* (ITV, 1956), *Maverick* (ITV, 1959), *Rawhide* (ITV, 1959), *Bonanza* (ITV, 1960), and later *Big Valley* and *The High Chaparral*.

"Deirdre" — ("Marriage Guidance Counsellor") Actually, the name "Deirdre" is most often associated with a sorrowing and pitiful maiden, so the incongruity (for those who could appreciate the etymology) is understood. This also illustrates Python's interest in unusual naming, usually for incongruous humor. Cf. the impressive Scottish enchanter "Tim" and the mercurial peasant "Dennis," both in *HG*, or the poet reader "Harness Wombat" in Ep. 17, as well as "Mitzie" and "Vicky" (both men) in Ep. 1.

"Descartes, René" — ("Pepperpots in Supermarket") Descartes (1596–1650) was a French mathematician, scientist, and philosopher, and is often called the father of modern philosophy. He is mentioned earlier in Gilliam's animation (when Rodin's "The Thinker" disappears in Ep. 1) and is also memorialized as a "drunken fart" in "The Philosopher's Drinking Song" (or "The Bruce's Song") on both the *Matching Tie and Handkerchief* and *Monty Python Live at Drury Lane* record albums. His influence is decidedly negative in Ep. 14, where Mrs. Simnel (Palin) will lament that children are being spoiled on Cartesian dualism. Descartes and "Cartesian Dualism" is also mentioned in the pre-Python song "Rhubarb Tart" in *At Last the 1948 Show* sung by Cleese. (See the "disappears too" entry below for more.) Descartes and fellow French intellectual Marcel Proust (Eps. 23 and 31) were names/clues in a number of period crossword puzzles as well.

desk — (PSC; "A Man with Three Buttocks") This is a standard BBC or ITV news/announcer set, complete with desk, chair, framing backdrop, and framed back-projection (BP) screen. A slide image of a walrus is projected on the BP screen behind the announcer, though it is never noticed or mentioned during the scene. Other slides that will appear without comment or context will include an illustration of an allosaurus, a naked sailor on a rug (photo by Robert Broeder, and which will be used again in Ep. 28), and the well-known 1934 photo taken by Dr. Robert Wilson, purportedly of the Loch Ness Monster. The photo was subsequently identified as a fake—it is in actuality a miniature floating model of the monster's head and neck.

disappears too — (PSC; animated link into "A Man with Three Buttocks") A clever play on Descartes's "Cogito, ergo sum," his famous summation of his belief in the significance of human thought as clear evidence of existence. The "gag" here is simple and profound: remove a man's thoughts, and you remove the man.

This image is a retouched photo of Rodin's statue *The Thinker* (1880).

This also indicates the power of the animator, the creator, in relation to the characters and worlds he creates. Gilliam's hands will often enter the seemingly sacrosanct diegetic world of the animation frame to manipulate that world before our eyes. This "figuration of the artist" in animation goes back to its earliest days. Pioneers J. Stuart Blackton, Winsor McCay, and Max Fleischer, among others, created animated cartoons where the hand of the animator can be seen to initiate the action, to create the cartoon world, to give the breath of life to inanimate drawings. In Fleischer's "Out of the Inkwell" series (c. 1919–1923), Fleischer's hand and pen create and/or set free Ko-ko the Clown from his inkwell, and the cartoon can only end when Ko-ko is returned to his capped home. In Later *FC* episodes, Gilliam will even insert his face and body into the frame, and in the feature film *Monty Python and the Holy Grail*, the audience gets to see the animator die of a heart attack, ending the animated sequence.

The "thought bubble" that is pricked in the Descartes/*Thinker* scene is an element used by cartoonists (and early animators like McCay, Wallace Carlson, William Nolan, Emile Cohl, et al.) to indicate a character's thoughts. The thought bubble often looks more cloudlike (fluffy around the edges) than a speech bubble. These bubbles were also present in the pages of *Private Eye*, reportedly suggested by Peter Cook to enliven the necessary but boring ministerial photos (Ingrams, 8).

• E •

"East Anglia" — ("The Wrestling Epilogue") The University of East Anglia is in Norwich, and in Ep. 20 is also the school where undergraduate village idiots matriculate. The university was established in 1962, and was thus a very "new" university in Britain in 1969, and therefore suspect. Oxford and Cambridge—where most of the Pythons studied—have been in existence since the thirteenth and fourteenth centuries, respectively.

Eek Eek Club — (PSC; "The Mouse Problem") This is a reference to clubs like Berlin's famous KitKatKlub, but may also reach back further, to the political and literary Kit Cat (or Kit Kat) Club founded in the eighteenth century in London. Whig politics and associations were the board of fare, and members included writers Congreve, Vanbrugh, Addison, and Steele, and politicians like the Duke of Marlborough and Sir Robert Walpole. The salacious and political possibilities, however, indicate a mixture of both references—meaning these sex clubs might be gathering places for Conservative Party deviants. (See the entries for "blue cheese films" and "blue corner" above for more.)

Caerphilly is a cheese originally from Caerphilly (Glamorgan, Wales), and "a go-go" indicates this is essentially a cheese strip club. This dance club's sign notes that it is actually located in Soho and is likely originally a sign for the "Whisky a Go Go" strip club at 33 Wardour Street, W1.

"Epilogue" — ("The Wrestling Epilogue") The signing-off show on early BBC-TV. A clergyman would read and then comment on scriptural passages. In *Hard Day's Night* (1964), the TV director (Victor Spinetti, 1949–2012) driven toward a breakdown by The Beatles' antics is certain that his failure will result in a career-ending *Epilogue* assignment.

Episode 2 — This is the second installment of the *Flying Circus* series, though it was recorded first on 30 August 1969, and broadcast 12 October 1969. (The calendar in the Marriage Counsellor's office indicates 28 August, incidentally, meaning they must have pulled it off of someone's office wall as they prepped the shoot.) The filmed portions (outside of the studio) would have been shot earlier, in July 1969.

Throughout most of this show's pre-filmed life this episode was known in internal BBC memos and communiqués as "Bunn, Wackett, Buzzard, Stubble, and Boot," not "Sex & Violence" (WAC T12/1,083). This obviously created some confusion in the middle management levels of the BBC, leading the Head of Light Entertainment, Michael Mills, to ask that any such subtitles be either de-emphasized or gotten rid of altogether (WAC T12/1,242).

In an in-house memo (probably from the desk of John Howard Davies), the delayed reaction to Episode 1 is recorded: "This week's episode [Episode 2] stars as usual John Cleese, Michawl [*sic*] Palin, Terry Jones, Graham Chapman and Eric Idle, and deals with the same idiotic rubbish as the first show but, we hope, will be funnier" (WAC T12/1,082).

"escape" — ("Flying Sheep") Perhaps even an obtuse reference to the recent hit film *The Great Escape* (1963), which is later satirized aptly in Ep. 28, as part of the "Trim-Jeans Theatre" sketch.

• F •

"farmer's wife" — ("The Mouse Problem") Reenactments of mouse roles in various fairy tales and children's rhymes characterize these parties, clearly. This last reference (the farmer's wife) hints at a pleasure/pain sadomasochistic theme, complete with a knife-wielding dominatrix and her willing, squeaking victims. See the "perverts meet" note for more on sadomasochism. The "matron" chasing these mice-men is Jones in drag, and with a full mustache.

These interiors were recorded inside the home at 48 Ullswater Road, where portions of the "The Funniest Joke in the World" (Ep. 1) were also shot.

"fellows" — ("The Mouse Problem") This seems to confirm that participants at these deviant gatherings were all male, thus supporting and escalating the homoerotic reading, where young white males seek illicit sexual thrills.

"Figgis, Arthur" — (PSC; "A Man with Three Buttocks") Character played by Cleese (Ep. 20) and Chapman (Eps. 2 and 6). In Ep. 20, Figgis is a village idiot; otherwise he seems to be an interviewer/announcer for the BBC. Figgis is mentioned here as if the audience would know him, though there isn't an accompanying laugh, so this may just be a setup for the cycling shot to come. It could be that Figgis is borrowing from the group over at *Private Eye*, who castigate *Punch* and its ancient librarian, "Figgis" (see the first issue of *Private Eye*).

"fight for it" — ("The Wrestling Epilogue") Classic confrontation between believers in God and believers in men, between religion and humanism, and probably a subtle comment on the "troubles" already under way among Northern Ireland's differing believers (Roman Catholic and Protestant), as well as recent religious conflicts in the Middle East where Britain found itself involved both militarily and diplomatically. There are also allusions here to the ongoing and often vitriolic debate between those who believe in a higher power and those who simply do not, and would have fit the contentions between men like Hilaire Belloc (see above) and Bishop John Robinson (see "books about belief" note above). The specter of two respected men wrestling for the existence of God isn't any less or more ridiculous, the Pythons seem to be saying, than two nations fighting and killing each other for essentially the same cause.

In the 5 April 1963 edition of *Private Eye*, cartoonist "Timothy" provides a two-page spread titled "Britain Gets Wythe Itte, 1963," a spoof on Tory attempts to make over the party's image from fussy and Victorian to hip and au courant. One placard attached to St. Martin-in-the-Fields reads: "Debate—Is There a God?" and lists two bishops who will be arguing the point in a repeat BBC show (Ingrams 80–81).

"film" — ("The Mouse Problem") In Ep. 18, the "*Blackmail*" sketch, the film presented is also of poor quality, as it is also a "hidden camera" film from the BBC.

Much of this footage was shot at or near 48 Ullswater Road, Barnes, with the police station shots being filmed at Barnes Police Station, Lonsdale Road (WAC T12/1,083).

film leader — (PSC; "The Wacky Queen") Correctly a "universal leader," since a film leader is actually just blank film that allows for the threading of the film through a projector. A universal leader is a "leader designed according to the ANSI [American National Standards Institute] document PH22.55 for the current projection rate of 24 frames per second (1-1/2 feet per second), and recommended for use on all release prints. It was designed to replace the Academy [of Motion Picture Arts and Sciences] leader originally conceived when the motion picture projection rate was 16 frames per second" (Pincus, 181).

"flying . . . slam" — ("The Wrestling Epilogue") The flying mare and full body slam are professional wrestling moves.

• G •

"Gladstone" — ("The Wacky Queen") William Gladstone (1809–1898) was a longtime and repeat British Prime Minister (1868–1874, 1880–1885, 1886, 1892–1894). His relationship with Victoria (see note below) soured late in his life, and in 1894 he tendered his resignation, rendering it highly unlikely that he would have cavorted about with his Queen for a silent comedy film. See *ODNB*. An early portrait of Gladstone is used by Gilliam for an animation in Ep. 6. There he's a bit effeminate and racing around in a criminal pram.

"Gosh" — ("Marriage Guidance Counsellor") Probably a slight swipe at the American version of English, and American colloquialisms. Also, it sounds very much like what the awestruck young Joey Starrett might say in *Shane* (1953).

"Greaves, Jimmy" — (film leader link into "The Wacky Queen") The name "Jimmy Greaves" takes the place of the number "5" in the leader as broadcast. Greaves was an English national team and professional football star, appearing in the 1962 and 1966 World Cup tournaments. England won the World Cup in 1966.

• H •

"Harold" — ("Flying Sheep") This very determined and clever "Harold" may be a reference to once Secretary of the Royal Aero Club, Commander Harold

Perrin, known as "Harold the Hearty." Harold, who ran the Royal Aero Club from 1906 to 1945, was characterized as "brilliant," and a man obsessed with the possibilities and inevitability of flight.

"have a go" — ("The Wacky Queen") This is much more a British phrase than American. All three citations in the *OED* are from Commonwealth sources. Again, just a slight malapropism as the Englishmen attempt an American monologue, obviously without consulting the lone American on the staff, Terry Gilliam. See entries for "hosepipe" and "wacky" for more.

"Hello Sailor" — ("The Wrestling Epilogue") A phrase used many times in *FC* (and at least once in *The Goon Show*), and always associated with homosexuality (see Ep. 14, as well). The phrase alludes to (ostensibly) women picking up sailors, but is adapted to the homosocial world of *FC*. Both men's sexuality is called into question, one by name (Gay) and the other by the title of his work ("Hello Sailor").

This motif will run throughout the series, where Her Majesty's sailors are, when mentioned, gay and usually rather effeminate. See later "sailor" references in Eps. 10, 20, 28, and 30 for more. Peter Sellers had created a sailor character for *The Goon Show* (in the early 1950s) who was poncy, neat, and easily irritated, and who spoke with the now-familiar lisp, a portrayal that seems a direct influence on the Pythons.

"hole" — ("The Mouse Problem") Can be read as either a homo- or heterosexual innuendo, especially in light of the secretive and perverse nature of the activity. Cf. Jonson's *Bartholomew Fair* where the puppet Leander tells Leatherhead to ". . . kiss my hole here, and smell" (5.4.135), suggesting the anal orifice, and the specter of love creeping "in at a mouse-hole" in Middleton and Rowley's *The Changeling* (3.3.100), to add the possibility of heterosexual encounters. See Henke's *Courtesans and Cuckolds* for more.

"holiday money" — ("Marriage Guidance Counsellor") During the postwar period, austerity measures enacted by the government to combat a badly slumping economy included the strict control of currency. British travelers overseas were at one time only allowed to take £30 with them, meaning most never could actually afford to leave the island(s). Thus, as Kenneth Morgan mentions: "People traveled to seaside holidays (especially on the fixed 'August Bank Holidays') in tightly packed and unmodernized rolling stock, or perhaps in ancient coaches" (*Britain since 1945*, 77). By 1969, that £30 figure had risen, evidently, under a Labour government. In a "Mrs. Wilson's Diary" entry in *Private Eye*, Chancellor Jenkins has just returned from a continental holiday, suntanned and confident, while the Scilly-refreshed PM Wilson, a bit parky over Jenkins's cheek, asks: "As a matter of interest, how did you fiddle the fifty pound limit?"

In the sketch Palin seems to be offering a character who knows this controlled, penny-conscious life intimately well; perhaps because Palin himself grew up in that environment, as did the rest of the troupe. Mates of the Pythons The Beatles broached this territory, as well, in McCartney's "When I'm Sixty-Four": "Every summer we can rent a cottage on the Isle of Wight, if it's not too dear / We shall scrimp and save . . ." (audio transcription from the McCartney/Lennon song, *Sgt. Pepper's Lonely Hearts Club Band* album, 1967).

See the entry for "sharing the interests" below for more.

"holiday or . . ." — ("Flying Sheep") Here the City Gent (Jones) looks the Rustic (Chapman) up and down from behind, doing a quick visual assessment of the rustic clothing, and by the look on his face, knows the answer to his own question—the man is a local. D.H. Lawrence approached this same kind of intercultural friction in the relationship between the gamekeeper Mellors and Lady Chatterley in *Lady Chatterley's Lover*:

> Mellors: "If yer want ter be 'ere, yo'll non want me messin' abaht a' th' time."
> Lady Chatterley: "Why don't you speak ordinary English?"

The Pythons will revisit this Lawrence-like world of haves and have-nots (of owners and workers) in the "Working-Class Playwright" scene later in this same episode, and throughout *FC*, whenever a toff meets a commoner.

"homosexual . . . drug-addict . . . footballer" — ("Working-Class Playwright") A reference inspired by the *Private Eye* staff's take on Tony Richardson's 1961 film, *A Taste of Honey*:

> We were lucky enough to find two exciting new cheap unknowns in Alfred Weights and Shirley-June Tush to play the lead parts of the *latently homosexual professional lacrosse player* Arthur Sidmouth, and Doreen, the girl who watches sympathetically from a bar stool in the film's opening shots as Arthur vomits up his half-pint of ginger shandy. (Ingrams 41; italics added)

The "homosexual nymphomaniac drug-addict" reference could also be an allusion to Chapman himself, who was known to struggle with alcoholism and his homosexuality (see Morgan [1999, 57, 68, 91]). Cleveland said of Chapman: "[He] always did everything to excess, everything he did: obviously his drinking and the way he flaunted his homosexuality . . . caused a certain amount of embarrassment at the time" (Morgan 1999, 68). Chapman's outré behavior may have been an embarrassment publicly, perhaps, but clearly not enough to steer clear of homosexual gibes throughout *FC*, many featuring Chapman chiming in with gusto.

This description of the father's play is also an amalgamation of "Angry Young Men" plots, including David Storey's *This Sporting Life* football theme (note the homosocial and even homoerotic post-match shower room scene), and homosexual themes and tension in many works of the period, including authors John Osborne (*A Patriot for Me*, 1965), Harold Pinter (*The Servant*, 1963), and Storey (*Radcliffe*, 1963). In *This Sporting Life*, the (anti)hero Frank Machin (played by Richard Harris) destroys himself and any relationship he may have been able to have with Margaret (Rachel Roberts) and her children with drink, angst, and self-doubt. (For more, see Aldgate's *Censorship and the Permissive Society* and Carpenter's *The Angry Young Men*.) *Private Eye* spoofs the critical fawning over the movement in its 4 May 1962 issue. Pinter, by the way, is also later lampooned in *FC* Ep. 10, the "Arthur Tree" sketch, as "Harold Splinter."

"**hosepipe**" — ("The Wacky Queen") A spigot or faucet, the term "hosepipe" isn't generally used in the United States, betraying the Pythons' British approach to American English.

"Hounslow" — ("The Mouse Problem") In the West London borough, near Heathrow Airport. "MIDDLESEX." is actually shortened to "MIDDX." on the caption card.

This caption spot may very well have been the place in this episode where the then-current home address of former mate and employer David Frost was included. Immediately after the initial broadcast of the episode on 12 October, Frost (or his people) must have called the BBC higher-ups (including Tom Sloan, Head of Light Entertainment, and even the Postmaster General) to complain about the direct reference, prompting a memo dated 14 October 1969 from producer John Howard Davies to director Ian MacNaughton, asking (tiredly, it seems, as if he were talking to or about naughty children) that the caption be changed. JHD asks that Cleese come in and record a new voiceover, so that after the repeats Davies won't have to get "castrated again" by the BBC (WAC T12/1,084). Contemporary phone books list a "Frost, DP" (completely, his name is David Paradine Frost) living at 84 Alexandra Road, NW8 with the phone number 01-624 1568. This is in the Camden suburb of London.

Davies was especially vexed since the Pythons had, in the previous episode, slipped Frost's phone number somewhere into the episode. Frost's *production* company, David Paradine Productions Ltd., had the phone number 01-584 5313 during this period, and his home number was MAIda Vale 1568, according to the British Telephone Historical Archives. Neither of these phone numbers appear or are mentioned in the first two *FC* episodes as they survive today, nor in the printed scripts, meaning the requested changes must have been made. (By 1971, according to BT records, Paradine and Frost had moved to swankier digs in Mayfair, all the more reason for the Pythons to dislike him.)

The Pythons would take infrequent potshots at Frost in *FC*, who had parlayed his Cambridge Footlights secretary position into satirical shows for the BBC, and who eventually became a fixture on British and even American TV as an interviewer and presenter. Frost's rather naked ambition seems to have rubbed a number of people, Pythons and *Beyond the Fringe* types included, the wrong way (see Humphrey Carpenter's *That Was Satire, That Was* for more). *Private Eye* cofounder and contributor Richard Ingrams characterized Frost in this warmly unflattering way in 1971:

> From the start Frost evinced a profound animosity from the founding fathers of the satire movement. There was something ungentlemanly about a man who was so obviously on the make. His astonishing industry ran counter to the spirit of public-school amateurism which characterized *Beyond the Fringe* and *Private Eye*. At the same time there was a strange charm about his barefaced ambition which was somehow endearing. (11)

It is no surprise, then, that the Pythons lump Frost in with the sexual deviants. By Ep. 19, Frost will be lampooned as Timmy Williams, an unctuous, insufferable TV hack.

• I •

"ici" — ("French Lecture on Sheep-Aircraft") Translation: "The travelers, the luggage, they are here!" Just prior to this, Jean-Brian (Palin) asks (in Franglish) where the passengers and baggage might be, and his partner (Cleese) answers the question.

interviewer — (PSC; Pepperpot link out of "French Lecture on Sheep-Aircraft") These are the same Pepperpots who in Ep. 1 couldn't tell the difference between Whizzo Butter and a dead crab; here they are able to appreciate the abstract and often difficult contributions of noted French philosophers. (See the entry for "Pepperpots" in Ep. 1 and "Jean-Paul Sartre" in this episode for more.) This scene is shot in the F.J. Wallis store in Acton, then located at Unit 9 Shopping Precinct, Acton High Street (WAC T12/1,242). Two Pepperpots (Mrs. Premise and Mrs. Conclusion) will discuss Sartre's worldview—and especially his writings on freedom and materialism—in Ep. 27, even traveling to Paris to confront him directly.

• J •

"Jackson, Arthur" — ("The Mouse Problem") Cf. Arthur "Two-Sheds" Jackson from Ep. 1. The address below this name on the caption may have been where the address of David Frost was broadcast, the inclusion of which caused a punch-up in BBC management, leading to JHD's memo to director Ian MacNaughton, and a change in the taped version for rebroadcast. See the entry for "Hounslow" above, and the entry for "*scoreboard*" in Ep. 1.

"Jehovah" — ("The Wrestling Epilogue") God of the Old Testament, and well chosen since it translates to "God the Almighty" in later Christian usage.

• K •

"Kargol and Janet" — ("The Mouse Problem") A hint of a narrative fracture here, especially as Janet (Cleveland) bursts into the frame, though acknowledgment of the rupture hasn't occurred, and the documentary atmosphere is still in force—at least at the diegetic level. In fact, the Linkman (Palin) will push the interview through/across this attempted narrative disruption by framing his questions to Kargol (Chapman) *the psychiatrist*, and not Kargol *the conjuror*. The smoothing over or resistance to the narrative disruption holds the presented diegetic world together, and the documentary can continue in earnest. This kind of fissure, in other episodes, will lead the narrative off into new directions, to "something completely different," as in Ep. 27, or stop it completely, as in Ep. 35, "Mortuary Hour," when an interruption by Badger (Idle) causes the sketch to be abandoned.

In the production notes for this episode, Janet's costume is supposed to look as if "she were assisting Mike and Bernie Winters" (WAC T12/1,083). The Winterses were comedians (and brothers) popular in the UK in the 1950s and 1960s, and who hosted their own TV shows in the early 1970s.

"Kierkegaard" — ("The Wrestling Epilogue") Søren Kierkegaard (1813–1855) was a Danish religious philosopher, a critic of "systematic rational philosophy," and is seen as the father of the existentialist trends in philosophy (Drabble 1985, 531). The continuing reference to Existentialist thought and thinkers should be noted, and displays the Pythons' debt to the Modernist period. For more on Kierkegaard and his influence on the Pythons (and the twentieth-century Existentialists), see notes to Eps. 14, 27, and 28, where his writings in *Either/Or* become significant, and specifically "Crop Rotation."

"kill 'em" — ("The Mouse Problem") It's not entirely clear whether all voices are talking about men who want to be mice, or actual mice. In any case, many of the solutions read like rodenticide—meaning men who act like mice can/should be treated as such.

• L •

Lawrence, D. H. — (PSC; "Working-Class Playwright") Lawrence (1885–1930), a Northerner himself, born in Eastwood in Nottinghamshire, was first recognized as that newest and brashest of literary breeds, the working-class novelist. The Oedipal elements of his works have been identified as early examples of the psychoanalyzing of characters in modern literature (see Ep. 43 for *Hamlet* on the psychiatrist's couch). The Pythons writing into the script "right out of D. H. Lawrence" obviates the need for a physical description of the set, for the production designers and viewers, and eventually taps into the acculturated viewer's knowledge of Lawrence, his tropes and characters/settings, and television and cinematic adaptations of his work. The viewer (or reader?) who understood these allusions could sport his/her "badge of acculturation," and "get" the in-jokes and allusions, just like one who "knows" Shakespeare can similarly claim acculturation (*MPSERD*, 24–25). This is an example of the Pythons' trotting out their academic credentials, where the similarly educated viewer can appreciate the allusions on multiple levels.

"Leamington" — ("The Mouse Problem") A city in the Warwick district, Warwickshire, and home to the Royal Leamington Spa.

little man — (PSC; "Marriage Guidance Counsellor") The Man (Arthur Pewtey) is described in the production notes for this episode as wearing a "Herbert Arkwright suit, eventually to be torn by a Buffalo," which is probably an oblique reference to the character created by Ronnie Barker, Arkwright, in *Seven of One*, a series of comedy pilots (WAC T12/1,083), and was probably a new iteration of an earlier Barker character. The BBC described the character as a "stuttering, miserly, lustful shopkeeper." The mentioned buffalo—perhaps meant to appear in relation to Cleese's Southerner—never did materialize in the episode. (This may just be that portions of the potential shows each week were elided for time or taste, and any production-related requests would also have been canceled.) Another short sketch—called the "Quickie Duel" in the show's notes—was also written and reportedly even recorded, but never made part of the broadcast episode (see WAC files for 1969 and the First Season). The elided scene may have finally appeared in Ep. 9, during "The Hunting Film." There, two duelers (Cleese and Chapman), take aim and fire at each other, but the second in between (Palin) is the one who drops dead. The scene seems slightly out of context as the duelers are costumed in more eighteenth- and nineteenth-century garb, while the hunters elsewhere are wearing their tweed and plus-fours. Johnson in *The First 20 Years of Monty Python* carefully notes the variations from printed script to recorded show (as do a number of fan websites), so most of these changes won't be addressed in these notes.

"London" — ("Working-Class Playwright") Again, a character defined by his speech, the way he talks and words he chooses. This satire is based entirely on the "Angry Young Men" and their "Kitchen Sink" dramas produced by young British novelists, filmmakers, and playwrights in the late 1950s and into the early 1960s, and often set in provincial mining and textile mill areas and featuring working-class antiheroes. Films like *Look Back in Anger* (1958), *Room at the Top* (1959), and *This Sporting Life* (1963) emerged from this social realist movement, a movement born of the British documentary "Free Cinema" of the postwar years. Significant playwrights of the period included John Braine, John Osborne, Harold Pinter, and David Storey. (See Aldgate's *Censorship and the Permissive Society* for more on the movement, as well as Carpenter's *The Angry Young Men: A Literary Comedy of the 1950s*.)

In *Room at the Top* (dir. Jack Clayton), for instance, the hero Joe Lampton (Laurence Harvey) wants nothing more than to stay out of his village and move up into the world of the upwardly mobile, and he's willing to do anything (and become anyone) to achieve his goals.

In the Pythons' world, though, instead of the working-class younger generation lashing out at the stultifying effects of life in the mines or mills, it's the older working-class artist blasting the effete notions of what real labor is, and where the really meaningful production is going on in Britain (on the stage, page, and screen). Python subverts expectations by almost reversing the Oedipal structure to favor the working-class playwright father over the "laborer" son. The Pythons are also subtly validating their own existence as artists—each from a working-class background.

The 4 May 1962 edition of *Private Eye* (1.10) spoofs this allegedly working-class literary and theatrical movement, as well, making fun of the "fee-paying school" grads like Osborne, and spoofing Richardson's *A Taste of Honey*.

• M •

"man's got to do" — ("Marriage Guidance Counsellor") A Marlovian "mighty line," of sorts. Cf. Marcus Aurelius Antoninus's *Meditations*: "In the morning, when you are sluggish about getting up, let this thought be present: 'I am rising to a man's work'" (Book V, 1). American Negro League baseball pitcher Satchel Paige spoke similarly when he said, discussing his use of multiple pitches and "looks": "Man's got to do what he's got to do." There's also some very similar dialogue throughout the 1952 Western *High Noon*, where Sheriff Kane (Gary Cooper) must go back and face the evil Frank Miller, simply because it's what he must do. This is also essentially the reason, Shane (Alan Ladd) explains, why he must go to town and face the gunman in black (Jack Palance) in *Shane* (1953).

"men now known to have been mice" — ("The Mouse Problem") "Veni, Vidi, Vici" ("I came, I saw, I conquered") were Julius Caesar's words (by his own account) at the defeat of Pharnaces in Anatolia. Caesar lived from c. 100 BC to 44 BC. He is also featured (as he dies) in Ep. 15, the "*Julius Caesar* on an Aldis Lamp" scene. Napoleon Bonaparte (1769–1821), emperor of France, stands in his familiar hand-in-coat pose. These inserts were shot in the dunes near Bournemouth.

If this sketch is actually about closet homosexuality, as it seems, then what the presenter is doing is what—according to Wayne Dynes in *Homosexuality: A Research Guide*—began to appear among "homosexual scholars in German-speaking countries" in the nineteenth century—namely, lists of noteworthy homosexuals in history (182). Dynes continues, identifying the historians' justifications for such (somewhat fanciful) listwork:

> Parallel tendencies occur with scholars representing other minority groups, where such lists seem to function to provide historical witness of the collective worth of an ostracized group. This "hall of fame" approach has recently been criticized as skewing homosexual and lesbian history towards an unrepresentative elite, effacing historical variety and class differences. The search for famous homosexuals also provokes a largely fruitless series of debates over whether figures of the past, such as Socrates or Caesar, were truly homosexual. (182)

Not historians by trade, the Pythons aren't trying to recuperate their chosen historical figures by creating a newfound "collective worth," they are instead ridiculing these same figures by tagging them with the sexual diminishment label used so often in *FC*. Again, for the Pythons, power and closet perversion go hand in hand as they here also favor the "unrepresentative elite"—Napoleon, Caesar—with their satiric attentions.

A portion of this sex-power connection must be attributed to the many lurid stories in tabloid newspapers of important (often political) men doing questionable things of a sexual nature. For instance, in December 1958 the political career of Ian Harvey, a Harrow East Conservative, was brought to an ignominious end when he was arrested in the bushes of St. James Park *in flagrante delicto* with a young member of the Coldstream Guards. Harvey even tried to make a break for it, contemporary reports say, but was easily caught. Both parties were eventually charged with "breaching the park's regulations," fined £5, and released. (This was also discussed, soberly and in respect to the Profumo affair, in *Private Eye* in the 12 November 1965 issue [Ingrams 129].) No surprise, then, that the Pythons can see both the Coldstream Guards–type organizations and any member of the government as potential closet perverts. In Ep. 14, for example, the Household Cavalry will be alluded to as a bastion of homosexuality. (The Goons also jab at the Household Cavalry in "The Telephone" and "The Starlings.")

"Mice and Men" — ("The Mouse Problem") Play on John Steinbeck novel title, *Of Mice and Men*, which is itself borrowed from noted Scotsman Robert Burns's 1785 poem, "To a Mouse": "The best laid schemes o' mice and men / Gang aft a-gley" (stanza 7).

monsignor . . . skull cap — (PSC; "The Wrestling Epilogue") This prelate is wearing black robes with red lining, including a short cape and matching skull cap. The actor is Terry Medlicote, from the Tough Guys Agency (WAC T12/1,083), and is obviously a professional wrestler, as he has noticeable cauliflower ear. Given the originally religious nature of *Epilogue*, this prelate character fits rather well.

Not so his opponent, a so-called old Don figure. This wrestler appears to be the prototypical Cambridge don, with tweedy conservative attire. An "old Don" is actually a college fellow or tutor. This would have been the "type" of lecturer the Pythons encountered at Oxford and Cambridge, and even in their prep schools. The actor is Brian Lancaster from Tough Guys Agency (WAC T12/1,083).

"mouse organ" — ("Musical Mice") Play on "mouth-organ," also known as a harmonica. This entire sketch was reportedly added to the episode's script after-the-fact (Johnson, *20 Years*, 49).

Mouse Problem — ("The Mouse Problem") According to Cleese, this sketch was originally written prior to *FC*, when Cleese and Chapman were writing additional material for a Peter Sellers film, *The Magic Christian* (1969; screenplay by Terry Southern). Sellers rejected the idea, eventually, and Cleese and Chapman retooled it for *FC* (Johnson, *20 Years*, 50). (The "Dead Parrot" sketch appearing later in Ep. 8 was also written prior to *MPFC*, beginning its life as a customer's attempt to return a "lemon" used car.)

"The Mouse Problem" sketch is also significant in that it is sustained satire without the self-consciousness characteristic of much of *FC*. This continuity may be attributed to its earlier incarnation as a proposed section of a complete, narratively fluid film. Additionally, the undercutting and acknowledgment of the artifice is missing here, with the exception of Kargol's (Chapman) attempt to perform as a conjuror, not a psychiatrist. The interviewer (Palin) refuses to let him do so, and the narrative moves on without interruption.

"Must Go" — (PSC; "The Mouse Problem") These placards are based on then-current anti-Vietnam posters like "Ho Ho Ho Troops Must Go," "SHHHAME," and "Put the Nix-On War—Bring Peace Now," seen in the streets of London and across the United States. Significant anti-war demonstrations had occurred in London in both March and October of 1968.

• N •

"National Theatre" — ("Working-Class Playwright") The National Theatre (actually several theater spaces) opened as a subsidized theater in 1962, on the South Bank of the Thames. Its inaugural play was *Hamlet*, starring Peter O'Toole, in 1963. The National Theatre was actually home to more conventional plays, including Shakespeare and other English Renaissance drama revivals, whereas the Royal Court Theatre (English Stage Company, St. Martin's Lane, London) staged works from this "new" group of playwrights, including Osborne (and the 1956 premiere of *Look Back in Anger*), Wesker, Arden, Storey, and others, as well as important foreign plays from Brecht, Ionesco, Beckett, Sartre, and Duras. (See royalcourttheatre.com.)

"Old Vic" is the colloquial name for the venerable Royal Victorian Theatre (Waterloo Road, London), which had to be rebuilt after the bombings of WWII. It's worth noting that this radical middle-aged playwright (as played by Chapman) would be hanging out with the more "establishment" types (Olivier, Redgrave, Gielgud, etc.) at both the Old Vic and National Theatre, and not the Angry Young Men types. This is either a mistake in venues from the Pythons, or yet another subversion, the latter being more likely.

newspaper headlines — (PSC; "The Mouse Problem") This headline has been physically replaced (cut-and-pasted by Gilliam) on what appears to be an actual contemporary edition of *News of the World*. (The Pythons requested that these newspapers look like, specifically, *News of the World, Daily Express*, and the *Times* [WAC T12/1,083].) Another (actual) story running in the same issue is titled "The Rise and Fall of the Kennedy Clan" (this hard on the heels of Ted Kennedy's 18 July 1969 Chappaquiddick incident). The "Peer Faces Rodent Charges" headline appears on the Friday, 15 August 1969 edition of the *Daily Express*, also a touched-up version, and replaced the original headline. Images of these newspapers are still available on microfilm.

A following headline ("Mouse Clubs on Increase") is pasted onto a retouched version of the Monday, 28 July 1969 (late London) edition of the *Times*, which also features a story on new test results from Apollo mission moon rock samples. (The Apollo frenzy will be treated in Ep. 28, "*Life of Tschaikowsky*.") The headline and story "Rocks of Moon a Puzzle" occupy the far right column of the paper; a photo of the astronauts' wives visiting their husbands in isolation has been replaced by the mouse photo. Feature stories on Edward Kennedy's post-Chappaquiddick difficulties were replaced by the "Mouse Clubs on Increase" headline and story. Gilliam (or the show's staff) has obviously manipulated these front pages, since one story seen here—"Boys help in plane hijack"—is actually lifted from the 18 August issue. In that issue, the hijacking story actually appeared on page five. The story under the "Mouse Clubs On Increase" headline is borrowed and edited (the opening paragraph is gone) from the 20 August edition, and discusses the precarious position of the new Sudanese government.

Northern couple — (PSC; "Working-Class Playwright") The son (Idle) is wearing a very nice business suit, while the Northern couple (Chapman and Jones) look like comfortable working folk. In the costuming notes for this particular episode, the costume designer is given this prompt for these characters: "Both look like Mr. and Mrs. Trevor Howard in *Sons and Lovers*" (WAC T12/1,083). Actor Trevor Howard (1913–1988) starred (with Dean Stockwell and Wendy Hiller) in the 1960 film adaptation of the Lawrence novel directed by Jack Cardiff. *Sons and Lovers* is the 1913 D.H. Lawrence novel based on his own childhood in Eastwood, Nottinghamshire. This visual dichotomy (again, here and throughout *FC* used as shorthand for the audience) will become quite important as the scene plays out.

The term "Northern" also covers quite a bit of territory, including just about everything north of London or, more specifically, north of the Humber, or anything north of a line from Bristol to The Wash ("the fordable portion of the estuary between Lincolnshire and Norfolk"—*OED*).

not applauding — (PSC; link into "The Wrestling Epilogue") Another bit of stock footage (though not accounted for in the WAC records), this time featuring Indian (and Asian) members of the Commonwealth. The fact that they aren't amused might be another example of Python's "othering" of everything and everyone not English. As Indians they are not part of the acculturated English club, thus they wouldn't "get" the joke, colloquial reference, etc. On the other hand, they could be unamused by the pranks of their colonizers, rendering this moment an indictment of the British Empire's presence in India, for example. Lastly, this clip could have been chosen only because it's kind of the "not applauding" version of the much-used Women's Institute clip.

"nowt" — ("Working-Class Playwright") A Northern colloquialism meaning "nothing." A section from Lawrence's 1913 novel, *Sons and Lovers*, gives a clear indication of where the Pythons lifted their Northern characters' speech patterns, and where the cross-cultural, class-to-class tension originated. In this scene from the novel, bullying father Walter Morel is decrying the "hateful" authority figures in his pit:

> Th' gaffer come down to our stal this morning, an' 'e says, "You know, Walter, this 'ere'll not do. What about these props?" An' I says to him, "Why, what art talkin' about? What d'st mean about th' props?" "It'll never do, this 'ere," 'e says. "You'll be havin' th' roof in, one o' these days." An' I says, "Tha'd better stan' on a bit o' clunch, then, an' hold it up wi' thy 'ead" So 'e wor that mad, 'e cossed an' 'e swore, an' t'other chaps they did laugh. (16)

Incidentally, the northern speech is much less distinct in the 1960 filmed version, likely due to the production company's (Twentieth Century Fox) desire to more easily distribute the film in the United States.

• O •

"offences" — ("The Mouse Problem") The same argument involving the legalization of drugs (thus making illicit drugs less attractive to young people) was made at the time and continues to be made today.

Perhaps the influence of former Harvard professor Timothy Leary (1920–1996) and his somewhat orgiastic advocacy of both clinical and recreational uses of marijuana, psilocybin, and LSD in the 1960s is significant here, as well. Leary was covered quite frequently in the *Times*, and often (as on 9 August 1969, for example) on the front page. (Leary is also mentioned and even profiled dozens of times in *Time* magazine between 1963 and 1970, and featured as one of the new age's "Three Wise Men" in an *Esquire* spread, along with Billy Graham [b. 1918] and Hugh Hefner [b. 1926], in 1966.) Kargol may be fashioned at least obliquely after Leary, especially in Leary's role as a high-profile ivory tower intellectual (1959–1963) and media celebrity more than willing to admit his own involvement in illicit drug use. By giving these and other psychedelic drugs to grad students, and then anyone who cared to share his life, Leary certainly got "it out in the open," as Kargol admonishes.

"Osborne" — ("The Wacky Queen") One of the royal family's residences during Queen Victoria's reign, Osborne is located on the Isle of Wight. After the Prince Consort's death, Victoria spent a great deal of time at Osborne and Balmoral—in other words, away from London and the demands of Westminster. This seclusion allowed her son, Bertie (later Edward VII, the "back marker" in "Famous Deaths" in Ep. 1), a more active role in the country's affairs. The Queen died at Osborne in 1901. This *FC* location, however, was obviously shot at Ham House (Richmond-upon-Thames), which would have been a much easier location to utilize. For more on Ham House see Ep. 1 notes. Parts of the later "Superman" sketch were also shot at Ham House.

For Python's on-location shooting, the cast and crew would typically shoot most if not all of the entire season's exteriors during one, extended trip. Location doubling would have saved time and money.

"other mice" — ("The Mouse Problem") Satirizing "probing" television documentaries, the writers have fetishized rodents, making dressing like a mouse akin to transvestitism, homosexuality, recreational drug use, or orgiastic sexual practices—or just about any other practice late-1960s British society might label as "deviant." The impetus for this sketch could have been documentaries about illicit drug use, spousal swapping, closeted homosexuals, etc., or, even more likely, a combination of many such documentaries dealing with obsessive-compulsive behaviors and alternative lifestyles of all kinds. Again, it's the unrelenting, unbroken (by irruptions of silliness or other narrative threads) nature of this narrative that sets this apart from most of Python's later work in *FC*.

It was in 1969 that groundbreaking documentary programs like *Civilization* (written and hosted by Kenneth Clark [1903–1983]) first went out in color on BBC2, then BBC1. David Attenborough (b. 1926) was running the show at BBC2 during this period (1965–1968), and his enthusiasm for documentary film of all kinds fueled this flowering of nonfiction broadcast.

"ovine" — ("Flying Sheep") Idle quite clearly says "avine" (of or pertaining to birds) and not "ovine" (of or referring to sheep), which may have been a slip of the tongue based on the following word ("aviation"), and simply missed during the editing and clean-up process. This voiceover would have been inserted after taping and playback, when the show was cleaned up for content, flow, and length. A later sketch ("Mouse Organ") was also inserted after principal recording had been completed.

• P •

paint on him — (PSC; "The Wacky Queen") There are hundreds of paint gags in silent comedy films and later cartoons, as well as Laurel and Hardy (*Towed in the Hole*, 1932) and the Three Stooges (*Tassels in the Air*, 1938) films.

The culminating "pie in the face" routine was a standard slapstick comedy bit from the music hall and vaudeville stage and myriad Keystone Cops (Mack Sennett) films, and especially later acts like Laurel and Hardy (*Their Purple Moment*, 1928; *The Battle of the Century*, 1927), the Three Stooges, and the Marx Brothers. The 1964 film *Dr. Strangelove*, co-written by Stanley Kubrick and Terry Southern, was originally supposed to end with an all-out pie fight in the War Room, but the scene was cut from the final release print of the film. The Pythons would later include a how-to "pie in the face" sketch in their live performance for *Live at the Hollywood Bowl* (1980).

Part 2 — (PSC; titles) This episode did end up as *Episode* 2, coincidentally, even though it was recorded first. This kind of mislabeling or purposeful misspeaking occurs throughout *FC*, and is evident much earlier in many *Goon Show* episodes, *At Last the 1948 Show*, on the pages of *Private Eye*, and then later in the feature film *Holy Grail* (Arthur replacing "5" with "3" over and over again).

"Pascal" — (Pepperpot link out of "French Lecture on Sheep-Aircraft") Blaise Pascal (1623–1662) was a French mathematician, physicist, religious philosopher, and writer. His principle of "intuitionism" had an impact on Rousseau and Henri Bergson, the latter being prominently mentioned several times in *FC*. Author Hilaire Belloc (noted above), who will be mentioned later in the episode, was also greatly influenced by Pascal.

"pathos" — ("Marriage Guidance Counsellor") From the Greek ("suffering," "feeling"). This mentioning supplements the use of "Deirdre" earlier, as well, adding a level to the allusion. Pathos may have actually been reached had the knight and chicken not appeared, prompting the caption and link, but then the Pythons wouldn't have been consistent in their undercutting of normal, expected dramatic structure and communication.

"Persian Radio" — ("A Man with Three Buttocks") The BBC has long held broadcast interests throughout the Middle East and Arabia, meant to serve the Empire's colonial presence. The Persian Gulf area is serviced by a shortwave relay station on Masirah Island near Oman (*EBO*).

"perverts meet" — ("The Mouse Problem") This entire satire—easily the most sustained satire in *FC*—is at least partially an allusion to the damaging Profumo scandal of just a few years earlier.

Elizabeth II's Secretary of State of War (1960–1963) John Profumo had an *affaire du coeur* with a young prostitute, Christine Keeler, who also happened to be bedding a Soviet naval attaché, Captain Eugene Ivanov. It was feared for years afterward that at the height of the Cold War the Soviets were given access to top secret "pillow talk" regarding the NATO alliance. There arose allegations (many reported also in publications ranging from *Private Eye* to the *New York Post*) that orgies were conducted in various palatial residences in and around London. These orgies included judges and ministers participating in acts of prostitution, sadomasochism, and the wearing of masks, according to *Lord Denning's Report*, compiled by Lord Alfred Thompson Denning (1963). The various young women involved also then sold their story to the London tabloids. Adding a sinister element to the whole fiasco, Profumo lied to the House of Commons about the affair. He resigned, but didn't have to do so ceremoniously, as was the norm. The U.S. FBI gathered 1,500-plus pages of documents as it quietly investigated the scandal that hobbled the Macmillan government.

"plummet" — (PSC; "Flying Sheep") An example of a word heavily accented but not depicted as such in the printed text. The Rustic lengthens the medial vowel, from an "uh" sound to the "oo" sound in "foot." He also delivers very hard [r] sounds in words like "birds" and "fair." Other such accentings occur on words like "much" (with the medial vowel pronounced like the vowels in "foot"), "my" ("mah-ee"), and "blind" (almost "blo-eend"). Other words, like "whole" and "Harold," are changed by aphaeresis, or the elision of the initial unstressed sound, resulting in "'oles" and "'arold," respectively. "Behavior" is altered in pronunciation via dissimilation, or the elision of the [h] due to its proximity to the medial [a].

The point here is not necessarily the eventual pronunciation, but to identify the speaker as a northern provincial, by his accent, and create a ready-made characterization (or caricaturization) at the same time. The Pythons do the same thing with the outrageous accents and delivery of "Upperclass Twits" in Ep. 12, so much so that the characters' speech must be subtitled for the viewer. A nod to G.B. Shaw and his well-known lament: "It is impossible for an Englishman to open his mouth, without making some other Englishman hate or despise him" (Preface to *Pygmalion*).

As will be seen, regional accents become very critical in *Flying Circus* as identifiers of class, education, and breeding, a trope borrowed, at least, from D.H. Lawrence. In *Sons and Lovers* (1913), for example, the significant class difference between young coal miner Walter Morel and the girl of his fancy, Gertrude Coppard, is evidenced simply by his listening to her:

> Walter Morel seemed to melt away before her. She was to the miner that thing of mystery and fascination, a lady. When she spoke to him, it was *with a southern pronunciation* and a *purity* of English which thrilled him to hear. (9; italics added)

Her speech gives her away, elevates her, endears him to her, engenders the distrust of her working-class neighbors, and eventually betokens the schism between husband and wife as they grow to loathe each other.

"PM" — ("The Wacky Queen") Prime Minister. Leader of the government in power, though the PM can be selected from a coalition government. See entry for Gladstone above, or depictions of Heath (Ep. 10), Macmillan (Ep. 12), and Chamberlain and Churchill (both Ep. 1).

"poncing" — ("Working-Class Playwright") As "ponce" means to be or act effeminately, the father here implies that a more effete laborer like his son must also be a homosexual.

pseudo — (PSC; "French Lecture on Sheep-Aircraft") With some foreign language training in their elementary educations, the Pythons could easily create pseudo-French or German dialogue, and supplement this pseudo-speak with gestures and bastardized English words. In his journal entry for the day of the taping of Ep. 2, Palin would call the moment "two Frenchmen talking rubbish" (Johnson, *20 Years*, 47–48).

Reminiscent of the bias against the French that seems to have existed in Britain since the Norman invasion, at least, this aversion to the French language is probably one of the "honest prejudices which naturally cleave to the heart of a true Englishman" that Addison wrote of in the *Spectator* (number 383, 20 May 1712). P.G. Wodehouse would much later describe the "look of furtive shame, the shifty, hangdog look which announces that an Englishman is about to talk French" (*The Luck of the Bodkins* [1936]). Shuffling off furtiveness, Python moves toward Anglicizing and sending up the French they speak, while caricaturing the French themselves, perhaps following Voltaire, who in *Candide* was quite nasty toward his countrymen, noting that their "principal occupations" were, in order, "lovemaking," "slander," and finally "stupid talk" (chapter 21).

"put my mind at rest" — ("Marriage Guidance Counsellor") Arthur Pewtey (Palin) is another in what will become a long line of Python characters who can't see what's going on in plain sight. Outrageous or absurd acts can be ignored entirely in the Python world. In Ep. 3 Cardinal Richelieu (Palin) is allowed to testify as a character witness in a modern courtroom; in Ep. 17 a family's living room is on a sidewalk; and in Ep. 6, "The Dull Life of a City Stockbroker" sketch, the stockbroker in question (also Palin) somehow can't see spear-throwing Africans, naked salesgirls, a guerilla war, and a hanged man over his desk.

The Pythons' Modernist impulse is apparent here, going right back to the work that announced the beginnings of Modernist Art, Manet's scandalous *Le déjeuner sur l'herbe* (*Luncheon on the Grass*, 1863). Manet placed a provocatively posed nude (whose gaze directly implicates and challenges the viewer/voyeur) in a modern setting *and* in the company of two dressed males—even the Salon des Refusés was scandalized, but a sensation followed nonetheless. The men in the setting seem impassive; the woman seems defiant. The world of art would never be the same. See Hughes's discussion of this transition in *The Shock of the New*.

• R •

Rodin's . . . The Kiss — (PSC; animated link into "The Mouse Problem") Auguste Rodin's (1840–1917) *The Kiss* was finished in 1886. A number of Rodin's works are on display at the Tate Gallery in London, including *The Kiss*. This version (commissioned by American E. P. Warren) had also spent a few years in Lewes, and went on public display in 1914. It immediately aroused a furor over its depicted sensuality and nudity, and opponents wanted the statue draped, screened from public view. The Tate would buy this version outright in 1952. Cf. "Tory Housewives Clean-Up Campaign" in Ep. 32, where statues, sculptures, and paintings at various galleries are covered—by Mary Whitehouse–type Pepperpots.

The erotic and troubling statue *The Kiss* is an apt transition into the following sketch, "The Mouse Problem," where men behave like mice.

The background behind the kissing, "musical" couple is appropriate for the presentational aspect of the imagery. The scene is a rendering for a theatrical production, drawn originally by Giuseppe Galli Bibiena (1696–1756), a noted "theatrical engineer and architect." Gilliam likely found this and several others (discussed elsewhere) in *Architectural and Perspective Designs*, a Dover publication from 1964. The original work was called *Architetture e prospettive dedicate alla Maestà di Carlo Sesto, Imperador de' Romani, da Giuseppe Galli Bibiena, suo primo ingregner teatrale, ed architetto, inventore delle medesime*, and was published in 1740 by Johann Andreas Pfeffel. (The V&A also owns a number of these prints as part of the Harry Beard Print Collection.) As the title indicates, the volume was dedicated to Charles VI (1685–1740), whose portrait is the first (unnumbered) plate, sort of a frontispiece, and which Gilliam will borrow for use in Ep. 14, in the animated sequence known as "*Vintage Model European Monarchs*."

The elaborate, columned theatrical backdrop—labeled as "Scene from the theatrical performance on the occasion of the nuptials of the Prince Elector of Bavaria," will be used twice more by Gilliam, in Eps. 19 and 23. Gilliam will use a total of at least five different plates from this text, meaning he likely had a copy of the Dover print in his work area. (He will use another period collection—*Perspective*, by Jan Vredeman de Vries—multiple times, as well, and likely owned a copy of that, too.)

rustic — (PSC; "Flying Sheep") The Rustic is a broadly drawn type, certainly meant to stand out in relation to the City Gent next to him. This "type" is universal, at least in Europe. The Rembrandt drawing *Portrait of Willem Bartholsz. Ruyter* (c. 1638) portrays the actor Ruyter in a burlesque costume of a yokel. The costume is clearly a smock and floppy hat, and represented, according to the Rijksmuseum, a popular leading role in the "boertigheden" playing in the theaters of Amsterdam (see Rijksmuseum.nl). The Pythons' knowledge of the Northern European (Holland, Germany, etc.) artists and their work is evident as early as Ep. 4 ("Art Gallery") and then Ep. 25 ("Art Gallery Strike"). There have been myriad paintings in the collections of the National Gallery from eminent Northern European artists (Rembrandt, Brueghels, Vermeer, et al.) since the 1830s, at least.

This rustic also looks very much like the village idiots characterized in Ep. 20, the "Idiot in Society" sketch, wearing the smock and floppy hat uniform. This uniform will also be worn by the "Bumpkin" character in Ep. 25, the "Art Gallery Strike" sketch, where he is supposed to be the figure from Constable's *The Hay Wain* painting (also in the National Gallery). The costume requirements were simply "smock, floppy hat" (WAC T12/1,083). In the actual painting, all that can really be seen are the figure's hat, kerchief, and smock, and those in minimal detail.

"rump" — ("A Man with Three Buttocks") Here begins a "thesaurus"-type sketch, where synonyms, metaphors, and variations-on-a-theme abound. Cf. the "Dead Parrot" sketch in Ep. 8, as well as the "What the Stars Foretell" sketch in Ep. 37, in which Cleese is himself being satirized (by others in the troupe) for his interest in thesaurus sketches. Voltaire provides an early example of this type of writing in *Candide*, when Martin has affirmed the constant foul nature of man, while Candide tries to see some hope:

> "Do you think," said Candide, "that mankind always massacred one another as they do now? Were they always guilty of lies, fraud, treachery, ingratitude, inconstancy, envy, ambition, and cruelty? Were they always thieves, fools, cowards, gluttons, drunkards, misers, calumniators, debauchees, fanatics, and hypocrites?" (chapter 21)

The Pythons (and especially writing partners Cleese and Chapman) will build on this foundation, adding a touch of the splenetic often, where the normally placid character—often the buttoned-down Cleese—will suddenly erupt into a vituperative verbal list. "Cheese Shop" in Ep. 33 is a textbook example of Cleese's escalation trope.

"runnin'" — (PSC; "Marriage Guidance Counsellor") Once again, the accent (here American, southern, which is as broad as saying England, northern) is partially implied by manipulating the written text. Also, this use of the "face up to the foe" verbal trope has a basis in Shakespeare, and involves both intestinal fortitude and a bridling of passions:

> *Nor*. Be advis'd;
> Heat not a furnace for your foe so hot
> That it do singe yourself. We may outrun
> By violent swiftness that which we run at,
> And lose by overrunning. Know you not
> The fire that mounts the liquor till't run o'er
> In seeming to augment it wastes it? Be advis'd;
> I say again, there is no English soul
> More stronger to direct you than yourself,
> If with the sap of reason you would quench,
> Or but allay, the fire of passion. (*Henry VIII* 1.1.139–49)

The formerly puling Arthur Pewtey will turn and face his fears and foe, but the ending isn't nearly as neat as it is in countless Hollywood movies, or even in a Shakespeare play. Pewtey will collapse at the first sign of resistance, perhaps a Python comment on the more contemporary Englishman.

• S •

sand dune — (PSC; "It's Man") According to BBC files, these opening and closing "It's Man" scenes were shot near the foreshore and cliffs near Covehithe, north of Southwold (WAC T12/1,083). Most of the location excursions during the four-season run of *FC* were planned to be as geographically varied as possible, meaning proximity to mountainous terrain, plains, and the seashore. Initially the Oban and Glencoe regions of Scotland provided the needed vistas (and later for *Holy Grail*, as well), then the Devon region (Dartmoor, Paignton, Torbay), then Norwich, and finally the island of Jersey.

"Sartre, Jean-Paul" — (Pepperpot link out of "French Lecture on Sheep-Aircraft") Sartre (1905–1980) was a French novelist, playwright, and Existentialist—triumphing individual beings' freedom. He became something of a darling to idealistic students and various anti-establishment types (like the young Pythons) when in 1964 he was awarded but refused to accept the Nobel Prize for Literature. The Pepperpots mention him here, along with Pascal, Voltaire, and Descartes. In Ep. 27 the intelligent, peripatetic Pepperpots Mrs. Premise (Cleese) and Mrs. Conclusion (Chapman) travel to Paris to visit Sartre and discuss his work. See the entries "Marxist" and "Revisionist" in Ep. 27 for a lengthier discussion of Sartre and his work and influence.

These "Aunt Edna" types (Rattigan's term, see "Pepperpots" entry in Ep. 1) are certainly "universal and immortal," but the Pythons obviously take umbrage at Rattigan's discounting of their intelligence and significance in the world of letters, and as participators in narrative decision-making (see Ep. 27 for more). Rattigan describes Aunt Edna's "lowbrow" nature:

> Now Aunt Edna does not appreciate Kafka . . . she is upset by Picasso . . . and she is against [William] Walton. . . . She is, in short, a hopeless lowbrow, and the great novelist, the master painter, and the composer of genius are, and can afford to be, as disregarding of her tastes as she is unappreciative of their works. (*Collected Plays, Volume 2*, xii)

The Pythons clearly have adopted the Aunt Edna type in their Pepperpots, but have more often than not gifted her with penetrating vision and encyclopedic knowledge, creating a very different "universal and immortal" type, perhaps closer to the Englishman that novelist and travel writer Evelyn Waugh (1903–1966) characterized in *Labels*. He watches his fellow passengers waiting to board their cruise ship in Monaco, seeing them as

> clearly diverse in origin and experience, but imbued, nevertheless, with a certain recognizable conformity of interests which makes them a necessary part of the study of any conscientious analyst of modern social conditions, for they are a type selected and developed by a series of conditions which are wholly peculiar to the present age, and must form part of our "period" . . . (33–34)

Waugh goes on to describe the world that created his fellow travelers, the "period" he's mining, and reads like it might even apply to the Oxbridge-educated Pythons themselves:

> It is a product of the English public school and University education; it is, in fact, almost its only product which cannot be acquired far more cheaply elsewhere. Cultured foreigners are lacking in it, and so are those admirably informed Englishmen whose education has been at secondary schools, technical colleges, and the modern Universities. . . . It consists of a vague knowledge of History, Literature, and Art, an amateurish interest in architecture and costume, of social, religious, and political institutions, of drama, of the biographies of the chief characters of each century. . . . All these snacks and tidbits of scholarship become fused together into a more or less homogenous and consistent whole, so that the cultured Englishman has a sense of the past, in a continuous series of clear and pretty *tableaux vivants*. This Sense of the Past lies at the back of most intelligent conversation. . . . (*Lables*, 34)

The Pepperpots and Pythons do, indeed, exhibit an uncanny Sense of the Past, their "living pictures" creating an overlapping, ever-present display of British history and society, where Admiral Nelsons can leap to their deaths from modern tower blocks.

"Scotsman on a horse" — ("A Scotsman on a Horse") This Scotsman will appear again in Ep. 6 and finish the sketch just begun here. The production design team for this location shoot may have also supplied three strategically placed thistle bushes near the Scotsman to create a believable ambience (the thistle being the heraldic emblem of Scotland). The stunt rider (except in close-ups) is Harry Woodley, not Cleese, and the church is The Old Place Chapel, Boveney, Windsor (WAC T12/ 1,083). The Old Place will be used again in Ep. 21, when the couple (Cleese and Cleveland) run into a church in the "Silly Vicar" sketch.

This obscure reference to a "Scotsman on" something is most likely borrowed from J. M. Barrie's play *What Every Woman Knows* (1918): "My lady, there are few more impressive sights in the world than a Scotsman on the make."

"sharing the interests . . . her feet" — ("Marriage Guidance Counsellor") Spaniard-American George Santayana (1863–1952) would, in 1922, describe the "British Character" thusly: "England is the paradise of individuality, eccentricity, heresy, anomalies, hobbies, and humours" (Santayana, 30). In the sketch there's really no indication that Deirdre and Arthur didn't actually share these stated interests—her encounter with the counselor notwithstanding—even though none of the interests may sound terribly interesting. Gardening, of course, is almost an English mania, and in most *FC* episodes even the tiniest yards behind row houses (see "The New Cooker Sketch," Ep. 14) feature carefully kept gardens. (During and after the war, for example, these gardens provided vegetables for a strictly rationed England, becoming ubiquitous by necessity.) Model aeroplane/airplane flying and clubs increased in popularity soon after the war, at places like Hibaldstow aerodrome (in North Lincolnshire, east of Doncaster), and remain a very popular family activity. The sheer number of hobbies and "spotting" societies in the UK is somewhat staggering, including trainspotters (Ep. 7), train switching box associations (Ep. 25), motorway interchange enthusiasts (Ep. 35), as well as bridge (foot, auto, and rail) and aerial antennae groups and websites.

The Pewteys might have been saving their money in a sixpenny bottle (see entry below) for a holiday to Brighton or Torquay, for instance. Postwar monetary controls limited the amount of money a British vacationer could take from the country, forcing many to find vacation spots in the UK (see Morgan's *Britain since 1945*). See the notes for "Brighton" and "holiday" above for more on these fiscal restrictions and travel/life during the postwar period.

Sheep — ("Flying Sheep") Ep. 1 offered the pig motif, and this episode will run with a sheep theme, the second major entry in the Python bestiary. Cf. Ep. 20, the "Killer Sheep" sketch. The presence of sheep in the economy and history of Great Britain could account for its significant presence in the *FC* episodes, though the frequent appearances and mentionings of penguins in the episodes aren't so easy (with the notable exception of the Penguin Books phenomenon, to be discussed later). Maybe it's just because penguins are (in Cleese's words) "comic, flightless web-footed little bastards" that they will additionally appear in episodes 5, 22, 23, and 38. See entries for those episodes for more.

showgirl's outfit — (PSC; "The Mouse Problem") This is Cleveland's second appearance in the series, and she is once again scantily clad and mute. Her role is an iconographic one—"pretty girl"—and thus far she has been objectified for her physical female attributes. There exists an early Monty Python publicity photo actually featuring the six Pythons and Cleveland—and she is not dressed scantily—though in the early part of the first season her contributions are purely gender-specific. See the "Kargol and Janet" entry above for a description of her outfit.

"sixpenny bottle" — ("Marriage Guidance Counsellor") A bottle of ale (or ink or wine, etc.) costing six pence. See Jonson's *Bartholomew Fair* 2.2.

"skirting board" — ("The Mouse Problem") Molding or base board installed along the lower part of an interior wall. In Ep. 20, the Killer Sheep also live behind the skirting boards and wainscotting.

"sparrows" — ("The Mouse Problem") The "Man" depicted here is dressed as a milkman, including black-and-white striped apron, a white uniform, and a peaked cap.

The "sparrows" this milkman mentions have been glossed as alluding to lechery. "Sparrow," according to Henke, was used by the Greeks "as a euphemism for the erected penis" (249). Using this terminology, the Milkman, then, is actually describing the act of fellatio. It is also interesting to note that the *OED* cites a December 1902 edition of the *Daily Chronicle*: "I should like to say a few words about the milkman's secret customers, otherwise 'sparrows.'" These are the (primarily female?) customers who benefit from the Milkman's visit in the form of illicit sexual congress. Cf. Ep. 3—where the siren traps milkmen in her attic—for the darker half of that equation.

Here again the accent issue comes to the fore, especially as a certain "type" is being forwarded. As this city "tough" (dressed as a milkman) speaks he substitutes the interdental fricative unvoiced "th" (q) sounds with the labiodental fricative unvoiced "f" sounds ("with" becomes "wif," and "throats" becomes "froats").

This Milkman scene was shot in the middle of the Town Centre of Walton-on-Thames, likely on the same day as the Whizzo Butter interview from Ep. 1. The Home Charms store visible over the Milkman's right shoulder was located at 125 Town Centre.

stock shot — (PSC; "A Man with Two Noses") The Pythons (and their researchers) culled the BBC archives and contemporary newspapers and magazines for still photos and film footage of politicians, royal events, and just everyday people, adding to the pastiche, collage effect of the series. See the "stock film" entry in Ep. 1. All of the stock film and photograph requests for the series are included in Appendix A.

stretching owls — (PSC; animated link into "Flying Sheep") The Gilliam animations here have nothing to do with owls, just as Ep. 1, titled "Whither Canada?," never actually answered that question, or even mentioned Canada after the title. *Owl-Stretching Time* was just one of the many show title possibilities bandied about by Chapman, Cleese, Gilliam, Idle, Jones, and Palin. *Owl-Stretching Time* finally ended up as the title for Ep. 4. Other possible titles for the entire series included *Baron Von Took's Flying Circus; Gwen Dibley's Flying Circus; The Circus; Flying Circus; A Horse, a Spoon and a Basin; Bunn, Wackett, Buzzard, Stubble, and Boot*; and *The Toad Elevating Moment*. (See Morgan's *Monty Python Speaks!*, and Roger Wilmut's *From Fringe to Flying Circus*.)

The *Bunn, Wackett, Buzzard, Stubble, and Boot* possibility was reportedly penciled onto the cover page of the Ep. 2 script, and *Owl-Stretching Time* was penciled through (Johnson, *20 Years*, 49).

Once again, very little prior knowledge of Gilliam's final product for these animated links was available to other cast members. Now and again, Gilliam would pull in a fellow Python to do a voiceover during the week of production rehearsal, but otherwise there was little contact, hence little clear description of the animations in the shooting script. See *Monty Python Speaks!* and *Gilliam on Gilliam* for more.

"Strewth!" — ("A Man with Three Buttocks") Cf. another character played by Chapman, Mr. Foster of Guildford, who dies suddenly in Ep. 1, uttering the same epithet. "Strewth" is a shortened version of "God's truth," and is used as an oath.

"succeed" — ("Flying Sheep") Note that all of the action in this sketch is described; it takes place off-camera. The occasional sound effect helps create and preserve the ambience, but there are no cutaways from the talking heads to nesting sheep, real or animated. The characters' perspectives, perceptions, and descriptions of the events are, then, the source of comedy, and not the actual events themselves. In *Beyond the Fringe*, the "Royal Box" sketch is performed by the three participants (Peter Cook, Dudley Moore, and Alan Bennett) sitting on chairs next to each other—facing the audience—and looking out over the audience toward an imaginary royal box. In *At Last the 1948 Show*, Chapman and Tim Brooke-Taylor perform the same "offstage" comedy in the form of a sheepdog trial, where Chapman speaks with a recognizable and broad Yorkshire accent:

> Brooke-Taylor: You have two dogs?
> Chapman: Ssh!
> Brooke-Taylor: (*whispering*) Where are they now?
> Chapman: Oh, ah, well one of them's over, now where is he? Oh, ah, over there by that pile of dead sheep. Magnificent brute, treacherous to a fault. ("Sheepdog Trial," Series 1, Program 3, 1 Mar. 1967)

All the action here is offscreen and therefore suggested, and when the dogs "Butcher" and "Crippen" attack and begin to eat the sheep, Brooke-Taylor recoils in revulsion, describing the rather graphic attack. (Cf. Ep. 33 notes for a Python reference to the infamous Crippen.) Another *At Last the 1948 Show* sketch, "Courier," features Cleese as a tour bus guide taking a busload of English tourists through myriad European capitals in record time. No other voices are heard at all, actually, just Cleese, pointing out distant capitals, barking instructions for photo opportunities, and threatening everyone with another hellish tour if they miss even one sightseeing opportunity.

This "observational" structure (far more presentational than representational) keeps this type of setting and writing more akin to stand-up or club comedy, which was enjoying a rise in popularity in the 1950s and 1960s, thanks to American performers including Lenny Bruce and Woody Allen. The physical and financial constraints experienced by the troupe in pre-Python days at various revues in Oxford and Cambridge would have also cultivated this referential or associative structure (as would the significant influence of BBC Radio's *The Goon Show*). Once they reached the BBC's television stages, budgets didn't allow for complicated sets or process shots, so the off-screen references would continue through the third season. (In the fourth season, when budgets skyrocketed to approximately £100,000 an episode, everything—the costumes, props, sets, location work, and special effects—became more elaborate, intricate, and expensive.) This is also not unlike Shakespeare's descriptions of the Battle at Agincourt in *Henry V*, actions that take place offstage and are merely referred to by characters onstage.

• T •

"talkin'" — ("Working-Class Playwright") The Northern, working-man accent here is quite pronounced, with the elision of words signaling at least part of this accent's particulars. Note, though, that a coarse accent (when compared, say, to the Queen's English spoken in London) doesn't mean the speaker is a rustic. Here it's quite the opposite. The coarse speaker turns out to be quite refined, in direct opposition to his *Sons and Lovers* "working-class" milieu, clothing, accent, etc., all reminiscent of Lawrence's brusque miner Walter Morel. Python undercuts its own undercutting on a regular basis. Significantly, the son has lost his Northern accent, in favor of English as spoken farther south.

"Tennyson" — ("The Wacky Queen") Alfred, Lord Tennyson (1809–1892) was an apt choice for this mock film, since Tennyson is considered to embody the Victorian age in his lyrical, often melancholic poetry. Tennyson spent most of his career in poetic pursuits, though he did attempt staged drama in 1874, somewhat unsuccessfully (*ODNB*). See notes to Ep. 17 for more on Tennyson, there installed in an East Midlands' bathtub. Tennyson was named Poet Laureate in 1850. See the "wax cylinders" entry below for more.

"That's a full working day, lad . . ." — ("Working-Class Playwright") Dialogue from the 1960 film *Sons and Lovers* obviously inspired this exchange. In the first kitchen scene, father Morel (Trevor Howard) harrumphs at his artistic son's efforts after smudging a sketch of his wife (Wendy Hiller):

> Father (Howard): Well he can soon knock off another, can't he? He's got nothing else to do but lie up there in bed . . .
> Mother (Hiller): He was up hours before you working on the sketch you just spoiled.
> Father: And how much were we going to get for that?
> Mother: He'll bring home his share when he starts work next week.
> Father: Work? That lad doesn't know what work is. Sitting on his bottom all week in an office. Scholarships and holidays and spouting algebra while we're sweating down there like suffocatin' bats . . . Now if that lad was to go down in the pits—
> Mother: He's not going down the pits and you know it. He's going to earn decent money one day.
> Father: Decent? What we get's indecent then I suppose? (*Sons and Lovers*, 1960)

"they're birds" — ("Flying Sheep") In Ep. 5, a cat is suffering from "the stockbroker syndrome, the suburban fin de siècle, ennui, angst, weltschmertz" and even "moping," and must be jarred from his "rut." This is Python's version of the classic beast fable, à la Dryden *The Hind and the Panther*, as certain animals take on qualities not generally associated with a particular species, and/or are anthropomorphized.

"thirty minutes . . . up" — ("The Mouse Problem") A moment where we can't be sure if the Linkman is referring to *The World around Us* show he's hosting, or the episode of *FC* we've been watching that contains the *World* show. Phenomenologically, the boundaries between these shows have disappeared during this segment.

"tit" — ("Working-Class Playwright") *OED*: "Fool."

"Trubshawe" — (PSC; "French Lecture on Sheep-Aircraft") Approximate translation: "Good evening, here we have the modern diagram of a French-English sheep. Now we have in the head, the cockpit. Here one finds the small English Captain Trubshawe." (Translations provided by Joshua Abboud.) This is clearly a reference to the then-famous Brian Trubshaw (1924–2001), Britain's first and very celebrated pilot for the new Anglo-French Concorde SST. In Ep. 37, the name "Concorde" will elicit quite a laugh from the audience, as there it will be given to Dennis Moore's horse. Lancelot's "horse" in *HG* (played by Idle) is also named Concorde.

This naming (or at least the spelling) could also refer obliquely to Michael Trubshawe (1905–1985), an actor who appeared in films such as *The Magic Christian* (1969; additional script material by Cleese and Chapman), *A Hard Day's Night* (1964), and *The Lavender Hill Mob* (1951). Trubshawe played an English aviator in *Scent of Mystery* (1960), and an armed forces officer in many other films. A prototypical role player—a type, even—Trubshawe seems a perfect choice for Python's sheep pilot. Cleese and Chapman would also later co-write *The Rise and Rise of Michael Rimmer* (1970), in which Trubshawe appeared.

"tungsten . . . operations" — ("Working-Class Playwright") Tungsten carbide–tipped drills are quite hard (on the Mohs Hardness Scale) and have been used extensively in coal mining operations since the 1920s. Preliminary operations might include drilling exploratory holes to mark the extent of the coal vein and preparing the face for the digging machinery. The coal face is the "working wall" of coal in a coal mine or the line of coal deposits followed by coal miners as they drill and remove, drill and remove, etc. Palin, who grew up in mining country, would probably have been familiar with the coal mining industry, tools, etc., and there's little doubt that the Pythons' lower-school exposure to such a significant and controversial industry in the history of Great Britain would be significant, as well.

Coal's significance to the economy of the UK has been well documented, but in this sketch, coal mining is being sent up as an escape for "laborers" and a neat way to hide from the work of the real world.

"two . . . a day" — ("The Mouse Problem") Sounds like a teenage masturbation statistic, possibly arising from David Reuben's 1969 book *Everything You Always Wanted to Know about Sex but Were Afraid to Ask*, or a similar quote from either Kinsey (*Sexual Behavior in the Human Male* [1948] and *Sexual Behavior in the Human Female* [1953]), or Masters and Johnson (*Human Sexual Response* [1966]). Reuben's book entered the mainstream culture, and was read by millions around the world. All of these landmark studies would have been prominently in the public view during this period, and could easily have influenced the Pythons' early lives and later writing.

• U •

"unique film" — ("The Wacky Queen") Even the earliest (and unsubstantiated) claims that motion pictures were exhibited to a royal audience in England weren't any earlier than 1891, making 1880 a date the Pythons probably chose out of the air. The film does share a resemblance with early British film pioneer Cecil Hepworth's and American Edwin S. Porter's staged, sight-gag approach in their "flicker"—*Rescued by Rover* (1905) and *The Great Train Robbery* (1903), respectively—but both were also working on such narrative-type films much later, around the turn of the century (1903–1905). It's also possible that the Pythons are referring to Leeds-based film maker Louis Le Prince (1841–c. 1890), whose early paper print films were known to have existed but were never played for large audiences. Specifically, his 1888 film *Roundhay Garden Scene* features scenes much like the Pythons offer in their Victoria film. Le Prince disappeared mysteriously from a train in 1890, and was not seen again. He was declared dead in 1897.

The "jolly American accent" called for in this film certainly isn't Tennyson (see note above) but is a recognition of the Hollywood pedigree that this type of film and film narration represent.

• V •

"Victoria" — ("The Wacky Queen") Queen Victoria (1819–1901) is considered by many to be Britain's most beloved monarch, and she reigned for sixty-three years. By the time films like the one in which the Pythons portray her could have existed (1895 and beyond), however, she would have been in her mid-70s, and rather frail. And since Gladstone (see note above) died in 1898, this fictional film would have to have been made between about December 1895 and May 1898.

"vole" — ("The Mouse Problem") Type of field mouse. The vole is the Pythons' American film studio parody logo during *FC*, depicted as "Twentieth-Century Vole," which will reappear in Ep. 6. Prior to *FC*, Cleese mentions the vole as a potentially comedic beast in the "Ant" sketch in *At Last the 1948 Show*.

"Voltaire" — (Pepperpot link out of "French Lecture on Sheep-Aircraft") "Voltaire" (1694–1778) was a pseudonym of François-Marie Arouet, an often acerbic but consistently astute observer of French culture, and French society in general. Voltaire's influence on the Pythons—perhaps in forming the English-ness they trumpet and the "characteristic qualities" of the English mind—is obvious as the alliterations, grotesqueries, narrative manipulations, and just the black-tinged satire (against tyranny, bigotry, narrow-mindedness) of their work are appreciated. Voltaire enjoyed taking pokes at religion and government, targets the Pythons consistently take aim at, as well. See notes throughout for allusions to Voltaire and *Candide* in *FC*.

Vox pop films — (PSC; "The Mouse Problem") Many of these inserts were shot in the Saxmundham meadows area on 22 August 1969, as well as near the foreshore and cliffs of Covehithe, and on or near the Harbour Pier, on 21 August (WAC T12/1,083).

• W •

"wacky" — ("The Wacky Queen") This is American slang (as are "a-plenty," "way-out," and "doggone it"), meaning Python was attempting to mimic not only the American accent, but also the use of American English idioms and colloquialisms. (See "hosepipe" and "have a go" notes for moments when the Pythons' Englishness betrays itself.)

The film as presented is reminiscent of the standard newsreel-type shorts popular in American movie theaters in the golden age of Hollywood, featuring slices of everyday life as well as news of the weird and celebrity from across the country and around the world. William Randolph Hearst, for example, had films made of his guests cavorting at Hearst Castle, his mansion in San Simeon, California, and audiences could see the likes of Mary Pickford, Douglas Fairbanks, Hal Roach, John Gilbert, and Charlie Chaplin engaged in the lives and leisures of the rich.

Waring, Arthur — ("The Wrestling Epilogue") Yet another Arthur character, though probably meant to build on the Eddie Waring reference in Ep. 1. Eddie Waring is such a strong allusion here because of his close connection to sport, and for so many years. He was a well-known Rugby League broadcaster, using phrases that were parroted by many in the South. Waring was either loved or hated as Rugby League commentator, and the Pythons seemed to have loved/hated him enough to caricature him more than once.

"wax cylinders" — ("The Wacky Queen") American inventor Thomas Edison had worked to perfect this type of audio recording and broadcasting technology, creating a working prototype by 1877.

In 1890, Poet Laureate Tennyson (1809–1892) himself recorded a version of both "Charge of the Light Brigade" (1864) and "Charge of the Heavy Brigade" (1882) on such wax cylinders, and the scratchy, sometimes inaudible (but still quite stirring) versions of both can be heard at poetryarchive.org. In Ep. 41, when John Hughman portrays Tennyson in the Victorian poetry sketch, his intonation and delivery ("Half an inch!") indicate he's most likely heard these recordings, as well.

"What's wrong wi' me? . . . yer tit!" — ("Working-Class Playwright") The two men nearly come to blows here, and, as this scene is "right out of D.H. Lawrence," it's clear that Lawrence's penned kitchen confrontation between eldest son William and drunk father Walter in *Sons and Lovers* is the inspiration:

> Paul never forgot coming home from the Band of Hope one Monday evening and finding his mother with her eye swollen and discoloured, his father standing on the hearth-rug, feet astride, his head down, and William, just home from work, glaring at his father. . . . William was white to the lips, and his fists were clenched. He waited until the children were silent, watching with children's rage and hate, then he said:
>
> "You coward, you daren't do it when I was in." But Morel's blood was up. He swung around on his son. William was bigger, but Morel was hard-muscled, and mad with fury.
>
> "Dossn't I?" he shouted. "Dossn't I? Ha'e much more o' thy chelp, my young jockey, an' I'll rattle my fist about thee. Ay, an I sholl that, dost see." Morel crouched at the knees and showed his fist in an ugly, almost beast-like fashion. William was white with rage.
>
> "Will yer?" he said, quiet and intense. "It 'ud be the last time, though." (56)

William's mother (Morel's wife) will break up the fight before it gets out of hand, just as Mother (Jones) does in the *FC* episode. The roles are cleverly reversed from the original, where Morel is the hard-bitten, uneducated, and now bitter coal miner, and son Paul is destined for schooling and a job in the city. Additionally, this scene is only hinted at in the 1960 film version, the abuse more emotional than bruise-making, and the film focusing on Paul rather than William.

"wheel" — ("The Mouse Problem") Exercise wheel often found in rodent cages. Also, a "run in the wheel" suggests copulation, with "run" glossed as energetic copulation and "wheel" meaning the female pudendum. See John Marston and George Chapman's 1605 play *Eastward Ho* (2.2.363).

"where's the water?" — ("The Wacky Queen") Reenactment of one of the seminal moments in film history, the Lumiere brothers' short film *Watering the Gardener*, or *The Sprinkler Sprinkled* (c. 1895). One of the earliest pseudo-narratives in surviving film, the action is based on a French comic strip of the period. Some of the Victoria-Gladstone film actually resembles these early slice-of-life "documentaries" (or "actualities") mixed with a healthy dose of silent comedy gaggery (which the French actually pioneered well before the Americans and then Hollywood came to the table).

"wherever you are" — ("French Lecture on Sheep-Aircraft") Reminiscent of American vaudeville, radio, and television performer Jimmy Durante's signature closing line: "Good night, Mrs. Calabash, wherever you are."

"Wigan" — ("The Wrestling Epilogue") West of Manchester, in Lancashire. Wigan is a coal and heavy industrial area, and probably more typically the home of a wrestler than a humanist. In 1936 George Orwell traveled north, eventually producing his *Road to Wigan Pier* (1937), a close look at unemployment in industrial Britain.

"Willie" — ("The Wacky Queen") A shortening of "William" that most Brits would likely avoid, except derisively, since it can be mistaken for the childish reference for "penis," and in the hearing is homonymic.

Women's Institute — ("A Man with Two Noses") Stock footage, probably from a Women's Institute gathering from the late 1940s or 1950s. This same footage is used many times in *FC*, and the women portrayed are at least partly the basis for the "look" of the Pepperpots as played by the Pythons. According to the weekly stock film and music requests cleared for usage (copyright clearance) by BBC staff for *FC*, this stock footage was paid for each time it appeared (see the Written Archives Collection files, *Monty Python's Flying Circus*).

The Women's Institute was originally established in Canada, and gained a foothold in England until just prior to WWI. Some of the Pythons' family members (mothers, aunts) may have been members, especially during the war years.

The World around Us — ("The Mouse Problem") A Python version of *Panorama*, the long-running current affairs show (BBC-TV, 1953–today), with elements of similar programs including Associated Rediffusion/ Thames TV's *This Week* (AR, 1956–1968; Thames, 1968–1992), *World in Action* (Granada TV, 1963–1999), and even *The World about Us* (BBC2, 1967–1986). *The World about Us* was a natural history series, which would account for the mice in "Mouse Problem," while *Panorama* employed in-depth, often abrasive (for the period) interviews and exposés. *World in Action* was Granada's popular and front-running public affairs program, and *This Week* served similar purposes for Associated Rediffusion, then Thames. (See Vahimagi's *British Television*.) Much of the material for *FC* came from the Pythons' growing up as the first television generation, and their satire often targets the confines and outlines of the television format and industry.

These public affairs–type programs together would produce, for example, at least eight filmed reports on the "troubles" in Northern Ireland during 1969 alone (see "Ten Years of TV Coverage," in *Belfast Bulletin* 6 [Spring 1979]: 20–25, published by the Belfast Workers Research Unit).

• Y •

Yorkshire — ("Working-Class Playwright") Northern county between the Pennines and the North Sea. Yorkshire changed from a largely agrarian to a heavily industrial economy during the Industrial Revolution, and has become well known for its factories, rowhouses, and wrenching work-to-live poverty. In the feature film *Meaning of Life*, one of the earliest sketches is set in a Yorkshire mill/mine town—specifically in one of the anonymous rowhouses—which the Pythons characterize as part of the Third World. Palin was born in Sheffield, South Yorkshire (D.H. Lawrence was also born in South Yorkshire), which may account for the significant attention paid to the region and its people, accents, and customs in *FC*. The neat suit Ken's wearing also subverts the expectations one might have of a caricatured Northerner, which is probably the intent, and fuels the humor of incongruity.

• Z •

"Zatapathique" — ("French Lecture on Sheep-Aircraft") Approximate translation: "Agreed, agreed. Now, I present to you my colleague, the celebrated poof Jean-Brian Zatapathique." Jean-Brian Zatapathique (Palin) and Cleese's Frenchman also appear in Ep. 14, introducing the French version of a Silly Walk ("Le marche futile"). A "poof" is a homosexual or effeminate male, and is, along with "fairy," Pythons' term of choice for the homosexual male in *FC*. The term "poof" was, as recently as 1957, one of the banned words on the English stage, being removed from John Osborne's play *The Entertainer* before a production license was granted (see Aldgate).

"zinc" — ("The Mouse Problem") This City Gent (Cleese) is as callous as his "type" can be, to the Pythons, with profit margins and capital being the essential elements of his final "solution." In regard to "widows and orphans" being commodified, in *ML* it is the laid-off Catholic laborer (Palin) who decides to sell all his children for medical experiments. Zinc also seems to be Python's mineral of choice (see Ep. 6).

Episode 3: "How to Recognize Different Types of Tree from Quite a Long Way Away"

"It's" Man fern forest intro; *Animation: Titles* (calm Cleese v/o); "Episode 12B: How to recognize different types of trees from quite a long way away" (slide No. 1: The Larch); Court scene ("Laurence Olivier" in the dock; Mrs. Fiona Lewis, Witness in Coffin, and Cardinal Richelieu); Inspector Dim of the Yard ("If I Were Not in the CID" song); Knight-and-rubber-chicken link; Slide No. 1: The larch; Bicycle Repair Man (Mr. F.G. Superman); Anti-communist link; *animated intro to*/and *"Children's Stories"*; *Animation: Link* into "Donkey Rides"; Butlin's redcoat intro (with Women's Institute clip), into "Restaurant Sketch"; Redcoat and knight link; *Animation: "Purchase a Past"*; Seduced milkmen; Stolen newsreader; Slide No. 1: The Larch; Slide No. 3: The Larch and the horse chestnut; Children's playground interview; **"Wink wink, nudge nudge"**; Referee whistle into "It's" Man closing credits

• B •

"bar" — ("Court Scene [Witness in Coffin/Cardinal Richelieu]") Simply, the barrier at which court business was transacted.

"barrister" — ("Court Scene [Witness in Coffin/Cardinal Richelieu]") An attorney. Cleese was, indeed, a student of the law, and would have made a career of it if it hadn't been for writing jobs for television. See the Cleese musings in McCabe's *The Pythons*.

"Bartlett" — ("Court Scene [Witness in Coffin/Cardinal Richelieu]") This same name will be used in Ep. 40 by a Glaswegian (played by Peter Brett) trying to see the Montgolfier brothers (Idle and Jones), along with another man posing as King Louis XIV, XV, and XVI (Palin).

"bloody" — ("Court Scene [Witness in Coffin/Cardinal Richelieu]") Less a swear word than a "vague epithet" (*OED*) in Britain today. See the complete *OED* entry for more on the word's history, which is varied and evolving. In the feature film *Life of Brian*, however, the word is clearly used as a serious imprecation:

> Mr. Cheeky (Idle): Do you mind? I can't hear a word he's saying.
> Mrs. Big Nose (Gwen Taylor): Don't you "do you mind" me. I was talking to my husband.
> Mr. Cheeky: Well, go and talk to him somewhere else. I can't hear a bloody thing.
> Mr. Big Nose (Palin): Don't you swear at my wife. (Scene 2)

The Pythons tend to use the word as more of a "vague epithet" throughout *FC*. This is not one of the words which, in Ep. 17, will be banned from use on the program.

In the 1948 BBC internal memo "BBC Variety Programmes Policy Guide for Writers and Producers," the law on swearing is laid down in the section entitled "Expletives":

> Generally speaking the use of expletives and forceful language on the air can only be justified in a serious dramatic setting where the action of the play demands them. *They have no place at all in light entertainment* and all such words as God, Good God, My God, Blast, Hell, Damn, Bloody, Gorblimey, Ruddy, etc., etc., should be deleted from scripts and innocuous expressions substituted.

Though produced a full two decades before *FC* was even created, the document (also known as the "Green Book") remained in full force and effect in 1969, and may have been read to the offending Pythons, chapter and verse, as they trounced all over its moralizing guidelines. A generation older than the Pythons, longtime BBC actor and then director/producer Ian MacNaughton would have been very familiar with the guidelines.

The Goons must have pushed up against this outright ban earlier (1951–1960), as well. Clearly, some latitude was granted by the time the Goons became popular, since they use most of the banned expressions listed above, as well as metaphoric crudities like "Pink Oboe," "Hugh Jampton," and "The Last Turkey in the Shop."

"bowler . . . innings" — ("Stolen Newsreader") Cricket terms: A "bowler" is essentially the pitcher on the cricket field. "Innings" means to proceed successively as batsmen, the first two as a pair together, to the wicket and try to make as many runs as possible against the bowling and fielding of their opponents. See "wickets" below. As an incredibly popular sport in the UK, cricket (and football) personalities and terminology will appear throughout the series. See cricinfo.com and Wisden for more.

"Bratbys" — ("Court Scene [Witness in Coffin/Cardinal Richelieu]") John Randall Bratby (1928–1992), a British painter affiliated with the social-realist Kitchen Sink School, is noted for producing hundreds of sketches and paintings even as his popularity declined. Bratby was quite active during this period, and could have been mentioned in the previous episode in relation to the "Working-Class Playwright" scene. He is at home, however, in the type of setting Mrs. Fiona Lewis (Chapman) describes—where goldfish could spit water on his work—as he was fascinated by the everyday, painting "cornflake packets," dustbins, kitchen table tops, and Monopoly boards (see Lambirth, *ODNB*).

bus — ("Bicycle Repair Man") The bus conductor is played by Al Fleming, and the driver is Dennis McTighe; this bus sequence was shot on Lammas Park Road, in Ealing (WAC T12/1,083). Other Supermen on the bus include John Dickenson, Lionel Sansby (*Doctor Who*), David Segger, and Peter Kaukus (*Doctor Who*) (WAC T12/1,242).

One of the Supermen behind F.G. Superman (Palin) is reading *Daltons Weekly*, a classified advertising paper.

• C •

Cardinal . . . beautiful robes — (PSC; "Court Scene [Witness in Coffin/Cardinal Richelieu]") Cardinal Richelieu (1585–1642) is fashioned here very much after the image available to the Pythons in the National Gallery, a full-body portrait by Champaigne (1602–1674), where the subject wears full-length, red-pink robes, white collar, an emblem of office on a blue collar, and a red skull cap. Richelieu also sports the recognizable upturned mustache and goatee. (This is also the same painting used by Gilliam in the opening credits animation for the first season. There Richelieu is on wheels and chasing a naked girl.) There is also a Champaigne triple portrait of the same subject in the National Gallery.

Continuing what will become a signature Python trope, no one seems to question the initial appearance of this long-dead historical figure, though Inspector Dim (Chapman) will eventually "out" him as an impersonator. See entry for "Dim" below.

Lastly, Richelieu is also carrying a microphone, which he holds like a lounge singer, and speaks here with a forced American/French accent. This characterization is somewhat out of character for the troupe, as French characters are usually forced to speak with thick French accents or in jabberwock French. This might be accounted for by the fact that this is an impersonator, and not the Cardinal himself.

children in playground — (PSC; link into "Nudge, Nudge") This quick interview scene was shot on the grounds of the then Ealing Technical College, St. Mary's Road, Ealing (T12/1,083).

"children's programme music" — (PSC; "Children's Stories") This is "Holiday Playtime" by King Palmer (WAC T12/1,084). The book Idle is allegedly reading from is actually the very popular children's book *What Do People Do All Day?*, published in 1968, by author/illustrator Richard Scarry (1919–1994).

chorus again with him — ("Court Scene [Witness in Coffin/Cardinal Richelieu]") This moment of Dim's unmotivated song is shared by all (including hand and body movements) and borrows from the genre of the American film musical, and of the 1950s, especially, but is quickly undercut as the Barrister (Cleese) takes over and is stared at, becoming nonplussed. In these musicals, the music tends to be non-diegetic (off-screen and *not* of the world of the film), and the passersby tend to "hear" the lead's music, as well, and join in the singing and dancing (see *Seven Brides For Seven Brothers* [1954], for example, as referenced in Ep. 18). See Rick Altman's *The American Film Musical*.

Church Warden — (PSC; "Bicycle Repair Man") Generally a layperson elected to assist the clerical staff in their duties.

"CID" — ("Court Scene [Witness in Coffin/Cardinal Richelieu]") Criminal Investigation Department, a branch of Scotland Yard. Members of this branch had carried out the investigation of the Kray brothers several years earlier. See entries in Ep. 14.

Clerk of the Court — (PSC; "Court Scene [Witness in Coffin/Cardinal Richelieu]") Though not listed in the printed script or in the credits for the show, this actor is Paul Lindley (WAC T12/1,084). Lindley had appeared in *Till Death Do Us Part* (1966) and the very popular *Dixon of Dock Green* (1965, 1970).

As this and the following seasons unfold, it will become clear that most of those who appear on screen (extras, walk-ons) will not get credit on screen. In fact, for most of the extras and walk-ons, this volume will be the first time after their initial appearances that their participation in *Monty Python's Flying Circus* will be publicly acknowledged. Most of these citations are culled from the cast lists for payment in repeats, by the way, and are part of the WAC records for the entire series. A special thanks to the BBC's Written Archives Collection (Caversham Park, UK) for their cooperation in this area.

Cleveland, Carol — (PSC; "Seduced Milkmen") This actress is *not* Carol Cleveland, but Thelma Taylor (WAC T12/1,084). Carol's name is included in the script, and there's no record of why she did not appear in this role. It could be that Cleveland simply wasn't available for this on-location shoot—a skeleton crew and cast would have made the trek for this scene. Taylor had small parts in other TV series, including *The Benny Hill Show* (1965), *Carry on Cleo* (1964), and *The World of Beachcomber* (1969). This sequence was shot on 16 July 1969 (WAC T12/1,242).

"CLINK!" — ("Bicycle Repair Man") These intertitles borrow from both the comic book and later TV traditions for campy American TV superhero shows like *Batman* (1966–1968) or *Mighty Thor* (1966).

Compère — (PSC; "Restaurant Sketch") The compère is both an organizer and a kind of director (for example, at Butlin's Holiday Camps) of music and entertainment activities. By the late 1960s, the compère is appearing as an introducer/presenter on television, and as a linking element, which is where the Pythons place him. The Pythons' compères are generally greasy, unctuous, and even salivating. See the compère (Palin) introducing the "Science Fiction" sketch in Ep. 7, and the compère (Idle) introducing Harry Fink in Ep. 9.

"Cornwall" — ("Stolen Newsreader") County in southwestern England, occupying a peninsula jutting into the Atlantic Ocean, and home to Penzance and Newquay. In Ep. 34, Jeremy Pither (Palin) will call Cornwall home, and the Chinese-British Ambassador (Chapman) will pretend to be familiar with the area.

"cruel to be kind" — ("Court Scene [Witness in Coffin/Cardinal Richelieu]") Cf. *Hamlet* 3.4.178. In the "Sheepdog Trials" sketch in *At Last the 1948 Show*, the sheepdog trainer (Chapman) admits how crucial cruelty is in training:

> Interviewer (Tim Brooke-Taylor): Well, how do you train the dogs?
> Trainer: Well that's very simple. We use a little kindness and a lot of cruelty.
> Interviewer: So you have to be cruel to the dogs?
> Trainer: Oh, yes, very cruel, very cruel indeed. I'm surprised it's allowed. Really nasty. Shocking! (*At Last the 1948 Show* album)

The Trainer is also obviously supposed to be a Yorkshireman, based on his accent (sounding very much like the rustic Chapman plays in Ep. 1), beginning most sentences with the regional "Ooh, ah. . . ."

• D •

"dead crab" — ("Court Scene [Witness in Coffin/Cardinal Richelieu]") Cf. "Whizzo Butter" sketch from Ep. 1.

"Dim" — ("Court Scene [Witness in Coffin/Cardinal Richelieu]") The incongruity between the inspector's name and his rather bare-faced cleverness (he's able to point out that Cardinal Richelieu died more than 300 years earlier) should be obvious. Dim's role as the unexpected resolution to the puzzle hearkens back to Dogberry's role in *Much Ado*, where the malapropistic (and, yes, probably dim) Constable actually ferrets out Don John's scheme (5.1).

Dim here is a CID man (Criminal Investigation Division), a branch of the Metropolitan police that had taken much of the blame for the drawn-out investigation, arrest, and prosecution of the noted Kray brothers just a few years earlier. Detective Chief Superintendent Frederick Gerrard, head of No. 3 District CID, had led the Kray investigation. The Kray arrests had been made in 1965, but convictions weren't achieved until March 1969, just weeks before the Pythons gathered to write the first season.

"Donkey Rides" — (PSC; link into "Restaurant Sketch") This is a silly sight or throwaway gag, of course, not unlike a Tex Avery or *Mad Magazine* gag, and shot on the beaches near Bournemouth. This gag will reappear in Ep. 35, where it's so dark it's nearly impossible to read the carried sign. In *Life of Brian*, a woman carrying a donkey on her shoulders walks past a stone-selling table saying she can't go to the stoning, her donkey's sick.

• E •

"East and West" — ("Stolen Newsreader") This refers to the Cold War division between the NATO countries (including the United States, UK, Western Europe, etc.) as "west," and as "east" the Soviet Bloc countries. These terms have lost much of their cultural significance recently, especially with the collapse of the Soviet empire in the late 1980s.

"engine driver" — ("Court Scene [Witness in Coffin/Cardinal Richelieu]") A train engineer.

Episode 3 — This episode was recorded third on 14 August 1969, and broadcast on 19 October 1969.

Some idea of the show's (a) middling popularity early and (b) its elevated level of corporate headache-inducement can be fathomed in another in-house memo—perhaps tongue-in-cheek (or just tired and cheeky)—from the office of John Howard Davies: "The third episode of 'Monty Python's Flying Circus' starring John Cleese, Michael Palin, Terry Jones, Graham Chapman and Eric Idle with animations by Terry Gilliam, please refer to episodes 1 and 2" (WAC T12/1,084). JHD will file another, similarly bleak memo for Ep. 4.

Walk-ons listed for this episode include Moira (or Moyra) Pearson, Elizabeth Broom, and Paul Lindley. Others being paid for appearing include Peter Blackburn, Philip Mutton, Joan Hayford-Hobbs, Peter Kaukus, Al Fleming, Thelma Taylor, Christine Young, and John Watters. See other entries in this episode for individual appearances by these actors (WAC T12/1,084).

• F •

"F.G. Superman" — ("Bicycle Repair Man") In the mid-1950s British Petroleum (BP) ran a newspaper ad campaign asking the question: "Are you a BP Superman?"

"fair cop" — ("Court Scene [Witness in Coffin/Cardinal Richelieu]") The phrase appears in *FC* (Eps. 3, 6, 27, and 29) and the later feature films, and is spoken by characters both historical and fictional. In *Holy Grail* it's the accused witch (Connie Booth) who mutters the phrase after she's been found a witch; in the "Salvation Fuzz" sketch (Ep. 29) the murderer (Idle) of various bishops is fingered by the hand of God, and replies: "It's a fair cop, but society's to blame." The *OED* indicates that the phrase "It's a fair cop"—meaning "to capture"—first appeared in print in 1891 (from a quote attributed to an apprehended thief), and has since become a part of the British vernacular. It's also heard in films where police work is simply a part of the plot, including Basil Dearden's *Victim* (1961), starring Dirk Bogarde (who's mentioned later in Ep. 29).

The phrase isn't just reserved for homey police shows like *Dixon of Dock Green*, either, or even just bad detective fiction, but can be found in a 16 July 1965 *Time* magazine article examining Tory vote-gerrymandering on a controversial capital gains tax cut amendment. It seems the Conservatives—who were in the minority 1964–1970, but by just three votes—lulled Labour to sleep in the wee hours of a legislative day, then surprised them by calling for a vote and showing up en masse to beat the sitting government, 180–166. Labour moaned and whinged, but eventually termed the successful surprise attack "a fair cop," and the Wilson government took its second parliamentary defeat as the majority party (www.time.com/time/magazine/article/0,9171,833977-1,00.html).

Fanfare of trumpets — (PSC; "Court Scene [Witness in Coffin/Cardinal Richelieu]") This fanfare music accompanying the entrance of the Cardinal is *not* accounted for in the usually comprehensive music rights requests (WAC T12/1,084). It may have been a public domain piece.

"freedom . . . much prized" — ("Court Scene [Witness in Coffin/Cardinal Richelieu]") Cf. John Quincy Adams's *Poem*. Also, see Shakespeare's *The Tempest* 2.2.186–87, and *Julius Caesar* 3.1.

• G •

"Glamorgan" — ("Stolen Newsreader") From the Welsh *Morgannwg*, Glamorgan is in southern Wales, and extends inland from the Bristol Channel coast between the Rivers Loughor and Rhymney. Swansea city and county are part of Glamorgan. This is the third Wales city mentioned in this sketch, including "Swansea" and "Porthcawl." Glamorgan's cricket club is a county team, and they play in Cardiff.

Noting that much of this newscast concerned Wales, this entire segment could be a jab at the BBC's regional news coverage, especially the silly details like a lost savings book somehow being of import to the entire region. In *Hard Day's Night*, the director of the TV special featuring The Beatles is certain that his failure will lead to a posting doing "news in Welsh," a most unfortunate eventuality.

"go" — ("Nudge, Nudge") Certainly a sexual reference as used here. See John Osborne's censor-exercising play *The Entertainer* (1957): "But I have a go, lady, don't I? I 'ave a go. I do." In the "Nudge, Nudge" sketch (written and performed by Idle), the sexual euphemisms include, "sport," "goer," "go," "games," "been around," "photographs," "Purley," "done it," and finally "slept with a lady," along with mildly suggestive hand gestures. Much of this sketch wouldn't have passed muster if the BBC's "Green Book" rules were still being strictly enforced. See the entry for "bloody" above for more on those restrictions.

"Gold Reserves" — ("Stolen Newsreader") Gold bullion or coin held by a government or bank, not individuals.

Grocer, The — ("Bicycle Repair Man") These titles represent Python's penchant for humor by incongruity, or the elevation of the mundane to the level of the heroic. See Fielding's *Tom Thumb* or Pope's *Rape of the Lock*, or even Simon Eyre and his "princely born" fellows in Dekker's *Shoemaker's Holiday*. Also, the Lord Mayor of London in Dekker's play, Sir Roger Otley, is a grocer by trade.

The satirical magazine *Private Eye* called Conservative PM Edward Heath (1916–1992) "The Grocer" or "Grocer Heath" from 1962 onwards. Heath would be PM 1970–1974, following the surprise-filled 1970 General Election, providing significant fodder for the *Private Eye* staff. See entries in Eps. 18 and 19 for much more on the tumultuous 1970 General Election.

"guv" — ("Bicycle Repair Man") Slang for "governor," often a term of deference to a more elevated, genteel person.

• H •

"hatchments" — ("Court Scene [Witness in Coffin/ Cardinal Richelieu]") This word appears in *Hamlet* 4.5, and nowhere else in Shakespeare's plays:

> *Laer*. Let this be so.
> His means of death, his obscure funeral—
> No trophy, sword, nor hatchment o'er his bones,
> No noble rite nor formal ostentation—
> Cry to be heard, as 'twere from heaven to earth,
> That I must call't in question. (4.5.213–18)

From the *OED*, there are two meanings, both rather obsolete: "1) An escutcheon or ensign armorial; esp. a square or lozenge-shaped tablet exhibiting the armorial bearings of a deceased person, which is affixed to the front of his dwelling-place," and "2) The 'hatching' with which the hilt of a sword is ornamented."

Both of these definitions can work for Python, but especially the latter, displaying the possible continuing cross-fertilization between art forms in Python's oeuvre. The Pythons were certainly aware of international cinemas, with the Japanese influence perhaps becoming apparent here. "The sword is the soul of the samurai" is part of the Bushido code, thus the "outward hatchments of his soul" operates on more than one level.

"hire purchase" — ("Court Scene [Witness in Coffin/Cardinal Richelieu]") Purchased on credit. The woman/witness (Chapman) is running through a laundry list of everyday gossip, none of which seems to have any connection to the case at hand.

There is also more than a hint of Eliot in this diatribe, specifically the section of *The Waste Land* where it's closing time at the pub. That lengthy, meandering, almost breathless incantation merits inclusion:

> When Lil's husband got demobbed, I said—
> I didn't mince my words, I said to her myself,
> HURRY UP PLEASE IT'S TIME
> Now Albert's coming back, make yourself a bit smart.
> He'll want to know what you done with that money he gave you
> To get herself some teeth. He did, I was there.
> You have them all out, Lil, and get a nice set,
> He said, I swear, I can't bear to look at you.
> And no more can't I, I said, and think of poor Albert,
> He's been in the army for four years, he wants a good time,
> And if you don't give it him, there's others will, I said.
> Oh is there, she said. Something o' that, I said.
> Then I'll know who to thank, she said, and give me a straight look.
> HURRY UP PLEASE IT'S TIME
> If you don't like it you can get on with it, I said.
> Others can pick and choose if you can't.
> But if Albert makes off, it won't be for a lack of telling.
> You ought to be ashamed, I said, to look so antique.
> (And her only thirty-one.)
> I can't help it, she said, pulling a long face,
> It's them pills I took, to bring it off, she said.
> (She's had five already, and nearly died of young George.)
> The chemist said it would be all right, but I've never been the same.
> You *are* a proper fool, I said.
> Well, if Albert won't leave you alone, there it is, I said,
> What you get married for if you don't want children?
> HURRY UP PLEASE IT'S TIME (lines 139–65)

The work of T. S. Eliot is referenced throughout *Flying Circus*, and he stands as one of the more important influences on the Pythons, especially as they contemplate their fractured modern world and the inefficacy of successful communication. See the index for more Eliot entries.

"his own hands" — ("Bicycle Repair Man") Also borrowed from the *Superman* (1940–1951) radio show's preamble: "Superman! Who can change the course of mighty rivers, bend steel with his bare hands. . . ."

horse chestnut — (link into "Nudge, Nudge") A large, ornamental, nut-bearing tree introduced to England in about 1550. See *OED*.

"Huguenots" — ("Court Scene [Witness in Coffin/Cardinal Richelieu]") Protestants in France in the sixteenth and seventeenth centuries, many of whom suffered severe persecution for their faith. Richelieu tolerated these non-Catholics until they presented a military threat to Louis XIII and, even though the Huguenots were supported by the English, including the Duke of Buckingham, he led a war against them in 1628–1629, destroying their power base and ending the threat.

This period will be broached again in Ep. 37, when the aristocrats being robbed by Dennis Moore discuss in detail the Thirty Years' War and England's embroilment in "continental affairs." The Pythons' source there, as here, seems to be eminent historian G.M. Trevelyan. See notes to Ep. 37 for more on this historical reference.

• I •

"immediatement" — ("Restaurant Sketch") A mangled French-ified version of "immediately." Cf. the "Flying Sheep" sketch (Ep. 2), or encounters with French soldiers in *Holy Grail* for Python's assault on the French language. The Goons (especially the character Moriarty, played by Milligan) had earlier provided many instances of travestied French. Also, see Shakespeare's similar treatment of the French language in *Henry V*.

"impersonator" — ("Court Scene [Witness in Coffin/Cardinal Richelieu]") Cf. the blancmange sketch, police station section, in Ep. 7, when the Detective Inspector (Idle) is eaten by a blancmange whom he's confused for "Riley." In Ep. 14, Cleese plays an admitted "female impersonator" (the only time such a cross-dressing is admitted in the series.)

Inside — ("Seduced Milkmen") The music that swells underneath as the man sees the other trapped milkmen here is Mantovani's version of "Charmaine" by Rupee (WAC T12/1,084).

Interesting Lives — (animated link into "Seduced Milkmen") Underneath this animated sequence, Gilliam utilizes "The Can-Can," as well as "Music Boxes 1–16" by Eddie Warner, and a portion of a Richard Rodger waltz (WAC T12/1,084).

"It's Bicycle Repair Man!" — ("Bicycle Repair Man") Based on "It's a bird! It's a plane! No, it's Superman!" from the *Superman* TV series starring George Reeves. The preamble to the 1940s radio show *Superman* also featured this tagline.

A number of political cartoonists and pundits in the UK were producing cartoons of "Wilman" (attacking PM Wilson), a weak and ineffective Superman-type able to defeat, barely, tiny islands like Anguilla, which British forces invaded in early 1969. See William Papas's panel cartoon for 24 March 1969 in the *Guardian*, and the British Cartoon Archive for more.

• J •

jetty — ("Stolen Newsreader") This is the end of Southwold Pier in Southwold, Suffolk. According to WAC records for the episode, Peter Lovell assists in pushing the Newsreader (Cleese) (WAC T12/1,083). Lovell would later work as a production assistant on *Goodies Rule—OK?* (1973) and *Some Mothers Do 'Ave 'Em* (1975).

• K •

"KGB" — ("Court Scene [Witness in Coffin/Cardinal Richelieu]") Former USSR secret police organization (Komitet Gosudarstvennoy Bezopasnosti ["Committee for State Security"]), 1917–1991. During this period, the KGB was very much a secretive and feared organization of political control. The KGB is mentioned again in Ep. 34, when Jeremy Pither (Palin) and his bicycle tour somehow make it from Devon and Cornwall to the Soviet Union. This is one of the words, when mentioned by the witness (Chapman), that prompts a direct look toward the camera by counsel (Cleese), the other key words being "leg" and "womb."

"kosher car park" — ("Court Scene [Witness in Coffin/Cardinal Richelieu]") Presumably, a place where Orthodox Jews (or Jewish cars?) can park without running afoul of Jewish law.

In *The Goon Show* episode "King Solomon's Mines," Bluebottle (Sellers) is thrown into the river, and shouts out: "Help! I've fallen into non-kosher water!" Other instances include "kosher margarine" in "The Tales of Old Dartmoor," "yellow kosher boots" in "The International Christmas Pudding," and "kosher wine gum" in "The Pevensey Bay Disaster."

• L •

"larch" — (opening credits) This slide image, though overexposed, seems to actually be a rather scraggly larch tree. This is also the only tree recognized during the episode, despite the title.

laundrette — ("Bicycle Repair Man") This is the Bendix Laundrette on Uxbridge Road in Acton, and the scene was shot on 14 July 1969 (WAC T12/1,083). Phone books for the period and area list the actual address as 261 High Street, which becomes Uxbridge Road.

"liver . . . head off" — ("Court Scene [Witness in Coffin/Cardinal Richelieu]") Cf. the "Live Organ Transplants" sketch in *ML*, wherein a man has his liver removed with kitchen and carpentry tools while he's alive.

"London town" — ("Restaurant Sketch") Probably the writing team of Cleese and Chapman, who had been writing together since their late Cambridge days. Neither were from London, however. Cleese was born in Weston-Super-Mare, Avonshire, and Chapman in Leicester, Leicestershire. All of the Pythons had been living in the Greater London area for most of the decade of the 1960s, writing for and performing in various TV shows.

lorry — ("Stolen Newsreader") A large truck for transporting goods. The troupe's gear was transported in such vehicles, one of which (a green panel truck) is featured in Ep. 15, after the "Spanish Inquisition" sketch. The driver of the lorry stealing the Newsreader (Cleese) is Peter Blackburn, and these scenes were shot on 15 July 1969 (WAC T12/1,242).

• M •

magic lantern — (opening credits) A precursor of the motion picture projector, the nineteenth-century "magic lantern" was often used to display slides during scientific lectures and demonstrations. Since the magic lantern—as a term—had been passé for a number of years in broadcasting, it's not clear why they chose the term instead of "slide projector." As early as the 1890s, "slide projector" was the preferred term.

man in the suit of armour — (PSC; link into "Children's Stories") The man in the uncomfortable-looking suit was almost always Terry Gilliam, and was a walk-on part, for which he would have been paid an additional £5/5, at least during the show's first season (WAC T12/1,083). These chestnut slapstick links become less and less frequent as the show progresses, seemingly as the Pythons feel more and more confident in their conception, writing, and performance skills.

"mangy" — ("Restaurant Sketch") *OED*: "Mean, stingy, niggardly; disappointingly small."

"men dressed as ladies" — ("Children's Stories") Certainly at least an intertextual reference to Python's own cross-dressing practices.

"Minister without Portfolio" — ("Stolen Newsreader") A minister of the government who may be a member of the Cabinet but who is not at the head of any particular department. In 1963–1964 Lord Carrington (b. 1919) was the Minister without Portfolio in Macmillan's government, and then was opposition leader in the House of Lords after the Conservatives fell from power in October 1964. Lord Carrington will be later mentioned in Ep. 42, and has already been mentioned—yes, unfavorably—a number of times in the pages of *Private Eye*.

"m'lud" — ("Court Scene [Witness in Coffin/Cardinal Richelieu]") A slang contraction of "My Lord," this is a term of respect for holders of office, specifically judges, as many were actually Lords. By the 1960s the usage is waning significantly, with overuse appearing obsequious and "patronising" (*OED*).

"Mungo" — ("Restaurant Sketch") *OED*: "A typical name for a Black slave. Hence, a Negro." This name could be used here as a play on the character's servile status (he is a cook), as either slave or kitchen worker. Most likely, however, given the Pythons' penchant for Modernist literature, the name probably comes from "Mungo Jerry," a character found in T.S. Eliot's well-known book *Old Possum's Book of Practical Cats* (1939, and republished more contemporarily by Faber in 1962).

• N •

"National Savings" — ("Stolen Newsreader") Currently England's second-largest savings institution, in business since 1861 when the Palmerston government set up the "Post Office Savings Bank" for ordinary workers across the UK. The loss of such a savings book and its mention on the national (even regional) news must be considered satirical, since it's highly unlikely the press would have much interest in such a trivial matter. Again, elevating the mundane to the level of the epic/heroic, or in this case, newsworthy, certainly applies here.

"NEDC" — ("Stolen Newsreader") Acronym for National Economic Development Council, which was set up in 1962 as a national (UK) economic policy forum.

"ODCN"—Perhaps Oil-Dri du Canada (ODCN), which has been in business since 1963, and may well have had opportunity or need to talk with the National Economic Development Council (NEDC). More likely this is one of the many made-up, official-sounding acronyms offered throughout the series. The satirical magazine *Private Eye* (and its Oxbridge precedents) also employed similarly made-up names and acronyms mixed in with actual names and acronyms; the magazine was sued for libel ("issued a writ" by the allegedly defamed) on many occasions, and paid out damages for many of those offenses.

"NO. 3" — ("The Larch") This is the same slide as image number one, clearly.

"nod's . . . bat" — ("Nudge, Nudge") Taken from an old Irish proverb: "A nod's as good as a wink to a blind horse." A bat doesn't rely on its eyes anyway, of course, which may be the reason for its inclusion here.

"not at all well" — ("Court Scene [Witness in Coffin/Cardinal Richelieu]") This phrase has become something of a Python trope—quoted or misquoted from its appearance in *HG* (see below). The phrase, however, is earlier mentioned in *The Goon Show* by Peter Sellers ("The White Box of Bardfield"), which is where the Pythons may have heard it first. In *HG*, cf. the "plague cart" scene:

> Dead Person (John Young): I'm not dead!
> Mortician (Idle): Here—he says he's not dead!
> Customer (Cleese): Yes, he is.
> Dead Person: I'm not!
> Mortician: He isn't.
> Customer: Well, he will be soon, he's very ill.
> Dead Person: I'm getting better!
> Customer: No, you're not—you'll be stone dead in a moment. (Scene 2)

The same sentiments are voiced in "Salvation Fuzz," when the rabbit fish is described in Ep. 29:

> Man (Idle): What, rabbit fish?
> Woman (Jones): Yes. It's got fins.
> Man: Is it dead?
> Woman: Well, it was coughin' up blood last night.

"Not so fast!" — ("Court Scene [Witness in Coffin/Cardinal Richelieu]") This exchange is probably based on extant crime and courtroom television shows like *Perry Mason*, where witnesses typically (and easily) confess on the stand under the examination of persistent counsel or investigators. *Perry Mason* (1957–1966) was available on British television as early as 1961, airing on BBC1 just before the 9:35 news.

• O •

Olivier impression — ("Court Scene [Witness in Coffin/Cardinal Richelieu]") Laurence Olivier (1907–1989) was a renowned English actor and director, whose delivery and intonation became both well known and much imitated. The balance of the soliloquy is a typically Pythonesque farrago of "Shakespearean" language and syntax, sometimes glossable, and sometimes not. Idle will mimic Olivier's delivery and posture, and the rest will be an authentic-sounding soliloquy as if from Shakespeare or Marlowe.

This section also reads very much like the *Beyond the Fringe* sketch "So That's the Way You Like It," which is a rather bouncy and jangled conflation of jabberwock English Renaissance drama-speak:

> Sustain we now description of a time
> When petty lust and overweening tyranny
> Offend the ruck of state.
> Thus fly we now, as oft with Phoebus did
> Fair Asterope unto proud Flander's court.
> Where is the warlike Warwick
> Like to the mole that sat on Hector's brow,
> Fairset for England, and for war! (audio transcription, *Beyond the Fringe*)

"Omsk . . . Krakow" — ("Stolen Newsreader") This is essentially fallacious geography, since Omsk is in Russia and Krakow is in Poland.

"Bulestan"—Not a country or a Soviet satellite, it is a term that appears in *Regesta Regis Æthelstani* (*The Anglo-Saxon Charters of King Æthelstan*, 924–39), and involving a land grant from the king to the brethren at Muchelney Abbey: ". . . on bulestan of bulanstane . . ." (Sawyer number 455). Obviously this name is supposed to sound like one of the Soviet Bloc regions (Kazakhstan, Kyrgyzstan, Tajikistan, Turkmenistan, Uzbekistan) but turns out to be very much of Old English derivation.

"Only . . . offence" — ("Court Scene [Witness in Coffin/Cardinal Richelieu]") Once again, Python elevates something minor to the epic level, not unlike Pope's *Rape of the Lock* (1712), Swift's description of the point of contention in Lilliput (ends of eggs) in *Gulliver's Travels* (1726), and Butler's *Erewhon* (1872). In the feature film *Life of Brian*, those who try and follow Brian as their messiah also argue over the spiritual significance of a gourd and a sandal, and one man wishes to be healed from thinning hair.

The appearance of Shakespearean terms and dialect in a petty offense court proceeding might be silly, but it also may refer to the recent (14 July 1969) quotation of *Richard III* in the celebrated trial at High Court against the makers of the damaging drug thalidomide.

QC Desmond Ackner quoted portions of Richard's opening speech—"Deform'd, unfinish'd, sent before my time"—and argued for significant compensation for his two clients, ages 7 and 8 (*Times*, 15 July 1969: 2).

"out of the TV Centre" — ("Stolen Newsreader") The thieves rush the Newsreader out of Studio 4 (*Flying Circus* was generally assigned to Studio 6).

• P •

"parking offence, schmarking offence" — ("Court Scene [Witness in Coffin/Cardinal Richelieu]") This is a common American colloquialism borrowed from many Yiddish words that, according to the *OED*, "begin with this sequence of sounds, fused with or replacing the initial letter(s) of a word, so as to form a nonsense-word which is added to the original word in order to convey disparagement, dismissal, or derision." In essence, a nonsense (and even nonce) word is created for each iteration of this phrase.

Piano starts playing — (PSC; "Court Scene [Witness in Coffin/Cardinal Richelieu]") Offscreen, Bill McGuffie (1927–1987) is playing this live piano accompaniment (WAC T12/1,084). McGuffie would also write and play original songs later in the series.

"point on it" — ("Court Scene [Witness in Coffin/Cardinal Richelieu]") Cf. Miguel de Cervantes' *La Gitanilla*: "Don't put too fine a point to your wit for fear it should get blunted."

"Porthcawl" — ("Stolen Newsreader") Another Welsh location, Porthcawl is a coastal resort, a Bridgend county borough, and also a part of the county of Glamorgan, Wales. Terry Jones was born in northern Wales.

"punch-line" — ("Restaurant Sketch") When the Pythons do deliver a punchline, they usually either (a) point it up to the audience, thus undercutting the effectiveness of any surprise (by definition) punchline in general; or (b) assault the deliverer of the punchline, either physically or with derision. Again, the Pythons' comedic inspirations The Goons did employ punchlines on occasion, and often dreadful puns (but lustily, unflinchingly, unapologetically delivered). The Goons, however, didn't pause and wait for audience reaction to the tried and true jokes, but raced right on with their rather dizzying barrage. Listen to, for example, the sketch "Napoleon's Piano" (*Collected Goon Show* CD), or this exchange in the episode "The Man Who Never Was":

> Prisoner (Secombe): Does your wife know this?
> Maj. Bloodnok (Sellers): Shut up! Achtung! Gebluten geblutz! Admit it, you're a spy!
> Prisoner: I'm not a spy, I'm a shepherd!
> Maj. Bloodnok: Ah! Shepherd's pie! You can't fool us, you naughty German!

"Purley" — ("Nudge, Nudge") An outer borough of southern London, in Surrey. When this sketch is performed in Los Angeles in 1980 for the film *Live at the Hollywood Bowl*, "Purley" is replaced by "Glendale," and to a healthy laugh from the LA audience.

• Q •

"Quantity Surveyor" — ("Bicycle Repair Man") *OED*: "A surveyor who estimates the quantities of labour and materials required for building and engineering work." Mentioned because it simply sounds dull, and not heroic.

"Queen, Michael" — ("Stolen Newsreader") A "queen" is slang for an effeminate homosexual man. See the description offered by Biggles's secretary (Nicki Howorth) in Ep. 33, "Biggles Dictates a Letter."

• R •

"red" — (link into "Children's Stories") Slang for Communist Party member or sympathizer, the usage also applies to "commies" uttered later in the diatribe. This originally referred to the color of the party badge (*OED*). Cleese is, if course, here depicting an over-the-top Enoch Powell, who had spoken of "reds in high places lighting their own funeral pyre" as he surveyed the left-leaning slump of England, his "green and pleasant land" (*Private Eye*, 31 July 1970: 10).

This period was significant in the history of the Cold War as both the United States and USSR struggled to keep control of their spheres of influence, especially in the face of the decolonization process throughout the Third World, and "Prague Spring"–type attempts at self-rule in Eastern Europe. The so-called Brezhnev Doctrine was implemented in November 1968, sending a distinctly chilly shiver into the world:

> When forces that are hostile to socialism try to turn the development of some socialist country towards capitalism, it becomes not only a problem of the country concerned, but a common problem and concern of all socialist countries. (Leonid Brezhnev, Fifth Congress speech)

Armed suppression of any such "development" was thereafter justified, and the Cold War got a bit colder. Though treated comedically here, the anxiety level of the Western world must have been significantly elevated between the time when Soviet tanks rolled through Budapest, Hungary, in November 1956, and Czechoslovakia in August 1968.

This ranting scene was shot in the backyard of a residence at 20 Edenfield Gardens, Worcester Park, Surrey, where the later "Confuse-a-Cat" sketch was also shot (see Ep. 5). Some of the "Bicycle Repair Man" sketch was also shot in the Worcester Park area (T12/1,083).

referee blowing whistle — (end credits) This stock film was taken from the recent Scottish Cup Final film, shot in 1969. This title is part of the list of stock film requested by the show for Ep. 3 (WAC T12/1,084). This type of obvious "ending" to an episode disappears as the first season progresses, often in favor of mock endings.

"Rhodesia" — ("Court Scene [Witness in Coffin/Cardinal Richelieu]") The subject of the African members of the Commonwealth comes up often in *Flying Circus*, and Rhodesia specifically in the fourth season's final episode (Ep. 45). See notes for Ep. 45 on "Rhodesia" and "Ian Smith."

Rhodesia was significantly in the news in 1969 when students at the London School of Economics (LSE) rioted and tore down newly installed security gates. Problems had begun in 1966 when the school appointed its new director, Dr. Walter Adams, who had come to LSE from the University College of Rhodesia, sparking immediate (then smoldering) student unrest. Adams was criticized for his cozy relationship with Ian Smith's government, and his perceived complicity with the continuation of white rule in Rhodesia. The LSE was closed for three weeks after the January 1969 riots (see bbc.co.uk for 24 January 1969, and entries in the *ODNB*).

"Rotarian" — ("Stolen Newsreader") A member of the Rotary Club, a philanthropic organization founded in the United States.

• S •

"saddle" — ("Bicycle Repair Man") A bicycle seat.

"savage" — ("Court Scene [Witness in Coffin/Cardinal Richelieu]") Cf. Shakespeare's *Merchant of Venice*: "Their savage eyes turn'd to a modest gaze / By the sweet power of music . . ." (5.1.78–79), and *King John*: "And tame the savage spirit of wild war" (5.2.74).

"scrubby" — ("Restaurant Sketch") *OED*: "Stunted, under-developed."

"send them back where they came from" — ("Mrs. Fiona Lewis") This had become the rallying cry for anti-immigration nationalists during this period, with National Front protestors carrying placards reading "Start Repatriation" and "Send Them Back" at myriad functions. The *Times* reports on one school meeting in Haringey where a controversial plan to separate immigrant children from native children (ostensibly to compensate for the immigrant students' lack of English skills) had been met with protestors for and against. National Front marchers called for the students and their families to be deported, while International Socialists chanted for racial tolerance and "Black and White unite and fight" (29 Apr. 1969: 1). The council passed the controversial separation plan easily.

And before coming to the subject of repatriation—voluntary or otherwise—in his address to his Wolverhampton, South-West constituency on 9 June 1969, Enoch Powell described the "dark and ever more menacing shadow" of immigrant birthrates:

> In a few years' time the proportion of coloured pupils in the secondary schools in Wolverhampton will have risen to 17 per cent; in a few years it will have risen to more than 23 per cent and higher. What reason is there to suppose that these pupils, when they grow up, will marry later or have fewer children than their schoolfellows? . . . Unless therefore the proportion of births falls soon and sharply—and I see no reason for expecting that—at least one quarter of the population of this borough will in course of time be Asian or West Indian. . . . This does not mean that every fourth house in every road will contain an Asian or West Indian family. It means, and we know that it means, that "whole areas" (to quote my own words again) "will be occupied by the immigrant and immigrant-descended population." (*Times*, 10 June 1969: 3)

So Mrs. Lewis (Chapman) is merely parroting the arch-conservative political rhetoric heard since at least the mid-1960s as Britain strained to deal with its inexorable population change.

"slept with a lady" — ("Nudge, Nudge") This rather tame sexual reference (the first of many to come) was only possible during the reign of BBC Director-General Hugh Greene (fl. 1960–1969), whose more liberal approach to programming possibilities allowed the Pythons a time slot. As the Pythons subsequently explored the boundaries of the BBC's newfound permissiveness, they seemed to litaneutically employ the handbook "Variety Programmes Policy Guide for Writers and Producers," written in 1948 but still in use more than twenty years later. The handbook's banned references for television presentation included "lavatories," "effeminacy in men," and "immorality of any kind," all of which the Pythons visited and revisited as the series rolled on. Also forbidden (and regularly targeted by the Pythons) were "suggestive references" to newlyweds (Ep. 8), fig leaves (Ep. 6), prostitution (Eps. 14, 33), ladies' underwear (Eps. 5, 9), animal sexual habits (Ep. 20), religion or religious figures (Eps. 15, 17), and commercial travelers (Eps. 22, 28). The government and politicians were also off-limits, two targets that became Python favorites. Humphrey Carpenter discusses the handbook in relation to early 1960s satire shows in *That Was Satire, That Was* (205–6).

song — ("Court Scene [Witness in Coffin/Cardinal Richelieu]") The tune borrowed here is "Someone Else I'd Like to Be" by Tom Sutton, sung by both Cleese and Chapman, with live piano by Bill McGuffie (WAC T12/1,084). McGuffie will figure in *FC* over the following several seasons, writing original songs for the performers and playing piano accompaniment, as he does here.

"soothe . . . quiet" — ("Court Scene [Witness in Coffin/Cardinal Richelieu]") Cf. Congreve's *The Mourning Bride*: "Music has charms to soothe a savage breast" (1.1), and Shakespeare's *King Richard II*: " . . . truth hath a quiet breast" (1.3.96). Congreve was a member of the Kit Kat Club in eighteenth-century London (see entry for "Eek Eek Club" in Ep. 2).

spanner — (PSC; "Bicycle Repair Man") A wrench.

"storm toss'd" — ("Court Scene [Witness in Coffin/Cardinal Richelieu]") Cf. *Romeo and Juliet*: "Thy tempest-tossed body . . ." (3.5.137).

"stuff and pith" — ("Court Scene [Witness in Coffin/Cardinal Richelieu]") Cf. similar phraseology found in both *Henry V* and *Hamlet*, with the latter reading: "The pith and marrow of our attribute" (1.4.22).

suburban house — (PSC; "Seduced Milkmen") This was filmed on location in Barnes, Richmond upon Thames, according to Palin. See Palin's presentation in *Pythonland* (DVD, dir. Ralph Lee, 1999). BBC records indicate that the house was precisely located at 48 Ullswater Road, Barnes, where portions of "The Mouse Problem" and "World's Deadliest Joke" were also filmed (WAC T12/1,083). Most of these sequences were shot on 16 July 1969.

Superboy — ("Bicycle Repair Man") There actually was a Superboy character (meant to be simply a young Superman) created in 1944. The boy playing Superboy here is John Watters (WAC T12/1,083), who also appeared in *Oliver!* (1968), *Z Cars* (1969), and *Footprints in the Jungle* (1970). Watters shot his scene on 14 July 1969 (WAC T12/1,242).

"Superman" — ("Bicycle Repair Man") American comic book character created in June 1938, written by Jerry Siegel and drawn by Joseph Shuster for Action Comics. Superman would appear on a radio show, TV cartoons, novels, a Broadway musical, several television series, and feature motion pictures. The American accents used by the commentator and those dressed as Superman remind the reader/viewer of the character's roots, and the credo by which he lives: "Truth, justice, and the American way." The American television show *The Adventures of Superman*, starring George Reeves (1914–1959), began to appear on British television (first regionally, then more widespread), as early as February 1956.

The accompanying music is not a generic "chase martial" as listed in the WAC records, but is a portion of "March of the Insurgents" by Jack Shaindlin (WAC T12/1,084). This music will also be heard in Ep. 6 as the Frankenstein monster (Cleese) attacks a bus queue.

"Swansea" — ("Stolen Newsreader") There are at least six nature reserves in the Swansea area. Swansea is a Welsh city in Glamorgan, southwestern Wales. It lies along the Bristol Channel at the mouth of the River Tawe (hence its Welsh name, Abertawe). Swansea is the second largest city in Wales.

• T •

"tangled web" — ("Court Scene [Witness in Coffin/Cardinal Richelieu]") Cf. Sir Walter Scott's *Marmion*: "Oh, what a tangled web we weave, / When first we practice to deceive!" (canto VI, stanza 17). Scott is mentioned/alluded to at least two other times in *FC*. His book *Redgauntlet* is woefully misread aloud in Ep. 38, and the other allusion is discussed below in the "Provost of Edinburgh" note in Ep. 7.

"Thinks—this is a job for . . ." — ("Bicycle Repair Man") This "Thinks" is borrowed directly from Bluebottle (Sellers) of *Goon Show* fame. In cartoon-like form, every time young Bluebottle needed a moment of inner monologue he'd start by saying "Thinks . . ."

"trap" — ("Court Scene [Witness in Coffin/Cardinal Richelieu]") Richelieu is now the woodcock to Dim's springe. See the entry for "woodcock" below.

TV Centre — ("Stolen Newsreader") Main British Broadcasting Corporation complex, located in Shepherd's Bush. This was where most of the BBC's sound stages were located, and where *Flying Circus* was primarily recorded, when *en-studio*. The then-state-of-the-art studio space opened to much fanfare in 1960.

• U •

"unturned" — ("Court Scene [Witness in Coffin/Cardinal Richelieu]") Cf. Euripides' *Heraclidae* (c. 428 BC). This is another insignificant moment elevated to high (mock) seriousness. Cleese, having read law at Cambridge, may have drawn upon his limited experience in the courts for this scene. In fact, in a publicity photo for *The Frost Report* (1966), Cleese appears dressed as a barrister.

"Uproar!" — ("Court Scene [Witness in Coffin/Cardinal Richelieu]") The others in this scene include Fred Berman and William Curran as the Ushers, Maurice Quick as the Counsel, as well as Bill Gosling, Jim Delany, Alan Granville, Moira Pearson, and Elizabeth Broom (WAC T12.1,084). Several of these are bit-part actors who appeared regularly in many British TV shows during this period. Maurice Quick, for example, appeared in *Dixon of Dock Green*, *Doctor Who*, and *Z Cars*, and Bill Gosling (a.k.a. William Gossling) appeared in *Z Cars* (1971), *Upstairs, Downstairs* (1972), and *Hearts and Flowers* (1970). Elizabeth Broom and Jim Delany would take other bit/walk-on parts in shows like *Some Mothers Do 'Ave 'Em* (1973), a show produced by Michael Mills, with technical folk like James Balfour (camera) and Bernard Wilkie (visual effects designer), late of the *FC* crew. Alan Granville was an uncredited extra on *Doctor Who*, as are others who appear often on *FC*, including Maurice Quick, Peter Kaukus, Cy Town, and Bernadette Barry (see *The Encyclopedia of Fantastic Film & Television*).

Any actor hired to appear in any *FC* episode is noted in the accounting portions of the surviving records, for repeat fee purposes, though the actor's precise role ("walk-on," "speaking," "extra") isn't always noted.

• V •

"very big" — ("Restaurant Sketch") This Cook looks very much like the hulking Cook figure appearing in Harold Lloyd's silent comedy film *Haunted Spooks* (1920), directed by Harold "Hal" Roach. The Cook in this silent comedy film is called out from the kitchen to help throw out an unwanted suitor.

"Voleschtadt" — ("Stolen Newsreader") Perhaps a homonym or just misspelling of Vollstadt, but may also be one of the earliest "vole" references in *FC*. It could translate essentially as "mouse city."

• W •

"wakes the drowsy apricot" — ("Court Scene [Witness in Coffin/Cardinal Richelieu]") Rousing a sleepy drupe? Cf. Shakespeare's *A Midsummer Night's Dream*:

> *Tit.* Be kind and courteous to this gentleman,
> Hop in his walks and gambol in his eyes;
> Feed him with apricocks and dewberries,
> With purple grapes, green figs, and mulberries;
> The honey-bags steal from the humble-bees,
> And for night-tapers crop their waxen thighs,
> And light them at the fiery glow-worm's eyes,
> To have my love to bed and to arise;
> And pluck the wings from painted butterflies
> To fan the moonbeams from his sleeping eyes:
> Nod to him, elves, and do him courtesies. (3.1.164–74)

The drowsiness is here attributed to the object of the four Fairies' attention, Bottom. In *King Richard II*, "dangling apricocks" are compared by the Gardener to unruly children who demand much of their master (3.4.29–32).

"What frees . . . owl of Thebes?" — ("Court Scene [Witness in Coffin/Cardinal Richelieu]") The phrase "owl of Thebes" does not appear in Shakespeare's corpus, and the owl, when mentioned by Shakespeare, is most often a harbinger of death or birth, or a sort of night watchman. (For medieval artist Hieronymus Bosch, owls represented evil and even Satan himself. Monstrous owls sketched by Gilliam appear several times in his preparations for the animated sequences in *Holy Grail*.) Perhaps, though, the gist of the phrase can be attributable to Fortinbras in *Hamlet*: "This quarry cries on havoc. O proud death, / What feast is toward in thine eternal *cell*, / That thou so many princes at a shot / So bloodily hast strook?" (5.2.364–67).

Or even to the Greek likeness of Cymbeline:

> *Gui.* Out of your proof you speak; we poor unfledg'd,
> Have never wing'd from view o' th' nest, nor [know] not
> What air's from home. Happ'ly this life is best,
> If quiet life be best; sweeter to you
> That have a sharper known; well corresponding
> With your stiff age; but unto us it is
> A *cell* of ignorance, travelling a-bed,
> A prison, or a debtor that not dares
> To stride a limit. (*Cymbeline* 3.3.27–34)

Perhaps an echo can be heard of Thomas Gray's *Elegy Written in a Country Church-Yard*, where are found the complaints of the "mopeing Owl," as well as the "narrow cell" containing "rude Forefathers" of the rural hamlet. Whatever the source, the Pythons consistently draw upon the rich panoply of English literature and literary figures for their comedy.

"What's-it like?" — ("Nudge, Nudge") This highly euphemistic sketch plays on the fact that the audience understands the lewdness of Norman's (Idle) questions and allusions, and the gent (Jones) misses the true meaning of every wink and nudge almost completely. Notice, too, that the punchline receives an appropriately fake laugh track response, signaling the Pythons' continuing sneer at what they considered to be typically restraining comedic structures. The lame-ness of the ending didn't stop them from including the sketch, of course, and it reappears to much acclaim in most of the troupe's live stage performances, including *Live at the Hollywood Bowl* (1980).

"wickets" — ("Stolen Newsreader") Cricket paraphernalia, a wicket consists of three stumps/stakes (about 28 inches tall) topped by two bails and arranged so that a ball cannot pass between the stumps. Two wickets are set up—the batsman defends and the bowler attacks. A cricket match will be depicted in Eps. 20 and 45, and two cricket teams will appear earlier in Ep. 20. Gilliam will use the image of a mustachioed cricketer (from a vintage team photo) in the title animations for the second season.

The match highlighted here (Yorkshire vs. Glamorgan) is an example of "county cricket," or matches between the various counties of the UK and a practice in place as early as 1827. These were also often amateur versus professional matches. Yorkshire dominated this inter-county play during the 1960s, probably much to the delight of South Yorkshire–native Palin.

"Wimbledon" — ("Court Scene [Witness in Coffin/Cardinal Richelieu]") Formerly a municipal borough of Surrey, though since 1965 Wimbledon has been part of Merton, a borough of Greater London. It is eight miles southwest of London. Most of Ep. 7 is centered on alien blancmanges playing for the tennis world crown at Wimbledon.

"woodcock in his springe" — ("Court Scene [Witness in Coffin/Cardinal Richelieu]") Cf. Laertes's too-late realization in *Hamlet*: "Why, as a woodcock to mine own springe, Osric: / I am justly kill'd with mine own treachery" (5.2.306–7). A "springe" is a trap for small animals, especially birds, like the woodcock.

• Y •

"Yard" — ("Court Scene [Witness in Coffin/Cardinal Richelieu]") Refers to Scotland Yard, headquarters of the London Metropolitan Police and located south of St. James's Park in Westminster. In *FC* episodes, appearances by characters from the Yard are generally greeted with some fanfare.

"Yorkshire" — ("Stolen Newsreader") Largest historical county of England, in the north-central part of the country between the Pennines and the North Sea. Palin was born in Sheffield, South Yorkshire.

Yorkshire's cricket club was founded in Sheffield in 1863, and many of its best years were had before WWII.

"you-know-what" — ("Court Scene [Witness in Coffin/Cardinal Richelieu]") This kind of non-reference usually means something of a sexual nature, here probably gynecological. The connection to Eliot's *The Waste Land* (see "hire purchase" entry above) is likely confirmed after this sexual reference. In the pub speech section of Eliot's poem, the speakers talk of multiple births, abortions, and ineffective contraception—lots of "you-know-what." See the sketch about taxation on "thingy" (sexual acts) in Ep. 15.

Episode 4: "Owl-Stretching Time"

"It's Man" thrown from cliff intro; *Animation: Titles* (calm Cleese v/o); "Episode Arthur, Part 7, Teeth"; "And Did Those Feet" (song); Art gallery; Art critic; "But it's my only line"; "And Did Those Feet" reprise; "It's a Man's Life in the Modern Army" and the Colonel; "This is my only line"; Undressing in public; "It's a pig's life" and the Colonel; Fruit self-defence class; *Animation: Tumor operation to palanquin link*; "And did those feet" link to "England's Mountains Green"; "It's a Man's Life in England's Mountains Green" rustic monologue (and the Colonel); Bookshop; Secret Service dentists; "Lemming of the BDA"; "It's a Man's Life in the British Dental Association"; The Colonel stops the program; Referee whistle into "It's" Man closing credits

• A •

"Albania" — ("Song [*And Did Those Feet*]") Zog ruled 1928–1939, when Italian fascists unseated him as they overran Albania. Zog lived in exile afterward.

"all the things you can read about in a book" — ("Secret Service Dentists") Meaning, these things just listed won't be seen in this sketch, or even on this show. This "faux intro" motif is also used to build up other sketches in other episodes, viz., Ep. 8, the "Army Protection Racket" sketch, as well as the "*Black Eagle*" sketch in Ep. 25. There is also the very sober, historically reasonable intro to *HG*, which is quickly undercut.

"ancient time" — ("Song [*And Did Those Feet*]") Here she stops his mouth with a kiss. Cf. Benedick to Beatrice in Shakespeare's *Much Ado*. The song is actually called "Jerusalem."

anti-tank gun — (PSC; "Secret Service Dentists") This is a weapon designed specifically to combat tanks in the field, featuring armor-piercing shells. The 1960s saw a significant increase in the interest in, production, and use of such weapons. The older model used in this episode looks very much like a version of the WWII-era M-20 bazooka. The rise in anti-colonial guerrilla actions in Africa and South America, for example, meant that these low-tech, shoulder-fired-type weapons became quite prominent.

The increasing size and lethality of the weapons in this sketch seems a comment on the then-current arms race, as well, where the United States and USSR (and, by association, NATO and the Warsaw Pact countries) were building and deploying ever larger and more destructive weapons in the race for global supremacy. Bugs Bunny and Elmer Fudd (and Bugs and Marvin Martian) had earlier spoofed this nihilistic build-up, as well, in the Warner Bros. cartoons *What's Opera, Doc?* and *Duck Dodgers*, respectively.

Great Britain's part in this arms race, for the most part, meant agreeing to host/deploy U.S. weapons systems, including nuclear submarines, B-52 bombers, and various missile systems. The decision to scuttle its own glitch-ridden Blue Streak missile project and cast in with the United States on the Skybolt system seemed a good idea in the very early 1960s, but soon thereafter the Americans announced the creation and deployment of long-range ICBMs, and the Skybolt system immediately became obsolete. Newspapers, Labour Party officials, and *Private Eye* had a field day skewering the seemingly shortsighted Macmillan administration for leaving the UK without a credible nuclear deterrent at the height of the Cold War.

"Art Gallery" — ("Art Gallery") Cf. *"It's the Arts"* in Ep. 1. Pythons' forays into the world of high art (and literature, music, etc.) display their acculturation, and their university training. Their "working mothers" here are also given significant knowledge and appreciation of fine art, well beyond what might be expected of the working class.

Pete and Dud (Peter Cook and Dudley Moore) had performed a sketch called "Art Gallery" for their 1965 TV show, *Not Only . . . But Also*. In it Pete and Dud meet and discuss the efficacies of Rubens's "fat ladies," da Vinci's cartoons (which aren't "funny" at all), and the unmatched skill of wildlife painter Vernon Ward (1905–1985), where the duck's eyes follow you as you pass the painting.

In the Python "Art Gallery," the women seem to be in a room of Constable-type (or at least nineteenth-century British) landscapes, and the Pythons had asked for the prop department to provide a copy of "Turner's *Bridge at Kew*." That prop painting can be glimpsed just behind the ladies, on an easel facing the camera. One of the paintings (third from left) may be a version of one of Constable's "Hampstead Heath" paintings (perhaps *Hampstead Heath with a Rainbow*, 1836); the painting on the far left resembles Turner's *Crossing the Brook* (1815). Most of the paintings can't be seen very well, but it's clear they're not eighteenth century or earlier. They may also be popularized prints of Constable followers, of which there were many.

See entry for "landscape artists" in this episode for more. Again, original versions of these English masters would have been available to the Pythons at the Tate, Victoria & Albert, and National Gallery museums, as they are today.

"Arthur" — ("Opening Captions") Cf. the multiple uses of "Arthur" in Eps. 1 and 2, and then throughout *FC*, appearing in twenty-one different episodes. This episode features the exploits of Arthur Lemming. See below.

• B •

"back at two" — ("Secret Service Dentists") Either a spoof on the dental profession for taking a regular lunch break no matter what they're involved with, or even the film/TV industry where actors can break character at the call for lunch and resume the situation later.

Not unlike the Warner Bros. cartoon characters (Ralph and Sam, a wolf and a sheepdog), who can be at each other's throats from 9 to 5 but come punch-out time they're friends again. The seven cartoons in which they appear and share this relationship date between 1953 and 1963. See Jerry Beck's *Looney Tunes and Merrie Melodies*.

"banana fiend" — ("Self-Defence") The specter of incongruity is apparent here, since attack by fresh fruit is rarely a real threat. But, the incongruity is almost ameliorated by the fact that the RSM type has a noticeable tic, as well as a fixation on fresh fruit. Perhaps the intimation is that the RSM suffers some sort of post-traumatic stress disorder after his military service. And before the "fresh-fruit-as-dangerous" scenario can be wholly discounted, it must be remembered that in the Python world, sheep, rabbits, and even blancmanges can be deadly.

The Goons had treated this subject in the episode "The Affair of the Lone Banana" (26 Oct. 1954), where a loaded banana is capable of killing a man.

"Baroque" — ("Art Gallery") Period defined by dramatic themes and stylistic complexity, and roughly coinciding with the duration of the seventeeth century, and including painters such as Rubens, Rembrandt, and Velazquez.

beach — ("Undressing in Public") Much of this sketch was shot at the beaches of Bournemouth, on Friday, 10 July 1969 (WAC T12/1,083).

"Big Cheese" — ("Secret Service Dentists") American underworld or film noir slang for a boss, or a self-important person. Used just this way by Raymond Chandler in a *Black Mask* story (July 1934): "So the big cheese give me the job" (64).

blank English stare — (PSC; "Undressing in Public") Another example of the Englishness of the text and its cultural referents/references. The authors are careful to note that there is no judgment in the look, no "disapproval," just another thing that "we" (as Englishmen and Englishwomen) can share, and in sharing are therefore English. Voltaire also commented on Englishness, characterizing the entire population as "eaten up with melancholy," and this penchant for watching blankly appears in *Candide*, chapter 23:

> As they were chatting thus together they arrived at Portsmouth. The shore on each side the harbor was lined with a multitude of people, whose eyes were steadfastly fixed on a lusty man who was kneeling down on the deck of one of the men-of-war, with something tied before his eyes. Opposite to this personage stood four soldiers, each of whom shot three bullets into his skull, with all the composure imaginable; and when it was done, the whole company went away perfectly well satisfied.

These selfsame kinds of stares can be seen in the location shots when passersby are watching the recording.

See the "Olympic Hide-and-Seek Final" in Ep. 35, and the somewhat disinterested bystanders in the "How to Give Up Being a Mason" sketch in Ep. 17, as well as holiday-goers in-shot during *Scott of the Antarctic* in Ep. 23.

This is also the same kind of look that often greeted Monsieur Hulot (Jacques Tati, 1909–1982) in films like *Mon. Hulot's Holiday* (1953) and *Mon oncle* (1958). Both are gentle commentaries on the display of private actions in public settings, with Hulot blithely stumbling through modern French society—a kind of throwback to a gentler, kinder era that may or may not have ever existed.

bookseller — (PSC; "Secret Service Dentists") Voltaire notes that the job of bookselling had no equal, with Candide deciding "that there was no trade in the world with which one should be more disgusted" (chapter 19). No surprise, then, that the bookseller (Cleese) as depicted here moonlights as a spy of sorts.

Cleese earlier played a perturbed bookseller in a sketch with customer Marty Feldman on *At Last the 1948 Show*. In the later Python version, Jones takes the part of the customer.

bookshop — (PSC; "Secret Service Dentists") There are posters on the walls of this shop for various current and popular titles, including:

1. A generic advertisement to read more Louis L'Amour books (noted American Western author), as well as a poster for the 1968 Mickey Spillane "Morgan the Raider" international spy novel, *The Delta Factor*. Spillane (1918–2006) is apropos to this scene by virtue of his dame-slapping, chain-smoking, tough-talking heroes (like Mike Hammer) and world of crime settings. *The Delta Factor* would be released as a feature film in 1970.
2. A title from a series of spy books featuring the cowardly Boysie Oakes, written by John E. Gardner, this one called *Madrigal* (1968). These books were quite popular during this period, and featured a super-spy who really wasn't terribly adept—not unlike the naughty dentists in the sketch.
3. *The Naked Ape* by Desmond Morris (published 1967, 1969) is prominently featured between Cleese and Idle (cf. Ep. 12, where the caption "The Naked Ant" appears.)
4. An advertisement for the latest book by Lobsang Rampa, *Beyond the Tenth* (1969), is also seen. Rampa had written *The Third Eye* in 1958, reportedly detailing his own life as a Tibetan lama, but he was later exposed as a Plympton-born Brit, Cyril Hoskin. He continued to write and live in this assumed monk character for many years. (See notes to the "*Erizabeth L*" sketch in Ep. 29 for more on Rampa.)
5. There is a poster for the Roderick Thorp novel *The Detective* ("An Adult Look at a Detective") near the door, and this a crossover poster for the film (1968) starring Frank Sinatra.
6. There are also several Penguin books, including a green "crime" series book, and an orange-jacketed "classic." See notes to Ep. 38 for more on the Penguin book series, and the cultural significance of Penguin Publishing in the UK. A paperback version (light blue cover) of Sir Ernest Gowers's influential style guide *The Complete Plain Words* (first published in 1948) can be seen in the bookrack under Brian's (Jones) bazooka. This is the Pelican Books edition from 1963.

This particular sketch was actually shot on Stage 8, not Stage 6, where the episodes were normally staged, perhaps because the size of the set and moveable machinery demanded a differently equipped space. There is also the possibility that this taping just got bumped by another show on this date, 21 September 1969, which will also happen later in the series on several occasions (WAC T12/1,086).

breakwater — ("Undressing in Public") *OED*: "A groyne or barrier on the beach to retain shingle." This breakwater seems to run from the top of the beach down to the low tide line.

"Bring me . . . chariot of fire" — (link into "It's a Man's Life in the Modern Army") The change of mood becomes very apparent here as the double-edged references appear. What was sacred in the hymnal setting must now be seen as sexual, especially as the girl enters. Henke notes that in English Renaissance literature "arrow" has been glossed as both "kiss" and a metaphor for "penis." He cites George Walton Williams (editor of the 1966 edition of *The Changeling*) who, following extant stage directions, glosses "arrow" as "kiss":

> *Ant*. No danger in me; I bring naught but love
> And his soft-wounding shafts to strike you with.
> Try but one arrow; if it hurt you,
> I'll stand you twenty back in recompense.
> [*Kisses her*.] (3.3.136–39)

(The format and spelling for quotes from Dekker, Middleton, Webster, et al., are included as found in Fraser and Rabkin's *Drama of the English Renaissance* [1976].)

Thus an arrow is merely a kiss, amorous but not overtly sexual. The ribaldry associated with the term is displayed by Robert Greene in *A Disputation between a Hee Cony-Catcher and a Shee Cony-Catcher* (1592), with Greene remarking that the harlot's "quiuer is open to euery arrow" (6). The allusion is even more pronounced in the next line from "Jerusalem," where the arrow has enlarged/engorged into a "spear," and the quiver is the "unfolding clouds" of the female pudenda. "Fire" also has sexual connotations, suggesting inflamed passions. So this hymn purportedly about Christ's visit to the British Isles here becomes—thanks to the fawning and fondling female presence—something of a torch song full of probably unintended double entendres and sexual allusions. The mood has indeed changed, and will continue to do so for the singer (Idle) and the amorous girl (Katya Wyeth).

"British Dental Association" — ("Secret Service Dentists") The BDA is the regulatory agency for the UK dental industry. This is one of the few times that an actual, active British organization is satirized, by name, in *FC*. Most of the time, the Pythons create a fictitious name for such things, perhaps to avoid litigation and/or libel entanglements. In Ep. 7, for example, a card that had been made to read "The President of British Footwear Ltd." was changed to "The President of Leisure Footwear Ltd."

bundle him out — (PSC; "Secret Service Dentists") Physically pushing him out the door (bundle meaning to go out in some disorder, according to the *OED*). Cf. the actions of the two interviewers in Ep. 1 who do the same to Arthur "Two-Sheds" Jackson.

• C •

"change the mood" — ("Song [*And Did Those Feet*]") The mood will get sexually charged in the singer's next appearance when a woman (Katya Wyeth) appears and begins to fondle the singer (Idle).

"clever dick" — ("Self-Defence") A smart, adept, adroit person (*OED*). In the "Top of the Form" sketch helmed by Cleese in *At Last the 1948 Show*, Cleese as moderator refuses to award points even as a contestant gives the correct answer, "Pyongyang," because the respondent is a "clever dick."

commissionaire — (PSC; "Undressing in Public") *OED*: "One entrusted with small commissions; a messenger or light porter; the designation of various subordinate employés in public offices, private businesses, hotels, etc., on the Continent." In an example of "the customer's always right," the commissionaire (Chapman) responds to the gentleman's mimed questioning by pulling his own pants down, a comic misunderstanding.

"Courtauld" — ("Art Gallery") Small but influential gallery in Somerset House, the Strand, London. The Courtauld houses an impressive collection that includes Manet, Rubens, and Tiepolo. This comment also indicates that this particular scene is set somewhere other than the Courtauld, most likely the National Gallery, but perhaps the Tate Britain or Victoria & Albert Museum. The Pythons would use the façade of the Tate Britain (on Millbank) again in Ep. 32, when the "Tory Housewives Clean-Up Campaign" race in to cover up the obscene art.

cut-out animation — (PSC; "Sedan Chair" animated link out of "Self-Defence") Gilliam's technique of using bits and pieces of photos, drawings, etc., arranged on an animations stand or table, then photographed one frame or a few frames at a time. Animator Lotte Reiniger (1899–1981) had been working with cut-outs in silhouette in animation since as early as 1919, while Hans Richter (1888–1976) worked with cut-out shapes in the 1920s. Cut-out animation continued to be successful in Eastern Europe and the USSR into the 1960s (see Khitruk's *Man in the Frame* [1966]). Gilliam's professed inspiration for the cut-rate and experimental animation seen in *FC* is Stan Vanderbeek (1927–1984), an animator and collagist (*Gilliam on Gilliam*, 38–40).

"cut to me" — ("It's a Man's Life in the Modern Army") Playing the role of the tyrant (cf. T.W. Baldwin's typology in *Organisation and Personnel of the Shakespearean Company*), the Colonel (Chapman) can for a moment take control of the narrative, become the director, and move the narrative off in a different direction.

For an almost completely successful attempt at narrative tyranny, look at Richard's power in Shakespeare's *Richard III* as both maker and director, able to transform friends into enemies and foes into allies, and able to direct the plots around him (see *MPSERD*, chapter 6). This power endures until the demands of historicity and simply the completion of the play make sure that Richard falls. Falstaff also attempts to wield such power, boasting that his influence over Prince Harry–cum–King Henry is such that he is a "maker," and that he possesses almost godlike abilities. Falstaff to Shallow: "I will *make* the King . . ." (*HIV* 5.5.5–8). The Colonel's influence will be overcome by the narrative, but the Colonel will have the last laugh, as he will eventually bring the program to a close, and even assist (off-screen) in tossing the "It's Man" back over the cliff.

• D •

"damsons . . . prunes" — ("Self-Defence") A damson is a black or purple plum, and a prune is simply a dried plum. This is an early iteration of the Chapman/Cleese "thesaurus"-type sketch that will be seen in full flower by Ep. 33, "Cheese Shop."

dentist's gear — (PSC; "Secret Service Dentists") The Big Cheese is wearing all-black, form-fitting clothing, and looks more like Dick Shawn's character Lorenzo Saint DuBois (LSD) from Mel Brooks's film *The Producers* (1968) than a prototypical megalomaniac, à la a James Bond villain. Still, the chair, the furry animal, and the diabolical laughter and equally diabolical acting (cf. "Spanish Inquisition," Ep. 15) are present to conjure up images of Bond villains like the cat-lover Blofeld (Donald Pleasence) from *You Only Live Twice* (1967). The Big Cheese is also wearing lots of hippie-jewelry, including a large flower-power necklace, nudging him closer to the LSD character, as well.

"do your worst" — ("Self-Defence") The supreme defensive challenge. Cf. the Old Woman (Bee Duffell) being accosted by Arthur and Bedivere (in relation to shrubbery) in *HG*. Also, see Jonson's *The Alchemist*: "Thy worst. I fart at thee" (1.1.2).

"Dresden Pottery" — ("Art Gallery") Pottery from the Dresden, Germany, area where fine pottery products have been created since the seventeenth century. The city was nearly bombed out of existence in the last days of WWII as the Allies switched from strategic targets to all targets of opportunity, hoping to shorten the war.

• E •

Episode 4 — Entitled "Owl-Stretching Time," which was one of the possible titles for the series, and was also considered as a possible title for Ep. 2, though it's still known by that title (in the WAC records). See the notes for "stretching owls" in Ep. 2, and Morgan (1999, 49).

This episode was recorded 21 September 1969, and broadcast on 26 October 1969.

Additional folk not included in the cast list for this particular episode—but noted as being paid for appearing in the show in WAC documents—include Frank Littlewood, Albert Ward, Barry Took, and Peter Lovell. Littlewood appeared in the sci-fi TV program *The Escape of RD7* (1961). Albert Ward was a longtime British TV figure, appearing in the radio and TV versions of *Welsh Rarebit* in 1952. Barry Took is given some credit for bringing all the Pythons to the BBC in 1969 for *FC*, and spent many years on BBC radio and TV as a writer and comedian. Peter Lovell was a production assistant on shows like *The Goodies*. Future episodes will include many more extras and walk-ons as the demands of the sketches increase and become more complicated and populated.

Still not convinced that they'd landed a winner in these earliest episodes, another John Howard Davies admittedly droll memo referencing Ep. 4 reads somewhat unflatteringly: "The fourth episode of 'Monty Python's Flying Circus' stars as usual John Cleese, Graham Chapman, Michael Palin, Terry Jones and Eric Idle. More rubbish" (WAC T12/1,084).

One indicator of the uncertainty with which the audience and BBC were reacting to *FC* could be that Ep. 4 is *listed* as having gone to air "Mono," meaning monochrome, and not as a "colour" broadcast, as the first three episodes clearly enjoyed. This was the period when bemused befuddlement was the overarching reaction to *FC*, and many regions were opting out of broadcasting the show in favor of more attractive local programming. The WAC files contain memos of Pythons' concerns about unfriendly broadcast slots, as well as audience shares compared to other BBC shows (see WAC T12/1,082 through T12/1,094 for *FC* first season information).

An additional memo in the file for Ep. 4 is from Michael Mills (Head of Comedy, Light Entertainment Television, BBC) to Ian MacNaughton and JHD patting the show on the back ("very meritorious and very funny"). Mills does give some tips for better editing, and ends by assuring IM and JHD that the show is better than most anything else currently produced through Light Entertainment. The memo is dated 29 September 1969, about one week prior to the airing of the first episode (WAC T12/1,085).

"evil" — ("Secret Service Dentists") Pronounced "ee-vil," with the schwa-sounding [i] replaced by the [i] as pronounced in "bid." Peter Sellers would use this same pronunciation in various character guises in *The Goon Show* (1951–1960).

"Excitement . . . Adventure" — (PSC; "Secret Service Dentists") The filmed black-and-white images that accompany each of these words are not accounted for in the WAC records of the episode or series.

explosion — (PSC; "Self-Defence") Undoubtedly part of Python's continuing satire on the nihilistic mentality of the military industrial complex of the world powers during this period. This same topic will be broached over and over again, including crime figures shaking down Britain's weakened military in "Army Protection Racket" (Ep. 8), the proliferation of nuclear weapons ("Piranha Brothers," Ep. 14) in an era when Britain was relying on the United States for its nuclear deterrent, wars and rumors of wars ("Blood, Devastation, Death, War and Horror," Ep. 30), the increasing Chinese threat (Gilliam animation and "Bingo-Crazed

Chinese," Ep. 34), the über-villain Richard Nixon (Eps. 5, 10, and 12; all written and recorded long before the Watergate revelations), and the soulless Soviet empire ("Mr. Pither," Ep. 34).

The *Beyond the Fringe* creative team had created a number of scathing Cold War skits in the early 1960s, as well, including "Civil War," "TV PM," and "Steppes in the Right Direction."

exposed again — (PSC; "Undressing in Public") This type of gag was Buster Keaton's stock-in-trade. In *Cops* (1922) he attempts an escape by climbing onto what appears to be a spare tire attached to a car. The car drives away, and we see that the tire is actually a display for a tire store. He also slips under a car to hide, and the car drives away, only to be replaced by another car before his pursuer can see him.

• F •

falling to the ground — (PSC; "Self-Defence") This lethality becomes the hallmark of the sketch, and is found throughout Python. Eventually, everyone in this sketch—including the RSM—is dead. The morbidity factor of Python's humor arose often from the troupe's attempts to "shock" or at least surprise the television audience, and must also be seen as a nod to the death and destruction seen on evening newscasts covering the recent civil and military disturbances around the world. In Ep. 8 the new recruit wants out of the military when he realizes that servicemen get "properly" dead; this could be a direct response to the Northern Ireland "troubles" featured on the front pages of all major English newspapers in 1969.

"Fighting Temeraire" — ("Art Gallery") A lesser-known 1838 Turner work, it is fully titled *The Fighting Temeraire Tugged to Her Last Berth to be Broken Up, 1838*. This painting still hangs in the National Gallery, though it's considerably larger than depicted, and couldn't have been carried around by the Pepperpots. *The Slave Ship* (1840) is considered Turner's masterpiece by most art critics, though pedestrian art lovers rank "Temeraire" higher, according to the NG. In "Fighting Temeraire," J.M.W. Turner (1775–1851) is said to be depicting the decline of the British navy, which may account for Python choosing the painting for the sketch. It may also have been chosen simply because it was a well-known painting by a well-known British artist, and one that would have been (and still is today) the subject of lectures for visiting grade school students as they tour the National Gallery.

"fillings" — ("Secret Service Dentists") In this parody, this mock epic, the Pythons have replaced the usual semantic elements of the spy thriller genre (international spies, nuclear weapons, microfilm, secret documents or tapes, etc.) with sillier items like fillings. They've even adapted the lingo ("appointment," "gas," "upper right two and four") from dentistry to tell their John le Carré, Alistair Maclean (or even Leon Uris) type spoof. In the usual Python genre-busting way, elements of American gangster films and pulp fiction novels also occupy this sketch, as will recognizable nods to Ian Fleming's "James Bond" novels and films.

"Flemish . . . Schools" — ("Art Gallery") Flemish Renaissance masters include Jan Van Eyck (more interested in multi-surfaced, realistic detail), while Mannerists attempted to combine Gothic and Renaissance styles with very different Flemish and Italian traditions, and many of the masterpieces of the latter school are unattributable (see *Gardner's*). The Van Eyck painting *The Arnolfini Portrait* (1434) is later featured in Gilliam's animation in Ep. 6, at the close of the lengthy "Johann Gambolputty . . ." sketch. The Bronzino *An Allegory with Venus and Cupid*—from which Gilliam borrowed the famous Python foot—is an example of stylized, affected Mannerist painting. (This painting will reappear, touched-up and animated, in a Gilliam animation in Ep. 6.) The Tate, National Gallery, and V&A all offered significant Flemish and Mannerist pieces and artists (Bronzino, Tintoretto, El Greco) for the Pythons' reference.

In the "Art Gallery" sketch performed by Pete and Dud for *Not Only . . . But Also* (1965), the boys have agreed to meet at the "Flemish masters" as the sketch begins.

"Flopsy" — ("Secret Service Dentists") Character from Beatrix Potter's *Peter Rabbit* (1901). The rabbit depicted in the sketch is obviously stuffed, looking no more alive than will the attack rabbit in *HG*, and is reminiscent of the white cat fondled by several Bond villains. In another genre-busting moment, the gun the Big Cheese will use to shoot the rabbit is a shiny, long-barreled American six-shooter.

"Florentine" — ("Art Gallery") Of or from Florence, Italy, including Raphael, who spent a short but important four years there (1504–1508). In the early fifteenth century, Florence was the locus of the learned and artistic world. According to historian John Symonds:

> Nowhere else except at Athens has the whole population of a city been so permeated with ideas, so highly intellectual by nature, so keen in perception, so witty so subtle, as at Florence. . . . The primacy of the Florentines in literature, the fine arts, law, scholarship, philosophy and science was acknowledged throughout Italy. (*The Renaissance in Italy*, 125)

The Pythons may have seen their London, and specifically their small digs at the BBC, as their own English version of that Florentine paradise. Florentine collections in the major museums and galleries in and around London had been significant and available for many years.

flunkey — (PSC; link into "Song [*And Did Those Feet*]") Originally, "flunkey" meant a male livery servant, with contempt implied (*OED*). Today, it refers to anyone who performs menial, drudge-like service.

• G •

"gelignite" — ("Self-Defence") A blasting gelatin invented by Alfred Nobel, who also invented dynamite. Comprising a topical, news-generated item for the Pythons as they wrote the first season, gelignite explosive devices were the weapon of choice for Provisional IRA Campaign–type attacks beginning in 1969, and often directed at British targets. In August 1969 hundreds of homes and businesses were destroyed in sectarian fighting in Northern Ireland.

gilt frame — (PSC; "Art Gallery") A gilt-edged frame is one that is ornately adorned.

Girl in a bikini — ("Undressing in Public") Probably walk-on Christine Young, as listed in the production records for the episode. This was shot on 10 July 1969 in Bournemouth (WAC T12/1,242). According to IMDb.com, Christine would also appear in 1970 in the television play *The Lie* (based on an Ingmar Bergman play), her only listed credit. (Where available, additional appearance credits for Python extras and walk-ons are primarily culled from the Internet Movie Database, as well as the British Film Institute archives.)

Graham knows the tune of — (PSC; link out of "Secret Service Dentists") Yet another unusual textual moment from the written scripts that would have no way of reaching any audience beyond the troupe and production personnel.

"greengages" — ("Self-Defence") A type of plum.

• H •

hiss him — (PSC; "Secret Service Dentists") One of the few moments where the studio audience is brought in on the structured humor during the run of *FC*. Cf. "The Queen Will Be Watching" sketch, Episode 26. This hissing also flexes the genre boundaries even more broadly, this time to encompass staged melodramas, where black-attired villains were regularly hissed, and heroes and ladies saved were applauded. The English pantomime audience, for example, would have been well used to such participatory moments.

The hissing goes along with the "Gone, and never called me mother" sentiment from the *East Lynne* melodrama noted below (see "never called me mother" entry below).

Hotel — (PSC; "Undressing in Public") The name on the front of the building identifies this location as the doorway of the Palace Court Hotel, which is actually in the heart of London (64-65 Princes Square, London, W2 4PX). This shot would have been recorded after the Pythons returned from their countryside/seaside excursions for filmed segments.

• I •

ice cream van — ("Undressing in Public") This is a Wall's ice cream company van. Wall's will be mentioned in the notes to Ep. 26, as one of Gilliam's cartoon characters eats an ice lolly. See "Swell's Goody" in Ep. 26 for more.

"It's a Man's Life in the . . ." — ("It's a Man's Life in the Modern Army") Slogan for the Royal Army (see Woodward). In *The Goon Show* episode "Dishonoured" (14 Dec. 1954), Neddie (Secombe), who is fleeing the country, takes to the sea exclaiming: "It's a man's life I tell ye!"

Also, an LP entitled "This Is Free Belfast: Irish Rebel Songs from the Six Counties" would be recorded in 1971, featuring a new traditional song from the time of the "Troubles," "It's a Man's Life in the Army," an anti-Crown folksong.

• J •

"Jerusalem . . . time" — ("Song [*And Did Those Feet*]") "Jerusalem" is a very English hymn adapted from a William Blake poem, with music by Charles H.H. Parry. The hymn is used several times in *FC*. Cf. Ep. 8, when bedding sales associates have to sing the hymn as an antidote to the utterance of the word "mattress." After the successful conclusion of the arrest in "Salvation Fuzz" (Ep. 29), the family is directed to sing this hymn, where it segues into the following sketch. The text of the hymn (from the Preface to *Milton: A Poem* [1804]) is as follows:

> And did those feet in ancient time
> Walk upon England's mountains green?
> And was the Holy Lamb of God
> On England's pleasant pastures seen?

And did the countenance divine
Shine forth upon our clouded hills?
And was Jerusalem builded here
Among these dark satanic mills?

Bring me my bow of burning gold!
Bring me my arrows of desire!
Bring me my spear! O clouds, unfold!
Bring me my chariots of fire!
I will not cease from mental fight,
Nor shall my sword sleep in my hand,
Till we have built Jerusalem
In England's green and pleasant land.

There is certainly a nineteenth-century and even Northern flavoring to the text ("satanic mills"). The text is dated 1804, and the music 1916. Its Englishness is apparent in the supposition that Christ visited England, thus Englishmen can lay claim to the Savior (just like an Englishman can claim Shakespeare and Monty Python). Teeth aren't mentioned anywhere in the actual hymn.

In the Pythons' May Day special shot for European television in 1971, the Cleese voiceover sonorously extols England's "green and pleasant land," as well, over bucolic images of Bray, Holyport, and Littlewick Green.

• K •

"know what I like" — ("Art Gallery") A paraphrase from several sources. First, Henry James's *Portrait of a Lady* (1881): "I don't care anything about reasons, but I know what I like" (ch. 24); and also (mentioned earlier) Max Beerbohm's 1911 novel *Zuleika Dobson*: "She was one of the people who say: 'I don't know anything about music really, but I know what I like'" (ch. 2).

Beerbohm (1872–1956) was a noted English author, parodist, and caricaturist (*ODNB*). His novel *Zuleika Dobson* was a burlesque of Oxford life, and should have been very familiar to all the Oxbridge Pythons. James's novel features Americans variously assimilating into English/European society, with the "hard, repellent" wife figure perhaps serving as inspiration for the women in this sketch, and Pepperpots throughout the Python oeuvre (Drabble 1985, 780).

Samuel Courtauld (see entries for "Courtauld," "Rubens," "Utrillo," "Van Gogh") gathered his enormous and influential collection (1923–1929) based on his own emotional responses to the works, and admitted his intense subjectivity (see courtauld.ac.uk). Courtauld "knew what he liked," and, as it turned out, what he liked happened to be shared by both critics and patrons.

Victor Weisz (pen name "Vicky") produced a UK political cartoon in February 1966 depicting Soviet Premier Khrushchev looking at a painting of PM Macmillan, with the caption: "'Well, I don't know anything about art, but I know what I like!' (The first major British art exhibition opened in Moscow yesterday)."

This phrase is also the trodden-upon punchline for the "Michelangelo" sketch in the Pythons' *Live at the Hollywood Bowl* concert film production.

• L •

"landscape artists" — ("Art Gallery") British nineteenth-century landscape artists included names like Turner and the prolific John Constable (1776–1837). Constable's *The Hay Wain* (1821) will figure prominently later in *FC*, in Ep. 25, when the central figure from the painting and many other painted figures go out on strike.

It's no surprise that the Pythons would choose these landscape artists for inclusion here. Both Turner and Constable separated themselves, to varying degrees, from the Italianate (or just continental) influence of the classical landscape, and, especially Constable, who focused on the English countryside for many years.

"Lemming of the BDA" — ("Secret Service Dentists") There was a classic BBC serial produced on the cusp of the silent-to-sound era called *Lloyd of the CID* (1932).

"Libya" — ("Song [*And Did Those Feet*]") The Cardiff Rooms would be the name of a lounge or restaurant setting at a hotel somewhere in Libya, perhaps Tripoli. Such venues would have been named after known, familiar locations in Great Britain, and would have attracted locals as well as significant numbers of nostalgic Brit expatriates working in the far-flung reaches of the Empire. Libya was promised by Great Britain in 1942 that the decades-long Italian rule would end and never reappear, and Libya became independent in 1952.

"loganberries" — ("Self-Defence") A hybridized fruit created from the raspberry and blackberry. Created in 1881 in California, the loganberry is also grown in England.

looks slightly outraged — (PSC; "Undressing in Public") Here the man looks directly at the camera, acknowledging its presence. He isn't outraged that the camera (and, by association, an audience) is sharing his private space, but the supposed peeping tom does raise his hackles. This is again a nod to the silent comedy and even classic cartoon trope where the character looks at the camera and both acknowledges and implicates the audience.

• M •

machine — (PSC; "Undressing in Public") A nickelodeon "peep show" machine that holds either a loop of film or a series of cards, both of which would be turned by a hand crank. (The Edison versions featured early and cumbersome electric motors and light bulbs.) Both also work on the same principle of providing successive images to the eye to create the illusion of motion. The view we see (as recorded by the Pythons) is from a different angle and distance-to-object than could have been provided by the machine, and the image is even reversed. The "flickering" effect provided by this projected image is what gave the earliest films their nickname—"flickers."

This "What the Butler Saw" (Mutoscope-type) machine is a fixture at seaside resorts, and is also seen in Osbert Lancaster's political cartoon of 16 July 1969 published in the *Daily Express*, where media campaigner Mary Whitehouse (1910–2001) is lampooned ("You can save your money—I'd say at a guess that this butler must have been in service with Mrs. Whitehouse"). Whitehouse and her group would lock horns with the Pythons in 1979, as *Life of Brian* was being produced and then distributed.

"Malaya" — ("Self-Defence") Actually, this was most likely learned from watching cartoons, where anvils and pianos and large rocks often fall from the sky and crush characters, including Blackie (Tex Avery) and Wile E. Coyote (Chuck Jones).

Malaya is now (and was at the episode's writing) called Malaysia (after 1963), is located in the South China Sea, and had a significant British presence until at least 1960. British troops and administrators were a significant part of that presence, since the beginning of the Communist (Chinese) guerrilla actions there in about 1948. Many National Service members just older than the Pythons would have served their tours of duty in Malaya during this postwar period, and many died in the hit-and-run attacks employed by the rebel forces (*Eyewitness: 1950–59*, "Malaya"). The many stirring accounts of British fortitude in the face of danger recounted in the newspapers and on the radio back home may account for the inclusion of Malaya and this RSM.

Spoofing the newest intercontinental ballistic missile (ICBM) technology sought by the British government in the 1950s, the Goons had launched a self-propelled guided NAAFI to British troops stationed in Malaya in "The Jet-Propelled Guided NAAFI" episode (24 January 1956). The Navy, Army, and Air Force Institutes were military canteens, where homefront goods could be purchased in far-flung locations.

"mangoes" — ("Secret Service Dentists") A return of the fruit obsession from the earlier "Self-Defence" sketch. These are tropical fruits, and would have been imported during this period from former members of the Empire like India.

"Mazarin . . . Versailles" — ("Song [*And Did Those Feet*]") Mazarin (1602–1661) was a cardinal (he followed Richelieu), as well as a tutor and minister to Louis XIV (1638–1715). Versailles is the massive palace built by Louis XIV, and was a palatial retreat for the French monarchy. References to Louis XIV (and XV and XVI) will reappear in Ep. 40.

"Mountains Green" — (link into "Secret Service Dentists") The glossing of "England's Mountains Green" as overtly sexual becomes much easier here, especially if "a man's life" is meant to include copulation. The color green has long been associated with sexual promiscuity and prostitution (Henke, 114), hence Spencer glossing "green women" as unchaste women (referencing Jonson's *Bartholomew Fair* 4.5. 127–29). "Mountains" can be either (or both) the female's breasts or pubic area. See Sidney's *Astrophil and Stella* and his object of lustful affection's "Cupid's hill." Also, cf. the Gardens of Adonis in Spenser's *Faerie Queene*, where the "stately Mount" is just one erotic section of this highly sexualized landscape:

> Right in the middest of that Paradise,
> There stood a stately Mount, on whose round top
> A gloomy groue of mirtle trees did rise,
> Whose shadie boughes sharpe steele did neuer lop,
> Nor wicked beasts their tender buds did crop,
> But like a girlond compassed the hight,
> And from their fruitfull sides sweet gum did drop,
> That all the ground with precious deaw bedight,
> Threw forth most dainty odours, & most sweet delight.
> And in the thickest couert oif that shade,
> There was a pleasant arbour. . . . (3.6.43–44)

See A.C. Hamilton's edition of *The Faerie Queene*, as well as his *The Spenser Encyclopedia*.

For more on this more Ovidian Sidney and his connection to Monty Python, see notes to Ep. 36, "Pornographic Bookshop" sketch.

"Mr. Apricot" — ("Self-Defence") Further proof that the RSM has lost touch with non-fruit-related reality. The apricot is also mentioned in Ep. 3, during the defendant's soliloquy.

"my only line" — (link into "Undressing in Public") Cf. Ian Davidson's appearances in Ep. 19, where he asks if he can mention that he's currently appearing on television. Otherwise, in an example of Python's "equal opportunity" tenet (where they try and offend everyone), the male character here is ridiculed just as the female character was earlier, though the consequences for the male character aren't nearly as fatal as for the female. See Ep. 8 where the Art Critic (Palin) strangles his wife. The woman (Katya Wyeth), at least, was intelligent enough to deliver a pun. Also, this line is accurate, in that Gilliam was given very little to do in the performance of the episodes, especially in the earlier episodes, and especially with any speaking roles. If he appeared, it was generally in full costume (i.e., he played the knight in armor a few times).

• N •

"natter" — ("Art Critic") To prattle, talk incessantly.

"naughty dentists" — ("Secret Service Dentists") There are naughty chemists in Ep. 17, and they get their comeuppance as well. "Naughty" is a descriptor used constantly in *The Goon Show*, especially by Sellers (as Major Bloodnok and Henry Crun) and Spike Milligan (as Minnie Bannister).

"never called me mother" — ("Secret Service Dentists") A phrase adapted from the nineteenth-century stage melodrama *East Lynne or The Earl's Daughter*, it is heard when the disguised heroine has returned home from her illicit romance only to have her formerly abandoned child die in her arms. The grief-stricken mother cries: "Gone! Gone, and never called me mother!"

Harry Secombe uses the phrase, as well, in *The Goon Show* episodes "Shifting Sands" (24 Jan. 1957), and "Scradje" (13 Mar. 1956). In these instances, sappy-violin-and-old-piano-style music ("Hearts and Flowers") accompanies the utterance, further supporting the "mellerdrammer" citation above. (In *FC* Ep. 11, the Goon word/name "F'tang" [from "The Call of the West," 20 Jan. 1959] is borrowed several times, and including Eps. 17 and 18.)

The pervasiveness of the reference is reinforced by other mentionings in popular culture, including Dashiell Hammett's *Red Harvest* (1929), where the unnamed lead character compares the soap opera–type goings-on in "Poisonville" to something out of "East Lynne."

"never used to like Turner" — ("Art Gallery") Equating art and food—both involve preferences and acquired tastes. The specter of the mass consumption of art is also addressed in Ep. 1, where Picasso races other artists, turning the relative singularity of a painter and his/her painting into a consumer-driven, mass-consumption form—a comment on the "acquisitive culture" that will reach its apotheosis in *FC* in Ep. 41. Walter Benjamin discussed this phenomenon—the loss of an artwork's "aura" and traditional "authority"—in his landmark essay, "The Work of Art in the Age of Mechanical Reproduction" (*Illuminations* 1968; also available in the third edition of the Mast and Cohen reader, *Film Theory & Criticism* [Oxford 1985]: 675–94.)

Python certainly violates the so-called natural distance that prior to the flowering of the Modernist period had existed between artwork and audience. They manipulate a reproduced image—segmenting, fragmenting, scrutinizing closer than the museum setting would ever allow. In this case, the characters get to actually *taste* the work of art, bringing to bear a sense that heretofore had no bearing on the artform or its appreciation.

This comment is also significant in that Turner himself and his work did, at least occasionally, suffer in comparison to others around and before him. In most of the texts written about him, he is described as taciturn and distant at best, and downright abusive when in a mood. His art would also cause an American investor to bemoan the artist's "indistinctness," so perhaps Turner was an acquired taste for many, including the Pepperpots in this scene (see Gage [1975] and Ackroyd [2006]). See the entry for Turner below for more on the influential English artist, and Herrmann's article on Turner in the *ODNB*.

"not good enough for you" — ("Self-Defence") This "taking on airs" ridicule is seen in Ep. 33, the "Biggles Dictates a Letter" sketch, when Biggles's secretary quibbles with him over whether she's a "courtesan" or a "harlot." The same theme is also seen in *ML*, when the Sergeant-Major wants to march "up and down the square," and none of his men do.

"number was on that one" — ("Self-Defence") A familiar colloquialism, primarily used in pulp fiction genres, meaning a lottery (or draft) number. The Third Man (Jones) is then rightly perplexed that one's number could be on something other than a bullet or the like—he's obviously familiar with the normal usage of the phrase. By Ep. 38, a character (played by Jones there, as well) won't be able to recognize a similarly colloquial and acceptable phrase, "No time to lose."

• O •

"out of them" — ("Secret Service Dentists") Cf. the cheese shop without any cheese in Ep. 33, as well the Tudor job agency offering no Tudor jobs (Ep. 36). This is one of many attempted transactions in the *Flying Circus* world that will go awry.

• P •

Part 7 — (Introductory link into "Song [*And Did Those Feet*]") *FC* often begins as if in medias res (Ep. 3 was numbered "12B" in the captions), probably a nod to the serialized histories (extended tellings of the Wars of the Roses, history of monarchs, etc.) available on British television and radio for many years. This structure will also apply to sketches throughout *FC*, where very few are allowed to play out to a logical conclusion, and especially to a punchline. And if the sketch involves a transaction ("Cheese Shop," "Dead Parrot," "Argument Clinic"), this same structural weakness almost always negates the successful transaction, sending the narrative, the customer, and the proprietor off into a completely new direction. In Ep. 22 the patient/customer (Chapman) manages to get the doctor/proprietor (Cleese) to agree to a homosexual encounter, but not plastic surgery ("Cosmetic Surgery").

The Monty Python feature films and live stage shows are a different matter. This same structure is more difficult, of course, in live settings, where the nature of the theatrical stage demands certain conventions—acknowledgment of the proscenium, opening and closing curtains, the inability to present inserts or cutaways at a moment's notice, etc. In these settings the sketches tend to dominate, naturally, and the stream-of-consciousness structure must necessarily recede. This is why the early feature film *And Now for Something Completely Different* (1971)—a collection of restaged and reshot (on film) sketches from the first two seasons of *FC*—seems to drag throughout, even though the funnier sketches are all included, and the performances are lively. What is missing are the quick cuts, the inserts, the interruptions from other sketches and characters, etc., that the television medium allows.

"passion fruit" — ("Self-Defence") The edible fruit of the Passion-flower (*OED*). The Passion-flower is named after the final events in Christ's mortality, so the passion fruit could actually be a fruit associated with suffering and death. This fruit, along with many on the list of dangerous fruits, would have been imported from tropical and subtropical Commonwealth countries.

"peckish" — ("Art Gallery") Hungry. Cf. the "Cheese Shop" sketch (Ep. 33), and the "Undertaker" sketch (Ep. 26).

"pig's life" — (link into "Self-Defence") Cf. Ep. 1 (and just a bit of Ep. 2) for the well-traveled pig motif.

"Pip" — ("Song [*And Did Those Feet*]") Python mentions a "Pip" (P.F. Jones) on several occasions, but almost always in relation to his more famous wife, tennis star Ann Haydon-Jones. Cf. Ep. 7, the "Blancmange" sketch, as well as notes to Eps. 19 and 22.

"pointed stick" — ("Self-Defence") This becomes the Fourth Man's (Idle) hobbyhorse, as he'll keep coming back to it; he's not unlike Uncle Toby (Sterne's *Tristram Shandy*) in his fixations.

This reappearing motif isn't foreign to Idle, who also plays a Scotsman in Ep. 35 who barges into sketches and demands payment to not interrupt the sketch, while in Ep. 19 he'll drone on and on about tourists and Watney's Red Barrel in his tourist monologue.

"pomegranates" — ("Self-Defence") Far from a threat, both the wandering children of Israel and the prophet Muhammad saw the pomegranate as the most desirable of fruits (*EBO*). The pomegranate is another fruit mentioned in the Self-Defence class that must be imported into the UK from former colonies, including Malaya, mentioned earlier.

"producer" — ("Rustic Monologue" link into "Secret Service Dentists") Referring to the well-known gossip that many eager but undiscovered Hollywood ingenues had sexual relations with studio higher-ups to get a foot in the door. Less known would be the male actor being forced to sleep with a producer—but it wasn't unheard of. This may also be a questioning of this rustic's sexuality.

promenade — (PSC; "Undressing in Public") Paved area at the top of the beach.

pulls them up — (PSC; "Undressing in Public") Here a musical score reminiscent of silent comedy films begins. The music is played on a movie palace–type Wurlitzer organ, and the song is the "Colonel Bogey March" from *The Bridge on the River Kwai* (1957). (Performed by Reginald Dixon [WAC T12/1,085].) The film itself—though not black and white or grainy—resembles a Roscoe "Fatty" Arbuckle film from his Mack Sennett days (c. 1917). The action also appears to be slightly faster than normal, meaning either the playback has been accelerated, or the camera was purposely "undercranked" when the film was shot. Either way, it's meant to look like a silent comedy film, which would have been shot at about sixteen to eighteen frames per second.

• Q •

"quinces" — ("Self-Defence") A yellowish pear-type fruit, also grown commercially only outside of Britain.

• R •

rabbit lying in his lap — (PSC; "Secret Service Dentists") This rather affected character with the associated affected performance (precise, exaggerated pronunciations, strange attire and mannerisms, etc.) is an interesting example of what Robert K. Jones described in his book *The Shudder Pulps*. The villains of the mid-'30s American detective stories began to overshadow the heroes, and the abominable nature of the villains (like Dr. Death) demanded a transformation of the hero. The so-called defective detective came about in response to these "weird menace" stories, and the morally, physically, ethically, or spiritually handicapped detective came to the fore (see Sam Spade's moral ambivalence in *The Maltese Falcon*, or Jeff Bailey's in *Out of the Past*).

Pythons' villain is of course an agglomeration of evilness from various genres, with a healthy dose of campiness, and the "hero" in this case is a dentist—not a detective at all. Garyn Roberts notes the penchant for pulp characters—both evil and good—to assume the characteristics of contemporary world leaders, with some adapting FDR's wheelchair-bound figure (see Happenstand, Roberts, and Browne, *More Tales of the Defective Detective in the Pulps*, 1–9). The most powerful man in the world, then, must be defective in some way. The Big Cheese appears in a chair, as do many of the early Bond villains—ruling from a permanently seated position. Python creates a whole host of "defective" characters—ugly Pepperpots, unassuming Pewtey-men, Gumbys, pieced-together animations—who just happen to be able to function in narratively strong and significant ways.

"Raphael's Baby Jesus" — ("Art Gallery") Perhaps referring to *The Madonna and Child* (c. 1508) or *The Madonna and Child with the Infant Baptist* (c. 1509–1510). Both Raphael works are displayed in the National Gallery; he and many other Renaissance artists painted similarly themed "virgin and child" pictures. Actually, considering the effects of time, pollution, misguided repainting and touch-up work, and even purposeful defacement, spilling ketchup on a painting might not be the worst a gallery could expect to endure.

"rat" — ("Secret Service Dentists") Almost a quote from a 1928 issue of *Collier's*: "'You're a double-crossing rat,' I said" (18 Aug. 1928). The terms "double-cross" and "rat" are aligned in a 1927 *Vanity Fair* issue where the term "rat" is glossed as "a double-crosser or a worthless person" (*OED*). No surprise, then, that the term would show up so prominently in the gangster, underworld, and pulp fiction–type films and novels of the late 1920s and through the 1940s. "Rat" is also glossed (in the *OED* and attributed to Lytton) as one who changes sides, so "double-crossing rat" is actually a doubled term.

"roscoe" — ("Secret Service Dentists") Quite a specialized term, actually, it is an American slang for "gun." Here the word is used by an obvious northern European (Van der Berg). In American gangster films of the 1930s and beyond, terms like "rod," "heater," "gat," even "bean shooter" are much more prevalent. (See the Hollywood gangster films *The Public Enemy* [1931], *Scarface* [1932], and *Little Caesar* [1931].)

One of the pulpiest of pulp fiction writers of the 1930s and 1940s, Robert Leslie Bellem (d. 1968), and his hard-nosed detective Dan Turner (in *Spicy Detective*), used the term "roscoe" constantly and seemingly without effort. Turner's milieu was the darker side of the Hollywood movie industry—fitting for the movie-like "Secret Service Dentist" sketch.

RSM — (PSC; "Self-Defence") Regimental Sergeant Major. Here he's (Cleese) even wearing his sergeant's stripes on both sleeves of his t-shirt. In Ep. 26, a hospital run by RSM-types features bandaged patients who have to work, perform calisthenics, and run races. Unlike their *Goon Show* predecessors, none of the Pythons served in WWII, nor would they perform National Service, meaning their "firsthand" exposure to such military types would have come through media depictions.

"Rubens . . . cherries" — ("Art Critic") Peter Paul Rubens (1577–1640) was a Flemish Baroque master. As for fruit in his paintings, there are grapes in *Bacchus* (c. 1638), miscellaneous fruit in *Minerva Protects Pax from Mars* (c. 1629), and even an overflowing cornucopia in *The Union of Earth and Water* (c. 1618)—but not an abundance of cherries.

The Pythons may have been familiar with Rubens through both the commissioned ceiling painting, *The Allegory of War and Peace* (1629), found in the Banqueting House, Whitehall Palace, as well as Rubens's works found throughout the National Gallery since the nineteenth century.

rustic accent — (PSC; link into "Secret Service Dentists") This does sound a bit like the rustic accent noted in Ep. 2, though the man is much less coarse in his dress.

The Rustic's aborted "rustic monologue" is perhaps an update of the pastoral-type piece that had become so popular in the seventeenth and eighteenth centuries in England, composed by John Gay and Alexander Pope, among others. That, or perhaps more akin to the rustic Scottish poetry uttered later in *FC* by the poet McTeagle in Ep. 16. See the note to Ep. 16 for more on this "coarse" poetry and its practitioners.

• S •

sedan chair — (link into "Song [*And Did Those Feet*]") Enclosed chair carried by two servants. This same chair and setup will be used again in one of the *Fliegender Zirkus* episodes made for Bavarian television.

This short scene was shot near Covehithe, Suffolk on 21 August 1969 (WAC T12/1,083).

shale beach — ("It's Man" link into "Song [*And Did Those Feet*]") Reminiscent of the "Famous Deaths" sketch from Ep. 1. The "It's Man," however, survives the fall here at Covehithe (WAC T12/1,083). A shale beach is a beach consisting of shale, the most common sediment on Earth, as opposed to sand. Shale tends to fracture along horizontal planes, creating a very rocky, uncomfortable beach.

singer . . . sitting on high stool with guitar — (PSC; "Song [*And Did Those Feet*]") This setting and the presentation/posture affected by Idle is very reminiscent of American folk singer Pete Seeger's appearances on television, perhaps specifically his 1967–1968 appearances on *The Smothers Brothers*, which was airing on Granada as early as February 1967.

"sixteen-ton weight" — ("Self-Defence") There appears to be no surviving record of this particular oversized, cartoon-like prop originally being requested from the BBC's property department. (Construction requests for other notable props—e.g., the giant penguin for "BBC Programme Planners," Ep. 38, or Mrs. Crump-Pinnet's green front door seen in Ep. 14's "New Cooker" sketch—are extant in WAC records for the various seasons.) This is the first time the weight prop is used in the show. It may have been destroyed afterward to conserve storage space, as another sixteen-ton weight is requested (to be built) of the design department's "Construction Organiser" for use in the studio on 19 December 1969 (WAC T12/1,093). This new weight will be the prop seen in Ep. 12, when it will be dropped on a Presenter (Palin) and clearly broken. It was obviously broken because, on 2 July 1970, a request was submitted to have it repaired (WAC T12/1,242). The show was on hiatus at this time, after the final broadcast of the first season on 11 January 1970.

"sloppy . . . plagiarism" — ("It's a Man's Life in the Modern Army") Could be Python's take on themselves. Idle wore shoulder-length hair throughout the run of the show, as did Gilliam, none of them performed National Service or served in the military, and they certainly felt free to pay homage to the parts of culture they liked, and to blast (by parody, satire) the parts of culture they didn't like.

"spits . . . again" — ("Art Gallery") The Pepperpots' priorities here are clearly in place. Public defacement and vandalism are regrettable but acceptable, while spitting clearly is not. The amoral capabilities of the younger generation—including its propensity for violence and anti-social behavior—is an occasional trope in *FC*, since the Pythons obviously still considered themselves to be youthful anti-establishment types. See the letter in Ep. 5 where the writer bemoans the loss of appreciation for traditional values and blasts the "young hippies roaming the streets, raping, looting and killing." This is a fine line the Pythons have to walk, between becoming their parents and decrying the younger generation, and remaining true to the youthful arrogance they've obviously cultivated.

striped . . . flannels — (PSC; "Undressing in Public") The man stands out at the beach wearing the black-and-yellow striped jacket, the straw hat ("boater"), and light flannel pants. It looks more like a period costume than everyday beach attire. The boater is called such because it was originally used as a boater's hat. This same type of costume will be used again in the "*Salad Days*" sketch in Ep. 33 , and is the male costume more often than not in Ronnie Barker's *Bathing Beauties* books, compiled from his vast collection of naughty postcards and boudoir photographs.

striptease routine — (PSC; "Undressing in Public") The accompanying music is the well-known "The Stripper" (performed by David Rose and Orchestra), and Jones is performing in a sort of casual theater setting in front of a complete, purpose-built interior set (WAC T12/1,085). This is the "pier pavilion" (Pier Theatre in Bournemouth) mentioned in the printed script, and can be glimpsed just before he enters the building. This scene was shot on 10 July 1969 (T12/1,242).

swarthy — ("Secret Service Dentists") Having a dark complexion, hair, etc.

"SW1" — (PSC; "Secret Service Dentists") London postal district, in this case the Westminster area, home to Parliament and, essentially, Her Majesty's government.

• T •

"Tarquin" — ("Song [*And Did Those Feet*]") Perhaps a reference to Laurence Olivier's son, Tarquin Olivier, who would have been just a little older than the Pythons (b. 1937). Or, the noted painting *Tarquin and Lucretia* (c. 1695) by Giuseppe Maria Crespi may have influenced the Pythons, especially when the following scene ("Art Gallery") is taken into account. Shakespeare also mentions Tarquin often, especially in *The Rape of Lucrece*, where he is "[b]orne by the trustless wings of false desire, / Lust-breathed Tarquin" (stanza 1). The change of mood mentioned by the singer might account for this inflamed desire.

"tastes a bit" — (PSC; "Art Gallery") So destroying the paintings and sculpture isn't acceptable, but eating them somehow is? Perhaps the distinction lies in the utility of the acts—one is mere destruction, and the other is nourishment, consumption, even acquisition (in an endlessly acquisitive culture). The Visual Effects department at the BBC declined to build the edible painting, referring the Pythons to the Catering department, instead (WAC T12/1,085).

In Ep. 10, Ron Obvious (Jones) attempts to eat the Chichester Cathedral, cannibalism is discussed in Ep. 26, and there is also significant consumption in Gilliam's animations. In *HG*, cold weather forces Sir Robin to eat his minstrels, and in *ML*, Mr. Creosote is the über-glutton who takes one bite too many.

"terrible joke" — ("Art Critic") This pun is actually no worse than any that the male Pythons have uttered, and actually fairly clever, but the female character here is singled out for derision, perhaps for violating the all-male club's rules by uttering a thoughtful witticism. The fact that she can pun may make her a threat, intellectually, to this boys' club.

terrible twitch on tic — ("Self-Defence") This tic may be due to the ex-RSM's unpleasant experiences in Malaya, where British forces (and civilians) were constantly sniped and targeted for bombing, forcing families to live in concrete bungalows, drive armored cars, and generally fear for their lives every day, and especially at night in the dark jungle. The account given by Mrs. Dorothy Lucy—of protecting her children and wielding a Bren gun against potential guerrilla marauders—is representative of the tic-inducing life in colonial Malaya (*Eyewitness: 1950–59*, "Malaya 3").

"Thompson" — (PSC; "Self-Defence") Name of a fruit, as well, as in Thompson Seedless grapes.

tiger — ("Self-Defence") The tiger appears again in the feature film *ML*, and there has taken a British officer's leg. The tiger here is obviously stuffed and mounted on wheels. This is also a somewhat rare example in *FC* of an actual, real-life predator (a wild, carnivorous animal) being used as a lethal—albeit stuffed—means of attack. Generally, it's the least likely animal (i.e., the rabbit) that poses the greatest threat in *FC*. The inclusion of the tiger indicates that the RSM may have actually served in Malaya, where tigers are endemic.

"tobacconist" — ("Secret Service Dentists") Proprietor of a shop that sells tobacco (cigarettes, cigars), and sundry convenience store items. Tobacconists are featured in *FC* a number of times, including the "Dirty Hungarian Phrase-Book" sketch in Ep. 25, and the "Silly Walks" sketch begins in a tobacconist's shop (Ep. 14).

to camera — (PSC; "Secret Service Dentists") Moreso than Ep. 2's faux epilogue, this resembles an actual epilogue, where the show is wrapped up, the loose narrative threads brought together.

"ton of bricks" — (PSC; "Self-Defence") Actually, the usual punishment from above in Python is either a sixteen-ton weight or a giant hammer. See the following "Self-Defence" sketch. The phrase "ton of bricks" refers to the past dangers associated with walking near a brick-façade building under construction, when the bricks would have been loaded on a flat board and hoisted via a pulley system. Warner Bros. cartoons featured this type of punishment, as did Hanna & Barbera's "Tom & Jerry" series, and Tex Avery in cartoons like *Bad Luck Blackie* (1947).

trippers — (PSC; "Undressing in Public") Slang for resort visitors, vacationers.

trousers — (PSC; "Undressing in Public") This furtive "peeping" is exactly what social and moral activists feared the movies would lead to in the early days of cinema, when storefront nickelodeons were seen as scurrilous dens of lower-class iniquity. See Musser.

"Turner" — ("Art Gallery") Joseph M. W. Turner (1775–1851) emotionalized nature (akin to a Romantic poet's literary work) in his English landscapes. Turner has consistently ranked at or near the top of "favorite artist" polls in the UK, being a favorite son for decades, probably for his attention to homegrown subjects and settings. Numerous Turner works have been on display in the National Gallery, including *Dido Building Carthage* (1815) and *Sun Rising Through Vapour* (c. 1807), both part of the Turner Bequest of 1856. *The Fighting Temeraire* (1839), glossed above, was also part of this significant bequest. For more on Turner see the *ODNB*.

"two-timed me" — ("Secret Service Dentists") The classic spy or film noir genre moment when a traitor is exposed, or a spy admits to counterintelligence, etc. In the film noir *Asphalt Jungle*, this type of exchange occurs when it's discovered that Emmerich (Louis Calhern) has double-crossed Doc Riedenschneider (Sam Jaffe) and Dix (Sterling Hayden). Gunfire, of course, erupts not long after, and both good guys and bad guys feel the "sting" of the coughing roscoe. (See the entry for "roscoe" above.)

• U •

"under the drill" — ("Secret Service Dentists") This has become something of a euphemism for any kind of suffering, and here it replaces other similar genre devices in Bond films like the laser in *Goldfinger* (1964), or the rocket engine in *Dr. No* (1962).

"up against the wall" — ("Secret Service Dentists") Probably a reference to the grisly St. Valentine's Day massacre in a Chicago garage in 1929, when men from Al Capone's gang killed men from Bugs Moran's gang over control of the illegal liquor trade (during Prohibition) in Chicago.

"Utrillo" — ("Art Critic") Frenchman Maurice Utrillo (1883–1955) is known for paintings depicting the streets of his hometown, Montmarte. Largely self-taught, Utrillo's brushwork was significant, as with "heavy, rich pigment he built up aging, cracked walls, often covered with large inscriptions" (*EBO*). The Art Critic is eating *Place du Tertre* (c. 1910), which is currently in the Tate Britain, and was originally purchased as part of the Courtauld Fund expenditures in 1926. See the entries for the "Art Gallery" sketch for more on these UK national collection purchases.

• V •

"Van Gogh" — ("Art Gallery") Vincent Van Gogh (1853–1890) was a Dutch-born painter who worked as an "expressionist" of color. There are a number of Van Gogh works in London public collections, including *Sunflowers* (1888), *Self Portrait with Bandaged Ear* (1889), and *A Wheatfield, with Cypresses* (1889).

Courtauld funds (c. 1924) purchased most of the better-known continental "modern" art for the UK national collection, including Cezanne, Degas, Gauguin, Manet, Monet, Renoir, Van Gogh, and others. Thanks as well to the National Gallery and Tate Gallery Act of 1955, paintings could be transferred back and forth between the museums, and may have been in either or both settings during this period.

"Vermeer's *Lady at the Window*" — ("Art Gallery") Not actually the name of the painting in question (see below). Vermeer will be mentioned by the Art Critic later in this episode, and the name *Lady at a Window* is mentioned in Ep. 25 as one of the paintings gone on strike. Vermeer shouldn't have been included in a Renaissance or Mannerist schools exhibition, however, since he lived much later (1632–1675) and was known as one of the "Little Dutch Masters."

Jan Vermeer (1632–1675) lived and worked in Delft, and only about three dozen paintings have been ascribed to him. The National Gallery owns two Vermeer paintings, *A Young Woman Standing at a Virginal* and *A Young Woman Seated at a Virginal*, both c. 1670–1672. See the National Gallery's website for images of the paintings.

The painting in question is actually called *Young Woman with a Water Pitcher* (c. 1665), and has been part of the Metropolitan Museum of Art's (New York City) collection for more than 100 years.

"Vogler" — ("Secret Service Dentists") Is this Arthur Lemming of the BDA betraying his real identity? To this point he's admitted only to being a tobacconist interested in books on false teeth, yet his is the first mentioning of "Vogler." None of the others notice the slip-up. There was a "Vogler" character (played by George Murcell) who appeared on the sleuthing show *The Saint* in 1963.

It's also likely that the recent success and notoriety of John le Carré's novels (and then films), including the film *The Spy Who Came in from the Cold* (1965, starring Richard Burton), and featuring colorful characters of international intrigue from East Germany, West Germany, the West, and the Soviet Bloc contributed to these over-the-top depictions of devious foreigners.

Vosburgh, Dick — (PSC; "Secret Service Dentists") An American actor and writer, Vosburgh (b. 1929) wrote for *The Frost Report* (1966) and appeared in *At Last the 1948 Show* (1967) and *How to Irritate People* (1968), working with several of the Pythons (especially Cleese) in both venues.

• W •

"Wait for it!" — ("It's a Man's Life in the Modern Army") Standard military-type leader line in Python (and British cinema in general, as will be evidenced below). Cf. Ep. 5, the "Confuse-a-Cat" sketch, as well as the crucifix party scene in *LB*.

This phrase is borrowed from many film sources, including the one movie produced by their comedy heroes, the Goons, called *Down among the Z Men* (1952). In a scene where Harry is mistaken for a new army recruit, he is hustled into rank, and a Sergeant readies the men for drilling. A dog barks offscreen, and the men mistake that for their Sergeant's command, and begin to move. He must call out "Wait for it!" several times before he is understood apart from the dog. The line also can be heard in the 1969 blockbuster *Battle of Britain*, when an old sergeant is maneuvering a squad of equally aged Home Guard types.

The Sergeant character in *Z Men* is very much copied by Palin for his drill sergeant portrayal in the feature film *Meaning of Life* (1983).

"Watteau" — ("Art Critic") Antoine Watteau (1684–1721) was a Rococo artist influenced by the lyrical commedia dell'arte and French comedy. The studio audience seems to miss entirely the homonymic pun, though they respond to the throttling scene later.

Watteau's *The Scale of Love* (1715–1718) has been part of the National Gallery's collection since 1912, and the chalk sketches *Study of an Antique Statue—Jason or Cincinnatus* and *Two Monkeys in Costume, Smoking* were received in 1952. See the online collections information for both the Courtauld and National Gallery.

wellingtons — ("Secret Service Dentists") A kind of waterproof boot designed by Hoby of St. James Street, London, for the Duke of Wellington in the nineteenth century. Initially a mark of high fashion, even foppishness, the Wellington soon became the footwear of choice for the working middle class.

Also known as "gum boots," the "Gumbys" will sport Wellingtons as part of their uniform throughout *FC*, the characters appearing first (but not yet named) in Ep. 5.

"Whatever Happened to Baby Jane?" — ("Secret Service Dentists") Play on the title of the 1962 Bette Davis film *Whatever Happened to Baby Jane?*, and based on the Henry Farrell novel.

"Wimpole St." — ("Secret Service Dentists") The address 22A Wimpole is the home of the Barretts in *The Barretts of Wimpole Street* (1934, 1957). Also, cf. Ep. 32 where Lake Pahoe is actually located at 22A Runcorn Avenue, and not 22 Runcorn Avenue.

Woman — (PSC; "Undressing in Public") This is a local woman, perhaps culled from the beachfront area as they shot, played by Joan Hayford-Hobbs of Bournemouth. The woman's "husband" in this scene is played by another local man, Philip Mutton (WAC T12/1,082).

working mothers — (PSC; "Art Gallery") Perhaps the "Pepperpot" term hadn't quite caught on by Ep. 4, since these two aren't dressed—nor do they act—much differently than Python's usual cross-dressed Pepperpots. The term "Pepperpot" makes its debut in an interview sketch in Ep. 2, the second episode broadcast but *written* as the first episode for the season. Whichever writing team (Chapman and Cleese, Jones and Palin, or Idle) contributed that scene seems to have coined the usage of the term for *Flying Circus*. They are officially called Pepperpots as early as Ep. 1.

• Y •

"You shot him!" — ("Self-Defence") It's not often in the Python world that an outrageous act like this one actually gets noticed or commented upon, and is akin to the transvestite in Ep. 14 identifying him/herself as such.

Episode 5: "Man's Crisis of Identity in the Latter Half of the Twentieth Century"

"It's" Man rowboat intro; *Animation: Titles* (silly Cleese v/o); Confuse-a-Cat (and pantomime show); *Animation: Pulling old lady apart;* The smuggler; A duck, a cat, and a lizard discussion on customs policies; Vox Pops on smuggling/customs policies; Knight-and-chicken link; "Ask Margaret Drabble"; Police raid; "Dear BBC" letters and Vox Pops; BBC newsreaders arrested; *Match of the Day*: Erotic Film and "What's on BBC 2"; *Animation: Charles Atlas' "Dynamo Tension"*; Silly job interview: Management Training Course; Careers Advisory Board; Burglar who is an encyclopedia salesman; Unsuccessful Encyclopaedia Salesmen; "It's" Man closing credits

• A •

A two-minute extravaganza constructed by Mr. Terry Gilliam of America you know — (PSC; "*Animation: Charles Atlas' Dynamo Tension*") This is one of the earliest animation sequences featuring characters and scenery drawn/painted by Gilliam, as opposed to his manipulating of "found" images. The exceptions here are the girls who hound the bulky Charles Atlas character. They are borrowed from Gilliam's collection of Edwardian nudes (a gift from Ronnie Barker), and several of these girls' images are used elsewhere in the series. The rest of the scene, including all characters (weakling, Charles Atlas, bikini girl, beach goon, and effeminate commentator), settings (beach, house), and sceneries are drawn and painted by Gilliam. The animation is still limited, of course, meaning new drawings aren't photographed for every frame (at 24 frames per second).

"all evening" — ("Erotic Film") The filmed sexually suggestive images are undercut by this admission, suggesting that the power of the image may occlude or even replace actual sexual experience. This sort of pop-Freudian allusiveness emerged between the wars, essentially, and worked its way into popular culture in movies, advertising, etc.

"All right!" — ("Police Raid") Chapman's typical blustery entrance as a police figure. This characterization is perhaps in purposeful opposition to the most beloved TV constable available to the great British viewing public, PC Dixon on the long-running *Dixon of Dock Green* (1955–1973). Dixon (Jack Warner) was warm, considerate, helpful, and the epitome of quiet, folksy strength. Chapman often seems to go out of his way to be the opposite of all these traits. (An exception will be seen in Ep. 7, when Chapman's constable actually turns to the camera and utters Dixon's well-known catchphrase: "Evening all.")

animation — (animated link into "The Smuggler") During the animation sequence, Gilliam hums snatches of "Up, Up and Away," a song made popular by the Fifth Dimension (and written by Jim Webb) in June 1967.

applauding — (PSC; "Erotic Film") All these images are meant to suggest successful male orgasm, of course, and not female sexual pleasure. (And as it turns out, he [Jones] is the only one being "pleasured" in this sketch, and outside the sexual relationship, as well.) These types of images are borrowed from Hitchcock, whose well-known usage of similar images (train into a tunnel, fireworks) in *North by Northwest* (1959) indicated the sexual congress of the characters played by Cary Grant and Eva Marie Saint.

The shot of planes refueling is a direct connection to the title sequence of Kubrick's *Dr. Strangelove* (1964), also suggesting copulation.

The inclusion of Richard Nixon was something of a running joke with the Pythons (and others, of course), especially since he was seen as unattractive and non-sexual, as compared to Jack Kennedy, for example. Nixon was mentioned earlier in Ep. 4, and will appear again in Eps. 10 and 12. Nixon had visited Britain in February 1969, and was lampooned in cartoons and caricatures in newspapers across the country (including, for example, *Guardian*, 21 Feb. 1969). See the British Cartoon Archive.

It's worth pointing out here that the Pythons shared "others" and "windmills" with these cartoonists, and with satirical gadflies, including noted caricaturist Gerald Scarfe (b. 1936). *Times* art critic Guy Brett describes Scarfe's targets and tactics, which should ring familiar:

> With his new effigies of well-known public figures, he has taken this physical insult to a new pitch, because the tactile sense is brought into play. Ian Paisley's mouth becomes an extravagant purple velvet cushion . . . Onassis, who Scarfe sees as an octopus, is given eyes in cloth sockets as big as beachballs . . . In this show [February 1969] his victims are the prime figures of newspaper coverage over the past months: Enoch Powell, Christian Barnard, de Gaulle, the Pope and the Pill, Nixon and others. . . . ("Scarfe's Effigies of Public Figures," *Times*, 17 Feb. 1969: 7)

Paisley, Onassis, Powell, Barnard, de Gaulle, the Pope, the Pill, and Nixon all find their way into the *Flying Circus* rogue's gallery (see the index). Scarfe's show at the Grosvenor Gallery ran, coincidentally, as the Pythons were beginning to gather and write the first season in spring 1969.

• B •

"Bagshot, Surrey" — ("Letters and Vox Pops") Located southwest of London, adjoining the River Thames. It's not clear why the letter writer would address the letter to someone other than the BBC, unless it was a direct response to a/the previous letter, in this case from Mr. Grisewood.

"Bakewell, Joan" — ("Erotic Film") Born in 1933, Bakewell was a presenter on BBC2's *Late Night Line-Up* (1964–1972). The Pythons will be admonished on 23 December 1970 by BBC higher-ups for "the further appearance of the programme team [the Pythons] on *Line-Up*, about which the producer" (JHD) hadn't informed superiors (WAC T47/216). Bakewell's TV work included shows at both the BBC and in independent television, with programs covering the arts, entertainment, and travel. Bakewell attended Newnham College, Cambridge, as did Margaret Drabble (see below for more on Drabble).

Bakewell is featured on the cover of the 29 November 1969 *Radio Times*.

battleship broadside — ("Erotic Film") This is stock footage of a WWII-era battleship firing its large guns from the side, hence "broadside." There is no specific request for this footage in the WAC files.

"BBC Home Service" — ("Letters and Vox Pops") The well-known 9 p.m. news (1939–1945) aired by the BBC attempted to provide accurate and honest information on the day's events during World War II, and was subsequently a bit of a thorn in the government's side. According to Wilson, Churchill consistently distrusted and attempted to corral the BBC during the war, calling the service "the enemy within the gates" (*After the Victorians*, 429). According to Geoffrey Wheatcroft, this period ushered in the "golden age" of the BBC (*Atlantic Monthly* 287, no. 3 [Mar. 2001]: 53–58). Many of *The Goon Show* episodes began with announcer Wallace Greenslade (1912–1961) uttering this phrase: "This is the BBC Home Service."

The cast of *Beyond the Fringe* had trod through this area in 1961 with their "Aftermyth of War" sketch, satirizing the alternating pluck and complacency of the British citizenry during WWII.

BBC Home Service would become Radio 4 in 1967.

"Berlin air lift" — ("Letters and Vox Pops") Vital postwar (1948) military airlift conducted by the United States into Soviet-occupied Berlin. The Soviet Union had closed the only road across East Germany and into Berlin (administered by U.S., UK, French, and Soviet forces in separate zones), hoping to squeeze the Allies out by starving the city of food, fuel, and supplies. Under the Marshall Plan, round-the-clock flights brought in everything a city would need to survive, until the Soviet and East German authorities relented.

"Bevis" — ("Erotic Film") Cf. Ep. 9, where the lumberjack's girl (Connie Booth) cries about her formerly "rugged" boyfriend of the same name.

bowler — (PSC; "Confuse-a-Cat") A recognizable domed hat, it became the way to identify a "City Gent" in *FC* and earlier in the pages of *Private Eye*. In *Hard Day's Night* (1964), Paul similarly dons a bowler (and affects a posh accent) to make a "pull" on two young ladies in the dining coach.

boxer — (PSC; "Letters and Vox Pops") The boxer character has reappeared from the "Confuse-a-Cat" sketch earlier. He is perhaps attacking the somewhat stentorian woman as the Pythons' version of a dowdy, unattractive New Left female.

bra and pants — ("Erotic Film") Cleveland is relegated to sexual object status again.

• C •

caber — ("Erotic Film") A test of skill and strength and Scottish in origin, the caber is a large pole or spar, and is tossed. In Ep. 7, the surfeit of Scotsmen forces the sharing of a single caber (which could be interpreted in a homosocial or homosexual way if we build on the image from the "Erotic Film").

"Camerer Cuss & Co." — (PSC; "Newsreader Arrested") This BP screen photo appears to be unretouched, and features the name of an actual business, Camerer Cuss & Co., founded 1788, and specializing in antique clocks and watches. This particular store was located at 186 Uxbridge Road, W12. Today, that space has been divided, and is occupied by a Snappy Snaps and Subway, at 188 and 186 Uxbridge Road, respectively. These photos were likely snapped for the production of the show as needed, and not requested from research.

"Camp, Sandy" — ("Police Raid") The pseudonymic Camp is referenced more than once in *FC*, including being noted as a "mighty fine director" by the Red Indian (Idle) in Ep. 6. (The Indian mentions that Camp is working at Leatherhead Rep.) This may also be an allusion to Sandy Wilson, a playwright who will be mentioned in Ep. 31, "Language Laboratory."

Also, the term "camp" may be important, as the man in question is both an artist (actor, director) and is in the company of another young man. The *OED* defines "camp": "Ostentatious, exaggerated, affected, theatrical; effeminate or homosexual; pertaining to or characteristic of homosexuals." So Sandy Camp may just be a catch-all name for the gay artist in Python's work.

For the specific significance of this police raid in a celebrity's home, see the entry for "found on the premises" below.

cardinal hat — (PSC; "Confuse-a-Cat") *OED*: The "cardinal" is one of the seventy in the College of Cardinals charged with electing the Pope. The cardinal's hat is a simple red skull cap.

"central London area" — ("Newsreader Arrested") BBC's Broadcast Centre was built for BBC Radio broadcasting in 1932, and was completely torn down and rebuilt in 2005. Broadcast House (BH), as it became known, is located at Oxford Street and Regents Park, adjacent to Nash's All Souls Church. The building was heavily damaged by German bombs during the Blitz, and was significantly remodeled and expanded in 1961. Television Centre, where *FC* was recorded, is farther from Central London, in Shepherd's Bush.

The BH building also purposely resembles a ship, and may have been an influence for the Python featurette *The Crimson Permanent Assurance* (1983), which features a Victorian office building that becomes a pirate ship. (See the feature film *Monty Python's Meaning of Life*.)

"check" — ("Vox Pops" link into "Police Raid") This is another example of Python's use of these Vox Pops moments as smooth, almost effortless modes of transition between scenes. The character Sandy (Idle) moves fluidly from Vox Pop contributor to participant in the following sketch.

circle each other — (PSC; "Confuse-a-Cat") One of Thomas Edison's earliest films is known as *Glenroy Brothers* (c. 1895), a comic boxing match. Edison staged numerous such events for his electric-driven, static camera. Python (Gilliam) would refer back to early motion picture depictions of boxing, probably drawn from surviving Eadweard Muybridge photographs in Ep. 40, "The Golden Age of Ballooning."

Cleveland — ("Letters and Vox Pops") This appearance for Cleveland (where she mentions Margaret Drabble) represents a second chance for a woman to "be one of the boys" and join in the humor. This will continue, to varying degrees, over the balance of the run of *FC*. Cleveland's usefulness as a sex object does not diminish, however, and she continues in that role as well.

crest — (PSC; "Confuse-a-Cat") This appears to be simply a BBC lorry, but the focus on a crest would indicate that it (the "Confuse-a-Cat" company) enjoys a Royal Charter, much like the BBC.

• D •

"dark days . . . wall" — ("Letters and Vox Pops") Cf. Winston Churchill's address at Harrow School on 29 October 1941:

> Do not let us speak of darker days; let us speak rather of sterner days. These are not dark days: these are great days—the greatest days our country has ever lived; and we must all thank God that we have been allowed, each of us according to our stations, to play a part in making these days memorable in the history of our race. (Churchill Centre)

The stated age of this correspondent, 60, would have meant he was about 30 years old when war was declared in 1939, and thus eligible for military service.

"Dean, Michael" — ("Erotic Film") Dean was also a presenter on *Late Night Line-Up*, along with Joan Bakewell, mentioned above. The other two members of the original *LNLU* staff were Denis Tuohy and Nicholas Tresilian (Vahimagi, 129). Bill Cotton, BBC Light Entertainment, will later complain about the appearance of the Pythons on *Late Night Line-Up* (and, perhaps, the presence of a *LNLU* camera on the Python set), permission for which the Pythons had not asked or received (WAC T47/216).

"Distract-a-Bee" — ("Confuse-a-Cat") Yet another "silly credits" motif, of which there will be many; see the "Timmy Williams" sketch, Ep. 19, and "*The Black Eagle*" (Ep. 25), as well as *HG*. The bee would also figure into Python humor, with the "Eric the Half-a-Bee" song sung by Cleese and originally found on *Monty Python's Previous Record* LP (and now CD). The song "Half-a-Bee," performed by the Fred Tomlinson Singers (and perhaps co-written by Tomlinson), was scheduled to be performed in Ep. 36, according to WAC records for that show. This performance was, however, either not recorded or not made part of the finished episode. The song was listed along with "Amontillado," which is performed as the episode ends. There is no record as to why the "Half-a-Bee" song was not included (T12/1,447).

"Drabble, Margaret" — ("Vox Pop" links) Noted British novelist and editor, Drabble was born in Sheffield, like Michael Palin, and attended Newnham College, Cambridge (graduating 1957, prior to Chapman or Cleese, both 1963). She joined the Royal Shakespeare Company upon completing university, where she understudied Vanessa Redgrave. Drabble's novels from this period include *A Summer Bird Cage* (1963), *The Garrick Year* (1964), *The Millstone* (1965), *Jerusalem the Golden* (1967), and *The Waterfall* (1969), and she also produced short stories and biographies (*ODNB*).

Interesting that rather than asking a lizard, the next best source would be author/historian Drabble, which seems a bit of a poke at the popular writer. Important as well is that this is really the first time in *Flying Circus* that a female character (played by a woman) is given a clever/funny line to deliver without some kind of textual, often violent retribution.

Dramatic music — (PSC; "Confuse-a-Cat" credits) The music clip here is "Action Station" by Dave Lindup, as played by the European Sound Stage Orchestra (WAC T12/1,086).

Drum roll and cymbals — ("Confuse-a-Cat") The percussion accompaniment is played by Tony Taylor (WAC T12/1,086).

"duck, cat and lizard" — ("A Duck, a Cat and a Lizard [Discussion]") The Montgolfier brothers—French balloonists later caricatured in Ep. 40—sent aloft a duck, a rooster, and a sheep in September 1783. Similarly, a section of the proposed Futurist film *Vita Futurista* (to be created by F.T. Marinetti) contained a section where "an argument between a foot, a hammer and an umbrella" was to take place (Weston, 86). The Futurists were part of the Modernist movement, and were active in Italy prior to WWI. Marinetti also made a number of memorable personal appearances in the UK, touting the Futurist movement (Wilson, *After the Victorians*, 162).

"Dunkirk" — ("Letters and Vox Pops") French beach from which thousands of Allied troops were rescued by civilian and military craft during WWII, May–June 1940. The name itself became a rallying cry, thanks to Churchill, to the unflagging spirit of the British people.

The Pythons, along with many their age, would have certainly grown up hearing this kind of litany from those that served during the "dark days" of the war, which is probably why it's being delivered here as more of a chanted liturgy than a rallying cry.

The grumpy man (Richard Vernon [1925–1997]) in *Hard Day's Night* (1964) who wants the train coach all to himself epitomized the sentiment:

> Man (Richard Vernon): And don't take that tone with me. I fought the war for your type.
> George: Yeah, and I'll bet you're sorry you won.

dustbin — (PSC; "Confuse-a-Cat") In this case, a large trash can. When two dustbins are presented moments later in the sketch, the scene looks very much like a performance of Beckett's Modernist and darkly absurd classic *Waiting for Godot*. (The play premiered in January 1953 in Paris.) The title of this third episode, "Man's Crisis of Identity in the Latter Half of the Twentieth Century" suggests yet another connection. Modern man's identity in an increasingly fragmented, technological world is a fundamental, vital concern for Beckett, certainly, and other Modernist figures of this period. In this world, successfully confusing a cat is the quintessential meaning given to the existence of these human characters—an absurd concept at which Beckett might have nodded approvingly.

• E •

"East Grinstead" — ("Letters and Vox Pops") Located south of London in the Mid Sussex district. The BBC studios are/were not located in East Grinstead, an area which has for many years, by the BBC's own admission, been virtually ignored (as a news source or place of interest) because of its proximity to London. (See the BBC's history section on the southeast at tvradiobits.co.uk.)

"encyclopaedia salesman" — ("Burglar/Encyclopaedia Salesman") This gag is also found earlier in the satirical magazine *Private Eye* (1961).

Episode 5 — This episode was recorded fifth on 10 March 1969, and broadcast 16 November 1969. Eps. 6–10 would be shuffled among themselves as the BBC tried to lift less-than-stellar ratings during this early period, though much of the problem could be blamed on the regional BBC entities opting for local programming instead of *Flying Circus*.

Early on, at least, the regions seemed to treat the show as a particularly and specifically *London* product, meaning a type of "city comedy" that might not appeal to (and may even offend) the historic counties. (This is ironic, in that none of the Pythons were actually from London, and the show did expend a great deal of time and energy mocking the life and people of London.) In the Elizabethan and then Jacobean city comedy, for instance, the wit and manners of the metropolis—often in comic juxtaposition to the rustic, backward provinces—provide the mirth and satire. Playwrights Dekker, Lyly, Middleton, and especially Jonson worked in the genre, bringing to the stage "deeds and language such as men do use" (*Every Man in His Humour*) and especially men of the City. See Larsen's *MPSERD* for a discussion of Dekker and Jonson.

As late as August 1970, all regions outside of the Greater London area were still intermittently opting out of *FC* transmissions according to BBC records (WAC T47/216).

"Esher" — (PSC; "Confuse-a-Cat") A part of Greater London, located on the southwest corner of the city's outskirts. Most of this sketch (the filmed portions), however, was shot at or near 20 Edenfield Gardens, Worcester Park, Surrey, on Monday, 18 August 1969 (WAC T12/1,083). In Ep. 36, Esher is the site where orgies seem to happen without much fuss, according to the "Man Who Says Words in the Wrong Order" (Palin). The city of Esher is mentioned in Eps. 5, 8, 28, 36, and 39.

"Excuse me a minute" — ("Newsreader Arrested") This multivalent moment is a very nice example of Python playing with the conventions of not only TV, but the supposed sanctity of time and space. And since the new Newsreader (also Idle) on the screen has taken over the balance of the newscast, it must mean that we from thence onward are watching the goings-on in the world of the BP screen, and not the original news set. There is a bracketed time and space inferred here, not unlike the layered brackets of time exhibited in Bergman's influential film *Wild Strawberries* (1960). (Very aware of the various New Waves and important film directors of this period, the Pythons will imitate the famous final scene from Bergman's *The Seventh Seal* [1957] in Ep. 7, "Science Fiction" sketch, and skewer the perhaps more self-important French New Wave directors like Godard in Ep. 23, the "French Subtitled Film.") The influence of Alain Resnais's enigmatic and difficult 1961 film *Last Year at Marienbad* is also felt here. (The Pythons will play with both the skewed temporality and medieval grotesqueries of these films—*The Seventh Seal* and *Last Year at Marienbad*, respectively—in their feature film *Monty Python and the Holy Grail* [1975].)

• F •

"fairy" — ("Vox Pops" link into "Police Raid") Once again, using effeminating names as put downs, part of the "othering" process of Python. Cf. the Biggles sketch in Ep. 33.

fast motion — (PSC; "Confuse-a-Cat") Filmed action exposed at fewer than twenty-four frames per second (for sound film), meaning the camera is "undercranked," which makes motion appear faster than natural when projected. Silent film would have run about sixteen to eighteen fps. See "jerky motion" note below for more.

fez — (PSC; "Confuse-a-Cat") A wool or felt cap. Several Gilliam-drawn characters will be depicted wearing fez in the first *FZ* episode in 1971, as the "Albrecht Dürer" story is morphed into a more Middle Eastern version.

"found on the premises" — ("Police Raid") This sketch is likely a composite reference to several much-celebrated celebrity arrests in 1968–1969:

1. In 1968, John Lennon—a Python acquaintance—was arrested by Police Sergeant Norman Pilcher for drug possession. Lennon would later say he was framed by Pilcher.
2. On 12 March 1969, George Harrison (who would later help finance *Life of Brian*) was arrested at home by Sergeant Pilcher (using police dogs), and more than 100 marijuana cigarettes were found. Harrison claimed a frame-up by Pilcher, as well.
3. And finally, there was the 1969 arrest of Mick Jagger (and then-girlfriend Marianne Faithfull) in Jagger's Chelsea flat for drug possession.

According to Jagger, local drug interdiction officer Detective Sgt. Robin Constable burst into Jagger's apartment, planted drugs, "found" them, and made an arrest. Jagger then said that Constable told him not to worry, that they could "sort it out," and a bribe of about $1,900 (£1,000) was allegedly solicited. Jagger was eventually fined about $200, and the police stood by their story of possession on Jagger's part, and found no malfeasance on Constable's part (see the National Archives, August 2005).

There was also, in fact, a police dog trained to sniff out drugs involved in the Jagger arrest. According to an affidavit in the National Archives, the dog handler was Sergeant Shearn. As for Pilcher, he would be indicted in late 1972 for planting evidence in other, unrelated cases and sentenced to more than four years in prison. (Pilcher's drug-sniffing dog was allegedly named "Willie.")

Tertiarily, there is also the case of Det. Sgt Harry Challenor, a West End Central officer who over a five-year period (c. 1958–1963) planted evidence of all sorts on myriad arrestees, and was eventually found to be schizophrenic and unfit for trial. (This characterization may have influenced the Pythons' rather loopy version of PC "Pan Am" in Ep. 17, also played by Chapman.) The fact that Challenor was a practicing and influential Freemason led many to believe that his psychiatric sentence as opposed to prison time was a fraternal favor. See freemasonrywatch.org for more. For the Pythons' take on Freemasonry, see Ep. 17, as well.

"Fulham" — ("Newsreader Arrested") An inner borough of London, home to Fulham Palace (early sixteenth century), the residence of the bishops of London until 1973, and now a museum. The BBC is headquartered in the Hammersmith and Fulham area, and many locations used by the Pythons for convenient film shooting were in this area.

(Incidentally, when the BBC studios were built in the Shepherd's Bush–White City area, corporation executives were adamant that "White City" not be used as the corporate address in internal communiqués—due to the BBC's acronym habit [i.e., Television Centre becomes "TC"]—as they didn't want to be constantly saying the BBC was in the "WC.")

• G •

"Gedderbong" — ("Confuse-a-Cat") Also used in Ep. 18, as the Master of Ceremonies (Palin) introduces the combatants in the Ken Clean-Aire Systems (Cleese) fight. Gedderbong is slang for "gentlemen." Goon Harry Secombe uses the term in the episode "The Last Tram (From Clapham)" (23 Nov. 1954) as he introduces the show.

"give the wife?" — ("Police Raid") One of the few actual punchlines delivered, sans retribution or undercutting, in all of *FC*.

"glib" — ("The Smuggler") Probably a reflexive moment, commenting on the writing, and not on the Man's (Palin) choice of words, per se. But if this can be construed as commenting on the comment itself, it could be that the Officer (Cleese) is reminding the traveler that he's in no position to be glib at all.

"Grisewood" — ("Letters and Vox Pops") Peter Grisewood was an actor in the popular *Quatermass and the Pit* TV series (BBC, 1958). A tad closer to home, the BBC Third Programme planner and eventual Controller during the Pythons' early lives was Harman Grisewood (1906–1997), who is credited with creating *The Money Programme*, which will be satirized by the Pythons in Ep. 29. Grisewood left the BBC for the *Times* in 1966, and was much talked about in the press of the time (*ODNB*).

• H •

he has a knotted handkerchief on his head and his trousers are rolled up to the knees — (PSC; "Vox Pops on Smuggling/Customs Policies") This man is very nearly costumed as a Gumby, wearing the rolled up trousers and Wellingtons, and even the knotted handkerchief as a cap. He's missing the smallish vest, braces, wire rim glasses, and rolled up workshirt.

"helping police" — ("Newsreader Arrested") Cf. Gilliam's later film *Brazil* (1985), where those under suspicion are "invited" by Ministry of Information officials to assist police in their investigations. In other words, it is a very polite euphemism for what might become a very unpleasant situation.

This isn't unusual language in the UK, especially in newspapers and on television. Duncan Campbell begins his report on a very recent "cash-for-peerages" scandal with the following: "One of the most enduring expressions in British policing is the phrase 'helping with inquiries.' A delicate euphemism, it can usually be taken to mean the exact opposite of what it says" (*Guardian Unlimited*, 1 Feb. 2007). More to the Pythons' period, when the Kray brothers were arrested in 1968, the BBC reported the following:

> They [Ronnie, Reggie, and Charlie Kray] are among 18 men currently being held at West End Central police station *helping with inquiries* relating to offences including conspiracy to murder, fraud, demanding

money with menaces and assault. (www.news.bbc.co.uk/onthisday/hi/dates/stories/may/8/newsid_2518000/2518695.stm, accessed 5 Feb. 2007)

For much more on the Krays, see notes to Ep. 14. There are almost sixty such uses of this iconic phrase after 1959 in *The Times* alone.

• I •

"I didn't want to be a barber anyway . . ." — ("Lumberjack Song") This "bad faith" moment is a Sartrean concept, where the "waiter" is unhappy serving bourgeois customers, and therefore abusive—he wants to be an "artist," instead. See notes for Ep. 13, "abuse you" for more on the conceit.

"I'm sorry, I'm confused" — ("Silly Job Interview") In this and other sketches like it—e.g., "Buying a Bed" (Ep. 8), and "Police Station (Silly Voices)" (Ep. 12)—the newcomer stumbles into a world he/she cannot comprehend, with lack of meaningful communication often the most obvious sign of this confusion. In all three, however, the novitiate can learn the rules that govern the world of the sketch and, with practice, even function in that world. Arthur and his knights learn how to deal with the Knights Who Say "Ni" in the same way.

"In Fulham this morning . . ." — ("Newsreader Arrested") The Newsreader (Idle) is fairly close here, since the store he's reporting on is located on Uxbridge Road in Shepherd's Bush, Hammersmith and Fulham, just two blocks from TV Centre.

"innit" — ("Vox Pops" link) Vulgar form of "isn't it."

into shot — (PSC; "Erotic Film") As a nosy Scotsman, Idle will interrupt sketches in Ep. 35, and Chapman's "Major" character will interrupt "silly" sketches many times in the series.

During "The Flea" episode of BBC Radio's *The Goon Show*, announcer Wallace Greenslade steps in front of the action twice to remind the audience that actual fleas are not being used in the program.

• J •

jerky motion — (PSC; "Confuse-a-Cat") What's shown here is a mishmash combination of both fast motion and jump cut—several short shots of an object in different positions presented in quick succession (a man "sliding" across stage without walking). The camera is turned on and off, exposing a few frames when the figure is in the desired position, then moving the figure, exposing a few more frames, etc. Scottish-Canadian filmmaker Norman McLaren pioneered this technique in the groundbreaking "pixilated" film *Neighbours* (1952). See the note for "pixilated motion" below.

"jolly good laugh" — ("Careers Advisory Board") This indicates that we might have been watching a promotional or training film, the kind of work that Cleese would move to (corporate training video) in the late 1970s. Cf. the currency discussion earlier between stuffed animals that followed on the heels of the customs sketch. Also, Cleese (with Chapman, Tim Brooke-Taylor, and Marty Feldman) had produced *How to Irritate People* in 1968—a David Frost production—a training film of sorts to teach and be able to identify irritating habits and people. Michael Palin, Connie Booth, and Dick Vosburgh also appear in this show.

jump cut — (PSC; "Confuse-a-Cat") A filmmaking term used to describe when something is filmed with a break in time—but appears to happen in real time—so that the action appears to "jump" impossibly to a new position. This phenomenon was reportedly "discovered" by French magician-turned-filmmaker Georges Méliès (1861–1938). See entry for "various tricks" below.

• K •

"killing" — ("Letters and Vox Pops") Perhaps a reference to the recent student riots seen in 1968 in Paris, the civil unrest in New York and Los Angeles of the same year, as well as many large cities globally, and the general increase in visibility of the "hippie" generation.

• L •

"Less race prejudice" — ("Letters and Vox Pops") This "child on the street" interview format is also seen in Ep. 3, where the "children" request Idle's "Nudge, Nudge" sketch.

Also, this moment draws on the still-current racial unrest in the United States (specifically, riots in Watts [Los Angeles], in 1965 and Washington, D.C., in 1968, to name two), the race-related unrest in the "Asian" and "Caribbean" neighborhoods of Greater London (including Notting Hill in the late 1950s), and might also refer to the religious "troubles" rising in Northern Ireland.

"Liddell, Alvar" — ("Letters and Vox Pops") A respected BBC newsreader, Liddell (1908–1981) was certainly known to the Pythons for his radio presence during the dark days of WWII, his guest appearance in 1968 on the popular *Dad's Army*, as well as his mention in the "Aftermyth of War" sketch from the *Beyond the Fringe* cast, "when, every night at nine o'clock, Alvar Liddell brought us news of fresh disasters."

See the entries for "BBC Home Service" and "Dunkirk" for more.

locked camera — (PSC; "Confuse-a-Cat") When a camera head is fastened to its mounting so that it will not move (pan, tilt, etc.), it is then "locked down." The locked, immobile camera is necessary for animating, or exposing one or a few frames at a time. The images would be far less stable if the camera head were allowed to remain loose during the pixilation sequences.

Long John Silver — (PSC; "Confuse-a-Cat") Character from Robert Louis Stevenson's novel *Treasure Island* (1883). The characterization here looks very much like it is patterned after Disney's 1950 film version, starring Robert Newton as Long John Silver. And either the costume was easy to come by (in the BBC's costume shop) or, thanks to the very popular Christmastime *Treasure Island* pantomime, Long John Silver loomed large in the Pythons' collective juvenile impressions (along with the Pantomime Goose, the Pantomime Princess Margaret, and Dobbin the Pantomime Horse). (See the entries for panto characters in Ep. 30.) This iconic pirate appears in multiple *FC* episodes, including Eps. 10, 23, 25, and 32, and is further mentioned in audio sketches on Python LPs.

The London region theaters Westminster, Mermaid, Palladium, Wembley Empire Pool, Thorndike (Leatherhead), Richmond, and Saville offered regular pantos and children's performances including *The Owl and the Pussycat, Aladdin, Queen Passionella, Sleeping Beauty, Give a Dog a Bone, Jack and the Beanstalk, Treasure Island* (this annually at the Mermaid Theatre, see below). See *Times* advertisements of the period for many more.

In the Goon episode "The Silver Doubloons" (21 Jan. 1960), a crusty, overacting pirate character finishes a speech by saying: "Excuse me, I've got to get back to the Mermaid Theatre, you know."

Pantomime performances had also been staples of the BBC's Christmas Day broadcast line-up for many years, airing in the early afternoons (usually around 2:15 p.m.) since at least 1956, when both *Puss in Boots* and *Pantomania* (featuring *Dick Whittington*) aired in the afternoon and evening, respectively (*TV & Radio Bits*). In the years that followed, *Babes in the Wood* (1957), *Puss in Boots* (1962), *Dick Whittington* (1963), *Robinson Crusoe* (1963), *Mother Goose* (1965), *Aladdin* (1966), *Cinderella* (1967), and *Humpty Dumpty* (1968) aired.

Long John Silver will reappear—for international viewers—in the Pythons' May Day short created for *Euroshow 71—May Day Special*. There, the fancifully dressed panto character will represent the good people of Beccles in Suffolk, where, the narrator (Cleese) intones, "May Day is marked by the traditional gavotte of the Long John Silvers, reliving the days when pirates ruled the seas." These characters are dancing on the green in Holyport, just two houses down from the The George on the Green.

• M •

"Match of the Day" — ("Newsreader Arrested") A sports show featuring regularly scheduled portions of a selected football match and commentary that premiered on BBC2 in 1964, then moved to BBC1 in 1966. *Match of the Day* would become a fixture on British television for many years.

"My husband, in common with a lot of people of his age, is fifty" — ("'Dear BBC' letters and Vox Pops") This sounds silly, of course, but like many such utterances in *Flying Circus*, it has some connection to an identifiable reality. In a letter to the editor published in the *Times* in April 1969, a Mr. Eric Linklater begins his letter with the following: "Sir,—By the accidents of time and the beneficence of a robust constitution, I am now an old age pensioner" (11 Apr. 1969: 11). The contributor goes on to ask why he is essentially being twice taxed, on his income and then on benefits in the form of a pension.

• N •

Napoleon — (PSC; "Confuse-a-Cat") The standard pose for depictions of Napoleon Bonaparte is hand in vest, and in full military uniform. Napoleon also appears in Ep. 2, the "Mouse Problem" sketch, where he pulls a wedge of cheese from his vest and takes a bite.

This image looks to be modeled on the famous portrait executed by Jean-Baptiste Isabey (1767–1855), *Napoleon at Malmaison* (1801).

"No" — (PSC; "A Duck, a Cat and a Lizard [Discussion]") For a very similar "no response" response in this same interview format (in fact, identical), cf. Ep. 36, where dead men are interviewed.

"No madam, I'm a burglar, I burgle people" — ("Burglar/Encyclopaedia Salesman") This scenario—an encyclopedia salesman pretending to be someone else—was precisely the impetus behind the "Doorstep

Selling Bill" introduced into the House of Commons in February 1966. From coverage of the proceedings: "The Bill imposed on itinerant salesmen the duty of identifying their purpose as salesmen on arrival at the house. Certain transactions would be subject to a written agreement and a four-day "cooling off period" ("Checking the Doorstep Rogues," *Times*, 25 Feb. 1966: 12). For more on this bill and comments in the Commons see the entry for "encyclopaedias" in Ep. 28.

• P •

Part of his signature gets away (animation) — (*"Animation: Escaping scribble* link into 'It's the Arts'") The map on which Gilliam's hand squashes the escaping scribble features portions of southern, coastal Spain—specifically, the Malaga and Granada regions—and coincidentally the area where many British tourists spent many holidays, including the ranting Tourist (Idle) in Ep. 31. "Torremolinos" can be glimpsed on the coast south of Malaga, for instance. There is no record in the WAC archives of this particular map being requested for use, or of any copyright clearance. Many of Gilliam's materials were used, obviously, without attribution.

penguin — (PSC; "Confuse-a-Cat") Significant to Python's bestiary, penguins in Ep. 38 are proven to be more intelligent than BBC program planners; and in Ep. 22, a penguin atop a TV set explodes. There is also a giant, tentacled, marauding penguin in Ep. 23. The prominence of Penguin Books in the UK as the Pythons grew up may help account for the presence of penguins. A Penguin title is clearly visible in the book rack during the "Secret Service Dentists" sketch in Ep. 4.

Silly references to penguins abound in period literatures as well. A satirical personal ad from the pages of *Private Eye*: "Old Penguins required by senile bird fancier and pervert" (Friday, 13 May 1966). Also, in a "Vickers Review" (an advertising section in the *Times*), a February 1965 headline reads "Pressurised Penguin." The ad goes on to detail how a Vickers hyperbaric chamber saved the life of a recently imported zoo penguin, Tot.

pixilated motion — (PSC; "Confuse-a-Cat") Photographing an image frame by frame, resulting in moving, seemingly "animated" objects, etc.

This type of animation (pixilation) is also called "stop-motion" animation, and is used again in Ep. 20 as furniture and appliances race at Epsom. The technique was utilized in animation by J.S. Blackton (*Haunted Hotel*, 1908), then Georges Méliès (fl. 1902–1912), and Ladislaw Starewicz (fl. 1912–1925). Scot-Canadian animator Norman McLaren would employ human figures in his pixilated animations as early as the 1940s, culminating in the celebrated *Neighbours* (1952). This particular work seems to be the predominant influence on the Pythons, as much of their animation work here very much resembles McLaren's "full body" pixilation.

pogostick — (PSC; "Confuse-a-Cat") Spring-loaded pole with foot rests, designed as a bouncing toy. In another early cinema connection, *Punch* magazine reported in 1921 that Charlie Chaplin intended to donate a pogo stick to each child attending the schools he'd attended in England.

More currently, a *Times* parliamentary correspondent reported on a Labour spokesman, Mr. Kenneth Robinson (1911–1996), mentioning derisively the Minister of Health Enoch Powell (1912–1998) "bouncing around Eaton Square on a pogo stick" to "give the impression that beneath his arid exterior a human heart beat on" (28 Mar. 1962: 12). See the index for the many references to Tory firebrand Powell during the run of the series.

"popularity" — ("Letters and Vox Pops") This is spoken by a City Gent, obviously representing the monied, business-enriched Conservative sector of the country. This callous, money-class characterization appears throughout Python, and is reminiscent of Voltaire's character Pococurante (meaning "small care"), who—after laying waste to women and fidelity, the art of Raphael, eighteenth-century music and drama, Homer, Virgil, Horace, Cicero, the sciences, and Milton—justifies his malaise-tinged opining: "Anyhow, I say what I think, and care very little whether other people agree with me" (*Candide*, ch. 25). (Voltaire has already been mentioned admiringly by the supermarket Pepperpots in Ep. 1.)

Enoch Powell and the more arch-conservative Tories of this period fit this mold, speaking strongly against immigration and foreigners on welfare rolls for the good of the country, as they would say, and not to court popularity. In June 1970, Tony Benn (b. 1925) spoke out against the Enoch Powells of the world, and against Powell and the Conservatives specifically:

> The flag of racialism, which has been hoisted in Wolverhampton [Powell's constituency and Idle's schoolboy home], is beginning to look like the one that fluttered twenty-five years ago over Dachau and Belsen. And if people don't speak up against filthy and obscene racialist propaganda still being issued under the imprint of the Conservative Central Office, by an official Conservative candidate, then the forces of hatred will mark up their first success, and mobilize for their next offensive.

(audio transcription from *Eyewitness: 1970–79*, "Racial Discrimination and Immigration")

It was also this very refusal to court popularity that served Churchill so well in the "dark days" of the war, but served to alienate him from his cabinet, party, and the postwar populace—and he was soundly voted into the opposition (Wilson, *After the Victorians*, 484–87).

"pre-sexual revolution" — ("Letters and Vox Pops") Characteristic of the changing times, this intellectual female journalist spouts the key terms of the late '60s and early '70s, calling for the shrugging off of the last vestiges of so-called Victorian morality. Being a sort of "stuffed blouse" she gets punched in the face for voicing her opinion.

"Profumo case" — ("Letters and Vox Pops") John Profumo, EII's Secretary of War (1960–1963), caused a scandal by having an affair with a prostitute who also happened to be seeing a Soviet naval attaché. The scandal and repercussions nearly toppled the sitting Macmillan government. See entry for Ep. 2, "Mouse Problem" sketch, for much more. There are also, not suprisingly, hundreds of extant political cartoons treating this sordid and entertaining subject (see the British Cartoon Archive).

proscenium — (PSC; "Confuse-a-Cat") The curtain, as well as the arch and framework holding the curtain up. This is an acknowledged, staged show, so the proscenium is not only visible, but expected.

• R •

"racialist" — ("Vox Pops" link) Racialism is a belief in one's own superiority to another race to the end that living anywhere near "others" can be threatening, in essence. A racialist, then, would be one who practices or believes in racialism. In this case, it's curious that this ur-Gumby somehow connects the eating of rodents to those who travel abroad.

Connecting this to the then-recent (April 1968) "Rivers of Blood" speech delivered by Enoch Powell (see entry for "taxpayers' expense" below) is possible through Conservative leader Edward Heath, who eventually called Powell a "racialist" when the storm over the inflammatory speech refused to subside, and finally sacked him. An editorial in the *Times* from 22 April 1968 sums up the general reaction to Powell's diatribe, calling the speech "disgraceful . . . because it was calculated to inflame hatred between the races, not only of white against black, but also of black against white" ("An Evil Speech," 22 Apr. 1968: 11). The Conservatives were still able to return to power in 1970, and under Heath.

This rift between Heath and Powell was also featured on the cover of the satirical magazine *Private Eye* on 19 June 1970. Heath and Powell sit next to each other at a dais:

> Heath: I give up. What is white and mad, sees blacks and reds all over the place and stabs me in the back at the last minute?
> Powell: (grinning) ME!

Private Eye was, of course, satirizing British culture and political figures, but also performing some first-rate investigative journalism. According to Bourke, the magazine welcomed hot potato stories the traditional press couldn't, including exposé work on the Ronan Point disaster (Ep. 17), early reporting on the Krays (Ep. 14), and Reginald Maudling's financial improprieties ("*Private Eye*" on BBC Audiobook *Eyewitness: 1960–69*).

recovers — ("Careers Advisory Board") Chapman and Cleese both endured career changes. Chapman had qualified to practice medicine, and Cleese was on his way to a life in the courts as a barrister when both surrendered those careers for work on stage and in television. See Morgan *Speaks!* and McCabe's *The Pythons*.

• S •

"satire" — ("Letters and Vox Pops") Which is, of course, what Python is doing, and how, for example, Doug Piranha will inspire fear in the London underworld in Ep. 14, causing grown men to "pull their own heads off" rather than face his sarcasm.

sedan chair — (PSC; "Confuse-a-Cat") In Ep. 4, a well-dressed eighteenth-century gentleman (Idle) arrives at the beach in a sedan chair, emerges, strips to his trunks, then gets back into the chair and is carried into the water. The sedan chair will reappear in the second episode of *Fliegender Zirkus* (1971), the two episodes written and recorded for Bavarian TV.

Several people get out — (PSC; "Confuse-a-Cat") The "crew" setting up the Confuse-a-Cat stage includes Palin, Idle, and Jones, and also Len Howe (*The Professionals*), Marcelle Elliott (*Doctor Who*), and Ian Elliott (*Paul Temple*) (WAC T12/1,086).

"Sherrin, Ned" — Sherrin (b. 1931) was producer of *That Was the Week That Was* (1962, 1964–1965), the current events comedy show where Cleese had worked as a writer.

"silly billy" — ("Vox Pops" link into "Police Raid") *OED*: "A foolish or feeble-minded person; used specifically as a nickname of William Frederick, Duke of Gloucester (1776–1834), and of William IV (1765–1837)." The phrase—as an answer to a question—also found its way into an Isle of Man schoolboys' holiday exam during World War II, where the young Pythons may have encountered it. The Campaign for Nuclear Disarmament (CND) also used the phrase on posters protesting the 1967 London visit of Dr. Billy Graham (b. 1918), who had recently toured the war effort in Vietnam at the request of President Lyndon Johnson (1908–1973). Given the term's etymology, it's not clear why a French au pair (Cleveland) would use it.

stage whisper — (PSC; "Confuse-a-Cat") Loud enough to be heard by an audience; a purposely loud whisper.

Stetson — (PSC; "Confuse-a-Cat") John B. Stetson (1830–1906) was an American hat manufacturer whose broad-brimmed hats became popular in the American West, and became popularly associated with cowboys and the frontier life. The Southerner (Cleese) in Ep. 2 wears a black Stetson-type hat, as do the characters in the Dodge City version of "Albrecht Dürer" in the first *FZ* episode.

This obvious Americanism would also have run afoul of the BBC's "Variety Programmes" handbook, as well, as it makes it very clear that both making fun of Americans and adopting Americanisms is out of bounds. The goal was to keep the BBC from being culturally pillaged by the attractive and surging American culture already occupying the majority of England's movie screens, magazines, and music venues. See Barry Took's *Laughter in the Air* for more/most of the contents of the handbook.

"Stig" — ("Silly Job Interview") The term (from Old Norse) actually means "to start in alarm," which comes pretty close to the character's reactions in this sketch. It is also perhaps an oblique reference to the work of Stig Kanger, a Swedish philosopher who was interested in logical necessity, possibility, and behaviors (*EOB*). The Stig in the sketch has a very difficult time following (perceiving, interpreting) the logic of his interviewer's actions.

Most likely, however, this is a casual reference to the character "Stig" from the very popular children's book *Stig of the Dump*, written by Clive King, and first published in the UK in 1962. King had graduated from Downing College, Cambridge, just as Cleese would later.

A "Stig O'Tracy" will appear as a character (played by Chapman) whose head is nailed to the floor by Dinsdale Piranha in Ep. 14.

"stoat" — ("Confuse-a-Cat") The European ermine, just one of the many small animals tossed into Python's mix regularly. The stoat is also mentioned a number of times—all in silly ways—in the pages of *Private Eye*.

"stockbroker syndrome" — ("Confuse-a-Cat") *Not* a reference to the Stockholm Syndrome, or the tendency for captives to bond with their captors during a period of detention, since that term wasn't coined until 1973. Instead, this is a clever turn-of-a-phrase that proffers a medical explanation for a career choice, and is akin to the gibing that chartered accountants receive in the Python opus, as well as stockbrokers (see "Dull Life of a City Stockbroker" in Ep. 6). This phrase begins a short "thesaurus" moment identified with Chapman and Cleese's team writing.

stove-pipe — (PSC; "Confuse-a-Cat") A tall, cylindrical hat, the description of such a hat is originally American. President Abraham Lincoln (see Ep. 1, "Famous Deaths") wore such a hat, as do a number of tertiary characters in the animated film *The Yellow Submarine* (1968).

"strip" — ("The Smuggler") Vicars and churchmen in general are almost always suspect in the Python oeuvre, just as they were for Ben Jonson, Voltaire, et al.

In *FC*, vicar types dip into church funds, engage in perverse "mouse" activities, are entrées ignored by the careful diner, act as henchmen for bishops, keep nude ladies, drink gallons of sherry, etc. On *The Contractual Obligation Album* (LP, 1980) a Bishop performs voiceover work for energy drink commercials on the radio. (See the entry "*vicar with a suitcase*" in Ep. 28 for much more.) In Jonson it is the Puritan sect attacked for its hypocritical double standards and money-grubbing activities (see Jonson's *Volpone* and *The Alchemist*). In Voltaire, Candide echoes Swift's Gulliver (from *Gulliver's Travels*, 3.9) as Candide waxes incredulous over the absence of churchmen in El Dorado, Voltaire's perfect society: "What!" said Cacambo, "have you no monks among you to dispute, to govern, to intrigue, and to burn people who are not of the same opinion with themselves?" (ch. 18).

In other instances Voltaire's depictions of men of the cloth include forays into gluttony and sexual depravity of all kinds, and men generally immersed in the world's vices and pleasures. Chaucer, of course, had set the tone much earlier, in *The Canterbury Tales* (with characters like the Pardoner and Summoner), pointing out the vices and shortcomings of both the Catholic Church and its mumping, scrofulous clergy. The Pythons will observe this as well in Ep. 24, when new-age religious men ask for only wealthy members, offer sexual license as part of membership, and deal in stolen merchandise ("Crackpot Religions Ltd.").

"suburban . . . what you will" — ("Confuse-a-Cat") "Suburban fin-de-siècle ennui" is a "turn-of-the-century weariness and dissatisfaction" characteristic of changing epochs, but generally attached to the close of the nineteenth century and the increase in the presence and even threat of technology. Here it's relegated to the suburbs, as well, so less localized.

"Angst"—*OED*: "Anxiety, anguish, neurotic fear; guilt, remorse."
"Weltschmertz"—Essentially "world pain," a sorrow or sadness over the present or future evils or woes of the world in general; sentimental pessimism. The term first appeared in Johann Paul Friedreich Richter's *Selina; or, Above Immortality* (1827).
"Moping"—Dull and spiritless. This state has been attributed to animals before, including Drayton's *Eclogues* (1593) ". . . little moping Lambe of mine . . . ," and Gray's *Elegy* (1750) where the "moping owl" greets the evening.

All these terms certainly serve to anthropomorphize the cat, rendering it more like a moody teenager than a house pet.

• T •

"taxpayers' expense" — ("Vox Pops" link) This entire diatribe sounds very much like ultra-Conservative Enoch Powell's "Rivers of Blood" speech delivered in 1968 in Birmingham, at the Annual General Meeting of the West Midlands Area Conservative Political Centre. Powell's fear that the foreign cultures coming with foreigners would inevitably erode his own culture is clearly evident:

> It almost passes belief that at this moment 20 or 30 additional immigrant children are arriving from overseas in Wolverhampton alone every week—and that means 15 or 20 additional families a decade or two hence. Those whom the gods wish to destroy, they first make mad. We must be mad, literally mad, as a nation to be permitting the annual inflow of some 50,000 dependants, who are for the most part the material of the future growth of the immigrant-descended population. It is like watching a nation busily engaged in heaping up its own funeral pyre . . . [a]s I look ahead, I am filled with foreboding. Like the Roman, I seem to see "the River Tiber foaming with much blood." (*Observer*, 21 Apr. 1968)

Powell (1912–1998) supported an idea he and some Conservatives termed "re-emigration"—meaning repatriating former immigrants back to their home countries or to other countries of their choice, at some taxpayer expense. As a result of this speech—wherein ultimately Powell predicted an organized, incremental overthrow of England by "foreign nationals" (mentioned in Ep. 15)—Conservative leader Heath (calling Powell a "racialist") fired Powell from his Shadow Cabinet. Powell never returned to national political prominence. He will be mentioned again during the Tourist's rant in Ep. 31. A timely book about Powell had appeared in this same year (1969), *The Rise of Enoch Powell: An Examination of Enoch Powell's Attitude to Immigration and Race* (Cornmarket: London), by Paul Foot.

Cf. Voltaire's *Candide*, wherein the people of El Dorado have adopted this same xenophobic attitude, barring citizens from traveling or studying abroad:

> Those princes of their family who remained in their native country acted more wisely. They ordained, with the consent of their whole nation, that none of the inhabitants of our little kingdom should ever quit it; and to this wise ordinance we owe the preservation of our innocence and happiness. The Spaniards had some confused notion of this country, to which they gave the name of El Dorado; and Sir Walter Raleigh, an Englishman, actually came very near it about three hundred years ago; but the inaccessible rocks and precipices with which our country is surrounded on all sides, has hitherto secured us from the rapacious fury of the people of Europe, who have an unaccountable fondness for the pebbles and dirt of our land, for the sake of which they would murder us all to the very last man. (ch. 18)

The Pythons' take on xenophobia is noteworthy in that their "othering" throughout *FC* identifies plenty of suspect persons and belief systems, including homosexuals, attractive and/or intelligent women, foreigners, religious leaders, Conservative politicians, upper-class types, and so on.

"Thatcher" — ("Police Raid") Probably an allusion to Margaret Thatcher (b. 1925), by 1969 a well-known Conservative figure (the "Iron Lady") and subject of Python's barbs on more than one occasion.

Perceived now as the staunchest of conservatives, Thatcher was, according to biographers, during the late 1950s and through the 1960s quite liberal in contrast to her party, pushing for the decriminalization of homosexuality, the legalization of abortion, and the right for tenants to actually buy their Council Estate homes (*ODNB*). Her role in the elimination of a free milk program for low-income school children may be what the Pythons remember her for, however. In 1969, Thatcher was part of Heath's Shadow Cabinet. The fact that the policeman/authority figure "Thatcher" here is trampling on an artist's rights simply reinforces the more liberal bent of the troupe.

"things off" — (PSC; "Confuse-a-Cat") In between this bit of dialogue and the workmen is a wipe transition in the form of a "closing book, opening book." Wipes of this nature are characteristically used in television shows (as well as by contemporary filmmaker Akira Kurosawa) to denote the passage of time, so this is a form of ellipses. The wipe is not used often in *Flying Circus*.

"Thompson's Gazelle" — ("Confuse-a-Cat") Misspelled—it's *Thomson's*—the East African gazelle is also called a "Tommy." Inspector Flying Thompson's Gazelle of the Yard (Idle) will appear in Ep. 29.

to the knees — (PSC; "Vox Pops" link) The Man standing in the stream is a proto-Gumby, though not identified as such in the written scripts. Obviously the name "Gumby" or "Gumbie" hadn't sufficiently worked itself into the Python lexicon by the writing of the fifth script/episode, unlike "Pepperpot," which quickly found common usage.

The first written description of this particular costume is found in the costuming requests for studio shooting (to be provided as copies of costumes used on location for continuity purposes), and is dated 12 October 1969: "5 Mr. Gumbies: 'Wellies, long trousers rolled up to the knee, braces. Collarless shirts. V. necked sleeveless pullovers (fairisle). All too small for the wearers. White knotted hankies on heads'" (WAC T12/1,083). The original idea for the costume allegedly came on location (shot in the summer of 1969), and so would have prefigured this in-studio iteration (see McCabe's *The Pythons*). This makes sense, since the location shots were all completed (on film) by July 1969, before entering the studio to record the videotape portions of the episode.

The Gumby costume itself might be inspired by the Alec Guinness character Henry Holland in *The Lavender Hill Mob* (1951), who sports the knotted handkerchief, wire glasses, etc. There is also the possibility that this look and performance came from a TV commercial character speaking for Toffo Deluxe toffees, and described as a "pathetic, cowering and servile, Yorkshire process worker, speaking from the shop floor, in his white surgical cap, and wellies" (see *1950s British TV Memories*).

"two hundred cigarettes" — ("Vox Pops on Smuggling") Travelers entering Britain would have been considered smugglers (or "duty-not-paid" targets) if they carried 200 or more cigarettes and did not declare them for purposes of excise tax payment. Also, most law enforcement officials in Great Britain were *not* armed on a regular basis.

• V •

various tricks — (PSC; "Confuse-a-Cat") This entire scene is not unlike the early, presentational days of cinema, often called primitive cinema. In primitive cinema the spectacle is emphasized, the movement of the images, and the "to-be-looked-at-ness" of the images as entertainment. "Trickfilm" maker Georges Méliès utilized these editing elements to make objects and people appear and disappear, transmogrify, and "become" as an audience watches—cinematic sleight-of-hand, certainly. Borrowing on this tradition later would be Richard Lester, Peter Sellers, and Spike Milligan in their "home movie" *The Running, Jumping and Standing Still Film* (1959), where characters appear and disappear, and silly non sequiturs populate the disjointed narrative space.

viewer's letter . . . voice over — ("Letters and Vox Pops") This format was actually a BBC staple from as early as 1962, when Robert Robinson (see below) hosted *Points of View*, a five-minute filler between programs on BBC-TV. The show was dedicated to viewer letters, and was primarily a place and time to air complaints from viewers about BBC programming. The graphics used on *Points of View* to give out the BBC mailing address were copied precisely by the Pythons, even down to the font selected:

POINTS OF VIEW
BBC Television Centre
London W12

Letters to the BBC also appear in Ep. 11, while similar letters to the *Daily Mirror* appear in Ep. 10, and offers to help re-start the "Icelandic Saga" are also given a similar address in Ep. 27. *Private Eye* also employed alleged letters from alleged readers, though most were written by the magazine's staff.

The BBC's Robert Robinson (1927–2011) will be vilified in Ep. 32, when he comes to represent (for the moral Conservatives) all that is smutty on TV. See Ep. 32, the "Tory Housewives Clean-Up Campaign" section.

"vole" — ("Confuse-a-Cat" end credits) A type of mouse, the vole has been mentioned already in Eps. 2 and 3; "Twentieth-Century Vole" is Python's generic Hollywood film studio.

• W •

"wait for it" — ("Confuse-a-Cat") Phrase often used in a military parade kind of setting in the Python corpus, including the cross bearer contingent as they prepare to march to their crucifixion in *Life of Brian*, as well as the Colonel redirecting the show via camera two in *Flying Circus* Ep. 4. The phrase is uttered in a number of previous films (many British WWII pictures, of course), from the Goons' *Down among the Z Men* (1952) to *Battle of Britain* (1969), and even Noel Coward's short play *Red Peppers* (from *Tonight at 8:30*) (1935).

"what we . . . call" — ("Confuse-a-Cat") Kind of a Python verbal trope; see the doctor in *Meaning of Life* who is examining a fellow officer who's lost a leg:

> Perkins (Idle): So, it'll, ehh—it'll just grow back again, then, will it?
> Doctor Livingstone (Chapman): Uhh . . . I think I'd better come clean with you about this. It's, um—it's not a virus, I'm afraid. You see, a virus is what we doctors call very, very small . . . ("Fighting Each Other")

Also used in Ep. 35 (". . . what we scientists call, 'Sexy Underwear' or 'Erotic Lingerie' . . .") and Ep. 45 (". . . what we in the medical profession call a naughty complaint"). The word choice and tone is certainly condescending in these instances, as if the highly trained professional must "dumb down" the dialogue for the television viewing public—though this may actually be the case, and is probably based on actual BBC interviews familiar to the Pythons.

wimple — (PSC; "Confuse-a-Cat") Part of the nun's "costume," or habit.

window — ("Burglar/Encyclopaedia Salesman") This "out-the-window" sequence was shot at 79 Slade House, Hounslow, Middlesex (WAC T12/1,086). The first encyclopedia salesman is thrown from the south side of Slade House over the parking lot, and the two following dummies are tossed from the west side. Both of the windows used are on the second-to-uppermost floor, and on the same corner of the building (flat 79). Similar deaths occur in Ep. 1, "Famous Deaths," as well as the suicides in Ep. 12.

"wonders" — ("Burglar/Encyclopaedia Salesman") Other Python door-to-door salesmen items include naughty novelty gags (Ep. 15), "live" television documentaries (Ep. 32), Icelandic honey and Liberal Party candidates (Ep. 45), and the collection of liver donations (*Meaning of Life*). Items or services delivered to the front door in the Python world include dung and dead Indians (Ep. 19), psychiatric advice and dairy products (Ep. 16), new gas cookers (Ep. 14), and BBC linkman jobs (Ep. 15).

"wood" — ("Letters and Vox Pops") This same Scotsman will later be made entirely of tin. See Ep. 6. Scotsmen (and not the Welsh or Irish) will be consistent targets for the Pythons throughout the life of *FC* (cf. Ep. 7, the "Science Fiction" sketch, and Mr. Badger [Idle] in Ep. 35).

• Y •

Y-fronts — ("Erotic Film") "Briefs" underwear.

"You know I" — ("Silly Job Interview") Like Shakespeare's Prelude in *Henry V*, this is a theatrical setup, not unlike the cards used by the Marriage Guidance Counsellor in Ep. 2, or the characters pointing to the card reading "Life Insurance Ltd." later, in Ep. 26. The delivery is purposely clumsy in this case, and probably satirizing similar shows/sketches where the writing of the setup is sincere, but achingly barefaced.

Episode 6: "Crunchy Frog"

"It's" Man ringing phone intro; *Animation: Titles* (silly Cleese v/o); "How to Fling an Otter"; The BBC Entry for the Zinc Stoat of Budapest (Current Affairs)"; Expensive captions; Arthur Figgis; *Animation: Escaping scribble* link into *"It's the Arts"*: Johann Gambolputty . . . von Hautkopf of Ulm—A Profile; *Animation: Link out of "It's the Arts"*; Non-illegal robbery; Vox Pops on things illegal; **"Crunchy Frog" candy**, and Inspector Parrot link; "The Dull Life of a City Stockbroker"; *Animation: "Thrills and Adventure" comic book, "The Theatre Sketch" intro*; Red Indian in theatre; "Another Indian massacre at Dorking Theatre" link; Policemen make wonderful friends; "A Scotsman on a horse" for Mrs. Emma Hamilton; *Animation: Criminal pram, and Twentieth-Century Vole intro*; Twentieth-Century Vole big picture; "It's" Man closing credits

• A •

"acting and hunting" — ("Red Indian in Theatre") As opposed to "hunting and gathering."

"All clear" — ("Non-Illegal Robbery") The music beneath this lead-in to the garret set is borrowed from the film *From Russia with Love* (1963)—the title track—and is written by John Barry (WAC T12/1,088).

"anthrax" — ("Crunchy Frog") A "splenic fever" (*Bacillus anthracis*) in sheep and cattle, anthrax can afflict humans, causing pustules and death. In a country at least historically linked to and even dependent on sheep, anthrax (and FMD and like diseases) would have been a topic of some public conversation. Anthrax had been much in the news in 1963–1964, when multiple cases broke out across England and Wales, affecting primarily pigs. By 1967, foot-and-mouth outbreaks had reached historic levels across the Midlands, leading to the slaughter of hundreds of thousands of animals. The outbreak was being blamed on imported Argentine beef (*Times*, 17 Nov. 1967: 1).

More significantly, perhaps, is the World Health Organization's contemporary ongoing study into the devastating effects of weaponized anthrax. After WWII, several nations, including the Soviet Union, aggressively pursued weaponized (i.e., aerosol) versions of such bacteria for biological warfare ends. The WHO study's results—up to 250,000 killed in each large city without immediate vaccination—would have made sensational newspaper copy in the late 1960s and early 1970s. The *Times* also reported in early 1967 that American "new left" magazines were outing major research universities for their secret, advanced biological weapons programs funded by the government, including weaponized anthrax research ("Biological Warfare Allegations," 29 May 1967: 4). The U.S. supply of weaponized anthrax began to be destroyed in 1969 (*JAMA* 287 [2002]: 2236–52).

assegai — (PSC; "The Dull Life of a City Stockbroker") *OED*: "A kind of slender spear or lance of hard wood, usually pointed with iron, used in battle . . . extended by the Portuguese to the light javelins of African tribespeople generally, *and most commonly applied by Englishmen to the missile weapons of the South African tribes*" (italics added). This inclusion, then, would have been an artifact of Britain's colonial presence in South and Eastern Africa.

The Goons had earlier played on the word in "The Emperor of the Universe" (23 Dec. 1956), when Ned

"Bulldog Drummond" (Secombe) and his faithful man Algernon (Milligan) are describing the famed adventurer's collection of indigenous weapons:

> Bulldog (Secombe): I insert a fresh whisp and say, "Yes, there you see the Ghurka kukri."
> Algy (Milligan): Kukri.
> Bulldog: It's a cookery book! This is the Zulu assegai.
> Algy: An' assegai who done it.

This post-WWI playboy-detective character and genre will be featured prominently in Ep. 29, when a mock-director (Jones) blasts his actors' limited abilities and imperial tone as a "load of Bulldog Drummond crap."

"autograph" — (link into *"It's the Arts"*) The hand (likely Gilliam's) signs "Best Wishes, Arthur Figgis" and underneath in parentheses he begins to write "accountant," when the squiggle that was his first name gets away. (Figgis is the ancient librarian for *Punch* magazine, according to *Private Eye* contributors.) The squiggle runs wild for a bit, with the animator's hand trying to stop it, then it is squashed, displaying once again the ultimate power of the animator over his creation.

This trope—the visible, controlling hand of the animator—is as old as animation itself, going back to J.S. Blackton (*Humorous Phases of Funny Faces*, 1906), Winsor McCay (*Little Nemo*, 1911), Emile Cohl (*The Newlyweds*, 1912), Max Fleischer (*Out of the Inkwell*, 1919), and even through Chuck Jones (*Duck Amuck*, 1953).

• B •

"Bach" — (*"It's the Arts"*) Cf. a similar litany of masters, though of the art world, in Eps. 4 and 8 of *FC*. In Ep. 4, the Art Critic (Palin) discusses the painters as he eats the paintings. In Ep. 8, the Art Critic (also Palin) focuses on the "place of the nude" in art, though his slip of the tongue places the nude in his bed. In Ep. 1, of course, the painters and sculptors are listed (by Cleese) as they ride by during a bicycle race.

The composers (their birth and death dates, genre, and country) listed before Johann Gambolputty include: Ludwig van Beethoven (1770–1827; Classic and Romantic, Germany-Austria); W.A. Mozart (1756–1791; Classic, Austria); F. Chopin (1810–1849; Romantic, Poland/France); F. Liszt (1811–1886; Romantic, Austrian-Hungarian Empire); J. Brahms (1833–1897; Romantic, Germany-Austria); R. Schumann (1810–1856; Romantic, Germany); F. Schubert (1797–1828; Classic, Romantic, Austria); Mendelssohn (1809–1847; Romantic, Germany), and J.S. Bach (1685–1750; Classic, Germany).

"bahnwagen" — ("Johann Gambolputty . . . von Hautkopf of Ulm") "Bahn" can mean "alley" or "railway," while "wagen" generally means "car." This nonce word could mean automobile or railway car, then. In pronunciation, "eisen-bahn-wagen" seems to run together, perhaps meaning a "railway car."

"BBC Entry" — (link into *"It's the Arts"*) Two possibilites here. The first is that this is a reference to the Eurovision Song Contest that accepts entries from across Europe and the UK for the annual music competition. Sandie Shaw's "Puppet on a String" won the contest for the UK in 1967. The contest will be referenced again in *FC* in Ep. 22, and afterwards the Pythons will have to endure a copyright infringement lawsuit over the song "Bing Tiddle Tiddle Bong," sung by Chapman. See notes to Ep. 22 for more. The second (and more likely option) is the Golden Rose of Montreux Festival, where the Pythons submitted a compilation episode in 1971 (losing to an Austrian submission). In the guise of a greasy redcoat, compère Palin will apologize for the losing "Mon-trerx" performance in Ep. 35. Gallingly, *The Frost Report* had won in 1967, and *Marty Feldman's Comedy Machine* would win in 1972.

"Bell & Compasses" — ("Red Indian in Theatre") An amalgam of pub names like the extant "Bell & Crown" and "Axe & Compasses."

Bishop & Saint — (PSC; "Johann Gambolputty . . . von Hautkopf of Ulm" photos) Gilliam borrowed these figures from the right third of the *Predella of the Pistoia Santa Trinità Altarpiece* (1455–1460), a work created by Francesco Pesellino (fl. 1422–1457). The figures are, most likely, St. James the Great and Mamas, according to the National Gallery. The altarpiece has been on display in the National Gallery since 1937.

Botticelli Lover — (PSC; "Johann Gambolputty . . . von Hautkopf of Ulm" photos) The painting depicted is actually by Bronzino (1503–1572), and titled *An Allegory with Venus and Cupid* (1550). Bronzino was a Mannerist (mentioned in Ep. 4) working for Cosimo in Tuscany. The mistake can be attributed to most of the group writing the script and including the probably generic "Botticelli Lover" entry, and then Gilliam (on his own) finding his own way to represent that idea in animation. Gilliam also hand-tinted the figures of Cupid and Folly, green and blue, respectively.

This is also the painting where Gilliam earlier borrowed the "foot" (Cupid's right foot) for the opening credits to the show. The painting hangs in the National Gallery, London.

"Budapest" — (link into *"It's the Arts"*) The capital of Hungary, and the administrative center of Budai járás (district) and Pest megye (county). Situated astride the Danube River. The Montreux Festival—which this mention is satirizing—is set in Switzerland, and is perhaps being gibed by the Pythons for having the temerity to award the relentlessly ambitious David Frost the Golden Rose in 1967.

bus arrives — (PSC; "The Dull Life of a City Stockbroker") This is the "Old 666" bus, and is labeled as covering the Knightsbridge route. This same 1954 London Transport Leyland Titan PD2 RTL1557 bus also appeared in an episode of *The Avengers*, "False Witness" (November 1968) (see theavengers.tv). The driver is Dennis McTighe (WAC T12/1,242).

• C •

"camera" — ("Crunchy Frog") This response to Milton's (Jones) "It's a fair cop" once again acknowledges the artifice of the television production, reminding the viewer that a camera is recording actors on a set, etc. Also, seeing that Parrot (Chapman) will address the camera momentarily, perhaps the direct address here is reserved for those in authority. Python regularly reminds the viewer of the constructed nature of the presentation, both in TV and film formats.

In Ep. 7, the avuncular police constable (Chapman) addresses the camera directly with a warm "Evening all," à la George Dixon of *Dixon of Dock Green* fame. Praline (Cleese) will also address the audience during both the "Dead Parrot" (Ep. 8) and "Fish Licence" (Ep. 23) sketches, perhaps looking for moral support in his struggles with the proprietors (both played by Palin).

"Camp, Sandy" — ("Red Indian in Theatre") Cf. Ep. 5 where "Sandy Camp, the actor" is harassed by a policeman. This is likely a reference to well-known West End theatrical director Sandy Wilson. See the entry for Wilson in Ep. 31, "Language Laboratory."

"Canada" — ("Non-Illegal Robbery") Part of the greater Commonwealth, and a haven for many American draft evaders during and after the Vietnam conflict, when conscription was in place in the United States.

. . . captions alone — (captions link into "*It's the Arts*") Each week the graphics department at the BBC would provide a written estimate for title work for the upcoming episode. The total captions charge for this episode would come in at £76 (WAC T12/1,088).

The cost factors of BBC television production come into play often in *FC*, including the sketch "The BBC Is Short of Money" from Ep. 28, where programs are being broadcast from a family's flat due to BBC insolvency. The episodes themselves were being allotted about £4,500 each during this period, and the letters from the Pythons' various agents were already coming in, asking for more money, higher repeat fees, etc. The second season saw a bump to £5,000 per episode, but that didn't stop agent Jill Foster (of Foster & Dunlop Scripts Limited) from writing directly to David Attenborough (Controller, BBC2) and asking for a further budget increase (WAC T47,216).

Chaney, Lon — (PSC; "Johann Gambolputty . . . von Hautkopf of Ulm" photos) Chaney (1883–1930) was known as the "Man of a Thousand Faces," and this particular still photo is taken from the film *The Phantom of the Opera* (1925), specifically the "unmasking" sequence. (Gilliam probably utilized a publicity still, of course, rather than an actual film frame.) Gilliam has tinted this still, as well—the portion of the film it comes from is black and white, though there are significant color sequences in the classic film.

Chartered Accountant — ("Vox Pops") Simply an accountant who is a member of a royally chartered organization. Objects of much satire and poking fun in Python's oeuvre (cf. the tax on "thingy," which would make chartered accountancy a "much more interesting" job, Ep. 15), as well as significant mentions in Eps. 2, 8, and 10. Chartered Accountants will also become successful pirates on the seas of international finance in the 1983 Monty Python feature film *The Meaning of Life*.

"chocky" — ("Crunchy Frog") Praline obviously uses the term as a slang for "chocolate," but the *OED* gives the spelling variously as "choccy," "chockie," and even "choccky." Colloquially, the term is and has been in fairly common use.

Classical music plays — ("*It's the Arts*") The music beneath the *It's the Arts* title card is Chopin's "12 Etudien Op. 10" (No. 9 in F Minor) performed by Tamas Vasary (WAC T12/1,088).

"cockroach cluster" — ("Crunchy Frog") For a similar grotesquerie, see Swift's 1730 poem "The Lady's Dressing Room," where the "rogue" Strephon steals in to uncover Celia's cosmetic secrets. Strephon produces sweat-stained clothes, filthy combs, "A paste of composition rare, / Sweat, dandruff, powder, lead and hair," as well as grimy towels, scab ointments, and noxious personal items of every purulent kind. It is all enough to turn Strephon's (and our) bowels, and is meant to remain hidden under the lady's made-up façade, just as these "candies" are hiding under tasty chocolate.

In the later *Live at the Hollywood Bowl* stage version of this same sketch, Gilliam plays Parrot, who—after hearing what he's eaten—throws up into his hat.

"Cornish" — ("Crunchy Frog") Of or belonging to the Cornwall region, in southwestern England.

"Courtneidge, Cicely" — ("Red Indian in Theatre") Sydney-born British actress (1893–1980) of musical comedy and revue. She would be made a Dame of the British Empire in 1972.

"Cow and Sickle" — ("Non-Illegal Robbery") Probably a pub, and created by amalgamating other pub names. There is a "Sheaf & Sickle" on Coventry Road, and a "Cow & Plough" pub in Leicester.

"Cowdenbeath" — ("Policemen Make Wonderful Friends") Town in Scotland, northeast of Dumfermline, and north of Edinburgh. The street address is "Masonic Apron Road." Masonry will be lampooned in Ep. 17, "Architect Sketch" and "How to Give Up Being a Mason." Chapman will be photographed wearing a Masonic apron—and little else—for that episode.

credits — (PSC; "Twentieth-Century Vole") All these "Saltzberg" credits are a swipe at the megalomania seen in some Hollywood producers whose name appears throughout a film's credits.

One credit for this episode was penciled out prior to the show being taped, specifically one that suggests Saltzberg is also a drug pusher. Perhaps the "drug pushers" joke might be a bit inflammatory, or just in poor taste (WAC T12/1,087). This elision was probably performed by producer John Howard Davies, though the change isn't attributed, nor is there a memo discussing the change. Such censoring did occur throughout the run of the series, but wasn't profligate. In a later Gilliam animation (in Ep. 19) the word "cancer" will be removed, for example, an elision demanded by BBC higher-ups (see Morgan, *Speaks!*).

Cricket Team — (PSC; "Johann Gambolputty . . . von Hautkopf of Ulm" photos) A late nineteenth-century (or fin-de-siècle) photograph of an unidentified cricket team. All of these photos are at least slightly retouched—"animated"—by Gilliam so that the depicted character will "speak" the necessary words.

This photo has been used before, in the Ep. 3 "Purchase a Past" animation. The cricketer seated on a chair, second from the left (middle row), will also be used (his head, anyway) in the closing moments of the second season's animated titles sequence.

"crunchy frog" — ("Crunchy Frog") Not as unlikely as it may sound—there are popular confections with names like "Polar Bear Paws" and "Jelly Bird Eggs."

Cut to presenter in studio — (PSC; link into "Johann Gambolputty . . . von Hautkopf of Ulm") Though not mentioned in the printed script, the music that comes up under Mr. Figgis' (Chapman) meditation is Elgar's "Nimrod" from his *Enigma* variations, as conducted by Sir Adrian Boult (WAC T12/1,088). The particular orchestra and/or LP is not mentioned.

• D •

"Denison, Michael . . . Dulcie Gray" — ("Red Indian in Theatre") Husband and wife, she was born Dulcie Bailey in Malaysia, and married Denison in 1939. Denison, a Yorkshire native, died in 1998. They acted together on stage and in film, on occasion. Gray would appear in the play *Double Cross* in 1958. Denison's last film appearance was in *Shadowlands* (1993).

Both are also mentioned by the Goons in "The Last Tram (From Clapham)" (23 Nov. 1954), the reference following a protracted and meaningless dialogue between Henry Crun (Sellers) and Minnie Bannister (Milligan) on the subject of a bed Henry is *not* occupying.

"Dial M for Murder" — ("Red Indian in Theatre") Frederick Knott's 1954 play would become a Hollywood film in 1954, directed by Alfred Hitchcock and starring Ray Milland and Grace Kelly. The play was a fixture at many UK theaters in the late 1950s being staged, for example, in the Rugby Theatre in 1955.

"Dimitri" — ("Twentieth-Century Vole") The ". . . yes, yes, yes . . ." trope is revisited in the "Our Eamonn" sketch in Ep. 31. Perhaps "Dimitri" is Dimitri Tiomkin (1899–1979), the renowned Hollywood composer whose film score credits include *Duel in the Sun* (1946), *High Noon* (1952), and, coincidentally, *Dial M for Murder* (1954), mentioned earlier in this episode. Tiomkin was a resident of London in his later years.

Doctor — (PSC; "Johann Gambolputty . . . von Hautkopf of Ulm" photos) This is a cropped version of Sir Luke Fildes's (1843–1927) *The Doctor*, which was acquired by the Tate and originally exhibited in 1891. The painting was inspired by the death of Fildes's son in 1877, and depicts the boy's caring physician.

"Dorking Civic Theatre" — ("Red Indian in Theatre") Dorking is in the Mole Valley, part of Surrey county. Dorking Halls Theatre (Reigate Road) continues to host performances of all kinds, and has been home to the Dorking Dramatic & Operatic Society since 1947. In 1969, this theater was offering the musical *Call Me Madam*.

"dressing up, yes" — ("Vox Pops") Judges in Python are often effete, stereotypically homosexual, or seemingly transvestites—or all three. Cf. the *Dad's Pooves* scene in Ep. 38 (which survives in the printed scripts but not the finished episode), as well as Ep. 21, where two judges effeminately discuss their sexuality (and attraction to "butch" court personnel) as they disrobe, revealing women's underclothing. In Ep. 37, judges participate in a beauty pageant, and several are inconsolable when they lose.

"The Dull Life of a City Stockbroker" — ("The Dull Life of a City Stockbroker") This concept of dullness in everyday life in Britain will be visited and revisited in *FC*, and has been discussed at length by one of the philosophers mentioned often by the Pythons, Søren Kierkegaard. In his "Crop Rotation" chapter in *Either/Or* (1843), the aesthete denounces boredom and describes that purposeful idleness—without yielding to industry or boredom—can be the sensualist's answer to the boring life. Kierkegaard also singles out the English for their prolific boring-ness:

> Boredom is partly an immediate talent, partly an acquired immediacy. Here the English are, on the whole, the paradigmatic nation. One seldom encounters a born talent for indolence, one never meets it in nature; indolence belongs to the world of spirit. Occasionally you meet an English traveller, however, who is an incarnation of this talent, a heavy immovable groundhog whose linguistic resources are exhausted in a single one-syllable word, an interjection with which he signifies his greatest admiration and *most profound indifference, because in the unity of boredom admiration and indifference have become indistinguishable*. No other nation but the English produces such natural curiosities. (italics added; 231)

So the English City Gent Stockbroker can wander through all manner of fantastic and dangerous situations without noticing or being affected by them in the least, purely because nothing but the unreal, alternate world of the comic book can relieve his boredom.

Kierkegaard will be revisited in Ep. 14, where one of the Piranha brothers' associates named Kierkegaard amuses himself by "biting the heads off whippets," perhaps also to stave off boredom.

• E •

"East Africa . . . plastic surgery" — ("Non-Illegal Robbery") Following WWI, Tanganyika was controlled by Britain, and after 1964, parts of East Africa became Tanzania, and continued to be administered by Britain. It seems that extradition treaties were in place, as well, at least by 1968, so that for a British criminal, attempting escape to East Africa may have been a futile undertaking.

Nazi war criminal Martin Bormann was rumored to have endured a botched plastic surgery in South America, but DNA tests in 1999 confirmed that he died, probably by suicide, without leaving Germany.

Ironic, too, that at least originally, when plastic surgery was pioneered (c. 600 BC), it was in India and to reconstruct criminals' noses and earlobes—to assist in the rehabilitation process, and not assist in an escape from justice.

Episode 6 — Like most episodes to follow (Eps. 10, 11, and beyond, for example), this episode was *not* given a name / title separate from *Monty Python's Flying Circus*, probably in response to Michael Mills's request for this alternate naming to stop. Mills felt it was confusing viewers and regional programmers alike, making it less likely that the fledgling show would be given a chance outside of London. (See BBC WAC files for the first season for more.) See notes for the entry for "Episode 2" in Ep. 2.

Secondly, the success of the show (probably not in actual numbers, except in London, but in audience letters and surveys) prompted Michael Mills to already (as of 27 November 1969) ask Cleese whether another thirteen episodes could be considered (WAC T12/1,242). In short, the show was beginning to get its legs, and audiences were actually tuning in, looking for *FC*.

Also appearing in this episode are W.F. Fairburn and Dennis McTighe (WAC T12/1,087). (McTighe plays the bus driver in this episode.) The numbers of extras and walk-ons will increase as the series goes on, with upward of two dozen extras per episode being regularly contracted by the fourth season. This contributed to the rapidly rising budget for the series, along with more elaborate costumes and prop requests.

This episode seems to have been shunted off to Golders Green Hippodrome for taping, as happened several times when the studio space at Television Centre was needed for another production (WAC T12/1,087). The theater setting for "Red Indian in Theatre" also demanded a much larger space, and in this case, one with theater seats.

All of the music requests for this episode are for some reason found in the records for Ep. 7, in the folder WAC T12/1,088. It may be that there were so few music requests for the two episodes that they were consolidated.

Exterior of bank — (PSC; "Vox Pops on Things Illegal") The logo near the door indicates this location is at least somehow affiliated with Lloyds Bank.

• F •

Family Group — (PSC; "Johan Gambolputty . . . von Hautkopf of Ulm" photos) This family group portrait (where the infant is vaulted upward out of the mother's arms) is from Thomas Gainsborough, and is known as *The Baille Family* (c. 1784). It's part of the Tate Gallery collection. Gainsborough's work will be featured again in Eps. 14 and 25.

"Figgis" — (link into *"It's the Arts"*) Arthur Figgis is also featured in Ep. 2 as a man (Chapman) who can verify that Mr. Frampton (Jones) does indeed have three buttocks. In neither appearance is he characterized as an accountant. Under this section can be heard the strains of that quintessentially English composer, Edward Elgar, and his "Nimrod" from *Enigma Variations* Op. 36, as conducted by Sir Adrian Boult (WAC T12/1,088).

"fondue" — ("Crunchy Frog") Normally, a dish using melted eggs and/or cheese.

"foul the foot" — ("Non-Illegal Robbery") A colloquialism meaning a dog defecating on the sidewalk.

Frankenstein monster — (PSC; "The Dull Life of a City Stockbroker") Creature from Mary Shelley's 1818 *Frankenstein* novel, though this iteration looks more like the Boris Karloff version of the creature from the 1931 Universal film *Frankenstein* directed by Englishman James Whale.

"front stalls" — ("Red Indian in Theatre") Seats in the orchestra area and/or near the stage.

The music in the background is a section of Ivor Novello's "Vitality" (1951), *Gay's the Word* part two (WAC T12/1,088). The original London cast starred Cicely Courtneidge, whom the Red Indian will mention.

• G •

"Gambolputty" — ("Johann Gambolputty . . . von Hautkopf of Ulm") To "gambol" is to frolic, and "putty" is, of course, caulking adhesive, the combination of which almost demands a string of nonce or nonsense words to justify the portmanteau-ing.

garret room — ("Non-Illegal Robbery") A room in the uppermost portion of a structure. Under this early part of the scene, a portion of the score from the James Bond film *From Russia with Love* (1963) by John Barry, can be heard (WAC T12/1,088).

Cf. similar gangster "planning" scenes in films like William Wellman's *The Public Enemy* (1931), Robert Siodmak's *The Killers* (1946), John Huston's *Asphalt Jungle* (1950), and perhaps especially Stanley Kubrick's *The Killing* (1956). Cleese (as co-screenwriter) would resurrect this scene in a much later film, *A Fish Called Wanda* (1988), directed by Charles Crichton. Michael Palin acts in this later scene and film, as well, though his part as the stutterer is almost opposite to his smoothly loquacious "The Boss" here in Ep. 6. Palin performed this same service as the planner for the Judean People's Front assault on Pilate's palace in the 1979 movie *LB*. "Reg" (Cleese) was also part of that gang.

"German Baroque" — ("Johann Gambolputty . . . von Hautkopf of Ulm") The early Baroque-period (roughly the seventeenth century) Germans were led by the likes of Pachelbel and Froberger, keyboardists both, and both forenamed Johann, coincidentally. Later, organists such as J.S. Bach and Handel led German baroque music through the sacred (Bach's Passions, sonatas, etc.) and more secular realms (Handel's opera, oratorio, and secular cantata compositions). Python's ridiculously monikered hero might be the troupe's erudite jab at the increasing complexity of *music* as written and performed by Germans of the baroque period, as well as of the longer names some of these composers used professionally (i.e., Carl Philip Emanuel Bach).

It also should be noted that of all the composers reeled off by the presenter, Gambolputty is the only Baroque-period name, the rest coming much later, in the Classic and Romantic epochs.

"grumblemeyer" — ("Johann Gambolputty . . . von Hautkopf of Ulm") Just might be a play on Ben Jonson's "grumbledory" (an alteration of "drumbledory") in *Every Man Out of His Humour* (1599): "The Goggle-ey'd Grumbledories would ha' Gigantomachiz'd" (5.4).

This list actually reads very much like the alchemical nonsense Jonson conjures up for his charlatans to use against the greedy Puritans in *The Alchemist*:

> Subtle: Did you look
> O' the bolt's-head yet?
> Face: [Within.] Which? on D, sir?
> Subtle: Ay;
> What's the complexion?
> Face: [Within.] Whitish.
> Subtle: Infuse vinegar,
> To draw his volatile substance and his tincture:
> And let the water in glass E be filter'd,
> And put into the gripe's egg. Lute him well;
> And leave him closed in balneo.
> Face: [Within.] I will, sir.
> Surly: What a brave language here is! next to canting.

Subtle: I have another work, you never saw, son,
That three days since past the philosopher's wheel,
In the lent heat of Athanor; and's become
Sulphur of Nature. (Act II)

See the author's *Monty Python, Shakespeare and English Renaissance Drama* (sections on Jonson) for more on Jonson's language, targets of vilification, and the Pythons. The "city comedy" elements are also discussed in the sections on Jonson.

"gutenabend . . . hundsfut" — ("Johann Gambolputty . . . von Hautkopf of Ulm") This section is a mangled food order, asking for Nuremberg bratwurst with dog's feet, essentially.

• H •

"Hardy" — ("Red Indian in Theatre") In the film and stage versions of *Dial M for Murder*, the character is named Chief Inspector Hubbard, not Hardy. Probably a memorial mistake on the Pythons' part (they'll switch Walpoles in Ep. 33, as well).

"Hautkopft" — ("Johann Gambolputty . . . von Hautkopf of Ulm") Can be translated as "skinhead." Skinheads were already appearing in England by this time (late 1960s), especially in depressed areas (mill towns, inner-city neighborhoods).

"heap" — ("Red Indian in Theatre") The Red Indian (Idle) probably borrows his phraseology and delivery from early American film Westerns, where Indians rarely spoke in complete English sentences.

"Hemmings, David" — ("Twentieth-Century Vole") Actor, star of Antonioni's *Blow Up* (1966) and appearing in the unforgettable *Barbarella* (1968). Cleese made an unbilled appearance in the 1969 Hemmings's flop *The Best House in London*.

"He tells it . . . out of sight!" — ("Twentieth-Century Vole") Clichés, all, and a swipe both at Hollywood and American English colloquialisms. The American film industry had exerted a strong—even dominant—influence on the UK since the early days of cinema, causing culture czars in Britain to chafe at the overwhelming presence of things American. The British government had implemented restrictive quotas against foreign (read: Hollywood) films as early as 1927, demanding that a majority of British screens show British films. This led to so-called quota-quickies—domestic films made to satisfy the quotas, quality aside—but British audiences demanded Hollywood films anyway. In fact, most major Hollywood studios merely set up or reconfigured their London offices and operations to make "local" films for the quota market, so American films continued to fill screens.

By 1948, when the BBC laid down the law as to what "quality television" meant in the UK, there were specific warnings against the use of American slangs and colloquialisms. See the entry for "slept with a lady" in Ep. 3.

high street — (PSC; "The Dull Life of a City Stockbroker") In many English towns and villages, the "high street" was the major shopping and dining area, losing some clout only when malls, larger department stores, and big box stores began to build nearer motorway exchanges.

Many towns in the UK, large and small, still boast a "High Street," not unlike the abundance of "Main" streets in the United States. The Pythons will shoot in high streets often, in Ealing, Walton-on-Thames, Croydon, Exeter, etc.

"himbleeisen" — ("Johann Gambolputty . . . von Hautkopf of Ulm") The word "eisen" means "iron," though "himble" seems to be a nonce word (the Germanic spelling would be "himbel" anyway).

"hippy Gestapo" — ("Twentieth-Century Vole") Perhaps an allusion to the hippy/flower child influence in the *Springtime for Hitler* production within the film *The Producers* (1968), but also may be inspired by the times themselves, as the early 1960s and 1970s were the heyday of the "hippie" generation and "flower-power" movement. The "Big Cheese" (Chapman) in Ep. 4 dresses as an evil hippy dentist, complete with resplendent flower-power jewelry.

"horowitz" — ("Johann Gambolputty . . . von Hautkopf of Ulm") Pianist Valdimir Horowitz (1903–1989) was *not* performing publicly between late 1969 and mid-1974, having performed in Boston in October 1969, then taking a hiatus until May 1974, when he performed in New York. He had performed fairly regularly between 1965 and 1969, and to high praise. Prior to that time, Horowitz had taken a sabbatical from public performance between 1953 and 1965, when he returned to the Carnegie Hall stage to rapturous acclaim ("Horowitz Ends His Exile," *Times*, 15 May 1965: 6).

"How to Fling an Otter" — (link into *"It's the Arts"*) Not unlike the later *Blue Peter*-ish sketch "How to Rid the World of All Known Diseases" in Ep. 28 where hosts teach or promise to teach viewers "How to Do It"—how to play the flute, feed the world, and bring peace to Russia and China. The "Fish Club" ad man (Palin) also reminds viewers they've already learned "How to Sex a Pike," and then proceeds to illustrate how to feed a goldfish (with gazpacho and sausage) in Ep. 26. The great British public have prided themselves on their DIY ("Do It Yourself") moxie since at least the privations of the war years. See notes for the listed episodes for more.

• I •

"Indian brave" — ("Red Indian in Theatre") Once again, the specter of incongruity—an English-challenged Indian using critical and theatrical idioms—elevates the speaker above his perceived station.

"Intercourse Italian Style" — ("Twentieth-Century Vole") There were a series of films produced between 1960 and 1970 with this same genericized title, including *Love Italian Style* (1960), *Divorce Italian Style* (1961, starring Marcello Mastroianni), *Marriage Italian Style* (1964, dir. Vittorio de Sica, starring Sophia Loren and Marcello Mastroianni), and *Adultery Italian Style* (1966). Also cf. the American TV show, *Love American Style*, airing 1969–1974.

It's the Arts — (link into "*It's the Arts*") This episode was recorded on 5 November 1969, and was broadcast on 23 November 1969. It was actually recorded seventh in the season, but was broadcast after the fifth episode. The title *It's the Arts* does not appear in the script. This is the second (and final) official appearance of the *It's the Arts* sketch format in *FC*.

The title card also features a depiction of Michelangelo's *David* sporting a fig leaf. A full-size replica of this statue has been on display in the Cast Courts at the Victoria & Albert Museum since 1858.

• K •

"kalbsfleisch" — ("Johann Gambolputty . . . von Hautkopf of Ulm") Veal.

kirk — ("A Scotsman on a Horse") Scottish: "Church."

"kleenex" — (animated link into "The Dull Life of a City Stockbroker") This is actually the proprietary name of the facial wipe, but has become attached to the product inseparably, no matter the maker.

"knacker" — ("Johann Gambolputty . . . Hautkopf von Ulm") Can mean things as varied as a lively singer, something that makes a cracking noise, one who buys old horses or houses, a saddle maker, or even testicles, according to the *OED*. Coupled with the following word, "thrasher," "knacker thrasher" could presumably translate into the vernacular "ball buster," to speak in the slang. The term "apple banger" also supports this reading.

Lastly, the intrepid *Private Eye* policeman during this period was Inspector Knacker of the Yard, fashioned after "Slipper of the Yard," or Jack Slipper, the lead investigator on the 1963 "Great Train Robbery" case.

"kurstlich" — ("Johann Gambolputty . . . von Hautkopf of Ulm") Perhaps a purposeful Germanicization of "shortly," combining a bad version of "kurz" ("short") and adding "-lich" to fully Germanicize the word. When creating jabberwocky French, the Pythons have also created French-sounding words and phrases (see Ep. 1).

• L •

large African native — ("The Dull Life of a City Stockbroker") Later, an American Indian native will be featured in this same episode. Both will be broadly stereotyped, not unlike the City Gent, the Rustic, and the Pepperpot throughout *FC*. This look will return in the "Our Eamonn" sketch, when Eamonn (Chapman), in full Zulu tribal kit, appears at his home after a stay in Dublin (Ep. 31).

"lavatories" — ("Crunchy Frog") This "direct address" moment makes it seem as if the preceding performance were some sort of Public Service Announcement (PSA). Cf. Ep. 7, where the policeman (Chapman again) interrupts the sketch to remind viewers to report all alien sightings before sending them back to the exciting story.

"Leatherhead Rep" — ("Red Indian in Theatre") Leatherhead Theatre is located at 7 Church Street, Leatherhead, Surrey, and was receiving significant Arts Council grants/subsidies between 1963 and 1967, according to files at the V&A. Filmmaker Mike Leigh (b. 1943) got his start as a stage assistant at Leatherhead Rep.

"love story . . . frontal nudity . . . comedy" — (Twentieth-Century Vole") Seemingly pell-mell genre mixing here, with identifiable semantic elements listed in this rant including: a setting in nature ("snow"), Hollywood A-list stars (Hudson and Day), physical passion ("kissing" and "Intercourse"), naughty foreign film ("*Intercourse Italian Style*"), Brit-film (Hemmings, who had also appeared in *The Wednesday Play* and *Dixon of Dock Green*), counterculture art film ("hippy"), WWII-film ("Gestapo officer"), adult film ("frontal nudity"), as well as a "family picture" and a "comedy." Frankly, with the dramatic inroads being made into Hollywood's hegemony by television, inflation, and several years of unwatchable films thanks to changing studio fortunes and leadership, many films of this period were assaying into any genre or subject matter that might bring audiences back into theaters. This may be a comment on films like *Where Eagles Dare* and *Ice Station Zebra* (spoofed later in Ep. 23), featuring all-star casts, pretty girls, intrigue, etc.

• M •

"Masonic Apron" — ("Policemen Make Wonderful Friends") Part of the Freemasons' official ceremonial dress. Cf. Ep. 17, both the "Architect Sketch" and "How to Give Up Being a Mason," where Chapman's character is standing in a bus queue wearing an apron.

"massacres" — (link out of "Red Indian in Theatre") Possibly an oblique reference to the experiments underway in live theater in the late 1960s, that is, the radical "Happenings Theatre" (c. 1966–1968), where events and activities take the place of plot and action.

More specifically to this reference of a "massacre" at Dorking during a performance, Richard Schechner's "Environmental Theatre" comes to mind. Schechner—a lifelong New Theatre practitioner—attempted to erase the line between performer and audience, between performance and life, even. Schechner defined the six axioms of Environmental Theatre: (1) "the theatrical event is a set of related transactions"; (2) "all the space is used for performance," and "all the space is used for audience"; (3) "the theatrical event can take place either in a totally transformed space or in 'found space'"; (4) "focus is flexible and variable"; (5) "all production elements speak in their own language"; and (6) "the text need be neither the starting point nor goal of production—there may be no text at all." A fascinating quote from Schechner illustrates the free-for-all potential that a Happenings or Environmental Theatre "performance" could allow: "Unlike the performers, the spectators attend theatre unrehearsed. . . . Thus unprepared, they are difficult to mobilize and, *once mobilized, even more difficult to control*" (italics added; *The Drama Review* 12, no. 3: 41–65). It's easy to see how the Pythons could take such a statement of possible chaos and adapt it to their satiric ends.

More sobering might be an allusion to the infamous massacre of English women and children by (East) Indians in the so-called Great Revolt in 1857. When news reached England, the outrage was so pervasive that even churchmen called for retaliatory massacres. For a contemporary account, including a call for calm to both the combatants and the hostile English press, see an article by Charles Creighton Hazewell in *The Atlantic Monthly*: "The Indian Revolt" 1, no. 2 (Dec. 1857): 217–22.

Medieval Couple — (PSC; "Johann Gambolputty . . . von Hautkopf of Ulm") This is a version of the Flemish van Eyck's *The Arnolfini Portrait* (1434). Jan van Eyck's (1390–1441) figures are here given animation by Gilliam, as the bridegroom pushes like a button the stomach of his seemingly pregnant bride. This painting also hangs in the National Gallery, London.

"mittler-aucher" — ("Johann Gambolputty . . . von Hautkopf of Ulm") In the taped version, this is pronounced more as "mittel raucher," which might translate into "middle smoker."

"Mona Lisa" — (PSC; "Johann Gambolputty . . . von Hautkopf of Ulm") Iconic painting by Leonardo da Vinci (c. 1503–1506), which now hangs in the Louvre, Paris. Gilliam pored through art books for his animations, utilizing works both well known and obscure. He has slightly tinted the figure, and removed the background, replacing it with an incongruous alpine valley scene, so that it looks more like a Mannerist painting, and is better connected to the German and Austrian subject of the arts piece.

Modernist artist Marcel Duchamp (1887–1968) had applied a painted mustache to the *Mona Lisa* in 1919, both solidifying the da Vinci work as an icon, and also emphasizing the unquestionable change Modern Art was inflicting on the old masters, classical representation, and "authenticity."

"monosodium glutamate" — ("Crunchy Frog") Abbreviated MSG, it has been used as a food flavor enhancer since 1908, and is originally from Japan. The assertion by Mr. Milton (Jones) earlier that no "preservatives or additives of any kind" are used in Whizzo chocolates, then, is a misstatement. Glucose, the most common sugar in nature, is also a key ingredient.

The marvelous benefits of the flavor enhancer MSG are touted in the *Times*, with thanks given to the work of the American company Arthur D. Little ("Profile of a Flavour," 18 May 1965: 17). Just four years later however, in 1969, the papers are covering what's being called "Chinese restaurant syndrome," which turns out to be an adverse physical reaction to MSG from food served in American Chinese restaurants. In October 1969 (the month *MPFC* took to the airwaves), the American Food and Drug Administration began to take a serious look at MSG. The additive was being voluntarily removed from baby food by the end of October 1969 ("Suspicion Cast on Flavour Additive to Baby Food," 25 Oct. 1969). This means that by the time this episode was recorded (5 November 1969), "monosodium glutamate" would have found its way into fairly common parlance, and would seem a likely ingredient employed by the Whizzo Chocolate Company.

"more exciting" — ("Vox Pops") This robbery quickly becomes a Vox Pops moment, one of Python's regular motifs, and a well-used linking item. The "man-on-the-street" interviews were characteristic of TV and radio during this and earlier periods, including the very popular *The Dick Emery Show* (1963), Peter Watkins's *Culloden* (1964), and his film *The War Game* (1965). The perverse excitement of illegality is also discussed in Ep. 2, the "Mouse Problem" sketch.

"motion-picture history" — ("Twentieth-Century Vole") Not only is this the longest line of dialogue given to Gilliam in the run of the series thus far, but it's also a nod to obsequiousness à la "The Emperor's New Clothes," where no one save a child wants to disagree with the emperor over the beauty or even reality of his new "clothing."

The infiltration of fairy tales and fairy tale tenets can perhaps be attributed to Palin, Jones, and Idle, who worked together on a children's television show prior to *FC* (*Do Not Adjust Your Set*, 1967) as well as Jones's interest in and publication of fairy tales himself. For a somewhat fractured children's story time in *FC*, see Ep. 3, where Idle reads from a naughty storybook. In the second *Fliegender Zirkus* episode the Pythons will tell the story of Princess Mitzi Gaynor, Prince Walter, and their lives in Happy Valley.

Mum (Terry J) (reading newspaper) — (PSC; "'Another Indian Massacre at Dorking Theatre' link") The mother here is reading the *Daily Sketch*, a Conservative-leaning newspaper that in fall 1969 was on its last legs. It would close in 1971, and merge with the more popular *Daily Mail*. The headline announces a "Typhoid" outbreak and a "Hotel" (only bits of the headline is readable). In September 1969 typhoid cases appeared in England and were traced to a particular site—the Hotel El Bousten—in Hammamet, Tangiers. It was thought initially that contaminated water in the hotel's swimming pool had infected the 17 British tourists (and more than 30 other European tourists), but contamination on travel package excursions (to local ruins?) was also a likely suspect. The Tourist (Idle) will rant about the excursions and intestinal illness and Enterovioform tablets and "queuing for the toilets" in Ep. 31.

• N •

National health specs — (PSC; "Johann Gambolputty . . . von Hautkopf of Ulm") The NHS came about as part of the sweeping social change called for in the Aneurin Bevan (1897–1960) report, "In Place of Fear," and was officially instituted in 1948. The "specs" are the standard glasses provided by National Health, and would have been those provided to the Pythons as youngsters had they needed them. According to the *Times*, in 1954, when the Pythons were ages 11–15, such glasses would have cost 8s. 9d., 9s. 9d., and 10s. 4d. This was a slight increase from the previous year. Children "of school age" were still being given free glasses (18 Mar. 1954: 5). The bespectacled man stands next to a light-green panel van (lorry) that bears the BBC's (royal) crest.

"Nelson" — ("A Scotsman on a Horse") Nelson is found in Lancashire, northern England, though there is also a Nelson in Caerphilly, Wales. Both are a long distance from either Dorking or Leatherhead (both in Surrey).

newsagents — ("The Dull Life of a City Stockbroker") These are often very small shops selling newspapers, magazines, candy and soda, and sundry items, and are typically squeezed into narrow spaces along busy city streets, but can also be corner shops. Cleese buys a paper in and then walks out of one as the "Silly Walks" sketch begins on Thorpebank Road. (This same corner store is no longer extant, having been replaced by a home in the same space.)

According to BBC records, this newsagent shop was located at the corner of Brighton Road and Liberty Lane, Addlestone, Surrey, and was utilized on 22 October 1969 (WAC T12/1,242). Several Vox Pops segments were also recorded here.

newspaper — (link out of "Red Indian in Theatre") The newspaper where he reads about the theater massacre is a copy of the *Daily Standard*.

"Nicaragua" — ("Non-Illegal Robbery") The British formed alliances with local Miskit Indians as early as the seventeenth century, and even treated the Mosquito Coast region as a "dependency" between 1740 and 1786. In 1969, however, the radical, "popular front party" Sandinista National Liberation Front was active in Nicaragua, opposing the Somoza dictatorship, rendering Nicaragua as an unlikely hiding place for a British non-criminal.

"no time to lose" — ("Non-Illegal Robbery") This phrase will later propel much of Ep. 38, but is used here as just a tossed-off phrase.

"not at all well" — ("Crunchy Frog") Cf. *HG*, where the plague cart man refuses to take a victim who's "not dead yet."

• O •

"Ooh, I like that" — (*Animation: Criminal Pram*) The "swishy" character in the criminal pram appears to be based on an early portrait of William Gladstone (1809–1898), a Liberal politician as well as Prime Minister four separate times. Gladstone has been featured earlier, in "The Wacky Queen" silent film from Ep. 2. Gladstone is mentioned in at least four *Goon Show* episodes, as well.

The Indian euphonium player (taken from a full band image) is snatched from in front of what looks to be the sprawling Carlton House Terrace in London.

"over six feet tall" — ("Policemen Make Wonderful Friends") This could be either a height requirement, as many professions demand (fighter pilot, submariner, runway model) or just a personal preference. This height precludes most women, of course, so the hint of homoeroticism in the constabulary is evident again. There are no longer any height restrictions in the British police forces. See the note for "policemen . . . friends" below.

• P •

Part of his signature gets away (animation) — (*"Animation: Escaping scribble* link into *'It's the Arts'"*) The map on which Gilliam's hand squashes the escaping scribble features portions of southern, coastal Spain—specifically, the Malaga and Granada regions—and coincidentally the area where many British tourists spent many holidays, including the ranting Tourist (Idle) in Ep. 31. "Torremolinos" can be glimpsed on the coast south of Malaga, for instance. There is no record in the WAC archives of this particular map being requested for use, or of any copyright clearance. Many of Gilliam's materials were used, obviously, without attribution.

"Pawnee" — ("Red Indian in Theatre") North American Plains Indians.

"pen friend" — ("Policemen Make Wonderful Friends") A pen pal, exchanging letters.

"piddles" — ("Twentieth-Century Vole") Urinates.

pig — (PSC; "Johann Gambolputty . . . von Hautkopf of Ulm") Cf. Ep. 1 for the earlier pig appearances. This photo is of a multi-teated sow. A boar appears later in the episode.

Just prior to this photo there appears a photo of a policeman leaning over some kind of apparatus, though this photo is not listed in the printed scripts. The PC wears the traditional bobby's uniform, including the tall helmet (discussed in some detail in Ep. 43).

"pinko" — ("Twentieth-Century Vole") Primarily an American slang word for a Communist sympathizer ("pink" meaning not completely "red"). By using the sobriquet Larry (Chapman) is suggesting that the writer is an agitator.

One of the darkest periods in American cinema was the heyday of the House Un-American Activities Committee and the attendant ferreting out of suspected Communists or Communist-sympathizers, primarily from among the artists (and especially screenwriters) of Hollywood. Those who were called before the various committees to testify and name names were summarily blacklisted if they didn't cooperate to the committee's satisfaction (including the "Hollywood Ten": Alvah Bessie, Herbert Biberman, Lester Cole, Edward Dmytryk, Ring Lardner Jr., John Howard Lawson, Albert Maltz, Samuel Ornitz, Adrian Scott, and Dalton Trumbo). Those who testified were labeled as informants and stoolies for helping the investigations, similarly attacked by those implicated and those who managed to avoid prosecution (i.e., Elia Kazan).

A Cleese character (a commentator) has already erupted into a splenetic over the "red scum" threatening England's sovereignty, perhaps a nod to the racialist leader of Britain's Union of Fascists, Oswald Mosley (1896–1980). In the late 1950s, Mosley had instigated racist riots in West London, where white Teddy boys hunted out darker "others" for beatings and abuse. By 1969, the Cold War was very much alive and well, with the Brezhnev era in the Soviet Union recently under way, and Nixon in the White House, whom many (probably including the Pythons) considered jingoistic.

pitched battle — (PSC; "The Dull Life of a City Stockbroker") This battle in the streets is reminiscent of the gun battle depicted in Lindsay Anderson's film *If . . .* (1968), and must also be at least indirectly related to the evening news depictions of the fighting under way in Vietnam. Perhaps even more significant might be the increasing "troubles" in Northern Ireland, which held the daily headlines in most newspapers of the time, and which featured British soldiers running through British (Irish) streets, armed and fighting.

Anderson (1923–1994) was one of Britain's newer, politically and socially charged filmmakers, and will be discussed in the notes for Ep. 19.

"policemen . . . friends" — ("Policemen Make Wonderful Friends") The police force are regularly lampooned in *FC*, from fighting crime with fairy wands and engaging in homosexual liaisons (both Ep. 13), to pretending to be an airplane (Ep. 17), to incompetent-but-film-literate Flying Squad members (Ep. 29). Policemen are just one type of authority figure regularly mocked in the Python oeuvre, joining church leaders, big business, the upper-class, and others.

"praline" — ("Vox Pops") A browned almond (or other nut) and boiled sugar confection. Praline (played by Cleese) is a semi-regular character during the show's first season. He will reappear returning a dead parrot in Ep. 8, try for a linking job in Ep. 18, and try to buy a license for his pet fish in Ep. 23.

• Q •

QC — ("Vox Pops") A "Queen's Counsel" is a senior barrister in the UK, a position Cleese may have aspired to had he continued work in the law after Cambridge. See Morgan's *Monty Python Speaks!* for Cleese's version of that decision.

queue — (PSC; "The Dull Life of a City Stockbroker") People waiting in line, or "queuing up." This scene was shot in the Australia Road area of East Acton on 20 October 1969, as was the "driverless" taxi scene (WAC T12/1,242).

• R •

Red Indian — ("Red Indian in Theatre") Reportedly, one of the tableaux vivants staged by Vivian van Damm (cf. Ep. 1) at the very popular Windmill Theatre was a "Red Indian" scene, featuring nude, motionless models in Indian garb and *mise en scène*. A similarly costumed Red Indian will reappear in Ep. 9 in the "Hunting Film" scene.

The phrase "Red Indian" appears ubiquitously in media references to North American Indians on British TV, as well as newspapers and magazines of the first half of the twentieth century.

"Redfoot" — ("Red Indian in Theatre") No such Plains Indian tribe existed, so this could be just a slight racial slur, akin to "redskin." Python uses racially derogatory terms like "darkies" and "wop" occasionally in *FC*. This level of racial insensitivity was fairly common in this period, seen often in cartoons, in the blackface characterization of *The Black and White Minstrel Show* (1958–1978), and, also, the *Goon Show* (where the jokes about bandleader Ellington's skin color were common). The Goons also produced an episode, "Call of the West," where saxophones are being sold to the "smelly old . . . Knobbly Knees" tribe. Not surprisingly, Ellington plays "Chief Sitting Bull and Bear" (20 Jan. 1959).

"Reluctant Debutante" — ("Red Indian in Theatre") A 1955 play (a comedy) by Edinburgh-born William Douglas-Home (1912–1992), brother to Prime Minister Sir Alec Douglas-Home (later Lord Home). The play had actually been performed at Leatherhead Repertory Theatre in August 1957.

restoration-fund — (PSC; "Vox Pops") Donations for church-related restorations, especially older churches listed on historic registers.

"Rio de Janeiro" — ("Non-Illegal Robbery") Capital of Brazil, port city, and one of several well-known South American destinations where extradition difficulties could be expected. In the 1947 Jacques Tourneur film noir *Out of the Past*, Jane Greer flees to Mexico, for example, to escape the revenge of her former boyfriend (Kirk Douglas), and his hired detective (Robert Mitchum).

"Rock Hudson . . . Doris Day" — ("Twentieth-Century Vole") Quintessential 1960s Hollywood screen couple, appearing together in films like *Pillow Talk* (1960). In *Gilliam on Gilliam*, Terry Gilliam would describe this duo and their movies as the antithesis to his own style of filmmaking.

In *The Goon Show*, the "Who Is Pink Oboe?" sketch (12 Jan. 1959), Eccles (Milligan) will claim to be Rock Hudson to woo a ladyfriend.

"roll the credits" — ("Twentieth-Century Vole") Saltzberg is acting the part of the narrative tyrant here, managing to control the end of the episode. This level of awareness isn't given to many Python characters—most are clearly trapped in their fictional worlds while some few others have the ability to demand changes. In Ep. 1, for instance, Mrs. Stebbings is able to ask for and receive the death of Mr. Foster (Chapman) of Guildford ("Famous Deaths"); in Ep. 2 a man (Palin) calling for "a Scotsman on a horse" (Cleese) is granted that wish ("A Scotsman on a Horse"); in Ep. 30, a dissatisfied participant in a sketch (Idle) gets additional chances to find satisfaction in other sketch settings, and even as different characters ("Bus Conductor Sketch").

This is much like more textually or narratively dominant cartoon characters (e.g., Chuck Jones's Bugs Bunny, Tex Avery's Droopy and Screwy Squirrel) who can manipulate and control their animated worlds because they possess not only a self-awareness of their cartoony natures, but because they also understand the tenets and limits of that fictional world. The Pythons often treat their created world as if it were animated—plastic, pliable, and abruptly reformable.

• S •

safety curtain — (PSC; animated link into "Red Indian") A fire-proof curtain that can be lowered to protect the viewing audience from a fire onstage or backstage.

"Saltzberg, Larry" — ("Twentieth-Century Vole") A stereotypical portrayal of a Hollywood movie mogul as a Jew. (See Gabler's *An Empire of Their Own: How the Jews Invented Hollywood.*) This man is perhaps modeled closely on producer Harry Saltzman (mixed with a dash of 1930s-era MGM mogul Irving Thalberg), whose film *Battle of Britain* (dir. Guy Hamilton, 1969) was just such an over-the-top kind of superstar production. (Saltzman also produced James Bond films from 1962 to 1974, after which he sold his stake in the franchise.) Saltzman had also been very much in the news at the forefront of the British film censorship debate when he produced controversial Angry Young Men films like *Look Back in Anger* (1959), *The Entertainer* (1960), and *Saturday Night and Sunday Morning* (1960), arguing for greater freedom of sexual and even political expression in British films (see Aldgate).

A few other moments of caricatured Jewishness can be found in *FC*. In Ep. 7, there is a less-than-iconic Jew (Palin), who just shrugs and ends his single sentence on an upward inflection (mock-Yiddish). If the script hadn't identified this character as a Jew, then he may not have been recognizable at all (he's not caricatured). Cf. Voltaire's (Ep. 2) stereotypical characterizations of Jews (Don Issachar, whose two interests are women and banking; and miserly Jews who might swear by Father Abraham while robbing Candide blind in diamond transactions, etc.) in *Candide*. Jewish Hollywood producer Irving Thalberg (1899–1936) is well known for butting heads with big-name directors like Eric Von Stroheim, bringing strict, streamlined studio control to Universal and then MGM projects. Thalberg's personal manner, however, is not recorded as blustery and over-the-top, meaning Chapman's portrayal isn't meant to impersonate Thalberg.

The Jew here and elsewhere becomes a stereotypical "other" in the Python oeuvre, joining the host of Others (Indians, blacks, homosexuals, women, Tories, chartered accountants, England's upper class) similarly enshrined. These Others are generally not treated scornfully, but perhaps thoughtlessly and playfully, which seems to have been characteristic for the period. The humorous (satiric and just silly) treatment of "others" (and then the recovery of same) during this period is summed up aptly by Alan Bennett, of *Beyond the Fringe* fame:

> I don't know that we had any intentions—any overall intentions—I think, what it wasn't, it seems to me was "cutting" and "devastating" satire. There were things that were—I mean Peter did a thing, an imitation of a television broadcast of Macmillan which was very funny, *but it was also quite affectionate.* (Audio transcription, *Eyewitness: 1960–69*, "Beyond the Fringe")

Much of Pythons' work fits into this vein—rather than outright scorn, there seems to be a certain level of affectionate nostalgia attached to the lampooning of ridiculous City Gents and Rustics and Tories and Pepperpots.

"Scotsman on a horse" — ("A Scotsman on a Horse") The bagpipe music here is not accounted for in the WAC records. The "Scotsman on a horse" motif initially appeared, also as a request, in Ep. 2. The bagpipe music, which plays as the Scotsman rides through gorse and thistle, alternates with a sober harpsichord ("Bonny Sweet Robin") processional whenever there's a cut to the interior of the kirk (WAC T12/1,088).

The stunt rider here is Harry Woodley, and the Bride seen in a moment is played by Bernardine (or Bernadette) Barry (WAC T12/1,083). Others in this scene (shot on 9 July 1969) include Tobin Mahon-Brown (*Doctor Who*), David Billa (*Doctor Who*), Laurie Goode (*The Wednesday Play*), Evan Ross (*Emma*), and Elaine Williams (*Some Mothers Do 'Ave 'Em*) (WAC T12/1,242).

"she takes off her wrap" — ("The Dull Life of a City Stockbroker") The actress playing the Stockbroker's (Palin) unfaithful wife is Miss Eddy May Scrandrett, who will appear in Ep. 17, as well.

"shönedanker" — ("Johann Gambolputty . . . von Hautkopf of Ulm") This is a twisted version of "thank you" in German—"Danke schön."

"Sioux" — ("Red Indian in Theatre") North American Plains Indians. Perhaps beyond the incongruity of a period-garbed Indian attending the theater is the fact that he is an American Indian who, along with his Sioux tribe, somehow lives somewhere near Leatherhead and regularly attends an English repertory theater. It's also later offered that a Pawnee tribe (also American Plains Indians) lives in the Leatherhead/Dorking region, and also attends the theater.

Instead of wearing a "single strip of hair," as the script calls for—a.k.a. a "Mohawk"—the Indian (Idle) wears a long black wig parted in the middle, and a headband. This stereotype looks very much like what may have been seen on American situation comedies and variety shows of the period. American actor Lon Chaney Jr. (1906–1973) is coiffed very similarly in ITV's *Hawkeye and the Last of the Mohicans* (1957), though Scar (Henry Brandon) in *The Searchers* (1956) may have been the inspiration for Idle's costuming.

"snogging" — (PSC; "The Dull Life of a City Stockbroker") Kissing passionately, noisily, even messily. Cf.

Ep. 45, "*Most Awful Family in Britain*" sketch, and the character of Valerie (Chapman), a Member of Parliament and "snogger."

"spelltinkle" — ("Johann Gambolputty . . . von Hautkopf of Ulm") This could actually be interpreted as a command. In *Beyond the Fringe*, the monologue delivered by Jonathan Miller titled "A Piece of My Mind (The Heat-Death of the Universe)," creates similar disparate readings of a single phrase as he discusses his impressions of British Rail bathrooms:

> where they have a marvelous and somewhat mysterious unpunctuated motto printed on the wall over the lavatory: "Gentlemen lift the seat." Now what exactly does this mean? Is it a sociological description? A definition of a gentleman that I can either take or leave? Or perhaps it's an invitation to upper-class larceny? (Audio transcription, *Beyond the Fringe*)

"spelterwasser" — ("Johann Gambolputty . . . von Hautkopf of Ulm") Since "spelter" is a solder containing significant amounts of zinc, the word might mean a drink of sorts containing the solder, like mineral water, but not nearly as healthy. There are such things as a spelter-box, spelter-dust, spelter-heap, spelter-maker, and spelter-ore, according to the *OED*, so spelter-wasser isn't terribly far from actuality. The zinc reference above (as in the "zinc stoat of Budapest" award) shouldn't be forgotten here; also, one of the Upperclass Twits of the Year in Ep. 12 is also implicated, one "Simon-Zinc-Trumpet-Harris."

"splunge" — ("Twentieth-Century Vole") An archaic American slang term that means literally "to plunge." The *OED* dates the first recorded colloquial usage to 1839. There's no indication of where the Pythons might have come across the arcane word, though it may have been borrowed from a comic book, given the earlier comic book reference, and the fact that such onomatopoeic words populate action comic pages. (Roy Lichtenstein's "Wham!" [1963] is an example of this comic book trope finding its way into high art.) Also, the *OED* mentions that a form of the word appeared in J.A. Froude's *Life of Carlyle* (1884), which certainly might have found its way to an Oxford or Cambridge reading list. Lastly, it may also have merely been a nonsense word, not unlike the Goons employed, with words like "Hern" and "Spontellibons" ("The Call of the West").

"steel bolts" — ("Crunchy Frog") A description not unlike the booby traps and land mines being dealt with in the Vietnam conflict, and which had been much in the news since the mid-1960s. One such device, called a "cartridge trap," is fired from the ground as a victim steps over it, then explodes.

"still on film . . . studio" — ("Vox Pops") This mention of the very different formats—film stock versus videotape—reminds the viewer that a created, constructed thing is being watched. The aesthetic differences between the two media are glaringly obvious to the eye, and certainly would have been jolting to the viewer if, say, a dramatic program (not a comedy show) were to fluctuate between media without a similar "heads up" to the viewer. British audiences would have been quite accustomed to this seemingly odd juxtaposition—comedian Benny Hill had been employing it since at least 1957 (beginning with *The Benny Hill Show*), as had most comedy shows leading up to *MPFC*. For another reaction to the film/videotape dichotomy, see Ep. 18, "Society for Putting Things on Top of Other Things." Also, see Ep. 8, where the Colonel stops the hermit sketch, even though it's on film, and not in-studio.

"stoat" — (link into "*It's the Arts*") A European ermine. In Ep. 26, a character (played by Gilliam) will appear with a stoat through his head. This violation is certainly a borrowing from the world of cartoons, where characters are regularly dropped, crushed, stretched, minced, and impaled without permanent damage. All sorts of body horrors are inflicted on Python characters, especially in Gilliam's dismembering and re-membering animations, but the impalings of "live" characters indicate perhaps a cultural fascination with the sacrosanctity-versus-violation ethoi. In *FC* characters are skewered by giant nails and floor lamps (Ep. 14), arrows (Eps. 6 and 38), spear gun darts (Ep. 30), tennis rackets and keyboards (Ep. 33), and hunting spears (Ep. 45).

Of the major American animation studios during the Pythons' formative years (Famous Studios, Disney, UPA, Warner Bros., et al.), only Disney—under the direct orders of Walt himself—explicitly forbade any such violation of his characters' bodies. Not so other studios. Tex Avery's Nazi Wolf (produced while at MGM) is riddled by bullets (so that light can shine through him) in *Blitz Wolf* (1942), and Daffy Duck loses his beak more than a dozen times in the trilogy *Rabbit Fire* (1951), *Rabbit Seasoning* (1952), and *Duck! Rabbit, Duck!* (1953). There are also myriad explosions throughout WB and MGM cartoons, explosions that leave the victim looking much like the "It's Man" when he is handed a cartoony "anarchist's bomb" in Ep. 8. The Pythons (like the Goons previously) seemed to draw heavily and consistently from these more violent, aggressive, and frenetic cartoons throughout the run of *FC*. (Harry Secombe would later describe the Goons' antics as being "like an oral cartoon" ["Desert Island Discs Archives: Harry Secombe"].)

Superman-type — (PSC; animated link out of "The Dull Life of a City Stockbroker") Cf. Ep. 3, "Bicycle Repair Man" sketch, for an earlier Superman reference.

The British public awareness of this very American character had been high since World War II, when American GIs brought their comic books with them to their UK postings. There had also been a number of attempts to ban such comics, or at least regulate them, since that time as well. In 1952 (the year *The Adventures of Superman* debuted on American television, starring George Reeves) discussions in the House of Commons raised the issue of the "pernicious and harmful" effects American action comics were having on British youth, including an increase in juvenile delinquency and violence. Most of these concerns centered on "disreputable publishers" of violent, anarchic, and sexually suggestive comics, but the iconic American hero was dragged in by the suggestion that any "superman [who] should take the law into his own hands" was a real danger to the great British public.

The Under-Secretary from the Home Office, Sir Hugh Lucas-Tooth (1903–1985), then explained in some detail (and, as it reads, tiredly) that the Obscene Publications Act of 1857 couldn't be massaged or manipulated to fit comics such as those cited into its bailiwick, and that censorship wasn't the answer, nor was classifying the comics with a kind of "ratings" system used in the film industry ("American Style Comics—Plea for Official Inquiry," *Times*, 2 Aug. 1952: 7). The American *Adventures of Superman* TV show would appear on British television in 1956.

"swag" — ("Vox Pops") *OED*: "A thief's plunder or booty; gen. a quantity of money or goods unlawfully acquired, gains dishonestly made." Dennis Moore's (Cleese) bag loaded with reapportioned goods in Ep. 37 is labeled "Swag," but with the pound sign (£) in place of the "s," thus spelled "£wag."

"sweetmeat" — ("Crunchy Frog") The *OED* identifies the term as primarily archaic, and referring to virtually any kind of sweetened (sugary) cake or tart or filling.

• T •

tab — (PSC; "Red Indian in Theatre") A "tableau curtain," one that is either drawn up or to the sides as the show begins.

"thrasher" — ("Johann Gambolputty . . . von Hautkopf of Ulm") Can mean one who threshes.

Three Naked Ladies — (PSC; "Johann Gambolputty . . . von Hautkopf of Ulm") Gilliam's "naked lady" photos come from a large collection of Victorian and Edwardian "boudoir" photographs given to him in the mid-'60s by comedian Ronnie Barker. The images appear hundreds of times in *FC* episodes. See *Gilliam on Gilliam* (1999). Several of the images can be seen in the pages of *Ronnie Barker's Book of Bathing Beauties*, including one on the "Foreword" page. See the entries in Ep. 8 for more.

Thrills and Adventure — ("The Dull Life of a City Stockbroker") *Thrills and Adventure* is not an actual DC comic from this period. This new title has been placed over the actual title, *Captain Action*, a DC comic from Gil Kane (1926–2000) that had enjoyed a limited five-issue series run beginning in July 1968. The character and comic were simply based on an existing action figure from Ideal Toy Company, which may have accounted for its brief life. The music beneath this portion of the film is from Jack Shaindlin's "March of the Insurgents." Shaindlin is one of many light music composers who—during the 1940s through 1960s—penned music specifically for programmed music needs on radio and then TV (WAC T12/1,088). This type of music was used by a wide variety of shows, and was available on LPs (records). This particular music is also heard in the "Bicycle Repair Man" sketch of Ep. 3.

"ticolensic" — ("Johann Gambolputty . . . von Hautkopf of Ulm") A "tico" is a Costa Rican. "Ticolens" is a medical term having to do with oral microbiology and immunology, and may have been contributed by Chapman, the troupe's only medical doctor.

"time for that later" — ("Twentieth-Century Vole") Another allusion to the moral price of Hollywood-style fame and success. Cf. the rustic (Cleese) in Ep. 4 who, after having his rustic monologue interrupted, resolves to not "sleep" with another producer.

"tin" — ("Vox Pops") In the Scotsman's previous appearance (also Palin, in Ep. 5), he was made "entirely of wood."

"treble" — ("Crunchy Frog") Triple, threefold.

"12/6D" — (link into "*It's the Arts*") Monetary figures in the UK are given as "pounds, shillings and pence" (£.s.d.). The "D." stands for the Latin *denarious*, or penny. The shilling disappeared only after the contentious 1971 move to decimal coinage. Since this episode was written in 1969, the Pythons would be expected to still use the term. Also since 1971, the pound has equaled 100 new pence (*OED*). "New pence" (the newly valued pence, post-1971) is mentioned in Ep. 27.

"Twentieth-Century Vole" — ("Twentieth-Century Vole") Play on the name of the American film studio Twentieth-Century Fox, which was established as

Fox Studios by William Fox in 1913. This trademark is followed by another animated trademark, this time the Metro Goldwyn Mayer (MGM) "roaring lion" design. (MGM, another storied Hollywood studio, was formed in 1924 by Louis B. Mayer from Metro Pictures and Goldwyn Studios.) In the lion's place, however, is a mangy, weedy-looking vole. (A vole is a short-tailed field mouse, and has been mentioned in Eps. 2, 3, and 5 already.) The "Ars Gratia Artis" ("Art for Art's Sake") part of the trademark is left unchanged.

Twentieth-Century Fox wasn't experiencing a terrific 1969, releasing few films of note until September and *Butch Cassidy and the Sundance Kid*, and ending the year with one of Hollywood's most expensive flops, *Hello, Dolly!* MGM could claim *Ice Station Zebra* (cf. Ep. 23) and *Where Eagles Dare* in 1968, as well as a *Goodbye, Mr. Chips* redux in 1969, but the late '60s weren't kind to the top-heavy, idea-poor, throwback Hollywood film studios. Foreign film, independent film, and the blockbuster film were changing the movie landscape, and television continued to offer more reasons for audiences to just stay home. Many studios changed ownership during this period, as well. Taken together, the major Hollywood film studios looked quite scraggly (like a wet vole) in 1969.

The music underneath the celebrated logo is Jack Shaindlin's "Spectacular," one of the many bits of program music written and/or performed by Shaindlin, Eric Coates, Ron Hamer, and Keith Papworth, and others, and created for television, radio, and low-budget film use in the 1940s and beyond. Most of the musical score for the Pythons' feature film *Holy Grail* came from such music, specifically the DeWolfe collection.

Two Dancers — (PSC; "Johann Gambolputty") This appears to be a photograph of any one of myriad two-man vaudeville/music hall song-and-dance acts, and could be from either a publicity still or captured from a film.

• U •

"Ulm" — ("Johann Gambolputty . . . von Hautkopf of Ulm") A city in southwestern Germany on the Danube River and opposite the Bavarian town of Neu Ulm. This entire "name" sketch is reminiscent of the "John Jacob Jingleheimer Schmidt" children's song, as well, the origins of which are quite obscure.

• V •

vicar — (PSC; "Vox Pops") This vicar steals from his own parishioners, while other churchmen already presented have or condone bizarre sexual practices (Ep. 2) and are suspected of being smugglers (Ep. 5). Later, in Ep. 13, a vicar will be an ignored entrée at a trendy restaurant, and by Ep. 28 the local vicar sells biros, Cup tickets, water heaters, etc.

The pilfering vicar insert was shot at Holy Trinity Church, Lyne Lane, Chertsey, Surrey (WAC T12/1,085).

Viking — (PSC; "Johann Gambolputty . . . von Hautkopf of Ulm") The Viking character appears several times in *FC* as a linking element, often speaking just a single word on the way to other links or the next sketch. Gilliam often plays the Viking, though the part gets spread around to other Pythons, as well (Palin and Cleese, for example). The identification of the linking item is also a significant aspect of Python upsetting the agreed-upon conventions of TV, including hiding such links in the quest for smooth, invisible continuity.

• W •

weedy — (PSC; "Johann Gambolputty . . . von Hautkopf of Ulm") A tall, lanky, and weak man or boy. Cf. the "weedy" and also bespectacled lance corporal (Jones) in Ep. 1, who easily succumbs to the funniest joke in the world.

"We present 'The Dull Life of a City Stockbroker'" — ("The Dull Life of a City Stockbroker") The background music that swells beneath this scene is a popular light classical music piece from the "London Suite" titled "Knightsbridge (March)" by Eric Coates (WAC T12/1,087). This is essentially "city" music, composed with the bustling Knightsbridge shopping area of London as its inspiration.

This long sketch begins at the front door of 49 Elers Road, near Lammas Park Road, Ealing, where portions of "The Funniest Joke in the World" were also filmed (WAC T12/1,087). The initial exterior shots for "City Stockbroker" were shot at 49 Elers (in the front yard), while the kitchen interior was also inside this address (fairly unusual, as location interiors are harder to secure and then even harder to light properly) (WAC T12/1,242).

"whizzo" — ("Crunchy Frog") *OED*: "An exclamation expressing delight," and "excellent, wonderful." Whizzo Butter was a product mentioned in Ep. 1. A *Private Eye* ad (13 May 1966) offers the following confection advertisement:

> For the appallingly greedy.
> Chocolates filled with gnat's pee.
> Stuff these black gobbets into your

maw and you'll be the envy of
other snobs. Send 88gns. for
illustrated catalogue to:
Boris Chocolates, Bumhole St. W8. (Ingrams, 133)

Women's Institute applauding — (PSC; link out of "A Scotsman on a Horse") This is the first time that the WI footage has been officially requested in the weekly copyright clearance requests for film footage and musical clips (WAC T12/1,088).

"write it" — ("Twentieth-Century Vole") All Larry's (Chapman) lines are delivered with an exaggerated American accent, characterized by very hard [r] sounds. All the writer characters in this scene attempt, with varying degrees of success, American accents.

Episode 7: "Science Fiction Sketch"

"It's" Man running/falling intro; *Animation: Titles* (silly Cleese v/o); Camel spotting (Yeti spotting, trainspotting); "You're no fun anymore" vignettes (and *animated photo*); Knight and chicken; The Audit; Vicar tied to railroad tracks; Complaint letters address; "Licence fee" and "Leave your radio on during the night"; **"Science Fiction Sketch"** (Men Turn into Scotsmen; Charles and "Darling"; "Soon Scotland was full of Scotsmen"; Mr. and Mrs. Angus Podgorny; Tennis doubles with five players; The Blancmange attacks; Avuncular policeman, and knight-and-chicken; Police station and Riley, a "Blancmange impersonator and cannibal"; Charles discovers the plot: "They mean to win Wimbledon"; Blancmanges and the "plucky Scotsman" playing Wimbledon; Mr. and Mrs. Samuel Brain Sample eat the Blancmange and save the Earth); Closing credits

• A •

abacus — (PSC; "Science Fiction Sketch") An ancient calculation tool, and right at home in this rustic Scottish "men's wear shop" as conjured by the Pythons. This is perhaps akin to ethnographic filmmaker Robert Flaherty's insistence that Eskimos depicted in his 1922 film *Nanook of the North* put away their twentieth-century accoutrements (rifles, utensils, etc.) in favor of the more romantic, traditional tools like spears and whale bone knives. An outdated abacus in this Scottish men's wear shop—rather than an adding machine or calculator—would be just such an item to instantly denote rusticity, backwardness, Scottishness, etc.

absurdly sexy — (PSC; "Science Fiction Sketch") The woman-as-attractive-prop is also endemic to the sci-fi genre. The characterization here seems more like Altaira (Anne Francis) in *Forbidden Planet* (1956), Irish Ryan (Naura Hayden) in the unintentionally funny *Angry Red Planet* (1960), or the intelligent but marginalized (and ogled) Pat Medford (Joan Weldon) in *Them!* (1954). Perhaps the best (or worst) example is the mute Nova (Linda Harrison) in *Planet of the Apes* (1968). A more local example might be Janet Munro's appearance in *The Day the Earth Caught Fire*, a British apocalyptic sci-fi film from 1961, directed by Val Guest (1906–2011), and also starring Leo McKern (1920–2002) and Edward Judd (1932–2009). And though narratively she is more than window dressing in this end-of-the-world tale, the film's producers do manage to give Janet (1934–1972) sensual bath and layabout time, breasts casually exposed—something mainstream American films of the same period, no matter how pulpy, could never risk.

"allay suspicion" — ("Science Fiction Sketch") The detective may be playing the role of skeptic here, or naysayer, the one who tries to explain away the fantastic in purely rational or reasonable terms in many sci-fi and fantasy films. In *The Thing from Another World*, Dr. Carrington (Robert Cornthwaite) sees the creature only as a superior being, while in *Forbidden Planet* Dr. Morbeus (Walter Pidgeon) refuses to believe that it is his own subconscious creating the killer monster. Both, of course, suffer for their shortsightedness.

"a lot faster" — ("Science Fiction Sketch") Perhaps an allusion to the reduction of some cricket match lengths in the UK in the 1960s from five days to just one day, a move brought about by sagging attendance and what was considered overly defensive play. One-day cricket began as early as 1962 in county play in England, in the "Midlands Knock-Out Cup" (where Northamptonshire won), and where rules were also adjusted to encourage faster play, more careful bowling, and aggressive batting. League one-day cricket would begin in 1969 in England, and was met with significant opposition from players, fans, and teams, including the venerable "MCC," the Marylebone Cricket Club. See the entry "calling it doubles" for more.

American Voice — (PSC; "Science Fiction Sketch") Meant to send up the very popular U.S. science fiction cinema of the 1950s, from classics like *The Day the Earth Stood Still* (1951) and *The Thing from Another World* (1951), to marvelous cult-flops like *Plan 9 from Outer Space* (1959). The sober, authoritative narrator (Cleese with an exaggerated American accent) was certainly one identifiable semantic element of the sci-fi genre syntax. This allusion continues to illustrate the significant effect that film, and especially Hollywood genre film, had on the Python troupe.

"And this . . . in the final" — ("Science Fiction Sketch") So the alien blancmanges can win Wimbledon but that win won't be recognized because they aren't human. Therefore, the invasion will have been unsuccessful. In sci-fi/horror the invading creatures' "Achilles Heel" is often something just that simple, a tiny backdoor waiting to be discovered by the intrepid scientist or the open-minded civilian (it's almost never the military in these films). In *War of the Worlds* (1953), the Martian invaders succumb to a common human virus; in *Forbidden Planet* (1956), the death of one man (Dr. Morbeus and his Id) is enough to destroy the marauding creature; in *The Blob* (1958), teenager Steve discovers the creature's simple temperature sensitivity, and passes the information on to a grateful world. In this *FC* episode, the blancmanges will be undone by the fact that they're not human, so a technicality would keep them from winning Wimbledon anyway, as well as the fact that they're both edible and quite tasty to humans.

Similarly, in Ep. 35, people living in high rises created by Mystico (Jones) can remain safely there as long as they simply believe in the buildings—the moment they doubt, the tower blocks begin to fall.

animation — (PSC; animated link out of "You're No Fun Anymore") As the animation finishes (members of an Indian brass band move up and down like piano hammers to music), two of the members disappear, with one man saying to the other that they have to "stop meeting like this." The other answers with this episode's catchphrase, "You're no fun anymore." This is yet another homoerotic moment, and one that will be followed closely by an image of two naked men cuddling in Ep. 8. The implication seems to be that if there is an all-male band, then there must be some sodomitical activity going on.

The quick scenes that follow continue the at least homosocial subtext, including a whipping on a nineteenth-century Royal Navy ship, and a Dracula figure (Chapman) who loses his teeth when confronted with the exposed neck of a pretty woman—both scenes end with the "You're no fun anymore." Incidentally, it wasn't until after the publication of the Wolfenden Report in 1957 that the depiction of homosexuality became possible in British film and on stage, and then only as long as there were no embraces, for instance (Aldgate, 128–29).

Incidentally, Gilliam has earlier used the image of the euphonium player (seated just right of the bass drum) in the "Criminal Pram" sequence from Ep. 6. This "personal" photo—like so many others Gilliam employs—is not accounted for in the WAC records.

". . . ate his wife" — ("Science Fiction Sketch") Not unlike similar moments in American gangster films like *Scarface* (1932) or *Asphalt Jungle* (1950) where an authority figure (newspaper editor, police chief) lectures both the diegetic and film audience regarding the evils of criminality, to disabuse listeners of any romantic notions of crime, and to reinforce the "crime doesn't pay" mantra. In the science fiction genre, these moments are reserved for the surviving participants to lament man's recklessness as he dabbles with the powers of God, as Dr. Frankenstein (Colin Clive) says himself in *Frankenstein* (1931), and Captain Abrams (Leslie Nielsen) reminds us in *Forbidden Planet* (1956).

"Australia" — ("Science Fiction Sketch") Australia, of course, by 1970 had a rich tradition of international tennis success, including Norman Brookes, John Bromwich, Tony Roche, and many others. The fact that Australia was a part of the Commonwealth but not English allowed them to be rendered here (and elsewhere in *FC*) as Other. The successful Aussies will reappear in Ep. 38, as respected penguin scientists dressed as (and named for) tennis players.

• B •

"be gentle with me" — ("The Audit") See Ep. 5, the "Erotic Film" sketch, where this line is actually spoken by a female character. Here in Ep. 7, though, there is a curious cutaway here to the Bishop (Jones) seated at the table, who leers in a rather unseemly way, as if he's responding in a sexual way to the accountant's (Palin) last line. It doesn't seem to be a moment for the audience (they don't respond to the insert). This sexual moment would fit Python's normal questioning of the libidinal capacities of authority figures in *FC*, churchmen and otherwise. In Ep. 20, three bishops will attack the gowned gong girl (Chapman) on the set of *Take Your Pick*.

"Berwick-on-Tweed" — ("Science Fiction Sketch") A slightly shortened version of Berwick-upon-Tweed, a town in the northernmost portion of England, in the Scottish borderlands. Historically a part of Berwickshire, Scotland. Dr. Johnson traveled through Berwick-on-Tweed, according to Boswell, on his way to Edinburgh on his tour to the Hebrides (*Life of Johnson*, 276).

"Big Business" — ("Science Fiction Sketch") Like "You're no fun anymore," this is another catchphrase. These kinds of phrases were at least partly discouraged in *FC*, probably since they had been (and continued to be) staples of other comedy shows on British radio and TV. The next person who utters the phrase, the Bishop (Jones), will end up tied to a railroad track (in the Feltham Marshalling Yards) for "pinching" the phrase, then lying about it. Later, another phrase will emerge, this time in reference to the afflicted Scotsmen under alien attack. See the entry for "destinies" below.

"billion" — ("Science Fiction Sketch") "Billion" is certainly an American term, comparable to the older English term "thousand millions" (or even "milliard"), and hence fits better in this American sci-fi film spoof. The terms mean a one followed by nine zeroes (or noughts or ciphers). See Schur. "Billion" was one of the Americanisms insinuating its way into British culture during this period. Interestingly, the postwar debt owed to the United States may have helped this increased usage along. In 1945 the British government owed the United States and allies about "£4,000 million," or £4 billion. The United States would have kept count in billions, of course, and the newspapers and government memos went back and forth between the terms as the debt was discussed and serviced (Wilson, *After the Victorians*, 507).

bishop bound and gagged and tied across a railway line — (PSC; "You're No Fun Anymore") The lack of respect accorded members of the Anglican clergy in *FC* is partly attributable to the anti-authority zeitgeist of this period anyway, but there's certainly more. In *Postwar* Judt notes a pan-European groundswell of antiauthoritarianism thanks to a perceived collusion between the power of the state and the will of the church:

> The spiritual authority of the Protestant pastor or the Anglican vicar was by convention offered not as a competitor to the state, but rather as its junior partner . . . [and] the distinction between church and state as arbiters of public manners and morals became rather blurred. The late forties and early fifties [when the Pythons came of age] thus appear as a transitional age . . . where the modern state was beginning to displace church and even class as the arbiter of collective behavior. (229)

Henceforth in these episodes churchmen will generally appear as thieves, drunkards, and sexual perverts, as well as in very close proximity (as in this sketch) to members of the ruling power and class.

"black pudding" — ("Man Turns into Scotsman") Traditional Scottish fare, it is sausage made with blood and suet (solid fat).

"blancmange" — ("Science Fiction Sketch") A boiled milk and gelatin sweetmeat. A dessert, then, is attacking the Earth and turning men into Scotsmen. In the production notes for this season, Terry Jones was scheduled to have played the blancmange (WAC T12/1,088). The blancmange will be mentioned again very late in the series, in Ep. 41 as a possible food for ants ("Michael Ellis"), and will elicit a healthy laugh of recognition from the audience. Earlier, the folks at *ISIRTA* (including Cleese) had mentioned an "incredible singing blancmange" in "The Desert Song" episode (23 July 1967).

The BBC Radio show *The Goon Show* (1951–1960) had earlier created a sketch where Old Age Pensioners are being attacked at the seaside by "hurled batter puddings" ("The Dreaded Batter Pudding Hurler," 12 Oct. 1954), as well as an episode where Neddie, Moriarty, Bluebottle, Gryptite Thynne, and Bloodnok must track and trap the "most savage part" of the "International Christmas Pudding" (15 Nov. 1955) running amok in Africa. There, the pudding is consumed in the end, as well.

Similar diminutions (lofty purpose/stakes, trivial object/means) have occurred in English literature, of course, with the "mock epic" leading the way. Swift in *Gulliver's Travels* (c. 1725), for example, created wars and rebellions based on which end of an egg should be broken first (part I, ch. IV), and it was a single lock of hair that caused nearly fatal familial strife in Pope's *Rape of the Lock* (1712).

Finally, in describing the kind of Britain that the Angry Young Men were rebelling against in the 1950s, novelist Edward Pierce inadvertently points up the incongruity the Pythons created when employing their "fatal blancmange" image:

> Having heard from parents, mostly, about pre-war agitation, read the books in school—the Old Left book publications—having faint memories of the war and the cause it was all about, and then everything having settled in to a sort of *blancmange*-like existence: common sense, tolerance, and a sort of half-a-grain-change

as it were, and being resentful that life was less exciting. (Audio transcription, *Eyewitness 1950–59*, "Angry Young Men II")

"Buenos Aires" — (link into "Science Fiction Sketch") Capital city of Argentina, and nowhere near Thaxted.

"But I must" — ("Science Fiction Sketch") Angus says this as if making a fool of himself *is* his ultimate destiny as a Scotsman, a destiny over which he has no control. Refer back to the beginning of the sketch, where it was pointed out that Scotsmen have no control over their own destinies. There are myriad political cartoons from this period equating the possibilities of Scottish home rule and the existence of the Loch Ness Monster—both, of course, far-fetched unrealities.

"Butley Down" — ("Science Fiction Sketch") If a legitimate reference, then it could be a misspelling of either "Bewley Down" (200 miles southwest of London) or "Butley Town" (20 miles southeast of Manchester). She clearly pronounces "Butley" as "Bucky," however.

• C •

"caber" — ("Man Turns into Scotsman") *OED*: "A pole, or spar . . . used in the Highland athletic exercise of throwing, tossing the caber." Probably here must also be recognized for its sexual connotations, as the lament has been that real men don't/couldn't turn into Scotsmen—these three Scotsmen aren't man enough to even have their own caber/penis. Conversely, in Ep. 37 in the "Ideal Loon Exhibition" there is a Scotsman attracting significant Pepperpot attention in the "Nae Trews" exhibit.

"calling it doubles" — ("Police Station") So playing with five players in a doubles match is all right, but *calling* it doubles is the problem. As is so often the case in the Python world, names and naming become a crucial issue, and the power of language is such that simple words can have significant textual power (e.g., "Ni!" in *HG*), and attributed names also can transform a person or situation into something or someone entirely different. In Ep. 36 a police inspector *becomes* Sir Philip Sidney simply because he is called by that name; in Ep. 37, a dull customer becomes a funny bus passenger and then a music hall straight man, etc. In Shakespeare's world Richard and Henry both name and transform in *Richard III*, and both *1 Henry IV* and *2 Henry IV*, creating and re-creating their worlds/friends/enemies to suit their purposes. See chapter 6 in the author's *MPSERD* for more on this subject.

The policeman's concern here—that playing the game differently means it's somehow not tennis anymore—is echoed in period newspaper articles discussing the one-day cricket fuss. One promoter said that the new, shorter matches (played on Sundays) "were not a cricket promotion [as much] as a financial operation"—like cricket wasn't cricket anymore, but the fiscal health of the game demanded the change.

"camel spotting" — ("Camel Spotting") A play on the pastime of trainspotting, where the train enthusiast watches for and notes trains and their numbers passing any given point. (The author has seen these hobbyists along the Paddington-Swansea and York–St. Pancras lines, for example, taking notes on each and every passing train.)

centre court — (PSC; "Blancmanges Playing Tennis") Centre Court, Wimbledon, is where the finals of the men's and women's singles matches are played. Scheduling of centre court assignments certainly also depends on the television appeal of the participants.

Monty Python's grass court tennis sequences were likely shot at the Ealing Lawn Tennis Club on Daniel Road, not far from Ealing Studios, Lammas Park, etc., where many of the series' exteriors were recorded.

"Chairman yet" — ("The Audit") Almost a tried-and-true punchline, but it's completely ignored by the other characters, perhaps because he's about to be "outed" as an embezzler.

"CID" — ("Police Station") Criminal Investigation Department. See Ep. 3, where Inspector Dim sings about another, more desirable profession outside of CID, that of a window cleaner.

"civilization" — ("Science Fiction Sketch") This can be directly connected to H.G. Wells's *War of the Worlds* (1898), which also takes place in a small English town, Woking, and features aliens from outer space bent on global destruction and domination. The American radio and film adaptations of the novel are set in the United States. The campiness of the writing and production value owe a great deal to Ed Wood's cult masterpiece *Plan 9 from Outer Space* (1959), called by many the worst film ever made, but also the myriad low-budget sci-fi coming from both the United States and UK during this period. The UK-based Planet Film Productions, for example, produced camp classics like *Devils of Darkness* (1965), *Island of Terror* (1966), and *Night of the Big Heat* (1967), fun sci-fi/horror/exploitation schlock, all.

collage — (PSC; "Science Fiction Sketch") A collection of filmed and often juxtapositionally edited shots; elsewhere in *FC* this process has been referred to as "montage," which is actually a more accurate term than collage, since mixed media isn't being used here.

"Covent Garden" — (caption link into "Science Fiction Sketch") Originally a convent garden, Covent Garden was laid out as per the design of Inigo Jones (see below), and was the first such residential square in the city. It was also London's principal fresh fruit, flower, and vegetable open market for three centuries (finally moving in 1974). It's also the site of the Covent Garden Theatre established by John Rich in 1732, which could account for the "7.30," "Saturday (near Sunday)," and "afterwards" quips. The eighteenth-century theater-going custom was for a show, then refreshments afterwards at local inns or pubs. See Pepys and Evelyn for more on London's theater history as experienced in the seventeenth century.

credits — (PSC; closing credits) Under the closing credits an unidentified Scottish tune plays, not the customary "Liberty Bell," something of a nod to the significance of the Scottishness of the episode.

cricket blazer . . . fussy print dress — (PSC; "Science Fiction Sketch") Mr. Brainsample (Chapman) wears a "cricket blazer," which is a light jacket, often brightly colored, along with "grey flannels"—trousers made of flannel and to be worn for boating or cricket (*OED*). Chapman's character Reg will wear very similar attire as he delivers Mr. Wentworth's message in the "Spanish Inquisition" sketch, even though the scene is set in 1911; he will then be able to move into another, more contemporary sketch when the "Spanish Inquisition" sketch sputters to a halt, at least for his character. See Ep. 15.

Mrs. Brainsample's (Idle) "carrier bag" is simply a handled paper shopping bag (it does look as if the Brainsamples have just gotten off the train from a day in the city).

Mr. Potter (Palin) sports the "briefcase and pinstripes," which, as has been seen, comprises portions of the typical attire/uniform of Pythons' City Gent. In this case, he is leaving the New Pudsey train station for home after work somewhere in London's financial district, probably the City of London.

All these clothing details are meant to create the "typical" characters employed by the Pythons by using already well-known and identifiable items. It's only the seventh episode (sixth, as recorded), and these codes are firmly in place. She's a Pepperpot, and he's one of the rarely seen Pepperpot husbands. Also, as in most sci-fi films, the events center around normal, everyday folk, like the young boy and his parents in *Invaders from Mars* (1953), the wandering orphan girl in *Them!* (1954), or the small-town doctor in *Invasion of the Body Snatchers* (1956). In a more local science fiction story, John Wyndham's 1957 novel *The Midwich Cuckoos* (which would be filmed as *Village of the Damned* in 1960), an entire normal, unexceptional English village becomes involved in an alien invasion.

"crofter" — ("Science Fiction Sketch") *OED*: "One who rents and cultivates a croft, small holdings especially in the Highlands and Islands of Scotland." In Ep. 37, Queen Victoria will be characterized as a "simple crofter's daughter" who became queen; when Neddie (Secombe) becomes Prime Minister in "The Gold Plate Robbery" (16 Feb. 1959), he is also characterized as a "crofter's son." *Private Eye* has also used a version of the sobriquet to describe PM Macmillan (see notes to Ep. 37). Macmillan had been born in Chelsea of well-to-do parentage.

"Czechoslovakia" — ("Science Fiction Sketch") Tennis in Czechoslovakia—in 1970 a Soviet-controlled satellite following the 1968 "Prague Spring" invasion—had produced Wimbledon champions like expatriate Jaroslav Drobny in 1954, and his coach (also a former player) Karel Kozeluh. (See wimbledon.org.)

• D •

"debenture preference stock" — ("The Audit") *OED*: "A bond issued by a corporation or company (under seal), in which acknowledgement is made that the corporation or company is indebted to a particular person or to the holder in a specified sum of money on which interest is to be paid until repayment of the principal." In a Wimbledon connection, debentures are available for the acquiring of seat options around center court. The Pythons are probably just throwing finance jargon around here, as well.

"destinies" — ("Man Turns into Scotsman") Cf. the sign in the boardroom, "There's no place in big business for sentiment" earlier in this same episode. This point, that the Scots have no control over their own destinies, is significant as the issues of sovereignty and self-rule are broached within the Commonwealth.

It won't be until the late 1970s when Scotland will gain some independence from England (and primarily based on the increasing importance of Scottish oil reserves, following North Sea oil discoveries in 1969), including an assembly with limited legislative and executive power. Harold Wilson's Labour government of the 1960s had taken the paternal approach and attempted to bring Scotland into the modern age by updating its economy and industry, perhaps a rather heavy-handed (and less than successful) way to keep Scotland from having control over its own destiny. Wilson's moves were also meant to quell a rising autonomy movement within the country (*ODNB*). This point is almost missed in the rapid-fire Python delivery, but salient and sensitive political issues of the 1960s and 1970s were regularly broached.

"Deutschmark" — ("The Audit") The West German unit of currency, officially instituted in 1948.

"Dimples, The" — (link into "Science Fiction Sketch") There is a Dimples in Lancashire, near Garstang. In this citation, the Pythons have indicated that "The Dimples" has some sort of geographic significance, like a dell, glen, or knoll, or the like. In D.H. Lawrence's *Sons and Lovers* (1913), the location of the colliery worker homes is known as "The Bottoms"; in fact, "The Bottoms" are the first words of the novel (1). Also, cf. the vacation spot known as the Wisconsin Dells, for instance. There is also a Dimples Lane in Garstang, Preston.

"dinna" — ("Science Fiction Sketch") Scottish slang for "do not," as "wilna" is for "will not."

"do that to a man" — ("Science Fiction Sketch") This same question is a rephrased version of similar hyperbolized and fear-ridden questions in *Them!*, *Forbidden Planet*, *The Blob*, and many other sci-fi films, asked when the full power and destructiveness of the "it"—giant ants, alien invaders, monsters from the Id—is finally, fully realized.

"Dr. Finlay" — ("Man Turns into Scotsman") Character on a Scottish TV series (*Dr. Finlay's Casebook*) that ran from 1962–1971 on BBC, and based on Archibald Cronin's stories. *Flying Circus* director Ian MacNaughton was working for the *Dr. Finlay* show, which he termed a "very turgid drama" and "too dramatic," when he was given the chance to move over to BBC Light Entertainment and Spike Milligan's *Q5* (Morgan 1999, 32).

Dr. Finlay's Casebook ("Sundays on BBC1") is the cover feature on the BBC's 8 March 1969 *Radio Times*.

"dromedary" — ("Camel Spotting") Also known as the Arabian Camel, the one-humped Dromedary is found in northern and eastern Africa (*EBO*). The silliness of this sketch (including and especially the ending) echoes the Ogden Nash poem, "The Camel":

> The camel has a single hump;
> The dromedary, two;
> Or else the other way around,
> I'm never sure. Are you? (*Bad Parents' Garden of Verse*)

(Incidentally, a camel can have either one or two humps.) A camel will also appear a number of times in the "Albrecht Dürer" sketches in the first episode of *Fliegender Zirkus*.

"dull" — ("Camel Spotting") Cf. the "dull. Dull. *Dull*. My God it's dull" life of a chartered accountant in the "Vocational Guidance Counsellor" sketch in Ep. 10.

"Dunbar" — ("Science Fiction Sketch") Located about fifty miles east of Edinburgh. The photo used here is pointedly rustic and Scottish—a humble cottage with thatched roof in a windswept countryside populated by sheep—befitting the backwardness the Pythons demand of their northern neighbors. It looks like a crofter's cottage, of course, and not a men's wear shop. The photo is not listed in the requests for this episode, though as mentioned later (in the "Scottish crofter's cottage" entry), it depicts a portion of the Skye Cottage Museum (WAC T12/1,088).

• E •

"earnest" — ("Science Fiction Sketch") A down payment, made so as to indicate that the deal is imminent, and being done "in good faith."

Episode 7 — This episode was recorded sixth on 10 October 1969, and broadcast on 30 November 1969. Also appearing in this episode: Donna Reading (*Softly Softly*), Constance Starling (*Dig*), Sandra Setchworth, J. Neill, and Flanagan (Eps. 11, 12; *Benny Hill*).

Flanagan, by the way, is the same Maureen Flanagan who was during this period a personal friend of the infamous Kray twins, East End gangsters who will be featured pseudonymously in Ep. 14 (as the Pirhana Brothers). See notes to Ep. 14 for more. There is no indication that Flanagan (also a former *Sun* "Page Three Girl") had any qualms with the Pythons spoofing her notorious friends.

Incidentally, in this episode Cleese's voiced "Monty Python's Flying Circus" line (to finish It's Man's utterance) is not included in the printed script, but is heard on the show as recorded. By the tenth episode, the Pythons will clearly be tiring of the "same old, same old" structure for opening the show. See notes to Ep. 10.

"everything depends" — ("Blancmanges Playing Tennis") In *Planet of the Apes* (1968), the fate of what's left of humanity rests on Charlton Heston's broad, suntanned shoulders; in *The Day the Earth Stood Still* (1951), a boy must show the alien that Earth has some value, or humanity is doomed; in *Metropolis* (1927), only young Freder's actions will bring change; and in *Doctor Who* (1963–1989) the earth is saved countless times by the title character (often with some assistance, as Podgorny will receive from the Brainsamples).

• F •

fangs fall out — (PSC; "You're No Fun Anymore") Since *Dracula* was at least partly a tale of perverse sexual profligacy (the vampire only "satisfied" when he is [en]gorged with blood), the loss of fangs is a sign of sexual impotency or at least inadequacy, especially when the woman's response—that he's "no fun any more"—is noted. Also significant is the fact that the troupe's only homosexual—Chapman—is portraying this emasculated, incapable vampire.

"Fields, W.C." — (link into "Science Fiction Sketch") This is a play on (1) the name of the well-known American vaudeville and film comedian (1880–1946), (2) the British use of the term "fields" in addresses, like St.-Martin-in-the-Fields, and (3) the meaning of "WC" in regional jargon—"water closet." Also, in newspaper advertisements of the period, any listing of addresses ending in "St.-Martin-in-the-Fields, W.C." or "Lincoln's Inns Fields, W.C." look like odd versions of the comedian's name.

Film of . . . along street — (PSC; "Man Turns into Scotsman") Typical shots of the "wasteland effect" of alien invasion, or, in this case, aliens turning normal people into Scotsmen and the infected Scotsmen leaving for Scotland. Similar shots can be seen in *The Day the Earth Stood Still* and the British film *The Day the Earth Caught Fire* (1961), for example. Once again, the Pythons are aware of the generic conventions of sci-fi and can either use them faithfully or undercut them, or both.

This sci-fi set-up is most likely borrowed from the very popular Richard Matheson novel *I Am Legend* (1954), wherein a bacterial pandemic has wiped out humanity (at least in Los Angeles, where the action is set), turning most into vampire-like creatures. The first film version of that novel, *The Last Man on Earth*, starring Vincent Price (1911–1993), appeared in 1964.

"Finchley" — ("Science Fiction Sketch") Finchley is a London suburb, northwest of the metropolis. The character Bluebottle (Peter Sellers) of *The Goon Show* hails from East Finchley, and is constantly bemoaning his plights on the playgrounds there.

"five people" — ("Police Station") The policeman (authority figure) here is more interested in the specter of uneven teams in tennis than in the portent of worldwide destruction. See the police officer in *The Blob* (1958), who spends much of his time making sure Steve McQueen and friends don't drive recklessly, as well as the misguided scientist Dr. Arthur Carrington (Robert Cornthwaite) in *The Thing* (1951) who only sees the scientific marvels of the marauding creature, not the imminent threat. The guards at the door of Swamp Castle as well as inside Herbert's room in *Holy Grail* are also more concerned with the trivia of their duties, and most end up skewered by Lancelot.

"Flight Lt." — (link into "Science Fiction Sketch") "In the Royal Air Force a flight lieutenant ranks below a squadron leader and above a flying officer" (*EBO*).

football stadium — ("Science Fiction Sketch") Stadium where club soccer teams regularly play. This stadium is the Bradford City Stadium (spectator Idle is also wearing Bradford FC colors). Part of this stadium would burn down in 1985, killing 56 people.

Contrary to what the printed script calls for, the play is already in progress when we cut to the scene, the spectator is standing with his noisemaker, and *then* the player scores and celebrates. Most of these are extreme long shots, emphasizing the emptiness of the stadium. (In shooting *Omega Man* in 1970–1971—another version of Matheson's popular novel—producers utilized downtown Los Angeles on weekends, when virtually no citizens visited the inner-city streets, and captured a handful of extreme long shots showing almost no human activity.) There is no slow pan around the stadium—also called for in the script—the long shots of the player and referee accomplish this task. These directional specifics, again, may have been provided by Jones, who was more interested in the camera movement and frame composition than the others (excepting, perhaps Gilliam) seemed to have been. Jones will go on to help edit much of the series (see McCabe; Morgan 1999), as well as co-direct *Holy Grail*, and direct *Life of Brian* and *Meaning of Life*.

"frog trampling" — (link into "Science Fiction Sketch") In the Python bestiary, frogs and toads appear quite often. One of the discussed names for the show originally was *The Toad Elevating Moment* (which would become a link in the episodes), and Idle mentions a band named "Toad the Wet Sprocket" in a Monty Python album sketch. In Ep. 14, the *Panorama*-type show exposing the Piranha brothers is called *Ethel the Frog*. There is also a "five frog curse" (like a five-car pile-up) occurring in Gilliam's animations in Ep. 17, crunchy frogs are eaten in Ep. 6, and "S. Frog" (Idle) is being fired for ruining an advertising firm in Ep. 24.

This reference is also heard earlier, prior to *FC*, in an episode of *At Last the 1948 Show*, when Joan Shock mentions "Dr. Bartle's Frog Trampling Institution."

• G •

"Galaxy of Andromeda" — ("Science Fiction Sketch") A spiral galaxy in fairly close proximity to Earth.

"Gonzales, Pancho" — ("Blancmanges Playing Tennis") Gonzalez (1928–1995) was an American tennis player of the 1950s and 1960s who won multiple singles championships. Gonzalez would play his famous 112-game match at the Wimbledon Championships in 1969, finally defeating Charlie Pasarell—he was, in fact, playing as well as he had ever played (as described the announcer [Idle]). Gonzalez won 22–24, 1–6, 16–14, 6–3, 11–9. The match was played 25 June 1969. (See wimbledon.org.)

• H •

Hackforth, Norman — (PSC; "Science Fiction Sketch") Hackforth (1908–1996) was a broadcaster, biographer, and songwriter. Hackforth's character (voiced by Jones) here acts like a game show host, speaking to audience members watching the show. Hackforth played the "mystery voice" on *The Twenty Questions Murder Mystery* (1950)—what the Pythons probably borrowed for their purposes—and earlier was a writer for *Halesapoppin* (BBC, 1948).

The traditional game show format for "clue"-type games is employed here, where the audience gets to see the answers before the contestants. It is rather incongruous to insert this format into a sci-fi sketch, of course.

"He . . . left them" — ("Science Fiction Sketch") Sort of a "meanwhile, back at the ranch" scenario used in serialized dramas in the early days of film, then television.

"He's right you know" — ("The Audit") The character Norman echoes this on the *Monty Python Live at the Theatre Royal Drury Lane* LP, in the sketch called "Election Special," and the sketch just fades away. Ron Vibbentrop (Chapman) will say the same thing to potential National Bocialist Party voters, though with a bit of a German accent, in Ep. 10.

• I •

"inadequate brain capacity" — ("Man Turns into Scotsman") Typical sophomoric jab at the Scots, displaying Pythons' penchant for both high and low comedy.

"incidental music" — ("Man Turns into Scotsman") In film, TV, and radio this music tends to be connected to the "incident" at hand (the setting), and can be either diegetic or extradiegetic, meaning created in the world of the film (where the characters can hear it or even create it) or beyond that world. In this scene the characters actually hear the extradiegetic music, which isn't usually the case, and the girl is simple enough to think it's the doorbell ringing. The conventions of the sci-fi genre, then, are being both upheld *and* undercut at a dizzying pace. Also, the traditional separation of the score or musical sound effects (extradiegetic sound) from the world of the film (the diegesis) is played with, reminding the viewer of the artificiality of the production.

The incidental music used throughout "Science Fiction Sketch" is not accounted for or even mentioned in the surviving papers held at the BBC's WAC records. This is unusual, as virtually every other episode in the series (and file in the WAC) contains such copyright clearance pages. This one may simply have gone missing in the intervening forty years.

"Institute" — ("Science Fiction Sketch") The presence of science and scientists—either as megalomaniacs fooling with the powers of God, or as the only answer to the alien threat—appear as necessary semantic elements in many sci-fi films. Charles (Chapman) is the type of scientist who did not create the global or cosmic disaster, but who is poised to (a) uncover the plot of the aliens or reasons for the disaster and (b) possibly offer solutions, thus saving the Earth. Later Charles will discover the aliens' insidious plot, but the invasion will only be countered when seemingly ordinary folk (the Brainsamples) take on the blancmange invaders.

"It's British sir" — ("The Audit") Perhaps not the answer the Board Member was looking for, as he (Cleese) looks back to his notes, but the sketch keeps going. Could be a reference to "British sterling," but that's not entirely clear.

• J •

Jewish figure — (link into "Science Fiction Sketch") This character isn't dressed in any caricatured style, actually, so the viewer may not comprehend the racial/ethnic gist. Not sporting a hooked nose or rubbing coins together, this rather vague caricature might be missed by viewers, unless the upward inflection of the character's voice is recognized. Again, this is a shorthand way for Python to identify racial Others. The character is also, of course, concerned with rising costs, which might also be a hint at his stereotyped Jewishness.

"Jocasta" — ("Science Fiction Sketch") The name is of nominal interest, as Jocasta is both the odd-woman-out in the doubles match, and, in literature, the widowed queen in Sophocles' *Oedipus the King* (c. 427 BC).

"Jones, Inigo" — (link into "Science Fiction Sketch") Jones (1573–1652), a renowned British painter, architect, and designer, is credited with founding the English classical tradition of architecture. Jones designed the Queen's House, the Banqueting House at Whitehall, and the Queen's Chapel at St. James's Palace (cf. Ep. 40, when George III [Chapman] wants to schedule a banquet at the palace). Jones is not known to have designed any fish emporia.

• K •

"ken" — ("Science Fiction Sketch") Scottish vernacular for "understand" or "recognize."

"King, Billie Jean" — ("Blancmanges Playing Tennis") Female American tennis player King (b. 1943) helped bring women's tennis into the public eye with the creation of the women's professional tennis tour. King was named "Outstanding Female Athlete of the World" in 1967, and had also beaten Ann Haydon-Jones (mentioned again in Ep. 22) for one of her six Wimbledon titles that same year.

knight in armour — (PSC; "You're No Fun Anymore") The knight in armour appears in several other *FC* episodes, and was usually played by Gilliam. If the punchline delivered happened to be off-color, purposely unfunny, or an acknowledged and hoary chestnut the knight would appear. This rather obvious visual gag, from the music hall and television stages, will soon disappear and not return to *FC*, especially as the Pythons' writing acumen sharpened.

• L •

"Lady Chairman" — ("The Audit") There are no women present, and the Chairman is played by Chapman.

"lager and limes" — ("Science Fiction Sketch") Light (pale) beers with lime or lime juice added. This could also be a cockney rhyming scheme, where "lager and limes" has replaced a more common word that would rhyme with "limes," and might be built on the near-rhyme with "spine" earlier. See Schur's *British English, A to Zed*, 424–25. Ringo orders this drink for himself and his mates in *Help!* (1965).

"Laver" — ("Blancmanges Playing Tennis") Rod Laver (b. 1938), successful Australian tennis player, won four singles championships at Wimbledon (1961–1962, 1968–1969). He is also mentioned in the "Australian Wine" sketch for the Python album *Monty Python's Previous Record* (1972), performed by "Wine Expert" Eric Idle:

> The Australian Wino Society thoroughly recommends a 1970 Coq du Rod Laver, which, believe me, has a kick on it like a mule: 8 bottles of this and you're really finished. At the opening of the Sydney Bridge Club, they were fishing them out of the main sewers every half an hour. (side 2)

The "Laver Institute" is mentioned in Ep. 38, where penguins are being studied by tennis players, including Bartkowicz, Ken Rosewall (b. 1934, Australia), and Jack Kramer (b. 1921, United States). See the entry for "Stolle, Fred" below, as well as Ep. 38, for more.

"leave your radio on during the night" — (link into "Science Fiction Sketch") As television programming would halt at night (and during the war, cease entirely), radios were often left on through the nights to hear civil defense news, warnings, evacuation announcements, etc.

A 1963 article in the *Times* on *Dixon of Dock Green* and its long-lasting popularity notes the importance of such "home-made" shows and characters, and how they worked their way into the hearts and minds of the British listening and viewing public. It also defines the background against which the Pythons would create their own characters and settings, their images and actions of authority—they came of age under the influence of these shows:

> In one category come *Dixon of Dock Green* and *Z Cars*, both of which derive in a way from the example set by sound radio many years ago. During the war, especially, the B.B.C. was indefatigable in producing feature programmes on sound which were designed to inform us about our duties and responsibilities: documentaries about Careless Talk, growing onions in the window-box, playing our part in Civil Defence. These dramatizations of our social obligations were intended, first, to inform us of what was expected of us and, second, to create a familiar and agreeable image of our responsibilities. The "nick" at Dock Green is, in the same sense, an image of how law and order are maintained, and a reminder to us to do all those things which assist the police. Dixon and the rest of them are there to protect us; if we trust them and help them the miscreants will always be brought to book. Failure is unknown, indeed unthinkable, in the Dock Green station, and the blue lamp is the comforting symbol of their infallibility. . . . This well-made serial is propaganda of the most palatable kind. ("Case for the Home-Made Detective," 2 Feb. 1963: 4)

"license fee" — (link into "Science Fiction Sketch") This is the mandatory fee paid annually by all TV and radio owners, and which funds the BBC. The subject of the requisite television license fee appears often throughout May 1969 in political cartoons. The license fees as of 1 January 1969 are displayed in Ep. 20, as the credits roll.

The "Jewish Figure" (Palin) seems less concerned about the rising fee than for the quality of the broadcast material it's paying for.

"lira" — ("The Audit") Italian denomination, indicating this corporation does business (and/or has a business presence) internationally.

"London Road, Oxford" — (link into "Science Fiction Sketch") London Road actually runs through Oxford, approximately east-west to/from Headington, which at least the Oxfordians of the troupe (Jones and Palin) would have known, and probably very well.

The "silly address" motif will reappear throughout *FC*, and is a response to the BBC's (and other local networks' and even newspapers') policy of airing letters from patrons. See entry for "viewer's letter" in Ep. 5, as well as the entry for "East Grinstead" in that same episode. (*Private Eye* also published mostly farcical letters made to look like ones sent to the BBC and *Daily Mirror*, etc. They did publish one or two proper letters of complaint from angry readers, as well, which were just as funny.) The BBC often went out of its way to promote regional viewership by catering to those more provincial areas.

". . . look after yourselves" — ("Police Station") The very picture of the paternal, all-embracing police or government presence in postwar Britain—powerful enough to interrupt BBC broadcasts, funny and perhaps chilling at the same time. This type of policeman harks back to the warm, avuncular PC Dixon (see Morgan below), and the "direct address" mode is borrowed directly from the beginning and ending of the beloved *Dixon of Dock Green* television episodes. Also, the postwar welfare society instigated and expanded by consecutive Labour (Attlee, 1945–1951) and Conservative (Churchill, 1951–1955; Anthony Eden, 1955–1957; Macmillan, 1957–1963) governments posited a similar warm embrace, but at the national level (e.g., "British restaurants," cradle to grave health care, nationalized industries).

In *Britain since 1945*, Kenneth Morgan characterizes the postwar English police force this way:

> In no country did the unarmed police enjoy a more natural respect, with the folk imagery of the "bobby on the beat," later to be given support in the film *The Blue Lamp* [1950] and later still in the highly popular television serial *PC 49* [BBC Radio and TV, 1947–1953]. The policeman was less a custodian of order . . . than a servant of the community who retrieved lost dogs and helped old ladies across the road. (60–61)

So this is the type of police force the Pythons would have all grown up with, and had reinforced in myriad TV and film depictions. For more on this topic, see notes to Ep. 29, under the "Evening all" entry, or earlier, in Ep. 5, under "All right!"

• M •

"Mary" — ("Science Fiction Sketch") A most Catholic name choice (in a most Popish country), just as Angus might be the stereotypical Scottish male name of choice. In Ep. 22, Mary, Queen of Scots will be murdered (in two eerily similar radio drama episodes).

McWoolworths — ("Man Turns into Scotsman") Satirizing the frequent Scottish use of the prefix "Mc" or "Mac" in front of their proper names. (The prefix "mac" or "mc" is Gaelic for "son," and can be properly McDonald, MacDonald, Macdonald, etc.) This is, then, another typal instance, a shorthand way to identify or apply Scottishness in humor, and especially satire. This is the very type of belittlement that the Pythons will not employ in regard to the Irish, who won't be mentioned at all except in the "Our Eamonn" sketch. See notes to Ep. 31 for more on this conspicuous absence.

Woolworths is the proprietary name of a chain of department stores in Great Britain and the United States and founded in 1878.

"mebbe . . . gi'" — ("Science Fiction Sketch") More Scottish colloquial spellings for Podgorny's approximate pronunciations. His accent is much thicker than even these special spellings indicate. A word like "has" is pronounced "hah," for instance.

mid-shot — (PSC; "Science Fiction Sketch") Medium camera shot, generally from the waist to just above the top of the subject's head. This is one of the few instances where camera directions, especially camera-to-subject distance, are mentioned in the written scripts. It could be that Terry Jones, who always had an interest in the actual direction and editing of the program, influenced this inclusion.

Mix to picture of same thing in newspaper — ("Mr. Attila the Hun") This newspaper was created for and used much earlier in Ep. 2, specifically the "Mouse Problem" sketch. The headline "Peer Faces Rodent Charges" can be seen.

moor — ("Science Fiction Sketch") Unenclosed wasteland, essentially, often covered in heather or gorse, depending on the latitude. A "moor" is often used symbolically or poetically to depict loneliness and distance from civilization, and is, for example, typically a Sir Walter Scott novel setting (Ep. 38). The Goons used the "lonely moor[s]" as settings for many episodes, including portions of "Around the World in Eighty Days" (21 Feb. 1957), and "The Yehti" (8 Mar. 1955).

"Mr. Llewellyn" — ("Man Turns into Scotsman") This gets a big laugh, perhaps because the specter of a Welshman turning into a Scotsman is even more outrageous than an Englishman doing the same. A well-known referent might be Richard Llewellyn (1906–1983), a Welsh-born novelist, and author of *How Green Was My Valley* (1939). Also, the American ambassador to the Soviet Union during this period was Llewellyn Thompson (1904–1972).

"mummy" — ("Man Turns into Scotsman") British slang for "mommy." The *OED* notes "mummy" as a childish version of "mommy," which would fit the already infantile, pouty, and obviously sexual depiction of the girl in this scene, a "Lolita" figure (Nabokov novel, 1954; Kubrick film, 1962).

music rises — (PSC; "Science Fiction Sketch") The sweating and rising creepy music are also significant generic components of the sci-fi and horror film genres, building tension for the inevitable surprise moment. See entry for "incidental music" above for more.

• N •

New Pudsey — ("Science Fiction Sketch") The train station where we meet the Brainsamples (Chapman and Idle) and Mr. Potter (Palin) is actually New Pudsey, just east of Bradford, where other exteriors for "Science Fiction Sketch" were also shot. The station, opened in 1967, hasn't changed much in the intervening forty-plus years.

newspaper — ("Man Turns into Scotsman") Actually, this is just a sandwich board–type sign with a handwritten headline under the *Daily Gazette* banner. These boards are still seen on London streets advertising the day's headlines.

"nip" — ("Science Fiction Sketch") *OED*: "To move rapidly or nimbly."

"no fun anymore" — ("You're No Fun Anymore") An admission that the "comic misunderstanding" characteristic of Renaissance comic history (where, for instance, a commoner is confused with a king) is necessary for the structure of Python humor to stand in this instance (see *MPSERD*, 132). Once the absurdity of the situation is noticed or identified by one of its participants, the narrative must move on to something else, some other constructed absurdity. Cf. the sketch where members of "The Society for Putting Things on Top of Other Things" realize how silly their society really is (and all other similar societies)—they halt the meeting and disband—only to discover they are trapped on film as opposed to video, and a new silliness begins.

• O •

oil lamps etc. — (PSC; "Science Fiction Sketch") The cottage interior seems as rustic as it can get, missing only any visible sign of the oats (or perhaps grazing animals) that both Dr. Johnson and Python would have connected inseparably with a tatty Scottish household.

In his *Dictionary* Johnson defines "oats" as a "grain which in England is generally given to horses, but in Scotland supports the people." Johnson's biographer Boswell, a Scot himself, would later note: "It was pleasant to me to find that 'oats,' the 'food of horses,' were so much used as the food of the people in Dr. Johnson's own town" (*Life of Johnson*, v. 1). Here the interior of the purported "men's wear shop" (a studio set) is made to match the rustic exterior (a photograph of the Skye Cottage Museum), a crofter's cottage surrounded by gorse and grazing sheep.

". . . ought not to go, Angus" — ("Science Fiction Sketch") Foreshadowing, or the prescience that characters often display in sci-fi and horror films that something nefarious, creeping, unforeseen, or calamitous is about to happen. In *Invasion of the Body Snatchers* (1956), Wilma (Virginia Christine) knows that her uncle isn't her uncle anymore, but can't prove it before she, too, is "changed"; in the even earlier *The Invisible Man* (1933), Flora (Gloria Stuart) begs Griffin (Claud Rains) to stop experimenting, certain that it will destroy him. Usually, though, these are the characters that survive, while those who ignore such warnings almost inevitably die. Again, since Mrs. Podgorny (Jones) herself will soon be consumed, Python is undermining audience expectations of the genre.

over the head — ("Man Turns into Scotsman") Just one of many examples where females (actual females, not cross-dressed males) in *FC* are treated with violence that is less cartoon-like. See also the Art Critic (Palin) strangling his wife (Ep. 8) and the shooting of Brian (Cleveland) in "The Lost World of Roiurama," Ep. 29.

• P •

"pelote" — ("Man Turns into Scotsman") Any of a number of ball games played in France, Spain, Mexico, the Philippines, etc.

photo — (PSC; link into "Science Fiction Sketch") This quick photo of a somewhat grizzled farmer-type, coupled with the voiceover reminding viewers to leave their radios on during the night, elicit a laugh from the audience—perhaps as a result of the incongruity of the moment. This photo is not accounted for in the WAC records for the episode.

This also follows the "license fee" reference, and radios were also subject to license fees until 1971, as a result of the Wireless Telegraphy Act of 1904 (licensed by the Postmaster General).

"pinches" — ("You're No Fun Anymore") Steals, purloins.

pitch — ("Science Fiction Sketch") Usually associated with cricket, but any playing field or surface can be called a pitch. In this case, the players are moving onto the tennis court.

plainclothes man — (PSC; "Police Station") Policeman not wearing a uniform. This is unusual for *FC*, since this out-of-uniform policeman isn't instantly recognizable, and therefore more difficult to identify as a type. In this scene, then, the policeman (Idle) must identify himself by personality and actions. His anger (he slaps Angus) at being mistaken for a lowly sergeant—"Detective Inspector!"—only happens because he isn't uniformed, and Mr. Podgorny (Palin) can't rely on visual cues to determine rank and status.

"plucky" — ("Blancmanges Playing Tennis") *OED*: "Characterized by pluck; showing determination to fight or struggle; brave, courageous, daring." This usage is also probably somewhat paternalistic and meant to diminish, as these Englishmen note the tenacity of even the lowly Scots. "Pluck" was the general character trait of many figures in the Ealing comedies of the postwar era, including *Passport to Pimlico* (1949), and *The Man in the White Suit* (1951), all brimming with English eccentricity and pluck. The rueful joke was that these characters had little else in the postwar years of austerity and rationing.

"Podgorny" — ("Science Fiction Sketch") Another name in the news at the time of this episode's writing was Nikolay Viktorovich Podgorny, a well-known Soviet statesman and Communist Party official. Podgorny traveled significantly, and was involved in a much-publicized power struggle for Soviet leadership—viz., the eventual overthrow of Nikita Khrushchev—along with Leonid Brezhnev in the mid-1960s. See Ep. 20 for a still photo and another mention of Podgorny. Podgorny is mentioned dozens of times in London newspapers in mid-to-late 1969 alone, when the Pythons were writing and recording this first season. And even earlier, an assassination attempt in January 1969 (where Soviet cosmonauts or party secretary Brezhnev may have been targeted) brought Podgorny prominently into the headlines ("How Lieut Ilyin Came to Moscow," *Times*, 4 Feb. 1969: 8). Curious that Angus would have such a non-Scots name, too, unless there is also a subtextual reference to the "them" of the Communist conspiracy of the period.

"Potter, Harold" — ("Science Fiction Sketch") This could be an oblique reference to Harold Potter, the author of the substantially soporific *The Principles and Practice of Conveyancing* (London, 1934). "Harold Potter" is also the name of a hoist company in existence in Nottingham (East Midlands) since 1921. Thirdly, Cleese could have contributed the name, as the very prominent Harold Potter had taught, practiced, and written in the area of English law for many years at Kings College, London. This Potter (author of *The Quest of Justice*) was cited as a legal scholar on English law many times in period newspapers (*Times*, 27 Jan. 1967: 11).

The name itself, "Potter," may be significant: *OED*: "Trifling action or (in Scott) talk. Also, a gentle stroll or saunter." Harold Potter, as underplayed by Palin, does fit these descriptions nicely.

Potter's front gate — (PSC; "Man Turns into Scotsman") The appropriately bad flying saucer scenes (looking every bit as accomplished as those found in Ed Wood's acclaimed *Plan 9 from Outer Space*) were shot in the BBC's puppet theater at TV Centre.

The backdrops in the puppet theater are composited (retouched) still photos of the central London area. Portland House (a very rectangular, International Style skyscraper built in 1963) can be clearly seen in the distance in the first photo, before Mr. Potter is changed. The second photo (when the aliens' "changing beam" fires down from the bouncy, dangling little ship), is also at least partially of the central London area, but appears to be even more of a composite photo, with a Lincoln Cathedral–type structure looming in the distance over London-area rooftops.

The scene just at "Potter's front gate" was shot at 19 Southmere Terrace in Bradford, even though this address is not listed in the WAC records as an approved location (which was often the case). It's the corner house, and the street corner Mr. Potter (Palin) and the Inspector (Jones) march around is and was a dead end, though now an adjacent tract of homes can be reached via this street. The troupe were filming in locations in and around Bradford, 10–14 November 1969. There is no specific address information in the WAC records, except that they were set to shoot in Bradford, Addlestone, and Ilkley Moor. See T12/1091, T12/1092, and T12/1242 for these mentions. Many of the locations used in the filming but not accounted for in the WAC records have been identified in the following pages.

"Provost of Edinburgh" — ("Science Fiction Sketch") Historically, provosts collected taxes and fines, and served as military leaders and judges. A very curious outburst, this might be an oblique reference to an incident described in Sir Walter Scott's novel *The Antiquary* (1816):

> "Alarm?" said Edie, "troth there's alarm, for the *provost's* gar'd the beacon light on the Halket-head be sorted up (that suld hae been sorted half a year syne) in an unco hurry, and the council hae named nae less a man than auld Caxon himsell to watch the light. Some say it was out o' compliment to Lieutenant Taffril,—for it's neist to certain that he'll marry Jenny Caxon,—some say it's to please your honour and Monkbarns that wear wigs—and some say there's some auld story about a periwig that ane o' the bailies got and neer paid for—Onyway, there he is, *sitting cockit up like a skart upon the tap o' the craig, to skirl when foul weather comes.*" (italics added; chapter 43)

Roughly translated, the final sentence describes the man as sitting proudly (cockit) like a cormorant (skart) on the top or point (tap) of the crag (craig). (The heavily pleated kilt was actually known to have often helped turn aside spear and sword thrusts.)

Sir Walter Scott will be mentioned significantly later, in Ep. 38, the "*A Book at Bedtime*" sketch, where multiple cast members attempt to read aloud excerpts from Scott's novel *Redgauntlet* (1824).

• R •

railway line — ("The Audit") This is a comic variation of the stereotypical silent gag (from early Biograph films—Griffith's *The Lonedale Operator* [1912], for example) of the "lady in distress" lying across a railroad track. Also popularized in the cartoon world of Bill Scott and Jay Ward, *Rocky and Bullwinkle and Friends* (1959–1967), where heroic Dudley Do-Right saved Nell more than once from a similar fate. (*The Bullwinkle Show* first appeared on Granada TV on 22 August 1962, and was scheduled to air late in the evening). These American cartoons were very deft social and especially political satires, poking at the Cold War powers, the space and arms race, Middle Eastern contentions and contenders, TV and advertising, and so on, puncturing many of the same targets the Pythons would draw down on just a few years later.

"Rayners Lane" — (link into "Science Fiction Sketch") Rayners Road runs through Putney, a London suburb.

red coat — ("Science Fiction Sketch") An oily compère, usually played by either Idle or Palin. Here, Palin takes the role. Probably just a well-known type here, but the Butlin's Holiday Camps employed ubiquitous redcoats as camp directors. The Goons had mentioned Billy Butlin and his camps as well, including "The Call of the West" (20 Jan. 1959). The scene is shot at the Staines Recreation Ground (WAC T12/1,086).

"refreshment . . . collector" — ("Camel Spotting") All parts of a normal passenger train operating in the UK to this day. The restaurant car serves full meals, the buffet is for lighter fare, and the ticket collector simply ensures that all passengers are ticketed. This fixation on trains and train travel is something of a British national mania, probably due to the indelibly scored images of and experiences with train travel so important to the UK since the mid-nineteenth century.

"rhetorically" — ("Man Turns into Scotsman") Here Charles is speaking rhetorically, a moment of higher thinking, while just two lines before he is extremely literal as he responds, "Hello mummy." Cf. the RSM in the "Self-Defence" sketch, who can teach his students about the dangers of fresh fruit one moment, and react in horror the next when one of those same students mentions a fruit by name.

"Riley" — ("Police Station") "Doghouse Reilly" is the fake name Marlowe offers to the flirtatious Carmen Sternwood in Raymond Chandler's novel *The Big Sleep* (1939).

Rise and Fall of the Roman Empire — ("Police Station") At the time of the writing of this episode, there were no extant books featuring this specific title. What the Pythons may have been referring to was the quite old *Reflections on the Causes of the Rise and Fall of the Roman Empire*, by Montesquieu (1689–1755), first published c. 1725. The book seems to have been fairly popular, being republished in both London and Scotland in the nineteenth century, probably for university library use.

Not an authoress, Googie Withers (1917–2011) was an actress, one of the many "plucky" Ealing Studios starlets of the postwar period (appearing in the comedy horror film *Dead of Night* in 1945, for example). She had not appeared in a feature film since 1956, taking up the craft again in 1971.

Runs to stop and puts out hand — ("Man Turns into Scotsman") The lonely shot where businessman Jones gets on and drives the bus was recorded at the corner of Commonwealth Avenue and India Way, Hammersmith and Fulham, in the same large housing project the WAC records indicate (off of Bloemfontein Road; T12/1,088). White City Stadium (now demolished) was just beyond the housing area, and BBC Television Centre isn't much farther. Once again the bus is the OLD 666, seen earlier in Ep. 3.

• S •

"Saturday (near Sunday)" — (link into "Science Fiction Sketch") Perhaps an oblique reference to the title of the film *Saturday Night and Sunday Morning* (1960), starring Albert Finney and directed by Karel Reisz. This Saturday night to Sunday morning stretch of time is also key to the conflict in part of Cunegonde's tale in *Candide*, wherein she is being shared by the Jew and the Inquisitor. Also, see the entry above for "Covent Garden."

Scotsman — (PSC; "Man Turns into Scotsman") The implication here is that a Scotsman isn't a man to begin with. This carries on the age-old, Dr. Samuel Johnson–led assault on all things Scottish, assaults happily reported and countered by his biographer Boswell. Johnson admitted to Boswell that he purposely tried to "vex" the Scots people by his definition of oats in his *Dictionary*. This is a good example of Python's Other characterizations—anything non-English is suspect.

Perhaps the Pythons' penchant for drawing down on Scotsmen and Scotland (Scotsmen on horses, Scotsmen wearing no underwear, Scotsmen as inept skyjackers, Scotsmen with inadequate brain capacities, Scotsmen as kamikaze bombers, etc.) can be traced back to their comedy heroes the Goons. The Scotsman is for the Goons a consistent target, whether just the use of an outrageous Scots accent, or the setting/subject matter of an entire episode, including "The Treasure of Loch Lomond" (28 Feb. 1956) and "The Curse of Frankenstein" (27 Jan. 1958). The Goons embrace and celebrate Scottish stereotypes—from thriftiness to diminished intelligence to country manners to a penchant for violence. The almost complete absence of *Goon Show* references to the Irish or Ireland, however, is also worth mentioning—a very similar lack seen in *FC*. More on this structuring Irish absence in the notes to Ep. 31, the "Our Eamonn" sketch.

In the *Goon Show* episode "Emperor of the Universe," incidentally, it's Englishmen who are leaving England in droves.

Scottish crofter's cottage on a lonely moor — (PSC; "Mr. and Mrs. Angus Podgorny") The photo used here is unattributed (not accounted for in the WAC records for the episode), but it is clearly an image of at least a portion of the Skye Cottage Museum near Portree, Scotland. The opening of the thatched roof museum was covered in the *Times* in May 1965 ("Skye Cottage Now Museum," 29 May 1965: 10).

Seventh Seal — (PSC; "Man Turns into Scotsman") A 1955 Swedish film written and directed by Ingmar Bergman. The Pythons were well aware of both European art films and Hollywood fare. The latter would have been available through the first-run movie houses across the country; during the postwar years Hollywood films were far outpacing British films on British screens. The Oxbridge university settings of the period happened to house the target audiences for filmmakers of the French New Wave (1959–1967), Das Neue Kino (1962–1982), and even Akira Kurosawa's internationally influential years (1950–1985). The famous shot from Bergman's masterpiece isn't quite realized here—the distance from subject and the position of the sun don't allow for the proper silhouette effect Bergman was able to create.

The high seriousness, artsy-ness, and Dark Ages setting of *Seventh Seal* would help inspire *Monty Python and the Holy Grail* almost two decades later.

"shareholders" — ("The Audit") Owners of stock (shares) in a company or corporation. The Pythons are/were, themselves, shareholders in *FC* and the films and merchandise that have followed.

"shilling" — ("The Audit") *OED*: "A former English money of account, from the Norman Conquest of the value of 12d., or of a pound sterling." The shilling would disappear in 1971 with the new monetary system. See the entry for "12/6D" in Ep. 6. The new monetary system is discussed in Ep. 27. See the "new pence" entry there for more on the change.

"shivers" — ("Science Fiction Sketch") A response generally reserved for the horror genre, though in the 1950s hybridizations of the horror and sci-fi genres occurred (see *The Beast from 20,000 Fathoms*, *Them!*, and *Tarantula*), creating more frightening technology-spawned creatures.

"sixpence" — ("The Audit") Obsolete monetary unit equal to six pennies. Mr. Pewtey has mentioned the sixpenny bottle in which he and his lovely wife save money during the "Marriage Guidance Counsellor" sketch in Ep. 2.

"Sol" — ("Science Fiction Sketch") The sun personified. The starscape background used in the opening portion of this sketch was 35mm stock film secured from Technicolor (WAC T12/1,088).

"Sopwith" — (PSC; "Camel Spotting") The Sopwith Camel, designed by Sir Thomas Octave Murdoch Sopwith (1888–1989), was Britain's premier fighter plane during WWI. The comic character Snoopy flew this "plane" (his doghouse), as well, as he portrayed the World War I Fighter Ace in "Peanuts."

"sporrans" — ("Science Fiction Sketch") The "kilt" reference is self-explanatory, but a "sporran" is a bit more specialized: "A pouch or large purse made of skin, usually with the hair left on and with ornamental tassels, etc., worn in front of the kilt by Scottish Highlanders" (*OED*).

spotting gear — (PSC; "Camel Spotting") The camel spotter is wearing hunting cap, plaid coat, etc., and uses binoculars. He could be a bird or train spotter, easily.

"Stolle, Fred . . . Haydon-Jones" — ("Blancmanges Playing Tennis") More than just a list of great British tennis players, this is a current sports page featuring the best players from around the world at that time. Fred Stolle (b. 1938) was the undefeated Australian Wimbledon Champion in 1966; Tony Roche (b. 1945, Australia) was a world Top Ten tennis player between 1965 and 1971; Charlie Pasarell (b. 1944, Puerto Rico) was U.S. Singles Champion in 1967; Cliff Drysdale (b. 1941, South Africa) was founding president of the Association of Tennis Professionals and credited as the first player to use the two-handed backhand swing; and Jane "Peaches" Bartkowitz (b. 1949, United States)—misspelled by the Pythons "Jane 'Peaches' Bartcowicz"—was one of the founders of the women's tennis tour in 1970. Bartkowicz will appear (played by Palin) in Ep. 38, the "BBC Programme Planners" sketch. (Also, Bartkowicz was playing a tournament in the middle of May 1969 in Athens, and winning, when the Pythons were writing/recording these episodes.) Finally, Ann Haydon-Jones (b. 1938, Birmingham) was a Brit who won Wimbledon (in 1969) as the first female left-hander. Haydon-Jones's husband's name was actually P.F. Jones. (See wimbledon.org.)

• T •

"Thaxted" — (link into "Science Fiction Sketch") Thaxted is found in Uttlesford, and in the county of Essex.

"Them!" — ("Man Turns into Scotsman") Title of a 1954 sci-fi classic about atomically mutated ants in the southwestern United States. In *Them!*, a little girl survives her family's massacre by marauding mutant ants, her first words upon emerging from catatonia being "Them! Them!" In the mock sci-fi case here, the "them" are the blancmanges, and by association the "othered" Scotsmen.

"There is no place for sentiment in Big Business" — ("The Audit") According to *Private Eye*, this was an oft-repeated Heath-ism during his years in the leadership of the Tory Opposition (*PE*, 4 Dec. 1970: 17). In a period review of a 1966 episode of Rediffusion's *The Rat Catchers*, the critic laments the drama's turgid dialogue, including gems like: "There's no place for sentiment inside this room—or outside it, for that matter" (*Times*, 12 Apr. 1966: 13).

"They" — (Man Turns into Scotsman") Throughout the episode the female character has not been and will not be given a name at all, rather identified by her gender, "She." Grammatically, then, this puts her into the same category as "they," the aliens. "She" is singular nominative, while "they" is plural nominative ("them" being plural objective). So the text categorizes her really only different in number from the blancmanges—she is an Other with "them."

thrilling chord — (PSC; "Man Turns into Scotsman") Generic to the horror/sci-fi genre(s). Also used by Python to announce the appearance of the Inquisitors in Ep. 15. Used again in *Holy Grail* to accompany shocking moments like the appearance of the killer rabbit.

"throw them under a camel" — ("You're No Fun Anymore") The phrase "you're no fun anymore" has itself been pinched (and slightly rephrased) from Ep. 1, where the Nazi officer tells his uncooperative British captive, "Ah . . . you're no fun." Such intertextuality is characteristic of the Python oeuvre; they, like Shakespeare, quote themselves often, creating afresh history and texts. See the "dull" note above.

"toon" — ("Science Fiction Sketch") *OED*: "Northern dialect for town." Palin, from the north, would have been quite familiar with the local accents, and often took on the northern parts. See Morgan's *Speaks!*.

"tough abrasive look" — ("Camel Spotting") Again, the no-holds-barred approach to journalism à la interviewer Robin Day, the declining "refinement" characteristic of much of the TV documentary tradition in British broadcasting of the period. See Ep. 1, *"It's the Arts"* sketch.

"trainspotter" — ("Camel Spotting") One who, as a hobby, looks for, identifies, and often notes trains (numbers, styles, names). This hobby has moved well beyond the purview of just young boys, and is enjoyed by many of all ages. There are spotters of all kinds, not just for trains. Buses, ships, canal boats, and even cars can be spotted as a hobby, and individual information recorded. In the Basil Dearden film *League of Gentlemen* (1960), the intricately plotted heist is unraveled by a small boy—he's innocently spotting license plates (he's excited to see an "Alabama" plate in London) and notes the thieves' getaway car.

"Tristram and Isolde" — (link into "Science Fiction Sketch") A play on the characters Tristan and Isolde (but also spelled Tristram and Tristrem, and Iseult, Isolt, or Yseult), a medieval love-romance based on

Celtic legend, itself based on an actual Pictish king. Matthew Arnold wrote "Tristram and Iseult" (1852), a three-part poem; "Tristram and Isoud" is Malory's fifth of eight *Works*; and Swinburne published his "Tristram of Lyonesse" in 1882, a poem in heroic couplets.

twizzles — (PSC; "Science Fiction Sketch") Rotates rapidly.

"two goes" — ("Science Fiction Sketch") Two trips. The comment here may be that even though the Scotsman Angus isn't terribly bright, his industry, dedication, and work ethic are laudable. He will also figure prominently in overcoming the alien invasion by defeating the blancmange at Wimbledon. The Pythons' trope will become obvious: they will jab and attack, then ultimately recover their target. The Scots are a backward and rustic people, but they alone will be able to defeat the global threat. Pepperpots, homosexuals, even Conservatives—all are skewered and embraced, skewered and embraced. This paradigm runs throughout *FC*. See Larsen's *MPSERD*.

• W •

"wasna" — ("Science Fiction Sketch") Contraction/conflation of "was not," part of Palin's continuing take on "Scottishness." "Na" is a variation of "nay."

"Waterloo" — ("Camel Spotting") Railway station in Lambeth, London. Heavily damaged in WWII, then rebuilt. Now part of this station serves as a terminus for the Channel Tunnel service.

weird electronic music — ("Man Turns into Scotsman") Again, as with all of the music heard in this episode, this electronic composition is not accounted for in the WAC records for this episode (WAC T12/1,088).

Popularized in sci-fi films by Bebe and Louis Barron in the 1956 movie *Forbidden Planet*, electronic music (tonalities) is a twentieth-century art form made possible by the creation of early synthesizers, which began to appear as early as 1909. RCA created its Electronic Music Synthesizer in 1955, releasing albums of electronic music (music made without musical instruments) soon thereafter.

"Who are Them?" — ("Man Turns into Scotsman") This scene, where the hero (scientist, military man, or normal citizen) thinks aloud, is also a staple of the sci-fi genre. It's also an example of the genre's tendency to be overly and overtly expository.

"Wimbledon" — ("Science Fiction Sketch") City located about eight miles southwest of London, and is the site of the annual All-England Championships, known as the Wimbledon Championships.

"Wimbledon fortnight"—The two-week run of the Wimbledon Championships. In 1969, Wimbledon began 23 June 1969, and the Pythons had begun meeting and writing by late May 1969. They continued to work, together and in teams, through June and July 1969, with a 24 August deadline set up by BBC. This episode was taped 30 November 1969.

It's clear that the significant presence of Wimbledon figures and news in the press and on TV during this period accounts for the genesis of this sketch. This isn't an isolated example for the Pythons—writing about or being influenced by current events—as will be seen in Ep. 28, *"Life of Tschaikowsky,"* where the hysteria over the Apollo missions is sent up.

"win Wimbledon" — ("Man Turns into Scotsman") Certainly a reference to the recent paucity of home-grown players (read: English) at the Wimbledon Championships. English tennis player appearances in the final rounds and championship games dropped dramatically in the Python formative years. No English male had won the men's singles since 1936 (when F.J. Perry won); during that same period, just two English women (Ann Haydon-Jones, 1969, and Angela Mortimer, 1961) had won the ladies' singles championship. So the reference to aliens on Wimbledon's courts is a very real complaint that it had been more than thirty years since an Englishman had won Wimbledon—the winners were aliens, all.

At the Wimbledon final in 1961, Rod Laver (Australia) beat Chuck McKinley (USA), but that's as close as England would come to a men's singles championship. Laver would be celebrated as "British" thereafter, just as Sir Edmund Hillary had been after he conquered Everest (he was from New Zealand).

• Y •

yardarm — (PSC; "You're No Fun Anymore") Part of a square-rigged ship, the yard is "a wooden (or steel) spar, comparatively long and slender, slung at its centre from, and forward of, a mast and serving to support and extend a square sail which is bent to it" (*OED*). A yardarm is either end of that yard, then.

Corporal punishment in the Royal Navy had been regularly practiced for generations, with the cat-o'-nine-tails the punishment of choice, and multiple lashes to the bare back (for an adult) or the buttocks (for a child). See the entries "burnt at the stake" and "cat of nine tails" in Ep. 15 for more on corporal and capital punishment in the UK and South Africa.

"Yes . . . she was . . . yes" — ("Police Station") The entire police station exchange is perhaps an allusion to the light and airy banter—liberally spread around to the principal characters, male and female—found throughout sci-fi films like *The Thing from Another World* (1951) and *The Day the Earth Caught Fire* (1961), both featuring fast-talking newspaper types.

"yeti" — ("Camel Spotting") The Tibetan "abominable snowman," a mythical creature. Buddhist monk-wannabe and former plumber Cyril Hoskins (in the guise of Rampa Lobsang) claimed to have encountered a yeti in his Himalayan travels. See notes to Eps. 4 and 29 for more on this diverting character, whose bizarre tales may have provided the Pythons with significant creative inspiration.

• Z •

"zillion" — ("Science Fiction Sketch") A large, hyperbolized number, meant to suggest an unfathomable amount.

Zoom through the galaxy — ("Science Fiction Sketch") The atmospheric music used underneath this setup is not accounted for in the WAC records for this episode. In fact, all the music requests that eventually appear in Ep. 6 are part of the Ep. 7 file, and the Ep. 7 music requests have since disappeared. The episodes were recorded in reverse order.

Episode 8: "Full Frontal Nudity"

"It's" Man and bomb intro; *Animation: Titles* (silly Cleese v/o); "Episode 12B: Full Frontal Nudity," and Vox Pops; "History of Warfare" intro for "Unoccupied Britain 1970"; Army Protection Racket ("I'd like to leave the army," the Vercotti Brothers, and "This is silly!"); The Colonel cues the "telecine" cartoon; *Animation: "Full Frontal Nudity Vol. 2"* and *"An Intimate Review"*; "Full Frontal Nudity" Vox Pops; Art critic—"The place of the nude" malapropisms; "But it's my only line!"; Art critic strangles his wife; Buying a bed ("Don't say mattress"), "Jerusalem"; "Full Frontal Nudity" Vox Pops; The Colonel's "silly" link; Hermits; The Colonel stops a sketch; *Animation: Meat grinder to dancing Botticelli's Venus link*; **Dead parrot**; "A Similar Pet Shop in Bolton," British Rail complaints, and "Notlob" gets too silly; "And now frontal nudity": The Flasher; "And now Notlob": ***Hell's Grannies* documentary**; "This film's got silly"; "Unisex"; "It's" Man exploding bomb credits

• A •

anarchist's type bomb — (PSC; "It's Man" link into opening credits) This bomb is a duplicate version of those seen in cartoons (especially Warner Bros. and MGM during the Chuck Jones and Tex Avery tenures) for many years—round, with a lighted fuse on top. The fact that the bomb is labeled makes the cartoon connection even stronger. It's more a recognizable icon than a threat, of course.

"Apart from that he's perfectly all right" — ("Buying a Bed") Here Mr. Verity (Idle) admits that he's at least aware of Mr. Lambert's (Chapman) perceptual shortcomings, but not his own. So again there are several levels of reality working at once in these sketches, and successful communication or transaction means navigating these levels.

"armoured division" — ("Army Protection Racket") A division consisting of tanks and supporting equipment and men. The British Army's Third Division fits this description.

Art Critic — (PSC; "Art Critic—The Place of the Nude") This is the Art Critic's second appearance in *FC*. We first met him eating paintings and getting Vermeer all over his shirt in Ep. 4. Here he is leering at the painting, attempting to get a better view of the Rubens-like nude from angle-on. (The "Rubens-like" nude was requested in the production files, and was created for the episode.) This type of angle would work very well for the Hans Holbein (1497–1543) work *The Ambassadors* (1533), wherein the anamorphic (oblique) skull created by the artist can only be viewed in its lifelike form from a skewed angle. Holbein's *The Ambassadors* has been on display in the National Gallery since 1890.

• B •

"bag" — ("Hell's Grannies") *OED*: "A disparaging term for a woman, esp. one who is unattractive or elderly." "Rat bag" is also thrown about a few times in *FC*, especially directed at loud, unattractive Python women (like the vulgar and incontinent Mrs. Equator [Jones] in Ep. 9).

"Barbara" — ("Vox Pops") As early as Ep. 1 (during the bicycle race sketch), male characters are given female names. The use of this practice in this situation does lend a sodomitical air, of course, and the moment Barbara (Jones) leans his head on Man's (Chapman) shoulder underlines the point.

"beautiful plumage" — ("Dead Parrot") Much of this exchange sounds familiar, and may have been at least inspired by a scene from the Goons' "The Missing Scroll" episode, where two Yorkshiremen (Sellers and Secombe) discuss a bird with "plumage":

> Sellers: It's in a cage, you say.
> Secombe: Aye. It were innit when I bought it, you know.
> Sellers: Aye. What kind of bird is it?
> Secombe: Well, I'm not sure, really. You see I got it off a sailor, you know.
> Sellers: Oh aye. I say, what's the color of its plumage?
> Secombe: Oh, you can't see it. It's covered with feathers.
> Sellers: Nature's wonderful, isn't it?
> Secombe: Aye.
> Sellers: I don't know what they'll think of next.
> Secombe: Sailor gave it me, you know.
> Sellers: Oh aye?
> Secombe: Aye. A sailor. It's got a red beak at one end, and a tail at the other.
> Sellers: And . . . ?
> Secombe: And a bird in between.
> Sellers: It's in between, then, is it?
> Secombe: Aye.
> Sellers: Aye. That's a good place for it, you know.
> Secombe: Well, he seems to be happy there, you know.
> Sellers: Well then, I wouldn't move him.
> Secombe: I don't think I shall, really.
> Sellers: You know I had one the same build. Beak one end, tail the other and the bird dead in between, it were.
> Secombe: They're like that, aren't they? Funny that, aye. (audio transcription, "The Missing Scroll")

The "Dead Parrot" sketch has been cited as one rewritten from a used car setting, of course, but the hint of the Goons can't be missed.

"barley cross fingers" — ("Army Protection Racket") Kind of a "safe" or "time-out mode" in children's play.

bikini — (PSC; "It's Man" link into opening credits) Prototypical depiction of women as objects in *FC*, with the added element of lethality (a femme fatale notion) borrowed from American pulp cinema (film noir) and novels. See Ep. 22 where both the Announcer (Cleese) and the It's Man (Palin) wear similarly sexy attire which undercuts, at least momentarily, the objectification process, since both men make profoundly unattractive bathing beauties.

"blimey" — ("Army Protection Racket") Shortened form of "blind me" or "blame me."

"blue in the mouth" — ("Dead Parrot") Generally phrased as "blue in the face," meaning talking until one runs out of breath and turns blue. As will be demonstrated in his later memorable appearances in Eps. 19 and 23, Praline (Cleese) is just the type of character to conjure these kinds of portmanteau sayings. In Ep. 31, another character (Chapman) will further mangle the phrase, saying "blue in the breast."

"Bolton" — ("Dead Parrot") Bolton is in Greater Manchester, Lancashire. Bolton is also reportedly home to a Mrs. Teal's lover as exposed on the air during the "*Blackmail*" sketch in Ep. 18.

In the *Euroshow 71—May Day Special*, Bolton, Lancashire is noted as the home of a particularly odd May Day ritual, the "annual return of the overdue library book, a much-loved ceremony that somehow captures the spirit of all that is most colorful, exciting, and indeed exotic in the north of England," according to Cleese's hushed narration. The film footage—of a Pewtey-like Palin marching along a high street, book in hand—was actually recorded not in Bolton but in Greater London, specifically Ealing, and he is returning the library book to the former Pitzhanger Manor/Library. Palin walks along New Broadway, Ealing, past the Squire Records shop (at 28 New Broadway) as he goes to return a book. Portions of Ep. 15 will also use the Pitzhanger building.

"boo" — ("The Flasher") The expectation is that the man is "flashing" those on the street, exposing himself. The payoff of the sign around his neck—"boo"—is a direct borrowing/steal from the 1945 Warner Bros. cartoon featuring Daffy Duck and Elmer Fudd, called *Ain't That Ducky* (dir. I. Freleng). In the cartoon, Daffy and Elmer attempt to see what's inside a valise being held by a young duck—who cries every time he looks inside, yet violently refuses the others even a peek. The payoff (from the valise) is a title card reading "The End." The influence of American animation on the Pythons and especially their use of speed, violence, and gaggery can be seen throughout *FC*, and will be noted where it appears.

"bother" — ("Army Protection Racket") *OED*: "To give trouble to; to pester, annoy, worry." Here, though, Dino pronounces the word as "bovver," which the *OED* identifies as appearing in relation to the disturbances created by skinhead (or "crophead") gangs of the late 1960s. The Pythons are thus hybridizing the age-old Mafia-type violence and threats with the more recent skinhead phenomenon, conflating images from their collective past knowledge and contemporary experience.

Botticelli Venus — (PSC; link into "Dead Parrot") Sandro Botticelli (1445–1510) was a Florentine Renaissance painter who worked for the de Medici court. He painted this most famous painting (*Birth of Venus*) in about 1485. This image of Venus is used often by Gilliam as part of his animations, including a recurring facial image in the opening credits. Soviet animator Fyodor Khitruk (1917–2012) also uses the image in his 1966 short *Man in the Frame*. The cut-out image Gilliam uses here eventually falls into the fish tank on the pet shop set, completing the transition between scenes.

The music underneath is "Gonna Get a Girl" by Harry Bidgood and His Broadcasters (Fox Trot) (WAC T12/1,089).

"bracken" — ("Hermits") Dead undergrowth. Arthur and his knights must bring shrubbery to the Knights Who Say "Ni" in *Holy Grail*; and in the later feature film made by Palin and Gilliam, *Time Bandits* (1981), the heroes will be God's shrubbery and bracken makers.

"British Rail" — ("Dead Parrot") Britain's national railway system, publicly held since passage of the Transport Act of 1947, and which at its largest employed almost 500,000 and operated trains on as many as 17,500 miles of tracks.

• C •

Cartoon rubbish entitled "Full Frontal Nudity" — (PSC; animated "Full Frontal Nudity" link into "Vox Pops") The five Pythons not involved in the animation process regularly had no idea what Gilliam was producing during their week of rehearsing and taping, just that he would fill the allotted time slot with often thematically contiguous animated images: "*Cartoon rubbish entitled 'Full Frontal Nudity': Written, created and conceived off the back of a lorry by a demented American*" (Ep. 8).

Incidentally, "rubbish" is producer John Howard Davies's description of the early episodes, on more than one occasion, in BBC memos. See the BBC Written Archives Collection for the first season.

The music Gilliam uses underneath this animated segment is Mantovani's "The Most Beautiful Girl in the World" by Rodgers and Hart (WAC T12/1,089).

The final image of nudity in this sequence—when the animated compère turns, naked, and "her" behind can be seen—is borrowed from the extensive Ronnie Barker postcard collection. The image is also used in the 1974 book *Ronnie Barker's Book of Bathing Beauties*, page 4, on the "Foreword" page. There is no attribution for these photos. This is the same model used earlier in the sequence, the third woman who turns away as the page is turned ("Full Frontal Nudity Vol. 2").

Chartered Accountant — ("Vox Pops") Cleese wears the recognizable uniform of a City Gent here. Chartered accountancy is implicated often in *FC* as dull, so it's no surprise that a chartered accountant might be looking for any kind of stimuli, including "full frontal nudity" scenes.

"chastise" — ("Hermits") This element of self-flagellation (whether emotionally or physically) still indicates hermit types in seclusion for religious purposes, seeking an ascetic lifestyle in the wilds—a sort of a John the Baptist, locusts-and-honey life. There is a significant scene in Bergman's *The Seventh Seal* (cf. Ep. 7, "Science Fiction Sketch") depicting medieval flagellants. Living with other hermits, of course, makes this more like the suburbs than the wilderness, and closer to some *monastic* lifestyles, where self-chastisement and self-flagellation were employed for penance.

"closing for lunch" — ("Dead Parrot") See Ep. 4, where the entire sketch involving international dental intrigue comes to a halt when lunch break is called. Like the wolf and sheepdog characters in Warner Bros. cartoons, when the whistle blows, the day's work is over and characters drop their business personas and go their separate ways. In Ep. 32, the characters decide to simply abandon the "silliest sketch" they've ever done, then get up and leave the set. In *HG*, the historical epic itself will be stopped by the appearance of the modern constabulary, and a hand over the camera lens.

colonel — ("Army Protection Racket") London gangster Ronnie Kray's nickname was, ironically, "The Colonel." For more on the Kray brothers see notes to Ep. 14.

"Commission" — (end credits) Actually, picking at nits, it was announced at the beginning of the show that a piece of wood would serve as David Hemmings for the show, meaning Hemmings himself wasn't even appearing. The last voiceover might have more accurately said, then, "The piece of wood portraying David Hemmings appeared by permission of the National Forestry Commission." See the entry below for "David Hemmings" for much more on the general critical reception of Hemmings's films and performances.

"crochet" — ("Hell's Grannies") A needlework hobby, and often associated (at least iconically) with sedate, harmless older women. So it's an addiction to crochet instead of heroin or hashish; the grannies have a "habit," and they steal to support that habit. This turnabout—the young feeling responsible for how their elders turned out—is an incongruous reversal of the expected, but might be explained by the distance created between generations after the war years. Many more young people left home for school and work than had prior to the war, making their own way in the world, meaning that as the parent generation aged, the traditional structure of child assuming responsibility for parent was more alien, more strained.

"cuttlefish" — ("Dead Parrot") A cuttlefish is a relative of the octopus and squid. In the audio (LP, CD) and live versions of this sketch, Cleese often replaces "cuttlefish" with "banana." The Pythons would have encountered cuttlefish as a food item on trips to Spain, undoubtedly, especially the coastal (resort) areas.

Cut to two naked men — (PSC; "'Full Frontal Nudity' Vox Pops") This Vox Pops scene was shot during the production of the "Dull Life of a City Stockbroker" sketch for Ep. 6. The Pythons scheduled and filmed inserts well in advance, often, making the most of a particular location, camera setup, and characters.

• D •

Davies, Rita — (PSC; link out of "Hell's Grannies") Davies appears in *FC* occasionally (see Eps. 19, 27, and 29), and also plays the murdered historian's wife in *HG*.

"demised . . . late parrot" — ("Dead Parrot") This begins the thesaurus portion of the sketch in earnest. The phrases "passed on," "no more," and "ceased to be" are all euphemisms for death, as are "expired," "gone to meet its maker," and "late parrot." "Stiff" is an irreverent reference to a corpse, accounting for the rigor mortis (stiffening) which sets in to a dead body hours after death. As Praline tried to demonstrate earlier the parrot's condition, this stiffness was apparent. In Ep. 26, Man (Cleese) will bring his dead mother in a bag into a funeral home, where she will immediately be identified as a "stiff."

The thesaurus sketch format will return in "Fish Licence" (Ep. 23), "Cheese Shop" (Ep. 33), and "What the Stars Foretell" (Ep. 37).

department store — ("Buying a Bed") The store was then a John Sanders department store, but is now a Marks & Spencers, and is in Ealing on The Broadway. There is no record in the BBC archives of the Pythons getting permission to shoot near or in the store (as they had for the F.J. Wallis store in Ep. 1). The camera is set up well across the street, so permissions may not have been needed.

"didn't have to say it" — ("Buying a Bed") "It's my only line" is now the false safe haven for transgressing female characters. Once again, it is the female who is treated more contemptuously and with less latitude than any (straight) male character. This is the same response the Art Critic's wife gives in Ep. 4 and earlier in Ep. 8.

"dog kennels please" — ("Buying a Bed") The bride and groom are certain that they've mastered the language, logic, and in-references necessary to function in this strange mattress-buying world, though they will fall short, as will be seen. Cf. the difficulties of communication as exhibited in the conversation between policemen in Ep. 12, where frequency and volume are the keys to communication, or in *Life of Brian*, where the Centurion (Palin) and Jailer (Gilliam) can't seem to communicate at all without comic misunderstandings.

In this reliance on miscommunication, the Pythons echo many Modernist authors, including and specifically T.S. Eliot, whose *The Waste Land* (1922) mourned the futility of communication—Man's ability to communicate with Man, and even God—after WWI.

"doing all right" — ("Army Protection Racket") A euphemism for "making good money" or being successful in business, and is a way for mafioso to justify the collection of protection money.

"done over" — ("Army Protection Racket") Beat up, roughed up.

"don't they" — ("Army Protection Racket") Dino's (Jones) Cockney accent is especially thick, pronouncing "fings" for "things" and "dunnay" for "don't they." It used to be that a Cockney accent indicated growing up within earshot of the bells of St. Mary-le-Bow in Cheapside, in the City of London proper, meaning this accent is both regional and, more specifically, urban-centered. (See Ackroyd, *London*.)

• E •

Episode 8 — "Full Frontal Nudity" was the eighth installment in the first season. It was recorded eighth on 25 November 1969, and broadcast on 7 December 1969. Kathja (also "Katya") Wyeth (Ep. 4; *The Avengers*), Jean Clarke (Ep. 39), and Rita Davies appear as extras in this episode (WAC T12/1,089).

"Full Frontal Nudity" is also a variation of contemporary (1969) phraseology used by the MPAA (Motion Picture Association of America) to categorize at least one reason for giving a "mature" or "for adults only" rating to a film. The standards were fairly new at the time of the episode's creation, having been instituted just the year before (November 1968), and were probably still new enough to be in the news.

Lastly, Cleese and the troupe at *ISIRTA* had been using "Full Frontal Radio" as the catchphrase for their own fictional "Radio Prune" series for several years.

"Esher" — ("Vox Pops") Located approximately thirty miles southwest of London. This also must be something of an incongruous moment, as there are probably few African natives in tribal dress living in any part of Esher. Esher will be mentioned again, this time as a haven for orgiastic middle-class couples (Ep. 36), and Eps. 28 and 44.

"eyeties" — ("Army Protection Racket") A slang reference to Italians. Originally used by the military as a disparaging remark. Python also employs racially derogatory terms like "dago," "wop," "darkie," etc.

• F •

"fifteen bob" — ("Army Protection Racket") The Colonel reacts to the silliness, yes, but may also be offended by the cut-rate price the Vercottis are demanding—just fifteen shillings a week to protect an entire modern army base. This currency system was done away with in 1971.

Film of grannies on motorbikes — ("Hell's Grannies") This shot—Grannies on motorcycles roaring down a deserted street—appears to have been shot in Bradford. The spire of St. John's Church looms in the background.

"five bob" — ("Army Protection Racket") The haggling motif will reappear in *Holy Grail*, where the "Knights Who Until Recently Said 'Ni'" demand and then cadge for additional offerings; in *Life of Brian* as Brian (Chapman) first tries to buy a beard, then sell a gourd. In Ep. 35 ("Bomb on Plane" sketch), the bomber (Idle) demands £1,000 for the location of the bomb, then realizing he'll be blown up, too, asks for just £1. Eventually, he pays the pound himself.

The Colonel is again acting as arbiter of good taste, and also—as a replacement for a punchline or a traditional link—he is a transitionary tool. His outbursts remind the viewer of the constructedness of the performance, of its artificiality, and of the fact that it can be directed and redirected by characters and elements within the diegetic world. This narrative chicanery is the Pythons' tilting at Auntie BBC—the ancien régime of Light Entertainment to be rebelled against—and will come to characterize the narrative structure of *Flying Circus*.

"fjords" — ("Dead Parrot") Glaciated valleys (steeply V-shaped) inundated with seawater, fjords are found throughout northern Scandinavia.

four or five of them — ("Hell's Grannies") This is an absurd, incongruous moment, where the specter of aged grannies (dressed typologically, again, in black dresses and caps) knocking about younger people is as ludicrous as the image from Ep. 17 of the tough-looking Bishop (Jones) and his vicar henchman clearing their own path along busy city sidewalks.

There may be an earlier television inspiration for this sketch. A Salada Tea commercial from the late 1960s features a motorcycle gang of senior citizens (à la *The Wild One*) roaring into a diner for tea (see Ellsworth).

This sequence was reportedly shot near the rear entrance to Walpole Park, Lammas Park Road, Ealing, on 20 October 1969. Lammas Park is just south of Walpole Park in Ealing. Also, the scenes where the Grannies are knocking about pedestrians, stealing the telephone kiosk, and dropping the sociologist (Idle) into the coal hole were shot on or near Lammas Park Road. All the park scenes were shot in Walpole and Lammas Parks. (See WAC T12/1,242.)

Fourth Hermit — ("Hermits") It is by this time obvious that these hermits have retired from the world, but are living as a community. This qualifies them technically as "cenobites," and not religious ascetics, or "eremites." So what the Pythons constructed perhaps as a joke of incongruity—reclusive, even misanthropic hermits living together, chatting, etc.—is actually historically accurate. Certain "common life" hermits did live together in communities separated from the rest of the world, leading to institutionalized monasticism. See entries in the *OED* and *EBO*.

• G •

"general inspection" — ("Army Protection Racket") Daily fallout for inspection of troops, barracks, arms, etc.

"get out of it" — ("Hell's Grannies") Chapman as the authority figure again, this time as a policeman. In Ep. 14, Chapman plays another policeman, Hawkins, and plays him as a drag queen in police gear and makeup prior to a sort of "gay police" revue. He camps it up until they exit the dressing room and enter the street, then he's all business, the stoic authority figure again. The implication, then, is that prior to any appearance onscreen or on the street as the sober authority figure, all manly and no-nonsense, Chapman is an outrageously poncing and campy homosexual, only assuming the role of straight policeman for the narrative, and the general public. Perhaps this is a not-so-unconscious allusion to his real life as a gay man in a still very straight world.

"giveaway" — ("Art Critic—The Place of the Nude") This same phrase used in *HG* when Chapman (as King) calls Palin (as beggar) a "bloody peasant." To "giveaway" is to reveal, perhaps unconsciously, one's true intent or meaning. In this flavoring it's not unlike the Freudian "faulty action," where an unintended thought/word escapes, causing an embarrassing social situation.

"goat" — ("Hermits") The goat is, of course, an ancient symbol of lechery, and fits right into this same-sex hermitage.

grannies harassing an attractive girl — (PSC; "Hell's Grannies") This scene is shot in the Australia Road area, specifically Canada Way, in White City, Shepherd's Bush, Hammersmith and Fulham. In Ep. 7, the lone City Gent figure (Jones) waits for and then drives the empty city bus in this same White City housing estate. The Our Lady of Fatima Catholic Church can be seen in the left background. The area looked decidedly more run-down in October 1969 when the Pythons chose the location.

grannies on motorbikes — (PSC; "Hell's Grannies") These motorcycle shots were captured in Bradford, West Yorkshire, far away from the other street scenes for the film, which were shot in and around Ealing.

"grim" — ("Hermits") An escape from the luxuries of the world was certainly a part of the hermit lifestyle. Grimness could be described as a necessary element of the truly ascetic lifestyle. The most noted English hermit was Roger Crab (1621–1680), who wrote *The English Hermite* and moved to Uxbridge, selling his worldly possessions. (It's perhaps ironic that the Pythons shot many of their *urban* exterior locations in the same area Crab had gone to escape modern industrial life.) He was actually sought out for many years for his views on health, diet, and spiritual issues (*ODNB*).

This sketch may also have been at least partly inspired by the less than grim lifestyle of the Maharishi Mahesh Yogi, with whom The Beatles studied Transcendental Meditation (TM) in 1967–1968 and to whom they may have eventually been expected to contribute a sizeable portion of their incomes for the maintenance of the Maharishi's enlightened lifestyle.

• H •

"ha, ha, ha" — ("Buying a Bed") Understanding the rules of a Python situation can allow for navigation through that situation. The rules, however, may only function at the level of the sketch, and not at the level of the particular episode, the *FC* show in general, or especially the real world. In "The Argument Clinic" one can argue successfully without realizing an argument is under way; in the "Silly Job Interview," responding in a silly way scores points, and honest, sober answers are marked down, etc. In the "Buying a Bed" sketch here in Ep. 8, it's a matter of mathematics and avoiding a certain very potent word: "mattress" (cf. the entry for "mattress"). Cf. the police station sketch in Ep. 12 where each policeman responds to a different speaking voice (high or low pitched, slow or fast paced, etc.), and the man reporting a crime must speak differently to each to be understood. The policemen already speak each other's languages, of course, and don't recognize or comment upon the phenomenon during the sketch.

"Han" — ("Hermits") This can be a feminine term of address/endearment, which would add to the level of aberrant sexuality in this scene (effeminate and "butch" men living together, loincloths, absence of female sexual companionship, etc.).

"happen to it" — ("Army Protection Racket") These cryptic allusions are characteristic of media portrayals of Mafia types, especially Hollywood movies like *The Killers* (1946) and *Capone* (1959), Ealing comedies like *The Ladykillers* (1955), and dime pulp novels featuring underworld figures and lower-class elements.

"healthy outdoor sketch" — (link into "Hermits") Interesting that the Colonel is able to direct even the settings of the sketches, it seems, though he has little control over their content or eventual outcome. It's as if his sketch starts out well, grows unruly, and ultimately gets away from him. The Colonel is also acting the part of the Greek or Elizabethan "chorus," narrating action, qualifying actions, and moving the scenes along to his (and perhaps the authors') inevitable conclusions.

Hell's Grannies — ("Hell's Grannies") A play on "Hell's Angels," the infamous American motorcycle gang. This may have provoked at least some concern at the BBC, especially since the episode was first broadcast less than one day after the infamous events at Altamont (near San Francisco, California), the Rolling Stones concert appearance on 6 December 1969, where a young black fan, Meredith Hunter, was stabbed to death by Hell's Angels "security" personnel hired to police the show. The proximity of the two events might have precluded anyone involved at BBC, including the Pythons, from being able to do anything about the broadcast of what might have been seen as a tasteless, thoughtless comedic reference to a tragic death. (The episode had been recorded on 25 November, and would be broadcast on 7 December 1969.) Perhaps, though, the less violent persona of the UK Hell's Angels chapters as opposed to their U.S. cousins was the source for this humor, and the rest was an unfortunate coincidence. (Though there had been, coincidentally, arrests made at a Hell's Angel fracas in September on the Isle of Wight, as well as an accidental death at a Hell's Angel [Bristol chapter] party that same month, so their violent tendencies were in the news.)

"Hemmings, David" — ("Full Frontal Nudity") A film actor, director, and producer, Hemmings (1941–2003) was best known during this period for his role as the photographer Thomas in Michelangelo Antonioni's *Blowup* (1966). (Antonioni will be referenced later, in Ep. 29.) Significantly, the film received an X-rating in the UK, and was released unrated in the United States. Hemmings's characterization of the wandering photographer has been described by some as "wooden." Hemmings is also mentioned in Ep. 6, and appeared six times on *Dixon of Dock Green* early in his career.

The more recent role that may have spurred the Pythons' attack is Hemmings's performance in *Alfred the Great* (directed by Clive Donner [1926–2010]), which was met with almost universally bad reviews. Critic Michael Billington (b. 1939) calls Hemmings "a major piece of miscasting" in a historically suspect film:

> Although David Hemmings has done some good work in contemporary roles, he does not remotely suggest the division in Alfred's nature between warrior and monk. As the former, he is never the "wild boar" of historical record; as the latter, he lacks any hint of scholarly introspection. Although there are good performances [from other actors in the cast] . . . they cannot make up for the gap at the centre. ("The Epic That Never Was," *Times*, 17 July 1969: 9)

Alfred the Great was showing at the Empire Theatre by 26 July 1969, and was reviewed (above) more than a week earlier, all when the Pythons were shooting exterior footage in the Bournemouth area, meaning the inclusion of jabs at Hemmings when they recorded the episodes in October and November was entirely possible.

"hermit" — ("Hermits") He is one who has chosen to live in solitude, and the choice can be for religious or just anti-social reasons. A hermit who is a social butterfly, then, would be incongruous, and a perfect Python character. See the entries for "grim" and "Fourth Hermit" for more.

Peter Ackroyd has noted the significance of the hermit in the history of the city of London, identifying them as elements of continuity and touchstones for the city masses. They are "lonely and isolated people who feel their solitude more intensely within the busy life of the streets" (*London*, 41). The Pythons have merely transported these hermits and their tendencies into the wild, an outcrop populated entirely by like souls.

Noted Modernist poet W.B. Yeats's work must also have inspired this back-to-nature setting, especially his paean to the hermetic life, "The Lake Isle of Innisfree" (published 1893):

> I WILL arise and go now, and go to Innisfree,
> And a small cabin build there, of clay and wattles made:
> Nine bean-rows will I have there, a hive for the honey-bee,
> And live alone in the bee-loud glade.
> And I shall have some peace there, for peace comes dropping slow,
> Dropping from the veils of the mourning to where the cricket sings;
> There midnight's all a glimmer, and noon a purple glow,
> And evening full of the linnet's wings.
> I will arise and go now, for always night and day
> I hear lake water lapping with low sounds by the shore;
> While I stand on the roadway, or on the pavements grey,
> I hear it in the deep heart's core.

Yeats would later say that the poem arose from his homesickness for the wilds of Ireland, especially as he found himself lost on the crowded streets of London, where he self-pityingly "planned out a life of lonely austerity, and at other times mixed the ideals and planned a life of lonely austerity mitigated by periodical lapses" (Yeats, *Four Years*). The Python hermits also coveniently mix hermetic austerity with the "lapses" of conversation, gossip, and camaraderie, meeting Yeats's goal of the truly balanced life.

high street — ("Buying a Bed") *OED*: ". . . a highway, a main road, whether in country or town; now, very generally, the proper name (High Street) of that street of a town which is built upon a great highway, and is (or was originally) the principal one in the town." In many towns and cities in England, High Street tends to be a main business street today.

This particular high street is The Broadway in Ealing, just a few blocks from Walpole Park, Lammas Park Road, and Ealing Studios, where myriad exterior location work was performed.

hop off — ("Buying a Bed") This hopping indicates that even another level of reaction has been reached, beyond singing en masse in the tea chest, and that such consequences could continue to build and expand as transgressions continue. The groom is quick to join in, as well, and the bride (the sole female) is left out of the solution for her verbal "mattress" transgression.

• I •

"in his room" — ("Hell's Grannies") Both of these young men are dressed as "toughs," wearing black leather biker gear (Second Young Man, played by Chapman) and a biker jacket (Third Young Man, played by Jones). In other words, they're dressed as if *they* should be the ones causing the crime, and hence the subject of just such a crime documentary. The type of decorated helmet worn by the Jones character can be seen in a still image in the 1968 film *Yellow Submarine*, and these uniforms can also be seen in the short documentary *Chelsea Bridge Boys* (1965), which looks at the teenage motorcycle mania in London.

Beginning in the 1950s with the antics of the Teddy Boys, there was great concern in the UK (England, Scotland, and Northern Ireland) with the rise in teen violence, gang activity, delinquency, and a general disaffection among the youth for the traditions of British paternal, familial culture. Blame was placed on both the scarcity and plenty of the postwar rationing years, the move away from child labor to child leisure time, rock and roll music, and the appearance of a bored younger generation flush with discretionary income (*Eyewitness: 1950–59*, "Teenagers" and "Teddy Boys").

"innit" — ("Dead Parrot") Vulgar form of "isn't it."

"Inter-City Rail" — ("Dead Parrot") Government-run rail service serving Britain's major cities, part of the larger British Railways, or British Rail (see note above) system.

"Ipswich" — ("Dead Parrot") Ipswich is a North Sea port town north and east of London, in Suffolk, while Bolton is north and west, well across the country, from London. This would have been quite a time-consuming (and illogical) ruse for Praline (Cleese) to fall for.

"irrelevant, isn't it" — ("Dead Parrot") Not surprising that Praline would acknowledge the porter's meanderings, since Praline has already made a habit of addressing the camera (effectively breaking the fourth wall) on several occasions, and will continue to do so in his later appearances in Eps. 18 and 23.

"It's dead, that's what's wrong with it!" — ("Dead Parrot") According to Cleese in *Monty Python Speaks!*, this sketch began as a used car sketch written by Palin prior to *FC*. Like the earlier "Mouse Problem" sketch (Ep. 2), this idea was updated and rewritten for Python's needs and *FC*. A few sketches from pre-Python days (from *The Frost Report*, *At Last the 1948 Show*) also made the transition to the Monty Python collection, primarily as part of the various LP recording sessions (e.g., "The Bookshop," *At Last the 1948 Show*, 1.3).

This sketch has entered the cultural lexicon like almost nothing else from *Monty Python's Flying Circus*, and has enjoyed memorialized popularity since its initial broadcast. In 1990, for instance Prime Minister Margaret Thatcher—subject of the Pythons' pokes and jabs on several occasions—included in a political speech a comparison between the Liberal Democrat Party "flying bird" symbol and Python's "Dead Parrot." (Her speechwriters were quite certain she was the only one within earshot who had no idea what the reference actually meant.) Just two years later a former "Thatcherite minister" compared the demise and attempted resuscitation of the Maastricht Treaty to a dead parrot being re-nailed to its perch (Larsen, 23–24). The acculturation to Englishness can be measured, John Diamond would write in 1995, by an appreciation of, for one, the "Dead Parrot" sketch, and being able to respond appropriately to a Spanish Inquisition reference (21, 26). The "Dead Parrot" comparison has been used as a reference (by journalists, politicos, et al.) literally hundreds of times in the intervening years (see *MPSERD*).

• J •

"Jerusalem" — (PSC; "Buying a Bed") Popular Church of England hymn, with text by Blake. Cf. Ep. 4 for another extended usage of the hymn. This version of "Jerusalem" is arranged by Blake-Parry, and performed by the Royal Choral Society and Philharmonia Orchestra (WAC T12/1,089).

• K •

keep left signs — ("Hell's Grannies") This scene was shot in the Australia Road area in East Acton on 20 October 1969, as were the exterior shots for the council house interviews in "Hell's Grannies" (WAC T12/1,242).

"Keep Left" was also the name of a proposal penned by Michael Foot (b. 1913) and other democratic socialists as a third way to deal with Europe—without allying Britain to either the USSR or U.S. demands for foreign policy collusion. Between 1945 and 1951 the left in the Labour movement vociferously used the slogan to remind voters (and party leaders) of the need to stay true to the ideals of the welfare state, as well as set a course left of the United States (*Eyewitness: 1950–59*).

"kiosks" — ("Hell's Grannies") Red telephone booths. This one is stolen from Lammas Park Road, which is not far from BBC's Television Centre, and just down the street from where "The Funniest Joke in the World" (Ep. 1) and parts of "Dull Life of a City Stockbroker" (Ep. 6) were shot.

"kipping" — ("Dead Parrot") *OED*: "To go to bed, sleep. Also, to lie down."

• L •

"Lancs." — (PSC; "Dead Parrot") Short for Lancastershire, or Lancashire.

"leaving you cold" — ("Hermits") This conversation might as well be taking place over a brick fence separating row house yards in any London suburb, including the earlier mentioned Esher. Note, though, that there are no female hermits, and that the males we hear from the most have affected, somewhat effeminate accents and mannerisms. Discovering that Mr. Robinson and Mr. Seagrave are "lodging" together adds to the homosocial and even homoerotic subtext already present.

"look after" — ("Army Protection Racket") Not unlike the avuncular policeman (Chapman) in Ep. 7 reassuring the viewing public that Her Majesty's government was watching after everyone. Here the paternalistic, patriarchal Mafia "godfathers" (Jones and Palin) offer similar protection and peace of mind, and for a sliding scale price. In 1965 the Kray brothers were arrested and charged with running just such a protection racket in North London. Specifically, they were charged with "demanding money with menaces" from local businesses.

• M •

Mafia — (PSC; "Army Protection Racket") "Mafia" has become the generic name for Italian American crime organizations based around family structures in the United States. Organized crime was also a significant problem in Britain (see "Vercotti" below, and "Piranha Brothers" entries in Ep. 14). In 1962, Genovese crime family member Joe Valachi turned state's evidence, for the first time exposing the structure and influence of organized crime in the United States. His memoirs, published in 1968, became a bestseller.

Python's Mafia types dress very much like those in Seijun Suzuki's popular gangster films of this period, *Tokyo Drifter* (1966) and *Branded to Kill* (1967).

As the 1960s waned there was an increased interest in and fascination with the "Mafia" in Great Britain, with various newspapers offering exposés and histories of the organized criminal enterprise in both the Old Country and in the United States, where diasporic Italian immigrants had established their criminal "families" generations earlier. (Organized crime's notoriety had been recently raised to uncomfortable, unprecedented levels thanks to the McClellan Hearings in the U.S. Congress in 1963, where Genovese crime family button man Joseph Valachi [1904–1971] spilled on the secretive and fascinating world.) An influx of foreign Mafia influence in Britain's gaming industry was debated in newspapers, current affairs programs, and even in Parliament. In February 1969, Home Secretary James Callaghan (1912–2005) answered questions about U.S. money and influence in London casinos:

> With regard to reports about the Mafia I obviously have no idea of what they are planning, but if they were to try to establish a foothold in this country there are many weapons in our armoury for repelling that undesirable organization. ("Repelling the Mafia," *Times*, 14 Feb. 1969: 4)

"mattress" — ("Buying a Bed") One of the miraculous, totem-like words in the Python world. The young married couple here have transgressed the laws of the sketch world—she's mentioned the unmentionable word—and all participants must endure even more elaborate rituals to set things right. This also exhibits once again the power of language and the presence of shibboleths in Python's oeuvre. Use (or abuse) of even a single word can send Python narratives off in wildly different directions, or can immediately "out" an interloper like a woman or anyone who doesn't understand the internal logic of the situation.

In an animation for Ep. 2, for example, Rodin's "Thinker" disappears when his thought bubble ("I think, therefore I am") is popped—he can't exist without those words. See the power of "Ni" in *Holy Grail*, or of Brian's badly memorized but beatific phrases in *Life of Brian*, or even the power of assuming Brian's name at the end of the film, when a man is saved from crucifixion just by saying, "I'm Brian!"

military music — (PSC; link into "Army Protection Racket") More musical selections culled from the vast BBC archives, as were literally hundreds of items—from newsreel stock to publicity stills to sound effects. In particular, this music is "Roll Out the Barrel," performed by the Band of the Scots, from "Music of the Two World Wars" (Part I) (WAC T12/1,089).

The military stock footage here is VISNEWS footage of the British Army, and "British Movietone News" footage of a peacetime army drill (WAC T12/1,089).

"miss" — ("Dead Parrot") The Shopkeeper (Palin) actually notices that he's been referred to by a feminine title, which is unusual for Python. In Ep. 7, the Chairman (Chapman) doesn't react at all when he's referred to as "Lady Chairman," for example. In Ep. 8 Praline claims a cold made him say "Miss" instead of "Sir" or "Mr.," and later the Shopkeeper will account for his misspeaking by claiming to have meant a "pun," and then a "palindrome" ("Notlob" for "Bolton"). Again, the miscommunication issue comes to the fore, as will be seen throughout Monty Python's works.

"Monty Python's Flying Circus" — (titles) This iteration of the tagline is delivered by Cleese in his "silly" (affected) voice. Earlier episodes featured Cleese speaking the title in a more sober, BBC announcer-type voice, which of course belied—purposely—the absurdities about to be presented. Cleese—the best known of this fledgling comedy troupe—was also the voice for the BBC radio comedy *I'm Sorry I'll Read That Again*.

"moving in" — ("Hell's Grannies") This kind of structure and tone is usually reserved for stories about gang infiltration into neighborhoods, drug use, racial tension, etc. Shows like *Panorama* (1953–2000) treated these topics during this period. Interviewer Robin Day (Ep. 2) worked for *Panorama* beginning in 1967, delivering hard-hitting reports on myriad social and political problems until 1972. Topics tackled by lead interviewers Day (1923–2000) and Richard Dimbleby (1913–1965) included the Suez Crisis, the hydrogen bomb, drug abuse, the Cuban missile crisis, and the first on-camera interview with a member of the royal family, the Duke of Edinburgh (1961).

Thematically, this could be a verbatim pseudo-copy of any period BBC or ITV documentary (or exposé) on the Teddy Boy, punk, and/or skinhead movements in London and the larger industrial cities. One such program, "Hells Angels and Skinheads," a *Man Alive* "inquiry," was broadcast on 10 December 1969 on BBC2, just days after the fateful events at Altamont. *Man Alive* (BBC, 1965–1981) is later mentioned by Mr. Herbert Mental (Jones) in Ep. 26, calling it a show that had become "all serious."

mustache — (PSC; "Dead Parrot") In the sketches where Palin and Cleese play Frenchmen, they share a mustache, taking turns speaking and wearing the mustache (Eps. 2 and 14). In the department store section of the "Michael Ellis" episode (Ep. 41), the salesman attempts to hide his identity by donning a large "Fu Manchu" mustache. This often suffices in the cartoony Python world to disguise the individual completely, but not in this case.

"my only line" — ("Art Critic—The Place of the Nude") Carol Cleveland uses this same line in the next sketch. This also takes us back to the "Watteau, dear?" joke in Ep. 4, and the acid response from the Art Critic. Equally bad puns from the male Pythons don't generally elicit such vitriolic responses (perhaps a chicken on the head).

The Goons offer puns (primarily through characters played by Milligan and Sellers) without apology, and with much gusto, including:

> Moriarty: The sky over England is leaking, and that's why the rain is getting in.
>
> Seagoon: Wait! You two men claim the sky is leaking. What proof do you have?
>
> Moriarty: Water proof! (from "Queen Anne's Rain," 22 Dec. 1958)

• N •

"nirvana" — ("Hermits") *OED*: "In Buddhist theology, the extinction of individual existence and absorption into the supreme spirit, or the extinction of all desires and passions and attainment of perfect beatitude." Another hybridization, this time of certain Christian ascetic practices and Buddhist universalism. The Hermits here are, of course, not extinguishing their individual selves, instead forming another community away from the one they've all left behind.

"Norwegian Blue" — ("Dead Parrot") This is probably funny just because of the incongruity between the dark, frozen north of Norway and the colorful, tropical bird that supposedly lives there. Cf. the end of Ep. 40, where the Norwegian Party is given time on British television for a party political broadcast.

Specialized animals occur throughout Pythons' work, including Dinsdale's enormous hedgehog (Ep. 14), a dangerous, swimming llama with a beak for eating honey (Ep. 9), pantomime horses and geese (Ep. 30), flying sheep (Ep. 2), moping cats (Ep. 5), fish terriers and tucked Airedales (Ep. 10), and a killer rabbit (*HG*). Gilliam also provides numerous animated examples of dismembered and re-membered animals throughout.

"Notlob" — ("Dead Parrot") Later in this same episode, when the Announcer (Idle) is surprised that the camera has come back to him, "Notlob" is mentioned again. This is a demonstration of a sort of cross-fertilization—from the acknowledged fictional worlds (sketches) and the acknowledged "real" or documentary worlds (news sets, which can also be called the often unacknowledged fictional worlds), as the newsreader accidentally uses a nonsense palindrome from the preceding sketch. Cf. Ep. 13 for a reappearance of this backward name.

nudges him — (PSC; link out of "Dead Parrot") The Colonel (Chapman) also has no compunction regarding entering the fictional worlds created via sketches and nudging them away from silliness, never surrendering his military character persona, either. He and Praline (Cleese) exhibit certain levels of narrative control in this regard. The Pythons are also, perhaps unconsciously, acknowledging the real-world influence of such a character representing the established authority system (a military-industrial complex operating with tacit government support). The Colonel may be a fuddy-duddy, but he is certainly able to force the narrative at least in the general direction he feels will be more redemptive, and less silly and "long-haired."

• O •

"on film" — ("Hermits") Perhaps an acknowledgment of the permanence of the filmed as opposed to the taped image. (Many early television concerns like the BBC regularly cleaned house by "wiping" expensive, reusable video tape, which is why so many episodes and even entire series of significant television shows no longer exist.) Also, this is an acknowledgment of the different media used in the *FC* episodes. The Colonel notes that the media matters little to the audience, which may or may not be true (like the world of a Turner or Constable landscape, it's a choice), depending on the purist sensibilities of particular viewers. However, if an audience is schooled on mixed media (from film to tape to film without acknowledged breaks in continuity), then they are less likely to be bothered by the image quality fluctuations.

"ours" — ("Hermits") This first person plural possessive pronoun (as opposed to any singular pronoun like "mine" or "yours") should be a major clue that the standard hermit lifestyle is being sent up here.

• P •

"pacifist" — ("Army Protection Racket") In the years leading up to the Second World War, with Germany ratcheting up both its military and its belligerent tone, the calls for pacifism rang across Britain. The pacifist sentiment was so pervasive, it seems, that arguing for a strong Britain in the face of Hitler's continental aggression was, ironically, asking for real trouble. The Bishop of London (Dr. Winnington-Ingram) preached a pro-readiness sermon in February 1937, and received "50 abusive letters the following week":

> Those people told me how annoyed they were in no uncertain fashion, but it is obvious they do not understand. We are all pacifists. Christians must be pacifists. But there is a difference between the policies of pacifism and non-defence. Democracy must not be at the heels of dictators, and despite those letters I still advocate we must be strong. ("Fifty Abusive Letters to a Bishop," *Times*, 15 Feb. 1937: 9)

This term is especially significant during the Vietnam War years, when the numbers of pacifists or conscientious objectors rose dramatically in the United States in response to the ever-widening Selective Service draft. In the UK, the period of National Service (1948–1960) saw many applicants for conscientious objector status, but relatively few were granted. Watkins (Idle) could have served as a noncombatant, of course, but the terms (and fairness) of National Service meant that, one way or another, service was going to happen. Artist David Hockney (Ep. 14), for example, performed hospital work during his National Service time, as opposed to any combat or combat support-type service.

"pad out" — ("Dead Parrot") *OED*: "To extend or increase." Again, reminding the viewer that this is a show, a play, a constructed thing. In Ep. 10, characters will wait around on-set for the "walk on" part actor to arrive, making the show longer than it should have been. In Ep. 33, the show actually runs short, and the "padding" is purposely clumsy, with Cleese in Conquistador uniform and sword (seen again later in Ep. 36) at the seashore apologizing and explaining why some shows run short.

In "The Choking Horror" episode of *The Goon Show*, the "padding out" of the show is mentioned, as well, and called "filling-in-time type dialogue" (14 Feb. 1956).

"pall" — ("Hell's Grannies") This kind of gloomy language was heard during WWII, for example, especially during the Battle of Britain. The *Beyond the Fringe* group painted newscaster Alvar Liddell as one who, on the regular evening newcasts on BBC Home Service, "brought us news of fresh disasters" from the warfront ("Aftermyth of War").

This slow panning establishing shot for "Hell's Grannies" was recorded just where the first men-cum-Scotsmen disappeared in Ep. 7—at the top of Southmere Terrace in Bradford. The camera was set up just beyond the backyard of 19 Southmere Terrace, on what was a dead end road at the time. The spire of the St. John the Evangelist (C of E) church can be seen in the left distance.

"pension day" — ("Hell's Grannies") The day that Old Age Pensioners (OAP) pick up their government checks, rather than drugs, alcohol, or lottery tickets, which might be expected in other such documentaries on a *Man Alive*, *Review*, or *Panorama*-type show.

"people, chat, gossip" — ("Hermits") The balance of the sketch is comprised almost completely of people, chat, and gossip—the very ills of society from which these hermits are allegedly escaping.

"permissive society" — ("Vox Pops") The phrase "permissive society" was oft-used in the media of the period (in more than fifty separate articles in the *Times* alone in 1969, for example) to describe the eroding morality seen by many as typifying especially London life. The "mod" movement; the increased availability, use, and abuse of marijuana and psychedelic drugs; and the advent of the birth control pill in 1960 all contributed to this perceived explosion of hedonism, and all played a significant role in the so-called satire boom of the late 1950s and into the 1960s. For more on the "permissive society" and its effects on the entertainment industry in the UK, see Aldgate's *Censorship and the Permissive Society*. (The allures of the "Permissive Society" were featured prominently on a *Newsweek* cover on 13 November 1967—subtitled "Anything Goes"—along with a naked image of Jane Fonda in *Barbarella*.)

This element of televised sexuality is a response to religiously and politically conservative anti-pornographer figures like Mary Whitehouse, who campaigned for stricter standards on television in Britain beginning in 1964. Whitehouse formed the "Clean Up TV" campaign in 1964, and in 1965 created the National Viewers and Listeners Association (NVLA). (The troupe at *ISIRTA* would refer to her as "Mary Whitewash" in the early portion of the episode "The Six Wives of Henry VIII" [29 Mar. 1970].) The Pythons would later have to face Mrs. Whitehouse in response to the public outcry over the "decency" and blasphemic elements of *LB*, especially as the film might offend Christians. See Hewison's *Monty Python: The Case Against*.

"pining" — ("Dead Parrot") To pine is to waste away, physically or emotionally. The use of a word like "pining" instead of something of more modern usage is an indication that this is indeed one of Cleese/Chapman's "thesaurus" sketches, where they may have literally consulted a thesaurus as they wrote. See Morgan's *Speaks!* Literary precedents also exist for the usage. See Gerard Manley Hopkins's (1844–1889) *Felix Randal*:

> Felix Randal the farrier, O he is dead then? My duty all ended,
> Who have watched his mold of man, big-boned and hardy-handsome,
> Pining, pining. (No. 53, stanza 1)

"public relations" — ("Hermits") A rimshot moment, in music hall terms, it is the payoff for this sketch, the punchline, even, and the Colonel interjects just as the sketch is about to move off somewhere else, or even conclude on its own. This is curious, in that he rarely lets the sketch reach a punchline status.

"pun" — ("Dead Parrot") A pun is a play on words, and in this usage is a good example of Python's oft-employed catachresis (using words improperly, abusing metaphors or tropes). Cf. Ep. 29, when "great expedition" is punned into "Great Exhibition," complete with a photo insert of the Crystal Palace. (The Pythons' comedy forebears, the Goons, employed puns often, and without apology.)

• Q •

Queen's Park Rangers — (PSC; "Hell's Grannies") The corrugated metal fence behind the policeman (Chapman) features some existing graffiti that identifies the actual location for this shot. Earlier, the announcer told us we were in Bolton, but the spray-painted scrawl tells us the local football team is clearly the Queen's Park Rangers, who play in a stadium just around the corner from Television Centre, at Loftus Road (London W12). QPR have been a football club since 1882.

The graffiti painted by the Grannies reads, "Make tea not love," a play on the then-fashionable anti–Vietnam War (and Campaign for Nuclear Disarmament) sentiment, "Make love not war." This graffiti sequence also features the fan scrawl "Rangers great Rodney" in plain view at the right side of the frame, likely a reference to Rodney Marsh, who played for QPR 1966–1972.

This scene was shot in the Australia Road, East Acton area, just a few blocks northwest of Television Centre, on 20 October 1969 (WAC T12/1,242).

• R •

reporter walking along the street — ("Hell's Grannies") This subject—Hell's Angels, skinheads, and delinquency—had obviously been covered ad infinitum on British television, given this *Times* December 1969 Julian Critchley (1930–2000) television review:

> Failure has its hazards. Line up in freezing fog under Waterloo Bridge for a cup of soup and a bed and the chances are that Desmond Wilcox will ask you to sing for your supper. *Man Alive*, BBC2, took its turn with the skinheads and hell's angels, two groups of the deprived from whom it is now almost impossible to escape. A month ago *Review* filled its studio with them, they were on again last night, and now *Man Alive* paid court . . . Where will it end? ("Fruits of Success," 11 Dec. 1969: 11)

So the cause célèbre (or du jour) in 1969 for BBC documentaries was criminal delinquency, meaning the Pythons would have plenty of opportunity to gather material for a new on take on the subject. (Desmond Wilcox [1931–2000] was a contributor to *Man Alive*, while *Review* was a BBC current affairs show airing in 1969.)

"right out" — ("Dead Parrot") A common British colloquialism, used emphatically to mean "no." Cf. *HG*, where a section from the Book of Armaments is being read aloud, and the number "five is right out."

• S •

"senile delinquents" — ("Hell's Grannies") A simple wordplay on "juvenile delinquents," and probably something of an oxymoron, since delinquency requires at least a modicum of deliberate action, which might not be possible for someone suffering from senility or diminished mental capacity due to advanced age. Social psychologists in this period (including Oxford's John Michael Argyle) noted the troubling increase of juvenile delinquency, calling it one of Britain's "most pressing problems" (see *Psychology and Social Problems*), meaning the discussion would have been much in the news, as well.

There were also a number of films and television programs produced on the subject of teen delinquency, including the narrative cinema verité–type *Bronco Bullfrog* (1969), to which the Pythons may be referring indirectly, or *Cosh Boy* (1953), which paints a picture of menacing teens (which the Pythons adapt into menacing grandmothers), not outcast anti-heroes. The skinheads had been sort of "officially" recognized in September 1969 by being so named in the *Guardian*, and *Bronco Bullfrog* was released not long after. The 1965 documentary short *Chelsea Bridge Boys* looked at this motorcycle and teenaged delinquency phenomena, but was more observational than those appearing on *Panorama* or the like. The head-on interview style is also used almost exclusively in the *Chelsea Bridge Boys* short, which appeared on Rediffusion television, late night, in December 1966.

several grannies walking aggressively along street — (PSC; "Hell's Grannies") This sequence was shot along Uxbridge Road, at about 46-50 Uxbridge Road. The Ealing Fire Station (60 Uxbridge Road) can be seen in the background.

"shagged" — ("Dead Parrot") Generally meaning weary, exhausted. To say both "tired" and "shagged out" might seem a bit redundant, though the thesaurus nature of this sketch will soon become apparent, and the redundancy more acceptable. The word "shag" also has copulative connotations, of course, which might account for the laugh from the studio audience at its use.

Shot of two grannies replacing manhole cover — (PSC; "Hell's Grannies") This is shot on Acton High Street, with the manhole located just in front of number 84. The Acton Town Hall can be seen in the background across the street.

This location is just down the street from one of the show's first locations, the F.J. Wallis store used in Ep. 1.

"silly line" — ("Army Protection Racket") The military authority figure as played by Chapman often comments on and even stops sketches in *FC* when he deems they've reached a certain unbearable level of silliness. He is often used as a linking element between sketches in this manner, a sort of purposeful narrative transition. See Ep. 4 for earlier appearances of the character, and later in Ep. 8 in the "Hermits" sketch.

"small part" — ("Vox Pops") The genital reference is intended, certainly.

"sociologists" — ("Hell's Grannies") This is a kind of usual suspects list of occupations that have been and will be lampooned in *FC*—usually as insipidly dull—or occupations that tend to attract those with some sort of perverted proclivity, and who hide behind the façade of dull respectability. The City Stockbroker in Ep. 6 must escape into the fictional life of superhero comic books, for example, and vicars tend to be thieves or sex deviants, etc. The sociologist's implication is that the older generation feels it has failed to raise its children properly, in that they've chosen such gainful but perhaps emotionally tepid employment. Incidentally, these are some of the occupations the Pythons avoided by entering the world of show business.

In the Pythons' contribution to *Euroshow* 1971—*May Day Special*, "A Sociologist" (Idle) and then "A Better Sociologist" (Cleese) try to explain the May Day rituals.

"Sound of Music" — ("Hell's Grannies") A Rodgers and Hammerstein musical, filmed in 1965 by Robert Wise and starring Julie Andrews and Christopher Plummer. The implication is that classic Hollywood musicals are the favorite films of senior citizens, especially older women (which was demographically accurate). The cast of the *Sound of Music* will appear in Ep. 42, as a show-jumping obstacle.

"stopping it" — ("Army Protection Racket") There are various levels of awareness here. The Colonel (Chapman) is stopping the sketch, but he is still in character as the Colonel, thus on some level the sketch continues. So he is not an actor playing a colonel acting in a sketch, he is a colonel acting in a sketch, and without any funny lines. Below it will be seen that he knows enough as a colonel to identify the TV milieu ("telecine," "director," "close-up," etc.), yet he isn't just an actor. Both Vercottis (Jones and Palin) have fallen out of character, as well, as has Watkins (Idle), but not the Colonel. Note the similar levels of reality as he later stops the hermits, and the "keep left signs" silliness in mid-sketch.

St. Peter's Square — (PSC; "Buying a Bed") These clips are of St. Peter's Basilica, which is in the heart of Rome. This is once again BBC stock footage, and the assembled Roman Catholic crowd is most likely not singing the Anglican hymn "Jerusalem." This footage was *not* on the weekly request list for this episode.

"strangle his wife" — (link out of "Art Critic—The Place of the Nude") The retribution for such a bad joke on her part is obviously death. The implication is that the critic will also, once his wife is dead, be able to move on "to pastures new." The music beneath (which is almost inaudible) is a portion of Debussy's "Jeux de Vagues" (WAC T12/1,089).

• T •

"tart" — A colloquial name for a prostitute. This mention could be explained away as just a malapropism, like most everything Dogberry utters in Shakespeare's *Much Ado*. Also, see Arthur Figgis's "panties" slip-of-the-tongue as he lists significant composers in Ep. 6. These so-called Freudian slips (Freud's "faulty action" or *"Fehlleistung")* would have been "discovered" popularly and entered the cultural lexicon between the wars, when Freud's work found its way into the mainstream media.

"telecine" — ("Army Protection Racket") The broadcasting of filmed images. The countdown (see "film leader" note in Ep. 2) runs a normal 7, 6, 5, and 4, but then a still photo (a passport or identification photo) of a blonde, *clothed* woman is inserted by Gilliam for just a few fleeting frames. The photo may be Maggie Weston, a makeup artist for *FC*, who would later become Gilliam's wife.

"that's as maybe" — (link into "Army Protection Racket") A variation on the "and now for something completely different," and isn't very different from such diverse and purposely misleading elements like giving titles to episodes that have no connection to the contents of that episode ("Whither Canada?"), providing random episode numbers (this episode is subtitled "12B"), and offering conflicting information between voiceover narration and provided captions, etc. This 1943 wartime intro might have fit the "Funniest Joke" sketch in Ep. 1, but here leads into a decidedly unheroic military shakedown sketch by London Mafia members. This is as misleading as the elaborate introduction to Ep. 25, the *"Black Eagle"* film credits, which goes into the episode, and not the promised film.

"This man's hair is too long for a vicar" — ("This Film's Got Silly") Keeping the youth of Britain affiliated with the Church had been a major concern since at least the postwar years, when myriad other distractions confronted Britain's children. The answers ranged from Church-run youth clubs of all sorts (including motorcycle and motorbike clubs) to cooler young vicars with longer hair to what the "Beyond the Fringe" boys saw as a monumental watering down of everything the Church used to stand for, including the majesty of the Almighty:

> "Dick" the Vicar (Jonathan Miller): "God is exactly the same as you and I. Once we can get away from the idea of thinking of God as something divine, you youngsters will come flooding back into church!" ("Man Bites God," 1961–1962)

"toddle" — ("Hermits") To take a leisurely walk, meaning he's not on his way anywhere in particular, and that the hermit's life is often one of pleasant idleness.

"travel, sir" — ("Army Protection Racket") This description fits some of the television commercials and print ads of the time period that depicted glamorous ports of call, camaraderie, and excitement as the whole of military life. The U.S. Army's slogan during the 1960s, for example, was "Fun, Travel, Adventure." The specter of the Vietnam War, which was raging through 1969 and would continue until at least 1973, provided news fodder of the fighting and the dying and would have certainly undercut the benign, even playful commercial images.

• U •

"unisex" — (link out of "Hell's Grannies") Anything (especially fashions) that can be utilized by both males and females. The term came into vogue in the late 1960s.

• V •

"valid" — ("Vox Pops") The implication, then, is that this policeman would appear in a nude scene if it was, indeed, valid (probably meaning the nudity was somehow germane to the plot, and not "gratuitous"). This has been a moral maxim used by many actresses, especially, to account for their appearances in various states of undress on camera. In Ep. 4 of *FC*, Chapman plays a nude man in a discussion on censorship.

And nudity is also valid, in Python's oeuvre, whenever it can shock or be considered incongruous. However, the full frontal nudity moments are reserved for female figures, not male.

"Vercotti" — ("Army Protection Racket") Probably based at least loosely on Ronnie and Reggie Kray, London's infamous gangsters born ten minutes apart in October 1933, Reggie being the older. They dressed in this slick, dapper way, spent most of their time together, and participated in criminal shakedowns—either together or separately—on a regular basis into the 1960s. There were other brothers in London's underworld, including Greek brothers (Tony and Chris Lambrianou), as well as Sicilian mobsters, including Charles "Darby" Sabini. A conflation of these characters might have created the Vercottis. See Thomas Jones's *The Kray Brothers* at "The Crime Library," as well as entries in the *ODNB*. See notes to Ep. 14 for more on the Krays, and their similarities to Python's Piranha brothers, as well.

"Verity" — ("Buying a Bed") *OED*: "Without article. Truth, either in general or with reference to a particular fact; conformity to fact or reality." Mr. Verity's "conformity to fact or reality" is at the heart of this bit.

The Pythons had requested name labels be created for "Mr. A. Lambert" and "Mr. F. Verity"—but those do not appear in the episode as recorded (WAC T12/1,086). These names are obviously borrowed from an actual man named Verity Lambert, producer of *Doctor Who* episodes (1963–1966), and the *W. Somerset Maugham* series (1969–1970) on BBC2.

vox pops — ("Full Frontal Nudity") Reoccurring "voice of the people" or "man on the street" sound bites. These were earlier staples of *The Dick Emery Show* (BBC, 1963–1981), a sketch and character comedy show, and were also found in far more serious works, including Humphrey Jennings's documentary *Listen to Britain* (1942).

• W •

walking aggressively — (PSC; "Hell's Grannies") The music dubbed to this film is an orchestrated section from the James Bond film *Thunderball*, by John Barry. Cf. the use of the "Peter Gunn Theme" to accompany strutting vicars and "The Bishop" in Ep. 17.

"waterskiing" — ("Army Protection Racket") There are a number of similarly themed recruitment posters extant, including a WWI-era British poster declaiming, "The Army Isn't All Work" that depicts three versions of one soldier: one in full combat kit, one wearing cricket togs and carrying a bat, and one sporting football gear and a ball. A more contemporary reference can be found in a recruitment cartoon made for the U.S. Navy in the early 1960s. The cartoon promotes the exotic ports and good money and, of course, depicts happy seamen waterskiing near a pristine beach: "Like action? On water, on land, under the sea? Like to travel? To have adventures in the far corners of the world? Join the Navy!"

In Ep. 38 one of the Kamikaze Scotsmen (Idle) notes that he's only in the program because of the waterskiing.

"wattles" — ("Hermits") *OED*: "Rods or stakes, interlaced with twigs or branches of trees, used to form fences and the walls and roofs of buildings." The wattle will also be cited as the "emblem" of the proud people of Australia in Ep. 22.

"What are they in it for, these old hoodlums, these layabouts in lace?" — ("Hell's Grannies") In the somewhat staged "documentary" *Primitive London* (dir. Arnold Miller, 1967) a gang of motorcycle toughs are interviewed, and their answers are as hazy as the Grannies (they ride and fight and drop out of society out of boredom, for fun, one boy admitting to simply being a "bad egg"). These riders are allied with the 59 Club, which had developed an internecine rift between those who rode motorcycles and those who chose scooters—often simplified as a "Rockers" versus "Mods" antagonism, which the Pythons might be alluding to as they sent up of the whole enterprise. (Ironically, the "gang" was begun as a C of E East London youth club in 1959, a point perhaps not lost on the Pythons.) The music track used to underscore this setting is The Beatles' "Can't Buy Me Love," interestingly.

"what's all this about" — ("Army Protection Racket") The Colonel doesn't understand the brothers' shakedown language, and the brothers continue to verbally dance around their actual threats and demands. As a military figure representing order and strict regimentation, the Colonel is much more literal, characteristically, tending to interrupt when puns, satire, or double entendres begin to crop up, prodding the show toward more sober, straightforward themes.

• Y •

yoghurt — (link into "The Flasher") Just a variant spelling of "yogurt."

It's worth pointing out in this scene that this assumedly professional BBC announcer-type is flustered when addressing the camera, and with what must be a common broadcast snafu—the unexpected "back to the studio" moment—while the average citizen Praline seems to feel perfectly comfortable in his numerous asides to the camera and viewing audience. Clearly there is a demarcation here between the acknowledged world of the news set as separate and distinct from the audience, and the acknowledged world of Praline, where "crossing over" is possible, and even necessary. The fictionality of the sketch world as opposed to the "real" news set world is essential in this demarcation, and is displayed often in *FC*. Both, however, are contrived and operate by agreed-upon paradigms that the Pythons consistently attempt to undermine. Cf. the manipulation of these structures via the filmed insert of the announcer (Idle) taken for questioning, then returned, and the on-set announcer then goes in his place in Ep. 5, "Newsreader Arrested."

Episode 9:
"The Ant, an Introduction"

"It's" Man exploding forest intro; *Animation: Titles* (silly Cleese v/o); "Part 2: The Llama" (Live from Golders Green); Ada's Snack Bar, "And Now for Something Completely Different": "A man with a tape recorder up his nose"; "And Now for Something Completely Different—The Office of Sir George Head, O.B.E.": Kilimanjaro expeditions; "And Now for Something Completely Different": "A man with a tape recorder up his brother's nose" (and in stereo); *Animation: Encyclopaedia Salesman, Kewpie Doll Carnival Game*; Homicidal barber; **"I'm a Lumberjack" song**; Letters; Vox Pops: "Sex on the television," Britain's entry joke for the "Rubber Mac of Zurich Award"; Gumby crooner: "Make Believe"; The refreshment room at Bletchley: Ken Buddha and his inflatable knees; *Animation: Brian Islam and Brucie*; Homicidal barber introduces "The Hunting Film"; Knight-and-chicken not needed; "And now for something completely different": The Visitors; "It's" Man "Cuidado llamas!" closing credits

• A •

Ada's Snack Bar — (PSC; link into "Kilimanjaro Expedition [Double Vision]") The sign is one provided by or in cooperation with a soft drink corporation seen on many older cafés, in this case advertising Barr's soft drink. Barr has been making soda drinks in the UK since 1875, including such popular drinks as Irn-Bru and Tizer. (Tizer is also mentioned on the sign, and will be discussed at some length in Ep. 34 by Jeremy Pither [Palin].)

There was an Ada's Snack Bar located at 60b Victoria Road South, Southsea, Portsmouth, during this period, according to the British Telephone archives.

animated sequence — (*"Animation: Encyclopaedia Salesman, Kewpie Doll Carnival Game"*) The animated sequence is preceded by a lonely shot of an empty, old football stadium, the same stadium used in Ep. 7 (where one player, one referee, and one spectator) make a lonely football match), Bradford's stadium, home to the Bradford Football Club. The troupe shot many scenes—including very recognizable sketches like the various "Undertakers" films (Ep. 11) and portions of "Hell's Grannies" (Ep. 8) in the Bradford area. The animation itself features a manipulated version of Francisco del Cossa's *Saint Vincent Ferrer* (1477–1478), which has been part of the National Gallery's collection since 1858.

The backgrounds behind the characters are often modeled directly after the de Vries *Perspective* work, specifically Plate 28. Gilliam will repurpose the three-walls-and-ceiling perspective (and occasionally include the floor) over and over again as inhabitable space for his action and characters.

• B •

"bang" — ("Kilimanjaro Expedition [Double Vision]") In this instance, to do something forcefully; namely, trashing the application.

BBC microphone — (PSC: link into "Kilimanjaro Expedition [Double Vision]") This is an angular, stand-mounted (on desk) microphone, and is probably bidirectional in capacity. The Announcer, Cleese, is dressed in DJ ("dinner jacket") evening attire, the uniform of the "old-fashioned" BBC announcer.

"bells are ringing" — ("The Visitors") A Christmas song in this most un-Christ-like setting. The carol is known as both "Ding Dong Merrily on High" and "Hosanna in Excelsis."

"Bevis" — ("Lumberjack Song") Cf. Ep. 5, where the Bevis featured there also is a sexually dysfunctional male, preferring to show metaphoric films to his underwear-clad girlfriend instead of engaging in actual intimacy. This name may also have been inspired by an Oxford classmate, Bevis Hillier (b. 1940), who had written a well-received book on the Art Deco period in 1968.

"bird" — ("The Visitors") Slang for a woman or girl. Cf. other instances in *FC* where women are referred to pejoratively as bits of "tail" (Ep. 33, "Biggles Dictates a Letter"). This is an ancient reference that the *OED* traces back to 1400 or before.

"blasting their heads off" — (link into "Hunting Film") The characters (Customer and Barber) have descended from leading status to linking elements. The transition away from them is one used as early as Ep. 2, where the camera zooms in on a still photo, then there is a dissolve to film footage of that scene. In this case, the photo is of a country house. The following sketch will end with another "photo freeze," and the camera will pull back into the new scene. This type of transition can be seen in the popular Ealing comedy *Kind Hearts and Coronets* (1949), with a transition from a still photo of a manor house to a live shot of the actual house.

"Blenkinsop" — ("Kilimanjaro Expedition [Double Vision]") John Blenkinsop, born in Yorkshire (1783–1831), invented the first practical locomotive (*ODNB*). The more likely reference is to Ernie Blenkinsop, born in Cudworth (1900–1969), who was a successful footballer for Sheffield Wednesday, compiling a 58 percent lifetime winning percentage. The fact that Ernie died within months of this episode (April 1969) would have put him in the news, and make him a more likely candidate for Python's name borrowing.

"Bletchley" — ("The Refreshment Room at Bletchley") Town located in Buckinghamshire, since 1967 Bletchley has been a part of greater Milton Keynes.

"botanists" — ("Kilimanjaro Expedition [Double Vision]") Botany is the study of plant life, and thus an interesting inclusion for a midwinter volcanic mountain assault, where precious little flora can exist. Beyond about 12,000 feet above sea level the scarce rainfall, thinner atmosphere, and very porous volcanic soils discourage most plant life.

"brace" — ("Kilimanjaro Expedition [Double Vision]") A matched set, often referring to dueling pistols.

braces — (PSC; "Gumby Crooner") Braces are suspenders, but the key here is that the "Gumby" moniker hasn't found its way indelibly into the written scripts. The character still must be described by his appearance. The braces were also to become a significant part of the uniform of the "hard mods," soon to be known as skinheads (emerging in the late 1960s). See notes to Ep. 8 for more on the juvenile delinquent fears of the period.

"British Columbia" — ("Lumberjack Song") The westernmost Canadian province, BC became a "crown colony" in 1849.

"Brown, Arthur" — ("Kilimanjaro Expedition [Double Vision]") Three interesting possibilities here: The first is Arthur Brown, a musician, born in Yorkshire (as Arthur Wilton) in 1942, who would later appear in *Tommy* (1975). Brown had released a very popular album, *The Crazy World of Arthur Brown*, in 1968. The second reference possibility is the Arthur Brown (1914–2003) who was an Oxford-educated, well-published local labor history scholar. Brown taught at the Colchester Royal grammar school for many years, and published books on the working class in the Essex area.

The third and most interesting, if not challenging possibility might be the central figures in a book released in 1966, *The Solid Mandala* by celebrated Australian author Patrick White. The characters are *twins*, Waldo and *Arthur Brown*, and the narrative follows the very different reminiscences of the two, as old men looking back across their lives. The book was favorably reviewed in the *Times* in summer 1969.

"Buddha" — ("The Refreshment Room at Bletchley") Means "awakened one," and represents the founder of Buddhism, the predominant religion in much of Asia. As an allusion, this is perhaps a nod to the pseudonym assumed by Beat poet Allen Ginsberg (1926–1997), "Rabbi Buddha Whitman/Ginsburg."

• C •

"change the record" — ("The Visitors") Mr. Name (Idle) takes the more romantic record off and replaces it with an American march (see entry for "Washington Post March" below). This is perhaps worth mentioning because it's a Dudley Moore recording that's being replaced—"I Love You Samantha" from the album *Genuine Dud* by the Dudley Moore Trio (WAC T12/1,090). Moore, of course, was part of the immediately preceding generation of university wits that includes fellow *Beyond the Fringe* castmembers Peter Cook, Alan Bennett, and Jonathan Miller, a generation that also included Marty Feldman. The Pythons would replace the *Fringe* comedians (and the satire movement in general) at the forefront of British comedy.

Compère — (PSC; "The Refreshment Room at Bletchley") This character is played by both Palin and Idle in *FC*, but here is much more salacious and unctuous than depicted before. Cf. the introduction to "Restaurant Sketch" (Ep. 3) and "Science Fiction Sketch" (Ep. 7) for previous appearances. These figures are meant to resemble the ubiquitous redcoats of the Butlin's Holiday Camps, where many cost-conscious Brits spent their bank and school holidays. Also, the kitschy and bizarre "documentaries" *London in the Raw* (1965) and *Primitive London* (1967) feature dank, sweaty clubs like this one, featuring equally greasy compère-types.

"crème de menthe" — ("The Visitors") A syrupy liqueur. The *OED* offers two citations wherein this type of drink is matched to a gender or sexuality:

> 1903 *Daily Mail* 11 Sept. 3/3 Crême de menthe, with its strong peppermint flavour, is the one almost exclusively favoured by ladies. 1930 E. WAUGH *Labels* 26 Shady young men in Charvet shirts sit round the bar repairing with powder-puff and lipstick the ravages of grenadine and crême de cacao. (*OED* 2003)

crooning — ("Gumby Crooner") Cf. the chanting monks in *HG*, who hit themselves in the foreheads as they walk. These self-flagellants are depicted in Bergman's *Seventh Seal* (1957), though they are there actually whipping themselves.

Customer sits in barber's chair — (PSC; "Homicidal Barber") Though not mentioned in the printed script, the magazine the Customer (Jones) is reading in this sketch is the men's magazine *Mayfair* (title mostly obscured), volume 4, number 12, from 1969. There is a Tio Pepe (sherry) ad on the back cover. The magazine was launched in 1966.

• D •

"down there" — ("Kilimanjaro Expedition [Double Vision]") This language betrays what was a fairly pervasive "them" mentality, especially shared by those who might have had vested interests in Britain's far-flung colonial holdings, including the British Raj in India (1858–1947). One of the deformations expected with long-term colonialization would be the assumption that the colonizers' language (in this case, English) would always be sufficient to get along in-country, especially in government, business, and the courts. African countries Kenya and Tanzania, for example, had only been independent since 1963–1964.

• E •

Episode 9 — "The Ant, an Introduction" was transmitted ninth but recorded tenth. The date of recording was 7 December 1969, and the date of broadcast was 14 December 1969. As for the title, ants aren't mentioned at all in this episode. The ant won't become a key narrative figure until Ep. 41, "Michael Ellis."

This is the last episode to be subtitled, probably as a result of Michael Mills's 29 July 1969 memo request that such additional titling was confusing to both programmers and audiences alike (WAC T12/1,242).

Also appearing in this episode are: Fanny Carby (*Dixon of Dock Green*), Connie Booth, Fred Tomlinson and His Singers ("I'm a Lumberjack"), with Jennifer Partridge on piano. The extras are Joanna Robbins (*Emma*), Hunter Clark, Jean Dempsey, and Tricia Peters; walk-ons include Clive Rogers (*Plateau of Fear*), Mike Briton (*Doctor Who*), Tina Simmons (*Doctor Who*), and Maxine Casson (*Z Cars*) (WAC T12/1,090).

• F •

"film society" — ("The Visitors") Weekly or monthly gatherings where the latest art films or classic films could be discussed. Film clubs arose in France, Great Britain, and elsewhere across Europe not long after WWII, and flourished during the heyday of Nouvelle Vague movements like Italian Neo-Realism, the French New Wave, Das Neue Kino (West Germany), and Britain's Free Cinema. All of these movements had significant impact upon Python's writing, stylizations, and parodic structures/targets.

There are and have been film societies across Britain, including, for example, the extant Swindon Film Society (est. 1947). The umbrella organization British Federation Film Societies (BFFS) was established in 1925.

The bothersome, prattling, and thick-skinned intruder Arthur Name (Idle) must also be a comment by the Pythons on the "types" who frequent such local film societies. One such type wrote a letter to the *Times* in December 1968, bemoaning the lack of quality films and "civic cinemas" in areas outside London:

> What we need is a nationwide chain of civic cinemas. Much has been done by the British Film Institute in establishing provincial theatres, but most are limited to one week in four. There is no film theatre in the west Midlands conurbation and it is left to groups like the Wolverhampton Film Society, which has a membership of 500 to help fill an appalling gap, which means two film nights a month and none in the summer. ("Hard-Hitting Cinema," 20 Dec. 1968: 9)

The letter writer hails from Wombourne, Staffordshire. The fact that Idle is playing this pushy film society type, and that he himself went to school in the "west Midlands conurbation" (in Wolverhampton, a handful of miles from the letter writer's home) is likely no coincidence.

"Fink, Harry" — ("The Refreshment Room at Bletchley") The name, of course, doesn't fit the superlatives that have just been uttered, much like "Tim" doesn't seem the normal name for a powerful enchanter (see *HG*). Harry Julian Fink was an American TV writer (*Ben Casey* and *The Dick Powell Show*, both 1961), and went on to write for Rock Hudson, John Wayne, and Clint Eastwood. Fink wrote with Peckinpah on *Dick Powell*, and Peckinpah will later be satirized in *FC* (cf. "Cheese Westerns" and "Sam Peckinpah's *Salad Days*," Ep. 33).

"forget all about it" — ("Homicidal Barber") Often in lurid tales of the period the impulsive killer or rapist will regret his actions and loathe himself for giving in to his depravities—but will go on anyway until he is stopped. The character in Robert Wiene's *The Cabinet of Dr. Caligari* (1919) is haunted by words and images telling him he is Caligari, and that he must become Caligari ("Du muss Caligari werden!"); the Peter Lorre character in Fritz Lang's chilling 1931 film *M* also wants to be able to stop killing, but cannot, and will do so whenever the voice tells him that he "muss"; and Mr. Craig (Mervyn Johns) in *Dead of Night* (1945) finds that he cannot escape his dreamed destiny of becoming a killer again and again, giving in to the urge to kill each time he dreams a certain dream.

This barber/serial killer character is most likely based on Sweeney Todd, the so-called Demon Barber of Fleet Street, made famous by a number of lurid stories and theatrical productions beginning in the mid-nineteenth century. The barber-killer may have actually lived at the end of the eighteenth century, and his exploits lived on in music halls for many years. There was even an early film based on the characters, *Sweeney Todd: The Demon Barber of Fleet Street* (1936). This film was playing on the BBC occasionally through the 1960s, often as part of "Gaslight Theatre."

frail . . . rebel maid — (PSC; "Lumberjack Song") Played by Connie Booth, an American and John Cleese's second wife (married 1968–1978), and his partner in *Fawlty Towers*. She is dressed to resemble Nell (Fenwick), the heroine from the American *The Dudley Do-Right Show* cartoons (Jay Ward Studios, 1969–1970), as well as myriad "meller-drammers." The Mounties are dressed in typical RCMP attire, and just like Dudley, as well. "Mountains" [*sic*] films were somewhat saccharine, innocuous late-Weimar (thus post-expressionist) films produced in Germany between the wars (and even during WWII), such as *Das Blaue Licht* (1932), starring Leni Riefenstahl, and *Die Weiße Hölle vom Piz Palü* (1929).

The "rebel maid" allusion is based on the character Lady Mary Trefusis, the titular character in the light opera *The Rebel Maid* (music by Montague Phillips; lyrics by Gerald Dodson; libretto by Alexander M. Thompson and Gerald Dodson). The opera premiered in 1921 at the Empire Theatre in London, and had been produced as recently as 1957 by the St. Albans Operatic Society in St. Albans, Hertfordshire. The light opera was also something of a recurring staple on the Home Service as late as 1966.

• G •

"ghastly place" — ("The Visitors") A snap judgment rendered by Mr. Freight (Gilliam) as he scans Victor's (Chapman) home, this fulfills the social stereotype of homosexual men being meticulous in personal habit and uncannily adept at interior design.

"Giant redwood . . . scots pine" — ("Lumberjack Song") This list of varying trees is an answer to the Barber's (Palin) hated sameness found in barber college. The giant redwood is only found in California, and only in portions of the northern Sierra Nevada mountains (so, not as far north as British Columbia). The larch—previously featured in Ep. 3—is found in Canada and much of North America. The Douglas fir tree is found throughout the mountain regions of Oregon and British Columbia. The scots pine is also called a fir in Great Britain, and is the only native British pine, hence not endemic to the British Columbia region. (See *EBO*.)

"glacier" — ("Kilimanjaro Expedition") Of the peaks at Kilimanjaro, only Kibo features a year-round snowcap (*EBO*).

goat — ("The Visitors") Both a sign of lechery and just plain animal filth, the goat fits right in with the rest of the group converging on Victor and Iris. The goats used in *FC* (see Ep. 27, as well) came from Animal Kingdom (WAC T12/1,242), and will reappear—eating revolutionary pamphlets—in the Sartre apartment in Ep. 27.

"Golders Green" — ("Llamas") Portions of episodes 8 and 9 were recorded at the Golders Green Hippodrome (on Sunday, 19 October 1969) (WAC T12/1,090). Golders Green is located in North London, near Finchley, Hendon, and Hampstead. The Hippodrome (est. 1913) was acquired by the BBC in the late 1960s and converted to a television recording studio. Taping of the *FC* episodes occurred primarily on Stage 6 at BBC-TC, but other shows could and did force the Pythons and crew to move—to TC Stage 8, to Ealing Studios, and to Golders Green on this occasion. The Hippodrome is located on North End Road in Golders Green, London, W13.

"go much" — ("The Visitors") Obviously a sexual allusion, as it's voiced to Iris (Cleveland) by the lecherous Mr. Equator (Cleese). Cf. the "Nudge, Nudge" man, who asks "knowingly" whether the gent's wife is "a goer" (Ep. 3). See the *OED* for the sexual connotations of the phrase in literature.

"Good questions" — ("Kilimanjaro Expedition [Double Vision]") Note the pluralizations that are creeping in: "Yes, *we* are leading. . . ."; "And what routes will you *both* be taking?," etc. Arthur Wilson (Idle) is figuring out the rules of this seemingly illogical man (Sir George Head) and setting, and is able to communicate effectively once those rules are followed.

"Gumby, Prof. R.J." — ("Gumby Crooner") Cf. Ep. 11, where Prof. *R.J.* Canning unsuccessfully attempts to narrate a Black Plague documentary. This use of initials for academics (and casting Gumbys to represent them) lampoons the luminaries and eminent scholars the Pythons would have read in school, such as A.J.P. Taylor (satirized in *HG*, as well), G. Wilson Knight, L.C. Knights, C.S. Lewis, and perhaps especially E.M.W. Tillyard, the progenitor of the well-known "Elizabethan world picture" thesis (1943).

Additionally, there may be a built-in reference here to the older tradition of "Gentlemen vs. Players" in cricket matches at Lords, where forename initials were used to distinguish between professional and amateur players.

• H •

hand-held camera — (PSC; link out of "Llamas") This simply means that the camera is not mounted on a tripod or "gyrocam" support, thus the image often appears bouncy, unsteady, more frenetic. The technique was used often in foreign film of the time, especially as an answer to Hollywood's fluid, flowing cameras mounted on tracks and dollies.

"Hitchcock, *Psycho*" — ("Homicidal Barber") The director and his trendsetting 1960 horror film, starring Janet Leigh and Tony Perkins, and for the first time in a major Hollywood film conflating sexuality, disturbed pathology, scopophilia, and violence into a popular and controversial hit.

The film features significant moments of cross-dressing, voyeurism, and violence—all of which would become essential to Python's métier. In *Psycho* Norman (Perkins) dresses as his dead mother and kills "naughty," transgressing women he's guiltily spying upon. In the Python sketch, the Barber has perhaps killed someone (there's plenty of blood as circumstantial evidence) as a result of his mother's negative influence, and will cross-dress once he's happily a lumberjack. See the entry for "mother" below for more on the negative maternal influence.

"Hurst" — ("Homicidal Barber") Geoff Hurst scored a celebrated hat trick in the 1966 World Cup final win over Germany. Hurst began playing for West Ham in 1960 as a nineteen-year-old wing half, but was soon moved to a striker position, where he stayed. Hurst replaced Jimmy Greaves in the '66 Cup during the knock-out phase, allowing for the four-goal performance. (The Greaves name is flashed in a film leader in Ep. 2.) The audio account of the thrilling final seconds of the match can be heard on the BBC's *Eyewitness: 1960–69*, "1966 World Cup."

• I •

"I keep falling off" — (link into "Gumby Crooner") This is a moment of extreme literality, when this comment actually refers back to the "permissive society" moments mentioned in Ep. 8, and the "full frontal nudity" theme. Also, cf. the appearances of Mary Whitehouse types who tilt at the liberal society in *FC*, as in the "Tory Housewives" sketch in Ep. 32. The Goons employed a multitude of such "literal" jokes.

This is also a straight-ahead joke—set-up and payoff, and could fit into a stand-up routine. There are very few of these in the Pythons' oeuvre, and fewer still that aren't undercut or punished. Here, the following title card points up the lameness of this joke, as it is Britain's entry into a Eurovision- or Montreux-type contest for jokes. The Pythons will be invited to enter a cobbled-together episode into the Golden Rose of Montreux contest in 1971, where they'll come second. WAC information for the reshooting of that episode can be found in WAC T12/1,413.

into the fire — (PSC; "The Visitors") Another instance where cats are made the object of violence in Python. Cf. the cat choking to death on lupins in Ep. 33, the cat as doorbell and another being ironed flat in Ep. 45, and the cat being dust-banged against a wall in *HG*.

"inviting them along" — ("The Visitors") The simple plot is beginning to resemble Dr. Seuss's children's book, *The Cat in the Hat* (1957), where an uninvited guest (the cat) appears and causes all manner of havoc as the children try to keep the house in shape for the mother's imminent return. Several of the Pythons (Gilliam, Idle, Jones, and Palin) did work together on a children's show (*Do Not Adjust Your Set* [1967–1969]) prior to *FC*, and also cf. the use of a Richard Scarry book in Ep. 3. This sketch, of course, takes a much more sexual, devious, and lethal turn than Theodor Geisel's works.

In walks . . . necklace — (PSC; "The Visitors") Mr. Freight (Gilliam) looks very much like a glam-rocker of the period. Glam-rock (also glitter rock) featured men dressed effeminately and outlandishly, with the "suggestion of sexual ambiguity or androgyny" (*OED*). The sexual ambiguity issue is key, since Equator (Cleese) mentions that his friend's wife has just died, then Freight shows up with a male companion (Palin), and is called a "great poof." His behavior is also stereotypically gay (a lisping, effeminate voice and poncing, affected posture, etc.).

According to A.C. Hamilton, most "antique and Renaissance" works featuring bisexual figures utilize an effeminate male as representing androgyny, which may have influenced Python's choice here. British glam-rock artists included David Bowie (as Ziggy Stardust), Gary Glitter, and members of Slade, among others. See *EBO*.

Gilliam will dress like this again in Ep. 33, as "Ginger," and be quite offended when it's implied that he might be gay.

"Islam" — (link into "Jug Dancing" animation) The Muhammadan religion established in the seventh century. Islam is monotheistic and follows strict religious practices. In the animation, neither character appears characteristically Islamic (either by race or dress, etc.). This and "Buddha" seem to be used here as just recognizable and silly throwaway names.

The name "Brian" has been and will continue to be utilized in *FC* and beyond, like the name "Arthur," and starting back as early as Ep. 2 (see notes to Ep. 2 for more on these myriad nominal appearances). "Bruce" will also appear again, especially in the "Drunken Philosophers" sketch, where everyone except the new faculty member is named Bruce.

"It's . . ." — (PSC; titles) The "Monty Python's Flying Circus," voiced by Cleese in his "silly" voice, is not noted in the written script.

• J •

jug band music — (PSC; "Jug Band Dancing" animated link out of "The Refreshment Room at Bletchley") A jazz sound characterized by simple, even homemade instruments, like a whiskey jug, washtub, etc., as well as typical jazz combo instruments. Most of this music would have been culled from the BBC's massive archives, and used gratis. This particular piece of music is called "Banjerino," and is a jug, washboard, and kazoo composition (WAC T12/1,090).

• K •

"Kilimanjaro" — ("Kilimanjaro Expedition [Double Vision]") Found in Tanzania (near the Kenyan border), it features the highest point(s) on the African continent, and was first climbed in 1889. Head's idea to build a bridge between the two summits of Kilimanjaro isn't as farfetched as the text would have us believe, as Kilimanjaro is actually a three-peak volcanic massif, with cones called Kibo (the highest), Mawensi, and Shira, from east to west (*EBO*). Head could have been thinking, then, of building a bridge between two of the cones, as unlikely as that might be (discounting his double vision, of course). Much like the intended incongruity of hermits living in happy communal groups in Ep. 8, this intended silliness has a basis in reality.

• L •

Letter — (link out of "Lumberjack Song") Letters of this type can be found in many period newspapers and periodicals, including both actual and created ones in *Private Eye*, and in *Spectator*, many responding to previously published letters:

> Sir: Is Sir Richard Acland (21 June) thinking of W.B. Yeats's saying: "Science is the religion of the suburbs"?
>
> *T.A.M. Jack*
>
> Preston-next-Wingham, Canterbury, Kent (5 July 1969)

This same type of "letter to the editor" is still characteristic of major newspapers to this day, and this format will appear throughout *FC*. (See Eps. 5, 10, and 11 for more letters.)

"Llama" — ("Llamas") A relative of the camel, and native to South America. Mutated as it becomes a part of Python's bestiary, the llama does not have a beak, nor does it eat honey (it is a ruminant), have fins, or pose much of a threat to humans. Llamas will later figure prominently in the "silly" opening titles for *Monty Python and the Holy Grail* (1975).

low sexy lighting—ha ha — (PSC; "The Visitors") The "ha ha" is certainly another in-joke, here indicating the remote possibility of achieving mood lighting on this particular stage set with the available light technology. With the entire show working on a very thin budget and on the least choice of available TC sets (usually TC 6, to this point, but perhaps Golders Green), the lights available would have been those most often used for news sets and the like, meaning bright, broad illumination from 5K and 10K overhead lights. More than that, Martin Kempton indicates that TC 6 was the *only* studio space not gifted with a new light control package in 1969 (a dimmer control called a "Thorn Q-File"), which allowed all the other Television Centre studios significantly more control over light levels (see *An Incomplete History of London's Television Studios*). Finally, mood lighting would require not only lights capable of lesser, manipulable illumination, but in-studio cameras that could successfully capture clear video images in such a low light environment.

It's clear that on many of the exterior shoots (on film) to gather inserts and the like the troupe traveled with even less complicated lighting packages, demanding lots of shooting in full daylight. For the kitchen sequence in "Dull Life of a City Stockbroker," however, the show actually used a kitchen in a council house in the Australia Road, East Acton area, which was unusual, as it would have demanded at least some onsite, indoor lighting.

• M •

"Machin" — ("Kilimanjaro Expedition [Double Vision]") Richard Harris played Frank Machin, the coal miner who tries to escape to football (rugby) stardom in Lindsay Anderson's tragic "Angry Young Man" film *This Sporting Life* (1963). See notes to Ep. 2 for more on the movement and film, and notes to Ep. 19 for more on Anderson.

Another Machin, Arnold (1911–1999), designed the most recognizable and oft-used effigy of the Queen to be used on British stamps from 1966 onward; and noted English author G.I.T. Machin (*The Catholic Question in English Politics, 1820 to 1830*, published in 1964) could have also prompted this name.

"Mama" — ("Lumberjack Song") Cf. the "mother" issues discussed in the entries "Hitchcock, Psycho" and "mother" in this episode. Here, rather than castration anxiety, the Barber-cum-Lumberjack seems to have castration envy.

Marseillaise — (PSC; "A Man with a Tape Recorder Up His Brother's Nose") Fitting for Python that the French national anthem would play in this instance where a finger is up a nose. This rendition is performed by the Band of the Grenadier Guards (WAC T12/1,090). The BGG also performs the version of "Liberty Bell Suite" used in the show's credits.

"Matrons" — ("Kilimanjaro Expedition [Double Vision]") The *OED* notes that there is a class-specific definition for the term "matron," and it fits the "Sir George Head, OBE" and later "Upperclass Twit" theme nicely: "A married woman, usually with the accessory idea of (moral or social) rank or dignity." But then the dictionary goes on to distinguish between Roman and British matrons, defining the British matron thusly: ". . . jocularly taken as the representative of certain social prejudices and rigorous notions of conventional propriety supposed to be characteristic of married women of the English upper middle-class."

moorland — (PSC; "Hunting Film") Land that has not been cultivated, fenland, etc. This looks to be the same Bournemouth area used in earlier episodes.

moped — (PSC; "Llamas") A "motorized pedal cycle," and used to be called an autocycle. Mopeds are also featured in Ep. 29, the "*Erizabeth L*" sketch.

"mother" — ("Homicidal Barber") Perhaps the Customer (Jones) is also a victim of his mother. The images of razors and scissors also invoke the specter of Freud's castrating mother figure, especially as the figurative emasculation renders Norman (Tony Perkins) incapable of natural sexuality, and prevents the Barber (Palin) from successfully cutting hair. None of these three, then, have entered the "genital phase." It seems that all three men (Norman, the Barber, and the Customer) are far too involved with their mothers to achieve sexual normalcy elsewhere. Later, after the Barber has refused/failed to cut the Customer's hair, the presence of an offscreen domineering, castrating mother is confirmed when he laments his mother forcing him into barber school, forcing him to cut hair, which repulses him.

Mounties — ("Lumberjack Song") Members of the Royal Canadian Mounted Police (RCMP), Canada's federal peace force, and here wearing their recognizable red jackets and peaked hats, another Python shorthand to remind the viewer that the plot is moving into Canadian territory.

Most of the Mounties here are actually members of the Fred Tomlinson Singers, semi-regular musical guests on *FC* (Ep. 22).

• N •

"Nairobi" — (Kilimanjaro Expedition [Double Vision]") Capital of Kenya. Nairobi is approximately 150 miles north and west of Kilimanjaro. Kenya had been much in the British newspapers and public consciousness during the earlier Mau Mau uprisings, when British settlers were attacked and often killed, some quite gruesomely. See the entries for "armed communist uprising . . ." (Ep. 31) and "Mau Mau" in Ep. 43 for other references.

"Name by name but not by nature" — ("The Visitors") A Dudley Moore character—Mr. Spigot, a one-legged actor auditioning for a Tarzan role—introduces himself as "A spigot by name but not by nature" (*Beyond the Fringe,* "One Leg Too Few").

• O •

"OBE" — ("Kilimanjaro Expedition [Double Vision]") Stands for Officer of the British Empire, and is one of the "Most Excellent Order of the British Empire" honors, though *not* an admission into knighthood.

The orders were instituted by George V in 1917, made available to many who served the empire during the Great War, including women and foreigners. This broadened application of royal recognition could be part of the reason the Pythons created the perceptually challenged Head—just about anyone could be considered for OBE status. The Order was in the news at this time, as well, when the Chapel for the Order was dedicated in 1969 at St. Paul's, the Queen and the Duke in attendance. The "affected" depiction of Head might be attributed to the fact that the easily targeted Duke of Edinburgh (the Queen's husband, Prince Philip) has been and remains Grand Master of the Order.

Noteworthy Order members of this era include other explorers like Sir Earnest Shackleton, CVO; Sir Edmund Hillary, KG, KBE; yachtsman Sir Francis Chichester, KG; as well as TV actress Violet Carson (*Coronation Street*). Chichester—who circumnavigated the globe solo—was knighted in 1967 on national TV, and with the Queen wielding Sir Francis Drake's sword. Cleese himself would decline the CBE in 1996.

"Odeon" — ("The Visitors") The Odeon would have been one of the cinemas built by Oscar Deutsch in Great Britain in the 1920s, then purchased by J. Arthur Rank and greatly expanded in the 1930s. He may be referring specifically to the Odeon at Leicester Square, an Art Deco movie palace.

"old days" — ("Gumby Crooner") Reflecting the "Yorkshire Gentlemen" sketch where four northern gentlemen sit about and swap hyperbolized stories of childhood privation and hardship, and generally agree that the older days were far more challenging. That sketch was originally written and performed on *At Last the 1948 Show* by Chapman, Cleese, Tim Brooke-Taylor, and Marty Feldman.

"One stain could be the mark . . ." — (PSC; "Homicidal Barber") Here again the script addresses the reader, not the viewer, mentioning that one of the blood streaks seen on the Barber's clothing could have been caused by a "hand slipping downward." This isn't clear at all in the performance itself—the Barber just looks blood spattered.

"Only make believe . . ." — ("Gumby Crooner") Lyrics from "Make Believe," from the Broadway musical *Showboat* (1927) by Jerome Kern and Oscar Hammerstein. The entire stanza:

> Only make believe I love you,
> Only make believe that you love me.
> Others find peace of mind in pretending,
> Couldn't you? Couldn't I? Couldn't we?
> Make believe our lips are blending
> In a phantom kiss, or two, or three.
> Might as well make believe I love you,
> For to tell the truth I do.

The musical was restaged on Broadway several times, as well as a celebrated 1966 version staged at Lincoln Center, New York. *Showboat* would be brought to the UK in 1971, and enjoyed a record run of more than 900 shows.

"only one" — ("Homicidal Barber") West Ham United Football Club (est. 1895) was a Division One team between 1958 and 1978—to date West Ham have won no Premiership titles or league championships, but can claim three FA cup wins.

"on the carpet" — ("The Visitors") This sketch is becoming a precursor to the troupe's final episode, wherein "The Most Awful Family in Britain" is profiled (Ep. 45). The squalor and debauchery here are certainly examples of Python's stated attempts to shock its audience. Mr. Cook (Palin) will change only slightly and reappear in Ep. 12 as Ken Shabby (also Palin), equally vile and debased.

• P •

"Palace" — ("Homicidal Barber") Crystal Palace Football Club was formed in 1905, and was named for the glass Crystal Palace the team originally occupied (built for the 1851 Great Exhibition). The team was promoted to Division One by 1969 on the heels of beating Fulham, which is when the Customer (Jones) would have been watching them. An illustration of the Crystal Palace will be seen in Ep. 29, "The Lost World of Roiurama."

Part 2 — (titles) One of the many misleading introductory numbers used by Python in *FC*. Cf. episodes 2, 3, 4, and 8 for similar meaningless mis-numberings.

"poof" — ("The Visitors") Slang for homosexual. Used often in *FC* (variations "pooftah," "poove"). Here the poof is acknowledged, welcomed, and accepted by the assembled crowd. In Ep. 33, Biggles will kill Alvy (Palin) when he admits his homosexuality. Ginger (Gilliam) then ponces in and is offended at being mistaken for a poof. The popular BBC television show *Dad's Army* (1968–1977) will be lampooned in Ep. 38 (printed script version only) as *Dad's Pooves*, and feature prancing, cross-dressing sadomasochists.

"press wild flowers" — ("Lumberjack Song") The practice of "pressing" flowers into books, albums, etc., is listed here probably because it might be considered an artistic, effeminate pastime. The following line then cements the effeminization motif. This specter of effeminization—on the stage and among the audience—is just the vice the anti-theatricalists were railing against at the height of the Tudor and through the end of the Stuart monarchies. Significant anti-theatricalist literature was produced by the likes of Gosson, Stubbes, Northbrook, and Prynne. There was a fear that acting on the stage and watching such play-acting prompted men to become effeminate and more likely to violate sumptuary laws (dressing above their station), as well as indulge in ingles, catamites, and all manner of sodomitical practices. In this sketch Palin's character disdains the "natural" love of his obviously willing female companion in favor of transvestism and even homosexuality, and is willing to play the less-dominant female part of some male-male relationship generated from a bar visit. See Stephen Gosson's *Schoole of Abuse* (1579) and Philip Stubbes' *The Anatomie of Abuses* (1583), both Puritan attacks on the falseness of the stage; see also William Prynne's *Histriomatrix* (1632). (For more on the subject see *MPSERD*, chapter 6.)

This is also a somewhat rare example in Python wherein the transvestism is not only noted textually, but takes on a sexual and even licentious tincture. Usually, cross-dressers (like Pepperpots) are textually treated as female figures (albeit ugly, dowdy, shrill, etc.). In Ep. 14, an admitted "female impersonator" (Cleese) will be gangster Dinsdale Piranha's object of affection.

• Q •

"quadruped" — ("Llamas") Any creature employing four-legged locomotion. Here, at least, the Pythons are correct.

• R •

"Radio Times" — (letter link out of "Lumberjack Song") The BBC's programming magazine has been in publication since 1923. The publication would feature *FC* on the cover only once, in 1974, when the final, abbreviated season was about to debut. (Idle is reading from this edition at the end of the final episode, Ep. 45, as he begs "Mr. Cotton" for a few more minutes of mayhem.) Cleese appears on the 11 January 1969 cover of the *Radio Times*, but for *I'm Sorry I'll Read That Again* (1964–1983).

"rat-bag" — ("The Visitors") *OED*: "A stupid or eccentric person, a fool; an unpleasant person, a trouble-maker. Also . . . stupid, idiotic, uncouth." In Renaissance terms, "baggage" could mean a worthless woman, as well. The term will be used again in Eps. 21, 27, and 37.

"rather sharply" — ("Kilimanjaro Expedition [Double Vision]") Actually, since Kilimanjaro is made up of three volcanic cones, unlike an Alpine formation the summit topography here is much more gentle, with a saddle at the 15,000-foot level connecting cone rims, and a gradual slope (influenced by past flows) leading to the plateaus below the formation. No mountaineering equipment is necessary to climb even the tallest peak (*EBO*). In a later episode (Ep. 33), the Pythons will attempt to climb the north face of the Uxbridge Road. There is also an aborted mountaineering sketch in Ep. 26, and in Ep. 31 Mt. Everest is climbed by hairdressers.

The description of the summit as tending to go up and up and then to "slope away rather sharply" is silly, yes, but this is very much like Sir Edmund Hillary described the summiting of Everest in one of his earliest recorded accounts of the ascent:

> at first glance it was most impressive, and even rather frightening. *Great* cornices—which are *great* overhanging masses of ice and snow—thrust out to the right, and hung over the two-mile drop of the Kan Chung face. If you held too far to that side it would be disaster. . . . I levered my way backwards up [an ice] chimney, praying the cornice would stay in place. . . . Beyond each stretch of the ridge there was always another one curving away beyond it, until we finally realized that the ridge ahead, *instead of rising, dropped sharply away*. (Audio transcription, *Eyewitness: 1950–59*, "The Conquest of Everest")

It should be noted that both Hillary and Richard Dimbleby—who was reverently describing the new Queen's coronation as Everest was being conquered—employ very similar phraseologies (a cornucopia of "great" moments) in their accounts. The more hushed and reverential Dimbleby will be parodied in Ep. 23, beginning in the "Fish Licence" sketch.

"real entertainment" — ("Gumby Crooner") This is probably a belief shared by many of the generation. The advent of television did nearly cripple feature filmmaking, causing Hollywood to streamline and innovate to survive. Television also replaced radio and newspapers, to a great degree, as the source of news and entertainment for postwar generations. Evening programming would have also kept more folk at home, and away from the cinema, a stroll, the pub, the musical revue, etc. As early as 1961 the head of the U.S. Federal Communications Commission (FCC), Newton Minow, had called television a "vast wasteland."

Red Indian — ("Hunting Film") Another appearance by an American Indian in Britain (cf. Ep. 6), this time also played by Idle. Like the City Gent and Pepperpot, the character is iconicized and reduced to a visual stereotype. In this instance, however, there is no opportunity for the character to overcome that liminalization, as he just plays the part of startled game and scampers off. The Pepperpots are allowed, often, knowledge and narrative control well beyond their appearance and station, and the previous appearance of the Red Indian revealed a literate theatergoer very much up on modern, British theatrical performance. The marginalization created by stereotypical behavior, dress, and speech can be trespassed by certain of these characters, perhaps finding its ultimate realization in the depiction of Dennis (Palin), the uppity peasant in *Holy Grail*. See entries in Ep. 2 for "city gent," as well as "Pepperpots" in Ep. 1.

"Rubber Mac Award" — (link out of "Lumberjack Song") A rubber mac is a rubber or synthetic material raincoat, as worn by Praline in the "Dead Parrot" sketch in Ep. 8. For the award, cf. the titles to Ep. 6, for the BBC's Eurovision- and Golden Rose of Montreux–like "entry for the Zinc Stoat of Budapest." For information on the Eurovision Song Contest, see entries in Ep. 22.

This image of a battered trophy may be a reference to the infamous "lost" World Cup trophy, which went missing in 1966, the year England won the celebrated title. The trophy was later discovered by a dog in a suburban home garden in South London.

runs out — ("The Visitors") P.G. Wodehouse actually used the film term "iris out" (meaning the use of an iris action to leave a scene) as an interesting way to exit characters from a scene. From *Plum Pie* (1966): "After a terrific struggle the hood called it a day and irised out" (177). In the Python sketch, Iris (Cleveland) puts up with as much as she can, then quickly exits.

• S •

"So are we" — ("Kilimanjaro Expedition [Double Vision]") There is the implication here that we as an audience now share Head's pathology—we can see the other side of the doubled world that only he has seen until this point. The influence and nominal significance of supernatural author Arthur Machen (1863–1947) can't be overlooked here. In his novella *The Great God Pan* (1894), Machen describes a world beyond or behind the perceived world:

> Look about you, Clarke. You see the mountain, and hill following after hill, as wave on wave, you see the woods and orchard, the fields of ripe corn, and the meadows reaching to the reed-beds by the river. You see me standing here beside you, and hear my voice; but I tell you that all these things—yes, from that star that has just shone out in the sky to the solid ground beneath our feet—*I say that all these are but dreams and shadows; the shadows that hide the real world from our eyes. There is a real world, but it is beyond this glamour and this vision, beyond these "chases in Arras, dreams in a career," beyond them all as beyond a veil.* I do not know whether any human being has ever lifted that veil; but I do know, Clarke, that you and I shall see it lifted this very night from before another's eyes. You may think this all strange nonsense; it may be strange, but it is true, and the ancients knew what lifting the veil means. They called it seeing the god Pan. (chapter 1; italics added)

In the sketch, Python seems to have given Head (Cleese) the ability to see this other world, which in the novella is only accessible by surgically altering the gray matter with a "slight lesion," according to Dr. Raymond. Upper-class folk, in Python's world, do tend to suffer from brain maladies, as exhibited by the actions and unintelligible (requiring subtitles) speech patterns (Ep. 12), and even brain shifting, requiring a sharp jostle to realign the tiny, off-center brain ("*Mortuary Hour*," Ep. 35).

"somehow" — ("Kilimanjaro Expedition [Double Vision]") At this moment, it seems that the absurdity has been controlled by the introduction of a character who—dressed like a credible mountaineer—assures Bob / Arthur Wilson (Idle) in something of an aside that everything's going to be fine. It takes just moments, though, for that calming effect to disappear as the guide (Chapman) climbs the walls, furniture, etc. A later example of this phenomena can be seen in Ep. 43, where Hamlet is accosted by a series of doctors, each saying that the one before was not a real doctor, only for the new scenario to quickly unravel with the appearance of the next "real" doctor. It's this "no safe ground" idea (where the proverbial rug of reality can be pulled out over and over again)—the fact in Python there is not a return to normalcy, just a new absurdism—that keeps their comedy from being precisely termed "Brechtian." In *MPSERD* the author notes:

> Kristin Thompson points out in "Sawing Through the Bough: *Tout va Bien* as a Brechtian Film" (*Wide Angle* 1:3, 1976), that Brecht separated himself from the Dadaists and surrealists and their interpretations of alienation. Ben Brewster's article "From Shklovsky to Brecht: A Reply" (*Screen* 15:2), quotes Brecht: "Their objects do not return from alienation" (Thompson 30). Brecht saw those practitioners essentially paralyzing the function of their art, so that "as far as its effect is concerned, it ends in an amusement" (30). Much of Python's work (especially the *Flying Circus* episodes) is explicitly created to undercut any return, to deny any progress other than that which leads to a comedic, shocking and often open-ended end. In other words, to end in an amusement. (311)

sportin' gentlemen dressed in huntin' tweed — ("Hunting Film") The printed script offers this vernacular spelling ("huntin'") throughout the scene description. This is an allusion to a character type created by Arthur Conan Doyle, the blustery Lord John Roxton, an ambitious big game hunter looking to bag a dinosaur in *The Lost World*:

> A sportin' risk, young fellah, that's the salt of existence. Then it's worth livin' again. We're all gettin' a deal too soft and dull and comfy. Give me the great waste lands and the wide spaces, with a gun in my fist and somethin' to look for that's worth findin'. I've tried war and steeplechasin' and aeroplanes, but this huntin' of beasts that look like a lobster-supper dream is a brand-new sensation. (chapter 6)

The music beneath (dubbed to the film) is a lively version of Melodious Brass' "Waltzing Trumpets" by the Fairey Band (WAC T12/1,090).

"stage with him" — ("The Refreshment Room at Bletchley") This is not unlike some of the serious prologues written for Restoration or eighteenth-century dramas, especially in their hyperbolic praise; also see the tongue-in-cheek version offered by H. Scriblerus Secundus (Fielding) as the "Preface" to his *Tom Thumb (The Tragedy of Tragedies)* (1731).

"Strong, Arthur" — (letter link out of "Lumberjack Song") Note the connection between the girl's misunderstanding about "rugged" appearances equaling heterosexual virility, and the name and title/rank of the letter writer. The implication that manly, uniformed, and/or titled men mask "swishy" personas is a consistent Python trope (fairy policemen, campy soldiers, swishy judges). The inclusion of "Mrs." also indicates that even protesting, letter writer Arthur Strong may share some of the Barber's proclivities.

"Swahili" — ("Kilimanjaro Expedition [Double Vision]") More accurately "Kiswahili," since "Swahili" are the Bantu peoples themselves. It is the principal language of the entire region, though hundreds of tribal dialects are still spoken, as well as English. See the entry above for "down there" for more on English colonial expectations, deformations, etc.

swish — (PSC; "The Refreshment Room at Bletchley") Slang for an effeminate man, or a homosexual, but here used to describe a posh, upscale club. See *OED*.

sync — ("A Man with a Tape Recorder Up His Brother's Nose") Out of synchronization, which would actually mean that rather than two channels where the sound is divided (voice, instrumentation, etc.), there are two perhaps mono recordings being played back almost simultaneously.

Following this performance, there appears a filmed shot of a single spectator, in long shot, in an otherwise empty football stadium. (This shot is not indicated at all in the written scripts.) The fan is clapping, and obviously taking the place in this instance for the stock Women's Institute footage, but not in stereo. The shot is part of the footage used in Ep. 7, where the lone spectator watched a single player and referee during the blancmange invasion. The stadium is the Bradford City Stadium in Bradford. The Pythons shot a significant number of exteriors for the first season on this trip to West Yorkshire, between 10 and 14 November 1969 (WAC T12/1,242).

• T •

tape recorder — (PSC; "Homicidal Barber") The intermediary that prevents actual contact or normal intimacy, here the tape recorder performs the role of a hole in a wall, a mask or role-playing mechanism, or even a peeping camera—in this case allowing the Barber the distance he needs from the actual act of hair cutting (from performance, from intimacy). Cf. the 1960 Michael Powell film *Peeping Tom*, where the 16mm camera performs a similar function, and the killer even uses the camera's tripod as his penetrating weapon/phallus.

"this week" — (link out of "Hunting Film") Perhaps an unconscious indication that the days of the armored knight and chicken were numbered. Gilliam (in the armor) will appear later in the episode in a significantly flamboyant part, and his out-of-armor appearances will increase into the second season. The slapstick knight character will appear only twice more, in Eps. 13 and 35, an indication that Pythons' writing prowess has gone well beyond the need for such a stock continuity figure.

This kind of silly, interruptive *and* transitionary character can be seen in cartoons the Pythons would have grown up watching. In Chuck Jones's *The Dover Boys* (1942) a bathing-costumed man saunters through the frame every few moments—to the tune of "The Fountain in the Park"—interrupting the narrative flow as both the characters and the audience watch. A mynah bird serves the same purpose in Jones's *Inki and the Minah Bird* (1943), as does the creepy character "Egghead" in Tex Avery's *A Day at the Zoo* (1939). These are early works by these talented directors, as well, and as their confidence increased they relied less and less on such gimmicks.

"tins of beans" — ("The Visitors") Cf. the Gilliam character (Kevin) in the Garibaldi family in Ep. 45 ("*Most Awful Family in Britain*"), who lays on the couch throughout the sketch, eats beans, passes gas, and screams for more beans.

Mocking the editorial and advertising commingling in the *Daily Express*, *Private Eye* (on Friday, 6 August 1965) ran a mock news story headlined "The Biggest News of the Day" in the *Daily Getsworse*, which was a "full-page colour ad" for Loosebowl's Baked Beans, a product that has "carried the good name of Britain all over the world" (Ingrams, 120). The story is penned by "Squire Barrowboy," a *Private Eye* pseudonym for the powerful *Express* publisher Lord Beaverbrook (1879–1964).

"Totnes" — ("Homicidal Barber") A town in Devon on the Dart River, essentially due west of the beachside resort town Paignton. A significant portion of the exteriors for the second season were shot in and around Paignton.

"two men" — ("Kilimanjaro Expedition [Double Vision]") It appears that Head's dictionary was either written by him, or the visual (and, eventually, cognitive) malady afflicts Head and his entire class, including authors of dictionaries. This kind of shared class affliction will reappear in more virulent terms in the "Upperclass Twit" sketch (Ep. 12). The class consciousness is also apparent in the consistent anti-Conservative bent the *FC* program takes, including aligning the Tories in Britain with Germany's National Socialist party, also in Ep. 12.

• V •

very small bird — ("Hunting Film") This hunting film is structured like a Keystone silent comedy, or the musical montage segment of a show like *The Monkees* (NBC, 1966–1968), but perhaps especially the contemporary (and naughty) *Benny Hill Show*. Hill had been on the air since 1955 (for BBC, ATV, and Thames), and was obviously an inspiration to the Pythons as they attended school and began work in the TV industry. Hill moved to Thames TV in 1969, and would spend the next twenty years there. The Pythons would move in to Television Centre as Benny Hill was leaving, and the shared props and set decorations can be seen when episodes from both shows are examined. Also, the rickety caption or title roller machine was shared by both shows. It can be seen in *Flying Circus* at the end of Ep. 26.

The images of the landed gentry blasting everything in sight is also reminiscent of the hunt sequence in Jean Renoir's scathing *Rules of the Game* (1938), a rich criticism of France's disinterested and disintegrating social elite in the inter-war years.

See the entry for "sportin' gentlemen dressed in huntin' tweed" above for more on the literary inspiration for this depiction.

• W •

"Washington Post March" — ("The Visitors") Actual title "The Washington Post," this is a march written by American John Philip Sousa (1854–1932) in 1889, and was culled from the BBC's audio archives (WAC T12/1,090). The tune had been used previously by Cleese for *At Last the 1948 Show*, the "I've Got a Parrot Up My Nose" song.

Welsh miners — (PSC; "The Visitors") The Welsh miners will reappear in Ep. 26, the "Coal Mine" sketch. Most of them here are the Fred Tomlinson Singers, who have appeared on the show previously, and will again. They will sing their version of "Summarizing Proust" in Ep. 31. Singers in female Welsh national costumes along with a Welsh harpist will appear in "*The Money Programme*" in Ep. 29.

"wet 'em" — ("The Visitors") Incontinence jokes also characterize the Garibaldi family sketch in Ep. 45, including references to flatulence and bowel regularity.

"Wilson, Arthur" — (PSC; "Kilimanjaro Expedition [Double Vision]") Idle is here called "Arthur Wilson," in spite of the fact that the script as printed has been calling him "Bob" from the outset. (For an earlier instance of this conflict between the written script's character identification and the character's professed identification—noting, of course, that both names would have been written by the script writers, building in the confusion at the written textual level—see

Ep. 5. There, "Stig" sits down for an interview, only to give his name moments later as "David Thomas" ("Silly Job Interview"). In both cases, the textual confusion would be apparent at the level of the *reader*, not the *viewer*. This structure makes for a far more writerly text (borrowing Barthes's term), demanding that the reader of the scripts perform some cognitive gymnastics as he/she tries to keep separate the written text from the performed text.

Perhaps, however, there are actually two of these men—Bob and Arthur Wilson, both played by Idle. This is another example of the "in-joke" level of the printed scripts, where information that never ends up on screen is included. The viewing audience, then, wouldn't know that the script had already named this character "Bob," and would accept the name he gives as his own, "Arthur Wilson." Perhaps at the *printed* textual level, then, the presence of two personalities is a given, but not at the *visually recorded* textual level. Later, after Arthur Wilson leaves in a huff, someone else (Bob?) is still in the room with Head.

Note the use of the "Arthur" name again, as was common in the early episodes and will continue throughout *FC*.

winces — ("Homicidal Barber") A typical Hitchcock motif, the use of a particular word or sound to remind the protagonist and the viewer of an event, and usually a crime. In *Blackmail* (1929), it's the image of and word "knife," since the heroine (Annie Oondra) had earlier used a knife to kill the artist (Cyril Ritchard) who attacked her.

"with an L" — ("The Visitors") There is, of course, no "L" anywhere in his name. Perhaps the "L" can stand for latitude, in relation to the equatorial reference? Also, cf. Ep. 19 where the character "Raymond Luxury Yacht" announces that his name is actually pronounced "Throatwobbler Mangrove," no matter the spelling.

• Y •

"your honour" — ("Homicidal Barber") Reading this as a so-called Freudian slip (or "faulty action"), it would appear that the Barber is at least subconsciously thinking about the consequences of his alleged crimes, and an appearance before a magistrate, and/or this is proof that he's perhaps committed a similar atrocity before.

The Art Critic (also Palin) exhibits a similar response in Ep. 8 when the woman catches him trying to get a better look at a Rubens nude, calling her, among other things, "Your honour."

Episode 10: "The League for Fighting Chartered Accountancy"

"It's" Man abattoir intro; *Animation: Titles* (silly Cleese v/o); Walk-on part in sketch; Bank robber: Lingerie Shop ("Adopt, adapt and improve"); Announcer David Unction and "A special good evening to you"; *It's a Tree* with Arthur Tree; *Animation: A Chippendale Writing Desk, intro for Vocational Guidance Counsellor;* Vocational Guidance Counsellor (Mr. Anchovie: Chartered Accountant or Lion Tamer?); "The League for Fighting Chartered Accountancy"; David Unction reads *Physique;* Ron Obvious: Jumping the Channel, eating an Anglican Cathedral, tunneling from Godalming to Java, splitting a railway carriage with his nose, and running to Mercury (with manager Dino Vercotti); "This is satire" Pepperpot transition; Pet conversions; "Predictable" Vox Pops; Gorilla librarian; Letters to *Daily Mirror;* Strangers in the night; *Animation: Humor, the new permissiveness, and animals eating animals;* "It's" Man taken from the meat hook, and closing credits

• A •

"Adapt . . . round table" — ("Bank Robber [Lingerie Shop]") "Adopt, adapt and improve" is, indeed, the motto of the Round Table organization, founded in 1927 by Louis Marchesi. The goal of the organization was to give eighteen- to forty-five-year-old men a place to gather, and provide service, initially, for the citizens of Norwich. The motto for the Round Table was derived from a speech made in 1927 at the British Industries Fair by the Prince of Wales (later Edward VIII):

> The young business and professional men of this country must get together round the table, *adopt* methods that have proved so sound in the past, *adapt* them to the changing needs of the times and wherever possible, *improve* them. (Round Table National Association)

"Airedale" — ("Pet Conversions") Short for "Airedale terrier." "Putting a tuck in" may mean somehow seaming or hemming the dog. "Let out" usually refers to letting down hems or opening pleats to increase length or girth on a garment. These alterations are essentially verbal descriptions of what Gilliam's dismembering and re-membering animations accomplish with photos of humans, animals, landmarks, etc.

"American . . . violence" — ("Arthur Tree") Cf. the duck, cat, and lizard *not* discussing affairs in Ep. 5. Also probably satirizing the propensity for such entertainment shows to invite celebrities to talk about significant topical issues, including David Frost's own *Frost on Saturday, Frost on Sunday*, etc. (See entry at "David Frost type" below for much more.) There were many BBC, ATV, ITV, Granada, and Thames TV shows of a similar nature, including the BBC's flagship panel discussion show *The Brains Trust* (1955–1961).

Anchovy — ("Vocational Guidance Counsellor [Chartered Accountant]") Saltwater, schooling, herring-like fish. This characterization by Palin is very much like the nebbish Arthur Pewtey, seen earlier in the "Marriage Guidance Counsellor" sketch.

animation of various strange and wonderful creatures — (PSC; "*ANIMATION: Humor, the new permissiveness, and animals eating animals*") The menagerie in this culminating feeding frenzy includes a goat eaten by a crocodile which is eaten by an ostrich (with two lady occupants) eaten by two pigs, one of which then consumes the other, only to be eaten by a third pig. The third pig (representing the government as he talks about "the new permissiveness" and "balance of payments") is carried off by a robin and both are eaten by a flying bowhead whale. The whale (a vintage illustration) is swallowed whole by a shrew. The shrew is then squashed by a "The End" box.

applause over — (PSC; "Arthur Tree") The forest, then, as the audience for this tree/wood show. But perhaps this is also an intentional double entendre, as the "block of wood" mentioned earlier can also be taken as not just a piece of wood, but as a block (an area, a portion of land) of trees, hence the photo of the forest.

shot of a forest—The color transparencies used here are called "In the Lael Forest" and "Easter Ross" (WAC T12/1,242). Easter Ross is a lush area in the highlands east of Ross, Scotland, while the Lael Forest is in the Ullapool area of Highland, Scotland. Some of the exterior work for season one and two would be shot in the Oban and Glencoe areas of Scotland.

"as near as dammit" — ("Pet Conversions") Used here as a comparative phrase, and found somewhat regularly in (especially) interviewee quotations in period newspapers. The *OED* offers this citation: "1961 *Guardian* 24 Apr. 9/7 'The score standing as near as dammit at two.'"

"Attendants" — ("Trailer") Cf. the *Up Your Pavement* TV show featured in Ep. 42. All of these shows (*Up Your Pavement*, *It's a Tree*, and *Yes It's the Sewage Farm Attendants*) feature less-than-noteworthy characters as the shows' foci, an example of the "leveling" aspects of Python's satire. See chapter 5 of *MPSERD*, as well as Dekker's *Shoemakers Holiday* (1599).

Aztec — (PSC; "Strangers in the Night") Central American Indian culture, and known as such since c. AD 1100. The printed script reveals its own level of textual meaning when it gives similes and metaphors (read: examples) for the reader only, and specifically the production design team charged with costuming the show. This "Aztec" character is supposed to resemble Christopher Plummer (b. 1929) as he appeared in *Royal Hunt of the Sun* (1969), according to the script. *Royal Hunt of the Sun* actually depicts Incan culture and chief Atahualpa (Plummer) as they interacted with the Spanish explorer Pisarro (Robert Shaw). The *Times* review of the film appeared three days before the first night of *Flying Circus* broadcast (2 October 1969)—with a large picture of the costumed Plummer—calling the film a "creditable but ineffective in-between" (John Russell Taylor, "Lack of a Bold, Clear Line," 14). Plummer also appeared in *Battle of Britain*, also in 1969.

And rather than the sketch being curtailed due to the husband's wandering off, the script mentions that Vera cuts the Aztec off "owing to lack of money," referring to the cost of speaking actors versus mute walk-ons. This is yet another tidbit for the reader(s) only. See Ep. 28, where the fiscal health of the BBC is in question, and speaking roles are discouraged (and the shows are being broadcast from a nice couple's home).

• B •

"bally froggie" — ("Strangers in the Night") Slang for "bloody Frenchman," probably originally from RAF types during World War I. Biggles (Chapman) comes in here as if he's saving the damsel in one of his many adventures. See "Biggles" entry below.

beach — ("The First Man to Jump the Channel") These scenes were filmed at the beaches beneath the cliffs of Covehithe. Most of the (beachside) Ron Obvious sketch was shot in the Covehithe, Southwold, and Saxmundham areas of Suffolk (WAC T12/1,083). Portions in the city were shot at the Brighton Road and Liberty Lane intersection, Sayes Court Fields, Addlestone, Surrey, on 22 October 1969 (WAC T12/1,242).

bedroom of a middle-aged — ("Strangers in the Night") The music beneath this introduction into the bedroom scene is "Creepy Clowns" from the Crawford Light Orchestra, by Ronald Hamer (WAC T12/1,091).

"Biggles" — ("Strangers in the Night") Based on the aviator character James Bigglesworth created by author Captain W.E. Johns, and who appeared in ninety-six books. Chapman plays Biggles in Ep. 33 as well, while Jones takes the Biggles part in the "Spanish Inquisition" sketch in Ep. 15.

"Algy"—Full name Algernon Montgomery Lacey, Biggles' best friend and companion in his adventures. Ginger, the third member of their team, isn't mentioned here, but will appear in Ep. 33, in the "Biggles Dictates a Letter" sketch, where he's a glam-rock poof. The script notes that Ian Davidson is playing the Algy part, but Davidson clearly enters moments later as the leader of the Mexican band. The actor playing Algy may be Barry Cryer, who was contracted a handful of times by the BBC to warm up the studio audience during this initial season. (Cryer [b. 1935] had also appeared, unbilled, as an advertising executive in a section of the Soho pseudo-documentary *Primitive London* [1967], referenced earlier.)

Lastly, "Braithwaite" is not Algy's last name (and Biggles is given an incorrect first name in the scene), but Ginger's last name was similar: "Hebblethwaite."

"big jump" — ("The First Man to Jump the Channel") This is all perhaps an allusion to the hype and hysteria promulgated by boxing promoters of the time for lightning-rod fighters like Muhammad Ali, but is more certainly connected to the daredevil grabbing headlines in the western deserts of the United States, Evel Knievel. By 1967 Knievel (1938–2007) was jumping lines of cars and buses in very popular events, including the well-documented Caesar's Palace jump/crash in 1968 that left him with multiple fractures and in a coma for nearly a month. The filmed footage of the spectacular jump aired hundreds of times, becoming a staple on ABC's Wide World of Sports—and Evel Knievel became the household name for daredevilry. While this *FC* episode was being created, Knievel would have been promoting his greatest jump ever, a Grand Canyon rocket cycle jump. He never received permission for this jump, opting for the spectacularly flawed Snake River attempt in 1972.

Knievel didn't have a Vercotti figure—he was his own promoter, though just as dangerous.

There's also the possibility that the Pythons stayed closer to home for their inspiration for Ron Obvious—namely, British speedster Donald Campbell (1921–1967). Between 1949 and his race-related death in 1967, Campbell had set and re-set land and water speed records, and was remembered for being "a showman, with the inherent flair that would have probably carried him to the heights of the theatrical world" ("Mr. Donald Campbell," *Times*, 5 Jan. 1967: 10).

Boring old It's Man — (PSC; link into "Walk-On Part in Sketch") By Episode 10 it appears that some of the new and incongruous elements Python created for their show have begun to wear thin. Cleese would later complain that by the middle of the second season, he felt as if the troupe had already exhausted its originality (see Morgan's *Speaks!*). Note also the "*Animated titles as per usual*" note just below—conspicuously absent are the expected witty rejoinders from the scriptwriters in regard to Gilliam's work. This element of boredom and staidness would be addressed with a "ratcheting-up" of the satire, grotesqueries, and shock value of the writing in some of the following episodes and later seasons.

"bricks" — ("The First Man to Jump the Channel") There is no comment here on the absurdity of carrying anywhere between fifty and fifty-six pounds of bricks during a sporting activity. Ron (Jones) will also be carrying a passport with him—in hand—as he jumps, as seen later.

It is possible that this incident is based on the American astronauts' penchant for taking trinkets along for short space rides in the 1960s—including Gus Grissom (dimes, figurines) and Alan Shepherd (golf balls)—for use as novelty gifts or to be sold or auctioned later.

buttress — ("The First Man to Jump the Channel") It's not clear that Obvious is biting anything but a wall of the cathedral. And since this isn't actually Chichester Cathedral, but Holy Trinity Church, there are no buttresses to bite, anyway.

• C •

"cabaret . . . New Forest" — ("Arthur Tree") Cabaret is generally a floor show, often at a dining establishment. The New Forest refers here specifically to newly planted forests, or reforestations, but also can mean the new forests (frontiers) of America, where Frost was keen to make a name for himself. New Forest is also an area southwest of Southampton.

"Caesar's Christmas show" — (link out of "Pet Conversions") The precedent for performing holiday (holy day) shows for royalty or the powerful goes well back in England. Theaters at Oxford, Cambridge, and the Inns at Court were in operation since the sixteenth century, with Christmas revels going back into the fifteenth century (Cox and Kastan, 59–76).

During the English Renaissance period troupes were "owned" and allowed to operate by the Queen, the Lord Admiral, the King, etc. (The Queen's Men, e.g.), with some of their performances expected to be at court, and others in theaters licensed by the state where the sovereign could appear, if she/he chose, for a royal performance. This official performance structure would continue after the Interregnum and well into the eighteenth century. See Gurr, Larsen.

"Calais" — ("The First Man to Jump the Channel") Across the English Channel from Dover, essentially, and is France's main cross-Channel port for both passengers and mail. The Goons had made for Calais in their "Napoleon's Piano" sketch (11 Oct. 1955) for *The Goon Show* (1951–1960).

camply — ("David Unction" link out of "Bank Robber [Lingerie Shop]") In a campy way.

"Channel" — ("The First Man to Jump the Channel") The English Channel separates the British Isles from mainland Europe, and is at its narrowest in the Dover-Calais area, about twenty-one miles. The Channel has become an enduring symbol of Britain's separation from the rest of Europe, acting as a defensive moat, essentially. The Pythons shot this on a shale beach in the Covehithe area, however, quite some distance north of Dover and the white chalk cliffs. Ron would have been jumping at least ninety miles to cross the Channel if he started at Covehithe.

Competitors had been swimming the Channel since 1875, when Captain Matthew Webb completed the swim, leaving from Admiralty Pier in Dover (see Sprawson's article on Webb in the *ODNB*). Webb would later be killed as he attempted to swim below Niagara Falls in 1883, a very Ron Obvious–like stunt. Perhaps more appropriately for this Ron Obvious attempted crossing, the first recorded *attempt* to swim the Channel came in 1872, when J.B. Johnson made it one hour and three minutes into the Channel before giving up. See The Dover Museum Online Exhibition for more.

"Chichester Cathedral" — ("The First Man to Jump the Channel") Located in Chichester on West Street, between Chapel and Tower streets. This location, however, is actually Holy Trinity Church, Lyne Lane, Chertsey, Surrey (WAC T12/1,086, 16 Nov. 1969).

The Chichester Cathedral photo is borrowed from *English Cathedrals in Colour* by A.F. Kersting, page 89, originally published in 1960 by Batsford.

"Chippendale" — ("Arthur Tree") Thomas Chippendale, born in Yorkshire (1718–1779), English furniture designer (*ODNB*).

"Chippenham Brick Company" — ("The First Man to Jump the Channel") Located in Wiltshire, between Bath and Swindon. Chippenham did have significant brick manufacture going on in its vicinity to provide brick for a boom in new housing in the nineteenth century.

By 1974–1975 stuntman and daredevil Evel Knievel was jumping to the sponsorship of Chuckles Candy, Harley-Davidson, and Mack Trucks. See the entry above for "big jump" for more on Knievel and his Obvious-like feats.

"Chipperfield" — ("Vocational Guidance Counsellor [Chartered Accountant]") Chipperfield is a city in Hertfordshire, near Watford.

Cincinnatti — (PSC; "Letters to *Daily Mirror*") Misspelled in the text and taped version, this should read "Cincinnati," which is located in Ohio. These spelling errors can apparently be blamed on the Pythons themselves, since they almost always appear in the writers' requests to the graphics department for captions and title cards, and the captions folk simply create the cards precisely as requested.

As for the mining reference, in 1963 geochemical explorations of Baffin Island revealed enormous deposits of iron ore; natural gas was discovered in the North Sea in 1965; and the Deep-Sea Drilling Project gets under way around the world in 1965–1968. And perhaps most closely linked to this reference is the discovery of oil in the North Sea in 1969. The relatively expensive exploitation process (extracting, delivery, refining, distribution) of North Sea gas and oil kept Britain dependent on foreign sources well into the 1980s, when higher prices worldwide made North Sea reserves more affordable. See the notes for the "New Cooker Sketch" in Ep. 14 for more on this transition.

Coelocanth — (PSC; link out of "Strangers in the Night") This animated figure looks much more like a northern right whale. The *OED* notes that the right whale has been applied to the Bible's "great fish" that swallowed Jonah, making its inclusion in Gilliam's animation (where each animal is eaten in turn) quite apropos. The word is actually misspelled, as well, in the printed scripts, and should read "coelacanth," which is a primeval fish thought to have been extinct until one was caught off the coast of Madagascar in 1938.

conga — (PSC; "Strangers in the Night") Latin American dance.

"cut motor taxes" — ("Letters to *Daily Mirror*") This phrase (and topic) found its way onto bumper stickers, window decals, and into political cartoons of the day, and was much-discussed in newspapers' op-ed pages (see the British Cartoon Archive). A £35 motor tax (a "Road Fund" fee) had been proposed by the Wilson Labour government, a tax flamboyant Conservative MP Gerald Nabarro fought against in the press and on the stump. See Keith Waite in the *Sun* (6 Feb. 1969), as well as David Langdon's panel strip in the *Sunday Mirror* on 6 April 1969.

• D •

David Frost type — (PSC; "Arthur Tree") The Pythons would satirize Frost more than once in *FC* (here portraying him as wooden as a tree), including the rather scathing "Timmy Williams" sketch in Ep. 19. Frost's high-pitched laugh, his "super, super" and "can't be bad" lines are part of Idle's spot-on impersonation here. The fact that most of the Pythons had worked with and for Frost at some point prior to *FC* is also significant—familiarity breeding, it seems at least some contempt. Cleese wrote for *That Was the Week That Was* (1962); Chapman, Cleese, Idle, and Palin appeared on/wrote for *The Frost Report* (1966–1967); and Chapman and Cleese wrote for *At Last the 1948 Show*, which Frost executive produced in 1967. By 1970 Frost was the preeminent television personality among Oxbridge grads, and wasn't afraid to toot his own horn, according to most of his (perhaps a mite jealous) contemporaries.

(See McCabe, Morgan [1999], and Wilmut for more on Frost's relationship with the Pythons.)

And it wasn't just the Pythons who took shots at Frost: *Private Eye* featured mock coverage of the ubiquitous, self-promoting presenter on a number of occasions (Ingrams, 11, 242–43, and 271). Cleese and friends poked at Frost in *ISIRTA* a number of times, including a characterization in "The Return of the Son of the Bride of Frankenstein." Frost is a "furry little animal," a "vampire rabbit" who may be a "bloodsucker with big front teeth" and who's "hungry for publicity" (12 Apr. 1970). See notes for "Hounslow" in Ep. 2 for much more on Frost and his ambitions.

Davidson, Ian — (PSC; "Strangers in the Night") A mistake in the printed script, as Davidson won't enter the scene as "Algy" but moments later as the "Mexican," asking directions to Vera (Jones). Davidson's name does not appear in the WAC records for this episode. Davidson is a writer, producer, and actor who appears in small roles on *FC* in Eps. 6, 10, 18, 19, and 26. He does not appear in any episode in either the third or fourth seasons of *FC*.

At this same time (1970–1971) Davidson was writing for other television shows, including *The Two Ronnies* and *The Kenneth Williams Show*. He had also helped produce *Do Not Adjust Your Set* in 1967, where he probably worked with the future Pythons for the first time. Davidson had also worked under Barry Took (notes to Ep. 4) on *Comedy Workshop: Love and Maud Carver* (1964), and may have been brought into the *FC* world through Took. Lastly, between 1971 and 1973 Davidson was busy producing a series of shows on Yorkshire Television, which likely accounts for his absence from the Python set.

"dead butch" — ("David Unction" link out of "Bank Robber [Lingerie Shop]") The implication, of course, is that the "manly" Vikings were just as prone to at least homosociality and probably homosexuality as the campy David Unction (Chapman). "Butch" generally implies tough characters and/or mannish lesbians, the second of which implicates the Viking's aberrant sexuality, and by his own admission. The *OED* cites the usage of both "fairy" and "butch" in the same instance, where a gay male could be both a fairy and look butch, or tough. This seems to be the point being made by Unction—that the tough-as-nails Vikings were actually mincing queens.

dolly bird — (PSC; "Strangers in the Night") Colloquially, a pretty girl. The *OED* cites "dolly" as emerging during London's swinging days in the mid-1960s, likely on the same wave that brought in The Beatles (and the Merseybeat), the Mods, and the new, free sexuality.

This particular "dolly bird" is identified as Carolae Donaghue in BBC records (WAC T12/1,091). The word "dolly," meaning handsome or attractive, was also part of the London "gay underworld" slang vocabulary, where—not unlike in Cockney rhyming slang—sexual words or phrases that could betray partakers in/of illegal sexual acts were substituted by slangy terms. (The hairdresser figure [Palin] in Ep. 28 speaks a similarly slangy and affected language.) The underground language was called "Polari," and would have been fading out of vogue in the 1960s and 1970s, having both been co-opted by straight groups and deemed increasingly demeaning by members of the emerging political gay community. Other terms from this vocabulary included "drag" (meaning to dress like a woman), "fruit" (homosexual), and "mince" (to walk suggestively). "Mince" will be mentioned in Ep. 33 when Biggles, Alvy, and Ginger are working out their sexuality.

"Dull" — ("Vocational Guidance Counsellor [Chartered Accountant]") Once again chartered accountancy takes it on the chin in *FC*, and will continue to do so through the last Python work, *The Meaning of Life* (1983), where high-spirited pirate-accountants are eventually destroyed by corporate-America-like big business realities. See Gilliam's *The Crimson Permanent Assurance* featurette appended to *ML*. Also, see the description below of an accountant's qualities. Perhaps if the "tax on thingy" mentioned in Ep. 15 were to be instituted, Mr. Anchovy (Palin) wouldn't be looking to switch jobs. The Pythons do seem to make an effort to increase the excitement level of chartered accountancy, including sex taxes and pirate dreams.

"dung" — ("Trailer") Cf. Ep. 9 where Arthur Name (Idle) tells a dung joke, and Ep. 19, where "Book of the Month Club" membership comes with buckets of dung. Excretory humor is also present in Eps. 9 and 45, and significantly in *HG*, where the best way to identify a king is by the fact the he doesn't have "shit all over him." In fact, the episodes of *Flying Circus* offer jokes about defecation (Eps. 15 and 19), urination (Eps. 6 and 42), expectoration (Eps. 3 and 4), masturbation (Eps. 2 and 31), and even ejaculation (Ep. 15), with the last two either censored or just hinted at via possible taxation.

This fascination with the body and especially its elemental/excremental functions in *FC* is indicative of a sort of Ovidian cultural fixation on the body as impure and a locus of change and degradation, rather than the sacred vessel of the spirit. This is the period of the emergence of women's reproductive rights—sexual permissiveness, the birth control pill in 1960, calls for more liberal abortion legislation in the 1950s and beyond—as well as sex change surgery, which began in 1969 in the United States, and major organ transplant surgery beginning in 1967 in South Africa. There is also a childish, sophomoric element to this type of humor—giggling at naughty words and bodily functions—that the Pythons (and many comedians, artists, and literary types of this period) embraced as an answer to the seemingly impenetrable veneer created by High Art and Culture. This, then, is a return to the carnivalesque humor of the Middle Ages, and the delightful indelicacies of the "grotesque." (See Bishop's "Bakhtin, Carnival and Comedy: The New Grotesque in Monty Python and the Holy Grail," and the author's chapter 5 in *MPSERD*.)

• E •

"East Grinstead" — (letter link out of "Gorilla Librarian") In Ep. 5, another letter is addressed to East Grinstead, that time to the BBC. East Grinstead is in West Sussex.

"eat ants" — ("Vocational Guidance Counsellor [Chartered Accountant]") This sort of transmogrification of beasts will be revisited later in the episode in the "Pet Conversions" sketch. In that case, animals will actually be modified to physically resemble other animals.

"Englishmen . . . nations" — ("The First Man to Jump the Channel") Indicating the Britishness of the farthest inhabitants of the Empire, as well as the long reach of colonialism and imperialism.

Episode 10 — Episode 10 was recorded ninth in order during the first season, but broadcast in the tenth position, swapping places with Episode 9. Episode 10 was recorded on 30 November 1969, and was broadcast 21 December 1969.

Also paid for appearing in this episode: Carolae Donaghue (the "dolly bird"; *Holidays on the Buses*), Sheila Sands (*Troubleshooters*), Des McGovern (studio guitarist who may have been a friend of Idle's), Stuart Gordon, Gordon Turnbull, Barry Cryer (*Doctor in the House*), Betty Martin (lady in library sketch), and a dog named Phoebe ("Gorilla Librarian" sketch). *Flying Circus* crew members George Clarke and Roger Last appear as themselves in the lingerie shop sketch.

"exploiting Ron for your own purposes" — ("Tunnelling from Godalming to Java") These Guinness-type stunts are ironically aligned with the inspiration for the Guinness Book of World Records itself. In 1955 the Guinness (stout) company came up with its own initial publicity stunt, creating a trivia book for each pub in the UK. The book was meant to settle bar bets, and was compiled by Norris and Ross McWhirter.

• F •

"Fin de Cross-Channel" — (PSC; "The First Man to Jump the Channel") The banner they are holding in Calais translates "End of Cross Channel" jump, essentially. Some of the Frenchmen waiting for Obvious to complete the jump include Mike Seddon, John Howard Davies (*FC* producer), and Peter Kaukus (*Doctor Who*). Seddon was a comedy writer well known to the Pythons for his work on *It's Marty* (1968) and *Joint Account* (1969) (bbc.co.uk). Chapman, Cleese, Gilliam, Jones, and Palin had all contributed to *It's Marty* (for Marty Feldman), while Michael Mills (BBC Light Entertainment) produced the latter show. Peter Willis, a BBC cameraman, may also have participated in this short scene. In the WAC records for the episode, these characters are termed "froggies" (WAC T12/1,083).

Not included as an official request or permission in the WAC records, this shot was taken in front of 52 Hill House in Market Square in Wickham Market, Suffolk. However, the nearby car park for the White Hart Hotel is mentioned as an approved location (WAC T12/1,083). The camera is set up in the car park across the street from Hill House.

Floor Manager — ("Bank Robber [Lingerie Shop]") George Clarke, Python's actual floor manager, also appears in Ep. 19.

french loaf — (PSC; "Strangers in the Night") These two items—the beret and the bread—typify the character as a Frenchman; he's wearing a "French costume" in the Python world (including "continental nylon mac"). In Ep. 27, when Mrs. Premise (Cleese) and Mrs. Conclusion (Chapman) go to France to meet with Jean-Paul Sartre, most of the folk seen around them are similarly/iconically dressed.

• G •

"get the job" — ("Gorilla Librarian") This is a turnabout on the "Silly Job Interview" set-up from Ep. 5, where the Interviewer has deceived the interviewee, Stig/David Thomas (Chapman). It is also, once again, a failed transaction in the Python world.

"give generously" — ("Vocational Guidance Counsellor [Chartered Accountant]") More like a plea for donations for starving children or abused animals seen on late night television. Chartered accountants, then, aren't capable of helping or saving themselves, and an interdiction must be arranged. (In Ep. 45, a similar plea for very rich people is broadcast.) The inability to do anything beyond chartered accountancy also seems to be a symptom of the disease. The emphasis on "young people" nudges this plea toward a substance abuse message for those dabbling in recreational drug use—use that can have lifelong residual effects. "The Mouse Problem" in Ep. 2 also plays on this theme (there for sexual deviances).

"Godalming" — ("The First Man to Jump the Channel") Located in Surrey, south of Guildford. The filming location is, more precisely, just outside of Saxmundham, Surrey.

"great impetus" — ("The First Man to Jump the Channel") A sort of mind-over-matter scenario also used in the "Amazing Mystico" sketch in Ep. 35, where tower blocks will remain standing as long as occupants believe in them. As soon as doubt emerges, however, the buildings begin to fall.

"grotty" — ("Walk-On Part in Sketch") A shortened, slangy form of "grotesque." George Harrison's character "George" in The Beatles' film *A Hard Day's Night* (1964) appalls a mod teen fashion consultant with his take on hip clothing: "I wouldn't be seen dead in them. They're dead grotty." The out-of-touch consultant Simon (Kenneth Haig) has to ask what the term means.

• H •

"Harrods" — ("Vocational Guidance Counsellor [Chartered Accountant]") Major British department store founded in 1849. Harrods is still on Brompton Road in fashionable Knightsbridge.

Hartebeest — (link out of "Strangers in the Night") South African antelope.

"Heath, Edward" — ("Chippendale Desk" animated link out of "Arthur Tree") Prime Minister and leader of the Conservative Party in Great Britain, 1970–1974. As a very visible, even iconic Conservative, Heath (1916–2005) is a consistently easy target for the more liberal Pythons. Gilliam uses Heath's image in his animations on many occasions. The "hello sailor" is an equally easy attack on Heath (who was unmarried), calling into question his sexual orientation, and is a phrase used throughout *FC*. Cf. Ep. 14, *"Face the Press"* and "New Cooker Sketch," where other government leaders are similarly portrayed.

On the covers of the 13 February and 22 May 1970 issues of *Private Eye*, Heath's ability to have any kind of sexual relationship with a woman is called into question.

"hedgehog" — ("Strangers in the Night") Curious term of endearment—the hedgehog is also utilized by Python as the giant nemesis of Dinsdale Piranha in Ep. 14, and as newsman Robin Day's pet in Ep. 1.

It's worth noting that biographer Anthony Sampson had characterized former Tory PM Macmillan—simplistically, to contemporary reviewer Lord Egremont (1920–1972)—as "a fox who wanted to be a hedgehog ('the fox knows many things, but the hedgehog knows one big thing'). To pursue the analogy," the reviewer goes on, "whoever heard of a Celt, even with blood diluted from other breeds, wanting to be, in this sense, a hedgehog?" ("Portrait of Mr. Macmillan," *Times*, 29 June 1967: 7).

Macmillan (1894–1986) had been a consistent target of the Goons, *Beyond the Fringe*, and frankly any anti-establishment group or performance for many years.

"Hill, Lord" — ("Walk-On Part in Sketch") Lord Hill of Luton, Charles Hill (1904–1989) was Chairman of the BBC from 1967 to 1972, and, before that, the well-known "Radio Doctor" heard during the wartime information program *Kitchen Front*. (It was for this role that the Goons mention "Lord Hill," who's sent them a congratulatory note.) Hill did not, of course, write and sign every letter to every walk-on participant for all BBC shows. It was reported (by the BBC) that he usually communicated with BBC Director-General Hugh Greene (1910–1987) through a secretary, and not personally.

Hill had been in charge of the Independent Television Authority, the body making policy for Britain's commercial television networks, and he was, according to Cockerell, brought in by PM Wilson to reign in the permissiveness of programs and programmers, to "humiliate BBC senior executives," and, most importantly, to hopefully force then Director-General Greene to resign (qtd. in Freedman, 28). Clearly, if Hill had been the man making the final decisions on programming in 1969, *Flying Circus* would likely have never seen the light of day. (For more on Wilson's antagonistic relationship with Greene and the BBC, see notes to Ep. 28, and Freedman's informative article "Modernising the BBC.")

For a photo of Lord Hill, see the cover of the *London Times* evening edition for 11 July 1969.

"howl a bit" — ("Pet Conversions") This is another "gross-out" sketch meant to shock, not unlike the proposed eating of "gammy"-legged sailors or freshly dead corpses in Ep. 26. Cleese comments on that diminishing shock value in Morgan (1999). See notes to Ep. 26.

• I •

"in a skin" — ("Gorilla Librarian") This "dressing as an animal" routine will be revisited in Python's final feature, *The Meaning of Life* (1983). In the "Zulu Wars" episode, two men (Palin and Idle) have been caught wearing a tiger suit, after making off with an officer's leg.

"It's a Tree" — ("Arthur Tree") Yet another "It's" title. Cf. *"It's the Arts"* (Eps. 1 and 6), and *"It's Wolfgang Amadeus Mozart"* in Ep. 1. The connection can be traced back to the It's Man, as well, since for many episodes he appends the word to the title of the show. See similarly titled shows on British TV, like *Yes, It's the Cathode Ray Tube Show* (1957, Peter Sellers); *It's a Square World* (1957, Ronnie Barker); *It's a Man's World* (1962); *It's a Woman's World* (1964); *It's Sad about Eddie* (1964); *It's Dark Outside* (1964–1965); *It's a Knockout* (1966, Eddie Waring); *It's a Long Way to Transylvania* (1967); and *It's Only Us* (1968). See Vahimagi for more on these shows.

The impact of radio should also be noted, with the very popular Tommy Handley show *It's That Man Again* (1939–1949) preparing the way, thematically, for both *The Goon Show* and the Pythons (see Grafton and Wilmut's *The Goon Show Companion*).

The music used here to introduce this David Frost–type show and character is "By George," the "David Frost Theme" (WAC T12/1,091).

• J •

"Jack and the Beanstalk" — (link out of "Pet Conversions") A well-known fairy tale (and especially Christmas pantomime show in the UK) featuring a boy, a giant, and a beanstalk. Like many fairy tales, this one includes moments of a graphic nature and/or grisly violence (implied or otherwise), such as "grinding" victims' bones to make food for the giant. So in perspective, the somewhat horrific images conjured up by Python involving cannibalism, pet mutilation, and maulings by wild animal librarians aren't far at all from many children's stories.

"Jacobs, David" — ("Letters to *Daily Mirror*") A radio and TV personality born in London (1926), hosting *Juke Box Jury* (1959–1967), and prior to that appearing on *The Golden Disc* (1958). In 1969 Jacobs was hosting *It's Sunday Night*, but the Pythons would have undoubtedly known him from his many years as a radio disc jockey.

"Janson, Hank" — ("Gorilla Librarian") Pseudonym for English pulp gangster novelist Stephen Frances, whose licentious work brought charges against him under the Obscene Publications Act in 1954. Covers to his novels featured scantily clad women in provocative poses, and were regularly censored in the UK. It was the 1959 update of this Act that prompted Penguin to publish Lawrence's *Lady Chatterley's Lover* for the first time in the UK. Penguin was charged and taken to court for the obscenity, but were able to now argue the literary merit of the book, and win the case.

For more, see Holland's *The Mushroom Jungle: A History of Postwar Paperback Publishing*, as well as Holland's *The Trials of Hank Janson*.

"Java" — ("The First Man to Jump the Channel") A Malaysian archipelago island. Tunneling under such a large body of water might have seemed ridiculous until the completion of the Channel Tunnel in 1994. Plans for such a tunnel had been discussed since at least Napoleon's time.

• L •

lady with a pince-nez — ("Gorilla Librarian") The third member of the interviewing panel is Betty Martin (WAC T12/1,091).

"larch" — (link out of "Vocational Guidance Counsellor [Chartered Accountant]") Cf. Ep. 3, which prominently featured the larch.

"Last Exit to Brooklyn . . . or . . . Groupie" — ("Gorilla Librarian") The works in question: *Last Exit to Brooklyn* (1964), written by Hubert Selby, and *Groupie* (1969), written by Jenny Fabian. *Brooklyn* features sexuality and language unparalleled for the time, and was set in Brooklyn's seedy lower-class tenements. *Groupie* is a depiction of the real-life exploits of a nineteen-year-old rock groupie in the late 1960s, where the author's described escapades include a "pulling" session with a noted musician, and where depictions of the London counterculture abound. Both books would have been relegated to "locked shelf" status, or not carried at all by many public libraries in the UK and United States. The panel members are obviously just interested in whether such sexually charged books would be available should the gorilla become librarian, and are willing to risk the potential wild animal attacks to have such titles in circulation.

"learning to read" — ("Arthur Tree") Probably satirizing the instances of celebrities who toot their own horns on such shows, especially their "unpublicized" charity work and philanthropic efforts. This could be a specific jab at the recent *David Frost Presents . . . Frankie Howerd* (February 1969), made for American television, meaning Frost was already successful on both sides of the Atlantic.

lingerie shop — ("Bank Robber [Lingerie Shop]") Even at such a feminine place, where one would naturally expect female employees, Python provides only a male assistant, though one obviously familiar with the feminine wares he sells.

"lions" — ("Vocational Guidance Counsellor [Chartered Accountant]") In an unusual twist, for *FC* and Python in general, the Counsellor here is actually asking very rational, reasonable questions, and not demanding that the supplicant before him jump through absurd hoops. Cf. the job interview in Ep. 5 where Cleese's character antagonizes Chapman's character without mercy, and without real reason. The "Vocational Guidance Counsellor" sketch ends up being fairly straight-faced satire, without slouching toward absurdity for shock.

The photo with which the Counsellor frightens the applicant is listed as a color print, "Animals 2548 Roaring Lion" L.404 by N. Myers (WAC T12/1,242).

"London, SW3" — ("Vocational Guidance Counsellor [Chartered Accountant]") This address actually exists (Lincoln House on Basil St.), located near the junction of Sloane and Brompton roads, and just up the road from Harrods (also mentioned in this sketch). This isn't terribly far from the actual headquarters of The Institute of Chartered Accountants in England & Wales, found at the corner of Great Swan Alley and Copthall Ave., in the City of London.

The letter to Conrad Poohs (Ep. 23) is addressed to 55, Lincoln House, SW3, which appears to have been a leasehold for quite some time. Lincoln House is on Basil Street.

Long John Silver — ("Chippendale Desk" animated link into "Arthur Tree") Another popular Christmas pantomime character looming large in the Pythons' collective nostalgia. Cf. Ep. 5, the "Confuse-a-Cat" sketch, the Long John Silver Impersonators football club (Ep. 23), as well as Ep. 32, where the interviewer (Cleese) transforms into a Long John Silver figure as the interview progresses.

A contemporary review (18 Dec. 1969) of a *Treasure Island* performance at the Mermaid Theatre raves about the "exciting spectacle," exulting that "[t]he blood and thunder are utterly whole-hearted. It would be sad to have grown so far from cheerful boisterous juvenility that we could not enjoy it" ("Hispaniola Sails Again," *Times*, 18 Dec. 1969: 13). The tried-and-true pantomimes were clearly still relevant, and not only to the Pythons.

• M •

"man's life" — ("Vocational Guidance Counsellor [Chartered Accountant]") Cf. the "copyrighted" Army slogan "It's a man's life in the modern army" used and abused throughout Ep. 4. The balance of Anchovy's (Palin) ebullient description supports this sloganeering: "Banking, travel, excitement, adventures, thrills, decisions affecting people's lives." Watkins (Idle) fell for this kind of line in Ep. 8, joined the army, then asked to be released before his portion of the sketch was identified as "silly" and halted.

"Melton Mowbray" — ("Pet Conversions") Located in Leicestershire, northeast of Leicester. Cf. the "Dead Parrot" sketch in Ep. 8 for a precursor to this pet shop set-up. That sketch also featured Palin and Cleese. Chapman attended Melton Mowbray Grammar School before entering Cambridge.

"Mercury" — ("Tunnelling from Godalming to Java") Planet closest to the sun. Just prior to the period when the Pythons were creating these episodes, the Mercury space program (pre-lunar flights) had been very active, and much in the world news. And even as the Apollo test flights continued, newspapers covered the successes and failures of the Gemini and Mercury programs over and over again.

"Mexican rhythm combo" — ("Strangers in the Night") The music played live is a portion of the "Mexican Hat Dance" (WAC T12/1,091).

"*Mirror* View" — ("Letters to *Daily Mirror*") Section of the *Daily Mirror* newspaper where letters from and to readers were posted. The *Mirror* has been a UK tabloid newspaper since the late 1930s, and is later mentioned in the printed script for Ep. 25.

"Motspur Park" — ("The First Man to Jump the Channel") Near New Malden, in Greater London. The University of London Athletics Ground (featuring a track) is found there, as are the BBC Sports Ground, the Sir Joseph Hood Memorial Playing Fields, and the Manor Park Recreation Grounds, all within blocks of each other.

The Pythons will film in Motspur Park for Ep. 40, "The Golden Age of Ballooning," when the "least talented Zeppelin brother" Barry (Jones) attempts to fly balloons in the shadow of the enormous gas collection tanks.

"Mrs. Brando . . . *Wild One*" — ("Walk-On Part in Sketch") Marlon Brando (1924–2004) starred in this 1954 film directed by László Benedek, which, due to its violence and political undertones, wasn't screened publicly in the UK until 1968. (As early as 1963 the film was screening at "members only" gatherings in London at the Arts Theatre in Great Newport Street, Westminster, however.) By 1954, though, Brando had already risen to international stardom with *Viva Zapata!* (1952) and *A Streetcar Named Desire* (1951). According to imdb.com, Brando did work briefly as an elevator operator prior to stage and screen fame. His mother was Dorothy Brando, of Nebraska.

"Mrs. Newman . . . *Sweet Bird of Youth*"—Paul Newman (b. 1925) starred in the 1962 film directed by Richard Brooks. Newman was also well known by this time, having starred in *Cat on a Hot Tin Roof* (1958) and *The Hustler* (1961) prior to 1962. Also according to imdb.com, young Newman labored in the family sporting goods store and sold encyclopedias door-to-door before taking to the stage. His mother was Theresa Newman, of Ohio.

• N •

"Neaps End" — ("The First Man to Jump the Channel") There are a few "Neap" locations in the UK, though most are located in Shetland. There is a Neap Ho (or Neap House) in Lincolnshire.

"nickel" — ("Letters to *Daily Mirror*") A chemical element (Ni), and ferromagnetic metal. There are nickel deposits on the Isle of Skye, for instance, and there had been significant mineral and petrochemical discoveries in and around the UK during this period. See the entry for the misspelled "Cincinnatti" for more.

There had been a significant nickel investment scheme making banner economic headlines in some of the major UK newspapers (as well as the more bold *Private Eye*). With the world in the throes of a Canadian nickel-producers' strike, Poseidon NL company had announced the discovery of impressive nickel deposits in Wandarra, Australia, in September 1969, and these reports bolstered the value of Poseidon stock from 20s all the way to £120, with City investors buying in as much as they could. Coverage in the *Times* expressed amazement that much of this furore came from the announcement by Poseidon of a minor nickel strike in "one borehole, I repeat one," mining editor Berry Ritchie noted ("Poseidon and the Bull Run," *Times*, 31 Oct. 1969: 29). Other nickel-mining companies also shot up in value, based on announced finds across Australia, but inflated estimates of the value of the deposits soon toppled all these mining concerns, and Poseidon fell as well (*Private Eye*, 6 Nov. 1970: 5). For about a year the skyrocketing values of nickel (and other war-related minerals) kept the London stock market busy, before confidence was outpaced by miserly returns and the headlines turned sour.

"Nixon" — ("Letters to *Daily Mirror*") Richard M. Nixon was in the first year of his first administration (beginning January 1969) at the time of this episode's writing and broadcast. He appears often in UK newspapers of the time in regard to the escalating war in Vietnam, relations with China and the Soviet Union, etc. He was also decidedly unpopular with the Pythons and members of the left everywhere as a right-leaning conservative Republican.

Nixon is probably also very significant because as vice president to Eisenhower (depicted in Ep. 44) he was the face and voice of the U.S. government overseas. Between 1953 and 1961 Nixon toured the world at the behest of his president, becoming especially visible in appearances with "enemy" countries, including volatile talks with Nikita Khrushchev in 1959, and bloody, protest-filled visits to Central and South American countries agitated by Communist activists.

Jonathan Miller had described the far left-ness and liberality of Britain's political middle, especially as compared to the United States, in the *Beyond the Fringe* sketch "Home Thoughts from Abroad":

> Cook: Of course one thing you'll notice about America is that it is a very young country, rather like Ghana in that respect.
> Miller: Except for the fact that they have inherited our two-party system.
> Moore: And how does that work?
> Cook: Well they have the, um, the Republican Party which is the equivalent of our Conservative Party, and the Democratic Party which is the equivalent of our Conservative Party.

No surprise, then, that a truly conservative American politician like Nixon with international influence and perhaps Monroe Doctrine and gunboat diplomacy designs on portions of what had been the British Empire would not be a popular face with the UK Left, except as a target.

"No, sir" — ("Bank Robber [Lingerie Shop]") The Robber's success rate here is an echo of the available books at the book shop in Ep. 4, the lack of cats at a pet shop (Ep. 10), and the unavailability of fish licenses (Ep. 23), and will be almost repeated in Ep. 33, where the customer tries to buy cheese at a cheese shop. In fact, very few transactions are successfully completed in *FC* shops, probably an ongoing comment on not only customer service in British society, but the specter of scarcity and limited choices for consumers in specifically *postwar* Britain, stretching all the way to about 1956 (see Morgan's *Britain since 1945*).

Prior to the "Silly Walks" gent (Cleese) successfully purchasing his newspaper in the newsagent's shop in Ep. 17, the customer (Idle) attempts various unsuccessful transactions, and fails because he is seeking sexually affiliated items, succumbing to understood metaphors ("chest of drawers," "a bit of pram," "pussycat," etc.). In that same episode various chemists fail to dispense their products successfully. In these settings the narrative generally tends to wander off in another direction when the transaction isn't successful.

• O •

"Old Codgers" — ("Letters to *Daily Mirror*") Perhaps the last bit of evidence necessary to confirm the age and out-of-touchness of the general readership and ownership of the *Daily Mirror*. This had been the popular paper when the Pythons were growing up, and one that *Private Eye*, for example, had been lambasting since 1961.

"old queen" — ("Trailer") Literally, an aging homosexual, and generally affixed to the more effeminate partner in a homosexual relationship. See the *OED*.

This is also an example of what others in the troupe have described as Chapman's "out-ness" in terms of his sexuality. See Morgan's *Speaks!* There may have been no better way for an admitted, practicing homosexual to hide such an unacceptable lifestyle than to overplay that out-ness in character.

This outré behavior is reminiscent of Quentin Crisp (1908–1999), the flamboyant author of *The Naked Civil Servant* (1968), whose public behavior may have given Python the license to camp up their depictions of homosexuals. Crisp described himself as "one of the stately homos of England" in his above-mentioned autobiography. See Ep. 12 for other Crispian allusions.

"open shelves" — ("Gorilla Librarian") Meaning the books are in open circulation, not behind the desk or in a locked case. In *Private Eye*, the editors include this short note of admonition to the Librarian at the British Museum: "In the Reading Room's locked case, reserved for pornography, you will find a copy of *Fire in the Flesh* by David Goodis . . . this is a book about a pyromaniac, and can very safely be placed on the open shelves" (22 May 1970: 4).

In a special for the *Times*, the Scottish correspondent visited local libraries in the Edinburgh area for their open shelves policies. He found that even though northerners were considered to be more morally restrictive, the books in locked cases were few, including *A Green Tree in Gedde*, *Lolita*, *The Group*, *Fanny Hill*, and *The Tropic of Capricorn*, though the rules for such choices varied from place to place, and many libraries had no restrictions on any titles at all. The Glasgow city librarian, C.W. Black, concluded: "We have no right to withhold from the public what the law of the country allows" ("Library Books Not on Open Shelf," *Times*, 5 Dec. 1967: 3). No permissive gorilla librarians here, but open shelves nonetheless.

"ordinary . . . jump" — ("The First Man to Jump the Channel") The standing long jump, or broad jump. Actually, Obvious takes a running start for his jump, which is the type of jump still a part of international track and field competitions. For comparison, the long jump record for the period was held by American Bob Beamon, and was set in the high altitude of Mexico City in 1968 (29 feet 2 inches).

Oxley, Mel — (PSC; "Trailer") Oxley was an announcer for Southern TV (1959–1961), as well as ATV and ABC Television. He was also a voice announcer for BBC-TV between 1965 and 1972.

• P •

"parrots" — ("Pet Conversions") The mention of "parrots" elicits a cheer from the studio audience, obviously attesting to the success of the "Dead Parrot" sketch just two episodes earlier.

In 1999, journalist and broadcaster John Diamond wrote that as teens he and his friends defined themselves as British and part of the "in" crowd in relation to the recognizability factor (and in-joke-ness) of their mutual Monty Python interest:

> I knew I was British because when I met other people who called themselves British we found we had things in common. They would look at the chicken in my fridge and say "This parrot is dead!" and I would come straight back there with "It's not dead it's only resting!" and my, but how we would laugh. For I knew that as I was watching Monty Python, so was every other 17-year-old in the country. I knew I could stand at the door of the sixth-form common room the next morning and shout, "No-one expects the Spanish Inquisition!" and only a boy called Kessler, who didn't have a television, would think I'd found Jesus. ("Once I Was British," 1)

The Pythons' studio audience obviously shared this mutual appreciation, meaning the intertextual references were all the more significant to these true fans who'd "found" Monty Python.

"payments" — (link out of "Strangers in the Night") Perhaps a version of a water cooler discussion that most certainly could have occurred sometime, somewhere during the run of *FC*. The topics broached—originality, topicality, predictability, absurd versus more conventional humor, and public tastes—are those the troupe did hear about from the higher-ups at the BBC, according to people like Barry Took and Cleese, as well as the letters and memos in the WAC records. There was concern that "normal" viewers wouldn't understand the absurd or archaic references ("They wouldn't understand that in Bradford"), and that such reactionary or shock humor had to be consistently updated to avoid repetition, or would almost certainly be short-lived. See Morgan (1999); also Wilmut, 196.

The "balance of payments" comment refers to buying a TV on hire purchase (cf. Ep. 3), but also to the woeful state of the British economy in relation to its foreign debt and the strength of its currency during the early 1970s.

Pearson — (link into "Gorilla Librarian") Canadian Nobel Peace Prize winner Lester Pearson (1897–1972) had delivered the BBC Reith lectures earlier this same year, in January 1969, his subject being a move away from violence and toward "creative social change." See the CBC Archives. See also the BBC 4 Radio Archives.

"permissive" — ("Gorilla Librarian") See earlier instances of Python tilting with the "permissive" society, in Eps. 2, 8, and 9.

***Physique* magazine** — (PSC; "David Unction" link out of "Bank Robber [Lingerie Shop]") The title has been obscured here by a piece of tape (as *Mayfair* had been obscured in Ep. 9), and is actually a March–April issue of *The Young Physique*. The photo foldout at the center of the magazine was characteristic of *Young Physique* and purposely positioned the magazine to be more like *Playboy*, but for young gay males. This younger "beefcake" magazine was one of many men's bodybuilding or health magazines that proliferated in the 1950s and beyond. The brown paper bag indicates that Unction is leering over the magazine, so it must be treated more like pornography—contraband—than a health magazine. (Most of these earlier magazines featured chiseled male models with genitalia discreetly covered—not unlike Gilliam's retouching of the Edwardian photos of, primarily, females he uses in his animations.) There was a fine line walked during the 1950s and 1960s as gay men's publications found both readership with interested gay men and attention from government and watchdog groups intent on stopping the purveyance of indecency. See Waugh's *Hard to Imagine* for more.

picture — ("Gorilla Librarian") The assumption is that the picture was titillating, which, in addition to the Vicar's later preferred book titles, reveals a penchant for perhaps deviant sexuality on the part of this man of the cloth. (It isn't necessarily erotic, of course, but the fact that it's being held discreetly renders it illicit.) Jones creates the same effect earlier in Ep. 7 when he leers after the plea "Be gentle with me." This continues Python's representation of churchmen as closeted postlapsarians always game for the opportunity to dip into the restoration funds (Ep. 6), to drink heavily (Ep. 36), engage in smuggling (Ep. 5), keep a naked lady (Ep. 15), and even have perverted "mouse" tendencies (Ep. 2).

This transition—from scene to scene via dissolve—is another photo-type linking element, as seen already in "Working-Class Playwright" in Ep. 2 and "Hunting Film" in Ep. 9.

"piece of wood" — ("Vocational Guidance Counsellor [Chartered Accountant]") This is like signaling a commercial break. And since the previous sketch was by and for wood products, this may well be a commercial, of sorts. From the earliest days of commercial TV in the UK the government demanded that Independent Television Authority (ITA) stations schedule commercials only in "natural breaks" of the narrative action—this intrusion might have prompted letters and calls from angry viewers (see "Modernising the BBC").

pince-nez — (PSC; "Gorilla Librarian") Glasses held to the face on the bridge of the nose rather than over the ears. These are probably used emblematically to imply a stuffy, Victorian librarian type.

"predictable" — (link out of "Pet Conversions") Not really all that predictable, since the Man in the sketch hadn't shown any predilection toward deviant behavior, just the Shopkeeper. It could be that Cleese is commenting on the Pythonesque-ness the sketch has embodied, which by the tenth episode could have already started to become business as usual rather than cutting edge. The punchline is undercut, of course, which may be why the Vox Pops responses are included.

"pulling the birds" — ("Arthur Tree") Slang for "picking up" females. See John Lennon's comment in *A Hard Day's Night* (1964; dir. Richard Lester) when, seeing two young women alone, he tells Paul McCartney to try a "pull" with them.

"pussy cat" — ("Pet Conversions") What's actually being proposed here is nothing more than what Gilliam does on a regular basis with his polymorphous animations—taking bits and pieces of figures and creating new, often monstrous beings. The earliest iterations of the opening credits feature a wheeled Cardinal Richelieu and a part-man-part-chicken, for example.

• R •

railway track — ("The First Man to Jump the Channel") Shot on location at the Feltham Marshaling Yards, Feltham, south of Hounslow (WAC T12/1,086).

"razor-sharp claws" — ("Vocational Guidance Counsellor [Chartered Accountant]") Cf. Cleese as the Enchanter Tim in *HG*, describing the killer rabbit. The

Zulu Wars scene in the film *ML* also features a large predator, whose carnage is there mistaken for first a mosquito and then a virus.

"Renaissance bit" — ("Arthur Tree") A Renaissance man is one who learns in many areas, who is multitalented, and the meaning of the term originally emerged from the Italian Renaissance and men like Leon Battista Alberti (1404–1472). Alberti was an architect, musician, and painter, as well as being actively involved in the humanist tradition and contemporary politics.

"Rhodesia" — ("Letter to *Daily Mirror*") This is a reference to Ian Smith (1919–2007) and the contentious period when Rhodesia sought white minority home rule. Rhodesia (formerly Southern Rhodesia) declared itself free from Great Britain on 11 November 1965, with Ian Smith and a minority white government in charge. The "Support Rhodesia" slogan would have been in support of this continuation of minority rule, as well as a demand that the UK (and UN) recognize the new state and support Britain's colonial empire. See notes to Ep. 45 for more. Smith was pilloried in the press by the left and right, of course, and appears in caricatured form in the pages of *Private Eye*.

Confirming the topicality of this reference, in the *Times* in 1969 alone there were more than 130 stories or news releases quoting, covering, or vilifying Smith and the deteriorating Rhodesia situation.

Robber — ("Bank Robber [Lingerie Shop]") Dressed in cartoon-like attire, with eye mask, striped shirt, black pants, etc. This same get-up will be used for another robber in Ep. 13. A 9″ figure dressed just like this, including holding a gun at arm's length, was commissioned early in the series, and appears on the map table (for no apparent reason) in the "Dobson's bought it, sir" link in Ep. 1 (WAC T12/1,082).

"Robinson, Eric" — ("Vocational Guidance Counsellor [Chartered Accountant]") Eric Robinson (1908–1974) was a BBC conductor whose show *Music for You* was a popular radio/TV program. This was a live program airing once a month on Wednesday evenings (often shot in Studio E at Lime Grove studios, where *Blue Peter, Steptoe & Son, Doctor Who, Panorama,* and *Nationwide* were also shot). Robinson and his Orchestra also appeared regularly on *New Faces* in 1947 (BBC), so he would have been a very familiar name to the Pythons by the time they reached maturity.

"rollocking" — ("Trailer") Boisterous (variant spelling of "rollicking").

Ron leaps off — ("Tunnelling from Godalming to Java") The fanfare beneath this jump is "Fanfare on the RAF Call" by O'Donnell (WAC T12/1,091).

"royalty on the loo" — ("Arthur Tree") The practice of procuring illicit photos of celebrities—including royalty—in private, compromising, or just embarrassing situations of all kinds has been alive since the inception of modern photojournalism.

"running-in" — ("Letters to *Daily Mirror*") The *OED* notes that running-in refers to "the process of operating a new machine (specifically the engine of a motor vehicle) at reduced power in order to establish proper working." This further supports the supposition that the letter writer is an older man, as he obviously drives slow enough on a regular basis to ask other drivers to pass.

• S •

"Save the Argylls" — ("Letters to *Daily Mirror*") Geographic area in Scotland, but also the name of a Scottish regiment much decorated since 1794. The latter is certainly the reference here, since the letter writer appears to be a retired military man. After service in Aden was completed (1967) the Argylls were brought home and told, unexpectedly, that the unit was being disbanded in the wake of budget cuts and slowing recruitment. A grassroots "Save the Argylls" campaign erupted (garnering more than a million signatures), and with the help of promises from opportunistic Tories the Argylls were saved and Labour was out after the next general election (see Chamberlain).

Cf. a similar angry letter from Brigadier Gormanstrop (Mrs.) in Ep. 5. Also, see notes to Ep. 26 for more on the trials of the Argylls in Aden.

"seen . . . zoo" — ("Vocational Guidance Counsellor [Chartered Accountant]") Cf. Mr. Sopwith as he tries to spot camels, dromedaries, and Yetis ("I've heard about them") in Ep. 7.

"Sicily" — ("The First Man to Jump the Channel") Largest of Italy's islands, and obviously used here as the acknowledged birthplace of organized crime, or the Mafia. Mario Puzo's betselling novel *The Godfather* had recently been published (February 1969), bringing the American crime organization into the international spotlight.

"sinks his fangs into their soft . . ." — ("Gorilla Librarian") This splenetic is characteristic of Cleese and Chapman's writing, where the careful, proper establishment type suddenly erupts with a stream of invectives or outrageous behavior. Roger Wilmut calls these scenes "escalation" sketches, and we'll see Cleese fly off the handle similarly in Ep. 24, in the

"Conquistador Coffee Campaign" sketch (*From Fringe to Flying Circus*, 198).

"Sir Francis . . . Antarctic" — ("The First Man to Jump the Channel") All noted English explorers and/or military men:

"Drake"—An explorer and seaman, Drake (1540–1596) commanded the phenomenally successful defeat of the vaunted Spanish Armada in 1588, bringing the English navy and England in general into a position of world superpower.

"Captain Matthew Webb" swam the Channel in August 1875, the first person to do so. Webb also swam from Dover to Calais, just as Ron plans to do. See "channel" above for more on Webb.

"Nelson"—In Ep. 1, Admiral Nelson is thrown from the upper floors of a high-rise building in a "Famous Deaths" sequence. See notes to Ep. 1 for Nelson's bio.

"Robert Falcon Scott" (1868–1912) reached the South Pole in January 1912, the first Brit to do so, one month after Norwegian Roland Amundsen made the first visit.

Record-breaking may have been in the news, as well, as in April 1969 (when the Pythons were writing the initial episodes) Sir Robin Knox-Johnston (b. 1939) was the first man to sail solo and non-stop around the world.

sleep again — ("Strangers in the Night") Once again, we are presented with a Python character who can't see the absurdity going on around him. In Ep. 6, the City Stockbroker (also Palin) goes to work amidst the chaos of societal breakdown, and sees none of it, only diverted by his comic book.

"Splinter, Harold" — ("Chippendale Desk" animated link out of "Arthur Tree") A play on the name of Harold Pinter (1930–2008), noted English playwright and screenwriter who tackled themes of class consciousness, social alienation, and gender issues. Pinter is most likely included because his name happens to rhyme with a wood product, though his creative work tends to poke the Establishment—identifying and enervating sexual, political, social, and class hypocrisies in contemporary British culture. Pinter was part of the "permissive society" cultural malaise so feared by Mary Whitehouse, the NVLA, and others. Cf. Ep. 2 for more on Pinter and his importance not only to this period, but to the Pythons' worldview as well.

"sponsor" — ("The First Man to Jump the Channel") The practice of companies sponsoring athletics is and was found in football, rugby, and especially auto racing, where decals dot both car and driver. American baseball players even promoted cigarettes and alcoholic beverages at one time, carrying and using the products. The official sponsors for the Chippenham Football Club, for example, include a vending machine company. See the entry for "big jump" for more.

"spruce . . . Bole" — ("Arthur Tree") Spruce trees are evergreens native to cooler climates like Britain and Holland. Gum trees include any tree that exudes gum, and which would be nonnative, hence "making their first appearance" in Britain. "Scots pine and the conifers" sounds much like a 1960s musical group (cf. Buddy Holly and the Crickets, Gerry and the Pacemakers), with the scots pine (a fir tree) being the only native British pine, and conifers being any cone-bearing tree.

For "Elm Tree Bole," cf. the 1832 Tennyson poem "A Dream of Fair Women" (1832): "Enormous *elmtree-boles* did stoop and lean / Upon the dusky brushwood underneath / Their broad curved branches, fledged with clearest green, / New from its silken sheath" (stanza 15). Also, see Robert Browning's *Home Thoughts, from Abroad* (1845), which features the prominence of things English, and must have appealed to the Pythons:

> Oh, to be in England now that April's there,
> And whoever wakes in England sees, some morning, unaware,
> That the lowest boughs and the brushwood sheaf
> Round the *elm-tree bole* are in tiny leaf,
> While the chaffinch sings on the orchard bough
> In England—now! (stanza 1, italics added)

A bole is the trunk of a tree, specifically. In Tennyson's *Mariana*, a poplar tree figures prominently, as well. The Pythons join Tennyson and Browning, as well as such luminaries as Shakespeare, Milton, and Longfellow in utilizing trees as significant textual tools.

Tennyson (played by John Hughman) will reappear in Ep. 41, "Michael Ellis," reading from his *Charge of the Ant Brigade*.

starts the sketch — ("Vocational Guidance Counsellor [Chartered Accountant]") This acknowledges the artifice of the television medium—here we're seeing the "before" moments—moments which are most often sacrosanctly concealed for the sake of continuity and to facilitate the viewers' suspension of disbelief. This hearkens back to the introductory sketch ("Lingerie Shop") where the actors dressed as characters and on a set waited for the walk-on to arrive. The character before us even participates in the sketch's theme song, breaking down the barrier between the "bookends" (opening credits with theme; closing credits with theme) normally found in the television format.

In a scene that appears in the printed scripts but somehow did not make it into the following video or

DVD versions of *Flying Circus*, "Party Political Broadcast" in Ep. 38 offers campy Tory-types rehearsing for their party political broadcast message, as if they were part of a 1930s backstage musical.

Stock film. Quick cuts. Plane arriving at night. Showbiz lights. Film premières — (PSC; "*It's a Tree* with Arthur Tree") The stock footage includes shots of the brightly-lit Piccadilly Circus area at night, specifically from late 1966. The William Holden/Richard Widmark western *Alvarez Kelly* began its London run at the London Pavilion (seen at the left of the screen) on 3 November 1966, to pleasant if not warm reviews. The second shot features the large Coca-Cola sign also at Piccadilly Circus, and is likely from the same newsreel footage. The third shot—of the Drury Lane Theatre, at the corner of Russell Street and Catherine Street—might also be from the same footage, as well. Dora Bryan (b. 1923) was appearing as the titular character in *Hello, Dolly!* in 1966, having taken over for Mary Martin (1913–1990) from 16 May 1966.

"stroppy" — ("Vocational Guidance Counsellor [Chartered Accountant]") *OED*: "Bad-tempered, rebellious, awkward, obstreperous, unruly."

• T •

"television license" — ("Letters to *Daily Mirror*") Cf. Ep. 20, where the BBC's license fees for 1969 are actually posted and readable. Each television owner (for purposes of viewing broadcast television) must purchase the license, each year, the funds raised going to support the BBC. See also the note for "license fee" in Ep. 7, as well as the entry for "cat detector van" in Ep. 23.

"335C" — ("Vocational Guidance Counsellor [Chartered Accountant]") Anchovy reverts to his more natural self, the accountant, more interested (at least subconsciously) with the numbers involved than with the act of lion taming.

tombstone — ("Tunnelling from Godalming to Mercury") The "Funniest Joke in the World" (Ep. 1) sketch ended similarly, with a tomb for the "Unknown Joke" somewhere in the Berkshire countryside. This tombstone scene is back at the north side of the Holy Trinity Church, Chertsey, used earlier in place of Chichester Cathedral.

"to the camera" — ("Strangers in the Night") The same warning given in Ep. 6 by Praline (Cleese) to Mr. Whizzo (Jones), acknowledging the self-consciousness by denying it. Insider comments about the existence of a sketch, pages of scripts, and character reactions also drag the artifice out into the light of the set.

tweedy colonel type — (PSC; link out of "Pet Conversions") This description must have something to do with Chapman's now accepted role as the Colonel, here dressed down in conservative tweed, like a Cambridge don.

• U •

Unction — ("Trailer") Probably an indication of his smoothness, oilyness, etc. It's likely no accident that his first name happens to be "David" (as in David Frost), either. This is the character that the script earlier mentioned was not to be confused with BBC announcer Mel Oxley.

"Upper Science Library" — ("Gorilla Librarian") Probably a reference to the Bodleian Library at Oxford, where Jones and Palin studied. The Library features Upper and Lower designations for study rooms, collections, etc.

• V •

"Vercotti, Luigi" — ("The First Man to Jump the Channel") Luigi (Palin) has appeared earlier in Ep. 8, with his brother Dino (Jones), there shaking down the Army for protection money; he will also appear in Ep. 13, as owner of the La Gondola Restaurant and purveyor of back-room pornography. See notes to Ep. 8 for the Vercotti brothers resemblance to the real-life Kray brothers.

"very talented" — ("Tunnelling from Godalming to Java") One of the catchphrases heard many times during the long run of *The Goon Show* often referred to the earnest but inept Neddie Seagoon (Harry Secombe) character, "He's very good, you know."

vin ordinaire — (PSC; "Strangers in the Night") Simple French wine; table wine.

• W •

"walk-on" — ("Walk-On Part in Sketch") Again, this Pepperpot-type is given significant—even technical—information which her husband does not possess. She's also familiar with the films of Brando and Newman, American actors.

For these walk-on types of roles (often noted as "w/o" in the BBC paperwork), Terry Gilliam, for example, was making £5/5 from the BBC (WAC T12/1,082).

"watch" — ("Pet Conversions") The specter of voyeurism, again, as the seemingly respectable customer (Cleese) reveals his disturbing proclivities. Also, once we reach the "Undertaker's Sketch" in Ep. 26, the son of the deceased (also Cleese) is included in the proposed cannibalistic feast. Through and with Gilliam's dis-membering and re-membering animations, too, the audience are watching, eagerly, these types of grotesqueries.

"wonderful unpublicized work for charity" — ("*It's a Tree* with Arthur Tree") This might be a rather direct (and peevish) allusion to the very prominent but seemingly sincere former England football captain Billy Wright's well-publicized UNICEF campaign of 1969. Wright's ad in the February 1969 *Times* personal columns was headlined "Seven Reasons Why a Child Should Die—in Nigeria/Biafra," followed by a thanks for contributions and a continuing appeal for more funding. Wright (1924–1994) appeared on ATV on 16 February 1969 with interviewer David Lloyd to hash out those seven reasons, and to raise more money for the starving in Africa.

And as for the later set-up in the "Literary Football Discussion" in Ep. 11—a hyperbolic interviewer (Idle) and common man's player (Cleese)—it's also likely no accident that Wright captained Idle's Wolverhampton Wanderers during the organization's most memorable years, a club "whose players were perhaps the finest exponents of the shrewd long-ball and the full-blooded attack ever known," and who "set pulses tingling over half of Europe" ("Fame by the Foot," *Times*, 30 Dec. 1969: iv).

• Z •

"zany madcap humour" — ("Tunnelling from Godalming to Java") Cf. the BBC Man (Cleese) in Ep. 15 as he describes *Flying Circus* ("a bit madcap funster . . . frankly I don't understand it myself"). The BBC had similar difficulties characterizing this show for its regional broadcasters and viewers. See notes for the first few episodes, including memo comments from producer/director John Howard Davies regarding the rubbishy qualities of the series.

"Zatapathique" — ("Letters to *Daily Mirror*") Perhaps Python's catchall name for any Frenchman. Cf. Eps. 2 and 14, for Jean-Brian Zatapathique, Ep. 22 for Chief Inspector Jean-Paul Zatapathique, and Ep. 23 for Brianette Zatapathique.

Episode 11: "Eighteenth-Century Social Legislation"

"It's" Man hit by cars intro; *Animation: Titles* (silly Cleese v/o); The Royal Philharmonic Goes to the Bathroom; Letters ("obvious lavatorial turn," Mary Bignall, and "cheap laughs"); Royal Philharmonic photo; *Animation: Flushing head;* Interruptions by Undertakers: "The World of History"—The Black Death; Agatha Christie sketch (also interrupted by undertakers); Literary football discussion; Detective sketch revisited; Undertakers film; *Animation: Violent nudes;* "Interesting People" (tiny Howard Stools, Mr. A. Bayan, the Rachel Tuvey Bicycle Choir, a man who can give a cat influenza, and Mr. T. Walters, who is totally invisible); "Interesting Sport": All-In Cricket; "Interesting People" (A man who shouts, his wife, a man who tosses his cat, and Mr. Keith Maniac); Another undertakers' film; *Animation: Tenement Coffins;* "Eighteenth-Century Social Legislation"; The Battle of Trafalgar with Prof. R.J. Canning; Prof. R.J. Gumby (and friends); **Batley Townswomen's Guild presents "The Battle of Pearl Harbour"**; Yet another undertakers' film; "It's" Man closing credits

• A •

Agatha Christie type — (PSC; "Agatha Christie Sketch") Christie, born in Torquay (1890–1976) was a noted prolific mystery writer. The drawing room setting and assembled suspects are a standard Christie motif, and have been seen in St. Martin's Theatre (Trafalgar Square, in London's West End) where *Mousetrap* (1952) has been playing since 1974. The play first took the stage at Ambassadors Theatre, London, in November 1952. An "Inspector" character is also featured in many of Christie's stories.

This particular set-up—wherein a body is discovered in the living room—is reminiscent of Christie's 1954 play *Spider's Web,* which was filmed in 1960. The character names in *Spider's Web* also ring familiar, including "Clarissa and Henry Hailsham-Brown," "Sir Rowland Delahaye," "Miss Peake," "Jeremy," "Elgin," "Pippa," "Hugo," "Mrs. Elgin," "Oliver," and, of course, "Inspector Lord." Cicely Courtneidge (mentioned by the Red Indian in Ep. 6) appears as Miss Peake in the 1960 film.

"albodyduce" — ("Agatha Christie Sketch") Cf. the misspeaking in the "Spanish Inquisition" sketch (Ep. 15), as well as various characters who speak beginnings, middles, or ends of sentences or in a roundabout way (Ep. 26), in anagrams only (Ep. 30), who is alternately rude and polite (Ep. 18), or who inserts malapropisms without knowing it (Ep. 36). A significant portion of Python humor deals with the inefficacies of communication.

"all-in cricket" — ("Interesting People") No holds barred, like professional wrestling, for instance. All-in wrestling appears in Ep. 2, "Epilogue," when a monsignor and an academic wrestle to determine the existence of God. Colin "Bomber" Harris (Chapman) will famously wrestle himself in live appearances like *Live at the Hollywood Bowl* (1980). (The All-In Cricket sketch will also be included in the short episode created by the Pythons for the *Euroshow 71—May Day Special* broadcast in 1971.)

In the 1969–1970 cricket season there were multiple protests and even riots at cricket and rugby matches across England. Protestors were angry that England's ruling sports organizations (including the MCC) had allowed South African cricket and rugby teams to tour the UK. The fact that the South African athletic teams were chosen with a racial bias in place (no blacks on "white" national teams) had caused a furore from the time the proposed tours were announced. The Treasurer of the Liberal Party and MP for Cornwall, John Pardoe, called for disruptions wherever possible:

> Sit down all over the pitch if you have to . . . the anti-apartheid movement has been fighting for a long time the idea of visits to Britain by South African sports teams selected on a racial basis. . . . If we can make enough row, be a big enough menace and be bloody-minded enough, we may be able to destroy totally the concept of sporting exchanges between South Africa and this country. ("Call to Disrupt the Springbok Tour," *Times*, 18 Sept. 1969: 4)

(See notes for Ep. 15 for more on the South Africa and apartheid situation.)

One political cartoon from the period mentions that cricket and rioting together might actually make cricket entertaining (Sidney William Martin, *Sunday Express*, 15 Feb. 1970). See the British Cartoon Archive.

The crowd noise over the all-in cricket match is borrowed from British Movietone News, "Football Crowd Cheering" (WAC T12/1,092).

Animation — ("Interruptions") In the printed script, this animated sequence is described for the reader as "beautiful and not zany," meaning they wanted Gilliam to create an intro that seemed more at home in Kenneth Clark's *Civilization* program, not *Flying Circus*. The more sober and serious the introductory piece, it seems, the more apparent the incongruity of what's to follow.

What's not mentioned is the few animated moments prior to the new program's introduction. The "sound of flushing" mentioned in the printed script is set under the stock film of the orchestra, and an animated sequence follows. The Royal Albert Hall, it's top opening, emits a large balloon labeled "Acme Toilets: As Used by the Royal Philharmonic Orchestra." Acme, of course, had been the firm where Wile E. Coyote (of the Warner Bros.' Coyote and Roadrunner cartoon fame) had ordered his host of weapons and gadgets, none of them performing to his expectations. There were also several dozen companies in Greater London alone during this period named "Acme," selling everything from ball castors to industrial cleaning services to typewriters. Perhaps closer to Gilliam's purposes here is the fact that functioning animation stands produced by the Acme Corporation could be found in most animation studios.

arrow through his neck — ("Agatha Christie Sketch") Cf, Ep. 30, where the pantomime goose kills Terence Rattigan (also played by Cleese) with an arrow through the neck. See notes to Ep. 30 for more on Rattigan.

• B •

"Batley Townswomen's Guild" — ("Batley Townswomen's Guild Presents the Battle of Pearl Harbour") Batley is in West Yorkshire, and such "association and mutual interest" guilds are still present in English towns and regions, including the Nene Valley region and Portsmouth.

This scene will be borrowed for inclusion in *Euroshow 71—May Day Special*, a one-off asked for by the BBC as representing British light entertainment for a Pan-European May Day celebration broadcast. In that short episode, the narrator (Cleese) notes that the "industrial conurbation of Batley . . . celebrates the first day of May in a very special way with their reinterpretation of the renewal of all forms of life in the miracle called spring." Then, there's a mud wrestle.

"Battle of Pearl Harbour" — ("Batley Townswomen's Guild Presents the Battle of Pearl Harbour") Significant turning point in WWII, when the Japanese attacked the American Pacific naval forces stationed at Pearl Harbor, Hawaii, in an attempt to both destroy the American Pacific naval fleet and discourage the United States from entering the war against the Axis. What the Battle of Britain was to the English population (and the young Pythons), Pearl Harbor was to Americans.

"Battle of Trafalgar" — ("The Battle of Trafalgar") Significant British naval victory (21 October 1805) led by Admiral Nelson (see Ep. 1), and where he lost his life. The battle cemented Britain's naval superiority for many years to follow.

The requested Trafalga colour print behind Prof. Canning (Chapman) is noted in the WAC records as the still "La Gloria Di Trafalga No. 942," or "1805 Trafalga," and is reportedly from the Colour Plate BBC Reference Library. On close inspection it appears to be a reversed version of the William Clarkson Stanfield (1793–1867) original, painted c. 1836. That original hung in the United Service Club, a gentlemen's club in Pall Mall, for many years.

"before his death" — ("Interesting People") Perhaps an oblique allusion to Lord Frederick Charles Cavendish

(1836–1882), who also lost his life just as he undertook a significant endeavor. Cavendish (newly installed Chief Secretary to the Lord Lieutenant) was murdered by Irish nationalists on 6 May 1882, when goodwill for England and England's representatives was at a low point in Northern Ireland.

"Bigbottie, Ivor" — (letter link into "Literary Football Discussion") *Ivor the Engine* was an English children's show about a Welsh train, 1958–1963, made for Associated-Rediffusion. In Ep. 13, Eric (Idle) is a child being interviewed, and he mentions that Raquel Welch has a "big bottom."

"Bignall, Mary" — ("Letters [Lavatorial Humour]") Some memorial and spelling mistakes evident here. The Rome Olympics were actually held in 1960; the 1964 Games were played out in Tokyo, Japan. Mary D. (Bignal) Rand took the gold in the same event in 1964 at the Tokyo Games; Brit Sheila Sherwood took a silver medal in the long jump at the 1968 Mexico City games. Rand's winning jump was 6.76 meters, or 22 feet, 2-1/4 inches. Rand (b. 1940) is credited as the first British athlete to win an Olympic gold medal in track and field (*EBO*).

The film footage is of Mary Bignal Rand, and was requested from BBC archives (WAC T12/1,092). Her name (Bignal) is misspelled in the archives as well.

"The Black Death . . . plague" — ("Interruptions") The Black Death pandemic afflicted Europe between 1347 and 1351, and both bubonic and pneumonic types were rampant. It is estimated that roughly twenty-five million died worldwide. The Pythons will revisit the plague theme in the later *Holy Grail* feature film.

"Bologna" — ("Literary Football Discussion") Bologna FC was formed in 1909, and would win the Italian Cup in 1969–1970.

"boutique" — ("Literary Football Discussion") This perhaps betrays the actual footballer the Pythons are satirizing, George Best. Irishman Best (1946–2005) was considered by many to be the best footballer of his generation, and played primarily for Manchester United, winning the Football League Championship in 1965 and 1967, and the European Cup in 1968. During his peak in the late 1960s, Best acted and spent money like a rock star, including opening several unsuccessful boutiques and even a nightclub.

Friends of the Pythons, The Beatles had also opened a boutique in 1967 in Baker Street in London, to much media fanfare. "Apple," as the trendy boutique was called, would close not long afterward.

BP — ("The Battle of Trafalgar") Back projection screen. Used often on news or current affairs–type sets in *FC*. The same set-up can be seen anytime the actual *Nine O'Clock News* (1970–) or *News at Ten* (1967–) sets are depicted. The first news set is seen in Ep. 30, and the latter in Ep. 13, when the Queen has reportedly switched over to watch the evening news.

"Brian" — ("Literary Football Discussion") Perhaps a reference to English sports commentator and interviewer Brian Moore (1932–2001). The effete and intellectual timbre of the interview/er, however, point more toward a critic who will be directly lampooned in Ep. 33, Philip Jenkinson (1935–2012). See notes to Ep. 33 for more. This may also be an allusion to the 16 February 1969 interview between ATV presenter David Lloyd and former footballer Billy Wright. See the entry for "wonderful unpublicized charity work" in Ep. 10 for more.

"Buzzard" — ("Literary Football Discussion") Character name brought to the group by Cleese, who had earlier created an imaginary football front line of "Bunn, Wackett, Buzzard, Stubble, and Boot." (See Morgan 1999, 26.) *FC* Episode 3 had been known by this longer title through most of its pre- and production life in BBC communications. As mentioned earlier, Jimmy Buzzard is likely an amalgam of footballer interviewees, but he also can be connected to George Best and Billy Wright. See the index for additional references to these players.

"By jove" — ("Agatha Christie Sketch") An epithet used by, for example, Tommy (among many other Christie characters) in *The Secret Adversary* (1922):

> "Lost her memory, eh?" said Tommy with interest. "By Jove, that explains why they looked at me so queerly when I spoke of questioning her. Bit of a slip on my part, that! But it wasn't the sort of thing a fellow would be likely to guess." (chapter 18, "The Telegram")

This was Christie's second novel. Coincidentally, and perhaps subconsciously conflated on the Pythons' part, the Pickering featured in another play, Shaw's *Pygmalion*, also utters the "By Jove" epithet.

• C •

"Camp on Blood Island" — ("Batley Townswomen's Guild Presents the Battle of Pearl Harbour") Title of 1957 film from England's Hammer Studios, directed by Val Guest, and depicting a Malaysian POW camp run by the Japanese in the closing days of the war.

"Canning, Prof. R.J." — ("Interruptions") Cf. the reference to R.J. Gumby and Canning in the notes to Ep. 9, and the allusion to noted historians of the time, including the *FC*-referenced A.J.P. Taylor, who after

1950 made regular appearances on the BBC, and Kenneth Clark, famous by this time for the immensely popular *Civilization* series first appearing on BBC, then PBS in America.

There is also an R.J. Canning Ltd. company in Berkshire.

"cat sat on the mat" — ("The Battle of Trafalgar") This, of course, sounds very much like a line from a Theodor Geisel learn-to-read book, and may well be a comment on the real-world knowledge of such learned academics. Later, in Ep. 40, George III (Chapman) will be read to from a Little Golden book.

"clearly not written by the general public" — ("Letters [Lavatorial Humour]") This is the first example in the series where the façade of reality over the letter-writing trope is removed/acknowledged, and it's given to an imagined viewer to write in and identify the "man behind the curtain," as it were. Generally, once the sent-up material (parody) is itself sent-up (acknowledgment of parody), the effectiveness and appearance of that material diminishes. Silly letters will continue to be a part of a number of *FC* episodes (as they were during this period in the pages of *Private Eye*), most of which purport to be from actual viewers.

Colonel Pickering — (PSC; "Agatha Christie Sketch") Name of a character in G.B. Shaw's play *Pygmalion* (1913), specifically, the man who bets Henry Higgins that he cannot properly refine Eliza Doolittle. No explanation is given here as to why he's appearing in an Agatha Christie–type sketch, nor is his name mentioned by any of the characters.

contemporary picture . . . Trafalgar — (PSC; "The Battle of Trafalgar") This still—"La Gloria Di Trafalga No. 942: 1805 Trafalga"—is from the Colour Plate BBC Reference Library (WAC T12/1,092). As mentioned in the "Battle of Trafalgar" entry above, this image is a version of Stanfield's 1836 painting.

• D •

"Dorking" — ("Interesting People") A theater massacre (by Red Indians) occurred at the Dorking Civic Theatre in Ep. 6. Dorking is in Surrey, south of London, and just south of Leatherhead, also mentioned in the "Red Indian" sketch. East Grinstead (mentioned earlier) is southeast of Dorking.

• E •

"Elementary" — ("Agatha Christie Sketch") Sherlock Holmes's signature word, and usually spoken to Watson. The characters were by Englishman Sir Arthur Conan Doyle (1859–1930). It's now obvious that Python is mining a number of more well-known British authors, rather than parodying Christie alone.

"entire Bible" — ("Interesting People") Later in the episodes there will be an attempt to summarize Proust, as well (Ep. 31). All of Ron Obvious's attempted sporting feats in Ep. 10 are also impossible, including jumping the English Channel and tunneling to Java. And by the *Fliegender Zirkus* episodes (made for Bavarian television), contemporary characters will appear on a similar show—*Stake Your Claim*—and claim to have written Shakespeare's plays and sonnets, to have built the Taj Mahal, to be Catherine the Great, and to possess the ability to tunnel through an elephant.

Episode 11 — This episode was recorded on 14 December 1969, and broadcast just two weeks later, on 28 December 1969. Note that mention of the Announcer is omitted from this episode's script, as is the standard "It's" utterance (at least in print). This is just one episode after the "It's Man" was termed "boring" in the printed script itself.

Also scheduled to appear in this episode, according to BBC records: Flanagan (Ep. 12; *Benny Hill*), Sheila Sands (Ep. 10; *Troubleshooters*), Alan Fields, Nigel Tramer, Anton Morrell, Kurt Muller, Beulah Hughes (Eps. 12, 33, 34; *Hands of Orlac*), Susan Marchbanks, Kay Baron, June Collinson, Bernadine Barry (Ep. 6; *Doctor Who*), Perrin Lewis (*Wednesday Play*), Joe Santo (*Dixon of Dock Green*), Dennis Balcombe (*Timeslip*), Leslie Weekes (*Z Cars*), Alan Troy (*Target*), and Peter Robinson (his appearance was eventually cancelled, according to surviving pay records) (WAC T12/1,092).

"existentialist football" — ("Literary Football Discussion") This theme of philosophical football will be approached later by Python in a more lengthy and visualized way, via "The Philosopher's Football Match," where German and Greek philosophers face off on the football pitch. This sketch will be introduced in the second *Fliegender Zirkus* episode (September 1971), then reappear in the Pythons' *Live at the Hollywood Bowl* performance in 1978.

• F •

"fellow historians" — ("The Battle of Trafalgar") This is a rather clever ridicule of the then-current academic debate surrounding A.J.P. Taylor's book *The Origins of the Second World War* (1961) examining the reasons behind and responsibilities for World War II and the infamous Western (read: English) appeasement of

Nazi aggression. Here, then, all historians are equally "thick," and equally misinformed on even the facts of history (and certainly the then-culled historical facts).

film of four undertakers struggling up a hill — (PSC; "Another Undertakers Film") This is the second undertakers' film, and this time the undertakers are struggling up Harrogate Street in Bradford. Existing council houses are visible behind them, as well as the spire of St. James Bolton Church in the far background. The open field next to the undertakers has since been filled with housing. At the upper end of this road is Otley Road, where the hearse will eventually speed away in the third undertakers' sequence. The undertakers will emerge from the gates of the Bradford Cemetery on Otley Road and get into the hearse.

fling her — ("Interesting People") Eighteenth-century English novelist Tobias Smollett used such an image to describe the size of his hero Humphry Clinker's London quarters: ". . . pent up in frowsy lodgings, where there is not room enough to *swing a cat*" (*The Expedition of Humphry Clinker*, vol. II).

• G •

"German . . . fleet" — ("The Battle of Trafalgar") Drake was involved with the defeat of the *Spanish* Armada in 1588, and had been dead since 1596. His naval skirmishes were primarily against Spanish vessels and holdings, not German.

gravediggers . . . surfboarder — ("Undertakers Film") Like a clown car at a circus, this resembles any of a number of similar *Benny Hill* scenes, as well as *The Monkees* (1966–1968) and *Rowan & Martin's Laugh-In* (1967–1973) on American television. Cf. Ep. 9 for more on Hill's "silly" influence on the Pythons.

Gumby . . . handkerchief, etc. — ("The Battle of Trafalgar") Here the script concretely (and for the first time in *Flying Circus*) identifies both the costume characteristics of the Gumby characters, and also attaches the "Gumby" name to the description. The appellation "Gumby" didn't even appear until Ep. 9, affixed to Chapman's "Gumby crooner" (Prof. R.J. Gumby).

• I •

"I'm off" — ("Interruptions") Like the historian lecturing in *HG*, Canning is cut short by other narrative elements. In this case the interruption is simply an annoyance. In *HG* the historian is killed by a marauding knight as he attempts to control the narrative by his own descriptions and proscriptions.

"Inspector Tiger" — ("Agatha Christie Sketch") Almost certainly at least a reference to Scotland Yard inspectors in general (as visible authority figures), but may also be a nod to the many television and film iterations of "Inspector" and "Detective Inspector." For instance, see the cast of the 1962 British TV series *Z Cars*. (*Z Cars* is one of the several shows—along with *Doctor Who*, *Softly Softly*, and *Dixon of Dock Green*—casting from the same talent pool for extras with *FC*.) In the 1947 film *Whispering City* there is an "Inspector Renaud" (loosely translating to "fox"), giving rise to "Inspector Fox." (The instance of "Renaud" as an early variation of "Reynard" is taken from the fourteenth-century epic poem *Sir Gawain and the Green Knight*. See the *OED*.)

Also, veteran English actor Michael Bates (*Patton*; *Battle of Britain*) played Inspector Mole in the 1964 TV series *Cluff*. Bates's inspiration to the Pythons is even more cemented when it's noted that he also appeared in *The Rise and Rise of Michael Rimmer* (1970), co-written by Chapman and Cleese (and others), and co-starring Cleese in a small role.

In Ep. 29, finally, Cleese plays Inspector Leopard (who has changed his name from "Panther"), and Idle plays both Inspector Thompson's Gazelle and Inspector Baboon, and Chapman plays Inspector Fox.

"interesting sport" — ("Interesting People") This film footage of various sports is from "*Sportsview*" (WAC T12/1,092). *Sportsview* (Eps. 35 and 39) appeared on the BBC beginning in 1957, and was hosted by Ken Wolstenholme (Ep. 21), Peter Dimmock, and Brian Johnston (Eps. 20, 21), among others.

• J •

"Jarrow" — ("Literary Football Discussion") Working-class town northwest of Sunderland, on the Tyne, and featured in Ep. 15 as the setting for "The Spanish Inquisition" sketch. East Jarrow United football club (a Catholic school league) was part of Jarrow & District League. See the entry for "smart interviewer and footballer" below.

• K •

"Kantian" — ("Literary Football Discussion") Of or pertaining to the works of philosopher Immanuel Kant (1724–1804). The sheer level of thinking exhibited by the names mentioned overwhelm the "midfield cognoscento" Buzzard, who may know football, but not nineteenth- and twentieth-century philosophy. The Interviewer (Idle) is just doing what many such interviewers and critics do—overanalyzing what Buzzard (Cleese) knows is nothing more than the kicking of a ball into a net. And if the Interviewer thinks Buzzard is, indeed, an "arch-thinker," then the Interviewer's state of mind must also be called into question.

Private Eye ran a regular short column called "Pseuds Corner" where readers could submit clippings from various respected British newspapers, clippings that featured the cream of euphuistic pretentiousness. One such entry from the 31 January 1969 issue, discussing the recent Leeds United versus Manchester United match:

> Leeds United . . . . . 2 Manchester United 1
>
> The bitter malevolence that erupted in the funeral dolorousness of the first half was blessedly relieved, although never expunged in the more intense legitimate conflict of the second.
>
> ARTHUR HOPCRAFT
> *Observer* (qtd. in *Private Eye*, 31 Jan. 1969: 4)

A similarly florid description of a cricket match in the offing appeared just a short while later in the *Times*:

> It was a hot, hazy, sometimes steamy day, the kind of day to win the toss. The Edgbaston field looked lovely, with its broad strips of dark and light green, rippling *crepe de chine* rather than velvet. The drab scar of the concrete wicket was unbearably poignant.
>
> ALAN GIBSON
> *The Times* (qtd. in *Private Eye*, 22 May 1970: 4)

(The entire story above appeared in the *Times* on 7 May 1970, page 17.) And finally, the cake is taken by one Brian Chapman writing for the *Guardian* as he gushes over an epic cricket match:

> Middlesex beat Yorkshire by three wickets at Lords yesterday with only one ball of the final 20 overs remaining. A match that for two days had dragged its leaden feet rose in the end to heights of drama. Reluctant heroes on both sides buckled on Homeric armour. The lotus-eaters, in Tennysonian idiom, rose from their soporific banks of Amaranth and gave battle.
>
> BRIAN CHAPMAN
> *Guardian* (qtd. in *Private Eye*, 14 Aug. 1970: 4)

Given these actual splendiferous rehearsals of sporting events, Idle's Interviewer sounds rather tame, even understandable.

"Kendal . . . Westmorland" — ("Interesting People") Kendal is in the county of Westmorland, at the edge of the Cumbrian Lake District.

"Keith Maniac" — ("Interesting People") Perhaps a reference to the then-rising paranormalist star Uri Geller (b. 1946), who by 1969 was becoming known for his highly publicized "abilities" to practice telekinesis (spoon-bending, watch-starting) and foresee the future.

In Ep. 35, a character played by Jones (Mystico) and dressed/acting in a similarly strange fashion is able to build high-rise housing simply by hypnosis.

Lastly, *Private Eye* had labeled longtime BBC presenter Jack de Manio "Mr. de Maniac," mock-lauding him for his "amazingly high standard of childish patter day after day," as well as for his performance in dog food commercials (*PE*, 1 Jan. 1971: 11).

kitted out — (PSC; "Interesting Sport") Wearing the complete cricketer's gear, including padding and sweater, etc.

• L •

"Lobotomy" — ("Agatha Christie Sketch") Radical surgical procedure where parts of the brain's frontal lobe are removed. The surgery hasn't a history of being used for treating confusion, rather schizophrenia and depression. This type of caption is also used often in *FC* as a means of ellipses, or the removal of time. Cf. Ep. 29, where "dead unjugged rabbit fish" and "rat tart" are consumed during the ellipses.

"Lookout" — ("Agatha Christie Sketch") Like Python's humor in general, this sketch, rather than resolving itself, continues on to the next absurdity, in this case the next appearance of an authority figure who also happens to be stuck in a literal mode.

This continuing reference to "So and so of the Yard" is a reflection of the ubiquitous presence of police shows like *Dixon of Dock Green*, but must also be connected to Jack "Slipper of the Yard" Slipper (1924–2005), Detective Chief Superintendent of the Metropolitan Police during this period. "Slipper of the Yard" hounded the "Great Train Robbery" gang for many years, and in several countries. Slipper was tall and sported a pencil mustache, the latter copied by the Pythons as various inspectors burst into scenes throughout *FC*. See the various detective entries in Ep. 29 for the "type."

"Lord Hill" — (link into closing credits) Previously a radio doctor, Charles (later Lord) Hill (1904–1989) of Luton led the BBC (as chairman 1967–1972) during this period, and enjoyed a close relationship with Labour Party PM Harold Wilson (1916–1995). Wilson was PM from 1964 to 1970, and also 1974–1976. It was even reported (by the BBC's Peter Scott) that Hill was appointed by Wilson just to force political foe Director-General Hugh Greene out of the BBC, though

Greene held firm until 1969 (allowing, for example, the Pythons a shot at a television contract).

See the entry on Lord Hill in Ep. 10, where he personally invites a walk-on to appear in a BBC sketch. Hill is also earlier mentioned by the Goons as being one of their own who's moved on to better things.

• M •

masculine voice — ("Eighteenth-Century Social Legislation") Generally, if Python is going to abrogate a female's speech or presence she is either presented as a mute sexual object, or given facile, dimwitted dialogue that marginalizes her narrative significance (cf. Episodes 4 and 7). In this case, her own voice is muted and replaced with a voice representing the patriarchy, but she is still able to "perform" her feminine role as the sexual object (writhing in orgasmic pleasure). This might be characterized as a somewhat disturbing hermaphroditic moment, or just another attempt at a new shock value level.

"Men of Harlech" — ("Interesting People") A martial song characterized as an unofficial anthem of Wales. Harlech Castle is in northern Wales, and was originally designed to play a part in the subjugation of the Welsh. The castle was built in 1283 under Edward I. The music became well-known after its use in the film *Zulu* (1964), the heroic story of an undermanned Welsh detachment fighting in the Zulu Wars in 1879. See the website data-wales.co.uk/harlech.htm. The Pythons will revisit this film and setting in the feature film *Meaning of Life*, the "Fighting Each Other" section.

"Municipal Baths, Croydon" — ("Interesting People") Outer borough of London, in Surrey. The only public outdoor pools/baths in Croydon were (they have since closed) Wandle Park and Purley Way Lido. Indoor baths were built in 1926. Croydon's Grants Department Store will be the location for most of the "Michael Ellis" sketch in Ep. 41.

• N •

"Nazi War Atrocities" — ("Batley Townswomen's Guild Presents the Battle of Pearl Harbour") These came to complete light during the Nuremberg Trials just after WWII. In Ep. 12, a fully uniformed Hitler, Himmler, and Von Ribbentrop (here renamed Hilter, Bimmler, and Ron Vibbentrop) will attempt to win a by-election in North Minehead. Hitler has already been lampooned in Ep. 2 (he is admittedly an easy target), and was a consistent target during WWII for cartoonists (like Tex Avery, Walt Disney, and Chuck Jones) across the Allied world.

More recently, the trial of former Nazi SS Lieutenant Colonel Adolf Eichmann (1906–1962) had occupied the headlines in 1961. Eichmann's control of transportation of Jews and other "undesirables" to concentration camps during WWII meant the trial revealed a steady stream of "atrocities" for eager readers and viewers during the early 1960s. Additionally, Hitler's "architect" Albert Speer (1905–1981) was released from prison in 1966, having served a twenty-year sentence as a war criminal. The books that Speer had written during his imprisonment and the interviews he gave (to *Der Spiegel*, for instance) just after his release offered up even more tantalizing and lurid details of the inner workings of the Third Reich.

"notice me" — ("Interesting People") Like Ellison's character in *Invisible Man*, Mr. Walters (Idle) notices that he is not noticed. In 1958 Incorporated Television had created a thirteen-episode series *HG Wells' The Invisible Man*, which may have inspired the Pythons. In that series, the title character tries to fit into society as he seeks a cure for his own invisibility, helping police solve crimes and friends in distress. Idle's characterization here of the "problems of the Invisible Man at home" aren't, then, far from television reality.

• O •

oilskins . . . sou'westers — ("Interesting People") These bell ringers are all wearing yellow rain gear, much like Vicky (Idle) in Ep. 1. The hat is the "sou'wester," and the coat is the "oilskin." The costuming will reappear in Ep. 33, in the "Lifeboat" sketch.

"old one like that" — ("Agatha Christie Sketch") Inspector Theresamanbehindyer (Jones) is the only inspector character so far not suffering from extreme literality. Each of the other inspectors treats his own name as either a command or a threat, and responds violently when hearing it.

out of frame — (PSC; "Eighteenth-Century Social Legislation") This "linkman from on high" seems to be at least a somewhat derisive comment on the elevated status of intellectuals like the fictional Canning, and especially the very real A.J.P. Taylor (1906–1990) and colleagues (including C.S. Lewis, 1898–1963) at Oxford, Cambridge, etc. The implication is clear: Inspiration comes from the hand of God to men like Taylor and Canning.

"out of the yard" — ("Agatha Christie Sketch") An example of a character's literality. She assumes he's giving her a command, rather than his name, and he has obviously never heard a pun on his own very punnable name. Cf. Mr. Smoke-Too-Much in Ep. 31, who finally "gets" the double meaning of his name, long after the "getting" can be funny.

This "of-the-yard" trope may be at least partly attributable to Harry Secombe's character in *Down among the Z Men* (1952), "Bats of the Yard," and will reappear in myriad episodes throughout *FC*.

"Over here Hughie" — ("Interesting People") A reference to presenter Hughie Green (1920–1997), known for *Double Your Money* and especially the talent show *Opportunity Knocks*.

• P •

pile of dead policemen — ("Agatha Christie Sketch") The dead policemen, including Ian Davidson, when he hits the top of the pile, also include Lesley Weekes, Dennis Balcombe, Peter Roy (*Englebert with the Young Generation*), and Alan Troy (WAC T12/1,092). (See the note above for "*Episode 11*" for more on these other actors.) This pile of bodies is yet another visual moment drawn from the cartoon world.

"plain wrapper" — ("The Battle of Trafalgar") Perhaps this image of the eminent historian and BBC personality as seductive siren is a comment on the allure of the "flavor-of-the-month" new theories in history. It seems to be a look at the splash that new historical readings and revelations can often make—especially when an event as fresh and raw as Nazism is the subject—before the newness wears off thanks to the next reading, a mis-reading, or even a discrediting of the previous "find" that sets the table anew. The fiery/frosty critical reception to A.J.P. Taylor's book *The Origins of the Second World War* likely "sparked" this sketch. See the entry below for "Taylor" for more on the critical imbroglio.

Also, see the entry for "sparked a wave" below for more on this revisionism.

"plastic arts" — ("Literary Football Discussion") Art forms that utilize some kind of malleable medium, including sculpture, woodworking, ceramics, even painting and sometimes film, etc. The use of the term itself identifies the interviewer as something of an effete intellectual.

"poison" — ("Agatha Christie Sketch") The daughter of a surgeon and a WWI nurse herself, Agatha Christie included significant uses of poisons in her mysteries. The three means of murder (poison, arrow, gunshot) are also each characteristic of Christie's novels.

"programme" — ("Interruptions") Professor Canning doesn't seem to mind the irreverent comedic takes on historical events depicted, treating them quite respectfully, just the interruptions he has to endure.

"Proustian" — ("Literary Football Discusssion") Of or pertaining to author Marcel Proust (1871–1922), a prominent literary figure whose work is mentioned several times in *FC*. Proust is best known for his seven-volume *À la recherche du temps perdu* (1913–1927; *Remembrance of Things Past*). In Ep. 31, there is a contest to determine who can summarize the entire novel set, and in Ep. 23 Praline nearly comes to blows with a man who hints that Proust might be a "loony."

The "Proustian memory" trope is significant to this discussion and this annotated work in general, since the Pythons clearly draw on "involuntary memory" throughout *FC*. The "recovery of the past" so important to Proust allows for a more structured reading of the seemingly random and chaotic *Flying Circus* world, where university reading lists and cherished historical figures and cartoon violence and contemporary, topical faces and foibles come together in a sort of noisome ever-present. This is why long-dead figures like Mozart or Julius Caesar can share screen space and time with Gumbys and Pepperpots, and why a "throes of orgasm" lady can discuss eighteenth-century social legislation in a man's voice—rather than treating time as an uninterrupted line, the Pythons stack discrete events/people into one jumbled "now."

psychedelic flowers — ("Undertakers Film") A nod to the "flower generation," or hippie culture prevalent as a subculture in the United States and UK during the 1960s and early 1970s. Such displays were often visual symbols of the "peace" movements opposed to the war in Vietnam, or British imperialism in Africa, etc.

The music under this change is a sped-up version of "There's No Business Like Show Business" from *Annie Get Your Gun* by Irving Berlin, as performed by Werner Muller and His Orchestra (WAC T12/1,092). The hearse has turned around on Otley Road at the corner of Harrogate in Bradford, just near the Bradford Cemetery.

• R •

"Regius Professor" — ("Eighteenth-Century Social Legislation") This is a professorship established by royalty in the older British universities, like Cambridge, Oxford, Dublin, Edinburgh, etc. Hugh Trevor-Roper, for example, was the Regius Professor of Modern History at Oxford (probably over Jones, specifically) between 1957 and 1980.

"Rijksmuseum" — ("Eighteenth-Century Social Legislation") This famous "state museum" hasn't been in The Hague since the museum's contents were moved to Amsterdam in 1808. The Hague is the seat of government of The Netherlands, and Amsterdam is the official capital city. Many of Rembrandt's best-known works can be found at this museum, including *Portrait of Willem Bartholsz Ruyter* (c. 1638), mentioned in the notes to Ep. 2 earlier.

"roomself" — ("Agatha Christie Sketch") The Constable (Palin) also responds *literally*, mimicking Inspector Tiger as precisely as he can.

"Royal Philharmonic Orchestra" — ("Letters [Lavatorial Humour]") The London-based orchestra was founded in 1925 by Sir Thomas Beecham, and resides at the Royal Albert Hall. None of the recordings during the run of the show were created by the RPO.

• S •

"shirty" — ("The Battle of Trafalgar") Ill-tempered.

"Shut up!" — ("Interesting People") Cleese's characters often try and control their environments by resorting to this (shutting off or shouting down opposition), including the nervy interviewer (Ep. 1), the ex-RSM (Ep. 4), the psychiatrist (Ep. 13), Praline (Ep. 18), Jim the TV commentator (Ep. 20), and so on.

On *The Goon Show*, "Shut up, Eccles!" had become a catchphrase, while Minnie Bannister and Henry Crun often shouted "shut up" to each other.

side of the head — ("Agatha Christie Sketch") Cf. Ep. 35 where the Attendant (Cleveland) must jar the Peer's (Palin) brain back into position, otherwise His Grace just stammers without end.

"Sir Gerald" — ("Agatha Christie Sketch") One of several references to Sir Gerald Nabarro (1913–1973), who was a Tory MP standing for South Worcestershire. Nabarro is also mentioned in Eps. 19, 21, and 23 (twice), and in the notes for Eps. 15, for example. In the mid-to-late 1960s Nabarro was also a fixture in the political cartoon panels across the Empire, with many hinting not-so-subtly that he, not PM Harold Wilson, was in charge.

Nabarro was a noted old school Conservative, who at different times, according to Joan Sutherland, "opposed Europe, the abolition of capital punishment, drugs, students, pornography and pop music. He supported Enoch Powell on immigration and white rule in Rhodesia [see notes to Eps. 10 and 45]. If he could have, he would have stopped the calendar at 1959" (*Guardian*, 27 Dec. 1999). His obituary says it quite well:

> In the Commons Nabarro cut a dash as a backbencher whose opinions might be ignored—for a time—but whose panache could never be. With Falstaffian aplomb he played a buffoon-like propagandist; the handlebar moustache, resonant voice, and silk topper were part of an idiosyncratic presence easily recognizable to the populace at large. ("Sir Gerald Nabarro: Coloyrful Tory with the Common Touch," *Times*, 19 Nov. 1973: 17)

He would have been a ripe target for Python, of course, and his fall from grace following a compromising auto accident with his female secretary—there were conflicting reports as to who was at the wheel, etc.—made Nabarro even more vulnerable.

Smart interviewer and footballer — (PSC; "Literary Football Discussion") The Pythons are more than likely skewering the still-current tradition of analyzing and overanalyzing athletic contests, this time comparing international league football to existential philosophy of the nineteenth and twentieth centuries. They will return to this subject in a very effective short filmed sketch, "The Philosophers' Football Match," which appears in one of the German episodes (*FZ*), and later in *Live at the Hollywood Bowl*, where Greek and German philosophers (and one actual footballer, Franz Beckenbauer) face off.

Jarrow can't boast a significant national or international football reputation, meaning the "Stadium of Light, Jarrow" (see below) mention is obviously a swipe at this working-class town. (The actual Stadium of Light, Estádio da Luz, was built in 1954 and was home to SL Benfica in Lisbon, Portugal.) Jarrow has a number of school-age teams (Catholic, public, etc.) that have been in place since the late nineteenth century. There are and have been popular professional football clubs in the region, however, including teams in Sunderland (est. 1880) and Newcastle (est. 1892).

The supposedly obsolete "catenaccio" defensive system was quite feared for many years on the continent—it involved an additional defensive man, a "sweeper," behind four defenders—and had been pioneered by an Austrian coach in the late 1930s. The system was employed contemporarily (and run very well) by Helenio Herrera's Inter Milan in the late 1960s, to which the Pythons probably allude by mentioning "Signor Alberto Fanfrino's Bologna FC" squad (see Motson and Rowlinson; Gray and Drewett).

The Pythons may have been indirectly referring to the rather storied 1967 European Cup, described by Andy Gray and Jim Drewett as:

> the biggest clash of footballing styles you could . . . imagine . . . a meeting of two teams who inhabited opposite ends of the tactical spectrum. Jock Stein's Celtic

played in the traditional Scottish way with two out-and-out wingers and a basic philosophy of all-out attack while Helenio Herrera's Inter Milan, the pioneers of *catenaccio* . . . defending, with four man markers and a sweeper, excelled at grinding out 1–0 wins. For many this game was more than a battle for the European Cup, it was a kind of good versus evil contest with Celtic on some kind of crusade to save free-flowing attacking football from extinction. (*Flat Back Four*)

Celtic won the match 2–1, incidentally, which was held in Lisbon's National Stadium. There was also, of course, no Jimmy Buzzard on the team, just Simpson, Craig, Gemmell, McNeill, Clark, Johnstone, Auld, Murdoch, Lennox, Wallace, and Chalmers. Real Madrid (Spain) won five straight European Cups (1956–1960), and then again in 1966, which may have felt like a stranglehold to UK fans. And when Real Madrid wasn't winning, AC Milan (Italy) took the prize twice in that decade (1962–1963 and 1968–1969).

The fact that a British team (Jarrow/Celtic) could go on the offensive and overcome the staid entrenchment of defensive continental football (Bologna/Internazionale) is a celebration of Britishness, of course, but it's worth noting that the Jarrow winners (and the Pythons) are employing the works of continental philosophers such as Kant and Proust, so it must also be a victory of new, enlightened thinking over the old.

"Positivism" stressed immediate experience as opposed to more structured (abstract, formalist) approaches to experience put forth by Idealists, and was very much in line with the "creative force" of nature and the emerging/exploding technologies of the nineteenth and twentieth centuries. The "obsolescent" Idealism was being overthrown on the fields of (philosophical) play as Kant (1724–1804) wrestled with the "deficiencies" of Rationalism and Empiricism in his three "critiques."

The "thrusting and bursting" is also "an almost Proustian display" of the formative significance of the "creative energies of past experience" formerly lodged in the unconscious emerging to affect the expression of the artist (Drabble 1985, 794). The significance of Proust (1871–1922) to the Pythons and their generation of university wits can't be overstated, as he and/or his works are mentioned and mimicked throughout *FC* and even their feature films. See the entry for "Proustian" above for more on Proust's "involuntary memory."

"social betterment" — ("Eighteenth-Century Social Legislation") The lecturer here ventures from English social legislation to Dutch matters, employing a German as opposed to a more proper Dutch accent, and he leaves the eighteenth century in favor of the fifteenth century, before abandoning the lecture altogether.

"sparked a wave of controversy" — ("The Battle of Trafalgar") The specter of revisionist history and revisionist historians shadowed this period, with the first significant Holocaust denials (or emendations) appearing in the 1960s, this on the heels of revisionist looks at Japanese and German atrocities committed during WWII, as well as the Allies' "real" reasons for going to war in the first place. David Hoggan's *The Myth of the Six Million* was published in 1969, and a firestorm erupted over the book's factual soundness, neo-Nazi point of view and support, and anti-Semitic slant. (The American historian's earlier book, *The Enforced War* [1961], had removed most of the blame for the war from Hitler, transferring the culpability to the British, generally, and Lord Halifax specifically [*Times*, 4 May 1964: 13].) This was a period when many shared national "myths" were taken to task by historians, and careful re-examination of neglected, new, or just ignored records cast long-held and often much-cherished beliefs into doubt. By casting dimwitted Gumbys as these learned men of letters, the Pythons belittle the entire revisionist undertaking, even though they themselves participate, at least comedically, in this type of revision.

"Stadium of Light, Jarrow" — ("Literary Football Discussion") This may be a clever passing allusion to the Nationwide *Festival* of Light organized by anti-permissive society campaigners Malcolm Muggeridge and Mary Whitehouse, among others. One of the stated goals of the event(s) was to counter the rising incidence of sex and violence in the media in the UK, which may be directly connected to the Interviewer's (Idle) "thrusting and bursting" descriptions of Jarrow's play. The first gathering was in Westminster, and regional meetings followed in fall 1971.

"Stools" — ("Interesting People") Medical terminology for human feces.

"Superintendents 9" — (link out of "Agatha Christie Sketch") Cf. the scorekeeping in Ep. 1, where the results are based on equally fatal acts: "Pigs 9–British Bipeds 4."

• T •

"Taylor, A.J.P." — ("Eighteenth-Century Social Legislation") Taylor (1906–1990) is the Oxfordian author of *English History 1914–1945* (1965), the final volume from the Oxford History of England, as well as the very controversial *The Origins of the Second World War* (1961), where Germany was blamed for the war, but where both France and England also came under fire for "vacillation" and appeasement policies. The reception of the book's thesis led to "a mixture of international obloquy and acclaim" for Taylor, according to Thompson (*ODNB*). See notes to Ep. 9 for more.

Also, for an example of perhaps some kind of shared mindset between Taylor and the Pythons, note just the title of Taylor's 1956 work: *Englishmen and Others*. Taylor's painting of all Conservatives and any conservative thought or policy with a negative, socially regressive brush betrays his own politics, and may actually be quite in line with those of the Pythons.

Tchaikovsky piano concerto — (PSC; link into "Letter [Lavatorial Humour]") This is Tchaikovsky's "Piano Concerto No. 1 in B Flat Minor, Op. 23," performed by Julius Katchen with the London Symphony Orchestra conducted by Pierino Gamba (WAC T12/1,092). Cf. this same concerto used in Ep. 28, where a concert pianist (Jones) plays the piano as he escapes a chained bag.

"Tiddles" — ("Interesting People") Cf. Arthur Waring and his musical mice in Ep. 1 for similar animal treatment. "Bing Tiddle Tiddle Bong" is the name of the song performed at the end of Ep. 22. Cats continue to be the household pet that suffers the most in *FC*, and will be detonated later in Ep. 22, ironed and inserted into a wall in Ep. 45, and beaten against a wall (to shake out the dust, presumably) in *Holy Grail*.

"tie" — ("Literary Football Discussion") *OED*: ". . . a match played between the victors in previous matches or heats."

"Tired of life?" — (link out of "Interruptions") Spoofing the television medium again, this like a commercial for bath oils, suicide, or just imminent, blissful death.

"Toovey" — ("Interesting People") Roy Tuvey is a British TV and film comedy writer (*Up the Front*; *Whoops, Baghdad!*). The latter show was produced by John Howard Davies, a director and producer for *FC*.

torchy music — (PSC; "Eighteenth-Century Social Legislation") This "torchy music" is "Night Train" from the album *David Rose and His Orchestra play "The Stripper" and Other Fun Songs for the Family!* (WAC T12/1,092).

"tuts" — (PSC; link into "Letters [Lavatorial Humour]") *OED*: "An ejaculation (often reduplicated) expressing impatience or dissatisfaction with a statement, notion, or proceeding, or contemptuously dismissing it."

• U •

undertakers — ("Undertakers Film") Most of these sketches—interruptions—are staged to be similar to silent comedy film routines. When the undertakers carry the coffin between the "Agatha Christie Sketch" and "Literary Football Discussion," the music utilized is from the Lansdowne Jazz Series Traditional Parade, "Oh, Didn't He Ramble" by Terry Lightfoot and His New Orleans Jazzmen. Bits of "The Dead March" are also used in other links (WAC T12/1.092).

undertakers leaving graveyard — (PSC; "Yet Another Undertakers' Film") This is another mixed scene, edited together from separate location shots. The graveyard they are leaving is the Bradford Cemetery, though the initial shot (of the church-like portico) is from elsewhere. The undertakers get into the hearse on Otley Road (at the cemetery's north entrance) eventually turning around at Harrogate Street and heading east along Otley Road.

• V •

very mad way — ("Interesting People") The treatment of foreigners (here "Ali Bayan") continues to be somewhat one-dimensional, and will be later replicated on the short-lived BBC series *Whoops, Baghdad!*, produced by John Howard Davies in 1973. Ali Bayan is actually a city in Iraq. A Middle Eastern setting will be visited in the first *Fliegender Zirkus* episode (1971), where Red Riding Hood (Cleese) has taken a job with Telefunken in the United Arab Republic ("Vereinigte Arabische Republik"), and is approached by a dingy Arab ("schmuddeliger Araber") selling Arab-themed Albrecht Dürer pictures.

Voice — (PSC; "Interesting People") Not credited in the scripts, but Jones provides the voice characterization for Mr. Stools. Some of this type of voice work may have been parceled out on the fly as the episode was being staged, then recorded.

• W •

"West Hartlepool" — ("Interesting People") In the county of Durham on the North Sea coast, and just north of North York.

"West 12" — W12 covers the Hammersmith and Fulham areas, the area surrounding BBC Television Centre.

"what it's like being invisible" — ("Interesting People") Perhaps a reference to the 1952 novel *Invisible Man* by Ralph Ellison, about the invisibility of the black man in a white world. The "Dull Stockbroker" (Palin) depicted in Ep. 6 isn't invisible, though catastrophic events around him have no effect on him, and he scurries through life missing and getting missed by everything. This is certainly a look at the impersonal, dehumanizing effect of modern industrial society, and the fact that "dull" types get marginalized, or just aren't interesting enough to be featured on shows like *Man Alive* (Ep. 26) or *Tomorrow's World* (Ep. 20).

Wife — ("Interesting People") The voice characterization is delivered here by Chapman, though he's not credited in the written text.

Winn, Anona — ("Agatha Christie Sketch") Anona Winn (1904–1994) was an Australian-born actress and singer who appeared in the 1934 film *On the Air*, and participated in the radio shows *Just a Minute* and *Twenty Questions*.

World of History — ("Interruptions") The music behind the titles and introductory graphics is "Music for Vive L'Oompa" Funeral March by Chopin, played by The London Brass Players (WAC T12/1,092).

The image used here is likely borrowed from an illuminated manuscript (a rich source Gilliam will plunder again and again for *Monty Python and the Holy Grail*). The original image is enclosed within a large letter "D" (an inhabited initial), and Gilliam (or production personnel) has cleverly overlaid the prison window edges, hiding the letter completely. Even the small camera movement as the title appears stops short of revealing the bottom edge of the letter.

The image depicts a religious procession, with bishops carrying a holy relic under a canopy, and candle-bearers all around. The original setting may be a waterfront town like Ghent or Amsterdam. If Amsterdam, the artist may have been depicting the medieval church Oude Kerk at the upper left.

"woven in the woof" — ("The Battle of Trafalgar") Cf. Thomas Gray's 1757 poem "The Bard":

> Weave the warp, and weave the woof,
> The winding sheet of Edward's race.
> Give ample room and verge enough,
> The characters of hell to trace. (2.1.1)

Perhaps the real question is whether Python is saying that such eminent historians are "characters of hell" in their quest for academic and popular acclaim. The evidence seems to support such scornful treatment.

• Y •

"Yorkshire" — ("The Battle of Trafalgar") Describing, really, a central aspect of *FC* itself. Almost nothing was shot "on location," with areas in and around London (and especially Ealing and Acton) standing in for far-flung and exotic locales. The actual Cudworth is northeast of Barnsley (where the coal mining son went "poncing off" to in Ep. 2) in South Yorkshire.

"You Jane" — ("Agatha Christie Sketch") Reference to the stilted dialogue spoken by Tarzan, the Ape-Man, an Edgar Rice Burroughs (1875–1950) character from the novel *Tarzan and the Apes* (1912), in the Hollywood movie version of the story.

• Z •

"zoom in" — ("Interruptions") Canning is aware of both the medium's capabilities and the "meaning" of such a camera movement—the zoom creates more of an intimacy, but is also more intrusive. Holding the long shot, then, would have been less threatening, allowing Canning to exit without "following" him and without preemptive action from him. Chapman's Colonel character also exerts narrative authority as he commands the camera (and the switcher board in the studio) in Ep. 4 earlier.

Episode 12:
"Upperclass Twit of the Year"

"It's" Man pinball intro; *Animation: Titles* (silly Cleese v/o); "Episodes 17–26: The Naked Ant"; A signal box somewhere near Hove; Falling from building (in an office off the Goswell Road); *Animation: Falling people, the Great Fred; Spectrum*—Talking about Things; Railway footage and Hove signal box; Visitors from Coventry; Messrs Hilter, Ron Vibbentrop, and Bimmler; **The Minehead By-Election**; National Bocialist Vox Pops; Police station (silly voices); "Silly voices" Vox Pops; **Upperclass Twit of the Year**; Letters; *Animation: Falling apart, Animals from a pipe*; Ken Shabby, and "story so far" photos; "A Corner of a Bed Sitter" link; "A Party Political Broadcast on Behalf of the Wood Party": How far can a minister fall?; "Has anyone anything else to say?"; "It's" Man pinball closing credits

• A •

animation (possibly incorporating falling) — (PSC; link into "*Spectrum*—Talking about Things") The fact that the Pythons writing the episode (all except Gilliam) didn't know what their animator had planned wasn't unusual, his work generally happening while the others rehearsed and blocked the week's show. More than likely, the writing team had told Gilliam of the falling sketch, without giving too many details, and the animator went from there. See Morgan *Speaks!* and *Gilliam on Gilliam* for more.

The bathing suit–clad woman whose stomach saves those falling is borrowed from another of Barker's postcards/photos, and can be seen in *Ronnie Barker's Book of Bathing Beauties*, page 13, in "The Costume" chapter. Stamped "Ostende," it is likely one of the many French seaside resort postcards so popular in the fin-de-siècle period, and which Barker collected by the thousands.

"annex Poland" — ("Mr. Hilter") Hitler's Nazi forces overran Poland in a matter of days beginning 1 September 1939, which was part of Hitler's systematic efforts to control all of Prussia, and even all of Europe and Soviet Asia.

"Armstrong-Jones" — ("The Minehead By-Election") Tony Armstrong-Jones (officially Snowdon, Antony Armstrong-Jones, 1st Earl of) was Princess Margaret's husband from 1960 to 1978, and is an award-winning photographer and filmmaker. Armstrong-Jones's photos appeared on the set of the 1958 John Cranko revue *Keep Your Hair On*, a disastrous London revolution epic set in a hairdresser's shop. Perhaps this bizarre juxtaposition inspired the Pythons to place Hitler planning his own revolution in Minehead. A photo of Armstrong-Jones appears in Ep. 30.

Additionally, the 23 March 1969 *Sunday Times* published the results of an opinion poll asking readers to gauge the "relative popularity" of members of the royal family. *Private Eye* also published the poll results, but wondered why Lord Snowdon had been left off the list, even though it was discovered he'd scored a 20. (The Queen came first at 63, then Philip at 55, the Queen Mother at 48, etc.) Snowdon would have come eighth, after Princess Anne (26) but before his wife, Princess Margaret, who was only able to score 2. The Duke of Kent (satirized in Ep. 30), managed a dismal –4. *Private Eye* pointed out that Snowdon happened to be a contributor to the *Sunday Times*, coincidentally, hence his mysterious omission from the list (Ingrams, 227).

attacked by a bear — (PSC; link into "Falling from Building") Signal boxes have long been points of social, political, and just plain criminal attention, including acts of violence. In the pre-WWI era, suffragettes claimed or were accused of myriad railway and signal box bombings; in the 1920s, it was the "troubles" in Northern Ireland that led to similar attacks; in the later 1920s organized labor caused considerable unrest on railway lines in attempts to bring attention to their cause; and finally, anarchists in the pre-WWII days planted numerous bombs and fired shots in and around railway buildings and trains.

During WWII, the Luftwaffe targeted Britain's railways often, especially in the early days of the conflict, and significant damage was recorded.

At this moment past the café come Hitler, Von Ribbentrop and Himmler on bikes — (PSC; "The Minehead By-Election") On bicycles, the Nazis emerge from Woodlawn Road and onto Crabtree Lane, past Den's Café (still a dining establishment today) and on to Holyport Road.

"Axis Café in Rosedale Road" — ("The Minehead By-Election") The primary Axis powers during WWII included Germany, Italy, and Japan. There is no Rosedale Road in Minehead. The closest such road is located in Bristol, near where Cleese grew up.

This café is actually Dens Café on the corner of Crabtree Lane and Rainville Road, Fulham, London W6 (WAC T12/1,094). In the filmed episode a secretive Mussolini figure (Jones) is nailing a campaign poster to the front door of the Axis Cafe—"Vote for Hitler"—with the "t" and the "l" marked up to be switched. Just above the door and almost unreadable thanks to the swift pan down is a small sign affixed to the door jam, reading "Prop. K. Tussolini," and then his license to sell spirits, etc.

• B •

bear — (PSC; link into "Falling from Building") Another entry into the Python bestiary, this bear is obviously a man (perhaps Gilliam) in a bear costume. Why a bear would be in a Hove signal box isn't addressed. Cf. the librarian in the gorilla suit (Ep. 10), or the equally out-of-place Pantomime Goose and Pantomime Horses (Ep. 30).

Incidentally, the Pythons asked for a polar bear costume in the original costuming requests, but obviously had to settle for a brown bear (WAC T12/1,093).

"Bed-Sitter" — (PSC; link into "How Far Can a Minister Fall?") The printed script identifies this shot as a "corner of a bed-sitter." A room that serves a dual purpose—bedroom and sitting room, and here simply used as a transition from one sketch to another. The *OED* notes that this usage is considered university slang, which might account for Python's usage. The actress in the scene is Flanagan (Eps. 11–13, 22).

"Bell and Compasses" — ("Mr. Hilter") A fictitious pub already mentioned in Ep. 6 where the Indian tribe often relax after seeing a stage show.

"Bideford" — ("Mr. Hilter") In Torridge, Devon, on Bideford Bay. Bideford is south and west of Minehead, across Exmoor, and would be at least a forty-mile hike as the crow flies. Following a prescribed trail would certainly be significantly longer.

As Cleese hails from Weston-Super-Mare, not far north of this area, much of this rather precise geography could be attributed to his influence.

"Bloody heck!" — ("How Far Can a Minister Fall?") This kind of slip-up must've happened quite regularly, but a recent obvious instance would be on-scene reporter Michael Charlton (b. 1927) covering the announcement of Ted Heath's successful defense of the Bexley seat in the wee morning hours of the June 1970 General Election. Cliff Michelmore sends the camera over to Bexley, and there's clearly chaos as Heath is just entering the room. Off-camera Charlton can be heard saying something like "can't we fix this bloody thing really" to someone, likely complaining about some technical difficulty. The remark went out live across Britain thanks to the BBC's much-heralded blanket coverage of the election. A long-time *Panorama* reporter, Charlton had the year before assisted with the equally active BBC coverage on the Apollo 11 moon landing broadcasts.

"board meeting" — ("Falling from Building") In the aftermath of Black Tuesday and the onset of the Great Depression, gallows humor flourished, not surprisingly, and one running joke became the specter of distressed, bankrupt brokers and business types leaping to their deaths from tall buildings.

"Bobby . . . Peters" — ("Mr. Hilter") Both men were on the 1966 England World Cup team. Bobby Charlton (b. 1937) played for Manchester United, and Martin Peters (b. 1943) for West Ham United. Mr. Bimmler (Palin) is merely displaying his credentials as a true Englishman.

Fittingly, England had beaten Germany 4–2 in the 1966 Cup, meaning Bimmler had to pretend to be happy that his "native" country had lost.

brown mackintoshed — (PSC; "Ken Shabby") Wearing a brown "mac" overcoat. The black, opaque "rubber mac" is the outerwear of choice for Praline in the "Dead Parrot" sketch in Ep. 8, as well as "Fish

Licence" in Ep. 23. This same type of brown, soiled mac will be part of the costume for the wild rapists in the first *Fliegender Zirkus* episode.

"brush" — ("Ken Shabby") Another veiled punchline, delivered without retribution or even comment. Rosamund's father (Chapman) doesn't even react to the news, but then he also doesn't notice that Mr. Shabby (Palin) is a sex-starved shambles who gropes his precious "English rose" (Connie Booth) and gobs on the carpet.

budget — (PSC; "How Far Can a Minister Fall?") Yet another instance where the script's writerly aspects are exposed, where text meant for the reader only (in this case, the director, Ian MacNaughton) is included: *"He thumps on the desk and he falls through the floor. (Yes Mr Director you did read that right: he fell through the floor and added a fortune to the budget)."* Moments later, the camera has to be turned upside down, as well—another challenge to the normally straight-ahead, three-camera set-up the Pythons (and most of the BBC) employed. This note from the Pythons also implies that a trap door didn't exist early in the show's run, at least in a studio space normally available to them. Perhaps this scene was eventually shot in a neighboring studio featuring a trap door, such as Ealing or even Golders Green (or one of the more elaborate TC studios). Such trap doors were fairly typical on British television stages, being holdovers from similar devices used in major theater spaces like the Rose and the Globe and beyond. Cf. the TV stage trap door (at the Scala Theatre) used to elevate Paul's Grandfather (Wilfrid Brambell) onto the soundstage in the penultimate scene of *Hard Day's Night* (1964). By Ep. 30, a trap door is obviously in place for the Merchant Banker (Cleese) to get rid of Mr. Ford (Jones) who is soliciting donations.

"by-election" — ("The Minehead By-Election") Any parliamentary election held off-year, or outside of a General Election. Very often the sitting government will lose some of its seats during these off-year elections, which is why Hilter and friends may have chosen to run during this election period, hoping to pick up disaffected voters.

• C •

"cake hole" — ("Mr. Hilter") A British military slang term for "mouth," and picked up by children after the war. Sellers's *Goon Show* character Grytpype-Thynne uses the term in "The Sale of Manhattan" episode (29 Nov. 1955).

The Pythons would revisit this type of banter in Ep. 42, the "RAF Banter" sketch. This might also serve to reassure the assembled folk that these three are as English as they claim to be.

"Camber Sands" — ("Police Station [Silly Voices]") Camber Sands is located in East Sussex, north of Hastings and Bexhill.

"cat's boil" — ("Visitors from Coventry") This in the category of "more information than absolutely necessary," another example of a Python character treading beyond accepted social boundaries—literally, a faux pas—and another character (Idle's Mr. Johnson) not seeming to notice. Perhaps Johnson's forthcoming loquacity is his own version of that same social boundary violation, since the Landlady (Jones) seems to put up quite pleasantly with his account of their trip to her home. Cf. Ep. 27 where Mrs. Conclusion (Cleese) admits casually to trying to bury her still living cat, as well as Ep. 4 where priceless art is destroyed and even eaten without guilt or recriminations.

"conservative then?" — ("The Minehead By-Election") Aligning Britain's Conservative Party with the Nazis (the National Socialist party in Weimar and WWII Germany) is no surprise considering the Pythons' left-of-center politics. Even purportedly impartial historians like the eminent A.J.P. Taylor spouted similarly veiled anti-Conservative biases in works such as *Englishmen and Others* (1956).

In the 1966 elections, Somerset North (where the sketch is set) retained its Conservative seat by about 2,300 votes, as would Weston-Super-Mare (where Cleese was born and raised). North Somerset, not coincidentally, is one of the towns mentioned in the Pythons' *Euroshow 1971—May Day Special*—along with Leighton Buzzard and Hereford—where "bugger-all" goes on during May Day celebrations.

In June 1970—just six months after the recording of this episode—the third-party Liberals under Jeremy Thorpe (mentioned repeatedly in Ep. 45) would lose half their seats to the Conservatives under Edward Heath in a political downturn for both Labour and the Liberals. This would have been a bit of a surprise to the Pythons, as well, as all opinion polls indicated a comfortable Labour victory in 1970.

"coons" — ("The Minehead By-Election") Pejorative term for blacks, but also used to describe members of the Whig party in the United States. See *OED*. This possible (but oblique) double meaning is interesting, since the reference can work both ways. The Nazis would have been anti-black, certainly, since the blacks aren't part of the Aryan race, but also anti-Whig, which translates into anti-Liberal.

Here the offensive term is delivered in what would be considered a racist (or racialist) way, but the sting is quickly removed as the woman (Jones) admits she's "a bit mental."

couple — (PSC; "Visitors from Coventry") Perhaps this description—*"a typical holiday bourgeois couple"*—more than any other betrays the Pythons' general take on contemporary English society and politics, and just where they might be found on the political spectrum. Words like "typical" and "bourgeois" are the give-away terms, and are used as both clues to the production design team (for costuming purposes) as well as handy "type" descriptions for the actors themselves, hinting at expected performance, for example. The couple will prove to be as dim or bright as anyone else, however, when they, too, are unable to realize that they are interacting with three infamous and allegedly long-dead Nazis.

Mrs. Johnson is played by Gillian Phelps, according to BBC records (WAC T12/1,093). She will also appear in Ep. 25.

"Coventry" — ("Visitors from Coventry") This is actually one of the few times that the Pythons carefully laid out directions from one place to another—this Coventry-to-Minehead route explained by Mr. Johnson (Idle) is spot on. Such accuracy is unusual for the troupe, who lean toward memorialized directions and history-off-the-cuff, meaning memory or factual errors can and do creep in. In the first episode, for instance, Picasso's cycling race route traced out by Eddie Waring and others does not follow such a clear path, nor does Head's proposed Kilimanjaro route in Ep. 10. Coventry lies east of Birmingham on the M6, in Warwickshire, and the distance from there to Minehead is about 132 miles.

"M5 . . . Droitwich"—The M5 runs between Bromsgrove and Worcester, and through Droitwich, in Worcestershire.

"before Bridgwater"—The A38 leaves the M5 corridor at Bridgwater, heading west to Williton, where it becomes the A39 to Minehead. There does appear to be a potentially major traffic situation where the A39 and A38 meet in the north part of Bridgwater (Bristol and Bath roads meet to become Monmouth Street).

"A372 . . . Stogumber"—Taunton is south of Bridgwater, and the A358 runs northwest out of Taunton. Both Crowcombe and Stogumber are small towns off of the A358, and don't appear to be potential traffic generators, to any great degree. The possibility that the small towns of the region empty toward the seaside on holidays and weekends may be what Mr. Johnson is talking about, or the very real possibility that penny-pinching weekenders from the north (like the Johnsons) crowd into this resort area on a regular basis.

current-affairs-type music — (PSC; *"Spectrum*—Talking about Things") Other shows of this nature from the period include *Nationwide* (1969) and *Panorama*, and given the name similarities, *Spectrum* might have been Python's direct adaptation of *Panorama* (1953–). Robin Day (1923–2000) appeared on *Panorama* between 1967 and 1979 (Ep. 1). Another connection to the Pythons is the presence on *Panorama* of Michael Barratt (b. 1928), who also appeared in *The Magic Christian* (1969) as a TV commentator, to which Cleese and Chapman contributed material (and in which both appeared). Alan Whicker also appeared in this film (cf. Ep. 27) as a TV commentator.

The music used for this section is the "Prelude to Richard III" from Walton's "Shakespeare Film Scores for Henry V, Hamlet, Richard III," with Sir William Walton conducting the Philharmonia Orchestra (WAC T12/1,093).

• D •

debs — ("Upperclass Twit of the Year") "Debutantes" are young women who have just emerged into high society. These three young women are played by Beulah Hughes, Ciona Forbes, and Sue Marchbank, according to BBC paperwork (WAC T12/1,093). This may be a bit of an anachronism by 1969, as the day of the young society woman's official visit to the court seems to have been waning by the late 1950s, according to former deb Fleur Hansen:

> The real question is what's the point of it? Of course it means you're "out"—I'm not quite sure what coming out entails, except that it's okay to be seen at a nightclub, although that's a doubtful advantage, too. Of course it gives point to the season. I suppose the season of dances and dreary all-female tea parties will go on. But without being presented at court it won't be as exciting, and it is exciting, now there won't be any anymore. I know debs are supposed to be silly and pampered and so on, but to be invited by the Lord Chamberlain to curtsy alone to the Queen of England, the latest of a line of monarchs going back for over a thousand years is an invitation I have no hesitation in saying I was deeply honored to accept. (*Eyewitness 1950–59*, "Life in the Fifties")

• E •

"Earth's crust" — ("How Far Can a Minister Fall?") Perhaps just a literal depiction of the "fall" of various political parties or politicians. In the Pythons' lifetimes, administrations and coalitions had fallen from time to time, including Churchill's rousting in the 1945 General Election, Macmillan's landslide election in 1959 (a majority of more than 100 seats), the rather sound thrashing that the Conservatives later took from Labour in 1964, and then Harold Wilson's Labour government was about to be voted out in the June 1970 elections in a surprise turnabout of political fortunes. Wage controls, the devaluation of the pound, the ever-diminishing British influence overseas, the embarrassment of/in Suez and Rhodesia, and rising taxes were all precursors to this fall, rendering the Pythons somewhat prescient in their satire.

All things considered, however, the stiff minister (Chapman) handles the situation surprisingly well, another example of the Pythons attacking, bloodying, but then recovering their target. Over and over again the Pythons will send up characters and points of view and, with perhaps the exception of actual women and the upper-class (in this episode, especially), they eventually re-embrace those characters. See Larsen, chapter 6.

This may also be directly referencing the precipitous fall of John Profumo (Ep. 2), who toppled from the highest levels of government as a Cabinet member to actually cleaning toilets at an East London charity house. See notes to Ep. 2 for more on the scandal.

"eating . . . Piccadilly line" — ("Mr. Hilter") A mishmash of Englishness which Himmler recites rather badly. "Fish and chips" are of course a noted English food; a "toad in the hole" is sausage baked in a batter, as well as a name for at least two children's games; "Dundee cakes" are rich fruit cakes covered with split almonds; "Piccadilly" is the well-known London tourist mecca, where such food items could have been bought and consumed.

This could be a play on the WWII-era practice (by American POWs, often) of identifying an enemy plant via his knowledge of American cultural trivia, specifically sports figures and World Series winners.

"Elsmore, Mrs." — (link out of "Ken Shabby") Philip Elsmore (b. 1937) is an English actor, born about the same time as the Pythons, in Worcestershire. Elsmore performed many linking and continuity duties for ABC and then Thames TV during this period. In 1969 Elsmore was narrating for *Two in Clover*.

The following narrated name, "Doug," is accompanied by a photo of a large sow, a still also used in Ep. 6. The inclusion of the sow photo may reflect back on Elsmore, as *Two in Clover* was a comedy set on a farm, where two city boys try and make it in rural life (read: lots of manure, farm machinery, and livestock jokes).

English rose — (PSC; "Ken Shabby") The phrase appears in describing the pink-skinned, blonde-haired English beauty as early as 1902 (according to the *OED*). Ironically, this "English rose" is portrayed here by the American Connie (or Constance) Booth, who earlier played the "rebel maid" in Ep. 9, the "Lumberjack" sketch. Booth and Cleese were married 1968–1978, and would go on to co-write and appear in *Fawlty Towers* (1975–1979) together.

Episode 12 — Recorded on 12 December 1969, and broadcast on 4 January 1970. In the WAC records, the dates for the entire episode (broadcast demands, costume requirements, etc.) are given as 4 January 1969, not 4 January 1970, a typo that seems to have gone unnoticed.

Also, official references (meaning beyond the walls of the BBC) to the program seem to have begun as early as January 1970 (when this episode aired), when an Ulster Unionist MP, Rafton Pounder, asked for a copy of a *Flying Circus* script so that he could use portions of it in his debate on accountants in the House later in January. The BBC sent him the copy straight away, though it's not indicated in the WAC files the precise episode requested (WAC T12/1,242). More than likely, however, the description of the dull life of a Chartered Accountant and efforts to "save" same in Ep. 10, "Vocational Guidance Counsellor," was the sketch remembered by the MP.

"extraordinary personal magnetism" — (link out of "Ken Shabby") This moment launches a soap opera–type narrative that had previously been employed by the Goons in the "Silent Bugler" episode (23 Feb. 1958). In a "the show so far" scenario, a Goon character rehearses what has gone before (none of which, of course, actually did go before):

> Narrator (Sellers): Helen Lovejoy, beautiful heiress to the Halibut millions, has been jilted at the altar by Villian de Paprikon, son of Louis the XIV. Peter, Villian's Eton boating friend, has heard this, but being in Tibet has embarrassed Mary, his fiancée, who being the only cousin of Sir Ray Ellington has passed the title on to Baron Geldray, also heir to the Halibut millions. Now read on . . .

These "show so far" moments often have little or nothing to do with the show at all, for both the Goons and the Pythons. In Ep. 33, however, the "show so far" moment will be accurate, up to and including the assault by giant "cartoony" hammer of the narrator (Jones).

"extraordinary way" — ("Vox Pops" link into "Upperclass Twit of the Year") In other episodes where they appear, these Upperclass Twits often have to be subtitled, their speech is so affected. They are treated as Other by the Pythons, as much as actual foreigners, and their speech (and affectations) is often the giveaway. See *MPSERD*, chapter 6.

• F •

. . . film of man falling out of window — ("Falling from Building") This dummy is tossed from the window of Slade House (off Hanworth Road, Hounslow, Middlesex) from a thirteenth-floor window. This was likely recorded early, along with the encyclopedia salesmen who also jumped (or were thrown) to their deaths in Ep. 5.

"Fiver?" — ("Falling from Building") There is a slight pause here as the line of impropriety is considered, then quickly crossed. Up to this point, the behavior has been within expected—if cynical—parameters, but with the wager on someone's death, the threshold into black humor is broached. The "rooting" to follow just ups the ante. Cf. a similar pause during the journey between normalcy and black comedy in Ep. 26, when the character (Cleese, again) is considering whether or not he should eat his recently deceased mother.

"Frampton Cottrell" — ("Visitors from Coventry") Actually spelled "Frampton Cotterell," this village lies northeast of Bristol.

"frothing and falling" — ("*Spectrum*—Talking about Things") This paragraph owes much to the Modernist writers Gertrude Stein and Virginia Woolf, as well as Lewis Carroll, where words aren't chosen for meaning, necessarily, but for sound, for how well they fit in with the previous word and the following word and the entire sentence. The Pythons' willingness to create nonce or psuedo-words and nonsense words ("zalling" and, later, "Dibbingley") and stream-of-consciousness sentences and paragraphs is a direct reflection of the Modernist literature and even art they'd grown up reading and experiencing.

"Führer" — ("Mr. Hilter") Typical title and respectful means of address for Hitler, especially after he became Chancellor of Germany in 1934. It means "leader," and is the less formal version of the official *Führer und Reichskanzler* (*OED*).

Later, Bimmler will call Hilter "Führer cat," mimicking the "Mod"-speak heard in swinging London and the "London hipster" films of the 1960s. His later "Soon baby" is another nod to the younger generation.

"fun in Stalingrad" — ("Mr. Hilter") Referring to the German army's miserable siege of Stalingrad (now Volgograd) which lasted seven months in 1942–1943 and, thanks to the tenacity of the Russian people and the especially harsh winter, turned the tide of war against the Nazis. Almost two million people (military and civilian) are believed to have lost their lives during the battle.

• G •

"Gervaise . . . basket" — ("Upperclass Twit of the Year") The name Gervaise Brook-Hampster might be an oblique reference to Tim Brooke-Taylor, who worked with various Pythons on *I'm Sorry I'll Read That Again* (1964–1973), *At Last the 1948 Show* (1967), *Marty* (1967), and *How to Irritate People* (1968).

"gobbed" — ("Ken Shabby") Slang term. To gob is to spit a clump of slimy substance—in this case, probably phlegm. In the earlier appearance of the Shabby-like Mr. Cook (also Palin) in Ep. 9, it was the goat that "did a bundle" on the carpet.

"God himself is made of" — ("How Far Can a Minister Fall?") Perhaps a swipe at the "enthusiastic" reporting being provided by American (and British) television news personalities as the Apollo 11 lunar mission results were discussed—including the importance of soil samples from the Moon's surface providing clues to the origins of not only the Moon, but the Earth, Solar System, and even the universe. (The BBC had created and broadcast some twenty-seven hours of coverage over the ten-day period in July 1969.) The cover of the 28 July 1969 Late London Edition of the *Times* carries a story titled "Rocks of Moon a Puzzle," and the subject was covered numerous times in other period newspapers, television reports, editorial pieces, and cartoon/comic panels. (See the British Cartoon Archive as well.) In 1969 there were more than 750 mentions of the various Apollo missions in the *Times* alone, and hundreds more in other British newspapers.

It also looks as though Third Robert (Cleese) is made up to appear to be upside down, just as the Minister (Chapman) was earlier.

goes back to wrestling with bear — (PSC; link into "Falling from Building") Cf. the film *HG* where a hairy beast reaches in to the "Book of the Film" section to snatch away the maiden's hand.

Elizabethan crowds enjoyed (and officials tolerated) bull- and bearbaiting, public performances which often outdrew even the most significant plays of the period, and were performed in "bear gardens." Producer Hounslowe even seems to indicate that he might have made more profits from such staged events than from producing plays (Gurr).

"going to die" — ("Mr. Hilter") This is precisely the same structure we saw when the façade dropped completely in Ep. 4, the "Secret Service Dentists" sketch.

"Goswell Road" — ("Falling from Building") North of the Thames in London, between Farrington and City roads. High-rise buildings dot the road. It's probably no accident that the headquarters of the Institute of Chartered Accountants in England and Wales is also on Goswell Road.

gramophone — (PSC; "The Minehead By-Election") Alluding to the manufactured crowds, enthusiasm, and support for the Nazi party in Germany prior to and even during the war. The 1934 Nazi Party Congress, for example, was a staged, theatrical event designed to impress and embolden Germans (as seen in Leni Riefenstahl's *Triumph of the Will* [1935]), and strike fear and respect in the rest of the world.

The music being played is the German national anthem "Deutschland Über Alles," this specific recording by the Band of Grenadier Guards, and conducted by Harris (WAC T12/1,093).

"gremlins" — ("How Far Can a Minister Fall?") According to the *OED*, this was originally an RAF term, which might explain the minister's (Chapman) usage as well as his character's military background.

• H •

"Hardacre" — ("*Spectrum*—Talking about Things") Paul H. Hardacre is the author of *The Royalists during the Puritan Revolution* (1956).

"'Hearts of Oak'–type music" — ("Ken Shabby") Music written by William Boyce (1711–1779), with lyrics by renowned actor David Garrick (1716–1779) in 1759. The song is a chest-thumping English naval hymn:

> Come cheer up, my lads! 'tis to glory we steer,
> To add something more to this wonderful year;
> To honour we call you, not press you like slaves,
> For who are so free as the sons of the waves?
> Heart of oak are our ships, heart of oak are our men;
> We always are ready, steady, boys, steady!
> We'll fight and we'll conquer again and again. . . .
> (www.contemplator.com/folk2/heartoak.html)

The "hearts of oak" phrase was adapted from a Rabelais work, *Gargantua and Pantagruel* (1548).

The music actually used for this transition is "The Rose"—Selection Myddleton, by the Band of Grenadier Guards, conducted by Harris (WAC T12/1,093).

"Henley" — ("Upperclass Twit of the Year") On the Thames in South Oxfordshire (Oxfordshire). Henley also boasts Stonor Park, the ancestral home of Lord and Lady Camoys and the Stonor family for more than 800 years, and to whom the Pythons may have been referring when creating the Nigel Incubator-Jones character.

The Goons had already employed this seemingly out-of-place rhyming word in their "Junk Affair" episode (7 Oct. 1957), when Milligan's character says: "See you later, incubator."

"Hilter" — ("Mr. Hilter") By simply rearranging/replacing letters in their names (Hilter, Bimmler, and Ron Vibbentrop) these characters are able to live and work openly (even dressed as Nazis) in North Minehead without fear of detection.

This is not unlike the Elizabethan stage practice of breech roles or the donning of flimsy disguises that rendered the character completely unrecognizable, even to lovers, spouses, and close family members. In those cases, the disguise was often used to elicit more emotionally honest responses from others in the play, who felt more free to speak, etc. Cf. Benedick's disguise (and the soothsaying results) as he discusses himself with Beatrice in *Much Ado*. Actually, the Nazis in this sketch also tend to reveal more about themselves even in disguise, though the rather dim guests and locals never seem to quite catch on. The Rustic on the street, however, doesn't seem to be taken in, nor are the children terribly impressed. The Conservative Vox Pops responders take to the message, of course.

Lastly, and most sinister, former Nazis determined to escape war crimes tribunals changed their names and appearances, and eventually fled Europe after the war. None of the biggest names in the Nazi party made it to any kind of postwar freedom, of course, but infamous others—including former doctors Josef Mengele (who later died in Brazil) and Aribert Heim, who disappeared into hiding in 1962, and Eichmann's former aide Alois Brunner—lived (or are living) long lives in concealed freedom.

"hire bombers by the hour" — ("Mr. Hilter") This bargain-basement approach to new fascism may have been inspired by a noted London fascist, a Mr. Robert Bloomfield, who had founded the National Action Party in June 1969, and was interviewed for the *Times Diary* in September of that same year. Bloomfield had been allied with Mosley's Union Movement (see Eps. 6, 25, and 32), and more recently the British National Party and National Democratic Party. As Mr. Bloomfield describes his organization and their capabilities, the image of silly, pathetic bike-riding Nazis seems quite apropos:

> [H]e takes pride in not disguising his fascist beliefs. "The number of members is a secret, but it is very small I can tell you. We can't afford a duplicator [mimeograph or copy machine], and have to pay for all our printing out of funds. I have been canvassing on my own, and with two other blokes—and I personally have only had the door slammed in my face three times," he says. (PHS, *Times Diary*, 15 Sept. 1969: 8)

The article concludes by pointing out that as a proud descendant of a Confederate soldier, Mr. Bloomfield remembers and honors his secessionist grandfather by displaying a Confederate flag in his den—a flag he had to paint himself.

Hitler ranting in German on a balcony — (PSC; "Mr. Hilter") The physical affectations, and especially the crossing of the arms and slight hunch, are borrowed from the surviving film footage of Hitler's address given at the Sportpalast in 1938, where he didn't have a podium to lean on or stand behind.

"Hitler . . . Ribbentrop" — ("Mr. Hilter") Adolf Hitler (1889–1945) was, of course, the leader of the Third Reich during the reign of the National Socialist Party in Germany (1933–1945). Hitler would commit suicide in a bunker in 1945 as the Russians closed in on Berlin.

Heinrich Himmler (1900–1945) was Hitler's right hand, especially during the war, leading all Nazi police forces, including the feared SS. Himmler would commit suicide the night before his Nuremberg trial was set to begin.

Joachim Von Ribbentrop (1893–1946) was a pseudo-aristocrat and Nazi foreign delegate who orchestrated the German-Soviet Nonaggression Pact of 1939, providing the way for the attack on Poland in September 1939. He was foreign minister 1938–1945, and was hanged as a war criminal after Nuremberg.

The *Private Eye* writers had created an exclusive in their 3 January 1969 issue, leading with the headline: "Hitler Arrested in Torquay." The article goes on to say that Hitler has been living in this sleepy resort town since the end of the war, that his neighbors just think he's a nice foreigner, and that both Goebbels and Mussolini were visiting friends (Ingrams, 212).

"Hove" — (link into "Falling from Building") Seaside town just west of the resort town Brighton, both in Sussex.

"Hunt Ball Photograph" — ("Upperclass Twit of the Year") A hunt ball is a ball given by those organizing a fox hunt. The photograph would be the traditional pre- and/or post-hunt posing for cameras. The photo with the young ladies would have been one destined for a Kensington reader's newspaper society page.

"Hurlingham Park" — ("Upperclass Twit of the Year") In the Greater London area (Fulham) on Hurlingham Road, SW6. Much of Eps. 11 and 12 were shot within a few square miles of this part of greater London. The park does feature a large grassy area, as well as a track, as depicted in the episode. The park is about six miles southeast of BBC TV Centre, and is one of the few times that a specific location is both named in the episode and then actually used as a setting.

In several of the camera angles facing northeast, the looming Battersea Power Station can be seen over the houses, well in the distance. The interior of the power station will be used for the "Find the Fish" sketch location in *Meaning of Life* (1983).

• I •

"Ilfracombe and Barnstaple" — ("Mr. Hilter") Barnstaple is at the junction of the A39 and A361, and Ilfracombe is north of Barnstaple, at the mouth of the Bristol Channel. Both are in Devon.

in a very deep voice — ("Police Station [Silly Voices]") This is much like the "Buying a Bed" sketch in Ep. 8, where the young couple have to speak and even listen differently, depending on the salesman they are confronting.

All these characters (Mr. Lambert, Mr. Verity, et al.) have learned to communicate among themselves, leaving only the Man (Jones) to get up to speed, like the audience. The importance (and, often, difficulty) of communication in *FC* is a significant trope. In Ep. 14, the Minister delivers his answer in his "normal voice, and then in a kind of silly, high-pitched whine." Other characters only speak parts of words, so that only in a group can they utter complete sentences; one character speaks in anagrams; and one insults the listener with every other sentence, etc. In a nicely visual twist on the trope, in Ep. 30, gestures are offered to denote "pauses in televised talk."

Incidentally, the poet T.S. Eliot titled the first two sections of his epic modernist poem *The Waste Land* "He Do the Police in Different Voices," a quote from Dickens's *Our Mutual Friend* (1864–1865).

Iron Cross — (PSC; "Mr. Hilter") Prussian military award instituted in 1813, and reinvigorated in 1939 by Hitler. Von Ribbentrop received his Iron Cross for service in WWI, as did Hitler.

"It's" Man intro — (PSC; "Titles") The "It's" Man is treated like a ball in a pinball machine in this opening. The pinball machine itself is a Bank-a-Ball machine created by Gottlieb from about 1965.

• J •

"Johnson" — ("Falling from Building") A "Johnson" may have been the man who actually jumped from the board meeting earlier, rather than Parkinson. The First Man (Idle) has already bet that Parkinson would jump next, while Second Man (Cleese) bets against Parkinson. They then cheer for or against "Parky," and even after the letter writer falls, and Second Man celebrates (that it's Parkinson), Second Man calls out, "Johnson!"

• K •

"Kensington and Weybridge" — ("Upperclass Twit of the Year") Part of Greater London, Kensington lies west of London, and is home to Kensington Palace, which still acts as a private residence for royals. Kensington and Chelsea have been home to kings, queens, royalty of all kinds, and "people of quality and note" since at least the fifteenth century, and remained the home of the fashionable upper class into the Pythons' era. Weybridge is in Surrey, directly south of Heathrow Airport, and is home to the annual Royal Regatta.

"Kicking the Beggar" — ("Upperclass Twit of the Year") A game that the more socialist-minded might attribute characteristically to more conservative folk. In other words, the monied upper class ignoring or even harming the poor, or anyone outside of their class.

"Know what I mean . . ." — ("Ken Shabby") In this case, the character of the father (Chapman) does not seem to appreciate Shabby's intentions. This is another example of a sketch wherein the characters can't see (or refuse to see) the absurdity of the situation, much like in an upcoming episode (Ep. 14), where the Minister (also Chapman) is cross-dressed, and a patch of liquid is allowed to "argue the case against the government." Shabby (Palin) will also use very clear sexual euphemisms throughout, much like the "Nudge, Nudge" man in Ep. 3, but Rosamund's father will miss those, as well.

• L •

"Lady . . . Smith" — ("Upperclass Twit of the Year") Cf. Ep. 18, where the names of candidates for the various parties are recited including: "Tarquin Fintim-lin-bin-whin-bim-lin-bus-stop-F'tang-F'tang-Olé-Biscuitbarrel." Actual names obviously generated this reference, names from the peerage (like Eustace Gervais Tennyson-d'Eyncourt and Kenneth Oliver Musgrave St. John et al.) that also graced the society pages during this period.

"lampshade time" — ("Mr. Hilter") Probably a euphemism for death, meaning to cover or diffuse the light (life). Sounds like a borrowing from a pulp fiction novel, perhaps. For Tex Avery, a lampshade on the head (and a bulb in the mouth) of the temporarily stunned Wolf is used as a blackout gag, a payoff before the next set-up (see *Red Hot Riding Hood*, 1942). Noting the Pythons' awareness and use of cartoon elements (and Hitler's admitted fondness for Mickey Mouse cartoons, as well), this is a possible, glancing referent.

Lancet — (link out of "Ken Shabby") Significant British medical journal founded in 1823. The Gumby Brain Specialist (Cleese) is looking in vain for his copy of *The Lancet* in Ep. 32.

"Leeds University" — ("*Spectrum*—Talking about Things") Located in Leeds, Yorkshire, the university is one of the "new" schools, and was officially established in 1904.

"leg-before-wicket" — ("Mr. Hilter") Cricket terminology. The batsman can defend the wicket with his leg or any part of his body, but can also be dismissed for same for not using his bat. The French guard (Cleese) who taunts Arthur and his knights in *HG* also disparagingly uses this phrase to taunt the "silly English 'kuh-niggets.'"

"Local Government Bill" — ("How Far Can a Minister Fall?") The extreme localization indicated here was part of the reason that the Conservatives were in trouble in 1962 as they approached defeat by Labour in 1964, a defeat that would end thirteen years of Tory rule. The international reputation and trading power of Britain had suffered under the Conservative government, and the former colony, the United States, had risen to superpower status in the interim; Britain found itself having to consult with the United States before embarking on any kind of significant monetary or military endeavor, which was quite galling to many (*Eyewitness 1950–59*).

London-Brighton train journey — (PSC; link out of "*Spectrum*—Talking about Things") The signal box where the episode began near Hove is near Brighton. There is no indication in the WAC records for this episode that this "stock film" was hired, so it may actually have been shot by BBC/Python personnel on the trip to Brighton.

Additionally, this film clip is reminiscent of the short live-action section of George Dunning's *Yellow Submarine* (1968), where filmed images and still photos are manipulated to appear as if the camera is racing through/over them.

• M •

"Mainwaring" — ("Upperclass Twit of the Year") Captain George J. Mainwaring was the lead character in the popular television show *Dad's Army* (1968–1977). The show was a fictional treatment of a small seaside town (not unlike Minehead) and its WWII Home Guard unit, the local voluntary militia.

Many of the names chosen for the "Upperclass Twit" sketch are straight from the list of the most gentrified families in the UK. There are currently more than sixty "Mainwaring" entries at peerage.com, for example, as well as myriad families named "Brooke," "Smith" and "Smythe," "Harris," "Jones," and "St. John."

"McGoering" — ("Mr. Hilter") Here Hermann Goering is cast as a Scotsman. The actual Goering (b. 1893) committed suicide at Nuremberg in 1946, and had been the rather flamboyant head of the Luftwaffe (Nazi air forces) during the war.

"Meinhead" — ("The Minehead By-Election") Note the Germanic spelling of the first syllable, which now connotes possession ("my"), and probably meant to refer to Hitler's prewar magnum opus, *Mein Kampf* (1925).

"Minehead, Somerset" — ("Visitors from Coventry") On the Bristol Channel, Minehead's principal industry is, not coincidentally, tourism.

"Mr. and Mrs. Phillips" — ("Visitors from Coventry") Gilliam plays Mr. Phillips, and Connie Booth plays Mrs. Phillips.

"Mr. Farquar's" — (link out of "Ken Shabby") At this point, a still from *The Phantom of the Opera* (1925; Lon Chaney) appears. The same still was used in Ep. 6. Gilliam used a number of photos and cutouts over and over again, whether for familiarity or just time considerations. The balance of the narration reads like an update to a long-running soap opera.

• N •

The Naked Ant — (PSC; captions for "Signalbox" link into "Falling from Building") Cf. Desmond Morris's 1967 book *The Naked Ape*, a poster of which is seen in Ep. 4 in the bookshop. See notes to Ep. 4. Also, the allusion to the openly gay Quentin Crisp's 1968 autobiography *The Naked Civil Servant* can't be overlooked, especially when the "poncing" campiness of Python's homosexual or effeminate characters are discussed. See David Unction (Chapman) in Ep. 10 for such behavior.

Napoleon — (link out of "Ken Shabby") This is a black and white portrait of Napoleon. It is a photocopy of "The Emperor" by Meissomer, and was borrowed from *The Life of Napoleon Bonaparte* by S. Baring-Gould (Methuen & Co., First Edition 1896, Second Edition 1908—Abridged), according to BBC archives (WAC T12/1,093).

"National Bocialist" — ("The Minehead By-Election") Again, a single letter replaced or misplaced and the meaning is lost completely. In Idle's harangue as a potential tourist in Ep. 31 he also replaces the letter [c] with [b], as in "Hotel Bontinental," "bolor supplements," and the eventually censored "silly bunt."

In Gilliam's 1985 Orwellian-nightmare film *Brazil* (co-written by Gilliam, Tom Stoppard, and Charles McKeown), a single misplaced letter—where "Tuttle" becoming "Buttle"—sets in motion a change of events that wreaks havoc, ruins lives, and propels the narrative to its dystopic climax.

"Nigel . . . stockbroker" — ("Upperclass Twit of the Year") These first three competitors—Simon, Nigel, and Gervaise—also all share the seeming inability to form and keep normal familial / fraternal relationships. Simon's spouse is a piece of furniture, Nigel has a tree for a best friend, and Gervaise acts as a waste receptacle for his father.

If there is a modicum of scorn meted out by the Pythons, it's often doled out along class lines, with the upper crust male getting the lion's share. This could simply be a matter of sour grapes, as none of the Pythons came from anything but working-class backgrounds, though each would have rubbed shoulders (or noses) with such upper-class types at Cambridge and Oxford.

Nixon — (PSC; "Vox Pops" link out of "Police Station [Silly Voices]") Perhaps thanks to Gilliam's American background, Nixon appears several times, and may have been alluded to earlier as a Nazi ("Dickie old chum"). Also, Nixon's international presence during his term as vice president to Eisenhower put him in the British news (and the political cartoons) of the period regularly.

"Nürnberg" — ("Mr. Hilter") City where the postwar Nazi war crimes trials were held. Himmler didn't actually make it to the trials, having committed suicide (by poison) after falling from Hitler's grace as the war wound down. Von Ribbentrop was found guilty on all four charges brought against him, and was sentenced to death. He was hanged soon thereafter.

• O •

"old men" — ("How Far Can a Minister Fall?") Likely a swipe at the Conservative Party, seen as the stodgy party of the status quo, representing the landed, monied, titled interests, etc. This treatment also indicates that such politicians have trouble functioning without carefully written scripts, and that minor technical difficulties can prevent the delivery of the party message. (See the printed script version of Ep. 38 for a rehearsed, choreographed party political broadcast.) Labour's Harold Wilson was in his late forties when he took office in 1964; Edward Heath was fifty-four when he assumes the post in 1970. Harold Macmillan was the nearly-retirement-age of sixty-three when he took office in 1957, and wouldn't retire until he was sixty-nine. The Pythons were part of the rebellious postwar generation, of course, all between about twenty-four and thirty-one years old in 1970, so anyone over forty must have seemed quite ancient and out of touch.

"Oliver . . . twit" — ("Upperclass Twit of the Year") "Harrow" is a public (independent) school attended by such notables as Robert Peel, Henry John Temple (Lord Palmerston), Richard Brinsley Sheridan, Lord Byron, John Galsworthy, Lord Shaftesbury, and Winston Churchill. Rather than simply producing Conservative graduates, Harrow was considered to be a nursery for the cultured elite, as indicated by the list above.

"The Guards" refers to the Queen's Household Cavalry Mounted Regiment (Life Guards, Blues and Royals), and this progression—from a school like Harrow or Eton through the Guards and into country life retirement—was the chosen path for many aristocratic young men. This ideal progression is embodied in Oliver here, and he is characterized as the "outstanding twit" of the year.

As for "Mollusc," there is a mollusc documentary acted out in Ep. 32.

"121 . . . SE21" — ("Police Station [Silly Voices]") Dulwich is located in the Greater London area, not far from Wimbledon and Crystal Palace. Dulwich is a part of the SE21 zip code. There is no Halliwell (Street, Road, Lane, etc.) in the SE21 postal code area. The nearest Halliwell Road is near Brixton Prison in the Lambeth area of Greater London.

127th — ("Upperclass Twit of the Year") Indicating that Upperclass Twits as a definable, contesting group have been recognized since about 1842. This could be a reference to the changing times signified by the rise of the Conservative Robert Peel to the PM position in 1841. The Opium War also ended the following year, leaving Britain in control of significant Chinese territory (China ceding Hong Kong and opening other ports to British trade) and cementing its reputation as a gunboat diplomacy nation. These types—"Eton, Harrow and the Guard"—would have been just the fellows to fill the plum military and civil service positions both at home as well as abroad in the far-flung British Empire.

"Oxfam" — (link out of "Ken Shabby") *OED*: "An organization for the distribution of food, funds, etc., in disaster areas and to poor countries."

• P •

"Pagoda" — (link out of "Ken Shabby") Asian temple or spiritual building.

"Parkhurst" — ("Police Station [Silly Voices]") Parkhurst Prison is located in Parkhurst on the Isle of Wight.

"Parkinson" — ("Falling from Building") Perhaps an allusion to noted British television presenter Michael Parkinson (b. 1935). Parkinson had also appeared on *World in Action* (1963), *Cinema* (1964), and *The Morecambe & Wise Show* (1968). Parkinson was presenting for *Cinema* in 1969, when this first *Flying Circus* season was produced.

"Party Political Broadcast" — ("How Far Can a Minister Fall?") Party political broadcasts involve television (and/or radio) airtime allotted to the major parties prior to elections. The "Wood Party" probably wouldn't have qualified for the time, though may be connected to other "wooden" characters like Arthur Tree and his guests (Ep. 10), David Hemmings (Ep. 8), and certainly the stuffy old Conservatives like former PM Macmillan and his successor, Alec Douglas-Home, who was sixty when he became PM. Other parties were extant but generally not allowed TV time (inclusion of parties was based on a certain level of performance at previous elections, number of seats contested and won, etc.). Participating parties have included Whigs, Workers (socialist), Conservatives (Tory origins), Labour, Liberal, and Social Democrats, etc.

Conservative, Labour, and Liberal would have been the three parties seen and heard on most party political broadcasts during the Pythons' lives, but in the 1966 General Election the increasing political spectrum in Britain was acknowledged. Broadcasts including the Communist, Scottish National, and Plaid Cymru (Wales) parties were offered.

"Peterborough, Lincolnshire" — ("Mr. Hilter") The real Von Ribbentrop actually spent some time in Canada prior to WWI (1910–1914), selling wine. Ron Vibbentrop is obviously flustered, since Peterborough is actually in Cambridgeshire, not Lincolnshire.

"piledriver" — ("Upperclass Twit of the Year") *OED*: "A very strong or powerful hit, stroke, kick, etc., in various games; something of great strength or power." It has also become known as a professional wrestling move, which may be more apropos in this setting.

"pluck" — ("Upperclass Twit of the Year") *OED*: "The heart as the seat of courage; courage, boldness, spirit; determination not to yield but to keep up the fight in the face of danger or difficulty." This term is often heard when the character of the (mostly common) British citizenry is being lauded, especially as they conducted themselves during the war years.

"Plunkett, Arabella" — ("Upperclass Twit of the Year") Arabella Fermor was the name of the young woman whose hair was snipped by an impulsive suitor, unleashing bad blood between aristocratic families and providing the inspiration for young Alexander Pope's "The Rape of the Lock." The poem is itself an indictment of the propensity for the elevation of a trivial matter to the heroic, tragic level—such elevations are, of course, part and parcel of Python's satire.

"polecat" — ("Ken Shabby") A weasel, essentially. Playwright John Gay also speaks of killing polecats in his *What d'ye call it* (1714).

• R •

"racialist" — ("The Minehead By-Election") Cf. the Gumby (Cleese) in Ep. 5 who rails against foreigners and any Englishman who might leave the country, and who also swore he wasn't a "racialist." Conservative MP Enoch Powell had made similar claims in his infamous "Rivers of Blood" speech, also discussed in the notes for Ep. 5.

Coincidentally, the British fascist leader Sir Oswald Mosley (1896–1980) was also active during this period, having returned from self-imposed exile in France to contest Kensington North in 1959 and 1966, hoping to capitalize on the smoldering sentiments after the race riots in Notting Hill. He was unsuccessful in both races.

"rallies" — ("The Minehead By-Election") A reference to the National Socialist rallies and party congresses where hundreds of thousands of Germans celebrated their new leader, Hitler. These gatherings began as early as 1921, when Hitler rose to power in the party and scores or hundreds would gather, and would culminate, in the early years, at enormous rallies in places like Nuremberg (1927). Leni Riefenstahl's 1935 film *Triumph of the Will* "documents" the 1934 Nazi Party Congress in Nuremberg.

The Pythons create an audience for Hilter and friends out of several children, a Rustic (Jones), and bemused onlookers. This balcony scene was staged at a building near the corner of Greswell Street and Stevenage Road, just across from the Fulham FC grounds (WAC T12/1.094). This is just around the corner from the "Axis Café" location seen in a previous shot.

rapid montage — (PSC; link out of "How Far Can a Minister Fall?") The fact that many of these characters hail from earlier episodes illustrates the careful preparation not only each episode but the entire series demanded. It means that they were planning the end of Ep. 12 much earlier. These characters are, in order of appearance: Second Robert (Idle), Third Robert (Cleese), Switchman (Jones), Bear (who shakes his head), Second Sergeant (Chapman, singing), Sergeant (Cleese, low register), Pepperpot (Idle), Stockbroker (Cleese), Gumby (Jones), Cassowary (animated), Gumby (Jones again, but no "no"), Fairy (Idle), City Gent (Chapman), Pepperpot (Jones), Gumby (Palin), Twit (Cleese, who struggles to say "no"), Ron Vibbentrop (Chapman), Hilter (Cleese) and Bimmler (Palin), an animated right whale, Madd (Chapman's foaming-mouth City Gent), and finally the *Spectrum* Presenter (Palin).

This last character is crushed by the cartoony sixteen-ton weight created by the BBC Property department for the show. Palin's head clearly breaks the top of the primarily Styrofoam prop, and a request to have the prop fixed can be found in the archival material. The prop will be broken again on 2 July 1970, while taping portions of Ep. 15, though, curiously, the scene where the weight is used (and clearly again broken) won't appear until Ep. 16, as a "Vox Pops" insert.

"Reginald" — ("Mr. Hilter") So his assumed name is Reginald Bimmler, and below we see that Hitler is actually Richard (or Dick) Hilter. It shouldn't be surprising that Python would choose these names—Reginald and Dickie—for their Nazis' pseudonyms. The "Reginald" is certainly an allusion to Reginald Maudling, the much-lampooned Tory MP and Cabinet member. His sometimes arch-Conservatism made him a Python target, of course. Maudling's "naughty bits" are pointed out in Ep. 22, for instance.

The "Dickie" can be none other than Richard Nixon, then president of the United States and consistent target of Britain's Left-leaning press and socialist government members. Nixon is also mentioned or depicted a number of times throughout *FC*, including later in this same episode during a Vox Pops section. Nixon had figured prominently in the international public eye since the early 1950s, when he served as Dwight Eisenhower's vice president (1953–1961), traveling widely throughout the world.

"Rosamund" — ("Ken Shabby") Rosamund the Fair (de Clifford), 1140–1176, was Henry II's mistress/concubine whom the king kept safely hidden away in a garden bower in Woodstock, Oxfordshire, near Blenheim Palace. The Pythons describe their Rosamund as an "English rose" (meaning fair-skinned and attractive), and period descriptions of the historical Rosamund agree: "A sweeter creature in this world

/ Could prince never embrace" (see Somerville). Artists Rossetti and Waterhouse painted famous images of Rosamund in 1861 and c. 1905, respectively. (See Drabble's *Oxford Companion to English Literature*, 846.)

Taken together, these descriptions of Fair Rosamund and the romantic historical and royal atmosphere of the story make the presence of Ken Shabby—and his "haven't had it for weeks" intentions—all the more incongruous.

"Rt. Hon. Lambert Warbeck" — (PSC; "How Far Can a Minister Fall?") The title "Rt. Hon." is described in the *OED*: "Right Honourable is applied to peers below the rank of Marquess, to Privy Councillors, and to certain civil functionaries, as the Lord-Mayors of London, York, and Belfast, and the Lord Provosts of Edinburgh and Glasgow; sometimes, also, in courtesy, to the sons and daughters of peers holding courtesy titles."

Here it's the titled authority figure Python renders ridiculous. The sight of a proper, Conservative gentleman hanging upside down on national television sends up not only the Tories but the entire political process. In the 1951 party political broadcast, Labour leader Lord Samuel (1870–1963) delivered a wooden, made-for-radio address that ran boring and long and may have helped inspire this sketch. The 1955 party political broadcasts saw gaffes that fit the new medium of television to a tee: the Conservative candidate (Harold Macmillan) fumbled through prop malfunctions and blown lines; the Labour candidate (Clement Attlee) interviewed much shorter than expected, flustering his interviewer.

As to the name "Lambert Warbeck," in 1491 Perkin Warbeck, a Flemish merchant, infamously posed as a prince of the House of York (as Richard, the younger son of Edward IV), and claimed the English throne held by Henry VII. Warbeck was eventually executed in 1497. (A previous claimant to the same throne, coincidentally, had been one "Lambert Simnel." He was deposed and—considered harmless—allowed to work for the king.) Python's use of the name might be a subtle comment on the "pretender" political parties vying for airtime and parliamentary seats during the late 1960s and early 1970s. "Lambert" was also the name of the afflicted mattress salesman in Ep. 4, also played by Chapman.

"running sores" — ("Mr. Hilter") Himmler here is not unlike the cat whose boil was being attended to as the sketch began. There is no record of Himmler having suffered any physical malady that might keep him from military service; in fact he briefly served in a Bavarian regiment at the end of WWI.

As alleged WWII Nazi war criminals were tracked down and brought to justice many years after the war ended, one of the consistent (and pitiful, but not pitiable) defenses espoused by many was their unfitness for trial, their infirmity due to advanced age.

• S •

"sap" — (link out of "Ken Shabby") Generally considered a pejorative term, the *OED* reports that in Eton College slang a "sap" is one who studies a great deal. This is another script-only comment, and wouldn't have been available to the viewers, and reads:

> Cut to strange PHOTO CAPTION SEQUENCE (to be worked out with Terry 'the sap' Gilliam) (if he can find the time).

The seeming impatience and frustration implied in the commentary may be attributable to the fact that this piece would have to have been created in addition to Gilliam's normal contributions (interstitial animations), and his time and energies (and patience) may have been stretched thin.

"Shabby, Ken" — ("Ken Shabby") This character seems an adaptation of an earlier Palin character appearing in Ep. 9, Mr. Cook, whose goat fouls the carpet, and looks forward to the street dwellers from "*Up Your Pavement*" in Ep. 42. Shabby is the lower-class figure thrust into upper-class society, and is reminiscent of G.B. Shaw's *Pygmalion* scenario, and especially including Eliza's father, whom Shaw describes as

> an elderly but vigorous dustman, clad in the costume of his profession, including a hat with a back brim covering his neck and shoulders. He has well marked and rather interesting features, and seems *equally free from fear and conscience*. He has a remarkably expressive voice, the result of a habit of giving vent to his feelings without reserve. His present pose is that of wounded honor and stern resolution. (2.196–99; italics added)

Shabby is just as out of place in fair Rosamund's world as Alfred is in Higgins's. These clashes of culture (ever more apparent in a class society like Britain's) are utilized to humorous ends throughout *FC*. See the entry for "Rosamund" above. G.B. Shaw (played by Palin) will be later featured in Ep. 41, the "Poetry Reading (Ants)" sketch, fending off the verbal barbs of both Whistler (Cleese) and Wilde (Chapman).

signalbox — ("Signalbox" link into "Falling from Building") Small buildings where railroad switching levers are located. Trainspotters and locomotive enthusiasts in general would (and still do) take/ swap/ discuss photographs of such boxes, and surviving photos of Somerset-area boxes look remarkably like the box depicted in this episode. Most of these boxes were built by Saxby & Farmer.

The BBC released *Engines Must Not Enter the Potato Siding* in 1969, a collection of short railway films including *Signal Man*, which looked at life and work at "one of the loneliest and busiest jobs on the railway line," and which also happens to be set in Northern England. (Also, the Goons prominently feature the Pevensey Bay signal box in "The Pevensey Bay Disaster" [3 Apr. 1956], where a bomb is being planted to derail the Hastings Flyer.)

The signal box in Minehead had been removed by British Rail in 1966, and the next year would see the closing of the Crowcombe signal box. These closings and consolidations—which prefaced a great deal of local consternation, given the number of rail enthusiasts—may account for the inclusion of this somewhat bizarre section in *FC*.

There are today signal box web pages across the Internet, dedicated entirely to the signal boxes, past and present, of particular regional railways in the UK.

"Simon . . . lamp" — ("Upperclass Twit of the Year") This character's name sounds like a Cleese creation, much like his "Bunn, Wackett, Buzzard, Stubble, and Boot" football line from pre-Python days. Simon Harris was a character (a doctor) on the American daytime drama *The Doctors* (1963–1982), which may have been known by at least Cleese from his work in NYC; Gilliam, an American; and perhaps even Chapman, a doctor himself. Both Cleese and Chapman wrote for a doctor television show in 1969, as well. The "Simon Harris" character appeared in 1968. The "zinc" reference may qualify that chemical element as Python's favorite, already mentioned in Eps. 2, 3, and 6.

The hyphenated or just plain silly name tropes are also seen in English literary tradition, including "Catsmeat Potter-Pirbright" and "Gussie Fink-Nottle" in Wodehouse's *The Code of the Woosters* (1938). The Pythons' immediate comedy predecessors, the Goons, created the oddly monikered Hercules Grytpype-Thynne, Bluebottle, and the Frenchman Count Jim Moriarty, among many others.

"A Small Boarding House in Minehead, Somerset" — ("Visitors from Coventry") The front door of the home where the Johnsons (Idle and Gillian Phelps) are to be greeted by the Landlady (Jones) looks to be right about 50 Ellerby Street, Hammersmith and Fulham, not Creswell [*sic*], as indicated in the WAC records for the episode. The shot was likely scheduled for *Greswell* Street, two streets over from Ellerby. Ellerby Street is not mentioned in the WAC records. The neighborhood is walking distance from Fulham FC stadium, and very near the "Axis Café" location.

"Somerset" — ("Mr. Hilter") Somerset—home to Minehead—is where Ron Vibbentrop says he was born, denying the Düsseldorf address. Von Ribbentrop was actually born in Wesel, Niederrhein, though both Düsseldorf and Wesel are in North Rhine, Westphalia.

"Stock Exchange" — ("The Minehead By-Election") Again, a representative of the Conservative class, the established and monied elite here supports the fascistic policies of a growth-spurred government. The fact that Enoch Powell, for example, remained a staunch Conservative infuriated many in the party (who saw him as a dividing demagogue), while it bolstered others who feared the Lib-Lab approach to immigration policy would lead to a tidal wave of "colour" into Britain in the 1950s and 1960s.

This may also be a reference to the significant support the National Socialists enjoyed in the 1930s in the UK (including the British Union of Fascists, banned in 1940), especially among people of note, many admiring the Nazi government's ability to drag Germany out of its financial straits and toward full employment and unmatched industrial production in the late 1930s.

. . . strange beasties climb out of it — ("*Animation: Falling Apart, Animals from a Pipe*") The creatures emerging from the pipe include a crested penguin (likely a southern rockhopper), a shrew, a raptor fossil drawing, a balloon designed by Francesco Lana in 1670 (which will be seen again in Ep. 23), a flea, and a right whale. The parade of beasties marches past the house where Ken Shabby will ask for Rosamund's hand.

• T •

tatty — (PSC; "Visitors from Coventry") Somewhat neglected or run down.

"Television Doctor" — ("Mr. Hilter") This reaction is probably a tongue-in-cheek allusion to doctor shows in general, and specifically the show *Doctor in the House*, for which Chapman (a nonpracticing doctor himself) and Cleese wrote the pilot episode in 1969. (See Wilmut, 187–88.) The show was produced by Humphrey Barclay, and ran through several iterations. Wilmut reports that Chapman and Cleese used actual names of friends and real people for characters, something they would continue to do as Pythons (187).

Though neither Himmler nor Hitler were actors, nor were they alive when commercial television was pervasive, archival footage from various Nazi rallies and addresses was used regularly in films and on TV. Significant Himmler/Hitler footage appeared in the 1956 TV presentation, *The Twisted Cross*, and they "acted" (as themselves) in Leni Riefenstahl's films *Victory of the Faith* (1933) and *Triumph of the Will* (1935).

This mention may have emerged from the Nuremberg trials, as well, since there was a special section of the proceedings set aside for doctors who had participated in human experiments, executions, etc., and much was made of the "missing" doctors, including the infamous "Der Weisse Engel" Josef Mengele.

Noteworthy television doctors from this period include Chapman himself from *Doctor in the House* (1969), Dr. Finlay (mentioned in Ep. 7), and Dr. Kildare. Lastly, the earlier-mentioned Lord Charles Hill was the well-known (and sexually saccharine) "Radio Doctor" in the 1950s, hosting a staid, rehearsed teenaged chat show ostensibly about sex, but focusing more on morality (*Eyewitness 1950–59*, "Sexual Attitudes").

3.48 seconds — (PSC; "Signalbox" link into "Falling from Building") The printed script mentions that the signalman (Jones) "wrestles [the bear] for 3.48 seconds," a comment meant for the reader only, of course. The "wrestle" actually lasts a little over 12 seconds.

"Tiddles" — ("*Spectrum*—Talking about Things") Also the name of the cat in Ep. 11, and would become the name of a cat living in a ladies' bathroom at Paddington Station just months after this episode aired for the first time.

"Twit of the Year" — ("Upperclass Twit of the Year") If comedy comes from below, as has been said, then so might certain population controls. This type of "eugenics" might also have its inception in the lower or middle classes, in the Python world, as opposed to the ruling class attempting to manipulate the physical and racial makeup of Man (well, Poorer, Lower-Class, and Third World Man). The significance of eugenics for many Modernists—at least, before ethnic cleansing became practicable and then brutally practiced in the twentieth century—was the promise of social elevation, the reduction of congenital disease and genetic weakness, and just a better world.

Success in this "Twit" competition, then, is defined as eliminating the Upperclass Twit (more specifically, the upper-class males) from society, and erasing the flawed bloodline from the English genetic pool. Gumbys and Pepperpots and even Ken Shabby can live and procreate, but not the upper class. Twits Simon (Jones) and Nigel (Cleese) will also prove successful at taking their own lives, joining Gervaise (Palin) in "winning."

• U •

"Uberleben muss gestammen . . ." — ("The Minehead By-Election") The German used here is a mixture of actual German and mangled English-German as has been used before in Ep. 1 ("The Funniest Joke in the World") and like those for French (Ep. 2, "Flying Sheep") and Spanish (Ep. 9, "Llamas"). This jabberwock concoction of German and English is also used—and is perhaps where the Pythons were inspired—in WWII-era cartoons lampooning Hitler, including *Blitz Wolf* (1942, MGM), and *Daffy the Commando* (1943, WB). Various British (and American) radio comedians also employed the "Germlish" language in comedy broadcasts lampooning Hitler and the Nazis.

Essentially, Hilter here is telling the people of Minehead that they have a historical claim on the Taunton region. Taunton is southeast of Minehead, along the A39, then A358, and seems to be of little strategic value, except as a tourist destination. Hitler made similar claims on much of Central Europe in the years leading up to WWII, including the Rhineland, which he flooded with German troops in 1936, claiming Germany's historical right to the area.

"Und . . . Somerset" — ("The Minehead By-Election") Rough translation: "And Bridgwater is the last desire we have in Somerset." In other words, appease us with Taunton and Bridgwater, and there will be peace, Hilter assures his listeners. (Bridgwater is north and a bit east of Taunton.) This is of course what Hitler and Germany claimed in regard to the Sudetenland prior to the eruption of WWII. From Hitler himself, in 1938:

> I hope that in a few days the problem of the Sudeten Germans will be finally solved. By October 10 we shall have occupied all the areas which belong to us. Thus one of Europe's most serious crises will be ended, and all of us, not only in Germany but those far beyond our frontiers, will then in this year for the first time really rejoice at the Christmas festival. It should for us all be a true Festival of Peace. (From Hitler's address of 5 Oct. 1938 at Sportpalast, Berlin)

These filmed speeches were played over and over again during the Pythons' young lives, as propaganda for the war effort, and later as propaganda for a strong England in the face of the specter of expanding international Communism, for example.

"Upperclass Twit" — ("Upperclass Twit of the Year") A particular target of the Pythons, these characters will be ridiculed at unprecedented length in the fully narrated sketch. These representations might be built on literary precursors like Bertram "Bertie" Wooster in the P.G. Wodehouse (1881–1975) book series featuring the exploits of the foppish upper-class Wooster and his clever man, Jeeves. The first of this series was *The Man with Two Left Feet* (1917). Python, employing the "rules" of satire, distorts the "amiable, vacuous" Wodehouse characterization with their almost unmitigated scorn of the Upperclass Twits (Drabble 1985, 1084). Also, Agatha Christie's Captain Hastings character (*The Disappearance of Mr. Davenheim* [1924]) might be an early reference.

These twittish upper crust characters may also be updated versions of the fops so essential to Restoration and eighteenth-century comedy, including Sir Fopling Flutter (from Etherege's *The Man of Mode*) and Lord Foppington (from Vanbrugh's *The Relapse*, Sheridan's *A Trip to Scarborough*, and Cibber's *The Careless Husband*). See Nettleton and Case, *British Dramatists from Dryden to Sheridan* (1939) for more on this character. The pages of fashionable mags like *The Tatler* and *Country Life* are also replete with such characters, posing for photos at mansion galas, debutante balls, cricket and fox hunting outings, and receiving the myriad "orders" (OBE, DSO) from HRH.

According to BBC records, this portion of the show was shot on 3 December 1969 at Hurlingham Sports Ground, Hurlingham Road, W6 (WAC T12/1,094). See the entry above for "Hurlingham Park" for more on this location.

• V •

"verges" — ("Visitors from Coventry") The grassy areas bounding the roadway might here be squeezed between road and some structure, like the hospital he mentions, for instance.

These verges, as well as the homes and businesses on or near them were threatened (and many eventually torn down) as the Greater London Development Plan was implemented, widening miles of city and village roads and creating motorways and interchanges throughout Greater London. See notes to Eps. 27 and 35 for more on this contentious issue.

via the miracle of cueing — (PSC; "Police Station [Silly Voices]") This acknowledges that the timely entrance of the detective inspector isn't serendipitous, but carefully planned and staged for the maximum comedic/dramatic effect. Such "cues" are meant to be invisible in most Western theatrical practices, and only become evident when there is a mistake in the transition, or the more modern/postmodern theatrical standards are applied. The Pythons are certainly commenting on the artifice of the production, the acknowledged practices of the television format, and are aligning themselves with the more overtly barefaced and theatrical stage conventions in vogue at the time. This is also another bit of information (an aside) that is only for the reader of the scripts, not the viewer.

"Vivian . . . chemo-hygeine" — ("Upperclass Twit of the Year") Vivian Anthony Stanshall (1943–1995) was the lead singer for the Bonzo Dog Doo-Dah Band, the "house band" for the Jones/Palin/Idle 1967 show *Do Not Adjust Your Set*.

An "O-level" ("ordinary level") is one of the standardized exams administered to students in UK secondary schools, the other being the "A-level" ("advanced level"). Respective scores for these exams are asked of Mr. Bee (Jones) in the "Job Hunter" sketch in Ep. 24.

• W •

"warm and wet" — ("Visitors from Coventry") Idle's characters tend to spout many of these idiomatic aphorisms. Cf. Arthur Name in Ep. 9 ("Name by name but not by nature"); or Ep. 3, where Norman tells the Gent that "a nod's as good as a wink to a blind bat" in the "Nudge, Nudge" sketch. The oily compères in *Flying Circus* tend to use similar phraseology—"lager and limes," etc. In *HG*, Cleese's Lancelot is very concerned with utilizing the proper idiomatic expressions and behaviors for his character, including manly escapes and knightly speeches.

"Was . . . bewegen" — ("Mr. Hilter") Probably supposed to be interpreted as "What's the word for hike?," especially when the answer is taken into account. Python's dubious command/application of the German language renders the question almost meaningless, however. "Hiking" would more likely be translated as "Wanderung." "Rückreise" could be what they meant, meaning "return journey," which would have ironically fit Hitler's yearning for a return to power.

"window cleaner" — ("Mr. Hilter") Himmler actually studied agriculture before joining right-wing organizations prior to allying himself with Hitler and the National Socialists (finding time to be a failed poultry farmer, too); Von Ribbentrop was a sparkling wine salesman in Canada; and Hitler was, of course, a failed painter.

"wouldn't have had much fun in Stalingrad" — ("Mr. Hilter") Actually, it isn't at all clear that the Landlady (Jones) could be capable of making such a subtle historical-political reference, and since she doesn't really seem to appreciate that the leaders of the Third Reich are in her drawing room, the possibility is even more remote. (She also could be referring to contemporary Stalingrad, which may have been equally bleak under the current General Secretary, Leonid Brezhnev. In 1961 the name of the city had been changed to Volgograd, incidentally.) On the other hand, it's the seemingly common character (like the plumber/narrator later in "The Montgolfier Brothers" sketch) who is able to make the salient comment, the clever and illusive connection, and the historical or political allusion in the Python world.

"writing to complain" — (PSC; "Falling from Building") The printed script uses this "falling" ellipses format shown in the letter itself, as well. It's a simple but effective visual complement to what happened with the Voice Over (Chapman) voice as he "falls" off-screen. The structure isn't unlike the recently named "concrete" or "shape" poetry, where the poem's text can be shaped and arranged to assist/comment on the "meaning" of the verbal images.

This is also a moment built into the script for the reader only, of which there would have been very few (the other Pythons, the production team, and a handful of BBC higher-ups, perhaps). Cf. the "Beast of Aaarrrrggh" scene in *HG*, where the last words/moans of Joseph of Arimathea are reportedly inscribed on the cave wall.

• Y •

"Yes that's better" — (animation link into "Ken Shabby") The music used behind a portion of this animation is a version of "Hallelujah" (from Handel's *Messiah*), performed by the London Philharmonic Choir with the LP Orchestra conducted by Susskind (WAC T12/1,093).

yokel — (PSC; "The Minehead By-Election") This yokel is played by Jones and is dressed just like the man in Constable's *The Hay Wain*, as seen in Ep. 25, the "Art Gallery Strike" sketch. Also, see the "real rustic" depicted in Ep. 2, there played by Chapman. The Village Idiots are dressed similarly in Ep. 20.

Episode 13: "A History of Irish Agriculture"

"It's" Man in coffin; "There will now be a short intermission"; *Animation: Titles* (silly Cleese v/o); "There will now be a medium-sized intermission"; *Animation: Feeding the birdman*; Restaurant Sketch (abuse, cannibalism, "Don't play with your food"); "There will now be a whopping-sized intermission"; Cinema Adverts (Luigi Vercotti and La Gondola restaurant); **Albatross**; More Cinema Adverts; A policeman near Rottingdeans: "Come back to my place"; "Me Doctor" (knight and rubber chicken); Vox Pops: "I'd like to see . . ."; "Historical Impersonations" (Petula Clark, Eddie Waring, Brian London, W.G. Grace, the R-101 disaster, Graham Hill, and Marcel Marceau); Schoolyard Interviews; "More fairy stories about the police"; "Probe-Around" on crime; Stonehenge sacrifice; Mr. Attila the Hun; Letters; *Animation: Ambulance on the loose*; Psychiatry—Silly Sketches; Operating theatre: Squatters; *Animation: "What a terrible way to end a series!"*; "It's" Man chased by undertakers closing credits; Intermission: "A History of Irish Agriculture"

• A •

"abuse you" — ("Restaurant [Abuse/Cannibalism]") Reference to the notion that waiters (especially at upscale restaurants) can be rude and condescending, especially toward more obviously petit bourgeois or provincial couples.

This is probably a Sartrean conceit at its core (from *Being and Nothingness*), and builds on the Homicidal Barber who actually wants to be a Lumberjack (Palin) in Ep. 9. In that case, the Barber chooses to act on his total freedom, not allowing social class or breeding (or his mother) to determine his life choices, and he launches into his "Lumberjack Song," accessing and embracing those freedoms. To Sartre, the obsequious or surly waiter (or barber or a porter [Ep. 8]) escapes into "bad faith" when the total freedoms of the world create anxiety, and the waiter then blames and abuses others for his situation, for his inability to act. The Butcher (Idle) in Ep. 18 also abuses his customer, though he is alternately rude and polite, as if still on the cusp of his Sartrean decision—freedom or bad faith. In this "Abuse/Cannibalism"episode, however, the Head Waiter will likely continue in his bad faith ways, as he laments arriving late to a wife-swapping party (and getting a bad second wife), he still wets his bed, still defers to his old Headmaster, etc.

"Albania" — ("*Probe-Around* on Crime") Ex-King Zog (1895–1961) was also referenced in Ep. 4. See notes to Ep. 4.

"albatross" — ("Restaurant [Abuse/Cannibalism]") Reference to Samuel Taylor Coleridge's use of the metaphor in *The Rime of the Ancient Mariner* (1798): "Instead of the cross, the albatross About my neck was hung" (2.14). Likened to a millstone here, and representative of the way the husband has been treating the wife throughout this sketch.

Cleese will actually wear an albatross around his neck as he tries to sell albatross later in this episode, and popularly at various Python live shows, including *Live at the Hollywood Bowl* (1980). The albatross is the largest of sea birds, and will be mentioned later as the only type of refreshment he has for sale, though as soon as he sells one, he offers "gannet on a stick" (a gannet is a type of goose). This set-up can be heard earlier in *ISIRTA*, when the cinema salesman is hawking "great hairy spiders" and the customer keeps asking for more traditional treats (season 1, episode 2).

"All men are the same" — ("Restaurant [Abuse/Cannibalism]") A common epithet heard among the more radical elements of the women's liberation movement of the period. The husband (Cleese), Head Waiter (Palin), and Headmaster (Chapman) in this scene would have been described as blinkered "male chauvinists" (a term in the 1960s appropriated from its more nationalistic heritage), or men who treat women as less than equal. See *EBO*.

"all sorts of lines in here" — ("Restaurant [Abuse/Cannibalism]") Sounds very much like the atmosphere in Rick's café in *Casablanca* (1942), or the group settings in a John Ford Western (*Stagecoach*; *My Darling Clementine*). This also could be a comment on the unpredictable nature of *Flying Circus* itself, where interloping characters or animations can propel the narrative in different directions at any time.

"almost human" — ("Restaurant [Abuse/Cannibalism]") An interesting paraphrase of a sentiment from a Robert Lowell (1917–1977) poem, "To Mother" (1977): "It has taken me the time since you died / to discover you are as human as I am . . . / if I am." Earlier, in 1964, Saul Bellow had expressed a similar sentiment: "I am simply a human being, more or less" (*Herzog*). Taking these readings into account, the husband's assessment of his wife as "almost human" is almost an affirmative.

"anyway" — ("Restaurant [Abuse/Cannibalism]") This last line spoken as an aside to the camera. The suggestion is here, as well, that there might be something more devious going on out of sight, like the Barber (Palin) who happens to be homicidal in Ep. 9, or the funeral parlor workers who eat corpses in Ep. 26.

"arrive late" — ("Restaurant [Abuse/Cannibalism]") These last few lines, delivered in fairly detached manners, signal an end to any cohesion the scene may have had. This line as spoken by the Head Waiter (Palin) is also by definition a one-liner, as is the previous retort from the wife, both of which are somewhat uncharacteristic of the Pythons' writing style, and run counter to their "tyranny of the punchline" credo. (This slavishness to the demands of a punchline, though trifled and tampered with significantly, was still a key ingredient for the Goons, *Benny Hill*, *Beyond the Fringe*, and *ISIRTA*, all leading up to *Flying Circus*.) This entire scene, however, is more cynical and glib than most of their work in *FC*.

Similarly, in *Private Eye*, columnist "Jolly Sooper" wrote of meeting her "second husband at a wife-swapping party given by his third wife" (Ingrams, 238).

"Attila the Hun" — ("Mr. Attila the Hun") King of the Huns, he died in 453. Ep. 20 will begin with a spoof of American situation comedies called *The Attila the Hun Show*, and, in *HG*, it is St. Attila who has left instructions as to the operation of the "Holy Hand Grenade of Antioch." Footage from a movie titled *Attila the Hun* (provenance unknown) will also be used in Eps. 20 and 36.

• B •

back on — ("Mr. Attila the Hun") Another "man-behind-the-curtain" moment, when a bit of costuming (here a mustache) is noted as such, and the artificiality of the construct is acknowledged. Jones also seems to be attempting to keep the mustache in place—it's popping off as he speaks—and he eventually pulls it off and pops it into his hat.

Ballantyne, David — ("Restaurant [Abuse/Cannibalism]") This actor plays both the Prologue and the waiter who announces the dead bishop. The dead bishop scenario will appear in Ep. 29, the "Salvation Fuzz" sketch. Ballantyne, incidentally, was paid £42 for his work in this episode (WAC T12/1,094). Ballantyne will also appear in the 1971 Montreux special episode.

David Ballantyne was something of a minor singing sensation on the UK pop music charts, releasing "I Can't Express It" and "Love around the World" in 1966. He may have been brought into the Python mix by Idle, a musician himself and very connected to the London music scene during this period.

"Beryl" — ("*Probe-Around* on Crime") Beryl Reid (1919–1996) starred in the 1968 television series *Beryl Reid Says Good Evening*. She also appeared in the *Before the Fringe* series, which, as its name implies, predated the *Beyond the Fringe* iteration. Both Ronnie Barker and Cicely Courtneidge appeared in the *Before . . .* series. Barker worked with the Pythons on *The Frost Report*, and Courtneidge is mentioned prominently in Ep. 6 by the Red Indian (Idle).

"botherkins" — ("*Probe-Around* on Crime") Pronounced "bodkins," and is an oath derived from "God's dear body." As spelled in this episode, the word doesn't appear in the *OED*.

breath test — ("Mr. Attila the Hun") A test administered by law enforcement officials to determine a suspect's blood alcohol level. The test, using a "breathalyser," made its debut in the UK in 1960, and the test's effectiveness and usefulness became subjects of much op-ed and Parliamentary discussion the entire decade.

This image of a breathalyzer that can "out" certain people is earlier seen in a political cartoon panel from 1968. The *Daily Express* published a cartoon by Michael Cummings depicting PM Harold Wilson kicking out a female figure labeled "The Conscience of the Left." She is carrying a breathalyzer labeled: "Moralyzer test—Racialist breath turns crystals white" (British Cartoon Archive). The Wilson government's favorable policies toward continuing military sales to the apartheid government of South Africa was treated regularly in the daily news across Britain during this period. For more on the South Africa situation, see notes to Ep. 15.

"bunches of five" — ("Psychiatry—Silly Sketch") Cf. Dylan Thomas for an earlier appearance of this imagery, in the poem "The Hand That Signed the Paper" (1936):

> The hand that signed the paper felled a city;
> Five sovereign fingers taxed the breath,
> Doubled the globe of dead and halved a country;
> These five kings did a king to death.

burglar's outfit — (PSC; "Quiz Programme—*Wishes*") The cartoonish, visually iconic representation of a burglar in *FC*, and could have been lifted right out of an early Mack Sennett film, a music hall or vaudeville stage, from *Benny Hill*, etc. (Python Frenchmen, interestingly, are given very similar dress.)

• C •

"Cardinal . . . Clark" — ("Historical Impersonations") This revisits a moment from Ep. 3, where Palin played Richelieu in a courtroom setting, using what appears to be the same handheld microphone. This very short scene may even have been shot for the earlier episode, then held for an opportune moment later in the series (many links would have been shot, catalogued, and archived for upcoming episodes).

Petula Clark (b. 1932) was a very popular singer/actress whose career spanned five decades. "Don't Sleep in the Subway" was written by Tony Hatch, and reached well into the top twenty most popular songs in both the United States and UK in 1967. Clark is also mentioned later in Ep. 37. This particular recording is from the album *These Are My Songs*, and is arranged and conducted by Ernie Freeman (WAC T12/1,094).

"care about me" — ("Restaurant [Abuse/Cannibalism]") Cf. the Catholic mother in *ML*, who gives birth while doing housework (the baby drops to the floor), adding to her scores of children. This is also the period of the so-called zero-population move (a term coined by Kingsley Davis), when groups were calling for a worldwide zero growth policy to save the planet's resources for future generations.

"Chelsea . . . Scrubs" — ("Advertisements") Carefully chosen prison-related restaurant sites, mingling Vercotti's underworld activities and the dining experience. Chelsea is actually a flower show to which Leyhill Prison has contributed for many years, though this may also be a slighting reference to the posh neighborhoods of the Upperclass Twits (see Ep. 12); Parkhurst is on the Isle of Wight, site of Parkhurst Prison; Dartmoor Prison is in Devon, and is located in Princetown near Plymouth; and "the Scrubs" is actually Wormwood Scrubs Prison in west London.

"choc-ices" — ("Albatross") *OED*: "A brickette of ice-cream covered with chocolate." Lyons Maid and Wall's ice creams and treats would have been available in British cinemas of this period.

"Cockfosters" — (link out of "Albatross") Cockfosters is a part of Greater London, and is northwest of London proper.

"come back to my place" — ("Come Back to My Place") Homosexual activity between even consenting adults had been a criminal offense in the UK since passage of the "Offences against the Person Act" in 1861. The Wolfenden Report (released 1957) recommended decriminalizing such acts between those over 21, leading to the passage in 1967 of the "Sexual Offences Act." The Wolfenden Committee had convened after a number of high-profile men were arrested and convicted of criminal activity in the early 1950s as a result of their active homosexuality.

The Goons refer to the report in the episode "Spon" (30 Sept. 1957), noting that Bloodnok has secured "the film rights of the Wolfenden Report," and they're certain that "Walt Disney will never forgive him" for the intrusion.

"court order" — ("Operating Theatre [Squatters]") Referencing the invocation of the Forcible Entry Act of 1381, which demanded a court order prior to any eviction in Britain. Without proof of a *forcible* entry, police were unable to prove a crime, and proper names of those being indicted had to be secured, as well, which was no easy task. Further, the law provided that once peaceable entry was undertaken, a squatter could place his own lock on the dwelling door(s), thus making it illegal for even the building's owner to enter and evict. Squatters were able to have owners then prosecuted for forcible entry violations into their own buildings. (See Andrew Friend, squat.freeserve.co.uk/story, chapter 14.) The continuing lack of affordable housing for many in Britain, especially in the urban areas (and made all the worse in the postwar years), certainly fueled both the emboldened squatters and the law's reluctance or even inability to deal harshly with displaced persons in an era of elevated social liberality. The charity Shelter estimated that as many as three million British citizens were in desperate need of better housing in 1969 (see "1969: Shelter Exposes Slum Homelessness" at news.bbc.co.uk).

During 1970–1972 the laws would begin to swing back toward actual owners, easing the process for eviction, news of which would have made the papers and other media, and on into the Pythons' written grist-to-the-mill. See the entry for "squatter" below for more.

According to contemporary reports, the Lord Chancellor's office began looking into revising the laws in relation to squatting and owners' rights as early as March 1970, just about four months after this episode was broadcast ("Squatters Law Under Review," *Times*, 12 Mar. 1970: 4).

• D •

"Dank Cinemas" — ("Cinema Adverts") The "Dank Cinemas" is a reference to Rank Organization cinemas, which owned most of the screen spaces in the UK during this period.

"diamante" — (PSC; "Quiz Programme—*Wishes*") *OED*: "Material to which a sparkling effect is given by the use of paste brilliants, powdered glass or crystal, etc." The Minister for Home Affairs (Chapman) will wear a diamante necklace in the following episode, where housing (see "Operating Theatre [Squatters]" sketch for more) will also be the subject.

Dick Barton — ("Quiz Programme—*Wishes*") Titular character in a BBC radio serial and several films, including *Dick Barton Strikes Back* (1949) and *Dick Barton at Bay* (1950), the music written by Rupert Grayson and Frank Spencer. Barton was a post-WWII radio hero fighting foreign criminals and femmes fatale.

This music ("Devil's Gallop" by Queens Hall Light Orchestra, directed by Charles Williams) is also used in other "chase" moments, including the hurried climax of the "Spanish Inquisition" sketch in Ep. 15. The Goons also employ this same recognizable, even iconic tune in the wrap-up to their episodes "The Plasticine Man" (23 Dec. 1957) and "The Whistling Spy Enigma" (28 Sept. 1954). *ISIRTA* also references "Dick Barton," the signature theme music, and the thriller show in general several times.

"Do Not Open 'Til Christmas" — (PSC; "Quiz Programme—*Wishes*") A typical cartoon moment—a large wooden box and the affixed signage—one that continues the cartoonish feel of the short film. This same gag was used in myriad Warner Bros. cartoons, for example, including an ur-Bugs Bunny short, *Prest-O Change-O* (1939).

Dr. Kildare *theme* — ("Psychiatry—Silly Sketch") Dr. Kildare is the titular character in an American TV series (NBC and MGM-TV) which was broadcast 1961–1966, as well as a number of feature films from the 1930s and 1940s. Lionel Barrymore and Lew Ayres appeared in many of the feature films, while Richard Chamberlain starred in the TV series, which appeared on BBC1 in the early to mid-1960s. Dr. Kildare is mentioned a number of times in American cartoons, including Tex Avery's *Blitz Wolf* (1942), where the Nazi wolf calls for him as he's about to die, and just after he's shrieked "Mein kampf!"

The theme here is played by Johnnie Spence and His Orchestra (WAC T12/1,094).

Dr. Larch — (PSC; "Psychiatry—Silly Sketch") The larch (a pine tree) is featured prominently in Ep. 3. There was a character Dr. Lench (played by James Edwards) on *Dr. Kildare* in 1965.

"ducks and drakes" — ("Psychiatry—Silly Sketch") A continuation, in a sense, of the thesaurus nature of the sketch already introduced by the Cleese psychiatrist. This phrase is possibly adapted from the Mother Goose rhyme:

> A duck and a drake,
> And a halfpenny cake,
> With a penny to pay the old baker.
> A hop and a scotch
> Is another notch,
> Slitherum, slatherum, take her.

"Ducks and drakes" is also an idiom that fittingly means "messing or playing about with," etc., as well as a stone skipping game. See the *OED*.

• E •

Episode 13 — Not titled in the script version, this episode was recorded on 4 January 1970, and was broadcast one week later on 11 January 1970. This was the final episode of the first season, and the Pythons wouldn't resume recording (the second season) until July 1970.

An "Audience Research Bulletin" taken on Sunday, 11 January 1970, 11:15–11:45 p.m., BBC1, estimated that 4.8 percent of the UK were watching *Monty Python's Flying Circus*, and the 104 respondents rated the show as follows: A+ (21%); A (37%); B (26%); C (7%); and C– (9%). The respondent comments ranged from "load of rubbish" to "inspired lunacy" (WAC T12/1,094).

Also appearing in this episode, according to the repeat fee schedule: Flanagan, Pat Prior, Beulah Hughes (all three playing Judges), Neil Fraser, Matthew Gray, Sheila Sands, and Rosemary Lord.

"Euphemism" — ("Me Doctor") The Doctor (Idle) isn't speaking euphemistically or metaphorically, but simply rattling off words and names that start with a "you" sound.

• F •

"Flight . . . (Mrs.)" — (letter link into "Psychiatry—Silly Sketch") Many letters to the program are from military personnel, retired and active, and many are WWII veterans. In this instance, "Lieutenant" is pronounced the British way "lef-tenant," and his name is borrowed from Mary Shelley's fictional doctor, Frankenstein, who created a monster/man from salvaged body parts. It also seems that many times it is actually the spouse of the writer who pens these letters "(Mrs.)," though the voiceover is usually performed by one of the male cast.

"Florence . . . London" — ("Historical Impersonations") Florence Nightingale (1820–1910) was considered to be the founder of modern nursing, and she did gain international fame serving during the Crimean War.

Brian London (b. 1934) was an English boxer (fl. 1955–1970; record: 37–20–1) who in the recent past (1959 and 1966) had been knocked out by Floyd Patterson and Cassius Clay, respectively. In this section, long-dead historical figures are reaching forward in time to impersonate still-living personalities like Hill, Waring, and London.

folk songs — ("Psychiatry—Silly Sketch") Often acoustic, guitar-based music that was very popular during the "hippie" generation times, and which wouldn't have included Bacharach-penned tunes (those being pop music). Acts like Peter, Paul and Mary; Bob Dylan; Woody Guthrie; the Kingston Trio (and Julie Felix, in the UK) were particularly well known. Many of the songs were socially progressive and reactionary, railing against war, hunger, capitalism, corporate greed, etc., and would have been the antithesis of what most of the WWII generation felt music and patriotism should be.

In an advertisement for a new poetry anthology in *Private Eye*, "Doves for the 70s," Julie Felix (a David Frost favorite) is highlighted as a special musical guest at the anthology's publication party on 30 December 1969 (19 Dec. 1969: 8).

"formica" — (Restaurant [Abuse/Cannibalism]") "Formica" is the proprietary name for a man-made counter-top material. But it is also a play on the "heart of gold" saying. This is a good example of one of Python's negative portrayals of a female, especially in relation to her husband, who is portrayed as quite affable. The wife is also allowed to ramble without much interference or even notice by others, until the husband apologizes and, later, bemoans his marital fate.

These unlikeable and slightly acrid "Husband/Wife in the Restaurant" characters are clearly reminiscent of the "John and Mary" skits from *ISIRTA*. These short skits starred Cleese as John, and Jo Kendall as Mary. An exchange from one particular skit in the third *ISIRTA* series ("Tim Brown's Schooldays") is quite familiar:

> Mary: Oh, John—why don't you admit it? You don't love me any more.
> John: All right, I admit it.
> Mary: John, once we had something that was pure, and wonderful, and—and good . . . what's happened to it?
> John: You spent it all. (audio transcription, *ISIRTA* 3.12)

In other skits featuring these same characters, Mary gets the best of John, so the spousal abuse turns both ways. These characters first appeared in Cambridge Circus performances.

Four undertakers — (link into "Intermissions") The music clip used under this funereal moment is, specifically, the London Brass Players performing Music for "Vive L'Oompa" Funeral March, by Chopin (WAC T12/1,094). The scene looks like a carryover from Ep. 11, where funeral sketches abounded. No music cue is mentioned in the printed script, but the snippet was obviously requested anyway.

The Undertakers carrying the coffin moment was shot in Hurlingham Park, northwest corner, near where "Upperclass Twits" were also recorded. The playground interviews (with children and City Gents) seen in Ep. 13 are also shot here, at the play equipment (tennis courts seen in the background). Homes along Hurlingham Road can be seen in the distance.

• G •

"giveaway" — ("Restaurant [Abuse/Cannibalism]") The "slip of the tongue" (or faulty action, to Freud) appears quite often in *FC*. David Unction (Chapman) wants to be thought of as an "Old Queen" (Ep. 10), the Art Critic (Palin) mentions naughty bits when discussing art (Ep. 8), and the Interviewer (Jones) can't help but notice (and comment on) his subject's enormous teeth (Ep. 24). The word chosen here, "giveaway," is characteristic of Palin's work, and used by the Art Critic in Ep. 8, and Dennis the Peasant in *HG*, as well as several Cleese characters in *ISIRTA*.

Golden . . . Torremolinos — ("Advertisements") The Golden Palm is a merit award of the Cannes Film Festival, which has been held in France since 1946. Films including *If* (1968, Lindsay Anderson), *Blowup* (1966, Michelangelo Antonioni), *Signore & Signori* (1965, Pietro Germi), *Un homme et une femme* (1966, Claude Lelouch), *Knack . . . and How to Get It* (1965, Richard Lester), *Umbrellas of Cherbourg* (1964, Jacques Demy), and *The Leopard* (1963, Luchino Visconti) had won the award in the recent past. Of these, the Pythons make references in *FC* to *If*, David Hemmings (the star of *Blowup*), director Antonioni, and both Visconti and *The Leopard*. Torremolinos is a resort city in southern Spain.

Grace — (animation in "Historical Impersonations") W.G. Grace (1848–1915) was considered one of the finest cricketers to ever play the game. He is credited with popularizing cricket around the world (at least within the Commonwealth countries). His bearded image will also be used in *Holy Grail*, where he, probably appropriately, plays God.

"Great, A.T." — ("Mr. Attila the Hun") Alexander was referenced earlier in this same show, attacking and bisecting a sales assistant at Freeman, Hardy and Willis.

• H •

Harley Street — ("Psychiatry—Silly Sketch") The Harley Street surgeons carried this vaunted reputation for many years according to A.N. Wilson:

> The British Medical Association was holding its annual meeting in its headquarters in Tavistock Square. This was a building where clerical staff, as late as the 1930s, were *instructed that they must vacate the lift, rather than share it with the frock-coated, top-hatted consultants who had arrived from Harley Street* to conduct business. Deference towards doctors in the great hospitals rivalled the reverence shown towards the higher clergy in Rome. (italics added; *After the Victorians*, 510)

The Surgeon (Chapman) plays a gramophone record for effect as he soliloquizes, with the music being "The *Dr. Kildare* Theme" as played by Johnnie Spence and His Orchestra (WAC T12/1,094).

Historical Impersonations — (PSC; "Historical Impersonations") This sketch is a direct relation to the "Famous Deaths" sketch from Ep. 1, where Mozart (Cleese) hosts a show featuring the deaths of historical figures. Most of the season would have been written within a several-week period, making the appearance of similarly themed sketches understandable, and even expected. The practice was not to get rid of such similarities (or variations on a theme), but pepper the sketches throughout the run of the season, so they don't jumble one atop another in a single episode.

hits him over the head — ("Me Doctor") The novelty of this type of ending/transition is wearing thin by Ep. 13, perhaps at least partly due to the live audience's lack of response to the Knight and chicken. In this case, there is almost complete silence after the gag. Other recurring characters, like the Gumbys or Praline or Cardinal Ximinez get appreciative, recognizing laughs when they appear. Not so with the Knight. The woman (Idle) complaining about a lack of "proper punchlines" earlier in the episode seems somewhat less annoying and more prescient, perhaps, by this time.

"how's it work?" — ("Mr. Attila the Hun") Cf. the Holy Hand Grenade section of *HG*, where King Arthur (Chapman) is able to understand the significance of the weapon that is the Holy Hand Grenade, but when it's in his hand he has no idea how to work it, nor does Lancelot (Cleese). They consult the scriptures and figure it out. Arthur then throws the hand grenade, destroying the killer rabbit. This later feature film scene benefited significantly from the comedic structure in the above "breathalyser" section.

"Hun, Norman" — ("Mr. Attila the Hun") A combination of conquerors—the Huns and the Normans—that could produce an ideal warrior, though this nebbish-like, Pewtey-ish man (also played by Palin) belies that potentiality.

• I •

"I'll never fall in love again" — ("Psychiatry—Silly Sketch") A 1969 number one hit written by Burt Bacharach (b. 1929) and lyricist Hal David (b. 1921) for the Broadway musical *Promises, Promises*. Not really a folk song, of course, but certainly more at home on the easy listening (and pop) AM dial of the period.

"Imagine . . . construe" — ("Restaurant [Abuse/Cannibalism]") A jabberwock take on the Prologue from Shakespeare's *Henry V*, where the Chorus asks his audience to imagine "vasty" fields, prancing horses, and men at arms:

> But pardon, gentles all,
> The flat unraised spirits that hath dar'd

> On this unworthy scaffold to bring forth
> So great an object. Can this cockpit hold
> The vasty fields of France? Or may we cram
> Within this wooden O the very casques
> That did affright the air at Agincourt? (1.1.8–14)

Idle's character (Prisoner) in Ep. 3 has already launched into a Laurence Olivier–like speech on freedom, mentioning the "owl of Thebes" then, as well.

"I'm sorry" — (PSC; link into "Psychiatry—Silly Sketch") The full line in the printed script reads: *Cut to letter (as used for* Xmas night with the stars *after pet shop. I'm sorry . . . as not used in* Xmas night with the stars"). This seems more like a marginal comment than a part of the finished script—a very first person moment as the script/sketch writer takes the time to not only write something in error, but then keeps that error and adds a rejoinder. These are comments available to the reader only, meaning a very limited audience prior to the 1989 publication of the scripts.

There is no letter inserted after either pet shop setting, in Ep. 8 or 10, as seen on *A Christmas Night with the Stars* or any other show, of course. Scenes, links, and inserts were often changed and rearranged, put in or elided as the shows came into shape during the writing and then taping processes.

"into consideration" — ("Mr. Attila the Hun") This to perhaps gain some leniency in sentencing. Cf. Ep. 29, where the father (Idle) asks the Church Police (Palin and Gilliam) to take the three dead bishops by the bin "into consideration," as well.

"Irish agriculture" — (link out of "Operating Theatre [Squatters]") The *Radio Times* (official publication of the BBC) had originally described *FC* as a "show to subdue the violence in us all."

"ironing" — ("Mr. Attila the Hun") In this episode alone, policemen have been characterized as homosexual, transvestites, and effeminate (often assuming female roles). The publication (it became an instant bestseller) of the so-called Wolfenden Report, *Report of the Departmental Committee on Homosexual Offences and Prostitution* (3 Sept. 1957), certainly put homosexuality and its illegality and social stigma into the public eye. The image later of the policeman (Cleese) agreeing to a homosexual encounter with a citizen (Palin) may be a very boldfaced acknowledgment of the changing public perception of homosexual relationships between consenting adults in the UK. See more at the "come back to my place" entry above.

"It's" Man chased by undertakers — (PSC; "'It's' Man chased by undertakers closing credits") This chase scene is also set in Hurlingham Park, where the episode began. The "It's" Man is running toward Hurlingham Road.

"Ivan . . . Willis" — ("Historical Impersonations") Ivan IV (1530–1584) was the first Russian monarch to assume the "czar" title. "USSR" stood for the Union of Soviet Socialist Republics, the name given Russia (and its satellite countries) in 1922.

"Freeman, Hardy and Willis" sounds like a fictional law firm, but there are likely two sources here. The first and most obvious ("sales assistant") is to the shoe retailer Freeman Hardy & Willis, which during this period had stores on Edgware Road and Putney High Street in Greater London. The second may be a more subtle, indirect connection to *Kes*, the 1969 Ken Loach film referenced earlier (in Ep. 2). The three kestrels used in the film were named Freedom, Hardy, and Willis, according to critic Graham Fuller.

Another shoe retailer, Saxone, will be mentioned in Ep. 31, along with Dr. Scholl's sandals, while a reference to Deirdre's feet (Ep. 2) and a caption for "British Footwear" in Ep. 7 began this fetishistic narrative thread.

• J •

"Janet" — ("Restaurant [Abuse/Cannibalism]") Hopkins is speaking to a male waiter. The male presenter played by Idle in Ep. 1 is called "Vicky," and Jones plays "Barbara" in "Full Frontal Nudity" in Ep. 8. Neither are characterized as drag performances.

"jelly babies" — ("Operating Theatre [Squatters]") Nickname for marijuana or hashish cigarettes. Also, though, these are the type of candies that schoolboy Bluebottle (Peter Sellers) often asks for in return for his services in *The Goon Show* from BBC Radio (1951–1960).

"John . . . Hill" — ("Historical Impersonations") John the Baptist was, of course, the biblical prophet who "prepared the way" for the coming of Christ. Charlton Heston had recently portrayed John the Baptist in *The Greatest Story Ever Told* (1965); John had been played by Mario Socrate in Pier Pasolini's 1964 *The Gospel according to St. Matthew*; and even earlier by Robert Ryan in *King of Kings* (1961), meaning the image of the Baptist's severed head on a platter would have been a familiar one to the Pythons and their audience by 1970.

Graham Hill (1929–1975) was the British winner of multiple Grand Prix events, as well as the Indianapolis 500.

"Join the scene and other phrases" — ("Operating Theatre [Squatters]") This hippie lingo can be found in period interviews of flower children kipping, for example, in Green Park, next to Buckingham Palace, in August 1969, where "squares" are hiding in their comfortable homes and the "fuzz" are always looking to cause trouble (*Times*, 14 Aug. 1969: 2)

"Julius . . . Waring" — ("Historical Impersonations") Both Caesar and Waring have appeared in *FC* before. Caesar (Chapman) appeared as a closet mouse in the "Mouse Problem" sketch (Ep. 2), as well as a quick Vox Pops moment in Ep. 10. A Waring-like figure (Idle) played the scorekeeper during the "Famous Deaths" sketch in Ep. 1. Eddie Waring was a well-known, oft-imitated television sports broadcaster in Britain. See notes to Ep. 1.

• L •

"Lazarus" — ("Psychiatry—Silly Sketch") Cf. the Biblical account of Lazarus who was raised from the dead by Christ.

"light show, baby" — ("Operating Theatre [Squatters]") The Squatter sounds very much American, like a Haight-Ashbury district (of San Francisco) hippie or flower child. (A cartoon panel from 17 September 1969 features squatters borrowing a cup of sugar from Buckingham Palace, while a newspaper headline nearby reads "Hippie Squatters Move in Near Palace" [Mac *Daily Sketch*].) The lights would be "showy" if the Squatter is experiencing an "acid trip," or the effects of ingesting the psychedelic hallucinogen LSD. See the many cartoons poking fun at squatters and the squatters' movement at the British Cartoon Archive.

As he continues, the Squatter (and friends) spout many of the well-known terms/maxims of the period, including "groovy," "bread," "great scene," "baby," "fuzz," "man," and "fascist." All of these connote a certain membership status, as well as articulating just who the "others" are as opposed to the counterculture movement. If you're in the groove and part of the scene (recreational drug use, no acknowledgment of property rights, "tuning out" of the status quo culture), then the terms of endearment apply; otherwise, you're a fascist and uptight. It's no accident that the newest edition of *The Little Oxford Dictionary* (fourth edition, published October 1969) accepted into its pages new and "trendy," even "with-it" words, including:

> the fuzz, pill (the pill), permissive (as in society), a fix, dropout and hippy—"a person (appearing to be) given to the use of hallucinogenic drugs." (*The Times Diary*, 10 Oct. 1969: 10)

Timothy Leary's "Tune in, turn on, drop out" mantra certainly applies here. (Remember, a subtitle for the first episode was included in the show's paperwork, but not in the show itself: "A new comedy series for the Switched On." Perhaps this was the Pythons' aborted attempt to connect with their younger, more "hip" viewers?) In November 1970, the *Listener* noted that "thought of a traditional kind . . . is the recognised enemy of the counter-culture," so it is the status quo being rebelled against here (622–23). Interesting that in this era of blossoming freedoms, including a woman's right to control her own body, the Pythons are suggesting that even one's body (albeit a white male's body) isn't something over which personal control can be exercised in the welfare state environment of 1960s Great Britain.

• M •

man in an ice-cream girl's uniform — (PSC; "Albatross") The uniform Cleese wears is likely a version of the Lyons Maid "Fruit Parfait Girl" outfit worn by salesgirls in cinemas of the period. The uniform can be seen in contemporary cinema adverts for Lyons Maid products.

"Marceau, Marcel" — ("Historical Impersonations") Marceau (1923–2007) was an internationally famous French mime performer. Marceau's name will reappear in Ep. 27, where he lives in the same apartment as Jean Genet and Jean-Paul Sartre.

"medium-sized intermission" — ("Intermissions") The music here is again Steiner's theme from *A Summer Place*, as played by the Percy Faith Strings (WAC T12/1,094). See the entry "seven seconds" below for more. The music is used again for the "whopping great intermission" later. In the days of double features and longer, epic films, such intermissions were more common.

model of a burglar — ("*Probe-Around* on Crime") This model prop was requested much earlier, and is seen in Ep. 1, during the "Funniest Joke in the World" sketch, but not used or acknowledged there (WAC T12/1,082).

"muggins" — ("Restaurant [Abuse/Cannibalism]") A fool, a simpleton.

• N •

Napoleon — ("Psychiatry—Silly Sketch") Jones earlier dressed as Napoleon in Ep. 2 (as a closet mouse) and earlier in this episode (as the R101 disaster). See notes below for more on that infamous crash.

"no money" — (Restaurant [Abuse/Cannibalism]") A reference to the fading practice of the bride bringing a dowry into the new marriage, and which was often provided by the bride's father.

"Notlob" — ("Psychiatry—Silly Sketch") Like the "Rottingdeans" reference earlier in this same episode, mentioning "Notlob" is a Python intertextuality, a moment of self-reference that loyal viewers tend to pick up on and enjoy. It is, again, Bolton spelled backward, and mentioned in Ep. 9 by the Shopkeeper (Palin) and Praline (Cleese).

"Nova" — ("Operating Theatre [Squatters]") A popular and trendy women's art, fashion, and photography magazine for/from London and the UK, published 1965–1975. From a contemporary listserv wherein an oral history of the magazine and its cultural significance is currently under way:

> *Nova* employed cutting edge writers, designers and editors who mixed an enthusiasm for sex, fun and fashion with editorial issues such as gender equality, contraception, and racism in a way that challenged the idea of what a woman's magazine 'should' be. Alongside the importance of its editorial legacy *Nova* is now seen as a style bible for a new generation of designers, stylists and musicians. (Alice Beard)

One issue of *Nova* from 1967, for example, included articles on Ossie Clark and Quorum (popular fashion designer and his shop), Barry Fantoni (comic artist for *Private Eye*), inflatable houses, and Terence Rattigan (Ep. 30).

"'Nuff said?" — ("Restaurant [Abuse/Cannibalism]") An American colloquialism meaning enough information has been given, and in this case, it takes the place of a "know what I mean?" phrase. Often shortened to "N.S." The phrase appeared in Al Capp's *Li'l Abner* comic strip, which was published regularly in newspapers from 1934.

Later, Sunleys (London) Ltd.—builder of sports grounds, pavilions, and grandstands—employed the phrase in its display print adverts in the 1950s. Ad copy in the *Times*, for example, included a vibrant image of two running cricketers, and the following quotes:

> "What a fine pavilion!"
> "Grand wicket too!"
> "Sunleys, of course!"
> "'Nuff said!" (15 July 1950: 5)

"Nurse me" — ("Me Doctor") Patterned after classic vaudeville-type patter, such as the "Who's On First?" (Abbott and Costello) routine. Also, this is another moment of a character's extreme literality, where a question ("Me, Doctor?") can be perceived as a statement ("Me Doctor.") It's as if the Doctor cannot appreciate either the upswinging pitch of the questions as questions, and/or he isn't understanding the comma (pause) between "me" and "doctor." Again, simple miscommunication leading to complete misunderstanding, a Python trope.

• O •

Ouija board — ("Quiz Programme—*Wishes*") *OED*: "A proprietary name for a board having the letters of the alphabet and other signs used for obtaining messages and answers in spiritualistic séances and in the practice of telepathy."

• P •

"padre" — ("Restaurant [Abuse/Cannibalism]") Probably a chaplain gone missing from the grammar school setting, the man who had formerly controlled the boys. The implication later—that the boys had descended into, perhaps, masturbation or homosexuality—signals the absence of a consistent authority figure. The Headmaster's (Chapman) speech here is cryptic and scattered, at best, so conclusions are difficult. Notice that he doesn't answer the Head Waiter's (Palin) question to begin with, continuing on in his own unilateral monologue.

In Ep. 18, "*Seven Brides for Seven Brothers*" sketch, the Padre (Palin) is late arriving for his role in the school production of *Seven Brides for Seven Brothers*, and his "wrestling with Plato" excuse is taken as a sexual metaphor ("What you do with your private time is written on the vestry wall").

Panorama — ("*Probe-Around* on Crime") Very popular and long-running (1953–present) interview and reporting television show. Cf. Ep. 2, "The Mouse Problem" sketch, for notes on the show. Presenters on *Panorama*—to this point in late 1969—included Max Robertson (1915–2009), Richard Dimbleby (1913–1965), and Robin Day (1923–2000). Both Dimbleby and Day are referred to in *Flying Circus* (see, for example, notes for Eps. 23 and 2, respectively).

The "*Panorama*-type" music behind this transition is Rachmaninov's "Symphony No. 1 in D Minor Op. 13," "Allegro Con Fuoco," as played by the USSR Symphony Orchestra, with Yevgeny Svetlanov conducting (WAC T12/1,094).

"part-time notice board" — (letter link into "Psychiatrist—Silly Sketch") A comment on the uselessness of the WWII veteran generation? The specter of aging men reminding the younger generation of the sacrifices they made during the war, and the unspoken debt owed to the war participants by subsequent generations, is a subject that surfaces often in letters and even sketches throughout *FC*.

In *Hard Day's Night*, the grumpy establishment-type City Gent on the train (played by Richard Vernon) reminds the young Beatles that he had "fought the war" for their type, and Ringo wonders aloud whether he's sorry he won. It's conceivable that the Pythons and their peers could have grown weary of hearing these "Yorkshire gentlemen" dressings-down, and these same veterans and their spouses were obviously in the editorial pages of the period, lamenting the changing, perhaps frightening values in the 1960s and 1970s.

Lastly, the letter writer claims to have spent the war in India, which means he would have been serving in a colonial capacity (helping rule the colonies), a trainer for Indian regiments, or busy with the supply and logistical aspects of the war. In any case, he probably didn't actually fight. These types of letters from retired career military and/or WWII vets can be found throughout the pages of traditional UK newspapers of the era, as well as in *Private Eye*.

"Pearls for Swine" — ("Advertisements") Reference to the biblical mentioning (Matthew 7:6) of giving precious things to those ill-prepared for such. Here used as a means of insulting an audience in a movie theater. Gilliam, at least, was obviously unhappy with the current cinematic offerings in and around London, and especially the "dank" theaters themselves; he was also likely rhyming as a reference to the well-known *Rank* Cinema Organization, a major controller of cinema screen spaces in the UK during this period.

Also, the "Pearls for Swine" cinema advert (which gets a hearty audience laugh) is an allusion to the ubiquitous Pearl & Dean advertising company, founded in 1953, and prominent in period British cinemas. Gilliam does not use the company's very recognizable theme music "Asteroid" by Pete Moore. It was likely expensive to borrow and actionable if used without permission.

"pill" — ("Restaurant [Abuse/Cannibalism]") Birth control pill. Introduced in 1960 by G.D. Searle, the pill (called Enovid)—as a birth control tool—would have been disallowed for Catholics, among others, meaning the couple here are probably Anglican, if they're churchgoers at all.

The Lambeth Conference of the Church of England (1930) had agreed that contraception was allowed when abstinence was "impractical," while that same year the Pope (Pius XI) reaffirmed the Catholic Church's position against such measures. Just months before the Pythons gathered to create *Flying Circus*, Pope Paul VI had underscored (in 1968) via his encyclical letter *Humanae Vitae* ("Human Life") the Catholic position against all forms of contraception, with the exception of "total abstinence, and the unreliable rhythm method" (see "rhythm method" entry below).

This somber and sweeping papal decree set off a firestorm of not only public and private debate, but had a concussive effect on the flock. In the words of the BBC's *Eyewitness: 1960–69* (written by Joanna Bourke and narrated by Tim Pigott-Smith), "the Catholic Church imploded," and many, many British Catholics simply continued using the pill and attended confession on a weekly basis (*Eyewitness: 1960–69*, "*Humana Vitae*" parts 1 and 2).

The Wife (Idle) in this sketch doesn't take the pill simply because it's "nasty," and not—presumably—because it's forbidden by church edict. Cf. the lecture given by the Protestant husband (Chapman) in *ML* as to the significance of contraception and its relationship to personal and religious freedoms.

Lastly, the most recent edition of *The Little Oxford Dictionary* (fourth edition, October 1969) included the word "pill" as a common, specific reference to birth control for the first time.

"pinny" — ("*Probe-Around* on Crime") A colloquialization of pinafore.

"pith . . . marrow" — ("Psychiatry—Silly Sketch") Cf. Ep. 3, the defendant's Olivier-like soliloquy.

pixilated motion — (PSC; "Quiz Programme—*Wishes*") Adjusting the speed of the film as it travels through the camera. In this case they are probably exposing a single frame or two, then the grouped actors move forward, then another exposure, and on. The amount of light available for each shot varies (thanks to moving clouds, rotation of the earth, etc.), betraying the pixilation technique, as well. Cf. Ep. 5, where the same technology is used to create the performance for the confused cat, as well as Ep. 7, where Englishmen are turning into Scotsmen. Fellow Brit and television funny man Benny Hill employed this technique often on his *The Benny Hill Show* (1955–1968), and it was pioneered creatively by Canadian filmmaker Norman McLaren in *Neighbours* (1952).

"Portnoy . . . Piccadilly" — (link out of "Albatross") Piccadilly is a historic section of London known for many years as the location for those seeking "casual sex" (Ackroyd, *London: The Biography*). (Not unlike Times Square in New York City, the Piccadilly area has more recently become a tourist mecca for shopping, dining, and entertainment.) The fact that a dank cinema featuring suggestively posed models is connected to the area is fitting. The nearby Charing Cross Road (on the edge of Soho) used to be the home to many sex shops (adult bookstores, novelties, etc.), which Jonathan Miller mentions in his "Porn Shop" monologue for *Beyond the Fringe*.

Movie theaters have been part of the Piccadilly scene for many years. The Plaza Cinema opened in 1926, seating about 1,900, but by 1967 was being remade into two adjoining cinema spaces, known as the Paramount and the Plaza. (Redesigned, interestingly, by a Mr. Frank *Verity* . . .) Gilliam will use a circa-1961 still image depicting a third cinema, the London Pavilion, also in Piccadilly (elaborate cinema façade and marquis clearly visible), in the "Atomic-Mutated Cat" animation, Ep. 22. See "story of the killer cars" note in Ep. 22 for more.

"profits" — (link out of "Albatross") Fairly accurate, actually, as theater owners—especially of single or just a few screens—paid (and still pay) very high rates for the rental of feature films, and tend to make their profits on concession sales alone.

projector and film — ("Advertisements") The viewing medium of choice, during this period, for non-theatrical pornographic film exhibition. The term "8mm" refers to the size of the film stock. Even as late as 1983 and *The Meaning of Life*, the birth of the child seen in part one, "The Miracle of Birth," is available "on Super-8."

prologue — (PSC; "Restaurant [Abuse/Cannibalism]") From the Greek, meaning "before speech." Shakespeare's Prologue in *Henry V* speaks often, begging the audience be patient in watching the unreal stage version of action and reality. Chaucer's prologue to his *Canterbury Tales* is also significant. Here in the restaurant, of course, the characters see prologue as a nuisance, adding misinformation—the waiter's hissed "No, it doesn't!"—not illumination to the scene.

David Ballantyne plays the Prologue character, and also plays the "Indian Head" later, in the squatter sketch. See the entry for "Ballantyne, David" above for more on this actor/musician.

"proper punchline" — ("Restaurant [Abuse/Cannibalism]") So Shirley (Idle) supports the staid, formulaic mode of comedy writing that Python came out against from the initial episode, but they still slouched into whenever the opportunity for a zinger presented itself.

• R •

"R101" — ("Historical Impersonations") The R101 was a British-built airship that crashed near Beauvais, France, on 5 October 1930, killing everyone aboard. Cf. Ep. 40 for an entire episode devoted to airships (not balloons). The music behind the stunt is "Le Marseillaise" as played by the Band of the Grenadier Guards (WAC T12/1,094).

"Rainwear through the Ages" — (link out of "Albatross") Perhaps a reference to the "dank" nature of some cinemas referred to in this link, or the seemingly constant need for rainwear in the London area, but may also be a slap at the international cinema of the period. Many recent "New Wave" films dealt with seemingly trivial or pedestrian or overtly oneiric (and therefore more personal) subjects and people, no longer focusing on kings and exciting historical events and larger-than-life Hollywood figures. Resnais's *Last Year at Marienbad* (1961) examines memory and desire in long, slow, undramatic (and for many, unwatchable) takes; Truffaut's *Jules and Jim* (1961) focuses on three normal young folk looking for sex and love; and Godard's 1967 film *Weekend* is as disconnected and narratively nontraditional a film as had been seen outside of the avant garde movements of the 1920s and 1930s.

Rainwear appears often in *FC*, which shouldn't be surprising considering the climate in and around London. Occasionally, rainwear figures into a character or sketch significantly. Cf. Eps. 8 and 23, where Praline (Cleese) wears a rubber mac, or Ep. 33, where the crew of a lifeboat find themselves in Mrs. Neves's (Jones) kitchen.

"rhythm method" — ("Restaurant [Abuse/Cannibalism]") Spoken directly to the camera. The rhythm method is a method of birth control (or to gauge fertile periods) using a woman's menstrual cycle to pinpoint ovulation. It is said to be the preferred method of pregnancy prevention even among those opposed—for religious reasons—to artificial forms of birth control.

This inflammatory subject had sparked quite a bit of controversy on the David Frost show *Not So Much a Programme, More a Way of Life* in November 1964, when a birth control sketch was featured. *NSMP* was a follow-up to Frost's popular *TW3*, which had been taken off the air as General Elections approached in 1964. Ned Sherrin (Ep. 5) again produced the show, but it seems none of the future Pythons contributed any material.

"Rottingdeans" — ("Come Back to My Place") Rottingdean (not "Rottingdeans") is south and east of Brighton, on the seashore. It's also not far down the coast from Hove, mentioned as the location of the "bear attack signalbox" in Ep. 12. It's perhaps fitting that the activity following is happening in a resort area.

This is also an intertextual moment, as there is no "Rottingdeans" in the UK, only in the Python world of Ep. 9, from which Sir George Head (Cleese) embarked to Africa: "The A23s through Purleys down on the main roads near Purbrights avoiding Leatherheads to the A231s entering Rottingdeans from the north. From *Rottingdeans* we go through Africa." The Pythons create the world of action, and then reference that same world, much as Shakespeare "quoted" himself (see Bergeron and/in Larsen's *MPSERD*).

Just before the transition to the policeman being propositioned by the man there is a filmed image of the Queen with accompanying music, "Great Britain: God Save the Queen" by National Anthems of the World, Band of the Grenadier Guards (WAC T12/1,094).

• S •

"salt of the earth" — ("Restaurant [Abuse/Cannibalism]") Phrase also used by Biggles (Chapman) to describe Ginger (Gilliam) in Ep. 33. This is also an indication, again stereotypically, that the wife (Idle) is overly attached to her mother.

"second form" — ("Restaurant [Abuse/Cannibalism]") English school vernacular. *OED*: "One of the numbered classes into which the pupils of a school are divided according to their degree of proficiency. In English Schools the sixth form is usually the highest; when a larger number of classes is required, the numbered 'forms' are divided into 'upper' and 'lower,' etc." Previous mentions of the levels of school include "Upper Science library" (ep. 10) and, later, lamentations over stock deals going on in "big school" (Ep. 28).

second interviewer — ("*Probe-Around* on Crime") Narrators usurping narrators is something of a Python staple, and is probably a comment on the competitive nature of the modern media. Cf. the "Whicker Island" sketch in Ep. 27, the documentary figures attacking each other in Ep. 30, the "Rival Documentaries" segment in Ep. 38, and even the killing of the Learned Historian (John Young) in the feature film *HG*. The power of the narrator is paramount—the controlling, leading voice, the forwarded point-of-view, the support or undercutting of the status quo, etc., all figure into this control—and lethal means are often used to secure such a privileged position of communication and power.

The adversarial and confrontational interviewing (almost interrogating) style of Robin Day, for example, so new to British television, is a significant influence here (see notes for Ep. 1 for more).

"second wife" — ("Restaurant—Abuse/Cannibalism") Cf. Euripides' characterization of a second wife as a hateful viper (*Alcestis*, line 309).

"seen it and seen it" — ("Psychiatry—Silly Sketch") Commenting on the kind of narrative and/or structural predictability in the television medium that the Pythons sought to parody, lampoon, and overthrow in *FC*. Actually, the sketch has already subverted expectations by not only allowing us to see the "out-of-character" exchange between the Receptionist (Cleveland) and Psychiatrist (Cleese), but giving us another out-of-character reaction by the Napoleon figure (Jones)—this kind of subversion had already come to be Python's signature in *FC*. Reacting against tradition—the hallmark of Modernism—works well until the reaction becomes traditional, then constant subversion is required.

Thus entrenched, the Pythons were trapped by their own demands for new approaches and the subsequent normalization/codification of those new moments. Audiences would have by now been tuning in and requesting live tickets to see more of this anarchic brand of humor, fully expecting to see more of the *same*. The subversive moments become the norm, and another predictable structure is created—an interesting paradox confronted by all things new in art. This is part of the reason, Cleese admits, that he left the show after the third season, and earlier why Michael Bentine (1922–1996)—one of the original Goons—left *The Goon Show* after just two increasingly successful seasons. See Wilmut and Grafton. For the remaining Pythons, the fourth season would be new by virtue of the episodes' thematic continuity, building on the success of Ep. 34 and Pither's "Cycling Tour," as well as the absence of Cleese's influence/presence, and the minimal use of outside writers, including Douglas Adams (1952–2001) and David Sherlock. See notes to the fourth season for more on the structural and tonal changes brought on by this increased attention to a single, overarching theme, as well as the new creative personnel.

seven seconds of (slightly) speeded up Mantovani — (PSC; "Intermissions") The music that fills this spot is actually Percy Faith's version of the theme from *A Summer Place* by Max Steiner, and not Mantovani (WAC T12/1,094). The show's theme music follows immediately.

Mantovani—Called Monty by friends, Mantovani (1905–1980) was a first-chair-violinist-cum-light-orchestra-conductor, and a naturalized Englishman. His music is heard in other episodes (Montreux compilation episode; Eps. 3, 16, and 35), but not this one.

In May of 1969 Mantovani had been a special guest at the Music Publishers' Association luncheon (Ivor Novello Awards were handed out), where he opined on the changes in popular culture and music, and gave credit to the Beatles, in a backhanded sort of way, for his own continuing success: "They [the Beatles and other pop groups] all sound more or less the same, have a driving beat and are so loud that anything I play must come out as a bit of fresh air" (*Times Diary*, 23 May 1969: 10). Mantovani and His Concert Orchestra appeared on BBC2 regularly, as well.

Other music heard during the animated and live action "movie theater" filmed sections include: Robert Hartow in "Sunday Night at the Palladium" by the London Palladium Orchestra, conducted by Cyril Orandel; "On the Button—Quick Mover" by The Studio Group, directed by Keith Papworth; "Happy Harp" from Johnny Teupen and His Harp; "Sweet & Singing" by Gene Herrmann and His Orchestra; Musical Boxes 1–8; and from "TV & Radio Commercials," "Mother & Baby," and "Bossa Nova Beat" (WAC T12/1,094).

"sherry" — ("Restaurant [Abuse/Cannibalism]") Originally, a Spanish fortified wine. Cf. the "Sherry-Drinking Vicar" sketch in Ep. 36, as well as the besotted Old Lady (Chapman) in Ep. 40.

"Shirley" — ("Restaurant [Abuse/Cannibalism]") The wife's first name first uttered at this point. Later the husband will be identified, as well—"Douglas." Shirley Douglas (b. 1934) is an actress who appeared in Kubrick's *Lolita* (1962) as the piano teacher. Peter Sellers also appeared in the film, as Clare Quilty, which may have provided Python's link to the "Shirley" and "Douglas" names.

"Sicilian delicacies" — ("Advertisements") The balance of this narration will deal in double entendres, making the link between food and sexuality utilized in many works, from the fourteenth-century Spanish work *Libro de buen amor* through more contemporary filmmakers Von Stroheim, Bunuel, Fellini, Godard, and beyond.

Popular and controversial New Wave film director Jean-Luc Godard would bring food, sex, politics, and death together in 1967 in the film *Week End*, where pre-Pythonesque absurdities include rape, cannibalism, and Marxist political speechifying accompanied by a live drummer. *Week End* was called "a film found on a dump" in one of the film's intertitles, which the Pythons will spoof directly in Ep. 23, "French Subtitled Film," shooting the episode on a rubbish tip. See notes to that episode for more on the significance of this film, filmmaker, and the various New Waves in general to/on the Pythons.

"sixteen stone" — ("Historical Impersonations") About 224 pounds. It's not clear what Cardinal Richelieu actually weighed. Another Python referent, Hilaire Belloc (Ep. 2), wrote a biography of Richelieu published in 1929.

"slit you up a treat" — ("Operating Theatre [Squatters]") A colloquialism meaning to cut him "extremely, excessively." See *OED*, "treat," entry 5b. The Piranha brothers will be "slit up a treat" in Ep. 14 when they attempt to strong-arm the MCC.

"Soho" — ("Advertisements") Soho is a district in the West End of London, known for many years for its population of foreigners, ladies of the night, and restaurants, and "latterly for its night clubs, striptease shows, [and] pornography shops" (*OED*). It's fitting that Mr. Vercotti would set up a restaurant here, then, and that all sorts of questionable activity could be taking place in the back rooms. Another period description of the parish mentions the sordid but colorful world of Soho:

> Untidy, full of Greeks, Ishmaelites, cats, Italians, tomatoes, restaurants, organs, coloured stuffs, queer names, people looking out of upper windows, it dwells remote from the British body politic. (qtd. in Ackroyd, *London*, 526)

One of the female "models" is astride one of the cars in the advertisement, much like a pub sign described by Ackroyd in *London*:

> A once famous inn known as the Mischief, in Charles Street, had as its sign a drunken courtesan straddling a man's back while holding a glass of gin with the legend "She's Drunk as a Sow" inscribed by her. (527)

Ackroyd concludes that it was the very "foreignness" of the area that allowed for such significant (illegal) sexual activity, and the Pythons, by employing Vercotti and his restaurant's "delicacies" and "specialities," acknowledge and even embrace and celebrate that foreign influence many years later.

"Soho Motors 2nd Floor" — (PSC; "Cinema Adverts") The "2nd floor" mention is accurate, since the walk-ups to find prostitutes in Soho during this period were above the shops below. Advertisement cards and suggestive flyers would be at street level, as seen in the "Tobacconists (prostitute advert)" sketch, Ep. 14. Here the girls' name cards include "Monica—French Comfort" and another girl advertising "Indian Styles." Later the secretary (Cleveland) in the "Travel Agent" sketch (Ep. 19) will invite the client to "come upstairs," before quickly changing the subject.

"smile, a conquest, and a dagger up your strap" — ("Historical Impersonations") Perhaps a nod to the old comedic "rule of threes." Julius Caesar was stabbed to death on 15 March (44 BC) in the senate house in Rome. Caesar (Chapman) also appeared in Ep. 2 as a closet mouse, and in Ep. 10 in relation to his Christmas show. The moment Caesar gets a dagger up his strap is re-enacted in Ep. 15, the "*Julius Caesar* on an Aldis Lamp" sketch.

"squatter" — ("Operating Theatre [Squatters]") A "squatter" is someone who occupies lands or property without legal ownership, and this is originally an American term. Portions of the counterculture movement of the 1960s in the United States adopted a sort of aboriginal notion of property rights, claiming the earth belonged to everyone, and that ownership wasn't allowed by/in Nature. This was primarily a sociopolitical argument, as most of the hue and cry happened to be against corporate, big business, and big money entities/persons.

In England, conversely, the London Squatters Campaign of the 1960s was fueled by the critical housing shortage experienced after the end of WWII, and squatting en masse became a familiar practice, especially in London. Each sitting and hopeful government (Labour and Conservative alike) promised more council houses, year after year, but demand far outpaced the government's ability to build affordable (and livable) homes for all qualified citizens. (This problem led to some of the ill-advised tower estates built in the 1960s; one of these collapsed in 1968, and the entire right-headed but shoddy endeavor is satirized by the Pythons in Ep. 17, and *Private Eye* in 1968 and 1969 issues.)

Andrew Friend characterizes the years 1969–1977 as the high water point in London squatting, a time when the "adroit use of the law by squatters [had] frequently delayed evictions and provided time for organisation and negotiation." Later in the sketch, the Surgeon (Chapman) confesses that he can't remove the squatters without a court order. According to Friend, the squatter in England benefited from the fact that under English law squatting was trespassing, which was not a criminal act, meaning police found themselves a bit powerless to enforce property rights if the squatters were in situ. The sketch plays on that notion throughout. By 1970 that balance began to shift, and landlord rights were more often upheld. (See the entry for "court order" above.)

For more on the housing problem and the adequate/inadequate governmental response to the situation in postwar Britain, see the entry for "build . . . houses" in Ep. 14.

sticking pins — ("*Probe-Around* on Crime") A voodoo practice of the West Indies, where the intended victim is pained by the pins inserted into his/her likeness. The doll seen here was ordered very early in the production of the season, perhaps because the scene was intended for earlier broadcast (WAC T12/1,082). See the entry for "model of a burglar" above for more on this curious prop.

strops — (PSC; "Operating Theatre [Squatters]") Meaning to sharpen a blade on a razor strop.

• T •

"television" — ("Restaurant [Abuse/Cannibalism]") Blaming the media for the crumbling of whatever society she pictures, Shirley is glumly, unattractively espousing the Mary Whitehouse line. A conservative, moralistic media watchdog group, Whitehouse's National Viewers' and Listeners' Association (NVLA) tilted long and loud against England's "permissive society," and especially the potential damage done by loosened moral standards on television, in films, and in books and magazines. See notes to Ep. 32, "Tory Housewives," for more.

As the Pythons were writing and prepping this first season, meetings were being held to discuss the possible repeal of the obscenity laws of 1959 and 1964 on publications, as well as the 1968 theater law. (These laws didn't have as much to do with television or even film, those being policed in-house, as it were, by the BBC and Independent Television Authority, and the British Board of Film Classification, respectively.) The Arts Council had convened these conferences, and Mary Whitehouse (and many others, including law enforcement bodies, social groups, parent organizations) were invited to contribute. The participants voted almost unanimously (97–3) to recommend repeal of the laws, and the proceedings were forwarded to the Home Secretary. Conservative MPs Sir Gerald Nabarro and Sir Cyril Osborne (1898–1969) were both on record as being *against* any repeal ("Obscene Stage and Book Laws Should Go, Report Says," *Times*, 16 July 1969: 2). Whitehouse didn't actually attend, saying two weeks later in a letter to the *Times* that "on receipt of the details of the organizations invited to the original conference it became clear to me that any recommendation made by the working party was likely to be "loaded"—meaning she thought the group had already made up its mind ("The Obscenity Laws," 1 Aug. 1969: 7).

Whitehouse and NVLA would in September 1969 seek to have television brought under the purview of the obscenity laws, and organized protests against shows like Frankie Howerd's *Up Pompeii!*, which they labeled "sordid and cheap" (*Times*, 18 Sept. 1969: 3).

test card — (link out of "Operating Theatre [Squatters]") *OED*: In "television, a diagrammatic still picture transmitted outside normal programme hours and designed for use in judging the quality and position of the image on any particular screen." Test cards have disappeared almost completely from today's television, as programming tends to run on around the clock, even on local stations.

theatre audience — ("Quiz Programme—*Wishes*") Stock footage of an applauding opera audience (simply termed "Opera Audience"), with the camera positioned at stage left looking out into the house (WAC T12/1,094).

thesaurus — ("Psychiatry—Silly Sketch") A self-deprecating comment on the type of sketches written, often, by Chapman and Cleese, and eventually parodied by others in the troupe. See Ep. 33, "Cheese Shop," and Ep. 37, "What the Stars Foretell."

"These hands . . . German bands" — ("Psychiatry—Silly Sketch") For the spirit of the entire speech, cf. the structure of the soliloquy given by John of Gaunt to the Duke of York in Shakespeare's *Richard II* (1595):

> This royal throne of kings, this sceptred isle,
> This earth of majesty, this seat of Mars,
> This other Eden, demi-paradise,
> This fortress built by Nature for herself
> Against infection and the hand of war,
> This happy breed of men, this little world,
> This precious stone set in the silver sea,
> Which serves it in the office of a wall,
> Or as [a] moat defensive to a house,
> Against the envy of less happier lands,
> This blessed plot, this earth, this realm, this England.
> (2.1.40–50)

In Ep. 3, the defendant's soliloquy, Python also waxes Shakespearean, and the psychoanalyzing of the character Hamlet will comprise most of Ep. 43.

"Tota . . . Hull Kingston Rovers" — ("Historical Impersonations") Translation: "Gaul (or France) is divided into three parts, Wigan, Hunslett and Hull Kingston Rovers."

The first portion of the quote is actually from Julius Caesar, writing in regard to the justification for the sacking of Gaul: "Gallia est omnis divisa in partes tres" (*Commentarii De Bello Gallico*, I.1).

"Wigan"—The Wigan rugby league (Greater Manchester area) is still active.

"Hunslett"—A misspelling of Hunslet, the Hunslet Rugby Club being formed in 1883, in South Leeds, Yorkshire.

"Hull Kingston Rovers"—Hull Kingston Rovers rugby team began in 1882, and won the Yorkshire Cup in 1966–1967, and 1967–1968. A noted matchup between Wigan and Hull occurred in May 1959, when Wigan beat Hull 30–13. Wigan also defeated Hunslet in May 1965 by a score of 20–16. Both matches were played at Wembley. See notes for Wembley below.

"two bricks" — ("Historical Impersonations") In Ep. 9, the Gumby Crooner (Chapman) sings a song while hitting himself in the head with two bricks, and later Ron Obvious (Jones) attempts to jump the Channel carrying a load of his sponsor's bricks (Ep. 11), and Ken Maniac (also Jones) puts a brick to sleep in Ep. 10.

• V •

"vegetarian" — ("Restaurant [Abuse/Cannibalism]") Vegetarianism generally means eating only fruits and vegetables, and avoiding animal flesh of any kind. This, of course, seems to run foul of the obvious fact that the restaurant serves human flesh, which might be a comment on the place of humans in relation to animals in the eyes of the more fervent animal rights activists.

The "smug" comment is perhaps a slap at the animal rights activists and/or vegetarians of the time who may have assumed self-righteous attitudes about their life choices as opposed to those who disagreed with them. The early 1970s saw the beginnings of Greenpeace (to combat over-whaling) and a significant rise in the number and activity of anti-vivisectionist groups.

Vegetarianism was in the news at this time, as well. Keith Waite had produced a cartoon in April 1969 for the *Sun* showing a vegetarian gone begging. See the British Cartoon Archive. In October 1969 the two long-competing societies in the UK, the Vegetarian Society and the London Vegetarian Society, had publicly joined forces to become The Vegetarian Society of the United Kingdom Limited. And finally, a chain of vegetarian restaurants—Slim Inns—were boldly announced in June 1969, the first having opened in the West End in October 1968, at 16 Maddox Street.

"Vercotti, Luigi" — ("Advertisements") Cf. Vercotti's equally oily appearances in Eps. 8, 10, and 14, each time as a shady underworld businessman with something or someone to sell. The Vercottis are loose, comedic versions of the real-life Kray brothers, East End gangsters who dealt in racketeering, prostitution, drugs, influence, and all manner of illegal activity, and who were sentenced to long prison terms in December 1969.

vestibule — (PSC; "Restaurant [Abuse/Cannibalism]") In the coat check room, the actress Flanagan (*Groupie Girl*) can be seen. She also appears in Eps. 7,

11, 12, and 22. A "vestibule" is a transitional entrance area.

vicar sitting thin and unhappy in a pot — ("Restaurant [Abuse/Cannibalism]") Believe it or not, there is a *direct* reference for this scene. Harold Davidson (1875–1937), the Rector of Stiffkey, Norfolk, had been leading a double life. In addition to his work as the vicar of the small coastal town of Stiffkey, he also visited the Soho district in London (between 1921 and 1931) to minister to the prostitutes there, where he was eventually arrested and charged (under the Clergy Discipline Act, 1892) with illicit activities unbecoming his position. It was never satisfactorily *proven* that he actually did anything untoward with the soiled doves of London, and one young woman in question would subsequently retract all traducing statements, but the publicity cost him his position, reputation, etc. He was found guilty by the diocesan Chancellor (of Norwich) on five counts, though acquitted of several other charges. In either a fit of pique, a paroxysm of mental stability, or just to point up the absurdity of his arrest and conviction in September 1932, he climbed into a barrel on the Blackpool Pier and caused mob-like crowds to gather while he was on display. Fittingly, Davidson would eventually die as a result of a lion attack on stage in a freak show (*ODNB* and *Eyewitness 1930–39*, "The Rector of Stiffkey" and "The Return of the Rector of Stiffkey").

There are also many lengthy articles detailing the proceedings of this splendidly sordid trial in the *Times* between January and July 1932. His appeals and further struggles for exoneration and clerical reinstatement occupy almost three dozen additional *Times* articles between 1932 and 1937, when he dies. The former rector's obituary appears in the 31 July 1937 edition, on page 14.

• W •

"wafers" — ("Albatross") A good question, since ices would be commonly served with wafers. Ice cream sandwiches also consist of ice cream sandwiched between wafers.

"Warner . . . Cuppa" — ("Restaurant [Abuse/Cannibalism]") "Warner House" and "Badger House" would be residence halls in Eton or Harrow-type schools (for Upperclass Twits), or even a school like the Pythons themselves had attended. Badger is located in Shropshire, and a Badger House is found there. The "headmaster" would be principal master of such a school.

The Pythons school backgrounds make such references quite understandable:

- Chapman attended King Edward VII Grammar School in Melton Mowbray
- Cleese boarded at Clifton College in Bristol, where the individual houses included Oakley's, North Town, Watson's, and Wiseman's (Cleese lived in North Town)
- Idle attended the Royal Wolverhampton School (Wolverhampton), where the houses are called Dartmouth, Rogers, and Victoria
- Jones attended the Royal Grammar School, Guildford, where the houses are called Austen, Beckinghan, Hamonde, Nettles, Powell, and Valpy
- Palin was enrolled at Shrewsbury School in Liverpool, where the individual houses include Churchill's, Ingram's, Moser's, Oldham's, and Rigg's.

"Second Cuppa"—The interval (halftime) during cricket matches gives players and umpires the opportunity to rest and enjoy tea and cucumber sandwiches, with a "second cuppa" being possible only if there's sufficient time.

"Welch, Racquel" — ("Quiz Programme—*Wishes*") Actually spelled "Raquel." Hollywood starlet who appeared in *Fantastic Voyage* and *One Million Years B.C.* (1966), and, perhaps most significantly, *The Magic Christian* (1969), where she played the Priestess of the Whip. Chapman and Cleese contributed written material to this Peter Sellers film.

Wembley — (PSC; "Historical Impersonations") Sports stadium located in Wembley, Greater London. The stadium was the site for both the British Empire Exposition of 1924–1925 and the 1948 summer Olympics. Wembley is home to the FA Cup Finals, has hosted many European cup finals, the 1966 World Cup, and Rugby League Challenge Cup Finals. The footage is from a "Cup Final" film (WAC T12/1,094).

"We're All Going to the Zoo Tomorrow" — ("Psychiatry—Silly Sketch") According to BBC records, this Julie Felix song is titled "Going to the Zoo" and performed here by The World of Harmony Music (WAC T12/1,094). *ISIRTA* had earlier used a portion of this same song in the episode "Inimitable Grimbling" (9 July 1967). Julie Felix's songs were also heard on various David Frost programs during the 1960s, and she was appearing weekly on BBC 2, hosting her own show *Once More with Felix* (1967–1970)—in short she was very high profile during this period.

"wet my bed" — ("Restaurant [Abuse/Cannibalism]") The barefaced honesty displayed by Shirley's (Idle) rantings, along with Donald's (Cleese) assessments of his wife's qualities, seems to have allowed the Head Waiter (Palin) to speak more freely than usual, offering one of the Pythons' many social faux pas that tend to go unnoticed by other characters, or are even subsequently built upon, narratively.

"What a terrible way to end a series" — (*Animation: "What a terrible way to end a series!"*) The animated character here is an image of British General Charles Cornwallis (1738–1805), and Gilliam's version is likely based on the Benjamin Smith (after John Singleton Copley) stipple engraving, part of the National Portrait Gallery collection.

This is the same head / face that Gilliam will use later in the feature film *Holy Grail*, when the monk / scribe is unsettled by the noisome, "bloody weather."

"without a pudding" — ("Restaurant [Abuse/Cannibalism]") Interestingly, most puddings would have been made using animal entrails and animal stuffing, meaning this restaurant wouldn't have served them (unless they substituted human or vegetable ingredients).

• X •

"Xmas night with the stars" — (PSC; link out of "Mr. Attila the Hun") *Christmas Night with the Stars* (1958–1994) was a long-running television special in the UK, starring, among others, Ronnie Barker (1929–2005) and Rolf Harris (b. 1930). Here the script writers reference this show, then admit the reference may be wrong, but leave the entire passage in the script anyway.

It was held by many that writing "Christ" over and over again—in words like Christmas, Christian, etc.—was very nearly taking the Lord's name in vain. As early as the 12th century scribes employed "X" in its place.

• Y •

"Yew Tree . . . U Thant" — ("Me Doctor") Yew trees are found throughout Europe and Asia, and often planted in churchyards. Utrecht is a town in Holland. (Cf. the mention of the Treaty of Utrecht in Ep. 2.) Utrillo is an artist—also mentioned elsewhere in *FC*—his paintings among those eaten by the Art Critic (Palin) in Ep. 4. Burmese diplomat U Thant (1909–1974) was the Secretary-General for the UN between 1961–1971.

This passage is very much reliant on the sounds of the words as opposed to any meaning or interconnectivity they may share or create. In this the Pythons are referencing the works of Modernist writers including T.S. Eliot (Ep. 28), James Joyce, and especially Gertrude Stein. Stein's ability to write for sound as opposed to meaning is manifest in many of her works, and exhibits the "modern" removal away from word signification toward less symbolic associations based on sounds. This decreased dependence on what words (or images, in art) "mean" was indicative of the Modernist period, where virtually all closely held truths of art and representation were called into question, upended, turned inside-out, or ignored altogether. From Stein's "Melanctha," from *Three Lives* (1909):

> Every day now, Jeff seemed to be coming nearer, to be really loving. Every day now, Melanctha poured it all out to him, with more freedom. Every day now, they seemed to be having more and more, both together, of this strong, right feeling. More and more every day now they seemed to know really, what it was each other one was always feeling. More and more now every day Jeff found in himself, he felt more trusting. More and more every day now, he did not think anything in words about what he was always doing. Every day now more and more Melanctha would let out to Jeff her real, strong feeling. (394)

Idle characters will often fall into this kind of "Stein meditation," where the outside world/narrative seems to have little or no influence on the phraseology being uttered, and the recitation can be repetitive, but actually builds and builds on previous lines. (See Ratcliffe for this discussion in relation to Stein.) The Pythons clearly embraced the linguistic and referential freedoms made possible by Modernist poets, novelists, and artists.

SEASON TWO

Episode 14: *"Ethel the Frog"*

(New) "And now for something completely different" Man, and "It's" Man in zoo cages; (New) *Animation: Titles* (silly Cleese v/o); "Face the Press"; **New Cooker Sketch**; *Animation: Vintage model European monarchs, Straight razor shave*; The Tobacconist (prostitute advert) **The Ministry of Silly Walks**; Silly walkers silent film; "Le Marche Futile"; "And now, a choice of viewing on BBC television"; ***"Ethel the Frog"*: The Piranha Brothers**; Spiny Norman looking for Dinsdale; "And now . . ." Man and a skeletal "It's" Man in zoo cages

• A •

a foot thick — (PSC; "The Ministry of Silly Walks") No character wears such shoes in the film clip. "Little Tich" is the stage name of Harry Relph (1867–1928), a Cudham-born music hall and pantomime performer. Tich's 28-inch (in length) boots are on display in Cudham today. In *The Goon Show* episode "The Mountain Eaters" (1 Dec. 1958), Bloodnok (Sellers) addresses Neddie (Secombe) as his "dear little Welsh Tich of no fixed trousers."

"Air Chief Marshal" — (link into "New Cooker Sketch") During this period, this would have been the second-highest ranking for an RAF officer. Other noted Air Chief Marshals included ACM Charles Portal (1893–1971), and ACM Sir Norman Howard Bottomley (1891–1970).

"Forster"—The character mentioned ("Air Chief Marshal Sir Vincent 'Kill the Japs' Forster") is yet another WWII-era veteran who obviously served in the Pacific Theatre and who, in 1969–1970, could very well have written the kind of angry/obtuse letters mentioned earlier. The depiction here, though, is likely based on the infamous head of RAF Bomber Command during WWII, Sir Arthur "Bomber" Harris (1892–1984), who engendered both respect and infamy for his advocacy of "carpet," or seemingly indiscriminate bombing on civilian targets like Cologne in 1942 and Dresden much later in the war. Harris had been the subject of much heated talk in the years following the war, and even found himself as the central character in German playwright Rolf Hochhuth's scathing drama *The Soldiers* in 1967. Harris's name didn't survive the first draft of the play, but critics and audiences knew whom the character Dorland was meant to represent ("Hochhuth Bends History to Serve the Higher Truth," *Times*, 10 Oct. 1967: 7).

There was also an actual General Forster, though he was head of the German Luftwehr (Air Defense) during WWII.

"Allied Bomber Command" — (link into "New Cooker Sketch") WWII-era organization in charge of the (primarily) American and British bomber squadrons operating out of Britain. Britain's Bomber Command merged with fighter forces in the late 1960s, its demise covered extensively in the news.

"Anglo-French" — ("The Ministry of Silly Walks") The British and French have endured rocky relations for centuries, going from outright war to uneasy peace by the nineteenth and twentieth centuries. Recently, Britain's attempted entry into the EEC (European Economic Community) had already been vetoed twice by this time by de Gaulle (rebuffing Macmillan and Wilson separately), and it wouldn't be until 1973 (and under a Tory government) that Britain would finally join the continental organization. In political cartoons of the period, the phrase is often found in panels lampooning the failed Anglo-French foreign policy endeavors in North Africa, the Middle East—especially in relation to the oil-rich states of the Gulf—the touchy EEC issue, the Concorde SST (Ep. 2), and, of course, the Channel Tunnel. The reinvigorated concept of the Channel Tunnel (c. 1957–1963) had become an enormously expensive (publicly and bi-laterally funded) and cooperative undertaking with the French, as the Concorde program had been. In an Abu Abraham panel, de Gaulle and Macmillan meet in the tunnel under the Channel, just to thumb their noses at each other (*Observer*, 22 Sept. 1963). See the British Cartoon Archive for this cartoon and many more.

animated titles — (PSC; "[New] *Animation: Titles* [silly Cleese v/o]") The face/head on the man and then chicken in these new opening credits (each season features reworked opening credits) is a Civil War figure, Union General John Alexander Logan (1826–1886). (This "Chicken Man" will reappear in the pages of *Monty Python's Big Red Book* in 1971.) In Ep. 15, several more Civil War–era photos will be used in Gilliam's "Civil War Cannons" animation sequence, and then they'll appear sprinkled throughout the balance of the series. See the lengthy "*animation*" entry in Ep. 15 for much more.

The mechanical or technical drawings are copied from an industrial design book, one like *The Growth of Industrial Art* by Benjamin Butterworth, published in 1892 and again in 1972, which Gilliam will sketch from in preparation for Monty Python's feature films. Similar images will be seen in the opening credits to *Meaning of Life*. See Larsen's *Monty Python and the Holy Grail* book for more on Gilliam's sources.

animation — (PSC; "*Animation: 'Colour Separation' Link*") The walking Civil War robot figure is actually the (reverse-image) torso of Lt. Col. William B. Hyde, already seen loading a cannon in an animation found in Ep. 15. The sword his right hand rests on in the original photo has been removed.

The drum corps that enters and exits the scene is also from the *Divided We Fought* book (as are all of the Civil War photos). These men are from the 93rd New York Infantry, and the photo was taken near Germantown, VA (page 205). The image has not been reversed.

The second marching general robot is the torso of Confederate Brig. Gen. Beverly H. Robertson (1827–1910), whose brain will be eaten in a later episode (Ep. 26). Robertson's original portrait is on page 111, in *DWF*, and the image has not been reversed. (When the two general torsos fight, they move like the popular "Rock'em Sock'em Robots" game, which appeared in 1964.)

When Sir William's (Chapman's image) animated body is ejected from the torso, he lands on the table in a version of da Vinci's *The Last Supper* (c. 1495–1498). The diners' clothing and poses, as well as the visibility of the nimbs (and Christ's feet) means this is more likely borrowed from the Giampietrino version (c. 1520), which is part of The Royal Academy of Arts collection. This version has had a significant place at Magdalen College, Oxford, for many years, as well. *The Last Supper* (and *The Penultimate Supper*) will be the nexus of a Monty Python sketch in the *Live at the Hollywood Bowl* performance.

"argh!" — ("Tobacconists [Prostitute Advert]") At the mention of the possibility of giving blood, the shabby man offers a subtle hand/arm gesture to indicate sexual penetration. Blood is "often synonymous with sexual passion," according to Henke in *Courtesans and Cuckolds*.

as she opens the door — (PSC; "New Cooker Sketch") As usual for the series, the props and set decorations of these interior sets are carefully composed and chosen to reflect the typical—in this case middle-class—British Midlands home. (Most of the Pythons' references and influences and settings emerge from the Midlands, interestingly, from London northward to York, the "middle" of the country where the working class are the representative population.)

Behind her, on the far wall are framed prints of paintings, including Thomas Gainsborough's portrait *The Marsham Children* (1787), and an unidentified landscape. The décor of the room (set in a "G-Plan," see below) includes what appears to be a mass-produced, drop-shoulder version of a "Devon" 1940s fireplace (Art Deco, cream-gray tile), and inside that a faux-Edwardian copper or brass stove (probably coal-burning).

• B •

backyard of terraced house — (PSC; "New Cooker Sketch") This location is not the Thorpebank Road house, since the backyards are much smaller. This long backyard is located behind a home on Goodhall Street, very near the Willesden Junction Station, less than two miles north of the Thorpebank Road location (WAC T12/1,416).

"Baldwin, Stanley" — ("The Piranha Brothers") Baldwin (1867–1947) was a Conservative British Prime Minister 1923–1924, 1924–1929, and 1935–1937. It's no surprise that the sexuality of a Tory PM would be called into question by the Pythons. Also, as Baldwin died in 1947, Dinsdale would have been under eighteen when this alleged affair took place.

This consistent blurring of past and present in *FC*—here the mention of a political figure now dead for twenty-three years—reminds us that, as Judt mentions in *Postwar*, the Pythons had been reared in a time as Edwardian as modern, living through a postwar "suspended time" where "daily life . . . would have been thoroughly familiar to men and women of fifty years earlier" (226). The Victorian and Edwardian emblems were everywhere: the almost total dependence on coal for power and heat and the concomitant blackened fog shrouding London; the popularity of Terence Rattigan's throwback plays and Ealing Studios' quirky "nineteenth-century" comedies; and the dance halls and "working-men's clubs" (226–27). This is the ancien regime the Pythons' both reveled in and rebelled against, and the war had merely extended the period's lease in the British public's collective conscience.

"Bath Chronicle" — ("The Piranha Brothers") Both of these papers—the *Bath Chronicle* and the *Bristol Evening Post*—are still being published. Bath is southeast of Bristol, on the River Avon. The *Western Daily News* is also extant.

"BBC2" — ("The Piranha Brothers") The second publicly owned channel began broadcasting in 1964, and produced shows including the groundbreaking documentary series *Civilization* (1969), *Late Night Line-Up* (1965–), and *The World about Us* (1967–). BBC2 would also pioneer color television in the UK in 1967, a move which benefited the Pythons and *Flying Circus* greatly.

Ben Hur — (PSC; "New Cooker Sketch") A 1959 biblical epic starring Charlton Heston and directed by William Wyler, and based on the popular 1880 Lew Wallace novel. The title is, indeed, made to look like letters chiseled from enormous stone blocks. Gilliam would revisit this look in the titles for *Life of Brian*, another "biblical" epic.

The music used for these impressive titles is the programmatic music "Epic Title" by Jack Shaindlin (WAC T12/1,417).

Putting such a seemingly simple and mundane bit of modern life—the new cooker—at the center of an epic presentation (worthy of "artistic" treatment) has an earlier context, interestingly. British painter Spencer Gore's *The Gas Cooker* (1913) is a quiet work celebrating both the artist's wife and her work in the modern kitchen. The painting has been part of the Tate's collection since 1962. Moving away from the strictures of classical art, modern art and artists often examine the everyday, the mundane, and find those subjects as compelling as any hero, myth, or legend. W. P. Sickert's commentary from this period and his own motivations for common subject matters and settings is illuminating:

> The more our art is serious, the more will it tend to avoid the drawing-room and stick to the kitchen. The plastic arts are gross servants, dealing joyously with gross material facts. They call, in their servants, for a robust stomach and a great power of endurance, and while they flourish in the scullery, or on the dunghill, they fade at a breath from the drawing-room. (From Sickert's "The Idealism News" in *A Free House! Or The Artist as Craftsman; Being the Writings of Walter Richard Sickert*, ed. Sitwell.)

Being the center of the typical English home, the kitchen is the center of not only many so-called kitchen sink dramas of the postwar British stage and screen, but in the parodic versions of that world created by the Pythons. See the Man and Wife (Palin and Jones) discussing a walk-on BBC part over breakfast (Ep. 10), the couple (Davidson and Jones) discussing the Indian massacre at Dorking Theatre in Ep. 6, the "Salvation Fuzz" sketch with "Strawberry Tart" in Ep. 29, and *"The Most Awful Family in Britain"* in the final episode. In the feature film *The Meaning of Life*, a man will donate his liver on his own kitchen table, and the delights of sex for enjoyment will be discussed over the morning's eggs and toast.

"Binkie" — ("The Piranha Brothers") Certainly a reference to Hugh "Binkie" Beaumont (1908–1973), the noted West End theater impresario who produced plays for Terence Rattigan (Eps. 24, 30) and Noel Coward (Ep. 35). The Goons mention him earlier as a financial backer of staged battles in "The Battle of Spion Kop" (29 Dec. 1958).

"Birmingham" — (link into "New Cooker Sketch") Large city in Warwickshire, called England's "second city," the BBC maintains studios in Birmingham at Pebble Mill. Much of the action and people described in the Tourist's tirade in Ep. 19 center on the greater Birmingham area, where Idle grew up and went to school.

"bit of pram" — ("Tobacconists [Prostitute Advert]") A play on the phrase "bit of tail," mentioned in several episodes, and refers to, again, the female pudendum. Cf. Ep. 33, where Biggles calls his secretary a "bit of tail."

"bless him" — ("The Piranha Brothers") This affectionate, nostalgic look at very real gangsters as portrayed by the Pythons would be reinforced in life. From the time of the Krays' arrest and convictions there were demonstrations for the brothers' release (they were folk heroes to many East Enders), and latterly by the presence of an estimated 100,000 funeral procession attendees for Reggie's 2000 funeral, "standing six deep along Bethnall [*sic*] Green Road," according to Jones, and this quote from a local female onlooker: "It's an East End event," said a woman. "I think they were a legend. The public liked them. They were gangsters, fun" (see Jones's article at "The Crime Library," and entries for the Krays in the *ODNB*).

"Block . . . Voice" — (PSC; "The Piranha Brothers") These two speeches aren't credited in the printed scripts, but are delivered by Jones and Palin, respectively.

"boot in the groin" — ("The Piranha Brothers") Reggie Kray developed a favorite assault mode, as well, formulating a sucker punch that reportedly broke many unsuspecting jaws. See Jones, chapter 3. Again, the Pythons are staying fairly close to actuality as they tell the tale of their fictional Piranha brothers. The Pythons were also likely emboldened by the fact that the Krays had very recently been handed lengthy prison sentences, as well as that the editors of *Private Eye*—who had "outed" the brothers in the national press for the first time—had not themselves suffered physical retribution.

"born on probation" — ("The Piranha Brothers") The Krays were born in 1933, not 1929, in Hoxton, Hackney, Greater London, in the heart of the crime-rich East End. At the turn of the twentieth century philanthropist/researcher Charles Booth (1840–1916) would describe the area as "the leading criminal quarter of London, and indeed of all England" ("Poverty in England").

"boxer" — ("The Piranha Brothers") Both Kray boys and their older brother, Charlie—not their mother—became accomplished amateur boxers in the East End.

"Boys' Clubs . . . Household Cavalry" — ("The Piranha Brothers") Ronnie Kray was an admitted and practicing homosexual, and was said to have had a fondness for younger men of any color. See Jones.

As for "household cavalry," these are the troops specially assigned to protect the sovereign, and favorites of the royal family generally fill these positions. These are the kinds of organizations that the Upper-class Twits also represented in Ep. 12.

The Kray brothers did, however, curry favor with their friends and neighbors by, for example, arranging boxing tournaments to raise money for local old folks' charities.

"Bristol Rep" — ("The Piranha Brothers") Bristol is also across the Severn from Cardiff, but almost due east. "Bristol Rep" probably refers to a smaller regional theater, like the Dorking Civic Theatre mentioned in Ep. 6. This also may be a reference to the prestigious Bristol Old Vic, the renowned local repertory company, or the Rapier Players, another repertory group in the area. Cleese grew up in this area.

Cleese's reverent narration for the *Euroshow 71—May Day Special* created by the Pythons for European television mentions that Bristol ("city and county") is home to the May Day tradition of "nun boiling week."

"build . . . houses" — (*"Face the Press"*) The subject of housing comes up again and again in post-WWII Britain, and these shortages led to documentaries (*Housing Problems*, 1935, directed by Edgar Antsey and Arthur Elton), prefabricated housing movements, so-called New Town constructions, as well as a significant squatters' movement. The 1951 Conservative government, for example, back in power after losing leadership in 1945, promised to build 300,000 new houses every year. Election-year promises aside, during 1950–1954 there were actually just 912,805 local authority houses (not including private-built homes) constructed in England and Wales (Cook and Stevenson, *Modern British History*, 171–72). Cf. Ep. 13 for more on the squatters' movement, which was quite active in postwar London, especially. Leading up to the 1964 election, both Labour and the Tories promised more and more houses, with the announced Labour number reaching 500,000 (*Labour Manifesto*). See notes to Ep. 35 for more.

According to the "London Housing Unit—History of Social Housing," more than four million homes were built in England and Wales in the two decades following WWII. Additionally, the pre- and postwar emphasis on local control for new housing led to supply bottlenecks and many fewer houses being built than had been optimistically announced/planned (Morgan, *Britain since 1945*, 39). By 1947, however, these difficulties were being overcome, according to Morgan, and houses were being built at the rate of about 200,000 per year (40). Between 1952 and 1956, more than 939,000 homes were built under the Conservative government (elected 1951), and 1956 saw the beginning of the move toward high-rise housing. (Morgan points out that it was the Labour government of the 1940s who designed and built terraced council estates "homes," while it was the Conservative government of the 1950s primarily responsible for the high-rise "projects" of the 1950s and 1960s [39–40].) By 1969, 400 high-rise blocks had been built in the Greater London area, but the Ronan Point disaster in 1968 signaled the end of enthusiasm for such structures (until very recently), and by the end of the century, they were being demolished in many towns.

These same high-rise blocks are mentioned in Ep. 17 ("Architect Sketch") and Ep. 35, where such structures are created thanks to Mystico's imagination. In Ep. 17, the satire is such (a high-rise model like Ronan Point bursts into flames) that the Pythons felt they had to perhaps protect themselves from prosecution by highlighting (using flashing captions) the satirical bent of the sketch. See notes for Ep. 17. For more on Greater London government-subsidized housing, see lhu.org.uk/history.htm, as well as "New Housing" on the *Eyewitness: 1950–59* collection.

Lastly, this depiction may be a direct connection to Sir Kenneth Robinson (1911–1996), Wilson's minister for Land and Planning, who had opined in 1968—during the worst of the squatting turmoil in London—that Britain's housing problems would be solved in just three years. This optimism was met with significant derision, especially from those on the front lines of Greater London's housing quagmire ("London Squatters Take Over Four Houses in Protest," 10 Feb. 1969: 2).

"buy a fruit machine" — ("The Piranha Brothers") The real Krays were charged in March 1965 with attempting to extort protection money from a Soho club owner, offering him doormen (bouncers) for a hefty percentage of the club's receipts (*ODNB*).

"fruit machine"—A "fruit machine" is a coin-operated slot-type machine, and would have been a machine installed as a profit-making device for the Krays/Piranhas, not the club owner. The easing of postwar rationing, as well as the legalization of gambling, had opened new vistas for corruption and shakedowns in the London underworld.

• C •

"Cardiff" — ("The Piranha Brothers") Jones was born in Colwyn Bay, on the northern coast of Wales (near Liverpool and Manchester). Cardiff is in southern Wales, south and east across the Mouth of the Severn from Weston-Super-Mare, Cleese's birthplace. Crossing the geographical borders of England for the wilds of Wales or Scotland had been practiced by those on the lam for centuries.

"Cartesian dualism" — ("The Piranha Brothers") René Descartes's dualistic belief in "the physical world [external] as mechanistic and entirely divorced from the mind [internal world], the only connection between the two being by intervention of God." See *EBO*. In other words, the "intervention" or presence of God might be what Mrs. Simnel (Palin) sees as the problem with youth of her day.

"case against" — (*"Face the Press"*) This is a prime example of Python's "fair play" rule, since the case against the obviously Conservative government is to be argued by a stain, in essence. The normally Conservative-bashing Pythons here put the more socially progressive Labour and/or Liberal parties into the seat of derision, as well. This follows, for example, The Beatles' naming of both parties—Heath's Conservatives and Wilson's Labour—as responsible for perpetuating the onerous tax burden in "Taxman" (1965), and by *Private Eye*'s by then eight-year bash against any silly or thick government figure, policy, or party.

More specifically to the housing crunch in the late 1960s, the razing of derelict housing tracts and factories and the building in their place of new housing facilities was a major plank in the Labour Party's platform as early as the 1930s, thanks to the 1930 Greenwood Act, which indelibly connected demolition to new housing starts. See "build . . . houses" note above.

Also, *Monty Python: The Case Against* is the title of Hewison's book on Python's struggles with censorship and obscenity charges.

"Chamberlain, Richard" — ("The Piranha Brothers") Richard Chamberlain (b. 1934) appeared in many television miniseries, and would have been known to the Pythons thanks to his famous role as Dr. Kildare (ABC, 1961). The music for *Dr. Kildare* will feature prominently in Ep. 26.

"Peggy Mount"—Peggy Mount (1915–2001) was a veteran character actress, appearing in *Oliver!* (1968).

"Billy Bremner"—Billy Bremner was a star football player for Leeds United and Scotland, and died in 1997 at the age of fifty-four. In 1970, Bremner was a midfielder for Leeds.

"cheque had bounced" — ("The Piranha Brothers") A notorious slum landlord in the Notting Hill area, Peter Rachman (1902–1962), had attempted to pay the Krays the first installment of protection money with a bad check. Instead of waiting around for the thugs to return and demand payment, Rachman went underground, and eventually found a way for the Krays to make money from investments he was connected to, without having to succumb completely to the brothers' thuggery (*Eyewitness: 1960–69*, "Rachmanism 1" and "Rachmanism 2"). See also the entry for Rachman in the *ODNB*.

The Kray brothers' trial was the longest in English legal history, and perhaps the trial that garnered the most (and mostly salacious) attention.

"chest of drawers" — ("Tobacconists [Prostitute Advert]") Volpone employs this same double entendre stratagem in Jonson's *Volpone* (1606), continuing a long tradition of sexual double entendres in English theatrical performance. Drawers is, of course, slang for underwear.

The customer's confusion here is understandable. It was well known in 1960s London that adverts in Soho of these types were most often metaphoric—phrases like "Studio Model" and "Large chest for sale" indicated willing, working girls waiting for customers. This way a solicitation could be made short of out-and-out solicitation, which was a chargeable offense under the Street Offences Act of 1959.

"Chief Constable" — ("The Piranha Brothers") The Krays were known for attempting to bribe police officers, and for providing fringe benefits in their clubs for same. They even finagled publicity photos with "Nipper" Read and Lord Boothby (much like American gangster John Dillinger had posed, smiling, with his captors/prosecutors), pictures that were attempts at either legitimacy or blackmail, whichever worked out.

Lord Boothby (1900–1986) had also on at least two occasions in the House of Lords argued for the brothers' release from custody pending their trial, and been shouted down both times, it seems ("Lord Boothby Angers Peers," *Times*, 12 Feb. 1965: 17). News of Boothby's bisexuality, his liaisons with young men arranged by Ronald Kray, and the two-way street of favors between this Lord and the gangster underworld was suppressed by the *Sunday Express* (a Conservative paper), but published by both the *Sunday Mirror* (a Labour-leaning paper), and the German magazine *Stern*. These revelations in 1965 likely contributed to the Pythons' continuing depiction of government figures as sexual deviants.

city gent leaves the shop — (link into "The Ministry of Silly Walks") This was a corner store called Pickfords, and was used on 25 May 1970. The permissions for the location usage cost the show £10, and the address was 107 Thorpebank Road (WAC T12/1,242). Period phone books give the owner as an "R. Pickford," and the space is listed as a newsagent's shop (precisely: "Pickfords, Nwsagts, 107 Thorpebank Rd W12 . . . 01-743 5752"). (See the British Telephone Archives.)

Cleese will walk out onto and across Thorpebank Road, then continue west on Dunraven Road. The corner store has since been converted into a single-family home.

"Clerkenwell" — ("The Piranha Brothers") Neighborhood in the borough of Islington in Greater London, and where St. Bartholomew's Hospital—where *Doctor* Graham Chapman interned—is located. More appropriately, Clerkenwell has been the site of a prison (or a series of prisons) for several hundred years. Islington is also the area where Black Power leader and sometime-terrorist Michael X was attempting to set up a peace commune, of sorts.

The school used in this interview scene is actually St. Hubert's School. There is no record in the WAC material for this episode that permission was either requested or received to shoot so near the school. St. Hubert's Secondary School was located at Mellitus St., Shepherd's Bush, W12, but is now known as the Old Oak Primary School. The interview is being recorded at the Erconwald Street entrance to the school grounds.

"clip joint" — ("The Piranha Brothers") A bar or club that charges excessively, and just the kind of establishment that the Krays were known for running. The term is used often in gangster and film noir (see *Detour* [1946]; *Asphalt Jungle* [1950]).

"colour supplements" — ("The Piranha Brothers") Portions of the newspaper with added color. See the entry for Harry "Snapper" Organs below for more on the significance of the "colour supplements." Cf. the "Travel Agent" sketch in Ep. 31, where "bolour supplements" are mentioned.

"combination of violence and sarcasm" — ("The Pirhana Brothers") The Krays were quite wily, actually. Rather than rely on violence and intimidation alone, which likely would have had the authorities at their door posthaste thanks to eager, bruised informants, the Krays instead balanced beatings with beneficence. The charitable work they performed for the poor and elderly of their neighborhood kept many mouths shut, it appears.

"completely different" — (titles) Cleese and Palin (It's Man) are in zoo cages here, shot at Chessington Zoo, Epsom Road, Chessington, Surrey (WAC T12/1,416). Cleese continues to deliver the tagline "And now for something completely different" in the BBC's received pronunciation, typical of BBC announcers.

The title tagline, however, is delivered in Cleese's "silly" voice, a change from the very sober kind of southern (read: London) "received pronunciation" earlier in the series, and employed whenever a BBC announcer is depicted. Palin will later take over this tagline duty. This "silly" version is more reminiscent of the delivery Cleese employed when he performed the same work for the radio series *I'm Sorry I'll Read That Again*.

"cooey" — ("New Cooker Sketch") A call originally used by Australian aborigines, then adapted by British colonists as a way to bring attention to the caller. See *OED*. Jones is the only one who uses the term in the show (see Ep. 27).

"CookEasi" — ("New Cooker Sketch") Probably a fictional proprietary name. The appliance used in the sketch looks to be a New World "Solaire"-type Gas Cooker.

"creosote" — (*"Face the Press"*) *OED*: "A colourless oily liquid, of complex composition, with odour like that of smoked meat, and burning taste, obtained from the distillation of wood-tar, and having powerful antiseptic properties."

"crimes of violence" — ("The Piranha Brothers") Even though the Krays were known to have engaged in money laundering, drug dealing, terrorism (especially against immigrant families), racketeering, intimidation, multiple assaults, illegal gambling, and a laundry list of felony charges, they were only brought to trial and eventually convicted for murder. See Jones, chapters 16 and 17.

• D •

"Deptford" — ("New Cooker Sketch") In Lewisham, a part of Greater London, and key to London's shipping industry for many generations. Peter Ackroyd reports in *London: The Biography* that the Deptford area in the nineteenth century was described as "the worst part of the great City's story," and that it was "muddy," melancholy," and "empty" (543). The enormous buildings of industry—including sprawling warehouses and dockside quay houses—contributed to this dehumanizing effect.

"Dinsdale" — ("The Piranha Brothers") Dinsdale Landen (1932–2003; Margate, Kent) was an English character actor who appeared in shows like *Doctor Who* and *The Guardians*. Dinsdale is also a well-known area in Darlington, where the Pythons shot portions of Ep. 25 for the second season.

This may also be a more direct reference to Tim Dinsdale (1924–1987), a man fascinated/haunted by the Loch Ness Monster phenomena, and who in 1960 claimed to have captured footage of the creature. The images were never absolutely substantiated, of course, and Dinsdale spent the better part of the rest of his life chasing that elusive proof. By the time this episode was written and recorded Dinsdale had published two books on the subject—*Loch Ness Monster* (1960) and *Leviathans* (1961)—and had received a £1230 grant (in 1967) from Kodak for further photographic research. Dinsdale and his efforts were also discussed in London papers of the period.

"Doug" — ("The Piranha Brothers") Of the twins, Ronnie may have been notably unpredictable, but Reggie was the heartless killer, according to Jones. Reggie was the lethal enforcer when Ronnie might only want to threaten and harm.

"drag" — (PSC; *"Face the Press"*) A man dressed as a woman; transvestitism. From the very first episode when Pepperpots were interviewed on the street, Python has eschewed the typical notion of casting women, or even including a woman in the troupe (Cleveland somewhat excepted), in favor of dressing the parts themselves. This is definitely a holdover from their revue days at Cambridge and Oxford, where there were few females either writing or performing, and men consistently took on female roles. (Cambridge actually had a sort of ban on women performing with Footlights, according to Idle.) This practice is also a significant throwback to the male-only Elizabethan stage practices. What is unique about this particular instance is that the man in drag is actually acknowledged, textually, which doesn't happen often in Python's oeuvre. Usually, a man dressed as a woman (e.g., a Pepperpot), is treated/perceived as a woman. Transvestitism is acknowledged twice in this episode, and again in Ep. 33, where Biggles (Chapman) admits that he sometimes dresses as his wife.

• E •

"Eastend" — ("The Piranha Brothers") The eastern end of London, known for its immigrant population, rough living and working conditions, and high crime rates. Major employment prior to WWII was located in the "London Docklands." Specifically, the East End is located "east of Shoreditch High Street, Houndsditch, Aldgate High Street, and Tower Bridge Approach. It extends eastward to the River Lea and lies mainly in the Inner London borough of Tower Hamlets, part of the historic county of Middlesex" (*OED*). See Ackroyd's *London* for more on the "perilous region's" troubled history.

"Egernon Road" — ("New Cooker Sketch") No such street exists anywhere in the UK, though there is an "Egerton Road" just off of Stamford Hill, and an "Egerton Crescent" in SW3. This is unusual for the Pythons, as they commonly choose existing street names then set them in different towns, probably culling such names from memory. Perhaps also it is a particular pronunciation of "Algernon," though the spelling in the scripts doesn't support this. It could also be a simple typo, which crept in regularly, often going unnoticed.

The frontal exteriors of this sketch were actually shot on Thorpebank Road, which intersects Uxbridge

Road, London, W12. Because of its proximity to Broadcast Centre, this neighborhood was used many times for exterior shooting, including the opening section of the "Silly Walks" sketch.

"English" — ("The Piranha Brothers") Reggie Kray purportedly "excelled" in English at Daniel Street School (Jones, chapter 2).

Episode 14 — This episode was the first episode recorded for the show's second season, and is known throughout WAC records as "Series 2, Ep. 1." It was taped on 7 July 1970, and was the fourth episode recorded, but the first aired. It was broadcast on 15 September 1970.

Other actors scheduled to appear in this episode, according to WAC records, included so-called Tourists, other period credits given where available: Paul Lindley (*Dixon of Dock Green*), Raymond St. Claire (sound, *Ginger*, 1971), Eric Lindsay (*Play for Today*), Cy Town (*Dad's Army; Star Wars*), Jonathan Gardner (*Warship*), Elizabeth Broom (*Dixon of Dock Green*), Deborah Millar, Philip Howard (*Dixon of Dock Green*), Michael Channon (Southampton FC), Moyra Pearson, Daphne Davey (*The Troubleshooters*), Paul McNeill (folk singer), and Morris Terry (WAC T12/1,242). David Ballantyne, Stanley Mason, and John Hughman (each appearing in the "New Cooker Sketch" in Mrs. Pinnet's [Jones] front room) were also scheduled to appear in small roles (WAC T12/1417).

exterior of police station — ("The Piranha Brothers") This was one of the pick-up shots recorded while the troupe and personnel were on the coast, here specifically recorded on 12 May 1970 at the Paignton Police Station (WAC T12/1,416).

"extroverted suicide" — ("The Piranha Brothers") Chapman makes an earlier appearance as this same kind of borderline psychiatrist character in the "Mouse Problem" sketch in Ep. 2, where perverted, masturbatory "mouse tendencies" are reinforced, not discouraged.

• F •

"Face the Press" — (*"Face the Press"*) Perhaps inspired by similar shows like *Face to Face* (1960), an interview-format show hosted by John Freeman and directed by Hugh Burnett. Freeman was also a presenter on *Panorama*. On American television, NBC's *Meet the Press* has been a news/talk staple since 1947.

The music behind the description of the Minister's (Chapman) dress is "Warm Hands," performed by the Watt Peters Orchestra (WAC T12/1,417).

"family of sixteen" — ("The Piranha Brothers") The Kray twins had an older brother, Charles Jr. (1927–2000), also an accomplished boxer and repeat felon, who spent most of his adult life in prison as well.

"February 22, 1966" — ("The Piranha Brothers") The specific date doesn't seem to be significant to the Krays, though on 8 March 1966, a gun battle between gang members resulted in a Kray cousin's death, setting the Krays on the path to murder. For the Krays, it would be when the brothers graduated from strong-arm tactics to gangland murders that would demand police "take notice."

In fact, by the end of 1966, Ronald Kray was still a bit of a mystery to the general public and even the police, as his only real appearance in the newspapers that year involved a police officer being charged with shaking him down for "looking the other way" money. By 22 December 1966, Ronald Kray was listed as "missing" as the police struggled to build a corruption case against one of their own (*Times*, 22 Dec. 1966: 7).

Also, there is the very real possibility that the in-depth reports on the Krays and the criticism of the lethargic police investigation into the Kray empire later appearing in the pages of the non–Fleet Street publication *Private Eye* actually spurred/shamed authorities into action.

"female impersonator" — ("The Piranha Brothers") One of the rare occasions in *FC* where a cross-dressed character is identified as such. Another is in the opening sketch (*"Face the Press"*) of this same episode.

Fifth Gas Man — ("New Cooker Sketch") Not credited in the script at this point, this is David Ballantyne, who also appears in Eps. 13 and 17. The Sixth Gas Man is Gilliam (misidentified as the Fifth Gas Man in the script), and the Seventh Gas Man is actor John Hughman. Hughman also appears in Eps. 17, 27, 28, and 41. The Eighth Gas Man is also unnamed in the script at this point—he is Stanley Mason (Ep. 17).

"film producers" — ("The Piranha Brothers") The Krays attracted significant celebrity attention during the early 1960s, cavorting with both American and British entertainment and crime figures.

"fiver" — ("Tobacconists [Prostitute Advert]") A five pound note. See *OED*.

"four hundred years" — ("The Piranha Brothers") The Kray twins went on trial officially (at the Old Bailey, seen at the end of the "Spanish Inquisition" sketch) in January 1969, and were sentenced to life in prison in March 1969. Jones notes that "life" at the time generally meant ten to twelve years, but that the judge in the case demanded actual sentences of not less than thirty years for both Krays. Reggie was sent to Parkhurst Prison (mentioned in Eps. 12 and 13), and Ronnie went to Durham Prison.

• G •

Gilliam — (PSC; "New Cooker Sketch") This is incorrect, as Gilliam does not speak this particular line, though he will appear, with many others. This line is spoken by David Ballantyne, who also appeared in Ep. 13 as Prologue, a waiter, and an Indian Head. Gilliam is the Sixth Gas Man, mentioned above.

"giveaway" — ("The Piranha Brothers") The Krays did lay low after the two murders, traveling on the continent and avoiding the limelight, as "Nipper" Read and his men tracked their movements and painstakingly built a solid case against them (Jones).

At the gang's sentencing, Mr. Justice Melford Stevenson (1902–1987) said to Detective-Superintendent Read: "I cannot part with this case without saying that the debt owed to Detective-superintendent Read, and the officers who served under him, cannot be overstated and never discharged" ("At Least 30 Years Gaol for the Kray Twins," *Times*, 6 Mar. 1969: 1).

"Gloucester . . . Lear" — ("The Piranha Brothers") Character in Shakespeare's play *King Lear*. Gloucester is blinded by Regan and Cornwall for supposedly supporting Cordelia. Organs's (Jones) other characterizations include:

A "pork butcher"—This still shot was taken in the tobacconist's shop seen earlier in the episode. The sexualized "chest of drawers" is just behind him.

"Blind Pew"—Evil character in Stevenson's *Treasure Island*, Pew will be mentioned again in Ep. 32. *Treasure Island* and its characters are mentioned often in *FC*, probably based on the familiarity of the *Treasure Island* Christmas pantomime, both live and on the BBC. See entry for "*Long John Silver*" in Ep. 5 for more.

"Ratty . . . *Toad Hall*"—*Toad of Toad Hall* was a 1946 television production based on Kenneth Grahame's popular novel *The Wind in the Willows* (1908). "Ratty" was the character Water Rat.

"Sancho . . . *La Mancha*"—Sancho is Don Quixote's servant in the book (1605, 1615) and Broadway play (1965). (The film version would not appear until 1972.) Notice, also, that all of Organs's roles are supporting, not leads.

It was noted by many pundits of the period that the high profile inspector "Nipper" Read was as much playing for the cameras and press as he was performing his job. *Private Eye* would satirize him as the intrepid "Knacker" of the Yard.

"go" — ("Tobacconists [Prostitute Advert]") Cf. the Idle-penned "Nudge, Nudge" sketch in Ep. 3, also filled with double entendres of familiar words given sexual connotations ("go," "sport," "games"). See *Shakespeare's Bawdy* for more on this rich allusiveness. D.H. Lawrence uses the term "go" similarly in *Lady Chatterly's Lover* (1928), a scurrilous text that pushed the boundaries of decorum in publishing as late as 1960, when Penguin Books was sued for obscenity. Penguin would win the case (see notes to Ep. 10, "Gorilla Librarian," for more). Lawrence figured prominently in Ep. 2 in relation to the "working-class" sitting room (borrowed from *Sons and Lovers*) and the coal mining family life.

goat with a hat — ("New Cooker Sketch") The goat was obtained from Animal Kingdom for the taping (WAC T12/1,417). Animal Kingdom Ltd., Animals for Hire, was located at 179a High Street, Uxbridge.

"good condition" — ("Tobacconists [Prostitute Advert]") Referring to the "bit of pram" he'd like to have, this would mean young and free from sexually transmitted diseases, in the shabby man's (Idle) estimation.

"Government" — ("*Face the Press*") Meaning the sitting government. When this episode was recorded (9 July 1970), the Tories (Conservatives) were in power, having won a majority in the 18 June 1970 elections. When the episode was written, however, Labour would have still been seated, so the "small patch of brown liquid" mentioned later would likely have been representing the Conservative Party.

G-plan type — (PSC; "New Cooker Sketch") A "G-plan" means a home designed/built on the design of Messrs. E. Gomme, Ltd., including the mass-produced utility furniture so prevalent in postwar Britain (and Europe, to a certain extent). Along with food and fuel, a nationwide shortage of industrial products (wood, plastic, metal) after the war (c. 1945–1954) meant that furniture designed for the thousands of new homes and apartments had to be as spare as possible, but without completely sacrificing attractiveness and comfort.

The G-Plan, introduced in 1952, featured modern style furniture that could be affordably purchased by British consumers into the 1970s. There were a limited number of items to choose from, and consumers could buy in a "modular" way for individuality. Houses became coordinated from room to room. This would have been the furniture that the Pythons grew up with (mixed in with handed-down antiques), building on the Utility Scheme furniture of the war and postwar years, and which the BBC prop department obviously carried in quantity. (The Utility Scheme had been instituted by the government during the early years of the war to make the best use of limited raw materials—furniture, appliances, and even toys fell under its rubric.) There were a number of other manufacturers of modern (even minimalist) furniture of the period, including Avalon and Meredrew. Large, eye-catching advertisements for E. Gomme Ltd. G-Plan furniture—"All a bedroom should be"—can be found in many period newspapers.

See Attfield's *Utility Reassessed* (1999) for more on the various government utility programs during and after WWII.

gravestone — ("The Piranha Brothers") This gravestone scene was one of the pick-up shots taken while the troupe was in Torquay (WAC T12/1,416).

• H •

"Hawkins" — ("The Piranha Brothers") Jim Hawkins is the young boy's name in *Treasure Island*, the novel-cum-Christmas pantomime that obviously so fixated the young Pythons they refer to it over and over again in *FC*.

"Hello Sailors" — (link into "New Cooker Sketch") The clarion call of the homosexual or effeminate male in *FC*. Cf. the swishy David Unction (Chapman) in Ep. 10, as well as the title of Tom Jack's book in Ep. 3. The Goons also used the phrase earlier. It can be heard in "The Great Bank of England Robbery" (2 Mar. 1958), for example. The phrase can probably be attributed to "working girls" at dockside calling to newly disembarked sailors.

"help me" — ("Tobacconists [Prostitute Advert]") What follows is a characteristic Idle sketch where double entendres and misunderstandings rule. Here the shabby character (Idle) misinterprets harmless posted adverts for sexual enticements. After some back-and-forth between the customer and proprietor, the façade is dropped and the advert the customer seems to have been searching for is presented. Cf. the "Pornographic Bookshop" in Ep. 36 where a Tudor storefront masks a pornographic bookstore.

"Hockney, David" — ("New Cooker Sketch") Hockney (b. 1937, Bradford) is a Pop Art and photography-inspired painter, printmaker, and stage designer who would have been something of a flamboyant peer of the Pythons. Ironically, Hockney was a conscientious objector, meaning he expressed a fundamental opposition to combat-related service in WWII, and performed his National Service in a hospital, instead. (Cf. the entry for "National Service" below.)

Hockney spent much time in the United States in the 1960s, in the company of people like Andy Warhol, and may have come to Cleese's and/or Gilliam's attention there. (His public profile was elevated enough by this time, however, that he was appearing in newspapers, and being covered on TV and radio, etc.) He painted images of showers and swimming pools, so the utility/facility aspects of his work might have inspired the Pythons to name him as a bomb designer. His noted status as a conscientious objector makes this an ironic connection, as well.

Also, the acknowledged homoerotic content/context of his work (including *Man Taking Shower in Beverly Hills* [1964]) would have made him a perfect target. On the Sir Forster set (with Cleese and the attendant fan boy) there is a chaise lounge, which also appears in Hockney's painting *Three Chairs with a Section of a Picasso Mural* (1970).

"Home Affairs" — (*"Face the Press"*) The Home Affairs Committee stands as the examiner of the Home Office, including administration, policy, and expenditures.

• I •

Intercom Voice — ("The Ministry of Silly Walks") This woman (who will appear with the tray in moments) is Daphne Davey (*The Troubleshooters*).

• K •

"Kierkegaard" — ("The Piranha Brothers") Søren Kierkegaard (1813–1855) was a Danish religious writer and thinker, who argued, among many other things, that truth was finally subjective. His name will be mentioned again in the following sketch. The "Kierkegaard's Journals" title is a reference to the approximately 7,000 pages of journals Kierkegaard produced during his lifetime. There are twenty-three volumes of the journals.

Kierkegaard is obviously important to the Pythons' *weltbild*, and is discussed at length in notes to Ep. 28 and 42.

• L •

"Lauderdale" — ("The Piranha Brothers") Police Constable Lauderdale was a character on the long-running British police television show *Dixon of Dock Green* (1955–1978). Richard "Dickie" Attenborough played RSM Lauderdale in the 1964 film *Guns at Batasi*. Attenborough is satirized at length in Ep. 39, the *"Light*

Entertainment Awards" sketch. In that same film, Jack Hawkins played Colonel Deal.

line of gas men — (PSC; "New Cooker Sketch") These brown-coated men snaking down Thorpebank Road (starting at 94 Thorpebank, then stretching toward Dunraven Road, wrapping around the newsagents' shop at 107 Thorpebank) included the following, according to BBC records: Bernard Egan (*Plague of the Zombies*), David Grinaux, Eric Kent (*Doctor in the House*), Tony Maddison (*Doctor Who*), David Joyce (*Doctor Who*), Scott Andrews (*Tiffany Memorandum*), Anthony Mayne (*Z Cars; Play for Today*), Lesley Parker (*Softly Softly*), Ron Gregory (*Dixon of Dock Green*), Willy Bowman (*The Wednesday Play*), Michael Earl (*Dixon of Dock Green; Doctor in the House*), Norton Clarke (*UFO*), Walter Henry (*Public Eye; Doctor Who*), Alex Hood (*Play for Today*), Brian Nolan (*Paul Temple; Z Cars*), Garth Watkins (*The Guardians*), Neville Simons (*Doctor Who*), Harry Tierney (*Doctor Who*), John Caesar (*Paul Temple*), Derek Chafer (*Doctor Who; Softly Softly*) (WAC T12/1,242).

"Luton" — ("The Piranha Brothers") Mentioned often in *FC* as a representative bastion of middle-class values (and home to the BBC's Lord Hill, for example), Luton is northwest of London. The London Luton airport is located there. Cf. the Tourist's reference to Luton in his rant in Ep. 19.

• M •

"MCC" — ("The Piranha Brothers") Acronym for the Marylebone Cricket Club, which just continues (to the absurd) the brothers' (Kray and Piranha) penchant for attempting to subjugate all sport betting activities. The MCC is and has been the home of English cricket, and is located at Lord's Cricket Ground in St. John's Wood, well out of the Piranhas' (or Krays') actual sphere of influence. That the brothers were "slit up a treat" indicates that they were unable to take over by force the MCC; the oldest and stodgiest of establishment fixtures are too much for such lower-class types.

The tough reputation of the MCC, however, can also be attributed to the group's resolute stance in favor of continued play with South Africa's cricket teams, and completing a tour of South Africa in 1968–1969. There are myriad political cartoons depicting very old MCC types in full cricket gear threatening long-haired protesters and politicians into submission, including one from Jak (Raymond Jackson) in the *Evening Standard* on 21 January 1970. The depicted cricketers, with bats ready, are asking the hippie demonstrator—whom they're about to execute—if he wants to go "fast, medium, or slow off-spin." The controversial tour was eventually canceled.

"Minister . . . Ola Pola" — (link into "New Cooker Sketch") In the taped version, "Minister" is actually pronounced "Ministerette," an additional and diminutive emasculation of the armed forces/government personnel. The "-ette" suffix is usually appended to a name or title to indicate a female, or in this case, an effeminate male in "outrageous drag."

By the 1960s, the UK was struggling to maintain its air forces amid aircraft manufacturing slowdowns and the U.S. military taking key NATO roles for defense of Europe against the Soviet Union. The celebrated failure of a missile system (Blue Streak) and the early retirement of the V-Bombers (in the face of elevated Soviet AA missile technology and deployment) weighed heavily on the Air Ministry and its funding future.

The Ministry of Aviation itself was formed in 1959, at the height of the Cold War, but by 1967 the control of aircraft was transferred to the Ministry of Technology, and the Board of Trade assumed other of Aviation's duties.

The British military participated in a northern Norway NATO exercise termed "*Polar* Express" in 1968, at least partially meant to discourage the Soviets—who had recently rolled tanks across Czechoslovakia—to flex NATO's military muscle within shouting distance of the Soviet sphere of influence.

Ministry — (PSC; "The Ministry of Silly Walks") Name given to areas of British government, such as the Ministry of Food, Ministry of Information, Ministry of Health Economics, and the Ministry of Agriculture, Fisheries and Foods. The phrase "Ministry of Silly Walks" has become something of a catchphrase in Britain when government mismanagement and pork-barrel spending are discussed. See notes to *MPSERD*.

"mother" — ("The Piranha Brothers") It's unclear here whether Vercotti (Palin) is actually talking to his mother—and she's just ordered a Chinese prostitute—or to a client whom Vercotti calls "mother" to belay suspicion. There is a pause after he says "bye-bye," as if the "mother" is an afterthought.

"Mr. Pudey" — ("The Ministry of Silly Walks") Arthur Pewtey (also Palin) appeared in Ep. 2, and this type of characterization from Palin appears many times throughout *FC*, including the similarly mannered Mr. Pither in Ep. 34, "The Cycling Tour."

Mrs. Pinnet's house — (PSC; link out of "Tobacconists [Prostitute Advert]") This outdoor location (corner of Thorpebank and Uxbridge roads, London, W12) was seen earlier in the episode. The "Silly Walks" sketch will begin at the other end of Thorpebank Road, just north of this corner.

• N •

"nailed to the floor" — ("The Piranha Brothers") There is a Kray story involving a victim being stabbed so violently that the knife impaled him to the floor. This is one of the murders for which the Krays were eventually prosecuted (Jones).

More specifically apropos is the criminal history of the "Charlie Richardson Gang," five of whom, including Charlie (1934–2012), were sentenced to long prison terms in 1967 for "assault, grievous bodily harm, robbery with violence and demanding money with menaces," among other crimes ("Gang Leader Richardson Gaoled for 25 Years," *Times*, 9 June 1967: 2). The Richardsons' preferred tortures included beatings, stabbings, hot iron burns, electrocutions, and, yes, nailing victims to the floor with long nails, according to contemporary reports. Several of the Richardsons actually had a running feud with the Krays, and Ronald Kray would be cross-examined in regard to a 1967 murder of a Richardson gang associate ("Ronald Kray Denies Any Part in Murders," *Times*, 1 Feb. 1969: 3).

Like the Krays, the Richardsons forced fruit machines on frightened business owners, paid off police officers and officials, consorted with starlets and swells, and generally lived the high life until the law caught up with them. Charlie Richardson was sentenced to 25 years in June 1967.

"National Service" — ("The Piranha Brothers") In effect between 1939 and 1960, National Service included either active participation in the armed forces or commensurate service outside of military duties. (Artist David Hockney [mentioned above] performed hospital duties, for example.) All able-bodied young men were to serve in active duty for eighteen months (later two years), and then as reserves for an additional four years. Both Reggie and Ronnie were dishonorably discharged from the Army after spending significant time in military stockades for desertion, insubordination, and all manner of violence against fellow conscriptees and their guards (*ODNB*).

None of the Pythons performed National Service.

"No fear!" — (*"Face the Press"*) Idiomatic expression, used now as an exclamation.

• O •

"Operation, The" — ("The Piranha Brothers") The Krays' crime organization was known as "The Firm." Also, Peter Cook's satirical club (Greek Street, Soho) was called simply and ironically "The Establishment," a term that had been recently coined by *Spectator* columnist Henry Fairlie to refer to the government and its unseen operations (Carpenter 2000, 130).

"Organs, Harry 'Snapper'" — ("The Piranha Brothers") The policeman who doggedly led the investigation of the Krays from 1964 through their first major arrest and trial in 1965 and incarceration in 1969 was Detective Chief Inspector Leonard "Nipper" Read. His nickname—played up in the tabloids of the time—is attributed to a successful boxing career as a youth.

This depiction is certainly also connected to Sergeant Norman Pilcher, who made a number of high-profile celebrity arrests in the late 1960s, and may have followed the movements of these celebrities (including John Lennon, Mick Jagger, Donovan, George Harrison) through their coverage in the "colour supplements" of the tabloids. For more on Pilcher and his star-studded investigations, see the "found on the premises" note in Ep. 5.

"organza . . . tulle" — (*"Face the Press"*) "Organza" is described by the *OED* as "a thin stiff transparent dress-fabric of silk or synthetic fibre," and "tulle"—"a fine silk bobbin-net used for women's dresses, veils, hats, etc."

"diamante"—This would be a necklace made "sparkly" by adding powdered glass, crystal, etc. See *OED*.

"Bond Street"—Off of Chiswick Common Road, just south of Bedford Park in London. A fashion district, like Harley Street is a medical locus. In Wodehouse's *Code of the Woosters* (1938), it is revealed that the burly, masculine Spode actually runs a fashionable ladies underwear shop on Bond Street, and even makes the underthings himself (297).

"hair is by Roger"—Probably a reference to the then-popular Raymond Bessone of Mayfair, the celebrity hair stylist. Raymond will be mentioned by his nickname, "Teasy-Weasy," in Ep. 31.

"Out of her mind" — ("The Ministry of Silly Walks") It's not clear here why the minister (Cleese) would conclude this, unless he's responding to her calling him "Mr. Teabag." If he is, then her name, "Mrs. Two-Lumps," is equally absurd, though she responds to it without question. Perhaps it's in reference to his request for coffee, and her response with a tea-related answer. The woman is Daphne Davey.

outrageous drag — (PSC; link into "New Cooker Sketch") Characterizing the country's leadership—in this case the military—as highly effeminate, and of dubious sexual orientation. Earlier, the police suffered the same treatment, as have upper-class types and authority figures of all stripes. Later in *Flying Circus*, judges will be lampooned in a similar manner, and the effeminization of male (often, but not always, Conservative) leaders serves the satirical purpose of making small by ridicule and derision.

• P •

"Panama Canal" — ("The Piranha Brothers") As Organs (Jones) recites the liturgy of his unsuccessful tracking of the Piranhas, he makes a trip back from South America through the Canal. The Krays were known to have looked into both Africa and Latin America for investment opportunities. More to the point, the investigation into the Great Train Robbery defendants led Scotland Yard to Rio de Janeiro, Brazil, where they tried, unsuccessfully to first kidnap, and, failing that, to extradite Ronnie Biggs.

"Piranha, Arthur" — ("The Piranha Brothers") Continuing Python's affinity for this first name. The Krays' father was Charlie Kray, their mother, Violet. Arthur Piranha is also characterized as both a "devout Catholic" and often in trouble with the authorities (the real Kray patriarch was a proud WWII deserter and spent years on the run). This conflation can't be overlooked—that of a criminal and practicing Roman Catholic in this Anglican country. The Inquisition (enacted by the Catholic Church) is also a significant topic in this episode. See entries for Ep. 15.

"Piranha brothers" — ("The Piranha Brothers") Cf. Ep. 8, the Vercotti brothers (Jones and Palin), for a previous iteration of the gangster siblings milieu. Doug and Dinsdale are certainly characters based loosely on London's most famous crime twins, Ronnie and Reggie Kray. The Krays were born ten minutes apart in October 1933, Reggie being the oldest. Ronnie died in prison in 1995, and Reggie died in October 2000, having been paroled for medical reasons after thirty-two years in prison (*ODNB*). As mentioned in the notes to Ep. 8, the Krays spent all their (free) time together, and participated in various criminal shakedowns and enterprises—either together or separately—on a regular basis into the 1960s.

The Krays had been featured on the cover of the satirical magazine *Private Eye* on 14 March 1969, meaning their private, corrupt lives were becoming much more public. Most conventional (Fleet Street) London newspapers had ignored or buried Kray coverage to this point, at least partly because some well-connected Conservative and Labour figures were associated—politically, monetarily, even sexually—to one or both of the Krays or their empire.

"pussy cat" — ("Tobacconists [Prostitute Advert]") "Puss" (in its various forms) has been slang for both the female pudendum and "whore" since at least the seventeenth century, as in Jonson's *The Alchemist* (5.3.38), performed first in 1610. This is probably not a reference to bestiality, but the shabby man (Idle) misinterpreting a real cat for sale for a "sex kitten." This term was first affixed to Marilyn Monroe in the late 1950s, and later to Raquel Welch (Ep. 13), Brigitte Bardot, Anita Ekberg (*FZ*), and others.

• R •

"Reading" — ("New Cooker Sketch") Reading is in Berkshire, and is thirty-eight miles west of London. Reading's proximity to the Thames and railroad junctions makes it a good choice for a gas company distribution hub. The BBC's Written Archives Collection is also located across the river from Reading, in Caversham Park. The other locations mentioned in this rant include:

"Cheltenham"—Northeast of Gloucester, in Gloucestershire;

"Hounslow"—In Greater London, near Heathrow Airport, Hounslow will figure prominently in Ep. 28 (in the "Surbiton to Hounslow" trek), and is also the actual location of Slade House, the high-rise apartment building where encyclopedia salesmen leap to their deaths at the end of Ep. 5. In the "Mouse Problem" sketch in Ep. 2, the "Hounslow" title card insert was the made-up address of Arthur Jackson, mouse pervert, and was created after the episode aired once (to cover up David Frost's actual address). See notes to Ep. 2, "Hounslow" for more;

"Twickenham"—In Greater London, just southeast of Hounslow; in 1971 Twickenham Station doubled for Hounslow's train station for Ep. 28, along with Twickenham Bridge and multiple locations in the Twickenham area (WAC T12/1,428). For Ep. 27, St. Margaret's Road, Twickenham, doubles for a North Malden high street.

"Holborn"—In Camden (near where Idle lived during this period), Holborn is also part of Greater London, and mentioned later in Ep. 19;

"Hainault"—In Greater London, between Redbridge and Chigwell, and also prominently mentioned as part of Neville Shunt's play title in Ep. 24;

"Southall"—Southall is also in Greater London, near Ealing, in the area where the Pythons shot many exterior sequences;

"Peckham"—Part of Greater London, and home to Peckham Rye Station;

"Tottenham, Lewisham, Ruislip"—Tottenham, Lewisham, and Ruislip are also areas within Greater

London. (The map displayed later during the "*Ethel the Frog*" section of this episode depicts this same area, centering—as is often the case—the *FC* action in Greater London.) Tottenham will be mentioned in Ep. 35, "Olympic Hide-and-Seek Final," while Ruislip will be utterly destroyed in Ep. 44, when Mr. Neutron (Chapman) is attacked by a nuclear missile barrage from the United States.

As part of the postwar welfare state reform, the Gas Act of 1948 had nationalized the more than 1,000 natural gas concerns into twelve regional gas boards, controlling the delivery and prices of domestic gas as well as creating the inevitable bureaucratic mess as depicted by the Pythons. The changes and the new alignments were printed in British newspapers, and often, but the confusion settled in anyway. Some of the perturbations here must be as a result of the alignment and realignment of gas board region boundaries during the 1950s and 1960s, meaning there would necessarily be villages and gas distribution points shifting from one board's purview to another, and oftentimes more than once. The bureaucratic silliness is revisited in Ep. 17, when every home must have a poet installed, and that poet read by a poet reader under the auspices of the East Midlands Poet Board.

Additional confusion and expense certainly emerged in 1967, when North Sea natural gas was transported onshore to Easington terminal for the first time, sparking a ten-year conversion program that would see the conversion of every gas appliance in the country from "town gas" to the new "natural gas." This conversion involved thirty-four million appliances, eventually, and a reported thirteen million homes. (See gasarchive .org for more.)

"Reverend Smiler Egret" — ("The Piranha Brothers") The Reverend is given a name as if he is a gangster, not unlike classical musician Arthur "Two-Sheds" Jackson (also Jones) interviewed in Ep. 1. There was, actually, a Woolland Parish (Dorset) priest who passed away in 1968 named Reverend Ronald Flower "Smiler" Martyn (*Times*, 26 Sept. 1968: 18).

• S •

"sarcasm . . . satire" — ("The Piranha Brothers") A sophisticated level of humor and observation, sarcasm and satire might not have been possible (or indeed necessary) for the Krays, as at least Ronnie was characterized by a state psychiatrist as below average in intelligence. The subtleties of thought and speech required for a speaker/writer to use such figures of speech as parody, satire, and bathos are incongruous with the Krays' penchant for physical violence and deadly intimidation. These are all tools in Python's quiver, however, and are used throughout their work.

"dramatic irony"—When an audience, for example, knows more about a character's situation and/or fate than the character. This can create a sense of superiority, but also an empathy with and for the character based on the crushing effects of Fate that are certain to come. In the case of the Krays, dramatic irony came into play when they murdered associate James McVite—the brothers staged a party, had McVite invited, and killed him when he arrived (Jones).

"metaphor"—A common quality between two ideas, thoughts, or figures suggested by metaphoric reference ("men are sheep").

"bathos"—Interesting that Vercotti would include this figure of speech, as it is an *accidental* fall from perhaps the sublime to the ridiculous in vain attempts at elevated speech—Dryden's detractors used this claim against him on more than one occasion. Lower-tier or court/occasional poets of the seventeenth and then eighteenth centuries (the latter category including Dryden) tended to fall prey to the bathetic.

"puns"—A pun is a play on words, a deliberate confusing of terms, primarily—for example, a confusing of homonyms and synonyms. The Shopkeeper in the "Dead Parrot Sketch" (Ep. 8) tries to use a pun, unsuccessfully, and then flubs a palindrome, as well.

"parody"—The Pythons employ parody often, imitating epic works of art and literature, and especially parodying television shows and the paradigms of presentation and broadcasting in general.

A "litote"—like "no small tempest"—is an indirect affirmation by denial of the opposite, and another rather clever figure of speech (Baldick, 142).

"say any more" — ("*Face the Press*") In Ep. 17, Chapman (playing "Man"), asks Devious (Palin) if he has any more lines to say. When he hears that he is finished, he decides to leave the sketch. In Ep. 15, when Chapman is playing Reg, his questions bring on the Inquisitors. But when that sketch begins to fade, and Reg is out of lines, he agrees to answer the door in another sketch.

"says here" — ("New Cooker Sketch") This type of seemingly insignificant bureaucratic mistake—even a misunderstanding—can have lasting, even lethal effects in the Python world. Later in this episode, a man (Chapman) will be assaulted based on a mistaken identity (he's *not* "Clement"), and, further assaulted when he points out the mistake (that he's not Clement). In Ep. 17, "Motor Insurance Sketch" (with *Ben Hur* titles again), the fine print in the Vicar's (Idle) insurance policy clearly states that no claim he makes will ever be paid. In *Meaning of Life*, obtaining an organ donor's card obligates the cardholder (Gilliam) to surrender his liver—even if he's "still using it." And in Gilliam's later feature film *Brazil* (1985), which was co-written by Gilliam, Charles McKeown, and Tom Stoppard, the entire scenario is based on a single typo on a government work order. In a Python bureaucracy, the form's the thing.

"School" — ("The Piranha Brothers") The Kray twins attended Woods Close and Daneford Street School (Bethnal Green), and boxed at the Robert Browning Youth Club (Southwark). By age fifteen, however, they had quit school in favor of boxing and their "work."

Pythagoras was a pre-Socratic philosopher best known for his teaching of the transmigration of souls and theory of numbers. This may have been included by the Pythons as a reference to the Krays' much-publicized belief in fortune-telling, and the early predictions that the boys were destined for short, brilliant lives (Jones).

scrambles — (PSC; "New Cooker Sketch") After performing this somewhat tomboy-ish, un-ladylike feat, Pinnet (Jones) carefully straightens her dress, then crawls through the rear window. This is a good example of a cross-dressed character not afraid to perform role(s) somewhat hermaphroditically.

Second Policeman — (PSC; "The Piranha Brothers") Not noted in the text, but this actor appears to be actor/singer David Ballantyne, who also appears in Eps. 13 and 14, as well as the 1971 Montreux compilation episode.

"shot silk" — (*"Face the Press"*) *OED*: "Woven with warp-threads of one colour and weft-threads of another, so that the fabric (usually silk) changes in tint when viewed from different points. Also, applied to mixed fabrics (esp. of cotton and silk), dyed by a process which produces a variegated effect similar to that of 'shot silk.'"

"shtoom" — ("The Piranha Brothers") A Yiddish version of the German word "stumm," meaning silent or dumb. This is also a Cockney term, generally meaning "shut it." As with Cockney rhyming slang (and Palani slang), the goal in using these words and phrases was to communicate in public (and especially in front of authorities) without betraying one's intentions. Here, Vercotti (Palin) wants to communicate with the caller without giving away the illicit details of the transaction.

silent movie type — ("The Ministry of Silly Walks") The music used behind this black-and-white film is "Cockney Song" from "Silent Film Music" (WAC T12/1,417).

"Silly Walks" — ("The Ministry of Silly Walks") Futurist F.T. Marinetti (1876–1944) proposed an avant garde film called *Futurist Life* (c. 1915), where the successful futurist would learn to employ various walks, including "neutralist walk," "interventionist walk," and "the Futurist March." In regard to this last proposed new walk, see the mention of "Le marche futile" further on in the sketch.

The posted sign here says, "Ministry of Silly Walks," but as requested on the show's "Graphics Requirements" page, it should have read "Ministry of Silly Walkers." There is no indication as to when the requirement was changed (WAC T12/1,417).

"Simnel" — ("The Piranha Brothers") Simnel Cake is a fruity Easter cake, which would account for both the woman's last name and "April." Also, Lambaster Simnel was a pretender to the English throne in 1486–1487, and even though he was eventually exposed, he was thereafter employed in the king's kitchens. Cf. Mr. Lambert in Ep. 8. In Ep. 21, an archaeological dig at "Abu Simnel" will be mentioned.

This scene is also shot on Thorpebank Road, in front of number 102, and just across the street from number 107, where Pickford's corner store was located.

small ad — (PSC; animated link into "Tobacconists [Prostitute Advert]") The text of this small ad isn't included in the printed scripts, as it was most likely not known at the time of the script's writing (per Gilliam's modus operandi). The ad reads: "Vacancy: Pilot Needed to Fly Vintage Model Monarchs." The ad is written by the animator's hand, and is preceded by various royal figure cutouts (including Elizabeth I and Charles VI) sporting propellers and flying around.

The Charles VI image (he is the first monarch we see, and the last, as he lands and "opens") is a borrow from a book Gilliam will use regularly through the series, Bibiena's *Architectural and Perspective Designs*, which was first published in 1740, then republished by Dover in 1964. The book is dedicated to Charles, and the drawing is from the dedication page (no page number). Gilliam has colored the drawing, as well.

The flying Elizabeth source is a more obscure version of a 1589 engraving, and is likely from a 1950s photograph of that engraving. The image is part of the National Portrait Gallery's collection, and was acquired in 1958. In the William Rogers original, Elizabeth is holding an orb and scepter; in the version Gilliam uses (the one owned by the NPG), she is holding an orb and olive branch.

The only "couple" image in this sequence appears to be Elizabeth I and a courtier, perhaps Leicester (Robert Dudley), and they are likely dancing in the original engraving. This is not unlike an engraving (owned by

Oxford University) depicting the Queen and Edward de Vere (1550–1604), where he carries the Sword of State before her. Similarities include his stance—his legs are planted wide—and her dress, which trails behind in both works. Either image could have been inspired by the other, of course.

Lastly, the flying clergyman appears to be a Pope (maybe Paul II) or a Holy Roman Emperor, as both were depicted with the cross-orb and scepter, symbols of power and authority.

Monarch Airlines had been in business since 1967, headquartered in Luton, and would have been the type of airline that most British vacationers heading to the warmer continental destinations (Ibiza, Mallorca) would have flown. (See the Tourist in Ep. 19 for more on these package trips.) Monarch's only operating planes during this period were prop-driven Bristol 175s (from the early 1950s), certainly qualifying as "vintage" in the jet age.

"smashing bloke" — ("The Piranha Brothers") Even toward the end of the brothers' freedom, police could find very few people who would testify against the Krays, relying on the testimony of one henchman who had cut a deal with prosecutors. Their status as local heroes would be reaffirmed over and over again (thanks to a fascinating combination of fear and charity work), with people like Flanagan (Eps. 7, 11–13, 22) lobbying for their release, and by their well-attended funerals.

"Social Security" — ("The Ministry of Silly Walks") Actually, public spending typically consumed around 40 percent of the British government's total annual public spending during this period. In 1970–1971, for example, the total came to 42.7 percent of the gross domestic product (GDP). Health spending sat at about 9 percent GDP in 1969; education spending reached about 11 percent in the same year; and defense spending fell to about 13 percent in 1969. Defense spending in the UK had fallen as a percentage of GDP every year since 1955. (See "UK Postwar Spending.") The demands of the welfare state ("cradle to grave" coverage) precluded spending monies (to any extravagant degree) on areas outside of social security, health, etc.

"Southwark" — ("The Piranha Brothers") A borough in Greater London. Historically, since Southwark was south of the City of London and across the Thames, the long arm of the City's royal law didn't reach into its dark recesses. Public playhouses not licensed by the court and many businesses and inns—both nefarious and legitimate—set up shop within sight of London without having to answer to the City's authority. Southwark was also the location of Chaucer's Tabard Inn, where his pilgrims began their journey in *Canterbury Tales*. See Ackroyd.

There is no Kipling Road in Southwark, but there is one not far away in Warwick.

"special delivery" — ("New Cooker Sketch") This sketch is evolving into a satire on Britain's postwar socialist bureaucracy, and will soon escalate—a Python trope—into absurdity. The end result is that Mrs. Pinnet (Jones) has to agree to a new name (Crump-Pinnet) and even assisted suicide before her stove can be hooked up—notions to which she eagerly accedes. (Cf. the "Live Organ Donor" sketch in the feature film *Meaning of Life*.) The cooker sketch here has no real ending, and it can't, since the bureaucratic labyrinth also has no end. This is made clear later in the episode as "Silly Walks" begins, with the Minister (Cleese) walking past Mrs. Pinnet's home and the long line of brown-coated gas men still waiting in the street. Gilliam (with Palin) will revisit this endless, fatal paperwork scenario in his 1985 film *Brazil*.

"Spiny Norman" — ("The Piranha Brothers") Ronnie Kray was prone to fits of manic behavior and prolonged periods of meditation (or catatonia), and lived much of his later life in a prison mental hospital. He is believed to have suffered from undiagnosed paranoid schizophrenia. Cf. the description by Sir Isaiah Berlin in his *Hedgehog and Fox* (1953) of the so-called hedgehog mentality in life, or "those who relate everything to a single central vision." (Originally, from Archilochus: "The fox knows many things—the hedgehog one big one.") The realization of a giant, malevolent hedgehog might account for this vision for Dinsdale. Also, see the earlier entry "Dinsdale" for a well-publicized connection between an actual man named Dinsdale and a fruitless search for the fabled Loch Ness Monster.

A few years earlier Soviet premier Nikita Khrushchev had told the *New York Times*: "If you start throwing hedgehogs under me, I shall throw a couple of porcupines under you" (7 Nov. 1963).

Lastly, this name (Spiny Norman) might be an oblique reference to Sergeant *Norman* Pilcher, the man who arrested a number of Python associates, including members of The Beatles and the Rolling Stones and jazz saxophonist Tubby Hayes (1935–1973) on drug possession charges. See Ep. 5 ("Police Raid"), and the entry for "Harry 'Snapper' Organs" (above) in this episode. Pilcher would later find himself in the dock, accused of manufacturing arrest evidence, giving false evidence, manipulating official paperwork, etc. In 1973 he would be sentenced to four years gaol for perjury.

"Stoats, Brian" — ("The Piranha Brothers") This name seems to be an amalgam of Pythonisms, including the oft-used first name Brian, and a reappearance of the "stoat," which was mentioned in Ep. 6.

"support" — ("The Ministry of Silly Walks") A reference to the massive waste attributed to Whitehall and the government in general and discussed ad infinitum in the newspapers and periodicals of the period. Millions and even billions of pounds were being overspent annually thanks to ineffective oversight policies in the Civil Service, overlapping ministerial areas, and outright fraud. (See Dixon for more.)

One month before the 1964 General Election, Labour leader Harold Wilson laid out his government's priorities, should they be elected after five years of Conservative rule. The second plank mentioned at a Transport House briefing was meant to address economic issues, and included the

> creation of a Minister of Economic Affairs to coordinate physical, economic, and industrial planning [that] would enable the Chancellor [of the Exchequer] to get on with two jobs in which Tory Chancellors had been remiss: Tax reform *and the effective control over waste in Government expenditure.* (italics added; "Tax Reform and Check on Waste," *Times*, 12 Sept. 1964: 8)

Labour would successfully return to power on 15 October 1964. James Callaghan (1912–2005) would be named Chancellor in October 1964.

"Investment grants" had also become significant sources of easy money for what turned out be—in many instances—dubious business ventures. Also see the editorial in the October 1967 *Management Today* where the real problem blamed on Wilson and his economic policies is termed a "stopped economy" (18).

• T •

"tarts" — ("The Piranha Brothers") For a thesaurus-like list of other names for prostitutes, see Ep. 33, the "Biggles Dictates a Letter" sketch. Vercotti's (Palin) other work—representing Ron Obvious (Jones) in his ultimately deadly record-setting attempts—he also consistently characterizes as legitimate and above board.

"tatty office" — ("The Piranha Brothers") This same type of cheap restaurant/office setting is carried over from Ep. 13, where Vercotti runs a low-end restaurant in Soho, a clip joint with girls and pornographic films in the back. The décor is very similar to a contemporary Margaret Belsky cartoon panel, as well, featuring two Kray-types in an equally tatty restaurant discussing the just-finished Old Bailey trial (*Sun*, 6 Mar. 1969). See the British Cartoon Archive.

"This Week" — (PSC; "The Piranha Brothers") Popular and long-running Associated Rediffusion and then Thames TV show *This Week* (AR, 1956–1968; Thames, 1968–1992).

The music is actually not from a TV show, but is a portion of "Karelia Suite Op. II, Intermezzo" by Sibelius, performed by the Danish State Radio Symphony Orchestra (WAC T12/1,417).

"Times" — ("Tobacconists [Prostitute Advert]") The *Times of London* or just the *Times* was the flagship British newspaper, established in 1788. This would have been the paper of choice for many monied Conservatives of the day, including the City Gent type portrayed here by Cleese.

"Trubshawe" — (link out of "The Ministry of Silly Walks") Featuring the return of Zatapathique and Trubshawe as Frenchmen (Cleese and Palin) speaking "rubbish" or jabberwock French. See notes to Ep. 2. Note here that Zatapathique is still a celebrity "poof." The transference of the mustache still gives the bearer/wearer voice, or the floor, as it were.

"tv quizmaster" — ("The Piranha Brothers") Perhaps a reference to the scandal-ridden American television quiz show industry after the 1958 revelation that *Twenty-One* (1956–1958) contestant Charles van Doren was provided answers prior to the show.

• U •

usual grey suit and floral tie — (PSC; "The Piranha Brothers") The uniform of the "current affairs" television presenter, and which was common from network to network (BBC, ATV, etc.). This harks well back to the beginnings of the BBC, when Lord John Reith (1889–1971) made sure his announcers wore dinner jackets in the evenings (*Eyewitness 1920–29*, "John Reith Joins the BBC").

• V •

"various well-known London locations" — ("The Piranha Brothers") These shots are still photographs that Gilliam would have secured during production of the show (likely from un-attributable collections), with an enormous Spiny Norman emerging from hiding in each location, calling for Dinsdale. None of the photos was officially requested (meaning copyright/use fees assessed) in the production material for this episode.

The photographed locations are, in order of appearance: Trafalgar Square, the Houses of Parliament, Buckingham Palace, an older photo of Ludgate Hill (with St. Paul's in the distance), and the Chessington Zoo setting where the episode started.

"Vercotti" — ("The Piranha Brothers") Himself a shakedown artist from Ep. 8, Vercotti (Palin) here assumes the role of little fish in a big pond, just as frightened of the Piranhas as anyone else. This scenario is also reinforced by Jones as he describes Kray thugs muscling out other thugs in the quest for gangland control of the East End.

• W •

"Welsh accent" — ("The Piranha Brothers") Undoubtedly a comment on Jones's own "high-pitched Welsh accent." Goon Harry Secombe (1921–2001) was also Welsh-born, and the show poked fun at him often.

"What does that mean?" — ("Tobacconists [Prostitute Advert]") The final line links this sketch, structurally, to the "Nudge, Nudge" sketch, both featuring almost identical punchlines. The shabby customer (Idle), then, is only aware of innuendo and connotation, and fails to appreciate the *literal* meanings of the words and phrases. Other characters in the Python world—like Mr. Pewtey (Palin)—miss the literality of words, inflections, and situations, meaning that the most outrageous things can happen to and around him without much effect. This set-up and pay-off structure, then, is more reminiscent of the comedy the Pythons were ostensibly moving away from, including Morecambe and Wise, Monkhouse and Goodwin, *Benny Hill*, and much of *I'm Sorry I'll Read That Again*.

"What's all this then?" — ("The Piranha Brothers") Along with "Hello, hello!," this phrase has become the standard cry of an arriving policeman in *FC*. Phrase perhaps borrowed from Wodehouse, among others, in works like *The Code of the Woosters* (1938), where a constable appears as from nowhere to question Bertie (20). The latter ("Hello, hello!") is a borrow from Peter Sellers as he plays a Bow Street Runner in *The Goon Show*, "The Last Smoking Seagoon" (28 Jan. 1960).

Whitehall — (PSC; "The Ministry of Silly Walks") This area is and was home to a number of official offices, including the Admiralty Building, the Ministry of Defence, the Department of Health, and even 10 Downing Street, where the Prime Minister still maintains his official residence.

The Minister (Cleese) is in fact walking along in front of 12 Whitehall, specifically just south of the confluence of Pall Mall, Cockspur, Northumberland, and Strand avenues (just south of Trafalgar Square). Behind him can be seen the Whitehall Theatre (14 Whitehall), the Old War Office buildings complex on the east side of the street, and Big Ben's tower in the distance to the south. Confirming beyond a doubt the location and time, the Whitehall Theatre's marquee can just be glimpsed, advertising the rather scandalous *Pyjama Tops* "nudie" revue that occupied the theater space 1969–1974.

Though the Pythons often indicate they are shooting in one place and then make do somewhere else (e.g., Norwich Castle for Edinburgh Castle), there are obviously some locations that are so completely iconic that shadow locations won't do. The very recognizable Whitehall is one, and so is Trafalgar Square (Eps. 26 and 35), Television Centre (Ep. 32), and the Houses of Parliament (Ep. 20).

"win 'em all" — ("The Piranha Brothers") Chapman here delivers a very campy, stereotypically gay performance, complete with makeup and swishy affectations. The authority figure—here a policeman—is again depicted as a latent homosexual, and more, the indication is that the stern, manly figure he cuts in public is merely a well-staged, costumed, and powdered burlesque.

working-class sitting room — (PSC; "New Cooker Sketch") There is obviously a common picture in the mind of both the Pythons and the production personnel for the show, one so understood that just "working-class sitting room" and "G-Plan" suffice for description in the printed scripts. This understanding indicates a common background—as children, they grew up in the same postwar Britain in the same kinds of housing developments sitting on the same furniture, obviously, and they've even watched the same BBC adaptations and serials. For a more Northern description of this type of setting, see Ep. 2, the "Working-Class Playwright" sketch.

"wrong house" — ("New Cooker Sketch") First, the "in the wrong house" trope is heard earlier in the Goons' "Silver Doubloons" episode (21 Jan. 1960):

> Minnie (Milligan): I thought our piano was stolen.
> Crun (Sellers): What?
> Minnie: Stolen! Stolen!
> Crun: It was, Min! *(to piano tuner)* Pardon me, sir, I don't want to worry you but we haven't got a piano. You're probably supposed to be tuning the one next door.
> Tuner (Secombe): I *am* next door.
> Crun: Min!
> Minnie: Ah! What?
> Crun: We're in the wrong house again! (audio transcription)

Second, all this visual absurdity—which should, normally, have led into a sketch featuring Pinnet

(Jones) and the visitor (Gilliam)—is instead immediately undercut by the announcement she may be in the wrong house. A clever variation on the "wrong number" scenario. This is also a comment—again, along the lines of the housing situation in Greater London and country towns with council housing—on the indistinguishable nature of terraced houses, row houses, and the ubiquitous apartment tower blocks so prominent in the suburbs.

These terrace houses became popular (at least for councils and builders) in the early Victorian period, when myriad textile mills were popping up around the country and worker housing was needed. The homes were nearly identical to facilitate rapid and far-flung construction, allowing for a consistent use of materials and construction methods. The result, of course, was row after row of homes virtually indistinguishable not only from each other, but from similar tracts in neighboring villages and counties. The opening shot of the "Miracle of Birth: The Third World" section in *Meaning of Life* depicts a Yorkshire version of these endless tracts. Rows of these houses can also be seen in the backgrounds of the "Undertakers' Film" sections of Ep. 11, much of which was shot in Bradford.

Episode 15: "The Spanish Inquisition"

Man-powered flight; "And now . . ." Man on a rocky beach, and "It's" Man; *Animation: Titles* (silly Cleese v/o); **Jarrow—New Year's Eve 1911: The Spanish Inquisition**; BBC walk-on role link; Jokes and novelties salesman; "What's the punchline?"; "Borrow your head for a bit of animation?": *Animation: The Can-Can diversion, Civil War cannons, "We are not amused," and nudes with faucets*; Tax on "thingy"; Vox Pops on taxation; Photos of Uncle Ted; Return of The Spanish Inquisition "that makes a smashing film"; Torturing an Old Woman with "soft cushions" and "comfy chair"; *Animation: "I confess"*; "The Semaphore Version of *Wuthering Heights*," "*Julius Caesar* on an Aldis lamp," "*Gunfight at OK Corral* in Morse Code," and "The Smoke Signal Version of *Gentlemen Prefer Blondes*"; Court scene—Charades; Sentencing a naughty judge; The Spanish Inquisition, late to the Old Bailey

• A •

AA sign — (link out of "The Spanish Inquisition") The UK's automotive association. The sign constructed for the sketch is meant to be identical to the recognizable, yellow-and-black AA signs seen on UK roads since the 1930s. See the entry for "AA" in Ep. 1, "Picasso/Cycling Sketch," as well as Mrs. S.C.U.M.'s (Jones) questions about a dreadful post-apocalyptic world without an AA in Ep. 44, the "Mr. Neutron" sketch.

This sign is posted on a wall in Cairn Avenue where it meets Disraeli Road and Lammas Park Gardens. The BBC truck is driving between Pitzhanger Manor and 49 Elers Road, where Reg (Chapman) will answer the door in the following sketch.

"Aldis lamp" — ("*Julius Caesar* on an Aldis Lamp") A naval signaling lamp employing Morse code signals.

animation — (link out of "The Spanish Inquisition") In this animation, Reg's (Chapman) head is removed and used for the setting, and his right iris is eventually "borrowed" (in the animated diegetic world) for use as a cannonball. Gilliam's animations are often built on borrowing—on the dismembering and re-membering of the human figure, specifically. Recognizable faces from the world of politics (Nabarro, Heath), sport or entertainment (W.G. Grace, Greer Garson) are given new, often grotesque bodies and/or abilities in Gilliam's world, and normal, unknown folk from traditional family photos also appear. The wholeness of the human body is the expectation, and Gilliam takes every opportunity he can to dismember and make strange and monstrous that formerly sanctified figure. This "body horror" phenomena isn't new to Gilliam or the Pythons, having crept into feature films (Hammer horror, bloody Peckinpah Westerns, George Romero's *Night of the Living Dead*, etc.) and on the nightly news as the color images from the day's fighting in Vietnam was reported.

The music in this particular animation is from Offenbach's "Orpheus in the Underworld" (WAC T12/1,437).

Additional identifiable animated scenes:

1. The background behind Reg's head in the pram is another borrow from Jan Vredeman de Vries's book *Perspective*, already used in the titles for season 1. This is Plate 15, and is a reverse-image from the original. The plinth on which Reg's head is set holds a fountain in the original work; the balance of the perspective drawing is then recolored. As with the other de Vries images Gil-

liam has used, he alters them slightly, but doesn't bother, for example, to remove the "orison" lines or any other perspective lines de Vries included as teaching guides. (De Vries's work will be seen again in this episode during the "I Confess" animated sequence.) Interesting that with a single, borrowed image Gilliam can create a deep, inhabitable world his characters can populate.

2. There are about a dozen separate American Civil War photographic images that Gilliam uses in the series, representing both the North and the South combatants. The first was seen in the opening credits for this second season (the head of Gen. Logan, borrowed from *DWF*, 383). Gilliam most likely used the book *Divided We Fought* (edited by David Donald; Macmillan, 1952), a collection of war photos and minor text. *This is the only book that features **all** of the Civil War photos Gilliam employed*, though individually and in small groups they can be found in many other books.

   The first image is a composite of two Civil War photos and a Gilliam foreground landscape. The background image is of a Union encampment, with an officer walking across (carrying Reg's eye). The background is a reversed image of Camp Northumberland, Pennsylvania, and was taken in 1861, according to the National Archives and Records Administration (NARA). This image can be found on page 33 of *Divided We Fought*. The walking soldier is Lt. Col. William B. Hyde, of the 9th New York Cavalry (*DWF*, 47). Gilliam used Hyde's full-length portrait photo for this scene, and in place of gloves he carries Reg's eye. The following artillery image is taken from a James Gibson photo (also not accounted for in the WAC records). The c. 1862 photo (known as "Capt. John C. Tidball and Staff, Battery A, 2nd U.S. Artillery") has been reversed and retouched (the cannon faces toward the right in the original image). Gilliam has made the cannon barrel larger, and he's slightly tinted bits of the uniforms (69). The cannon is fired as a transition to the next scene.

   The image following is cobbled together from several sources, including a scale drawing of a period cannon, one of the horsed aides-de-camp to General Joseph Hooker, Capt. William L. Candler (he gives the order to fire; photo taken c. 1863 in Virginia), and a seated group of medicos, including Dr. Jonathan Letterman (1824–1872), taken in Virginia in 1862. Candler's photo is found on page 151 of *DWF*, while Letterman is on page 134. The two figure photos are also reversed from their normal orientation.

3. This is a late photo of Queen Victoria. The Goons also used the "We are not amused" gag in their "Crystal Palace" episode. This scenario will reappear in Ep. 41, when a more Germanic Victoria visits the poetry reading, Bertie's coffin in tow.

"answer the door in a sketch" — ("The Spanish Inquisition") In Ep. 10, Lord Hill (of Luton) has sent a letter requesting Man (Palin) appear as a walk-on in the "Bank Robber (Lingerie Shop)" sketch. Every week as *Flying Circus* episodes were taped and filmed, walk-ons and assorted actors/production personnel were needed.

As they leave the mill owner's manor house after the "Spanish Inquisition" sketch has slowed to a halt, the BBC Man and Reg (Cleese and Chapman) are actually outside the Pitzhanger Manor House at the edge of Lammas Park, where the BBC truck awaits. This Lammas Park area has been and will continue to be used for exterior shooting, mostly due to its close proximity to Ealing TFS.

In BBC records for this episode, additional hires (i.e., speaking or active parts) include Marjorie Wilde, Pat[ricia] Prior (*Doctor Who; Softly Softly*), Pam Saire (*Softly Softly*), and Philip Howard (*Softly Softly; Dixon of Dock Green*). Walk-ons for the episode—some who would also have significant film and TV appearances elsewhere—were Maurice Quick (*Dixon of Dock Green; Softly Softly*), Cy Town (who would go on to play a Storm Trooper in *Star Wars* [1977]), David Melbourne (*Softly Softly*), Eden Fox (appeared with Chapman in *Doctor in the House*), Jim Delaney (*Emma*), Anne Jay, Derek Glynne (*Brett: Investment—Long Term*), and Bill Johnston (WAC T12/1,437). Marjorie Wilde (an actual mature woman) will have the largest part in this episode, playing the Dear Old Lady in the "Spanish Inquisition" sketch.

appropriate film music throughout — (PSC; "The Semaphore Version of *Wuthering Heights*") This sweeping music seems to be a version of "The World Turns" by L. Stevens (WAC T12/1,437).

• B •

"Belsize Park" — ("Court Scene [Charades]") Belsize Park is located in Camden, part of Greater London. Idle visited a flat in the Camden area during part of the run of the series, in Camden High Street, specifically, at/above World's End. See notes to Ep. 19 for more.

"Biggles" — ("The Spanish Inquisition") Well-known children's book aviator character. Group Captain Biggles is featured in Eps. 10 and 33, in both places played by Chapman. Other obviously significant characters (based on myriad appearances in *FC*) from the Pythons' collective youth include panto characters like Long John Silver, Dobbins, and Puss in Boots.

Black Dyke Mills Band — (PSC; "The Spanish Inquisition") A brass band organized around 1833 in Queensbury, West Yorkshire, and featuring a French horn player who happened to own the Black Dyke Mills, John Foster. The music used here is Liszt's Hungarian Rhapsody No. 2, and it is actually performed by the Black Dyke Mills band (WAC T12/1,437). For more on the mill and band, see the entry for John's father, "William Foster" at *ODNB*.

"borrow your head for a piece of animation" — (link out of "Jokes and Novelties Salesman") This is precisely what Gilliam has been doing since the show's inception, and usually without asking or attribution. (See "*animation*" note above for more.) The BBC's records for the show almost always indicate when a piece of music or photograph or a bit of film stock is used outside of an animated sequence, but *not* when they were to be part of Gilliam's animations. Gilliam would use photocopies from the pages of art and history books, stills from popular and educational films, and even actual photographs of real people, living and dead, and the BBC never seems to have demanded a copyright review for any of these items. Some quite famous (and therefore recognizable) heads seen in *FC* include Venus (from the Botticelli painting), W.G. Grace (of cricket fame), and Queen Victoria.

Gilliam would get into trouble on at least one occasion for including material without permission or attribution, however. In December 1972 the animation company Halas and Batchelor (*Animal Farm* [1955]) complained in writing that an animated sequence in Ep. 35 contained a soundtrack element taken from a German television spot created (and owned) by H&B. The letter asks how and why such a borrowing could have happened (WAC T12/1,413). Rather than contest the matter, BBC higher-ups simply decided to edit the jingle out before it was rebroadcast (WAC T12/1,428).

Breugel — (PSC; link out of "Photos of Uncle Ted [Spanish Inquisition]") The portion of the famous painting depicted here is Pieter Brueghel's (the Elder) *Triumph of Death* (c. 1562), which is in the collection of the Museo del Prado, Madrid, Spain. Brueghel is a Flemish/Dutch Renaissance painter who will be mentioned again when his skating characters cause a "terrible bloody din" in the "Art Gallery Strike" sketch (Ep. 25). The section of the painting depicted is the upper right corner of the large painting.

"bugger" — (link out of "Court Scene [Charades]") A fascinating possibility arises from the inclusion of this invective, beyond its sodomitical context: "Bugger" was actually a specialized term used to describe an Albigenses heretic in the fourteenth century (*OED*). The Albigenses felt that marriage and procreation were grievous sins, meaning sexual intercourse where fertilization is impossible might be more acceptable—buggery, then, becoming the sin of choice, and one that might be on the lips of the Church's Inquisitors.

Used here for the first time in the series (before being heard again in Ep. 21), the word has a long and controversial history in British dramatic production. Over and over again in the late 1950s the term "bugger" and its variations ("buggery," "bogger," etc.) were consistently penciled through by the British Board of Film Censors (BBFC) and the Master of Revels for deletion from films and plays, respectively. As late as 1966 and the "British New Wave" film *Saturday Night and Sunday Morning* and the swinging 1960s film *Alfie* (and subsequent staged plays for each) the term was being elided, no matter the eventual rating or venue. It wouldn't be until *Up the Junction* (1967) that the BBFC would allow the use of the term "bugger" in British film and, somewhat coincidentally, full frontal nudity the following year in Lindsay Anderson's *If . . .* (1968).

"burnt at the stake" — ("Court Scene [Charades]") This type of punishment hasn't been practiced since the late eighteenth century, and by then only after the victim had been strangled first. Hanging had been the punishment of choice in England since at least the Romans went home in the fifth century, but later boiling and beheading also became popular. England was well known during the eighteenth century for attaching the death penalty to literally hundreds of offenses, many quite minor (pickpocketing, poaching), so the pseudo-contempt of court charge here ("do you for heresy")—and a religious charge at that—actually isn't out of bounds given historical precedent.

• C •

"Cardinal Fang" — ("The Spanish Inquisition") In *Oliver Twist*, Mr. Fang is a blustering magistrate caught up in his own authority and importance. *Fang* was also the name of a publication Gilliam contributed to while attending Occidental College in California.

"cat of nine tails" — ("Court Scene [Charades]") Under South African law during this period, corporal punishment was not only legal, but used quite liberally. One popular method was caning, originally reserved for younger offenders, and which was officially administered in 1968–1969 on more than 5,200 separate occasions in South Africa. The cat of nine tails (also "cat-o'-nine-tails") was for adult males, primarily, and was the corporal punishment weapon of choice in the nineteenth century. Public opinion (domestic and international) in the war years led to a reduction in its implementation, and it's believed that 1958 saw its last use, at least officially.

"Central Criminal Court" — ("Court Scene [Charades]") Located in the Old Bailey, City of London, which features prominently in relation to the final ("Oh, bugger!") scene of "The Spanish Inquisition."

"chartered accountancy a more interesting job" — ("Tax on Thingy") This is one of the few times that accountants—consistent targets in *FC*—are given something to hope for. Earlier iterations of these accountancy mentions feature timid, hopelessly oneiric, sexually frustrated/twisted types. In Ep. 10 there is even a call for intervention to save anyone falling into the inescapable trap of chartered accountancy. The popularity of this good-natured niggling was confirmed when an Irish MP asked for a script for quotation purposes in Parliament. See notes to Ep. 12 for more.

"cheap labour" — ("Court Scene [Charades]") There is a typically condemning cartoon (by David Low) in the *Manchester Guardian* (7 May 1954) linking Britain to South Africa economically—as Britain publicly decried the South African policies—through continuing investment and ownership of South African interests, and especially the abundant "cheap labour" available and utilized by British interests. See the British Cartoon Archive. Through the 1960s, and as African countries chafed under colonial rule and began agitating for freedoms and some slice of the economic pie, the "cheap labour" siren sign was somewhat diminished.

"comfy chair" — ("The Spanish Inquisition") This is perhaps an unintentional irony, since the Pythons were probably meaning to create humor via incongruity—viz., torture by soft pillow and comfy chair. During the days of the various Inquisitions, the term used when identified heretics were turned over (from church) to secular authorities was "relaxed," so that the church would have no blood on its hands (*OED*).

courtroom — ("Court Scene [Charades]") This courtroom set-up and the earlier drawing room for the "Spanish Inquisition" sketch are much larger than the usual *FC* sets, which is why much or all of this episode's interiors were shot on the Ealing TFS stages, and not at BBC Television Centre.

"CS" — ("Jokes and Novelties Salesman") CS gas is a riot gas invented in 1928 (*OED*). The reference here might be attributable to the very recent discovery (Autumn 1969) of a shipment of CS gas to South Africa—then enduring an arms embargo for its human rights abuses—a shipment that had managed to slip past the Foreign Office before being identified as containing banned items (*PE*, 31 July 1970: 16).

Also, significant concern had been voiced when it was learned that British police units had requested and been issued CS gas supplies as early as summer 1968, ostensibly to assist in quelling the sometimes violent protests and street riots that erupted in May 1968 ("British Police and CS," *Times*, 29 June 1968: 3).

• D •

"Des O'Connor . . . Tom Jones" — (link into "Jokes and Novelties Salesman") These comments indicate the "older" generation of music and performer to which this "arty" type is attracted.

Des O'Connor (b. 1932) appeared in *The Des O'Connor Show* (1963–1968), and with Morecambe & Wise (beginning in 1961), creating more familiar, traditional comedy and variety shows than the Pythons may have appreciated (and would have been rebelling against), which is why the "arty" BBC man would prefer the genre. O'Connor also appeared on *The Ed Sullivan Show* and in Las Vegas, making a fairly successful ripple across the pond.

Rolf Harris (b. 1930) starred in *The Rolf Harris Show* (1967), and is a TV presenter, singer, painter, and cartoonist, and also presented animal shows (*Rolf's Amazing World of Animals*), art shows, and children's shows. Again, the family-friendly nature of Harris probably put him on this list of Python TV pabulum.

Tom Jones (b. 1940) is a Welsh-born pop singer and entertainer then and still very popular with adult women and middle-of-the-road-trendy. During the mid-to-late 1960s he sported the fashionable Edwardian look (tight pants, billowy shirts), and appeared in his own very popular TV show *This Is Tom Jones* (1969–1971).

This link (the BBC man and Reg) is listed as being shot on 1 June 1970 at *39 Elers Road*, Ealing, a continuation of Lammas Park Rd. (WAC T12/1,416). This listed address was either a mistake or they simply changed shooting locations on the fly, which happened occasionally. Reg (Chapman) gets into the BBC truck at the front of Pitzhanger Manor; the truck is then seen turning on a bend in Cairn Avenue toward Disraeli Road (and Lammas Park Gardens), before coming to a stop at the next location, *49* Elers Road, not 39 Elers Road. These are all in the same general area surrounding Walpole Park in Ealing.

"Diabolical Laughter" — ("The Spanish Inquisition") This "superimposed caption" motif—a graphic intertitle commenting on the narrative action "on the fly"—will be revisited in Ep. 17, when the burning apartment block (made to resemble Ronan Point) image is tempered with a "Satire" caption. This intertitling allows for another level of humor and even meaning, and will appear throughout the series.

Dick Barton music — (PSC; link out of "Court Scene [Charades]") This theme, "Devil's Gallop" performed by Charles Williams, is borrowed from the *Dick Barton* radio and TV shows. The Goons also used the tune occasionally, and the Pythons have already employed its recognizability for Ep. 12. See notes for Ep. 12 for more on the theme.

DJ — (PSC; "Man-Powered Flight") "Dinner Jacket." This was the uniform of the BBC announcer, especially early in the BBC's life under first director general John C.W. Reith (1922–1938). As a BBC Announcer about to be thrown into the sea in Ep. 3, Cleese wears the prototypical DJ attire.

• E •

"emigrating . . . South Africa" — ("Court Scene [Charades]") The British empire had assumed control of the Cape in 1806 from the Dutch, and in 1910 the four colonies on the Cape were merged to form South Africa. In 1948 a rightist, anti-British coalition party—the Afrikaner National Party—won the general election, and the fifty years of apartheid policy began. The new regime was repressive by nature and necessity, as well as authoritarian, as the majority black population needed to be kept in check.

By 1970, when this episode was written and recorded, South Africa had become a republic, having left the Commonwealth in 1961. Political, economic, and familial ties and relations remained, of course, sometimes unofficially, between South Africa and Great Britain. So even as England moved away from authoritarian government and criminal punishment at home, South Africa was becoming all the more authoritarian, which would have given judges like Chapman depicts a clear choice between the two.

It's worth noting that during the permissive 1960s there were many letters to the editor bemoaning the lack of corporal punishment in England's schools, and even movements in parliament to reintroduce caning, for example, as a way to deal with the new pre-teen and teenage delinquency in schools and in the court systems. A report released in 1968 indicated that youth crime in Cardiff had risen precipitously in the twelve months since caning was outlawed, and many (adults) were clamoring for its reinstatement ("Boys Misbehave after Cane Ban," *Times*, 24 Feb. 1968: 4).

As early as 1948 political cartoons began appearing in British newspapers regarding the nationalist political agenda in South Africa, and its attractiveness to many hard-line Conservatives in the UK. One such cartoon from the 27 June 1950 *Daily Express* features a prim, Conservative, upper-middle-class woman who laments: "I can tell you that but for the fact that Labour got in by only a *tiny* majority, I should have emigrated to S. Africa." In other words, if Labour had won handily, she was off to the more politically conservative former colony.

Tony Judt reports that in the immediate postwar years (1946–1948) more than 150,000 Brits emigrated to (predominantly white) Commonwealth countries, mostly due to the privations demanded by the austerity programs as the welfare state struggled through its infancy (163).

Epic film music — ("The Spanish Inquisition") According to WAC files, this music is "Aggression" by Eric Towren, as played by the International Studio Orchestra (WAC T12/1,437).

Episode 15 — The second show of season 2 (BBC listing Series 2, Episode 2), recorded on 2 July 1970, and broadcast on 22 September 1970. This episode was recorded third in the second season, but broadcast second. Extras and walk-ons for this episode are listed above in the "answer the door in a sketch" entry.

"Et Tu Brute" — ("*Julius Caesar* on an Aldis Lamp") Famous line borrowed from Shakespeare's version of the life and death of Caesar (*Julius Caesar* 3.1.77).

The production that may have gotten the Pythons' minds turning in this absurd direction is the 1970 film production *Julius Caesar* starring Charlton Heston as Marc Antony, Jason Robards as Brutus, and John Gielgud (Ep. 33) as Caesar. The film was directed by Stuart Burge, and received scathing contemporary reviews for its acting, staging, directing, and even poor set construction and sound mix (see Roger Ebert's 1971 review, for one).

• F •

"fanatical devotion to the pope" — ("The Spanish Inquisition") The church men who carried out the work of the Inquisition may have less a devotion to the sitting pope—Sixtus IV, who was against the zealousness of the endeavor—than to their worldly sovereigns, Ferdinand and Isabella, and the eradication of any religious dissent within the ranks of the Holy Church itself.

"find something new to tax" — ("Tax on Thingy") The income tax rate in the UK was steep—above 90 percent during and just after the war at its highest, with monies going to the creation and support of the welfare state. Just a handful of the national taxation sources in the UK included: Income, National Insurance, Value Added Tax (VAT), Corporations, Fuel, Councils, Business, Stamps and Tobacco, Vehicle, Spirits and Beer/Cider, Inheritance, Capital Gains, Gaming, etc. In the late 1960s and early 1970s the tax pinch would have felt quite strong, with most middle-class incomes disappearing before paychecks could even be cut. (See Her Majesty's Treasury figures for more.)

In 1969 political cartoonist Keith Waite lampooned Chancellor of the Exchequer Roy Jenkins, who was the face of the Labour government seeking a new series of revenue streams. The cartoon text reads: "Wealth tax; 'Young people have far too much money these days,' says Chancellor, introducing licences for bicycles and tricycles, goldfish and white mice" (*Sun*, 1 Jan. 1969). See the British Cartoon Archive.

front door of the house — (PSC; link into "Joke and Novelties Salesman") The location here is 49 Elers Road, situated just across the street from Lammas Park and Walpole Park, Ealing. The homeowner who gave permission for the Pythons to shoot here (and later to come back and reshoot for the 1971 Montreux episode) was, according to the WAC records, a "Mrs. Korobro." This was a misspelling of "Korobko," as it turns out. Period phone directories list an "M. Korobko" living at 49 Elers Road, Ealing, between, at least, 1961 and 1983. (See T12/1,413 for the notation, and British Telephone books for the period.) The Ealing TFS is just a half-mile north and east of this location. This park setting (and surrounding area) has been used previously for portions of "Bicycle Repair Man" (Ep. 3), "Hell's Grannies" (Ep. 8), and "The Dull Life of a City Stockbroker" (Ep. 6). (See WAC T12/1,242.)

• G •

Gentlemen Prefer Blondes — ("*Julius Caesar* on an Aldis Lamp") Popular 1953 Howard Hawks film starring Marilyn Monroe.

Gunfight at the OK Corral — ("*Julius Caesar* on an Aldis Lamp") A 1957 Hollywood film directed by John Sturges, starring Burt Lancaster and Kirk Douglas (both Lancaster and Douglas will be referred to in the credits for *Timmy Williams* in Ep. 19).

Morse code is a dot-and-dash communication method developed first for the electric telegraph, but soon became useful as a silent, sight-only communication method for military purposes. In this scene, the gunfighters use Morse signalers instead of guns, delivering electronic dots and dashes instead of bullets. The means of communication has become the weapon, then, unlike the previous scene from *Julius Caesar*. By the time we transition to the Criminal Court for charades, the code (charades) will be employed for communication again, and not as a weapon.

• H •

"heresy" — ("The Spanish Inquisition") *OED*: "Theological or religious opinion or doctrine maintained in opposition, or held to be contrary, to the 'catholic' or orthodox doctrine of the Christian Church, or, by extension, to that of any church, creed, or religious system, considered as orthodox." In 1979, some would make similar charges against the Pythons for heretical utterances and blasphemous depictions in *Life of Brian*.

• I •

"I confess" animation — (*Animation: "I confess"*) There are three identifiable source elements here. First, the perspectival rooms. The beamed room where the constable has the chair repeatedly pulled from under him is "Plate 7" by Jan Vredeman de Vries (1527–c. 1604), from his 1604–1605 book *Perspective*. Gilliam has colored the image, and removed the doorways in the far background. He's also removed one window and wall at the immediate right, but left the rest of the walls and ceiling untouched (excepting tincture). He's left the dashed perspective lines, the "orison" (horizon) line, and de Vries's notations on the bottom of each column (they are lettered "a" through "f" in the original). The *Perspective* book was reprinted in 1968 by Dover, laid out just as de Vries's first edition, and it's likely Gilliam kept a copy near his work desk—he uses it in *Flying Circus* and *Holy Grail*.

The second room, where the "I confess" man is inflated/deflated repeatedly is also a retouched version of a de Vries plate, this time "Plate 28," and also from his teaching book on drawing with perspective. Plate 28 also features three persons for reference—one lying on the floor, one entering the door at the right, and one entering the door at the rear. Gilliam's removed them all, but left behind the numbering, 1 through 6, on the squares next to them, which had indicated relative height in perspective. He's gotten rid of the floor completely. Gilliam will go back to de Vries in *Holy Grail*, when the scribe, being disturbed by the "bloody weather," walks downstairs. That interior image is "Plate 39" from the same book. Most of the rest of the "found" material used in *Holy Grail* comes from period (Gothic) illuminated manuscripts. (See the author's book on *Monty Python and the Holy Grail* for more.)

Additionally, the "wandering hand woman" animation is from a nineteenth-century Cadbury's "Cocoa

Essence" advertisement. The advertisement first appeared in an 1892 edition of the weekly *The Black and White*. It's a full-page advertisement (with doctor testimonials about the product's medical benefits).

"I haven't had any for weeks" — ("Sentencing a Naughty Judge") This is the same excuse given earlier by Ken Shabby (Palin, Ep. 12) for wanting to marry the fair Rosamund (Booth) so quickly.

• J •

jarring chord — ("The Spanish Inquisition") The now-famous "jarring chord" used to herald the appearance of the Spanish Inquisition is from "Openings and Endings No. 2," by Robert Farnon (WAC T12/1,437).

"Jarrow" — (PSC; "The Spanish Inquisition") In Tyne, Jarrow is a northern industrial town, about 300 miles northeast of London. Jarrow had been significant in the strife-ridden, labor-management relationship since at least 1932, when "hunger" marchers left Jarrow for London to protest high unemployment, scarce unemployment benefits, and the "means test," which often further reduced a family's benefits.

The local *Newcastle Daily Chronicle* for 4 January 1912 reports with much chagrin the closing of the nearby Wardley Colliery (*not* the Jarrow Colliery), and notes that the Wardley Village built up around the colliery was already becoming a ghost town. The notice had gone out just two weeks earlier, right around Christmas, which would explain the Pythons placing this scene on New Year's Eve 1911 and New Year's Day 1912. According to *Whellan's 1894 Directory of County Durham*, *all* of the working villagers living in Wardley Village were miners.

• K •

"kids seem to like it" — (link into "Jokes and Novelties Salesman") This is a bit ironic, as Cleese was himself over thirty by this time (born in 1939), the age over which one became "untrustworthy" to the younger, hipper generation. This may be part of the reason Cleese was keen to move on from Monty Python much earlier than the others, leaving after the third season to prepare for his instructional video work as well as *Fawlty Towers* (1975–1978).

• L •

"life imprisonment" — ("Court Scene [Charades]") Capital punishment had been suspended throughout the UK in October–November 1965, for a period of five years. In mid-December 1969, when episodes from season 1 were still being broadcast, the suspension of the death penalty was made permanent, and executions were abolished for all crimes excepting piracy and high treason. During this same period in South Africa (especially after 1967), death penalty cases were being heard and carried out in record numbers.

"life-size winkle" — ("Jokes and Novelties Salesman") A "winkle" is a childish reference to the penis. In this same year, poet Ted Hughes (1930–1998) published this stanza from the epic poem *Crow*:

> O do not chop his winkle off
> His Mammy cried with horror
> Think of the joy will come of it
> Tomorrer and tomorrer
> Mamma Mamma.

Hughes was a West Yorkshire–born poet, coincidentally (see "One on't . . . treddle" below), and attended Pembroke College, Cambridge. Idle also graduated from Pembroke, as did earlier-mentioned folk including Peter Cook, Tim Brooke-Taylor, and Stephen Greenblatt (Ep. 27).

The tiny doll Mr. Johnson (Idle) calls "wicked willy" is also a troll doll, this one a much smaller version than the "naughty Humphrey" (see note below) he held up earlier.

• M •

mechanical wings — (PSC; "Man-Powered Flight") This Victorian inventor-type image was probably culled from actual history, specifically the attempts at man-powered flight (vehicles like the ornithopter) by men like Edward Purkis Frost. Frost's attempts in 1902 were using wings made to resemble a crow's, and were constructed of willow, silk, and feathers, according to the Science Museum of London. One wing of Frost's last ornithopter is on display in the museum, as is a scale replica of the Montgolfier brothers' hot air balloon (see Ep. 40). There are myriad surviving short films capturing failed attempts at early flight, and in Ep. 40 the Pythons offer a fin-de-siècle film piece featuring Barry Zeppelin (Jones) attempting balloon flight.

This flying/falling scene was shot at Seaford Cliffs, Seaford, on 9–10 June 1970 (WAC T12/1,416).

"MP . . . nem. con." — ("Tax on Thingy") Playing on the governmental affinity for acronyms. "MP" stands for Member of Parliament; "PM" is Prime Minister;

"AM" and "PM" are, of course, time indicators (L. *ante meridiem*, before noon, and L. *post meridiem*, afternoon); "LSD" is both an abbreviation for pounds, shilling, and pence, as well as the then-popular psychedelic drug Lysergic acid diethylamide; "PIB" is the Prices and Incomes Board; "PPS" is Parliamentary Private Secretary; "NBG" is "no bloody good"; and "nem. con." is an abbreviation of the L. *nemine contradicente*, "(with) no one contradicting" (*OED*).

This convoluted mess translates rather simply into "more money (or LSD) from the Prices and Income Board is needed."

"My old man said . . ." — ("The Spanish Inquisition") The beginning of this song is heard from Gilliam, though without the printed scripts it isn't clear at all what he's saying. The verse is borrowed from the Cockney English music hall song "My Old Man":

> My old man said "Follow the van,
> And don't dilly dally on the way,"
> Off went the van with me 'ome packed in it,
> I walked behind with me ol' cock linnet,
> But I dillied, I dallied,
> I dallied and I dillied,
> Lorst the van and don' know where to roam.
> And you can't trust the specials like an old time copper,
> When you can't find your way 'ome!

The song was made popular by Marie Lloyd (1870–1922), a Cockney English music hall entertainer later lauded by T.S. Eliot and others. She popularized the singing for and about common folk in England, much as Eliot and the Modernists would preach the significance of the mundane, of the everyday.

• N •

"naughty Humphrey" — ("Jokes and Novelties Salesman") This appears to be one of the "troll" dolls that became wildly popular in the mid-1960s. Mr. Johnson (Idle) will pull out another, slightly smaller troll doll toward the end of his threshold spiel. The "Humphrey" reference may be a nod to Python chum Humphrey Barclay (b. 1941), who will be mentioned again (by complete name) in Ep. 19. See notes to Ep. 19 for more on Barclay. This may also be a poke at the Tory MP Humphrey Atkins (1922–1996), who represented Merton and Morden, Greater London, 1955–1970.

Nurse — (PSC; "The Semaphore Version of *Wuthering Heights*") The Nurse is played by Jean Clarke, and the Old Man is played by Albert Ward. Call time for these shots (at Ealing TFS) was 1:30 p.m. on 29 May 1969 (WAC T12/1,242).

• O •

"Oh! Heathcliffe" — ("The Semaphore Version of *Wuthering Heights*") The dialogue here is not lifted directly from the novel or the film, but is an approximation of the heightened emotionality of the entire story, characters, setting, period, etc. The Pythons play the scene as if it's right out of the overtly melodramatic *East Lynne*, a much-staged (and filmed) nineteenth-century novel and stage play. (The play's oft-quoted line "Dead, and never called me mother" is voiced by The Big Cheese [Chapman] in Ep. 4.)

Lines like "Oh, Catherine" and "hark" do appear, but not in the overly emotional way the Pythons imply, and the following "You've been seeing Heathcliffe" exchange is completely fabricated.

"Old Bailey" — ("Court Scene [Charades]") The home of the Central Criminal Courts in London, the Old Bailey is near London's financial district and St. Paul's Cathedral. Judges are called "My Lord" (or "M'lud") in this court. Once again, Ximinez—asking for two, then three tickets—has confused his numbers.

These exterior shots were recorded on 3 June 1970 (WAC T12/1,416).

As the three Inquisitors finally exit the bus, Cardinal Fang (Gilliam) is carrying a copy of *The Encyclopedia of Witchcraft and Demonology* by Rossell Hope Robbins, first published in 1959.

"One on't . . . treddle" — ("The Spanish Inquisition") Delivered in a thick northern accent, and obviously not understood by the more affluent, patrician wife of the mill owner. The scene in D.H. Lawrence's *Sons and Lovers* (mentioned so prominently in the production notes and final script for Ep. 2) where a boy from the mine rushes to Mrs. Morel to tell of her husband's mine accident, is staged very much like this one (80–81). As for the accent, cf. one of Morel's very Northern rejoinders as he and his wife argue over his drinking and the constant frittering away of their money:

> "Then get out on it—it's mine. Get out on it!" he shouted. "It's me as brings th' money whoam, not thee. It's my house, not thine. Then *ger out on't—ger out on't*!" (21, italics added)

Clearly, the more angry Morel gets, the more "northern" his talk becomes, the façade of being married to a southern woman and yearning to talk like her evaporating with the heat of rage.

In the "Spanish Inquisition" introductory material here, not only does Lady Mountback (Cleveland) not understand Reg's (Chapman) northern accent, once he does translate into "proper" English for her, she still has no idea what the phrase means. It's clear this is a barefaced set-up for the narrative intrusion that is to follow (the Inquisitors), and that perhaps the absent Lord Mountback (ostensibly, the mill owner) was the intended recipient of this message. Yet another example of a failed communication in the Python world, this time—as is often the case—leading to reprisals and narrative punishments.

In a textile mill (cotton, for example), treddles (or treadles) were often foot-operated devices used "to produce reciprocating or rotary motion" (*OED*). Water, steam, and electric power would eventually take most of the treddle work from laborers.

opulent sitting room — (PSC; "The Spanish Inquisition") This room looks as if the BBC designers and propmasters simply watched *The Edwardians* (Granada, 1965), and copied the drawing room depicted in the episode "The Madras." (See Vahimagi's *British Television*.) Many of the interior sets and props used in the early *Benny Hill* episodes can be seen on various Python sets, since they were culling from the same prop department. Hill had only recently left BBC for Thames in 1969.

A source of significant and ongoing consternation for laborers, unions, and even government figures was the lavish lifestyle often enjoyed by mill and mine owners, especially in relation to the living and working conditions of their employees.

Much of the fire in the bellies of the "Angry Young Men" writers arose from this imbalance they saw in many northern towns. There are photos of many of these managers'/owners' homes and even castles in Colum Giles's *Yorkshire Textile Mills, 1770–1930*.

Finally, the size and layout of this set demanded that the show relocate to Ealing Television Film Studios (Ealing TFS) for most of this episode (WAC T12/1,437).

"our *three* weapons" — ("The Spanish Inquisition") This "counting problem" will reappear with King Arthur in *Monty Python and the Holy Grail* (1975).

• P •

"Phelps, Brian" — ("Court Scene [Charades]") British diver who won the bronze medal in the 1960 Rome Olympics. In 1970 (when this episode was written and recorded) Phelps was performing in a dive show at the Aquadrome on the Isle of Man. (Another Brian Phelps, also a Brit, won the three-metre springboard in the 1932 Perth Olympics.)

"playing fields" — ("Vox Pops") The need for additional playing fields may be a reference to the continuing destruction and vandalism of cricket fields across England by protestors angry that South Africa cricketers were being allowed to tour in the UK. The protestors would invade the pitches at night, often armed with shovels, and dig holes and furrows, generally destroying the playing surface. See other entries relating to South Africa for more.

"Program Planning" — (link out of "The Spanish Inquisition") The swipes at the mentality and creative acumen of BBC types appear over and over in *FC*. Cf. Ep. 38, where BBC Programme Planners are compared (unfavorably) with penguins and non-English-speaking foreigners. The fact that BBC Man (Cleese) can boast a university degree automatically disqualifies him for BBC creative employment. Later in the episode, the Programme Planner will read a missing punchline and decide to "make a series out of it."

Throughout the run of the first three seasons, at least, there is constant, simmering unrest over the scheduling for various *FC* episodes, as evidenced in memos in WAC files. The Pythons and their representatives ask for and sometimes demand clarification as to broadcast time slots, broadcast regions, the frustrations of opt-out agreements, and just changes—sometimes week-to-week—in what time slot the *FC* epsiodes would appear.

• R •

"rack" — ("The Spanish Inquisition") A frame-and-roller torture device where the vicitm is tied down and stretched, eventually suffering socket dislocation. In this case, of course, it's a dish drying rack. Inquisitor torture methods included water torture and hanging by the wrists. See the *Catholic Encyclopedia*—which offers a very thorough and surprisingly candid section on the Inquisition—for more.

Roman chariot race — (PSC; "*Julius Caesar* on an Aldis Lamp") This film footage is borrowed from P. Jenkinson's *Chariot Race* (WAC T12/1,417). Jenkinson (b. 1935), a film critic, writer (*Marty*), and television presenter, is lampooned by name and depiction in Eps. 23 and 33.

• S •

"Semaphore Code" — ("The Semaphore Version of *Wuthering Heights*") Semaphore is a code using differing positions of the arms (sometimes holding flags), with each separate position indicating a particular letter. (There is a very similar scene in Chuck Jones's 1942 cartoon *The Dover Boys of Pimiento U* where boy scouts, within talking distance of each other, use signal flags and semaphore instead.)

The code as delivered by the Pythons is accurate to a certain point, though that accuracy depends on the signaler. Instead of "Oh, Catherine," for example, Heathcliffe (Jones) signals just "Oh," twice, but accurately. Both Jones and Idle (the Husband) can signal with very close approximations to the actual code, erring only in precise placement of the flags, on occasion.

Catherine (Cleveland), however, was obviously just instructed to move her arms and flags as the mood of the scene struck her, as her first longer signal translates (letter-by-letter) "e, (incomprehensible signal), t/u, h, j, x, y, i" and a break, and then "o, e, (incomprehensible signal)." (The "incomprehensible signals" are those that represent flag positions used by the actors that are *not* part of semaphore code.) As part of Python's consistent "othering" of the female characters this may also be something of a slight—only the men in the scene either knew or learned the code for the sketch. This isn't much of a conjecture, as previous females (actual women, that is) have failed to understand facial cues, aural cues, and metaphoric language (Ep. 7), not been allowed to pun along with the boys (Ep. 8), and punished for uttering the unutterable word "mattress" (Ep. 4).

Continuing along this thesis, the Husband (Idle) fairly clearly signals "Catherine," transposing only a "p" for the "i" in the name, probably due to the speed of the signaling. He also emphasizes the break or stop after/between words (both flags held against the legs, pointing straight down to the ground), as if this were the visualization of yelling in semaphore. Catherine answers, spelling out "p, h (wrong hands again), y/v, r, k, r" and a break. Her husband then, using larger flags, starts her name again, and gets through "c, a, t, h, and e," before there is a cut to the baby crying (signaling gibberish, not "waaaagh"). The Nurse (Jean Clarke) signals "s" (not "sssh"), and the Old Man (Albert Ward) "z" and "h" for sleeping sounds.

The gibberish takes over from here all around. When asking if she's been seeing Heathcliffe, the Husband spells out "y, q, n, e, r, j, h/b, e, u" and a break. But it's Catherine who gets to rant on in meaningless (but entirely watchable) semaphore, for, as she paces around her husband, defending her relationship with Heathcliffe, she clearly spells out "o, q, j, r (break), r, z, h (break), r, j, j, r, r (break), r, f, r, (incomprehensible signal), r, f, r, j, r (break), r, z, r (break), r, j, r, f, r," and on and on. At this point her signaling is so fluid that each incomprehensible signal blends into the next, for complete gibberish, at least at the semaphoric level. It may just be, finally, that emotion wins out, and words (and letters threatening to become words) grow meaningless in the presence of such strong feelings, and with such iconic characters.

small hills, in rolling countryside — ("The Semaphore Version of *Wuthering Heights*") This looks to be filmed on or near Hookney Tor on Dartmoor, Devon, which is near Headland Warren, the long house where the building scenes were shot for this episode. The show was, according to WAC records, shooting in Devon for this episode (WAC T12/1,437).

"smashing film" — ("The Spanish Inquisition") Delivered like a film promo, bringing attention to the entertainment value of this tragic period in history, and reminding the viewer that television—even public television—is aware of and dependent on ratings/viewership. Cf. Ep. 25, where the *Black Eagle* film is triumphantly introduced, then fizzles out.

"Spanish Inquisition" — ("The Spanish Inquisition") Probably working from memory, the Pythons came close to historical accuracy in this introduction. Originally proposed to root out converted Jews, then Muslims, who might stray from the Catholic faith, the Inquisition was instigated in 1478 by Spanish heads of state Ferdinand and Isabella, and was actually opposed by Pope Sixtus IV. Sixtus consistently tried to limit the scope and ferocity of the endeavor, his "let and hindrance" being actively engaged. Eventually, however, all members of the Spanish church were potential subjects to Inquisitors' attentions. Tomas de Torquemada was the first well-known leader of the Inquisition. Why the inquisitors would be in the north of England in 1912 isn't explained. (See the *Catholic Encyclopedia* for more on the period and participants.)

The obvious influence on the Pythons of Voltaire (Ep. 2) and *Candide* may also have an influence here, as Candide describes the auto-da-fé (public trials) of the Spanish Inquisition in great detail and with equally great satire.

Interestingly, recent scholarship had called into question the actual scope and levels of violence perpetrated, with very low percentages of those called before Inquisitors reporting any torture at all. This, of course, wouldn't have prevented the Pythons from beefing up the violent details, anyway.

Lastly, this fixation on the Spanish Inquisition may be attributable to the then-current talk of so-called Spanish practices in industrial settings. Trade unions (the bane of PM Wilson's existence) could promote overstaffed shops, increased overtime, shorter hours, etc., which came to be known as "Spanish practices"—by definition good for the workers and unions, but bad for management. These unions would be accused of "holding to ransom" all of Great Britain by both the Wilson and then Heath administrations, especially as inflation began to erode consumer spending and saving abilities, but certain wages continued to spiral. For the Pythons, (worker) Reg's trouble communicating effectively with (owner) Lady Mountback leads to the appearance of the loud Spaniards, and they intrude (with varying degrees of effectiveness) throughout the episode.

"Stage, The" — ("Jokes and Novelties Salesman") *The Stage* is a weekly newspaper published since 1880, and focusing on the entertainment industry (and specifically theater) in the UK.

Stock . . . mill town — (PSC; "The Spanish Inquisition") This is a still photo of an unidentified industrial concern. The Pythons wouldn't, certainly, have spent much time making certain that their researcher provided them with an actual photo of a Jarrow-area mill, or even a mill at all, so an industrial-looking, turn-of-the-century photo obviously served the purpose. The cooling towers and the four-chimney structure in the background indicate that at least portions of this complex may have comprised a coal-fired power station. There is no record in the BBC archives for this episode of where the photo was obtained.

• T •

"tax all foreigners living abroad" — ("Tax on Thingy") The British colonial empire was, historically, a very effective means of gathering tax monies from, yes, foreigners living abroad. They may have become subjects of His/Her Majesty, but they were never Englishmen. The fact that this taxation request is delivered by a Conservative City Gent type (Jones) is expected. In fact, the City Gents and businessman types in this Vox Pops section are primarily concerned with (1) increasing Britain's colonial presence and profit, (2) sexuality and taxation, (3) capital punishment and the profiteering possible in that business, and (4) getting rid of the body's naughty bits—these Pythonesque Conservative types are, as ever, a strange and twisted lot.

"tax . . . thingy" — ("Tax on Thingy") Technically, since prostitution behind closed doors and where no third party is acting as manager or pimp was and is not illegal in the UK, there were many men and women probably at least eligible to pay taxes on their sexual incomes.

As for taxes on pleasure items, there was a joke going around (in cartoons of the day) that if cannabis could just be legalized the government would have a significant new and very reliable tax revenue. See "Jon's" cartoon in the *Daily Mail* for 9 January 1969. Another cartoon lists the recent rise in taxation, addressing the uproar Sir Gerald Nabarro instigated, as well: "New moustache tax / Nab[arro] for PM / Import tax up! / Postage up 6d / S.E.T. [Selective Employment Tax] doubled / Car tax up! / Dog tax up! / Jenkins [Chancellor of the Exchequer] is a jerk / The Pill Tax / Petrol up Whisky up Every bloody thing up" (Papas, *Guardian*, 4 Feb. 1969). Other items (fictional and not) suggested for taxation or increased taxation in the political cartoons of the day include handlebar mustaches (as the one worn by Conservative MP Gerald Nabarro), land betterment projects, tissue paper, betting, personal wealth, beer, retail sales taxes to pay for new roads in London, death duties, income tax, and capital gains. See the British Cartoon Archive.

As a barometer of the tax burden in the UK, and therefore the significance of its effect on the public conscience, it's worth noting that in the period 1964–1970, the so-called tax freedom day (indicating the number of days in a year it takes to pay the tax burden) lurched forward from 23 April to 26 May. Pundits of the period were well aware of this increasing tax burden, and their cries are heard in newspapers, magazines, and interviews.

Many have concluded that this egregious financial burden led directly to Wilson's Labour government being surprisingly ousted by the Heath-led Conservatives in 1970, though a change of government didn't presage a significant change in the economy (and the Tories lost in 1974).

Torchlight dungeon — (PSC; "Photos of Uncle Ted [Spanish Inquisition]") This large and seemingly multileveled set makes it clear the show is being recorded at Ealing TFS, not back at Television Centre.

"Trouble at mill" — ("The Spanish Inquisition") This introduction—a hurried, Yorkshire-accented worker trying to tell his betters there's been trouble down at the mill—appears earlier in the *ISIRTA* episode "Incompetence" (5 May 1968). There, though both Fozz Wackett mill owner (Mr. Arkwright) and mill worker speak with similar northern dialects, neither can understand the other. Their conversation devolves into an exchange of apostrophe-laden portmanteau words and sounds.

• W •

"We are not amused" — (animated link into "Tax on Thingy") Gilliam includes this line in the "Reg's head" animation. The phrase is somewhat apocryphally attributed to Queen Victoria (in *The Notebooks of a Spinster Lady*, 1919), in several settings and in relation to several possible events. The Goons employ the phrase in the "Crystal Palace Project" (5 Feb. 1952), where Victoria—Albert in tow—wanders into the construction of the Crystal Palace. They are shooed off by Captain Pureheart (Bentine), and Victoria responds coolly: "Young man, we are not amused. Come Albert." *Private Eye* had picked up on the saying, as it appears in a 7 August 1964 Gerald Scarfe panel cartoon depicting the ailing *Punch* as the central character in Hogarth's *The Rake's Progress* (Ingrams, 108).

The phrase and its connection to Victoria return in Ep. 41, when the Queen appears at a department store Victorian poetry reading to complain about ants. There is even dispute as to whether the Queen was employing the royal "we" or merely referring to herself and the ladies of the court. See notes to "We are not . . . amusiert"? in Ep. 41 for more.

"week 39.4" — (link out of "Jokes and Novelties Salesman") This week in 1970 would have been the last full week of September, the twentieth through the twenty-sixth. The Pythons were actually in the studio during this week, recording the final version of Ep. 22 on Friday, 25 September. The location sequences (at 49 Elers Road) were shot in May 1970 (WAC T12/1,242).

"Welch, Raquel" — ("Vox Pops") Mentioned earlier in Ep. 13, some of the Pythons may have run into Welch on the set of *The Magic Christian* (1969), to which Chapman and Cleese had contributed.

"we're on film" — (link out of "The Spanish Inquisition") Another moment—"It's a link, is it?"—where the artifice of the production is acknowledged. During this period, 16mm film cameras were the primary "out of studio" recording devices for television production, not bulky, more sensitive videotape cameras. (One of these new studio color video cameras, model EMI 2001, can be seen in Ep. 2, in the "A Man with Three Buttocks" sketch.) These video cameras were used in the studio setting, and the filmed and taped images were then cut into a single episode, obvious picture clarity and medium differences notwithstanding.

Wilde, Marjorie — (PSC; "Photos of Uncle Ted [Spanish Inquisition]") The "Dear Old Lady" Wilde (1902–1988) is an actual older woman playing that very part, one of the few times the Pythons went this route. Like many of the other extras and walk-ons employed by the troupe, Wilde had appeared in several familiar television shows prior to this appearance, including *Troubleshooters* and *Z Cars*.

Wuthering Heights — ("The Semaphore Version of *Wuthering Heights*") The popular 1847 Emily Brontë (1818–1848) novel. The BBC had broadcast a version of *Wuthering Heights* in 1967, starring Ian McShane (*Z Cars*) and Angela Scoular (*Casino Royale*).

• X •

"Ximinez" — ("The Spanish Inquisition") The Grand Inquisitor chosen by Ferdinand and Isabella was Tomás de Torquemada (1420–1498), known as "the hammer of heretics." For more on Torquemada see the *Catholic Encyclopedia*.

• Y •

"You will get expenses" — (link out of "The Spanish Inquisition") The Pythons did employ local walk-ons and extras in much this manner, hiring local actors for location shooting in Bournemouth and Norwich, at least (WAC T12/1,445).

Episode 16: "Déjà Vu"

Tower flat striptease, "And now . . ." Man on a window cleaner's platform, exploding animals, and the "It's" Man intro; *Animation: Titles* (silly Cleese v/o); Exploding animals; The long walk; A bishop rehearsing: "Oh, Mr. Belpit"; Flying lessons; "Two years later"; BALPA interruption; "Four years later"; BALPA corrections; Plane hijacked to Luton; Bus hijacked to Cuba; **The Poet McTeagle**; St. John Limbo, Poetry Expert; Ian McKellan-figure performs McTeagle; A Very Good Playwright; Exploding animals; A Highland spokesman offers corrections; *Animation: "I am somebody's lunch hour"* and *Blossoming hands*; Psychiatrist milkman; Complaints; Mrs. Pim takes a walk to see Dr. Cream; "It's the Mind": Déjà vu; Closing credits

• A •

"aeroplane" — ("Flying Lessons") Curious, since this was (and is) a word still in very common usage in the UK. It may just be that Anemone (Chapman) is simply picking on Chigger (Jones) for not using the newer, trendier (perhaps more American) "airplane," determining "aeroplane" to be more effete, uppercrust, and old-fashioned.

and an owl — (PSC; link into opening titles) Actually, no lion is visible in this menagerie, but there is a cobra, a rabbit, a boar, and perhaps a monkey visible besides what's listed in the printed scripts. It's the ferret that explodes, not the owl, as indicated in the printed scripts.

Anemone — (PSC; "Flying Lessons") An anemone is both a plant with beautiful flowers or a sea creature, named so for its flower-like appendages. There often seems to be no pattern for the naming of characters, besides the silliness of silly names. Mr. Anemone (Chapman) isn't addressed this way by any of the characters or himself, meaning he is named simply for the amusement of the writers and to differentiate him from Mr. Chigger (Jones).

announcer rises up in front of the window — (PSC; "Girl in the Window" link into opening titles) This sexually suggestive shot seems to have been recorded on 21 May 1970 (WAC T12/1,416). WAC records don't indicate the specific building used for this shot, nor the usual permissions to use a device like the cleaner hoist. Further research determined, however, that the building used was one of the Wellington Close towers in Walton-on-Thames. This same building was the setting for Admiral Nelson's fall in Ep. 1. (The encyclopedia salesmen in Ep. 5 were thrown from 79 Slade House in Hounslow.)

"ask anyone" — ("The Poet McTeagle") This continual begging was also the modus operandi of the American cartoon character Wimpy, who appeared in the *Popeye* series. Wimpy always asked for a hamburger, with the promise that he would make good the loan the next Tuesday. After its initial run as a theatrical cartoon series, which had begun in 1933, *Popeye* appeared on American TV 1956–1963. Popeye theatrical shorts began appearing in UK cinemas as early as 1935, and by 1958 could be found on ITA broadcasts on television.

• B •

badly — ("Girl in the Window" link into opening titles) This dialogue is dubbed, meaning they may have shot on location without sound equipment, though it's actually dubbed fairly well. (The sound will be recorded live later, as Cleese appears on the hoist.) The script call for bad dubbing may have been an attempt to mimic earnest but poorly made pornographic films of the period (e.g., *I Am Curious Yellow* [1967]), or even some of the more respected (but also technically challenged) New Wave films from the neo-realists onward. Hong Kong exports of this era (*Come Drink with Me*, e.g.), were also distributed in the West in badly dubbed versions.

In the printed script for *Monty Python and the Holy Grail* (1975) the scene description for the Rabbit of Caerbannog fight scene calls for shots reminiscent of "kung fu and karate" films.

"bally" — ("Hijacked Plane [to Luton]") "Bally" is the mild epithet of choice among Python (and jolly RAF) aviator types, hence Zanie (Chapman) here calling himself a "flying man, you know." (Chapman's character's name—but not his characterization—has changed between sketches, from Anemone to Zanie, A to Z.) This also refers back to the character Captain Biggles, from Ep. 10, and who will be featured again in Ep. 33 (both Chapman). A close look at such RAF banter will be seen later, in Ep. 42.

"BALPA" — ("Hijacked Plane [to Luton]") BALPA is the British Airline Pilots' Association, the guild that speaks for most of Britain's pilots. It was founded in Croydon in 1937.

The airline industry had spent a good deal of time on the nation's front (and op-ed) pages in 1970, including the much-celebrated and much-poo-poohed arrival of the first Boeing 747 jumbo jet, hijackings to Cuba and terrorist bombs on European airliners, and a threatened strike by airline unions if British United Airways did not merge with BOAC. See myriad cartoons, for example, at the British Cartoon Archive.

"Basingstoke" — ("Hijacked Plane [to Luton]") Basingstoke is at least forty miles southwest of Heathrow, meaning it's probably well in line with a London-Cuba flight path. Basingstoke will be referenced again in Ep. 42, when it somehow becomes part of Westphalia.

"Belpit" — ("A Bishop Rehearsing") Not a very common name anywhere in Britain or Wales, there were just a handful of Belpits living, for example, in the Paddington area in London according to the 1891 UK census, and none in the Greater London area in the late 1960s.

big pile of straw — ("Hijacked Plane [to Luton]") This exterior shot (where Zanie [Chapman] falls from the plane) was recorded on 3 June 1970 at the public restrooms at Old Oak Common, Acton. The Pythons were booked for rehearsals into the Old Oak Club in Acton during this season (WAC T12/1,093).

Bishop — ("A Bishop Rehearsing") The Bishop (Palin) is dressed much like Terry Jones's character "The Bishop" will be in the following episode. A "mitre" is a bishop's staff. This costume will reappear in Ep. 20, "*Take Your Pick*," when the Bishop (Palin) will assault a cross-dressed game show hostess (Chapman).

"bladder trouble" — ("The Poet McTeagle") Cf. "Biggles Dictates a Letter" in Ep. 33 for a similar letter, with similar sentiments.

"bloody Midland Bank" — ("The Poet McTeagle") Gilliam will later include an older photo of a branch of the Midland Bank in Ep. 20, where the killer sheep rob and then blow up the building.

"bob" — ("The Poet McTeagle") A "bob" is one shilling.

"British Psychiatric Association" — ("Psychiatrist Milkman") The British Psychiatric Association will be mentioned again in Ep. 43, when a bogus psychiatrist (Palin) is trying to prove his credentials. The British Psychological Society (Tavistock House, South Tavistock Square, WC1) had been overseeing Britain's mental health industry since the early part of the twentieth century. The British Psycho-Analytical Society was also extant, housed at 63 New Cavendish, W1.

"British Sugar Association" — ("Psychiatrist Milkman") The British Sugar Corporation was formed by an Act of Parliament in 1936, and was from its inception a nationalized industry. Its corporate headquarters during this period were found at 134 Piccadilly, W1.

"building society" — ("The Poet McTeagle") According to the *OED*, a building society is "a society in which the members periodically contribute to a fund out of which money may be lent to any of their number for the purpose of building (or purchasing) a house." Technically, then, McTeagle (Jones) shouldn't have been able to use his divvy money for anything but a house purchase or construction.

Bus moving away from camera — (PSC; "Bus Hijacked to Cuba") The transition between the semi-urban haystack at Old Oak Common, Acton, to the bus stop in rural Devon is made certain by the inclusion of this bus, a green Western National bus. Western National operated in South West England, and had very recently (January 1969) been made part of the nationalized bus system, the National Bus Company.

Not surprisingly, this bus has its own website, with its complete operating history. See the bibliography, under "Western National."

"buttered scones" — ("Flying Lessons") Scones are soft cakes made of barley or oatmeal. The Lumberjack (Palin) sings of having "buttered scones for tea" in the "I'm a Lumberjack" sketch in Ep. 9. He also happens to be a transvestite, which may be flavoring Anemone's appraisal of Chigger's flying inabilities in this sketch. In the "Flying Lessons" setting, however, the scones are a symbol of Mr. Chigger's alleged snobbery.

• C •

"Cameron tartan" — ("The Poet McTeagle") There are myriad Cameron tartans representing Camerons from different regions in Scotland. Incidentally, McTeagle (Jones) doesn't appear to be wearing a Cameron tartan, either, meaning this particular entry (and many others in these volumes) is performing a service similar to that of both the BALPA spokesman (Idle) and the Highlander (Cleese) in this episode.

This "fact-checking" (to which the Pythons clearly weren't wed) would come back in another form during the following season. For Ep. 33, a 30 September 1971 letter from the Royal National Life-Boat Institution—to whom the Pythons had directed a request to shoot on a lifeboat, and obviously submitted a script of the sequence, as well—granted the request but asked simply if they intended showing a Shoreham life-boat then it should be named specifically, and that the script reference to "Ramsgate" be eliminated, as Ramsgate had "no self-righting life-boat" (WAC T12,1,428). See notes to Ep. 33 for more on the locations and equipment used in this scene.

"certain involuntary muscular movements" — ("Hijacked Plane [to Luton]") This sort of narrative devolution—from confident assertion to qualification to equivocation to outright backpedaling—will reappear as Dennis Moore (Cleese) tries to rob a coach in Ep. 37. Idle's Mr. Sopwith in Ep. 7 also goes from spotting all yetis to seeing just one to spotting a little one to seeing a picture of one to just hearing about yetis—all in one dialogic decrescendo of diminution.

Chigger — (PSC; "Flying Lessons") A harvest mite, which fastens itself to the skin, causing irritation.

"Cooper, Tommy" — ("Hijacked Plane [to Luton]") Tommy Cooper was a British music hall comedian and sometime magician who died in 1984. Cooper was also a television personality, appearing on many shows and having his own show (twice) on ATV. There is no record of Cooper appearing in any of the many versions of *Sherlock Holmes* produced for television.

"crofter" — ("The Poet McTeagle") A crofter is essentially a Scottish tenant farmer or sharecropper. Again, this is the shorthand way to identify the rustic Scottishness of the character, and the Scots in general, in the Python oeuvre. This same approach was used in Ep. 7, when aliens were turning normal Englishmen into alien Scotsmen, and probably can be connected back to Samuel Johnson's similar marginalizing of the Scots even as he enjoyed their countryside and the company of one of their own, his biographer James Boswell.

This same photo of a "crofter's cottage" was earlier used in Ep. 7 to identify the rustic "Dunbar Menswear Shop," home of the "plucky Scotsman" Angus Podgorny. The photo is not accounted for in the WAC records, but it is clearly at least a portion of the Skye Cottage Museum near Portree, Scotland. See the Ep. 7 entry for "Scottish crofter's cottage" for more.

• D •

"divvy" — ("The Poet McTeagle") A "divvy" is a colloquial abbreviation of "dividend," or a payout from a common fund or investment.

"don't anybody move" — ("Hijacked Plane [to Luton]") What follows is a sort of postmodern deconstruction of the shopworn movie, TV, and dime novel criminal's phrase "don't anybody move." The point here is that in Python's world (and in this transitionary Modern-Postmodern world in general) no word or phrase (or meaning) is stable, especially those words that may have entered the *cultural* lexicon and come to mean the same thing to everyone—in Python, these most common utterances are the best targets, always already ripe for the cycle of misreading and reinvestment and misreading.

In Ep. 8, the word "mattress" has been connected not to something to sleep on, but to a ritualized set of bizarre behaviors enacted by Mr. Lambert (Chapman) and counteracted by his co-workers, where the "something to sleep on" is to be known as a "dog kennel." Later, in Ep. 38, the phrase "No time to lose" will be worried over until it becomes meaninglessness, completely detached from its context, its connotative and denotative moorings, as Man (Palin) can't even figure out which word or syllable to stress, and the RSM (Jones) doesn't recognize the phrase at all. Successful communication, therefore, continues to evade most person-to-person transactions in the Python world.

The Goons may have kick started this word-worrying in one of Milligan's more cerebral episodes, "Six Charlies in Search of an Author," where characters are controlled by and can control narrative trajectories simply by controlling the typewriter. In one exchange, the meaninglessness of word associations in a typical sentence is pointed up, as the speakers simply emphasize (put an accent on) different words:

> Ned (Secombe): (gulps) I haven't got any bones.
> Grytpype-Thynne (Sellers): Nonsense, nonsense, you'd fall down without them. You'd fall DOWN without them.
> Ned: You'd fall down without THEM.
> Grytpype-Thynne: YOU'D fall down without them.
> Peter (Sellers): Take yer choice. (*The Goon Show*, 26 Dec. 1956)

The concept is based, of course, on Pirandello's Modernist masterpiece play *Six Characters in Search of an Author*, from 1921, a reflexive work quite influential to the Pythons.

"dormice" — ("Hijacked Plane [to Luton]") "Dormice" is the (folk) plural of "dormouse," which is a small, hibernating rodent (*OED*). It also can mean a sleepy or dozing person. The Second Pilot's (Cleese) questioning response probably arises from the Hostess's uses of "dormice" rather than perhaps "churchmice." The rodent also makes a sleepy appearance in Lewis Carroll's *Alice's Adventures in Wonderland*, a text and author the Pythons have often leaned toward in their absurd visual and linguistic constructions.

• E •

Episode 16 — Given no specific title in the printed scripts, the episodes wouldn't be titled again regularly until the fourth and final season in 1974. This is the third show of the second season, broadcast 29 September 1970, and recorded fifth on 16 July 1970.

The BBC records for this episode indicate only one official extra or walk-on, Jeanette Wild (*Z Cars*; *Up Pompeii*). She plays Second Secretary in the "Flying Lessons" sketch, and has a very brief speaking part (including a voiceover in the "Hijacked Plane" sketch).

"Eton and Madgalene" — ("Flying Lessons") Eton is an ancient college (high-school-aged pupils) founded by Henry VI in 1440, a so-called public school where Britain's elite were and are nurtured. One of Harold Wilson's oppositional complaints about the ruling Tory government between 1951 and 1964 was both the fact that so many blue-blooded Conservatives had attended Eton, and took care of their own, essentially:

> We take the view that everyone should be equal in the matter of selection and yet, well, the last three Prime Ministers have all been to one school, and there are forty-thousand schools in this country. Nearly half the Cabinet comes from that school. I think it still shows I think that the Conservative party is out of touch with the times in which we live. (*Eyewitness 1960–69*, "Macmillan Resigns")

"Madgalene" [*sic*] is a misspelling of Magdalene (probably just a typo [and pronounced "Maud-lin"]), part of Cambridge University (est. 1542). There is also a Magdalen College in Oxford. All of these schools have been associated with producing the elite, ruling class of Britain for centuries. (Ironic, since five of the Pythons attended these very same institutions.)

The Pythons were able to attend Oxford and Cambridge, yes, but none of them were in the social or financial class for Etonian matriculation. Many of the political and/or society characters lampooned in the series follow this same educational trail, including Ludovic Kennedy (Ep. 37); Liberal leader Jeremy Thorpe (Ep. 45); Prime Ministers William Gladstone (Ep. 2); a Liberal, and Conservative Alec Douglas-Home (Ep. 30); and Lord Snowdon, Antony Armstrong-Jones (Ep. 19).

"exaggerated, violent movements" — ("Hijacked Plane [to Luton]") The characters have to put a finer and finer point on the original catchphrase (an absolute: "don't anybody move"), narrowing, refining, and then winnowing out the obvious and the not-so-obvious variations of "movement" as they are identified. A sort of relativism has been broached here, rendering the phrase "don't anybody move" not only moot, but somewhat ridiculous and physically, even cosmically impossible. The solid, knowable days of Modern art (where a pear could still look like a pear) were rapidly being undermined by the Postmodernism of abstraction, nonrepresentation, and metamorphosis—the separation of the signifier from the signified was well under way during this period. Dennis Moore (Cleese) will find this as he attempts to convince his victims that he practices every day, then most days, then whenever he can, etc.

• F •

"fags" — ("The Poet McTeagle") "Fag" is a slang term for cigarette. In Ep. 15, the acronym-spouting Politician (Cleese) demands a fag so he won't "go spare."

"Fly Me to the Stars" — ("Hijacked Plane [to Luton]") This made-up title is probably a play on the Frank Sinatra standard "Fly Me to the Moon," penned by Bart Howard in 1954, and recorded by Sinatra in 1964.

"fly the plane to Luton" — ("Hijacked Plane [to Luton]") A turnabout on the familiar skyjacking destination of Cuba, which many considered a haven for radical Leftist revolutionaries since Castro's forces overthrew the dictator Batista in 1959.

Hijacking (or skyjacking) had become a real danger in the 1960s, with smaller political groups reaping very high public exposure via these essentially low-tech crimes. There were nine reported hijackings in January 1969 alone, most rerouted to Cuba. In September 1969, the International Federation of Airline Pilots' Association was even considering a worldwide strike to draw attention to the hijacking situation.

Political cartoons of the period treat the subject a number of times, with one in particular jabbing at similar targets as the Pythons. Keith Waite in the *Sun* (2 Sept. 1969) is certain that no one would be interested in hijacking any Monarch-like airline (he calls it "Busy Bee") destined for the continent, for example, and in another panel an air hostess tells a gun-wielding hijacker: "We can't possibly fly you to Syria, we're already flying to Cuba." See the British Cartoon Archive for more.

• G •

"Gilbert and Sullivan" — ("Psychiatrist Milkman") Noted nineteenth-century English light opera partnership. The Gilbert and Sullivan Society was formed in London in 1924. See the notes for "I want to marry you too sir" in Ep. 19.

glen — (PSC; "The Poet McTeagle") A "glen" is a "mountain-valley, usually narrow and forming the course of a stream," and was initially applied only to such places in Scotland and Ireland, according to the *OED*. A "scar" is a rocky crag or steep, rocky precipice. A "coot" is a swimming/diving bird, and a "moorhen," also called a water-hen, is a bird that favors watery areas. A "tarn" is a small mountain lake, while a "loch" is a lake or inland sea, often land-locked. These are Sir Walter Scott (1771–1832) locations, words, and phrases, really, whose *Redgauntlet* had been very recently produced as a popular eight-part miniseries for Scottish television in January 1970.

The Pythons will read aloud (with great difficulty) from Scott's *Redgauntlet* (1824) in Ep. 38.

Good mornings — (PSC; "Flying Lessons") This entire "arty shot" is elided from the filmed version of the sketch. Ingmar Bergman's 1957 film *The Seventh Seal* was a well-known art film of the recent past, and featured a much-copied silhouette shot of the type described above (and perhaps borrowed by Bergman, as well, from Griffith's *Birth of a Nation* forty years earlier, frankly). In the case of *Seventh Seal*, it was Death personified leading the mortals along the brow of the hill toward their ultimate destination. This same shot/film source is mentioned in Ep. 7, as transformed Scotsmen enter Scotland, and will be revisited in some detail in the Pythons' final feature film, *The Meaning of Life* (1983), where Death leads the motorcars and passengers into heaven (there specifically modeled after the Hieronymus Bosch work *Ascent of the Blessed* [after 1490]).

Most likely, the demands of an "evening" shot (waiting for the right silhouette light, the "golden hour") as called for in the script precluded this scene, given the time and budget constraints the show would have been under, especially on location.

"Gordon" — ("Flying Lessons") Possibly a reference to Gordon Campbell, Heath's Secretary of State for Scotland between 1970 and 1974. Heath's Conservative government had replaced the Wilson Labourites after a successful 18 June 1970 General Election.

GPO tent — (PSC; "Flying Lessons") A small fabric or plastic covering for General Post Office employees working in manholes, etc. A portion of the GPO's work includes communications, meaning this tent depicted was probably being used over a manhole where land line work was under way. This same type of tent appears in *A Hard Day's Night* (1964), when the Beatles use it to help sneak into the recording studio (from a vehicle) and away from screaming fans. The GPO was essentially dissolved in 1969, just as the Pythons were writing these initial episodes. The name ("GPO tent") would understandably have remained in consumers' minds long after the dissolution of the GPO.

"gynaecologist" — ("The Poet McTeagle") This said as if being a gynecologist isn't actually being a doctor, and/or that on the side, this woman's doctor examines male patients (and/or that Scottish males aren't men). This will be repeated later in the episode. The latter charge would seem to be refuted by Ep. 37, when in the "Ideal Loon Exhibition" there is a revealing "Nae Trews" exhibit that seems very popular to female visitors.

• H •

"Harpenden" — ("Hijacked Plane [to Luton]") Harpenden is another London borough, situated five miles southeast of Luton.

haystack in a field — ("Hijacked Plane [to Luton]") This haystack was also shot at Old Oak Common, just as the previous haystack scene, but the restrooms are not visible. A quick jump cut on the gunman's hand as he flags the bus takes us instead to the same area where the "rocky highlands" of the wandering poet McTeagle (Jones) were shot, at Newbridge, Dartmoor on 14 May 1970 (WAC T12/1,425). In one cut the action moves more than 175 miles away, from the London suburbs to Devon.

He is Mr. Boniface — ("Déjà Vu") This character's name is never mentioned by another character, but included (and pointed out) in the printed script. In literary tradition, Boniface is the well-known character from Farquhar's *Beaux' Stratagem* (1707), the good-natured innkeeper. In the unsettling *It's the Mind* world sketch, Palin's Boniface struggles mightily to live up to the eponymous nature of his name.

"High Chaparral" — ("Hijacked Plane [to Luton]") *The High Chaparral* was an American television Western airing 1967–1971, and appeared in color on BBC2 in December 1967. *Bonanza* and *Big Valley* were also popular on ITV and BBC, respectively. *High Chaparral* is featured on the 22 March 1969 *Radio Times* cover.

highland gentleman — (PSC; "The Poet McTeagle") Here the Pythons employ obvious visual cues to identify a Scotsman. He wears a kilt, as well as a "tam-o'-shanter," which is a circular woolen bonnet originally worn by Scottish ploughmen. He also carries a "knobkerry," a "short thick stick with a knobbed head, used as a weapon or missile by South African peoples. Also extended to similar weapons used by other peoples, e.g., in Polynesia and Australia." There's no indication in the *OED* that such a cudgel was ever characteristic of Scotland, though there are significant evidences that such cudgels were carried by Irish priests (as they taught rowdy schoolboys), among others. The etymology of the word ("knobkerrie") is even African.

In the 1948 Warner Bros. cartoon *My Bunny Lies over the Sea* (dir. Chuck Jones), several Scottish-type characters carry similar cudgels as walking canes, including a disguised Bugs Bunny.

"Holmes, Sherlock" — ("Hijacked Plane [to Luton]") Shows starring the Sherlock Holmes character were on British television in many iterations, including a 1951 series, a 1964 installment (eventually starring Peter Cushing by 1968), and then even 1967 in West Germany. The character was created by Sir Arthur Conan Doyle.

• I •

"I am somebody's lunch hour" — (animated link into "Psychiatrist Milkman") The music Gilliam uses in this animation includes the International Studio Orchestra playing the "Flute" Promenade by Eric Towren, and then "Long Trail" from "Far West Suite" by Eddie Warner (WAC T12/1,436).

In this animated sequence, a portion of a Civil War photo already used in Ep. 15 is used again. The cowboy character riding the hand is a face borrowed from the "Captain John C. Tidball and Staff, Battery A, 2nd U.S. Artillery" photo, the second officer from the right (in the original photo, found in *DWF*, page 69), wearing the broad-brimmed hat. Gilliam's matched the man's jauntily cocked hat quite well. (The window he throws the lasso through is in a modern London building.)

The Union officer hanging from the cowboy's rope (in the scene just following) is once again Gen. Logan, who is part of the second season credit sequence.

Ian Mckellan figure — ("The Poet McTeagle") Actually spelled "Ian McKellen"—now Sir Ian—he is a respected English stage and screen actor, who in 1970 performed the one-man show *Keats* for the BBC. Born in 1939, McKellen is a member of the Python generation, attending St. Catharine's at Cambridge. McKellen had played Richard in *Richard II*, Edward in *Edward II*, and T.E. Lawrence in Terence Rattigan's *Ross* in 1970, as well, and all for the BBC. The costume chosen by the Pythons for this "Ian Mckellan figure" looks a bit like the one he wore for the *Richard II* production.

"If I could . . ." — ("Psychiatrist Milkman") Both the Milkman (Idle) and Milkmaid (Chapman) hold up a warning index finger to the Lady (Cleveland), a joke and gesture that will be seen again in Eps. 17 and 18. The indication, again, is that the "rimshot" joke of the past—the well-known set-up and punchline payoff—is indeed to be left in the past. This "If I could walk that way . . ." joke is a hoary chestnut from music hall and vaudeville days, when verbal comedians would patter through a series of "Doctor, Doctor" jokes in burlesque shows.

These farm scenes were shot on 21 May 1970 in the area around Torquay (WAC T12/1,416).

inspiring Scottish music — ("The Poet McTeagle") These selections—heard beneath the various portions of the McTeagle (Jones) scenes—include performances by the Pipes and Drums of the Royal Scots Greys of "Scotland's Pride," "Skye Boat Song," and "Road to Isles" (WAC T12/1,436).

"Inverness pantomime" — ("The Poet McTeagle") Inverness' variety theater during this period was the Empire Theatre, which offered pantomime shows through at least the 1950s and 1960s. (Inverness is in the Scottish Highlands area along the Moray Firth coast.) These pantomimes are children's entertainments featuring well-known fairy or nursery tales, songs, slapstick, and stock characters "such as a pantomime 'dame,' played by a man, a leading boy, played by a woman, and a pantomime animal, e.g., horse, cat, goose, played by actors dressed in a comic costume, with some regional variations" (*OED*). A pantomime goose, horse ("Dobbins"), Princess Margaret and Puss, and even Long John Silver make appearances in *FC*, a testament to the entertainment's cultural significance to the young Pythons. (In 1967–1968, for instance, *Aladdin* was the pantomime running in Glasgow's King's Theatre, while in the early 1960s the *Jamie* series [e.g., *A Wish for Jamie*]—pantomimes in full Scottish dress—played to packed houses.) These panto performances were also reviewed regularly and thoroughly in period newspapers, and by established critics.

The "leading boy played by a woman" and the panto animal will both make appearances in Ep. 28, while other pantomime characters including Margaret, a goose, and horses are featured throughout *FC*. See entries for Ep. 30 for more.

"Isn't!" — ("Flying Lessons") This meaningless, repetitive argument is much like both the "Dead Parrot" exchange in Ep. 8, especially when the Shopkeeper (Palin) hits the cage, and most of the "Argument Clinic" dialogue found in Ep. 29. The obvious fakery is also present—and equally defended—in the feature film *HG*, where a woman (Connie Booth) has been forcibly dressed up as a witch, complete with false nose and witch's clothing.

It's the Mind — ("Déjà Vu") The illustration in the opening title sequence for *It's the Mind* is from *Gray's Anatomy*, page 868, figure 743, and is called "The veins of the right side of the head and neck" (33rd edition, published 1962, and edited by Davies and Davies). The show paid £5/51 for the rights to use the illustration (WAC T12/1,242). The photos used in this title sequence are not accounted for in the archival material for this episode. This also continues the long tradition on British TV of the "It's" title (see Ep. 1).

The weird music beneath this title sequence (and the reiterations of the titles) is from P. Wilsher and K. Chester's "Eye of Horns" from the "Electroshake" album (WAC T12/1,436).

• J •

"Jeez" — ("A Bishop Rehearsing") "Jeez" is a particularly American colloquialism, though neither the character (Bishop) nor the actor (Palin) affect an American accent or delivery. (The Bishop follows this reading with a Scottish and then Japanese version of the phrase.) The word also appears in a "Barry McKenzie" cartoon in the 2 January 1970 edition of *Private Eye* (12).

• K •

"Kirby, Kathy" — ("Hijacked Plane [to Luton]") Kathy Kirby never did sing on *High Chaparral*, but did have her own show, several hit records, and in 1963 was voted the top female British singer. She would take second two years later in the popular Eurovision Song Contest, singing "I Belong." See Ep. 22 for the Pythons' version of the Eurovision Song Contest.

• L •

"Lassie O'Shea" — ("The Poet McTeagle") Here the Scotswoman (Idle) isn't even given a true name, but simply called "Lassie," meaning a young girl.

"lurex" — ("Hijacked Plane [to Luton]") "Lurex" is "the proprietary name of a type of yarn which incorporates a metallic thread; also, fabric made from this yarn" (*OED*). Since proprietary, it could/should have been capitalized in the printed scripts. There is no indication as to what kinds of "fun" the BALPA man (Idle) would be using the dancing tights for, but the uniform and air of authority would point us toward some sexually deviant activity, given the Pythons' previous depictions of such "types." Perhaps the BALPA Man is hinting at the homosocial/homosexual atmosphere with the "chaps at BALPA House."

"Luton" — ("Hijacked Plane [to Luton]") Luton, about twenty miles north and west of London, has been and will be mentioned a number of times in *FC*, and was most notably the place where the Pirhana brothers detonated a nuclear device in Ep. 14, specifically at Luton's airport. Luton was also the jumping-off point for many continental package tour excursions, the type that the Tourist blasts in Ep. 19.

The Pythons' ultimate boss, Lord Hill (mentioned in Eps. 10, 11, and 18), the former "Radio Doctor," was created a life peer as Baron Luton, after successfully standing for parliament for Luton in 1950.

• M •

"Mater" — ("Flying Lessons") The Latin word for "mother," "mater" was an in-vogue term for British public schoolboys (along with the later-mentioned "pater" for "father") from the nineteenth and twentieth centuries. This tradition of the higher-born boys leaving for boarding school is lampooned by radio comedian Tony Hancock (1924–1968) in *Hancock's Half Hour*:

> Mother: Come along, Anthony; lift your cases down.
> Hancock: Right-ho, Mater, I'm ready.

Mother: This is the first time you've been away from home, you must be a brave little soldier.
Hancock: I will, Mater, I will.
Mother: Promise to write to me every week, study hard and don't get into bad company.
Hancock: I'll try jolly hard to make myself a credit to you and Pater. (Series 4, Ep. 15, Jan. 1957)

"Maudling" — ("Flying Lessons") Yet another reference to Reginald Maudling (1917–1979), Home Secretary under Heath, and much-maligned Conservative figure throughout this period. What it is Maudling wouldn't do for fifty shillings isn't clear, but a reputation for financial promises delayed or not kept (i.e., promises to move from direct to indirect taxation) dogged Heath's government, as did a moribund economy. As early as 1966, however, Maudling's alleged involvement with companies that engaged in kickbacks, bribery, and influence peddling found its way into the press and, obviously, the Pythons' quiver.

During the 1968–1974 period, major newspapers featured 260 political cartoons depicting Maudling and Tory comrades, and Maudling found himself on the cover of *Private Eye* eight times between 1962 and 1974, with his pecuniary improprieties making prime, real news fodder for the satirical magazine.

Mercer, David — (PSC; "The Poet McTeagle") Mercer (1928–1980) was, in fact, a respected playwright, having created *Emma's Time* (1970), *On the Eve of Publication* (1967), *The Parachute* (1967), *In Two Minds* (BBC, 1967), and *Morgan: A Suitable Case for Treatment* (1966) prior to this *FC* episode being written. Mercer contributed often to the "Wednesday Play" TV series, which were commissioned plays presented by the BBC between 1964–1970. (Many *FC* extras also found work during this period on the various "Wednesday Play" productions.) The type of sincere, dramatic performance evinced by both McTeagle and the "Mckellan" character was characteristic of the "Wednesday Play" series.

"milk-float" — ("Psychiatrist Milkman") A "milk-float" is a wagon or vehicle for distributing milk products. In this sketch, psychiatry is being dispensed.

In the following episode (Ep. 17), the "Architect Sketch" offers a "deck access"–type apartment block designed by Mr. Wiggin's (Cleese) firm. These elongated developments were given very wide entry decks ("streets in the sky") just so milk-floats could maneuver down them easily, delivering dairy products door-to-door, obviating the need for inhabitants to even leave their apartments on grocery errands. This led many to feel all the more trapped in these intricately planned and efficient but joyless gray structures, and levels of depression, apathy, and crime climbed in most such developments. A psychiatrist milkman would have been most welcome and needed, then, in these oppressive and depressing flats.

Milkman — ("Psychiatrist Milkman") Idle often plays the intrusive man-at-the-door, including a nudging pub visitor (Ep. 3), a vicar selling sundries (Ep. 28), an encyclopedia salesman pretending to be a burglar (Ep. 5), and a novelty joke salesman (Ep. 15).

Mr. Chigger follows — (link into "Flying Lessons") The light, jaunty music underneath this long walk is Eric Coates and the Philharmonic Promenade Orchestra playing the "Knightsbridge March" from "London Suite" (WAC T12/1,436). This same music is used in Ep. 41, "Michael Ellis."

"mush" — ("Flying Lessons") "Mush" is actually a term of address, though here it may take the more pejorative meaning as found in the phrase "mush-head," or "a person of a yielding disposition; one lacking in firmness" (*OED*). The American usage can mean "idiot," and the Pythons have been known to employ American vernacularisms when necessary.

• N •

"New Guinea" — ("The Poet McTeagle") To continue the "correctional" motif of this episode, the practice of lip plate insertion isn't common to New Guinea (an island in the Melanesia chain), but is found in many areas of East Africa (e.g., the Mursi tribe of Ethiopia).

"No. They're all number three" — ("Psychiatrist Milkman") In this case, another example of "it's not what you say but how you say it" in the Python world. Often, in the Python world, the correct answer isn't the answer, since the question may change before the answer is provided in the emerging Postmodern world. The "Silly Job Interview" in Ep. 5 is an example of the shifting relationship, again, between signifier and signified, and between expectation and experience.

This is also perhaps a comment on the seeming randomness of psychiatry's standard, subjective, and interpretive diagnoses (the interpretable Rorschach ink blot, for example). The diagnosis is based on the Lady's *need* for dairy products, and is thus perhaps a slap at the then-emerging (the early 1970s) and flourishing books and trends (and fads) in sexuality, gender studies, self-help and self-improvement, etc. See notes to Ep. 2, "The Mouse Problem," for more. Note also that the psychiatrist milkman's diagnosis only confirms the woman's suspicions that he's actually a milkman.

"not in this show" — ("A Bishop Rehearsing") The Bishop (Palin) here immediately steps out of the fictional world of the sketch and identifies the setting for what it is, a show. It's not made clear whether he's actually a bishop auditioning/practicing for a part, or an actor dressed as a bishop doing the same. (In an audio sketch created for *The Contractual Obligation* album [1980], the Bishop of Leicester [Palin] reads radio commercial voiceovers—happily taking the paycheck, and quibbling only slightly with the evolutionary nature of the text. The radio personnel [Chapman and Idle] wish aloud that they could have secured the Bishop of Bath and Wells, who's busy doing a frozen peas advert, or the Bishop of Worcester, instead.)

Chigger (Jones) doesn't seem ready or willing (or able) to step out of the fiction, continuing to press the "flying lessons" agenda, even as the Bishop, on another narrative level, can't or won't help him. So there are at least two sketches going on with the Bishop and Mr. Chigger—and they intrude on one another only momentarily. Either way, the "fiction within a fiction" structure—so endemic to Python—emerges again.

The Pythons could have been inspired by the Goons, again, for in "The Great Spon Plague" episode (10 Mar. 1958) a Scottish character (played by Sellers) introduces himself, begins to recite his family history, and then quickly bids the audience good night because he has nothing more to do with/in the episode.

• O •

"'oop" — (PSC; "Flying Lessons") An *initial "h" dropping*, characteristic of a number of English dialects in the UK, including Cockney and what's now known as "Estuary English" (a working-class accent spoken along the Thames). A G.B. Shaw moment, certainly, where one Englishman identifies and pigeonholes another Englishman the moment the other speaks. This is a class-based determination set in "proper" or accepted English pronunciation, often assumed to be centered in London and modeled by the BBC and Oxbridge schools. Here the affected upper-crust accent will re-emerge, with Anemone (Chapman) assuming Chigger (Jones) didn't/couldn't understand his provincial, lower-class pronunciation of "hoop." Anemone also employs the more formal "an," even though Chigger didn't use it himself. The italicized "*h*" is provided in the scripts, as well as being emphasized in the speaking.

Other common characters, like blustering constables, also h-drop with their characteristic "Allo, allo" (or "Ello, ello") as they enter various Python sketches. Palin's First Gas Man in Ep. 14 also clearly h-drops ("'ere" and "'ave"), indicating his working-class status.

"orf to play the grahnd piano" — (PSC; "Flying Lessons") Here the uppercrust accent is indicated by phonetic spelling in the scripts. Such precision is almost never the case in the *FC* scripts.

• P •

"Pancho" — ("Hijacked Plane [to Luton]") Pancho (Jones) used to be Mr. Chigger, of course, though his first name may have been "Pancho." The name could be a reference to Pancho Gonzalez, the American tennis player, who is mentioned a number of times in Ep. 7. More likely, however, since "Pancho" in this scene is a co-pilot or sidekick, this is a reference to the character Pancho in the long-running American Western television show *The Cisco Kid* (1950–1956), starring Duncan Renaldo as Cisco, and Leo Carillo as Pancho. *The Cisco Kid* was picked up by ITA for Granada (Northern) television.

"Pat-a-cake . . ." — ("Psychiatrist Milkman") Perhaps this rhyme simply continues the pantomime thematic thread from the previous sketch. The instances of such irruptions into present sketches of previous themes or characters are seen throughout *FC* (see Ep. 27, for example). Also, according to the *OED*: "Hence pat-a-cake *v., nonce-wd.,* to superintend or direct any one's action as the nurse does the baby's hands in this game." The Lady (Chapman) is being directed by the Milkman (Idle) into purchasing his goods or accepting his pat psychiatric diagnoses—and preferably both.

perfectly calm and friendly — (PSC; "Hijacked Plane [to Luton]") This textual comment—that no one seems to notice the potential danger of the hijacking situation—is unusual for Python. Most of the scenes where this kind of absurdity occurs aren't commented upon at all in the stage directions. This same kind of drifting away from the danger at hand into tangential semantics happens often in *FC*, notably later in a similar hold-up scene featuring Dennis Moore (Ep. 37).

pillar box — ("The Poet McTeagle") A "pillar box" is a receptacle for receiving mail. Similar boxes will be commissioned throughout Ep. 44, stretching around the world.

"Pim, Mrs." — ("Psychiatrist Milkman") Mrs. Pim (Chapman) was previously called Mrs. Ratbag.

posh accent — (PSC; "Flying Lessons") This "imitation posh accent" is used often in *Flying Circus*, especially when one character is deriding the allegedly high-bred manners or speech of another character. See the RSM (Cleese) in Ep. 4. Biggles (Chapman) uses this type of accent in all his speeches and dictations in Ep. 33. In

The Goon Show, the gang often made fun of announcer Wallace Greenslade (1912–1961) for his "posh talk," acknowledging BBC training, which began in 1945. Having been born in Formby, Lancashire, he likely didn't grow up with such a refined accent.

"pottery" — ("The Poet McTeagle") A malapropism or "faulty action." The author may actually be, however, rejecting the "traditional cliches of modern pottery" as he pursues his poetry. As an Art Critic in an earlier episode, Palin also tried to comment on the "place of the nude" in his bed, rather than art (Ep. 8).

pouffe — (PSC; "The Poet McTeagle") A somewhat obsolete usage, a "pouffe" is usually an overstuffed ottoman or seat. In this case, the pouffe is a blue inflatable chair which looks like it belongs on the set of a trendy arts program.

"Puss in Boots" — ("The Poet McTeagle") The pantomime *Puss in Boots* is referenced again during Ep. 28, when an adaptation of *Puss in Boots* attempts to take over the show. The female lead there is played by Julia Breck.

• R •

Radio Voice — (PSC; "Hijacked Plane [to Luton]") Not credited in the printed scripts, this voiceover sounds like Jeannette Wild, who appears at the beginning of this episode.

"rejecting **all the typical clichés of modern pottery"** — ("The Poet McTeagle") This rejection places the poet more in line with the unconventional, doggerel verse of the "Mersey Sound" poets, who had actively attempted to bring poetry down from its lofty perch using vernacular language and common, everyday settings and characters. See the entry for "simple, homespun verses" for more on these so-called Liverpool Poets.

"right on my uppers" — ("The Poet McTeagle") This is a colloquialism (from "down on my uppers") meaning "down on my luck." Uppers were wrappings worn above the ankles, and could be wrapped around the bottom of the foot as boots wore out. The Scottish poet Burns—though talented and much respected—spent most of his life in dire financial distress, which probably prompted this characterization.

rises up — (PSC; "Girl in the Window" link into opening titles) An obvious sexual element here—"rises up"—this scene with the cleaner's hoist was shot on 5 June 1970, at the Wellington Close buildings in Walton-on-Thames.

rocky highland landscape — ("The Poet McTeagle") This "rocky highland landscape" depicted means they are clearly far from Basingstoke and Hampshire in general (home to the flatlands around the Basingstoke Canal), and actually filming somewhere in the rougher Devon countryside. The WAC records for this episode confirm this, indicating that these "Scottish" scenes were shot on 14 May 1970 in the Newbridge, Dartmoor, area near Ashburton (WAC T12/1,416).

• S •

"scheduled flight to Cuba" — ("Hijacked Plane [to Luton]") Interestingly, this is a near copy of an existing political cartoon detailed above in the "fly the plane to Luton" entry.

"Seasons of mists . . ." — ("The Poet McTeagle") Drawn from John Keats's *To Autumn* (1819–1920), and titled much like many of Burns's poems. (It's actually "Season" and not "Seasons," by the way.) Keats (1795–1821) toured Scotland in July and August 1818, and the rugged scenery inspired his later *Hyperion* (1820). (Keats will, ironically, be named as an emblematically *English* poet in the Cleese voiceover narration for the Pythons' contribution to *Euroshow 71—May Day Special*.)

"I wandered" is from William Wordsworth's "I Wandered Lonely as a Cloud" (1804). Wordsworth (1770–1850) will be mentioned later (for his "bloody daffodils") in Ep. 17.

For some reason the Pythons also chose epic Restoration poet John Milton (1608–1674) to group here with these Romantic poets. Milton flourished in the mid-to-late seventeenth century, creating *Paradise Lost* (1667), among others. Milton's characters (Satan, Eve, Gabriel) will later also appear as crew building a new motorway (Ep. 35).

Second Secretary — (PSC; "Flying Lessons") Though not credited in the printed scripts, this actress appears to be Jeannette Wild. (She is given a credit at the end of the taped performance.)

secretary some yards away — (PSC; "A Bishop Rehearsing") The journey to a flying appointment Mr. Chigger (Jones) and the Secretary (Cleveland) are about to embark upon was quite circuitous—shot in and around the Torquay area (beaches, Dartmoor), as well as in Ealing/Acton comprising a period of about six weeks (WAC T12/1,416).

The Secretary leads Mr. Chigger finally to the Crown House building in High Street (at Church), Walton-on-Thames, Surrey KT12. The building and corner intersection look remarkably the same some forty years later. The stores to the left (panned across)—AC Bell Ltd. and Walton Carpets (at 4a Church Street), have given way to Barclay's, an opticians', and a charity shop, respectively.

She starts to undress — ("Girl in the Window" link into opening titles) The music swelling beneath the disrobing "busty girl" is Mantovani's "It's 3 O'clock in the Morning" by Robledo/Terriss (WAC T12/1,436).

"show five" — ("A Bishop Rehearsing") Coincidentally, this episode was actually recorded fifth in the second season, but broadcast third. Throughout the WAC records it is known as "Series 2, Episode 5." Ep. 19 would be recorded as the eighth show of this season, where Palin will also show up as a bishop, but wearing a suit and "dog collar." In Ep. 20, the robe-wearing Bishop played by Palin will finally show up, though he won't mention "Mr. Belpit"—he'll assault a game show hostess with two other (dog-collared) bishops, instead.

"simple, homespun verses" — ("The Poet McTeagle") This may be a comment on the still-trendy "Liverpool Poet" movement, a Beat-inspired collection of poets and poems whose inspirations and subject matters were down-to-earth, everyday, contemporary, and often quite playful (see Drabble's *Oxford Companion to English Literature*). The Liverpool Poets Adrian Henri, Roger McGough, and Brian Patten co-published *The Mersey Sound* in 1967. See the entry for "McGough" in Ep. 37 for more on the movement and Idle's relation to these poets/performers.

This is also a reference to fellow Scotsman Robert Burns's penchant for the provincial Ayrshire dialect of the Lowland Scots in many of his works.

"skint" — ("The Poet McTeagle") To be "skint" is to be penniless or broke. This is a term used a number of times by the Goons as well.

stuffed animal which explodes — ("Déjà Vu") It is a stuffed rabbit that explodes here. A killer rabbit will be destroyed by the Holy Hand Grenade in the 1975 feature film *HG*. The script calls for a lion, tiger, cow, elk, leopard, two ferrets, and an owl. What makes it into the finished scene are a tiger, cow, elk, cobra, rabbit, monkey, and a boar.

• T •

"Trident" — ("Hijacked Plane [to Luton]") The Trident was a de Havilland-built commercial airliner that flew primarily in the 1950s and 1960s. The "vanguard" is the leading edge of an army, just as the middle tine of a trident would lead the way in a thrust. Ironically, the Trident was not an attractive plane to international buyers, and did not have a long life.

Additionally, British European Airways (BEA) and a Trident airplane were in the news in July 1969 when a plane on a passenger route (and with passengers) took part in a commercial aerial display. Several political cartoonists, including Osbert Lancaster for the *Daily Express* (26 July 1969) and Keith Waite for the *Sun* (25 July 1969), satirized the moment of profoundly bad judgment. See the British Cartoon Archive.

trolley — (PSC; "Flying Lessons") A trolley is a tea service cart, and is featured in Eps. 17, 22, and 23, as well. Other trolleys, a.k.a. "gurneys," appear in Eps. 25, 34, and 35.

"two poems" — ("The Poet McTeagle") The respected poet Burns wrote to favorite women, as well, including Alison Begbie and Mary Campbell, and a "Mrs. M'Lehose."

• U •

"unique style first flowered" — ("The Poet McTeagle") Most likely a two-sided commentary, referring to at least two noted Scotsmen, William McGonagall and Robert Burns. The first was the flamboyant Scottish poet and tragedian William McGonagall (1830–1902), called by many the "worst poet" who ever lived, and who was satirized by the Goons as William J. MacGoonigal ("The Tay Bridge Disaster," 9 Feb. 1959). McGonagall asked for and eventually received two guineas (perhaps his only successful poetic transaction) for a short poem meant to sell soap:

> Gentlemen you have my best wishes, and I hope
> That the poem I've written about Sunlight Soap
> Will cause a demand for it in every clime
> For I declare it to be superfine.
> And I hope before long, without any joke,
> You will require some more of my poems about Sunlight Soap.
> And in conclusion, gentlemen, I thank ye—
> William McGonagall, Poet, 48 Step Row, Dundee.

McGonagall would also dress up in full Scottish kit in any public performance, though contemporary accounts say the raucous, booing crowds often led to fights and the throwing of fruit at the earnest poet (McGonagall Online). The BBC Home Service would bring the "poet and tragedian" into people's homes in June 1940, when *The Great McGonagall: A Study in Invincible Ineptitude; Based on Authentic Incidents in the Life of William McGonagall of Dundee* premiered at 3:45 p.m., 26 June 1940. Rachel Reynolds is the listed playwright.

But this characterization could also be an oblique, clever reference to the well-regarded eighteenth-century Scottish poet Robert Burns, who utilized careful observation and detailed minutiae of Scottish customs, nature, dialect, and folkways in his poetry. Burns's financial hardships throughout his life—even as a celebrated poet and songwriter—are well known, and perhaps inspired the financial bent of McTeagle's poetry here. As Burns was a lifelong ploughman, the use of the tam-o'-shanter in Python's depiction of their "typed" rustic Scottish poet might be particularly apt. "Tam o' Shanter" was Burns's last major poem, as well.

• V •

"vanguard" — ("Flying Lessons") Definitely a bit of an in-joke for the "chaps at BALPA House," the Vickers-built Vanguard was a turboprop airliner developed and introduced (in 1959) just before commercial jets took the lead for good in passenger and cargo aviation. Because of the appearance of jets, the Vanguard was never a big commercial success, nor was the Trident, also mentioned by BALPA Man. See "Trident" above for more.

"Project Vanguard" was also the name of the U.S. government's earliest artificial satellite program.

• W •

"walk on the moon . . . hire purchase agreements" — ("Hijacked Plane [to Luton]") Apollo 11 had successfully landed on the moon to great worldwide fanfare in July 1969, prompting the first significant overnight coverage on the BBC.

"Hire purchase agreements" are contracts to buy goods (e.g., appliances) on credit, making regular payments. Mrs. Conclusion (Chapman) will wonder later about anyone being free in a world where "nine installments" are left to be paid on a refrigerator (Ep. 27). These agreements had become very popular after WWII, when thousands of new homes needed new furnishings, and money was tight.

"Whittington, Dick" — ("The Poet McTeagle") A familiar panto figure, Whittington is based on the real-life Richard Whittington who would become Lord Mayor of London several times. A song that accompanied this panto character:

> Turn again, Whittington,
> Once Mayor of London!
> Turn again, Whittington,
> Twice Mayor of London!
> Turn again, Whittington,
> Thrice Mayor of London!

Another Dick Whittington was a contemporary comedian and a regular on *Rowan & Martin's Laugh-In* from 1968 to 1969. Both *Laugh-In* (which debuted on BBC2 on 8 Sept. 1968) and the contemporary rise of stand-up comedy in general were significant influences (from the American side of the pond) on Monty Python.

• Z •

Zanie — (PSC; "Bomb on Plane") "Zanie" is actually the Shakespearean spelling of "zany": "A comic performer attending on a clown, acrobat, or mountebank, who imitates his master's acts in a ludicrously awkward way; a clown's or mountebank's assistant, a merry-, jack-pudding; sometimes used vaguely for a professional jester or buffoon in general" (*OED*). For Shakespeare's usage, see *Love's Labours Lost* 5.2.463 and *Twelfth Night* 1.5.96. Jonson would also spell it this way (see *Every Man in His Humour* 2.3.) In the case of the man entering the cockpit, he seems more of a hanger-on, a parasite, which is the second *OED* entry.

Zanie (Chapman) had been Mr. Anemone just moments before, in the "Flying Lessons" sketch. In the same sketch, Chigger (Jones) becomes Pancho in the transition to the cockpit.

Episode 17: *"The Bishop"*

Animation: Cocoon to Compere Butterfly; "And now . . ." Man in propellered desk, and "It's" Man; *Titles* (silly Cleese v/o); "The BBC would like to apologize" by the **Gumbys**, a link; **The Architect Sketch**; "What other ways are there of recognizing a Mason?"; *Animation: How to give up being a Mason*; "The BBC would like to apologize" by the Gumbys, a link; Motor Insurance Sketch; **"The Bishop"** titles and film (and titles and film); "This is where we came in"; Living room on a pavement; Poets (and *Animated Poets advert*); Poet reading; "And now on BBC television, a choice of viewing"; Poet Reader Wombat Harness; Derek Hart interviewing Nude Man; "The Bishop" titles; "The BBC would like to apologize . . ."; *Animation: Bouncing on a naked lady, Jack and the Beanstalk,* and *Five Frog Curse*; Gumbys introduce "The Chemist sketch"; The Chemist Sketch: An Apology; "Words that are not to be used again on this program"; A Less Naughty Chemist: After-shave; "A toilet requisite: Something fishier"; Vox Pops on aftershave; Police Constable Pan-Am; "The BBC would like to apologize . . ."; Buzz Aldrin photo and closing credits; Gumbys and "The End"

• A •

"abattoir" — ("Architect Sketch") Abattoirs were cattle slaughterhouses on the continent. The term didn't enter the common English lexicon until the later nineteenth century (*OED*).

"Aberdeen" — ("Chemist Sketch") There is an Aberdeen near Bradford, but the Chemist may also be referring to the Aberdeen much farther north, on the Scottish coast.

"Aldrin, Buzz" — ("Police Constable Pan-Am") Edwin Eugene Aldrin Jr., U.S. astronaut and second man to set foot on the moon on 20 July 1969. The photo the Pythons use is Aldrin's official astronaut photo (most likely made available long before to the BBC for Apollo news coverage) taken prior to the Apollo 11 mission in 1969. Aldrin will also figure prominently in the German-language *Fliegender Zirkus*, Ep. 2, made for Bavarian TV in 1972.

A version of "The Star-Spangled Banner" can be heard under this image, as well. WAC records only record that the piece is used, and not the performing band, though it sounds like the British Grenadier Guard version.

all-in wrestlers — (PSC; *"The Bishop"*) "All-in" means "without restrictions," or anything goes, in wrestling. "Cauliflower ear"—a thickening and disfiguring of the ear tissue—results from repeated abuse in boxing, wrestling, etc. These all-in wrestlers/actors include Anthony Powell (*Softly Softly*) and John Lord (*Doctor Who*) (WAC T12/1,418). All-in cricket (featuring robust beatings and even impalings) will be depicted in Eps. 11, 18, and 45, as well as the short May Day episode created in 1971 for the *Euroshow 71—May Day Special* broadcast on the BBC and European networks.

American car — (PSC; *"The Bishop"*) The car driven by the Bishop and his henchmen appears to be a 1967 Pontiac Firebird convertible, a popular American "muscle car" of the period. In the Hollywood movies of the day, it was the "tough guys" who drove these muscle cars. The prototypical screen tough for this period, Steve McQueen, drove a fastback Ford Mustang in *Bullitt* (1968). Pontiac Firebirds are featured prominently in *Bullitt, Le clan des siciliens* (1969), and

Le cercle rouge (dir. Jean-Pierre Melville, 1970). Hamlet (Jones) will drive another big American car in Ep. 43, an obvious betrayal of his deep-seated desire to be a "private dick."

animated item (the Butterfly) — (link into opening titles) The two pieces of music Gilliam includes underneath this opening animation are "Grazing Land" (for the pastoral moment) followed by "Vistavision Title" (when the butterfly emerges), both by stock music composer Jack Shaindlin. The Pythons will continue to employ stock music as linking, mood-setting, and titling material throughout the series. During this period, many British television shows did the same, paying for broadcast rights for stock music rather than employing a composer.

The stock music industry was a thriving one as the BBC (radio and TV) and the British commercial television stations greatly expanded programming after 1955. For the feature film *Monty Python and the Holy Grail*, the Pythons will cull the DeWolfe music archives for most of the film's incidental music.

Animation: An Advertisement — (*"Animated Poets Advert"*) The row of houses seen in the "Poet Jingle" ad animation looks to have been shot near Lammas Park Road, where portions of Ep. 15 were shot.

Animation: an advertisement — (PSC; "Poets") The Shakespeare image Gilliam uses in this "Poets" animation is a retouched version of the famous "Chandos" work (National Portrait Gallery).

"Architects Sketch" — ("Architect Sketch") Once again the Pythons illustrate their awareness of current events, here referencing the recent revelations regarding the architectural firm John Poulson Associates and the influence of Freemason membership. It seems that Poulson and then Opposition deputy leader Reginald Maudling (majority shareholder and chairman, respectively, of International Technical and Construction Services) were part of an insider deal to award public works contracts to fellow Freemasons, in this case a contract to build Bradford's city center (*Private Eye*, 22 May 1970: 19–20). The article lists at least six Freemasons who also happen to be in on the deal in some way, and "would be among those reluctant to give a clear denial that they are complete strangers to the collar, the trowel, and the knotty handshake" (20). Poulson eventually fell prey to tax evasion difficulties, and declared bankruptcy; Maudling would later be forced from office in 1972 (as Home Secretary) in the wake of this influence-peddling scheme.

"Aston Martin" — ("Motor Insurance Sketch") British racing car firm established in 1914. The valuable Aston Martin series available during this period (1967–1972) was the "DB" series, named after newer (1947–1972) company owner David Brown.

"avant-garde . . . namby-pambies" — ("Nude Man" link out of "Poets") A typical Cleese/Chapman farrago of invectives, in this case aptly illustrating the Pythonesque "attack-then-defend" motif. Here the Pythons attack the more left-leaning point of view that they might otherwise defend, being less than conservative themselves. (In this they follow the stated positions of the *Beyond the Fringe* cast and the creators and contributors to *Private Eye*—any reckless or feckless power, from any point along the political spectrum, can be dangerous and should be tilted at.) Immediately, though, the Pythons undercut the attack by having the position delivered by a nude man and, in reality, a nude gay man (Chapman). These are the kinds of diatribes the Pythons themselves heard (from viewers and media pundits) during the run of *FC*, but especially in 1978–1979 as *Life of Brian* was being produced. (See Hewison's *Monty Python: The Case Against*.) In-house memos will also reveal that by the end of this second season the show was upsetting mid-level BBC managers, who term portions of Ep. 26 "disgusting," "over the edge," and "in appalling taste" (WAC T12/1,469). See notes to Ep. 26 for more.

"Namby-pamby" is a slur attributed to critics (including Carey and Pope) of Ambrose Philips (d. 1749) and his writing style, which some considered childish, though Samual Johnson greatly appreciated the "pleasant" language usage. The term has now come to mean "ineffective" and "wishy-washy." See Drabble (1985) and the "Ambrose Phillips" entry at *ODNB*.

• B •

"BBC TV Action Replay" — ("Architect Sketch") Instant replay was first used by the BBC for the Grand National in 1964.

"be a Mason?" — ("How to Give Up Being a Mason") The practicing (and antler-wearing) Mason (Chapman) is offered visual enticements in the animation to surrender his Masonic tendencies—these dangled carrots include photos of nude ladies, to which he eventually says "no," calling into question the sexual preference of this and all Masons (and bowler-hatted City types, and all authority figures, including Churchmen, etc.).

"behavioural psychotherapy" — ("How to Give Up Being a Mason") Clinical attempts to modify behavior via "talking" (Freud) and reinforcement of positive habits, or punishment for negative habits, as seen here. Journals and newspapers during the 1960s are replete with articles and editorials espousing (or eviscerating) behavior psychotherapy, pharmaceutical and even spiritual treatments for "abnormal" behaviors of all kinds, from truancy to depression to homosexuality.

Bishop's crook — (PSC; "*The Bishop*") *OED*: "The pastoral staff of a bishop, abbot or abbess, shaped like a shepherd's staff; a crosier." The Bishop wields it here like a weapon, and also uses it as a phone device. The costume used here is similar but not identical to the one worn by Palin's bishop in Ep. 16.

A mitre is the recognizable tall cap, an embroidered head-dress in the Church of England (and the Western Church).

This Bishop also has a Y-shaped scar on his cheek, which could have significance in archaic terms, and wouldn't be beyond the well-read Pythons. The *OED* gives this possibility: "Used for the Greek letter Y (*upsilon*), esp. as a Pythagorean symbol." The dictionary goes on to cite numerous instances where the "spreading branches" symbol is used to indicate the Pythagorean "life on earth is short, but life is eternal" motif, and a "y" is metaphoric for virtue (see below), which is "small at the foot but broad at the top." For more, see the *OED*.

So this tattoo or scar could be the tough Bishop's way to remind himself and others of the divergent ways of God and man, and that "to obtaine vertue is *verie painefull*, but the possession thereof passing pleasant" (Greene's *Morando, the Tritameron of Love*, 96).

"Bishop of Woolwich" — ("Nude Man" link out of "Poets") This link takes us right back to the crime-fighting character of "The Bishop," and forward to the dual-roled (and very real) Bishop of Woolwich, then Liverpool.

The Bishop of Woolwich during this period (1969–1975) was David Sheppard (1929–2005; Trinity Hall, Cambridge), a former professional cricketer (Cambridge, Sussex, and England) who was named Wisden Cricketer of the Year in 1953. This is a cricketer the Pythons would have grown up with, followed in the news, and perhaps even been able to watch. Sheppard had been ordained in 1955, and played test cricket until 1963. He was called an active "campaigner," as a member of the clergy, for the betterment of inner-city conditions, as well as actively working against the UK participating in apartheid-era South African cricket matches. So Sheppard was a Bishop who could put down his staff and pick up a cricket bat, if necessary, and a ripe influence for the Pythons' crime-fighting clergyman.

See the other entries for "*The Bishop*" sketch and character for more.

"bit the ceiling" — ("*The Bishop*") Expectedly, the Bishop speaks in TV and film noir clichés, not unlike some of the pot-boiler dialogue from classic pulp films like *Double Indemnity* (1944), *T-Men* (1947), *Pickup on South Street* (1948), and even *Shock Corridor* (1963). Television crime shows like *The Untouchables* (1959) also can be mentioned. "Bit the ceiling" is obviously a variation on "bit(e) the dust": "To bite the dust, ground, sand, etc.: to fall in death, to die; also, to fall to the ground, to fall wounded; to be abased" (see *OED*).

"blinkered . . . ignorance" — ("Architect Sketch") Being "blinkered," figuratively, means being limited in outlook or vision; the term "philistine" can be "applied to persons regarded as 'the enemy,' into whose hands one may fall, e.g., bailiffs, literary critics, etc."; and "pig ignorance" means having the characteristics of one so pig-headed (stubborn, obstinate) that nothing new or enlightened can penetrate. See the *OED*. The diatribe rambles on, with Mr. Wiggin (Cleese) carrying off a classic Python splenetic that includes:

"non-creative"—The specter of conformity and uniformity as anathema to youth, the artist, and freedom is a theme that runs consistently through *FC*. It seems that Wiggin is the voice of the Modernist, attacking the Establishment way of seeing art and architecture, and asking that conventional ideas and forms be reimagined. This is also a defining, delimiting comment—the creative types are "us," and the non-creative are "them."

"tinker's cuss"—Historically held in low repute, to be said to do anything like a "tinker" constituted a degrading insult (*OED*).

"toadies"—A toady is a "servile parasite; a sycophant, an interested flatterer" (*OED*). The "hypocritical toadies" comment also connects back to Wiggin's Modernist tendencies. In their design wants the City Gents (Palin and Jones) are clinging to the conventional, the usual, the "simple block of flats" mode of architecture that the Bauhaus group and other Modernist artists had been reacting against since the 1920s. Wiggin's design doesn't look terribly cutting edge, but it's the creative, innovative usage of the building—as a slaughterhouse—that separates him from the norm.

"colour TV sets"—Color TVs were more expensive and the license fees were higher, as well, proving here that perhaps only the (relatively) wealthy could afford such a luxury. It was only in 1969 that BBC shows began to be broadcast regularly in color, which certainly benefited *Flying Circus* a great deal in assuring both its survival (in videotape format) and legacy. (The BBC and other networks regularly "wiped" videotape for re-use, meaning many pre-1970 shows, including those featuring the Pythons, no longer exist in any viewable format.)

"Tony Jacklin golf clubs"—Jacklin (b. 1944) is an English golfer who won the U.S. Open in 1970, the first Brit to claim the title in fifty years. Jacklin had played successfully on the European and American professional golf circuits during the 1960s. Clubs bearing his name, then, would have been quite a status symbol. Jacklin will be mentioned again in Eps. 21 and 28. Jacklin and Ann Haydon-Jones (Eps. 7, 19, 22) had been named Sportsman and Sportswoman of the Year, respectively, in November 1969.

"masonic handshakes"—Secret handshakes of ancient origin used by the Freemasons to identify other members of the order. The Pythons, of course, will later make them appear quite ridiculous.

Freemasonry is a secret, fraternal society with associated rituals, handshakes, signs, knocks, ceremonial apparel, etc. These masons were initially connected to the building trades, including architecture. (Coincidentally, but certainly not lost on the Pythons, the development in which the Ronan Point building was constructed in Newham is called "Freemasons Estate." The other eight blocks were built between 1968–1970, and all are now demolished. There were no other collapse failures in this type of building, partly because concerned councils went back and performed expensive retrofits on the other buildings.)

"blackballing"—*OED*: "To exclude (a person) from a club or other society by adverse votes, recorded by the placing of black balls in the ballot-box, or in other ways." Because membership in the Masonic organization often provided critical business and social opportunities ("It opens doors. I'm telling you."), chapters could be quite selective, even exclusive. Many Freemason chapters have historically employed the black and white ball ballot box, as well.

"purulent"—Having the qualities of pus.

Finally, Cleese and Chapman are known for writing such vitriolic, end-to-end vituperative imprecations (a kind of "escalation" format) for their formerly mild-mannered characters to suddenly spew, with Cleese himself often being cast in this role.

"block of flats" — ("Architect Sketch") *OED*: "A suite of rooms on one floor, forming a complete residence." In this case, a vertical city block of such structures, the type of which can still be seen across the UK (i.e., Barbican Centre, built 1964–1975). These structures (inspired by the Modernist architect Le Corbusier, and Bauhaus principles) were very popular across not only the UK but into Europe, Eastern Europe, and the Soviet Union. The efficiency, locations, and city views offered by these types of buildings were initially attractive, but in the long term building and neighborhood decay tarnished the blocks' image. The 1968 fire and collapse at Ronan Point sealed the public's negative opinion of the structures. (Only recently has the slide reversed, as the flats are remodeled and now trend "hip.") See notes below for more, as well as the entry for "milk-float" in Ep. 16.

Wiggin's (Cleese) version of the "block of flats" looks more like a Robin Hood Gardens (Poplar) design, or Park Hill (designed by Lynn and Smith in Sheffield) than a tower block as proposed by Mr. Leavey (Idle). Robin Hood Gardens is a long, low block of flats designed by Alison and Peter Smithson, and was being constructed as these episodes were being written and recorded. Park Hill was finished in 1961.

The magazine *Private Eye* also satirized these monuments to what it called "New Barbarism" in its architectural columns.

(blows raspberry) — (PSC; "Architect Sketch") A raspberry is a derisive sound made using the tongue and lips, also called a "Bronx cheer" (*OED*), and Wiggin (Cleese) employs it in his entreaty to the City Gents (Palin and Jones). Instead of a carefully placed raspberry, though, the original script actually called for Mr. Wiggin to say "sod" (see Morgan's *Speaks!*). BBC censors asked that the word not be used, determining the term to still be too offensive for the British viewing public. (It may be that since the word was being used anatomically rather than adjectivally, it was more offensive.) By Ep. 27 they are able to get away with "Intercourse the penguin!" without much concern. And by the final *FC* episode, Ep. 45, they offered up "get off my sodding wick" without influence or interference of the censors, meaning either that times had changed or it was acknowledged that this was the last show of the series (or both).

• C •

"cement" — ("Motor Insurance Sketch") Death by cement is a typical method employed by underworld hoodlums, by whom the Devious (Palin) character seems inspired. The presence of organized crime-types in the building trades, especially as suppliers of material, including cement, has perhaps allowed for the death-by-cement scenario heard so often in film and TV. Generally, though, the victim's feet are placed in cement and then he is dumped into a river, or the body is (allegedly, perhaps even apocryphally) thrown into a new building's cement pour.

See the entry for "Devious" below, and this sketch's relation to the infamous Emil Savundra.

"central . . . concrete" — ("Architect Sketch") What the architect is describing here is another Modernist influence, the International Style (what many call "Brutalist") type architecture, Le Corbusier-inspired, and which is often defined by massive, geometric blocks of concrete and very little baroque ornamentation. A "central pillar" (probably of steel and concrete) would have carried the weight of the cantilevered floors, meaning structural support (load-bearing) at the inner ("dividing") and outer walls was deemed unnecessary. The explosion and collapse of the Ronan Point block indicated that this design—precast, reinforced concrete blocks brought onsite and "slotted" into place—left something to be desired, especially as the onsite construction seems to have been substandard.

"chemist" — ("Chemist Sketch") British term for "pharmacist." A chemist shop in the UK can provide sundries, as well, including film development (Ep. 19).

cinema — (PSC; "Living Room on Pavement") A large sign can be seen on the front of the cinema (though isn't referred to by the characters or the text itself), actually a marquee advertisement for the Peter Sellers film *Hoffman* (1970), directed by Alvin Rakoff. Peter Sellers and the other Goons (Milligan and Secombe) were admittedly influential to Python and the style and structure of *FC*.

This cinema is the ABC Cinema that used to occupy a lot on New Zealand Avenue in Walton-on-Thames. The building and several around it were torn down and replaced with a mixed use development. It is just down the street from where the Bishop and his henchmen were strolling confidently.

"C. of E." — ("*The Bishop*") The Church of England or Anglican Church, the official church of the state since 1534, when Henry VIII separated himself and the country from the Roman Catholic faith.

congregation — (PSC; "*The Bishop*") Members of the congregation in "*The Bishop*" include Roger Tolliday (*Special Branch*), George Ballantyne (*Emma*), Mary Maxted (*Miss Bohrloch*), Elizabeth Broom (*Dixon of Dock Green*), Elaine Williams (*Studio 4*), Joyce Freeman (*Play for Today*), and Joanna Robbins (*Emma*). These scenes were shot in the larger spaces of Ealing TFS (WAC T12/1,418).

crime-series-type titles, suitable music — (PSC; "*The Bishop*") The music under these titles is Dave Lindup's "Superperformance (Impact and Action)" (WAC T12/1,431).

Cut to Gumbys as at start of show — (PSC; "Gumbys and 'The End'") The Gumbys (and then their female counterparts) are standing in front of the now demolished Elmbridge Town Hall on New Zealand Avenue in Walton-on-Thames. This shot and location have been repeated from the beginning of the episode.

• D •

"Devious" — ("Motor Insurance Sketch") Devious (not unlike another shady Palin character, Dino Vercotti) sports a couple of facial scars, greased hair, inner-city accent, and here is reading an erotic book, probably from a pornographic series published in Germany or the Netherlands, or even Soho. The latter location is connected to the work of Harrison Marks (1926–1997), a Gerrard Street glamor photographer active during the 1950s and 1960s, whose work appeared in *Kamera*, *Solo*, *Focus*, et al. Some of these titles can be glimpsed in the footlocker of the defrocked padre in the Basil Dearden (1911–1971) caper film *The League of Gentlemen* (1960), and are likely the kinds of "photography magazines" Major Bloodnok (Sellers) is referring to whenever he's trying to discreetly order back issues in a plain brown wrapper. (*League of Gentlemen* was written by Bryan Forbes, who is mentioned in Eps. 20, 23, and 36.)

This entire incident is likely a reference to the notorious Emil Savundra (1923–1976), a Sri Lankan businessman who pioneered the auto insurance fraud industry in the UK in the 1960s. Savundra took in far more premium-paying customers (offering "cut-rate" policies) than he could ever hope to service if any number of claims were made, and he was eventually grilled on national television by none other than David Frost on *The Frost Programme* (3 Feb. 1967). Idle was working on the Frost program at this time. The encounter helped make Frost's reputation as a dogged interviewer.

"Dibbingley Road" — ("Architect Sketch") No such road or street exists in the UK. Just the onomatopoeic appeal of this and similar names—Dibble, Dibley, Dibbingley—perhaps account for their recurring appearances in *FC* (more mentions in Eps. 18 and 19). These all "sound" like silly places and names, not unlike Carroll's fanciful language: ". . . slithy toves / [Could] gyre and gimble in the wabe; / All mimsy were the borogoves, / And the mome raths outgrabe" (final stanza, *Jabberwocky*).

The Modernist author Gertrude Stein—according to Mabel Dodge in her 1913 essay "Speculations, or Post-Impressionism in Prose"—was particular in choosing "words for their inherent quality, rather than for their accepted meaning." The Pythons would even choose their sentences for similar reasons, as was seen earlier, when the Presenter (Palin) launches into his *Spectrum* tirade in Ep. 12. The new and unorthodox wordsmithing of Stein and Carroll, of Virginia Woolf and James Joyce are clearly influential throughout *FC*.

"dirty books" — ("Motor Insurance Sketch") In the "Tudor Jobs Agency" sketch, Ep. 36, dirty books are the real products for sale in the job agency.

"documentary" — ("Living Room on Pavement") One of the major television formats satirized by Python throughout *FC*, the others including TV news, sitcoms, quiz and game shows, commercials, and BBC serial dramas. These kinds of on-the-scene-reporter documentary shows were being produced by *Panorama* during this period.

dog collars — (PSC; *"The Bishop"*) This is a derogatory term for the clerical collar.

"Don't say the text!" — (*"The Bishop"*) Each time the Bishop (Jones) intervenes in these filmed segments, it is on behalf of a Church of England clergyman, and as that clergyman is performing one of his sacerdotal (and specifically ordinance) duties. The preaching of a sermon, an infant baptism, a wedding, a bell ringing, and a graveside service are all moments when the Bishop attempts to thwart Italian-looking (hence, Roman Catholic?) thugs from killing C. of E. vicars—and importantly, as the vicars attempt to ritually administer to their respective flocks. The Bishop (Jones) is always too late, of course. When he intervenes on behalf of Reverend Morris (Idle) in Devious's office, though, it is in response to cries for help, as if Morris was trapped in a burning building. The question of where *"The Bishop"* film begins is questionable, eventually, perhaps even Alpha and Omega, without beginning or end.

"do you for heresy" — ("Police Constable Pan-Am") A slang phrase, to be "done" here means he'll be arrested for crimes against the church. Generally (in England) this would indicate the Christian Church, but in the case of the text and its reflexivity, is probably referring to the Roman Catholic Church as indicated by the Inquisitor allusion. (Though, of course Elizabeth I had her own inquisitor, Richard Topcliff [see the *ODNB*], who performed very similar functions, but for good Queen Bess, England, and the Anglican Church.)

This is a rather ancient form (c. 1000) of "do," as well, according to the *OED*: "To impart to, bring upon (a person, etc.) some affecting quality or condition; to bestow, confer, inflict, to cause by one's action (a person) to have (something). In later use, associated more closely with the notion of performance."

Duke of Edinburgh — (PSC; "Chemist Sketch") The printed script describes Gilliam as walking into the chemist's shop "with hands clasped behind him à la the Duke of Edinburgh." The Queen's husband, Prince Philip (b. 1921), has adopted the "arms behind the back" pose for most of his official career. For two examples, see Illingworth's cartoon published in the *Daily Mail* on 10 November 1969, or Jak's in the *Evening Standard* eight days later. Even today in political cartoons he is very often depicted in this characteristic, even iconic pose. See the British Cartoon Archive.

• E •

"East Midlands" — ("Poets") The East Midlands region includes the counties of Lincolnshire, Northamptonshire, Derbyshire, Nottinghamshire, Leicestershire, and Rutland. Chapman is from this area, having attended elementary school in Melton Mowbray. This portion of the episode, however, was recorded in Walton-on-Thames, along New Zealand Avenue. The office and light manufacturing building behind Cleese is still in situ, while the ABC Cinema behind the camera has been torn down.

Episode 17 — This episode was recorded as the ninth episode of this second season on 18 September 1970, and then broadcast on 20 October 1970. It was broadcast as the fourth episode, however. There must have been some confusion or the episode or even sketches were jumbled along the way—the WAC records sometimes refer to actors appearing in this episode as appearing in "Ep. 8," even though it eventually was recorded ninth.

Denton De Gray (*Quatermass II*) and Julie Desmond (*Casanova, The Goodies*) also appeared in this episode, though the WAC records don't identify their roles (WAC T12/1,431).

• F •

female Gumbys — (PSC; link out of "Police Constable Pan-Am") These are actually women, and the sounds they make are trilling sounds, not unlike the Arab women during a battle in *Lawrence of Arabia* (1962). Again, the mere presence of a real woman becomes a bit more unusual, especially with so much cross-dressing in *FC*. This shot is still set in front of the (now demolished) Elmbridge Town Hall on New Zealand Avenue, Walton-on-Thames. Portions of "The Bishop" and "Living Room on a Pavement" were also shot on this street.

Floor manager — (PSC; "After-Shave") One of the on-set TV production team members, the floor manager normally stands between cameras (off-camera), and indicates with hand signals which camera is "hot," etc., and usually is wearing headphones and carrying a clipboard with a shot sheet attached. The show's actual floor manager appears in Eps. 2, 10, and 19. The position has some less significance today, as a director can communicate with on-screen talent directly through hidden ear pieces, and cameras are often remotely controlled.

four henchmen — (PSC; "*The Bishop*") These four toughs/vicars are Michael Stayner (Eps. 17–19; *Billion Dollar Brain*), Brian Gardner (Ep. 18; *The Fabulous Frump*), Bill Leonard (Eps. 18, 19), and Tom O'Leary (Ep. 18; *A Man Called Shenandoah*). These actors were all hired from Cagneys Agency (WAC T12/1,418).

"Frankincense" — ("Vox Pops") A pleasant resin for burning. Ximenez (Palin) is appearing again as the Cardinal (in front of the Old Bailey and to audience cheers) after Ep. 15's "Spanish Inquisition" success.

The biblical frankincense-and-myrrh theme is revisited in the opening scene of the Python feature film *Life of Brian* (1979), where the Three Wise Men (Cleese, Chapman, and Palin) accidentally deliver their valuable gifts to the baby Brian, and not Jesus.

"Freemasonry opens doors" — ("Architect Sketch") It was generally agreed that such fraternal orders did (and even do) offer members significant networking opportunities in the business world, "opening doors" to promotions and other advancements thanks to the desire for members to help members whenever possible. See the note above to "blackballing" for more.

"f'tang" — ("Police Constable Pan-Am") A word borrowed from the Pythons' comedy inspirations, the Goons, which can be heard in the episode "The Call of the West" (20 Jan. 1959) several times in the phrase "Fort F'tang."

furnishings of a bathroom — (PSC; "Living Room on Pavement") In the first, establishing shot of this scene, Alfred, Lord Tennyson is not yet in the tub. He won't appear until Mrs. Potter (Chapman) goes to draw a bath.

• G •

gets script out — ("Motor Insurance Sketch") This breaking of the illusion of the world of the sketch will become common in *FC*, as well as in the later feature films. When the "Man" (Chapman) asks if he has any more to say, he is reminding the audience they are watching an act, a sketch. The script is consulted on a number of occasions in *FC* episodes, including "Lost World of Roiurama" (Ep. 29) and at the unsuccessful ending of the "Jokes and Novelties Salesman" sketch (Ep. 15).

Participants in the inspirational *The Goon Show* (1951–1960) would on occasion pause and consult the script, or address the audience as audience, or even acknowledge that they are each playing multiple characters. In "The Jet-Propelled Guided NAAFI" episode, Sellers picks up and reads from the script for a moment, moving the sketch from one scene to another (*The Goon Show*, 24 Jan. 1956).

"Grimsby" — ("*The Bishop*") The printed script reads "Grimsby," though the video (and eventually DVD) version uses "Gromsby," and includes a hyphen afterward. Gilliam would have produced this title sequence, and the physical disconnect between Gilliam's work/working space and the rest of the troupe probably accounts for this error. Grimsby is a city in Lincolnshire, and in archival sources (genealogy records, for instance) it seems that the Grimsby/Gromsby confusion goes well beyond the Pythons. "Urqhart" is the name of a castle in Scotland, to push the Scottish motif of these titles a bit further.

group of Gumbys — (PSC; link into "Architect Sketch") These Gumbys are standing in front of the Elmbridge Town Hall in Walton-on-Thames. The building was demolished in 1988. The building had been finished in 1966, so it was fairly new when the Pythons used the location. This hall was also on New Zealand Avenue, where portions of *The Bishop* and the old couple living on the pavement were filmed.

Gumbys — (link into "Architect Sketch") This could have been a name derived from the boots the characters wear, though the *OED* doesn't mention "Gumby" at all when defining "gum-booted" in its latest edition. Additonally, the Gumbys sport napkins or kerchiefs tied to their heads, wire-rimmed glasses, Hitler-like mustaches, too-small vests, white shirts with rolled-up sleeves, rolled-up trousers, and, of course, the rubber boots. They characteristically shout everything, and first appeared in the first season's Ep. 5 (see notes there).

Another strange possibility (at least for the nomenclature) has to be the popular American animated character "Gumby," created by Art Clokey, and who began appearing regularly on the children's show *The Howdy Doody Show* on ABC in 1956. *The Gumby Show* then appeared on NBC in 1957, and new episodes appeared sporadically in 1962, and 1966–1967.

• H •

"Halitosis" — ("Vox Pops") Foul breath.

hammer — (animated link out of "Architect Sketch") The large hammer, both animated and in prop form, is used often in *FC*, especially to end a sketch or act as a link. This is certainly a cartoony prop, not unlike the sixteen-ton weight and the round, black ("anarchist's") bomb prop. The hammer acts much as the iconic crook did for the music hall/vaudeville stage decades earlier—in this case bringing the act to a close with a resounding "thud." In this way the hammer is both a nontraditional replacement for the purposely avoided punchline, a punishment for the delivery of a punchline, as well as the more traditional linking element so key to the sketch/musical variety show structure. Using the prop in myriad ways ensures that the Pythons are able to have their cake and eat it, too.

"Hardy, Thomas" — ("Poets") Thomas Hardy (1840–1928) was both a novelist *and* a poet, producing eight volumes of poetry which were somewhat tepidly received during his lifetime, though greatly appreciated since. Hardy's admitted dislike of flowery speech, the "jewelled line," accounts for why the housewife disdains her Hardy and seeks the "garden of love" with Wombat (*MPSERD*, 98n).

"Hart, Derek" — ("Nude Man" link out of "Poets") Derek Hart (1925–1986) was a respectable member of the newscast for the *Tonight* program (1957–1965) created by the legendary TV producer Grace Wyndham Goldie (1900–1986), and also starring Ned Sherrin (mentioned in Ep. 5), and Alan Whicker (Ep. 27).

"Hendon" — ("Architect Sketch") In the borough of Barnet, Greater London, Hendon is a stone's throw northwest of Golders Green, which figures prominently in Ep. 9, and the Pythons recorded studio portions of several episodes at the Hippodrome there. The nearest Masonic hall to Hendon seems to have been in Watford, Hertfordshire, to the northwest.

high window . . . where vicar is looking out — (PSC; *"The Bishop"*) Idle's close-up (as the wailing Vicar) is shot in the upper right window of the building where the Bishop enters, at 123 New Zealand Ave.

hoarding — (PSC; "How to Give Up Being a Mason") *OED*: "A temporary fence made of boards enclosing a building while in course of erection or repair; often used for posting bills and advertisements; hence, any boarding on which bills are posted." This appears to be a purpose-built billboard, and is situated next to another billboard with an actual advertisement (for cognac) on it.

"housing problem facing Britain's aged" — ("Living Room on Pavement") The subject of adequate housing comes up again and again in *FC*, and the problem is a consistent feature in newspapers of the period.

An example from Birmingham: The local council was building as many as 2,000 new homes every year by 1968, but the waiting list for homes stood at about 60,000, which helped lead to Ronan Point–type buildings. For more on the chronic housing shortage in postwar Britain, see notes to Ep. 14, as well as Morgan's *Britain since 1945*, Judt's *Postwar*, and Wilson's *After the Victorians*. (Housing shortage was a chronic problem across all of Europe in the wake of the Allies' indiscriminate bombing, and Goebbel's "total war" responses.) By Ep. 43, unscrupulous Python characters (there played by Palin) are advocating the easy removal of the elderly from their homes to make way for businesses and younger, higher-income tenants.

In the political cartoons of the period, the wrangling debate over Britain's support of the United States in Vietnam is tied directly to inattention to domestic matters like inadequate housing (e.g., Illingworth, *Daily Mail*, 8 Dec. 1969). See the British Cartoon Archive.

humming and harring — (PSC; "How to Give Up Being a Mason") The Gumbies are moving about and muttering to themselves, getting situated for the link. The printed scripts sometimes include these bits of business, but usually not.

hymn is heard — (PSC; *"The Bishop"*) The hymn that ends as the Bishop (Jones) and his cronies approach the church is a version of Blake's "O, Jerusalem," which has been heard earlier in Eps. 4 and 8, and will be featured again in Ep. 29.

• I •

"Ironside and Malone" — ("Architect Sketch") Edmund Ironside (c. 993–1016) was king of England for a short period in 1016, and died trying to repel Danish invaders. Also, the American crime drama *Ironside* (1967–1975), starring post–*Perry Mason* actor Raymond Burr, was a current popular hit. (*Ironside* appeared on Telefis Eireann—Irish TV—in September 1967, before moving to BBC1.) A prominent Malone included another Edmund—Edmund Malone (1741–1812)—a noted editor of Shakespeare's corpus. Malone attended Trinity College, Cambridge.

• K •

"Kensington" — ("After-Shave") Part of the Royal Borough of Kensington and Chelsea, Greater London, and fashionable home (to the Pythons, at least) of Upperclass Twit types.

"kn*ckers" — ("Chemist Sketch") Though "knickers" (short pants/underwear) would fit here, this is probably meant to be "knockers," since the word is given twice. The Pythons resort to such bodily/schoolboy (or even "carnivalesque") humor as often as their lofty predecessors Jonson, Swift, and Voltaire (see *MPSERD*, chapter 2.) The Goons also employed vulgar euphemisms, but within the more restrained limitations imposed by the BBC ("Auntie Beeb") of the 1950s. In just moments, another word—"Semprini"—will also be banned based on an assumed sexual connotation. See the entry for "Semprini" below for more.

• L •

"Leviticus 3-14" — (*"The Bishop"*) This is probably not meant to indicate all chapters between and including 3 and 14, though that's how it's written in the printed script. The fourteenth verse of the third chapter of Leviticus reads as follows: "And he shall offer thereof his offering, even an offering made by fire unto the LORD; the fat that covereth the inwards, and all the fat that is upon the inwards" (King James Version).

"lifts" — ("Architect Sketch") British term for "elevators."

"longeurs" — ("Words Not to Be Used Again") *OED*: "A lengthy or tedious passage of writing. Also in extended use, of music, etc." As the customer (Idle) waits for the Chemist (Palin) there is a rather lengthy passage of time, of dead air, which actually had become fashionable in various New Waves of the recent past. French films, especially, had begun experimenting with "lived" or "perceived" time (inspired by Henri Bergson's musings on *duré*) as opposed to cinematic time, which can be quite elliptical. (See notes for Bergson and his significance to the Pythons in Ep. 20.) See the long and often repeated tracking shots in Alain Resnais's *Last Year at Marienbad* (1961), or the empty pauses in Jean-Pierre Melville's *Le samourai* (1967). The *OED* also identifies this particular spelling as incorrect, with "longueur" being the accepted spelling.

"lunar module" — ("Police Constable Pan-Am") The portion of the Apollo 11 spacecraft that actually landed on the moon's surface, containing Armstrong and Aldrin, was called the "Eagle." Michael Collins (b. 1930) orbited in the command module. The U.S. Apollo space missions had been front-page news in British newspapers since the earliest "destination: Moon" flights. Also, in 1969 alone there were almost 120 op-ed cartoons referencing the Apollo missions in British newspapers. See the British Cartoon Archive.

In Ep. 28, an Apollo-inspired three-stage model of Tchaikovsky will be examined during the *"Life of Tschaikowsky"* sketch. Models of the various Apollo crafts were used by BBC presenters during these broadcasts.

• M •

"mainly design slaughter houses" — ("Architect Sketch") Peter Ackroyd notes in *London: The Biography* that the designer of the Holloway Prison (opened 1852), James B. Banning, also designed buildings for both the Coal Exchange (Lower Thames Street) as well as the Metropolitan Cattle Market (Caledonian Road, Islington), and utilized similar design principles from building to building (253).

"moderator" — (PSC; *"The Bishop"*) In the Presbyterian churches: A minister elected to preside over any one of the ecclesiastical bodies, for example, the congregation, the presbytery, the synod, the general assembly. In the Scottish church, historically, a Moderator was often appointed to "avoid confusion in reasoning," according to the *OED*.

"mush" — ("Architect Sketch") *OED*: "Man, 'chap'; hence also as a term of address."

• N •

"neo-Georgian" — ("Architect Sketch") A revival of eighteenth- (and nineteenth-) century British architectural styles, the neo-Georgian look was very popular in the late Edwardian era and into the 1920s. Clearly, the symmetry of Wiggin's (Cleese) design is characteristic of the reinvigorated style. The extant Grosvenor Square Marriott is an example of the neo-Georgian style; Mayfair is also home to a number of neo-Georgian buildings.

Neuk — (*"The Bishop"*) Small town / region of Scotland. The Goons also use the name, in a mention of "Mrs. Violet Neuk of 5 Sussex Road" ("The Last Smoking Seagoon").

"No I'm not" — ("Police Constable Pan-Am") Though not identified in the script, this is Gilliam speaking—acting the upper half of the mac—with the diminutive Stanley Mason (Eps. 14, 17, 19, and the Montreux special; *Doctor Who*) below.

"not meant to be luxury flats" — ("Architect Sketch") This rather offhand treatment and general lack of consideration for the would-be inhabitants of this structure lends credence to Mr. Wiggin's (Cleese) earlier outburst, and even to his assessment of them as "philistine" and uncaring, which was certainly Python's intent. This also goes right along with the general concerns voiced publicly and in government halls after the Ronan Point disaster, when it was thought that local councils and contractors were more interested in getting the more affordable experimental blocks finished and occupied than in the assurance of safe, quality housing.

Nude Lady — ("Motor Insurance Sketch") This actress appears to be Mary (Maxted) Millington (1945–1979) who would go on to become a "Page Three" girl in the *Sun*, and star in a number of celebrated "adult" films.

• O •

Outside a cigarette shop — (PSC; "*The Bishop*") This cigarette shop is still a newsagent and cigarette store (an AAQ Newsagent and Confectioners), and is located at 4, Simpson House, New Zealand Avenue, Walton-on-Thames. The window where the vicar (Idle) wails is just a few storefronts down the street (123 New Zealand), and the cinema where the old couple live on the pavement is just beyond that.

• P •

"Pan Am" — ("Police Constable Pan-Am") A U.S. airline, Pan American Airways was formed in 1927, and pioneered the transpacific, transatlantic, and around-the-world flights. Pan Am also purchased the first jet (Boeing 707) for commercial airline use. The citation of a prominent American airline continues the episode's Yankee trend that includes mentions of astronaut Buzz Aldrin and the "Raindrops Keep Fallin' on My Head" refrain from a popular Hollywood movie (*Butch Cassidy and the Sundance Kid* [1969]).

"Peter Gunn Theme" — ("*The Bishop*") The "Peter Gunn Theme" was composed by another American, Henry Mancini, and the theme originally appeared in 1958. It has become almost generic in its application to crime stories/themes on TV and in film. The theme kicks in when the Bishop and henchmen are walking down the street, knocking everyone aside as they go. This same effect was created in Ep. 8, when the "Hell's Grannies" characters strut down the street to the theme from the James Bond film *From Russia with Love* (1963).

"plumped" — ("Motor Insurance Sketch") This means to pay for at once, as well as "to fall for," making a poor choice. See *OED*. Both definitions fit the Vicar's situation as he tries to make a claim on a worthless policy.

"poet in every home" — ("Poets") There had recently been socially responsible movements calling for natural gas in every home, a nationwide change to North Sea natural gas, as well as the denial of gas for those living in recently built high rises (following the Ronan Point disaster in 1968). See entries in Ep. 14 for more on the gas situation in the UK.

The "Poet Jingle" song heard during the short Gilliam animation was composed by Bill McGuffie and sung by Jones and Cleveland (WAC T12/1,431). McGuffie also plays live accompaniment for Cleese and Chapman in Ep. 3 ("Someone Else I'd Like to Be"), and composed songs for Eps. 22 and 25, also in this second season (WAC T12/1,242).

The "Poet Board" interview (Cleese) is recorded on the same block where the Bishop (Jones) and his henchmen emerge from the newsagent's shop and strut up the street (toward the cinema, where Cleese stands, at about what is now 111-115 New Zealand Avenue). The office/industrial bldg. over Cleese's shoulder is still in situ, just across from where the ABC Cinema once stood, and today is relatively unchanged.

"pox" — ("Chemist Sketch") Any venereal disease. Here we can identify sufferers and their complaints by their postures and/or appearances. Note that no one wants to admit to having the transmittable disease, leading to the reticent raised hand (Idle). The man (John Hughman) with the boil on his "botty" is standing, of course; the very busty woman (Julie Desmond) has the chest rash; and the man suffering from flatulence (Jones) is keeping himself as far away from the others as he can.

"Prebendary 'Chopper' Harris" — (PSC; "*The Bishop*") A prebendary: "The holder of a prebend (portion of the revenues of a cathedral or collegiate church granted to a canon or member of the chapter as his stipend); a canon of a cathedral or collegiate church who holds a prebend"; and "chopper": "One who barters or exchanges . . . in ecclesiastical benefices" and/or "chops logic" (*OED* 1989). This is a character that has both access to the church funds and the ability to divvy out favors and spiritual gifts—so he sounds very much like a combination of both the Pardoner and the Monk from Chaucer's *Canterbury Tales*, for example.

There are several other similarly monikered Python characters, Colin "Bomber" Harris (a wrestler), Harry "Snapper" Organs (a police inspector), and Colin "Chopper" Mozart (a ratcatcher). (This type of nickname was often garnered as a result of a boxing background.)

The character's actual namesake is most likely Detective Chief Inspector Leonard "Nipper" Read, who was instrumental in bringing the Krays to justice. See notes to Ep. 14 for more on the Krays.

• Q •

"quid" — ("Architect Sketch") A sovereign, or one pound sterling.

• R •

"raindrops . . . my" — ("Police Constable Pan-Am") "Raindrops Keep Fallin' on My Head" was written and performed by B.J. Thomas (b. 1942) for the 1969 film (and fitting there somewhat anachronistically) *Butch Cassidy and the Sundance Kid*. The song went on to become an international hit, crossing over to radio, sheet music, and elevator music fame.

"recessed . . . grooves" — ("Architect Sketch") *OED*: "Magnalium": "A light aluminium-based alloy containing some magnesium."

"flange"—"A projecting flat rim, collar, or rib, used to strengthen an object, to guide it, to keep it in place, to facilitate its attachment to another object, or for other purposes."

In lay terms, these are inset walls, ostensibly slotted into (but not affixed to?) the central pillar. This was similar to the construction of the Ronan Point tower which partially collapsed in 1968. See the entry for "SATIRE" below.

rubber mac — (PSC; "Poets") A rubber, dark-but-still-see-through overcoat also worn by Cleese in the "Dead Parrot" sketch and other Praline character appearances, including Ep. 19. The "Mackintosh" is named for Charles Mackintosh (1766–1843), who invented the cloth and rubber cement overcoats. More recently, the name "Mackintosh" has been used to designate any type of rain-proof coat, and is very often shortened to "mac."

• S •

"Sandalwood" — ("Vox Pops") A fragrant wood often used for perfume. Myrrh and frankincense were also used in perfumes. Chanel No. 5 (not "Rancid Polecat number two") was a very popular and expensive perfume in the early 1970s. Chanel had introduced with great fanfare a No. 19 perfume in early 1970.

"SATIRE" — ("Architect Sketch") This inserted caption could be just a slap at the typical, mindless television viewer who wouldn't know satire unless it were captioned. More pessimistically (and perhaps realistically), this could be the Pythons' weak attempt at avoiding any kind of legal action from the building trades, the Freemasons, City Councils, etc., given Britain's rather draconian libel laws in place at the time. The satirical magazine *Private Eye* had already attacked the subject with vigor the previous year, but the *Eye* also had a history of being served with myriad writs, and paid out thousands of pounds in damages, and even accepted donations from readers to help pay for legal fees. As at least nominally a traditional organ of the government, the BBC was quite unwilling to suffer similar exposure.

Specifically, this points back to the Ronan Point disaster of 1968—a relatively small gas explosion destroyed a corner of a high rise in Newham, top to bottom—where at least four died and seventeen were injured (a first-person account can be heard on *Eyewitness: 1960–69*, "Ronan Point Tower Collapses"). Charges were tossed about that shoddy building practices were used—since the flats were for public housing—and the segmental design itself was ultimately admitted to be compromised by improper installation. (There were at least 429 such buildings in Birmingham alone, for example, and more than one million people living in these structures throughout Britain.)

The BBC carried the flag on a number of these exposé programs, prompting ministerial calls for a more cautious, less profligate broadcast approach to the topic. *Private Eye* seemed to apply the pressure early and with consistency, posing some of the toughest questions for those responsible (Ingrams, 192–93). In November 1968 a high rise under construction in Sheffield also partially collapsed, bringing calls for increased tower block inspections, review of designs, inspection of already-built structures, and many, many op-ed pieces and biting political cartoons (including a cartoon by Jak, *Evening Standard*, 15 Nov. 1968). See the British Cartoon Archive, as well as Pearson and Delatte, and *Private Eye*.

See Hewison's *Monty Python: The Case Against* for more on Python's brushes with the law and the religious orthodoxy, especially after the release of *Life of Brian* (1979).

"saw the light" — ("*The Bishop*") Play on the phrase "seeing the light," with an emphasis on the explosion and even heaven's brightness as Reverend Neuk (Chapman) crosses to the other side. Generally, however, to "see the light" means to come to some better understanding.

"scaly" — ("Vox Pops") The "Ken Shabby" character is also here making a return appearance, having been introduced in Ep. 12.

"second-hand apron" — ("Architect Sketch") An apron worn by Freemasons as part of their ritual clothing, it has certain symbolic meanings in the organization, including the representation of the wearer's soul. Wiggin (Cleese) appears to have bought his used, or inherited it. When Chapman appears in the animation to follow he is also wearing a Masonic apron, and little else.

"Semprini" — ("Words Not to Be Used Again") A.F.R. Semprini (1908–1990) was a British pianist who became a fixture on BBC Radio. His *Semprini Serenade* made its debut in 1957 and ran at least through 1969 (on Radio 1 and 2). This reference, of course, could also be an "othering" by Python of something non-English, in this case an Italian. This would also continue the theme established earlier in "*The Bishop*" film, where Italian-looking gangsters were the threat.

The young woman who appears here and asks, "Semprini?" is actress Sandra Richards.

"shouts out of window at gumbys" — ("Architect Sketch") In this exchange there is a cutting back and forth between the very separate and distinct worlds of the videotape and film stock image. The image quality difference of the filmed as compared to the taped image is very evident, though the Pythons make no attempt to hide or even blur the rather obvious transitions. Often, the transition from videotaped to filmed image is a simple cut from inside the studio to the outside, from one sketch to another, but not always. In this case the continuity of the scene might seem to be in jeopardy, but it's likely the viewing audience is quite accustomed to these transitions, as they are clearly evident in earlier BBC shows like *Benny Hill*, *Do Not Adjust Your Set*, etc. The difference there is, of course, that those shows were all broadcast in monochrome (black and white), meaning the distinct image qualities were less noticeable. In color transmission (which BBC2 pioneered in 1968), the color quality of the 16mm filmed images and the studio-bound videotaped images is quite distinct, but these noticeable, self-conscious transitions continued anyway.

The script also calls for just "two gumbys" outside, but all five (Chapman, Cleese, Idle, Jones, and Palin) are included throughout. Gilliam is missing because this scene was shot in the Greater London area (Walton-on-Thames, specifically), not in a far-flung Devon or Norwich location—and most likely during the week leading up to the show's taping—when the animator would have been busy with his own contributions to the episode.

"Show 8" — ("Architect Sketch") This is of course Ep. 17, the fourth show of the second season, and is called Episode 4 by the folks at Light Entertainment. This episode was recorded ninth, then moved up to fourth in the broadcast line.

"Spanish Inquisition" — ("Police Constable Pan-Am") Again, an Ep. 15 reference, but here no one leaps out dressed as an Inquisitor, and none of the characters wait in anticipation. Cardinal Ximinez (Palin) has already appeared in the Vox Pops section of this episode counting off his favorite aftershave lotions. This episode was recorded more than two months after Ep. 15 was completed.

"standing in the garage" — ("Motor Insurance Sketch") *OED*: "That remains at rest or in a fixed position." The car, essentially, was parked, legally, then hit by a lorry (delivery truck), seemingly an open-and-shut insurance claim for the Vicar (Idle). The Vicar isn't likely to have been the type that Emil Savundra (see the entry for "Devious" above) would have insured, since he doesn't fit the high-risk profile, but then again being a Vicar he might be the ideal customer—timid and less likely to complain about shoddy insurance coverage.

"Straight Man" — ("Motor Insurance Sketch") This continues the subtitling motif already established, though the actions of these characters also betray their roles. In a comedy sketch, the straight man is the member of the team who sets up the funny lines. Bing Crosby often played straight man to partner Bob Hope, for example. Idle will play a straight man wanting to be a funny passenger in Ep. 30, "Bus Conductor Sketch."

straight through the balsa wood door — (PSC; "*The Bishop*") The script comments on the particulars of the stunt here, which is rare, and would only have been intended for the other Pythons as readers. The walls of the set begin to fall over, as well, meaning this entire hallway was purpose-built on the studio floor for this one scene.

"strengthening a bit" — ("Architect Sketch") All high-rise blocks built to May 1968 and to similar standards as the one which collapsed at Ronan Point were inspected and strengthened in the months following the explosion. Repairs included concrete where, sometimes, only crushed newspaper had been stuffed, and the bolting of slotted pillars (Pearson and Delatte).

"Swinburne . . . Shelley" — ("Poets") Algernon Charles Swinburne (1837–1909) was a Pre-Raphaelite poet, a so-called decadent poet, writing of life and love, before easing into middle-aged respectability.

Percy Bysshe Shelley (1792–1822) was called "Mad Shelley" at school (University College, Oxford), where he was a writer of Gothic horrors and politically reactionary (and prescient) works on revolution and reform. See Drabble (1985) and the *ODNB* for more on both poets. Shelley (or "Sherry") will reappear in Ep. 41 in the department store's Victorian poets reading room.

Harness could have found complaint with either of these Victorian and pre-Victorian poets, of course, as he will with Wordsworth's "bloody daffodils."

• T •

Tennyson, Alfred Lord — ("Living Room on Pavement") Tennyson (1809–1892) is considered by many to be the father of Victorian poetry; he became Poet Laureate and was the first poet raised to peerage (1884). (See Ricks's article on Tennyson in the *ODNB*.) The Tennyson in the tub (Jones) is reading from *The Princess: A Medley* (1847, 1850):

> The splendour falls on castle walls
> And snowy summits old in story:
> The long light shakes across the lakes,
> And the wild cataract leaps in glory.
> Blow, bugle, blow, set the wild echoes flying,
> Blow, bugle; answer, echoes, dying, dying, dying.

In keeping with the Masonic tendencies of the episode, it's worth noting that Tennyson was a member of the Cambridge Apostles, a secret society at Trinity College, Cambridge (*ODNB*). Tennyson (played by John Hughman) will also appear in the Victorian poets reading room scene in Ep. 41.

"Thank you" — ("Architect Sketch") This tirade by Mr. Wiggin seems to have had no effect on the Gents, who sit quite passively, even pleasantly. In fact, it isn't until Wiggin mentions Freemasonry that they seem nonplussed at all, and subtly indicate it's time for him to leave.

"third party" — ("Motor Insurance Sketch") This means insurance to cover injuries/damages to someone/something not directly involved in the accident.

Threadneedle Street — (PSC; "Architect Sketch") The printed scripts indicate that this is to be shot on a crowded city street "e.g., Threadneedle Street." Threadneedle is a thoroughfare running through the heart of London's financial district; both the venerable Bank of England and the Stock Exchange are located here. They're actually a few blocks away, hopping up Ludgate Hill, passing in front of The Wren Church of St. Martin Within Ludgate (40 Ludgate Hill), and approaching an ABC (Aerated Bread Company) teashop. The ABC (at 38 Ludgate Hill) has gone of course, but the church, either cleaned or repainted, remains. They're just a block or so from St. Paul's, as well.

"torch" — ("Poets") A flashlight, and in this case one that assumes a sexual connotation for She (Jones).

trolley — ("Motor Insurance Sketch") In this case, the trolley is a shopping cart. Tea trolleys and hospital trolleys are seen in other episodes.

"twenty-eight storeys" — ("Architect Sketch") Interestingly, these are just the types of public housing blocks that would later be demolished or, as very lately, become fashionable apartments for the new wealthy. The blocks had become centers and symbols of urban blight, drug use, and crime prior to recent renovation and neighborhood change (including a dramatic increase in immigrant populations, often from other Commonwealth countries). The Barbican Estate (begun in 1965), for example, features three such buildings, each of which rises to forty-two stories. What many occupants of these concrete behemoths lamented (especially in the New Towns) was the move away from a village setting, where going to the shops or the pub had been such a significant part of the social day (*Eyewitness 1950–59*, "New Housing").

• V •

voice of God — (PSC; *"The Bishop"*) Though the voice of God is promised in the credits to *"The Bishop,"* it's never heard in this short—and repeated—film.

• W •

WW**** — ("Words Not to Be Used Again") The use of asterisks (or other symbols) in place of letters is a common practice when objectionable words are displayed in both print and televised journalism.

In 1948 the BBC had produced a lengthy list of "do nots" for its writers, producers, and its television and radio shows in general. The "Variety Programmes Policy Guide for Writers and Producers" became compulsory reading for any hopeful creative type at Auntie Beeb in the decades afterward, and was still in at least nominal effect in 1969. Inappropriate language and social, political, and cultural taboos are very clearly defined in the document. (See notes to "slept with a lady" in Ep. 3 for more.)

"Walton Street" — ("Living Room on Pavement") Perhaps the Walton Street in the Brompton (SW3) area, near Brompton Road. Walton Street runs north and eastward toward the Harrods block, and is near the Egerton streets mentioned in the notes to Ep. 14. During much of this period, the "hard drug" area of West London was centered in Piccadilly. And since this shot was recorded on location in Walton-on-Thames, it may have been simply convenient to use this name; there are and were dozens of streets, businesses, and place names in the area beginning with "Walton."

"wee-wees" — ("Words Not to Be Used Again") This nursery word can refer to both the act of urination and the penis itself, especially for children.

"West Country . . . Pennines" — ("Poets") The major weather movement over the UK is from the West Country and across southeast England, generally affecting London last before moving out to sea and on toward the continent.

"whatever we happen to have down there" — ("Police Constable Pan-Am") Cf. a very similar police reaction in Ep. 5, where the actor Sandy Camp (Idle) is confronted by a constable (Chapman) looking for "certain substances of an illicit nature." He eventually tries to plant the "illicit" substances, but ineptly. See the notes for Ep. 5 for the historical reference connected to this "creative" police work and Det. Robin Constable. (On 6 May 1970, incidentally, Constable would be officially cleared of any corruption charges by an *internal* review board, news sardonically delivered by *Private Eye* in an article entitled "Carry on Constable!" [22 May 1970, 19]).

"What's all this then?" — ("After-Shave") This is a reflexive moment, wherein the fiction of the show refers to itself, another fiction. The Chemist character (Palin) here notes that this catchphrase has become synonymous in *FC* with police officials (including constables, detectives, inspectors) as they enter a room. See Eps. 5, 7, and 11 for earlier PC entrances. Python often quotes itself, accessing its own history, just as Shakespeare did in his histories. Falstaff recalls the events of Gad's Hill, Bergeron notes, though as a fictional character himself he is actually accessing Shakespeare's version of history as laid out in *1 Henry IV*. See Bergeron, Larsen.

"Wombat" — ("Poets") A wombat is a nocturnal Australian marsupial. In Ep. 20, the "News for Wombats" is delivered by the helpful BBC newsreader (Palin).

"Wordsworth" — ("Poets") William Wordsworth (1770–1850) was a Romantic-era poet, and eventually made poet laureate of England (1843–1850). His *Lyrical Ballads* (1798), written with Samuel Taylor Coleridge, helped launch the English Romantic movement.

working-class lounge is arranged on the pavement — ("Living Room on Pavement") This cinema location is just down the street from the cigarette shop where the Bishop (Jones) and his Vicars stroll like toughs down the crowded sidewalk, along New Zealand Avenue. The cinema has since been demolished.

• Y •

"yus" — ("Police Constable Pan-Am") Colloquialization/regional variation of "yes."

Episode 18: "The Linkman"

BBC 1 announcement: Live from the Grill-o-Mat snack bar, Paignton; *Titles* (silly Cleese v/o); Linkman announcing the "item"; **"Blackmail"** (phone calls and film); Society for Putting Things on Top of Other Things; Escape from film; *Animation: Monopod woman* and *Men escaping the film*; Snack bar linkman links to the "next dish"; Praline's current affairs show (interrupted); *Animation: Colour separation link (Walking general robots, Last Supper ruined, Hand of God rescues Sir William, and WWI fighter cloud)*; Snack bar linkman interrupted; "Prawn Salad": Accidents sketch; A bishop rehearsing; Snack bar linkman surprised; "Seven Brides for Seven Brothers" by the Dibley School for Boys; *Animation: Teddy and Neddy want to hunt piggybanks*; The man who is alternately rude and polite; Documentary on boxer Ken Clean-air Systems; Snack bar linkman on the bus

• A •

Animation — (PSC; link out of "Escape [From Film]") This is one of the very few times that a complete description of the animation is included in the printed scripts. Usually, the animation is being completed as the show is prepared, and Gilliam is away from the rest of the troupe. In this case, however, the matte work necessary for the videotaped versions of the escaping men to blend into the animated world would have required significant preparation, so the animation would have to have been completed earlier than normal. The following animated sequence in the episode is, as usual, not described. See *Gilliam on Gilliam* for more on the animation process in *FC*.

Animation sketch links us to a butcher's shop — (PSC; link out of "*Seven Brides for Seven Brothers*") The music used in the animation is a rough piano version of "Keep the Home Fires Burning" by Ivor Novello.

Animation: various adventures of the Society members — (PSC; link out of "Current Affairs") The "Neddy" and "Teddy" characters are both images of Civil War Union General Benjamin Franklin Butler (1818–1893), known to many as "Beast Butler" for his administration of New Orleans during the war. The image Gilliam uses is a copy of the Matthew Brady print held by the Library of Congress. Gilliam employs a number of Civil War photos (most manipulated in some way) throughout the series.

"Australasia" — ("Society for Putting Things on Top of Other Things") Australasia includes Australia, New Guinea, Tasmania, New Zealand, and many other area islands. For this Society, however, it's most likely that "Australasia" refers just to the "white islands" Australia and New Zealand, the rest of the area being far too aboriginal.

• B •

"Babbacombe" — ("Linkman" link out of "Documentary on Boxer") Babbacombe is a seaside town in Torbay reached by the main road between Newton Abbot and Torquay. It is about five miles north of Paignton, along the A3022. For this episode and several others shot during this stretch most of the exterior (and filmed) scenes/sketches were actually shot in this resort region. The snack bar interiors were shot on 22 May 1970 (WAC T12/1,416).

Big showbiz music crashes in — (*"Blackmail"*) The music used in this scene is listed as "Bright Lights" by Sam Fonteyn (WAC T12/1,430). Fonteyn was one of the many stock and light music composers the Pythons would employ for the incidental music during the series, along with Keith Papworth (Eps. 6, 13), Eric Coates (Eps. 6, 42), Trevor Duncan (Ep. 33), and others. See notes to these episodes for more on the light music composers and their significance not only to the Pythons but British television, radio, and film between 1940 and the 1960s.

Bishop in the field — (PSC; link into *"Seven Brides for Seven Brothers"*) The Bishop is making an unscheduled reappearance, after having an equally unscheduled appearance in Ep. 16. In both instances he reminds us that he won't be appearing until a later episode, even though he *is* appearing in this episode.

This field and the following school hall exteriors were shot in Torquay (WAC T12/1,430).

"Bolton" — (*"Blackmail"*) Southeast of Preston, Bolton is earlier mentioned in Ep. 8 and spelled backward, becoming "Notlob."

"Brazilian dagger" — ("Accidents Sketch") The fact that this prop is named just means that the owner is a wealthy collector of sorts, as the layout of the room already indicates. Larger-than-life characters like Bulldog Drummond (Ep. 29) fit the bill. The dagger is obviously a prop with a retractable blade.

This set piece is a bit unusual for the Pythons, especially as it plays more like an action-reaction Danny Kaye scene (until the deaths) than a Python sketch. At this level, however, it is also what Wilmut characterized as an escalation-type sketch, with the levels of violence escalating as the sketch progresses (in other sketches, the dialogue or anger levels of characters can rise as well). This is not unlike the favored Tex Avery cartoon structure, as seen in *King Size Canary* (1947) and *Bad Luck Blackie* (1949). In the latter film, a bulldog smitten with increasing bad luck is nearly crushed—in turn—by a sink, a tub, a piano, a steamroller, a plane, a city bus, and a battleship.

The cartoony-ness of *FC* has already been pointed out, including the cartoon props (giant hammer, sixteen-ton weight, anarchist's bomb), as well as the levels of cartoon violence and even the rendering of characters (in this very episode) into cartoon cutouts for animation purposes.

"Bromsgrove" — (*"Blackmail"*) Bromsgrove is in the county of Worcestershire, south of Birmingham, and would have been familiar to Idle, who attended the Royal Wolverhampton School, founded by a noted Freemason (see Ep. 17).

Politically, Bromsgrove had been a Conservative stronghold (and so a natural Python target) since at least the 1951 General Election, when John Higgs held the seat, garnering more than 52 percent of the vote. In 1955, Bromsgrove went even more Conservative with a 55.2 percent win by James Dance, who also won in 1959 with a 58 percent polling. Even in the swing year of 1964 when Labour took the reins of power, Bromsgrove returned their Conservative candidate (Dance) by the largest majority (more than 11 percent) over the Labour candidate. Bromsgrove would remain Conservative in 1966 and 1970, as well.

For all General Election results see Keele University's Election Results website at www.psr.keele.ac.uk.

• C •

"cheeky and lovable Cockney sergeant" — ("Escape [From Film]") This scene and "cheeky" character are most directly borrowed from the British POW film *The Wooden Horse* (1950). The character of Peter as played by Leo Genn (1905–1978) in this POW film may be the actual sergeant character the Pythons were referencing. In the book version, however, it's Paul's "cheeky" mouth (not Peter's) toward his German captors that lands him in the cooler again and again. See the note for "horse" below.

"city of London ex-public school type" — (PSC; "Society for Putting Things on Top of Other Things") The printed script calls for a very precise character type, but it is identifiable (and seen as early as Ep. 2, "Flying Sheep"). The "City of London" reference means these are bankers or otherwise financial types—those who wear trilbies, carry brollies, speak with polished accents, and belong to exclusive clubs—these epitomize the "City Gent" for the Pythons. These types are found within the confines of the City of London, a rather small place (about one square mile) that acts as the heart of England's financial industry.

The "public school" reference means these types were educated at the expensive, class-rigid schools like Dulwich, Eton, and Harrow, and not state-supported schools. For many years these public schools had acted as nurseries for leadership positions in the empire, including royalty, Prime Ministers, MPs, cabinet members, colonial sinecures, etc.

All this history and acculturation is summed up—for the Pythons and their viewers alike—with an iconic, recognizable shorthand description ("city of London ex-public school type") that is interpreted by the show's dressers into an equally recognizable costume. This level of cultural awareness would most certainly be missed by the unacculturated (non-English) viewer, and even the native viewer given sufficient passage of time. In fact, the brolly and trilby (or bowler hat) look was already dated by 1970, meaning the studio audience knew they were seeing a throwback reference to a bygone day, to the City Gent look of the Pythons' youth.

"colour separation" — ("Current Affairs") This is a television chroma key process that allows for the combination (usually as a superimposition) of images, and is accomplished by a blue- or green-screen effect.

"cotton head" — ("Current Affairs") Something of a misnomer, as the term is usually applied to a dotty elderly person, i.e., an older person who drives too slowly in the fast lane.

"current affairs issues of burning import" — ("Current Affairs") This may be a swipe at such newer and trendy news shows including *The World at One*, which made its BBC debut in 1965. The "softer" and flashier format reportedly angered old-timers in the BBC's news organization. The even softer news and current affairs show *Nationwide* also made its debut in 1969, which the Pythons spoof in Ep. 35, "Olympic Hide-and-Seek Final." *Nationwide* is remembered for human- and pet-interest stories often bordering on the silly, including skateboarding ducks, for example.

• E •

Edwardian gentleman — (PSC; animation link out of "Escape [From Film]") This "Edwardian gentleman" is a medical chart type. The usual Edwardian and Victorian images in this series are the female nude postcards that Gilliam uses in the title sequences and animated links. Gilliam collected the images from friend and comic mentor Ronnie Barker in the late 1960s. See *Gilliam on Gilliam* (41).

The Edwardian era dates from approximately Queen Victoria's death (1901) through at least King Edward VII's passing in 1910. (The Pythons had, in Ep. 1, put the death of Edward VII as the "back marker" in their "Famous Deaths" poll.) The era saw a flourishing of appreciation for the arts and architecture, following the monarch's passions for Continental Europe, entertainment, and travel.

"eighteen . . . weight" — ("Documentary on Boxer") Eighteen stone (one stone equals fourteen pounds) comes to about 252 pounds, much heavier than the very thin Cleese, obviously, and much, much heavier than the 112- to 119-pound bantamweight classification.

Episode 18 — Not titled in the original scripts. This episode was recorded seventh (on 10 September 1970) in the second season, and aired fifth on 27 October 1970.

As so much of this episode (and Ep. 19, as well) was (1) scheduled to be shot on film, (2) already recorded on film in Torquay in May and June, and (3) scheduled away from BBC Television Centre (on location and at Ealing TFS), the studio time for the two episodes were combined, freeing up a full week of studio time for other shows at the BBC (WAC T12/1,242). As a result, some of the participants in this and Ep. 19 are included in the same WAC file. Curiously, one of the Pythons' agents, Jill Foster (of Fraser & Dunlop Scripts Ltd., 91 Regent Street, London), complains in a letter dated 20 August 1971 written to "David Attenborough Esq" that because of budgetary constraints the Pythons had to tape two shows in one evening and asks that the budget for the show be raised "because of lack of money." (They were already receiving £5,000/show in late 1971, up from £4,500 the season before [WAC T47/216].) In the memo, Foster neglects to mention the greatly reduced in-studio needs for these two episodes—needs determined by the troupe's writing/compiling for the episode—angling for a raise, instead.

The list of additional, often uncredited participants in this episode, according to BBC files, include: Connie Booth, Denton De Gray (Ep. 24; *Quatermass II*), Corona, Eddie May Scrandrett (Eps. 17, 19), Bill Leonard (Eps. 17–19), Michael Stayner (*Billion Dollar Brain*), Stephanie Marrian (*Benny Hill*), Barbara Smith, Bunny Saunders (likely of the "Bunny Saunders Pop Singers & Orchestra" fame), Colin Skeaping (*Star Wars*), Barbara Lindley (*Benny Hill*), Ian Davidson (and Mrs. E. Toller, Mr. D. Grice, Mr. P. O'Brien, Mrs. G. Dewhurst, Mrs. I. Docherty, and Mrs. Barbara Ball—these last six seem to be the parents for the boys in the "School Prize-Giving" sketch), Neil Innes (studio audience warm-up; *Do Not Adjust Your Set*; later contributor to *FC*), Terry Williams, Reuben Martin (*Carry On Up the Jungle*), and Roy Scammell (stuntman/actor, *Benny Hill; A Clockwork Orange*) (WAC T12/1,242).

"Everything seems to be in order" — ("Escape [From Film]") The "cheeky" character seems to have been a staple of most of these POW films, from Renoir's *Grand Illusion* to *The Wooden Horse* to *Stalag 17*, so the Pythons' entry in the POW genre couldn't be complete without his appearance.

• F •

finger gesture — ("Escape [From Film]") Once again, the punchline is forbidden. In Ep. 17, when this same joke is started and successfully completed, the man who delivers the punchline is immediately arrested and hustled off.

frail and lovely — (PSC; "Documentary on Boxer") The printed script describes Connie Booth in this way, much as her earlier appearance as the "rebel maid" in the "I'm a Lumberjack" sketch for Ep. 9 ("a frail adoring blonde, the heroine of many a mountains film, or perhaps the rebel maid"). Booth was married to Cleese during this period.

"freemason" — (*"Blackmail"*) Cf. Ep. 17 for a more direct assault on Freemasonry. For the Pythons, such accepted fraternal organizations are natural breeding grounds for sexual deviants. Here the term is used as a descriptor for a successful, respected member of society who'd rather not be outed, and is likely to pay quickly.

• G •

gates of a hospital — (PSC; "Documentary on Boxer") This sequence was originally shot (or scheduled to be shot) at Glenfield, Old Torwood Road, Torquay, on 22 May 1970 (WAC T12/1,416). WAC records indicate that the scene between Ken (Cleese) and the gesturing doctor (Chapman) was later shot/reshot on 2 June 1970 at Hammersmith Hospital, near Wormwood Scrubs. Old Torwood Road connects to Babbacombe Road, mentioned by the Waitress (Chapman) later in the episode.

"gedderbong" — ("Documentary on Boxer") Slang for "gentlemen," this term is also used in Ep. 5, in the "Confuse-a-Cat" sketch. The Goons also mangle the word "gentlemen" in a number of similar introductions.

"germoline" — ("Documentary on Boxer") Misspelled here, "Germolene" is the proprietary name for a first aid (antibiotic) ointment still popular in Britain.

gonk — ("Documentary on Boxer") A Gonk is actually a proprietary name for an egg-shaped doll that was the rage in the UK from about 1964, meaning the innocent young boxer (Booth) would certainly have collected a few for her bedroom.

"great white hope" — ("Documentary on Boxer") *Great White Hope* was a 1970 film starring James Earl Jones and directed by Martin Ritt, depicting the life of boxer Jack Johnson. Johnson (1878–1946) was the first black heavyweight champion of the world, and his various opponents were often called "great white hopes" as they fought and inevitably lost to him.

The British, Commonwealth, and European champion during this period was Henry Cooper, according to the International Boxing Hall of Fame. In March 1970, Cooper had defeated Jack Bodell (featured later in Ep. 37) to regain his British heavyweight crown. (The American and world heavyweight champion during this period was Joe Frazier.) Cooper would also appear on *A Question of Sport* (BBC, 1970–), a sports quiz show very popular during this period.

The "great white hope" moniker is quite fitting for Cooper, as he managed to knock Cassius Clay (who would later become Muhammad Ali) to the canvas in the fourth round of their 1963 fight at Wembley Stadium. Clay would recover in between rounds and go on to win by TKO. Their 1966 rematch was not so favorable for Cooper, with the fight being stopped in the sixth round.

green baize apron — (PSC; "Accidents Sketch") Baize is a coarse woolen material, often used for linings on shelves where clothes were stored.

The "man in the green baize apron" is an emblematic, humble, old man serving figure from a number of sources, including Joseph Conrad's *Arrow of Gold* (1919) and *The Secret Agent* (1907), as well as Virginia Woolf's *The Waves* (1931), and perhaps the most significant Victorian literature source, Dickens's *Bleak House* (1852–1853). The "green baize door" is also used as a literary trope depicting the dividing line between the two sides/levels of the manor house—between the landed family and their domestic help.

Grillomatic snack bar — (PSC; "Linkman" link out of "Documentary on Boxer") In the printed script, the final mention of this snack bar is spelled quite differently from previous iterations. As a matter of fact, the name of the snack bar is spelled severally as "Grill-o-Mat," "Grillomat," and, finally, "Grillomatic" in the printed script.

• H •

"horse" — ("Escape [From Film]") This is a vaulting horse used for calisthenics, and would seem to have no place in a Royal Society meetinghouse. In the transition to the WWII prisoner-of-war camp setting, however, the horse does actually fit, as a number of POW camp films included sports/calisthenic activities for the prisoners, including baseball in *The Great Escape* (1963).

Specifically, however, a film set in Stalag-Luft III where the actual "Great Escape" took place, *The Wooden Horse* (1950) is the real basis for this part of the sketch. In Stalag-Luft III the prisoners would carry a large vaulting horse out into the exercise yard nearer the perimeter fence, two men hiding inside, and as the other prisoners exercised, the hidden men would dig an escape tunnel. The hole entrance would be hidden at day's end and the horse returned, men and sand inside, to the barracks, the sand then broadcast around the compound. See Williams's *The Wooden Horse* for a first-person account of this camp, the tunnels, and the eventual mass escape. See the entry for Williams at *ODNB*.

"Humperdinck, Englebert" — ("Documentary on Boxer") Two men, actually. The first Engelbert Humperdinck (1854–1921) was a German composer known for his opera *Hansel and Gretel* (1893). The second is an Indian-born popular singer of the same name who was raised in Leicester (as was Chapman) and has sold millions of records. In the late 1960s Humperdinck's records were outpacing The Beatles' albums in sales, and his fans were legion. In 1970, *The Engelbert Humperdinck Show* was airing on London Weekend Television.

• I •

"I'm more of a visual performer" — (link out of "Documentary on Boxer") Cleese is of course being reflexive again, reminding the audience of the already much-loved sketch ("Ministry of Silly Walks") that had aired just a few weeks earlier, on 15 September 1970. Reappearances of non-typed characters—including Ken Shabby and Cardinal Ximinez (both Palin)—elicit applause and sounds of recognition from the studio audience, indicating the show had generated a significant following by this time, less than a year into its existence, and that the home viewers were making efforts to secure tickets and see the tapings live. Contemporary fans like Jeremy Paxman and John Diamond (mentioned in notes to Ep. 8) attest to this cult of familiarity in the teens and twenty-somethings of the Greater London area in 1969–1970.

In subsequent interviews Cleese mentions that he and Chapman (often as writing partners) tended to create the more verbal sketches based on wordplay and escalation of character/setting temperament, while Jones and Palin contributed more surreal, often bizarre sketches. For audience members familiar at all with Cleese's previous work (prior to *Flying Circus*), of course, Cleese had become the picture of a sober, straight-laced type who could be egged into outbursts of splenetic rage, as earlier seen in the "Architect Sketch" (Ep. 17), as well as a talented wordsmith. (See Cleese's work in *The Frost Report* [1966] and *At Last the 1948 Show* [1967], for example.) The "Silly Walks" scene, then, would have been a novel bit of a departure for the sober, respectable former barrister Cleese, which probably accounts for its continuing appeal. See Morgan's *Monty Python Speaks!* and McCabe's *The Pythons*.

This entire sequence is shot as the bus drives along Torbay Road. Toward the end of the scene, both the South Sands Hotel and the Avon Guest House can be seen. Both are along Torbay Road in greater Paignton.

• K •

Ken jogging . . . trees — (PSC; "Documentary on Boxer") According to the BBC, most of this footage, including the council houses, streets, and village areas were shot in and around Torquay (WAC T12/1,430).

Ken's house is located at Glenfield, Old Torwood Road, Torquay (WAC T12/1,416). Parts of this sketch were also shot quite far away in the Richmond and Norfolk areas.

• L •

Linkman — (PSC; "Live from the Grill-o-Mat Snack Bar, Paignton") This is the first time that a Linkman has been so prominently featured in *FC*, though links are consistently, pointedly, even clumsily pointed out across the series. The linking character is probably something of a holdover from the days of radio, when such transitions were necessary, as there were no graphics or picture transitions available. The Pythons are clearly lampooning the stodgy role of the unctuous or inept linkman—his witticisms forced and puns all bad. Such linkmen in the BBC world are obviously important figures in the Pythons' collective viewing experiences as they grew up—they appear throughout *FC*, often as greasy compères, as well.

"live from the Grill-o-Mat Snack Bar" — ("Live from the Grill-o-Mat Snack Bar, Paignton") This, of course, would have been recorded on film long before the episode was recorded in the studio on 10 September 1970. This snack bar location (in Torquay) was used on 22 May 1970.

"load them up with cutlery" — ("Escape [From Film]") In the "Great Escape" from Stalag Luft III, prisoners used utensils, bowls, and hand-fashioned spades to dig the escape tunnels "Tom," "Dick," and "Harry." See Williams's *The Wooden Horse*.

"Lord Hill" — ("Current Affairs") Lord Hill (of Luton) was in charge of the BBC during this period.

He is mentioned earlier in Ep. 10, in the "Bank Robber (Lingerie Shop)" sketch, as well as Ep. 11, by the miffed Professor Canning (Chapman). Lord Hill had allegedly intervened not long before as the new, color-format *Newsroom* appeared on BBC, arguing that the sheer number of satellite-spewed pictures from around the world could convince the British public that the world was in a state of "greater ferment" than it actually was. (See the BBC's information on *Newsroom* at news.bbc.co.uk.) *Newsroom* was presented by Peter Woods (1930–1995) and John Timpson (1928–2005). Woods will make an appearance in *Flying Circus* Ep. 42, announcing that World War II has entered a "sentimental phase."

This is the second time that a character has been included in a show where either there is no time for it or he's not scheduled to appear. In Ep. 16 (and later in Ep. 18), the Bishop (Palin) can't answer questions since he's not scheduled to appear in the episode in which he is appearing. Later in this episode (Ep. 18) this same rehearsing Bishop will appear as the gentlemen from the Royal Society make their way to the *Seven Brides for Seven Brothers* play. The Bishop is still not scheduled to appear, he tells the gentlemen. In Ep. 19, the Announcer (Cleese) also mentions that he's not scheduled to appear in that episode, and yet there he is (he realizes the irony, however).

• M •

Man Alive — (PSC; "Documentary on Boxer") *Man Alive* aired on BBC2 from 1965 to 1982, and was a hard-hitting current affairs program covering topics including molestation, marriage, and agoraphobia (Vahimagi, 138). The show was designed to offer the viewpoint, often, of the common man. In the printed scripts, "camera noise" is mentioned, meaning the sound of the whirring film spools should be heard as the interview progresses.

Man Alive will be mentioned again, by Herbert Mental (Jones), in Ep. 26, as the show he'd hoped would invite him for an interview.

"Maybe it's because I'm a Londoner . . ." — ("Escape [From Film]") This recently penned pub song (written by Hubert Gregg [1914–2004] during the blitz but not popularized until after the war) is the song the men are attempting to sing as they vault:

> Maybe it's because I'm a Londoner, that I love London so.
> Maybe it's because I'm a Londoner, that I think of her wherever I go.
> I get a funny feeling inside of me, just walking up and down.
> Maybe it's because I'm a Londoner, that I love London Town.

A curious choice, since the Stalags and their Allied prisoners were liberated in 1945, prior to the song's composition. (It may be that the Pythons are remembering another Gregg hit, "I'm Going to Get Lit Up When the Lights Go On in London," which was popular during the war.) Actor/singer Bud Flanagan would popularize the song in a musical revue called *Together Again* that ran for several years on the West End after the war.

Finally, *Dixon of Dock Green* would also use the tune for its titles song, George Dixon whistling the tune as the show begins. See entries in Eps. 5 and 7 for more on this iconic police show.

"Medwin" — ("Escape [From Film]") Michael Medwin (b. 1923) appeared in *The Bruce Forsythe Show* (1967), as well as Lindsay Anderson's *If . . .* (1968), which will be mentioned prominently in Ep. 19. There were also several characters named "Medwin" in the *Doctor at Large* series, for which both Chapman and Cleese contributed at least eight episodes (writing) together.

Mr. Cutler runs up . . . — ("Escape [From Film]") Here the characters cement the *Wooden Horse* homage by tapping on the vault (Cleese) and pretending to begin to hide in it, before following Sir William (Chapman) out of the scene.

"my mother" — ("Society for Putting Things on Top of Other Things") In Ep. 2, "The Mouse Problem," Dino Vercotti also pretends to have been speaking to his mother on the phone—when actually he was confirming a Chinese prostitute appointment ("the Chinese watch") for that evening.

• N •

"no need for me to interrupt at all" — (link into "*Seven Brides for Seven Brothers*") But of course he is interrupting as well as creating a link, not unlike Praline (Cleese), whose current affairs show was earlier canceled, though he appeared anyway, and the rehearsing Bishop (Palin) who appears but is always scheduled for a later show.

• O •

"on film" — ("Escape [From Film]") Continuity did not seem to be a problem for British viewers when a TV show switched from video format to film format, even in this kind of interior/exterior match cut, which really doesn't match at all. It is possible that since 1968–1969 was the year that the transition from black-and-white to color broadcasts was undertaken at the BBC—and that in black-and-white broadcast the clarity difference between a filmed and videotaped image is much less noticeable—audiences for *Monty Python* and news shows, for example, would have taken the image dissimilarities as par for the course, as it were.

Portable video cameras were a bulky rarity during this period, with most news field reporting being done on film. The trade-off, of course, is that the graininess, depth, and color quality of the 16mm image contrasts greatly to the sharp but shallow video images. Again, audiences new to color television would have known nothing else for comparison. But the Pythons knew. Cf. Ep. 15, where the linking element of film is mentioned as the Hermits' sketch is stopped and the Major (Chapman) cues the show back to the studio. This acknowledgment of the world of film as separate and distinct from the world of the studio is yet another example of the Pythons not only breaking the traditional barrier between the audience and what goes on behind the scenes of a TV show—in this case, identifying the differing visual formats—but making sure that audiences are aware of these artifices.

The white, portico-and-column exterior shots for this scene were recorded at Thorne House, Ham Common, Richmond, on 4 June 1970 (WAC T12/1,416).

• P •

"Paignton" — ("Live from the Grill-o-Mat Snack Bar, Paignton") Paignton is in South West England, and is part of the "English Riviera" coast country. Portions of "*Scott of the Antarctic*" (Ep. 23) are shot at the Paignton Pier. The snack bar location is actually in Torquay, according to BBC records (WAC T12/1,430), and was utilized on 22 May 1970. The Pythons will return to this area for many of the fourth season exteriors.

"piano stool" — ("Current Affairs") Praline (and Brooky) will reappear, piano stool in hand, to accompany both the *Seven Brides for Seven Brothers* performance as well as the animated "Hunting Piggybanks" animation that follows.

"poovy po-nagger" — ("The Man Who Is Alternately Rude and Polite") These variations on effeminating homosexual insults, including "poofta," "pillock," and "spotted prancer"—appear elsewhere in *FC* as "poove," "wee wee," and "mincing fairy."

This structure—here alternately rude and polite—will be revisited in Ep. 26 with a man who speaks only the middle of words, except every third and fourth sentence where he speaks full sentences.

"population explosion" — ("Current Affairs") The Nobel Peace Prize for 1970 was awarded to Norman Borlaug (1914–2009), whose area of study was the population and world food crisis.

Birth control methods in China, for instance, weren't significantly encouraged until the early 1970s, several years after this episode, and China's population (under Mao's encouragement) had been growing prodigiously, reaching a birth rate of about 34.3 in 1970. The *China Statistical Yearbook* (2003) notes that China's population grew from 806.7 million in 1969 to 829.9 million in 1970. (For reference, the population of the entire UK stood at only about 55 million in mid-1970, or about 6.6 percent of China's population.) Also, given the fact that when Mao Tse-tung called up the Red Guard as recently as 1966, and 11 million young people had descended on Peking to participate in demonstrations, the impression of a motivated, fervent, and "alien" mass must have made quite an impression in the First World ("China's Youth 'Volunteer' for Rural Life," *Times*, 2 Jan. 1969: 4). In 1991, the future date mentioned in the sketch, China's population had reached about 1.16 billion.

Gilliam's animation in Ep. 24 depicts yellow Chinese characters overwhelming a young secretary, with an animated Mao leading the way. The references to China throughout *FC* indicate a mix of fascination and fear in the Western world of this inscrutable, emerging superpower.

"posh talk" — ("The Man Who Is Alternately Rude and Polite") Reaffirming George Bernard Shaw's belief that one Englishman will inevitably despise another Englishman the moment he opens his mouth—a maxim based on the level of sophistication of language and diction in "Southern" English (read: London) as opposed to the coarser, earthier Northern or Western dialects. The Gent (Palin) here isn't dressed to the nines, however—e.g., trilby and brolly—but does sound a bit more refined than the average customer ("I'd care to purchase a chicken").

"prep" — ("*Seven Brides for Seven Brothers*") The standard thirty minutes of homework in secondary schools, often conducted in a study hall setting before or after classroom instruction (*OED*).

"Preston . . . Lancashire" — ("*Blackmail*") Preston in the county Lancashire lies along the River Ribble near the coast of the Irish Sea northwest of London. Preston North and South had gone Labour in the 1964 and 1966 General Elections, but both went Conservative in the 1970 General Election in June. This would have allowed the Pythons to take some solace in the Labour loss when they finally recorded the episode in September, locating their sexual deviants in comfortable Conservative neighborhoods.

"prospective Tory MP" — (*"Blackmail"*) This man would be someone standing for Parliament for the Conservative Party, as opposed to the Labour, Liberal, or one of the myriad fringe parties. The fact that he is a Tory earmarks him, in the Python world, for sexual deviancy.

There is the very real possibility that this sketch is yet another reference to the still-fresh Profumo sex scandal that essentially toppled the Macmillan government in 1964, and helped give Labour its control of the government until 1970. Cf. Ep. 2, "The Mouse Problem" for an earlier, more in-depth treatment of this sex-and-political-intrigue scandal. In the Profumo case of 1963, highly placed and well-respected Conservative politicians—and especially Secretary for War John Profumo—engaged in sexual improprieties (including costumed sadomasochism) and then lied to the House of Commons about their involvement. (The latter was seen by many as the more egregious sin, by the way.) The government change ushered in the much more liberal Harold Wilson (a so-called New Age Labourite) government, a change always seen as at least indirectly precipitated by Profumo's sexual shenanigans.

• R •

"Reigate" — ("Documentary on Boxer") Located in Surrey, near Gatwick airport. This location is actually on Old Torwood Road, Torquay, according to BBC records (WAC T12/1,416).

"Pesticide Research Centre at Shoreham"—Shoreham is in Kent, south of Dartford. There has been a pesticide research center at Silwood Park since 1955, known as the International Pesticide Application Research Centre. Silwood Park is in the Royal Borough of Windsor and Maidenhead.

"Reading"—Reading is in Berkshire, on the Thames west of London. It was mentioned in the "New Cooker Sketch" in Ep. 14. The BBC written archives are also "near Reading," in Caversham Park.

"Bangkok"—Capital and largest city of Thailand. The distance between London and Bangkok is about 6,000 miles.

"Kyoto"—Ancient capital of Japan.

"return of post" — (*"Blackmail"*) An idiom that can just mean as soon as possible, though more precisely, a response delivered at the next available posting of the Royal Mail.

"Richard, Cliff" — ("Documentary on Boxer") British pop musician Richard (b. 1940) had been popular since 1958, and was the type of teenage heartthrob that young girls like Petula (Booth) would have swooned over surrounded by her Gonk collection. Richard's image and record sales had suffered since the appearance of The Beatles (and the Mersey sound, and skiffle groups), but he was still a popular draw, managing high ratings (for "Congratulations") in the 1968 Eurovision Song Contest, for example.

roadside diner — (PSC; "Documentary on Boxer") This scene was shot at the base of the Walton Bridge, on Walton Bridge Road, Shepperton, Middlesex. A Gingham Auto Diner Restaurant—it's sign obviously changed from Gingham Kitchen Restaurant—can be seen behind the crouching Ken (Cleese). Gingham Kitchen Limited was a pioneer in microwave-assisted catering, and owned at least seven stores in the London area alone. This is near Walton-on-Thames, where the Pythons were scheduled to shoot portions of this sketch, and had already shot scenes for Eps. 1 and 2 (WAC T12/1,083).

Robin Hood hat — (PSC; *"Blackmail"*) The script calls very specifically for a "Robin Hood hat" on this character. The hat's brim is slightly turned up at the back and down at the front. According to one entry in the *OED*, this type of hat made something of a comeback in 1960: "*News Chron*. 11 Apr. 8/4 Gone are the heavy-looking trilbies . . . in their place have come the delta and the Robin Hood." The trilby is the hat of choice for Pythons' stereotyped City Gents (Ep. 17), though the "Eton, Harrow and the Guard" Upperclass Twits (Ep. 12) sport the Robin Hood–type hat, and City of London types often wear a bowler.

"rota" — ("Escape [From Film]") A "rota" is a rotation of persons or routines, and here is used much like the escape procedures in *The Great Escape* (1963), with some men digging the tunnels, some standing guard, some resting, and some acting as distractions to the prison camp guards. The *Great Escape* motif will be revisited more plainly (including the well-known theme music) in Ep. 28, the "Trim-Jeans Theatre" sketch.

The rota in *The Wooden Horse* (which inspired the inclusion here) included vaulting, initially, then medicine ball, calisthenics, and even running as the long process of digging went on beneath them. See Williams's *The Wooden Horse*.

"Royal Society" — ("Society for Putting Things on Top of Other Things") There are myriad Royal Societies, for arts and letters, sciences, husbandry, etc., which is probably why the Pythons could lampoon the idea. Just some include: the Royal Society for the

Protection of Birds, the Royal Commonwealth Society, the Royal Agricultural Society, as well as Royal Societies of chemistry, medicine, etc. To qualify as a "royal" society, the group must receive a charter from the sitting monarch. (The BBC, for example, possesses such a charter.) The original Royal Society was found in 1662 during the reign of Charles II, and was designed as a bastion of scientific learning.

Swift satirizes the Royal Society in his *Gulliver's Travels*, specifically in the third book, on the flying island of Laputa.

"rubs gravel into his hair" — ("Documentary on Boxer") A bit of comedic overkill here as Ken (Cleese) performs a silly act—rubbing gravel into his hair—and the narrator describes the act as it's being performed for us. This obviates at least one level of possible incongruity, that between the visual and the spoken. Earlier in the sketch, for example, Ken inexplicably runs from his home to the Pesticide Research Centre, but the visuals just offer generic running shots, leaving the viewer to make the connection between the visual and aural suggestions.

Comedian Woody Allen (b. 1935) slips into this same reiterating trap in his early comic film *Take the Money and Run* (1969)—when the narrator mentions Orthodox Jews in prison, then cuts to praying Orthodox Jews in a cell—as well as the man having sex with a loaf of rye bread in *Everything You Always Wanted to Ask about Sex but Were Afraid to Ask* (1969). The incongruity of the gags is significantly undercut when the ridiculous payoffs are rendered so concretely.

• S •

"Sabine School for Girls" — (*"Seven Brides for Seven Brothers"*) Turned into "sobbin' women" in the Benet short story, the "Rape of the Sabine Women" is depicted by Livy and Plutarch, among others. The story involves Romulus' Romans abducting Sabine women to become brides. Here the Dibley boys have convinced just two Sabine girls to appear in the stilted performance.

same stupendous sound effects as for all-in cricket — ("Documentary on Boxer") An example of the Pythons being reflexive and intertextual, mentioning the all-in cricket sketch in Ep. 11, and offering the production crew (in this case, the sound team) a quick reference to effects already used and available. The resulting sound effects are, needless to say, hardly stupendous, meaning the direction was glib. This glibness is seen earlier in Ep. 9 when mood lighting is requested ("Ha!") in the printed script, the writers knowing such lighting isn't available. This sketch also appears as part of the Pythons' *May Day Special* show for 1971.

"Satellite Five" — ("Documentary on Boxer") Probably meant to be a play on *Saturn V*, the enormous rocket used by NASA to conduct moon launches for the Apollo program (1967–1973). The proliferation of satellites in the 1950s and 1960s may also account for this reference, with the United States and USSR launching multiple satellites for weather observation, communication, military, and surveillance activities. The UK wouldn't send up its first British-made and -launched satellite until 1971.

The fact that Britain's extraterrestrial program had lagged behind both the USSR and US also becomes significant here. After Sputnik went up and the US followed not long after with its own satellite program, there were the expected calls in the public fora in Great Britain for a British satellite venture. The Pythons might be commenting here on the irony that presented itself in July 1959, when it was announced that the first British satellite—"Ariel"—might be lifted into orbit by an American rocket as early as spring 1962. In fact, the first scientific and military British satellites were launched this way.

Schoolmaster — (PSC; *"Seven Brides for Seven Brothers"*) This is Palin speaking this line, off-camera, though he is not credited. He will appear in a few moments as the Padre.

"semi-detached house" — ("Documentary on Boxer") This location is 67 Broughton Avenue, Ham, Richmond, Surrey, and the interior and exterior footage was shot on 3 June 1970 (WAC T12/1,242).

"Seven Brides for Seven Brothers" — (*"Seven Brides for Seven Brothers"*) A popular Hollywood film musical from 1954 (dir. Stanley Donen), the significant singing and dancing demands (and large cast requirements) of *Seven Brides* make it an unlikely (and therefore funny) choice for an all-boys school production. The original story was written by Stephen Vincent Benet, and was called *The Sobbin' Women*. The popular MGM film had actually enjoyed a recent London revival at the Odeon Marble Arch, appearing in a 70mm (widescreen) print version in February 1969 (*Times*, 22 Feb. 1969: 20).

School shows in the UK had been common since at least Shakespeare's youth, when his Stratford Grammar School would regularly perform plays like Nicholas Udall's *Ralph Roister Doister* (1553), featuring an all-boy cast. The Pythons variously acted in school plays in their grammar school experiences as well.

"shop where you bought the equipment" — (*"Blackmail"*) These kinds of sex shops, according to one of Alan Bennett's *Beyond the Fringe* monologues ("The

Porn Shop"), were located in the Charing Cross Road area of the West End, London, and were especially pervasive in the 1950s and 1960s.

"Silly! I suppose it is" — ("Society for Putting Things on Top of Other Things") There aren't many occasions in *FC* where the character admits to the silliness of the set-up or situation, a sort of "Emperor's New Clothes" scenario where the Emperor's nakedness is pointed out. More often, the silliness is reinforced, then built upon, then undercut or supplanted by yet another silliness, etc.

"Smith Major" — ("*Seven Brides for Seven Brothers*") This is a specialized, public school usage, according to the *OED*, where such a phrase designates "the elder or senior of two pupils with the same surname or the first to enter the school (used especially in British public schools)."

"Smith brothers"—The family name for the brothers in the 1954 feature film *Seven Brides for Seven Brothers* as well as Benet's short story is actually "Pontipee."

"southpaw" — ("Documentary on Boxer") A boxer who leads with his/her left hand.

"Staffordshire" — ("Society for Putting Things on Top of Other Things") Staffordshire is a West Midlands county south of Manchester. The Pythons continue to find their locus of provinciality in the Midlands regions, which will become irrefutably evident in Ep. 19, when the Tourist (Idle) waxes pleniloquent about nightmarish package tours originating in Luton.

stately rather than modern — (PSC; "Accidents Sketch") This paneled, Tudor-like set (found at Ealing Television-Film Studios) is the same one used in Ep. 29 for the "Erizabeth L" sketch.

stock film . . . blown up — ("Accidents Sketch") The post-explosion sequence (where Idle holds the doorknob in a pile of rubble) following the stock film explosion was shot in the London area, according to the BBC (WAC T12/1,430).

• T •

"ten bob" — ("Current Affairs") "Ten bob" usually referred to the ten-shilling note, until that note was removed from circulation in 1971, when British currency "went decimal." In 1969–1970, the BBC was paying walk-ons (at least for the *Flying Circus* series) about five pounds and five shillings, according to WAC records (WAC T12/1,082).

"Thames Ditton" — (PSC; "*Blackmail*") This exterior was actually shot in the London area, according to BBC records (WAC T12/1,439). Thames Ditton is in Surrey, South East England, on the Thames near Esher. In the printed script, the writers placed a "[*sic*]" after "Thames Ditton," though there was no misspelling. This could be an acknowledgment that the scene was not or would not be shot in Thames Ditton, but somewhere closer to home—most likely Ealing or East Acton. (Though difficult to see clearly, the setting looks very much like the 49 Elers Road, Ealing, location [near Lammas Park Road], where portions of the first season were recorded.) This is yet another example of a scripted moment available only to other readers, and not the eventual viewer, and is meant to be an in-joke.

Also, the inclusion of "[*sic*]" could be a reference to the "anomalous or erroneous" (*OED*) use of such a setting as Thames Ditton in the first place, since nearby Esher had remained overwhelmingly Conservative in the 1966 general election, garnering more than 55 percent of the vote. The *Private Eye* editors occasionally included a "[*sic*]" after a properly spelled word or name, usually to draw unwarranted attention to it.

These exterior scenes were shot on 1 June 1970, according to WAC records (WAC T12/1,416).

tin helmet — (PSC; "Escape [From Film]") This ubiquitous tin helmet was worn in combat, by civil defense workers, and even miners, but is probably most associated with British soldiers serving in Burma during World War II.

Two Girls — (PSC; "*Seven Brides for Seven Brothers*") These girls are Connie Booth and Lynn Idle. Booth was married to Cleese at this time (1968–1978), and Lynn was Eric Idle's wife (1969–1978).

• U •

underneath she wears black corsets — ("*Blackmail*") This actress appears to be Helena Clayton, who also played the Dominatrix in the *Flying Circus* Montreux episode compilation in 1971 (WAC T12/1,413).

• V •

"vestry" — ("*Seven Brides for Seven Brothers*") A room in a church setting often adjacent to the chapel, where vestments and church records are kept (*OED*).

"Victoria Station" — ("*Blackmail*") Victoria Station is located in Westminster in the heart of London. It is perhaps ironic that blackmail demands for the prospective Tory MP's sexual deviancy should be paid in the station named for the virtuous Victoria, the eponymous representative of Britain's supposedly buttoned-down sexual period.

• W •

"we're really out this time" — (link out of "Accidents Sketch") If what Sir William (Chapman) is referring to is the fact that they were caught on film, then they are clearly not "out," since this scene is also shot on film. They are out of the Edwardian gentleman's entrails, of course, but that was shot on both videotape and film.

whip — (*"Blackmail"*) With the whip and black corsets she is obviously playing to the man's domination fetish, commenting on the sexual proclivities of the Conservative types. The Profumo confessions included details of sadomasochistic orgies. This is also another interesting portrayal of women for the Pythons, in this case, as an armed, seductive dominatrix bent on humiliation of the submissive male.

• Y •

"youth organization to which they belong" — (*"Blackmail"*) Dinsdale Piranha is also described as being fond of such younger groups, including "Boy's Clubs . . . Chorister's Associations . . . [and] Scouting Jamborees" as part of his sexual deviancy. The host (Palin) hints here that the Conservative "Mr. S. of Bromsgrove" is a sexual fetishist who enjoys pederasty and perhaps bondage. Continuing this theme later in the episode, the Butcher (Idle) will castigate his customer (Palin) with all manner of sodomitical epithets, including "pillock," "trollope," and "poovy po-nagger."

Episode 19: "Election Night Special"

"It's a Living"; The time on BBC 1; *Animation: Enoch Powell head, Lights out, and Titles;* "And now . . ." Man in smithee; Interruptions; School prize-giving—Bishop(s) of East Anglia; *if . . .* a film by Mr. L.F. Dibley (and *2001*, and *Midnight Cowboy*); *Rear Window*—a film by Mr. Dibley; *Finian's Rainbow* by Mr. Dibley starring the man from the off-licence; The Foreign Secretary tells about canoeing; Industrial relations reorganization's human pyramid; Industrialists, bicycle racers, and singers thrown into a river; Dame Irene Stoat reads before being thrown into a river; Dinner party, Book-of-the-Month Club, and dung; Dead Indian with a new cooker; Milk Marketing Board gives away the M4; Prize in a police raffle; *Animation: Additional Prizes, including a deadly samurai made into a meal;* "Personally, I prefer more classical dishes"; *Animation: Michelangelo's Adam in a sandwich;* **"Timmy Williams Coffee Time"**; Raymond Luxury Yacht interview; *Animation: Train and naked girl, "Welcome All Sexual Athletes," Mona Lisa says "Hello Tiger";* Registry office—The Five-Man Couple; *Animation: Bloody lipstick, and the story of The Prince and the Black Spot;* **Election Night Special (Silly and Sensible Parties)**; Closing credits

• A •

"Additional Material By" — ("PSC; "Timmy Williams Interview") This long, fast laundry list of names is a hodge-podge of well-known entertainment and sport figures, lesser-known figures from the same areas, characters/authors from Oxbridge academic reading lists, and assorted people known only to the individual Python who contributed the name.

According to one person so named, Jonathan Ashmore, the bulk of the "unknowns" on the list were "layabouts" at a flat at World's End (in Camden High Street, London) during this period. See the entry for Ashmore below.

"agent" — ("Election Night Special") One who represents the candidate, in this case.

"all five of them" — ("Registry Office") What begins as a characteristic, Pythonesque misunderstanding between characters eventually becomes a rather sly comment on heterosexual marriage and the volatile sexual liberation movement of the 1960s and 1970s. Homosexuality in the UK had only been (partly) decriminalized three years earlier, but was still quite stigmatized. In fact, sexual acts between consenting men (aged twenty-one and above) had been legalized, but even a third person anywhere in the home recrimininalized the act, so the five Pythons would have still been subject to arrest. See the restrictions of the Sexual Offences Act of 1967 for more.

"Allied Technician's Union" — ("Foreign Secretary") The very powerful Trade Union Congress (TUC) was an umbrella organization representing many unions and was quite active in 1970. The pressure applied to management and government in the late 1960s would help bring Wilson's Labour government down (and encumber the incoming Heath government, as well) with threatened or actual strikes at industrial concerns like Ford Motors, by newspaper publishers, miners, and even a national dock strike. Strike activity was at its highest during the 1970–1974 period in the UK, as the Tories tried to rein in the power of organized labor, and the TUC is referenced more than sixty times in UK newspaper op-ed page cartoons in 1968–1970 alone. See the British Cartoon Archive.

Animation: for a minute or two strange things happen — (animated link out of "The Time on BBC 1") The animated head Gilliam uses in this sequence is a still photo of Wolverhampton MP Enoch Powell (1912–1998), whose "Rivers of Blood" immigration speech (see notes to Ep. 25) had bounced him from Cabinet status but into very high popularity with Conservative voters (and many others who feared unfettered immigration). The fact that Powell was an outspoken and blunt Tory painted him a perfect target for the Pythons. Powell would have been representing Idle's former constituency.

The background behind and around Powell is a reversed, colored version of Plate 15 from the de Vries book, *Perspective*, which Gilliam has used already. Powell's head has replaced a large fountain from the original drawing. The character who walks in and enters Powell's head features the head of Gen. Logan (*DWF*, 383), again, who can be seen in the second season opening credits which follow immediately.

Animation: "The Spot" — (PSC; "link into Election Night Special") As is often the case, this animation is a mix of found images and Gilliam artwork. Several of the images employed are identifiable.

Just as the storyteller begins narrating the story of the unlucky prince, an image of portions of the Kremlin can be glimpsed on the distant hillside, likely the Prince's home. The following scene—when the Prince discovers "the spot"—is framed in front of one of Giuseppe Galli Bibiena's prints, specifically "Scene from the theatrical performance on the occasion of the nuptials of the Prince Elector of Bavaria" (*Architectural and Perspective Designs*, Part IV, Plate 9). This backdrop has already been used in Ep. 2, behind Rodin's *The Kiss*. Gilliam will use this book often during the *Flying Circus* series run.

In the following scene the Prince dies of gangrene ("cancer" had been the original cause of death, but the BBC thought that too callous), and the black Spot begins its own adventures.

The next scene sees the Spot making his way "To the Big City," and here Gilliam has used as a background an actual background. He borrows the background scene from Bellini's *Madonna of the Meadow* (c. 1500), removing the Madonna and child figures completely. This painting has been part of the National Gallery collection for many years. (This same painting, figures intact, will appear later in Ep. 25.)

The laughing general in the following "Book of the Month Club section is Brigadier General William Farquhar Barry (1818–1879), yet another Civil War image Gilliam's borrowed from *Divided We Fought* (382). Barry will reappear as a wind-up doll in the "*Animation: Communists under the Bed, Putrid Peter Doll*" sequence in Ep. 31.

"Applied Mathematics" — ("School Prize-Giving") Mathematics used in the sciences, including astronomy, physics, etc.

Arabs — ("Foreign Secretary") Stereotypically attired in flowing robes and head coverings, the "Arabs" whoop and leap about as they toss various characters into the river. Between 1967 and September 1970 (when this episode was recorded), the Palestinian Liberation Organization (PLO) along with the Popular Front for the Liberation of Palestine (PFLP) had operated as a militant terrorist organization in Jordan, kidnapping and killing foes and foreigners, and the PFLP eventually hijacking planes and destroying them. A handful of Brits were on the three planes hijacked in September 1970, and were eventually rescued by Jordanian army troops on 26 September (Office for National Statistics).

"Ashley, Len" — ("Timmy Williams Interview" credits) Perhaps the sibling of Lyn Ashley, who was Mrs. Idle between 1967 and 1979.

"Ashmore, Jonathan" — ("Timmy Williams Interview" credits) Ashmore was a child actor who appeared in the 1955 film *A Kid for Two Farthings*, directed by Carol Reed. Ashmore is more recently Professor Jonathan Ashmore, FMedSci FRS, Department of Physiology, University College London. From Ashmore: "It's just that I happened to share a house c. 1970 in World's End, London with some good friends of Eric Idle . . . some of the other people in those high speed rolling credits were drunks/layabouts/crazies/hangers-on too . . ." (from e-mail correspondence with the author).

"at the rate of knots" — ("Election Night Special") A British colloquialism meaning "very quickly."

"Avery, Charles" — ("Foreign Secretary") Charles Avery was one of the original Keystone Kops at Mack Sennett's Keystone studio, appearing in (and even directing) dozens of early Hollywood knockabout comedies. It is no surprise that the Pythons would offer a bumbling screen comic as the employers' representative in this sketch.

• B •

bank of a river — ("Foreign Secretary") These riverbank scenes were shot while on location in the Easton Lodge area, Easton, at River Bank, on 24 August 1970

(WAC T12/1,413). The following day, the crew moved farther north to shoot in and around Norwich.

"Barclay, Humphrey" — ("Timmy Williams Interview" credits) A friend and employer to the Pythons, Barclay produced several shows involving various members of the troupe, including *Complete and Utter History of Britain* (1969), *Doctor in the House* (1969), and *Do Not Adjust Your Set* (1967). Barclay was also active in the Cambridge Footlights events, writing, directing, and producing.

"Barrow-in-Furness" — ("Election Night Special") Situated on the Irish Sea, and west of Lancashire. The entertainer Engelbert Humperdinck never stood for this (or any) constituency, hailing from Leicester. In the General Election of 1970, Albert Booth (the Labour candidate) held his seat in this constituency, and would remain in that position until 1983.

"BBC2" — ("The Time on BBC 1") On 20 April 1964 BBC2 came on the air, quickly earning a reputation for fostering edgier, often more daring programming than BBC1. Hit shows on BBC2 would often then make the jump to BBC1 (especially when any hint of inappropriateness had worn off).

"Beach, James" — ("Timmy Williams Interview" credits) Jim Beach was a fellow Cambridge Footlights member with Eric Idle in 1964, an entertainment lawyer who went on to eventually manage the band Queen and produce TV, theatrical performances, and films. Beach also produced the Pythons' "Monty Python at Drury Lane" and "City Center New York" projects.

"Beamish, Adrian" — ("Timmy Williams Interview" credits) A graduate of Christ's College, Cambridge, in 1962, Beamish would go on to become British ambassador to Mexico, and is now Sir Adrian Beamish.

"Bishop of East Anglia" — ("School Prize-Giving") East Anglia was *not* an Anglican diocese during this time, which may be why the Pythons chose the location. East Anglia is an area northeast of London comprising (primarily) the Norfolk and Suffolk regions, and where the Pythons shot some of the location material for the second season. It is so named because it was the easternmost part of the ancient kingdom of Angliæ.

The Idiots later (Ep. 20) will be trained at the University of East Anglia (Norwich, Norfolk), one of the oft-maligned "new" universities set up as a result of the government's Robbins Report released in October 1963. See entries for the "Idiot" sketch for more.

"Bloggs, David" — ("Timmy Williams Interview" credits) Probably a nonsense name, since "Joe Bloggs" (and sometimes "Fred Bloggs" or "Mr. and Mrs. Bloggs") is a British place-holding name, like "John Q. Public" in the United States. The character is played here by John Hughman (Eps. 14, 17, 28).

"Board of Trade" — ("Foreign Secretary") This episode was recorded in October 1970, just when the major alterations in the Board of Trade were front-page news. Created in 1761, the Board of Trade had gradually changed functions by 1970. In October 1970, the Department of Trade and Industry was formed from remnants of the Board of Trade and the Ministry of Technology.

Roy Mason (b. 1924) and then Michael Noble (1913–1984) were presidents of the Board of Trade in 1969 and 1970, respectively, just before the Board was reformulated.

"Book of the Month Club" — ("Dung") Concern founded in 1923, where "outstanding" books are chosen monthly and provided to paying subscribers. Accompanying items are usually limited to tote bags and the like, not dung or dead Indians.

Gilliam will use a copy of a Book of the Month Club ad (featuring titles like *The Rise and Fall of the Third Reich*, *The Naked Ape*, etc.) in his animation "The Spot" later in this episode.

"Bradshaw, Elizabeth" — ("School Prize-Giving") Dressed in a trench coat and hat, Inspector Bradshaw looks very much like the prototypical Scotland Yard official who often breaks in on *FC* sketches. The use of the female first name for a male character is also, of course, a Python trait of diminution for authority figures.

"breach of promise" — ("Registry Office") Under British law, engagements had been treated as enforceable contracts until almost the twentieth century, meaning a woman—after accepting a man's proposal of marriage—could seek damages if he backed out. Part of the consideration was that the woman could lose her virginity (and, hence, her future marriage value) in such a breach. (In *Hard Day's Night* [1964], Paul mentions that his philandering grandfather has cost the family "a fortune in breach of promise cases.") The twist for this scene, of course, is that British law did not recognize a homosexual marital relationship, and the injured party (the Registrar) couldn't technically have demonstrated breach.

"Brian!" — ("Timmy Williams Interview") This actor appears to be David Kempton (WAC T12/1,434).

"Bristols" — ("Election Night Special") "Bristols" is a word of rhyming slang: "Bristol cities" becomes "titties" (breasts), hence "Bristols." This reference elicits quite a laugh from the studio audience. Similarly,

"Jethro Q. Walrus*titty*" was the Silly candidate for Leicester earlier in the sketch.

The Goons would get away with similar veiled vulgarities. In "The Battle of Spion Kop," the name "Hugh Jampton" is actually read "huge Hampton," from "Hampton Wick," which is a rhyming slang for "prick" or "dick."

"buzzing noise" — ("Election Night Special") Sending up the "earpiece" news flashes and off-camera direction broadcasters receive while on air. The buzzing itself would have been interference or microphone feedback, and newscasters often have to remove the earpiece if the noise or director's messages get too jumbled and distracting. For more, see "loud buzzing noise" entry later.

• C •

"Can I just butt in at this point . . ." — ("Election Night Special") Colin (Ian Davidson) may be mimicking to a point one of the BBC's in-studio reporters, Graham Pyatt. Though on the same set level as Michelmore and the others during the 1970 election night coverage, Pyatt seems to get on camera less than others, and when he does, he tends to begin with "I'd just like to say here that," and the like.

"charabanc" — ("Timmy Williams Interview") A kind of motor coach, and one that might even be open to the air. The openness of the vehicle seems to fit Timmy Williams's/David Frost's need for being in sight at all times (as if he's royalty on parade). Also, traveling with the Timmy Williams/David Frost entourage would seem to demand such a vehicle.

"chemist's" — ("*If*—A Film by Mr. Dibley") Drugstores were the primary drop-off point for undeveloped film (including still film and 8mm and 16mm motion picture film), and is where Dibley's film was evidently being developed.

Coffee Time — ("Timmy Williams Interview") The intimation now is that the entire "chance" encounter between Timmy and Nigel was all part of the Timmy Williams schedule of shows and events. In just a four-year period Frost himself appeared on *The David Frost Show* (1969), *Frost on Saturday* (1968), *Frost on Sunday* (1968), *David Frost Presents* (1967), *The Frost Programme* (1966), and *The Frost Report* (1966). He was also executive producer for *The Rise and Rise of Michael Rimmer* (1970), *The Ronnie Barker Playhouse* (1968), and *At Last the 1948 Show* (1967): during the same period, he also appeared twice on *Rowan & Martin's Laugh-In* in 1968. It wouldn't be surprising if the Pythons' unflattering treatment of Frost didn't smack of at least a modicum of professional jealousy—Frost was, after all, the face of popular British TV at this time.

"Coleman, George" — ("Timmy Williams Interview" credits) George Coleman b. (1935) is an American saxophone player who appeared with the likes of Miles Davis and Herbie Hancock during the 1960s, and may have been known to Idle, who mingled in the popular London music scene.

Compère — ("*It's a Living*") A TV host figure, usually sequined and brashy in *FC* episodes.

"complete with silly walk" — (animated link out of "Dead Indian") This "Stop Press" animated section includes three separate sections created by Gilliam. The first is a full-page Madame Dowding advertisement from a fin-de-siècle publication (one of these same corseted models appeared in the title animations for the first season as well); and the second is a pig photo that's been used before, but this time attached to a piston engine borrowed from an industrial art schematic book.

The third is a combination page, as well. The Civil War general performing a silly walk across the scene of "Arabian splendour" is a member of Brigadier General George Stoneman's staff. The group photo can be found on page 67 of the *Divided We Fought* book used so often by Gilliam. (*DWF*, de Vries's *Perspective*, and Bibiena's *Architectural and Perspective Designs* were all Gilliam source books.) The "Arabian splendour" scene is another borrow from Bibiena, this time Plate 10. The more classical, columned portions of the scene are removed so that the bay or canals are the focus, and only the end portion of one of the buildings on the right hints at what's missing in the foreground edges. (Gilliam will manipulate a Bibiena plate for Ep. 33 similarly, removing portions as needed to place his action in those areas.) The edge of the scene as presented by Gilliam is just outside the tallest (nearest) towers on either side. The scene has been colored, as well. Bibiena's work appears in Eps. 2, 14, 19, and 33.

(could they be soldiers?) — (PSC; "School Prize-Giving") This is an in-joke moment for the readers of the script only, and is probably just an example of the Pythons finding ways to make the writing and communicating process (between themselves and the production personnel for the show) more interesting. There are comments about boredom and tediousness peppered throughout the printed scripts, especially in relation to the repeated appearances of characters like the "It's Man," for example.

"council estate" — ("Registry Office") Local municipal councils are responsible for planning and building homes for their citizens, and have included row-houses, semi-detached homes, and even tower blocks (as in Birmingham).

• D •

Dead Indian — ("Dead Indian") This Dead Indian appears to be played by Ian Davidson, who is noted as having appeared in (and been paid for) this episode in the BBC records (WAC T12/1,242).

"Dibley" — ("*If*—A Film by Mr. Dibley") "Gwen Dibley's Flying Circus" was a name floated early on as a possible title for the show, and was the name of the boys' school in Ep. 18, the "*Seven Brides for Seven Brothers*" sketch. The name allegedly came from an obituary. Versions of Dibley—including Dibbingley, Dibble, and even Richard Dimbleby—appear throughout the series. Dibley is not a terribly unusual name, however, appearing more than a dozen times in the 1968 edition of the Greater London area phone book (*British Phone Books*).

"Driffield" — ("Election Night Special") Situated in the Yorkshire Wolds, east of York and north of Kingston upon Hull. This report originated at Harpenden, but somehow moved to the village of Driffield in the middle of the delivery.

In the 1964 General Election, nearby Bridlington remained Conservative, easily, and even gained a few percentage points in the 1970 election.

"due to the number of votes cast" — ("Election Night Special") Said in jest, but at least partly true. With the voting age dropping to eighteen for the first time in a general election (thanks to the Representation of the People Act 1969), turnout dropped to the lowest rate since 1935, by percentage of possible votes. A larger turnout would have assured Labour the win, historians seem to agree (Clarke, 318).

"Dulwich" — ("Registry Office") A city in Greater London, Southwark, south of Westminster. In the 1970s, the once sleepy town where Dickens's and Wodehouse's characters could grow up and grow old had become a destination for the new rich, and probably more open to "special" marriages like the one depicted here. Conversely, ultra-conservative PM Margaret Thatcher bought a home there in one of the most upscale developments, Hambledon Place, Dulwich Common.

"dung" — ("Dung") Interesting that it's with a third book order that dung is merited, which may be a comment on the Fowles' novel (though *French Lieutenant's Woman* was a very popular book, selling millions of copies).

There were dung delivery attempts being made right around this time, but they were from angry National Farmers Union (NFU) farmers (demanding higher subsidies) delivering loads of offal to ministerial offices in London. *Evening News* cartoonist "Gus" depicted the protests in a cartoon on 21 March 1969. See the British Cartoon Archive.

• E •

Election Night Special — ("Election Night Special") The BBC coverage of the 1970 General Election was titled *BBC Election 70*, and was hosted by Cliff Michelmore, who had taken over in 1966 after the death of Richard Dimbleby. The frantic nature of the Pythons' version of the coverage is likely due to the BBC's zealous attempts to cover every region of the country as simultaneously as possible. The technical prowess needed for such blanket coverage—and the scores of personnel involved—were mentioned often by host Michelmore.

"Elstree" — ("Dead Indian") Elstree Studios is located in Elstree (and Borehamwood), Hertfordshire, and was a fixture in the British film industry for many years, producing, among many other titles, the *Star Wars* films.

"Emerson, Ralph" — ("Timmy Williams Interview" credits) Ralph Waldo Emerson (1830–1882) was an American philosopher and poet. Emerson had significant contacts with Python favorites Coleridge, Wordsworth, and Carlyle. This reference also connects back to Dame Irene's Emersonesque (via John Oxenham) poem mentioned in the "Foreign Secretary" sketch.

"Eyes down" — ("School Prize-Giving") A bingo term, meaning to look down at the card at the start of a game; here it could be meant more literally (and deviously); meaning attendees should look away as the "Chinaman" steals the school prizes. Bingo (or "Housey Housey") had swept through Britain in the postwar years, becoming a socially appropriate leisure activity for, especially, women (*Eyewitness: 1950–59*, "Popular Culture").

The appearance of Chinese references—all threatening—indicate that as of 1969–1970 the first sweeping Cultural Revolution had come to an end, that Mao was at least nominally in control with his zealous young Red Guard (and People's Liberation Army) cadres causing civil chaos, and foes like Deng Xiaoping purged into ineffectiveness. The escalating border confrontations with the Soviets (and North Vietnam) in 1968 and beyond had forced China's leadership to bury a few hatchets and take a more vocal, united approach to both foreign and domestic affairs, meaning the People's Republic of China (PRC) would have been much more in the public eye during this period.

• F •

"faulty cooker" — ("Dung") A quiet, almost tossed-off intertextual moment here. In Ep. 14, Mrs. Crump-Pinnet (Jones) is convinced that she can get the best gas company service if she's first overwhelmed by fumes—murdered—from a faulty cooker. The faulty cooker syndrome plagued Britain for years, with gas build-ups causing explosions or near-explosions in high rises (1968–1969), leading to the outlawing of gas cookers in such buildings. The Newham Borough Council, for example, cut gas deliveries to a development known as Abrahams Point in early August 1969, and decided to delay or even stop the gas hook-ups to another high-rise development in progress known as Merrit Point ("Council Turn Off Gas at Tower Block," *The Times*, 3 Aug. 1969: 1). A David Langdon cartoon from the *Sunday Mirror* published 17 November 1968 depicts faulty gas cookers being tossed from a high rise and at a Gas Board lorry (British Cartoon Archive). The ubiquitous gas-operated (as opposed to primarily electric) appliances across Britain—cookers, heaters, etc.—guaranteed a fair number of gas-related suicides, accidental asphyxiations, and explosions, and period newspaper coverage attests to the unsettling phenomena.

Finian's Rainbow — ("*Finian's Rainbow*—Starring the Man from the Off-Licence") A very late (1968) and somewhat clunky and self-conscious Warner Bros. musical (starring an aging Fred Astaire) directed by the very young Francis Ford Coppola as part of a multipicture arrangement with WB-Seven Arts.

The "her" Mr. Dibley mentions as being essential to a quality film is the character Sharon McLonergan, played in the original film musical by Surrey-born Petula Clark (b. 1932). Clark is also mentioned in *FC* in Eps. 13 and 37.

This memorable dancing scene was shot at Hurlingham Park, just near the tennis courts, where the undertakers were earlier carrying a coffin (Ep. 13 introduction).

"first result" — ("Election Night Special") In the actual BBC coverage of the 1970 General Election, Cliff Michelmore, Robin Day, David Butler, and Robert McKenzie led the way. The location for these scenes appears to be the St. Mary's Wing of the Whittington Hospital, Highgate Hill, London N19, and were shot on the night of 15 September 1970 (WAC T12/1,242).

"Fitzjones, Brian" — ("Timmy Williams Interview" credits) Brian Fitzjones contributed to the "television discussion program" *London: A New Look* (1960), including a filmed segment, according to the NFA Catalog at BFI.

"flog back" — ("*It's a Living*") Slang, meaning the prize can be sold for cash rather than kept, probably avoiding the significant tax bite on the value of the item.

"Forbes Minor" — ("School Prize-Giving") Based on the school reference ("Smith Major") in Ep. 18, it's likely this is a similar reference to the younger boy named Forbes enrolled in this "old school." Filmmaker Bryan Forbes will be mentioned later (Eps. 20, 36), and is also witheringly satirized in the pages of *Private Eye* (17 July 1970: 5).

"Foreign Secretary" — (link out of "*Finian's Rainbow*—Starring the Man from the Off-Licence) A Secretary of State, since 1945 this position has been responsible for foreign as opposed to domestic relations. In 1970, the Foreign Secretary was Sir Alec Douglas-Home (from 20 June, under Prime Minister Edward Heath). During this period, secret negotiations were under way for Britain's entry into the Common Market and the eventual adoption of the euro, the resumption of arms sales to South Africa and the controversial South African cricket team tour of the UK, as well as the escalating troubles in Northern Ireland, making the position of Foreign Secretary a significant flashpoint for controversy. Cabinet members Douglas-Home (known as "Baillie Vass" in the pages of *PE*) and "Reggie" Maudling were the lightning rods for the Opposition during this administration.

There seem to have been no attempts on the life of Britain's foreign secretary during this period, but there were several unsuccessful attempts made to assassinate King Hussein of Jordan by Palestine Liberation groups in 1970.

"Frankel, Dennis" — ("Timmy Williams Interview" credits) Dennis Frankel appears in the period London phone books living at 1 Northwood Gardens, N12 (*British Phone Books*, 1159).

Frost, David — (PSC; "Timmy Williams Interview") The script mentions that this may slightly resemble David Frost, but Idle carries off a spot-on impersonation and even caricature of Frost, so much so that the studio audience reacts uproariously to the rather acid-toned spoof. The audience is clearly enjoying the jokes at Frost's expense as the sketch unfolds.

Frost was a one-time collaborator, then employer for several of the Pythons, especially on shows like *That Was the Week That Was*, and they'd been at least familiar since their Oxbridge days, when Frost managed to get a secretary job with the Footlights. His aggressive personality was apparent even then.

Just two years earlier (September 1968), The Beatles had also taken Frost down a notch or two as guests on his own show, *The Frost Programme*. As Frost tries to introduce the band and be convivial, Paul, George, and especially John ignore him, needle him, and fret with their instruments as Frost vamps nervously, struggling to regain control.

By mid-1970, *Private Eye* is calling him "the odious Frost OBE," pillorying Frost's stepping backward into fame and fortune at every turn (17 July 1970: 4). Frost interviews "Lassie the Wonderdog" in this same *PE* issue.

"fully motorized pig" — (PSC; "Dead Indian") The printed script mentions that Gilliam is expected to create this insert. The motorized pig is reminiscent of the flying transport sheep in Ep. 2. This is followed by a Civil War Union general cutout "silly walking" across an Arabian-themed background.

"Fyffe-Chulmleigh" — ("School Prize-Giving") Chulmleigh is a small town found in Devon (where the Pythons shot significant location footage), while Fyffe Robertson was a presenter/reporter for *Tonight* on BBC. Robertson would work with other BBC types mentioned in *FC*, including Alan Whicker (Ep. 27) and Derek Hart (Ep. 17).

• G •

"gastroenteritis" — ("Election Night Special") An inflammation of the intestinal tract that can exhibit itself in vomiting and diarrhea, which is certainly what Gerald (Cleese) is referring to when he mentions the "very messy" possibility spreading across the countryside. Palin's "auntie" (in Australia, by then) will be mentioned again in Ep. 31.

"German television" — ("Timmy Williams Interview") Bavarian television officials also approached the Pythons about creating two shows, which eventually were written and recorded in German and English as *Der Fliegende Zirkus*.

"Gilbert, James" — ("Election Night Special") Gilbert (b. 1923) was a producer and director, producing various shows that included Python members as writers, including *Idle at Work* (1972), *The Two Ronnies* (1971; director and producer), *The Frost Report* (1966), and *Not Only . . . But Also* (1965). He would become head of BBC Comedy in 1973, while the Pythons were still on the air. Gilbert also worked with Sydney Lotterby (from the "Timmy Williams Interview" credits list) on *Me Mammy* (1969–1971). Gilbert also won several BAFTA awards in the 1960s.

Gone . . . Woman — ("Dung") *Gone with the Wind* was published in 1936 by Margaret Mitchell, and also garnered a Pulitzer prize; Hugo's *Les Miserables* was published in 1862; and *The French Lieutenant's Woman*, by John Fowles, was published in 1969. Of the three, the first two are admitted classics, while the third is the only one by a British author, and the most likely, being a contemporary novel, to be part of a Book of the Month Club listing. The novel would race up the *New York Times* bestseller list, and Fowles would be called "the most popular new British novelist" by *Times* reviewer Richard Jones ("Fiction in America: The Mood of the Times," 28 Mar. 1970: 14). Also, however, the parodic structure of the Fowles novel, wherein a nineteenth-century plot and characters (and the novel itself) are examined in a very twentieth-century way, offers much in comparison to the Pythons' similar parodic re-examination of television and historical and political figures.

According to a 1943 *Time* article on the burgeoning Book-of-the-Month Club market, popular "Club authors include Pearl Buck, Sylvia Townsend Warner, Sinclair Lewis, Ernest Hemingway, [and] Willa Cather," not to mention that year's most popular author and book, William Saroyan's *The Human Comedy* (15 Mar. 1943).

"Goschen, David" — ("Timmy Williams Interview" credits) David Goschen is also "one of the gang" with and around Idle in 1970 London, then in 1972 established Florian Studios (in Saxmundham, Suffolk) to create decorative tiles.

"Gosse, Edmund" — ("Timmy Williams Interview" credits) Gosse (1849–1928) was also an early Modernist poet (like Hovey, below) who worked as a librarian to the House of Lords, wrote academically on English poets Gray and Congreve, and for the *Sunday Times* (*ODNB*). Gosse lectured at Trinity College, Cambridge, and was awarded an honorary degree from Cambridge in 1886.

"Gowers, Michael" — ("Timmy Williams Interview" credits) Michael Gowers (1929–2008) was the TV critic for the *Daily Mail* during this period, and wrote and produced for ITV. Gowers also contributed to *The Frost Report*, where the Pythons may have encountered him.

"Granville Cup" — ("School Prize-Giving") There is a Granville Cup in which Bishop Vesey's Grammar School (Birmingham) participates.

gray suit and purple stock and dog collar — (PSC; "School Prize-Giving") According to the *OED*, a stock is "an article of clerical attire, consisting of a piece of black silk or stuff (worn on the chest and secured by a band round the neck) over which the linen collar is fastened." A "dog collar" is a colloquial, derisive term for a priest's neckwear. The Bishop's suit is actually dark blue or black, or perhaps charcoal gray. In short, the character is meant to portray the padre or headmaster (or both) of a public school, both figures seen earlier in Ep. 18, in the "*Seven Brides for Seven Brothers*" sketch.

"Grimwade Gynn" — ("School Prize-Giving") Peter Grimwade (1942–1990) was a writer and director, working on *Z Cars*, and especially *Doctor Who*. The Pythons and *Flying Circus* shared extras and walk-ons with both of these shows, almost on a weekly basis, between 1969 and 1974.

"Gulf of Amman" — ("Foreign Secretary") In 1969–1970, Egypt embarked upon a series of border conflicts with Israel, during which negotiations for a cease-fire were sought by British interests. Fighting in Amman, Jordan, drew U.S. warships (for Israel) and Soviet tanks (for the PLO) into the region. The strife in the region was the subject of myriad op-ed pieces and political cartoons across the UK.

• H •

"Harpenden" — ("Election Night Special") The Pythons give Harpenden to the Sensible Party by a single vote. The Hitchin & Harpenden electorate remained a Labour stronghold through the 1970 General Election, with Shirley Williams (Labour) garnering 48.53 percent, R. Luce (Conservative) at 44.18 percent, and the Liberal candidate, T. Willis, claiming 7.29 percent of the vote. Williams and Labour had earlier won the seat in 1964.

"Harris, Reg" — ("Foreign Secretary") Reg Harris (1920–1992) was a world champion cyclist, Olympic medalist, and World Amateur Sprint Champion in 1949–1952 and 1954. He was also awarded an OBE and named Sportsman of the Year, and would have been the premier English cyclist during the Pythons' formative years.

"Haydon-Jones, Ann" — ("Election Night Special") Ann was an English tennis player and has already been mentioned in Ep. 7, when the blancmanges played at Wimbledon. She was named UK Sportswoman of the Year in 1969. See notes to Ep. 7. Haydon-Jones will also be mentioned in Ep. 22.

"heap dizzy" — ("Dung") Standard Hollywood Indian-speak from hundreds of serial and feature westerns, and used by the Pythons in Ep. 6, the "Red Indian in Theatre" sketch. The Dead Indian is played by Ian Davidson, though he's uncredited in the printed scripts. Davidson will also appear in Eps. 18, 20, and 26 during this season.

He is dragged down by an unseen hand — ("School Prize-Giving") The appearance of the Mao-jacketed character (Chapman) indicates this is a send-up of the recent internal struggles in China as a result of Mao's Cultural Revolution. By 1967 Mao was publicly encouraging mid-level Party leaders and members (and even workers and military men) in the larger cities to regularly denounce counter-revolutionary activities and figures. The paranoia spread into the central leadership, with many embracing the CR as an opportunity to rid themselves of political enemies, since denouncement led to inevitable and quite often fatal purgings. The following years' struggle between Mao and Lin Biao (1907–1971)—where assassination attempts went both ways, each trying to supplant the other in the people's hearts and minds—only ended when, after a failed armed revolt, Lin died in a plane crash as he tried to flee the country.

The constant mention of Chinese political and military activity in international newspapers and newscasts probably accounts for the Pythons' (and the world's) seeming fixation on the subject. In larger UK newspapers there were, for instance, more than 200 political cartoons poking fun at the Chinese political situation published between 1967 and 1970 alone. See the British Cartoon Archive for more.

"held Leicester" — ("Election Night Special") In the (18 June) 1970 British General Election, Conservatives took 330 seats to Labour's 288 (with six seats going to the Liberals and six to Others, including the Communist Party, Plaid Cymru, Scottish National Party, and the Republican Labour Party). The Scottish National Party scored its first General Election seat in 1970, a triumph of a fringe party obviously not lost on the Pythons.

In the Derby-Leicester area, for example, a higher-than-average swing vote to the Conservative side was achieved, with two seats—formerly held by Labour fixtures George Brown and Jennie Lee—going "Conservative for the first time at a general election since the war" (see Butler and Pinto-Duschinsky's *The British General Election of 1970*). This trend toward Conservatism (a 4.7 percent boost to Conservatives between 1966 and 1970 in by-election races) would certainly have alarmed the left-leaning Pythons, and would certainly have flavored this sketch as a result. This swing followed a 7 percent swing to Labour during the preceding inter-election years, 1959–1966. In fact, according to Butler and Pinto-Duschinsky, suburban and rural areas like those around Luton and Leicester were Conservative's strongest areas by 1970, where they regained many of the seats they'd recently lost.

"Herbert, George" — ("Timmy Williams Interview" credits) Herbert (1593–1633) was a noted English poet, and a Trinity College, Cambridge, graduate. Another George Herbert was a character name in H[erbert] G[eorge] Wells's *War of the Worlds* (1898), and yet another George Herbert financed Carter's King Tut archaeological digs between 1907 and 1922. Lastly (and most likely the source of this reference), George Herbert was a local British actor appearing in such memorable cult films as *The Secrets of Sex* (1970) and TV shows like *Boy Meets Girl* (1967). A number of extras appearing in *FC* also appeared in *Secrets of Sex*.

"He's not dead!" — ("Dung") This exchange will be famously revisited in the feature film *HG*, in the "Plague Cart" scene.

"Holborn" — ("Timmy Williams Interview") Just outside the City of London, near the British Museum. There were a number of very fashionable, Italian-type coffee shops in this area in the 1960s.

"hot up" — ("Election Night Special") Variation of "heat up." The BBC broadcast of this particular (1970) election was also quite overheated, especially as the returns clarified the shocking turn-of-political-fortunes for the two major parties.

Noted BBC personalities covered the election—Cliff Michelmore, Robin Day (Ep. 2), Desmond Wilcox, Alf Garnett, David Butler, Alan Watson, and Bob McKenzie were in-studio as returns came in, while out among the constituencies were David Dimbleby (in Huyton), Michael Charlton (in Bexley), Keith Kyle (in Wolverhampton), Denis Tuohy (in Guildford), and James Burke (Ep. 35) in Cheltenham. There were on-air BBC personnel reporting from many other cities, as well. Cutting back and forth between the studio, the graphics, and live shots made for a hectic night, especially as the swingometer registered the surprising results—a Conservative victory. Opinion polls had predicted a comfortable Labour win. (Ian Jones provides an enlightening play-by-play of that tumultuous evening at offthetelly.co.uk.)

Lastly, Michelmore at one point mentions that the races are "warming up" (Jones).

"Hovey, Richard" — ("Timmy Williams Interview" credits) Richard Hovey (1864–1900) was an American Modernist poet and playwright. Hovey also wrote the Dartmouth Song "Men of Dartmouth," which connects him to another anthem-writer mentioned in this list, John Stamford (see below).

"how big a swing" — ("Election Night Special") Election night commentator McKenzie (see entry for "swingometer") was during the broadcast guessing a Conservative gain of about 6 percent, which was, technically, off the chart.

"Hughes, Geoffrey" — ("Timmy Williams Interview" credits) Geoffrey Hughes (1944–2012) was an actor who contributed Paul's voice in the animated film *The Yellow Submarine* (1968), and appeared on the wildly popular *Coronation Street* for a decade. He also guest-starred on *Dad's Army, Doctor Who,* and *Up Pompeii* in the 1960s, and produced Frost's *The Frost Programme* (1966).

"Humperdinck, Engelbert" — ("Election Night Special") British singer born Arnold George Dorsey in India, Humperdinck (played by Chapman) is identified as Ken Clean-Air Systems' (Cleese) manager in Ep. 18. Humperdinck was raised in Leicester (as was Chapman). *The Engelbert Humperdinck Show* appeared on British television in 1969.

• I •

"ICI" — ("Foreign Secretary") ICI is "Imperial Chemical Industries," founded in 1926 to produce paints and specialty chemical products. ICI was considered a top company in Britain for many years.

"If" — ("*If*—A Film by Mr. Dibley") Lindsay Anderson's 1968 film is correctly printed *If. . . .*, and featured an assistant editor named Michael Ellis, whose name will figure prominently in Ep. 41, which is entitled "Michael Ellis." (All the episodes in the fourth and final season were given titles, and several were even monothematic.) The film starred Malcolm McDowell (b. 1943), and was deemed so controversial it was given an "X" rating in the United States.

"if . . . 2001 . . . Midnight Cowboy" — ("*If*—A Film by Mr. Dibley") These three films form a significant portion of the core of "new wave" films emerging from the United States and UK in the late 1960s, some ten years after the advent of France's New Wave. These would have been just the type of cutting-edge films that astute cinephiles like the Pythons (and their university and workplace pals) would have frequented in the many London-area cinemas offering international fare. Other foreign new wave films and filmmakers mentioned in *FC* include the Italian directors Visconti and Antonioni (Ep. 29), American Sam Peckinpah (Ep.

33), and they clearly satirize the films of Frenchman Jean-Luc Godard in the "French Subtitled Film" sketch (Ep. 23).

"I get so bloody bored" — ("The Time on BBC 1") The BBC employed myriad announcers and linkmen to introduce shows, lay out programming for the evening, etc.—they were ubiquitous before the days of prerecorded sound bites. In Ep. 30, in the "Neurotic Announcers" sketch, the BBC announcer (Cleese) works through his confidence problems with the help of an announcer friend (Palin) and his wife (Cleveland), all on the air.

The reference to dullness and being "bloody bored" has already been broached in Ep. 6 with a look at "The Dull Life of a City Stockbroker"; in Ep. 7, when Sopwith (Idle) admits that camel spotting is "dull"; and Ep. 10, where the Chartered Accountant (Palin) wants to become a lion tamer because his work is "desperately dull and tedious and stuffy and boring." Philosophers referenced often by the Pythons in *Flying Circus*—including Schopenhauer and Heidegger (*FZ*), and especially Kierkegaard (Eps. 2 and 14)—all point to boredom in the Industrial Age as a particularly affecting malady. In Kierkegaard's "Crop Rotation" essay, boredom is the fundamental reason humans exist, and seems to define the world of the Pythons quite accurately:

> So all people are boring. The word itself indicates the possibility of a subdivision. "Boring" can describe a person who bores others as well as one who bores himself. Those who bore others are the plebeians, the mass, the endless train of humanity in general. Those who bore themselves are the elect, the nobility; and how strange it is that those who don't bore themselves usually bore others, while those who do bore themselves amuse others. The people who do not bore themselves are generally those who are busy in the world in one way or another, but that is just why they are the most boring, the most insufferable of all. . . . The other class of men, the select, are those who bore themselves. As remarked above, generally they amuse others, outwardly occasionally the mob, in a deeper sense their fellow initiates. The more profoundly they bore themsleves, the more powerful a means of diversion they offer others, when boredom reaches its zenith, either by dying of boredom (the passive form) or (the active form) by shooting themselves out of curiosity. (*Either/Or*, 230)

It is for this reason—the ineluctable boredom of modern life—that characters like the Waiter (Jones) in Ep. 13 can (or must) go off and commit suicide, but "not because of anything serious." Clearly, the "busy in the world" people defined as "most insufferable" by Kierkegaard are the chartered accountants and city stockbrokers and City Gents that populate the Python world, and they end up killing themselves not out of curiosity (see the Upperclass Twits in Ep. 12), but because they are too addled to do anything else. However they die, though, it's a blessing.

For his part Heidegger would write: "For if life, in the desire for which our essence and existence consists, possessed in itself a positive value and real content, there would be no such thing as boredom: mere existence would fulfill and satisfy us" (from *What Is Metaphysics?* [1929]). Well, in the twentieth century—and especially in the Python world where "positive value and real content" are replaced with a postmodern pastiche of nostalgia and cultural malaise and television-encouraged consumerism—the simple joy of "mere existence" is *not* enough, and the Python character (and narrative) tends to be adaptative and elusive, to become and become and become, constantly undercutting and reinventing itself.

ignore him — (PSC; "Foreign Secretary") Again, absurdities playing out for the audience while most of the characters miss them entirely, or treat them as matter-of-fact.

"impostor" — ("School Prize-Giving") Ep. 43 will feature several impostor psychiatrists, each seeking sexual details from Hamlet (Jones) about his relationship with Ophelia.

"interesting undergarments" — (link out of "Dead Indian") This is a fin-de-siècle advertisement page for "Madame Dowding" corsets. Madame Dowding's was located at 8 and 10 Charing Cross Road. One of these same corseted models appeared in the title animations for the first season, as well.

The Civil War general performing a silly walk across the following scene of "Arabian splendour" is a member of Brigadier General George Stoneman's staff. Stoneman (1822–1894) was a Union general, and acts as one of more than a dozen Civil War images included in the series' animations. The photo can be found on page 67 of *Divided We Fought*.

"interrupt" — ("Interruption" links out of "The Time on BBC 1") This series of interruptions is a jab at the characteristic interruptions of programming by BBC announcers and the like, which also happens in Ep. 7, where the constable (Chapman) interrupts the sci-fi sketch to reassure viewers at home. These narrative interruptions emerge often in *FC*, including the Major (Chapman) interrupting and prodding the show in different directions in Ep. 8, and the city of North Malden and two Pepperpots (Chapman and Cleese) repeatedly interrupting "Njorl's Saga" in Ep. 27. The sanctity of the fictional televised world is one of the medium's pillars, and one that the Pythons undercut on a regular basis.

"in toto" — (*"It's a Living"*) Latin phrase indicating totality, completeness.

"Israeli embassy" — ("Timmy Williams Interview") As part of *The David Frost Show*, Frost had already interviewed many noteworthy world leaders, including Israeli PM Golda Meir and Defense Minister Moshe Dayan (both July 1969).

It's a Living — (*"It's a Living"*) Reminiscent of many show titles from British television over the years (*It's a Knockout*; *It's a Square World*; and *Yes, It's the Cathode-Ray Tube Show!*), and is often satirized on *FC*, including several *It's the Arts* programs. The "It's Man" (Palin) himself was created by the Pythons to represent the hoary chestnuts of such show names and obvious links (he's haggard, frayed, and worn out).

"I want to marry you too sir" — ("Registry Office") The comic misunderstanding used so often in Python, and which is earlier seen in Shakespeare, Dekker, and Jonson (see *MPSERD*), where, in this case, the literality of one character almost renders impossible successful communication. Another noted English stage comedy team, Gilbert and Sullivan (mentioned earlier in Ep. 16), fell into this music hall prattle, as well, including the following exchange in *The Pirates of Penzance* (1879):

> General: I ask you, have you ever known what it is to be an orphan?
> King: Often!
> General: Yes, orphan. Have you ever known what it is to be one?
> King: I say, often.
> Pirates: Often, often, often. (Act I)

• J •

"Jones, Alan" — ("Election Night Special") A well-known Welsh cricketer, Jones scored more than 40,000 runs for Glamorgan between 1957 and 1983. England's selectors overlooked him for the series until 1970, which may account for Python's inclusion of his name in this sketch.

• K •

"Kerr, Malcolm" — ("Timmy Williams Interview" credits) A noted Islamic student and scholar of the period, expatriate-American Kerr (1931–1984) could have been known to the Pythons for several reasons. His wife attended Occidental College, where Gilliam had also been a student. Kerr would also later take a post-doctoral position at Oxford. Kerr's publications centered on the Arab political situation (having been raised in Beirut), and may account for Python's recurring use of the Arab motif in this episode.

"Kubrick, Stanley" — (*"If*—A Film by Mr. Dibley") Kubrick (1928–1999) was an American expatriate director who spent most of his career in the UK. Kubrick's first UK-based film was *Lolita* (1962). Like *If. . .*, Kubrick's *2001: A Space Odyssey* also came out in 1968, though to significant audience puzzlement, then cult and critical acclaim, before finding its honored place in film history.

• L •

Late Night Line-Up — (*"It's a Living"*) *Late Night Line-Up* debuted in 1964 as simply *Line-Up*, then in September 1964 became *Late Night Line-Up*, and ran through 1972. The show offered "slots for films, books, jazz, folk and progressive rock music," according to *British Television* (Oxford, 1996). The original cast included Denis Tuohy, Michael Dean, Nicholas Tresilian, and Joan Bakewell. Terry Jones contributed material to the show in the mid-1960s.

The day after the final episode in the *Flying Circus* second season (Ep. 26) was broadcast, 23 December 1970, the "TV Weekly Programme Review" team met at Television Centre to perform its regular post-mortem on the week's broadcast. Bill Cotton (Head of Light Entertainment) complained that the Pythons' unscheduled (or just unannounced) appearance on *Late Night Line-Up* in December had just exacerbated concerns about the vulgarity of the later *FC* episodes (WAC T47/216). See notes to Ep. 26 for more.

"Latin Elegaics" — ("School Prize-Giving") Misspelling of "elegiac." These are (often structural, as in coupleted) elegies written in Latin, and covering a wide range of subjects. A well-known English elegy is Thomas Gray's *Elegy Written in a Country Church-Yard*. Gray dwelt at Cambridge for several years, though not as either a student or professor.

Latin elegists include Tibullus, Catullus, Sulpicia, and Ovid. For a later reference to the Pythons' more Ovidian approach to sensuality, see notes to Ep. 36.

"Leicester . . . Luton" — ("Election Night Special") Leicester (Chapman's birthplace) is a northern city by geography, lying northeast of Birmingham in Leicestershire. Tom Boardman was elected MP for Leicester SW at a by-election in 1967. Luton is a borough in Bedfordshire. Luton figures prominently in many *FC* episodes, but especially as the hiding place for Spiny Norman, Dinsdale Piranha's enormous imaginary tormentor. Dinsdale eventually explodes a nuclear device at the Luton Airport (Ep. 14).

In the 1970 General Election, Luton and all districts of Leicester turned out more than 70 percent of their constituencies. Luton-area MPs in 1970 included Sir D. Madel (for then-South Bedfordshire). Will Howie (Labour) lost his seat in Luton in 1970, held since 1963. Luton East went to Labour (from Conservative) in the following 1974 General Election.

Lastly, Lord Hill, head of the BBC (1967–1972) during much of the Pythons' tenure there, was also from Luton.

"Lord Mayor, Lady Mayoress" — ("School Prize-Giving") The Lord Mayor is played by Evan Ross, while the Lady Mayoress is played by Eddy May Scrandrett (WAC T12/1,242).

"Lotterby, Sydney" — ("Timmy Williams Interview" credits) Lotterby (b. 1926) is a British producer and comedy director, who by the time of this episode's writing had created *Up Pompeii* (1970) and *The Liver Birds* (1969). In *At Last the 1948 Show*, Cleese, Marty Feldman, Chapman, and Tim Brooke-Taylor each play a character named Sydney Lotterby, and they all look and sound exactly the same. Lotterby was living at 55 Watchfield Ct., Sutton Court Road, Hounslow, during this period (*British Phone Book*, 2129).

"loud buzzing noise in my left ear" — ("Election Night Special") During *BBC Election 70*, there are a number of sequences where psephologist David Butler (b. 1924) talks result numbers, trying to correlate and then distill dozens of reporting districts in a live shot. At about 11:55 p.m. there can be heard all sorts of noises (overlapping voices, paperwork, mechanical sounds), and the human traffic behind and around Butler seems nothing short of a cacophonous distraction. To his credit, Butler plays the seasoned campaigner and pushes right through.

Luton Town Hall — ("Election Results") These night shots of the silly election results were all shot on the night of 12 May 1970, which would have made for a very long day. Also shot that day were the scenes for the All Blacks football match for the "Derby Council vs. All Blacks Rugby Match" sketch for Ep. 23. The following day portions of the "French Subtitled Film" sketch were shot, as was the soccer match between the gynecologists and Long John Silvers, all in the Torquay area. They also shot at Anstey Cove for Ep. 25 footage (see notes to that episode for more). They would keep shooting in the area until at least 22 May 1970, then take a week or so off before resuming the more local location work back in Ealing on 1 June (WAC T12/1,416).

"Luxury Yacht, Raymond" — ("Raymond Luxury Yacht") This character also appears in Ep. 22, where, instead of being a "leading skin specialist," he is seeking plastic surgery for his oversized false nose. The "false nose" bit will reappear in the feature film *HG*, when a medieval village mob puts a false nose on a woman (Connie Booth) to make her look like a witch.

"Lynn, Johnny" — ("Timmy Williams Interview" credits) Jonathan Lynn, a Cambridge alum, contributed to the *Stuff What Dreams Are Made Of* writing at the Cambridge Footlights in 1964, during Idle's time there. Lynn also contributed to the Cambridge Circus that played Broadway in 1964 (with Cleese and Chapman), and would later co-write both *Yes, Minister* and *Yes, Prime Minister*.

• M •

"Mail" — ("Timmy Williams Interview") Refers to the *Daily Mail* newspaper, a conservative tabloid often termed the "*Daily Hate Mail*" by *Private Eye*, and one the *PE* editors take to task for:

> its slavish adherence to every tiny fluctuation in the Conservative Party line, its progression of vacillating editors, its third-rate staff and fourth-hand ideas . . . all contributed to what is undoubtedly the dullest and most amateurish product that Fleet Street has ever known (barring only the *Daily Sketch* and the *Evening News*). Nothing can be served by prolonging the grisly farce of the *Mail*'s continued existence any longer. (Ingrams, 285)

Private Eye's wish hasn't come true: the *Daily Mail* continues today to enjoy large circulation and readership numbers, as well as a broad online readership.

man — ("Timmy Williams Interview") This "Man," as he's referred to in the printed script, is David Ballantyne, who also appears in Eps. 13, 14, and 17 in this season. At one point he's paid £42 for his scheduled appearances (BBC WAC T12/1,094).

"Mangrove" — ("Raymond Luxury Yacht") Though an unusual name, Mangrove is not completely made up. Graham Chapman writes of a young man he knew named (allegedly) Buzz Mangrove, who was a junior warden with passkeys to residence halls in London, where young medical students could billet (McCabe, 92). There are no surviving phone records indicating that a "Mangrove" (using this spelling) actually lived in the Greater London area, however.

There was also a restaurant in the Kensington area at 8 All Saints Road, W11, during this period called "Mangrove Restaurant." This Notting Hill-area restaurant had been much in the news—it was there on 9 August 1970 that police and West Indians (and other "people of colour") scuffled, leading to 19 arrests and 17 police officers injured. Ep. 19 was recorded less than one month later.

Mao jacket and cap — (PSC; "School Prize-Giving") The plain "uniform" worn by Chairman Mao Tse-tung (1893–1976), at this time the ailing leader of the People's Republic of China, and standard wear for Chinese men (and many women) during Mao's tenure. This character is also wearing the white "dog collar" under his Mao tunic, probably to indicate that he's purporting to be the Bishop of East Anglia.

In Ep. 30, a Chinese man (Chapman) will portray the English ambassador to Russia, complete with pidgin English and an overstated knowledge of the Cornish countryside and Devon and Cornwall leisure customs.

"Marwood, Reginald" — ("Timmy Williams Interview" credits) Reginald Francis Cheese was John Cleese's father, who would change the family name to "Cleese," while John's middle name was "Marwood."

"Massinger, Thomas" — ("Timmy Williams Interview" credits) This name could be an accidental conflation of the Jacobean playwrights and writing partners, Thomas Dekker (or Thomas Middleton) and Phillip Massinger.

"Matherson, Ian" — ("Timmy Williams Interview" credits) There was an Ian Matheson living in Hounslow during this period, at 20 Northcote Avenue, W5 (*British Phone Book*, 345).

"M4 motorway" — ("Dead Indian") The M4 stretches some 200 miles from London to Wales, and was fairly new at this period. The section of whatever roadway they've chosen for this scene seems to be near completion but not yet open. Construction on the actual M4 was under way in this period.

"Milk Marketing Board" — ("Dung") MMBs are regional controlling entities for the selling of milk products in the UK, and they were originally created in the early years of the Great Depression. Many MMBs have since been disbanded, allowing for competition in the milk production and distribution industries in the UK. MMBs were in the news often during this period, as the sitting governments attempted to balance the fair price of milk with the need for favorable export prices in the face of continuing subsidies. "Single cream" is cream with a manipulated low fat content.

"Millichope, Ray" — ("Foreign Secretary") Millichope was the film editor for *FC*, as well as *Not Only . . . But Also* and *The Two Ronnies*.

Mix through — (PSC; link into "*If*—A Film by Mr. Dibley") Television term for moving from one shot to another, in this case involving a cut from the live color film to a TV-produced filmed image of the same battle scene.

"more classical dishes" — ("*Animation: Michelangelo's Adam in a Sandwich*") This figure is Adam (given the gift of life) from the well-known Sistine Chapel ceiling painted by Michelangelo between 1508 and 1512. God's outstretched fingers and hand from this same work of art will be used later—in the "Salvation Fuzz" sketch, Ep. 29—to condemn a man for killing bishops and leaving them on the landing.

Muted music and sophisticated lighting — ("Dung") Actually, the lighting looks as even and featureless as ever—the Pythons quipped about the lack of lighting control in their studio space as early as Ep. 9, in "The Visitors" sketch. (The Pythons tended to share soundstage space with news and game shows, meaning the installed lighting packages in these stages were only minimally manipulable.)

As for the muted music, the background music seems to be "Late Night" by Roger Webb (WAC T12/1,434).

Muted trumpet plays a corny segue — (School Prize-Giving") This snippet of badly played music is "Comic Bugle Call" by Alan Langford (WAC T12/1,434).

• N •

"Nabarro" — (PSC; link into "School Prize-Giving") The character portrayed by Chapman is called "Nabarro" in the printed script. Sir Gerald Nabarro was a South Worcestershire MP until his death in 1973. Nabarro is also mentioned prominently in Ep. 23, where he is noted for having a pet prawn called Simon, and Ep. 21, by name only. His image is used as early as Ep. 2 by Gilliam in a "talking head" animation, where his "blah-blah-ing" is covered by ad-draped boarding. Nabarro was one of the old Conservatives that the Pythons and the Left loved to hate, and he appeared on the cover of the satirical journal *Private Eye* on 14 February 1969.

A prominent and often lightning rod politician, Nabarro tweaked the nose of the government—including his own party—more than once (e.g., the Motor Tax issue mentioned in Ep. 10). Nabarro is mentioned more than 200 times in political cartoons in UK newspapers between 1968 and 1974, and he would have been quite recognizable to *FC* thanks to his impressive trademark mustache.

"Negus, Arthur" — ("Election Night Special") Negus (1903–1985) was an antiques expert and a broadcaster. He came to BBC television in 1966 on *Going for a Song*, where he valued antiques for an audience. Negus won the Sir Ambrose Fleming Memorial Award in 1967 for service to television in the Bristol area (see entry for "Bristols" above for more), where he may have come to the young Cleese's attention. Negus will be mentioned again in Ep. 21, in the "*Archaeology Today*" sketch.

"new cooker" — ("Dung") This harks back to the "New Cooker Sketch" from Ep. 14, though there Mrs. Crump-Pinnet (Jones) doesn't get the free dead Indian. This man (Chapman) is wearing the same uniform that Cleese wore as the East Midlands Poet Board man in Ep. 17.

"New Haven . . . Continent" — ("Foreign Secretary") Crossing point for tourists over the English Channel to France.

"Nigel" — ("Timmy Williams") John Cleese would sometimes write under the pseudonym Nigel Farquhar-Bennett, while Terry Jones's older brother is Nigel Jones (Ep. 27).

No reaction . . . guests — ("School Prize-Giving") Again, this non-reaction is a moment in the Python world where characters ignore completely the outlandish goings-on, just adding to the absurdity of the scene.

The Mayor is played by Evan Ross (*Emma; Dad's Army*), and the Mayoress by Eddy May Scrandrett (Ep. 17); others at the table include Peggy Scrimshaw (*Yes, Honestly*), Hazel Cave (*Upstairs, Downstairs*), Brian Gardner (Ep. 17; *The Fabulous Frump*), Tom O'Leary (Ep. 17), Michael Stayner (Eps. 17–18; *Billion Dollar Brain*), and Bill Leonard (Eps. 17–18). The soldiers are played by Gordon Winter and David Melbourne (*Softly Softly; Z Cars*). The row of boys watching the awards (not mentioned at all in the printed script) include Robert Toller, Brian Ball, Garry O'Brien, David Docherty, Nigel Grice (*Oliver!*), and Keith Dewhurst (*Z Cars*) (WAC T12/1,242). The boys' parents (mothers, primarily) are noted as being on the set, as well, during filming.

"Nought" — ("Election Night Special") The forty-seven parties standing candidates for the 1970 General Election each received some votes, though at least eighteen scored a statistical nil (0.00 percent) of the total vote, with six more registering just 0.01 percent each. Keele University figures indicate that 408 candidates forfeited their £150 deposits in 1970, failing to garner the requisite minimum votes. The Anti-Abortion Party received the fewest votes, claiming just 103. The Liberal Party lost many of the seats (7 of 13) won in the by-election years. Welsh and Scottish nationalists also fared very poorly in 1970, and the Communists were only able to claim 1.2 percent of the vote (see Keele; Butler and Pinto-Duschinsky).

The "lost deposit" embarrassment will be revisited in Ep. 45, where the Liberal Party candidates (the Pythons themselves) will, in the closing credits, all forfeit their deposits.

• O •

"off-licence" — ("*If*—A Film by Mr. Dibley") A licensed liquor store in the UK that sells alcohol for consumption off the premises (as opposed to a pub or tavern).

"old school" — ("School Prize-Giving") For the schools attended by the Pythons, see notes to Ep. 13. This "Nabarro" fellow is obviously referring to a public (fee paying) school, where Britain's elite are trained. Most of these schools keep and promote lists of celebrated graduates, and do invite those grads back for these annual award-giving ceremonies.

ordinary interview set — ("Raymond Luxury Yacht Interview") The music beneath this transition is Gerry Mulligan's "Jeru" (WAC T12/1,434).

• P •

"Pennycate, John" — ("Timmy Williams Interview" credits) His last name actually spelled "Penycate," John Penycate (b. 1943) is a BBC reporter and producer who began as a researcher for *The Frost Programme*.

"people have drawn comparisons between your film" — ("*If*—A Film by Mr. Dibley") During the 1960s, AIP (American International Pictures) kept up a steady stream of very low budget and often salacious knock-off films, including *Angel Unchained* (1970), which drew its inspiration from Kurosawa's *Seven Samurai* (1954), and *Strawberries Need Rain* (1970) from Ingmar Bergman's *Seventh Seal* (1957).

"phone to America" — ("Timmy Williams Interview") The awful Garibaldi family will also be making a deal with American film/TV people in Ep. 45, and American film producers make a trans-Atlantic call to the idiots' banker (Chapman) in Ep. 20. Clearly there is an equating here of moronic, self-absorbed behavior with American entertainment, as well as a new level of success if the lucrative American market can be broached. Many British musicians and performers, including Cliff Richard, Frankie Howerd, and The Beatles set their sights on success in the States—and only The Beatles managed to accomplish this success.

Frost himself had been commuting (often on the Concorde, no less) between New York and London since 1963 when his *TW3* produced a very popular tribute to John F. Kennedy, and he became a known face in America. The American version of *TW3* increased that high profile, and subsequent interview shows with President Richard Nixon, for example, elevated Frost to international celebrity status. One of the concerns voiced by many who knew him during this period was that he tried to be everywhere, do everything, and have some kind of relationship with everyone in the world of television in both the UK and United States (see Morgan's *Speaks!*, as well as the introduction to Ingrams's *The Life and Times of* Private Eye for more).

"Picksley, Frank" — ("Timmy Williams Interview" credits) Frank Pixley (1867–1921) was, like Hattie Starr below, an early American composer. Pixley had co-written *King Dido*, a musical comedy that premiered in 1902. Pixley was also a member of the Royal Geographical Society in London. The misspelling (of his name, albeit phonetically) is characteristic of the show, where faulty memorial misspellings occurred in original material submitted to the graphics department as well as subsequent mistakes on the title cards.

"polling's been quite heavy" — ("Election Night Special") Voter turnout in the 1970 General Election reached almost 72 percent, down about 3 percent from the 1966 General Election.

"polystyrene" — ("Raymond Luxury Yacht") Most of the props used in *FC*, and especially the larger ones (the sixteen-ton weight, for example) are made from polystyrene, according to the requisitions and constructions forms extant in the WAC collection for the show.

"Portman, Lord" — ("Foreign Secretary") Character in Anna Austen Lefroy's book, and mentioned by Jane Austen in 1814 letters to Anna concerning suggestions for editorial work on the manuscript.

In life, the actual Lords Portman had been members of the peerage since Henry VIII's time, with Edward Henry Berkeley Portman, ninth Viscount Portman occupying the title in 1969–1970. The Lords Portman would have been peers in the House of Lords, having less political power than their elected counterparts at this time (and significantly less today).

"pyramid" — ("Foreign Secretary") According to WAC repeat fee records, these three performers are Terry Williams, Colin Skeaping (stuntman, *Star Wars*), and Bunny Saunders. The script calls for each to be wearing shorts, but they are clearly dressed in business attire, which adds to the incongruity.

• R •

"Raymond, Paul" — ("Timmy Williams Interview" credits) Paul Raymond (1925–2008) was a publisher of erotic magazines and producer of "nudie" revues, the latter (Raymond called it "Vaudeville Express") of a type Idle describes in his biography section of *The Pythons* (McCabe). Raymond also produced the theatrical show "Pyjama Tops"—a live, all-nude farce—in the Whitehall Theatre, the marquee for which can be glimpsed in the "Ministry of Silly Walks" sketch (street scene) in Ep. 14.

Rear Window — ("*If*—A Film by Mr. Dibley") Feature film directed by Hitchcock in 1954 and starring James Stewart and Grace Kelly. Incidentally, Hitchcock's last "silent" film was *Blackmail* (1929), which was initially shot as a silent, then partially reshot and dubbed for sound release.

"repeat fee" — ("*It's a Living*") Fees generated for the actors whenever the episodes are rebroadcast. By February 1971, the Pythons were commanding £80 per BBC repeat. Many of the memos and letters surviving in WAC records discuss repeat schedules and fees, and careful cast lists were compiled by the BBC primarily to make sure repeat fees were distributed properly.

"Report on Industrial Reorganization" — ("Foreign Secretary") In 1969 a number of "white paper" proposals were being considered for the formation of an Industrial Reorganization Corporation during the Harold Wilson Labour administration. The 1969 white paper "In Place of Strife: A Policy for Industrial Relations" created by Employment and Productivity Secretary Barbara Castle for the Labour government called for strict controls of unions (the bane of Wilson's existence during this period), but never did become law. Castle and Wilson were demonized by union leaders for this attempt at big labor control.

With the passage of the Monopolies and Mergers Act of 1965 there was also much public focus and discussion on/of any industrial reorganization that involved two or more UK companies, especially if gross assets of the target company exceded £5 million or a monopoly (approximately one-third control of a market) could emerge from the union (Pickering, 123).

"result for Leicester" — ("Election Night Special") There were four Leicester voting districts in the 1970

General Election, with Labour taking two and the Conservatives taking the other two. Both parties held their seats. The fringe parties Anti-Immigration, National Democrat, and National Front all registered votes in Leicester, with Anti-Immigration leading the way at 5.25 percent (Keele).

"Returning Officer" — ("Election Night Special") This official conducts the various elections and reports the results (*OED*).

ripple effect — (PSC; "Interruption" link into "School Prize-Giving") An electronic transitional tool in television production—a dissolve, actually—where under a "rippling" transitional effect the scene "dissolves" from the Nabarro character shot to the shot of the boy playing the trumpet.

"rumourlette" — ("Timmy Williams Interview") This appears to be a word created here by / for Timmy Williams, and characteristic of the way "Frostie" himself talked.

• S •

Samurai warrior — ("Foreign Secretary") The samurai class were Japanese feudal warriors attached to great lords and houses in ancient Japan. The proliferation of internationally known Japanese films featuring samurai—including *Yojimbo* and *Sanjuro* (Kurosawa, 1961 and 1962), *The Loyal 47 Ronin* (Inagaki, 1962), and *Seppuku* (Kobayashi, 1962)—would have firmly planted this figure in the public's consciousness. The continuing references to international film and art movements and figures throughout *FC* attests to the Pythons' awareness of these foreign filmmakers (see Eps. 23 and 29 for more on current, referenced French and Italian filmmakers).

"Savage, Richard" — ("Timmy Williams Interview" credits) There are two Englishmen of note who could have been on the Pythons' minds. Richard Savage, the eighteenth-century poet discussed by Dr. Johnson in his *The Lives of the English Poets*, and who was the author of *The Wanderer* (1729) and *The Bastard* (1728). The other, more contemporary Richard Savage wrote the novel *Stranger's Meeting* in the late 1950s, which was made into a 1958 film.

"Schlesinger, John" — ("*If*—A Film by Mr. Dibley") British filmmaker Schlesinger (1926–2003) directed one of the quintessentially American films of the late 1960s, *Midnight Cowboy* (1969). In the film, Ratso Rizzo was played by Dustin Hoffman (b. 1937).

"semitic" — ("Raymond Luxury Yacht") Characteristic of a Semite, or Python's shorthand way of identifying a "Jewish-type" nose, a "hooknose." The only other script-identified "Jewish" character appears for a moment in Ep. 7. His only identifying trait was the spoken inflected upswing—Yiddish-like—at the end of his sentence. There are also several references to "kosher" car parks, a phrase that also can be heard in *The Goon Show*. In Ep. 37, there is an unmentioned but visual reference to Jewishness, when the "Chairman of the Amalgamated Money TV, Sir Abe Sappenheim" (Chapman) is depicted with a larger-than-normal nose.

"sensible constituency" — ("Election Night Special") Luton (home to Lord Hill, the Pythons' boss) was a narrow Conservative gain in 1970, with C. Simeons taking 50.99 percent of the vote, followed by the Labour candidate W. Howie (48.04 percent) and Communist candidate A. Chater (0.98 percent).

"Shand, Neil" — ("Timmy Williams Interview" credits) Shand was a writer for various BBC shows, including Spike Milligan's *Q5* (1969), and *The World of Beachcomber* (1968).

"Shaw, Joe" — ("Timmy Williams Interview" credits) Shaw (1928–2007) was a star defender for Sheffield United between 1948 and 1966—through all of Palin's (a Sheffield native) formative early life.

"silly" — ("Election Night Special") Used here in the northern (or Scottish) sense, since Leicester is the setting, which would mean a person "deserving of pity, compassion, or sympathy," and one who is "weakly, feeble, sickly, ailing."

The sheer number of parties eligible to participate in elections in the UK during this period merits the "silly" appellation. In 1970, votes were registered for at least forty-seven separate parties, including the well-known major parties, as well as these smaller vote-getters (some with platform definitions, where necessary): Anti-War, Anti-Common Market, Anti-Election, Anti-Immigration, Anti-Labour, Anti-Party, Anti-War Radical, Unity (Irish nationalists), Independent, Communist, Protestant Unionist (Northern Ireland unionists), Republican Labour, Independent Labour, Independent Conservative, Democratic, National Democratic (right-wing extremist), National Front (extremist, anti-immigration), National Democrats, Vectis National (seeking Isle of Wight freedoms), Independent Liberal, World Government, Mebyon Kernow (seeking Cornwall freedoms), British Movement (British neo-Nazi), Independent Progressive, Socialist Party (Marxist), Young Ideas, Ratepayers, and British Commonwealth. (Keele University maintains a complete record of the General Elections results in the UK.)

Incidentally, a more local version of the Silly Party managed to put up 50 candidates at Manchester University for the president of the student union, forcing the university to raise the bar on how many signatures were required to make it onto the ballot, and later how many eventual votes were necessary to qualify for the candidate's allowance of £10. PHS of the *Times* noted wryly that the uncomfortable situation was "not, it [was] believed, uninfluenced by Monty Python" (*Times Diary*, 19 Feb. 1971: 14).

"silver cup" — ("School Prize-Giving") Representative of the various trophies and other awards given by public schools in England, including, for example, the Gold Duke of Edinburgh Award at the Bromsgrove Upper School, as well as the Tony Limbert Trophy, Paul Sawtell Trophy, Ben Showell Memorial Rose Bowl, and various Headmaster prizes also given at Bromsgrove and similar schools. The schools the Pythons attended would have had their own prizes to be annually awarded. Palin's school, Shrewsbury, for example, offers multiple academic and related scholarship awards for its third and sixth form students.

"skinhead" — ("Dead Indian") Youth gang members characterized by heavy boots and workingman's clothing, the skinheads were known to cause significant troubles during this period, especially in poorer neighborhoods and at sporting events (*OED*). Aggressive youths do appear in *FC*, including leather-wearing "Teddys" (Ep. 8), but never a skinhead, perhaps because the movement was (a) fairly new at the time and (b) the Pythons were too old to have gone through the skinhead phase themselves.

The skinhead phenomenon had been profiled in the 3 September 1969 issue of the *Daily Mirror*, and appeared as subject in more than a dozen political cartoons in major UK newspapers in 1969–1970. (Many of the cartoons, incidentally, were comparing the Conservative government to the violent, bovver-booted skinheads.) See the British Cartoon Archive.

On the floor of parliament in late October 1969, Mr. William Hamilton of West Fife (Labour) somewhat famously said the following: "I have great regard for Mrs. Thatcher, but we think she is going to be the skinhead of the Tory Party in educational matters" ("Parliament," *Times*, 1 Nov. 1969: 3).

"Smith, Arthur J." — ("Election Night Special") The Sensible Party candidate and his agent both wear a green rosette (ribbon). The Silly Party candidates wear yellow rosettes. Indicating party affiliation, red rosettes have been worn by Labour candidates, and blue by Conservative. The rosettes can be as elaborate as the candidate desires.

"Smith, Sidney" — ("Timmy Williams Interview" credits) Probably meant to be "Sydney Smith," a well-known cricketer. Smith (1881–1963) was born in Trinidad but would eventually play in England, notably for Northamptonshire, and be named as a Wisden Cricketer of the Year in 1915. The Pythons will exhibit a fan(atic)'s knowledge of English cricket and cricketers throughout the series. Northamptonshire borders Leicestershire, home to Chapman.

"Smith, Simon" — ("Timmy Williams Interview" credits) Simon Smith was a barrister in London, his office located in the Queen Elizabeth Building, Temple EC4 (*British Phone Books*, 3157). There was also a popular Randy Newman–penned song, "Simon Smith and the Amazing Dancing Bear" covered by the Alan Price Set in 1967. The song reached number four on the UK charts that year.

"Snowdon" — ("Timmy Williams Interview") Lord Snowdon (Antony Armstrong-Jones, b. 1930) was a respected portrait photographer in the 1950s, creating portraits of the royal family before marrying the Queen's sister, Princess Margaret in 1960. A 1970 *Time* magazine article notes that Snowdon was well known for his own "wicked" impersonation of David Frost (6 July 1970).

Armstrong-Jones attended Jesus College at Cambridge, where he studied architecture, while Frost attended Caius College, Cambridge.

"Something Silly's Going to Happen" — ("Foreign Secretary") This title heralds the now-expected Python version of the "set-up and payoff" comic formula, where the mundane and normal quickly turns absurd. The Pythonesque undercutting of traditional humor structures would eventually need to be undercut if the Pythons were to continue exploring their medium. (The subversive, tradition-usurping Modern Art movements active since the turn of the century suffered from similar demands for the "new and fresh"—creating the need for perpetual turnover, constant renewal, perpetual undercutting.) This consistent need for change and reevaluation would send Cleese shopping for something new as early as the second season. See Morgan's *Speaks!*

"Special Branch Speech Day Squad" — ("School Prize-Giving") There will be a special branch investigating foreign film directors in a later episode (Ep. 29). The "Special Branch" section of the Criminal Investigation Department (CID) is generally involved with political security.

In UK public schools, "Speech Day" is the day at the end of the school year when prizes (and commencement speeches) are given. The influence of Lindsay Anderson's 1968 film *If. . .* is already apparent by this point. See notes for *If. . .* above.

"Spike" — ("Election Night Special") Spike Milligan (1918–2002), the comedic idol of the Pythons, seems to have been watching during this evening's taping somewhere off-camera. Milligan will later appear with the Pythons in the feature film *Life of Brian* (1979).

"Spoon" — ("School Prize-Giving") Perhaps an ironic award, since at Cambridge it was the student who performed worst in math who was awarded a wooden spoon, and later any academic or sport contestant/team could be eligible for such an honor. The sometimes very large spoons were last officially awarded in the early twentieth century, but live on unofficially at the Oxbridge schools and in public life (and are especially favored by UK consumer affairs gadflies).

At Cambridge, for example, "Sir William Browne's Medals" are awarded annually for best Greek Ode and Greek Elegy, Latin Ode and Latin Elegy, Greek Epigram and Latin Epigram; the "Montagu Butler Prize" goes to the best Latin Hexameter Verse; and there are also dissertation and translation prizes for Greek and Latin subjects.

"Spot, The" — (animated link into "Election Night Special") Subject of one of the few real censorial dilemmas faced by *Flying Circus*, this animated cancer spot originally narrated by Carol Cleveland was ordered changed by BBC higher-ups so as not to offend or disturb cancer patients, victims, and their families. Instead of dying of "cancer," the young prince pictured dies of "gangrene." The new word was dubbed, and badly, by someone—and with a male voice, to boot—other than the Pythons, perhaps John Howard Davies or Ian MacNaughton.

In Hogarth's *Marriage à la mode* (1743), "The Inspection," both central figures bear prominent black spots, both suffering from sexually transmitted diseases. In the painting (displayed in the National Gallery since 1824) the afflicted are being treated by a quack healer. Hogarth significantly paved the way for the Pythons, examining theatrical convention and the joy and misery of everyday life in his work, satirizing the French and Catholicism, and displaying a fascination with London's low and prurient lifestyles and neighborhoods.

"Stamford, John" — ("Timmy Williams Interview" credits) John Stamford was the editor and founder of the *Spartacus International Gay Guide*, a gay travel guide, which began publishing in 1970.

"Starr, Hatty" — ("Timmy Williams Interview" credits) Hattie Starr was a Tin Pan Alley singer and songwriter in the 1890s, and later a Theodore Dreiser character from the novel *Titan* (1914), where she was "plain Hattie Starr, the keeper of a more or less secret house of ill repute" (chapter 40). See the entry for "Frank Picksley" for more.

"Stoat, Dame Irene" — ("Foreign Secretary") This may be an oblique reference to Dame Irene Ward (1895–1980), a Pepperpot-type Conservative politician representing the Tyne and Wear area in the 1940s and into the 1970s, serving thirty-eight years. Not a noted poet, there is a collection of her own poems included in her manuscripts and papers held at the Bodleian Library at Oxford.

The lowly stoat continues to be a favorite in the Python bestiary, and will be mentioned again in the very long name of the Very Silly candidate in the "Election Night Special" sketch later. And likely thanks to Cleese's influence, the stoat is also mentioned more than once in *ISIRTA* episodes.

"Stop-Press" — (link out of "Dead Indian") A printing term. A "stop press" in the printing run of a newspaper is an interruption in the run for the insertion of last-minute material. The presses had to actually be stopped, the material inserted, then the presses were restarted. Usually, this meant that the papers that had already been printed would have been destroyed.

"straight fight" — ("Election Night Special") A "straight fight" is an election where there are just two candidates vying for the office. This happened somewhat rarely during this period in the UK, though there were many races where the fringe candidates lost their deposits by polling well below the minimum percentage.

"Super, super!" — ("Timmy Williams Interview") Apart from being just an admitted Frostian characteristic, this repetitive phraseology can be found in a number of British period films, including Jack Clayton's "Angry Young Man" film *Room at the Top* (1959), where it's used quite sardonically. (Cleese will perform a very similar Frost impersonation in the *ISIRTA* "Macbeth" [9 June 1968], including the nasally tone, the "supers," and the penchant for recording the achingly awkward personal moments of his guests.)

swingometer — ("Election Night Special") An actual BBC device used during the 1970 election broadcast, it had to be "extended" to account for the unexpected results toward the Conservatives. The BBC version featured a background of the British Isles (in green) and a red and blue (Labour and Conservative, respectively) pendulum track. Robert McKenzie operated the swingometer during this broadcast, and correctly predicted the Heath and Conservative win at 11:43 p.m. GMT. The BBC website offers video clips from the 1970 British General Election.

"swong" — ("Election Night Special") Both "swong" and "swang" are certainly meant to be silly variations of "swing," but they also both have meaning.

"Swong" means "thin, lean," while "swang"—in Northern dialect—is a marshy bog (*OED*).

• T •

"that's the game" — (*"It's a Living"*) In Ep. 37, an interview show about the necessity of a fourth TV channel (BBC 4) is settled when the four panelists issue single word answers, and the show is over.

"the book" — ("School Prize-Giving") Though it sounds silly, this could actually be a reference to any Church of England *Clergy List* (of which there are many) including *Kelly's Clergy List*, which made available the information for each member of the Anglican Clergy in all the British Isles, as well as the Colonies and in military service anywhere.

"three-cornered fight" — ("Election Night Special") A "three-cornered" contest is one where two similar candidates can draw significant vote percentages while a third, more distinct candidate can actually win the election. In 1966, for instance, the Scottish National Party (SNP) contested its most seats ever (twenty-three), and took 14.3 percent of the votes in those races. In the following by-election (November 1967), SNP candidate Winnifred Ewing was able to win the Hamilton seat by effectively splitting the Conservative and Labour vote (see *Westminster Target Seats* at alba .org.uk/nextwe/snp.html). Labour had won the seat in the previous election by a convincing majority.

"Fin-tim-lin-bin" — ("Election Night Special") There have been and continue to be a fair number of longer-than-average-named candidates in any UK election. In the 1970 General Election, just a few include Sir Frederic Mackarness Bennett, Norman St. John-Stevas, Sir Brandon Rhys Williams, and Christopher Brocklebank-Fowler. The longer names tend to be from those whose families come from older money, which also makes them certain targets for the Pythons.

Following are explanations of some of the less gibberished sections of these candidate names (though in toto the names are meant to read as Lewis Carroll–like nonsense):

"lin-bus"—Idle actually pronounces this "limbus," separating it from the following "stop." "Limbus" means "limbo," or a place for the unbaptized.

"Biscuitbarrel"—Not a nonce word, "biscuit barrel" is actually a purpose-made barrel for, especially, biscuits.

"Bong"—Perhaps a drug paraphernalia reference, but also looks forward to the song "Bing Tiddle Tiddle Bong" sung by Inspector Zatapathique in Ep. 22, and for which the Pythons were sued for copyright infringement. See Ep. 22 notes for details. As for the name Phillips-Bong, the number of hyphenates in the 1970 General Election were myriad, including Robin Chichester-Clark, Sir Alec Douglas-Home, and Sir R. Grant-Ferris, and others.

"Tarquin . . . lin"—Certainly a phonetic game, where words are chosen in a Modernist, Gertrude Stein kind of way (for how well they sound together, not what they mean), but several of these words/utterances also have their own meanings. A "fin" is both a fin-like appendage on an animal or vehicle, as well as a five-dollar note (U.S.); "tim" is variously an insult word (used by English Renaissance playwright/poet Ben Jonson), and "a Protestant nickname for a Roman Catholic [and especially] a supporter of Glasgow Celtic football club" (*OED*). "Lin" means to leave off or desist from; "bin" is of course a container of sorts, and is also short for loony bin, which fits well here; "whin" is both a gorse-type shrub as well as (in Northern dialect) short for whinstone. A "Bim" is slang for a Barbados resident. Lastly, Tarquin Olivier is the son of actor Laurence Olivier. Tarquin appeared as a child actor in *Eagle Squadron* in 1941, and the name is also mentioned in Ep. 4.

"F'tang"—Used here as part of a nonsense name, but also found in several episodes of *The Goon Show*, including "The Call of the West." "Tang" can mean the sting (or bite) of an insect or snake, and may be the source of this variation, and the word is used threateningly in Ep. 17 by Constable Pan Am (Chapman).

Finally, the editors of *Private Eye* create a faux "Letter to the Editor," making fun of their own long-standing penchant for such names, offering a writer complaining about the use of long names for a "so-called joke." The letter is signed: "KAISER-BILLY B'UNTER-DEN-LINDEN-BAINES-JOHNSON'S-BABY-POWDER-ROOM-FOR-THREE-MORE-STANDING-INSIDE-STORY-OF-MY-LIFE-BY-ALAN-HERBERT-GUSSETT" (20 Nov. 1970: 13).

"three drinks at the BBC" — (*"It's a Living"*) The castmembers of the BBC satire show *That Was the Week That Was* acknowledge that there was indeed a set-up for drinks not unlike the one described here, and that because they were working for the "news" section and not "light entertainment," they were able to have drinks and food catered by a Mrs. Reynolds after the tapings. See Carpenter (2000) for more.

"Three hundredweight" — ("Dung") A hundredweight can actually vary from 100 to 120 pounds.

The Goons were here first, no surprise. In "The Mystery of the Fake Neddie Seagoon," where it's not dung but rubbish:

> Crun (Sellers): What is it, gentlemen?
> Spriggs (Milligan): I'm sorry to interrupt you in the middle of the day like this, sir, but I have a load of rubbish for you outside.

Crun: It's a music publisher, Min.
Spriggs: You don't understand, sir and Maurice Burman. What I mean is—we have a dustbin of selected rubbish especially for you.
Crun: You mean it's free?
Spriggs: Yep, not a penny piece to pay!
Crun: Oooohhyyooooo—Min! Min!
Minnie (Milligan): There, steady, Hen. I hope you've got your binder on.
Crun: Yes.
Minnie: Ah, did he say rubbish? At last we can look our neighbors in the face. We've got our own rubbish!
Crun: Yes.
Minnie: Ooohh, hallelujah.
Crun: Would you just leave it in the hall here, Mr. Man?
Minnie: Yes, yes. Uh, you must excuse the mess, sir, but we've got *us* in.
Spriggs: Ah, there, madam—and there's plenty more rubbish where that came from. England's getting back on its feet, I tell you. Good day to you, sir. (29 Nov. 1956)

Incidentally, Maurice Burman ran the Maurice Burman School of Singing in London, and was an accomplished dance band leader.

trumpeter — (PSC; "School Prize-Giving") This young trumpeter is Garry O'Brien, one of the schoolboy-aged extras hired for the day (WAC T12/1,242).

"turkish bath" — ("Timmy Williams Interview") The Ironmonger Row baths are found just northeast of Holborn (where Woppi's is supposedly located) in Islington.

"TV Times" — ("Timmy Williams Interview") An ITV publication that made its debut in 1955, *TV Times* was a weekly listing of the ITV broadcast schedule, as well as media stories and advertising.

• U •

"unable to appear in the show this week" — ("Interruption" link into "School Prize-Giving") In Eps. 16 and 18, the character (played by Palin) rehearsing for the Bishop's part (or perhaps he is a Bishop rehearsing for some other part) also says that he doesn't appear in those particular episodes, though he obviously does appear in both.

Also, the vague way in which the script refers to this link (*"announcer in a silly location"*) indicates it was one of the many pick-up shots made during location shooting, and would later be inserted wherever it might fit. WAC records indicate that inserts and pick-up shots (including "It's Man," Vox Pops, and the Announcer bits) were on location shooting "to-do" lists.

This particular insert was filmed in the traditional blacksmith's shop at Heydon Village, a privately owned village (owned by the Bulwer-Longs since 1640) in Norwich. WAC records note that permission to shoot in the village was granted by a "Captain W.M. Bulwer-Long," and most of the filming was completed on 25 August 1970 (WAC T12/1,242).

"Unseen Translation" — ("School Prize-Giving") Common course/exercise in preparation for examinations in UK schools, where passages (in Latin, Greek, French, etc.) are given to students for translation, sight unseen. Entire courses are structured to prepare students for the exam.

• V •

Vatican crowds — ("Foreign Secretary") The shot is of a crowd in the vast St. Peter's Square in front of the Basilica in Rome. The footage is from the BBC Library, and was originally only scheduled for use in Ep. 22 (WAC T12/1,242).

"Velly solly" — ("School Prize-Giving") Standard Pythonesque (or, honestly, most period comedy television) shorthand characterization here, with Chapman squinting his eyes and adopting an "l" for "r" Chinese accent. See notes for Ep. 30 for more on this, as well as Ep. 34, where Jeremy Pither (Palin) is accosted by myriad Chinese characters pretending to be British diplomats. This "accent" was also typical of most Hollywood films of the sound era whenever a Chinese character was depicted.

"Very Silly candidate" — ("Election Night Special") This is certainly silly, and well over the top, but there have been a number of candidates whose lengthy names almost defy belief. Just a handful who contested the 1966 General Election included Labour MP Arthur Leslie Noel Douglas Houghton, Baron Houghton of Sowerby (1898–1996) and Conservative MPs Hugh Charles Patrick Joseph Fraser (1918–1984) and Alfred George Fletcher Hall-Davis (1924–1979). Hall-Davis was educated at Clifton College, where Cleese also attended.

Since the names chosen for this spiel might be just off-the-top-of-the-head, the following are approximations of where the references may have begun:

"Umbrella Stand"—In Ep. 20, the Third City Idiot (Chapman) acts as a "wastepaper basket" for his father.

"Jasper"—Ann Jasper was a designer for Cambridge Footlights in 1961–1962.

"Wednesday"—*The Wednesday Play* premiered in 1964 (and ran through 1970), and many of the *FC* extras/actors also found acting work in that series.

"Stoatgobbler"—Literally, one who consumes stoats, a favorite Python animal reference, also appearing or being mentioned in Eps. 5, 6, 26, and 30.

"Harris"— Richard Harris was a Cambridge Footlights member in 1966, and participated in the show *This Way Out*.

"Mason"—In 1965, John Hope-Mason was the revue director for the Cambridge show *My Girl Herbert*.

"Fruitbat"—This reference would find its way into *HG*, as the Book of Armaments passage is read aloud.

"We'll Keep a Welcome"—A traditional Welsh song composed by Mai Jones:

> We'll keep a welcome in the hillside.
> We'll keep a welcome in the Vales
> This land you knew will still be singing
> When you come home again to Wales.
> This land of song will keep a welcome
> And with a love that never fails,
> We'll kiss away each hour of hiraeth
> When you come home again to Wales.

"Raindrops Keep Fallin' On My Head"—B.J. Thomas song from the 1969 film *Butch Cassidy and the Sundance Kid*. By January 1970, the song had reached number one on the Billboard Hot 100, and would win the Academy Award for Best Original Song. At the time of this taping, however, the Pythons would have known the song for its place in the popular film, and probably as a single on the radio.

"Don't Sleep in the Subway"—Petula Clark hit from 1967, reaching number 5 on the U.S. charts. A Cardinal Ximinez figure (played by Palin) sings part of the song in Ep. 13.

"Mannering"—Col. Guy Mannering is Sir Walter Scott's titular character from the 1815 novel *Guy Mannering*, as well as the name of an immigrant ship. The character/novel will be mentioned again in Ep. 38.

• W •

"Waring, Guy" — ("Timmy Williams Interview" credits) Guy Waring is a character in Grant Allen's (1848–1899) novel *What's Bred in the Bone* (1898), and his first appearance is, coincidentally, at an inn in Holborn (see the entry for "Woppi's").

"Welcome All Sexual Athletes" — (*Animation* link out of "Raymond Luxury Yacht") The "Welcome All Sexual Athletes" idea is likely borrowed from the popular BBC play/TV drama *The Year of the Sex Olympics* (1968), written by Nigel Kneale.

In this animated sequence, the gleeful, bouncing man is at least a portion of yet another Civil War figure, this time a Confederate, Maj. Gen. Mansfield Lovell (1822–1884). Gilliam found Lovell's mustachioed face in *Divided We Fought*, page 91.

"What's all this then?" — ("Dead Indian") The catchphrase for many of Python's constabulary, and even mentioned reflexively by the Naughty Chemist (Palin) in Ep. 17.

"Whitehouse, Mary" — ("Election Night Special") Founder of the "Clean Up TV Campaign" in 1964, which became the National Viewers' and Listeners' Association (NVLA) in 1965, with the goal of raising standards on television in the UK. Upon the announcement of the filming of *Life of Brian* (1979), she turned her cannons on the Pythons, sending EMI (studio that funded the film) running for cover. Ex-Beatle George Harrison would step in and help finance the picture. See *Monty Python: The Case Against*.

"Who shall . . . eternal gain" — ("Foreign Secretary") Reminiscent of portions of Emerson's *Celestial Love*, and even William Cowper's (1731–1800) work, but this snippet is actually taken from the much more obscure John Oxenham's post-Edwardian poem "Profit and Loss," first printed in the collection *Bees in Amber: A Little Book of Thoughtful Verse* (American Tract Society: New York, 1913). Oxenham (born W.A. Dunkerley) was a native of Manchester, a novelist, journalist, and by WWI a successful poet.

Oxenham's work was included in numerous anthologies of the period—such as *The Oxford Book of English Mystical Verse* (1917)—as he wrote across genres and themes.

"Wonderful Mr. Williams, The" — ("Timmy Williams Interview") During this period (1969–1972), Frost was hosting and producing the very popular *The David Frost Show*, interviewing celebrities and world leaders.

"won you in a police raffle" — (link out of "Dead Indian") In the 6 August 1965 edition of *Private Eye*, female readers can win Conservative opposition leader Ted Heath, a weekend with Reginald Maudling, or a "lifetime with Enoch Powell" (Ingrams, 121).

"Woppi's" — ("Timmy Williams Interview") Probably a racial slur (based on "wop") as the printed script describes the setting as an "expensive looking coffee shop, Italian style." This also could be a reference to the restaurant chain "Wimpy's," popular in the UK for many years. There is a Wimpy restaurant in Holborn, on Kingsway Street.

The advent of the Italian-style coffee shop in London neighborhoods began as early as 1953 with the opening of Gina Lollabrigida's "The Moka," and the trendy coffee shops spread throughout the metropolitan area over the next two decades.

"wrench" — ("Registry Office") In this case, "wrench" means an unforeseen twist.

"Wright, Bill" — ("Timmy Williams Interview" credits) Billy Wright (1924–1994) was a talented footballer for Idle's Wolverhampton Wanderers, later a manager for Arsenal, and a presenter for *Youth Sportsview* (BBC, 1957–62).

"writing a book on me" — ("Timmy Williams Interview") Author Willi Frischauer (Austrian by birth) was preparing a book on Frost at this time, having, ironically, already published books on Nazis Hermann Goering and Heinrich Himmler, as well as the Aga Khans. Part of the reason the Pythons (and other Oxbridge grads) may have been unenthusiastic about Frost is just the fact that such celebrity biographies were under way less than a decade into Frost's very public entertainment career. *David Frost* would be published by Michael Joseph in 1972.

• Z •

"Zeigler, Anne . . . Webster Booth" — ("Foreign Secretary") "Zeigler" is a misspelling of "Ziegler." Anne Ziegler (1910–2003) and Webster Booth (1902–1984) were a popular British vocal duo. Teamed in the 1930s, their signature song was "Only a Rose." Ziegler also appeared in three postwar feature films. Booth was a tenor who began his career with an opera company in the mid-1920s. The fact that several characters in this season (Eps. 21, 22) have signature songs may account for this couple's inclusion. Several studio audience members (probably of the younger generation) applaud at the sight of the hampers containing Ziegler and Booth being tossed into the river, meaning the Ziegler-Booth duo probably appealed more to their parents' generation. The Goons, for example, had mentioned the duo several times more than a decade earlier.

Episode 20: "Killer Sheep"

Hun film stock; **"The Attila the Hun Show"**; "And now . . ." Man and "It's" Man; *Titles* (silly Cleese v/o); "Attila the Nun"; Sexy doctor's examination; The Peephole Club: Secretary of State for Commonwealth Affairs striptease; Register for Pensions and the Social Security belly dance; "Today in Britain": Vox pop on politicians; **Ratcatcher** (and Chairman of the Test Selection Committee); "Wainscotting" ("A Little Dorset Village"); "Is the Third Test in here?"; "He's got a gun!": **Killer sheep**; "Is the Third Test in here?"; *Animation: "Arthur X, leader of the Pennine Gang"*; BBC-TV News; *Animation: Parrots announcing television programs*; The News for Parrots; *A Tale of Two Cities* for parrots; The News for Gibbons; "Today in Parliament"; The News for Wombats; *Animation: "Attila the Bun"*; **"Idiots": The Idiot in Society**; Test Match: "Well Not-Played"; Furniture playing cricket; The Epsom 3:00 furniture race; *Take Your Pick*: "I'll take the blow on the head"; Licence fees and closing credits

• A •

"agricultural subsidies" — ("Secretary of State Striptease") The long-standing policy of government support for farm product prices in the UK had reached a crisis level in mid-1969 when the National Farmers Union (NFU) staged protests for higher prices for meat and wheat, as well as protections against lower-priced imports. A farmers' protest was held in Newton Abbot, Devon (just north of Torquay and Paignton), in December 1969, where the Pythons would shoot much of the early second season. Farmers and their families also marched outside the Ministry of Agriculture along the Strand, and across Waterloo Bridge. These fears would only escalate over the next few years, of course, as the Conservative government pushed and pulled the country closer to EU membership.

What the stripping minister is saying, essentially, is that a balance must be achieved between artificial (meaning government-inflated) support for local goods/prices and the need for consumer-friendly prices that imported products could provide. In essence, he is promising the Commonwealth countries that they will continue to receive MFN or Most Favored Nation status in trade matters.

This subject found its way onto op-ed pages across the country in 1969–1970 (see the British Cartoon Archive).

"Agricultural Tariff" — (*"Today in Parliament"*) Import fees attached to foreign agricultural products designed to protect domestic (UK) farmers and producers. See the "agricultural subsidies" note above.

"Alaric . . . Ostrogoth" — (*"The Attila the Hun Show"*) The Visigoths invaded Roman lands at the end of the fourth century, taking Spain. Vandals were Germanic and also invaded Western Europe during this period. Ostrogoths are "Eastern Goths" who conquered Italy in the late fifth century (*EBO*).

Here the Pythons are generally accurate historically: The Visigoths were led by Alaric (370–410) between 395–410 (even allying with the Romans against the Huns at one point); the Vandals by Genseric (c. 390–477, a.k.a. Gaiseric); and the Ostrogoths, by "Theodoric" (c. 454–526), not "Theodoris." Several of the Pythons read in history (including Jones, who has written texts in history since), and they probably depended on their collective memories as they wrote this scene.

"Allen, Gubby" — ("Test Match") Sir George Oswald Browning Allen (1902–1989) was another well-known cricketer, though born in Australia. Allen captained England in three series, with his Test debut in the England vs. Australia match at Lord's, 2nd Test, 1930. The "'32" reference indicates, rightly, that Allen participated in the infamous "Bodyline" tour of 1932–1933, when fast bowling aimed at the batters upset the Australian cricket team, officials, and fans, and even caused a diplomatic incident.

American-living-room-type set — (PSC; *"The Attila the Hun Show"*) The printed script describes the room (for the production designers), and the layout seems to fit the larger living rooms seen in the single-family homes typical of the suburban United States (as opposed to the council estate rowhouses in the UK). As a set, the room would have been larger than a typical living room, anyway, and missing the fourth wall, as seen in period Hollywood sitcoms like *I Love Lucy*, *The Honeymooners*, and *The Debbie Reynolds Show*.

"Ames, Leslie" — ("Ratcatcher [and Chairman of the Test Selection Committee]") Leslie Ames (1905–1990) was a wicket-keeper and batsman for England and Kent, and Wisden Cricketer of the Year for 1929. Ames also participated in the Bodyline tour, which is discussed elsewhere in these notes. Most recently, Ames had managed MCC tours to the West Indies, Sri Lanka, and Pakistan (1967–1969), and guided the Kent County CC to the championship in 1970.

Animation: perhaps even mixed with stock film — (PSC; "Killer Sheep") Again, at the time of the script's writing, the rest of the Pythons had little idea what Gilliam would be creating weeks or months later for the in-studio taping of the show. They do know, however, that rather than a linking element, this animation serves as a proscribed bridge in the story, so clues were obviously provided that Gilliam then had to follow with his "fevered mind."

In the animation, the sheep rob the Westminster Bank Limited, blow up and rob the Midland Bank Limited, then make good their escape in a 1930s-era convertible to the music "Banjo in the Hollow" from The Dillards' 1963 album *Back Porch Blue Grass* (WAC T12/1,433). (The London-area bank photos are obviously vintage, since by 1968 Westminster Bank had been merged out of existence, becoming part of National Westminster Bank.) See the note later for "Sheep executing . . ." for more on these photos. Also, Gilliam did not follow the scriptwriters' call for a "sheep with machine-gun coming out of its arse, etc." as he created his animation. That sort of sheep/machine was created and used much earlier, in Ep. 2, when the "possibilities of avine aviation" are presented.

The WAC records actually note that the banjo song used by Gilliam is by a "D. Allard," a slight typo.

"Armchairs!" — (*"Take Your Pick"*) This type of "bad answers to easy questions" scenario will be revisited in Ep. 22 ("Burma!"), as well as the feature film *HG*, where Sir Bedivere (Jones) asks what floats in water, and the peasants guess everything from bread to small rocks and churches.

"Arthur X" — ("Killer Sheep") Most likely a reference to the Trinidad and Tobago–born Michael X (born Michael de Freitas, 1933–1975), a revolutionary and sometime civil rights voice in London of the 1960s. Michael X had lived in the racially volatile Notting Hill area (where race riots erupted at the Mangrove restaurant) since 1957, and had initially been a drug dealer and even a thug for slumlord Peter Rachman (see "cheque had bounced" entry in Ep. 14), before taking up the black power revolutionary banner. He would be hanged for murder in 1975.

At the time this episode was being created, Michael X was trying to set up a commune in Islington, according to Joan Didion ("Without Regret or Hope," *NY Times Review of Books*, 12 June 1980). In 1969 and 1970, Michael X was also in and out of court, being arrested for marijuana possession and robbery.

"ate . . . eucalyptus leaves" — ("The News for Wombats") The Pythons have confused their Australian marsupials here. Wombats actually eat grass, roots, and bark. Koalas eat the eucalyptus tree leaves.

"Attila the Nun" — ("Attila the Nun") This appellation is previously mentioned by E.L. Wisty (a.k.a. Peter Cook) in his monologue "The World Domination League," originally taped for *On the Braden Beat* (ITV, 1964):

> There's been wonderful dominators in history, you know. Attila was one. He was a wonderful dominator, Attila the Nun. He was an amazing dominator. He had a Gothic horde, and he used to move about entire countries and strangle people completely to death. And then, when everybody woke up, they'd see a little note pinned to their chest, saying "You've been dominated. Ha, ha. Attila the Nun." (*Tragically I Was an Only Twin*, 60).

• B •

"back benches" — (*"Today in Parliament"*) These would be the lower-ranking members of either party in Parliament, and thus perhaps more likely to be such discontented rabble rousers, in the Python oeuvre.

"Baxter, Ray" — ("Ratcatcher") Raymond Baxter's (1922–2006) 1965 show *Tomorrow's World* introduced new technology developments on film and in studio reports. It was called a "science-future" show, and was initially transmitted live (see Vahimagi's *British Television*). See entries in Ep. 21 for more on Baxter and BBC colleagues David Coleman, Frank Bough, and Ken Wolstenholme.

"beautifully not done anything about" — ("Test Match") This is certainly a purposeful irony, since Colin Cowdrey was anything but a timid or unaccomplished batter during his long career. What this could be a reference to is the hold on a particular run that Cowdrey endured on the way to his maiden century in 1954. His Wisden obituary remembers Cowdrey's "wonderful maiden century . . . [where he] was becalmed on 56 for 40 minutes." This seeming eternity could certainly have elicited the Pythons' barb—"a superb display of inertia"—in the sketch.

The Goons mention another famous cricketer, Len Hutton (1916–1990), for "laying off the ball" in their episode "1985" (4 Jan. 1955):

> Seagoon (Secombe): I say! What's this old object?
> Shop Owner (Sellers): That, beautiful isn't it? It's called a cricket bat.
> Seagoon: Oh yes, yes . . . Did they have test matches way back?
> Shop Owner: Yes, that's . . . that's right. As a matter of fact, this bat was used in the very last test by Len Hutton. You can see it's quite unmarked. (*generous laugh and applause*)

"Bergson, Henri" — ("*Take Your Pick*") Frenchman Bergson (1859–1941) was a philosopher influenced significantly by Spencer, Mill, and Darwin, and who then based his career on opposing their "rationalist" systems. He won the Nobel Prize for literature in 1927. In his 1900 work *Laughter*, Bergson developed a theory of comedy and laughter which seems to have been an influential work on the Pythons, and perhaps especially Cleese. In doing so, the respected Bergson elevated the study of comedy to a more academic level, worthy of study in works looking at aesthetics and philosophies of art forms.

Being au courant with Bergson and his theories seems to have been quite fashionable during this period—and certainly when the Pythons were attending university. Cleese's Announcer character is discussing his "Bergsonian theory" of humor in Ep. 35 as the show begins.

bike crashing off camera — (PSC; "Attila the Nun") Taken from the opening moments of David Lean's epic 1962 film *Lawrence of Arabia*, when Lawrence is killed after a harrowing motorcycle ride and crash. The rider here appears to be Jones, though he's not credited in the printed script. This scene was shot in picturesque Heydon Village, Norfolk, where they were gathering filmed material in late August 1970 (WAC T12/1,430).

bishops — ("*Take Your Pick*") These rambunctious bishops are played by Ian Davidson, Palin, and Gilliam. Palin is dressed in the full attire (mitre and robes) he's worn before when practicing the "Mr. Belpit" line (see Ep. 16). The others are wearing black clerical outfits and "dog collars."

blacked up like Rochester — (PSC; "*The Attila the Hun Show*") In black-face, as was the tradition for playing performing blacks in U.S. vaudeville and UK music hall performances, etc. The BBC still offered the very popular *The Black and White Minstrel Show* (1958–1978), featuring singing and dancing black-face performers, this following the long-standing tradition of such shows on BBC radio and the fin-de-siècle music hall stages. See the article on the show by Sarita Malik at the Museum of Broadcast Communications for more.

As for the "Rochester" reference, Eddie Anderson (1905–1977), television personality Jack Benny's sidekick for twenty-seven years, was a black man, and not "blacked up." *The Jack Benny Show* was a spin-off of Benny's popular radio show, and ran for almost fifteen years on American television.

"Black Rod" — ("Vox Pops on Politicians") The "Gentleman Usher of the Black Rod" (he carries a black wand with a golden lion) is the usher to the House of Lords and part of the royal household (*OED*). The position of Black Rod in 1970 was occupied by George Holroyd Mills (18 June 1963 through 1 September 1970), followed by Frank Roddam Twiss (fl. 1970–1978). See Bond's *The Gentleman Usher of the Black Rod*. So at the time of this episode's writing, Mills would have been Black Rod, and the object of Second Girl's (Chapman) affections.

"blow on the head" — ("*Take Your Pick*") The prompting for this type of game show may have come from the very popular *It's a Knockout* (1966), a rough-and-tumble contest show where contestants performed fairly pointless physical feats (building giant hamburgers, running obstacle courses, etc.) as quickly as possible. Eddie Waring (Ep. 1) was one of the show's commentators. The shows will be spoofed again in Ep. 30, where a successful anagram quiz contestant (Jones, again) is bludgeoned with a giant hammer.

"bollard" — ("The News for Parrots") A "bollard" is a traffic island post. The *Beyond the Fringe* cast created an entire sketch (and song) around a fictional cigarette with the brand name "Bollard." The Goons earlier used the term in at least three episodes, including

"The Mystery of the Marie Celeste (Solved)," "The Man Who Never Was," and "Tales of Old Dartmoor."

"Bosanquet, Reginald" — ("Ratcatcher") An original *News at Ten* newsreader (ITN, 1967–), Bosanquet (1932–1984) also contributed to *Dateline* (ITN, 1961–1967). *News at Ten* was ITV's (Independent Television) first half-hour newscast. Bosanquet himself will appear briefly in Ep. 26 of *FC*.

"Brando, M." — ("The Idiot in Society") American actor Marlon Brando is also mentioned in Ep. 10. Mr. Brando (Chapman) stands in front of what is purportedly a branch of the Northwestern Provincial Bank, which would put this "idiot's bank" outside of London, of course, in the East Midlands or Lancashire area—the rustic north. Most of the footage for this sketch was shot in and around Heydon Village, Norwich. This particular shot was recorded in front of a house on The Street, just down from the Heydon Village Tea Room.

Brezhnev, Podgorny and Kosygin — (PSC; "The News for Parrots") Many historians name these three men among the moving force behind Nikita Khrushchev's rise to power in 1958 as well as his eventual ouster in 1964.

Leonid Ilyich Brezhnev (1906–1982) is actually in the middle of the trio as they stand on the reviewing stand, probably watching a recent annual celebration of the famed October Revolution (or a May Day parade). Brezhnev was Soviet leader from as early as 1964 to his death in 1982. Nikolai Podgorny (1903–1983, on the left), who helped Brezhnev to power, was ceremonial head of state, but was himself replaced by Brezhnev as President of the Presidum of the Supreme Soviet of the USSR in 1977. (In Ep. 7, the plucky Scots tailor [Palin] is named Angus Podgorny.) Aleksei Nikolaievich Kosygin (1904–1980) was another fellow anti-Khrushchevite who supported Brezhnev's ascendancy, and became Chairman of the Soviet of Ministers USSR. The solidarity among these leaders during this period (and among the highest government bodies in general) was quite unprecedented in Soviet history. See Rigby for more on this period.

• C •

Canned laughter — (PSC; *"The Attila the Hun Show"*) "Canned" laughter is a prerecorded laugh track (and often applause) that is laid over/under the live or animated action of a TV show, to give the illusion of a live studio audience. Many sitcoms utilized canned laughter and applause, as did almost all Hanna-Barbera and Filmation cartoons of the 1960s and 1970s.

The Debbie Reynolds Show (1969–1970) was a thinly veiled rip-off of the very successful *I Love Lucy* (1951–1957), where a live audience reacted well to the real laughs in the weekly filmed episodes. The fact that Reynolds's version followed *Lucy* by more than a decade may account for the staleness of the idea and forced delivery as performed by the Pythons. The producers of the Reynolds version of the show probably realized very quickly that their product was short on laughs, as well as hopelessly quaint, forcing them to add post facto laughter and applause. In the *Attila* case canned laughter and applause are purposely over-the-top, and being used to send up the Hollywood sitcom genre. *The Debbie Reynolds Show* premiered on BBC1 in January 1970.

"Cartesian dualism" — (*"Take Your Pick"*) Philosopher Bertrand Russell (1872–1970) characterized Descartes's "method of systematic doubt" as an attempt to doubt everything that couldn't be proved, that his doubt proved only his own existence, thus leading him to only believe in his own existence (*Problems of Philosophy*, 18–19). Descartes therefore could build a philosophical world based on this "duality." Opponents of the theory argue that mental events cannot cause or effect physical events, an immaterial effecting the material.

See the note on Descartes (referenced in a Gilliam animation) in Ep. 2 for more.

cashier — ("The Idiot in Society") This character is played by Eddy May Scrandrett, who also appeared in Ep. 19, and whose name is spelled at least three different ways in the surviving records for the show (WAC T12/1,242).

"Charles Crompton, the Stripping Doctor" — ("Secretary of State Striptease") A clever and fluid Pythonesque transition here, starting with Chapman's character (Crompton) acting the part of a doctor who appreciates/encourages stripping, and metamorphosing into Cabinet ministers who strip while mouthing government policy.

Charles Crompton contributed to the Marxist-Leninist publication *The New International* in the late 1930s.

Chief Commissioner of Police — (PSC; "Killer Sheep") The body in the drawer is supposed to have been played by Leslie Noyes (*Dad's Army; Z Cars*), according to WAC documents (T12/1,418), but the actor looks very much like Ian Davidson. Several times the official BBC records—especially for casting—indicate one actor in a particular role when it is obviously someone else entirely by the time they taped the show.

city gents in their own clothes — (PSC; "The Idiot in Society") This stock film footage is also from the BBC Library (WAC T12/1,242). This is also a wry comment on the "look" and clothing of both the Idiot and the City Gent. The Pythons have clothed the Idiots for this scene and then let them "work"; the City Gents don their recognizable costumes themselves and go shoulder-to-shoulder off to work.

"civil servants" — ("Vox Pops on Politicians") Government employees, especially those who serve in civilian capacities of the public administration, including the diplomatic corps, post office and communications, state-run educational institutions, the collection of revenues, etc. The term was originally only applied to employees of the East India Company (*OED*). This definition doesn't seem to necessarily include MPs, however.

Cleveland, Carol — ("The News for Parrots") This portrayal of a nurse who "parrots" with everyone else is an example of Cleveland getting in on the comedy, increasingly on equal footing with the boys. She is still used often for her more feminine attributes, but as the series moves on she more and more is allowed to display her comedic talents, as well. Cleveland had appeared in the earliest (1969) publicity photos with the rest of the troupe, but was never a named writing partner or material contributor to the show.

"coach party" — ("The Idiot in Society") Generally a tour group traveling by bus, or motor coach. In this case, the tourists would have been actual visitors to scenic Heydon Village, where most of this sketch was filmed.

"Common Market" — ("Secretary of State Striptease") An on-again, off-again initiative to join with Europe as trading partners in a "common market" had existed in the UK for many years. Two areas of contention from as early as 1962 included the agreements on agricultural price parity and the gutting of internal tariffs (and, additionally, that England was not "European enough" to satisfy de Gaulle). See the entry for "agricultural subsidies" above. The British Parliament would approve Britain's application for Common Market membership in 1972, and in 1975 voters approved the move by a two-thirds majority.

"Council Ratcatcher" — ("Ratcatcher") This is actually a position in many boroughs in the UK, including, for example, Doncaster and Stokes St. Milborough. There is a small display in the Chobham Museum of very old rat tails as caught by the Chobham municipal ratcatcher. The museum is on Benham's Corner, West End, London.

In Ep. 21, Colin Mozart (Palin), a ratcatcher, will be featured. His famous father has pushed him into the more respectable job of ratcatching, and away from the shameful world of composing.

"Cowdrey" — ("Test Match") Michael Colin Cowdrey (1932–2000) was a popular right hand bat and employed a "leg break" bowling style. "Leg break" is a pitch that is thrown almost like baseball's "screwball," and breaks into a batter's body off the bounce, from the batter's "leg" side. (See *Dictionary of Cricket Terms*.) Cowdrey played mainly for Kent, Oxford University, and England, with his Test debut coming at the England vs. Australia at Brisbane, 1st Test, 1954/55. Cowdrey was Wisden Cricketer of the Year in 1956. It's said that his father loved cricket, and chose his son's initials (MCC) appropriately. In retirement he was a noted cricket administrator. Cowdrey also participated in the "England and the Rest of the World XI" Test in 1970 (*ODNB*).

"crops go gey are in the medley crun" — ("The Idiot in Society") This provincial, northern version of English can be heard earlier in *At Last the 1948 Show*, specifically show five in the first season.

Cut through to a Cruikshank engraving of London — (PSC; "The News for Parrots") Not a Cruikshank engraving, the print is actually borrowed from 18th-century draughtsman Edward Dayes (1763–1804). This particular image is of Hanover Square, Mayfair (labeled "Fig. 183"), and is used in both Eps. 20 and 21. It's not clear from what book Gilliam copied this page. This print is not accounted for in the WAC records for the episode, meaning no copyright clearance was requested, and no royalty had to be paid for its use.

The graphic over the projected print, "London 1793," is off significantly. The events being depicted in *A Tale of Two Cities* involving Darnay, Lucie, and her father occur in 1780-1781, according to Dickens. This is yet another probably memorial mistake on the Pythons' part, as these events occur prior to the French Revolution in Dickens's tale. The events of the novel actually conclude sometime in mid-to-late 1790.

• D •

"darkies" — ("Test Match") In the past, a popular colloquial term in the United States for African Americans. The British public would have been introduced to the term through over-the-counter products, interestingly, like "Darkie" toothpaste, and the black-face images on Gollywog-brand jam. In this specific case, the cricketing reference indicates that "darkies" are members of teams representing West Indies, Pakistan, or India.

Debbie Reynolds Show, The — (*"The Attila the Hun Show"*) Appeared on American television (NBC, Tuesdays) 1969–1970, with twenty-six episodes recorded. Produced by an *I Love Lucy* writer, the show was based on that show's premise and situations. The show's musical theme was written by Jack Wilton Marshall, and was sung by Reynolds herself over the closing credits. The show appeared on BBC1 on Saturdays in January 1970.

The theme that plays beneath the titles is *The Debbie Reynolds Show* theme, here Mike Leroy's version of "With a Little Love" by T. Romeo (WAC T12/1,433).

"Did he have his head all bandaged?" — ("Ratcatcher") This may be an oblique reference to writer/presenter Raymond Baxter being injured in a punch-up between drivers Graham Hill and Jim Clark as Baxter covered the 1964 European Grand Prix held at Brands Hatch. *Private Eye* TV critic "George Millais" mentions that Baxter "suffered incurable brain damage in the pits at Brands Hatch" that day, though this didn't stop him from participating in what Millais derisively terms *Man Half-Alive* (actually, *Man Alive*, see notes to Eps. 18 and 26 for more) (Ingrams, 168).

"don't know" — ("Killer Sheep") Again, playing on the moment in many sci-fi and horror films when the scientist or military figure(s) attempt to explain the deadly phenomena. This is usually an expository moment for the audience more than anything else. This same sort of helpful moment endemic to the sci-fi genre is also employed in Ep. 7, the "Science Fiction Sketch."

"Dorset" — ("Wainscotting") A rural county at nearly the southernmost tip of England. Dorset was the inspiration for the bucolic setting "Wessex," central to Thomas Hardy's pre-industrial revolution England in many of his novels. This scene, however, was shot in the Heydon Village area, Norwich, not Dorset. The Village Idiot scenes will also be shot in Heydon Village.

• E •

Episode 20 — This episode was recorded 2 October 1970, and broadcast 10 November 1970.

"Epsom" — ("The Epsom Furniture Races") Epsom Downs is in Surrey, and is the racecourse where the Derby is run. The actual film location, however, is not Epsom, as they most likely would not have been granted permission to film there (just as in Ep. 7, when a local tennis court park gamely stood in for Wimbledon Centre Court). The former Alexandra Palace Race Course is the actual setting here (WAC T12/1,430), which closed officially in 1970.

"Eton, Sandhurst and the Guards" — ("The Idiot in Society") This has been the standard trajectory for important British diplomats and military men in the past. Eton is the largest ancient English college, founded by Henry VI on the Thames opposite Windsor; Sandhurst is the Royal Military Academy at Sandhurst; and "the Guards" refers to various members of the Household Cavalry, or troops employed to guard the monarch.

Exciting crime-type music — (PSC; "Killer Sheep") The music used by Gilliam in the early portion of the animation is Westway Studio Ensemble's "Woodland Tryst" by C. Watters (WAC T12/1,433).

• F •

"Farmer Ambushed in Pen" — (PSC; "Killer Sheep") This headline is placed on an altered copy of the Friday, 4 September 1970 edition of the *Daily Courier*.

"Merino Ram in Wages Grab"—This headline replaces the headline for the Friday, 18 September 1970 *Daily Echo*, a Dorset-area newspaper.

The printed script also calls for "eerie science fiction music" during this transition, but there is none in the finished film.

fast bowler — (PSC; "Test Match") A bowler who uses speed to overpower batsmen, as opposed to a spin bowler.

"Figgis, Arthur" — ("The Idiot in Society") Not perhaps a completely fabricated name or person, as there was at least one "Arthur Figgis" listed in the Greater London telephone books of this period. Figgis is also mentioned in Eps. 2 and 6, and is, in the pages of *Private Eye*, the ancient librarian of the maligned (and equally ancient) *Punch* magazine.

French Revolution type music — (PSC; "The News for Parrots") This music is a portion of the Orchestra of Amsterdam's performance of Berlioz's "Symphonie Fantastique, Fourth Movement" (WAC T12/1,433).

"front-bench" — (*"Today in Parliament"*) In both houses of Parliament, the front seats are where the most influential members (often spokesmen) sit. There are front and back benches for both the party in power and the opposition.

The Front Bench Spokesman for the opposition between 1964 and 1970 (when the Conservatives were in the minority) was Margaret Thatcher, mentioned in Eps. 21, 22, and 30.

• G •

"get a-head" — (*"The Attila the Hun Show"*) A purposely bad pun perhaps borrowed from a Hat Council (UK) ad slogan for 1965, "If you want to get ahead, get a hat" (*ODMQ*, 8). The Pythons are clearly lampooning the broad, less-than-deft comedy writing (and delivery) characteristic of most American television sitcoms of the period.

"get your hand off my thigh, West" — ("Test Match") There is no indication that Peter West (see below) ever "hit on" one of his broadcast partners, but the jovial, bon vivant atmosphere in the cricket broadcast booths certainly created a sense of companionship for and with listeners/viewers.

Groupie — ("Vox Pops on Politicians") This look and just the inclusion of these types may have been influenced by the recent (both August 1970) open air pop festivals in London and on the Isle of Wight, where Jimi Hendrix, Joan Baez, and many others performed, and "hippie" types attended in droves.

• H •

"Headingley" — ("Test Match") Headingley (Leeds) has been the home of the Yorkshire CCC since 1891. Brian Close (b. 1931), who will be mentioned later, played for Yorkshire.

"Home Secretary and mother won the Derby" — (link out of "The Idiot in Society") The Home Secretary is the Secretary of State for Home Affairs in the UK. The colloquial "Derby" (pronounced "darby") is the oldest horse race in the country, founded by the Earl of Derby in 1780, and run at Epsom. The fact that the mother figure could be referred to as a "horse" is reminiscent of the term "war-horse," which can mean a strong-willed woman. The Epsom racecourse will be the supposed site of the later "Epsom Furniture Race," and is actually shot at the Alexandra Park course, according to WAC records. The Fourth City Idiot's (Jones) mention of the Derby isn't out of place—this type of horse race has been supported by the gentry in England since at least the end of the eighteenth century.

"Hunlets" — (*"The Attila the Hun Show"*) A play on pop music names of the period, including the Ronettes (Veronica Bennett, Estelle Bennett, and Nedra Talley).

"Huns" — (*"The Attila the Hun Show"*) A fifth-century Asian tribe that, under Attila—the scourge of God—invaded and terrorized Europe.

Attila the Hun lived c. 406–453, was king of the Huns (c. 433–453), and was characterized as cunning and ambitious, even unpredictable. In the feature film *HG*, the young monk (Palin) reads from the Book of Armaments about St. Attila and the Holy Hand Grenade.

• I •

"Iceland" — ("Test Match") Iceland has no history of cricket, meaning England is now struggling to beat even the non-cricket-playing nations. This pessimism was well founded in 1970. The South African Test tour was canceled, and MCC had to scramble to put together cricket for paying audiences for the year. In June–August 1970, the "England and a Rest of the World XI" series of matches were played in the UK, pitting an English team against an international squad composed of players representing South Africa, Australia, West Indies, India, and Pakistan. England eventually lost 4–1.

As of 1970, there were only seven recognized Test-status cricket nations: England, Australia, South Africa, West Indies, New Zealand, India, and Pakistan.

"ICI have increased . . ." — ("The Idiot in Society") ICI is Imperial Chemical Industries, in 1970 one of the largest and most successful UK companies. This is one of the companies that Mr. Brando (Chapman) will term as a "big industrial combine," where a "really blithering idiot" can be found.

idiot gear with BA hoods — ("The Idiot in Society") The "BA hood" is part of the recognizable academic regalia, and traditionally worn with a cap and gown. The Pythons, as Oxbridge grads, would have worn prescribed clothing underneath their regalia, as well, and the "idiot gear" with the academic kit seems a comment on that strict dress code. The majority of the poking-fun, however, is obviously reserved for these graduates of the "new" and certainly more plebeian university system, where virtually any "idiot" could complete a degree and call himself a university graduate.

"I really just don't know" — ("Killer Sheep") This "I don't know" incantation is likely a send-up of cricket commentator Brian Johnston (1912–1994). Cleese and the *ISIRTA* folk perform a similar set-piece in their pilot episode (3 Apr. 1964).

"Is the third test in here?" — ("Ratcatcher") The difficulties surrounding the South African cricket team's tour of the UK in 1970 are covered in notes to Eps. 14 and 17. In short, the increasingly separatist and racist policies of the South African government toward its majority black population led to calls for boycotts of all but essential trade with South Africa, as well as bans on international sporting cooperation with Springbok teams. At one point, protestors were damaging playing fields in England so that matches could not be held, leading to rescheduling efforts (officials trying to find suitable alternate sites), and finally the cancellation of the tour.

It was also earlier this same year (in April 1970) that there had arisen a significant row over England's cricket team making a trip to South Africa, with the result that a broadcaster like John Arlott at BBC decided to not make the trip in protest of the regime's oppressive racial policies. Arlott explains himself in an open letter found in the *Guardian* on 17 April 1970, mentioning prominently the play of English cricketer Graeme Pollock with a West Indian team the previous summer, and what a marvelous experience it was (see *Guardian Century 1970–1979*).

The cricketers behind Cleese include walk-ons David Aldridge (*Doctor Who*), Steve Smart, David Gilchrist (*Dad's Army*), Jim Haswell (*Doctor Who; Z Cars*), and George Janson (*Mystery and Imagination*) (WAC T12/1,433).

• J •

Jenny and Robin — (*"The Attila the Hun Show"*) On Debbie Reynolds's TV show, the couple had no children, but the "two child" family was right for the American sitcoms of the period, as exhibited by both *I Love Lucy*, with children Desi Jr. and Lucie; *The Adventures of Ozzie and Harriet* (1952–1966), with sons David and Ricky; and *Leave It to Beaver* (1957–1963), with Wally and the Beaver.

"Joey Boy" — ("The News for Parrots") Name of a 1965 British film set during WWII, but also a traditional name for a parrot.

• K •

"killer" — ("Killer Sheep") As early as Ep. 2 (recorded first, however), sheep have been portrayed incongruously as clever by the Pythons, contrary to the popular (and literary) belief that they're quite dumb. Marianne Moore, for example, in her 1959 poem "The Arctic Ox (Or Goat)," calls camels "snobbish" and sheep "unintelligent" (stanza 9). In Ep. 2, Harold the Sheep was teaching other sheep to fly, and planning an escape from the rustic shepherd (Chapman).

"Knightsbridge" — (*"Today in Parliament"*) Located in the city of Westminster, and home to Harrods, Knightsbridge is probably mentioned due to its proximity to Parliament and the seat of government.

knitting — ("Ratcatcher") She's actually stuffing a chicken with what appears to be stuffing. She (Palin) then wears the chicken on her right hand throughout the scene.

• L •

"Licence Fees" — (PSC; link out of *"Take Your Pick"*) On 1 January 1969, the mandatory license fee—the annual fee paid by all television and radio owners in the UK—had been increased by £1. This fee helps fund the BBC.

"Little bastard" — (link out of "Vox Pops on Politicians") Kind of an oxymoronic statement, since both the Groupie's parents are there, but typical for the Pythons. This is an interesting parody of the then very topical "rebellious generation" syndrome, where flower children and the hippie generation sought something beyond their parents' ken. The satire rests in the fact that these young people are actually interested in politics and politicians, rather than "turning on and dropping out." This same turnabout can be seen in the upended "Angry Young Man" drawing room scenario in Ep. 2, "Working-Class Playwright."

"little joke" — ("Ratcatcher") As he puts on his workingman's hat, Mr. Ames's (Chapman) posh, obviously patrician, and MCC-appropriate accent changes to a much more rustic accent.

"lobbying" — ("Vox Pops on Politicians") Originally, this was an American term for the (legal) act of influencing political figures, legislation, etc. It seems to have appeared in the UK around 1894, as the term was used in the 4 April 1894 *Yorkshire Post* with quotation marks around it, as if it were a newer, less familiar, even specialized term (*OED*). The groupies seem to be using it in a sexualized way, of course.

One recent bit of lobbying had led to the Representation of the People Act of 1969, wherein the vote was given to those over the age of eighteen in the UK, meaning these groupies might have just recently achieved some measure of influence and access to their representatives. Some pundits have connected this expansion of suffrage to the distinct drop in voter turnout in the 1970 General Election, leading to the subsequent loss by Labour.

Lastly, *Private Eye*'s mention of Westminster's lobbyists is nothing short of bracingly scornful, employing the words "clowns," "deceiving," and "toadying," before concluding that "these drunks, toadies and geriatrics are as guilty by default as the politicians are for all the ills which beset our punk little, drunk little island" (*PE*, 1 Sept. 1970: 17).

"Look of fear!" — ("Killer Sheep") This is identified by the Professor (Idle) as another "strange line," this time because the line actually reads more like a stage direction than dialogue. The line could also be read as a shot sheet entry for the overacted reaction shot seen in many science fiction and horror films.

Lords cricket grounds — (PSC; "Test Match") They did shoot at the gates of Lords for this intro, but the cricket match itself was shot much earlier at the Norfolk County Cricket Ground (WAC T12/1,430). Lords is the home of English cricket, and is located in exclusive St. Johns Wood, and would likely have not welcomed the Pythons onto their pitch for the scene.

• M •

macs — (PSC; link into "Secretary of State Striptease") Mackintosh overcoats. Most shabby Python characters wear such a coat, though Praline's (Cleese) is always rubber. These same extras also appear in the "Killer Sheep" sketch as cricketers, and include David Aldridge, Steve Smart, David Gilchrist, Jim Haswell, and George Janson. The music played for their "observation" is "The Stripper" by Rose, as played by the Concert Band of Her Majesty's Lifeguards (WAC T12/1,433).

"maintain consumer prices" — ("Secretary of State Striptease") The Labour government rode this horse into the 1970 General Election, with sitting PM Harold Wilson sounding very much like a stripping Minister as he blasts the opposition's economic proposals:

> Conservative policies are deliberately designed to raise prices. To raise food prices by abolishing the food subsidies which protect the housewife and imposing levies—food taxes—on the food we buy from abroad. To raise almost all other prices by their Value Added Sales Tax. To raise rents, by getting rid of our present system of housing subsidies. By ending the protection which Labour's Acts of Parliament give to the householder in the face of rising council house rents. They would scrap all the controls we operate to restrain price increases. . . . The Conservatives have made it clear that they would scrap all we are doing. (transcribed from the "Labour Party Election Broadcast, 1970")

The Conservative position (voiced by Edward Heath) also touched on prices and social programs, but in the party political messages in 1970, neither party spent much time talking up agricultural subsidies or the Common Market—meaning, perhaps, that the bleak domestic situation outweighed foreign issues in the minds of potential voters.

The party election manifestoes for Labour and the Tories in 1966 also touch on the strength of the UK as part of the Commonwealth and an arm's-length participant in the Common Market (though the Conservative platform calls for a more active Common Market cause). (See the various manifestoes for recent UK elections at www.psr.keele.ac.uk.)

maybe they're brown coats — (PSC; "The Epsom Furniture Races") These men look like the line of gasmen depicted in Ep. 14, as part of the "New Cooker Sketch." Again, the writer(s) of this scene could have easily erased the "white coats" reference in the printed scripts and penciled in "brown coats," but the asides to the reader continue.

"Merino" — ("Killer Sheep") A merino is a type of sheep quite prized for its wool in the UK.

"Minister of Pensions and Social Security" — ("Secretary of State Striptease") The Ministry of Social Security was set up in 1966, and the Department of Health and Social Security followed in 1968. The Labour minister for this position (until June 1970) was Richard Crossman (1907–1974). Crossman was replaced in 1970 by Sir Keith Joseph (1918–1994), who would remain in the post until the Conservatives lost the 1974 General Election.

"Minister of Technology" — ("The News for Parrots") Tony Benn (b. 1925) was Minister of Technology (Labour government) from 1966 to 1970. On 19 June 1970, Geoffrey Rippon (1924–1997) took the position for the newly elected Conservative government. The photo included by the Pythons is of Benn. Benn is also remembered for losing his House of Commons seat after a by-election win from Bristol South-east in 1960 because he was Anthony Wedgwood-Benn—he had inherited an unwanted viscountcy. He would go on to press the cause of those who would renounce their titles to seek Commons seats, realized in the Peerage Act of 1963.

"Minister without Portfolio" — ("*Today in Parliament*") A government minister not in charge of a specific department of state, and perhaps relegated to the back benches.

"Shadow Minister"—Member of the opposition party (the party not in the majority in Parliament) nominated to be counterpart to the sitting minister. In late 1970, Labour assumed the shadow posts, having lost badly (and unforeseenly) in the summer General Election. See the entries for "Election Night Special" in Ep. 19 for more on that surprising political turnabout.

It's worth noting that in this monologue the Pythons are skewering *both* sides of the political aisle, front and back benchers, Conservative and Labour, at least. (Liberals will finally be lampooned in Ep. 45.)

modern box — (PSC; "Test Match") The script calls for the commentators to be sitting in a "modern box," which appears to be nothing more than a standard broadcast booth loaded with alcohol.

"M1" — ("The News for Parrots") The M1 is the major London-to-Birmingham motorway, which opened in 1959.

• N •

"*naturally* mad . . . I don't use any chemicals" — ("The Idiot in Society") English poet A.C. Swinburne (mentioned in Ep. 17) would comment in *Testaments* (1590) on the "naturall foole" who is idiotic by nature (meaning birth). The Upperclass Twits fit nicely into this category.

The "chemicals" reference is a pertinent comment during a period when experimentation with myriad drugs was rampant, including among the Pythons (see McCabe). In sports, the increasing use of performance-enhancing drugs (e.g., steroids, doping) is also significant. (The first drug disqualification in Olympic history came in 1968 when a Swedish modern pentathlete tested positive for "excessive" alcohol.) As early as the mid-1950s the Soviet weightlifting teams were being given testosterone injections, and the U.S. squad allegedly followed suit in the following Oympic games, spurring the East German sports machine into the fray, etc., opening the floodgates for drug use in myriad Olympic sports.

"new strain" — ("Killer Sheep") This is one of the foundational semantic elements of the 1950s sci-fi film genre, viz., the mutation of an existing species by either Man's or some unknown—often alien—interference. For example, see the mutated ants in *Them!* (1954), a tarantula and other animals in *Tarantula* (1955), *The Giant Gila Monster* (1959) mutant, and even mutated humans in *The Incredible Shrinking Man* (1957). These sheep begin to perform very human acts, all criminal, of course, which may also be a vague allusion to the human-like HAL 9000 computer in *2001: A Space Odyssey* (1968), and the Colossus computer in *The Forbin Project* (1970). The reason for the sheep's mutation is never made clear, unlike the more complete sci-fi sketch in Ep. 7, where it's revealed that alien blancmanges are attempting to win Wimbledon.

"nobody does that anymore" — ("The Idiot in Society") Certainly at least an oblique comment on the transition the Pythons were very much associated with—the move away from the traditional, music hall-ish Frankie Howerd or *Morecambe and Wise*–type (gag-rich, set-up-and-rimshot-payoff) school of television comedy.

"none surpassed . . . cruelty" — ("*The Attila the Hun Show*") This claim is supported by many sources, including (and not surprisingly) *The Catholic Encyclopedia*: ". . . plundering and devastating all in his path with a ferocity unparalleled in the records of barbarian invasions and compelling those he overcame to augment his mighty army" ("Attila").

"Northants" — ("Test Match") Short for Northamptonshire.

Northwest Provincial — (PSC; "The Idiot in Society") The sign behind Mr. Brando at the bank reads "Northwest Provincial," placing this scene in the Merseyside, Manchester, Lancashire, Cumbria, and Cheshire region. (It was actually shot in Norfolk, well across the country to the east, but still well north of London, and civilization.) Simply put, anywhere north of London can be considered provincial, which has been the bias of southerners for generations.

"not so many of them" — ("Ratcatcher") There were four into-camera newsreaders for the 1967 *News at Ten* (ITN) debut: Alastair Burnet (1928–2012), Andrew Gardner (1932–1999), Bosanquet, and George Ffitch (1929–2001); four foreign correspondents (John Edwards, Alan Hart, Richard Lindley, and Sandy Gall); and Gerald Seymour in the ITN studio, among others (see Vahimagi).

"Notts" — ("Test Match") Short for Nottinghamshire.

"now it's the North East's turn with the Samba" — ("Test Match") A direct reference to the popular BBC show *Come Dancing* (1949–1995) which the Pythons obviously were aware of as they grew up. The broadcast dance show began to promote competitions between regions in 1953, which accounts for the "North East" reference (Vahimagi, 25). The mention during cricket coverage is also significant—cricket commentator Brian Johnston appeared on *Come Dancing* as a presenter. *Come Dancing* will also be mentioned in Ep. 39, where it will be known as *Come Wife-Swapping*, though still hosted by Peter West (Idle).

• O •

"off stump" — ("Test Match") "Stumps" are the upright sticks behind the batsman, and the two "bails" laid on top of them complete the "wicket." The "off stump" is the stump to the keeper's far right, the "leg stump" is nearest the batsman's leg, with the "middle stump" in between.

"O'Nassis" — ("The Idiot in Society") Certainly a reference to the then in-the-news Onassis family, including Aristotle and wife Jacqueline Kennedy Onassis. With the apostrophe, the name is Gaelicized (specifically, to an Irish name).

outside loo — (PSC; "Vox Pops on Politicians") The script indicates that he is standing in front of the door to an "outside loo," which is an outdoor privy. However, when he turns to go in the door, the following match cut is the interior of his home (which may, of course, be a comment on the typical council estate home of the period).

• P •

"parrots" — ("The News for Parrots") The happy Commonwealth theme is carried on here, with animals native to distant but Commonwealth-member countries—parrots (Australasia, India), gibbons (the Indian Archipelago), and wombats (Australia)—being offered culture-friendly and species-specific news from the BBC.

This is also a play on the BBC's myriad broadcast offerings for specific regions/peoples like Devon and Wales, the Middle East, and all the far-flung corners of the former British Empire. One such offering, Persian Radio, has already been mentioned by Arthur Frampton (Jones) in Ep. 2. In the film *Hard Day's Night* (dir. Richard Lester, 1964), the TV director bemoans his fate after The Beatles' less-than-perfect taping session, certain that his next stop is the *News in Welsh* backwater.

Lastly, proto-BBC (then known as "2LO") broadcaster Arthur Burrows (1882–1947) was known to deliver the newscast twice, consecutively—once at a normal clip, and once "exceptionally slowly" (*Eyewitness 1920–29*, "Early Broadcasting"). Burrows was also known as "Uncle Arthur" on the BBC's *Children's Hour* for many years, which might at least partly explain the Pythons' fixation on that name. See Burrows's entry at the *ODNB* for more.

patriotic music — (PSC; "Vox Pops on Politicians") The music played beneath this shot is the first march of the "Pomp and Circumstance Marches" composed by archetypal English composer Edward Elgar in 1901. Also known as "Land of Hope and Glory," it became a sort of unofficial anthem of the Conservative Party, hence its inclusion here. It has since become associated with graduations, sporting events, and upper-crust pomposity in both the UK and United States.

"Peephole Club" — ("Secretary of State Striptease") Certainly modeled after one of the many clip joints and nudie clubs in the Soho area of the West End of London. The Soho neighborhood has been the center of London's sex trade for at least two centuries (Ackroyd, *London*, 527–28).

"Pennine Gang" — ("Killer Sheep") Pennine sheep are special in that they are "hefted," meaning they remain in a particular territory (on a hill or moor, for instance), and thus don't necessarily need to be herded or even fenced. This becomes ironic as we see the Pennine Gang breaking out of their territoriality to rob and pillage. The name is a play on the "Barrow Gang" of Clyde Barrow and Bonnie Parker (et al.), and the "pickin'" music used in the sequence supports that reading. Also, the printed script mentions "Basil Cassidy and the Sundance Sheep," whose real-life inspirations led the "Hole in the Wall Gang" (or the "Wild Bunch Gang"). *Bonnie and Clyde* was released in 1967, followed two years later by *Butch Cassidy and the Sundance Kid*.

"Peter" — ("Test Match") Peter West (1920–2003) joined the BBC in 1947 and became the voice of cricket coverage for a generation. He also starred on BBC's *Guess My Story* quiz show (1953–1954); he earlier presented for the BBC's *Come Dancing* (1949–1995). Brian Johnston presented in the early 1960s on this latter show. (See the note above for "now it's the North East's . . ." for more on the show.)

"Brian"—Brian Johnston (1912–1994) almost took the City Gent route (Eton, Oxford, and the Grenadier Guards) but joined the BBC instead in 1946, where he would work for almost fifty years. He covered cricket from the beginning, on both radio and TV, joining the Test Match Special team in 1970. Pictures indicate that he did have a rather large nose, and in several he is posing with glass conspicuously in hand. The request for the polystyrene prosthetic nose to be built can be found in the surviving WAC records.

"Naughton"—This could be a reference to Naunton Wayne (1901–1970), actually, a British actor who portrayed a cricket enthusiast in at least eleven films (several times partnered with Basil Radford), including Hitchcock's *The Lady Vanishes* (1938). Naunton died in November 1970.

"Knott"—Cricketer Alan Knott (b. 1946) played for Kent, Tasmania, and England, appearing on the national cricket scene in 1965 when he was considered the best young cricketer in the country. By 1967 he was a Test player, and in 1970 was the Wisden Cricketer of the Year. His first test was played, incidentally, at *Nott*ingham. Knott was part of the Kent County team managed by Leslie Ames (see above) that won the county championship in 1970.

"Newton"—Harry Newton (b. 1935) played for Sussex and England, participating nationally in 1966. Another Newton—Harold Newton (1918–2007)—was actually born in and would play for Northamptonshire (Northants).

"postcards for sale" — (*"Today in Parliament"*) Probably "naughty" Edwardian erotic postcards such as those Gilliam utilizes in his animations, and which the roguish Major Bloodnok (Peter Sellers) flogs in various *Goon Show* episodes. An "Arab" (Jones) tries to sell dirty postcards to Little Red Riding Hood (Cleese) in *Fliegender Zirkus* as well. The following "who likes a sailor, then" adds credence to the sexualized nature of the reference. Again, the straight-laced (and especially Conservative) MP types, in the Python world, are more likely to be sexual profligates and deviants than simple public servants.

• R •

rampaging bun — ("Attila the Bun") In this animated sequence, it's worth noting that the figure on the dining room table who eventually consumes the rogue bread is labeled "BBC."

"rhubarb" — (*"Today in Parliament"*) Both a vegetable often used in English summers as a fruit, as well as a canted word used by radio actors to imitate the sound of a large gathering—the Goons often "Rhubarb! Rhubarb!" heartily in their characterizations of Lords and Ministers in Parliament chambers, for instance. Here the rhubarb seems to be hinted at as a possible sex toy, as well, along with a dachshund. Also, Cleese had become quite well known for his "Rhubarb Tart" song from his *ISIRTA* days.

"rodental" — ("Ratcatcher") The word is actually "rodential."

• S •

"said it again" — ("Wainscotting") This gag is repeated to great effect in the second "Knights Who Say Ni" appearance in *HG*, reinforcing the power and significance of *words* in the Python world.

"Secretary . . . Affairs" — ("Secretary of State Striptease") This minister would have been in charge of relations with members of the Commonwealth, many former colonies now elevated to trading partner status. The striptease may be a comment at the ridiculous façade many saw Britain attempting to shore up as its international presence and influence continued to shrink in the postwar era. In many cases, Commonwealth members were flourishing even as Britain ebbed into international ineffectiveness.

In 1970, the Secretary of State for Foreign and Commonwealth Affairs was Sir Alec Douglas-Home. Members of the Commonwealth (with Britain) in 1970 included: Australia, Canada, New Zealand, India, Pakistan, Sri Lanka, Ghana, Malaysia, Nigeria, Cyprus, Sierra Leone, Jamaica, Trinidad and Tobago, Uganda, Kenya, Malawi, Malta, Tanzania, Zambia, Gambia, Singapore, Barbados, Botswana, Guyana, Lesotho, Mauritius, and Swaziland.

seedy strip club — ("Secretary of State Striptease") This milieu—the hanging curtains, potted plant, and general seediness—reflect many of the Soho district's strip clubs of the 1960s, including the Phoenix Club. The 1966 short film *Strip*—set in the Phoenix—takes an honest, unglamorous look at the lives of these working girls, and the depressing décor is quite visible throughout.

"Selfridges" — ("Killer Sheep") A UK department store chain in business since 1909. Its Oxford street store has been the site of numerous protests and demonstrations (anti-fur, anti-Israel, etc.) since at least 1967.

The BBC had broadcast *The Great Store Robbery* in 1970, a program looking at retail theft, and Selfridges was one of the establishments featured prominently. See the BFI Film and TV Database website for program information.

"self-taught idiot" — ("The Idiot in Society") The past decade had been a significant transitioning period between the few, elite (or very intelligent) students finding their way successfully through university, and the realization of higher education for just about anyone with the building of myriad universities and upgrading of technical colleges after WWII, and especially in the 1960s. These "New Universities" were often derided (especially by those who'd attended the Ancient Universities) as places where the great unwashed could pretend to higher learning. In late 1963, acceptance of the findings of the Robbins Report led to plans for multiple "plate glass" universities across the country, including the mentioned University of East Anglia in Norwich, which entered students beginning in 1963.

This was also the period when the "University of the Air" (and later "Open University") was under discussion, and political cartoonists were having great fun taking jabs at this radical, long-distance learning concept. See notes to Ep. 41 for much more on Open University.

Lastly, it was primarily during the Pythons' young lives that the significant transition from the apprentice to the university (or arts college) system was gathering steam. Filmmakers, animators, television personnel, and plastic artists and performers of all types were graduating from degree programs and entering the marketplace, rapidly replacing the "self-taught" types in the arts and entertainment fields. The Pythons themselves were certainly a result of this transition.

This Idiot's (Idle) "ooh arh" is the stereotyped Yorkshire accent heard much earlier in Ep. 2, from the Rustic (Chapman) in the "Flying Sheep" sketch.

sexily dressed girl . . . strikes a small gong — (*"Take Your Pick"*) The gong ringer for *Take Your Pick* was actually Alec Dane, a more-than-middle-aged man. This gong moment will be revisited in Ep. 25, the "Court (Phrasebook)" sketch.

Sheep executing dangerous raids — (PSC; *"Animation: 'Arthur X, leader of the Pennine Gang'"*) The branch of the Westminster Bank Limited being robbed by the killer sheep (an unattributed still photo employed by Gilliam) is located at 424 Hornsey Road, Greater London, N19.

Gilliam also includes a photo of a Midland Bank branch, which the sheep rob and then detonate. The "bloody Midland Bank" has previously been mentioned by the poet McTeagle in Ep. 16.

"sheep poison" — ("Wainscotting") There is no such thing, of course, though there is rat poison, which is often strychnine.

"simple country girl" — ("Attila the Nun") A Joan of Arc (c. 1412–1431) or even Bernadette of Lourdes (1844–1879) type of description, excepting the "brutality." Both Joan and Bernadette were simple country girls when they received their visitations and took up their individual vows.

soft breathy jazzy music — (PSC; "Secretary of State Striptease") The music beneath the stripping Secretary (Jones) is very muted, and is another "stripper"-type song, of which there are many. This song is not accounted for in the WAC records.

"Southcott, Joanna" — ("The Epsom Furniture Races") Southcott (1750–1814) was a Devon-area religious fanatic who wrote verse prophecies, and gathered quite a large following. Her "box" supposedly contained prophetic material necessary for Britain when a time of great crisis appeared, and was to be opened in the presence of all the sitting C. of E. bishops (*ODNB*). In the 1960s and early 1970s there were organized groups demanding that Southcott's wishes be followed and the box at last opened, which is why the bishops in the following sketch are screaming for "the box" to be opened.

"Spam" — (*"Take Your Pick"*) American pressed lunch meat referenced again in Ep. 25, and very popular in Britain both during and after WWII, when food rationing meant a limited supply of meat. Spam wasn't one of the regularly rationed items, meaning Britons could buy it, eat it, and even store it whenever it became available, without ration cards.

During the war, Spam (a ham-based product) and "Mor" (a pork shoulder-based product) were part of the Lend-Lease deliveries from America, and were quite popular (as far as tinned meats went).

"Speaker" — ("Vox Pops on Politicians") The Speaker of the House of Commons in 1970 was Dr. Horace King (1901–1986), and afterwards J. Selwyn Lloyd (1904–1978). This position is chosen by the House of Commons—and the party in power—and is charged with representing the Commons and presiding over debate—choosing those who will speak, among other duties.

stock film — (PSC; *"The Attila the Hun Show"*) There were at least three color feature films available by 1970 for this pillaged footage, including *La Regina dei tartari* (1961), *Tharus figlio di Attila* (1962), and the big-budget Anthony Quinn/Sophia Loren vehicle *Attila* (1954). The WAC records indicate that the film stock used was called *Attila the Hun*—no mention of where it came from, which probably means it was already somewhere in the BBC collection (WAC T12/1,242). This clip may have come from Philip Jenkinson's collection, as well.

stock film of fast moving Huns — (PSC; *"The Attila the Hun Show"*) The music underneath this stock footage is "Episodes from the Bible" by Derek Laren, and is played by the International Studio Orchestra (WAC T12/1,433).

"strange, strange line" — ("Killer Sheep") Commenting on the often hypertrophic dialogue and situations of the sci-fi genre, science fiction films are well known for offering arch, often over-the-top dialogue that, generically, could have no home in another genre. See entries for the "Science Fiction Sketch" in Ep. 7 for more on the Pythons' sci-fi genre acumen.

This is also a very self-conscious moment, of which there are many in *FC*. Period sci-fi films (featuring mutated creatures) that the Pythons might be lampooning include *Tarantula* (1955; rodents and arachnids grow to enormous killers), *Them!* (1954; killer ants), *It Came from Beneath the Sea* (1955; a giant octopus), *Beginning of the End* (1957; mutated grasshoppers), and perhaps especially films like *The Giant Gila Monster* (1959). Most of these films share the incongruous plot structure—formerly docile or just "too small to be real threats to humanity-type" creatures are mutated and run amok.

• T •

Take Your Pick — (PSC; "*Take Your Pick*") Quiz show (1955–1968) produced by Arlington Television and Radio, with Michael Miles (1919–1971) as host. The printed scripts describe Miles as a "grinning type monster." Not unlike the Python version of the show, the studio audience members for *Take Your Pick* would shout "Open the box!" to the contestant if they felt the proffered money wasn't sufficient.

Tale of Two Cities — ("The News for Parrots") Novel by Charles Dickens, published 1859.

"Test Selection Committee" — ("Ratcatcher") "Test" is short for Test Match, "an official two-inning match between two accredited national teams, usually spread over 5 playing days (30 hours)" (see *Dictionary of Cricket Terms*). Results of the Rest of the World in England, 1970, include England XI vs. Rest-of-the-World, played at Lord's, London on 17, 19, 20, and 22 June 1970 (a three-day match). The result: Rest-of-the-World won by an inning and eighty runs. See the "Association of Cricket Statisticians and Historians." There were four other England XI vs. Rest-of-the-World matches in 1970, played at Nottingham, Birmingham, Leeds, and The Oval (in Kennington).

The Test Selection Committee would have been in charge of selecting players to represent England in the planned international tests.

"third test" — ("Killer Sheep") Cleese is in black-face, and speaks with a vague Jamaican/West Indies accent in this appearance. (This is the second blacked-up character in the episode, following Rochester [Idle] in the "*Attila*" sketch.) The Jamaican cricket team played four matches in England in 1970: against Glamorgan at Swansea, 25–28 July 1970; against Lancashire at Manchester, 8–11 August 1970; against Sussex at Hove, 15–18 August 1970; and against Essex at Leyton, 19–21 August 1970. See the Association of Cricket Statisticians and Historians records for more.

Cricket was very much in the news during this period. MCC bore the brunt of national and international disapprobation as the South African cricket team prepared to tour the UK in 1969–1970. Protests included the destruction of cricket pitches across the country, meaning teams had to play in different stadia or cancel matches. The South African tour was eventually cancelled due to this uproar.

This Is Your Life — (PSC; "Killer Sheep") The printed script calls for a bit of the show's theme music. *This Is Your Life* was a radio series created by Ralph Edwards in the late 1940s. It led to a U.S. television series that ran on NBC from 1952 to 1961. The British version appeared on the BBC 1955–1964, then moved to Thames TV in 1969.

The snippet of music played as the Commissioner is rolled out is not from *This Is Your Life*, as requested in the printed script, but is instead the theme for the very popular *Sunday Night at the Palladium* (1955), a weekly musical variety show.

Today in Parliament — ("*Today in Parliament*") A BBC Radio program that has covered political proceedings at the Houses of Parliament since 1945, and had been broadcast from Westminster.

"tonight's star prize" — ("*Take Your Pick*") Michael Miles did offer a "star prize" on *Take Your Pick*, though the prize was more likely to be a lounge suite, as seen later in the "Communist Quiz" sketch (Ep. 25).

Turkish music — (PSC; "Secretary of State Striptease") The music here is borrowed from an LP and is performed by the Concert Band of Her Majesty's Lifeguards, featuring John Leach. The track is called "Arabian Belly Dance" (WAC T12/1,433).

"Ty Gudrun and Nik Con" — ("*The Attila the Hun Show*") Nik Cohn (b. 1946, Ireland) is a rock journalist whose works pioneered the critical appreciation of the rock music industry. By late 1970 he had published *I Am Still the Greatest Says Johnny Angelo* (1967), *Pop* (1969), *Awopbopaloobop Alopbamboom* (1970) and *Market* (1970). His magazine article "Tribal Rites of the New Saturday Night" led to the hit movie *Saturday Night Fever* (1977).

"Ty Gudrun"—The Baader-Meinhof Gang was active in Germany during this period (firebombing department stores, for example), and leader Gudrun Ensslin could have inspired the other name chosen here.

• U •

"Uncle Tom" — ("*The Attila the Hun Show*") Titular character in Harriet Beecher Stowe's *Uncle Tom's Cabin* (1851–1852), but also used allusively and derogatively for any servile black man, or even as a catch-all term for any black man.

"University of East Anglia" — ("The Idiot in Society") In Norwich, the university was set up in 1963, one of many new universities chartered as the Robbins Report was surfacing. The university's motto is "Do Different," which may account for the Pythons' placing of the idioting degree at UEA. The motto comes from the old Norfolk saying, "People in Norfolk do things different." It was also the first English university to adopt the modular, semester system.

Much of the location work for this part of the second season was shot in and around Norwich, meaning the Pythons' proximity to UEA could also account for its inclusion here.

University scarves — (PSC; "The Idiot in Society") Scarves that indicate a particular school matriculation. The fact that UEA also sits adjacent to Norfolk, seen as the best-preserved medieval English town in the country, is also significant as the sketch discusses the transition between ancient village life and the modern world. See UEA's website for more.

This dancing scene was shot in the green area of Heydon Village, just south of the St. Peter and St. Paul's Church. (WAC T12/1,242).

University setting — (PSC; "The Idiot in Society") This setting—where the Vice-Chancellor is awarding degrees to the Idiots—was filmed at Elm Hill, Norwich (WAC T12/1,242).

• V •

Viking — ("Killer Sheep") Various Pythons dressed as Vikings act as transitional (linking) or just interruptive elements throughout the series. Perhaps a nod to the Viking culture's history as marauders and plunderers up and down England's seacoasts and rivers, but more likely the Viking get-up just looks appropriately incongruous.

There is also a similar, perhaps ur-*Monty Python* moment in the popular Ealing comedy *I'm All Right Jack* (1959), where, at a television studio, two actors dressed as Vikings walk casually (and obviously) through the shot, then stop and stare.

"village idiot" — ("The Idiot in Society") This term may be no older than the Pythons' parents' generation, actually. "Village idiot" seems to appear in print first in G.B. Shaw's play *Major Barbara* (1907), so he's at least English, if not medieval. There are significant mentions of idiots in smaller villages and towns, in both American and British literature, but the term "village idiot" seems of more recent coinage.

The attire chosen for the village idiot here is identical to that chosen for the Rustic (Chapman) in Ep. 2, and later the Hay Wain (Jones playing yet another rustic) depicted in Ep. 25. The idiot's name, Arthur Figgis, was also used in Ep. 2.

Continuing their interest in English poets, this idiot motif might also be drawn from Wordsworth's *Lyrical Ballads* collection, specifically "The Idiot Boy" (1798), wherein a retarded child is sent into a village to fetch a doctor.

• W •

"wainscotting" — ("Wainscotting") Formerly, imported oak used for paneling, though now referring just to the paneling itself, whatever the wood type. The exteriors for these cutaways to the "little Dorset village" were shot in Heydon Village, where much of the "Idiot in Society" sketch was shot (WAC T12/1,242).

"Warner, Plum" — ("Test Match") Truly a "Grand Old Man" of English cricket (though not as early as 1732), Sir Pelham Francis Warner (1873–1963) was both a player and later administrator, founding *The Cricketer* magazine (now *Cricketer International*). Warner was also a batsman and Captain for Oxford University (Championship in 1920) and England, where he was captain for the successful 1903–1904 Ashes tour. He would go on to become a Test selector and Chairman of the Test selectors, as well as occupying various leadership positions in the MCC until his death. See the *ODNB* for more.

"WC Pedestal" — ("The Epsom Furniture Race") A water closet (bathroom) sink and pedestal.

Westminster — ("*Today in Parliament*") Westminster is the home of the Palace of Westminster (including the Houses of Parliament) and Westminster Abbey.

"What do penguins eat?" — ("*Take Your Pick*") This seemingly simple and innocent question elicits a barrage of wrong answers from Mrs. Scum (Jones), including:

"Cannelloni"—Rolls of pastry or pasta filled with cream or meat. The word "cannelloni" does sound like a sea creature, however.

"Lasagna . . . with cheese"—Moussaka is a traditional Mediterranean meat and potatoes dish, while lobster thermidor is a haute cuisine sauce-and-cheese, in-shell dish. The latter is also mentioned in Ep. 25, during one of the Spam menu recitations.

"Brian Close"—The cricket references continue. Dennis Brian Close (b. 1931) is a cricketer who played for Yorkshire, Somerset, and England; he was a left hand bat. Close was Wisden Cricketer of the Year in 1964, and will be referenced again in Ep. 21.

"Brian Inglis, Brian Johnson, Bryan Forbes"—Brian Inglis (1916–1993) wrote significantly on the Irish situation, especially in the 1950s and 1960s; Brian Johns(t)on was a longtime host of BBC's *Sportsview*; and Bryan Forbes (b. 1926) is a British actor/director/writer who appeared in *The Guns of Navarone* (1961) and wrote *King Rat* (1965). Forbes also directed *The Madwoman of Chaillot* (1969), which will be mentioned in Ep. 23. Johnston will be mentioned again in Ep. 21, and is castigated by the editors of *Private Eye* in late 1970.

"Nanette Newman"—Newman (b. 1934, Northampton) appeared in the 1970 film *The Raging Moon* for director Bryan Forbes (see above), which probably accounts for their proximity / inclusion here.

"Reginald Maudling"—Home Secretary under Heath's Conservative administration (1970–1974). Maudling is a consistent Python target, and will be mentioned again in Eps. 22 and 30.

If this were the portion of *Take Your Pick* known as the "Yes / No Interlude," where the contestant had to answer questions over a sixty-second period without saying either "yes" or "no," then Mrs. Scum performs very well. Most contestants (drawn from the studio audience) couldn't last more than a few seconds with either Johnston or Miles. The "Yes / No Interlude" gag will be revisited in Ep. 25, when Mr. Alexander Yahlt (Palin) is on trial for creating a "Dirty Hungarian Phrasebook."

wide-shot of Lords — (PSC; "Test Match") This footage of a match at Lords is drawn from the BBC Library's own collection of classic cricket film stock (WAC T12 / 1,242). Lords cricket ground is located at St. John's Wood, Greater London, and is named after founder Thomas Lord (1757–1832). It is the headquarters of the Marylebone Cricket Club (MCC), mentioned as being the only organization able to withstand the Piranha brothers in Ep. 14. The Pythons identify Lords as one of the pillars of the "idiot in society" world.

"Wildeburg, Bo" — ("Test Match") Bo *Wideberg* (1930–1997) was a Swedish director of the period, most notably directing *Elvira Madigan* in 1967, which appeared in London-area cinemas in early April 1968.

"wild slogging" — ("Test Match") A vernacular term for aggressive (or even overly aggressive) batting in cricket. The term is not covered in Lord's *Laws of Cricket*, but it is employed in contemporary newspaper descriptions of sloppy cricket batting. The "boundaries" indicate both the edges of the playing area and the scoring possibilities while batting (when the ball touches or goes over the boundary, or the fielder touching the ball does same, for example). Boundaries are discussed in Law 19 of the *Laws of Cricket* published by MCC (pages 42–45). The term "innings" (always plural when used in this way) indicate when one side is "in" or at bat, and / or any one batsman during his turn at bat. An "over" is a sequence of six balls bowled by one bowler from one end of the pitch.

"wolf's clothing" — ("Killer Sheep") Playing on the Aesopian and biblical allusions to the wolf in sheep's clothing (Matt. 7:15). In *HG*, it is a harmless white bunny that kills many knights, and has to be destroyed by the Holy Hand Grenade. In many Warner Bros. cartoons the smallest, least harmful-looking characters (chicken hawks, gremlins, mynah birds) often packed the biggest punch, which may have informed this *FC* scenario.

Episode 21: *"Archaeology Today"*

BBC 1 previews trailer (*Rain Stopped Play*, "Brian Close at The Talk of the Town," John Galsworthy's *Snooker My Way*, *Thirteen Weeks of Off-Spin Bowling*, *'Owzat*, *Panorama* with Tony Jacklin, Lulu climbing the Old Man of Hoy, and *Show of the Week* with a singing Kenneth Wostenholme); *Titles* (silly Cleese v/o); *Animation: Building and Decay, then Luxury Flats and a Toe-Elephant*; *Archaeology Today*: "That's what I call tall!"; *Flaming Star*: The Story of one man's vengeance . . . ; Archaeology (the musical); Silly vicar (The Reverend Arthur Belling); An Appeal on behalf of the National Truss; Leapy Lee; Women's Institute footage; Registrar (wife swap); Referee interrupts; Silly doctor sketch (immediately abandoned); *Animation: Giant ball in Wembley, Mugsy Spaniel, Eggs Diamond*, and *Raising Gangsters for Fun & Profit*; Mr. and Mrs. Git; "And now a nice version of that same sketch"; Nun KO'd; Mosquito hunters; Poofy judges; Mrs. Thing and Mrs. Entity (the drudgery of getting up, making tea, and looking out the window before shopping); **Beethoven's mynah bird**; "Shakespeare never had this trouble"; Michelangelo's "Fifth Symphony"; Colin Mozart, Ratcatcher; Beethoven finds "The Lost Chord"; More poofy judges and closing credits

• A •

"abolished hanging" — ("Judges") In the UK, the death penalty was replaced by life imprisonment by the Murder (Abolition of Death Penalty) Act of 1965, with the exception of acts of high treason and piracy. See notes to Ep. 15 for more on previous mentions of capital punishment.

"Abu Simnel" — (*"Archaeology Today"*) The site of the Temple of Abu *Simbel* in Egypt built during the reign of Ramses II, where four large, seated statues still guard the entrance. This site was much in the news during this period, which may account for its inclusion here. The building of the Aswan Dam (1960–1970) and the creation of Lake Nasser would have inundated the site, and between 1963 and 1968 the entire temple was with great fanfare disassembled and moved to higher ground. The entire decade-long process was covered extensively in period newspapers.

In Ep. 14, a Mrs. April *Simnel* (Palin) reminisces fondly about the young "boot-in" Piranha brothers.

Animation: A sketch about an archaeological find . . . — (*"Animation: Building and Decay, then Luxury Flats and a Toe-Elephant"*) This animated sequence features a clump of London buildings culled from various areas, and includes portions of St. Martin-in-the-Fields (the smaller spire), HM's Treasury building (the larger spire, Great George Street), perhaps the Limebank Building (Fenchurch Street), the then-headquarters for Barclays Bank, etc. The following building—labeled as "The British Museum"—is actually the British Museum.

Animation: Eggs Diamond — (*Animation: "Giant ball in Wembley, Mugsy Spaniel, Eggs Diamond,* and *Raising Gangsters for Fun & Profit"*) In the "Eggs Diamond" animation Gilliam uses a version of *Le comte de Vaudreuil* (1758), by François-Hubert Drouais. The painting has been part of the National Gallery collection since 1927. The Vaudreuil figure acts as the narrator of the film.

The map he's gesturing toward (and which gets shot and bleeds) is not the original. It looks to be a page borrowed from the *Geographers' A to Z Street Atlas of London* (Seven Oaks, Kent: Geographers' Map Co., 1968), which the Pythons will use as a source and reference as they later plot pick-up shot locations for *Monty Python and the Holy Grail*.

"Annaley . . . Softee" — ("Trailer") A great example of scriptwriting without checking for spelling or factual errors, this rider's name is actually "Anneli Drummond-Hay," and her mounts were Merely-a-Monarch and November Rain, among others. Drummond-Hay won the Burghley Three Day event in 1961, the Great Badminton in 1962, etc., and was a well-known rider of the period.

"Mr. Softee" was an award-winning Northern Ireland show jumping horse that competed in the 1968 Summer Olympics, and was ridden by David Broome. The show jumping theme will return to *FC* in Ep. 28, "The BBC Is Short of Money," when Mrs. Kelly's flat is being used for studio space, as well as Ep. 42, the "Show Jumping (Musical)" sketch.

archaeological dig — (PSC; "*Archaeology Today*") The Middle-Eastern atmospheric music used in the transition to the dig site is the London Studio Orchestra's version of "Casbah" by Keith Papworth (WAC T12/1,429).

"Archaeology Today" — ("*Archaeology Today*") An allusion to the show *Chronicle*—a fifty-minute, monthly program on BBC2 that took to the air in 1966, and focused on archaeology and history. Glyn Daniels (Cambridge archaeology lecturer) and Magnus Magnusson introduced the show. See notes below for "Silbury Dig."

"Arnold, P.P." — ("Leapy Lee") Born Patricia Ann Cole in Los Angeles, P.P. Arnold was "discovered" by Tina Turner, then by Bill Wyman and Charlie Watts (of the Rolling Stones), and she was off to a singing and acting career in England in 1966.

"awful bore" — ("Mr. and Mrs. Git") The obviously atrocious first names aren't noticed by the Gits, just their unfortunate last name, a structure of misunderstanding employed by the Pythons and English Renaissance dramatists Shakespeare, Jonson, and especially Dekker (see *MPSERD*). This is perhaps an allusion to the well-known "Ima Hogg" appellation from American (Texas) history. The last name was unfortunate enough (to the hearer), but when coupled with the choice of first names, American folkloric history was created. Ima's brothers were more carefully named William, Michael, and Thomas.

• B •

"Bailie" — ("Judges") Derivation of "bailiff," a bailie is now "a municipal magistrate corresponding to the English alderman" (*OED*). Used more in Scotland, according to the *OED*, which fits the Glaswegian allusions of this sketch.

"Baldwin, Mrs. Stanley" — ("Mrs. Thing and Mrs. Entity") Stanley Baldwin (1867–1947) was a Conservative MP and later Chancellor of the Exchequer, then PM in 1923 when Bonar Law resigned due to ill health. He had married Lucy (Mrs. Stanley Baldwin) in 1892.

See the entry for Baldwin in Ep. 14, where he's mentioned in regard to an alleged sexual relationship with Dinsdale Piranha. Baldwin and his Conservative government will again be mentioned in Ep. 24, when the stripping Ramsay MacDonald appears wearing ladies' unmentionables.

"bent" — ("Judges") The term often means corrupt or venal, but here it's given the obviously more British meaning of gay or effeminate.

"black cap" — ("Judges") *OED*: "That worn by English judges when in full dress, and consequently put on by them when passing sentence of death upon a prisoner." The last need for a judge to don the black cap came in November 1965, when David Stephen Chapman was sentenced to hang for murder. He would be reprieved thanks to the abolition of the death penalty, and remain in prison until 1979.

"body stocking" — ("Judges") A full body leotard, often worn in place of undergarments and, often, to give the illusion of nudity. Chapman appears to be wearing a black body stocking in Ep. 13, when he's pretending to be Marcel Marceau. The Lycra-based product appeared in about 1965, and quickly became fashionable.

brothers standing on a tank — (PSC; "Mosquito Hunters") This shot was taken at the main gate, Army School of Transport, Longmore, Liss, Hampshire (WAC T12/1,413). The Tory Housewives will also pose on the tank here for Ep. 32.

"bugger" — (end credits) Slang, meaning someone who participates in sodomy, or "buggery." This is the last word used, as an invective, in Ep. 15, as Cardinal Ximinez (Palin) fails to reach the Old Bailey in time.

"butch" — ("Judges") Originally an American slang, the *OED* defines "butch" as "a tough youth or man; a lesbian of masculine appearance or behaviour." In this scene the usually effeminate men are describing their more masculine moments using the term, especially a more "mannish" voice.

• C •

camp — (PSC; "Poofy Judges") A slang word meaning "ostentatious, exaggerated, affected, theatrical," and in this case stereotypically homosexual (*OED*). The Pythons often "camp it up" when depicting effeminate men—an affectation borrowed from the music hall, the Goons, and Benny Hill, among others, and which has become one of the hallmarks of Monty Python's over-the-top-ness. All the troupe members take it in turn "swanning about," including Gilliam as the flamboyant glam-boy in Ep. 9 and the equally poofy Algy in Ep. 33, Chapman as a policeman in makeup (Ep. 14) and as David Unction (Ep. 10), and all as gay army personnel (Ep. 22). Here, as elsewhere in *FC*, a stuffy or authority-type figure is undercut by lampooning or questioning (or outing) his sexuality, a technique used by screenwriter Terry Southern (a Python mate) in the 1964 satirical film *Dr. Strangelove*, as well.

"catarrh" — ("Mr. and Mrs. Git") Essentially, fluid from a runny nose (and eyes).

characters are in twenties' clothes — (PSC; "*Archaeology Today*") The costuming requests for this sketch describe Cleese's Eversley costume as "a Mortimer Wheeler type" (WAC T12/1,429). Sir Mortimer Wheeler (1890–1976) was an eminent English archaeologist who did significant work in the London area, and brought archaeology to the general public via radio and television shows including *Animal, Vegetable, Mineral?* (1952) and *Chronicle* (1966; with Magnus Magnusson). The young Pythons would have grown up with the dapper, mustachioed Wheeler as their image of a proper archaeologist, certainly.

"cheeky" — ("Poofy Judges") Common British colloquialism, meaning to be insolent or audacious. It's adapted from "cheek," meaning to talk insolently.

"Chopper" — ("Colin Mozart [Ratcatcher]") Could just refer to Colin's chosen killing technique, but also is slang for a machine gun, or one who operates such a gun. (A machine gun will figure in later in the sketch.) This term also means a fine, strapping child. This is probably also yet another intertextual reference to Detective Chief Inspector Leonard "Nipper" Read, responsible for arresting many celebrities during this period (see notes to Ep. 14).

"Close, Brian" — ("Trailer") Wisden Cricketer of the Year in 1964. See notes to Ep. 20 for more on Close.

cocktail party — ("Mr. and Mrs. Git") In this scene the camera first focuses in on a book being read by one of the partygoers: *Raising Gangsters for Fun & Profit*. The title is probably a reference to F.G. Ashbrook's *Raising Small Animals for Pleasure and Profit* (1951), or even a galley (or UK) version of Paul Villiard's book *Raising Small Animals for Fun & Profit*, which was eventually published in the United States in 1973.

In a second season episode of *The Bullwinkle Show*, Bullwinkle is reading "Barbering for Fun and Profit." *The Bullwinkle Show* (a.k.a. *Rocky & Bullwinkle*) came to British television in 1962.

The two featured extras in this scene are Patricia Prior (*Troubleshooters*) and Barbara Lindley (*Benny Hill*). Lindley also appears as the bride in the "Registrar (Wife Swap)" sketch.

"Coleman, David" — ("Trailer") Coleman (b. 1926) was a presenter of the World Cup Final in 1966, where Wolstenholme supplied commentary, for BBC1. See the entry for *Grandstand* below.

"Common Market" — ("Mrs. Thing and Mrs. Entity") A reference to the much-debated common pan-European trade market, where duties on trade were, ideally, either reduced or done away with altogether, creating a large, powerful trade zone able to compete with, for example, the exploding and rapacious postwar U.S. market. In the late 1950s France, West Germany, Italy, Belgium, Luxembourg, and Holland formed the consortium, with France (and specifically anglophobe President de Gaulle) tweaking Britain's nose by refusing to admit England into the group.

Many in Britain resisted membership for many years (see Marwick's comment about Britain's xenophobia in *British Society since 1945*, page 133), but it was Conservative PM "Mr. Heath" (1970–1974), ironically, who was instrumental in bringing the country to the CM table in the early 1960s. Full membership for the UK would come in 1973.

"Compton, Denis" — ("Trailer") Denis Charles Scott Compton (1918–1997) was a cricketer, and played for Middlesex, Holkar, Europeans (India), and England. His first Test appearance was in 1937, and two years later he was named Wisden Cricketer of the Year (*ODNB*).

• D •

Danielle joins in — (PSC; "*Archaeology Today*") The dig has become much like a Hollywood musical from the 1930–1960 period, where characters can un-self-consciously break into song at any moment to swelling, extradiegetic music. In critical terms, this would qualify as a fairy tale musical (see Altman), where "sex as adventure" and "sex as battle" are played out through song and dance. Here, the adventure is the dig and discovery, and the battle is between Sir Robert (Cleese) and his romantic interest Danielle (Cleveland), and the Interviewer (Palin) and his fawning "partner" Kastner (Jones). The melodramatic nature of the Silbury Dig itself (huge egos looking in vain for bits of history) certainly contributed to this sketch, as the Silbury dig was carried out in front of BBC cameras and a watchful nation. See notes for "Silbury Dig" below for more on the media event.

"Davis, Joe" — ("Trailer") Called the world's greatest snooker player, Davis (1901–1978) was a fourteen-time world champion before retiring, unbeaten, in 1946. Davis was awarded the OBE in 1963. See the *ODNB* for more on Davis.

"Day, Robin" — ("Registrar [Wife Swap]") A noted TV interviewer (*Panorama*), Day is characterized as helping usher in the more pointed, combative style of modern journalism. See notes to Ep. 2 for more, as well as the *ODNB*.

"deed poll" — ("Registrar [Wife Swap]") This means that Mr. Git's (Jones) name change attempt would be "made and executed" by just one party (*OED*).

"dirty version" — ("Mr. and Mrs. Git") This piling on of crudities is a precursor to the "*Most Awful Family in Britain*" sketch that will appear later in Ep. 45, the final original episode broadcast for the show.

"dolly sentences" — ("Judges") Actually a cricket (and gaming) term meaning easy, soft. In Ep. 15, the Judge (Chapman) was also complaining about the lack of real teeth in criminal case punishments, and was off for the more corporal South Africa the very next day.

Dulwich — (PSC; "Mr. and Mrs. Git") The city setting is only mentioned in the script, and not by any of the characters (or by subtitle). Dulwich is a city in Greater London, south of Westminster. Dulwich is characterized as a well-to-do, perhaps even Tory-friendly area, boasting, among others, Margaret Thatcher's residence. See notes to Ep. 19 for more.

Durante, Jimmy — (PSC; "Colin Mozart [Ratcatcher]") Durante (1893–1980) was an American vaudeville, film, and television entertainer. An accomplished musician, Durante also played in jazz bands for many years.

"I'm the guy that found the lost chord"—This is a multi-layered reference, to be sure. Firstly, light opera composer Arthur Sullivan (of Gilbert and Sullivan) wrote "The Lost Chord" as a serious work to offset his well-known lighter pieces. The gist, according to Sullivan, is the elusiveness of that "perfect" chord, found and then inevitably lost, which can only be reclaimed upon crossing the veil into the afterlife. Jimmy Durante later sang of finding that same chord as he sat at the "pianer . . . improvisin' symphonies." "Bing! Bing!" and he has the chord, then just as quickly—"Bong! Bong!"—and the chord is lost. Try as he might, he cannot find the chord again, remembering, lastly and ironically, that he normally plays "by ear" (Schroth). This entire Beethoven/mynah bird/ratcatcher scene, then, is based on this "lost chord" idea; if Beethoven truly played by ear, his deafness would have finished his composing career (it did not, of course).

This recording is from Jimmy Durante's *Schnozzles* record album (WAC T12/1,429).

• E •

"Egyptian tomb paintings" — ("*Archaeology Today*") If they are truly in the studio to discuss El Ara, then a scholar like Kastner is out of place. Abu Simbel is a temple site, not a burial site, and features bas-relief works and carved statues.

Episode 21 — Recorded as the eighth show of the second season on 9 October 1970. This episode was broadcast 17 November 1970.

Also appearing in or working for this episode are Barbara Lindley (*Benny Hill*), Pat Prior (*Doctor Who*), and Bill McGuffie (*Softly Softly*; *Doctor Who*) and his orchestra. Extras (uncredited) in this episode include Troy Adams (*Upstairs, Downstairs*), Gary Deans (*Doctor Who*), Barry Ashton (*Doctor Who*), Derek Hunt (*Z Cars*), Constance Carling (*Softly Softly*; *Z Cars*), and Jean Sadgrove (*Z Cars*).

"Eversley, Robert" — ("*Archaeology Today*") Loosely based on Prof. Richard Atkinson, leader of the Silbury Dig. See "Silbury Dig" notes below.

There also may be a reference to an earlier explorer of the Abu Simbel site, Giovanni Belzoni (1778–1823), who reportedly stood 6′ 7″ tall. The *Catholic Encyclopedia* reports that Giovanni performed in pantomime and music hall–type performances in London to support himself and his English wife earlier in his life, which may account for the musical references the Pythons include. Belzoni is credited with removing the sand from around the temple in the early nineteenth century, and reportedly removed most of the portable artifacts from the dig.

• F •

Fade into a bench in a public park, garden or square — (PSC; "Mrs. Thing and Mrs. Entity") The script calls for a park-like setting, though the backdrop used here is a painted/photographed flat, likely for a generic public house (a pub) that sells Truman's beer. The image may also be of an actual Truman's pub. The Truman's sign can be seen over Mrs. Thing's (Chapman) shoulder. Truman's was an East London brewing concern established in 1666.

fairly rough country location — (PSC; "Mosquito Hunters") Much of this scene was shot in the Easton, River Bank, and Ringland Woods area. The exterior work for "*Attila*" (Ep. 20) and Dame Irene ("Foreign Secretary," Ep. 19) was also photographed in this area, all on 24 August 1970 (WAC T12/1,413).

"fifth dynasty" — ("*Archaeology Today*") The Fifth Dynasty (2490–2330 BC) in Egypt is characterized as a period of relative decline, with smaller pyramids being built. Mentioned later, the Fourth Dynasty (2613–2494 BC) in Egypt was characterized by more significant pyramid construction. The Silbury Mound is thought to have been built c. 2750 BC. This proximity probably meant that news coverage of the Silbury Dig period highlighted the more familiar Egyptian dynasties for BBC viewer reference.

The Hittites were non-Semitic peoples in Asia Minor who flourished from approximately 1900 to 700 BC (*OED*).

first few notes of the fifth symphony — ("Beethoven's Mynah Bird") Historically, there doesn't seem to be any indication that Beethoven struggled with these well-known notes, nor that he ever married (so that his wife could constantly disturb him). His deafness was progressing rapidly as this symphony was being composed (1804–1808).

Flick Colby Dancers, Pan's People — (PSC; "Trailer") Dance troupe formed by BBC dancer/choreographer Flick Colby, as was the Pan's People troupe. The dancers appeared regularly on BBC's *Top of the Pops*. These dance troupes would perform to a well-known song when the song's performer was unable to appear.

"four corners" — ("*Archaeology Today*") An image of the measure of creation attributed to Coverdale's version of the Old Testament.

"funny he never married" — ("Mrs. Thing and Mrs. Entity") Heath (1916–1992) never did marry, but there doesn't seem to have been any real evidence that Heath favored men, according to his biographer John Campbell (1993). Mrs. Entity and Mrs. Thing seem to be positing a relationship between Heath's bachelor status and his unwillingness to hop into bed with France and the rest of Europe.

• G •

"Galsworthy, John" — ("Trailer") Galsworthy (1867–1933) was a Nobel Prize winner (1932), an actor, and playwright/novelist. This reference is undoubtedly connected to his epic *Forsyte Saga* that premiered on BBC in 1967 starring Nyree Dawn Porter—it was a critically hailed and very popular twenty-two-hour miniseries.

"Git" — ("Mr. and Mrs. Git") A slang term meaning a worthless or useless person. Originally from Scotland and northern England, "git" is a derivation of "get," and specifically refers to a bastard, or a brat (*OED*). The term will reappear in Ep. 29 as part of the "Abuse" section of the oft-quoted "Argument Clinic" sketch.

gobs — (PSC; "Mr. and Mrs. Git") Usually meaning "spits," but here she nearly throws up. Ken Shabby (Palin) earlier "gobbed" on Rosamund's father's (Chapman) carpet in Ep. 12.

Grandstand — ("Trailer") Billed as the longest-running live sports series, *Grandstand* took to the air in 1958 (BBC), and was hosted by David Coleman until 1968. The *Grandstand* tune was penned by Keith Mansfield, but the tune actually used in this transition (and just a snippet at that) is Burns's "Saturday Sport" (WAC T12/1,429).

• H •

"had" — ("Judges") Meaning he "had" him sexually, it would seem. This is an Old English usage, but certainly familiar to the Pythons.

Hammond organ accompaniment — (PSC; "*Archaeology Today*") The cheesy organ accompaniment to Eversley's obviously dubbed song is provided by the song's composer, Bill McGuffie, and members of his orchestra.

"Harrods" — ("Registrar [Wife Swap]") Giant, upscale department store in Knightsbridge, London, originally established in 1849.

"hen" — ("Judges") A diminutive term of affection, like "love" or "dear." Idle's floor director character will also use it in Ep. 12 as the minister (Chapman) hangs upside down.

"Hittite" — ("*Archaeology Today*") An ancient Iron Age civilization centered in what is today Turkey.

"Sumerian"—The Sumerian culture existed long before the Hittites in the ancient Near East.

"Hutton, Sir Len" — ("Leapy Lee") Leonard Hutton (1916–1990) was a cricketer who played for Yorkshire and England. His Test debut came in 1937; he was named Wisden Cricketer of the Year in 1938, and knighted for "services to cricket" in 1956. The continuing mentions of cricket legends like Hutton, Compton (see above), and W.G. Grace, among others, indicate the singular importance of cricket in the Pythons' collective youth. English football players also get this kind of star treatment in *FC*.

• I •

"I didn't like the colour" — ("Registrar [Wife Swap]") The Pythons' rather ambivalent attitude toward women is perhaps no better represented than here, where a wife's/woman's place as commodity, an article of trade, is reinforced. Elsewhere in *FC*, actual females are most often included for their physical attributes, with Carol Cleveland only occasionally being allowed a fair share in the funmaking. And if they're not being ogled, the female in *FC* is often the target of abuse, both verbal and physical.

"I'm six foot five and I eat punks like you for breakfast" — ("*Archaeology Today*") This connection between height and one's expertise or collegial respect in one's profession might be a veiled allusion to the "towering presence" of producer and director Tyrone Guthrie (1900–1971), who also stood six foot five, and whose height seems to never have gone without comment in appraisals of his stature in modern British theater. According to Shaughnessy in *The Shakespeare Effect*:

> "He was described as a founding father, as a pioneer, and, over and over again, as a 'giant' of the theatre," and "there was a quality to Guthrie's work, as well as his personality, that seemingly inevitably transformed his physique into metaphor, summed up in the phrase 'larger than life.'" (80)

This kind of two-fold admiration—where artistic accomplishment could only be matched by physical impressiveness—might have caused concern to Guthrie's colleagues of more average stature, just as Kastner (Jones) feels inferior to Eversley (Cleese).

"It's only a flashback" — ("Mrs. Thing and Mrs. Entity") Once again, the Pythons draw attention to the artifice of the television medium, in this case pointing out the very obvious but still "invisible" (to seasoned viewers) "ripple" that signals a temporal and often spatial shift. This ripple will appear again in Ep. 30, as a story of a ship's sinking is told. There, it doesn't transition anywhere, further exposing its artificiality.

• J •

"Jacklin, Tony" — ("Trailer") Internationally known British golfer, not a television announcer. Those who own Jacklin's "golf clubs" are excoriated by the architect (Cleese) in Ep. 17.

Jacklin had been named Sportsman of the Year in 1969, and appeared in February 1970 on the very popular *This Is Your Life* (1955–), significantly, as the Pythons prepared to write the scripts for the second season of *Flying Circus*.

Jewish accent — (PSC; "Colin Mozart [Ratcatcher]") It's unclear why the Pythons would give Mozart—born and raised as a German-speaking Austrian—a Jewish accent, except that it's a noticeable incongruity. See the note for Mendelssohn below for a more practicable usage of such an accent. Idle's portrayal of Shakespeare is also Jewish-accented, for perhaps the same reasons.

"JP's" — ("Judges") Semi-official shorthand for Justice of the Peace, so-called inferior magistrates for county or town legal enforcement. As representatives of the establishment, JPs are natural targets of the Pythons' ridicule, in this case by calling into question their sexual orientations.

• K •

"Kant" — ("Colin Mozart [Ratcatcher]") The list of occupants in this star-studded apartment include:

"Mr. and Mrs. Emmanuel Kant"—Kant (1724–1804) was an eminent philosopher whose belief in the *a priori* nature of certain, necessary, and determinable truths guided much of the trajectory of twentieth-century philosophy, and included the bridging of the Materialist and Idealist modes of philosophical thought. His belief in "things as we experience them" seems key to the Pythons' created world, where experience of a situation or reaction often flies in the face of the expected.

"Frau Mitzi Handgepäckaufbewahrung"—Roughly translates into "Mrs. Mitzi Carry-on Luggage Storage." For their Bavarian episodes, Connie Booth will play Princess Mitzi Gaynor in "Schnapps with Everything," the second *Fliegender Zirkus* episode.

"Mr. Dickie Wagner"—Given the "great man" motif employed thus far, this is most likely Richard Wagner (1813–1883), the nineteenth-century German composer.

"K. Tynan"—Kenneth Tynan (1927–1980) was a flamboyant, effete British theater critic seemingly devoted to smoking, sadomasochism, and regularly upsetting the status quo. Tynan was the drama critic for the *Observer* during the Angry Young Men heyday, and helped champion the movement. He also was the first person to use the word "fuck" live on the BBC—quite matter-of-factly, too—bringing upon himself the rage of myriad Conservative *and* Labour politicians, Mary Whitehouse, and many in Britain's "moral majority" of the period. He was seen by many as the flag-bearer for the so-called permissive society (Eps. 8 and 32), and a downward-trending moral barometer.

Tynan attended Magdalen, Oxford, and his in-your-face literary, sexual, and public style made him the ideal Python hero figure, especially as they chafed against the restrictions of the BBC and the television medium in *Flying Circus*. For more on Tynan, see the *ODNB* and the many references to the critic in the pages of *Private Eye*.

"Mr. and Mrs. J.W. Von Goethe"—Johann Wolfgang von Goethe (1749–1832) was a German Romantic writer. As for a "Mrs.," Goethe married Christiane Volpius late in life, in 1806.

"Herr E.W. Swanton"—E.W. "Jim" Swanton (1907–2000) was a legendary cricket broadcaster who's already been mentioned earlier in this episode. See notes to Ep. 20 for more on Swanton, as well as *ODNB*.

"Mr. and Mrs. P. Anka"—Paul Anka (b. 1941) is a Canadian pop singer and prolific songwriter and lyricist. He wrote the lyrics for Frank Sinatra's "My Way." Anka had appeared on *The Ed Sullivan Show* in 1969, and had toured the UK in the late 1950s at the height of his teen idol fame. "Mrs. Paul Anka" was Anne De Zogheb, whom he married in 1963. In September 1970, Anka was appearing in London at The Talk of the Town.

"Mr. and Mrs. Ludwig van Beethoven"—The lifespan is correct (1770–1827), but Beethoven was never married, though he seemed to have involved himself in a number of tempestuous romantic relationships, often with involved women.

This same kind of laundry list of celebrity names reportedly living in a nondescript apartment will be revisited in Ep. 27, when Mrs. Premise (Cleese) and Mrs. Conclusion (Chapman) travel to Paris to visit Jean-Paul Sartre.

There is something of a German theme to this particular apartment setting, supposedly the home of composer Beethoven (Bonn) and fellow Germanics Kant (born in East Prussia), Wagner (born in Liepzig), and Goethe (Frankfurt).

"Kastner, Prof. Lucien" — (*"Archaeology Today"*) Seems to be loosely modeled after Magnus Magnusson (1929–2007; Iceland), host of *Chronicle* and former reporter for *Tonight*. It's interesting here that Kastner (Jones)—the short, "weedy" man—is said to be from the University of Oslo, where the tall, athletic Thor Heyerdahl went to school. Eversley (Cleese) is given no alma mater in the sketch.

• L •

"Laker, Jim" — ("Trailer") James Charles Laker (1922–1986, Yorkshire) was a noted Test player who also appeared in the cricket-themed film *The Final Test* (1953), written by Terence Rattigan. (Rattigan will be mentioned again—killed, actually—in Ep. 30.) Laker played primarily for Surrey, Essex, and for England. His Test debut was 1947–1948, and he was named Wisden Cricketer of the Year in 1952 (*ODNB*).

Laker may also have been the model for the "Jim" character (played by Cleese) in the "Test Match" sketch in Ep. 20.

"Leapy Lee" — ("Leapy Lee") Comedian/singer whose real name is Lee Graham (b. 1942), Leapy had a close relationship with Ray Davies and the Kinks, and formed a backup group for himself called the Peppers in 1968. Davies wrote "King of the Whole Wide World" for Lee in 1966. Lee was appearing on *Beat Club* (German TV) in 1968–1969.

"Little arrows that will"—Lyric from the song called "Little Arrows" released in 1968-1969, and sung by Leapy Lee. The song was reissued three more times in the following years.

The boxer who appears and floors Leapy Lee (Idle) is played by Gilliam, who from the beginning of *FC* has taken on small walk-on roles as needed during taping. He has also played the ubiquitous Knight, a Viking, and a man with a stoat through his head in the early episodes. According to BBC records, Gilliam was paid stipends by the appearance for these roles.

"Lockheed Starfighter" — ("Mosquito Hunters") The F-104 was the state-of-the-art fighter/bomber built by the United States in the mid-1950s and part of the West German, Belgium, Japan, and Netherlands air forces well into the 1980s. Ironically, the Australian air forces don't seem to have deployed the plane.

"Lulu" — ("Trailer") A British pop singer, Lulu (born Marie MacDonald McLaughlin Lawrie in Scotland, 1948) sang the theme song for the film *To Sir, with Love* (1969) and became an immediate sensation. Lulu will appear in Ep. 28, with Ringo Starr and the It's Man (Palin), and she is featured on the *Radio Times* cover on 29 March 1969.

• M •

"Mao Tse-tung" — ("Leapy Lee") Leader of the People's Republic of China. Mao is also mentioned prominently in Eps. 19, 23, 24, and 25. See notes in those episodes for more on the international presence of China during this period.

"Maudling, Mrs. Reginald" — ("Mrs. Thing and Mrs. Entity") Maudling was a Conservative MP and Cabinet secretary, and is mentioned/ridiculed perhaps more than any other living politician in *FC*. "Mrs. Reginald Maudling" was Beryl Laverick Maudling, and they were married in 1939. A favorite lightning rod for the Pythons and the Left, then-Home Secretary Maudling appeared on the BBC (news, election coverages, current and political affairs shows) more than 200 times in the late 1960s and through the course of the run of *Flying Circus*. See the BBC Programme Catalogue for more. Also, confirming Maudling's status as a recognizable face of the Conservatives, just between 1969 and 1974 Maudling is lampooned in at least 275 political cartoons in newspapers of every kind in the UK. See the British Cartoon Archive. He is also mentioned (favorably and not) in hundreds of period newspaper articles.

"Mein Lieber Gott" — ("Beethoven's Mynah Bird") Beethoven's German expressions of frustration translate as: "My dear God" and "God in Heaven."

"Mendelssohns" — ("Beethoven's Mynah Bird") Felix Mendelssohn (1809–1847) was born into a Jewish family, but later converted. He wasn't alive when Beethoven was composing his Fifth Symphony. Mendelssohn became friends with Goethe in 1821 (see note for Goethe). Mendelssohn's wife was Cecile Jeanrenaud, and they would have five children.

"Michelangelo" — ("Michelangelo" link into "Colin Mozart [Ratcatcher]") Michelangelo (1475–1564) was an Italian Renaissance painter, poet, and sculptor, and preferred men to women, at least romantically.

"Mozart" — ("Colin Mozart [Ratcatcher]") Presumably Wolfgang Amadeus Mozart (1756–1791), he also appears in Ep. 1, as the host of "Famous Deaths." W.A. Mozart did have two sons (with Constanze Weber), Karl Thomas (1784–1858) and minor composer F.X. Mozart (1791–1844).

Wolfgang and Constanze had six children together, two of whom lived into adulthood, and both children pursued music-affiliated careers.

"Mrs. Thing" — (PSC; "Mrs. Thing and Mrs. Entity") Probably a reference to philosopher Nietzsche's work on the impossibility of a "thing-in-itself," and the importance of "relationships" and "actions" (see *The Will to Power*).

"Mugsy Spaniel" — ("*Animation: Giant ball in Wembley, Mugsy Spaniel, Eggs Diamond,* and *Raising Gangsters for Fun & Profit*") The gangster name here is a bricolage of references, including "Mugsy," who was a hulking Warner Bros. cartoon thug in the mid-1950s (*Bugsy and Mugsy*, 1957), which was also a variation on "Bugsy" Siegel (1906–1947), the American gangster credited with building Las Vegas.

The room behind Mugsy is another appearance of Plate 28 from de Vries's *Perspective*.

• N •

"Nabarro, Sir Gerald" — ("Leapy Lee") A rather flamboyant Conservative MP, Nabarro is mentioned and lampooned in *FC* more than once. See notes to Eps. 2, 11, and 15. Nabarro will also be mentioned by name in Ep. 23, and an image of him is defaced in Ep. 2.

"National Trust" — ("Silly Vicar") The National Trust was founded in the nineteenth century to preserve the UK's historic buildings and places. This type of publicized appeal isn't uncommon. In the late 1920s there was a concerted effort on behalf of the National Trust to save Stonehenge, for example, including newspaper advertisements and broadsides. In early 1969, the Benson Report was released, outlining "sweeping changes" to the management and implementation of the trust.

• O •

"Off-Spin Bowling" — ("Trailer") A cricket bowling term, this is a spin that moves the ball from the off side and toward the leg side. See Rundell's *The Dictionary of Cricket* (1995).

Old Bailey — (PSC; "Poofy Judges") "Old Bailey" is mentioned here as a setting, and not in dialogue. Home of the Central Criminal Court, the Old Bailey features prominently in Ep. 15 and the "Spanish Inquisition" sketch.

"Old Man of Hoy" — ("Trailer") A prominent sandstone sea stack landmark about 137 meters high, found in the Orkney Islands. The Old Man had been climbed in 1967, and BBC cameras were there. See notes to Ep. 31 and 33 for more on this media event.

ono — (PSC; "Trailer") This is an acronym included in the printed script, "o.n.o.," "or near(est) offer," and is a note to the Pythons themselves and the show's researcher. In other words, in the case of a needed photo of the Flick Colby Dancers or Pan's People, any contemporary dance troupe picture would do, and the Pythons weren't sure what their researcher would be able to find in the interim.

"Owzat" — ("Trailer") A colloquialism used in cricket, meaning "How's that?"

• **P** •

"Panorama" — ("Trailer") Long-running (1953–) BBC current affairs program. See notes to Ep. 2, the "Mouse Problem" sketch.

Party Hints — ("Leapy Lee") This could be a reference to the popular and long-running morning talk show *Girl Talk* (1963–1970), where the female hosts covered topics ranging from the Cold War to celebrity gossip to health and home issues.

"pikelets" — ("Beethoven's Mynah Bird") A pikelet is a Western and Midland name for a kind of tea-cake, refocusing the Python frame of reference on the areas north and west of London, where most of them grew up, and firmly placing the Beethovens in the provincial middle-class.

"Pitt the Elder, Mrs. William" — ("Mrs. Entity and Mrs. Thing") William Pitt the Elder (1708–1778) was the first Earl of Chatham. Pitt had married Lady Hester Grenville in 1754, and probably never had to go truffle hunting, especially with her snout. Female pigs were commonly employed to sniff out the buried tubers.

"Polynesian influence" — ("*Archaeology Today*") Explorer Thor Heyerdahl spent the better part of his long career proving that aboriginal peoples did indeed have the technological expertise to build rafts that could cross oceans successfully. As late as 1997, fifty years after his voyages began, Heyerdahl still held firm to the seafaring thesis, and blasted the ethnocentrism of his detractors:

> We Europeans are so one-track-minded when it comes to our own history that we say to the world that Europe discovered the whole world . . . I say that no European has discovered anything but Europe." (Interview posted at greatdreams.com/thor.htm, 18 Apr. 2002)

Heyerdahl's crafts, Kon Tiki, Ra, and Ra II are mentioned in Ep. 28.

"Porter, Cole, with Pearl Bailey and Arthur Negus" — ("*Archaeology Today*") American singer Bailey (1918–1990) released the composer Porter (1891–1964) cover album *Pearl Bailey Sings the Cole Porter Songbook* during this period. Arthur Negus (1903–1985), already mentioned prominently in Ep. 19, "Election Night Special," was a popular antiques expert and television personality. He had recently appeared on *The Jimmy Logan Show* in 1969.

"Porter, Nyree Dawn" — ("Trailer") Porter (1936–2001) was a New Zealand–born actress who starred in the 1967 BBC2 staging of Galsworthy's twenty-two-hour *The Forsyte Saga*.

• **Q** •

"QC's" — ("Poofy Judges") "Queen's Counsel," meaning in the service of the queen. Not called so because of Elizabeth, but thanks to the very long reign of Queen Victoria, and the appellation stuck. As one trained in the law, Cleese would have been very familiar with this world.

"Queen's evidence" — ("Judges") Play on the double meaning of the term "queen," of course. *OED*: "To turn King's (Queen's, State's) evidence (formerly also to turn evidence), said of an accomplice or sharer in a crime: to offer himself as a witness for the prosecution against the other persons implicated." Secondly, in Ep. 10, David Unction (Chapman) calls himself "an old queen" as he's caught reading a male physique magazine.

Quiet party type music — (PSC; "Mr. and Mrs. Git") This light, vibraphone-type music is from the Franco Chiari Jazz Quartet, and is called "Romantic Theme" (WAC T12/1,429).

• **R** •

"rat-bag" — ("Beethoven's Mynah Bird") Originally Australian and New Zealand slang, the *OED* defines it in terms ranging from "stupid" to foolish and even "uncouth." Used in Eps. 10, 16, 27, and 37 as well.

ratcatcher — ("Colin Mozart [Ratcatcher]") Cf. Ep. 20 for an earlier appearance of a ratcatcher.

Registrar — (PSC; "Registrar [Wife Swap]") The Registrar is the local official who keeps records for marriages, births, deaths, etc. (*OED*). The Registrar wouldn't actually perform the wedding ceremony.

"Reverend Arthur Belling" — ("Silly Vicar [The Reverend Arthur Belling]") Belling will be featured again in Ep. 36, there played by Palin, where he will smash plates and worry about disturbing those around him.

Roy Spim — (PSC; "Mosquito Hunters") Idle plays this character as a one-armed Australian big game hunter. This may be a reference to Alan John "Jock" Marshall (1911–1967), an eminent, larger-than-life Australian academic and zoologist who was a Reader at St. Bartholomew's Hospital, where Chapman studied.

• S •

"Scottish Assizes" — ("Judges") Assizes are periodic courts held throughout the United Kingdom since the twelfth century, but especially in England and Wales. The long-running joke of the well-endowed Scotsman is employed here, as well, as elsewhere in *FC* (including Ep. 37, the "Nae Trews" section of the "Ideal Loon Exhibition").

Shakespeare washing up at a sink — (PSC; "Shakespeare" link into "Colin Mozart [Ratcatcher]") What the Pythons are doing here is moving away from the "Great Man" approach to history, at least as it's usually pursued. The Pythons would have grown up with the historical approach of Thomas Carlyle (1795–1881) and undoubtedly read the *Encyclopedia Britannica Eleventh Edition* (1911), both of which focused on the noble and heroic endeavors of the greatest men in/on "History." History could be read and accessed, then, only through the exploits of such great men.

The Pythons are clearly responding to both the New Criticism rejection of biography in favor of close textual reading, the French New History movement of the late 1960s, as well as anticipating fellow Englishman Stephen Greenblatt's (Ep. 27) New Historicist movement, the second and third of which are more interested in the influence and deformative effects of culture and society on history. Also, the seemingly less significant events of history—ignored by the Great Man theorists—become much more visible and effective in such histories, where Shakespeare can participate in the housework; Beethoven can compete with his wife, household pets, and a sugar bowl; and Michelangelo can play wetnurse to his own brood. This is the elevating of the domestic to the (ig)noble, and where the Pythons spend a great deal of their time and energies in *FC*.

"Silbury Dig" — ("*Archaeology Today*") In 1967 an enormous archaeological dig was begun to determine the makeup and reasons for existence of Silbury Mound (or Silbury Hill, Avebury, Wiltshire), the largest man-made prehistoric mound in Europe. The mound had previously been explored at least three times, in 1732, 1776–1777, and sometime in the nineteenth century, the remnants of which were found in the 1967–1969 dig. BBC2 shot hours of documentary footage for its *Chronicle* program, and viewers by the millions tuned in to watch the findings. (Mortimer Wheeler was attached to this show. See the entry for "characters are in twenties'" above for more on Wheeler.) By October 1969, the excavation was ceremonially filled in, leaving more questions than answers. Prof. Richard Atkinson led the dig, and the BBC's Paul Johnstone headed up the footage compilation. Dr. John Taylor was the mining engineer. Many saw the whole thing as a major embarrassment and boondoggle, since a much hoped-for burial site was not unearthed.

The *Times* were a bit more kind, but still admitted some frustrations:

> On Saturday B.B.C. 2's *Chronicle* came up with another episode in that long-running serial *The Silbury Dig*. At last we were taken to the heart of this vast Wiltshire mound but, like Magnus Magnusson, I thought the most exciting part of the excavation was seeing subterranean blades of grass and moss that had grown in prehistoric times. . . . It was a fascinating programme but not without its oddities. For instance, the discovery of a squashed matchbox dating from 1915 generated a good deal of excitement. But Professor Richard Atkinson said that the worst thing that could happen during the dig would be for them to make a really dramatic find since that would hold up the excavation. I was rather surprised since I thought no devoted archaeologist would ever look a gift skeleton in the mouth. ("Farewell with Few Regrets," 29 July 1968: 7)

snooker cue — (PSC; "Trailer") A stick (like a pool cue) used in this billiard table game that combines pool and pyramids. Televised snooker is and has been a fixture on British TV for many years.

Snooker will be mentioned again by Mrs. Thing (Chapman) as she and Mrs. Entity (Idle) discuss the non-drudgery of married life, especially for wealthy Conservatives like Mrs. Reginald Maudling.

"sod" — ("Beethoven's Mynah Bird") An insult generally meaning one who practices sodomy. In this case, the term is used as a crude invective, essentially meaning "screw the sugar bowl." This same word was earlier censored by a nervous BBC before the taping of Ep. 17, in the "Architect Sketch," and was replaced (by Cleese then, too) with a blown "raspberry." The viewing audience's toleration of such crudities seems to have reached new levels by this time, and the word made it through.

"Stolle, Mrs. Fred" — ("Leapy Lee") Pat Stolle is the wife of British tennis player Fred Stolle (b. 1938, Australia) mentioned in Ep. 7. Stolle is winner of eighteen grand slam titles.

street with old-fashioned shops — ("Colin Mozart [Ratcatcher]") The music that creeps in under this transition is Mozart's "Eine Kleine Nachtmusik" (G-dur KV525) (WAC T12/1,429). This is the Rondo: Allegro movement.

This scene is shot at Elm Hill, Norwich, where a large number of early sixteenth-century Tudor homes and buildings can still be found (WAC T12/1,413).

"Swanage" — ("Mr. and Mrs. Git") A Dorset coastal village south of Bournemouth, where the Pythons performed significant location shooting.

"Swanton, E.W." — ("Trailer") "Jim" Swanton (1907–2000) was a longtime cricket writer for the *Daily Telegraph,* and a former player for MCC. He was also part of the first radio broadcasts of international cricket matches in the late 1930s, and made the transition to television cricket commentating (*ODNB*).

• T •

take the name — (PSC; link out of "Registrar [Wife Swap]") Referees in football (soccer) take names of those charged with infractions, keeping a record of the game and allowing for punitive action (i.e., disqualification) if additional penalties are incurred by the particular player. Those substituting must also be named with the officials. This moment continues the sporting theme of the episode.

"Talk of the Town" — ("Trailer") A very popular, trendy restaurant and cabaret (and general performance space) in London's Hippodrome that opened in 1958. The Talk of the Town billed itself as "the world's most modern theatre restaurant," and hosted the best dance troupes and bands. The venue was also a valuable recording and performing space. The Temptations, for example, would record a live album at the club in the summer of 1970, and Paul Anka (mentioned in this same episode) was performing there in September 1970.

tense music as they worm their way forward — (PSC; "Mosquito Hunters") This mood music is Ronald Hanmer's "Elephant Country" followed by bits of "Heroic Saga" (WAC T12/1,429).

"Thatcher, Margaret" — ("Leapy Lee") Idle does actually look like Thatcher here. Now Baroness Thatcher (b. 1925), she was in 1970 a leading Conservative politician, first elected to the House of Commons in 1959 as Member for Finchley (*ODNB*). She was a vocal front-bencher 1964–1970, in the opposition, and in 1970 in the Heath government was appointed secretary of state for education and science. Thatcher would have been the archenemy to Pythons' liberality during this period, and is often derided (usually in Gilliam's pictorials) as a heartless Tory.

theme and film titles as for a Western — (PSC; "*Archaeology Today*") The "Western-type" theme music here is "Overland to Oregon Part 1" (WAC T12/1,429).

"third dynasty" — ("*Archaeology Today*") (c. 2686–2575 BC) Representing the first part of the Egyptian "Old Kingdom," the Third Dynasty covers about six rulers and about seventy-five years. Pharaohs in this dynasty were the first to construct (step) pyramids as shrines to themselves. Imhotep was born during this dynasty.

"Today I hear the robin sing" — ("*Archaeology Today*") This song was written by Bill McGuffie, who received £20 for this and another composition heard in Ep. 17 (WAC T12/1,242). The script indicates that McGuffie plays a Hammond organ as accompaniment. McGuffie also plays accompaniment for Cleese and Chapman as they sing in Ep. 3.

"too sharp" — ("Judges") Meaning here too keen, too brisk, and too forward, even.

"treacle" — ("Silly Vicar") Variously a molasses-type syrup, and, anciently, a pharmacological concoction.

"trench" — ("*Archaeology Today*") Miss Vanilla Hoare (Cleveland) acts in a trench (and has acted previously in a furrow and syncline) in Ep. 23. The significant height difference between members of the troupe was the subject of some conversation, reportedly, and here finds its way into the final staged product. There is also the real possibility that what the Pythons are lampooning are the academic reputations of archaeologists diminishing as a result of Silbury-like frustrations, leaving other archaeologists "taller" in the profession.

"Truss" — ("Silly Vicar") Probably not a misprint, and the clever assumption would be that the Pythons meant to equate the work and value of the landmark-saving National Trust (est. 1895) with that of a hernia appliance. See the entry for "National Trust" above for more. Trusses will be mentioned again (and depicted) in Ep. 26, when the "Hercules Hold-Em-In" is pitched prior to *Fish Club*.

"two thousand years before" — ("*Archaeology Today*") A memorial mistake here, as the young Tut ruled about a thousand years before the temple at Abu Simbel was even built. Ramesses II commissioned the temple to commemorate his own rule, and it was completed in about 1264 BC.

• U •

"used to have to get up at midnight" — ("Mrs. Thing and Mrs. Entity") This oneupsmanship structure is reminiscent of the "Four Yorkshire Gentlemen" sketch first seen on *At Last the 1948 Show* in 1967.

• W •

"waggled" — ("Poofy Judges") Cf. Wodehouse's usage of the word in *The Code of the Woosters*, where its coquettish possibilities are highlighted: "She *waggled* her chin, like a girl who considers that she has put over a swift one" (192). Just a few pages later, this same character (the charming and scheming "Stiffy"), "*wiggled* from base to apex with girlish enthusiasm" (206).

"Washington Post March" — (PSC; "Beethoven's Mynah Bird") Composed by John Philip Sousa (1854–1932). Cleese had written lyrics for this tune for the *At Last the 1948 Show*, and called it "Rhubarb Tart." He also performed the song, though the audience reaction (a mild laugh) doesn't seem to indicate they recognize the intertextual reference. The *FC* theme song is a version of another Sousa composition, "Liberty Bell."

"Watutsi" — ("*Archaeology Today*") Actually spelled "Watusi," they are a minority racial group historically in Rwanda and Burundi (*OED*). The Interviewer (Palin) probably means the Maasai tribe, who often grow to more than six feet tall.

"well-hung" — ("Judges") Another sexual play on words. A hung jury is one that cannot agree on a verdict, while a well-hung man is one who possesses larger-than-average genitalia.

"West, Peter, and Brian Johnston" — ("Trailer") Both mentioned prominently in the previous episode. The significant presence of cricket in Eps. 20 and 21 certainly indicates the high media saturation level that Test cricket was enjoying as England played host to "Rest of the World" in the summer months of 1970. Johnston was called "the voice of cricket," and Peter West was also a much-loved cricket broadcaster. See notes to Ep. 20.

Women's Institute — (PSC; "Leapy Lee") Stock black-and-white footage of women applauding. See notes for "Women's Institute" in Ep. 2.

"Wostenholme, Kenneth" — ("Trailer") Kenneth *Wolstenholme* (1920–2002) was a sports broadcaster, his credits including the monumental and memorable 1966 World Cup final at Wembley. He also appeared on *Sportsview* with David Coleman, and hosted *Match of the Day* on BBC1 and BBC2.

For a contemporary review of these venerable BBC presenters, there is an illuminating discussion of the various merits of sports coverage on the up-and-coming ITA and the age-old, perhaps tired BBC:

> Now the smug complacency of the B.B.C. is being challenged, to the satisfaction of those who have come to resent the arrogance shown by the B.B.C., both on the screen and off it, to say nothing of the ludicrous overselling of an inferior article. . . . A frenetic commentary accompanying a spurious race among bits of motor cars on a mud heap makes us pine for more of Raymond Baxter [Ep. 20], and if we are ever spared the over-dimpled smile of Frank Bough [Ep. 35] there will probably be no escape from the fixed one of Kenneth Wolstenholme [Ep. 21] or the abrasive assault on our ear drums by David Coleman [Ep. 21]. ("Challenge to Complacency and Arrogance," *Times*, 19 Feb. 1969: 12)

The fight was on for coverage rights to the 1972 Olympics, and opinions (ITA vs. BBC) flew back and forth in the media.

Episode 22: "How to Recognize Different Parts of the Body"

Bikini girls; "And now . . ." Man and "It's" Man in bikinis; *Titles* (silly Cleese v/o); "How to recognize different parts of the body" (including naughty bits); **Bruces: The Philosophy Department of the University of Woolamaloo**; More naughty bits; The man who contradicts people; "And now . . ." Man and a pig; Cosmetic surgery; Doctor and patient relationship; The men of the Derbyshire Light Infantry: Camp square-bashing and close-order swanning about; *Animation: Dancing Generals, Suicidal Man, Bus Stop Eyeball, The Killer Cars,* and *Atomic-Mutated Cat*; Cut-price airline; Uninteresting tales of the sea; The "Where to put Edward Heath's statue?" competition; Batley Townswomen's Guild presents "The first heart transplant"; The first underwater production of "Measure for Measure" (and *Hello Dolly*, Formula Two car racing); More "How to recognize different parts of the body"; **The radio version of "The death of Mary Queen of Scots"**; Radio 4 explodes; Exploding penguin on TV set; More "How to recognize different parts of the body"; The interior of a country house: "There's been a murder"; **Europolice Song Contest**; "Bing Tiddle Tiddle Bong" (song); closing credits

• A •

"Abbos" — ("Bruces") A derogatory abbreviation of "aborigine," and in this period more commonly spelled "abos" (*OED*). The plight of the aboriginal people would have been much discussed in relation to the Queen's most recent visit to Australia, certainly. Aborigines had been enfranchised only recently, beginning in 1963, and in 1967 were included for the first time in legislative and census decisions and activities.

"And so on and so on and so on . . ." — (link out of "The Man Who Contradicts People") Cleese's acknowledgment of the familiarity and repetitive (and even tedious) nature of this interrupted sketch points up a growing disaffection for both the material and structure, as well as the difficulty the Pythons were already encountering (well into the second season) in generating afresh the "Pythonesque" elements. In this they are struggling as all Modern Art types struggle—with the constant need for new outrages, new definitions, new reactions.

a penguin . . . sits contentedly looking at them in a stuffed sort of way — (PSC; *"The Death of Mary Queen of Scots"*) Once again, the penguin appears as a source of incongruous humor. There's no rational reason for the penguin to be atop the TV, which is probably why they've included him, and just as little reason for it to explode later. Also, the printed script is once again creating in-jokes—references for the other *readers* only.

In Ep. 16 a sitting cat is pointed out (by an inserted arrow, no less) before it blows up. No explanation offered there, either, though our attention is drawn to it just before it explodes.

• B •

"Barley sugar" — ("Cut-Price Airline") Doses of barley sugar sweets have been known to help diabetics get the "sugar injection" they may need before stressful activities, and has been a traditional treatment for upset stomachs and sore throats for many years.

It might be just coincidental that Man (Idle) also crosses his fingers in a "barley cross" gesture, essentially indemnifying himself from whatever he's just averred. The barley cross fingers motif was earlier mentioned in Ep. 8, "Army Protection Racket," there also by Idle.

"Battle of Pearl Harbour performed by . . ." — ("Batley Townswomen's Guild Presents The First Heart Transplant") This messy sketch, with a new introduction, will appear as part of the Pythons' contribution to *Euroshow 71—May Day Special*, along with "All-In Cricket," "Fish Slapping Dance," and "*Match of the Day* (hugging)," as well as new linking material.

BEA, TWA, Air India, BOAC — (PSC; "Cut-Price Airline") BEA began as BEAC (British European Airways Corporation) on 1 August 1946, the European division of the British state airline, BOAC. In 1947 fourteen British airline companies were merged under BEA's control. TWA was Trans World Airlines, an American airline created as "Transcontinental & Western Air" in 1930. TWA was formed after a forced merger of regional airlines, as well. Air India began operations in 1948. BOAC was British Overseas Airways Corporation, and was Britain's state airline from 1939–1974.

The introduction of the new airline consortium Airbus in 1970 had something to do with the genesis of this sketch. There was a general fear of mongrelization from many in the UK as the Common Market became more and more real, and forced cooperation with the French and others loomed large.

"Birmingham . . . Burnley . . . Barclay's" — ("Eurovision Song Contest") Birmingham is a large northwestern city near Idle's old stomping grounds, while Burnley is much farther north in Lancashire, not far north of Bolton. Barclay's has been in the banking business in the UK since the seventeenth century.

"bit crook" — ("Bruces") Australian and New Zealand slang for bad or unpleasant.

"blank verse" — ("The First Underwater Production of *Measure for Measure*") Unrhymed verse, which was introduced by the Earl of Surrey in the early sixteenth century. The line of dialogue heard seconds later—"Servant ho!"—is found nowhere in *Measure for Measure*, incidentally.

"Board of Trade" — ("Cut-Price Airline") Very much in the news at this juncture, the Board of Trade ceased in some ways and continued unabated in others in the fall of 1970 as its duties were subsumed into the Department of Trade and Industry.

"both bodies flown back" — ("Cut-Price Airline") This treatment of the airline industry is probably generated by the instability of that industry in the late 1960s and early 1970s (see the "BEA" note above), as well as the still-recent crash of an Ariana Afghan Airlines 727 at Gatwick Airport, where fifty people died. Also, the number and frequency of hijackings continued to escalate, further discouraging Britons from air travel.

"Brandt, Willi" — ("Batley Townswomen's Guild Presents the First Heart Transplant") West German Chancellor "Willy" Brandt arranged and attended the first postwar German-German summit; his counterpart was the East German Prime Minister, Willi Stoph. The summit was held in the East German town of Erfurt in March 1970. East German crowds reportedly chanted "Willy!" in support of the visiting leader.

"Bronowski" — ("Exploding Penguin on TV Set") Dr. Jacob Bronowski (1908–1974) presented the popular BBC series *The Ascent of Man* (1973), but prior to that he appeared on *The Brains Trust* (1950), where the young Pythons most likely first encountered him.

"Brussels . . . Cromer" — ("Cosmetic Surgery") Brussels, Liege, Antwerp, and Asse are all cities in Belgium. Cromer is actually the name of a series of geologic features—freshwater deposits featuring abundant fossils, specifically—found at the coast of Cromer, Norfolk. The Pythons shot much of their second season location footage in the Norwich, Norfolk region.

• C •

"Camp Square-Bashing" — ("Camp Square-Bashing") "Square-bashing" is military slang for marching, drilling. In the feature film *Meaning of Life*, recruits who don't want to go "marching up and down the square" are allowed to beg out for piano practice, family time, the cinema, etc. "Bashing" can also carry a masturbation association, which fits the sexualized nature of the send-up.

"classical philosophy" — ("Bruces") Referring to noted ancien regime philosophers, including those who will later play on the Greek football team (Plato, Socrates, Aristotle, et al.) against the more "modern" Germans (Leibniz, Wittgenstein, Heidegger, et al.) in the Philosophers' Football Match created for the second *Fliegender Zirkus* episode.

"colour sergeant" — ("Camp Square-Bashing") A non-commissioned rank in the British Army infantry regiments.

"come on a camping holiday" — ("Cosmetic Surgery") This same type of alleged professional relationship (in this case, a simple doctor-and-patient two-set), followed by the pay-off of an aberrant (read: incongruous) sexual relationship is earlier explored with a policeman (Cleese) and victim (Palin) in Ep. 13, the "Come Back to My Place" sketch.

"confusion" — ("Bruces") The implication here, then, is that nonconformity is the cause of confusion, not conformity.

"Coronation Scot" — (PSC; *"The Death of Mary Queen of Scots"*) This theme (from the BBC's *Paul Temple* radio series) is performed by the Queens Hall Light Orchestra, and is by Vivian Ellis (WAC T12/1,432). *Paul Temple* was a crime novel detective show heard on British radio between 1938 and 1968, and in 1969 made for German TV, as well.

"crack the tubes" — ("Bruces") A "tube" is an Australian colloquialism for a beer can. The phrase simply means to open the cans of beer.

• D •

"Derbyshire Light Infantry" — ("Camp Square-Bashing") The term "light" is probably meant to signal a sort of "light in the loafers" connotation, meaning to be light on one's feet, originally, and later a prancing, poncing man.

There is an Oxfordshire and Buckinghamshire Light infantry unit in existence, among others, while light infantry units were often termed "irregulars," the othering being significant in this usage.

These "swanning about" scenes were shot at the Stanford Training Area, West Tofts Camp, Norfolk, where they also shot some of the mosquito hunt footage (Ep. 21), exercising patients (Ep. 26), and idiots for episode 20 (Wac T12/1,430).

dog-collar — (PSC; "Bruces") Clerical collar slapped on by the padre. See notes to Ep. 19.

"ducky" — ("Camp Square-Bashing") A term of endearment.

"duty-free" — ("Cut-Price Airline") Most international airports have duty-free shops, where items can be purchased with no customs or excise taxes collected.

• E •

"eccles cakes" — ("Cut-Price Airline") Small, grape-filled cakes, originally, and supposedly named after the town of Eccles, Salford.

eight soldiers — (PSC; "Camp Square-Bashing") The four in the back row clearly are Pythons, while those in the front rank are actual dancers, as they are much more fluid in their movements. These dancers were hired specifically for this episode, and are (in no discernible order) Roy Gunson (*The Avengers*), Ralph Wood, Alexander Curry, and John Clement (*Diary of a Sinner*) (WAC T12/1,432).

"elevenses" — ("Bruces") Light refreshment taken at about 11:00 a.m., also called "elevens."

Episode 22 — Recorded 25 September 1970, then broadcast on 24 November 1970. It was the tenth episode recorded, and the ninth broadcast. Previously unnamed walk-ons for this episode include Karen Kerr, Nick Moody, Malcolm Holbrooks, and John Freeman (*Adam Adamant Lives!*) (WAC T12/1,432). They each seem to have posed for "Naughty Bits" still photos, and were brought in from the Jaclyn Model Agency (WAC T12/1,432).

Eurovision — (PSC; "Europolice Song Contest") A very popular Pan-European song contest. On 24 March 1969, in Madrid, Spain (at the Teator Real), sixteen countries competed. Representing the United Kingdom was Lulu, singing "Boom Bang-a-Bang." (The Pythons would later be nearly sued for perceived infringement of copyright in relation to this song and their publication *Monty Python's Big Red Book* [see Hewison's *Monty Python*, 29–30].) In March 1970 the contest was won by Ireland's Dana singing "All Kinds of Everything." The presenter in 1970 was Willy Dobbe, and the show was hosted by the Netherlands.

Eurovision girl — ("Europolice Song Contest") The presenter in the 1969 Eurovision Song Contest was Laurita Valenzuela (b. 1931), a possible source for Pythons' Girl (Idle) host, but the 1968 host, Brit Katie Boyle (whom Idle seems made-up to resemble), is the more likely target here. See notes to Ep. 38 for another mention of Boyle, there as a possible "loony."

• F •

"fairly butch" — (*"The Death of Mary Queen of Scots"*) To be described as "butch" is to be perceived as either an aggressive, masculine woman, a tough youth, or, more appropriately for the Pythons, a non-mincing gay man.

"first heart transplant" — ("Batley Townswomen's Guild Presents the First Heart Transplant") The world's first heart transplant took place in Groote Schuur Hospital in South Africa. Professor Christiaan

Barnard performed the surgery on 3 December 1967. The recipient lived eighteen days with the new heart.

Also, Barnard was pictured on the cover of the satirical magazine *Private Eye* on 6 June 1969, and there are more than thirty mentions of the historic operation in the political cartoon pages of UK newspapers. The editors of *PE* follow the exploits of Barnard for a few issues, cataloging the deaths of his patients, his publicity stunts, and the general furore over the "miraculous" new technology (that seemed to signal a death sentence for each and every patient). In many interviews after the death of his first patient (Louis Washkansky) and just after the implantation of his second (Dr. Blaiberg), Barnard seemed, however, both hopeful and humble: "We give a patient a little extra life to sit in the sun again, to listen to the birds and that is the only reason for a heart transplantation" ("I Give Extra Life Barnard Says," *Times*, 10 Oct. 1969: 2). This was printed just five days after the first airing of episode one of *Flying Circus*. Less than three weeks earlier Barnard had been in London speaking about the palliative value of heart transplants, as well.

"flying philosopher" — ("Bruces") Perhaps referring to the dream of the philosopher Chang Tzou (c. fourth century BC), where he becomes the butterfly, or the butterfly becomes him. The "butterfly dream" has found its way into Western philosophy as well.

Also, when the Queen visited Australia in 1963 she toured the *Flying Doctor* Service base in Alice Springs. Pictures of that particular visit can be found in the National Library of Australia. The Flying Doctor Service brought modern medicine and physicians into contact with outback dwellers and aborigines alike.

"Formula 2" — (link out of "The First Underwater Production of *Measure for Measure*") An auto race circuit introduced in 1947 for those drivers who could not qualify for the Formula 1 circuit, and which served as a sort of minor league for the faster, more expensive, and more exclusive Formula 1 level.

Fred Tomlinson Singers — (PSC; "There's Been a Murder") The PCs in the drawing room sketch behind Sgt. Duckie are Tomlinson's singers, with accompanist Jennifer Partridge somewhere offscreen.

"F.R.S." — ("Cosmetic Surgery") Most of the acronyms on this rather long list are actual appellations, as follows:

"F.R.S."—Fellow of the Royal Society

"F.R.C.S."—Fellow of the Royal College of Surgeons

"F.R.C.P."—Fellow of the Royal College of Physicians

"M.D.M.S. (Oxon)"—Doctor of Medicine, Master of Science from Oxford University ("Oxon" indicates Oxford University, and is only used in titles)

"M.A., Ph.D., M.Sc. (Cantab)"—Master of Arts, Doctor of Philosophy, and Master of Science, Cambridge University (the last indicating Cambridge University, and also used only in titles)

"Ph.D. (Syd)"—Doctor of Philosophy, University of Sydney

"F.R.G.S."—Fellow of the Royal Geographical Society

"F.R.C.O.G."—Fellow of the Royal College of Obstetricians and Gynaecologists

"F.F.A.R.C.S."—Fellow of the Faculty of Anaesthetists of the Royal College of Surgeons

"Birm"—Degrees from University of Birmingham

"M.S. (Liv)"—M.S. degrees from University of Liverpool ("Liv"), Guadalajara University ("Guadalahara") in Mexico, the University of Karachi ("Karach") in Pakistan (originally part of pre-British India, and then the British Raj), and the University of Edinburgh ("Edin")

"B.A. (Chic)"—Bachelor of Arts, University of Chicago

"B.Litt."—Bachelor of Literature, Bachelor of Letters

"D.Litt."—Doctor of Letters

"Ottawa"—University of Ottawa, Ontario

"Medicine Hat"—In Alberta, Canada. There is also a Medicine Hat College, incidentally

"B.Sc."—Bachelor of Science

Chapman's training and qualification as a medical doctor were undoubtedly referenced as this sketch was created.

• G •

gorgeous lovelies in bikinis — (PSC; link into "*How to Recognize Different Parts of the Body*") These actresses/models include—in approximately this order—Flanagan (Eps. 7, 11–13, 20; *Benny Hill*), Beulah Hughes (Eps. 29, 33, 34; *Hands of the Ripper*), Marie (a popular erotic model of the day, Marie can also be seen in nudie posters advertised in *Private Eye*), Barbara Lindley (Ep. 18; *Benny Hill*), and Sandra Richards (Ep. 17) (WAC T12/1,242).

"great socialist thinkers" — ("Bruces") This would certainly include at least the Structuralist school so popular in the 1960s and 1970s in Europe, including luminaries such as Ferdinand de Saussure, Claude Levi-Strauss, Lacan, Foucault, and Althusser.

The seminal importance of language and linguistic structures as the foundation of contemporary philosophy cannot be overstressed, especially for its influence on the Pythons (and the arts in general during this period). The fact that the speaker is now structured by his speech resonates throughout *Flying Circus* and the feature films, allowing peasants to banter with kings, words like "it" to carry cosmic significance, and things to simply be or not be by mere invocation.

• H •

Harley Street — (PSC; "Cosmetic Surgery") Center of the high-end medical establishment in London, it will be mentioned again in Eps. 32 and 37.

"Haydon-Jones, Ann" — (link into *"The Death of Mary Queen of Scots"*) Popular tennis player Haydon-Jones has already been mentioned in Eps. 7 and 19. See notes to Ep. 7 for more.

"Hegelian philosophy" — ("Bruces") G.W.F. Hegel (1770–1831) was a post-Kantian German idealist who posited that "the rational alone is real."

"*Hello, Dolly!* is also doing good business" — ("The First Underwater Production of *"Measure for Measure"*) The stage run for the popular musical *Hello, Dolly!* had been doing good business, on Broadway and in the West End—it was the film version (starring Barbra Streisand, Walter Matthau, and Michael Crawford; directed by Gene Kelly) that was underwater, financially speaking. See the entry for "20th Century Vole" in Ep. 23 for more.

"Hollowood, Bernard, and Brian London" — (*"The Death of Mary Queen of Scots"*) Bernard Hollowood (1911–1981) was a writer and editor, publishing in the 1950s and 1960s in literary magazines including *Lilliput*. Hollowood also edited *Punch* magazine (1957–1968) and was resident pocket cartoonist for same. Hollowood's cartoons have been donated to the British Cartoon Archive at the University of Kent. Hollowood had published the book *Cricket on the Brain* in 1970.

Private Eye satirizes Hollowood in a Gerald Scarfe cartoon in the 7 August 1964 issue, where he is depicted being knighted as a wanna-be cricketer (Ingrams, 108).

Brian London has already been mentioned (Ep. 13), and was an English boxer (fl. 1955–1970). See the entry for Brian London in notes for Ep. 13.

"How to Recognize Different Parts of the Body" — (*"How to Recognize Different Parts of the Body"*) Reminiscent of the sketch *"How to Recognize Different Types of Trees from Quite a Long Way Away"* from Ep. 3. These may be references to the myriad WWII-era public information films created for the homefront on both sides of the Atlantic, including *Recognition of the Zero Fighter* (1943). It's also reminiscent of the various "how to"–type (now "DIY") shows on British television, and lampooned by the Pythons in Ep. 26 (*"How to Feed a Goldfish"*) and Ep. 28 (*"How to Rid the World of All Known Diseases"*).

• I •

"Inspector Zatapathique" — ("Eurovision Song Contest") Brian Zatapathique (Palin) is presented in Ep. 2 as a "French Lecturer on Sheep-Aircraft," and again in Ep. 14.

"intercourse the penguin" — ("Exploding Penguin on TV Set") Rather than say "sod," "intercourse" is used in this phrase, though Cleese still manages to nearly laugh aloud at the mention. They had tried "sod" back in Ep. 17, and had to replace it with a raspberry sound. BBC higher-ups would regularly view the episodes, make a listing of potentially offensive words/scenes/references, and suggest changes (*Monty Python: The Case Against* 38–39). The Pythons generally tried to ignore the suggestions. In the LP versions of many of these sketches, the more graphic curse words are kept in place.

• K •

Kamikaze — (PSC; "Cut-Price Airline") This actor is Vincent Wong (*Doctor Who*), who will also appear in Ep. 43 as a Japanese businessman.

killer cars, story of the — (PSC; *Animation: Dancing Generals, Suicidal Man, Bus Stop Eyeball, The Killer Cars,* and *Atomic-Mutated Cat*) Photos used by Gilliam in this sequence include the following (those identifiable):

The building the red car leaps from behind is Her Majesty's Theatre, specifically the northernmost corner of the structure (at the Charles and Haymarket intersection). The following photo (where the yellow car pounces) offers another angle of the same theater building, this time from the front, while across the street (at the left of the screen) is the Charles Street-side of the theater (but not including the Royal Opera Arcade). Thus, we're seeing two sides of the same historic building on opposite sides of the same street in this Gilliam world.

After an unidentifiable Georgian neighborhood photo, Gilliam provides an image from Trafalgar Square, facing approximately southeast, the Nelson statue base (with lions) in the foreground, and buildings on The Strand in the background. This is the first photo scene the "Mutated Cat" walks through.

The following photo from the Mutated Cat sequence is a fairly recent snap of the Piccadilly Circus area, specifically Shaftesbury Avenue. (The background is the sunrise title card from *"It's the Arts"* in Ep. 6.) The photo can be dated based on the feature film playing at the London Pavilion, the 1961 drama *The Hoodlum Priest*, starring Don Murray (b. 1929) and Keir Dullea (*2001: A Space Odyssey*; b. 1936), and directed by Irvin Kershner (1923–2010), later of *Empire Strikes Back* fame. *Hoodlum Priest* appeared in London in July 1961. Also visible are the advertising signs for Lemon Hart, Wrigley's, and Max Factor, and (well up the street) the black-faced Golly character known for selling Robertson's jam products.

The next photo (after the giant hand has overcome the giant cat) is a return to the fantastical street created by Gilliam, featuring portions of Her Majesty's Theatre on both sides of the street.

In the following sequence, when frightened Londoners are escaping the killer hand, the third conveyance (after a train and a sailing ship) is a rendering of the 1827 steam coach invented by Goldsworthy Gurney (1793–1875), which operated between London and Bath. The sailing ship (with red-and-white striped sails) will be used again, in the animated sequence "*Overrun by Chinese Communists*" and "*the Domino theory*" in Ep. 24. The train image is borrowed from *Divided We Fought*, page 338, and is a U.S. military engine (the Union army). The reversed-image photo was taken at City Point, Virginia. The biplane is an early model seaplane, and the jet looks like a Pan Am Boeing 727.

• L •

"like this one" — (link into "Batley Townswomen's Guild Presents the First Heart Transplant") Similar to Python's "deflating" announcements in other episodes, including the "*Black Eagle*" intro of Ep. 25.

"logical positivism" — ("Bruces") The school of philosophy emerging from the Vienna Circle in the 1920s and 1930s, and set against, primarily, the metaphysical (and ultimately all speculative) approaches to philosophical questions.

lyrical film . . . frolicking in the countryside — (PSC; "Cosmetic Surgery") This location footage looks as if it were shot in the same area where the nature scenes for "*The Attila the Hun Show*" (Ep. 20) were photographed.

• M •

"Machiavelli . . . Benaud" — ("Bruces") Why the new Bruce (Jones) in the Philosophy Department will be teaching political science isn't clear, but the confusion with eminent cricketers quickly moots the point anyway.

"Machiavelli"—An Italian Renaissance philosopher and writer, Niccolo Machiavelli (1469–1527) wrote on republicanism and realist political theory, citing "force and prudence" as the basis for a successful government.

"Bentham"—Jeremy Bentham (1748–1832) was a noted English philosopher and social reformer (*ODNB*).

"Locke"—John Locke (1632–1704) influenced Bentham, but this Englishman would oppose Hobbes's "state of nature" with a "will of the people" approach to legitimate government.

"Hobbes"—Earlier English philosopher Thomas Hobbes (1588–1679) published *Leviathan* in 1651, proclaiming the social contract theory of political/social philosophy.

"Sutcliffe"—Probably meant to be Herbert Sutcliffe (1894–1978), an English (not Australian) cricketer whose best years came in the 1920s and early 1930s, long before the Pythons' births. The English team did enjoy a very successful tour of Australia in 1928–1929, where Sutcliffe batted with talented teammate Jack Hobbs (1882–1963). (See cricinfo.com for more complete statistics.)

"Bradman"—Australian cricketer Don Bradman (1908–2001) was a Wisden Cricketer of the Year in 1931. During the 1930s and 1940s, most considered Bradman to be the greatest cricketer in the world.

"Lindwall"—Ray Lindwall (1921–1996) was also an Australian cricketer, and was named Wisden Cricketer of the Year in 1949.

"Miller"—Australian Keith Miller (1919–2004) partnered with Lindwall, and was named Wisden Cricketer of the Year in 1954.

"Hassett"—Lindsay Hassett (1913–1993) followed Bradman as captain of the Australian team, and was named Wisden Cricketer of the Year in 1949.

"Benaud"—Richard Benaud (b. 1930) came much later than any of the above-mentioned cricketers, captaining the Australian team in 1958–1959 against England. Benaud was named Wisden Cricketer of the Year in 1962.

Bradman, Lindwall, Miller, and Hassett played together against England at Kennington Oval in London in 1948, winning 4–0. The young Pythons—aged between about five and nine at this time—may have been uniquely aware of England's poor showing in this 1948 match.

Mary is getting the shit knocked out of her — (PSC; "*The Death of Mary Queen of Scots*") This is one of the very few places where the Pythons include an actual curse word—one of those generally not allowed on broadcast television—and not just a crudity. Granted, the word only appears in the printed text, and a non-spoken portion at that.

Contemporary reports indicate that it took at least three blows of the executioner's axe to sever Mary's head, and—going along with the Pythons' "No I'm not" from Mary—she was still alive and perhaps even conscious after the first two strokes. See the *ODNB* for more on Mary.

"Mary, Queen of Scots" — (*"The Death of Mary Queen of Scots"*) Mary (1542–1587) was the only child of James V of Scotland, descended from the Stuart and Tudor houses, and a devout Catholic. Serialized dramas on the royal families (Stuarts, Plantagenets, Tudors, et al.) were common on BBC radio and then television, including *An Age of Kings* (1960), which covered five Shakespeare history plays in fifteen parts.

There was a feature film in production at this time, *Mary, Queen of Scots*, starring Vanessa Redgrave and Glenda Jackson, which would be released in 1971.

"Maudling, Reginald" — ("Naughty Bits") Oft-jabbed (by the Pythons) Conservative politician Maudling (1917–1979) was the embattled Home Secretary during this period. A lightning-rod figure to many, during the initial run of *Flying Circus*, Maudling is pilloried in more than three hundred political cartoons in UK newspapers, and was a regular in the pages of *Private Eye*, especially for his alleged financial improprieties and influence peddling.

"Measure for Measure" — ("The First Underwater Production of *Measure for Measure*") Shakespeare's 1604 play was performed first at King James's court. This was Shakespeare's last comedy, and was followed by a series of tragedies. These seaside scenes were shot on 9–10 June 1970 near Seaford Cliffs, Seaford (WAC T12/1,416).

mincing — (PSC; "Camp Square-Bashing") To walk or act in a dainty or effeminate manner.

"Monaco is the winner" — ("Europolice Song Contest") Monaco did compete in 1970, placing eighth.

Muffin the Mule — (PSC; "There's Been a Murder") Muffin was a popular and long-running marionette puppet character (fl. 1946–1955) on early British TV children's programs. The character had been on TV since the mid-1930s, but not named "Muffin" until 1946. In 1950, Muffin was being used to help teach children how to look properly before crossing a street. These were to be short films shown in schools.

This is yet another example of the printed script proffering information to which the intended audience—namely, viewers at home—had no access. The name "Muffin the Mule" isn't spoken in the scene, nor is it included in a caption—it was included for the Pythons themselves.

• N •

"Nolan, Sydney" — ("Bruces") Sidney Nolan (1917–1992) was perhaps the best-known Australian artist of this period, and his work often focused on life in and the people of Australia. Sir Kenneth Clark (Eps. 25 and 37) had "discovered" Nolan in 1949, and provided the means for his introduction to London and the art world (*ODNB*).

"no pooftahs" — ("Bruces") Not an unusual or even bigoted statement, certainly, since same-sex sexual activity ("buggery") wouldn't begin to be decriminalized in Australia until 1975. The Campaign against Moral Persecution (CAMP) was formed in 1970 in Australia, with gay and lesbian demonstrations appearing in the following year.

This sketch theme may have been at least partly inspired by Australian comedian Barry Humphries's popular monologues, including "A Nice Night's Entertainment." Also, Humphries's comic strip "Barry McKenzie" had been appearing regularly in *Private Eye* during this period, featuring a flamboyant, crude Aussie. A collection of these strips appeared in November 1968, titled *The Wonderful World of Barry McKenzie* (from Macdonald), with the display ad in the *Times* proclaiming "Hey, Pommies!" Humphries (b. 1934) might be better known for his most popular creation, Dame Edna Everage. In 1968, he'd been appearing with Spike Milligan in a *Treasure Island* panto at the Mermaid, and in 1969, Humphries's Edna Everage breakout performance, *Just a Show*, was playing at the Fortune Theatre.

Watching the Pythons trot out one Aussie stereotype after another makes it feel as if one or all of them had caught Humphries's popular show the night before writing this sketch. Theater critic Irving Wardle bemoans Humphries's one-note song, "a single-minded essay on the awfulness of Australia":

> Mr. Humphries scores very few direct hits on his outsize target. Instead of picking out anything really wrong with Australian life, he simply parades a group of Australian stereotypes at whom we are supposed to laugh just because they are different. ("Stern Days for Revue," *Times*, 12 Apr. 1969: 21)

There's even a Sidney Nolan joke (see Nolan entry above) in Humphries's act.

• P •

"padre" — ("Bruces") Generally referring to a chaplain, a padre also appeared in the big school production, *"Seven Brides for Seven Brothers"* sketch in Ep. 18.

"parcel post" — ("Cut-Price Airline") Simply the branch of the UK postal service that deals with posted (mailed) packages.

"perhaps it comes from next door" — ("Exploding Penguin on TV Set") In the Python world, such things can, in fact, be just next door. In Ep. 32, it turns out that Lake Pahoe is found at 22A Runcorn Avenue (*not* 22 Runcorn Avenue), the "Argument" office is just one along from "Abuse" (Ep. 29), and in Ep. 33, Mrs. Neves (Jones) steps out her kitchen door and onto the deck of a lifeboat.

picture of the cabinet at a table — (PSC; "Naughty Bits") Conservative Ted Heath's cabinet in late 1970 (he was elected in June) included: Home Secretary—Reginald Maudling; Lord Privy Seal—Earl Jellicoe; Lord Chancellor—Lord Hailsham; Chancellor of the Exchequer—Iain Macleod, then Anthony Barber; Secretary of State for Foreign and Commonwealth Affairs—Sir Alec Douglas-Home; Secretary of State for Defence—Lord Carrington; Secretary of State for Scotland—Gordon Campbell; Secretary of State for Social Services—Sir Keith Joseph; Secretary of State for Education and Science—Margaret Thatcher; Secretary of State for Trade and Industry and President of the Board of Trade—John Davies; Minister of Housing and Local Government—Peter Walker; Minister for Public Works—Julian Amery; Secretary of State for Employment—Antony Barber, then Robert Carr; Secretary of State for Wales—Peter Thomas; Minister of Agriculture, Fisheries, and Food—James Prior; Minister for Housing and Construction—Julian Amery; Minister of Overseas Development—Richard Wood; Minister of Technology—Geoffrey Rippon, then John Davies et al.

In the photo provided by/for Gilliam for this "Naughty Bits" sequence, Heath, Barber, Maudling, Jellicoe, Douglas-Home, and Thatcher are clearly visible. The photo is grainy enough that others in attendance can only be guessed. Heath sits at the center on the right side of the table.

Most of these names and faces appear fairly regularly in the pages of *Private Eye*, where their various exploits (primarily involving cuts in services, government waste, and personal peccadilloes) are tracked.

"plastic surgery" — ("Cosmetic Surgery") Cosmetic (as opposed to reconstructive) plastic surgery of the nose—to approve appearance—was a relatively young practice at this time, having appeared at around the turn of the century.

"pommy bastard" — ("Bruces") Actually an affectionate term in Australian English, its use even ascribed to the Queen on the cover of the 8 May 1970 issue of *Private Eye*. The story covers the Queen's return from her extended (two-month) visit to Australia, and the cover shot gives her a balloon quote: "Greetings to all youse loyal pommy bastards!"

To be from "pommie land" means to be from England. This is probably a slangy reference to the potato-eating stereotype of the UK population (from *pomme de terre*).

"pooftah" — ("Bruces") An Australian slang term for an effeminate male, or a homosexual. Other derivatives heard in *FC* include "poof" and "poove."

Pope — ("Naughty Bits") The Pope in 1970 was Pope Paul VI (fl. 1963–1978).

"Prime Minister" — ("Bruces") The Australian PM in 1970 was the Rt Hon. John Grey Gorton (January 1968 to March 1971). The Queen had recently visited Australia, in March–May 1970, and before that in 1963 and 1954.

profile picture of strange person (provided by Terry Gilliam) — (*"How to Recognize Different Parts of the Body"*) The "nose" indicated here is borrowed from Dutch painter Quentin Matsys's *Portrait of an Elderly Man* (c. 1517), and it will be used again in the opening credits for the fourth season.

"pull" — (link into "Camp Square-Bashing") To "give a pull" is to attempt to hit on, romantically/sexually; the term is used by John Lennon in the train buffet car scene in *A Hard Day's Night* (1964).

• Q •

"quid" — ("Cut-Price Airline") A sovereign (one pound sterling).

• R •

"Radio 4" — (*"The Death of Mary Queen of Scots"*) One of the four extant BBC radio stations, BBC 4 came on the air in September 1967.

In 1970 all four radio stations were in the process of major revamping, with the goal being a clearer portrait of each channel as its own, discernible entity. The BBC's policy paper "Broadcasting in the Seventies" was the roadmap for this change, and was, in a way, exploding the somewhat confused and often overlapping areas of interest the four radio channels had been operating with, some since WWII.

"ratty" — ("Camp Square-Bashing") Here meaning irritated, angry.

"Raymond Luxury Yacht" — ("Cosmetic Surgery") Cf. Ep. 19 for the earlier appearance of this character.

"re-enactment" — ("Batley Townswomen's Guild Presents the First Heart Transplant") An example of Python's self-reflexivity, their references to their own corpus, in this case, footage from a muddy pasture where Pepperpots bash each other with purses. The audience usually reacts quite appreciatively when these moments appear, meaning the studio audience (at least by the second season) is made up of those who also watch the show on TV at home.

• S •

"safe as houses" — ("Cut-Price Airline") A British and Australian idiom meaning worry-free.

"Second Armoured Division" — ("Camp Square-Bashing") Ironically, this is the division that Elvis Presley trained under during WWII. The division was quite active during the early part of the war (December 1939–May 1941), but after most of the division were captured in Libya by the Nazis, the unit was disbanded. This ill-gained notoriety may account for Pythons' mention of the division in this campy setting.

"sheepdip" — ("Bruces") A place where sheep are washed, or the fluid in which they are washed.

"Sheila" — ("Bruces") A colloquialism for a young woman or girlfriend, and primarily used in Australia and New Zealand.

The Queen is also credited by these Bruces with not being "stuck up," which means to put on airs and be pretentious, or a "sticky beak," which is to be nosey. Her Majesty's lengthy 1954, 1963, and 1970 visits went quite favorably, and featured hospital openings, art exhibitions, opening of sports and government buildings and even an airport terminal. These very positive, even glowing images were played up on television back home in the UK.

"sherry" — ("Bruces") A high alcohol content wine commonly made in Spain. Cf. notes for Ep. 36, the "Sherry-Drinking Vicar" sketch, as well as the Victorian woman (Chapman) in Ep. 41.

show eleven — (PSC; "Batley Townswomen's Guild Presents the First Heart Transplant") See notes to Ep. 11 for more on this footage.

"someone gets stabbled" — (PSC; "There's Been a Murder") The printed script clearly spells the word "stabbled," not "stabbed." Probably a misprint, though there is such a word—to "stabble" means to tramp dirt around, as on a clean floor (*OED*).

"springbok" — ("Batley Townswomen's Guild Presents the First Heart Transplant") A nickname for a South African, but also referring to an antelope of the region. The term is used almost exclusively in the sports pages, political cartoons, and op-ed pages in English newspapers of the period when referring to South African white males, primarily, and especially those representing sports teams. See the entries for Eps. 14, 15, 19, and 20 for more on the South African references.

"Stewart, Michael" — ("Batley Townswomen's Guild Presents the First Heart Transplant") Referring back to Foreign Secretary Michael Stewart (later Lord Stewart of Fulham) who spoke for Harold Wilson's Labour government as he justified their support for interfering with Biafra's attempts at independence in the late 1960s. The Christian Biafrans had been struggling for independence from Muslim Nigeria since the country won its freedom from the UK in 1960.

swanning about — ("Camp Square-Bashing") "Swan" is actually a military term, meaning "an apparently aimless journey; an excursion made for reconnaissance or for pleasure." Here the men are swanning about in a very effeminate, campy way.

"Sydney Harbour Bridge" — ("Bruces") This bridge was erected in 1932, and is a single-arch bridge. There are retail and/or historical establishments in several of the four brick piers, incidentally, meaning a "Sydney Harbour Bridge Room" is possible.

• T •

"Thatcher, Margaret" — ("Naughty Bits") A cabinet member in Heath's 1970–1974 Conservative government, Thatcher (b. 1925) was already perceived as the "Iron Lady" of the Tories, meaning she was a consistent Python target.

"Thirty bob" — ("Cut-Price Airline") Thirty shillings. A shilling was worth 1/20 of a pound sterling, and was phased out of the British monetary system with the adoption of the decimal system in 1971, not long after this sketch first aired.

track along this name plate — ("Cosmetic Surgery") The stirring music underneath this extended tracking shot is "National Anthems (Eire)" as played by the Band of the Royal Engineers (WAC T12/1,432).

"Triumph Herald" — ("Cut-Price Airline") This small car was produced between 1959 and 1971 in the UK, with the original model featuring a 948cc engine that generated about 50 bhp. Luxury car manufacturer Rolls Royce was well known for producing both prop-driven and jet engines.

"two hundred each on the plane" — ("Cut-Price Airline") This is actually the ceiling for the number of cigarettes that could be brought into the UK by travelers—any more and there was a potential arrest for smuggling. Travelers could also have in their possession only half a bottle of spirits, and one bottle of wine. There are dozens of small news items detailing customs' arrests for travelers forgetting these restrictions. See the note for Ep. 5, "Vox Pops on Smuggling" for an earlier mention.

• V •

Venus de Milo — (PSC; *"How to Recognize Different Parts of the Body"*) Famous parian marble statue found in Milos, Greece, and dated to about 120–130 BC. An image of this statue will also be used in Ep. 25, "Art Gallery Strike," where she is the only statue to abstain in a "show of hands" vote. (This joke will be squashed by the audience laughter from the previous bit.)

• W •

"Waltzing Mathilda" — ("Bruces") Unofficial Australian national anthem written by Andrew "Banjo" Paterson (1864–1941), a bush poet and ballad writer. This arrangement is from Peter Dawson's album *My Life of Song*, and is arranged by Patterson-Cowan and Thomas Wood (WAC T12/1,432). Dawson (1882–1961) was an Australian bass-baritone.

"wattle" — ("Bruces") The golden wattle (or acacia) is an indigenous Australian tree, as well as the official flower/tree of Australia.

"Woolamaloo" — ("Bruces") Probably a misspelling of "Woolloomooloo," which has been a working-class, docklands area of greater Sydney. During her 1963 visit to Australia, the Queen had toured the University of New South Wales, and opened two schools on campus. She was also a visitor at the University of Western Australia and Australian National University on this trip. There is also a University of Wollongong, in New South Wales, which was established in 1951. The Queen visited Wollongong in May 1954.

This university-in-the-bush setting may be another nod to the eminent Australian zoologist Alan "Jock" Marshall, who taught at St. Bart's (London) for more than a decade and then joined the faculty at Monash University in 1960. See the entry in Ep. 21 for "Roy Spim."

Episode 23: "Fish Licence"

French subtitled film; Film critic; Later in the French subtitled film, with black and white inserts; More film criticism; ***Scott of the Antarctic* in Paignton**; On-set interviews; Acting on boxes and in trenches; Fighting a penguin or a lion?; *Scott of the Sahara*; Ensign Oates fights the electric penguin; Miss Evans loses her clothes; "And now . . ." Man at Paignton, and "It's" Man and *Titles* (silly Cleese v/o); *Animation: Stepping on people, Conrad Poohs and His Dancing Teeth, and a letter is undelivered*; Mr. Praline wants a **fish licence**; The third-tallest mayor in Derby history signs the "fishy exception"; Derby Council v. All Blacks rugby match; Rugby commentators: "And what about China?"; Watford Long John Silver Impersonators v. Bournemouth Gynaecologists; Sixteen-ton weight and destruction file footage, closing credits

• A •

"Aldermen" — ("Derby Council vs. All Blacks Rugby Match") Aldermen are ward officers, not unlike city council members. They can and do wear such official regalia in the course of their duties. Much of the aldermanic tradition would be done away with in 1972 with the passage of the Local Government Act.

"All Blacks" — ("Derby Council vs. All Blacks Rugby Match") The national rugby team from New Zealand. These All Blacks are actually Torquay Rugby FC members (WAC T12/1,416).

ANIMATION: Dancing Teeth — (PSC; "*Animation: Stepping on People, Conrad Poohs and His Dancing Teeth, and a Letter Is Undelivered*") There are a number of very recognizable images in this lengthy animated sequence, including:

The background behind Conrad (Gilliam) as he holds and then loses the letter is another borrow from Giuseppe Galli Bibiena, a theatrical designer whose work was used earlier in Eps. 2 and 19. The scene is from a "theatrical performance on the occasion of the nuptials of the Royal Prince of Poland, Prince Elector of Saxony," according to the text. It is labeled as Part II, Plate 6, and has been colored for Gilliam's purposes. The postman walks backwards and out the door at the right.

The scene following is the "Arabian splendour" print, again. This is earlier seen in Ep. 19, and is labeled Part II, Plate 10 in the Bibiena book. The cropping is a bit less severe in this version, but most of the classical architecture at the right and left are still elided. Gilliam has placed a red bridge across the water (for the peripatetic postman), which is not part of the original. The scene is also colored.

In the next scene, the mailman puts the letter back into the pillar box (this is a Gilliam-penned image, primarily), and the letter makes its way through pipes (industrial art schematics), and to a waiting hand.

The following sequence depicts a balloon designed by Francesco Lana in 1670. This balloon has been used already, in Ep. 12, the "*Animation: Falling Apart, Animals from a Pipe*" section. See that entry in Ep. 12 for more. Behind that balloon (the "room" it's seen to occupy) is a tinted version of one of de Vries's *Perspective* drawings, Plate 7. (This same image has also appeared before, as part of the "*I Confess*" animation in Ep. 15.) In this iteration Gilliam keeps the perspectival floor (the "tile") and tints the rest green and brown. The background wall and door are gone, but the "orison" line and dashed perspective lines remain. The following image borrows a metal coil or tube from the second season credit sequence (itself borrowed from an industrial art design text), for the balloon to travel through.

Finally, as the letter is being "undelivered," a tinted version of a portion of Albrecht Dürer's *Apocalypse of St. John, The Dragon with the Seven Heads* is seen. Dürer's St. Anthony will be part of an animated sequence in Ep. 35. Gilliam also sketches portions of Dürer's work in *The Brand New Monty Python Bok,* and the German artist will figure prominently in the first *Fliegender Zirkus* episode (1971). In Bavaria they were celebrating the 500th anniversary of Dürer's birth in 1971, and the Pythons became part of that remembrance.

"Anka, Paul" — ("Fish Licence") Canadian pop singer and songwriter Anka was known during this period for the number one song "Diana," as well as hugely popular songs written for Buddy Holly, Johnny Carson's *Tonight Show,* and Tom Jones. Anka (and his wife) have already been mentioned in Ep. 21.

"Ataturk, Kemal" — ("Fish Licence") Mustafa Kemal Ataturk (1881–1938) fought for and founded the Republic of Turkey, becoming its first president. Ataturk led the successful fight against the combined and ill-fated British and ANZAC forces at Gallipoli in 1915.

The fictional book mentioned (*"Kemal Ataturk, the Man"*) is supposed to have been written by E.W. Swanton, the noted English cricket broadcaster already mentioned (and pictured) in Ep. 21.

• B •

"blood goes pssssssssshhh in slow motion" — (*"Scott of the Antarctic"*) The success of Akira Kurosawa's pulpy samurai film *Sanjuro* (1962)—with its shocking and celebrated "fountain of blood" ending—led many younger filmmakers to ratchet up the blood and gore content in their own films in subsequent years. This level of blood and violence wouldn't reach Hollywood screens (due to the lingering effects of the Production Code) until the late 1960s, when Arthur Penn's *Bonnie and Clyde* (1967) and especially Sam Peckinpah's *The Wild Bunch* (1969), among others, made their debut.

"breakdown in communication in our modern society" — ("French Subtitled Film") In a nutshell, this defines *Flying Circus.* There are very few examples in the series of a *successful* communication or transaction. In most cases, the message is misunderstood, delivered improperly, or perceived incorrectly. A man who wants an argument gets abuse, complaints, and "being hit on the head lessons"; a man who wants to report a burglary has to speak louder, then lower, or he won't be understood; a visit to the doctor becomes a homosexual tryst; a man who seeks advice from a marriage counselor loses his wife to the counselor in the transaction, etc. In the *FC* world, successful transactions (robbing a lingerie shop, buying a converted pet, returning a dead parrot, buying cheese) are nearly impossible.

The communication issue is key for the Pythons, and is based on the recent interest in semantics and semiotics, the growing awareness that meaning isn't just "there," it is imbued by and for society/culture, and that meaning can and does fluctuate depending on *context.* The separation of a word from its "meaning" allows for new meanings and even multiple meanings to be temporarily affixed to a word—there now exists the possibility of "wiggle room" in the world of language. Modernist authors like Joyce, Stein, Pound, Woolf, and Eliot pushed this separation, this slippage, this interchangeability, and the Pythons came along at just the right time to explore that new ambiguity in the television format.

"Bullock, Alan" — ("Fish Licence") Bullock (1914–2004) was an Oxford grad, a British historian, and author of the influential *Hitler: A Study of Tyranny* (1952). Bullock had also founded St. Catherine's College at Oxford in 1962, and both Palin and Jones were attending Oxford at that time.

"But soft . . ." — ("Fish Licence") Oft-used Elizabethan dramatic phrase, and used as a transition or link in the speaker's thought pattern or attention (as when something/someone unseen is overheard), and found in Shakespeare's history plays *Richard II* (5.1), *1 King Henry IV* (1.3), *Richard III* (1.3), comedies *The Taming of the Shrew* (4.5), *The Comedy of Errors* (2.2; 3.1), *A Midsummer Night's Dream* (4.1), *The Merchant of Venice* (1.3), *Much Ado about Nothing* (5.1), and even his tragedies *Cymbeline* (4.2), *Titus Andronicus* (5.3), *Romeo and Juliet* (2.2; 3.4), *Julius Caesar* (1.2), and even *Hamlet,* when the ghost approaches Horatio in act one. Praline uses the phrase similarly to move from one grille to the next, hoping for success in attaining a fish license.

• C •

"Cardiff Arms Park" — ("Derby Council vs. All Blacks Rugby Match") The home stadium of the Welsh rugby union, and named after a pub nearby. These scenes were actually shot on 12 May 1970 at the Torquay Rugby Football Ground, with the All Blacks played by members of the Torquay RFC (WAC T12/1,416).

The match was filmed on the northernmost field of the club, likely a practice field.

"cat detector van" — ("Fish Licence") In the UK, a license must be purchased if a TV is going to be viewed in the home or business. This licensing fee helps fund the BBC (and local radio/TV), and has been bringing money to the BBC coffers since 1904 (initially, just for radio broadcast). To help encourage compliance with these mandatory fees, special "detection vans" had been patrolling British streets with the stated ability of detecting whether a TV in a particular home/office is receiving broadcast transmissions. (There is a small picture of the insides of one of these "G.P.O. television detection vans" in the *Times*, dated 2 February 1952, page 10.) Using a master address list of license holders, the detectors can allegedly identify if the address is legally watching TV. One license fee per single-family household covers all TVs in the home.

completely rigid stuffed lion — (PSC; *"Scott of the Sahara"*) This same kind of profoundly bad special effect work can be seen in many films of the 1950s and 1960s, but a particularly apt reference is the film *Hercules and the Captive Women* (1961). In this low, low budget Italian sword and sandals epic, Hercules at one point wrestles with a very obviously stuffed lion. In this film Hercules was played by the British actor Reg Park (1928–2007).

Conger — (*"Scott of the Antarctic"*) A conger is a type of eel found in the coastal regions of the UK (and caught for food), the mention of which may be a comment on this type of BBC coverage of these Hollywood superproductions, including the recent *Ryan's Daughter* (1970) and especially the often painfully unfunny *Casino Royale* (1967), which J. McGrath (see entry below) actually directed.

Conger's wardrobe cues are listed as "like Tony Bilbow, almost Regency" in the wardrobe requests for the episode, while Gerry Schlick is described as "American, like Marcel Hellman" (WAC T12/1,435). Bilbow (b. 1932) was writing for the show *Mind Your Own Business* in 1970 and presenting on *Late Night Line-Up* (and would later appear with Idle in *Rutland Weekend Television*), while Romanian-born Hellman (1898–1985) had produced a version of *Moll Flanders* for the big screen in 1965, and which was playing at the Plaza cinema in July of that year. The *Times* television critic Henry Raynor (1917–1989)—when commenting on late night shows, including *Late Night Line-Up*—made a point of mentioning Bilbow's "sartorial extravagance" in his review. The "Regency" (historically, between "Georgian" and "Victorian" in England) comment means Conger is to look a bit of a dandy, and very concerned with the neatness of his appearance.

cos lettuce — (PSC; "French Subtitled Film") Lettuce from the island of Cos, the lettuce is named in the script. See entry for "Webb's Wonder" below.

"crumb bum" — (*"Scott of the Antarctic"*) A term used, appropriately, by the prostitute ("Sunny") Holden visits in Salinger's *Catcher in the Rye* (1951). She calls him a "crumb-bum" when he pays her five dollars instead of ten.

• D •

"Derby" — ("Derby Council vs. All Blacks Rugby Match") A city in the East Midlands. These scenes were shot in Torquay, which is much farther south.

"Derby Council XV" — ("Derby Council vs. All Blacks Rugby Match") The "XV" indicating that this is rugby *union* football, where fifteen players per team are involved, as opposed to thirteen players for rugby *league* football. In the episode as filmed, however, there appear to be only eleven All Blacks and about twelve Derby Council players on the pitch.

"Derry and Toms" — ("Derby Council vs. All Blacks Rugby Match") An upscale department store initially founded in 1920 when two companies merged, then came into its own in 1932 with the building of its lavish, garden-topped headquarters in Kensington High Street. It will be mentioned again in Ep. 37. The Derry and Toms concern would close just months after the broadcast of this episode, in 1972.

"Devonshire resort will be transformed" — (*"Scott of the Antarctic"*) Typical of the money-saving practice for many Hollywood (and bigger-budget foreign) films. D.W. Griffith's *Birth of a Nation* (1915) was shot in southern California (not the southern United States); *55 Days at Peking* (1963) was shot in Spain; and parts of the *Lawrence of Arabia* (1962) sand dunes were also shot in California. The Hollywood blockbuster film that at least partly inspired the *Scott of the Antarctic* spoof here, *Ice Station Zebra* (1968), was shot entirely in sunny southern California, even though it is set entirely in the frozen Arctic.

"disappointing result" — ("Derby Council vs. All Blacks Rugby Match") In fall 1970 the fifth Rugby League World Cup was held in Great Britain. Played in late October and early November, the British team was strong and impressive early, but surprisingly lost 12–7 to an Australian team that had struggled to even qualify for the final match.

"Distel, Brian" — ("French Subtitled Film") Sacha Distel (1933–2004) was a French-born singer and guitarist who had many hits during the 1960s and 1970s, as well as television specials and even his own show. In October 1970 Distel was performing at the Palladium, and getting solid reviews. Idle's penchant for including music folk into his writing should probably be credited for Distel's sideways mention. "Brian," of course, is, along with "Arthur," one of the catch-all first names given to Python characters throughout not only *FC*, but into the feature films.

"Brianette Zatapathique" is a bit of silliness that keeps appearing in *FC*, with the name Zatapathique being mentioned prominently in Eps. 2, 17, and 22.

• E •

"edited highlights of the match" — ("Long John Silver Impersonators v. Bournemouth Gynaecologists") A reference to the practice of the BBC's popular *Match of the Day* since the 1960s, when edited highlights of Division One football (soccer) matches were shown on Saturday evenings to millions of viewers. David Coleman (Ep. 21) was the main presenter during this period.

"electric penguin" — ("*Scott of the Antarctic*") This bit of silliness is most likely a reference to the 1961 adventure film *Voyage to the Bottom of the Sea*, where a giant octopus attacks the intrepid submarine and crew. (Actually, it's a normal-sized octopus photographed in close-up and with miniature props.) That film also starred young and beautiful Barbara Eden (b. 1934), cast to attract the young male audience, not unlike Miss Vanilla Hoare (Cleveland).

The music played beneath this oft-seen fowl (at least in *FC*) is from The Machines, "Electronic Screams" by Eric Peters (WAC T12/1,435).

enters shot — (PSC; "French Subtitled Film") The New Wave filmmakers drew attention to the formal elements of cinema, in this case acknowledging the cinematographic frame, its existence and role as "divider" of photographed space. The fact that the boom mic drops into the shot is also a comment on the movement's inattention to some of the "finished" details of film, more interested in the visceral experience of the cinematic moment. Also, lower-budget films tend to suffer more continuity problems, as reshoots are more expensive than can be justified.

Episode 23 — Recorded 2 July 1970, and broadcast 1 December 1970. This episode was actually recorded second in the second season, but aired as the final episode of the season. This episode was also recorded on the same evening (2 July 1970) as what eventually would be known as Ep. 15, meaning there were fewer in-studio shots or scenes than usual.

"'E's an 'alibut" — ("Fish Licence") An example of class differentiation even among the middle class, the Post Office Worker (Palin) doesn't understand Praline's (Cleese) "common" English, his dropping of the initial "h," and Praline must speak more precisely: "He is an halibut."

"Exeter Amateur Operatic Society" — ("Derby Council vs. All Blacks Rugby Match") There is and has been an Exeter Operatic Society, and there exist many amateur societies, including the Barnstaple Amateur Operatic Society. Both of these are in Devon.

• F •

fanfare of trumpets — (PSC; link out of "Fish Licence") The fanfare is "Aggression" from Eric Towren, one of Britain's many light music composers whose work could be heard on British TV and radio throughout the 1950s and 1960s, and in countless low-budget films (WAC T12/1,435).

first of two grilles — (PSC; "Fish Licence") The name plates under these grilles are "Miss McCheane," "Mr. Balfour," and "Mr. Last." Mary McCheane is a producer's assistant on the show, James Balfour is a cameraman, and Roger Last is one of the show's floor managers.

In a side note, McCheane (*Top of the Pops*) and sometime *FC* musician/composer Bill McGuffie (1927–1987) were husband and wife. McCheane died in 2002.

"Fromage Grand, Le" — ("French Subtitled Film") French, literally "The Big Cheese." In Ep. 4, Chapman plays the part of "The Big Cheese," a Blofeld-type villain who intervenes into the "Secret Service Dentists" sketch. Ring Lardner (American novelist and screenwriter) is credited with bringing the phrase into common parlance in his hard-boiled small-town fiction from about 1914 (*OED*).

• G •

"geological syncline" — ("*Scott of the Antarctic*") A syncline is a downward-curving fold, which can create basins—meaning Miss Hoare (Cleveland) could certainly act in one.

"get his finger out and get going" — ("Rugby Commentators: 'And what about China?'") A common colloquialism meaning simply to stop mucking about and get some work done. It's still used regularly in sports columns and in reference to governmental bodies (Parliament, city councils) that regularly, maddeningly dither. See "What about China?" for more on the phrase.

Girl — (PSC; "*Scott of the Antarctic*") Not named in the script, this is Lyn Ashley, Idle's wife at this time.

• H •

hand-held camera — ("French Subtitled Film") One of the characteristics of the French New Wave (Nouvelle Vague) was a conscious move away from classical, prestige-film Hollywood aesthetics in favor of more genre-influenced styles. The manipulation of classical form included taking the camera off of the tripod and especially the dolly, where steady, beautiful shots had created a hallmark of Hollywood cinema. Hand-held camera work (inspired by documentary films and especially the combat footage of WWII), black-and-white film stock, elliptical editing and storytelling, sex and sexuality as integral to the narrative and characters, and topicality characterized the movement. Godard's 1959 film *Breathless* is a terrific example of these formal concerns.

• I •

"I don't know. I was getting confused." — ("*Scott of the Antarctic* in Paignton") There are a number of reports of friction, misunderstandings, and even physical altercations on and around the set of *Casino Royale*, which Joe McGrath directed in 1967 (before quitting), and which starred Peter Sellers, Orson Welles, and Woody Allen. McGrath's "confusion" started with the film's use of the Panavision process, a widescreen mode new to him and most everyone else on the set, the scope and complexity of the project, and included the egos of its major stars and their inability to get along. (Sellers early on asked to shoot his scenes with Orson Welles—across a gaming table—separately, meaning no establishing shots of both of them sharing a frame. It went down from there.) The mess that became *The Magic Christian* (1969) was also a disaster, with McGrath unable to direct his mercurial friend and lead actor, Peter Sellers. In *Scott of the Antarctic*, McRettin's surrender to Vilb's every demand, no matter how ridiculous, is supported by those close to McGrath-Sellers in 1966–1969. McGrath at best seems to have been in an unwinnable situation. See Peter Evans's *Peter Sellers: The Mask behind the Mask* for more.

Intercut . . . plane — (PSC; "French Subtitled Film") Jean-Luc Godard used stock documentary footage of student demonstrations, riots, and police and military actions in his 1968 compilation film *Cinétracts*. Much of the stock footage the Pythons used is culled from the BBC's own film archive. This particular shot isn't accounted for (by name) in the WAC records.

The live-action (starring the Pythons) insert portions were all shot in the Torquay city area; the few interiors were shot at Ealing TFS (WAC T12/1,435).

"I rewrote it" — ("*Scott of the Antarctic*") Joseph McGrath is credited (unofficially) with significant rewrites of the *Casino Royale* (1967) script, as were many other directors who had contact with the troubled project. See entry for "McGrath" below.

• J •

"John the Baptist" — ("*Scott of the Antarctic*") Cousin to Jesus, there is no indication in any surviving record that John was ever married or had a daughter named for him, meaning Vanilla (as Miss Evans) could be talking about a particularly bold casting move for the John the Baptist story in a previous film. It also could be that since she is playing against gender as a female Evans (both of the "Evans" participants on the actual Scott expedition were men) that she is merely continuing this intriguing casting, having played female versions of John the Baptist, Napoleon, Alexander Fleming, and the astronomer Galileo in what in the film industry were known as "biopics."

Fleming (1881–1955) was a Scotsman credited as discovering penicillin, and who won the Nobel Prize in 1945.

Significant Hollywood biopics the Pythons are referencing include Pual Muni's *The Story of Louis Pasteur* (1935), *The Life of Emile Zola* and *Juarez* (both 1937), as well as the star-studded *Becket* (1964).

• L •

Lawrence of Glamorgan — ("*Scott of the Antarctic*") A play on the very popular David Lean film (also a biopic) *Lawrence of Arabia* (1962), starring Peter O'Toole. Glamorgan is a traditional county in Wales, and is home to Cardiff, Caerphilly, and Swansea.

Bridge over the River Trent—This title adapted from Lean's *Bridge on the River Kwai* (1957). The River Trent runs through cities like Burton and Nottingham, and generally through the Midlands to the Humber Estuary.

The Mad Woman of Biggleswade—Reference to the *The Mad Woman of Chaillot*, a play (and then film) written by Jean Giradoux. The film, directed by Bryan Forbes, premiered in 1969, and starred Katharine Hepburn. (This is not the "Kate Hepburn" included in the semi-silly credits for *Monty Python and the Holy Grail*. One of Gilliam's animation assistants then was a Kate Hepburn, too.) Forbes has already been mentioned in Ep. 20, *"Take Your Pick,"* and is also unflatteringly referenced in *Private Eye* (17 July 1970, 5). Biggleswade is actually in Bedfordshire, north of London.

Krakatoa, East of Leamington—Another spoofed title, this time of the disaster film *Krakatoa, East of Java* (1969), starring Maxmilian Schell. Leamington Spa is in Warwickshire.

lid slams on his hands — ("French Subtitled Film") This stock film footage sequence is reminiscent of the recent and somewhat celebrated BBC-sponsored Tony Palmer film, *All My Loving* (1968). Palmer employed music of The Beatles and images of filmed violence from the twentieth century, eliciting rave reviews from the major newspaper critics of the day. *Private Eye*, of course, is the exception, blasting the film as nothing more than a vanity piece from "Tony Palmer-lotofsensationalfilmclipsonthepublicandtryandpretenditissomethingsignificant" (Ingrams, 204). The images used are fairly standard—Vietnam, burning monks, student protests, concentration camp footage, etc.

"Longueur, Jean Kenneth" — ("French Subtitled Film") Probably a portmanteau name comprising directors Jean-Luc Godard and Ken Russell (Eps. 29 and 31). A "longueur" is a tedious or lengthy passage or thing. Critics and viewers alike have complained that Godard's political agenda often outpaces and overwhelms his artistic accomplishments. The famous traffic tracking shot in *Week End* (1967) lasts at least eight minutes, well longer than most audiences expect, and demands that the viewer begin to think not only about the content but the shot itself.

"looks more like snow than snow" — (*"Scott of the Antarctic"*) Not really. *Times* critic John Russell Taylor (b. 1935) reviews *Ice Station Zebra* by lauding the performances of leads Rock Hudson (1925–1985) and Patrick McGoohan (1928–2009), but jabs at the rest: "None of the climax, set amid cardboard ice-floes and studio snow which chills no one and does not even condense breath, carries the slightest conviction, but the plot mechanics keeps one watching . . ." (*"Ice Station Zebra,"* 27 Mar. 1969: 7).

"Lord Mayor" — ("Derby Council vs. All Blacks Rugby Match") Part of the joke here, of course, is that the smallish East Midlands city (so awarded by the Queen much later, in 1977) Derby is not one of the cities in the UK to have a Lord Mayor.

• M •

McGrath, J. — (PSC; *"Scott of the Antarctic"*) The printed script actually mentions that this besotted character "McRettin" is supposed to resemble Scottish director "J. McGrath," a writer, director, and producer well known to the Pythons. Joseph McGrath produced television's *Not Only . . . But Also* (1965, starring Peter Cook and Dudley Moore), and directed the feature film *The Magic Christian* (1969, starring Peter Sellers, with writing contributions by Chapman and Cleese). McGrath also directed the TV version of *The Goon Show* in 1968. He was born in Glasgow, Scotland, in 1930 and, like *FC*-director Ian MacNaughton, is depicted as a bit of a drinker.

McGrath also co-directed *Casino Royale* (1967), a cult film known for its frenetic, frantic production, including outbursts from stars Peter Sellers and Woody Allen, and ongoing friction between Sellers and mercurial Hollywood star Orson Welles. The Pythons may well have been drawing on the much-publicized on-set shenanigans of *Royale* for their portrait of the confused, besotted McRettin.

"Ministry of Housinge" — ("Fish Licence") The Ministry of Housing and Local Government was established after World War II (January 1951) and was headed by Anthony Crosland in 1969–1970.

miserable attempt to capture joy and togetherness — (PSC; "French Subtitled Film") Again, the ennui of modern life tends to be the focus of much New Wave film, meaning "joy and togetherness," if ever realized, will inevitably be crushed by the weight of the real world. In *Breathless*, the Bogart-wannabe "hero" (Jean-Paul Belmondo; b. 1933) has a series of meaningless physical relationships before being gunned down by the police in the street, never achieving his goal of a solid relationship with the pretty American girl (Jean Seberg; 1938–1979); in *400 Blows*, Truffaut's alter ego escapes from reform school, only to realize there's nowhere to run; in *Jules et Jim* (1962), the fantastic prospect of a successful and lasting ménage à trois runs smack up against conventional morals and the crushing weight of fate. In other words, most of the New Wave films—from France, Italy, Poland, Hungary, West Germany—offer characters who reach for the brass ring, but eventually fall and are destroyed. (Frenchman Truffaut's characters, at least, can and do experience significant joy in the early stages of the narrative—making the inevitable fall all the more poignant.)

"Miss Evans?" — (*"Scott of the Antarctic"*) In the 1948 version of the film starring John Mills as Scott, the only significant female figure is Scott's wife, Kathleen, played by Diana Churchill. There are two actual people named Evans in the Scott story, Petty Officer Edgar "Taff" Evans and Lt. E.G.G. "Teddy" Evans, and Conger seems to pick up on this discrepancy when, upon being introduced to Evans, he repeats her name as if surprised to hear the "Miss."

montage of scenes of destruction — (PSC; link out of "Long John Silver Impersonators v. Bournemouth Gynaecologists") These filmed images of explosions and warplane strafing runs are not accounted for in the WAC records for the episode.

"Morgan, Cliff" — ("Derby Council vs. All Blacks Rugby Match") Morgan (b. 1930) is a Welsh-born former Cardiff RFC player, then sports analyst and enshrinee into the International Rugby Hall of Fame. The printed script even indicates that Morgan is to have a Welsh accent, an unusual (and textually rare) bit of direction considering the many variations of English spoken throughout *FC,* most of which aren't identified except by the speaker's dress or the accent itself. Morgan was a commentator on *Rugby Special* during this period.

• N •

"Nabarro, Sir Gerald" — ("Fish Licence") Conservative minister and cabinet secretary who was typically seen as a bit loony to the Pythons and the more liberal Left. Nabarro has already been depicted in an Ep. 2 animation, and mentioned by name in Eps. 11, 15, and 21. His very recognizable and prominent handlebar mustache is aped occasionally in City Gent Vox Pops characterizations, especially by Chapman.

"New Zealanders" — ("Derby Council vs. All Blacks Rugby Match") The New Zealand All Blacks handily beat the Welsh team in May and June 1969 in New Zealand; in the previous season they'd toured Australia and Fiji and gone undefeated in twelve games, many shutouts; and in 1967, the All Blacks had toured the UK, and gone 16–0–1. In short, they had trampled across most of the Commonwealth rugby fields and teams in the very recent past, and would probably have had little trouble, actually, defeating Derby Council, no matter how tall the Lord Mayor might be.

• O •

"Olympic pole vaulter" — (*"Scott of the Antarctic"*) Using a well-known athlete here is not unlike American footballer O.J. Simpson making guest appearances on American TV shows such as *Dragnet 1967, Here's Lucy,* and *Medical Center* in the late 1960s, and Super Bowl hero Joe Namath appearing in three films in 1970, including *C.C. and Company, The Last Rebel,* and *Norwood.*

The presence of retired American football star Jim Brown in films like *Ice Station Zebra* (1968) must also have fueled this parody, with Kirk Vilb (Palin) here playing the virile and hirsute Rock Hudson part. Also, the casting of NFL quarterback Roman Gabriel and lineman Merlin Olsen in the John Wayne 1967 film *The Undefeated*—which also features Rock Hudson—is certainly worth mentioning.

"oranges" — ("Derby Council vs. All Blacks Rugby Match") Eating slices of orange is a long-standing halftime tradition in rugby and football throughout the Commonwealth. The oranges were seen as a quick energy food. (Recent studies have indicated that the mango is the best fruit for such replenishment, and many teams and coaches have switched.)

organ music — (PSC; link out of "Fish Licence") This organ music played under the narrated "fishy exemption" section is by Helmut Walcha on the Church of Capperl Schritger Organ, and is the "Prelude & Fugue, D Major BWV 532" by J.S. Bach.

• P •

"Paignton" — (*"Scott of the Antarctic"*) Resort city on the English Channel, south of Exeter. Nearby Torquay is actually termed the "Queen of the English Riviera." Most of the location work for the second season was actually shot in this area. This is also one of the infrequent occasions where the Pythons shot just where they claimed to be.

"Palethorpe, Dawn" — ("Fish Licence") Dawn Penelope (Palethorpe) Wofford (b. 1936) competed for the British Show Jumping Olympic team in 1956 and 1960. In 1956 Palethorpe was riding Earlsrath Rambler. Later in the rugby match section of this sketch, Palethorpe will be riding a horse named Sir Gerald (referring to Tory MP Gerald Nabarro).

Paris riots and clubbing — (PSC; "French Subtitled Film") Obviously supposed to be film from the fairly recent May 1968 riots in Paris, when students took up a revolutionary cause and stormed various French universities. One of the leaders of the student movement, Daniel Cohn-Bendit, would later visit London in an attempt to urge English students into similar acts of civil disobedience, but managed only a few, relatively quiet appearances.

This section of film stock (and the remainder of the war-related footage in this scene) is not accounted for by name in the WAC records.

penguin is close to the camera in the foreground and appears huge — (PSC; "*Scott of the Antarctic*") This is a standard special effects composition for low-budget films of this period. Using a lens (with plenty of lighting) that both can focus on an object close to the camera *and* deeper in the shot, the illusion of a looming element can be achieved. Meaningful interaction between the two objects is the real trick, of course, and this is where most of these films show their seams, as the Pythons indicate when the script calls for the film to "intercut a lot of phoney reverses." The two separate objects never truly can interact or share the same space, even, so the illusion is often spoiled. The Pythons will re-employ this illusion in the feature films *Holy Grail* and *Life of Brian*, where miniature castle and city sets, respectively, are placed on small hills in the background.

pimply youth — ("French Subtitled Film") Played by Idle, the critic isn't pimply, but does affect a "swishy" tone and delivery. Identified as "Phil" in the scripts, there is the possibility that he is modeled on Philip French, a regular BBC contributor since 1960, and columnist for the *Observer* and *New Statesman* during this period.

More likely, however, he is Philip Jenkinson (1935–2012), who has earlier been mentioned in both the *FC* episodes and WAC notes, and who was, among other things, a writer for *Marty* (1968) and film reviewer for the BBC's *Radio Times*. Jenkinson also hosted *Film Night* beginning in 1970 (where Tony Bilbow also appeared), which is the context the Pythons give him in these appearances. Often lampooned by the Pythons (see his brutal murder in Ep. 33), Jenkinson was obviously a friend—he would appear in Idle's *Rutland Weekend Television* in 1975, and occasionally provided film clips from his own collection for later *Flying Circus* episodes.

"played by your very own lovely Terrence Lemming" — ("*Scott of the Antarctic*") The nominal Brit in the main *Ice Station Zebra* cast was Patrick McGoohan, playing David Jones.

post office — (PSC; "Fish Licence") The printed script calls for a "real" post office after the backward mailing animation, but this is actually a redressed Market Street Methodist Hall in Torquay (WAC T12/1,416). This building has since been torn down.

Praline — (PSC; "Fish Licence") One of the few *named* recurring characters in *FC*, Praline first appeared as a policeman in Ep. 6, then in the "Dead Parrot" sketch (Ep. 8), and as the host of a mysteriously canceled talk show in Ep. 18.

Proust, Marcel — ("Fish Licence") Proust (1871–1922) is one of the most influential (certainly to the Pythons) writers of the twentieth century, his *Remembrance of Things Past* or *In Search of Lost Time* (*À la recherché du temps perdu*) seen by many as the most significant novel ever written.

Proust has already been mentioned in *FC*, in Ep. 11, and will figure prominently again in the "Summarize Proust" competition in Ep. 31. Proust's interest in time and memory, and the essentiality of experience (the "essence" of the madeleine cookie) is obviously important to the Pythons as their characters experience the modern, nostalgic, and pastiche world.

• R •

reverent voice over — (PSC; "Derby Council vs. All Blacks Rugby Match") In this voiceover Cleese mimics the earnest but soft delivery (loaded with "greats" as well) of Richard Dimbleby (1913–1965), longtime interviewer and reporter for *Panorama*. Cleese is specifically channeling Dimbleby's well-known hushed, reverential broadcast description of Queen Elizabeth II's coronation on 2 June 1953, broadcast live from Westminster Abbey:

> Here in the Abbey Church of St. Peter in Westminster, a great congregation of seven thousand, come from every part of the world, awaits the arrival of Her Majesty. And we'll see very shortly the procession as it passes right up the great church. (*choir and organ begin*) As the choir begin their lovely anthem . . . there come into sight all the splendors of the great officers and their regalia. Behind the heralds, the scepter with the cross carried by the Master of the Royal Air Force, the Viscount Portal of Hungerford . . . Saint Edward's staff, borne by the Earl of Lancaster. . . . (Audio transcription, *Eyewitness 1950–59*, "Coronation 2")

On the *Goon Show*, Peter Sellers had also impersonated the mellifluous Dimbleby in several play-by-play-type commentaries in several episodes, including "The Starlings" (31 Aug. 1954) and "The Last Tram" (23 Nov. 1954).

"revolutionnaire" — ("French Subtitled Film") In French New Wave filmmaker Jean-Luc Godard's *Le vent d'est* (1969), there is a character named simply "La révolutionnaire." In Godard's 1967 film *Week End*, the estranged couple find cannibalistic revolutionaries in the woods. The events of May 1968 helped push Godard and other left-leaning artists into more overtly political artistic expression.

rubbish dump — ("French Subtitled Film") This setting is reminiscent of French New Wave director Jean-Luc Godard's film *Week End* (1967), where two garbage men rant about contemporary politics and the state of the capitalist world, and the film's somewhat self-aware heroes, Roland (Jean Yanne) and Corrine (Mireille Darc), argue about sex, cigarettes, traffic, and the lousy film they're having to slog through. The entire sequence in this "French Subtitled Film" sketch is obviously a parody of Godard's (and Chabrol's, and Resnais's et al.) often political, often overt, and certainly preachy and indicting French films of the late 1960s and early 1970s. A number of New Wave–type films from this period include garbage dumps as evidence of the detritus of modern capitalist society, including Luis Bunuel's *Los Olvidados* (1950) and Andrzej Wajda's *Ashes and Diamonds* (1957), where our "heroes" die ignominiously among the other trash.

A mention must be made of an older, more mature (and therefore, assumedly, more conservative) filmmaker, Akira Kurosawa, whose remarkable 1970 film *Dô dese ka den* is set entirely on a vast rubbish dump. Rather than making an overt political (meaning anti-West, anti-capitalist, anti-U.S.) statement, Kurosawa looks at the lives of society's lost people, the slum dweller, and tries to find nobility there.

The actual setting for the "French Subtitled Film" scene is a rubbish tip in Torquay, specifically the Lawsbridge Refuse Depot, and was shot on 13 May 1970 (WAC T12/1,416).

• S •

Scott of the Antarctic — (*"Scott of the Antarctic"*) There is a 1948 British film called *Scott of the Antarctic* starring John Mills and Diana Churchill.

The sweeping music heard underneath this sketch is from Sir Adrian Boult and the London Philharmonic Orchestra's "Sinfonia Antarctica," selections from the First, Third, and Fifth Movements by Vaughn Williams (WAC T12/1,435). The music cues are not mentioned in the printed script, just in the WAC records.

Scott of the Sahara — (*"Scott of the Sahara"*) The music played during this sequence includes the International Studio Orchestra playing "Aggression" by E. Towren, as well as "Pride of the Ride" and "Nathan le prophete" by Edward Michael (WAC T12/1,435).

She is walking in a trench — (*"Scott of the Antarctic"*) A jab at the well-known Hollywood practice of using camera angles, carefully chosen actors/extras, and "apple boxes" and trenches to make stars taller or shorter, including such diminutive A-list stars as Alan Ladd and Humphrey Bogart. In *Shane* (1953), for example, the (reportedly) 5′ 5″ Ladd had to hold his own—compositionally—against Van Heflin (6′) and Jack Palance (6′ 4″), so trenches were dug and apple boxes employed to negate the height differences.

Shot of a Spitfire — (PSC; "French Subtitled Film") This bit of film stock is called the "RAF Style Dog Fight," and is from VisNews, film number 13774 (WAC T12/1,428). This is one of the very few sections of stock film in this scene actually accounted for in WAC records.

"Sir Gerald" — ("Derby Council vs. All Blacks Rugby Match") Yet another reference to Sir Gerald Nabarro (1913–1973), the flamboyant Conservative politician. Obviously a popular and polarizing figure, Nabarro is mentioned/lampooned in more than one hundred political cartoons during this period. In this instance he's the name of Dawn Palethorpe's mount, though she was riding Earlsrath Rambler at the time.

sixteen-ton weight falls on him — (PSC; link out of "Long John Silver Impersonators v. Bournemouth Gynaecologists") The large prop was clearly broken in this shot (recorded 2 July 1970), and a request for it to be either repaired or replaced is found in the WAC records (WAC T12/1,242).

"Sixty quid" — ("Fish Licence") See the entry for "cat detector van." The most expensive license fee as of January 1969 (for color TV and radio) came to just £11.

"sort it out on the floor" — (*"Scott of the Antarctic"*) Meaning, they'll fix the problem in the editing room later. Filmed flubs or just bad or extra takes end up on the proverbial "floor" of the editing room.

"Stafford" — ("Fish Licence") Sir Richard Stafford Cripps (1889–1952) was the (Labour) Chancellor of the Exchequer in 1947–1950 under PM Attlee, and would have been much in the news during the Pythons' formative years.

Stig — ("French Subtitled Film") This character is wearing a tight shirt, wide belt, and scarf, almost identical to a character ("Man in Farmyard," played by Michel Cournot) standing in a farmyard in Godard's *Week End* (1967). Stig (Jones) will also wander out of shot, just as characters do in *Week End*—one of the garbage men, for example, is normally offscreen, yet still rants on.

The character Stig, not mentioned by name by any of the characters (but named in the printed scripts), may be based on an actual Stig, one Stig Dagerman (1923–1954). Dagerman was a Swedish existentialist, who immersed himself and his plays and novels in the despair and anxiety of the movement. After losing his marriage and suffering a nervous breakdown, Dagerman committed suicide in 1954. Dagerman was also attracted to the Syndicalist movement—where workers would control factories—a famous reference to which will appear in *Monty Python and the Holy Grail*. Dagerman's work could be heard on the BBC's "Third Programme" as early as 1950, his plays were being read and staged two years after his death (1956) at the Institute of Contemporary Arts, and collections of his works were published in 1960. The Swedish poet and novelist's play *The Shadow of Mart* was adapted for BBC television in summer 1963, and was reviewed quite favorably.

• T •

"Town Clerk" — ("Derby Council vs. All Blacks Rugby Match") The Town Clerk was often the senior administrator in towns and villages, and would have merited regalia befitting this high office.

"try" — ("Derby Council vs. All Blacks Rugby Match") A "try" in rugby is a grounding of the ball over the opponent's goal line (a "touch-down"). The Lady Mayoress (Cleveland) will end up scoring both tries in this match.

The "set-pieces" the New Zealanders are going to struggle with in the second half would include the "scrum," "line-outs," and "restarts."

"20th Century Vole are shooting their latest epic" — ("*Scott of the Antarctic* in Paignton") Ep. 23 was recorded in July 1970 and broadcast for the first time in December of that same year. In 1970, major Hollywood film studio 20th Century Fox was experiencing the ups and downs of a protean, shifting movie audience, with films ranging from safe bets to indie hopefuls, and box office successes fleeting, at best.

Fox had finished 1969 with the very expensive and marginally successful *Hello, Dolly!* (The film cost about $25 million and made roughly the same, meaning it may have broken even. More important, it had failed to do *Sound of Music*–type box office [$266 million gross on a $9 million budget], which Fox had depended on). Fox then saddled itself with the equally expensive and equally so-so successful "epic" *Tora! Tora! Tora!* in the late summer, and flops like *Myra Breckenridge* and *The Kremlin Letter*. The studio stayed afloat thanks to cheap exploitation (*Beyond the Valley of the Dolls*), sure-thing sequels (*Beneath the Planet of the Apes*), Oscar-worthy *rarae aves* like *Patton*, and revisionist histories like *MASH*. It was truly a roller-coaster year for Fox, and most of the major Hollywood studios.

• U •

"U.S. furlong" — ("*Scott of the Antarctic*") A U.S. furlong is 660 feet, or 220 yards.

• W •

"Watford" — (link into "Long John Silver Impersonators v. Bournemouth Gynaecologists") Watford is a town in Hertfordshire, and Bournemouth is on the South Coast in Dorset.

"Wayne, John" — ("French Subtitled Film") Wayne (1907–1979), the iconic Hollywood actor, had most recently appeared in *True Grit* (1969), *The Undefeated* (1969), *Chisum* (1970), and *Rio Lobo* (1970). None are particularly bloody, especially when compared with the newfound penchant for sex, violence, and gore in the films of Sam Peckinpah (Ep. 33; *The Wild Bunch*) and Arthur Penn (*Bonnie and Clyde*; still photo used in Ep. 33). The cast of *The Undefeated* featured, coincidentally, retired American football players Merlin Olsen and Roman Gabriel, as well as the rugged, hirsute, and Kirk Vilb–like Rock Hudson.

"Webb's Wonder" — ("French Subtitled Film") Actually "Webb's Wonderful," a crisp lettuce, which (significantly) is a cultivar that originated from France. This went to graphics not as "Webb's Wonder," but as "Cos Lettuce," before someone changed the request (WAC T12/1,435).

"What about China?" — ("Derby Council vs. All Blacks Rugby Match") In 1970, Mao Tse-tung was probably ailing, and Lin Biao (also Lin Piao; 1907–1971) had tacitly assumed power in China with the support of the military. Biao would die mysteriously a few months after this episode aired, however, when Mao began to fear his subordinate's rising influence. Liu Shaoqi (Lin Shao Chi) was considered quite powerful and perhaps even the heir apparent to Mao, but was purged in the late 1960s. The "second-half" hope Zhou Enlai (Chou Enlai; 1898–1976) was premier in China from 1949 to 1976, and considered the third most powerful man in China during this period.

Mao and China are mentioned significantly in *FC* a number of times, illustrating the increasing international presence the Communist country and regime were enjoying in the late 1960s and early 1970s. See notes for Eps. 24 and 25 for more.

To get one's "finger out" is a British naval term meaning to uncover the powder so a cannon can be touched off (*OED*). Colloquially, it means to get a move on. In the 5 April 1963 edition of *Private Eye*, the spread cartoon from "Timothy" depicts a hip new Britain under Tory leadership, and includes Prince Philip and the Queen on a float. Philip, in his customary hands-behind-back position, is whispering: "Ie must gette my bloodye finger out before she notices!" as if he's caught himself in an unseen Chinese finger trap (Ingrams, 80–81).

"wingers" — ("Derby Council vs. All Blacks Rugby Match") A winger is a forward whose place is on the back row of the scrum.

"Wintrex . . . on screen looks more like snow than snow" — ("*Scott of the Antarctic* in Paignton") In 1946 Frank Capra (1897–1991) and special effects man Russell Shearman (d. 1956) worked together to create a better snow substitute, specifically for shooting *It's a Wonderful Life* in the summer. They combined "foamite" (a fire extinguishing material) with sugar and water, reportedly, and the "snow" could be sprayed across the entire Bedford Falls set (built in southern California's desert heat).

Episode 24: "How Not to Be Seen"

Conquistador Coffee Campaign; "And Now . . ." Man at the seaside, repeating groove (gramophone), and "It's" Man; *Titles* (also skipping); Ramsay MacDonald striptease; Job hunter; *Animation: Overrun by Chinese Communists, the "Domino theory," and Crelm toothpaste and Shrill Petrol*; Agatha Christie sketch (Railway Timetables); "It All Happened on the 11:20 from Heinault . . ."; Mr. Neville Shunte; Gavin Millar, critic; Writer/dentist (Film director—Teeth): *The Twelve Caesars* (and *Trafalgar*); Audience and City Gents Vox Pops; "Must be one of them Crackpot Religions" link; **Crackpot Religions Ltd.**; Archbishop Gumby Vox Pops (and John Lennon, Archbishops Shabby and Nudge); Other religions, including The Most Popular Religion Ltd.); *Animation: Cartoon Religions Ltd*; H.M. Government, Public Service Film No. 42: ***How Not to Be Seen***; Crossing the Atlantic on a tricycle; Mr. Bent is in our Durham studios; Interview with Ludwig Grayson in filing cabinet; "Yummy, Yummy, Yummy, I've Got Love in My Tummy" (in boxes) under closing credits; BBC 1 Colour symbol: *Monty Python's Flying Circus* again in thirty seconds

• A •

Animation: An elderly secretary . . . — (PSC; animated link out of "Job Hunter") This is one of the few occasions where a Gilliam-rendered animated link is included in its entirety in the printed script. And even though it is included and reads like a traditional sketch, it's not given its own title. This might mean that Gilliam had completed the animation earlier, and perhaps for another show.

"anytime free men anywhere waver in their defence of democracy" — (animated link out of "Job Hunter") This gunboat diplomacy (or Monroe Doctrine) foreign policy practice meant that during the 1950s and 1960s there were significant and ongoing U.S. efforts in Asia, Africa, and perhaps especially Latin America (being so close to home) to support any administration that would fight Leftist insurgencies. Consequently, militaristic and often brutal Right-wing regimes were at least tacitly supported by U.S. funding and advisors, often through the CIA. This subject will be revisited more specifically in Ep. 33, the "Storage Jars" sketch.

Archbishop Shabby — (PSC; "Crackpot Religions Ltd.") Ken Shabby (Palin) has already appeared in Ep. 12, and Mr. Nudge (Idle) has also appeared, in Ep. 3. Both characters are greeted affectionately by the studio audience, indicating home viewers of the show were making efforts to get tickets and watch the show in person. Gumby characters are also recognized throughout the series.

Arnold, Malcolm — ("Repeating Groove") Arnold (1921–2006) was a composer who scored, among many other works, *The Bridge on the River Kwai* (1957) and was awarded a CBE in 1970. The "travelogue music" that the script mentions in relation to Arnold includes *Royal New Zealand Journey* (1954), a documentary on the Queen's trip to New Zealand that year. There were six such films made on the subject of the Queen's half-year visit to Australasia.

The music being played beneath the scene here is not from Arnold, but is a selection from "Overtures from Fingal's Cave" by Mendelssohn as played by the Vienna Philharmonic Orchestra (WAC T12/1,414).

"Arsenal's 1–0 victory" — ("Interview in Filing Cabinet") Arsenal FC is a football club which called Highbury home in 1970, and would win the FA Cup in the 1970–1971 season, defeating Liverpool 2–1. The Goons mentioned Arsenal quite a bit, though generally as the losing side in a blowout.

• B •

"Baldwin, Stanley" — ("Ramsay MacDonald Striptease") Already mentioned in passing in Eps. 14 and 21, Baldwin (1867–1947) was the Conservative PM chosen by George V, 1923–1924, then reclaimed the office 1924–1929. Ramsay MacDonald (1866–1937) led the Labour government (and the country as PM) both before and after Baldwin.

"battle against Caractacus" — ("Film Director [Teeth]") There is no evidence that Julius Caesar and Caractacus met on the battlefield (they were separated by a number of years). Claudius was Caesar when Caractacus was captured.

beach huts across to beach and sea — (*"How Not to Be Seen"*) This idyllic beach scene was shot in the Broadsands Beach area 11–13 May 1970 (WAC T12/1,416).

"Bishop of Dulwich" — ("Crackpot Religions Ltd.") There is no Bishop of Dulwich, of course, an area of London in the Southwark region, south of the Thames and, therefore, anciently, out of the influence of the monarchy and haven to all sorts of illegal activity. On the other side of criminality (but still suspect, in the Pythons' eyes), Conservative leader Margaret Thatcher owned a home on Dulwich Common.

"bishopric in a see of your choice" — ("Crackpot Religions Ltd.") The granting of sinecures is as old as such valued religious posts have existed. The Pythons will revisit one such arrangement in Ep. 28, "Trim-Jeans Theatre," Thomas Becket's placement as the Archbishop of Canterbury in 1162, ostensibly to be Henry II's ecclesiastical rubber stamp.

"Bishop's Stortford" — ("Crackpot Religions Ltd.") Yet another pun (see "North See Gas" below), Bishop's Stortford is a smaller town in Hertfordshire. On the old road between Cambridge and London, Chapman, Cleese, and Idle may have passed through the town in their student years.

"novice"—A "novice" is a person who's in probationary status in a religious order, a new entrant. The allusion here is that this "diocesan lovely" is anything but inexperienced.

bleak landscape — (PSC; animated link out of "Job Hunter") Staged very much like a Shell Oil commercial from 1964 titled "Mojave Run," which featured side-by-side cars driving across a barren desert. The oil additive being touted in these commercials was "Platformate." See the entries for "Crelm" and "Shrill" in this same episode for more on this commercial.

"Bonetti, Peter" — ("Crackpot Religions Ltd.") Bonetti (b. 1941) is a retired footballer for Chelsea and England.

"Bradshaw, Mr. E.R." — (*"How Not to Be Seen"*) Jones has played Inspector Elizabeth Bradshaw in Ep. 19, in the "School Prize-Giving" sketch.

• C •

"Chabrol stops at nothing" — ("Mr. Neville Shunte") Claude Chabrol (1930–2010) was a significant French New Wave film director of this period. Directing films in Italy and France, Chabrol had produced *Les Biches* in 1968, a daring look (for its time) at bisexuality, and a film that most likely had many more conservative types asking if he would stop at anything, indeed.

"Charlton, Jackie" — (*"Yummy, Yummy"*) Jack Charlton (b. 1935) wasn't a frontman for a pop group, but a star defender for Leeds United. He played for England between 1965 and 1970, and was part of the successful World Cup team in 1966.

Chinese for Business Men — (PSC; "Conquistador Coffee Campaign") The book cover reads *"Chinese for Advertising Men,"* while the printed script called for *"Chinese for Business Men."* Silly as it may sound, BBC Publications offered the very similar *Introduction to Chinese: A BBC Radio Course in Spoken Mandarin* (1966) by David Pollard, which was a companion piece to a BBC Radio program.

The continuing presence of China and Chinese references in *FC* indicate the expanding Chinese presence in the international community during this period, and most probably reflects the very real anxiety felt by many as China's population and economy boomed. This is the era of Chinese-American saber rattling and then diplomacy, with President Nixon's much-celebrated visit to China in 1972 affirming the growing significance of China in the First World of global politics, and eventually economics. See entries for Eps. 23 and 25 for more.

"cholera . . . athlete's head" — ("Conquistador Coffee Campaign") "Cholera" is a diarrheal illness caused by bacteria; "mange" is a skin condition caused by burrowing mites (often in pets); "dropsy" is soft tissue swelling due to excess water; "the clap" is a sexually transmitted disease; "hard pad" is a form of distemper in dogs; and "athlete's head" is a silly version of athlete's foot (*tinea pedis*, mentioned in Ep. 25), a fungal skin infection.

"clever people like me, who talk loudly in restaurants" — ("Gavin Millar, Critic") Cleese had earlier offered a very similar critical rant in the *ISIRTA* episode "Incompetence" (5 May 1968), employing precisely the same cant and phrasing:

> Well, there it is. Education is still the same teeming hotch-potch of half-formed conjecture, the same turmoil of conflicting opinion in the seething melting pot of emotion that it was last week. Tomorrow, who knows? Today, who cares? Yesterday, I went to the dentist. Has this country got the education it deserves or not? Perhaps yes, perhaps no, perhaps perhaps. There are still plenty of "ifs." If we go on the way we are, the system may collapse. If we change, we may not change wisely. If I ruled the world, every day would be the first day of spring. Well, who can sort out this sorry mess? Who can say? I can say, and here are some of the things I can say: Wallaby. Rumpus. Bee straddle. Cornucopia. Beech root. Oh dear, I think I've gone again! Fish. Corn plasters. . . . (*ISIRTA* transcription, "Incompetence")

coastline — (PSC; "Repeating Groove") This entire scene was shot above Broadsands Beach, South Devon, on 13 May 1970 (WAC T12/1,416).

"Conquistador Coffee" — ("Conquistador Coffee Campaign") A wry comment on the presence of European conquerors ("conquistadores") in Central and South America from the fifteenth century and beyond, introducing and then controlling the production and distribution of coffee for many years thereafter.

Also, in a section of the underground documentary-type film *Primitive London* (mentioned in the notes to Eps. 2 and 8), a (staged) advertiser's recording session is depicted, where the brand name of the product is "Señor Coffee."

"Crelm" — (animated link into "Agatha Christie Sketch [Railway Timetables]") Probably intended to sound like the proprietary and popular "Crest" toothpaste brand name, which had introduced its fluoride additive "Fluoristan" in 1955 (here called "Fraudulin") by announcer Idle. See more on Crelm and early British TV advertising in notes to Ep. 26. The two cars racing across an open landscape scenario is borrowed from Shell Oil commercials of the 1960s. The additive "Platformate" was claimed to give the car better gas mileage per tank, and the winning car (with Super Shell fuel) raced through the paper barrier first. Here, the car hits the barrier, which then crushes the car.

"cross the Atlantic on a tricycle" — ("Crossing the Atlantic on a Tricycle") This is likely a reference to the recent and celebrated crossing of the Atlantic by explorer Thor Heyerdahl on papyrus rafts (Ra I and Ra II). Heyerdahl and his exploits will be covered in much more detail in Ep. 28, "Emigration from Surbiton to Hounslow."

Also, Brit John Fairfax had recently rowed alone across the Atlantic, and had been featured on *This Is Your Life* in early 1970 for his troubles.

"crumpet over sixteen" — ("Crackpot Religions Ltd.") A "crumpet" is a slang term for a sexually available woman, in this case of legal age.

• D •

Daily Mirror — ("Crackpot Religions Ltd.") The *Daily Mirror* was by this time competing (and badly) with Rupert Murdoch's *Sun*—candid photos like this one of Bishop Sarah appeared regularly in both papers, and obviously appealed to the reading audience.

"deliberate ambiguity, a plea for understanding in a mechanized world" — ("Mr. Neville Shunt") This very concern fueled much Modern Art in the late nineteenth and early twentieth centuries. The dehumanizing effects of the Industrial Revolution found their way into the man-machine sculptures of Epstein, the horrors of the more efficient and gruesome slaughter in WWI, the antiseptic architecture of Gropius and the Bauhaus movement, the restless cacophony of Eliot's *Waste Land*, the cinematographical poetic images of Ezra Pound and Vachel Lindsay, and that same filmic influence in Duchamp's painting and sculpture, among many others.

In a number of works "the beast" embodied the heartless, relentless machine, and even earlier, of course, that mechanical marvel the train had been known as "The Iron Horse."

The "deliberate ambiguity" has also been a staple of avant garde film since the 1920s, and then New Wave film in the 1950s and 1960s, a reaction to the spot-on narrative clarity ("this means this") of most traditional (read: classical narrative) film. See Bordwell and Thompson for more.

"diagram of a tooth" — ("animated link out of "Job Hunter") This is the same image Gilliam used—his own smile—in the previous episode for the "Conrad Pooves's Dancing Teeth" animation.

Different Voice Over — (PSC; animated link into "Job Hunter") Uncredited in the printed script, this is Idle.

"Domino Theory" — (animated link out of "Job Hunter") Gilliam's narrator (Gilliam himself) describes this theory fairly accurately. Much U.S. foreign policy in this period was aimed at supporting anti-Communist governments, forces, or even rebels around the world, both covertly and, where necessary, in full view on the world stage, as in Vietnam. President Kennedy (1917–1963) had given the theory credibility in September 1963, when he'd discussed the dangers associated with the potential collapse of South Vietnam without U.S. aid (*Times*, 10 Sept. 1963: 8).

• E •

"Ecce homo" — ("Mr. Neville Shunte") Latin, the phrase translates to "behold the man" (John 19:5).

Episode 24 — Recorded as Episode 6 (Season 2, Episode 6), and broadcast eleventh in the season.

Also appearing in this episode, and uncredited, are Dilys Marvin (*Omnibus*), Lewis Alexander (*Doctor Who*), and Len Kingston (on film; *Play for Today*). The David Agency (located at 6 Holborn Viaduct, EC1) provided Willy Bowman (*The Troubleshooters*), George Feasey, and Philip Webb (*The Wednesday Play*), while the Blyth Agency sent over Marvin, Dorothy Watson (*Z Cars*), and Pat Dooley for small roles.

Exchange & Mart — (PSC; "Job Hunter") A long-standing buying and selling publication for all sorts of goods (cars, appliances, real estate), which now has a significant online presence in the UK.

• F •

"film's won a prize" — ("Conquistador Coffee Campaign") The worldwide film festival phenomenon came to life during the Pythons' formative years, with the major festivals—including those held annually in Cannes, Berlin, Moscow, and San Francisco—being established in the 1950s. It was at these festivals that many of the so-called New Wave films and filmmakers appeared for the first time, and the film festival became a very important venue for non-traditional (meaning outside the Hollywood studio or approved national film systems worldwide) films to find both a critical and then commercial audience. Filmmakers who obviously influenced the Pythons—including Truffaut, Godard, Pinter, and Antonioni—were discovered at such festivals.

"Football Special" — ("Agatha Christie Sketch [Railway Timetables]") Often an additional train put on just for days a football match is in the offing. This way, fans of a particular team can travel together and begin their merrymaking before reaching the stadium. (The author experienced this firsthand, watching as two Chelsea supporters consumed significant quantities of vodka—"hidden" in sports drink bottles—between Hammersmith/Fulham and Cardiff. Incidentally, a celebration was in order, as Chelsea beat Arsenal 2–1, and won the FA Community Shield.)

• G •

"get knotted" — ("Mr. Neville Shunte") A *New Society* article reported in 1963 that "get knotted" was an emerging phrase, and that younger people were using it to mean, essentially, "go to hell."

"GLC 9424075" — (animated link into "Agatha Christie Sketch [Railway Timetables]") Shell gasoline was advertised in 1954 with the new additive "ICA"—"Ignition Control Additive." Closer to home, "GLC" was the then fairly new acronym for the Greater London Council, an administrative authority for public works in Greater London, and which the Conservatives controlled in 1970.

Also, "942" was the telephone prefix for New Malden in 1968. See Ep. 27 for more on Malden.

"gradient signs" — ("Agatha Christie Sketch [Railway Timetables]") These are ground-level signs posted along railroad right-of-ways indicating the grade (up or down, ending or beginning) along the track ahead. The signs usually feature an upward or downward arrow and a number.

• H •

holds up a card saying "joke" — (PSC; "Conquistador Coffee Campaign") Returning here to the time-honored cartoon tradition seen in Warner Bros. cartoons of the 1940s and beyond, and especially in the self-conscious, gag-ridden cartoons of Tex Avery. These asides to the television (not studio) audience rather abruptly take the sting off particularly pointed barbs, or those just in really poor taste. In Ep. 17, the "Architect Sketch," captions ("Satire") are used to the same effect.

holidaymaker in braces, collarless shirt . . . — (PSC; *"How Not to Be Seen"*) Though quite a long way from the camera, the man (Chapman) doesn't appear to be dressed much like the costume description provided by the printed script.

"Holidaymaker Special" — ("Agatha Christie Sketch [Railway Timetables]") A train destined for a holiday spot, probably the southern coast, and likely making fewer stops along the way. These also could be additional trains put on during bank holidays, when pilgrimages are made south to the beaches.

"Hornchurch" — ("Agatha Christie Sketch [Railway Timetables]") As in the "New Cooker Sketch" in Ep. 14, the Pythons reel off a slew of locally known placenames, including:

"Hornchurch"—Located about fifteen miles north and east of Charing Cross, there is not a train station in Hornchurch. The nearest main line is located at Upminster.

"Basingstoke"—South of Reading, in Hampshire. By Ep. 42, Basingstoke will be in Westphalia.

"Caterham"—Both Caterham and Chipstead (both in Surrey) are on the Caterham and Tattenham Corner Services line and part of the Southern Railway.

"Lambs Green"—There is a Lambs Green in Dorset and Sussex, both well away from the Caterham and Chipstead line.

"Swanborough"—In Swindon (see below), it seems that Sir Horace's beloved railway has in fact been dismantled. The portion of the line that ran between Stanton Fitzwarren and Hampton (through Swanborough) is no longer in service.

"King's Cross"—Still a major hub in northeast central London, King's Cross is in Camden.

"Swindon"—Located in the southwest of England (Wiltshire), Swindon is also mentioned in Ep. 26.

"Wisborough Junction"—Wisborough Green is in West Sussex.

"Gillingham"—There is a Gillingham in both Kent and Dorset.

"Bedford, Colmworth"—Both in Bedfordshire.

"Fen Ditton"—Just outside Cambridge in Cambridgeshire, this station should have been well known to at least the two Cambridge alums, Chapman and Cleese.

"Sutton"—Also located in Bedfordshire.

"Wallington"—In the London Borough of Sutton, on the Southern rail line. The jumbled directions these stops would require indicate that the Pythons grabbed names from their collective hats as they wrote this sketch—the joke being the attention to detail the characters like Tony (Palin) and Lady Partridge (Chapman) exhibit for their beloved railway timetables.

"Hainault"—In the London Borough of Redbridge, Hainault lies at the very edge of Greater London, north and east of the City. Hainault was originally on the loop line to Ilford.

As in other sketches where directions or precise details are included, the Pythons tend to rely on memory as well as plainly contrived information, meaning the overall point here is the fixation Neville Shunt (Jones) exhibits for railway timetables, and not the specifics of the timetables themselves. The BALPA Spokesman in Ep. 16 (played by Idle), would disagree, of course, arguing the point for accuracy, as did a number of letter writers to *FC*.

• I •

"I inherited this religion from my father" — ("Crackpot Religions Ltd.") Almost certainly a slighting reference to the radio preachers Herbert and Garner Ted Armstrong, a father and son associated with the Worldwide Church of God. Beginning as the Radio Church of God in the 1930s, the organization grew rapidly with the rise of its medium, with the broadcast being named "The World Tomorrow" on the eve of WWII. Similar to Arthur Crackpot's church, the Worldwide Church of God solicited donations (tithes) of its membership, and was seen by many Christian pundits as a cobbled-together (and very profitable) cult:

> Small wonder that the church's annual income is estimated at around $55 million. Or that Founder Armstrong zips round the world to visit such leaders as Japan's Prime Minister Eisaku Sato or India's Indira Gandhi in a Grumman Gulfstream jet that gobbles up at least $1.5 million a year. Former W.C.G. members charge that the Armstrongs live like kings while members often live in poverty in order to pay their tithes. They maintain that each of the two Armstrongs has elegant homes in Texas, California and England; that Herbert sports a $1,000 watch and bought a $2,000 set of cuff links and tie tack for a Jerusalem trip. (*Time*, 15 May 1972)

The church operated a university in St. Albans, as well, and could claim chess champion Bobby Fischer (Ep. 35) as a sympathetic friend.

The son, Garner Ted, had taken over as the voice of the media church in the 1960s, but a power struggle came to a head in May 1972, and the church's inner politics became front-page news. The "devilish" animation provided by Gilliam reflects the charge presented by Herbert to the church faithful in May 1972—son Garner was "in the bonds of Satan," and had to be reined in. See the balance of the contemporary article in *Time* on the church, its history, finances, and its internecine strife (15 May 1972).

"In fact, he's shot himself" — ("Conquistador Coffee Campaign") This witty exchange is reminiscent of one from the *Goon Show*, the "Moriarty Murder Mystery" episode (20 Jan. 1958). First, the Python version:

> Boss (Cleese): Very unhappy. In fact, he's shot himself.
> Frog (Idle): Badly, sir?
> Boss: No. Extremely well.

And the Goons' earlier version:

> Grytpype-Thynne (Sellers): He's been murdered.
> Neddie (Secombe): Badly?
> Grytpype-Thynne: No. Very Well. He's dead.

"in our Durham studios" — ("Crossing the Atlantic on a Tricycle") The BBC had regional offices and studio space in Midlands cities like Norwich and Birmingham, where regional material could be put together and eventually broadcast. These were the areas that often decided to "opt out" of broadcasting *Flying Circus*, especially during the first season, in favor of more local programming. For the Durham area, the BBC regional offices are located in Newcastle upon Tyne.

"inside the distance" — ("Crackpot Religions Ltd.") A sports betting term from both racing and boxing, allying the work of Crackpot's bishops and archbishops with that of the influence-peddler and illegal gaming industries.

"international Chinese Communist Conspiracy" — (animated link out of "Job Hunter") Chinese historian Elizabeth Perry writes of the then-rabid Chinese Communist conspiracy talk, especially virulent in the United States in the 1960s. (And since this is an animated link, it's not surprising that the troupe's lone American, Gilliam, would broach the subject.) Those active in the anti-Chinese movements included men like Robert DePugh, founder of a militia in California, whose beliefs included the alleged presence of an enormous and hostile Chinese Communist army massing on the Mexican side of the California-Mexico border, according to Perry. This over-the-top American paranoia is the subject of the following animation, as well. DePugh had been arrested after being on the run for more than a year in New Mexico in 1970, which probably kept both him and his beliefs in the public eye during this period.

This level of concern over Communist China was not isolated to the United States, of course. A sampling of letters to editors in both major and minor British newspapers illustrates this widespread paranoia, and as early as 1950. The Shoreditch Labour MP Ernest Thurtle (1884–1954) wrote this to the *Times*, regarding China's "extra-constitutional means" of consolidating power, and the threat to a free South Korea and Asia in the balance:

> In the light of these facts it is surely right that the United Nations should not consider membership and voting powers of [China] on a mere head-counting basis . . . and thereby delight the Cominform [the Communist Information Bureau]. On the contrary, it should watch the operations of this body with the gravest suspicion, recognizing that this *international Communist conspiracy against the free world* is not less dangerous because it has its fellow-traveller partisans in many countries and in all sorts of political parties. ("Communist China," 17 Nov. 1950: 5; italics added)

To Thurtle and others like him, the Chinese Communists and their sympathizers were everywhere, including the House of Commons.

Additionally, the threat of Chinese communism in 1970–1971 (before Nixon's celebrated trip to China in 1972) is clear in speeches/writings from the White House where SEATO and pan-Asian interests are discussed, and any mention of China is conspicuously absent (see "Building for Peace: A Report by President Richard Nixon to the Congress, 25 February 1971"). The goal was to strengthen a buffer zone around China, hopefully preventing a "domino theory" scenario across the Asian diaspora.

"It All Happened on the 11.20 from Hainault . . ." — ("Agatha Christie Sketch [Railway Timetables]") The Hainault to Redhill via Horsham and Reigate route (all in the Greater London area) demands quite a bit of backtracking, not surprisingly. And while Carshalton, Tooting Bec, and West Croydon are more or less on the way, Malmesbury is well west in Wiltshire.

"I think it must be one of them crackpot religions" — ("Crackpot Religions, Ltd.") Voiced by Carol Cleveland as part of an "elderly couple," this is one of the very few instances where an actual woman plays the role of an elderly woman in the series. The Pythons have from the beginning kept the fun roles to themselves—the rat bags and crones were especially rewarding—but as the series moved on Carol was given more opportunity to work with the troupe in front of the camera in comedic (as opposed to merely sexualized) roles. By Ep. 41, for instance, she shows she can deftly handle physical comedy in the form of a hair-trigger flamethrower bought at a department store.

"I've been in the sea for thirty-three years now" — ("City Gents Vox Pops") This beach scene was shot at Broadsands Beach on 13 May 1970 (WAC T12/1,416).

• J •

"John the Baptist had the most enormous . . . dental appendages" — ("Film Director [Teeth]") This may be a rather clever comment on the very popular film theory of the period, the "auteur" theory. Propounded by French New Wave writers-cum-filmmakers like Godard and especially Truffaut in the pages of *Cahiers du cinema*, then expanded and championed by American critic Andrew Sarris in 1968, the theory essentially argues that the director of a seemingly generic film produced by the studio system can still exert significant and ultimately identifiable "personality" on/in that film, so much so that his body of work can be examined for those influences. Directors mentioned by these theorists include Howard Hawks, Orson Welles, Fritz Lang, Sam Fuller, etc.

The fact that all Curry's characters feature large teeth, like Curry, is significant for the auteur theory, as well. For Truffaut, his own autobiographical experiences tend to emerge over and over in his films, including *400 Blows*, creating personalized films that reveal as much, allegedly, about the director as the subject or time in which the film was created. For Hawks, his depictions of relationships—especially older and younger male, the homosocial benefits of the male group, and male-female—provide a commonality from film to film, across the many genres he attempted.

"Jones, Tom" — ("Mr. Neville Shunte") "Tom Jones" is of course (1) the titular character from the 1749 Henry Fielding novel, and (2) the more contemporary Welsh-born (b. 1940) pop singer. British director Tony Richardson (1928–1991) had produced a very popular film adaptation of the Fielding novel in 1963. In 1969–1971, the singing Jones was starring in his own very popular *This Is Tom Jones* TV show, airing on ABC and ITV.

• L •

Labienus — (PSC; "Film Director [Teeth]") Titus Labienus, known as "Caesar's Lieutenant," lived c. 100–45 BC.

"La Fontaine's elk" — ("Mr. Neville Shunte") This may be an oblique reference to Jean de la Fontaine (1621–1695), the seventeenth-century beast fabulist.

"Lambert, E.V." — (*"How Not to Be Seen"*) Verity Lambert (b. 1935) has already been mentioned in Ep. 8, the "Buying a Bed" sketch. Lambert was a producer for *Doctor Who* episodes.

late-night line-up — ("Film Director [Teeth]") The two-chair set-up was characteristic of many discussion-type shows of this period. Already mentioned in Ep. 19, *"It's a Living," Late Night Line-Up* (1964–1972) was a popular television discussion program whose cameras showed up at a *FC* taping (probably Ep. 26), much to the consternation of the BBC hierarchy (WAC T47/216).

"lead piping" — ("Crackpot Religions Ltd.") Lead products used in construction in the UK—including piping, gutters, and roofing tiles—have for generations been stolen for resale on the street (lead melts down and is reformed very easily), especially by low-end criminals and drug addicts looking for quick money.

Lennon, John — (PSC; "Crackpot Religions Ltd.") Python contemporary and friend John Lennon (1940–1980) and Yoko Ono (b. 1933) had staged a very publicized "sleep-in" (or "bed-in") in 1969 in an attempt to bring awareness to the misery going on in Vietnam.

"level crossing" — ("Mr. Neville Shunte") Simply an intersection on the same level of either a road and a railway, or two railways (*OED*). The trainspotting subculture would have appreciated this reference, along with "bogies" and "shunt," for example.

"lists her hobbies as swimming, riding, and film producers" — ("Crackpot Religions Ltd.") The gist here is, of course, that Bishop Sarah is engaging in sexual affairs with film producers—visiting the "casting couch"—to secure acting parts.

"Lord Langdon" — (*"How Not to Be Seen"*) A character from a "Biggles" adventure, *Biggles Sorts It Out* (1967). Biggles has already been mentioned in Eps. 10 and 15, and will figure significantly in Ep. 33, where he (played by Chapman) will dictate a letter and shoot his best mate Algy (Palin).

"Lower class—I can't touch it" — ("Crackpot Religions Ltd.") Again, as Crackpot (Idle) earlier admits that paid church membership will bring prizes, here he is refreshingly candid as to the preferred level of income his parishioners need to have reached for participation. In Ep. 26, the undertaker (Idle) is also quite honest with the man (Cleese) who's brought his dead mother to the funeral home, describing the nastiness of both cremation and burial, and then admitting she's "quite young" enough to be "an eater." The undertaker then good-naturedly invites the man to join in the feast. In both instances, the characters are defying the common language of a transaction by admitting their levels of self-interest.

• M •

"MacDonald, Ramsay" — ("Ramsay MacDonald Striptease") The image of a respected, sober, and even grave man-of-the-people wearing women's undergarments is the deflation-by-ridicule approach employed by the Pythons throughout *FC* and the feature films. And MacDonald (1866–1937) was not the monied, cultured elite, either—he was of illegitimate birth and a working-class Labour politician—his position of authority put him in the cross hairs.

"Manchester and the West Midlands, Spain, China" — (*"How Not to Be Seen"*) Not surprising anymore to see the conflation of two Midlands areas, both destroyed here by nuclear attack, along with two of the most notably dictatorial regimes in existence, Franco's Spain and Mao's People's Republic of China. Franco had been in power since 1939; Mao since 1949, or much of the collective Pythons' lives.

"Millar, Gavin" — ("Film Director [Teeth]") A writer, actor, director, and editor, Millar (b. 1938) co-authored (with filmmaker Karel Reisz) *Technique of Film Editing* (1968), and created documentary profiles on big-screen luminaries including American Busby Berkeley, Brits Powell and Pressburger, and Frenchman Jean Renoir. Millar was also the film critic for *The Listener* for many years, beginning in 1970, also contributing to periodicals like *Sight and Sound*, etc.

Miss Johnson — (PSC; link out of "Job Hunter") Though not credited in the printed script, this voice seems to have been provided by Carol Cleveland.

"Most Popular Religion Ltd." — ("Crackpot Religions Ltd.") By sheer numbers worldwide, this would clearly be the Roman Catholic faith, though in Britain, Anglican Church membership exceeded Catholic figures.

Mr. Frog comes in — (PSC; "Conquistador Coffee Campaign") Though not mentioned in the printed script, Frog (Idle) enters through the window, not the door. This may have been a last-minute change to the scene, as most such moments (even the silliest ones) are noted in the printed scripts as written prior to tapings. The backdrop outside the window makes it clear that the office is supposed to be at least one floor above street level, as well. As the Pythons move into the second and third seasons, especially, the standard set of television practices—including entrances and exits and transitions of all kinds—are more and more altered, done away with, or made visible to the viewing audience, bringing a self-consciousness to the show that fed on itself, reflexively, from week to week, and then from season to season.

• N •

"narrow traction bogies" — ("Agatha Christie Railway Sketch [Railway Timetables]") A bogie is the wheel-and-axle configuration beneath train cars and engines. The newest bogie introduced during this period had appeared in 1963.

"nasty, greedy, cold hearted, avaricious, moneygrubber . . . *Conservative*" — ("City Gent Vox Pops") In short, the Pythons' definition of the enemy during this period, the Tories. They tended to poke fun at politicians and authority types in general, irrespective of political affiliation, but the real barbs and low blows are always reserved for more conservative types (Heath, Thatcher, Maudling, Nabarro, et al.).

A similarly themed cartoon appeared in the pages of *Private Eye* and features two City Gents, one saying to the other: "It's simple really—pensions for the over 80's, then the Euthanasia Bill . . ." (17 July 1970, 5). Versions of a "Euthanasia Bill"—where "incurables" could voluntarily off themselves—had been introduced into parliamentary discussion since at least 1935 (the "eugenics era," yes).

Nesbitt — (PSC; *"How Not to Be Seen"*) A name used several times (see Eps. 26 and 37, as well) for the prototypical Pepperpot. "Nesbitt" is also used by Peter Cook in his "Sitting on the Bench" sketch for *Beyond the Fringe*.

"Harlow New Town" is in Essex, and is one of the "new towns" designed and built after the war in the surge for adequate housing for the displaced millions.

"nine out of ten small countries" — (animated link out of "Job Hunter") A play on the toothpaste advertising slogan of the period, "4 out of 5 dentists surveyed," it was actually true that scores of countries around the world were benefiting from the somewhat paranoid foreign policy of the United States, and enjoying the proffered money, CIA presence, and trade deals. This may also be a comment on the continuing presence of American military forces in Europe and Asia since the end of WWII.

"no names no pack drill" — ("Crackpot Religions Ltd.") A "pack drill" is a military term for a punishment that includes forced marching with a heavy pack. The phrase means he's not naming names. Arthur Crackpot (Idle) further asserts that most religions demand such spiritual and temporal activities from adherents, and promises that his religion will not.

"North See Gas" — ("Crackpot Religions Ltd.") One of those topical, very contemporary puns that can become illusory over time, Britain was in the late 1960s still fairly new to the dependence on North Sea gas (then North Sea oil in the 1970s), meaning petroleum products were finally coming from British sources, not overseas suppliers. The phrase "North Sea Gas" was appearing regularly in newspaper headlines and stories during this period.

"North Walsham, Norfolk" — ("Crossing the Atlantic on a Tricycle") North Walsham is some twenty-five miles north of Norwich, already mentioned in this episode, and the location for much spring and summer location shooting for the Pythons.

"Norwich City Council" — ("Crackpot Religions Ltd.) A significant mention only because the Pythons had shot a good deal of location and insert footage in the Norwich area, hiring local actors where necessary, etc.

"Not for sale, what does that mean?" — ("Job Hunter") Cleese will later play a Merchant Banker who has no understanding of charity, giving, or the meaning of "inner life" (Ep. 30). These are the same kinds of character traits that will also be seen in the "Argument Clinic," where each man only understands his own specific area of expertise—"abuse," "complaints," arguing, and "being-hit-on-the-head" lessons (Ep. 29).

Number 10 Downing Street — (PSC; "Ramsay MacDonald Striptease") Official residence of the PM since the eighteenth century, though many PMs have used it only as an official residence (more like an office), and actually lived elsewhere.

• O •

old fashioned gramophone — (PSC; "At the seaside, repeating groove [gramophone]") This gramophone and Cleese are sitting on a rise above Brixham Harbour, just near the railroad tracks, and just off Dartmouth Road (at the terminus of Cliff Park Road).

"O Levels" — ("Job Hunter") This is the "ordinary level (of the General Certificate of Education examination)" (*OED*). An "A Level" is the "advanced level." These General Certificate of Education exams were introduced in 1951, just when the young Pythons would have been encountering their rigors in school. Performance on the A-Level exam often indicated whether a student was an acceptable candidate for university.

• P •

"Paddington" — ("Mr. Neville Shunte") Major departure and arrival station for train travel west and south of London.

Photo of Aussie bishop with beer can — (PSC; "Crackpot Religions Ltd.") Not unlike the gifted churchman and cricketer David Sheppard, Bishop of Woolwich discussed in Ep. 17, this strange conflation—sporting prowess and organized religion—might be a reference to Australian rugby league star Father John Cootes (b. 1941), a Roman Catholic priest who scored two tries against New Zealand in the 1970 Rugby League World Cup. The Aussies would end up beating Great Britain at Headingley for the Cup.

"Public Service Film No. 42" — ("*How Not to Be Seen*") These public service films did, in fact, exist, and included titles like *Litter Defence Volunteers* (1968), showing how children can band together to clean up Britain; and *Teenagers Learn to Swim* (1972).

• R •

"Rio Tinto" — ("Crackpot Religions Ltd.") Rio Tinto is an international mining corporation, and would have been a solid investment for the "Most Popular Religion" priest/investor. "Allied Breweries" disappeared in a 1978 merger, but had been a large UK-based distillery corporation. The priest also appears to be reading a copy of the *Financial Times*, the voice of the marketplace and modern investor, and certainly meant here to take the place of a Holy Bible.

Rio Tinto was unwillingly in the news during this period when it was leaked that a secret uranium mining deal had been reached between the UK government's Atomic Energy Authority and Rio Tinto in South West Africa, an unofficial colony of South Africa (*Private Eye*, 31 July 1970: 16–17). All above board business dealings with the apartheid state had become news fodder, forcing such deals into backrooms and out of the public eye.

• S •

"SE5" — ("*How Not to Be Seen*") The postal code SE5 is in the Camberwell area of Greater London. There is only one Black Lion Road in the UK, and it's in Wales.

"S. Frog, sir" — ("Conquistador Coffee Campaign") The use of the initial can be seen as an attempt by Mr. Frog to ally himself with the more respected academicians, athletes, and highly placed social and political figures of Britain's nineteenth and twentieth centuries. Most noted nineteenth-century cricket players were known throughout their careers by initialed names, like "W.G. Grace," for example. Life in academe also merited such respect, including A.J.P. Taylor (referenced in Ep. 11 and *HG*) and E.M.W. Tillyard, to name just two.

Secondly, this may be yet another reference to the tradition of "Gentlemen vs. Players" in Lords cricket matches. There, forename initials were used to distinguish between the professional and amateur players. In this case, S. Frog (Idle) wants to be clustered in with the "Gentlemen" as opposed to the more plebeian

"Players" in the world of competitive advertising. See the note for "Gumby, Prof. R.J." in Ep. 9.

"Shrill" — (link into "Agatha Christie Sketch [Railway Timetables]") Shell Oil is a British-Dutch oil and gas consortium in business since the late nineteenth century. The word "shrill" (meaning a loud, strident sound) may also refer to the way in which the Shell Oil TV (and much American TV) commercials were delivered/perceived in the period.

Commercial television didn't appear in the UK until 1954, when ITV came on the air, and competition with the BBC was finally in place.

The "Shrill" Man (uncredited) is Palin.

"Shunt, Neville" — ("Agatha Christie Sketch [Railway Timetables]") An appropriate name for this train-obsessed playwright, as a "shunt" is a British railway term for "switching" individual cars into connected trains. Shunt is spelled "Shunt" and "Shunte" in the printed scripts.

This is certainly a reference to the writer Nevil Shute (1899–1960), an aeronautical-engineer-turned-author whose works often centered on the very technical. For example, his novel *No Highway* (1948) sets a fictional narrative within a discussion of aircraft structural integrity and design. It's reported that Shute's books were often on grade school required reading lists, where the young Pythons may have found them, and judged them exceedingly pedantic. In 1950, however, the *Times* book reviewer called Shute's work "indispensable" for young boys, ranking with *Tarzan* and Zane Grey ("What Boys Read," 15 Feb. 1950: 8). The Pythons would have been ages 7 to 11 at this time.

"Slough" — (*"How Not to Be Seen"*) There are a number of Leighton Roads in the UK, not surprisingly, though none in Slough, which is north of Windsor and south of Gerrards Cross.

"Smegma" — (*"How Not to Be Seen"*) A secretion from the sex gland areas of mammals, and here a rather sophomoric "naughty" word. A Mr. Glans (Cleese) appeared in the previous episode.

There is a "Belmont" in the very same area of Llanelli, Carmarthenshire as Black Lion Road. See the entry for "SE5" for more.

"soft-sell" — ("Conquistador Coffee Campaign") Advertising that attempts to be subtly persuasive, as opposed to loud and aggressive (*OED*). American television of the period was *not* considered to be a bastion of the soft-sell approach (see the entries for "Crelm" and "Shrill").

stock film of Ramsay MacDonald — (PSC; "Ramsay MacDonald Striptease") The stock film used here is nine seconds of MacDonald footage from VisNews. Ramsay MacDonald (1866–1937) was twice Prime Minister and the first Labour PM—in 1924, and then 1929–1935. See the entry for MacDonald above.

stock film of a small house — (PSC; *"How Not to Be Seen"*) The stock film of explosions is not accounted for in the WAC records for the episode, excepting a ten-second section from the Bond film *Goldfinger* (actually from a 1964 news report *about* the upcoming Bond film) from British Movietone "Goldfinger" E. 9536 (WAC T12/1,414).

"stopping train" — ("Agatha Christie Sketch [Railway Timetables]") In the UK, a "stopping train" is one that makes stops at smaller stations between larger cities. The express trains race right past most of these smaller stations.

• T •

"today's diocesan lovely" — ("Crackpot Religions Ltd.") This presentation is meant to mimic the well-known nude and semi-nude "Page Three Girls" feature of the tabloid the *Sun*, introduced by owner Rupert Murdoch in 1969. This same set-up is earlier used in the courtroom scene of Ep. 15, where Miss Rita Fang is introduced.

"tonight's star prize" — ("Crackpot Religions Ltd.") Yet another game show reference, this to the popular *Take Your Pick* (1955–1968), where the "star prize" could have been a lounge suite, home organ, or appliance, etc. *Take Your Pick* has already been satirized in Ep. 20.

This reference is certainly at least a jab at the emerging evangelical broadcasting phenomenon which would sweep across the Bible Belt of the United States in the 1970s, as well as the "older" churches' (Roman Catholic; Church of England) long-established practices of offering sinecures, forgiveness, absolution, and even guaranteed escape from damnation with appropriate contributions to the cause. What the Python characters seem to actually be doing—in barefacedly asking for contributions and aknowledging the quid pro quo nature of the modern church(es)—is pulling back the veneer of respectability to reveal a perfectly understandable business arrangement that can satisfy both parties. In this they propose and even make likely a *successful* transaction—a rarity in the Python world. They will revisit this particular area of spiritual hypocrisy in their controversial feature film *Life of Brian*.

trendy pop-music set — (PSC; *"Yummy, Yummy"*) This set is probably meant to look like *Top of the Pops* (1964–2002), which in 1970 was setting trends by highlighting current pop acts to an audience of millions.

"Turkish Champions FC Botty" — ("Interview in Filing Cabinet") The Turkish football champion in 1969–1970 was Fenerbahçe SK, and in 1970–1971 was Galatasaray SK.

"Twelve Caesars" — ("Film Director [Teeth]") Perhaps a reference to the 1968 Granada TV television series (six episodes) *The Caesars*, directed by Derek Bennett, and starring Freddie Jones.

• V •

various atom bombs and hydrogen bomb — (PSC; "*How Not to Be Seen*") A number of these film clips of mushroom clouds were already quite well known, many having been used in the closing credit sequence of the 1964 Kubrick film *Dr. Strangelove.*

"Vespasian" — ("Film Director [Teeth]") Vespasian was emperor of Rome from 69 to 79 AD.

• W •

waterbutt — (PSC; "*How Not to Be Seen*") A receptacle for gathering rainwater. In this case, it is a large barrel, and it's apparently where Ken Andrews is hiding before he's blown up.

"West End hit" — ("Agatha Christie Sketch [Railway Timetables]") London's West End has been the center of theatergoing in London for many years. There are multiple theatrical houses in this area that have featured everything from Christie's long-running *Mousetrap* to Terence Rattigan works to revivals to the most contemporary hits from playwrights including Harold Pinter (Eps. 2 and 10) and David Storey (Ep. 28).

"white card . . . black card" — (animated link into "Agatha Christie Sketch [Railway Timetables]") In the late 1950s and early 1960s Crest ran a commercial where half a school class reportedly brushed with Crest while half used ordinary toothpaste, with the Crest half displaying shining white teeth.

white flannels and boater — ("Agatha Christie Sketch [Railway Timetables]") This is the uniform (for the Pythons) of the "jolly upper class," and includes creased pants ("white flannels") and the straw hat ("boater"). This same uniform will be used in Ep. 33, "Salad Days," and was earlier seen in the "Undressing in Public" sketch (Ep. 4) shot on the Bournemouth beaches for the first season.

wide-boy type — (PSC; "Crackpot Religions Ltd.") A street tough, essentially, one who lives by his wits, criminality, etc. A "respray job" would be repainting a stolen car prior to selling it on the street. The printed script calls for Palin to also be dressed in a "small moustache and kipper tie," but he's instead dressed as a vicar, and just "acting" shady. (A "kipper tie" was a very wide tie.)

"Worplesdon Road" — ("*How Not to Be Seen*") There is a Worplesdon Road in Guildford, Surrey. "Ivy Cottage" is a very common place/home name, not unlike "The Dells." "Hull" (or Kingston upon Hull) is located in Yorkshire. Hull was first mentioned in Ep. 1, where Mrs. Violet Stebbings requests the death of Bruce Foster (Chapman), and will be mentioned again in Ep. 39 by the Eddie Waring character, played by Idle.

• Y •

"you won't catch the 3.45" — ("Agatha Christie Sketch [Railway Timetables]") This fixation on and fascination with railway timetables has some precedent in life, actually, as Peter Ackroyd points out in *London: The Biography*: "It [the railway, during the nineteenth century] became the great conduit of communication and of commerce in a world in which 'railway time' set the standard of the general hurry" (581). By 1849, Ackroyd continues, the enormous impact of the burgeoning railway system in and around London led to "the whole country" being "transfixed by the idea of rail travel." Mr. Shunt, mentioned above, is certainly one of those so transfixed.

Among poets more noteworthy than Shunt (or Shute), Alfred, Lord Tennyson would also "draw poetic images" from the railway in some of his work during the bustling nineteenth century (see Drabble's *For Queen and Country*, 116–17).

Philip Scowcroft has written an interesting piece on the history of railways and trains in music, which includes mentions of songs and even suites composed for train lovers, and in response to train experiences (musicweb.uk.net/railways).

"Yummy, Yummy, Yummy" — ("*Yummy, Yummy*") This cover version is from an album called *Autumn Chartbusters*, and the original song is written by Arthur Resnick and Joey Levine (WAC T12/1,414).

Episode 25: "Art Gallery Strike"

The Black Eagle; "And now . . ." Man and "It's" Man; *Titles* (silly Cleese v/o); "In 1970 the British Empire lay in ruins . . ."; **Dirty Hungarian phrasebook**; Constable runs to the scene; Court scene (Phrasebook—"Call Alexander Yalt"; "Call Abigail Tesla"); Page 3 profiles; *Animation: Picketers and* 2001: A Space Odyssey; *World Forum*: Communist quiz show; *Animation: "I wonder just how much Molly knew?"*; "In 1914 the balance of power lay in ruin" crawl; "Ypres 1914"—abandoned ("Knickers 1914"); Karl Marx and Che Guevara kissing, surprised; **Art gallery strike** ("The Man from the Hay Wain"); *Animation: Characters leaving paintings*; "Here is the news": Men sawing woman in half, strikers outside window; Sotheby's sells empty paintings; *Animation: Venus de Milo: ". . . bloody consultation!"*; Meanwhile at Television Centre: "Ypres 1914"; Drawing for it, and the Padre takes "the other way out"; Hospital for Over-actors; *Animation: Over-actors, bombs creating flowers*; Gumby flower arranging; **Spam**; Historian discusses other Viking and Spam victories; Closing "Spam" credits; Post-coital Marx and Guevara.

• A •

"acceptable legal phrase" — ("Court [Phrasebook]") At Gray's Inn (see "Gray's Inn" note below) dining sessions, "permission to smoke" or even permission to leave a room must be obtained from the most senior barrister present, meaning even a bathroom break could be put off almost indefinitely.

Adventure music as for buccaneer film — (PSC; *"The Black Eagle"*) The musical snippet used here is called "Battle at Sea," and is penned by J. Pearson (WAC T12/1,416).

"Afro-Asian Nations" — (link out of "Court [Phrasebook]") These would have generally been Third World nations with existing Commonwealth or potential trade status with Britain, including South Africa, India, Pakistan, etc. The term doesn't appear in official parlance until about 1954.

"A horse . . . a horse" — ("Hospital for Over-Actors") From Shakespeare's *The Tragedy of Richard III* (5.4.7). The part of Richard has been for generations played in a rather arch style, and Shakespeare himself contributed to this over-the-top-ness by giving Richard a hunched back and something of a cripple's manner that may have been completely fictional.

"All we bloody want is a little bloody consultation" — ("Art Gallery Strike") Probably a call for more equitable consultation in the NEDC, the National Economic Development Council, where government, trade unions, and management were supposed to be able to talk amicably. In June 1969, British Airport Authority drivers struck (and performed work-to-rule) for eleven days, claiming that new "self-drive" vehicles had been introduced into the workplace "without proper union consultations" (*Times*, 24 June 1969: 2). The return of "reformism" with the new Heath administration in 1970 meant that trade unions had become burdensome throwbacks, a more free market economy (and Thatcherism) was on the horizon, and labor unrest would only escalate with increasing global competition (falling prices, runaway production, etc.). This ongoing attempt to wrest control of production from wealthy, often distant owners to workers (via unions) is the same "anarcho-syndicalist" movement mentioned later by the peasant Dennis (Palin) in *Holy Grail*.

An unattributed Trade Union Congress (TUC) announcement after the Conservatives came to power in 1951 made it clear this crucial "consultation" would continue to be pursued during the Tory years:

> The range of consultation between both sides of industry has considerably increased, and the machinery of consultation has enormously improved. We expect of this government that they will maintain the full practice of consultation. (qtd. in Unit 20, *Britain: 1950–1990*)

It seems that by 1970, what workers still wanted (and weren't getting from their union leaders) was just a bit of "bloody consultation."

It's also probably no accident that in this episode—where recognizable communist leaders attempt to compete on a game show (and then two of them "snog")—there is a significant left-leaning, up-with-labor presence. In the UK, at least, the British Communist Party was inextricably intertwined with workers and trade unions, at least by empathy and influence, if not number of elected representatives.

Animation: Involving grotesque Hamlets — (*"Animation: Over-actors, Bombs Creating Flowers"*) The background for these dueling Hamlets is from de Vries's book *Perspective*, Plate 7, and it has been tinted. Gilliam has changed things up a bit—he's turned the image upside down from the original. See the index for other appearances of this and other de Vries works.

There is no indication why the character here is Hamlet and not Richard III. The other over-actors in this hospital include panto characters Long John Silver and Ratty, both mentioned elsewhere in these episodes, though both often expected to overact, to play to the last row in the popular pantomime performances.

The plane that follows this scene looks like a Handley Page Bomber, a British plane used during and after WWI. The bomb that emerges from the plane is much, much larger than it could actually handle, perhaps a tribute to the Tex Avery cartoon *Blitz Wolf*. The pig aviator drops an equally large bomb from a very small plane. The city being bombed in Gilliam's animation is clearly New York City, and a mushroom cloud of flowers erupts.

Animation: sketch leading to . . . — (link out of "Communist Quiz") The painting used by Gilliam for his "little joke" with Madonna and child (eyes open, eyes shut, eyes open, etc.) is Giovanni Bellini's *The Madonna of the Meadow* (c. 1500), which has been a part of the NG collection since 1858. When the Madonna and child are jerked away by the shepherd's crook, it reveals a complete background (no holes, like those when figures on strike leave their paintings). Gilliam had created a full background for use in "The Spot" animation back in Ep. 19, and clearly employs it again here.

At one of the "TV Weekly Programme Review Meetings" held regularly after the broadcast week, BBC executive Oliver Hunkin (of Religious Affairs) complained that he found this particular image objectionable (WAC T47/216). Incidentally, Hunkin (1916–2011) had not only dined as the guest of the Archbishop of Canterbury at Lambeth Palace in September 1970, his specialty (when it came to appearing on the BBC) seems to have been discussing depictions of sacred moments (Christ's birth, the Passion, Mary and Christ's body, etc.) as presented by the "Old Masters." He seems the perfect type to be offended by the Pythons' version(s) of irreverent divinity.

The other character in the animation is from a brightly recolored version of the Dürer work *Erasmus of Rotterdam* (1526), and was originally an engraving. This work is part of the Museum of Modern Art (MMA) collection. The Pythons would pay tribute to Dürer in a *Fliegender Zirkus* episode created for Bavarian Television in 1971, the 500th anniversary of the artist's birth.

"Assizes at Exeter" — ("Court [Phrasebook]") Assize courts were criminal courts held around England (and Wales) until 1972 (replaced by the Crown Court), where judges traveled from city to city, region to region, hearing cases and rendering judgments. Assizes were held regularly in Exeter, with cases heard including those charged with murder, religious heresy (including being a Quaker), witchcraft, etc. Having spent so much time shooting in the Devon area, it's no surprise that the Pythons mention Exeter (since Devon County assizes were typically held at Exeter).

"Aussies certainly know a thing . . ." — ("Court [Phrasebook]") Probably a reference to Australian-born Rupert Murdoch (b. 1931), owner and publisher of the rival to the *Daily Mirror*, the equally salacious tabloid the *Sun*.

• B •

"baked beans" — ("Spam") The "traditional English breakfast" as advertised on café and restaurant sandwich boards around London to this day consists of (primarily) the following: eggs, bacon, sausage, baked beans, mushrooms and tomato, and bread.

"beautiful lounge suite" — ("Communist Quiz") This was just the type of fabulous "star prize" offered on the popular game show hosted by Michael Miles, *Take Your Pick*.

Black Eagle — (*"The Black Eagle"*) Other pirate movies include *Captain Blood*, *The Sea Hawk*, and *Treasure Island* (the latter of which will figure prominently in this episode). There is a Western of the same name filmed in 1948, and directed by Robert Gordon, as well as a silent Indian film (1931) and a 1965 South Korean film.

The title here seems to be taken directly, however, from the 1942 swashbuckling film *The Black Swan*, based on the Rafael Sabatini novel and starring Tyrone Power and Maureen O'Hara.

"Blighty" — (*"Ypres 1914*—Abandoned") British armed forces slang term for "home."

Blue Eagle, The — (*"The Black Eagle"*) A 1926 film based on an O. Henry short story, directed by John Ford and starring George O'Brien and Janet Gaynor.

Noted author Sabatini (1875–1950) penned books that inspired the popular swashbuckling movies *The Sea Hawk* (1924), *Scaramouche* (1923), and *Captain Blood* (1924). Of Italian birth, Sabatini lived much of his later life in Wye, on the border of England and Wales. He did not write *The Blue Eagle*, but he did write the color-named stories/novels *The Red Mask* (1898), *The Red Owl* (1900), and *The Black Swan* (1931), etc.

"breach of the peace" — ("Dirty Hungarian Phrasebook") A legal term indicating a violation of the public peace by affray, riot, or similar disturbance (*OED*).

"Brentford Football Ground" — ("Art Gallery Strike") Extant stadium on Griffin Park, Braemer Road, Brentford. The Brentford Football Club still plays at this site.

"Bridge at Arles" — ("Art Gallery Strike") The Dutch Post-Impressionist Vincent Van Gogh (1853–1890) painted multiple versions of the *Bridge at Arles* motif, most in 1888.

"Bristol . . . Molineux" — (link out of "Communist Quiz") The Bristol Rovers are the football team Cleese grew up admiring.

"Molineux" is the home stadium of Idle's team, the Wolverhampton Wanderers.

"British Empire . . . ruins" — (*"The Black Eagle"*) By 1970, the British empire had changed drastically since Queen Victoria's day, and perhaps especially since the end of WWII. Australia, Canada, and New Zealand were granted "Dominion" status in 1926 (translating to autonomy in the Empire), followed in 1947 by Pakistan and India being granted a peaceful independence. Many others, including Cyprus, Zambia, the Seychelles, Zimbabwe (Rhodesia [Ep. 45]), and Malaysia also were separated (forcibly, often) from the British Empire in the twentieth century. So in the short lifetimes of the Pythons, the British Empire had indeed diminished in size and international significance.

This "devolution" figured prominently in election after election, with both major parties arguing time and again that each other were to blame. See Morgan's *Britain since 1945* and Marwick's *British Society since 1945* for more. The political cartoons of the era are also replete with the pundits' take on the British Empire's precipitous decline in both scope and influence. See the British Cartoon Archive.

In economic terms, the UK's inflation rate was up but not dramatically—reaching 6.4 percent in 1970, after a steady three-year rise. Though still relatively low, the inflation rate was the highest it had been in the UK since the very bleak days of 1952, and the depths of postwar paucity. And "tomorrow" won't be any kind of salve for the Pythons and the UK—by the last season of *FC*, in 1974, inflation will reach a burdensome 16.0 percent. Needless to say, Labour took full advantage of the Conservatives' bad luck with the economy during 1970–1974, whipping the "staggering economy horse" to a Labour victory in the 1974 General Election. Myriad labor strikes (including the first national dock strike since 1926) and trade union and worker unrest also helped fuel the "British Empire in ruins" fires in the early 1970s.

See the various pertinent entries in *Eyewitness: 1970–79* for more on this economically depressed era, when both Tory and Labour candidates shouldered significant voter blame, and the Liberals (and fringe parties) picked up many disaffected voters.

British Tommy — (PSC; *"Ypres 1914*—Abandoned") The British WWI infantryman. Short for "Thomas Atkins," or "Tommy Atkins," the typical private soldier, the name worked its way into official and unofficial military parlance by the early nineteenth century.

"Bromley" — ("Spam") Part of Greater London, and located south of the City.

"Brueghels" — ("Art Gallery Strike") Pieter Brueghel (or Bruegel) (c. 1525–1569) has been called the "greatest and most original Flemish painter" of his period, and his centers of interest were the "activities of man," especially in village and communal settings. Weddings, harvests, dances, group meals caught his attention, and ice skating is significant in at least three paintings—*Winter Landscape with a Bird Trap* (1565), *Numbering at Bethlehem* (1566), and *Winter, Hunters in the Snow* (1565).

Brueghel employed satire and humor in his work and, significantly, Brueghel "chooses the peasant, whom he sees as an uncomplicated representative of humanity; a member of society whose actions and behavior are open, direct, and unspoiled by the artificial cultural gloss that disguises, but does not alter, the city-dweller's natural inclinations" (*Gardner's*, 619). Monty Python's commoners (Rustics, Pepperpots, middle-class couples) are similarly open and straightforward, cutting through social niceties and mores without shame, pause, or self-consciousness. Python goes the step further, too, acknowledging the characters' postmodern surroundings, by "complicating" their peasants to such a degree that they can stand toe-to-toe with their betters in virtually any setting. It's also worth noting that myriad Flemish artists of this period included similar characters in their work, as there are skaters and laborers and shopkeepers in abundance in these paintings.

Interesting, too, that Brueghel would often be commissioned to paint people *into* existing landscapes/monument portraits by other artists. In the Monty Python world, those same characters are now walking out of some of these same paintings.

• C •

"canteen's open upstairs" — ("*Ypres 1914*—Abandoned") In the BBC's studios in Shepherd's Bush, the canteen *is* actually located on a floor above the studio spaces.

cherub — (PSC; "Art Gallery Strike") This figure is not in the original Titian painting, and has been placed there by Gilliam for the purposes of the narrative. (See the entry above for Brueghel—he would do the same thing for certain prestigious clients.) In fact, with the inclusion of the cherub, it seems that the focus of the adoration has moved from the Father and Son, who sit atop the painting, to the foregrounded cherub.

"Chichester Festival" — ("Spam") This theater was founded in 1962 under director Laurence Olivier, featured a thrust stage (no proscenium), and played host to virtually all Shakespearean actors of repute. The artistic director through the late 1960s and into the 1970s for Chichester was John Clement. There were no productions of *Richard III* between 1962 and 1972 at Chichester. (See the festival's website for more.)

"ChromaColour" — ("*The Black Eagle*") Probably meant to refer to the many early film color processes (Technicolor, ComiColor, CineColor, Brewster Color, etc.), since this is a film reference, but it is also a reference to the 1969 introduction of the Zenith "Chromacolour," a new television picture tube that greatly increased the color saturation of the picture. In other words, this is a TV picture tube that would have been much talked-about at the BBC and elsewhere.

"Clarke, Sir Kenneth" — ("Art Gallery Strike") This might be a bit of a doubled reference. The Sir Kenneth *Clark* (1903–1983) who would appreciate the state of the work of art had created *Civilization* (1969), the groundbreaking TV series looking at art and history. The other possibility (homonymically, but also by profession) is Python contemporary Kenneth Clarke (b. 1940), a Cambridge graduate and lawyer. Clarke contested Mansfield in 1964 and 1966 but lost, then took the Rushcliffe seat in 1970 from Labour. His focus in his early political career was industrial relations, making him a perfect fit for this sketch.

During his Cambridge years, Clarke offended many by inviting—in his capacity as chairman of the Cambridge University Conservative Association—the "fascist, Oswald Mosley, to speak there, provoking a near riot and the resignation of his contemporary, Michael Howard" (*Observer*, 5 Aug. 2001). Chapman, Cleese, and Idle likely at least knew of Clarke in school, and he was certainly the rising star in labor relations during this period, and would have been very high profile. Clarke would be called to the bar by Gray's Inn (see below) in 1963, and came to be known as one of the "Cambridge Mafia," a group of conservative-minded students who later served in Tory governments.

"Colwyn Bay" — ("Spam") Located in northern Wales, Jones was born in Colwyn Bay in 1942. The Jodrell Lecture Theatre, however, is located in Kew Gardens in London.

crash zoom — (PSC; "*Ypres—1914*") A rapid camera zoom in on a character or object. As the lens movement is very self-conscious, the shot has been little-used since the 1970s. Crash zooms can be seen in abundance in myriad Hong Kong cinema action pictures, however.

"Cup Final in 1949" — ("Communist Quiz") The Wolverhampton Wanderers (also called the Wolves) did win the 1948–1949 Football Association Cup on 30 April 1949, beating Leicester 3–1, with Arsenal winning the 1949–1950 FA Cup by beating Liverpool, 2–0.

Idle grew up in the Wolverhampton area, attending the Royal Wolverhampton School, and followed the Wanderers closely, which is probably why this fact is memorialized correctly.

• D •

"Déjeuner Sur L'Herbe" — ("Art Gallery Strike") A fitting choice to instigate a strike, as this painting is credited with breathing to life the Modernist movement in the arts. The painting was created by Edouard Manet (1863; Galerie de Jeu de Paume, Paris), who actually predates the Impressionist movement, and is known as a Realist. The painting features a classical setting and figures—a nude woman sitting with clothed men in a pastoral scene—but the facts that each of the figures depicted were actual people and not mythological characters, and that Manet utilized nudity unconventionally, outraged many.

Manet's "lot" might have been Gustave Courbet, Jean François Millet, and Honoré Daumier, and this group inspired the later Impressionists such as Monet, Renoir, and Manet himself. The Impressionists both associated with these Realists, as well as exhibited with them, according to *Gardner's* (760). Critical response to Realism was fairly harsh, and the public struggled to appreciate the limited palettes and bold use of paint.

"De Vere, Dino" — (*"The Black Eagle"*) The surname is perhaps a reference to animator Alison De Vere (1927–2001), who had been working for TV Cartoons as *The Yellow Submarine* progressed in 1967–1968. An example of a Python-rendered agglomerate name, "Dino" may be a reference to noted film producer Dino De Laurentis (1919–2010). De Laurentis was producing *Waterloo* (1970) during this period, and had produced the critically acclaimed Italian films *Bitter Rice* (1949) and *La Strada* (1954) from directors De Santis and Fellini, respectively.

• E •

"English portraits" — ("Art Gallery Strike") These would include Hogarth, Gainsborough, Joshua Reynolds, Thomas Lawrence, John Constable, George Romney, and others. All of these artists' works are featured in the National Gallery's collections.

Episode 25 — Recorded as Ep. 1 (Season 2, Episode 1) on 25 June 1970, and broadcast 15 December 1970. The Pythons (in consultation with Ian MacNaughton, John Howard Davies, and studio bosses like Michael Mills and Duncan Wood) would go through the scripts and the recorded shows and decide which were the strongest, and those would be placed at the start of the season. In September 1972 Wood watched and ranked the first nine episodes of the third season, then hinted very strongly that they should be broadcast in the order he suggested (WAC T12/1,428).

"Esher" — ("Court [Phrasebook]") The home of this sexually active judge has also been the alleged setting for "Confuse-a-Cat" and "The Dull Life of a City Stockbroker," meaning it was the epitome of Greater-London-middle-class-dom for the Pythons. In Ep. 36 an orgy is supposed to have occurred in the city. Python friend and later financier George Harrison lived in Esher during this period.

Esher is mentioned often elsewhere in *FC*, including Eps. 9, 28, 31, and 44.

• F •

famous statues — ("Art Gallery Strike") The statues depicted include: Michelangelo's *David* (1501–1504; Galleria dell Accademia, Florence), and *Moses* (1513–1515; San Pietro in Vincoli, Rome); the Venus de Milo (130–120 BC; Louvre); Rodin's *The Thinker* (1880; Metropolitan Museum of Art), and *The Kiss* (1886; Musee Rodin, Paris); the *Discus Thrower* by Myron (c. 485 BC–c. 425 BC); and *Laocoon* (Vatican Museum), among others.

"fisties" — (*"Ypres—1914"*) Child's game, also called "rock, paper, scissors."

"Flemish school" — ("Art Gallery Strike") Includes names like Jan van Eyck, Rogier van der Weyden, Hieronymus Bosch, Pieter Brueghel, Peter Paul Rubens, Frans Hals, Rembrandt van Rijn, and Jan Vermeer, and covers the end of the fourteenth through the seventeenth centuries. Van Eyck, Bosch, Brueghel, Rubens, Rembrandt, and Vermeer are all well represented in the National Gallery in London. (Gilliam will also sketch repeatedly from Bosch as he preps for the animated sequences in *Holy Grail.*) It's clear that in writing the sketch, the Pythons were basing their choice of paintings on those held by the National Gallery, and equally clear that Gilliam (working apart from the others) felt free to pick from whatever paintings struck his fancy, and were available in the art books Gilliam had at hand.

Floor Manager — (PSC; *"Ypres 1914*—Abandoned") The actual floor manager for *FC* during this period was George Clarke.

"Foreign Nationals" — (*"The Black Eagle"*) These are foreign visitors (and perhaps potential immigrants), many with the intent of seeking permanent UK residency. This mention follows the much-publicized "Rivers of Blood" speech given by Conservative Cabinet member Enoch Powell (and which would cost him his position in the Heath opposition government). See the notes to Ep. 5 for much more on Powell and the inflammatory racial issue in late 1960s Britain.

• G •

"Gainsborough's Blue Boy's" — ("Art Gallery Strike") Thomas Gainsborough (1727–1788) actually preferred landscape to portraits, though he worked in both. His "Blue Boy" is properly titled *Jonathan Buttall: The Blue Boy* (c. 1770).

"German woodcuts" — ("Art Gallery Strike") Most notably, the German woodcuts of Albrecht Dürer (1471–1528), who will be prominently featured in the first of Python's German episodes in 1971, *Monty Python's Fliegender Zirkus*. Other later German woodcut artists include Max Beckmann (1884–1950), and Franz Eichenberg (1901–1990).

"Gray's Inn" — ("Court [Phrasebook]") One of the four Inns of the Court (with Middle Temple, Inner Temple, and Lincoln's Inn) where English lawyers are called to the bar. Cleese, at least, would have been familiar with both the terminology and the profession, having read law at Oxford, and where he might have encountered another Gray's Inn call-up, Kenneth Clarke, discussed earlier.

"Grin and Pillage It" — ("Spam") "Grin and Bear It" was an internationally syndicated cartoon panel originally drawn by George Lichtenstein, as well as the title of a 1954 Donald Duck cartoon short from Disney.

group of famous characters from famous paintings — (PSC; "Art Gallery Strike") These protesting characters include Venus, Rembrandt (a version of his 1669 self-portrait), Arnolfini, Infanta Margarita, Mr. Andrews from Gainsborough's *Mr. and Mrs. Andrews* (1748–7149; National Gallery), and "La Goulue" from Toulouse-Lautrec's *La Goulue Arriving at the Moulin Rouge with Two Women* (1892). See the entry for "various famous paintings" below for more.

This strike action send-up may also have been suggested by the ongoing strike by ITV personnel that came to be known as the "Colour Strike." Technicians at all ITV companies refused to use the colour recording or broadcast equipment in 1970–1971, forcing dozens of newly colorful shows to go back to glum black and white for the duration.

group of paintings with picket signs pass by — (PSC; "Art Gallery Strike") As the men saw the woman in half while listening to the radio, the art gallery picketers passing the window outside include: Venus (from the Botticelli painting), Charles I (Anthony Van Dyck), Arnolfini (Jan van Eyck), Mr. and Mrs. Andrews (from Gainsborough's *Mr. and Mrs. Andrews*), Mona Lisa (da Vinci), and the Infanta (or Margarita, from Velazquez).

The Latin sign, "Ars longa vita brevis," carried by Venus, translates to "Art is long, life is short." The other signs read "Art for Art's Sake" (essentially, "Ars gratia artis") and "Equal pay for Cubists."

This last sign may be a reference to many in Britain who responded with puzzlement whenever the state-funded galleries would purchase (with tax dollars) "questionable" works of art—including those by twentieth-century artists who flouted traditional art forms and genres. On the open market during this period, modern art works (including Cubism) were fetching very attractive prices around the world.

• H •

"Ha, ha, ha, I got him" — ("Court [Phrasebook]") This "got you" moment is borrowed from the earlier mentioned *Take Your Pick*, specifically the "Yes/No Interlude" section where host Michael Miles or Brian Johnston try to trick the contestant into answering "yes" or "no."

"Hammers" — ("Communist Quiz") Nickname for the West Ham United football club, formerly the Thames' Ironworks club, hence the nickname.

"Coventry City"—Coventry would not even be involved in an FA Cup Final until 1987, when they would beat Tottenham Hotspur 3–2 at Wembley. This is probably a bit of a pranging from Idle, at least, toward a perennial also-ran in English football.

"FA Cup"—The Football Association's Challenge Cup was instituted in 1871 when fifteen teams vied for the small trophy cup, with the Wolverhampton Wanderers (Idle's hometown team) winning. More recently, 600 teams a year try for the FA Cup, with Manchester United leading the way with ten championships, followed by Arsenal and Tottenham Hotspur (eight apiece).

"Hay Wain" by Constable — (PSC; "Art Gallery Strike") John Constable (1776–1837) was one of England's most celebrated and prolific landscape painters of the late eighteenth and early nineteenth centuries. His *The Hay Wain* was painted in 1821, and was part of Constable's abiding interest in the English countryside and rural people.

And while it's clear the Pythons are using their memories of this painting to conjure this rustic image, even peering closely at the painting in the National Gallery it's impossible to tell what the haymaker standing near the hay wain is actually wearing. The haymakers in the far background actually look to be wearing at least the same colors as Pythons' version of the man. There is even a similarly clad figure in Constable's *The Cornfield* (1826).

Two other works in the National Gallery feature more prominently figures like this "bumpkin": Hart's *A Rustic Timepiece* (1856) features a smocked boy, and John Robertson Reid's *A Country Cricket Match* (1878) also features similar rustic costuming. The Pythons' continuing use of "normal folk" in *Flying Circus* indicates a similar (albeit comedic) interest in the English common man shared by these nineteenth-century landscape artists.

Lastly, a copy of Constable's famous painting will be used as set decoration in Ep. 39, in the Zambesi home.

He claps his hand to his mouth; gong sounds — (PSC; "Court [Phrasebook]") This game show "gong" moment (delivered by the Clerk) is a reference to the gong sounding if a character says either "yes" or "no" during Michael Miles's barrage of questions (the so-called Yes/No Interlude) on *Take Your Pick* (1955–1968). Alec Dane was in charge of the gong on *Take Your Pick*.

"Hepworths" — (*"The Black Eagle"*) Meant to invoke the fashionable designers and design houses who worked for the major Hollywood studios in the 1930s and 1940s, including "Adrian" (1903–1959), who designed costumes for Rudolph Valentino films, and for Cecil B. DeMille and MGM studios.

He starts running down the street, round corner . . . — ("Constable Runs to the Scene") This scene was likely shot in Richmond, and perhaps on the same day (or on the same trip) as the exterior still shots for "Cheese Shop" (Ep. 33), which were taken down in the King Street area. The fish and chips corner shop the policeman (Chapman) pauses near sells the *Darlington and Stockton Times*, a regional newspaper.

"Horton Terrace" — ("Court [Phrasebook]") There is a Horton Terrace in Halifax, near the intersection of Halifax Road and Denholme Gate Road.

"Hughes, Norman" — (*"The Black Eagle"*) A Lecturer then Fellow at Queens' College at Cambridge between 1952 and his retirement in 1985, Hughes (1918–1994) may have been a professor remembered by the Cambridge Pythons (Chapman, Cleese, and Idle) as they wrote this episode and cast about for names. Hughes was a palynologist, or one who studies plant microfossils—and primarily pollen and spores. Hughes was characterized as "outrageously authoritarian" by many who knew him, which may also account for his memorability to the Pythons.

• I •

"If there's any more stock film of women applauding . . ." — ("Court Scene [Phrasebook—"Call Alexander Yalt"]) Stock film is mentioned many times in the scripts and production notes, of course, but this is the first time a character has drawn attention to the practice directly. As the show moves along and matures (this being the second-to-last episode of the sophomore season), both the Pythons and the audience seem more willing to acknowledge the artificiality of the television presentation, and suspension of disbelief becomes less necessary.

"Impressionists" — ("Art Gallery Strike") Includes artists like Monet, Pissarro, Renoir, and Degas who depicted scenes from contemporary life and landscapes, and whose preoccupation with the immediacy of the moment actually sent them out-of-doors to paint in the elements (as opposed to eighteenth- and early nineteenth-century landscape artists like Constable and Turner who would paint from sketch books back in their studios). The Impressionists' fascination with light and its coloring effect on landscapes and structures characterized much of their work. Monet, for example, painted twenty-six different views of Rouen Cathedral.

The Impressionists are especially significant to the Pythons due to their collective rejection by the "Academy" of classical art in France—this snubbing signaled the beginnings of Modern Art, paving the way for nontraditionalists in the other artforms, including literature, comedy, and television, eventually.

"Industrial proletariat" — ("Communist Quiz") Marx's partner in ideology, Frederick Engels (1820–1895), wrote *The Condition of the Working Class in England* in 1845, a significant section of which (chapter 3) is entitled "The Industrial Proletariat." And as has been pointed out by a number of historians, Marx consistently discussed the condition of the industrial proletariat only in relation to a nineteenth-century capitalist paradigm, so applying his work to Maoism or even Leninism (or Trotskyism), for example, would be, to many, as silly and unsupportable as Marx appearing on a game show.

"In 1914, the balance of power lay in ruins" — (*"Ypres 1914*—Abandoned") This phrasing is a bit of a giveaway that the source of the material is actually World War I–era history and period writings. The term "balance of power" seems to have been used quite a bit to describe the European situation, as well as justify attack or retreat at the outset of the war. One noteworthy example: In economist John Maynard Keynes's *The Economic Consequences of the Peace* (1919), he writes of the devastating results of the recently concluded war, seeing very little to celebrate. Keynes (1883–1946)—a Cambridge man who ran in the same intellectual circles as Russell and Wittgenstein (both Ep. 32)—was especially concerned about the long-term effects the Versailles Treaty reparations would have on Germany and the world:

> England had destroyed, as in each preceding century, a trade rival; a mighty chapter had been closed in the

> secular struggle between the glories of Germany and France. Prudence required some measure of lip service to the "ideals" of foolish Americans and hypocritical Englishmen, but it would be stupid to believe that there was much room in the world, as it really is, for such affairs as the League of Nations, or any sense in the principle of self-determination except as an ingenious formula for rearranging *the balance of power* in one's own interest. (80; italics added)

By Ep. 37, the Pythons will be very nearly quoting historian Trevelyan as they write about the European wars for "Dennis Moore."

"International Court in the Hague" — ("Court [Phrasebook]") The International Court of Justice was created after WWII, and is connected to the United Nations. This "judging" theme will be revisited at the conclusion of Ep. 37, where judges who finished out of the money are consoled by mothers, spouses, etc.

"Italian Masters of the Renaissance" — ("Art Gallery Strike") See entry for "Renaissance School" below.

• J •

"Johnson, Teddy, and Pearl Carr" — ("Communist Quiz") Husband-and-wife contestants in the 1959 Eurovision Song Contest, Carr (b. 1923) and Johnson (b. 1920) performed "Sing, Little Birdie." Carr and Johnson came second in the contest, which features songs/singers from European countries. The contest began in 1956, and has already been featured at the conclusion of Ep. 22.

"jurisprude" — ("Court [Phrasebook]") A clever play on words, a "jurisprudist" (a somewhat archaic term) is one knowledgeable in the law, while a "jurisprude" adds a sexual connotation to the legal definition. In the Python world the conflation of illicit sex and legal figures (judges who wear female underwear beneath their robes, for example) has become something of a given. In Ep. 15, the accused judge (Jones) keeps a mistress in Belsize Park, while the sitting judge (Chapman) allegedly has a "Chinese bit" at "8a Woodford Square," the divulging of which leads to a capital punishment sentence, even though the death penalty's been abolished since 1965. Also, in Ep. 27, the judge (Jones) can't wait to get out of the courtroom and attend his Gay Lib meeting.

• K •

King Rats — (PSC; "Hospital for Over-Actors") King Rat is a character in the "Dick Whittington" pantomime. Panto characters obviously loomed large in the Pythons' collective youth—Dobbins, Puss, Principal Boy, Goose, Ratty, and Long John Silver (and the Pantomime Princess Margaret) appear throughout *FC*.

The Nurse in this scene is a walk-on part played by Barbara Shackleton (*Dixon of Dock Green*). In the BBC records the King Rats (and the others in this scene) are simply described as "9 male water rats," and they are: J. Neil, Neil Crowder, Donald Groves (*The Wednesday Play*), James Haswell (*The Wednesday Play*; *Doctor Who*), Roy Brent (*Some Mothers Do 'Ave 'Em*), Les Bryant (*The Wednesday Play*), Stuart Myers (*Doctor Who*; *Star Wars*), Aubrey Danvers-Walker (*Dixon of Dock Green*), and Alistair Stuart-Meldrum (*Brett*) (WAC T12/1,242). The scene was shot at Ealing TFS on 27 May 1970 (call was at 8:30 a.m., incidentally).

• L •

"Landseer, Edward" — ("Art Gallery Strike") This is a memorial mistake, as Landseer's first name is "Edwin." The Pythons do often write from memory, without checking for specifics.

Sir Edwin Henry Landseer (1802–1873) was an English animal painter. Many of his works were made into engravings, and he was very popular and much copied. The Tate Britain features many Landseer paintings; the National Gallery, none. His work depicted here, *Stag at Bay*, was created in 1846.

Long John Silver — ("Hospital for Over-Actors") Silver is a character from Robert Louis Stevenson's novel *Treasure Island* (1883). The book was filmed by the Walt Disney Company in 1950, starring Robert Newton as the Long John Silver character, and then re-filmed in half-hour episodes for television. The Pythons mention (and/or depict) the character several times in *FC*, including Eps. 5, 10, 23, and 32. Long John Silver's annual, seemingly unforgettable presence in the popular Christmas pantomime (also broadcast on the BBC) probably accounts for his constant inclusion in *FC*.

• M •

man . . . mouth — (PSC; "Art Gallery Strike") This character is meant to look very much like the Rustic (Chapman) character from Ep. 2; he is clearly a visual "type" borrowed from Rembrandt, Constable, and the Pythons' oeuvre, as well. See notes to Ep. 2 for more on the Rustic "type."

"Marx, Karl" — ("Communist Quiz") Similarly, a 1966 newspaper cartoon by Cummings features a David

Frost interview show with guests Charles de Gaulle, Lyndon Johnson, Alexei Kosygin, Mao Tse-tung, and Adolph Hitler (*Times*, 23 Nov.). See the British Cartoon Archive.

Marx was a German-born resident of London (after 1849) when he penned one of his most famous works, *Das Kapital* (1867). Marx (1818–1883) was the ideological inspiration for many in the later Russian Revolution of 1917, and his writings would be trumpeted (and reinterpreted) by followers of Lenin, Trotsky, and Stalin. Marx would live in England for almost thirty-four years, plenty of time for him to actually appreciate the exploits of various English football teams.

"Lenin"—Famed leader of the October Revolution in Russia in 1917, the figure of Lenin (1870–1924) is here played by Eden Fox (*Doctor in the House*, contributed to by Chapman and Cleese), who will also appear sawing a woman in half in "Art Gallery Strike."

"Che Guevara"—Latin American political activist, Guevara (1928–1967) would have been fresh news fodder during this period, after he was captured and executed in Bolivia. Gilliam takes this role.

"Mao Tse-tung"—Leader of the People's Republic of China, Mao is played by actor Basil Tang (*Doctor Who*). Mao seems a favorite reference point for the Pythons, having been mentioned previously in Eps. 19, 23, and 24, all in the second season.

Lastly, it shouldn't be a surprise by this time to see this jumble of historical figures in an incongruous setting, as the Pythons are clearly what French film maker Jean-Luc Godard would call "children of Marx and Coca-Cola," or a product of the pastiche, aggregate culture that was the late 1960s, the beginnings of the Postmodern period.

Miles, Michael — (PSC; "Communist Quiz") The prototypically unctuous and effusive host, Miles has already been mentioned by name—and called "a grinning type monster"—in the printed script for Ep. 20. The leering, often violent Michael Miles–type host/Priest also appears in Ep. 24, also played by Cleese, when Mrs. Collins (Palin) tries to win the star prize (of the Norwich City Council). In the later feature film *Time Bandits* (dir. Gilliam), Jim Broadbent (b. 1949) will play this same oily host type.

Mr. and Mrs. Bun enter—downwards (on wires) — (PSC; "Spam") In the 1960s American car commercial "Let Hertz put you in the driver's seat," the lucky smiling couple are lowered into the car as it's driving down the open road.

This entry is also acknowledging the general artificiality of the stage entrance, as well. In the first sketch of Ep. 24, "Conquistador Coffee," S. Frog (Idle) steps into the office through the window. As the show progresses the Pythons—whether from experiment or just boredom—will push the boundaries of suspension of disbelief.

". . . my bum" — ("Dirty Hungarian Phrasebook") Again, miscommunication is the fillip for the scene, with the unusual additional element being that here the miscommunication is textually acknowledged. Generally, the Python characters will push on through a scene—usually attempting some sort of communication or transaction—without mentioning the miscommunication at all (cf. the "Police Station" in Ep. 12). This may be an indication of the transition in various episodes during this series from the self-aware-but-silent Modernist approach (where Joycean dialogue, for example, can be delivered and responded to without any character batting an eye) toward the more brazen self-aware-and-trumpeting-the-fact Postmodernist approach to the artificiality of the constructed scene. The fact that the oft-used "Women's Institute" film clip has already been mentioned by a character acknowledges the artificiality (the "television-ness") of the setting.

"my company does publish" — ("Dirty Hungarian Phrasebook") This structure—repeating the question in the form of an answer—was typical of the *Take Your Pick* game show, specifically the "Yes/No Interlude" hosted by Michael Miles. As long as the contestant did not use the words "yes" or "no" in their answer, the game went on, with questions coming one on top of the next. Miles and *Take Your Pick* are mentioned in Eps. 20 and 24.

• N •

"National Gallery" — ("Art Gallery Strike") It was decided as early as 1824 that an art collection for the nation was needed, and Parliament funded the purchase of John Julius Angerstein's private collection (for £57,000), and even used his house on Pall Mall to display the paintings. Trafalgar Square was later chosen as the designated site for the purpose-built gallery, intended to be accessible to the wealthy and commoner alike. From the outset, the National Gallery has also encouraged students to use the Gallery, through which the field-tripping, school-blazered Pythons in their grammar school years may have traipsed.

***newspaper like the* Mirror** — (PSC; "Court" [Phrasebook]") The *Daily Mirror* is a sensationalist and (often) lurid daily tabloid published in London since 1903, and which adopted the tabloid layout in the late 1930s. The Pythons have already lampooned letters to the *Mirror* in Ep. 10, as well as the pin-up girl photos and commentary in Ep. 24. Another period tabloid newspaper "like the *Mirror*" is Rupert Murdoch's *Sun*, discussed in the notes to Ep. 24.

Nimmo, Derek — (PSC; "Dirty Hungarian Phrasebook") The printed script gives the only hint that this is an impersonation of an actual person. Nimmo (1930–1999) was a British character actor who by 1971 had appeared in the TV shows *All Gas and Gaiters* (1966); *The Bedsit Girl* (1966); *Blandings Castle* (1967); *Sorry I'm Single* (1967); and *Oh Brother!* (1968–1970). He had also appeared in small roles in the feature films *A Hard Day's Night* (1964) and *Casino Royale* (1967).

Nimmo is featured on the BBC's 17 January 1970 *Radio Times*, advertising a new series of *Oh Brother!* (1968–1970).

• O •

"over the top" — ("Hospital for Over-Actors") Playing a scene melodramatically, or "chewing the scenery," as the theatrical stage saying goes. The villains in the blood tragedies of the Elizabethan and Jacobean stage were often written for just such bombastic, snarling, over-the-top-ness—audiences accustomed to bear-baiting and cockfights reveled in the Tamburlinian carnage.

A contemporary review of a *Richard III* production staged in Nottingham starring Leonard Rossiter (*Oliver!*) as the renowned king celebrates this over-the-top-ness: "Mr. Rossiter assumes the stance of a maimed hero; he stalks about, lurches, and jerks his head bird-like from side to side. He is often quite still, and occasionally erupts into dangerous rages" (Frank Marcus, *Sunday Telegraph*, 1971).

In April 1970 Norman Rodway (1929–2001) was playing Richard in the Royal Shakespeare Theatre.

• P •

"Phillips . . . pen" — (*"Ypres 1914"*) Certainly a schoolboy's complaint, and perhaps even indicative of the young Pythons growing up in the immediate post-war years. Since "Phillips" is a fairly English name, the complaint that he is a "German" must also be an attempt at an insult (and would have been, certainly, when the Pythons were growing up in the shadow of the Second World War). If the child's nationality was not known at the time, this kind of betrayal could have landed him and his family in one of the British government's internment camps set up just before the war to protect the homefront from acts of sabotage (*Eyewitness: 1940–49*, "Internment").

The "yah boo" reference finally cements the origin of the invective, being an oft-heard English prep school witticism the Pythons would have known well. (Several legitimate letters to the editor in *Private Eye* also employ the word, accusing the editors of being priggish.) The term is also heard in several *ISIRTA* episodes, including the "Billy Bunter of Greyfriars School" episode (15 Mar. 1970). Cleese does not perform in this particular episode. (The episode begins with a rousing version of "Also Sprach Zarathustra," which Gilliam has also employed more than once.) The phrase can also be delivered as "yah boo sucks" on contemporary radio and in magazines.

A derivation of this phrase—"yarooh" ("hooray" spelled backwards)—was the catchword for Billy Bunter, the schoolboy literary creation of Charles Hamilton (as Frank Richards), published 1908–1940. See the entry for "Bounder" in Ep. 31 for more on Billy Bunter and friends.

"Privateers" — (*"The Black Eagle"*) Sir Francis Drake (1540–1596) was one such privateer, meaning a ship, captain, and crew commissioned by the sovereign to prey on foreign shipping. Drake (or "Dlake") will be mentioned in Ep. 29, in the "Erizabeth L" sketch.

• Q •

"QC" — ("Court [Phrasebook]") Queen's Counsel. Here used primarily to rhyme slyly with "cutie."

• R •

"radiator" — ("Art Gallery Strike") According to the National Gallery's Technical Services team, in 1836 there were a number of fireplaces scattered about, as well as hot water pipes running under the floors for heating, with water supplied from a central boiler. Two additional central boilers and ventilation were installed in 1876, with the heating for the building's wings *always* being provided centrally (with the exception of the individual fireplaces). Thus, individual radiators were never a part of the National Gallery's heating system.

"Renaissance School" — ("Art Gallery Strike") The Renaissance period is seen as a revival of arts and letters built upon the influence of classical models, and is the dividing era between the so-called Dark Ages and the modern world. Significant names in the Italian Renaissance School of art would be Giotto, Duccio, Donatello, Angelico, Botticelli, da Vinci, Michaelangelo, and others. (Other European countries also had their various Renaissance periods, mostly in the fifteenth and sixteenth centuries.) Titian was a sixteenth-century Venetian artist, part of the later "High

Renaissance," and was considered by many to be the father of modern painting. He was often imitated and had many followers, meaning his position as a shop steward for the paintings' union was an apt choice by the Pythons.

"Richard III" — ("Hospital for Over-Actors") Last of the Plantaganet monarchs, Richard maneuvered his way to the throne, reportedly, over the bodies of friends, kinsmen, and enemies. This crippled, hunched, overtly evil figure is probably a dramatic creation of Shakespeare based on earlier (and also literary as opposed to historical) works by Holinshed (1529–1580) and Thomas More (1478–1535). Many productions of the play have taken up this "crippled" standard, as it makes for better visual, metaphoric drama—the hunch and unsteady gait play well to the back rows.

round corner and down another street — (PSC; "Dirty Hungarian Phrasebook") This running section (with Chapman) starts and finishes in the same Thorpebank Road area where "Silly Walks" (Ep. 14) began and Mrs. Crump-Pinnet lived (Ep. 14). The stadium lights for the Queen's Park Rangers facility can be seen in the background of several of these shots.

• S •

"Schlack, Joseph M." — (*"The Black Eagle"*) Probably a reference to the noted Hollywood producer Joseph M. Schenck (1878–1961), who headed studios such as United Artists in the 1920s and Twentieth Century-Fox later, and was instrumental in bringing to market the Todd-AO widescreen process. Schenck produced many of Buster Keaton's most notable films, among others.

A younger, hipper, and more unctuous Hollywood producer type of a similar name—Gerry Schlick (Idle)—is featured in Ep. 23, *"Scott of the Antarctic."* Both "Schlick" and "Schlack" sound like Yiddish-type cousins to what the Pythons might really be intending—"schlock," or shoddy (movie) goods.

scudding clouds — (PSC; *"The Black Eagle"*) Essentially, being driven by the wind with little or no sail. A phrase used in various forms by such varied authors as Edgar Rice Burroughs, Leo Tolstoy, Bram Stoker, and Herman Melville.

Sheikh, a Viking warrior . . . Greek Orthodox priest — (PSC; *"Ypres 1914*—Abandoned") In the BBC studios, there would have been multiple comedy and game shows in production during this period, so there actually could have been colorfully costumed extras available. Dramas, however, would mostly have been shot in separate studio spaces.

For this particular sketch, the Sheik is played by Ishaq Bux (*Dixon of Dock Green*), the Viking Warrior by Steve Kelly (*Barlow at Large*), the Male Mermaid by Cy Town (*Doctor Who*; *Star Wars*), the Nun by Gillian Phelps (Eps. 12, 32, 39; *Microbes and Men*), the Milkman by David Melbourne (*Softly Softly*; *Z Cars*), and the Greek Orthodox Priest by Andrew Andreaus (*Doctor Who*). The Spaceman who appears momentarily is played by Fred Clemson (*Softly Softly*) (WAC T12/1,416).

"shore of England" — (*"The Black Eagle"*) That treasure had been coming home to England since at least 1588, when Drake defeated the Spanish Armada, signaling the beginning of the end of Spain's worldwide domination.

slowly and silently toward the shore — (PSC; *"The Black Eagle"*) This extended faux-intro scene was shot on the night of 13 May 1970 at Broadsands Beach, near Torquay (WAC T12/1,416). The pirate landing boat was hired from G. Dyer in Brixham (WAC T12/1,242).

Solomon — (PSC; "Art Gallery Strike") In the printed script, the character played by Chapman is named "Solomon." The two figures at the top of the painting are actually, however, the Father and the Son, with the Holy Ghost depicted as a dove. King David, bearing a harp, is also depicted toward the bottom of the painting, but not Solomon.

"Sotheby's" — ("Art Gallery Strike") Fine art auction house founded in London in the mid-eighteenth century.

"spam" — ("Spam") Pressed, canned meat product from Hormel that appeared in 1937. The UK has been the second-leading consumer of Spam for many years, according to Hormel. The Pythons may have included the reference due to Spam's very significant presence during the food rationing postwar years in England, when the tinned product would have been much more available than other meats—if it could be found to buy, it could be eaten without worrying about ration restrictions.

"spam, bacon, sausage and spam" — ("Spam") This menu delivery style was likely inspired by the Goons, no surprise, and specifically a scene from "The Thing on the Mountain" (6 Jan. 1958):

> Crun (Sellers): Here's the menu.
> Neddie (Secombe): Let me see now . . . elephant's eggs, elephant's eggs, elephant's eggs, elephant's eggs, elephant's eggs, elephant's eggs. . . hmm. Umm, I think I'll have some elephant's eggs.
> Crun: Elephants eggs are off, sir. They've gone off—PONG!

More recently, only two weeks after Ep. 25 was first broadcast, on 15 December 1970, *Private Eye* included a short, familiar passage in their 1 January 1971 issue that betrays the almost instantaneous cultural influence of *Flying Circus* by the end of the second season. An article describing the attractions of Neasden includes the "adventure" of eating out:

> Try the Fiesta (Tesco Road) just by the station. Specialities: Egg and chipps [*sic*] 3s 9d. Egg, chips and peas 4s 6d. Egg chips sausage and peas 5s 6d. Egg chips sausage bacon and peas 6s 9d. Egg chips sausage bacon tomato and peas 7s 11d. Egg chips sausage bacon tomato beans and peas 8s 9d. Eggs chips sausage bacon tomato beans fried bread and peas 12s 6d. ("*Off the Beaten Track* with Cyril Lord David Cecil B. De Mille," *PE*, 1 Jan. 1971: 13)

"Spanish Main" — ("*The Black Eagle*") This is what English traders (and pirates) called parts of Spain's holdings in the New World, including the northern coast of South America to the Caribbean Islands. It's actually a shortened version of "Spanish Mainland," which originally referred to what is now Columbia and Venezuela.

The Spanish empire had actually reached its height during the reign of Philip II (1556–1598), followed by a steady decline. During the eighteenth century, Spain fought a series of unsuccessful wars for territory (the Americas, Minorca, etc.) with Great Britain, and by 1742 (the date mentioned in the show) was greatly diminished in international significance.

"starter for ten" — ("Communist Quiz") A phrase used in the quiz show *University Challenge* (see *University Challenge* entry below).

stock film of goal being scored — (PSC; "Communist Quiz") The music under the closing credits of "Communist Quiz" is Johnny Scott's "News Titles" (WAC T12/1,416). This stock film footage is not accounted for in the WAC records.

Sunshine Sizzler — ("Dirty Hungarian Phrasebook") Miss Abigail Tesler (Carol Cleveland) was obviously photographed near the Walton Bridge on Walton Bridge Road. There is a Gingham's Auto Diner Restaurant across the street, seen when boxer Ken (Cleese) rubs gravel in his hair, and Ken also jumps into a bed in this same spot for Ep. 18, the "Documentary on Boxer" sketch. Earlier, some of the "Silly Walks" episode was filmed at this site. These kinds of alluring photos had been appearing both the *Mirror* and the *Sun*, and are mentioned in Ep. 24, when "diocesan lovely" Bishop Sarah is profiled.

• T •

"Tesler" — ("Court [Phrasebook]") The name "Abigail Tesler" is most likely a creation of the Pythons, though she may be a namesake of Brian Tesler (b. 1929), producer of *The Benny Hill Show*, and at the age of 32 he was named Television Programme Controller for A.B.C. Television. Tesler was an Oxfordian, Exeter College, and chummed around with Tony Richardson, Kenneth Tynan, and Lindsay Anderson. Featuring a plethora of historical impersonations, television send-ups, and off-color humor in general, *Benny Hill* was clearly an influence on the Pythons and the structure of *FC*.

"Thank you very much for the change" — ("Dirty Hungarian Phrasebook") The stiltedness of this delivery and the common dress (Fireman) of the character may be a reference to the similarly stilted "normal" folk who appeared often on British TV. Myriad "vox pops"–type moments featured people on the street answering questions, offering opinions, even reading lines—all with varying degrees of clumsiness and earnest stammering. In Peter Watkins's 1965 British docudrama *The War Game*, on-the-street interviews asking shoppers about emergency preparedness and the possibilities of nuclear attack produce some very self-conscious moments. Palin does a similar turn as a walk-on in Ep. 10, and as the "whiskery old porter" Hargreaves in Ep. 29.

"There'll Always Be an England" — (PSC; "*Ypres 1914*") This overtly patriotic song is employed here anachronistically, as it was later penned by Ross Parker and Hughie Charles, becoming a beloved World War II anthem. The Band of the Irish Guards plays this version (WAC T12/1,416).

"Tinea Pedis" — ("*The Black Eagle*") The medical term for athlete's foot. Probably offered by the troupe's only doctor, Graham Chapman.

"Titian" — ("Art Gallery Strike") Venetian painter Tiziano Vecellio (c. 1485–1576) was known as "Titian." This mocked-up version seems to be after either the Titian work *Gloria* (1551–1554, Museo del Prado, Madrid, Spain), or more likely of a painting done "after Titian" (perhaps in a workshop setting) which is part of the National Gallery's collection, called *The Gloria*, and probably produced after 1566.

Titian was perhaps the greatest painter in sixteenth-century Venice, and his influence was also pervasive, as his work affected such luminaries to follow as Michelangelo and Raphael, as well as Rubens, Velázquez, Rembrandt, Delacroix, and even the Impressionists, many of whose work is involved in this painting strike. In their praise, then, the art critics in the scene are correct—if slightly unctuous—as they laud the work.

"height of his powers"—Painted late in his career, about 1554, this painting would have indeed been Titian at his best.

"Trondheim" — ("Spam") A major port city in Sør Trøndelag, Norway, Trondheim was the point of departure for many Viking expeditions.

TV Centre — (PSC; "*Ypres 1914*") The BBC's broadcast headquarters at Shepherd's Bush, west of London. The building opened in 1949, and was designed in the shape of a question mark to fit its triangular plot of land.

When the Padre (Cleese) is carried out on the stretcher, he is taken to a waiting ambulance from BBC main reception, then along the Westway to Hammersmith Hospital (near Wormwood Scrubs) (WAC T12/1,416).

"28th day of May 1970" — ("Dirty Hungarian Phrasebook") During most of May 1970 the Pythons were shooting location, insert, and pick-up material (all on film) in the Torquay area. Between 22 May, when they shot "Ken Clean-Air System" and the snack bar (both Ep. 18), and 1 June 1970, when they were back on Elers Road, Ealing, they must have scheduled something of a break (WAC T12/1,416). This in-studio section (where Yahlt [Palin] is on trial for publishing the dirty phrasebook) would be shot nearly a month after this stated date, on Thursday, 25 June 1970.

• U •

University Challenge — (PSC; "Communist Quiz") Very popular quiz show that pitted teams of university students, the show made its debut on TV in the UK in 1962. Cambridge finally won in 1970, after three years of public universities (Sussex and Keele) taking the crown from Oxford in 1966. Either Cambridge or Oxford teams would win the next seven *University Challenge* contests.

• V •

various famous paintings whose characters suddenly disappear — (PSC; "Art Gallery Strike") These characters walk out of their various paintings in Gilliam's initial animation section: Venus from Sandro Botticelli's *The Birth of Venus* (c. 1482); the child Margarita from Velazquez's *Las Meninas* (1656); the white-frocked citizen (who flies away) from Francisco Goya's *The Third of May* (1808); Mona Lisa (who puts on a hat to leave) from Leonardo da Vinci (c. 1503–1505); the groom (after patting his bride's hand) from Jan van Eyck's *Giovanni Arnolfini and His Bride* (1434; National Gallery, London); the man (probably John) holding the Christ figure from Caravaggio's *The Deposition* (1604); Charles I from Anthony Van Dyck's *Charles I Dismounted* (c. 1635); and the dead Marat (who goes down the drain of his tub) from Jacques Louis David's *The Death of Marat* (1793). Most of these paintings aren't found in the National Gallery collections.

In the weekly postmortem discussion of BBC broadcast shows, this sequence was mentioned by several as being "unfortunately" offensive, specifically the animation where Christ is dropped (WAC T12/1,416).

"VC" — ("*Ypres 1914*—Abandoned") The Victoria Cross is a decoration for Army and Navy personnel awarded for exceptional personal valor, and was instituted in 1856.

"Vermeer's . . . Window" — ("Art Gallery Strike") The picture is not shown here, and there is no Vermeer painting of that title, though he did paint many female figures standing near a window, some writing, some just posing. Johannes Vermeer (1632–1675) was a skilled painter of genre scenes, landscapes, and allegories, and was mentioned in Ep. 4, the "Art Gallery" sketch (when the Art Critic [Palin] gets Vermeer all over his shirt).

Two Vermeer "lady at window" paintings are in the National Gallery: *A Young Woman Standing at a Virginal* (c. 1670); and *A Young Woman Seated at a Virginal* (c. 1670), the previous painting a part of the collection since 1892.

The painting here is sold for "two bob," or a single shilling.

• W •

"walk-out" — ("Art Gallery Strike") A labor strike where workers put down their tools and leave the factories, essentially. Labor in the UK has a long history of union activity and strikes, including the infamous 1926 General Strike, where up to three million railwaymen, transport workers, printers, dockworkers, and iron and steel workers struck on 3 May 1926. The Conservative Baldwin government had prepared for the strike, however, and was able to keep supplies and transportation flowing fairly well, undermining the effectiveness of the strike.

More significant for the Pythons may have been the French general strike of 1968, where a reported ten million people took to the streets in major French cities to demonstrate against poverty, high unemployment, and the stultifyingly conservative government.

Bus strikes in the UK came in 1950, 1954, 1955, 1957, and 1958, according to the UK's Public Record Office, and crippling rail strikes occurred in 1955 and 1962. A glance at the op-ed pages of contemporary British newspapers—overflowing with political cartoons and opinion pieces discussing trade union activity—indicate the cultural and political significance of Big Labor in postwar Britain. See the British Cartoon Archive.

The Pythons will revisit this topic in Ep. 26, when Welsh coal miners will call a strike based on management's ignorance of classic temple architecture construction.

"watch out for sharks, Abigail!" — ("Court [Phrasebook]") These fairly wretched double entendres were the stock-in-trade of the tabloid pin-up sections, probably delivered tongue-in-cheek, acknowledging the cheesecake aspects (but reveling in the naughtiness, nonetheless) of the "Page Three Girl" sections.

"WCA System" — (*"The Black Eagle"*) Meant to indicate a manufacturer of sound and equipment systems for film, and is probably an amalgam of RCA and Western Electric.

"Welles, Thornton . . . Laurent F. Norder" — (*"The Black Eagle"*) As seen before (Ep. 19), and as will be seen later (Ep. 27), these "lists" are generally a mix of identifiable individuals, made-up names, silly names, etc., created in much the same way as seen in the pages of the satirical magazine *Private Eye* since 1961. At least a portion of the list of individuals thanked in the "Timmy Williams" sketch include Idle's flatmates and friends of the time, for example.

"Thornton Welles"—This may be an amalgam of noted filmmakers/playwrights Thornton Wilder and Orson Welles.

"Wembley" — ("Art Gallery Strike") Stadium built in 1922 where FA Cup matches would be played (first game—April 1923).

"England beat Spain"—Another reference to the World Cup football matches held at Wembley Stadium. In 1966 England hosted and won (4–2) the World Cup at Wembley Stadium. The World Cup in 1970 featured Brazil beating Italy 4–1 in Mexico City.

"whence they sailed on May 23rd" — ("Spam") On 23 May 1970, the Pythons were most likely in transit back from Torquay to London, having wrapped location shooting the day before.

"women applauding" — ("Court [Phrasebook]") This is the first acknowledgment (in the diegetic world of the narrative) of the oft-used "Women's Institute" footage. In Ep. 29, a color insert of the Crystal Palace will also be noted by the characters, even though they are in no position to see the insert.

"workers' control of factories" — ("Communist Quiz") The following snippets voiced by the Michael Miles type (Idle) and Marx (Jones) are lifted from various Marxian writings and attributions, most of which had entered the cultural lexicon after the success of the October Revolution in Russia.

The "development" phrase is found in Marx's *The Class Struggles in France, 1848–1850*: "The development of the industrial proletariat is, in general, conditioned by the development of the industrial bourgeoisie" (chapter 1: "The Defeat of June, 1848").

The "struggle of class against class" discussion is also found in the above work, but is most perspicuously voiced in Marx and Frederick Engel's *Manifesto of the Communist Party* (1848): "But every class struggle is a political struggle" (10).

The "workers' control of factories" and the "struggle of the urban proletariat" are also discussed in the *Manifesto*. The phrase "urban proletariat" is also characteristic of Lenin's later phraseology, including *The Proletariat and the Peasantry*: "the common struggle of the rural and the urban proletariat against the whole of bourgeois society" (231–36).

World Forum — ("Communist Quiz") Granada Television had been producing the respected on-the-scene current affairs program *World in Action* since 1963, which quickly gained a reputation for taking alternate (non–status quo) editorial stances, while the BBC had been producing the studio-bound *Panorama* since 1953.

• Y •

young major—excruciatingly public school — (PSC; *"Ypres 1914"*) The "public school" sobriquet means the major is from a name family, and attended an upper-crust academy like Eton, Winchester, or Harrow. He's not one of the "blokes," he never will be, and it's no surprise that the Pythons consistently give him the shortest straw, nor that he consistently finds a way to wriggle out of being chosen.

"Ypres" — (*"Ypres 1914"*) The Battle of Ypres took place in Belgium, and was the first battle where the Allies (England, France, Belgium, et al.) stopped the German force on its "Race to the Sea." The battle began in October 1914, and lasted through November 1914, when both sides dug in, and trench warfare that would endure for the next three and a half years began. During the Second Battle of Ypres, in April 1915, the Germans would use poison gas for the first time. Britain would lose 908,400 in WWI, and 2,090,200 would be wounded.

Though staunchly against Britain's involvement in the war, Labour party leader Ramsay MacDonald (lampooned in Ep. 24) had visited Ypres in 1914.

Episode 26: "The Queen Will Be Watching"

"The Queen will be watching"; *Royal titles;* Royal Episode Thirteen, First Spoof, **A Coal Mine in Llanddarog** (historical argument); Caption: "HM the Queen still watching *The Virginian*"; News on the strikes; **"The Toad Elevating Moment"**; The man who says things in a very roundabout way; The man who speaks only the ends of words; The man who speaks only the beginnings of words; The man who speaks only the middles of words; *Animation: Crelm toothpaste*; Soap powder commercial; *Animation: The surgical garment*; How to feed a goldfish; "The R.S.P.C.A. wish it to be known . . ."; Tape recorded love; The man who collects birdwatcher's eggs; Racing pigeon fanciers; *Animation: The Madonna balloon bomb, and "Monty Python proudly presents . . ."*; "The Insurance Sketch"—interrupted by the Queen, who's tuned in; "She's switched over—she's watching *News at Ten*"; **Hospital run by RSM**—St. Pooves; Other hospitals—"And now the mountaineering sketch"; **The exploding version of "The Blue Danube"**; Girls' boarding school; Documentary Time: Invasion of Normandy; Pepperpots in submarine—"Standby to fire Mrs. Nesbit!"; *Animation: "Fire Mrs. Nesbit!"*; A man with a stoat through his head; **Lifeboat (cannibalism)**; Letters (Royal Navy cannibalism); *Animation: Cannibalism*; "Stop this cannibalism!" link; **Undertaker's sketch**—"Are you suggesting eating my mother?"; Closing credits, everyone at attention ("God Save the Queen")

• A •

"abacus" — ("Coal Mine [Historical Argument]") *OED*: "Arch. The upper member of the capital of a column, supporting the architrave; in the Tuscan, Doric, and ancient Ionic orders, a square flat plate."

Following are the balance of the rattled-off architectural terms:

"triglyphs"—The triglyphs are a simple pattern of three vertical lines located between the metopes.

"frieze section"—The frieze section is located above the columns and the architrave, and has simple patterns.

"entablature"—"The upper part of an order, consisting of cornice, frieze and architrave. Essentially the beam which spans between columns. Literally it means something laid upon a table, i.e., flat" (*Conservation Glossary*).

"classical Greek Doric temples"—The least ornamented type of Greek temples, and includes the Parthenon.

"metope"—The Foreman (Idle) and the Fourth Miner (Ian Davidson) are correct. The metope (plain, smooth stone section) is found between the triglyphs on Doric temples. The abacus is located below the frieze section, atop the column shaft, and helping to support the architrave.

"aechinus"—Spelled "echinus" in the *1911 Edition Encyclopedia*, it is the convex molding that supports the abacus in a Doric column. It's uncertain whether the Pythons knew that in Greek it could translate as "hedgehog."

"capital"—The abacus is the uppermost member of the capital of the column, and simply provides a larger support surface for the architrave. The capital is the top portion of the column.

In the Jan Vredeman de Vries book *Perspective* (1604–1605), which Gilliam draws from a number of times in both *Flying Circus* and *Holy Grail*, the final plate illustration is labeled *"Dorica: Prima origo quinque columnarum."* Plate 24 is essentially a breakdown of the Doric column in classical Greek temples, and may have served as the jumping off point for this sketch. Most of the architectural terminology used by the miners ("echinus," "triglyphs," "metope," etc.) are labeled on this very helpful page by de Vries.

"All through the Night" — ("Coal Mine [Historical Argument]") A Welsh lullaby that became associated with laborers in the UK's heartlands. This performance is from the Treorchy Male Choir from the album *The Pride of Wales* as arranged by Robinson (WAC T12/1,415).

Animation: Cannibalism — (PSC; "Cannibalism") These photos are again American nineteenth-century images. The Confederate general having his brains eaten by the lady is Beverly Holcombe Robertson (1827–1910); and the Union Brigadier General eating the "Swells Goody" girl ice lolly (popsicle) is Thomas W. Sherman (1813–1879). These last two are taken from *DWF*, pages 111 and 273, respectively.

Animation: Madonna Balloon Bomb . . . — (animated link out of "Racing Pigeon Fanciers") The painting used here is a version of Lorenzo di Credi's *The Virgin and Child* (1480–1485).

"Argylls ate in Aden" — ("Lifeboat [Cannibalism]") The Argyll regiment spent about three years in Aden (1964–1967), though they apparently never had to eat Arabs. There was a protracted stalemate between local "terrorists" and the British forces, as the lawless area known as the "Crater" was surrounded, cut off, and eventually stormed and retaken by British forces. The Argyll regiment has already been mentioned by one of the Old Codgers types who write to the *Daily Mirror* in Ep. 10. Also, a "Scottish" regiment will be recommended by the Brigadier (Cleese) in his lecture to the "Well-Basically Club" in Ep. 35.

***as per* Eamonn Andrews Show** — (PSC; "Man Who Says Things in a Very Roundabout Way") Andrews (1922–1987) was both a television presenter and, later, a broadcasting administrator. His most recognized shows included *What's My Line?* (1951), *This Is Your Life* (1955), *Pantomania: Babes in the Woods* (1957), and *The Eamonn Andrews Show* (1964), the latter referenced here in the printed scripts. *The Eamonn Andrews Show* ran from 1964–1969 for ABC-TV, and was preceded in 1956–1957 by a same-titled show running on BBC-TV. The formats for both were "late night medley(s) of talk and music," with Andrews entertaining up to five guests at once (Vahimagi, 125).

In Ireland, he also acted as television's first Chairman in the governing body, the RTE Authority. See Andrews's entry in *ODNB* for more.

"Avril" — ("Girls' Boarding School") Probably a nod to Avril Stewart—wife of Cambridge alum and budding mathematician Ian Stewart. Avril would later appear as Dr. Piglet in *Holy Grail*.

• B •

Babycham animal — (PSC; "How to Feed a Goldfish") An advertising deer character created for the Babycham drink product in the 1950s, the studio audience reacts appreciably to this obviously recognized character.

Babycham was initially a clear sparkling drink made from pears, and was test marketed in the Bristol area (where Cleese grew up). The drink was bottled in the trademark "baby champagne" bottles in 1950, and was launched nationally in 1953. This is approximately when the deer image became associated with the drink. This was also a drink marketed primarily to women.

"BBC wardrobe department" — (link out of "Insurance Sketch") This BBC department holds more than two million items, and was raided regularly by the Pythons to create their historical sketches.

"binomial theorem" — ("Coal Mine [Historical Argument]") This is another example of commoners exhibiting knowledge well beyond their seeming grasp or ken (cf. virtually any Pepperpot sketch, or the "Mollusc Documentary" sketch, or much of the feature film *Holy Grail*). The Pepperpots in Ep. 27, for example, will argue the finer points of Sartre's existential philosophies. The binomial theorem is an algebraic formula discovered by Newton (*OED*).

"Blue Danube" — ("Exploding Version of 'The Blue Danube'") "The Blue Danube" is a popular waltz composed by Johan Strauss (1825–1899) in 1867.

"Bradshaw, P.F." — ("The Man Who Collects Birdwatcher's Eggs") The Bradshaw name has been popular during the latter part of this second season, appearing in Eps. 19, 24, and now 26.

• C •

Carmarthen — ("Coal Mine [Historical Argument]") Llanddarog is in Carmarthen, Carmarthenshire, in south Wales, and was a rugged town at the end of the rail line.

Coal mining in Great Britain may go back as far as Roman times, and perhaps earlier (even the Bronze Age), but exploded in the nineteenth century to fuel Britain's burgeoning industry and empire. Entire cities and towns were built up around these mines, and these same settlements suffered as the mines later suffered. Most ore and metal mines in the UK had closed by WWI, as seams ran out or just became harder to follow, meaning it became much cheaper to import coal and metals from South America, the United States, etc. Much of the labor unrest during this period centered on either diminishing returns, like in the mines, or in heavy industry where newer, more efficient, and less manual labor–intensive machines were needed to maintain profitability. Both meant reduced employment figures, of course, and the trade unions fought the changes.

There does not seem to have been a pit head like the one described here in Llanddarog, though there would have been surface or near-surface mining works throughout the area, meaning collieries would have dotted the countryside.

"cave" — ("Girls' Boarding School") English public school slang meaning "hide, the headmaster (or butch mistress, in this case) is approaching."

"chicken man from the opening credits, the" — ("Racing Pigeon Fanciers *animation*") This is the chicken with the head of Gen. Logan (Union Civil War general) seen in every opening episode credit sequence for season 2. (For the Logan original photo see *DWF*, 383.) The background is a view of Trafalgar Square.

"coal face" — ("Coal Mine [Historical Argument]") The face of the coal seam where workers/machines remove coal, following the seam.

The coal mine and the coal town have been settings for many British films and novels, from novelists D.H. Lawrence (*Sons and Lovers*) and David Storey (*This Sporting Life*), to filmmakers Ken Loach (*Kes*), Lindsay Anderson (*This Sporting Life*), and even Hollywood film legend John Ford (*How Green Was My Valley*)—most of which examine the stultifying effects of the mines and mining town life. The Pythons have already treated a scene from *Sons and Lovers* in Ep. 2, "Working-Class Playwright."

"cold consommé" — ("How to Feed a Goldfish") A strong, clear soup. The other items and organizations mentioned include:

"gazpacho"—A cold Spanish vegetable soup.

"spring greens"—Leaves of young cabbage plants.

"RSPCA"—The Royal Society for the Prevention of Cruelty to Animals was created in 1824, though didn't achieve royal recognition until 1840.

"treacle tart"—A filled pastry. In the UK, treacle is the thick, dark residue left over in the sugar refining process, or "molasses" in the United States.

"breadcrumbs . . . pheasant"—Actually, goldfish are quite happy with some kinds of non-fish-food, including fresh foods like Romaine lettuce, cucumber, grapes, oranges, and spinach, as well as cooked peas, eggs, and even earthworms and insect larvae.

"collecting butterfly hunters" — ("The Man Who Collects Birdwatcher's Eggs") This unexpected incongruity—a man who collects those who collect—is a borrow from Tex Avery's cartoon visual gags, like a short phone for local calling and a tall phone for long distance, a short waitress for regular cigarettes and a very tall girl for "king size" cigarettes, etc.

colonial governor's helmet — (PSC; "Coal Mine [Historical Argument]") The character is dressed as if he is a ranking official in colonial India or Malaya, with the subtext being Wales depicted here as a Third World, colonized pit to be mined for its natural resources.

These coal mines were nationalized in 1947, following the costly war and even more despairing postwar malaise, and even though there was significant power in the hands of miners and their unions between 1947 and 1970, as Kenneth Morgan indicates, there was still a noticeable, even shocking difference between, for example, the homes built by the government for mine management (villa style, often), and the terraced rowhouses built by the same government for the miners themselves (*Britain since 1945*, 62).

The significance and relative impressiveness of official headgear is also discussed at length in Ep. 43, "Police Helmets."

"Crelm" — ("Commercials") Already mentioned in Ep. 24, where Gilliam parodies the very visible Crest and/or Colgate toothpaste commercials of the period, while the plot (cars racing across the landscape) is very much like an Esso (gasoline stations) commercial from the late 1950s, where the car running on clean Esso petrol runs farther, faster, than competitors. In this episode, the dragon who brushes with Crelm gets (to eat) all the girls.

Incidentally, the first commercial on British television in 1955 was a toothpaste ad, for Gibbs SR toothpaste (see whirligig-tv.co.uk for more).

• D •

"Dagenham" — (link out of "Coal Mine [Historical Argument]") East London location of a Ford Motor Company plant where labor strikes, slowdowns, and absenteeism curtailed production on a number of occasions during the 1960s and early 1970s. This plant was much in the news during the Pythons' lifetimes, making hundreds of appearances on op-ed pages and in political cartoons since the 1930s, almost all relating to labor actions, and with a disproportionate number appearing in 1968–1970. See the British Cartoon Archive.

deerstalker and tweeds — (PSC; "Man Who Collects Birdwatcher's Eggs") A Sherlock Holmes–type hat and tweed jacket, with pants. This is the uniform, obviously, of the Pythons' version of a birdwatcher.

Dr. Kildare — (PSC; "Hospital Run by RSM") Long-running and very popular ABC-TV show starring the young Richard Chamberlain (b. 1934). The show was a fan favorite in the United States and UK, providing stiff competition for *Dr. Finlay's Casebook*, mentioned in Ep. 7 as a source of deforming Scottishness. The theme music is performed by the Johnnie Spence Orchestra, and written by Jerry Goldsmith (1929–2004) (WAC T12/1,415).

Chamberlain's smiling face graces the cover of the 11 March 1966 *Radio Times*, and he has already been mentioned by the Pythons in Ep. 14.

"dump . . . Thames" — ("Undertaker's Sketch") Historically, of course, the Thames and its tributaries (some now gone completely or controlled, like the rivers Fleet and Tyburn) were dumping grounds for the detritus of the metropolis, including a number of murdered young prostitutes in the late 1950s and into the 1960s by a man dubbed by the press as "Jack the Stripper" (*Time*, 8 May 1964). Up to the nineteenth century, at least, the bodies of those executed at Wapping were consigned to the waters of the Thames, as well (see Mailik). Earlier, when London Bridge boasted houses and businesses, every bit of sewage and refuse from those establishments emptied into the river (Ackroyd, 331). In fact, it wasn't until the 1860s that purpose-built sewers were constructed to keep raw sewage out of the river, and that only after the so-called Great Stink of 1858, when many had to flee the city—the stench was that overpowering.

There is also a rather sardonic poster on the Thames seen in a *Quatermass* television episode that reminds Londoners: "It is forbidden to dump bodies in the river."

"Dunfermline" — ("Man Who Speaks Only the Middle of Words") The historic capital of Scotland, where Robert the Bruce is buried.

• E •

Episode 26 — Recorded 16 October 1970, and broadcast 22 December 1970. Also scheduled to appear in this episode were semi-regulars Ian Davidson and John Hughman, as well as Willi Bowman (*The Wednesday Play; Z Cars*), Eddie Connor (*The Wednesday Play*), Paul Fraser (*Half Hour Story*), Barry Kennington (*Doctor Who; Des O'Connor*), Troy Adams (*Upstairs, Downstairs*), Maurice Berenice, and Neville Bourne (WAC T12/1,415). Berenice and Bourne were brought in from Oriental Casting (239 Lancaster Rd. W11).

"equerry" — ("The Queen Will Be Watching") One of the Queen's "men," or servant/representative. In 1970 the Queen's Equerry was Lt. Commander Jock Slater, LVO Royal Navy (b. 1938).

"Essex" — ("Man Who Speaks Only the Beginnings of Words") A county in the east of England, and an area not mentioned much in *FC*. The bulk of the regional references are apportioned to the Midlands and Greater London.

"everybody out" — ("Coal Mine [Historical Argument]") Another labor strike (remember the painting subjects who went out on strike in Ep. 25), this time in an understandable place, a working coal mine, but for very odd reasons. The general strike-worthy complaints of the miners and their union included a shorter working week, reduced working hours, higher wages, better housing and health care, and improved safety in the mines.

This period (1958–1979) in the UK was particularly beset with antagonistic management-labor relations, with multiple strikes against Ford Motor Company (in 1968, 1969, 1970, and 1971), for example, over pay scale grades, equal pay for women, and parity with Ford workers at other plants in the UK (*Socialist Review* 243, July/August 2000). Miners, dockworkers, and transport unions also struck. During this period, successive governments—including Macmillan's Conservatives and Wilson's Labour—reached out to big labor, seeing it as a rather vibrant and politically powerful body. Heath's Tories saw organized labor as a threat, and acted peremptorily on that perception.

• F •

Feldman — ("Insurance Sketch") Certainly a nod to the Pythons' friend, inspiration, and sometime writing and performing partner, Marty Feldman (1933–1982). Chapman and Cleese appeared/wrote with Feldman in *At Last the 1948 Show* (Rediffusion, 1967), and Chapman, Cleese, Jones, and Palin contributed to his 1968 show, *Marty* (BBC2, 1968–1969).

First Butch Voice — ("Girls' Boarding School") This silliness actually has some grounding in television reality. In 1947, BBC broadcast *The Happiest Days of*

Your Life, a wartime farce wherein the Ministry has accidentally resettled boys and girls together in a boarding school setting.

five bedraggled sailors — (PSC; "Lifeboat [Cannibalism]") One of these sailors (Idle) is wearing a hat with the ship name HMS *Hopeful* stenciled across the brow. The "Hopeful" name may have been shared, as it seemed to have been a small nineteenth-century British "sealer" and warship, seeing service in the Falklands and then later during WWI. The name may have been used on more than one ship, of course.

"floods . . . pneumoconiosis" — ("Coal Mine [Historical Argument]") Coal mines (and other deep pit/tunnel mining operations) fight the battle against incoming groundwater for as long as the mines are in operation, while cave-ins are also a constant hazard, especially as large, rich seams are hewed out.

"English criminal law"—This is probably just a Python swipe at the alleged inborn criminality of the Welsh in general, like saying all Scotsmen have a "diminished brain capacity" in Ep. 7, or indicating that all white Rhodesians think like Ian Smith (Eps. 31 and 45).

"Carbon monoxide"—A colorless, odorless gas that can kill by replacing oxygen in the bloodstream. Canaries were used by miners to determine when the mine's air supply began to dwindle or sicken. Two canaries had been employed in each pit in the UK since 1911, finally phased out in 1986.

"Pneumoconiosis"—Also called "coal miner's disease," or "black lung," pneumoconiosis is a lung disease brought on by the inhalation of coal dust or other mineral/metallic particles.

"14th Marine Commandos" — ("Girls' Boarding School") Probably referring to the West Yorkshire Regiment, also known as "The Prince of Wales' Own," which may be a comment on the young prince (about 22 at this time), as well.

"Fractured tibia sergeant" — ("Hospital Run by RSM") There is actually a kind of precedent for this juxtaposition of the military and convalescing patients. When Victoria's son "Bertie" (Edward VII) decided to close most of his mother's beloved Osborne House on the Isle of Wight in 1903, he replaced the royal tenants with naval college cadets in training, and retired officers in convalescent settings (Wilson 2005, 5). Also, in the Humphrey Jennings documentary *A Diary for Timothy* (1945), the pluck of the wounded British military man demands that he can't wait to get back to fighting the enemy—the fighter pilot is even trying to get back into his cockpit, still bandaged and limping.

• G •

"gaffer" — ("Coal Mine [Historical Argument]") The foreman of a work gang.

"gammy leg" — ("Lifeboat [Cannibalism]") An injured leg, especially with the wound becoming infected.

"great grey suit" — (link out of "Insurance Sketch") This cadence (and the overuse of "great") is very much a spoof of revered British broadcaster Richard Dimbleby, as already spoofed by Cleese in Ep. 23 as the All Blacks play the Derby Town Council in rugby. Dimbleby famously covered the Queen's accession in 1953 with such reverence.

The traditional gray to black suit is worn by the Pythons whenever a character is meant to disappear, to blend away, to act the faceless, spineless salaryman, such as Arthur Pewtey (Palin, Ep. 2) or James (Cleese, Ep. 34). Artist Gerhard Richter wrote of grey in regard to his 1966 painting, *Two Greys Juxtaposed*: "Grey is the epitome of non-statement, it does not trigger off feelings or association . . . for me gray is the welcome and only possible equivalent for indifference, for the refusal to make a statement, for lack of opinion, lack of form" (comments included with the painting, National Gallery).

• H •

"Henry III was a bad king" — ("Coal Mine [Historical Argument]") Henry of Winchester (1207–1272) was a Plantagenet king who fought expensive wars, kept close ties to Rome, and eventually had to acknowledge the rule of law as his nobles consolidated their own power (*ODNB*). Dante even includes Henry in his *The Divine Comedy*, an ignoble accomplishment at best.

The silliness of this demand—"thirteen reasons why Henry III was a bad king"—as a plank in the strikers' platform is actually indicative of the damage done by such unofficial or uncoordinated strikes, or even by the fact that a strike in and of itself is often a public relations nightmare for the coordinating union. The rash of strike activity during the early 1970s in the UK certainly contributed to this inclusion.

A lengthy archaeological dig at Winchester—a significant Roman and then Saxon site and home to Henry III—was winding down in the late 1960s, after eight seasons of digging. A fourteen-volume monograph set was published in 1971, and both Henry and the dig were much in the news at this time.

"Her Majesty the Queen" — ("The Queen Will Be Watching") Queen Elizabeth II, who has occupied the throne since 1952.

• I •

identical hard-boiled eggs — (PSC; "The Man Who Collects Birdwatcher's Eggs") A comment on the English penchant for collecting / recording what might be considered odd things, such as the phenomena of trainspotting (cf. Ep. 7), photographing switching houses, or bottle collecting (Ep. 2), etc.

"Insurance Sketch" — ("The Insurance Sketch") This is the precise set-up used earlier (Ep. 24) for the "Conquistador Coffee" sketch (desk, window, etc.). That sketch didn't properly conclude, either.

"iron foundry at Swindon" — ("Hospital Run by RSM") A significant iron foundry was located in Swindon, connected to the booming rail industry (and the Great Western Railway) in the region in the nineteenth and twentieth centuries.

This may also be a swipe at successive postwar governments' attempts at "full employment" (what Beveridge [of NHS fame] would characterize as 3 percent or lower unemployment), schemes that always seemed to culminate in unwieldy, overheated economies, inflation, higher interest rates, balance of payment problems, etc. In a New Year's Day speech in 1969, PM Wilson had once again dangled the carrot of "full employment" as a long-term goal. Quotes from other party representatives on this New Year occasion—from the Tories and Liberals to the Welsh Nationalist Party—promised no such thing. The promise also has a place in most party platforms approaching every election in the UK during this period, but the realities of the British version of the capitalist system precludes full employment, frankly.

• K •

"kosher" — ("Lifeboat [Cannibalism]") "Kosher" food is food that is certified (rabbinically) to be fit for consumption by those of the Jewish faith. A human corpse would, of course, fly in the face of that striving for purity, whether he / she were "properly" killed or not. The terms "kosher" and "non-kosher" appear in British papers regularly during this period, and are especially visible after the formation of the state of Israel in 1948, and with the increased presence of kosher food operations in Great Britain.

The Pythons have also mentioned kosher car parks and kosher parking spaces in earlier episodes. Before them—and likely inspiring them—the Goons had also used kosher as a silly adjective a number of times. In "The Pevensey Bay Disaster" a character offers "kosher wine gum"; in "The Tales of Old Dartmoor" a character is paid "three shillings in kosher margarine"; in "The International Christmas Pudding" there are boxes of "yellow kosher boots"; and in "King Solomon's Mines" a character is drowning in "non-kosher water."

• L •

lifeboat — ("Lifeboat [Cannibalism]") Certainly a reference to the popular Hitchcock film *Lifeboat* (1944), but also to the wreck of the Dumaru during WWI (1918, off Guam), where survivors resorted to eating two of the dead sailors in the open boats. The men of the Dumaru were adrift for a total of twenty-four days. *The Wreck of the Dumaru* was a popular book written by Lowell Thomas in 1930, which sensationalized the event.

• M •

management man arrives — (PSC; "Coal Mine [Historical Argument]") The music used in this pompous entrance is from the Band of Corps of Royal Engineers, "National Anthems" (WAC T12/1,415).

Man Alive — ("Man Who Collects Birdwatcher's Eggs") *Man Alive* was a public affairs program that ran from 1965 to 1982 on BBC2, and at least initially looked at ordinary people in "situations that shaped their lives." *Man Alive* did take on more serious subjects as time went on, including child molestation, psychological phobias, and the inadequacies of Britain's public institutions (Vahimagi, 138).

"Mature, Victor" — ("Commercials") Hollywood actor Mature (1913–1999) starred in scores of films, including *My Darling Clementine* (1946), and became the embodiment of the screen *man* (and not at all the type to have to wear a surgical garment). Mature had starred in *The Egyptian* (1954), as well, which may acccount for the "sail down the Nile" comment from the Adman (Palin).

In a classic *Beyond the Fringe* sketch, "Porn Shop," Jonathan Miller talks a great deal about "curious" Charing Cross Road shops that sell these "rupture appliances."

"Maudling" — ("Lifeboat [Cannibalism]") Another of the many references to Gerald Maudling, Heath's Home Secretary during this period, who was one of the Pythons' (and the editors of *Private Eye*) favorite whipping boys. See the entry in Ep. 16, the "Flying Lessons" sketch for more.

"McGuffie . . . report" — (link into "Hospital Run by RSM") Probably named for sometime house composer Bill McGuffie, who was married to *FC* show assistant Mary McCheane.

Reports from special commissions were often the first public step toward change in the National Health Service (and any other publicly held organization), with White Papers and Green Papers functioning as findings/proposals from these inquiries.

In 1970, the *Daily Telegraph* notes that one particularly cantankerous issue was the fundamental, flawed structure of health care in the UK: "Doctors are divided over the second Green Paper on the future structure of the National Health Service ["National Health Service: The Future Structure of the NHS in England," London: HMSO, 1970] put forward for discussion, [which] proposes the scrapping of the present hospital boards and committees" (10 April 1970). This well-publicized discussion may have been the impetus for this sketch.

"North London hospitals" during this period would have included North London Nuffield Hospital, University College Hospital, St. Bartholomew's Hospital (where Chapman had worked before deciding on a career in television), Middlesex Hospital, Royal College of Physicians of London, St. Mary's Hospital, Northwick Park Hospital, etc.

motors and asdic — (PSC; "Submarine") These are simple "submarine sounds" as called for by the printed script, including sonar pinging ("asdic"), communication, and engine noises. The sound crew's job would have been to gather these effects from the BBC's sound archives based on this simple request.

• N •

National Anthem — ("Insurance Sketch") This version is played by the Band of Corps of Royal Engineers (WAC T12/1,415).

Nationwide — ("The Man Who Collects Birdwatcher's Eggs") Called a "populist current affairs" program, *Nationwide* (BBC1, 1969–1984) was an evening program that tried to reach every region of BBC TV, covering such topics as the "miners' strikes, hot pants fashions and glitter rock" (*BT*, 176). It was presented by Michael Barratt and Frank Bough (and later Richard Dimbleby). Bough will be caricatured in Eps. 35 and 39.

"Naughtiest Girl in the School" — (PSC; "Girls' Boarding School") The printed script mentions that this character is to be played "by one of us," when in fact oft-extra John Hughman takes the part. This still photo was taken by Joan Williams (WAC T12/1,416).

News at Ten — (link out of "Insurance Sketch") The first ITV extended news program (thirty minutes), it replaced the previous twelve-minute format program that had aired at 8:55 p.m. At its inception in 1967, the newsreaders were Alastair Burnet, Andrew Gardner, Reginald Bosanquet, and George Ffitch.

Reggie Bosanquet (the real one)—Newsreader Bosanquet (1932–1984) helmed *News at Ten* from 1967 to 1979, and was also mentioned in Ep. 20, in the "Ratcatcher" sketch. He was the son of noted cricketer Bernard Bosanquet.

• O •

"Oakdene . . . Science" — ("Girls' Boarding School") The Oakdene girls' school in Beaconsfield (Bucks) closed in 1992, having been in operation since 1911, while the same-named school in Gloucestershire remains open today.

"ones that are really ill do sport" — ("Hospital Run By RSM") The music here (not identified in the printed script) is "Saturday Sport" by Burns (WAC T12/1,415).

"only the ends of words" — ("Man Who Speaks Only the Ends of Words") A sketch about miscommunication once again. In this case, using their various idiosyncratic modes of speech, these guests are able to understand each other perfectly, as has been the case in earlier sketches, including "Police Station (Silly Voices)" (Ep. 12).

"O.W.A. Giveaway" — (link out of "Lifeboat [Cannibalism]") Meaning "Oh what a giveaway."

• P •

panto geese — ("Girls' Boarding School") The Pantomime Goose—of *Mother Goose* Christmas pantomime tradition in the UK—has made several appearances in *FC*, most recently in Ep. 30.

pastoral music — (PSC; "Commercials") These selections are from Neil Richardson, and are titled "Open Air" and "Fresh Breezes" (WAC T12/1,415).

pit head — (PSC; "Coal Mine [Historical Argument]") The top of the mine pit, an entrance and exit, for workers, ore, and detritus.

pompous music — ("The Man Who Says Things in a Very Roundabout Way") This "pompous" tune is "Culver City Title" (from "Signature Tunes and Titles") by Jack Shaindlin (WAC T12/1,415).

• R •

racing pigeon fanciers — (link out of "The Man Who Collects Birdwatcher's Eggs") These outdoor scenes in this "open field" were shot in the Ashburton and Newbridge areas of Dartmoor on 14 May 1970 (WAC T12/1,416). The music that appears when they switch to Trafalgar Square is Elgar's "P&C March," again, the same version as used in the opening credits.

"rat's bane" — ("Girls' Boarding School") Rat poison, arsenic.

"Rhondda" — ("Coal Mine [Historical Argument]") A city in South Wales that is home to coal mining, and specifically the Powell Duffryn Coal Company (est. 1864), the company that ran, owned, and operated many mines in Wales, employed thousands, and essentially owned the towns that sprang up around its works. The coal mining industry bottomed out in the area during the Pythons' lifetimes, with steep declines between 1946 and 1971 that were never reversed, and multiple strikes and well-publicized labor unrest characterizing miners' struggles against the loss of their livelihood.

A "typical bleeding Rhondda" might be a miner from the big city, if you will, who sees himself as more erudite and sophisticated (and better politically connected) than miners from smaller, end-of-the-railroad-line towns like Llanddarog. This seems to indicate that there's not equality even at the coal face.

"Royal . . . cannibalism" — ("Undertaker's Sketch") The evidence for cannibalism in the Royal Navy is scant, though Sir John Franklin's disastrous expedition into the Northwest Territories between 1819 and 1822 may have involved murder and cannibalism. The occurrences of tribal cannibalism encountered by James Cook and *Endeavour* in the eighteenth century—and Cook's reported indifference to the practice, seeing it as indigenous custom and not savagery—might also be significant here (see Salmond and the *ODNB*).

• S •

"senior . . . All Souls" — ("Coal Mine [Historical Argument]") All Souls College has been part of Oxford since 1443, and was created to serve postundergraduates who would "take Orders and . . . engage in higher studies," according to the College's own history. The school was becoming a known research institution for Visiting Fellows in the 1960s when the Pythons were Oxbridge students. The senior common room would have been a comfortable gathering spot for advanced students.

soap powder — (PSC; "Commercials") In the United States, "laundry detergent." The late 1950s period saw the British TV ad wars for various laundry detergents, including White Tide ("Get your clothes clean. Not only clean but deep-down clean") versus Surf ("Hold it up to the light. Not a stain and shining bright!") versus Domestos ("Killing all known germs in one hour"), all claiming to clean better than any competitor. (See "1950's Commercials," whirligig-tv.co.uk/tv/adverts/commercials.htm.)

"something decent . . . it's disgusting" — ("Undertaker's Sketch") There were letters, calls, and voiced complaints about *Flying Circus* after this particular episode aired on 22 December 1970, with the weekly review board (made up of heads of other BBC departments) leading the way (WAC T12/1,415). Several on the review board felt that the show had become crude for crude's sake, essentially.

"specimen" — ("Insurance Sketch") Some insurance policies require rigorous medical examinations, blood and urine samples, etc., before the policy will be enacted, especially life insurance policies, and then regularly afterwards. This scene suggests something a bit more nefarious.

Spiny Norman — (PSC; link out of "Man Who Collects Birdwatcher's Eggs") The giant hedgehog who appears in Ep. 14 to terrorize Dinsdale Piranha. The studio audience applauds enthusiastically, obviously recognizing the character from the earlier episode. Clearly by this time (the last episode of the second full season), the show had garnered a loyal audience who not only watched at home, but who requested tickets and then came to the live tapings of the show. (The BBC WAC records include several ticket requests, most of which seem to have been quickly honored.)

Stalin . . . Gandhi — (PSC; link out of "Girls' Boarding School") The images included here for this "documentary time" include Gandhi, Hitler, Mussolini, bomb-ravaged wartime London, Churchill's "V-sign" hand, a Nazi swastika flag, a sheep, a nuclear mushroom cloud, a wing of the White House, Neville Chamberlain and his infamous treaty (Ep. 1), a burning U.S. battleship at Pearl Harbor, and British General Montgomery. There is no record in the WAC archives of where these images were obtained.

"St. Bridget's" — ("Girls' Boarding School") St. Bridget's Catholic Primary School is found on St. Bridget's Lane in Egremont, Cumbria.

"St. Gandulf's" — ("Hospital Run by RSM") Gandulf (or Gundulf) was the bishop of Rochester in the late eleventh and early twelfth centuries. Chapman's hospital was St. Bartholomew.

Most of these shots were made, however, nowhere near a hospital, but (fittingly) at the Stanford Training Area, West Tofts Camp, Norfolk (WAC T12/1,413).

St. Martin-in-the-Fields — (PSC) Spiny Norman appears above this church in the short animation. Designed by James Gibbs in 1726, it is a parish church. It was originally surrounded by fields where livestock belonging to Westminster Abbey grazed, hence the name, and it is now on the east side of Trafalgar Square. (Note: Its columns are Ionic in design, not Doric, and thus would not have been part of the coal miners' argument earlier in this sketch.) This photo is not accounted for in the WAC records for this episode. Most of the photos utilized by Gilliam were not included in the copyright request portions of the paperwork for the episodes.

"St. Pancras" — ("The Man Who Collects Birdwatcher's Eggs") A "High Victorian" train station built 1864–1868, and designed by engineer William Henry Barlow in conjunction with R.M. Ordish.

string vest and short dibley haircut — (PSC; "Girls' Boarding School") The string vest is a mesh undershirt, often worn by military men, while the "dibley" haircut is a short, effeminate bob. In 1956 the British Ministry of Supply and War Office had commissioned a study of the military string vest in both hot and dry conditions. Results of that study are available in the National Archives. Mr. Bee (Jones) wears (and eventually barters away) his string vest in Ep. 24.

"Surrey" — ("The Man Who Collects Birdwatcher's Eggs") Terry Jones moved to this area with his family at a young age. Surrey is a county in southeast England, just south and west of greater London, and includes the *FC*-mentioned cities of Leatherhead, Reigate, Epsom, Esher, Walton-on-Thames, Godalming, Weybridge, Guildford, Surbiton, New Malden, and Purley. The Pythons would shoot a good number of scenes for the second season in and around Walton-on-Thames.

"Surrey hedgerows"—These are planted hedges that grow into walls, dividing properties from one another, and providing wildlife corridors throughout the Surrey Hills area.

"Swell's Goody" — (*"Animation: Cannibalism"*) The "Swell's" brand being consumed by the Union general is likely a reference to the popular British ice cream manufacturer Wall's, whose line of products included "Poparama" and "Big Tasties."

• T •

teleprinter — (PSC; "Coal Mine [Historical Argument]") Generates printed material for television display. This machine looks to be the very one used by the earlier occupants of this stage space, *The Benny Hill Show*. Hill and company had left the BBC for Thames TV in 1969.

"Thirty Years' War" — ("Coal Mine [Historical Argument]") Fought between 1618 and 1648 in the central European portions of the Holy Roman Empire, this was primarily a religious war between Protestants and Catholics. See the "Treaty of Westphalia" note below.

"Battle of Borodino"—Fought 7 September 1812, it was part of the Napoleonic Wars (1803–1815) with Napoleon commanding a force of some 600,000. Borodino was an indecisive, bloody battle that set the stage for Napoleon's unsuccessful and ultimately disastrous Russian campaign.

"tiger's bum" — ("Coal Mine [Historical Argument]") The relative tightness of a kangaroo's rectum is the subject of one scene in the first of two *Fliegender Zirkus* programs produced for Bavarian television in 1971.

"titles" — ("The Queen Will Be Watching') The music underneath is Elgar's "Pomp and Circumstance March" in D Major played by the London Symphony Orchestra (WAC T12/1,415).

"total cashectomy" — ("Hospital Run by RSM") Recent economic difficulties were forcing the Tory government to consider some very unpopular budget cuts in the welfare state, including Margaret Thatcher's adjustments to the elementary school milk program, and, more to the point of this sketch, Chancellor of the Exchequer Anthony Barber's proposed cuts to medical benefits coupled with increased charges for "free" medical services. Hospital beds were being considered for so-called hotel fees, for example, so that taxes wouldn't be raised, just fees.

traditional expanding square — (PSC; "Commercials") An electronic "wipe" (a transition in television broadcast) that originates in the center of the screen as a tiny square, then "opens" to reveal the following scene.

Trafalgar Square — (PSC; link out of "Man Who Collects Birdwatcher's Eggs") A very busy square that was, at the time of *FC*, a congested one-way traffic area, as well. Home to the National Gallery (cf. Eps. 4 and 25), St. Martin-in-the-Fields church (see above), Canada House, South Africa House, and Admiralty Arch, etc., the Square as pictured has traffic flow all around the area where the Lord Nelson statue stands. Today, the National Gallery is connected to the Square by a pedestrian mall.

The Square was designed (1829–1841) to be a place where the commoner (from South London) and the wealthy (from the West and North) could mingle. Nelson's Column was built in honor of Admiral Nelson for his victory in 1805 at the Battle of Trafalgar (cf. Ep.

1, where Nelson dies a "Famous Death"). The Column was designed by John Nash in the 1830s, and is 185 feet high, and supports a seventeen-foot high statue of Nelson. The lions around the base were added later, and designed by Landseer (mentioned in Ep. 25). The "Olympic Hide-and-Seek Final" sketch will commence at the foot of the column in Ep. 35.

"Treaty . . . 1713" — ("Coal Mine [Historical Argument]") This is not so simple as it seems. The Treaty was signed 11 April 1713 by France, Great Britain, Prussia, Savoy, Portugal, and the Netherlands, and then later by Spain (July 1713 and June 1714 and February 1715), then even later by others, even until 1725, when all parties seemed to be in agreement, including the Holy Roman Empire. See Trevelyan.

"Treaty of Westphalia"—The treaty (or series of treaties) that ended the Thirty Years' War on 24 October 1648, a conflict between Catholic and Protestant forces.

"Trevelyan, page 468" — ("Coal Mine [Historical Argument]") Fairly close, really. In both the 1926 and 1952 editions of George Macaulay Trevelyan's *History of England*, the Treaty of Utrecht is first discussed on page *486*, only a slight transposition. See Trevelyan's *History of England*. G.M. Trevelyan (1876–1962) was an eminent Harrow-then-Cambridge historian; he'll be nearly quoted by the Pythons in Ep. 37.

"tuck in" — ("Lifeboat [Cannibalism]") Colloquialism meaning to dig right in and eat.

"tuck shop" — ("Girls' Boarding School") A pastry or sweet shop, often in proximity or even connected to a school, and catering primarily to schoolchildren. Many secondary schools in the UK still have such shops. There would have been similar shops in Oxford and Cambridge, catering to the university population, including "The Tuck Shop" and now "The Alternative Tuck Shop" in Oxford. The cast of *I'm Sorry I'll Read That Again* mention a schoolkids' tuck shop—"a wonderland to my youthful gaze full of marvelous sweeties"—in their episode "Tim Brown's School Days" (30 May 1966). In this episode, Cleese plays Flashman, the school bully.

• U •

"uncompromising hell of one mile under" — ("Coal Mine [Historical Argument]") The subject of mine safety may have been a very sore one, this just three years after the infamous Aberfan disaster, where tons of an unstable coal waste tip slid into and over the mining town of Aberfan, Wales, killing 144, most of whom were children in the local elementary school (*Eyewitness: 1960–69*, "The Aberfan Tragedy").

"unofficial strike committee" — (link out of "Coal Mine [Historical Argument]") The Solidarity Federation (the current publication of the British Section of the International Workers' Association) has noted that a very high number of strikes in the UK during the postwar period have been so-called wildcat strikes—where single unions or even segments of unions (hence "unofficial") have struck without consulting national union leadership—diminishing the effectiveness of the concerted strike effort a trade union promises, and undermining the members in general, especially as such strikes were often painted negatively in the press. Striking for a definition of an architectural term, or for reasons why a monarch is "bad" probably qualify as less-than-useful strike actions, at least to the Pythons.

• V •

"Virginian, The" — ("The Queen Will Be Watching") American Western-themed TV series that ran from 1962 to 1971, starring James Drury, Lee J. Cobb, and Doug McClure. *The Virginian* was featured on the cover of the BBC's *Radio Times* on 22 March and 1 November 1969.

Private Eye reported (on its 7 November 1969 cover) that the Queen had decided to give up television, fearing "over-exposure."

• W •

Wales — (PSC; "Coal Mine [Historical Argument]") Python Terry Jones was born in Colwyn Bay, in northern Wales, and would early in life move to Surrey (see Herbert Mental later in the episode).

"War of Spanish Succession" — ("Coal Mine [Historical Argument]") Fought 1702–1713, the combatants were from across Europe, and the struggle was to ensure that France and Spain would not merge as a result of the succession of Louis XIV's grandson Philip V to the Spanish throne. The Treaties of Utrecht and Rastatt ended the war in 1713–1714. The portion fought in North America was termed "Queen Anne's War."

"Whacko the diddle-oh" — ("Girls' Boarding School") An Australian colloquialism, thus a bit out of place at an English girls' boarding school, unless it's a reference to/from the very popular Jimmy Edwards show *Whack-O!*, appearing 1956–1960.

The Irish song "Whiskey in the Jar" has lyrics that may help explain "Whack oh the Diddle O," as well: "Musha rig um du rum da, / Whack fol the daddy O, / Whack fol the daddy O, / There's whiskey in the jar."

Appendix A: Stock Film Clips and Still Images

Not all of the titles listed below were included in the finished episodes, nor are all of them cited in the pages of this book (though the majority of them are identified and/or discussed). This listing represents every *request* made for film stock and photos during the run of the series. Some requests made for one episode were actually aired as part of another episode, as well. Lastly, not every photograph and bit of film footage used in the series was officially requested, meaning public domain may have applied, or the show's researchers just neglected to ask. (For example, almost none of the myriad photographs, postcards, and film clips used by animator Gilliam are accounted for in the WAC records.)

Listed by BBC WAC file number:

T12/1,082 *Monty Python's Flying Circus* 1969–1971 TX 69.10.05
Episode 1—Film stock: "WWII Nuremberg Rally" from Associated British Pathé; 49 feet of Library Mt. footage (silent); Neville Chamberlain's piece from VisNews, Ref. No. 1450; Hitler footage from Pathé, Ref. No. 139

T12/1,083 *Monty Python's Flying Circus* 1969–1986 TX 69.10.12
Episode 2—No film stock or photo requests

T12/1,084 *Monty Python's Flying Circus* 1969–1971 TX 69.10.19
Episode 3—Film stock: 1969 Scottish Cup Final film, British Movietone News (BMN)

T12/1,085 *Monty Python's Flying Circus* 1969–1971 TX 69.10.26
Episode 4—No film stock or photo requests

T12/1,086 *Monty Python's Flying Circus* 1969–1971 TX 69.11.16
Episode 5—Photo: Chichester Cathedral plate from *English Cathedrals in Colour* by A.F. Kersting (London: Batsford, 1960); Film stock: "Girl Bosses Lions"

T12/1,087 *Monty Python's Flying Circus* 1969–1971 TX 69.11.23
Episode 6—No film stock or photo requests

T12/1,088 *Monty Python's Flying Circus* 1969–1971 TX 69.11.30
Episode 7—Film stock: "Women's Institute Applauding" (WI) first used/requested, 3 feet of film (about 48 frames, or two seconds at 24 frames per second); 35mm "outer space material" used in "Blancmange" opening ("Science Fiction Sketch") obtained from Technicolour

T12/1,089 *Monty Python's Flying Circus* 1969–1970 TX 69.12.07
Episode 8—Film stock: VisNews footage of the British Army; British Movietone News, peacetime army drill; "WI Applauding"

T12/1,090 *Monty Python's Flying Circus* 1969–1971 TX 69.12.14
Episode 9—Film stock: "Women's Institute again"; "*Casino Royale*" from the Shepperton Film Library

T12/1,091 *Monty Python's Flying Circus* 1969–1971 TX 69.12.21
Episode 10—Film stock: Unnamed stock film footage from the BBC Film Library; BMN clip of the Pope; Photo: Plate from *Gray's Anatomy*, 33rd edition, p. 868, figure 743, "The veins of the right side of the head and neck" (1962, edited by Davies and Davies)

T12/1,092 ***Monty Python's Flying Circus*** **1969–1971 TX 69.12.28**
Episode 11—Film stock: "Mary Bignall," "WI," "Orchestra," and "*Sportsview*," all monochrome; Audio clip: "Football Crowd Cheering," BMN; Photo: "La Gloria Di Trafalga No. 942, 1805 Trafalga" from the Colour Plate BBC Reference Library

T12/1,093 ***Monty Python's Flying Circus*** **1969–1970 TX 70.01.04**
Episode 12—Photo: "The Emperor" by Meissomer, from *The Life of Napoleon Bonaparte* by S. Baring-Gould (Methuen & Co., 1896 and 1908)

T12/1,094 ***Monty Python's Flying Circus*** **1970 TX 70.01.11**
Episode 13—Film stock: "Cup Final" and "Opera Audience"

T12/1,242 ***Monty Python's Flying Circus*** **1969–1970 GENERAL: SERIES 1**
Photos: Plate from *Gray's Anatomy*, 33rd edition, p. 868, figure 743, "The veins of the right side of the head and neck" (1962, edited by Davies and Davies); colour print "Animals 2548—Roaring Lion," L.404 by N. Myers; and colour transparencies "In the Lael Forest" and "Easter Ross"; Stock film request (from a penciled note): Speeding train in show 8—from A.B. Pathé GER 0444; the Pyramids from the British Movietone, Denham; the battleships (show 9), city gents (show 11), Lords cricket (show 11), swimming races (show 10), and Vatican crowds (show 10) all BBC Library; Hun shots are all from "Attila the Hun"

T12/1,413 ***Monty Python's Flying Circus*** **1971 TX 71.04.16 MONTREUX**
Montreux Special episode: The clips for "blue films" watched by Jones/Cleveland in "Match of the Day": Factory Chimney (427-430); pan up tall soaring poplars, waves crashing (2088-9); fountain (75756); explosion (47624); volcano erupting (45072); rocket taking off (NPA 15438); express train going into a tunnel (SKP 50); torpedo coming out of a tube (26634); dam bursting (99656); battleship broadside (95537); lion leaping through flaming hoop (Pathé); penalty kick into goal net (81800); Richard Nixon smiling (16 6A 48606); milking a cow by hand (K 14392); planes refueling in mid-air (NPA 8508); people charging a door with a battering ram, WI applauding (223/4); tossing the caber (SKP 700-702); plane falling in flames (Pathé); tree crashing to ground (92136); factory chimney (427-430); WI applauding, huge audience applauding (92027); and Wembley crowd applauding (NP 70674 and NP 71102)

T12/1,414 ***Monty Python's Flying Circus*** **1970 TX 70.12.08 SERIES 2 EP 11**
Episode 24—Film stock: VisNews, Ramsay Macdonald (9 secs.), and British Movietone "Goldfinger" E. 9536 (10 secs.)

T12/1,415 ***Monty Python's Flying Circus*** **1970 TX 70.12.22 SERIES 2 EP 13**
Episode 26—Film stock: "Women's Institute" footage

T12/1,416 ***Monty Python's Flying Circus*** **1970 TX 70.12.15 SERIES 2 EP 12**
Episode 25—No film stock or photo requests

T12/1,417 ***Monty Python's Flying Circus*** **1970 TX 70.9.15 SERIES 2 EP 1**
Episode 14—No film stock or photo requests

T12/1,418 ***Monty Python's Flying Circus*** **1970 SERIES 2: GENERAL**
No film stock or photo requests

T12/1,426 ***Monty Python's Flying Circus*** **1972 TX 72.10.19 SERIES 3 EP 1**
Episode 27—Film stock: "Plane taking off" from *Whickers World* (K1418); "Coral Islands" (SKRP65); "Eiffel Tower" and "French Street" from World Backgrounds, Elstree Studios

T12/1,427 ***Monty Python's Flying Circus*** **1972 TX 72.10.26 SERIES 3 EP 2**
Episode 28—Photos: "Pig" photos by Thomas A. Wilkie, AG3131 and AG6256; "Sailor on rug" photo by Robert Broeder; Tschaikowsky picture from the Mansell Collection; Film stock: BBC 48808, SKP 2874A/D, 2868A/B, 2850A/B, 2791A/C, and 2789A/B; Movietone Library of "Titanic" A17702-126, A17654-1076, A17709-126, and A17636-1073

T12/1,428 ***Monty Python's Flying Circus*** **1972 SERIES 3: GENERAL**
Episodes 27–31—Audience laughing (PL 049564 BBC B&W), Heath laughing (BBC K015049), audience applause (WI), Kremlin (Pathé "Moscow" or K 3028 BBC), volcanoes (BBC SKP 2812A-6), chimney stacks in brickyard (BBC SKP 1879-1880 or BBC SKP 1816-9), Houses of Parliament (BBC 3SKP20), Ark Royal (Movietone GR 526A), volcano erupting (BBC CL 45072), Torrey Canyon burning (Navy newsreel film), forest fires (BBC NPA 6688), sea lions fighting (BBC Bristol 8917), limpets ("Seashells" Educational Foundation for Visual Aids or (two just slightly moving on a rock), "Animals of the Rocky Shore" (Rank 5689222), wolf (static shot 34 seconds long) either slide or from

Windrose Dumont Time, honey bears (2 films from Phillip Ware), RAF style dog fight (VisNews 13774), trains crashing (P. Jenkinson "Casey Jones"), hotel blowing up (Movietone E9536 [1040]), car crashing and exploding (BBC SP1891 or EMI E1740 [red sports car]), train on collapsing bridge (P. Jenkinson), plateau of Roiurama ("South American Expedition" by David Bromhall, Dept. of Zoology, South Park Rd., Oxford), "Prehistoric Beasts Attacking" (P. Jenkinson), plane landing (BBC SKP 168), plane taking off (BBC SKP 168, "Air Safety: Unknown Factor"), boat traveling, listing, exploding (Pathé HMS Barham 45/55); Montreux holdover: Map: Phillips Contemporary World Atlas (1956), "The World—Political and Communications"

T12/1,429 *Monty Python's Flying Circus* 1970 SERIES 2 EP 8
Episode 21—No stock film or photo requests

T12/1,430 *Monty Python's Flying Circus* 1970 SERIES 2 EP 5
Episode 18—No film stock or photo requests

T12/1,431 *Monty Python's Flying Circus* 1970 SERIES 2 EP 4
Episode 17—No film stock or photo requests

T12/1,432 *Monty Python's Flying Circus* 1970 SERIES 2 EP 9
Episode 22—No film stock or photo requests

T12/1,433 *Monty Python's Flying Circus* 1970 TX 70.09.29 SERIES 2 EP 7
Episode 20—No film stock or photo requests

T12/1,434 *Monty Python's Flying Circus* 1970 TX 70.09.22 SERIES 2 EP 6
Episode 19—No film stock or photo requests

T12/1,435 *Monty Python's Flying Circus* 1970 SERIES 2 EP 10
Episode 23—No film stock or photo requests

T12/1,436 *Monty Python's Flying Circus* 1970 SERIES 2 EP 3
Episode 16—No film stock or photo requests

T12/1,437 *Monty Python's Flying Circus* 1970 TX 70.9.22 SERIES 2 EP 2
Episode 15—Film stock: Philip Jenkinson's "Chariot Race," from Film Finders Limited

T12/1,440 *Monty Python's Flying Circus* 1972 TX 72.12.07 SERIES 3 EP 8
Episode 34—Film stock: Pathé: Lenin; VisNews: Red Guards 1376/67, 961/67; Pathé: Kremlin.

T12/1,441 *Monty Python's Flying Circus* 1972 TX 72.11.16 SERIES 3 EP 5
Episode 31—Photo: Alfred Gregory Camera Press, Nepal 161A; BBC film stock: K26544, -45, and -46; EMI *Cowboy Western*

T12/1,442 *Monty Python's Flying Circus* 1972 TX 72.11.09 SERIES 3 EP 4
Episode 30 (See T12/1,428 above)—No film stock or photo requests

T12/1,443 *Monty Python's Flying Circus* 1972 TX 72.12.14 SERIES 3 EP 9
Episode 35—Photo: "Anthony & Cleopatra" B127, from the Mansell Collection

T12/1,444 *Monty Python's Flying Circus* 1972 TX 72.11.30 SERIES 3 EP 7
Episode 33—Photo: Colour Library International, G.V. La Paz 60914; Stock film: BBC: "Ark Royal" NP78078; EMI's *Cowboy* C2 859; and "Dog Fight" VisNews 2266

T12/1,445 *Monty Python's Flying Circus* 1972 TX 72.11.02 SERIES 3 EP 3
Episode 29—No film stock or photo requests

T12/1,446 *Monty Python's Flying Circus* 1972 TX 72.11.23 SERIES 3 EP 6
Episode 32—Film stock: BBC—"Christmas Lights," etc. (74630), "Ambulance" (NP/NT73292 and NP/NT65980), "Ramsay Macdonald" (BBC News WPA16133/A), "Jarrow Marchers" (Ktra514/5), "Red Arrows" (BBC News Southampton 458), and Ted Heath (*Omnibus*)

T12/1,447 *Monty Python's Flying Circus* 1972 TX 72.12.21 SERIES 3 EP 10
Episode 36—Slides: "Scottish Dancing" from Walton, and "Cactus in the Desert"

T12/1,460 *Monty Python's Flying Circus* 1973 TX 73.01.04 SERIES 3 EP 11
Episode 37—Still photo: Keystone Press CF 14728-3; Film stock: BBC's "Heath & Queen at Ideal Home Exhibition"; BMN Library No. 259-CY3, "Do It Now"

T12/1,461 *Monty Python's Flying Circus* 1973 TX 73.01.18 SERIES 3 EP 13
Episode 39—Film stock: BBC Film DO23/72/41 "Heath"; BMN Library "Hansom Cab"; EMI, "Theatre Audience"

T12/1,462 *Monty Python's Flying Circus* 1973 TX 73.11.01 SERIES 3 EP 12
Episode 38—Film stock: GR 2091A, Reduction Print from Thames Rediffusion

T12/1,467 *Monty Python's Flying Circus* 1974 TX 74.11.07
Episode 41—Film Stock: "Aerial Views London" from World Background, Elstree Studios

T12/1,468 *Monty Python's Flying Circus* 1974 TX 74.11.21
Episode 43—No film stock or photo requests

T12/1,469 *Monty Python's Flying Circus* 1974 GENERAL
Episodes 40–45—Photos: Fiat car factory and "Henry Kissinger"; Film Stock: Imperial War Museum footage; Pathé stock

Appendix B: Recorded and Live Music Cues

Not all of the items listed below were included in the finished episodes. This listing represents every *request* made for music cues during the run of the series. It is listed by episode.

EPISODE 1

"Liberty Bell" (J.P. Sousa) played by the Band of Grenadier Guard (BGG); "Tratalala Rhythm"; National Light Orchestra, "Saturday Sports" (Wilfred Burns); (89-key marenghi) "All the Fun of the Fairground" and "Baywood Villa"; Handel's *Messiah* Highlights No. 44, "Hallelujah Chorus"; "Rule Britannia"; "In the News" (Peter York); Funeral March (Beethoven, arr. Mayhew Lake); L'Oiseau-lyre: Gigue in G (Mozart) and Mozart Quartets: "Pression No. 3"; Hitler's Inferno "Deutschland Über Alles"; Beethoven Symphonie No. 4.; Miguel Lopez-Cortezo, guitar, "Quando Caliente del Sol"

EPISODE 2

Track from Chaplin's film "In the Park"; Handel's "Concerto No. 3 in G Minor, 4th movement, Allegro"; Rachmaninoff's "Symphony No. 1, Op. 13, Part 4, Allegro con fuoco"

EPISODE 3

Mantovani's Waltz Time—"Charmaine" (by Rapee); "Someone Else I'd Like to Be" sung by GC and JC, live piano by Bill McGuffie, written by Tom Sutton; "Chase martial" from Jack Shaindlin; Holiday Playtime, "King Palmer"; Famous Offenbach Overtures—Orpheus in the Underground, "The Can-Can"; "Music Boxes 1–16" by Eddie Warner; Richard Rodger's Waltzes

EPISODE 4

Fourteen Pictorial Sketches for Orchestra, "Eveil a L'Aube" by Edward Michael; Blackpool Favourites, "I Do Like to Be Beside the Seaside" performed by Reginald Dixon; Dubbed to film: Reg Dixon, "Colonel Bogey March" by Alford; David Rose and Orchestra performing "The Stripper"

EPISODE 5

"Action Station" by Dave Lindup, European Sound Stage Orchestra; "Stars and Stripes Forever," BGG (band 1, side 1)

EPISODES 6 AND 7

"Enigma" variations (no. 9, "Nimrod"), OP 36 by Elgar (conducted by Sir Adrian Boult); "From Russia with Love" by John Barry; "Gay's World" Part Two ('Vitality') by Novello; Dubbed to film: "March of the Insurgents" and "Spectacular" by J. Shaindlin, dramatic and scenic usage, respectively; 12 Etudien Op. 10 (No. 9 in F Minor) by Tamas Vasary; London Suite "Knightsbridge" (March) Side 1, Band 3; "Bonny Sweet Robin" on harpsichord

EPISODE 8

"Jerusalem" by Blake-Parry, performed by Royal Choral Society and Philharmonia Orchestra; Band of the

Scots playing Music of the Two World Wars, World War II, Part I, "Roll Out the Barrel"; Dubbed onto film: "Thunderball" by John Barry; "Gonna Get a Girl" by Harry Bidgood and His Broadcasters Fox Trot; Debussy's "Jeux de Vagues"; "Mantovani's "The Most Beautiful Girl in the World" by Rodgers and Hart; "True to the End" by Van Phillips

EPISODE 9

Dubbed onto film: Melodious Brass "Waltzing Trumpets" by the Fairey Band; "Banjerino" on jugs, washboards, and kazoos; On record: "I Love You Samantha" by the Dudley Moore Trio, from "Genuine Dud"; "Le Marsellaise" by BGG; "Ad Lib" by P. Reno and performed by the Quartet of Modern Jazz, The Studio Group; and Sousa's "Washington Post" march

EPISODE 10

On record: "Dead March" from "Saul" by Handel; "By George," the David Frost Theme and "Frost over London"; "The Dambusters" from the Central Band of the Royal Air Force; "Victory at Sea" by Richard Rodgers; "Fanfare on the RAF Call" by O'Donnell; "Creepy Clowns," Crawford Light Orchestra, by Ronald Hamer; "Mexican Hat Dance" played live

EPISODE 11

Tchaikovsky Piano Concerto No. 1 in B Flat Minor, Op. 23, performed by Julius Katchen with the LSO and Pierino Gamba; Handel's *Messiah*, "Hallelujah" by London Philharmonic Choir with the LPO and Walter Sisskind; Lansdowne Jazz Series, "Oh, Didn't He Ramble" by Terry Lightfoot and His New Orleans Jazzmen; "Music for Vive L'Oompa" Funeral March, Chopin, The London Brass Players; "I'm Gonna Make You Love Me" from "I've Gotta Be Me" by Peter Nero; David Rose and His Orchestra play the Stripper and other fun songs for the Family!, and "Night Train"; The Paris Studio Group, "Batterie pour une foule" by Renaud and Hermel; "Carols From the Kings" by The Choir of King's College Cambridge singing "Ding Dong Merrily," and conducted by David Willcocks; "There's No Business Like Show Business" from "Annie Get Your Gun" by Irving Berlin, performed by Werner Muller and His Orchestra; "Towers & Spires" by Spencer Nakin; "Song of the Universe" from "Seven Symphonic Preludes" from The Music of Edward Michael, The International Symphony Orchestra

EPISODE 12

"Deutschland Über Alles" by BGG, conducted by Harris; "Prelude Richard III" from Walton's "Shakespeare Film Scores for *Henry V, Hamlet, Richard III,*" with Sir William Walton conducting the Philharmonia Orchestra; "Hallelujah" from Handel's *Messiah*, London Philharmonia Choir with the LPO conducted by Susskind; "The Rose"—Selection Myddleton, by BGG, conducted by Harris

EPISODE 13

The London Brass Players performing "Music for Vive L'Oompa" Funeral March, by Chopin; Robert Hartow in "Sunday Night at the Palladium" by the London Palladium Orchestra, conducted by Cyril Orandel; "On the Button—Quick Mover" by The Studio Group, directed by Keith Papworth; Petula Clark's "Don't Sleep in the Subway" from "These Are My Songs," arranged and conducted by Ernie Freeman; "Le Marsellaise" by BGG; Rachmaninov Symphony No. 1 in D Minor Op. 13, "Allegro Con Fuoco," by USSR Symphony Orchestra, Yevgeny Svetlanov conducting; Julie Felix's "Going to the Zoo" by The World of Harmony Music; "The *Dr. Kildare* Theme" by Johnnie Spence and His Orchestra; Strings and Things Tilsley Orchestra playing "The Lump," "Return to Summer," and "Venus"; "Great Britain: God Save the Queen" by National Anthems of the World, BGG; "Devil's Gallop" by Queens Hall Light Orchestra, directed by Charles Williams; Theme from "A Summer Place" by Max Steiner, from Percy Faith; "Happy Harp" from Johnny Teupen and His Harp; "Sweet & Singing" by Gene Herrmann and His Orchestra; "Musical Boxes 1–8"; TV & Radio Commercials: "Mother & Baby" and "Bossa Nova Beat"

EPISODE 14

"Warm Hands," Watt Peters Orchestra; "Epic Title" by Jack Shaindlin; "Karelia Suite Op. II, Intermezzo" by Sibelius, Danish State Radio Symphony Orchestra; "Cockney Song" from Silent Film Music

EPISODE 15

"Lullaby" by Gary Hughes, Westway Studio Orchestra; Hungarian Rhapsody No. 2, Liszt, Black Dyke Mills Band; "Aggression," Eric Towren, ISO; "The World Turns," L. Stevens; "Ceremonial March No. 1," John Reids, ISO; "Openings and Endings No. 2," Robert Farnon; "Voice of the Jungle—Tribal Message,"

Freddie Phillips; Offenbach's "Orpheus in the Underworld" ("Can-Can"), Jean Martinau; "God Save the Queen," Synchrofax Music Library; "Devil's Gallop," Charles Williams

EPISODE 16

Music dubbed onto film: ISO "Flute" Promenade by E. Towren; "Long Trail" from Far West Suite by Eddie Warner; Eric Coates and the Philharmonic Promenade Orchestra playing "Knightsbridge March" from London Suite; Pipes and Drums of the Royal Scots Greys: "Scotland's Pride," "Skye Boat Song" and "Road to Isles"; Mantovani's "It's 3 O'clock in the Morning" by Robledo/Terriss; BGG "LB"; On record: Pete Wilsher and Keith Chester's "Eye of Horus" from "Electroshake"; P.M. MacLellan "Clan Campbell's" from Pibroch 1

EPISODE 17

"Star Spangled Banner"; "Grazing Land" and "Vistavision Title" by J. Shaindlin; "Superformance (Impact and Action) by D. Lindup; "Concert" by Concert band of HM's Lifeguards; "Peter Gunn Theme" by Mancini; "Poet Jingle" by B. McGuffie, sung by CC and TJ

EPISODE 18

"Keep the Home Fires Burning" by Ivor Novello; "Bright Lights" by Sam Fonteyn

EPISODE 19

On record: "Roving Report No. 2" by Jack Trombey; "Comic Bugle Call" by Alan Langford; "Late Night" by Roger Webb; "Jeru" by Gerry Mulligan; Dubbed onto tape: BGG "LB"; On film: "Hollywood Title" from "Signature Tunes and Titles" by J. Shaindlin; "News Titles No. 1" by J. Scott

EPISODE 20

On film: Mike Leroy's "With a Little Love" by T. Romeo; "Banjo in the Hollow" and "Back Porch Blue Grass" by D. Allard; "Episodes from the Bible" by Derek Laren and ISO; Westway Studio Ensemble, "Woodland Tryst" by C. Watters; On record: Concert Band of HM's Lifeguards, "The Stripper" by Rose and "Arabian Belly Dance" by John Leach; LSO, "The Land of Hope and Glory" by Elgar; "The Big Fuzz" from "Impact and Action" by Johnny Pearson; Orchestra of Amsterdam's "Symphonie Fantastique 4th Movement" by Berlioz; London Palladium Orchestra, "Startime"

EPISODE 21

On record: Jimmy Durante, "Schnozzles," "I'm the guy who found the lost chord" by Brent and Durante; LSO, "Casbah" by Keith Papworth and "Overland to Oregon Pt. 1"; LSO "Pomp and Circumstance," "Orb and Sceptre," and "Coronation March"; Franco Chiari Jazz Quartet, "Romantic Theme"; On film: Light scenic Pastorale "Assisi Byways" by J. Shaindlin; Black Bottom, "My Baby Loves to Charleston" by De Sylva, Brown, and Henderson; "The Hunt" (Music for Wind Quintet) by Adrian Bonse; Dubbed from tape to film: "Today" sung by TJ and composed by B. McGuffie with His Orchestra; On film: Symphonia Orchestra's "Elephant Country" and "Heroic Saga," and "Saturday Sport" by Burns; On tape: Mozart's "Eine Kleine Nachtmusik" (G-dur KV525)

EPISODE 22

On record: Peter Dawson's "My Life of Song" for "Waltzing Matilda," arranged by Patterson-Cowan and Thomas Wood; Queens Hall Light Orchestra, "Coronation Scott" by Vivian Ellis; Band of Corps of Royal Engineers "National Anthems (Eire)"; BGG "LB"; On film: "Horrific Sting" by Alan Langford; The Westway Studio Ensemble's "Woodland Tryst" by C. Watters; RCA Victor Symphony Orchestra's "Victory at Sea" by Richard Rodgers, and "The Sugar Plum Fairy" by Tschaikowsky

EPISODE 23

Music dubbed onto film: Sir Adrian Boult and the LPO, "Sinfonia Antarctica," First, Third, and Fifth Movements by Vaughn Williams; The Machines "Electronic Screams" by Eric Peters; BGG's "LB"; ISO, "Aggression" by E. Towren, "Pride of the Ride" and "Nathan le prophete" by Edward Michael; Helmut Walcha, Church of Cappel Schnitger Organ, "Prelude & Fugue D. Major BWV 532" by J.S. Bach

EPISODE 24

On record: Autumn Chartbusters "Yummy, Yummy" by Resnick/Levine (MAL 848); Music dubbed onto film: Vienna Philharmonic Orchestra played "Overtures from Fingal's Cave" by Mendelssohn; LPO, "Stars & Stripes" by Sousa (ACL33); ISO, "Man of Power" by J. Trombey (DW LP 2988)

EPISODE 25

On record: "Battle at Sea" by J. Pearson; Syd Dale's "Breaking Point"; Band of the Irish Guards, "There'll Always Be an England" by Parker/Charles; Music played live: Eric Idle on harmonica, "Keep the Home Fires Burning" by I. Novello; Music dubbed onto film: Vienna Symphony Orchestra from "Ace of Diamonds," "Thus Spake Zarathustra" by H. Van Karajan; Pearson's "Battle at Sea"; Johnny Scott's "News Titles"; ISO, "Pastoralia" by E. Towren and "Pastel Pastoral" by Neil Richardson; BGG "LB"

EPISODE 26

On record: Band of Corps of Royal Engineers, "National Anthems" (MALS 1141 Side 1, Band 1); Treorchy Male Choir, from "The Pride of Wales," "All through the Night", arranged by Robinson (HMV CLP 3653); ISO, "On the River" by John Snow (DW/LP 3068A); On film: LSO, "Pomp and Circumstance March" in D Major, Elgar (ACL 137), "Fresh Breezes" and "Open Air" by N. Richardson (KPM 1060), and "Culver City Title" (from "Signature Tunes and Titles") by J. Shaindlin (CMR 301A); London Variety Theatre Orchestra, "Blue Danube" ("Great Waltzes of J. Strauss") by Strauss (STM 6025); Johnnie Spence Orchestra, "The *Dr. Kildare* Theme" by Goldsmith (EMI CLP1565); "Saturday Sport" by Burns (BC 1269)

EPISODE 27

On film: "Quatorze esquisses pittoresques pour orchestra" side 2, track 1: "Au fil de l'eau" by Edouard Michael; BGG "LB"; National, "Monegasque" by Primo di Luca; ISO, "New World—Man of Destiny" by S. Fonteyn; Music on disc: Wally Stott and Orchestra "Rotten Row" from "London Souvenir"; Georgia Brown's "Theme from Roads to Freedom" by James Cellan-Jones and Herbert Kretzmer; BGG "LB"

EPISODE 28

On film: New Concert Orchestra Background Music, "Sinfonia Tellurica and Homines" by Trevor Duncan; USSR Symphony Orchestra, "Symphony No. 6 in B Minor Allegro non Troppo" by Tchaikowsky; Geoff Love and Orchestra, Big War Movie Themes, "The Great Escape" by Bernstein/Stillman; "Theme Suites Vol. 11, Under Full Sail" by J. Pearson; BGG "LB"; Music on record: Theatre Orchestra Light Intimations, "Days Work" by Mike McNaught; Theatre Overture Dramatic and Horror, "String Suspenses" by Paul Lewis; BGG "LB"; LSO, "Piano Concerto No. 1 in B Flat Minor Op. 23 "Allegro non troppo" and "molto maestos" by Tchaikowsky; Harp Solos, "Descending Glassando," Gareth Walters; "Openings, Closings, Links and Bridges" by P. Moore; Music dubbed onto film: "Theatre Overture" by A. Mawer; "Free Love" and "Man Is Born" by Peter Reno

EPISODE 29

On film: "Jimmy Smith Theme" from "The Carpet Baggers" by Bernstein; BGG "LB"; The Early Music Consort of London and the Morley Consort, "Passe & medio & reprise le pingue," "Basse danse," and "Bergeret sans roche"; Spencer Nakin "Trumpet Calls" from Towers & Spires; D. Lindup "Elephant Herd"; Guy Warren of Ghana, "African Drums"; The Folk Dance Orchestra, "The Shrewsbury Lasses" by Thompson; The New Concert Orchestra, "Background Music 'Stings'" by Alan Langford; LSO "Pomp and Circumstance" by Elgar; R. Sharples's "Shock Treatment" (Side A, Tracks 1 and 3); On record: Helmut Walcha, "Fantasia & Fugue in G minor" by J. S. Bach; Live song: "Money, Money, Money" sung by Idle and the Fred Tomlinson Singers and harpist, music by Tomlinson and lyrics by John Gould; Live performance of "And did those feet . . ."

EPISODE 30

Lansdowne Light Orchestra "Newsroom" by Simon Campbell; "Greensleeves," De Sik, "The Windmill Song," BGG "LB"; Selling Sounds "Droopy Draws" by Barry Stoller; Looney Tunes by Reg Wale, International London Studio Group; The Big Top "Acrobats" by Keith Papworth, ISO; "The Rite of Spring" by Stravinsky, L'Orchestra de la Suisse Romande; "Coach and Pair" by Merrick and Farran; "Camel Team" by Merrick Farran; "Orb and Sceptre" by Walton, Royal Liverpool Philharmonic Orchestra; "Theme and Variation" by R. Tilsley; Today's World "Walk Tall" by Papworth; "Gong Sinister" by J. Gunn; Waterbuck Koala by S. Sklair from Cartoon Capers; "Hearts and Flowers" by Alphons Czibulka, W. Warren, LSO;

"Prairie Vista" by Dudley Simpson; "Bright Lights" by Roger Webb; "Love in Slow Motion" by Tilsley and ISO; "Devil's Gallop" by Queen's Hall Orchestra; "Viet Theme" by Roger

EPISODE 31

Music: "Stage Struck" by Jack Parnell; BGG "LB"; "World Trip for Big Orchestra No. 1, Pizzicata Milanese" by H. Kressling; New Concert Orchestra "Pistons from Crankcraft" by T. Duncan; Tomlinson/Idle's "Proust" sung live, as well as "Boo Boopee Doo"; music dubbed to film: LPO "Sinfonia Antarctica" by V. Williams; BGG "LB" and "Theme from Glorious West"; London Studio Group "Inner Reflections Gentle Touch" by Reg Wale; ISO "Military Preparation" by Hugo de Groot, "Culver City Title" by Shaindlin, and "Dramenasuspence No. 5" by R. Sharples

EPISODE 32

On film: "Queen of the Fleet" by George Chase; BGG "LB"; Mantovani, "Mantovani's Golden Hits," "Charmaine" by Rapee/Pollack; Royal Marines "A Life on the Ocean Wave" by Russell; "Peter Pan" by Hugo de Groot; Main Titles and Openers: Wide Screen Title" by Shaindlin; J. Spence and Orchestra "*Dr. Kildare* Theme" by Goldsmith; LSO "P&C" by Elgar

EPISODE 33

On film: "String Quartet in G minor" by Debussy; BGG "LB"; Royal Liverpool PO, "Spitfire Prelude & Fugue" by Walton, "Riot Squad" from Standard Music Library by P. Gerard; ISO Sea Music "Ripcord" by J. Steffaro; Julian Slade "Salad Days"; "I Sit in the Sun" and "Oh! Look at Me," both by Slade; "This Division" by Shaindlin; live performance by Alan Parker, "Grecian Nights"

EPISODE 34

Terry Jones singing "Just an Old-Fashioned Girl" by Fisher; LSO "Gayaneh Ballet Suite: "Dance of the Young Kurds" and "Fire" by Khachaturian, "P&C" by Elgar (Marches No. 1 in D major), and Variety Playoff by M. Hunter; Unaccompanied Artists "Jack in a Box" by David Myers and John Worsley; Vienna Philharmonic "Waltz from Faust" by Gounod; ISO, Modern Transport "Long Haul" by K. Papworth

EPISODE 35

Music for Technology "Industrial Sounds" by Walter Scott; BGG "LB"; dubbed to film: ISO "March Trident" by J. Trombey; BGG "LB"; Pul Piotet et Son Grand Orchestre, Dance Mood Music, "Les fous de soleil" by St. George

EPISODE 36

FT Singers "Amontillado" and "Half-a-Bee" both by Tomlinson; Weller Quartet "String Quartet in G" (K.516) by Mozart; LSO Prokofiev's "Symphony No. 3"; ISO "David & Goliath" by Derek Laren; BGG "LB"; Ensemble de Cuivres de Paris, "Fanfares de tous les temps" by Gravure; "Lady Margaret's Pavan" and "Sir William Gaillard" by Gareth Walters; "Fanfare No. 8" by Rene Challan; and "Dark Passage" by R. Wilhelm

EPISODE 37

On record: Leningrad PO "Symphony No. 12 1st Movement" Shostakovich; Paul Bonneau Orchestra, Terpsichoreau Festival (Overture Period), F. de Boisvalle, and "Musique pour les fetes d'eau Face" 461; BGG "LB"; Johnny Pearson "Locations" and "Comedy"; music dubbed onto film: Scots Guards "Drum Majorette" by Steck; BGG "LB"; ISO "Early Dusk" (Pastoral Music) by Ivor Slaney and "Flashing Blade" (Arena March); Stanley Black "A Pretty Girl Is Like a Melody" by Berlin; Band of Royal Military Academy, Sandhurst, "Stars and Stripes Forever" by Sousa; Fred Tomlinson Singers with piano, "Robin Hood"

EPISODE 38

Music dubbed onto film: BGG "LB"; M. Burgess "Lament for Viscount Dundee"; Orchestra de Suisse Romande, French Overtures Orpheus Scenic and Romance "Desert Morning" by Cliff Johns, and "Industrial and War: Action Line" by David De Lara, and "Scenic and Romance: After Midnight" by James Harpham; Moscow PO "The Execution of Stepan Razin" by Shostakovich, and "Dramatic Background: Approaching Menace" by N. Richardson; "I Belong to Glasgow"; ISO Pastoral Music "The Big Country" by Papworth; "Locations and Comedy: Comic Giggles" by J. Pearson, and "Viennese Party" by Harry Wild; Ensemble de Guivres de Paris "Fanfares de Tour les Temps Face" by Paul Dukas; "Towers and Spires" Brandle de Bourgogne" by Spencer Nakin; Scholar

Canforiuno of Stuttgart "Lux Aeterna New Music for Chorus" by Ligeti, and "Blue Danube" by Strauss; (music on disc) English Chamber Orchestra "Welsh Music for Strings 5th Movement" by Gareth Walters; Ronnie Aldrich "Silent Movie Piano Suite No. 6: Hearts and Flowers" by Czibulka/Warren, and "Opening Number" by Len Stevens; Queens Hall Light Orchestra "Devil's Gallop"; BGG "LB"; London Big Sound "Big City Story: Beyond the Night" by Peter Reno

EPISODE 39

Music dubbed onto film: "Strauss at the Waltz" Harry Wild; Czech PO "Fight on the Ice from 'Alexander Nevsky'" Prokofiev; BBC SO Collages "La Nativite du Seigneru" Massaien; Edmundo Ros Orchestra, The Wedding Samba "Dance Again," Ellestein; London Festival SO "Nutcracker Suite" Tchaikowsky and "Time Marches On: Wide Screen Title" by Shaindlin, and "Soft Touch" by R. Tilsley; On records: ISO "Academy Awards: The Music of Stanley Black" by Stanley Black, and "Aces to Open" by Syd Dale; Band of Scots Guards "News Scoop" by Stevens; LSO "Enigma Variations" by Elgar

EPISODE 40

BGG "LB"; Vienna PO "Ride of the Valkyrie" by Wagner; Geoff Love and His Orchestra, "The Big Country" by Neff-Lewis-Moross; The New Concert Orchestra, "A Little Suite March" by T. Duncan; The Westway Novelty Ensemble, "Hawaiian Party"; Pro Arts Orchestra, "Vanity Fair" by Collins; Stuart Crombie and Orchestra, "The World about Us"; "George III" (Neil Innes)

EPISODE 41

On film: BGG "LB"; Royal Liverpool PO, "Knightsbridge" by E. Coates; "Elm Street" by Johnny Burt; music on disc: BGG "LB"; Members of the English Chamber Orchestra, "Lisbon" by Britten; "Devil's Gallop" and "Investiture Fanfare" by Charles Williams

EPISODE 42

B. McGuffie's "When Does a Dream Begin" sung by N. Innes; Johnnie Spence, "*Dr. Kildare* Theme" by Goldsmith; Neil Richardson "Full Speed Ahead"; LSO "P&C March" by Elgar; All Stars Brass Band, "Rule Britannia" by Siebert; George Malcolm "Bach before Breakfast"; Gordon Franks and Orchestra "La Dolce Vita"; Geoff Love and Orchestra, "The Dam Busters" and "633 Squadron"; Tony Adams and Singers, "Oklahoma" by Rodgers-Hammerstein; Black & White Minstrels, "Let's Face the Music" by Berlin; London Festival Orchestra, "Love theme from Ben Hur"; Ann Rogers with Ainsworth and His Orchestra, "The Sound of Music" by Rodgers-Hammerstein; Wurttenburg Chamber Orchestra, "A Musical Joke—Rondo" by Mozart; LSO, "P&C March" by Elgar; Terry Jones sings "Anything Goes" by Cole Porter

EPISODE 43

BGG "LB"; Johnny Scott and his Orchestra, "The Good Word"; Philharmonia Orchestra and Sir William Walton, "*Henry V* Suite—Globe Playhouse"

EPISODE 44

BGG "LB" and "Stars & Stripes Forever"; London Proms SO, "Finlandia Op. 26 No. 7" by Sibelius; All Stars Brass Band, "Rule Britannia" by Siebert; "Agony" by Ilhan Mimaroglu; Continental Theatre Orchestra, "In the Party Mood" by Jack Strachney; "Serenade for Summer" by King Palmer

EPISODE 45

BGG "LB"; Vienna PO "Ride of the Valkyrie" by Wagner; Geoff Love and His Orchestra, "The Big Country" by Neff-Lewis-Moross; The New Concert Orchestra, "A Little Suite March" by T. Duncan; The Westway Novelty Ensemble, "Hawaiian Party"; Pro Arts Orchestra, "Vanity Fair" by Collins; Stuart Crombie and Orchestra, "The World about Us"

Appendix C: Sketch, Animation, and Link Listing

This comprehensive listing of sketches, animations, and links in *Monty Python's Flying Circus* includes entries from both volumes of this book. To find more information about each episode, refer to volume 1 for episodes 1–26 (seasons 1 and 2) and volume 2 for episodes 27–45 (seasons 3 and 4).

"42nd International Clambake" Ep. 34
"Accidental Executions" Ep. 35
"Accidents Sketch" ("Prawn Salad Ltd.") Ep. 18
Ada's Snack Bar ("And now . . ." Man link) Ep. 9
"After-shave" ("Toilet requisite") Ep. 17
"Agatha Christie Sketch" Ep. 11
"Agatha Christie Sketch (Railway Timetables) Ep. 24
"Albatross" Ep. 13
"All-England Summarize Proust Competition" Ep. 31
"All-Essex Badminton Championship" (promo) Ep. 32
"All-In Cricket" Ep. 11
"Amazing Kargol and Janet" Ep. 2
"Anagram Quiz" Ep. 30
"Anagram Versions of Shakespeare" Ep. 30
"An Appeal on Behalf of the National Truss" Ep. 21
"And Did Those Feet" (song); Link into "England's Mountains Green" Ep. 4
"And Did Those Feet . . ." (arrest hymn) Ep. 29
"And now for something completely different" (links) Eps. 2, 9, 21
"And now for something completely different" Man (intros/links): Ep. 9—Ada's Snack Bar; Ep. 14—Zoo cage; Ep. 15—Rocky beach; Ep. 16—Window cleaner's platform; Ep. 17—Propellered desk; Ep. 18—Grill-o-Mat snack bar; Ep. 19—Smithee; Ep. 20—Projected over Hun film; Ep. 22—Bikini-clad; With a pig; Ep. 23—Paignton; Ep. 24—Seaside; Ep. 25—Night-time beach; Ep. 26—At attention (for the Queen); Eps. 27–33—Norwich Castle; Ep. 35—Interviewed in a flowery field; Ep. 36—Norwich Castle; Ep. 37—Boxing ring; Ep. 38—Norwich Castle; Ep. 39—Flowery field
"And then . . ." Man (link) Ep. 43
Animations (*in the order each appears, by episode*): Ep. 1—Escaping pig; Whizzo Butter; "Sit up!" photos; Ep. 2—"I think therefore I am"; Harold the flying sheep; Carnivorous pram; Ep. 3—Link into Donkey Rides; Purchase a past; Ep. 4—Tumor operation to palanquin link; Ep. 5—Pulling old lady apart; Charles Atlas's "Dynamo Tension"; Ep. 6—Escaping scribble; Link out of *It's the Arts; Thrills and Adventure* comic book; Criminal pram; 20th-Century Vole; Ep. 8—"Full Frontal Nudity Vol. 2"; "An Intimate Review"; Meat grinder to dancing Botticelli's Venus link; Ep. 9—Encyclopaedia salesman; Kewpie doll carnival game; Brian Islam and Brucie; Ep. 10—A Chippendale writing desk; Humor, the new permissiveness, and animals eating animals; Ep. 11—Flushing head; Violent nudes; Tenement coffins; Ep. 12—Falling people; The Great Fred; Falling apart; Animals from a pipe; Ep. 13—Feeding the birdman; Ambulance on the loose; "What a terrible way to end the series!"; Ep. 14—Vintage model European monarchs; Straight razor shave; Ep. 15—Can-can diversion; Civil War cannons; "I confess!"; Ep. 16—"I am somebody's lunch hour"; Ep. 17—Cocoon to compère butterfly; "How to give up being a Mason"; Bouncing on naked lady; Jack and the Beanstalk; Five Frog Curse; Ep. 18—Monopod woman; Men escaping the film; Color separation link (walking general Civil War robots, Last Supper ruined, Hand of God rescues Sir William, WWI fighter cloud); Teddy and Neddy want to hunt piggybanks; Ep. 19—Enoch Powell head; Lights out; Additional prizes, including a deadly samurai made into a meal; Michelangelo's Adam in a sandwich;

Train and naked girl; "Welcome All Sexual Athletes"; Mona Lisa says "Hello Tiger; Bloody lipstick; The Prince and the Black Spot; *Election Night Special* titles; Ep. 20—"Arthur X, leader of the Pennine Gang"; Parrots announcing TV programs; Attila the Bun; Ep. 21—Building and decay; Luxury Flats; A toe-elephant; Giant football in Wembley; Mugsy Spaniel and Eggs Diamond; *Raising Gangsters for Fun & Profit*; Ep. 22—Dancing generals; Suicidal man; Bus stop eyeball; "The Killer Cars"; Atomic-Mutated Cat; Ep. 23—Stepping on people; Conrad Poohs and His Dancing Teeth; A letter undelivered; Ep. 24—Overrun by Chinese Communists; "Domino Theory"; Crelm toothpaste; Shrill petrol; Cartoon Religions Ltd.; Ep. 25—Picketers and *2001: A Space Odyssey*; "I wonder just how much Molly knew?"; Characters leaving paintings; Venus de Milo: ". . . bloody consultation!"; Over-actors; Bombs creating flowers; Ep. 26—Crelm toothpaste; The surgical garment; Madonna balloon bomb; "Fire Mrs. Nesbit!"; Cannibalism; Ep. 27—Into the criminal body; Davis and the Inspector in the criminal body; Teleporting Mrs. Cut-out; Ep. 28—Surbiton to Hounslow map; Anatomical model walks off the edge of the cartoon; Compère's mouth escapes; Nazi fish swallows British fish; Chinese fish sinks ocean liner; Ep. 29—Police violence; Many-handed victim; Woman in the sun; Bouncy ball woman; Ep. 30—Pantomime flea eats man; Carnivorous dining and bed rooms; Killer houses; *The House-Hunters*; NCP Car Parks; Ep. 31—Communists under the bed; Putrid Peter doll; Ep. 32—The meaning of life, badly framed; Carnivorous baby; Groovy Royal Navy advert; Ep. 33—The domino effect; TV is bad for your eyes; Program Control fairy; Ep. 34—Monsters dance; Ep. 35—How to animate cut-outs; St. Anthony on a break; WWI helmets; A simple little push of a button; Two trees; Hitler; Ep. 36—Aldwych Theatre's *Gay Boys in Bondage*; Arcade target shooting; Mixing a drink; A kiss at the pub; Folding and posting a letter to the BBC; Ep. 37—Ambulance running over City Gent; Stealing cut-outs; moveable black hole; Ep. 38—No-Time Toulouse; 2001: A Space Odyssey; Penguin invasion; Ep. 39—Swell party and bathroom noises; Charwoman; Ep. 40—Washing with soap and water; *The Golden Age of Colonic Irrigation*; Ep. 41—Anatomy of an ant; Ep. 42—"What a lovely day"; Ep. 43—Anatomy monster at the city walls; Grape balloons; Ep. 44—Mr. Neutron; Ep. 45—Slow-motion cannon shell; Batsmen of the Kalahari

"Another Indian massacre at Dorking Theatre" (link) Ep. 6
"Ant Communication" ("Restaurant Sketch") Ep. 41
Anti-communist (link) Ep. 3
"Antonioni Career Review" Ep. 29
"Anything Goes In" (song) Ep. 42
"Apology for Violence and Nudity" Ep. 28
"Apology (Politicians)" Ep. 32
"Appeal on Behalf of Extremely Rich People" Ep. 45
"*Archaeology Today*" Ep. 21
"Architect Sketch" Ep. 17
"Argument Clinic" Ep. 29
"Army Captain as Clown" Ep. 30
"Army Protection Racket" Ep. 8
"Art Critic" Ep. 4
"Art Critic Strangles His Wife" Ep. 8
"Art Critic: 'The Place of the Nude'" Ep. 8
"Art Gallery" Ep. 4
"Art Gallery Strike" Ep. 25
"Arthur Ewing and His Musical Mice" Ep. 2
"Arthur Figgis" Ep. 6
"Arthur Tree" Ep. 10
"Arthur 'Two-Sheds' Jackson Interview" Ep. 1
"At Home with the Ant and Other Pets" Ep. 41
"*The Attila the Hun Show*" Ep. 20
"Attila the Nun" Ep. 20
"Audit" Ep. 7

"BALPA Interruptions" (and "Corrections") Ep. 16
"Banana and Cheese Sandwiches" Ep. 34
"Bank Robber (Lingerie Shop)" Ep. 10
"Basingstoke in Westphalia" Ep. 42
"Batley Townswomen's Guild Presents the Battle of Pearl Harbour" Ep. 11
"Batley Townswomen's Guild Presents the First Heart Transplant" Ep. 22
"Battle of Trafalgar with Prof. R.J. Canning" Ep. 11
"BBC 1 and 2 Promos" Ep. 37
"BBC 1 Colour Promos" (*Dad's Doctors* and *Dad's Pooves*) Ep. 38
"BBC 1 Previews Trailer" Ep. 21
"BBC Apology" (and the BBC's denial of that apology) Ep. 33
"BBC Entry for the Zinc Stoat of Budapest" Ep. 6
"BBC Head of Drama" Ep. 27
"BBC Is Short of Money" Ep. 28
"BBC News Handovers" Ep. 45
"BBC Newsreader(s) Arrested" Ep. 5
"BBC Programme Planners" Ep. 38
"BBC TV News" Ep. 20
BBC walk-on role (link) Ep. 15
"BBC Would Like to Apologize" by the Gumbys (link) Ep. 17
"*Beat the Clock*" Ep. 30
"Being Thrown into a River" Ep. 19
"Beethoven Finds 'The Lost Chord'" Ep. 21
"Beethoven's Mynah Bird" (and Shakespeare, Michelangelo) Ep. 21
"Bicycle Repair Man" (Mr. F.G. Superman) Ep. 3
Bicycling Picasso map (link) Ep. 1

"Gorilla Librarian" Ep. 10
"*Grandstand*" ("Match Highlights") Ep. 39
"Gumby Brain Specialist" (and "Gumby Brain Surgeons") Ep. 32
"Gumby Crooner" ("Make Believe") Ep. 9
"Gumby Flower Arranging" Ep. 25
Gumbys introduce sketches ("Architect Sketch," "Chemist Sketch") (link) Ep. 17

"*Hamlet*" (and Ophelia, and "Curtain Call") Ep. 43
"Harold the Clever Sheep" Ep. 2
"Has anyone anything else to say?" (conclusion) Ep. 12
"Hell's Grannies" documentary Ep. 8
"Here is the news" ("Art Gallery Strike") Ep. 25
"Hermits" Ep. 8
"A Highland Spokesman Offers Corrections" Ep. 16
"Hijacked Bus to Cuba" Ep. 16
"Hijacked Plane (to Luton)" Ep. 16
"Historical Impersonations" Ep. 13
"History of Warfare" (intro) Ep. 8
"HM the Queen still watching *The Virginian*" (caption) Ep. 26
"Homicidal Barber" Ep. 9
"*Horse of the Year Show*" (Kelly's flat) Ep. 28
"Hospital Run by RSM" Ep. 26
"Housing Project Built by Characters from Nineteenth-Century English Literature" Ep. 35
"How Far Can a Minister Fall?" Ep. 12
"*How Not to Be Seen*" (Government Public Service film) Ep. 24
"*How to Do It*" Ep. 28
"How to Feed a Goldfish" Ep. 26
"How to Fling an Otter" Ep. 6
"How to Give Up Being a Mason" Ep. 17
"*How to Recognize Different Parts of the Body*" Ep. 22
"How to Rid the World of All Known Diseases" (*How to Do It*) Ep. 28
"Hunting Film" Ep. 9

"Icelandic Honey Week" Ep. 45
"Icelandic Saga" (Erik Njorl) Ep. 27
"Ideal Loon Exhibition" Ep. 37
"The Idiot in Society" Ep. 20
"*If*—A Film by Mr. Dibley" (and *2001*, *Midnight Cowboy*, *Rear Window*, *Finian's Rainbow*) Ep. 19
"If I Were Not in the CID" (song) Ep. 3
"I'm a Lumberjack" (song) Ep. 9
"In 1914 the Balance of Power Lay in Ruin . . ." (link) Ep. 25
"In 1970 the British Empire lay in ruins . . ." Ep. 25
"Industrial Relations Reorganization's Human Pyramid" Ep. 19
"Inspector Dim of the Yard" Ep. 3
"Inspector Flying Fox of the Yard" (and Baboon, Leopard, Panther, and Thomson's Gazelle) Ep. 29
"Insurance Sketch" (interrupted by the Queen tuning in) Ep. 26
"Interesting People" Ep. 11
"Interesting Sport: All-In Cricket" Ep. 11
"Intermission: A History of Irish Agriculture" Ep. 13
"International Wife-Swapping" Ep. 39
"Interruptions" Ep. 19
"Interruptions by Undertakers: The World of History—The Black Death" Ep. 11
"Interview (w/Ludwig Grayson) in Filing Cabinet" Ep. 24
"Is the Third Test in Here?" (interruptions) Ep. 20
"*Is There? . . . Life after Death?*" Ep. 36
"It All Happened on the 11:20 from Heinault . . ." Ep. 24
"*It's*" Show (with Ringo Starr and Lulu) Ep. 28
"*It's a Living*" Ep. 19
"It's a Man's Life in the British Dental Association" Ep. 4
"It's a Man's Life in the Modern Army" (and "It's a dog's life" and "It's a pig's life . . .") Ep. 4
"*It's a Tree* with Arthur Tree" Ep. 10
"It's" Man intro/link clips: Ep. 1—Ocean, Poole Harbour); Ep. 2—Dunes; Ep. 3—Fern forest; Ep. 4—Thrown from cliff; Ep. 5—Rowboat; Ep. 6—Ringing phone; Ep. 7—Running, falling; Ep. 8—Anarchist's bomb; Ep. 9—Exploding forest; Ep. 10—Abattoir; Ep. 11—Hit by cars; Ep. 12—Pinball; Ep. 13—Coffin; Ep. 14—Zoo cage; Eps. 15–18, 20—Seaside (head shot only); Ep. 22—Bikini; Eps. 23–25—Seaside, head shot; Ep. 27— Foliage background (head shot only); Ep. 28—Foliage, head shot (nighttime); Eps. 29–33—Foliage, head shot; Ep. 35—Jersey field; Ep. 36—Foliage, head shot; Ep. 37—Boxing ring; Eps. 38–39—Foliage, head shot; Ep. 42—Boxing ring
"*It's the Arts*" Eps. 1, 6
"*It's the Mind*: Déjà vu" Ep. 16
"*It's Wolfgang Amadeus Mozart*" Ep. 1
"I won't ruin this sketch for a pound" (link) Ep. 35

"Jack in a Box" (song) Ep. 34
"Jarrow—New Year's Eve 1911" ("Spanish Inquisition") Ep. 15
"Job Hunter" Ep. 24
"Jerusalem" (song: "And did those feet . . .) Ep. 8
"Johann Gambolputty . . . von Hautkopf of Ulm" Ep. 6
"Jokes and Novelties Salesman" Ep. 15
"Judging" (JP Beauty Pageant) Ep. 37
"*Julius Caesar* on an Aldis Lamp" Ep. 15
"Jungle Restaurant" Ep. 29

"Kami-kaze Advice Centre" Ep. 38
"Kamikaze Scotsmen" Ep. 38
"Karl Marx and Che Guevara, Kissing" (and in bed) Ep. 25

"Ken Buddha as His Inflatable Knees" Ep. 9
"Ken Russell's *Gardening Club*" Ep. 33
"Ken Russell's *Gardening Club* (1958)" Ep. 29
"Ken Shabby" (and "the story so far") Ep. 12
"Kilimanjaro Expedition (Double Vision)" Ep. 9
"Killer Sheep" Ep. 20
Knight-and-rubber-chicken (link) Eps. 2, 3, 5, 7, 9, 13

"Language Laboratory" Ep. 31
"The Larch" Ep. 3
"Last Five Miles of the M2" Ep. 42
"League for Fighting Chartered Accountancy" Ep. 10
"Leapy Lee" Ep. 21
"Leave Your Radio On during the Night" Ep. 7
"Legendary Batsmen of the Kalahari" Ep. 45
"Le Marche Futile" Ep. 14
"Lemming of the BDA" Ep. 4
"Let's Talk Ant" (University of the Air) Ep. 41
"Letters" (cannibalism) Ep. 26
"Letters" ("I object to . . .") Ep. 13
"Letters ('Lavatorial Humour'; 'Mary Bignall'; 'Cheap Laughs')" Ep. 11
"Letters" (self-destruction) Ep. 12
"Letters to *Daily Mirror*" Ep. 10
"Licence Fees" Eps. 7, 20
"Life and Death Struggles" Ep. 30
"Life of Sir Philip Sidney" Ep. 36
"*Life of Tschaikowsky*" Ep. 28
"Lifeboat" (cannibalism) Ep. 26
"Lifeboat" ("It's not a lifeboat . . .") Ep. 33
"*Light Entertainment Awards*" Ep. 39
"Linkman at the snack bar" (and on the bus) Ep. 18
"Literary Football Discussion" Ep. 11
"Live from Epsom" Ep. 43
"Live from the Grill-o-Mat Snack Bar, Paignton" Ep. 18
"Living Room on Pavement" Ep. 17
"Long John Silver Impersonators v. Bournemouth Gynaecologists" Ep. 23
"Lost World of Roiurama" Ep. 29
"Louis XIV" Ep. 40
"Lumberjack Song" Ep. 9
"Lupins" Ep. 37

"M1 Interchange Built by Characters from *Paradise Lost*" Ep. 35
"Man-Powered Flight" (intro) Ep. 15
"Man Turns into Scotsman!" Ep. 7
"Man Who Collects Birdwatcher's Eggs" Ep. 26
"Man Who Contradicts People" Ep. 22
"Man Who Finishes Other People's Sentences" Ep. 45
"Man Who Is Alternately Rude and Polite" Ep. 18
"Man Who Makes People Laugh Uncontrollably" Ep. 30
"Man Who Says Things in a Very Roundabout Way" Ep. 26
"The Man Who Says Words in the Wrong Order" ("Thripshaw's Disease") Ep. 36
"Man Who Speaks Only the Beginnings of Words" (and "Middles" and "Ends") Ep. 26
"Man Who Talks in Anagrams" Ep. 30
"Man with a Stoat through His Head" (link) Ep. 26
"Man with a Tape Recorder up His Nose" (and up "His Brother's Nose") Ep. 9
"Man with Three Buttocks" Ep. 2
"Man with Two Noses" Ep. 2
"Marriage Guidance Counsellor" (Deirdre and Arthur Pewtey) Ep. 2
"Mary Recruitment Office" Ep. 30
"*Match of the Day*: Erotic Film" Ep. 5; "Players Hugging/Kissing," Ep. 32
"Me Doctor" Ep. 13
"Merchant Banker" (at Slater-Nazi) Ep. 30
"*The Mill on the Floss*" (by balloon) Ep. 40
"Minehead By-Election" Ep. 12
"Minister for Not Listening to People" Ep. 32
"Ministry of Silly Walks" Ep. 14
"*Molluscs*—'Live' TV Documentary" Ep. 32
"Money Programme" Ep. 29
Monsters dance (animated link) to "Jack in a Box" (song) Ep. 34
"Montgolfier Brothers" Ep. 40
"Morning Teas on the Lifeboat" Ep. 33
"*Mortuary Hour*" Ep. 35
"Mosquito Hunters" Ep. 21
"*Most Awful Family in Britain*" Ep. 45
"Motor Insurance Sketch" (Mr. Devious) Ep. 17
"Mountaineering Sketch" Ep. 26
"The Mouse Problem" (and Vox Pops) Ep. 2
"Mr. and Mrs. Brian Norris' Ford Popular" Ep. 28
"Mr. and Mrs. Git" (and the "nice version") Ep. 21
"Mr. Attila the Hun" (Who is actually Alexander the Great) Ep. 13
"Mr. Bent Is in Our Durham Studios" Ep. 24
"Mr. Gulliver Becomes Clodagh Rogers Becomes Leon Trotsky Becomes Eartha Kitt" Ep. 34
"Mr. Hilter" (and Ron Vibbentrop, Bimmler) Ep. 12
"*Mr. Neutron*" ("Loves Mrs. S.C.U.M.") Ep. 44
"Mr. Neville Shunte" Ep. 24
"Mr. Pither" (*Cycling Tour*) Ep. 34
"Mrs. Nigger-Baiter Explodes" Ep. 28
"Mrs. Premise and Mrs. Conclusion Visit Jean-Paul Sartre" Ep. 27
"Mrs. Thing and Mrs. Entity" Ep. 21
"Music Critic and Famous Hairdresser" Ep. 28
"Must be one of them crackpot religions" (link) Ep. 24
"Mystico and Janet—Flats Built by Hypnosis" Ep. 35

"*Nationwide*" Ep. 43
"Naughty Bits" Ep. 22
"Neurotic Announcer" Ep. 30

Bibliography

Abrams, Mark. "The Opinion Polls and the 1970 British General Election." *Public Opinion Quarterly* 34, no. 3 (1970): 317–24.

Abrams, M.H. *A Glossary of Literary Terms*. 4th ed. New York: Holt, Rinehart and Winston, 1981.

Ackroyd, Peter. *Albion*. London: Doubleday, 2003.

———. *J.M.W. Turner*. New York: Nan A. Talese, 2006.

———. *London: The Biography*. London: Doubleday, 2000.

Aldgate, Anthony. *Censorship and the Permissive Society: British Cinema and Theatre, 1955–1965*. London: Oxford University Press, 1995.

Aldous, Richard. *Macmillan, Eisenhower and the Cold War*. Dublin, Ireland: Four Courts Press, 2005.

Allen, Grant. *What's Bred in the Bone*. New York: Knight & Brown, 1898.

Altman, Rick. *The American Film Musical*. Bloomington: Indiana University Press, 1989.

Altman, Wilfred. "Harder Fight to Sell Air Time." *Times*, 2 July 1968: xi.

Anderson, Ronald, and Anne Koval. *James McNeill Whistler: Beyond the Myth*. London: John Murray, 1994.

Andors, Stephen. "Mao and Marx: A Comment." *Modern China* 3, no. 4 (1977): 427–33.

Araloff, Simon. "The Internal Corps—The Kremlin's Private Army." Global Challenges Research website: http://www.axisglobe.com/article.asp?article=178. Accessed 18 November 2006.

Argyle, John Michael. *Psychology and Social Problems*. London: Methuen, 1964.

Attfield, Judy. *Utility Reassessed: The Role of Ethics in the Practice of Design*. Manchester, NY: Manchester University Press, 1999.

"Attila" *World Encyclopedia*. Philip's, 2005. *Oxford Reference Online*. Oxford University Press. Brigham Young University (BYU). http://www.oxfordreference.com/views/ENTRY.html?subview=Main&entry=t142.e793. Accessed 1 May 2006.

Aylett, Glenn. "The Sporting Class." Transdiffusion Broadcasting System website: http://www.transdiffusion.org/emc/worldofsport/the_sporting_cl.php. Accessed 17 October 2006.

Bakhtin, Mikhail. *Rabelais and His World*. Trans. Helene Iswolsky. Bloomington: Indiana University Press, 1984.

Baldick, Chris. *Oxford Concise Dictionary of Literary Terms*. Oxford: Oxford University Press, 2001.

Baldwin, T.W. *Organisation and Personnel of the Shakespearean Company*. Princeton: Princeton University Press, 1927.

Barker, Ronnie. *Ooh-La-La: The Ladies of Paris*. London: Hodder & Stoughton, 1983.

———. *Ronnie Barker's Book of Bathing Beauties*. London: Hodder & Stoughton, 1974.

———. *Ronnie Barker's Book of Boudoir Beauties*. London: Coronet, 1975.

Barrie, J.M. *What Every Woman Knows*. New York: Scribner's, 1918.

Beck, Jerry. *Looney Tunes and Merrie Melodies: A Complete Illustrated Guide to the Warner Bros. Cartoons*. New York: Henry Holt, 1989.

Beerbohm, Max. *Zuleika Dobson*. New York: John Lane, 1911.

Benjamin, Walter. *Illuminations*. New York: Houghton Mifflin Harcourt, 1968.

———. "The Work of Art in the Age of Mechanical Reproduction." *Film Theory and Criticism*, 3rd ed. New York: Oxford UP, 1985.

Bennett, Alan, Peter Cook, Jonathan Miller, and Dudley Moore. *Beyond the Fringe*. New York: Random House, 1963.

Bergeron, David M. "Shakespeare Makes History: *2 Henry IV*." *Studies in English Literature* 31, no. 2 (1991): 231–45.

Bergson, Henri. *The Creative Mind: An Introduction to Metaphysics*. 1946. New York: Dover, 2007.

———. "Laughter: An Essay on the Meaning of the Comic." Trans. Brereton and Rothwell. London: Macmillan, 1911.

Biao, Lin. "Advance Along the Road Opened up by the October Socialist Revolution." Foreign Languages Press, 1967.

Bird, Peter A. *First Food Empire: A History of J. Lyons & Co.* Chichester: Phillimore, 2000.

Bishop, Ellen. "Bakhtin, Carnival and Comedy: The New Grotesque in Monty Python and the Holy Grail." *Film Criticism* 15, no. 1 (1990): 49–64.

Blake, William. *Milton: A Poem*. France: Trianon Press, 1815.

Bogle, Donald. *Toms, Coons, Mulattoes, Mammies, & Bucks*. New York: Continuum International, 2003.

Bond, Maurice Francis. *The Gentleman Usher of the Black Rod*. London: HMSO, 1976.

Boose, Lynda. "Let It Be Hid: The Pornographic Aesthetic of Shakespeare's *Othello*." *Women, Violence, and English Renaissance Literature*. Ed. Linda Woodbridge and Sharon Beehler, *Medieval and Renaissance Texts and Studies*. Phoenix: Arizona State University Press, 2003, 34–58.

Bordwell, David, Janet Staiger, and Kristin Thompson. *The Classical Hollywood Cinema*. London, Melbourne, and Henley: Routledge and Kegan Paul, 1985.

Bordwell, David, and Kristin Thompson. *Narration in the Fiction Film*. University of Wisconsin Press, 1985.

"Boxing's Loss, Too." *Boxing Monthly* 10, no. 3 (July 1998).

Bradman, Sir Don. *The Art of Cricket*. London: Hodder & Stoughton, 1990.

Brettell, Richard R. *Modern Art 1851–1929*. London: Oxford University Press, 1999.

Brontë, Anne. *The Tenant of Wildfell Hall*. Whitefish, MT: Kessinger, 2004.

Brontë, Emily. *Wuthering Heights*. 1847. New York: Bantam, 1983.

Browning, Robert. *Home Thoughts, from Abroad*. 1845. http://www.emule.com/poetry/?page=poem&poem=297. Accessed 28 November 2007.

Bruce-Briggs, B. *Supergenius: The Mega-Worlds of Herman Khan*. North American Policy Press, 2000.

Bryk, William. "Defender of the Faith." *The New York Press*. 16 March 2000.

Buscombe, Edward. *British Television: A Reader*. Oxford: Oxford University Press, 2000.

Butler, David, and Michael Pinto-Duschinsky. *The British General Election of 1970*. London: Macmillan, 1971.

Caesar, Julius. *Commentarii De Bello Gallico*. http://www.gutenberg.org/etext/10657. Accessed 26 November 2007.

Cambridge History of English and American Literature, The. New York: Putnam, 1907–1921.

Campbell, John. *Edward Heath: A Biography*. London: Jonathan Cape, 1993.

Canetti, Elias, and Michael Hofmann. *Party in the Blitz: The English Years*. New York: New Directions, 2005.

Carpenter, Humphrey. *The Angry Young Men: A Literary Comedy of the 1950s*. London: Penguin, 2004.

———. *A Great Silly Grin: The British Satire Boom of the 1960s*. London: Da Capo Press, 2003.

———. *That Was Satire, That Was*. London: Victor Gollancz, 2000.

Catholic Encyclopedia, The. http://www.catholic.org/encyclopedia. Accessed 19 November 2007.

Chamberlain, Gethin. "Threatened Regiments Take Courage from Past." *The Scotsman*. 10 July 2004. http://thescotsman.scotsman.com/index.cfm?id=789542004. Accessed 25 January 2006.

Chandler, Raymond. "Smart Aleck Kill." *Black Mask* (July 1934): 64.

Chapman, George, Ben Jonson, and John Marston. *Eastward Ho*. Ed. Schelling. 1903. Complete digital reproduction at http://books.google.com/books?as_brr=1&id=qlL1LVR0xj8C&vid=OCLC05138166&jtp=1. Accessed 27 November 2007.

Chapman, Graham, John Cleese, Terry Gilliam, Eric Idle, Terry Jones, and Michael Palin. *The Complete Monty Python's Flying Circus: All the Words*, 2 vols. New York: Pantheon, 1989.

Chapman, Graham et al. *The Monty Python Song Book*. New York: Harper Trade, 1995.

———. *Monty Python's Big Red Book*. New York: Contemporary Books, 1980.

Chesneau, Roger. *Aircraft Carriers of the World, 1914 to the Present: An Illustrated Encyclopedia*. Annapolis: Naval Institute Press, 1984.

Christie, Ian. *Gilliam on Gilliam*. London: Faber and Faber, 1999.

Clark, Kenneth. *Civilization: A Personal View*. New York: Harper & Row, 1970.

Clarke, Peter. *Hope and Glory: Britain 1900–1990*. London: Penguin, 1996.

Cockerell, Michael. *Live from Number 10: The Inside Story of Prime Ministers and Television*. London: Faber, 1989.

Coleman, Alice. *Utopia on Trial: Vision and Reality in Planned Housing*. London: Hilary Shipman, 1985.

Colledge, J.J. *Ships of the Royal Navy*. London: Chatham, 1969.

The Complete Works of Shakespeare and Monty Python. Eds. Graham Chapman, et al. London: Methuen, 1981.

Cook, Chris, and John Stevenson, eds. *Modern British History: 1714–2001*. London: Longman, 2001.

Cook, Peter. *Tragically I Was an Only Twin*. New York: St. Martin's, 2003.

Corner, John. *Popular Television in Britain: Studies in Cultural History*. London: BFI, 1991.

Cox, John D., and David Scott Kastan, eds. *A New History of Early English Drama*. New York: Columbia University Press, 1997.

Crab, Roger. *The English Hermite, or, Wonder of This Age*. London, 1655. http://wwwlib.umi.com/eebo/image/42017 (Huntington Library reproduction).

Crawford, Robert. *The Savage and the City in the Work of T.S. Eliot*. Oxford: Oxford University Press, 1991.

Creaton, Heather. *Sources for the History of London 1939–45*. London: British Records Association, 1998.

Crisell, Andrew. *An Introductory History of British Broadcasting*. New York: Routledge, 2002.

———. "Filth, Sedition and Blasphemy: The Rise and Fall of Television Satire." *Popular Television in Britain: Studies in Cultural History*. Ed. John Corner. London: BFI, 1991.

Crisp, Quentin. *The Naked Civil Servant*. London: Penguin, 1997.

Crowe, Brian L. "British Entry into the Common Market: A British View." *Law and Contemporary Problems* 37, no. 2 (Spring 1972): 228–34.

Dale, Iain, ed., *Labour Party General Election Manifestos, 1900–1997*. London: Routledge, 2000.

Davis, John. "The London Drug Scene and the Making of Drug Policy, 1965–73." *Twentieth-Century British History* 17, no. 1 (2006): 26–49.

DeAndrea, William L. *Encyclopedia Mysteriosa: A Comprehensive Guide to the Art of Detection in Print, Film, Radio, and Television*. New York: Prentice Hall, 1994.

Deighton, Len. *Blood, Tears and Folly: An Objective Look at World War II*. New York: HarperCollins, 1993.

Dekker, Thomas. *The Shoemaker's Holiday*. *Drama of the English Renaissance: The Tudor Period*. Ed. Russell A. Fraser and Norman Rabkin. New York: Macmillan, 1976.

D'Emilio, John. *Sexual Politics, Sexual Communities*. Chicago: University of Chicago Press, 1983.

Denning, Lord Alfred Thompson. *Lord Denning's Report, Presented to Parliament by the Prime Minister by Command of Her Majesty*. London: HMSO, 1963.

De Syon, Guillaume. *Zeppelin!: Germany and the Airship, 1900–1939*. Baltimore: Johns Hopkins University Press, 2002.

Deutscher, Isaac. *The Prophet Outcast: Trotsky 1929–1940*. New York: Verso, 2003.

De Vries, Jan Vredeman. *Perspective*. New York: Dover, 1968.

Diamond, John. "Once I Was British." *Times*, 14 January 1995: 1.

Dictionary of National Biography. Oxford: Oxford University Press, 2004.

Dixon, T. J. "The Civil Service Syndrome." *Management Today* (May 1980): 74–79, 154, 158, 162.

Dodge, Mabel. "Speculations, or Post-Impressionism in Prose." *Arts and Decoration* (March 1913).

Dollimore, Jonathan, and Alan Sinfield, eds. *Political Shakespeare: Essays in Cultural Materialism*. Manchester: Manchester University Press, 1999.

Donald, David, ed. *Divided We Fought: A Pictorial History of the Civil War 1861–1865*. New York: Macmillan, 1952.

Dover, Harriet. *Home Front Furniture*. England: Scolar Press, 1991.

Doyle, Arthur Conan. *The Lost World*. New York: Tor Classics, 1997.

Drabble, Margaret. *For Queen and Country: Britain in the Victorian Age*. New York: Seabury Press, 1978.

———. *The Oxford Companion to English Literature*. 5th ed. Oxford: Oxford University Press, 1985.

Duberman, Martin. *Stonewall*. New York: Dutton, 1993.

Dynes, Wayne. *Homosexuality: A Research Guide*. New York: Taylor and Francis, 1987.

Ebert, Roger. *Julius Caesar*. 17 March 1971. http://rogerebert.suntimes.com/apps/pbcs.dll/article?AID=/19710317/REVIEWS/103170301/1023. Accessed 28 November 2007.

Eirik the Red and Other Icelandic Sagas. London: Oxford University Press, 1999.

Eliot, T.S. *Murder in the Cathedral*. 1935. San Diego: HBJ, 1988.

———. "The Waste Land." 1922. *The Norton Anthology of World Masterpieces*. Vol. 2, 5th ed. Ed. Maynard Mack et al. New York and London: Norton, 1985.

Ellsworth, Scott. "Interview with Amil Gargano." *Advertising and Society Review* 2, no. 4 (2001). Website: http://muse.jhu.edu/journals/asr/archives/archives.html. Accessed 18 January 2006.

Esher, Lionel. *A Broken Wave: The Rebuilding of England, 1940–1980*. London: Allen Lane, 1981.

Evans, G. Blakemore, ed. *The Riverside Shakespeare*. New York: Houghton Mifflin, 1974.

Evans, Peter. *Peter Sellers: The Mask behind the Mask*. New York: Signet, 1968.

Evelyn, John. *The Diary of John Evelyn*. Trans. E.S. de Beer. Oxford: Oxford, 1955.

Eyewitness: 1940–1979. Wr. Joanna Bourke, narr. Tim Pigott-Smith. CD. BBC Books, 2005.

Fielding, Henry. *Tom Thumb (The Tragedy of Tragedies)*. http://www.gutenberg.org/etext/6828. Accessed 28 November 2007.

Fraser, Rebecca. *The Story of Britain*. New York: W.W. Norton, 2003.

Fraser, Russell, and Norman Rabkin, eds. *Drama of the English Renaissance, I and II*. New York: Macmillan, 1976.

Freedman, Des. "Modernising the BBC: Wilson's Government and Television, 1964–66." *Contemporary British History* 15, no. 1 (Spring 2001): 21–40.

Fuller, Graham. "Winged Hope." *Kes* (1969) Criterion Collection DVD liner notes.

Gable, Jo. *The Tuppenny Punch and Judy Show—25 Years of TV Commercials*. London: Michael Joseph, 1980.

Gabler, Neal. *An Empire of Their Own: How the Jews Invented Hollywood*. New York: Random House, 1989.

Gage, John. "The Distinctness of Turner." *Journal of the Royal Society of Arts* 123 (1975): 448–57.

Gardner's Art through the Ages, 7th ed. Horst de la Croix and Richard Tansey, eds. New York: Harcourt Brace Jovanovich, 1980.

Genette, Gérard. *Narrative Discourse: An Essay in Method*. Ithaca, NY: Cornell University Press, 1980.

Geographers' A to Z Street Atlas of London. Kent, Seven Oaks: Geographers' Map Co., 1968.

"Germany's Heart: The Modern Taboo." Interview with Jurgen Syberberg in *NPQ* 10, no. 1 (Winter 1993).

Giddings, Robert, and Keith Selby. *The Classic Serial on Television and Radio*. New York: Palgrave-Macmillan, 2001.

Gilbert, Martin. *The First World War*. New York: Owl Books, 2004.

Gilbert, W.S., and Arthur Sullivan. *The Pirates of Penzance*. 1879.

Giles, Colum. *Yorkshire Textile Mills, 1770–1930*. London: HMSO, 1992.

Gilliam, Terry. *Gilliam on Gilliam*. Ed. Ian Christie. London: Faber and Faber, 1999.

Gillispie, Charles. *The Montgolfier Brothers and the Invention of Aviation, 1783–1784*. Princeton, NJ: Princeton University Press, 1983.

Glendinning, Miles, and Stefan Muthesius. *Tower Block: Modern Public Housing in England, Scotland, Wales and Northern Ireland*. New Haven: Yale University Press, 1994.

Goon Show, The. Starring Spike Milligan, Peter Sellers, and Harry Secombe, 1951–1960. "*The Goon Show* Old Time Radio MP3 Collection," 2007.

Gordon, David. "Shavian Comedy and the Shadow of Wilde." *The Cambridge Companion to George Bernard Shaw*. Ed. Christopher Innes. Cambridge: Cambridge University Press, 1998.

Grafton, Roger, and Roger Wilmut. *The Goon Show Companion: A History and Goonography*. London: Robson, 1976.

Gray, Andy, with Jim Drewett. *Flat Back Four: The Tactical Game*. London: Macmillan, 1998.

Greene, Robert. *Morando, the Tritameron of Love. The Life and Complete Works in Prose and Verse of Robert Greene*. New York: Russell & Russell, 1964.

Grimm's Teutonic Mythology. Trans. James Steven Stallybrass. London: Routledge, 1999.

Gurr, Andrew. *The Shakespearean Stage, 1574–1642*. Cambridge: Cambridge University Press, 1992.

Hamilton, A.C., ed. *The Faerie Queene*. London and New York: Longman, 1977.

———. *The Spenser Encyclopedia*. Toronto: Toronto University Press, 1997.

Hazewell, Charles Creighton. "The Indian Revolt." *The Atlantic Monthly* 1, no. 2 (December 1857): 217–22.

Henke, James. *Courtesans and Cuckolds*. New York: Garland, 1979.

Henri, Adrian, Roger McGough, and Brian Patten. *The Mersey Sound*. London: Penguin, 1967.

Hewison, Robert. *In Anger: British Culture in the Cold War 1945–60*. New York: Oxford University Press, 1981.

———. *Monty Python: The Case Against*. London: Eyre Methuen, 1981.

———. *Too Much: Art and Society in the Sixties*, 1960–1975. New York: Oxford UP, 1986.

Heyerdahl, Thor. *Kon Tiki: Across the Pacific By Raft*. Chicago: Rand McNally, 1950.

———. *The Ra Expeditions*. New York: Doubleday, 1971.

Hillier, Bevis. "Colour, Fizz and Bubble." *Times*, 21 September 1968: 17.

Holland, Steve. *The Mushroom Jungle: A History of Postwar Paperback Publishing*. Wiltshire, England: Zeon, 1993.

———. *The Trials of Hank Janson*. Richmond, KY: Books Are Everything, 1991.

Hopkins, Gerald M. "Felix Randal." http://www.bartleby.com/122/29.html. Accessed 28 November 2007.

Hopkins, James K. *A Woman to Deliver Her People: Joanna Southcott and English Millenarianism in an Era of Revolution*. Austin, TX: University of Texas Press, 1981.

Hoppenstand, Gary, Garyn G. Roberts, and Ray B. Browne, eds. *More Tales of the Defective Detective in the Pulps*. Bowling Green: Bowling Green University Press, 1985.

Howard, Philip. "How Britain Drifted to Tragedy of Munich." *Times*, 1 January 1969: 8.

Hughes, Merritt Y. *John Milton's Complete Poems and Major Prose*. Indianapolis: Odyssey, 1957.

Hughes, Robert. *The Shock of the New*. New York: Knopf, 1991.

Hughes, Ted. *Crow: From the Life and Songs of a Crow*. London: Faber, 1970.

Index to the Times. London: Times Publishing Co., 1969–1974.

Ingrams, Richard, ed. *The Life and Times of* Private Eye: *1961–1971*. New York: McGraw-Hill, 1971.

James, C.L.R. *World Revolution, 1917–1936: The Rise of the Communist International*. New Jersey: Humanities P, 1937.

James, Henry. *Portrait of a Lady*. London: Macmillan, 1881.

James, Lawrence. *The Illustrated Rise and Fall of the British Empire*. New York: St. Martin's Griffin, 1994.

———. *The Rise and Fall of the British Empire*. New York: St. Martin's Griffin, 1995.

Jardine, Doug. *In Quest of the Ashes*. London: Methuen, 2005.

Jenkins, Steven. *Cheese Primer*. New York: Workman, 1996.

Johnson, Kim. *The First 20 Years of Monty Python*. New York: St. Martin's Press, 1989.

———. *The First 28 Years of Monty Python*. New York: St. Martin's Press, 1998.

Jones, Robert K. *The Shudder Pulps*. New York: Dutton/Plume, 1978.

Jonson, Ben. *The Alchemist. Drama of the English Renaissance II: The Stuart Period*. Ed. Russell Fraser and Norman Rabkin. New York: Macmillan, 1976.

———. *Bartholomew Fair. Drama of the English Renaissance II: The Stuart Period*. Ed. Russell Fraser and Norman Rabkin. New York: Macmillan, 1976.

———. *Volpone. Drama of the English Renaissance II: The Stuart Period*. Ed. Russell Fraser and Norman Rabkin. New York: Macmillan, 1976.

Joyce, James. *Ulysses*. New York: Vintage Books, 1990.

Judt, Tony. *Postwar: A History of Europe Since 1945*. New York: Penguin, 2005.

Keynes, John Maynard. *The Economic Consequences of the Peace*. New York: Prometheus, 2004.

"KGB's 1967 Annual Report, The." Woodrow Wilson International Center for Scholars, Cold War International History Project (TsKhSD f. 89, op. 5, d. 3, ll. 1–14). Trans. Vladislav Zubok (6 May 1968).

Kierkegaard, Søren. *Either/Or: A Fragment of Life*. London: Penguin, 1992.

Klein, Rudolf, M.A. "The Troubled Transformation of Britain's National Health Service." *NEJM* 355, no. 4 (July 2006): 409–15.

Koszarski, Richard. *An Evening's Entertainment: The Age of the Silent Feature Picture, 1915–1928*. New York: Scribner, 1990.

"Kurt Schwitters Retrospective." *The Times*, 16 October 1958: 4.

Larsen, Darl. "'Is Not the Truth the Truth?' or Rude Frenchman in English Castles: Shakespeare's and Monty Python's (Ab)Uses of History." *Journal of the Utah Academy of Sciences, Arts, and Letters* 76 (1999): 201–12.

———. *Monty Python, Shakespeare, and English Renaissance Drama*. Jefferson, NC: McFarland, 2003.

Lawrence, D.H. *Lady Chatterley's Lover*. London: Penguin, 1960.

———. *The Rainbow*. London: Penguin, 1915.

———. *Sons and Lovers*. New York: Signet, 1953.

———. *Women in Love*. London: Penguin, 1921.

Laws of Cricket, 2003. 2nd edition. London: Lord's, 2003.

Laxdaela Saga. Trans. Magnus Magnusson. London: Penguin, 1969.

Lenin, V.I. *Lenin Collected Works, Volume 8*. Moscow: Foreign Languages Publishing House, 1962.

Loemker, Leroy E., ed. *G.W. Leibniz: Philosophical Papers and Letters*. 2nd ed. Dordrecht, 1969.

Machen, Arthur. *The Great God Pan*. http://www.gutenberg.org/etext/389. Accessed 28 November 2007.

Mack, Maynard et al., ed. *The Norton Anthology of World Masterpieces*, vols. 1 and 2. 5th ed. New York: W.W. Norton, 1985.

Mailik, Zaiba. "Watery Grave." *Guardian*, 15 December 2004.

Malik, Sarita. "The Black and White Minstrel Show." Museum of Broadcast Communication. http://www.museum.tv/archives/etv/B/htmlB/blackandwhim/blackandwhim.htm. Accessed 29 April 2006.

The Maltese Falcon. Dir. John Huston, starring Humphrey Bogart. Warner Bros., 1941.

Man in the Frame. Dir. Fyodor Khitruk. Soyuzmultfilm, 1966.

Marwick, Arthur. *British Society Since 1945*. London: Penguin, 2003.

Marx, Karl, and Frederick Engels. *The Manifesto of the Communist Party*. Chicago: Kerr and Co., 1906.

Matyszak, Philip. *The Enemies of Rome*. London: Thames and Hudson, 2004.

McCabe, Bob. *The Pythons*. New York: St. Martin's, 2003.

Miller, Fredric. "The British Unemployment Crisis of 1935." *Journal of Contemporary History* 14, no. 2 (April 1979): 329–52.

Miller, Paul Allen. "Sidney, Petrarch, and Ovid, or Imitation as Subversion." *ELH* 58, no. 3 (Autumn 1991): 499–522.

Milligan, Spike. *The Goon Show Scripts*. New York: St. Martin's, 1972.

Mills, A.D. *A Dictionary of British Place Names*. Oxford: Oxford University Press, 2003.

Monty Python and the Holy Grail. Dir. Terry Gilliam and Terry Jones. EMI Films, 1975.

Monty Python's Fliegender Zirkus: Sämtliche deutschen Shows. Graham Chapman et al. Eds. Alfred Biolek and Tomas Woitkewitsch. Trans. Heiko Arntz. Zurich: Haffmans Verlag, 1998.

Monty Python's Flying Circus. Dir. John Howard Davies and Ian MacNaughton. BBC, 1969–1974.

Monty Python's Life of Brian. Dir. Terry Jones. HandMade Films, 1979.

Monty Python's The Meaning of Life. Dir. Terry Gilliam and Terry Jones. Universal Pictures, 1983.

Morgan, David. *Monty Python Speaks!* New York: Avon Books, 1999.

Morgan, Kenneth O. *Britain since 1945: The People's Peace*. Oxford: Oxford University Press, 2001.

———. *The Oxford History of Britain*. Oxford: Oxford University Press, 2001.

Motson, John, and John Rowlinson. *The European Cup 1955–1980*. London: Queen Anne Press, 1980.

Musser, Charles. *The Emergence of Cinema: The American Screen to 1907*. New York: Scribner, 1990.

Nelson, Russell. *English Wits*. London: Hutchinson, 1953.

Nettleton, George, and Arthur Case, eds. *British Dramatists from Dryden to Sheridan*. Boston: Houghton Mifflin, 1939.

Newman, Ray. "The Dialectic Aspect of Raymond Chandler's Novels." http://home.comcast.net/~mossrobert/html/criticism/newman.htm. Accessed 24 December 2006.

Nietzsche, Frederich. *The Will to Power*. New York: Vintage, 1968.

Nixon, Richard. "Building for Peace: A Report by President Richard Nixon to the Congress, 25 February 1971." http://www.state.gov/r/pa/ho/frus/nixon/e5/54812.htm. Accessed 28 November 2007.

Njal's Saga. Trans. Robert Cook. London: Penguin, 2002.

Nowell-Smith, Geoffrey. *The Oxford History of World Cinema*. Oxford: Oxford University Press, 1996.

Nuttgens, Patrick. "From Utopia to Slum." *Tablet*, 26 September 1998. www.the tablet.co.uk. Accessed 6 April 2006.

Orczy, Baroness. *The Scarlet Pimpernel*. 1905. First World Library, 2005.

Orlova, Alexandra. "Tchaikovsky: The Last Chapter." *Music & Letters* 62, no. 2 (1981): 125–45.

Ostrom, John. "*Archaeopteryx*: Notice of a 'New' Specimen." *Science* 170, no. 3957 (30 October 1970): 537–38.

Out of the Past. Jacques Tourneur, starring Robert Mitchum. RKO, 1947.

Oxenham, John. *Bees in Amber: A Little Book of Thoughtful Verse*. New York: American Tract Society, 1913.

Oxford Dictionary of Modern Quotations. Ed. Elizabeth Knowles. Oxford: Oxford University Press, 2003.

Oxford Dictionary of National Biography. Oxford: Oxford University Press, 2004. Online version at: http://www.oxforddnb.com.

Palin, Michael. *Michael Palin Diaries 1969–1979: The Python Years*. London: Weidenfeld & Nicholson, 2006.

Partridge, Eric. *Shakespeare's Bawdy*. London: Routledge, 1991.

Paxman, Jeremy. "The English." *Sunday Times*, 27 September 1998: 1–8.

Pearson, Cynthia, and Norbert Delatte, M.ASCE. "Ronan Point Apartment Tower Collapse and Its Effect on Building Codes." *Journal of Performance of Constructed Facilities* 19, no. 2 (May 2005): 172–77.

Pennell, E. R., and J., eds. *The Whistler Journal*. Philadelphia: Lippincott, 1921.

Pepys, Samuel. *Passages from the Diary of Samuel Pepys*. Ed. Richard Le Gallienne. New York: The Modern Library, 1964.

Perez, Joseph. *The Spanish Inquisition: A History*. New Haven, CT: Yale University Press, 2005.

Perry, Elizabeth J. *Patrolling the Revolution: Worker Militias, Citizenship, and the Modern Chinese State*. New York: Rowman & Littlefield, 2005.

Pickering, J.F. "The Abandonment of Major Mergers in the UK." *Journal of Industrial Economics* 27, no. 2: 123–131.

Pincus, Edward. *The Filmmaker's Handbook*. New York: New American Library, 1984.

Preble, Christopher A. "Review of E. Bruce Geelhoed and Anthony O. Edmonds, *Eisenhower, Macmillan and Allied Unity, 1957–1961*," H-Diplo, H-Net Reviews, February 2005. http://www.h-net.org/reviews/showrev.cgi?path=125481117220884. Accessed 29 November 2006.

Propp, Vladimir. *Morphology of the Folk Tale*. Austin: University of Texas Press, 1968.

Proust, Marcel. *In Search of Lost Time*. Trans. Lydia Davis. London: Penguin, 2004.

Quicherat, Jules. *Histoire du costume en France*. Paris, 1875.

Rainey, Laurence. "The Cultural Economy of Modernism." *The Cambridge Companion to Modernism*. Ed. Michael Levenson. Cambridge: Cambridge University Press, 1999.

Rampa, T. Lobsang. *The Third Eye*. 1956. New York: Ballantine, 1986.

Ratcliffe, Stephen. "MEMO/RE: Reading Stein." *Corner* 2 (Spring 1999). http://www.cornermag.org/corner02/page07.htm#anchor76741. Accessed 2 February 2007.

Rattigan, Terence. *The Collected Plays of Terence Rattigan*. Ed. Elizabeth Knowles. Oxford University Press, 2002. Oxford Reference Online. Oxford University Press. Accessed 6 October 2003.

The Renaissance in Italy. New York: Modern Library, 1935.

Rigby, T.H. "The Soviet Leadership: Towards a Self-Stabilizing Oligarchy?" *Soviet Studies* 22, no. 2 (1970): 167–91.

Robertson, Jean. "Philip Sidney." *The Spenser Encyclopedia*. Ed. A.C. Hamilton et al. Toronto: University of Toronto Press, 1990.

Rosenbaum, Martin. *From Soapbox to Soundbite: Party Political Campaigning in Britain since 1945*. London: Macmillan, 1997.

Ross, Charles. *The Wars of the Roses: A Concise History*. London: Thames and Hudson, 1986.

Rundell, Michael. *The Dictionary of Cricket*. 2nd ed. Oxford: Oxford University Press, 1995.

Russell, Bertrand. *The Autobiography of Bertrand Russell*. London: Routledge, 2000.

———. *The Problems of Philosophy*. Oxford: Oxford University Press, 1997.

Rutherford, Jonathan. *Forever England: Reflections on Race, Masculinity and Empire*. London: Lawrence & Wishart, 1997.

R v. Inwood. (1973) 2 All ER 645. http: //www.hrcr.org/safrica/arrested_rights/R_Inwood.htm.

Sachs, Albie. *Justice in South Africa*. London: Chatto & Heinemann, 1973.

Salmond, Dame Anne. *Two Worlds*. New Zealand: Penguin, 1991.

Santayana, George. *Soliloquies in England*. New York: Charles Scribner's Sons, 1922.

Sartre, Jean Paul. *Being and Nothingness*. Trans. Hazel Barnes. New York: Washington Square Press, 1966.

Schmidt, Steven C. "United Kingdom Entry into the European Economic Community: Issues and Implications." *Illinois Agricultural Economics* 12, no. 2 (July 1972): 1–11.

Schroth, Raymond A. "The One and Only." *National Catholic Reporter* 38, no. 14 (8 February 2002): 11.

Schur, Norman. *British English, A to Zed*. New York: Facts on File, 2007.

Scott, Walter, Sir. *Marmion: A Tale of Flodden Field*. London: John Murray, 1808.

———. *Redgauntlet*. Boston: Estes and Lauriat, c1894.

Shakespeare, William. *Cymbeline. The Riverside Shakespeare*. Ed. G. Blakemore Evans. Boston: Houghton Mifflin, 1974.

———. *Hamlet. The Riverside Shakespeare*. Ed. G. Blakemore Evans. Boston: Houghton Mifflin, 1974.

———. *1 Henry IV. The Riverside Shakespeare*. Ed. G. Blakemore Evans. Boston: Houghton Mifflin, 1974.

———. *2 Henry IV. The Riverside Shakespeare*. Ed. G. Blakemore Evans. Boston: Houghton Mifflin, 1974.

———. *Henry V. The Riverside Shakespeare*. Ed. G. Blakemore Evans. Boston: Houghton Mifflin, 1974.

———. *Henry VIII. The Riverside Shakespeare*. Ed. G. Blakemore Evans. Boston: Houghton Mifflin, 1974.

———. *Julius Caesar. The Riverside Shakespeare*. Ed. G. Blakemore Evans. Boston: Houghton Mifflin, 1974.

———. *King John. The Riverside Shakespeare*. Ed. G. Blakemore Evans. Boston: Houghton Mifflin, 1974.

———. *The Merchant of Venice. The Riverside Shakespeare*. Ed. G. Blakemore Evans. Boston: Houghton Mifflin, 1974.

———. *A Midsummer Night's Dream. The Riverside Shakespeare*. Ed. G. Blakemore Evans. Boston: Houghton Mifflin, 1974.

———. *Much Ado about Nothing. The Riverside Shakespeare*. Ed. G. Blakemore Evans. Boston: Houghton Mifflin, 1974.

———. *The Rape of Lucrece. The Riverside Shakespeare*. Ed. G. Blakemore Evans. Boston: Houghton Mifflin, 1974.

———. *Richard II. The Riverside Shakespeare*. Ed. G. Blakemore Evans. Boston: Houghton Mifflin, 1974.

———. *Richard III. The Riverside Shakespeare*. Ed. G. Blakemore Evans. Boston: Houghton Mifflin, 1974.

———. *Romeo and Juliet. The Riverside Shakespeare*. Ed. G. Blakemore Evans. Boston: Houghton Mifflin, 1974.

———. *The Tempest. The Riverside Shakespeare*. Ed. G. Blakemore Evans. Boston: Houghton Mifflin, 1974.

Shaughnessy, Robert. *The Shakespeare Effect*. London: Palgrave Macmillan, 2002.

Shaw, George Bernard. *Pygmalion*. 1916. http://www.bartleby.com/138/2.html. Accessed 28 November 2007.

Shaw, Harry E. *Critical Essays on Sir Walter Scott: The Waverley Novels*. London: Prentice Hall, 1996.

Shelley, Percy Bysshe. "Ozymandias." *Shelley's Poetry and Prose: Authoritative Texts, Criticism*. New York: Norton, 1977.

Shepherd, John. *Continuum Encyclopedia of Popular Music of the World*, Vol. 1. London: Continuum, 2003.

Sherrin, Ned. *I Wish I'd Said That*. Oxford: Oxford University Press, 2004.

Sidney, Sir Philip. *Astrophil and Stella*. Garden City, NY: Anchor Books, 1967.

Sickert, Walter P. "The Idealism News." In *A Free House! Or The Artist as Craftsman; Being the Writings of Walter Richard Sickert*, ed. Oscar Sitwell. London: Macmillan, 1947.

Smethurst, William. *The Archers—The True Story: The History of Radio's Most Famous Programme*. London: Michael O'Mara Books, 1996.

Smith, Alexander. *A Complete History of the Lives and Robberies of the Most Notorious Highwaymen* (1714). London: Routledge, 1926.

Smollett, Tobias. *Humphry Clinker*. Ed. James L. Thorson, Norton Critical Editions. London: W.W. Norton, 1983.

———. *The Letters of Tobias Smollett*, ed. L. M. Knapp. Oxford: Clarendon Press, 1970.

Somerville, Christopher. "Woodstock Oxfordshire Walk." *Weekend Telegraph*. http://www.woodstock-oxfordshire.co.uk/pages/sport_and_entertainment/walk/walk.htm. Accessed 31 January 2007.

Spraggs, Gillian. *Outlaws and Highwaymen: The Cult of the Robber in England from the Middle Ages to the Nineteenth Century*. London: Pimlico, 2002.

Springer, Steve. "The City Was Full of Fight." *Los Angeles Times*, 30 March 2006. Website accessed 24 November 2006.

Stam, Robert. *Reflexivity in Film and Literature: From Don Quixote to Jean-Luc Godard*. New York: Columbia University Press, 1992.

Stein, Gertrude. "Melanctha." *Three Lives*. New York: Vintage, 1909.

Stevenson, Robert Louis. *Treasure Island*. 1883. http://www.online-literature.com/stevenson/treasureisland. Accessed 29 November 2007.

Stewart, Gordon. "Tenzing's Two Wrist-Watches: The Conquest of Everest and Late Imperial Culture in Britain, 1921–1953." *Past & Present* 149 (November 1995): 170–97.

Swift, Jonathan. *Gulliver's Travels. The Writings of Jonathan Swift*. Robert A. Greenberg and William B. Piper, eds. London: Norton, 1973.

———. *The Lady's Dressing Room. The Writings of Jonathan Swift*. Eds. Robert A. Greenberg and William B. Piper. London: Norton, 1973.

Tansey, Richard, et al. *Gardner's Art through the Ages*. 7th ed. New York: HBJ, 1980.

Taylor, Basil. *Constable: Paintings, Drawings, and Watercolours*. London: Phaidon, 1973.

"Ten Years of TV Coverage." *Belfast Bulletin* 6 (Spring 1979): 20–25, published by the Belfast Workers Research Unit.

Tennyson, Alfred Lord. *A Dream of Fair Women*. 1832. http://whitewolf.newcastle.edu.au/words/authors/T/Tennyson Alfred/verse/ladyshalott/dreamfairwomen.html.

———. *Mariana*. http://www.web-books.com/Classics/Poetry/anthology/Tennyson/Mariana.htm.

———. *The Princess: A Medley*. 1847, 1850. http://classiclit.about.com/library/bl-etexts/atennyson/bl-aten-princess.htm.

This Sceptred Isle: The Twentieth Century. Wr. Christopher Lee. CD. *BBC Radio 4 Series*, BBC Audiobooks, 1999.

Thompson, John O. *Monty Python: Complete and Utter Theory of the Grotesque*. London: BFI, 1982.

Tillyard, E.M.W. *Shakespeare's History Plays*. London: Chatto and Windus, 1944.

Took, Barry. *Laughter in the Air*. London: BBC, 1981.

Trevelyan, G.M. *History of England*. 2nd ed. New York: Longmans, Green and Co., 1926.

———. *History of England*. 3rd ed. New York: Longmans, Green and Co., 1952.

Trotsky, Leon, and Isaac Deutscher. *The Age of Permanent Revolution: A Trotsky Anthology*. New York: Dell Publishing 1964.

Unger, Roberto. *Passion: An Essay on Personality*. New York: Free Press, 1986.

Vague, Tom. *Bash the Rich: The Class War Radical History Tour of Notting Hill*. Notting Hill, London: Bash the Rich Press, 2007.

Vahimagi, Tise. *British Television*. Oxford: Oxford University Press, 1996.

Veblen, Thorstein. *The Theory of the Leisure Class*. 1899. New York: Dover, 1999.

Voltaire. *Candide*. London: Penguin, 1950.

Warburton, Nigel. *Philosophy: The Classics*. 3rd ed. London: Routledge, 2006.

Warwick, Charles, and John R. Neill. *Mirabeau and the French Revolution*. Whitefish, MT: Kessinger, 2005.

Watson, Peter. *The Modern Mind: An Intellectual History of the 20th Century*. New York: HarperCollins, 2002.

Waugh, Evelyn. *Labels: A Mediterranean Journal*. London: Duckworth, 1930.

———. *Waugh Abroad: Collected Travel Writing*. New York: Knopf, 2003.

Waugh, Thomas. *Hard to Imagine: Gay Male Eroticism in Photography and Film from Their Beginnings to Stonewall*. New York: Columbia University Press, 1996.

Webster, Charles. *The National Health Service: A Political History*. Oxford: Oxford University Press, 2002.

Weintraub, Stanley, ed. *Bernard Shaw on the London Art Scene, 1885–1950*. Penn State: University Park University Press, 1989.

Wells, Stanley, and Gary Taylor, eds. *The Oxford Shakespeare: Histories with the Poems and Sonnets*. Oxford: Oxford University Press, 1994.

Westman, Andrew, and Tony Dyson. *Archaeology in Greater London, 1965–1990*. London: Museum of London, 1998.

Weston, Richard. *Modernism*. London: Phaidon, 1996.

Westwood, J.N. *Railways of India*. Newton Abbot, UK: David & Charles, 1975.

"What Will the 1970's Bring?" *Awake!* 8 October 1969, 14–16.

Williams, Eric. *The Wooden Horse*. New York: Harper, 1949.

Wilmut, Roger. *From Fringe to Flying Circus*. London: Methuen, 1987.

Wilson, A.N. *After the Victorians: The Decline of Britain in the World*. London: Picador, 2005.

Wilson, J. Dover. *What Happens in Hamlet*. Cambridge: Cambridge University Press, 1935.

"Witnessing the End." *Time*. 18 July 1969. http://www.time.com/time/magazine/article/0,9171,901074-1,00.html. Accessed 28 October 2006.

Wodehouse, P. G. *The Luck of the Bodkins*. Boston: Little, Brown and Co., 1936.

Wolfe, Tom. *From Bauhaus to Our House*. New York: Farrar Straus & Giroux, 1981.

Wooden Horse, The. Dir. Jack Lee, 1950.

Woodward, Rachel. "'It's a Man's Life!': Soldiers, Masculinity and the Countryside." *Gender, Place and Culture: A Journal of Feminist Geography* 5, no. 3 (1 November 1998): 277–300.

Wynne-Thomas, Peter. *Hamlyn A–Z of Cricket Records*. London: Hamlyn, 1983.

SELECTED INTERNET RESOURCES

1970 General Election, review of the rebroadcast: http://www.offthetelly.co.uk/reviews/2003/election70.htm

Affected "gay" speech (by Caroline Bowen): http://www.speech-language-therapy.com/caroline.html. Accessed 16 August 2006

All Blacks Rugby: http://www.allblacks.com

"Anarcho-Syndicalism, History of." *Self-Ed Education Collective*, http://www.selfed.org.uk/units/2001/index.htm

Argyll Regiment: http://argylls.co.uk/today.html

At Last the 1948 Show information: http://orangecow.org/pythonet/1948show

Avengers, The, TV show: http://theavengers.tv/forever

Barr Soft Drinks: http://www.agbarr.co.uk

Baths, UK: http://www.localhistory.scit.wlv.ac.uk/interesting/htbaths/htbaths04.htm

BBC History: http://www.tvradiobits.co.uk

BBC Programme Catalogue: http://open.bbc.co.uk/catalogue/infax

BBC Radio (1967): http://www.radiorewind.co.uk/1967_page.htm. Accessed 1 January 2007.
BBC Radio (1971–1972): http://www.radiorewind.co.uk/1971_page.htm
BBC Television Centre history: http://www.martinkempton.com/TV%20Centre%20history.htm#stage%206
Best, George obituary: http://www.timesonline.co.uk/article/0,,2-1890892,00.html, and http://www.manutdzone.com/legends/GeorgeBest.htm
BFI Film and TV Database: http://www.bfi.org.uk/filmtvinfo/ftvdb
Board of Trade: http://dti.gov.uk/history/board.htm
British Broadcasting Corporation: http://www.bbc.co.uk
British Cartoon Archive: http://opal.kent.ac.uk/cartoonx-cgi/ccc.py
British Telephone Historical Archives (accessed through ancestry.com): http://content.ancestry.co.uk/iexec/?htx=List&dbid=1025&offerid=0%3a7858%3a0
British TV, anecdotal history: http://www.whirligig-tv.co.uk
British TV, history: http://www.teletronic.co.uk
Brown, Arthur, obituary: http://www.guardian.co.uk/obituaries/story/0,3604,969745,00.html (penned by Andrew Phillips).
Cambridge University prizes in Classics: http://www.admin.cam.ac.uk/reporter/2003-04/special/05/b5.html
"Catenaccio defense": http://naccio.cs.virginia.edu/catenaccio.html
Celtic FC: http://www.lonestarceltic.com/25_may_1967.php
Chichester Festival history: http://www.cft.org.uk/content.asp?CategoryID=1107.
Churchill Centre "darker days" speech: http://www.winstonchurchill.org/i4a/pages/index.cfm?pageid=423
Clergy Lists, UK: *Kelly's Clergy List, 1909*: http://midlandshistoricaldata.org
Commonwealth Immigration Act of 1968: http://britishcitizen.info/CIA1968.pdf
Corporal punishment in South Africa: http://www.corpun.com/jcpza9.htm
Courtauld Gallery collection search: http://www.courtauld.ac.uk/index.html
Cowdrey, Colin, obituary (by John Thicknesse): http://content-www.cricinfo.com/ci/content/player/10846.html
Cricket info.: http://content-usa.cricinfo.com/england/content/player/20159.html
Crystal Palace FC: http://www.cpfc.co.uk
"Desert Island Discs Archives: Harry Secombe." BBC Radio 4 podcast: http://www.bbc.co.uk/programmes/p00943sz
DeWolfe music: http://www.dewolfe.co.uk
Dorking Dramatic Society Archives: http://www.ddos.org.uk/archives.asp
Encyclopedia Britannica: http://www.ebo.com
Encyclopedia of Fantastic Film & Television: http://www.eofftv.com
Everest Climbing History: http://www.everestnews.com/everest1.htm
FBI files on Burgess, Maclean: http://foia.fbi.gov/filelink.html?file=/philby/philby1a.pdf
Forestry Commission UK: http://www.forestry.gov.uk
Freemasonry watchdog: http://freemasonrywatch.org
Gas Boards history: http://www.gasarchive.org/Nationalisation.htm and http://www.centrica.co.uk/index.asp?pageid=397
Gay characters on British TV: http://www.queertv.btinternet.co.uk
Gay men's magazines: http://www.planetout.com/news/history/archive/09271999.html
Guardian Century: http://century.guardian.co.uk
Highwayman Humphrey Kynaston: http://www.bbc.co.uk/shropshire/features/halloween/kynaston.shtml
Hitler's speeches: http://hitler.org/speeches
Homelessness in the UK in 1969: http://news.bbc.co.uk/onthisday/hi/dates/stories/september/11/newsid_3037000/3037650.stm
An Incomplete History of London's Television Studios: http://www.tvstudiohistory.co.uk/tv%20centre%20history.htm
Keele University General Elections Results, http://www.psr.keele.ac.uk.
"Kray Brothers" (by Thomas Jones): http://www.crimelibrary.com/gangsters_outlaws/mob_bosses/kray/index_1.html
Labour Manifesto, 1966: http://www.psr.keele.ac.uk/area/uk/man/lab66.htm
Labour Market Trends, Office for National Statistics, June 1999: http://www.statistics.gov.uk
London School of Economics riots (January 1969): http://news.bbc.co.uk/onthisday/hi/dates/stories/january/24/newsid_2506000/2506485.stm
Lord's (MCC) Laws of Cricket: http://www.lords.org/laws-and-spirit/laws-of-cricket
"Men of Harlech": http://www.data-wales.co.uk/harlech.htm
MPFC Scripts: http://www.ibras.dk/montypython/justthewords.htm
National Film Theatre: http://bfi.uk.org
National Gallery collection archive: http://www.nationalgallery.org.uk
National Portrait Gallery collection search: http://www.npg.org.uk/live/collect.asp
North Yorkshire photos (Unnetie Digitisation Project) http://www2.northyorks.gov.uk/unnetie
Man Alive: http://www.offthetelly.co.uk/features/bbc2/forty1.htm
McGonagall Online. http://www.mcgonagall-online.org.uk/articles/awful-poet-who-didnt-know-it.
McGuffie, Mary (McCheane) information, Farnon Society: http://www.rfsoc.org.uk/jim3.shtml
Mont Orgueil Castle: http://www.bbc.co.uk/jersey/content/image_galleries/mont_orgueil_one_gallery.shtml?5
"Northern Ireland Conflict and Politics (1968 to the Present)": http://cain.ulst.ac.uk/othelem/media/tv10yrs.htm
Notting Hill "pop" history (by Tom Vague): http://www.historytalk.org/Tom%20Vague%20Pop%20History/Tom%20Vague%20Pop%20History.htm
Nova (magazine) listserv: http://listserv.uel.ac.uk/pipermail/centrefornarrativeresearch/Week-of-Mon-20050411/000319.html
Online Medieval & Classical Library: http://omacl.org

Open University ("From Here to Modernity"): http://www.open2.net/modernity
"Overcrowding in London" (March 2004): http://www.lhu.org.uk
Oxford English Dictionary: http://dictionary.oed.com
Party Political (or Election) Broadcasts: http://www.psr.keele.ac.uk/area/uk/peb.htm
Peerage listings: http://www.thepeerage.com
Pinball machines, vintage: http://dguhlow.tripod.com/pinballs/htmls/bankaball.html
Pontiac Firebirds in movies: http://www.imcdb.org/vehicles_make-Pontiac_model-Firebird.html
Positivism: http://radicalacademy.com/philpositivists.htm
Postwar fireplaces (and fireplace inserts): http://www.c20fires.co.uk/fireplaces/original/postfires.htm
Pound devaluation, 1972: http://news.bbc.co.uk/onthisday/low/dates/stories/june/23/newsid_2518000/2518927.stm
"Poverty in England" (by Charles Booth): http://booth.lse.ac.uk
Proust, Marcel and *À la recherche du temps perdu*: http://tempsperdu.com
Queen's itinerary and speeches, 1970: http://www.nla.gov.au/ms/findaids/9174.html#1970
Queen's Park Rangers FC: http://www.qpc.co.uk
"Radio Rewind." http://www.radiorewind.co.uk.
Radio Times official website: http://radiotimes.beeb.com
Radio Times (unofficial) cover art site: http://www.vintagetimes.org.uk
Railroad music: http://www.musicweb.uk.net/railways_in_music.htm
Railway signal boxes: http://www.signalbox.org/gallery/be.htm
Railway violence: http://btp.police.uk/History
Reith Lectures: http://www.bbc.co.uk/radio4/reith/reith_history.shtml
Richter, Sviatoslav (chronology): http://www.trovar.com/str/dates/index.html
Rijksmuseum Rembrandt collection: http://rijksmuseum.nl/index.jsp
Rock climbing jargon: http://www.myoan.net/climbing/jargon.html
Roiurama Expedition: http://www.lastrefuge.co.uk/data/adrian2.html
Royal Scottish Forestry Society: http://www.rsfs.org
Scott, Peter entry at WordIQ: http://www.wordiq.com/definition/Peter_Scott
Scottish politics: http://www.alba.org.uk/nextwe/snp.html
Semaphore signals: http://www.cs.dartmouth.edu/~rockmore/semaphore.jpg
Shakespeare listserv: http://www.shaksper.net/www.shaksper.net
Julian Slade obituary (by Dennis Barker): http://arts.guardian.co.uk/news/obituary/0,,1801400,00.html
Society of Film and TV Arts (UK): http://www.bafta.org
"Squatting in London" (Andrew Friend): http://squat.freeserve.co.uk/story
St. Albans Operatic Society: http://www.saos.org.uk
Strike activity in the UK: http://www.eiro.eurofound.eu.int/1999/07/feature/uk9907215f.html
Tate Gallery Collection: http://www.tate.org.uk/britain
Tax Freedom Day in the UK: http://www.adamsmith.org/tax/short-history.php
Tennis information: http://www.tennisfame.org/enshrinees
Time Magazine online archives: http://www.time.com/time/magazine/archives
The *Times* (London) Digital Archive, 1785–1985: http://infotrac.galegroup.com/itw
UK Announcers archive: http://tvannouncers.thetvroomplus.com/channel-19.html
UK General Elections (including results since 1832): http://www.psr.keele.ac.uk/area/uk/edates.htm
UK motorway exchanges: http://www.cbrd.co.uk/reference/interchanges/fourlevelstack.shtml
UK Parliament: http://www.parliament.uk
UK postwar politics: http://politics.guardian.co.uk/politicspast/story/0,9061,471383,00.html
UK postwar spending: "Long-Term Trends in British Taxation and Spending" (Tom Clark and Andrew Dilnot) from the Institute for Fiscal Studies: http://www.ifs.org.uk/bns/bn25.pdf
UK street maps: http://www.streetmap.co.uk
Victoria & Albert Museum collection: http://www.vam.ac.uk/collections
Vladimir Horowitz concert information: http://web.telia.com/~u85420275/index.htm
Western National bus number 350 EDV: http://www.bristolsu.co.uk/Su/operatordetails/westernnational/350edv.htm
Wimbledon archives: http://www.wimbledon.org
Wisden Cricketer, The: http://www.cricinfo.com/wisdencricketer
YMCA in Russia: http://www.ymca.ru/english/history

Index

*Page numbers for both volumes are listed in each entry, with page numbers preceded by a Roman numeral to distinguish those in volume one from those in volume two (e.g., 10 Downing Street, **I**-xi, 17, 238, 368; **II**-xi, 53, 66, 67, 181, 200). For each entry, all the pertinent page numbers for volume one are listed first, followed immediately by those in volume two*

About the Author

Darl Larsen was born in California in 1963 and has been part of the film faculty at Brigham Young University since 1998. He took degrees at UC Santa Barbara, Brigham Young University, and Northern Illinois University. At BYU he is professor of media arts and animation and teaches film and popular culture studies. He lives in beautiful Provo, Utah, with his family.